LOKI
AGENT OF ASGARD

THE COMPLETE COLLECTION

D1430207

River Forest Public Library
735 Lathrop Avenue
River Forest, IL 60305
708-366-5205
January 2020

LOKI: AGENT OF ASGARD — THE COMPLETE COLLECTION. Contains material originally published in magazine form as LOKI: AGENT OF ASGARD (2014) #1-17, ORIGINAL SIN (2014) #5.5 and ALL-NEW MARVEL NOW! POINT ONE (2014) #1. First printing 2019. ISBN 978-1-302-92073-9. Published by MARVEL WORLDWIDE, INC., a subsidiary of MARVEL ENTERTAINMENT, LLC. OFFICE OF PUBLICATION: 135 West 50th Street, New York, NY 10020. © 2019 MARVEL No similarity between any of the names, characters, persons, and/or institutions in this magazine with those of any living or dead person or institution is intended, and any such similarity which may exist is purely coincidental. Printed in the U.S.A. DAN BUCKLEY, President, Marvel Entertainment; JOHN NEE, Publisher; JOE QUESADA, Chief Creative Officer; TOM BREVOORT, SVP of Publishing; DAVID BOGART, SVP of Business Affairs & Operations, Publisher & SVP of Talent Affairs; DAVID GABRIEL, VP of Print & Digital Publishing; JEFF YOUNGQUIST, VP of Production & Special Projects; DAN CARR, Executive Director of Publishing Technology; ALEX MORALES, Director of Publishing Operations; DAN EDINGTON, Managing Editor; SUSAN CRESPI, Production Manager; STAN LEE, Chairman Emeritus. For information regarding advertising in Marvel Comics or on Marvel.com, please contact Vit DeBellis, Custom Solutions & Integrated Advertising Manager, at vdebellis@marvel.com. For Marvel subscription inquiries, please call 888-511-5480. Manufactured between 10/30/2019 and 11/20/2019 by LSC COMMUNICATIONS INC., KENDALLVILLE, IN, USA.

10987654321

LOKI
AGENT OF ASGARD
THE COMPLETE COLLECTION

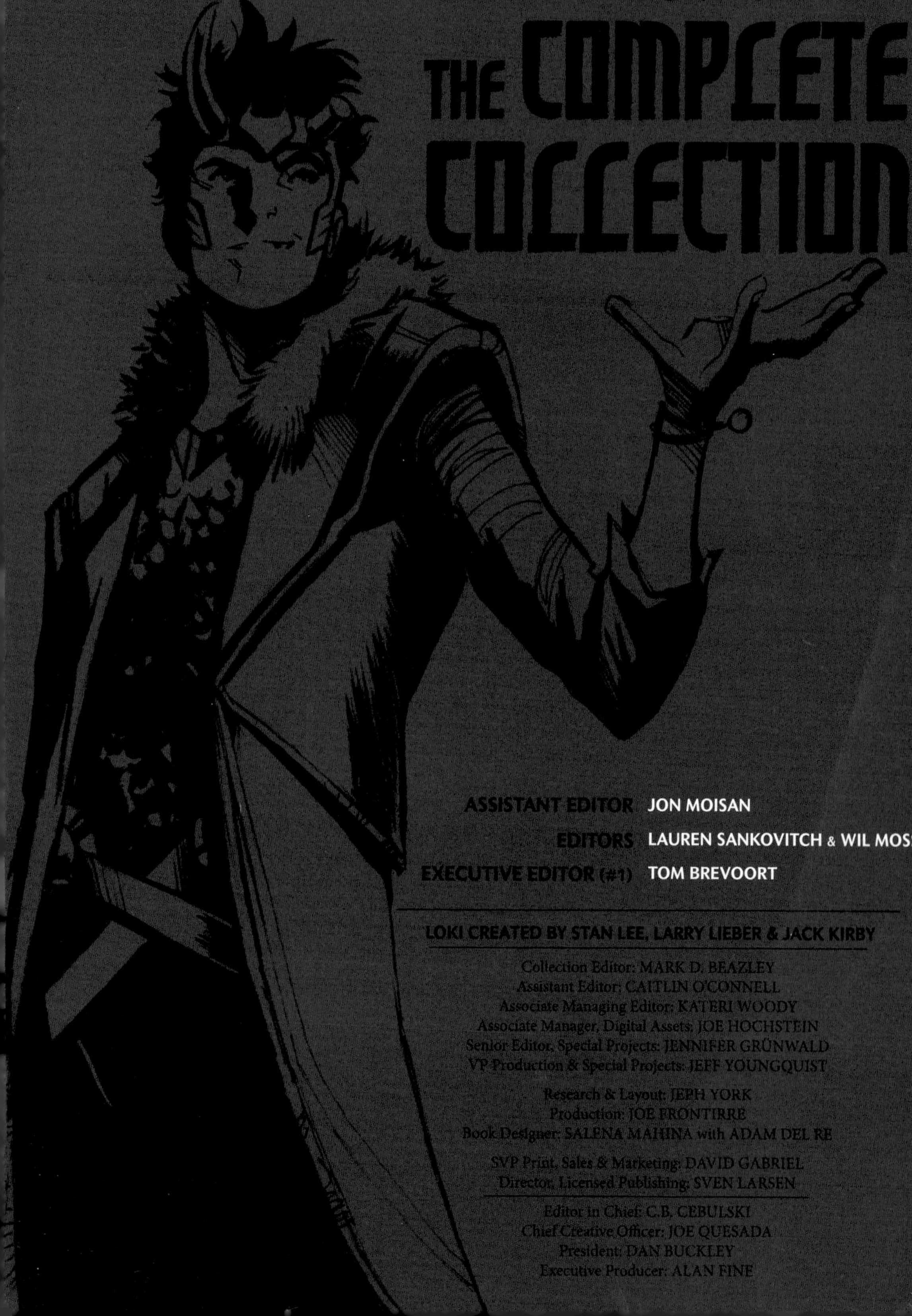

ASSISTANT EDITOR JON MOISAN
EDITORS LAUREN SANKOVITCH & WIL MOSS
EXECUTIVE EDITOR (#1) TOM BREVOORT

LOKI CREATED BY STAN LEE, LARRY LIEBER & JACK KIRBY

Collection Editor: MARK D. BEAZLEY
Assistant Editor: CAITLIN O'CONNELL
Associate Managing Editor: KATERI WOODY
Associate Manager, Digital Assets: JOE HOCHSTEIN
Senior Editor, Special Projects: JENNIFER GRÜNWALD
VP Production & Special Projects: JEFF YOUNGQUIST

Research & Layout: JEPH YORK
Production: JOE FRONTIRRE
Book Designer: SALENA MAHINA with ADAM DEL RE

SVP Print, Sales & Marketing: DAVID GABRIEL
Director, Licensed Publishing: SVEN LARSEN

Editor in Chief: C.B. CEBULSKI
Chief Creative Officer: JOE QUESADA
President: DAN BUCKLEY
Executive Producer: ALAN FINE

WRITER **AL EWING**

WITH **JASON AARON** (CO-PLOT, *ORIGINAL SIN* #5.1-5.5)

ALL-NEW MARVEL NOW! POINT ONE — "BEFORE THE TRUTH HAS ITS PANTS ON" LOKI: AGENT OF ASGARD #1-5

ARTIST **LEE GARBETT**

COLORIST NOLAN WOODARD

ORIGINAL SIN #5.1-5.5 — "THOR & LOKI: THE TENTH REALM"

ARTISTS **LEE GARBETT & SIMONE BIANCHI** WITH

SZYMON KUDRANSKI & **MARCO CHECCHETTO** (#5.5)

ADDITIONAL INKS (#5.4-5.5) RICCARDO PIERUCCINI

COLORSTS NOLAN WOODARD WITH ADRIANO DELL'ALPI (#5.2-5.5),

SIMONE BIANCHI (#5.1), SIMONE PERUZZI (#5.3)

& PAUL MOUNTS (#5.5)

LOKI: AGENT OF ASGARD #6-7 — "MARCH TO AXIS"

ARTIST **JORGE COELHO**

COLORIST LEE LOUGHRIDGE

LOKI: AGENT OF ASGARD #8-10 — "AXIS"

ARTIST **LEE GARBETT**

COLORIST NOLAN WOODARD

LOKI: AGENT OF ASGARD #11-17 — "LAST DAYS"

ARTIST **LEE GARBETT**

COLORISTS ANTONIO FABELA WITH ANDRES MOSSA (#14)

LETTERERS **VC'S CLAYTON COWLES**
(ALL-NEW MARVEL NOW! POINT ONE,
LOKI: AGENT OF ASGARD)

VC'S JOE SABINO
(ORIGINAL SIN)

COVER ART **SALVADOR LARROCA**
& LAURA MARTIN
(ALL-NEW MARVEL NOW! POINT ONE)

JENNY FRISON
(LOKI: AGENT OF ASGARD #1-5)

DALE KEOWN & JASON KEITH
(ORIGINAL SIN #5.1)

DALE KEOWN & IVE SVORCINA
(ORIGINAL SIN #5.2)

SIMONE BIANCHI
(ORIGINAL SIN #5.3-5.5)

LEE GARBETT
(LOKI: AGENT OF ASGARD #6-17)

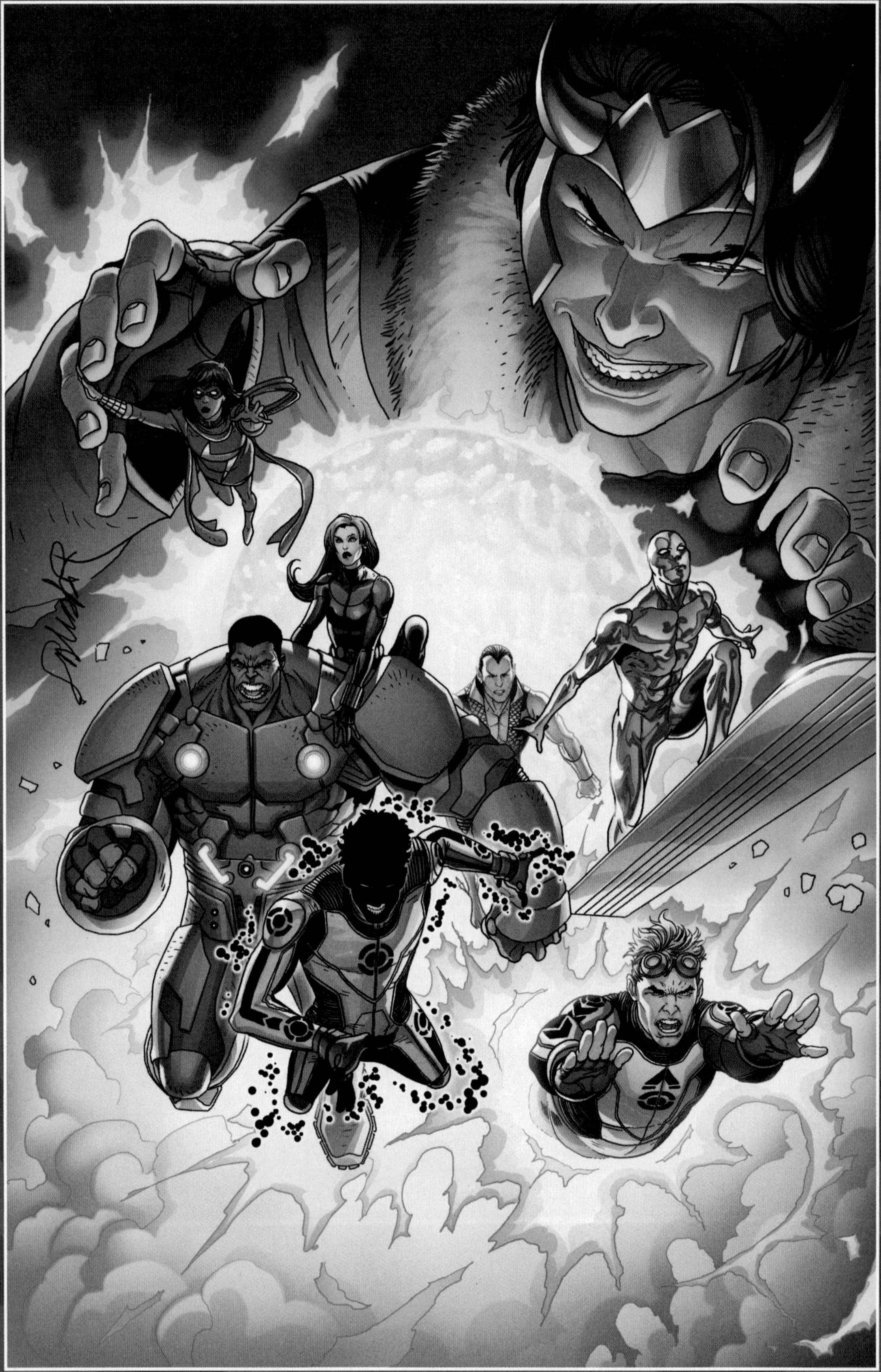

ALL-NEW MARVEL NOW POINT ONE #1

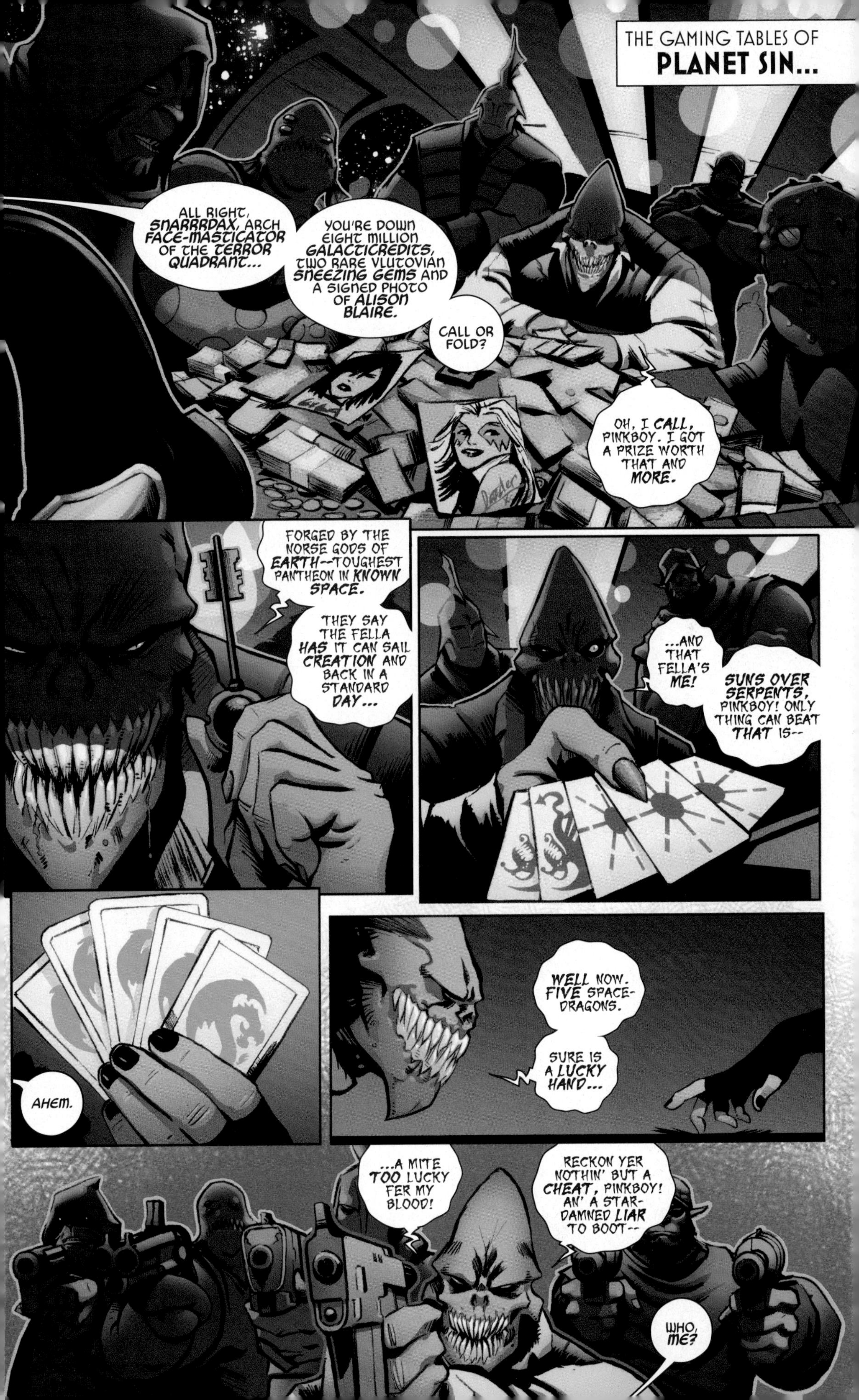

THE GAMING TABLES OF PLANET SIN...
ALL RIGHT, SNARRRDAX, ARCH FACE-MASTICATOR OF THE TERROR QUADRANT...
YOU'RE DOWN EIGHT MILLION GALACTICREDITS, TWO RARE VLUTOVIAN SNEEZING GEMS AND A SIGNED PHOTO OF ALISON BLAIRE.
CALL OR FOLD?
OH, I CALL, PINKBOY. I GOT A PRIZE WORTH THAT AND MORE.
FORGED BY THE NORSE GODS OF EARTH--TOUGHEST PANTHEON IN KNOWN SPACE.
THEY SAY THE FELLA HAS IT CAN SAIL CREATION AND BACK IN A STANDARD DAY...
...AND THAT FELLA'S ME!
SUNS OVER SERPENTS, PINKBOY! ONLY THING CAN BEAT THAT IS--
AHEM.
WELL NOW. FIVE SPACE-DRAGONS.
SURE IS A LUCKY HAND...
...A MITE TOO LUCKY FER MY BLOOD!
RECKON YER NOTHIN' BUT A CHEAT, PINKBOY! AN' A STAR-DAMNED LIAR TO BOOT--
WHO, ME?

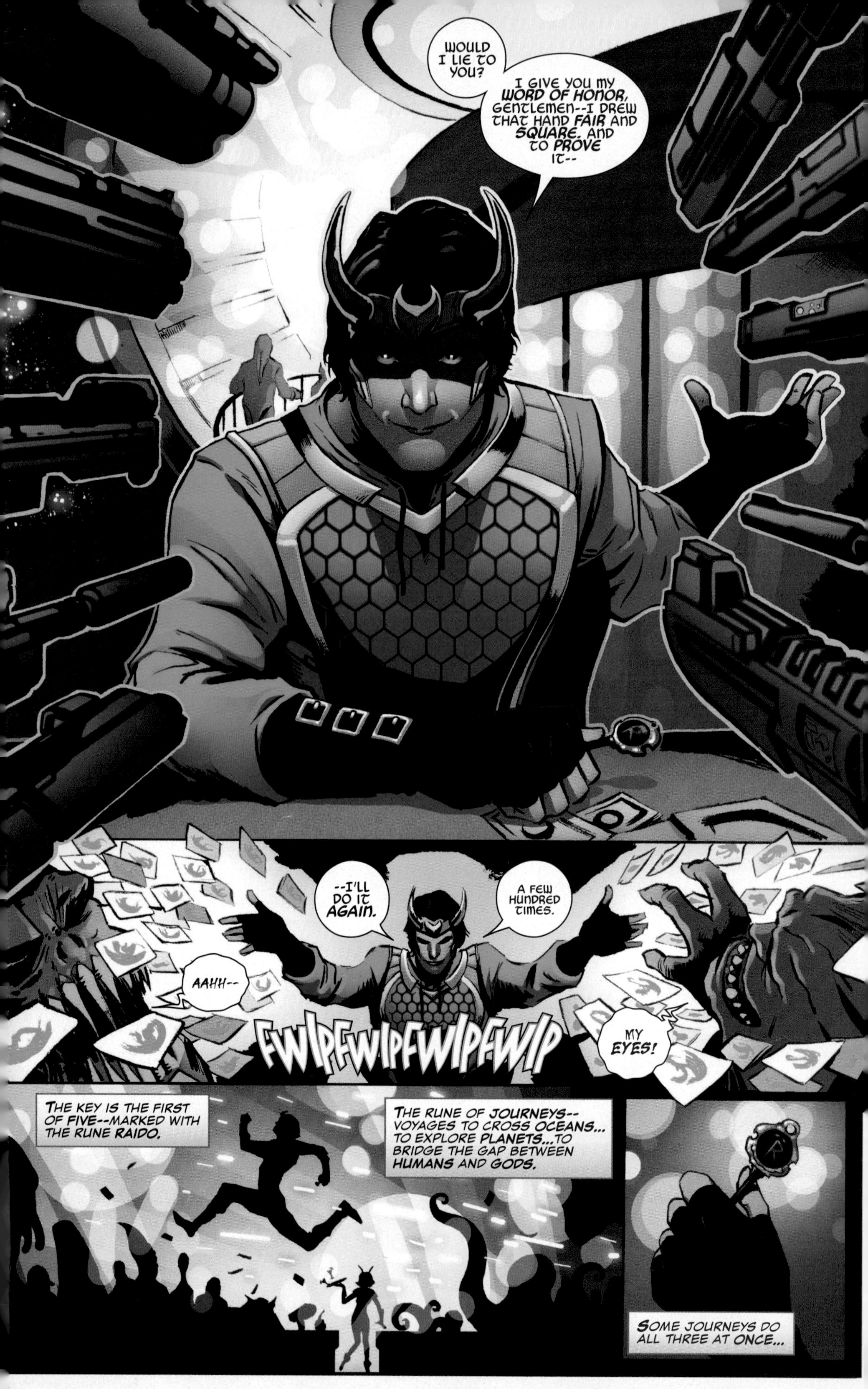
WOULD I LIE TO YOU?
I GIVE YOU MY WORD OF HONOR, GENTLEMEN--I DREW THAT HAND FAIR AND SQUARE. AND TO PROVE IT--
--I'LL DO IT AGAIN.
A FEW HUNDRED TIMES.
AAHH--
FWIPFWIPFWIPFWIP
MY EYES!
THE KEY IS THE FIRST OF FIVE--MARKED WITH THE RUNE RAIDO.
THE RUNE OF JOURNEYS--VOYAGES TO CROSS OCEANS...TO EXPLORE PLANETS...TO BRIDGE THE GAP BETWEEN HUMANS AND GODS.
SOME JOURNEYS DO ALL THREE AT ONCE...

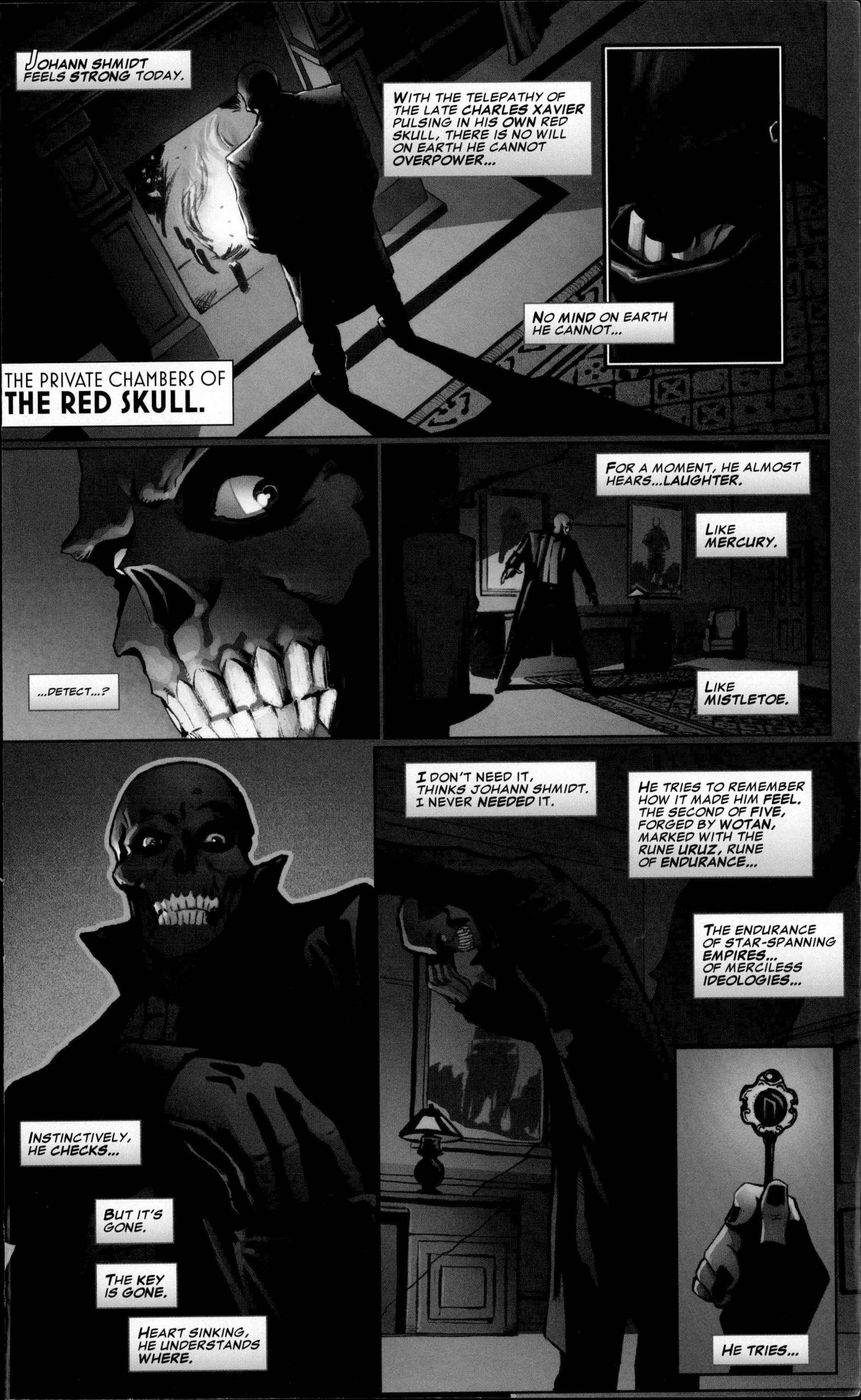
JOHANN SHMIDT FEELS STRONG TODAY.
WITH THE TELEPATHY OF THE LATE CHARLES XAVIER PULSING IN HIS OWN RED SKULL, THERE IS NO WILL ON EARTH HE CANNOT OVERPOWER...
NO MIND ON EARTH HE CANNOT...
THE PRIVATE CHAMBERS OF THE RED SKULL.
...DETECT...?
FOR A MOMENT, HE ALMOST HEARS...LAUGHTER.
LIKE MERCURY.
LIKE MISTLETOE.
INSTINCTIVELY, HE CHECKS...
BUT IT'S GONE.
THE KEY IS GONE.
HEART SINKING, HE UNDERSTANDS WHERE.
I DON'T NEED IT, THINKS JOHANN SHMIDT. I NEVER NEEDED IT.
HE TRIES TO REMEMBER HOW IT MADE HIM FEEL. THE SECOND OF FIVE, FORGED BY WOTAN, MARKED WITH THE RUNE URUZ, RUNE OF ENDURANCE...
THE ENDURANCE OF STAR-SPANNING EMPIRES... OF MERCILESS IDEOLOGIES...
HE TRIES...

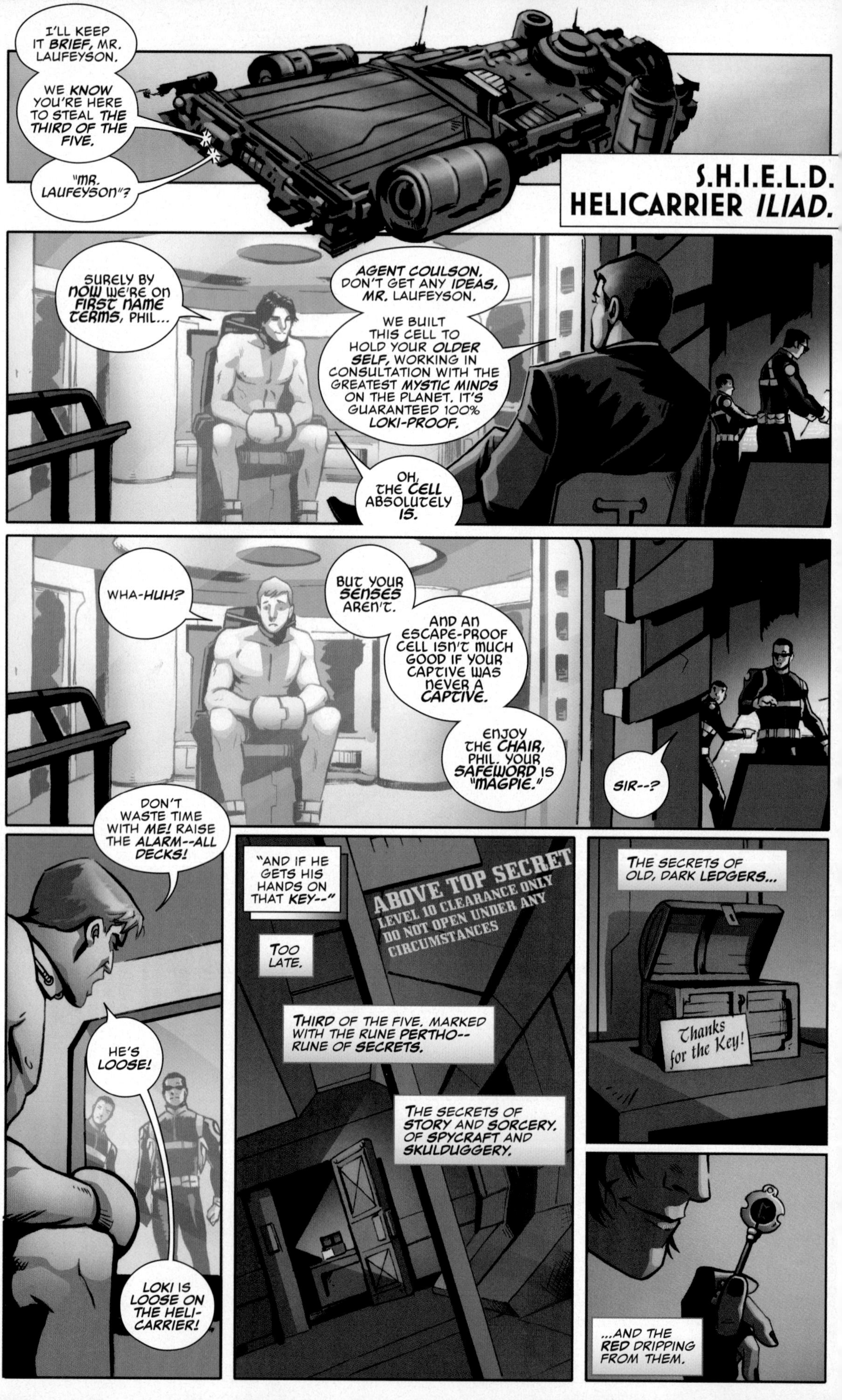
I'LL KEEP IT BRIEF, MR. LAUFEYSON.
WE KNOW YOU'RE HERE TO STEAL THE THIRD OF THE FIVE.
"MR. LAUFEYSON"?
S.H.I.E.L.D. HELICARRIER ILIAD.
SURELY BY NOW WE'RE ON FIRST NAME TERMS, PHIL...
AGENT COULSON. DON'T GET ANY IDEAS, MR. LAUFEYSON.
WE BUILT THIS CELL TO HOLD YOUR OLDER SELF, WORKING IN CONSULTATION WITH THE GREATEST MYSTIC MINDS ON THE PLANET. IT'S GUARANTEED 100% LOKI-PROOF.
OH, THE CELL ABSOLUTELY IS.
WHA-HUH?
BUT YOUR SENSES AREN'T.
AND AN ESCAPE-PROOF CELL ISN'T MUCH GOOD IF YOUR CAPTIVE WAS NEVER A CAPTIVE.
ENJOY THE CHAIR, PHIL. YOUR SAFEWORD IS "MAGPIE."
SIR--?
DON'T WASTE TIME WITH ME! RAISE THE ALARM--ALL DECKS!
HE'S LOOSE!
LOKI IS LOOSE ON THE HELI-CARRIER!
"AND IF HE GETS HIS HANDS ON THAT KEY--"
ABOVE TOP SECRET
LEVEL 10 CLEARANCE ONLY
DO NOT OPEN UNDER ANY CIRCUMSTANCES
TOO LATE.
THIRD OF THE FIVE. MARKED WITH THE RUNE PERTHO-- RUNE OF SECRETS.
THE SECRETS OF STORY AND SORCERY. OF SPYCRAFT AND SKULDUGGERY.
THE SECRETS OF OLD, DARK LEDGERS...
Thanks for the Key!
...AND THE RED DRIPPING FROM THEM.

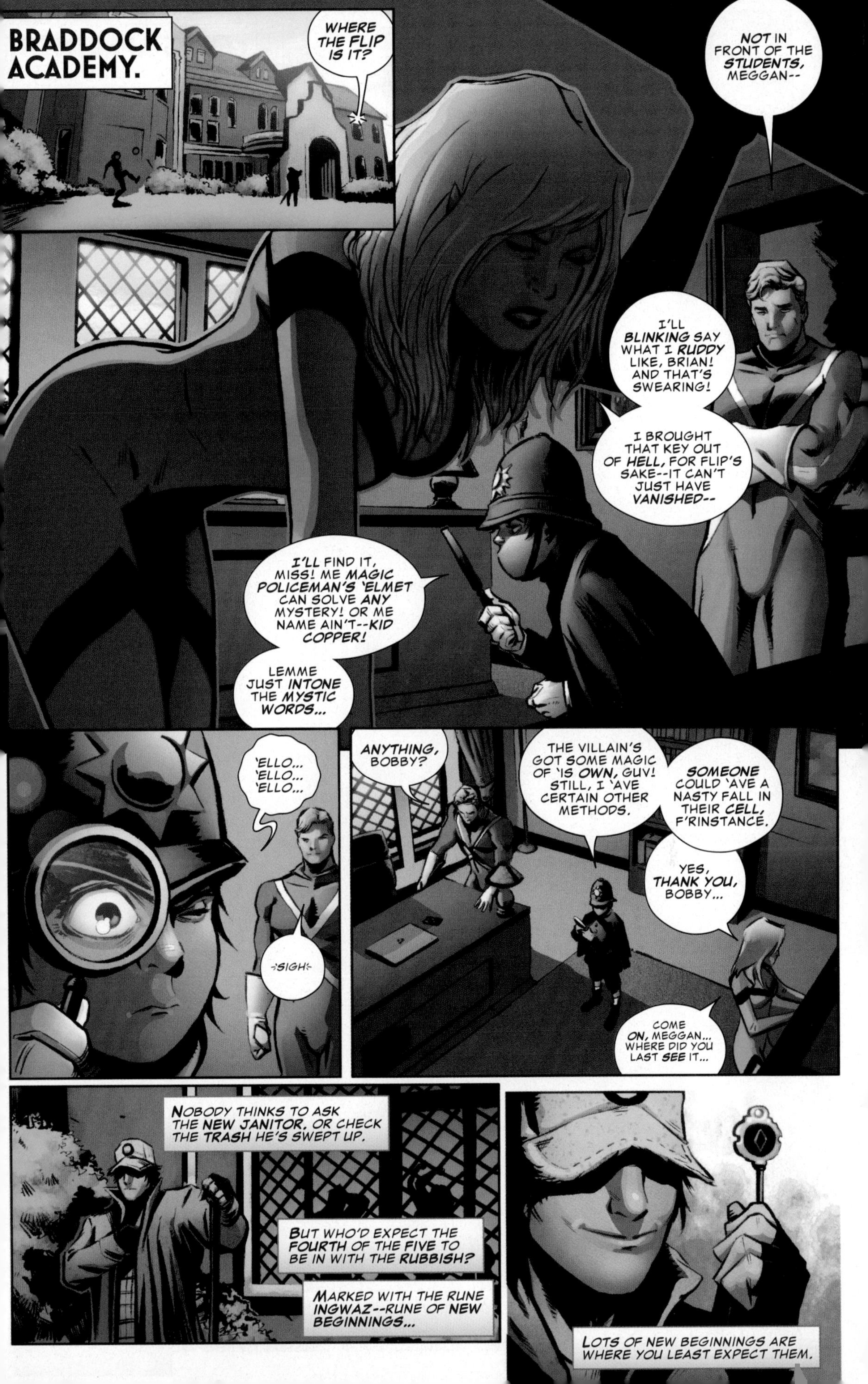
BRADDOCK ACADEMY.
WHERE THE FLIP IS IT?
NOT IN FRONT OF THE STUDENTS, MEGGAN--
I'LL BLINKING SAY WHAT I RUDDY LIKE, BRIAN! AND THAT'S SWEARING!
I BROUGHT THAT KEY OUT OF HELL, FOR FLIP'S SAKE--IT CAN'T JUST HAVE VANISHED--
I'LL FIND IT, MISS! ME MAGIC POLICEMAN'S 'ELMET CAN SOLVE ANY MYSTERY! OR ME NAME AIN'T--KID COPPER!
LEMME JUST INTONE THE MYSTIC WORDS...
'ELLO... 'ELLO... 'ELLO...
SIGH
ANYTHING, BOBBY?
THE VILLAIN'S GOT SOME MAGIC OF 'IS OWN, GUV! STILL, I 'AVE CERTAIN OTHER METHODS.
SOMEONE COULD 'AVE A NASTY FALL IN THEIR CELL, F'RINSTANCE.
YES, THANK YOU, BOBBY...
COME ON, MEGGAN... WHERE DID YOU LAST SEE IT...
NOBODY THINKS TO ASK THE NEW JANITOR, OR CHECK THE TRASH HE'S SWEPT UP.
BUT WHO'D EXPECT THE FOURTH OF THE FIVE TO BE IN WITH THE RUBBISH?
MARKED WITH THE RUNE INGWAZ--RUNE OF NEW BEGINNINGS...
LOTS OF NEW BEGINNINGS ARE WHERE YOU LEAST EXPECT THEM.

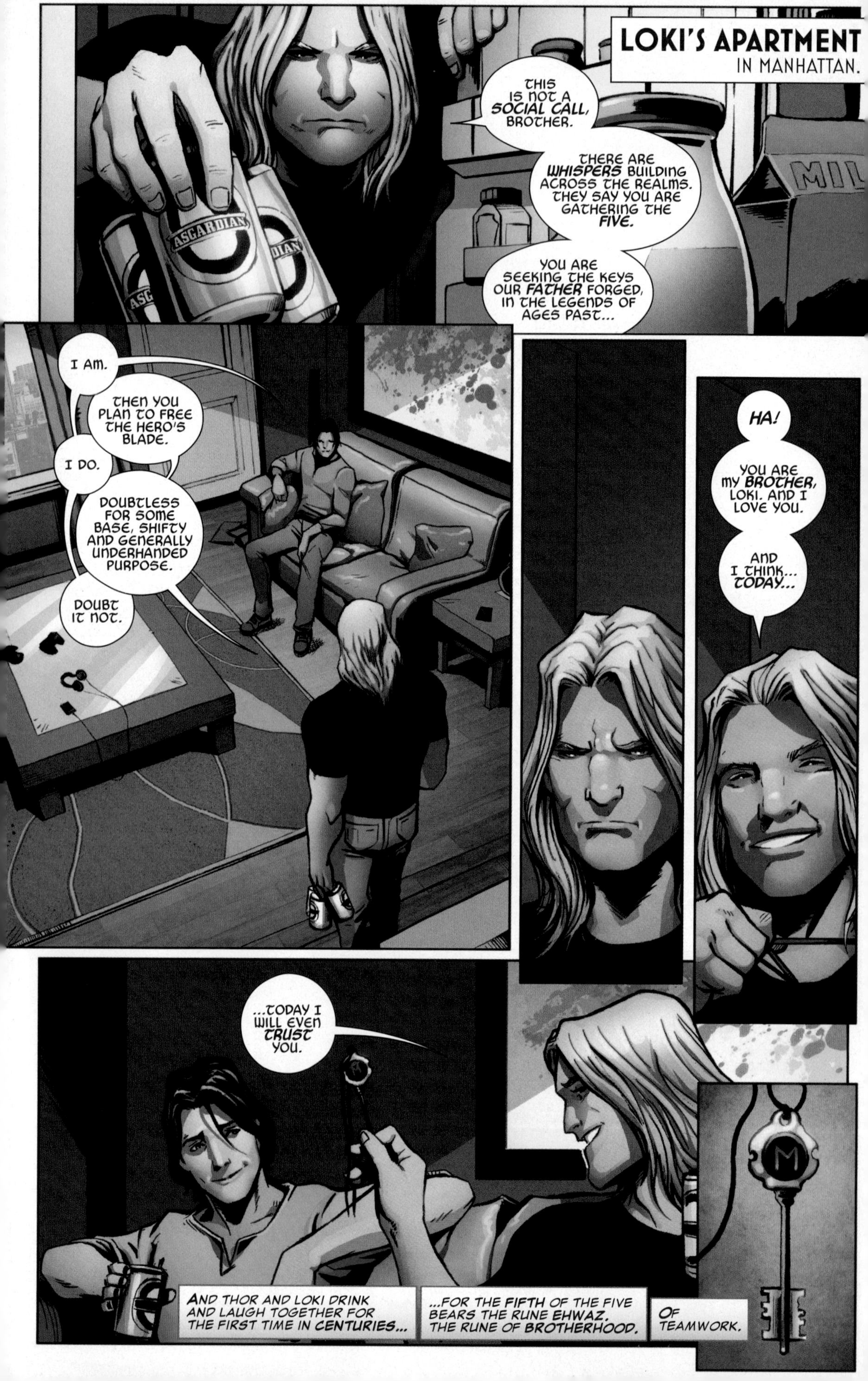
LOKI'S APARTMENT IN MANHATTAN.
THIS IS NOT A SOCIAL CALL, BROTHER.
THERE ARE WHISPERS BUILDING ACROSS THE REALMS. THEY SAY YOU ARE GATHERING THE FIVE.
YOU ARE SEEKING THE KEYS OUR FATHER FORGED, IN THE LEGENDS OF AGES PAST...
ASGARDIAN
I AM.
THEN YOU PLAN TO FREE THE HERO'S BLADE.
I DO.
DOUBTLESS FOR SOME BASE, SHIFTY AND GENERALLY UNDERHANDED PURPOSE.
DOUBT IT NOT.
HA!
YOU ARE MY BROTHER, LOKI. AND I LOVE YOU.
AND I THINK... TODAY...
...TODAY I WILL EVEN TRUST YOU.
AND THOR AND LOKI DRINK AND LAUGH TOGETHER FOR THE FIRST TIME IN CENTURIES...
...FOR THE FIFTH OF THE FIVE BEARS THE RUNE EHWAZ, THE RUNE OF BROTHERHOOD.
OF TEAMWORK.

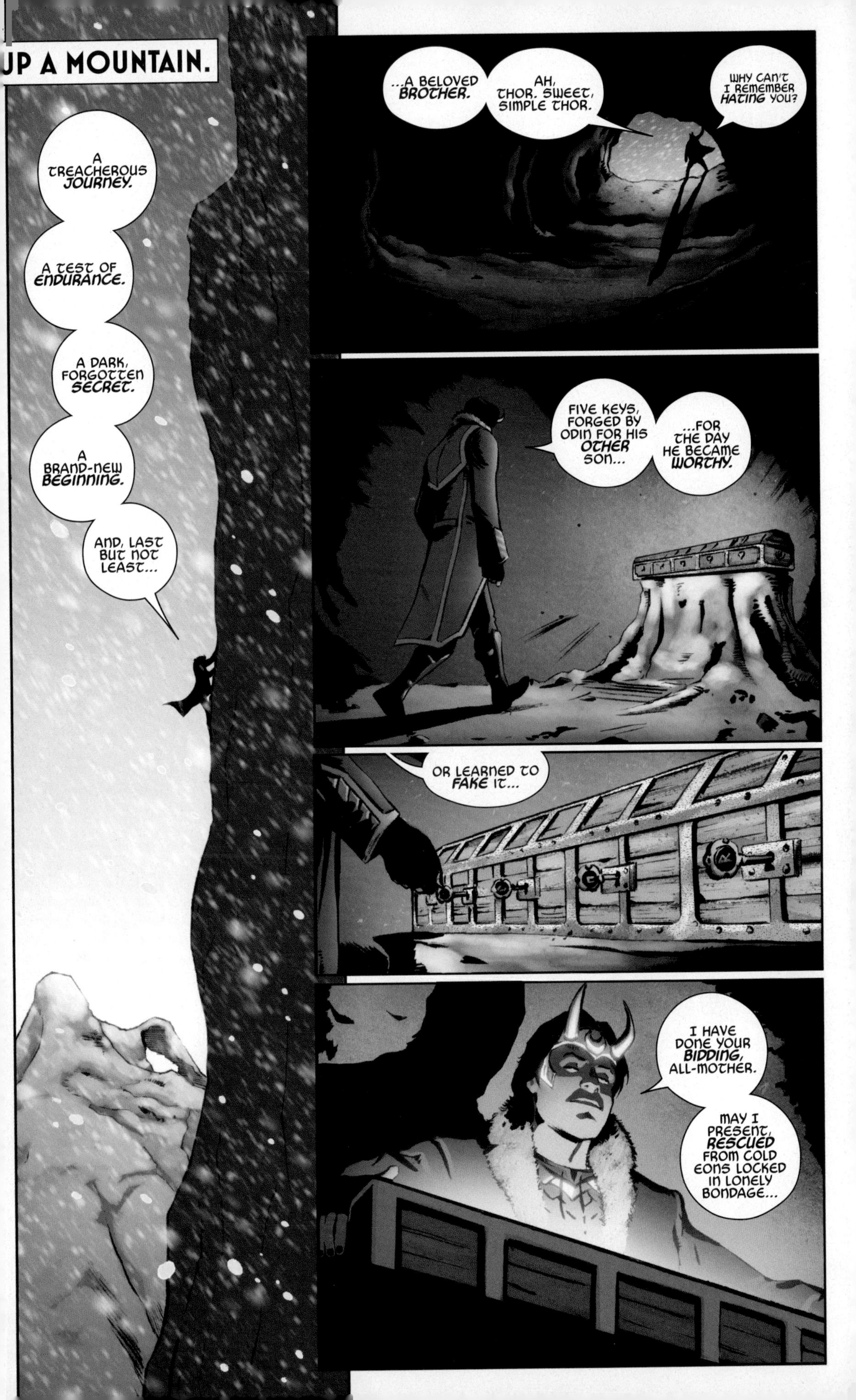
UP A MOUNTAIN.
A TREACHEROUS JOURNEY.
A TEST OF ENDURANCE.
A DARK, FORGOTTEN SECRET.
A BRAND-NEW BEGINNING.
AND, LAST BUT NOT LEAST...
...A BELOVED BROTHER.
AH, THOR. SWEET, SIMPLE THOR.
WHY CAN'T I REMEMBER HATING YOU?
FIVE KEYS, FORGED BY ODIN FOR HIS OTHER SON...
...FOR THE DAY HE BECAME WORTHY.
OR LEARNED TO FAKE IT...
I HAVE DONE YOUR BIDDING, ALL-MOTHER.
MAY I PRESENT, RESCUED FROM COLD EONS LOCKED IN LONELY BONDAGE...

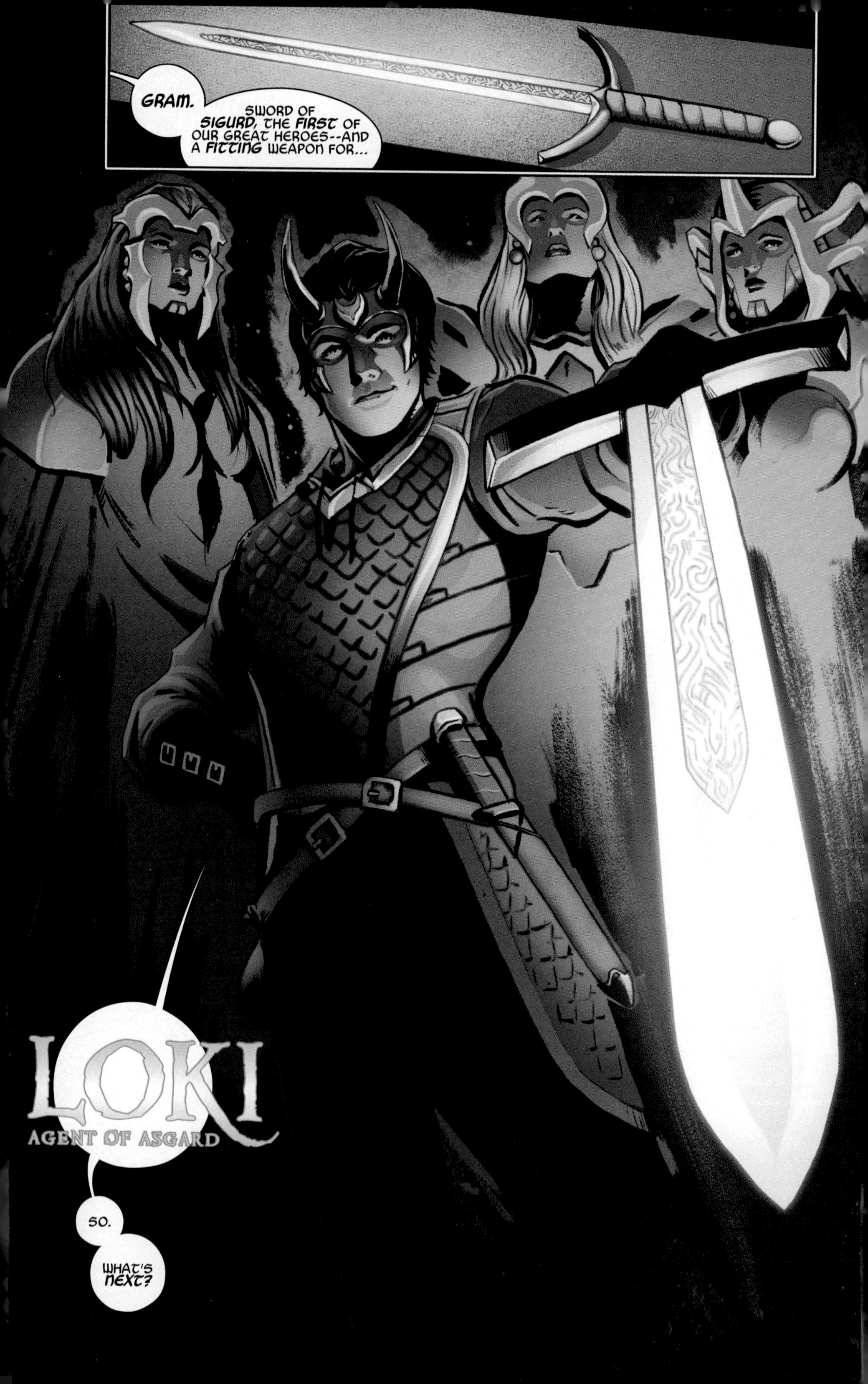
GRAM.
SWORD OF SIGURD, THE FIRST OF OUR GREAT HEROES--AND A FITTING WEAPON FOR...
LOKI
AGENT OF ASGARD
SO.
WHAT'S NEXT?

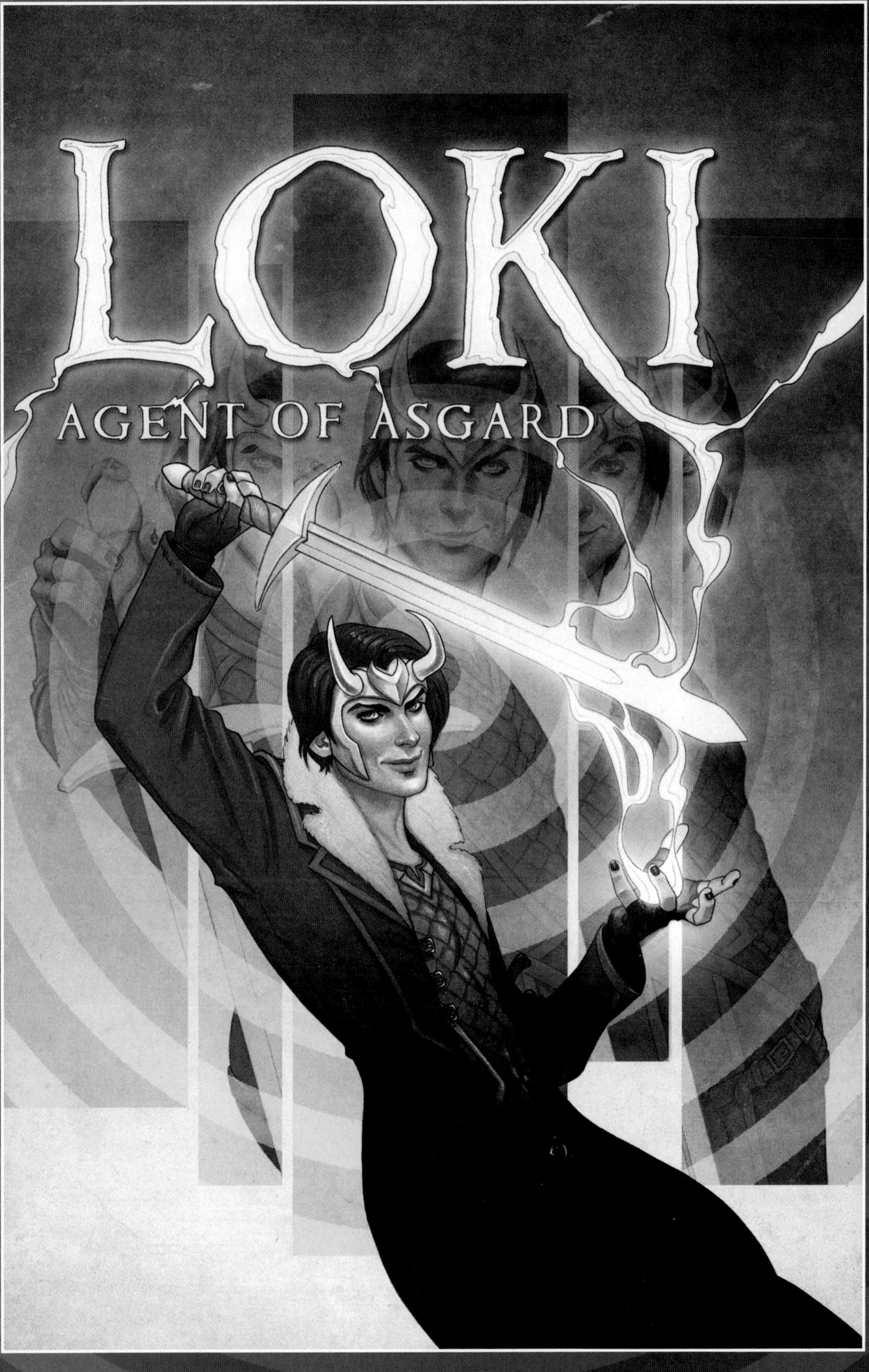
LOKI
AGENT OF ASGARD

LOKI: AGENT OF ASGARD #1

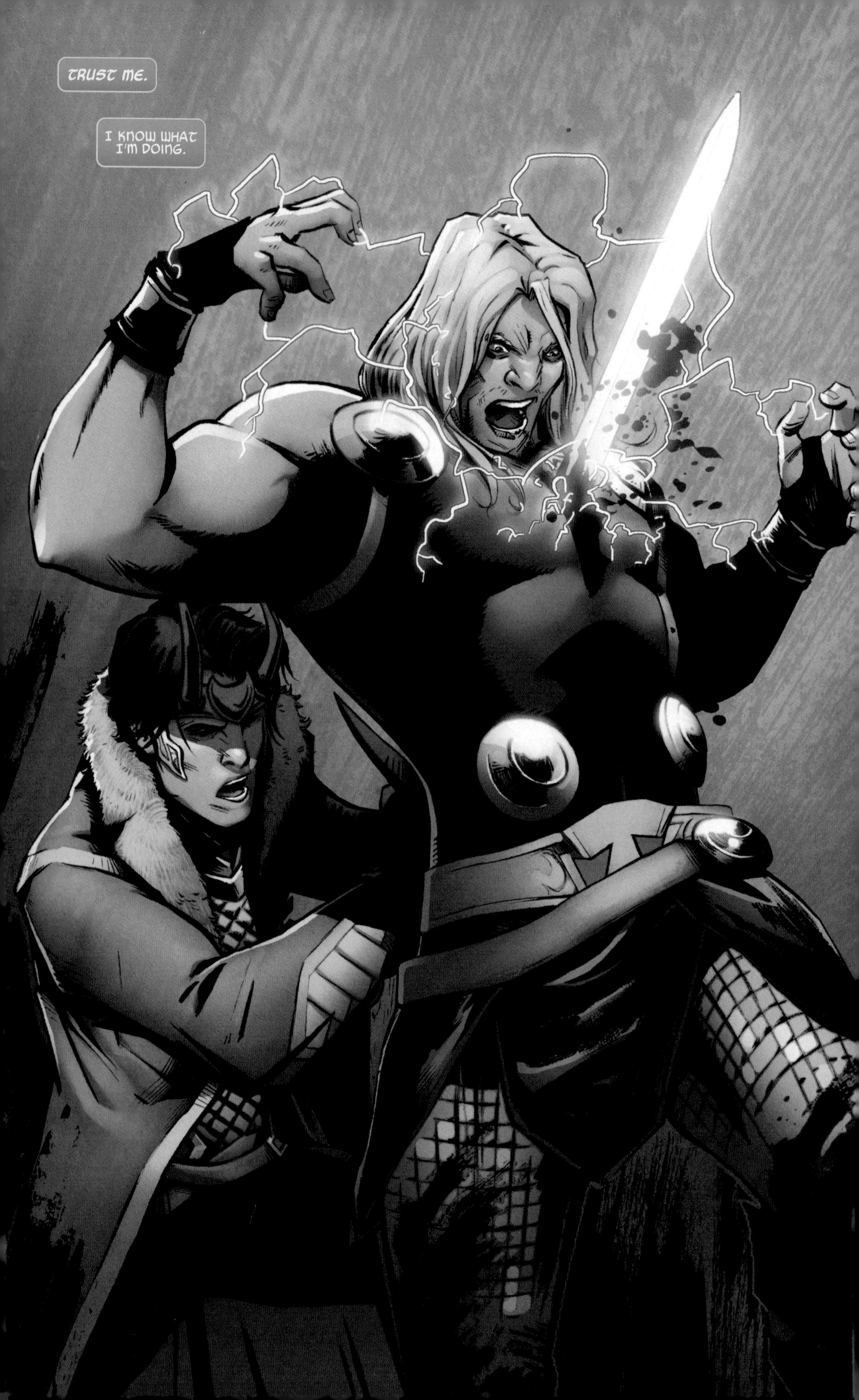
TRUST ME.
I KNOW WHAT I'M DOING.

THIS IS THE STORY OF LOKI.

ADOPTED ON THE BATTLEFIELD BY ODIN, KING OF ASGARD, LOKI WAS THE FOSTER BROTHER OF THOR. THEY DIDN'T ALWAYS GET ALONG.

ADMITTEDLY, THAT WAS BECAUSE LOKI BECAME INVOLVED IN INCREASINGLY WICKED SCHEMES OVER THE LONG CENTURIES, UNTIL EVENTUALLY, HE WAS KNOWN BY ALL AS THE GOD OF EVIL.

AND HE WAS TRAPPED BY THAT DEFINITION – SPIRALING DEEPER INTO INFAMY WITH EACH NEW MISDEED, UNABLE TO ESCAPE HIS ROLE, UNABLE TO ESCAPE HIMSELF. DOOMED TO NEVER BE ANYTHING BUT LOKI – LOKI THE BAD SON, LOKI THE VILLAIN – UNTIL THE DAY HE DIED.

SO...HE DIED.

WHICH WAS, OF COURSE, HIS GREATEST SCHEME OF ALL.

FOR SOON HE WAS REBORN INTO A NEW, YOUTHFUL BODY, FREE TO CHOOSE HIS OWN FATE. WITH THE SWORD OF ASGARD'S EARLIEST HERO IN HIS HAND AND MISSIONS FROM THE ALL-MOTHER, RULING TRIUMVIRATE OF ASGARDIA, TO HELP POLISH HIS SPARKLING NEW REPUTATION.

SO OBVIOUSLY, AFTER ALL THAT, HE WOULDN'T JUST STAB HIS BROTHER RIGHT IN THE BACK.

SURELY.

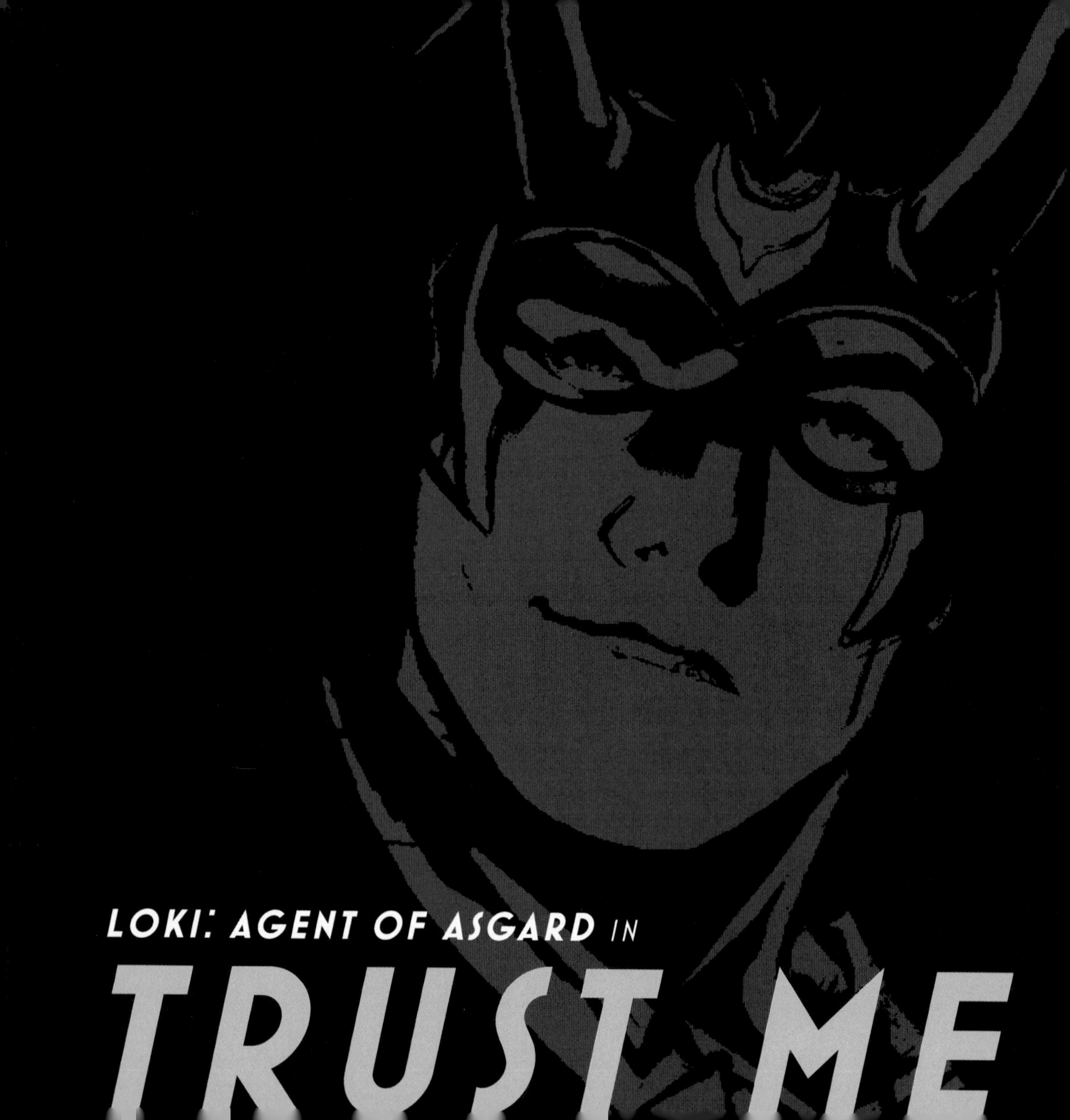
LOKI: AGENT OF ASGARD IN
TRUST ME

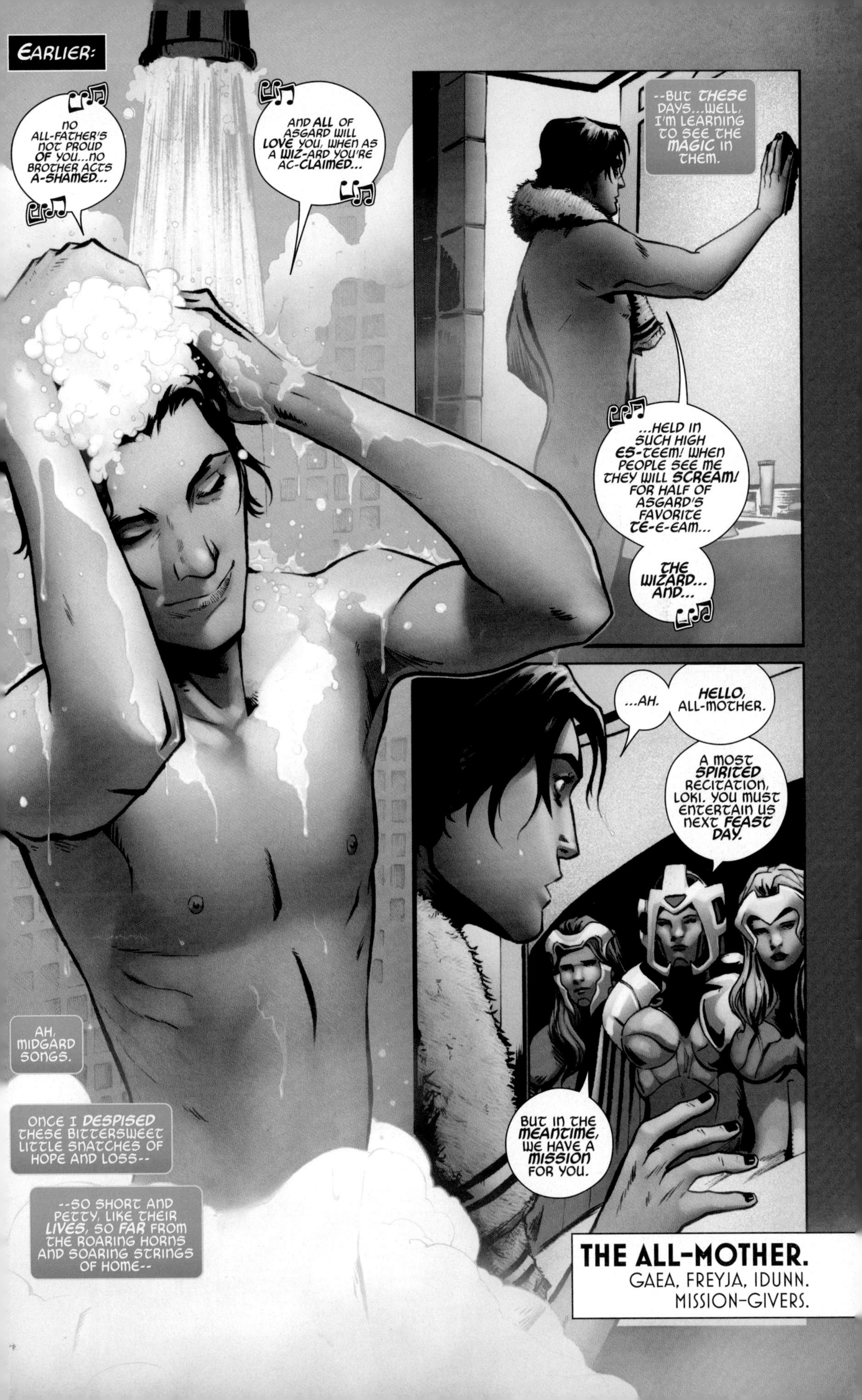
EARLIER:
NO ALL-FATHER'S NOT PROUD OF YOU...NO BROTHER ACTS A-SHAMED...
AND ALL OF ASGARD WILL LOVE YOU, WHEN AS A WIZ-ARD YOU'RE AC-CLAIMED...
--BUT THESE DAYS...WELL, I'M LEARNING TO SEE THE MAGIC IN THEM.
...HELD IN SUCH HIGH ES-TEEM! WHEN PEOPLE SEE ME THEY WILL SCREAM! FOR HALF OF ASGARD'S FAVORITE TE-E-EAM...
THE WIZARD... AND...
...AH.
HELLO, ALL-MOTHER.
A MOST SPIRITED RECITATION, LOKI. YOU MUST ENTERTAIN US NEXT FEAST DAY.
BUT IN THE MEANTIME, WE HAVE A MISSION FOR YOU.
AH, MIDGARD SONGS.
ONCE I DESPISED THESE BITTERSWEET LITTLE SNATCHES OF HOPE AND LOSS--
--SO SHORT AND PETTY, LIKE THEIR LIVES, SO FAR FROM THE ROARING HORNS AND SOARING STRINGS OF HOME--
THE ALL-MOTHER.
GAEA, FREYJA, IDUNN.
MISSION-GIVERS.

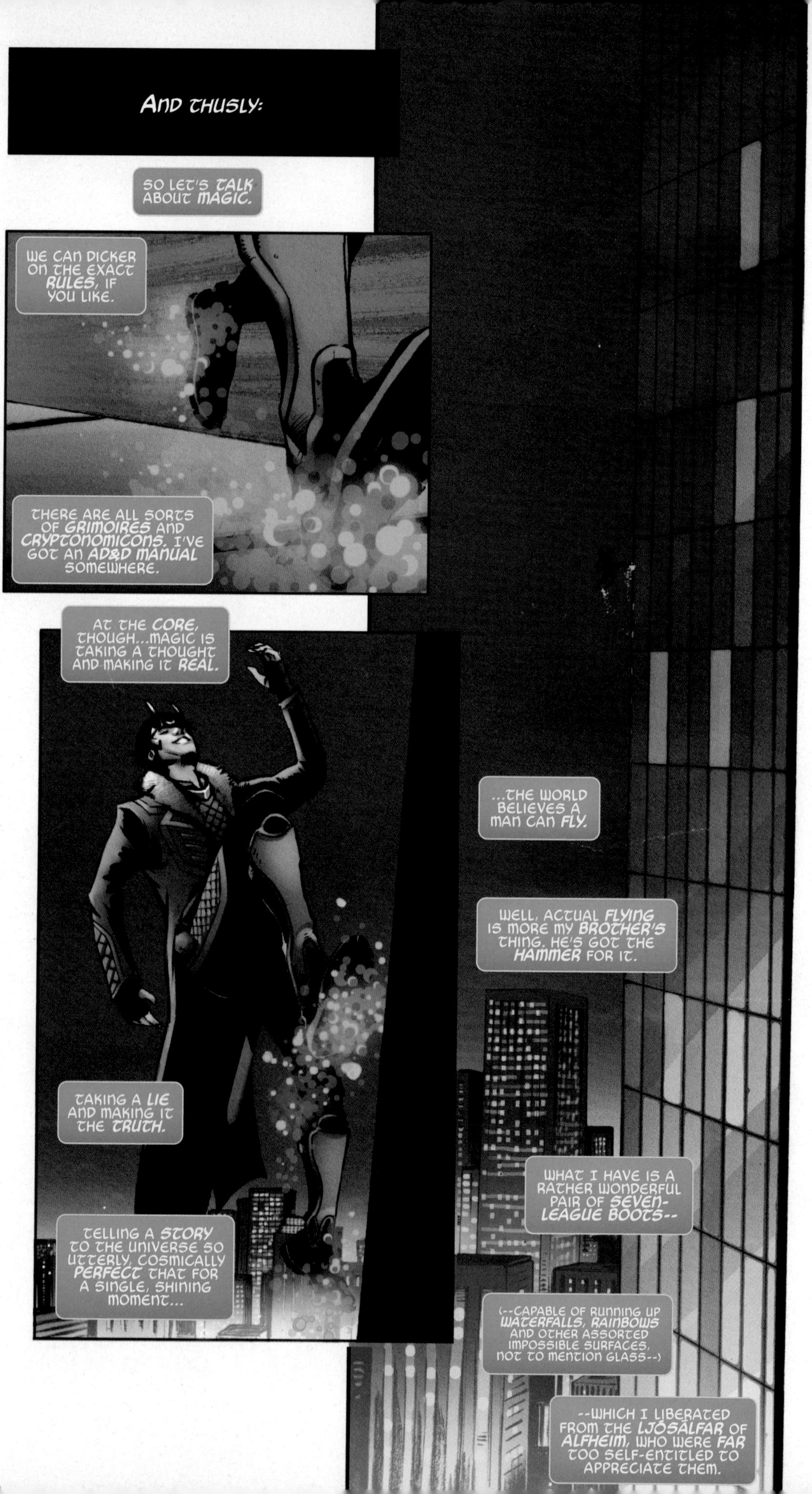
AND THUSLY:
SO LET'S TALK ABOUT MAGIC.
WE CAN DICKER ON THE EXACT RULES, IF YOU LIKE.
THERE ARE ALL SORTS OF GRIMOIRES AND CRYPTONOMICONS. I'VE GOT AN AD&D MANUAL SOMEWHERE.
AT THE CORE, THOUGH...MAGIC IS TAKING A THOUGHT AND MAKING IT REAL.
TAKING A LIE AND MAKING IT THE TRUTH.
TELLING A STORY TO THE UNIVERSE SO UTTERLY, COSMICALLY PERFECT THAT FOR A SINGLE, SHINING MOMENT...
...THE WORLD BELIEVES A MAN CAN FLY.
WELL, ACTUAL FLYING IS MORE MY BROTHER'S THING. HE'S GOT THE HAMMER FOR IT.
WHAT I HAVE IS A RATHER WONDERFUL PAIR OF SEVEN-LEAGUE BOOTS--
(--CAPABLE OF RUNNING UP WATERFALLS, RAINBOWS AND OTHER ASSORTED IMPOSSIBLE SURFACES, NOT TO MENTION GLASS--)
--WHICH I LIBERATED FROM THE LJÓSÁLFAR OF ALFHEIM, WHO WERE FAR TOO SELF-ENTITLED TO APPRECIATE THEM.

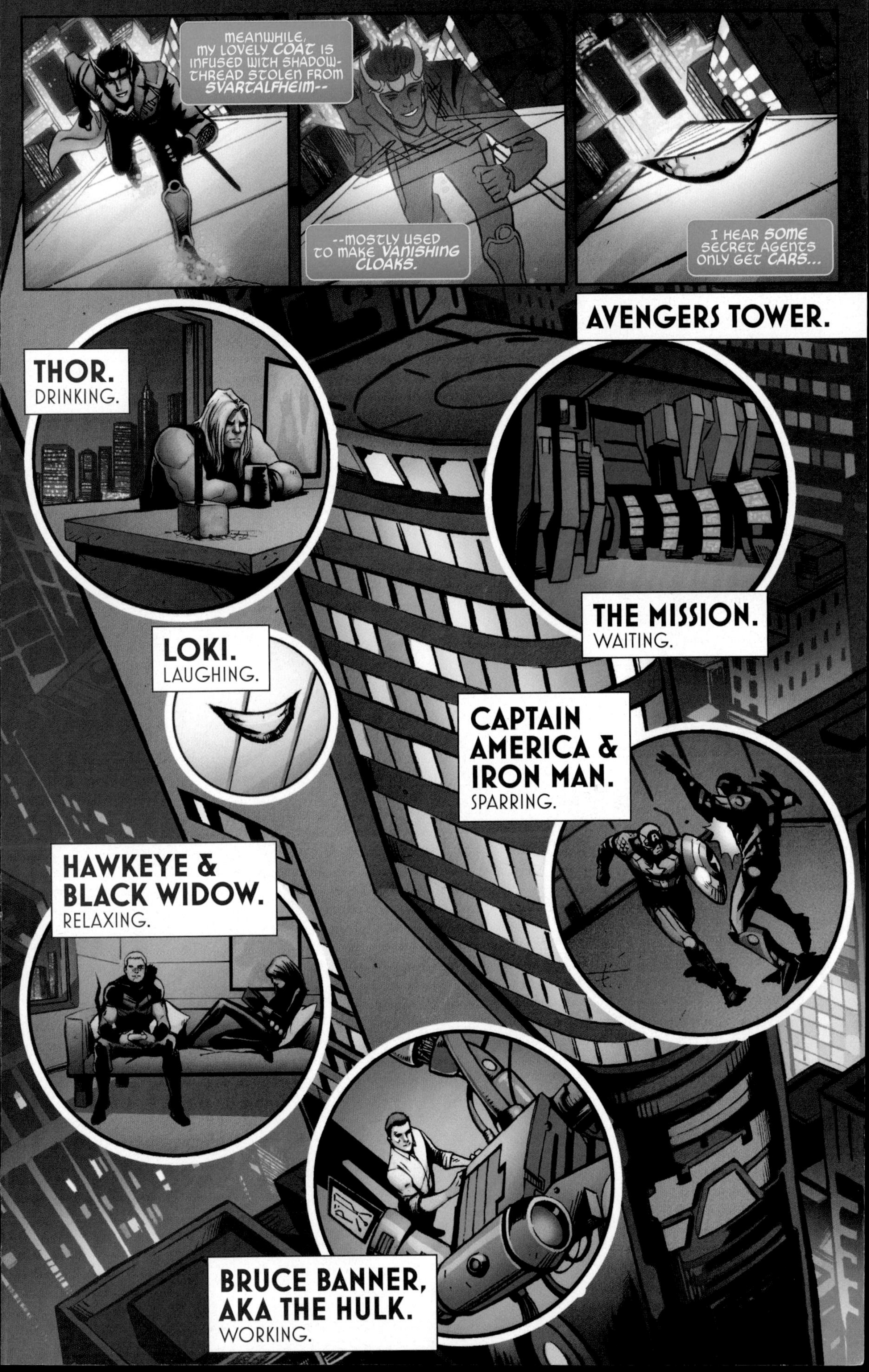
MEANWHILE, MY LOVELY COAT IS INFUSED WITH SHADOW-THREAD STOLEN FROM SVARTALFHEIM--
--MOSTLY USED TO MAKE VANISHING CLOAKS.
I HEAR SOME SECRET AGENTS ONLY GET CARS...
AVENGERS TOWER.
THOR. DRINKING.
THE MISSION. WAITING.
LOKI. LAUGHING.
CAPTAIN AMERICA & IRON MAN. SPARRING.
HAWKEYE & BLACK WIDOW. RELAXING.
BRUCE BANNER, AKA THE HULK. WORKING.

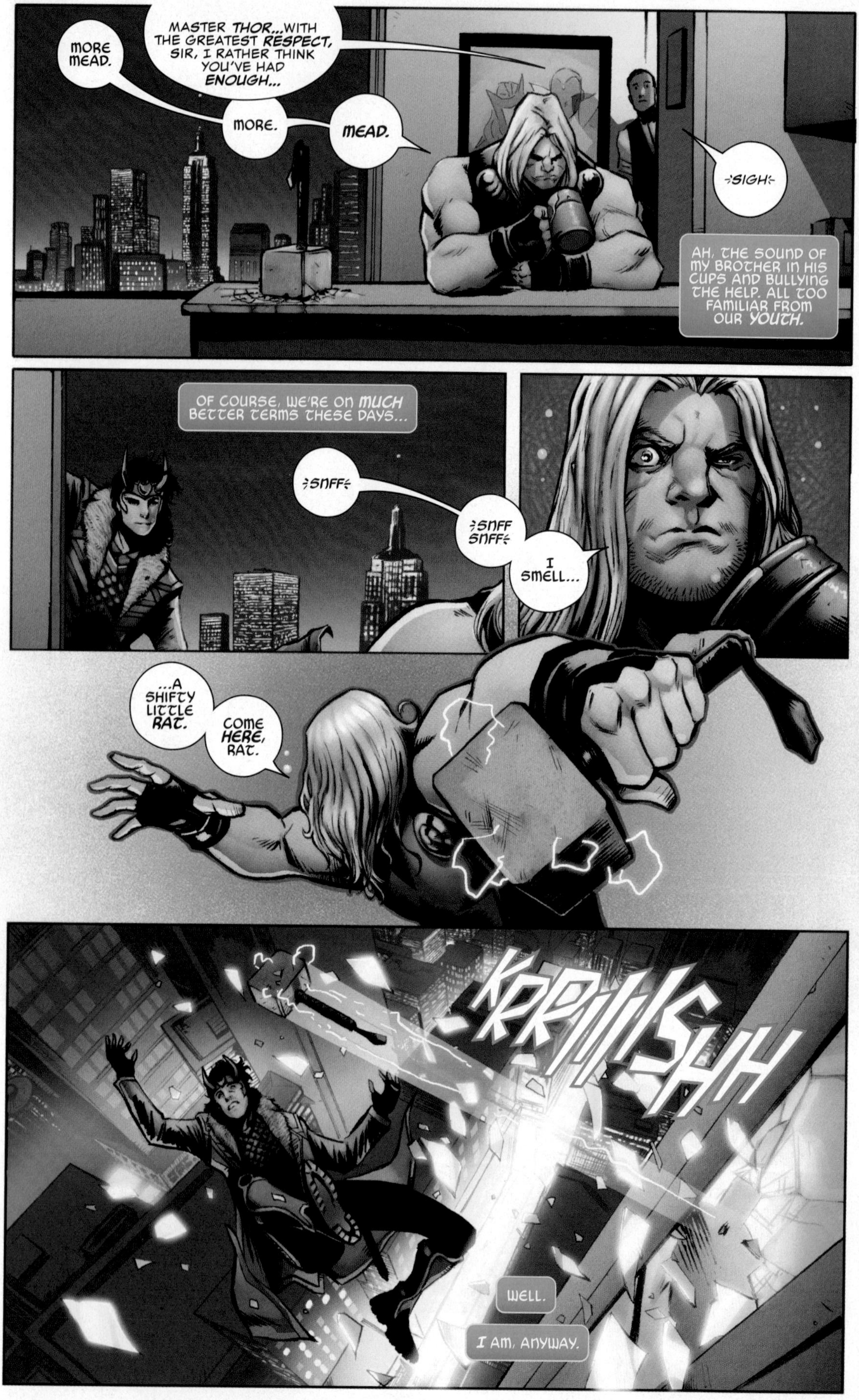
MORE MEAD.
MASTER THOR...WITH THE GREATEST RESPECT, SIR, I RATHER THINK YOU'VE HAD ENOUGH...
MORE.
MEAD.
SIGH
AH, THE SOUND OF MY BROTHER IN HIS CUPS AND BULLYING THE HELP. ALL TOO FAMILIAR FROM OUR YOUTH.
OF COURSE, WE'RE ON MUCH BETTER TERMS THESE DAYS...
SNFF
SNFF SNFF
I SMELL...
...A SHIFTY LITTLE RAT.
COME HERE, RAT.
KRRUUSHH
WELL.
I AM, ANYWAY.

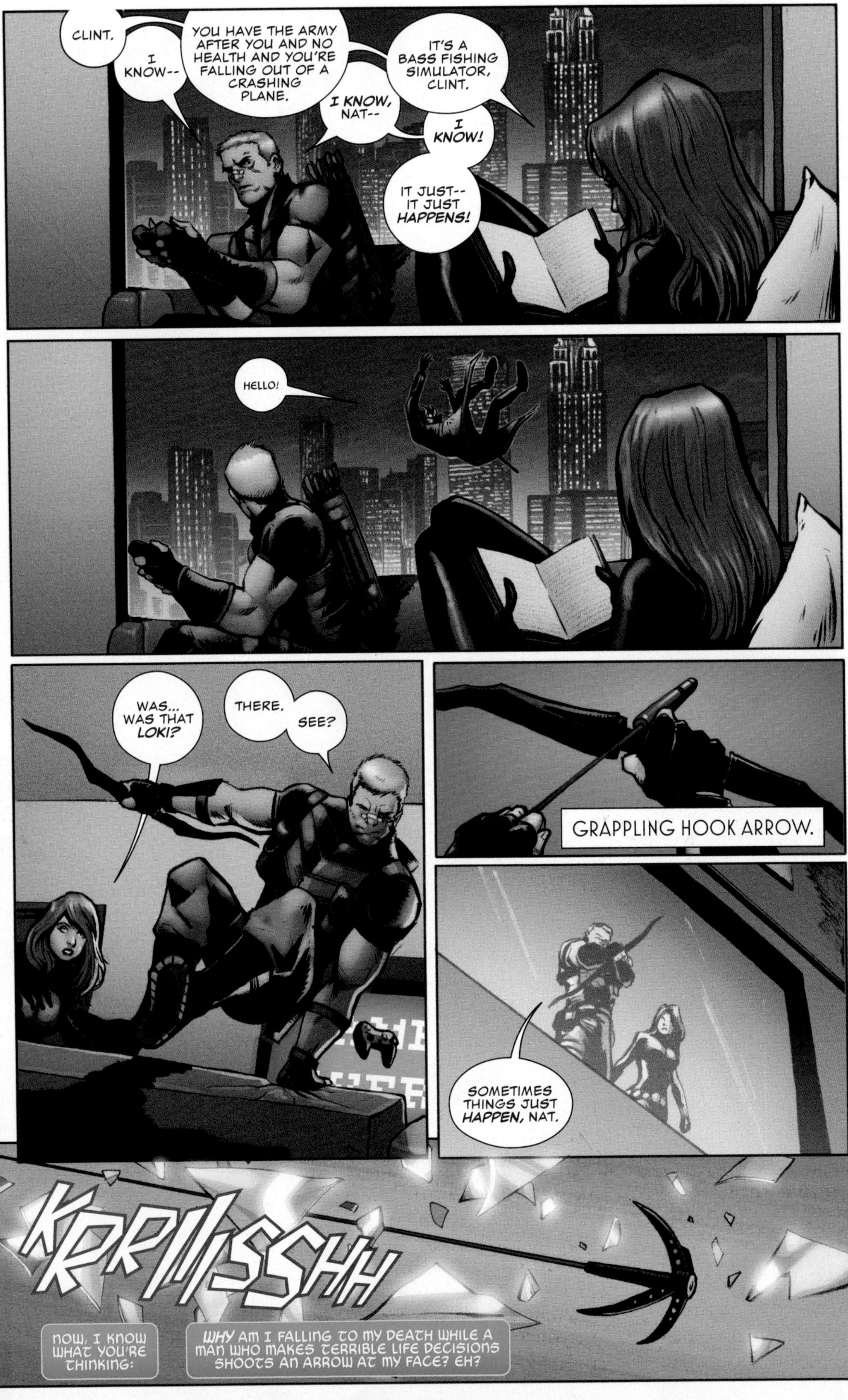
CLINT.
I KNOW--
YOU HAVE THE ARMY AFTER YOU AND NO HEALTH AND YOU'RE FALLING OUT OF A CRASHING PLANE.
I KNOW, NAT--
IT'S A BASS FISHING SIMULATOR, CLINT.
I KNOW!
IT JUST-- IT JUST HAPPENS!
HELLO!
WAS... WAS THAT LOKI?
THERE.
SEE?
GRAPPLING HOOK ARROW.
SOMETIMES THINGS JUST HAPPEN, NAT.
KRRUSSHH
NOW, I KNOW WHAT YOU'RE THINKING:
WHY AM I FALLING TO MY DEATH WHILE A MAN WHO MAKES TERRIBLE LIFE DECISIONS SHOOTS AN ARROW AT MY FACE? EH?

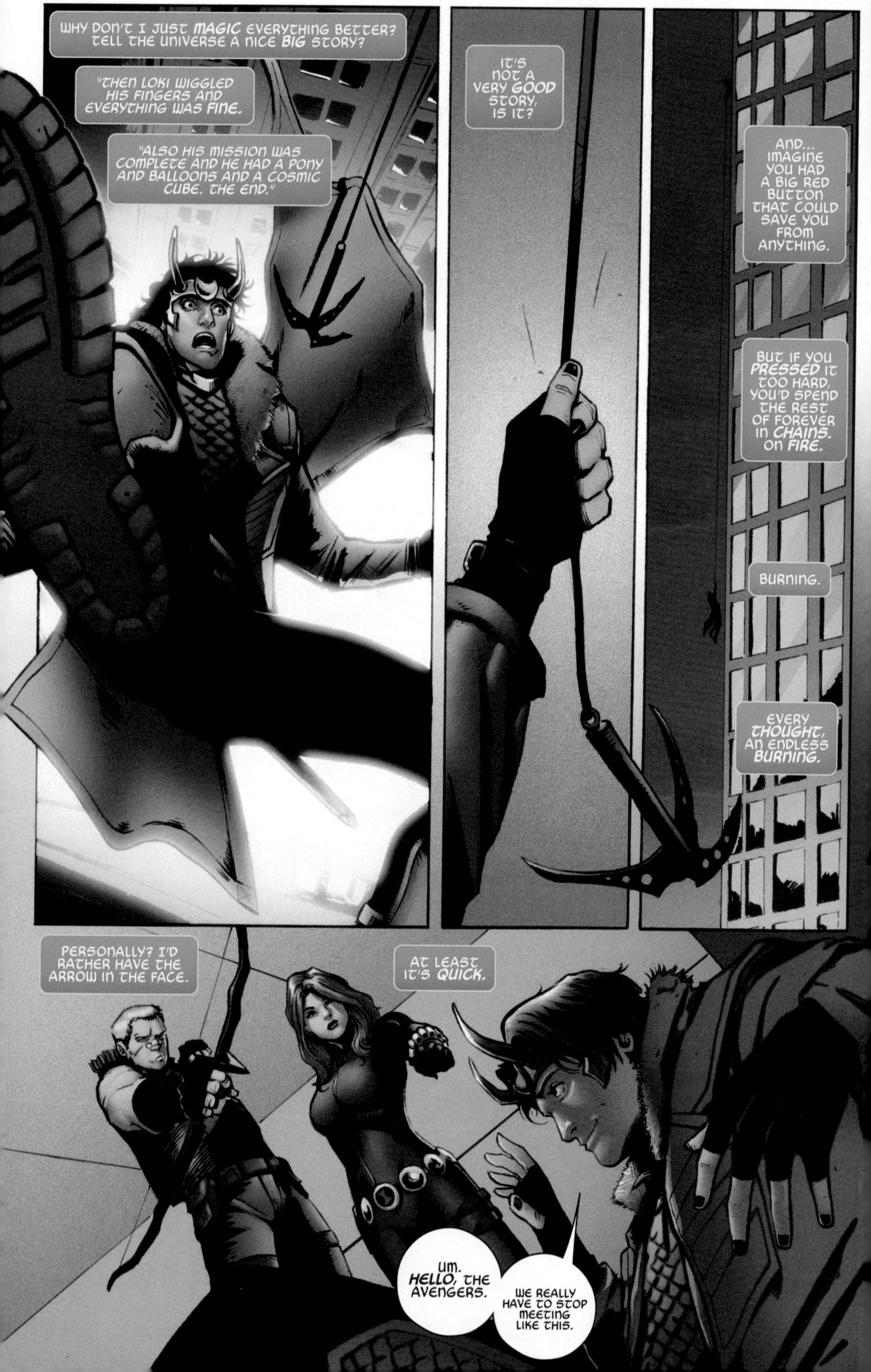
WHY DON'T I JUST MAGIC EVERYTHING BETTER? TELL THE UNIVERSE A NICE BIG STORY?
"THEN LOKI WIGGLED HIS FINGERS AND EVERYTHING WAS FINE.
"ALSO HIS MISSION WAS COMPLETE AND HE HAD A PONY AND BALLOONS AND A COSMIC CUBE. THE END."
IT'S NOT A VERY GOOD STORY, IS IT?
AND... IMAGINE YOU HAD A BIG RED BUTTON THAT COULD SAVE YOU FROM ANYTHING.
BUT IF YOU PRESSED IT TOO HARD, YOU'D SPEND THE REST OF FOREVER IN CHAINS. ON FIRE.
BURNING.
EVERY THOUGHT, AN ENDLESS BURNING.
PERSONALLY? I'D RATHER HAVE THE ARROW IN THE FACE.
AT LEAST IT'S QUICK.
UM. HELLO, THE AVENGERS.
WE REALLY HAVE TO STOP MEETING LIKE THIS.

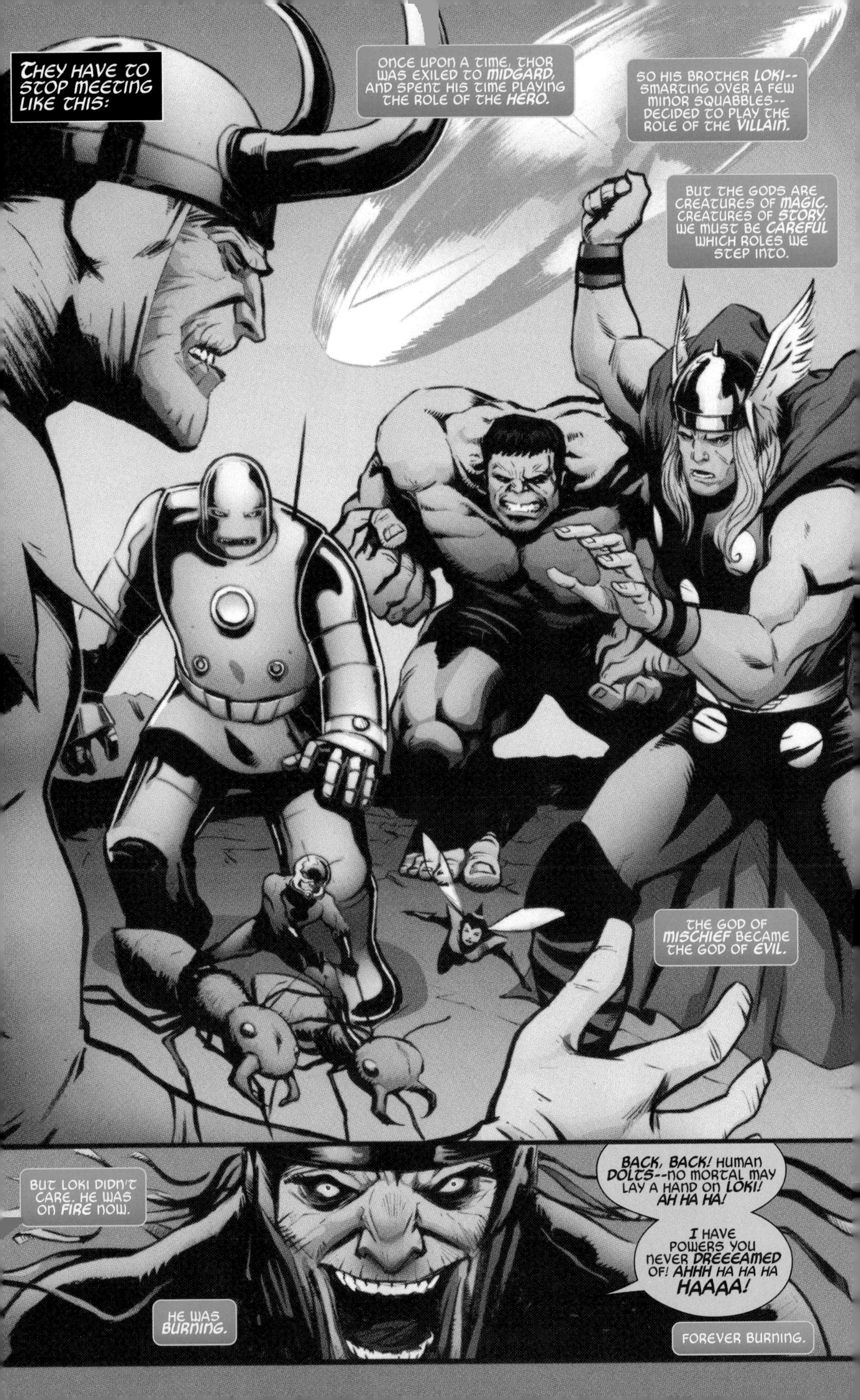
THEY HAVE TO STOP MEETING LIKE THIS:
ONCE UPON A TIME, THOR WAS EXILED TO MIDGARD, AND SPENT HIS TIME PLAYING THE ROLE OF THE HERO.
SO HIS BROTHER LOKI--SMARTING OVER A FEW MINOR SQUABBLES--DECIDED TO PLAY THE ROLE OF THE VILLAIN.
BUT THE GODS ARE CREATURES OF MAGIC. CREATURES OF STORY. WE MUST BE CAREFUL WHICH ROLES WE STEP INTO.
THE GOD OF MISCHIEF BECAME THE GOD OF EVIL.
BUT LOKI DIDN'T CARE. HE WAS ON FIRE NOW.
BACK, BACK! HUMAN DOLTS--NO MORTAL MAY LAY A HAND ON LOKI! AH HA HA!
I HAVE POWERS YOU NEVER DREEEAMED OF! AHHH HA HA HA HAAAA!
HE WAS BURNING.
FOREVER BURNING.

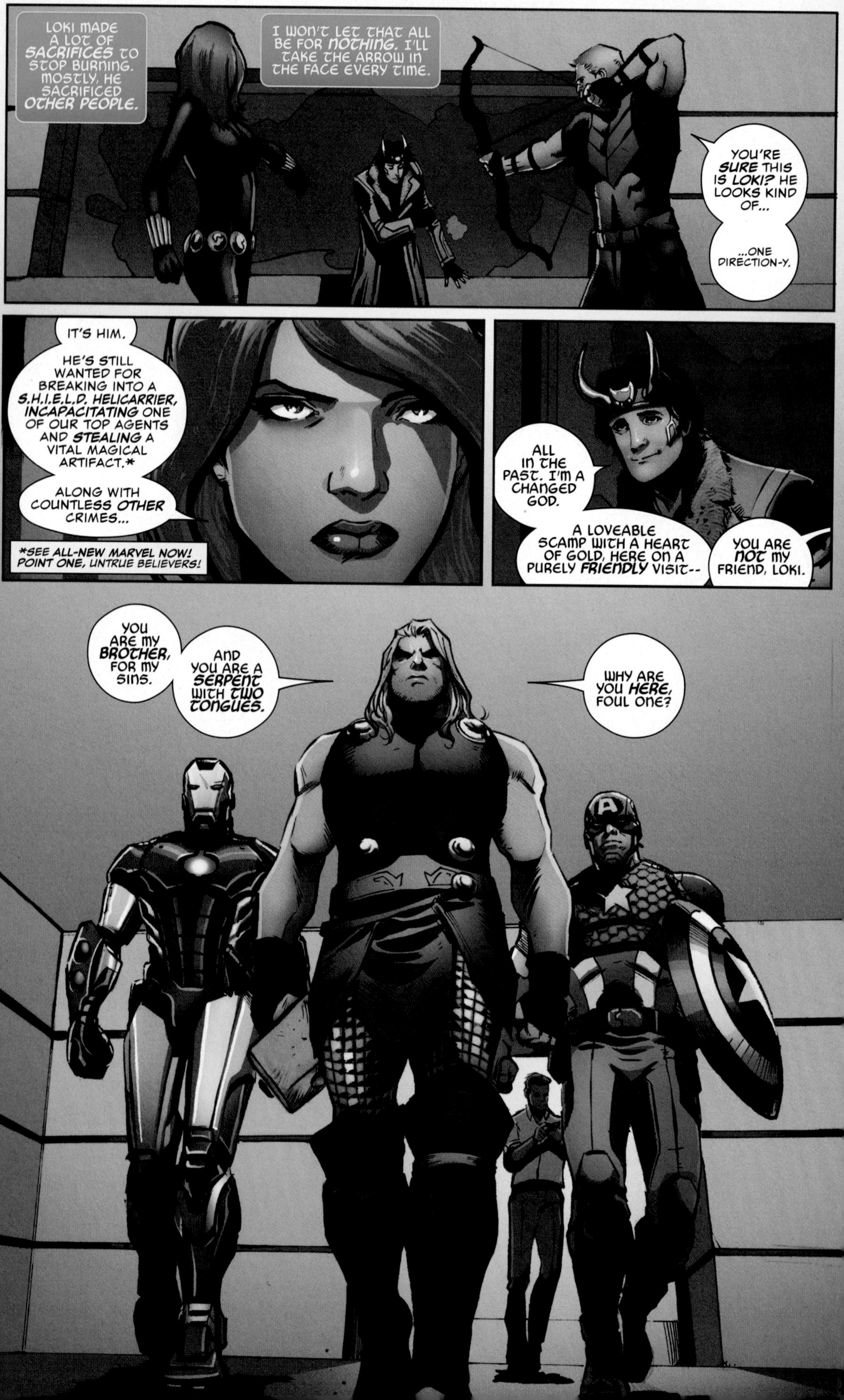

LOKI MADE A LOT OF SACRIFICES TO STOP BURNING. MOSTLY, HE SACRIFICED OTHER PEOPLE.
I WON'T LET THAT ALL BE FOR NOTHING. I'LL TAKE THE ARROW IN THE FACE EVERY TIME.
YOU'RE SURE THIS IS LOKI? HE LOOKS KIND OF...
...ONE DIRECTION-Y.
IT'S HIM.
HE'S STILL WANTED FOR BREAKING INTO A S.H.I.E.L.D. HELICARRIER, INCAPACITATING ONE OF OUR TOP AGENTS AND STEALING A VITAL MAGICAL ARTIFACT.*
ALONG WITH COUNTLESS OTHER CRIMES...
*SEE ALL-NEW MARVEL NOW! POINT ONE, UNTRUE BELIEVERS!
ALL IN THE PAST. I'M A CHANGED GOD.
A LOVEABLE SCAMP WITH A HEART OF GOLD, HERE ON A PURELY FRIENDLY VISIT--
YOU ARE NOT MY FRIEND, LOKI.
YOU ARE MY BROTHER, FOR MY SINS.
AND YOU ARE A SERPENT WITH TWO TONGUES.
WHY ARE YOU HERE, FOUL ONE?

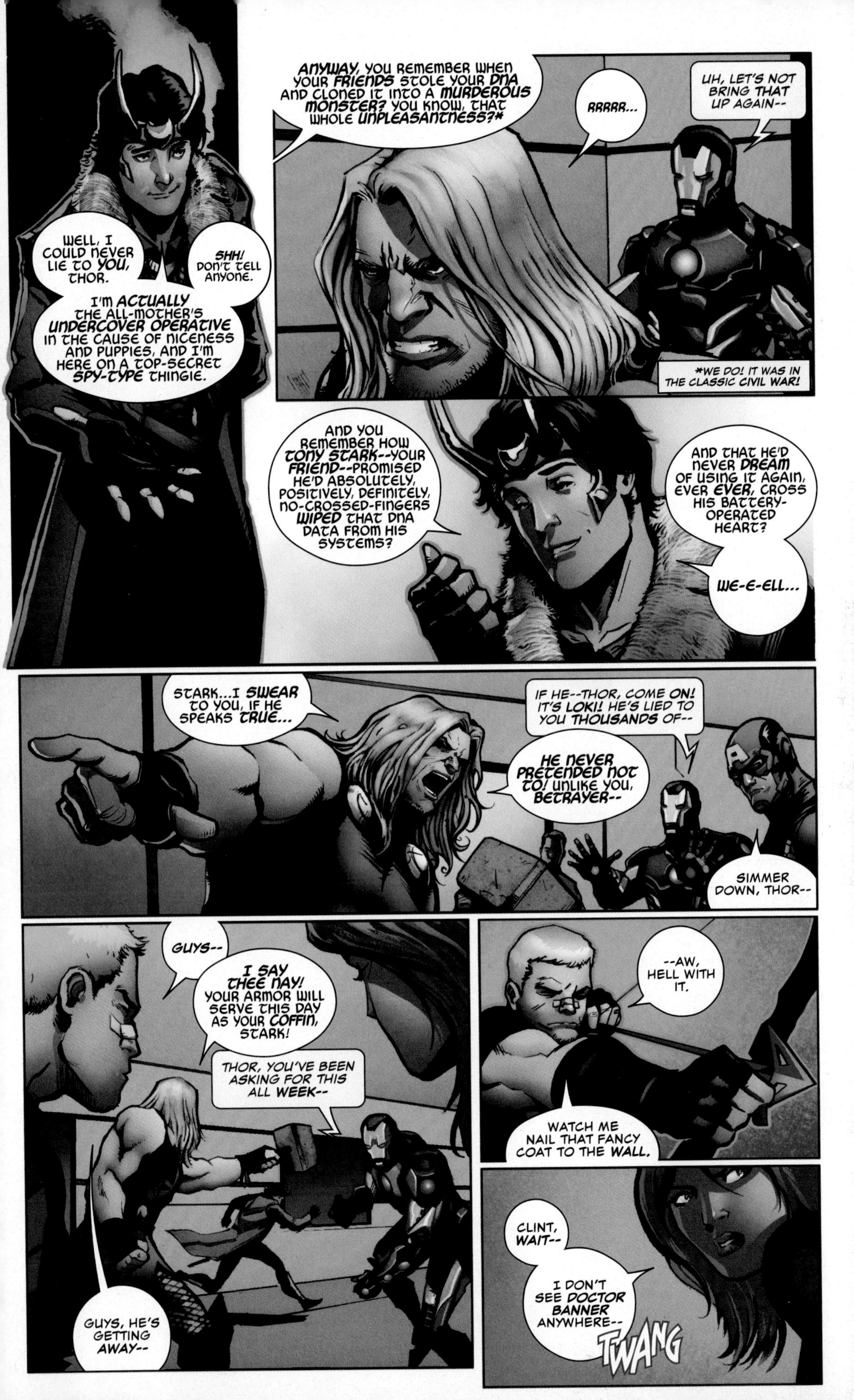
ANYWAY, YOU REMEMBER WHEN YOUR FRIENDS STOLE YOUR DNA AND CLONED IT INTO A MURDEROUS MONSTER? YOU KNOW, THAT WHOLE UNPLEASANTNESS?*
RRRRR...
UH, LET'S NOT BRING THAT UP AGAIN--
*WE DO! IT WAS IN THE CLASSIC CIVIL WAR!
WELL, I COULD NEVER LIE TO YOU, THOR.
SHH! DON'T TELL ANYONE.
I'M ACTUALLY THE ALL-MOTHER'S UNDERCOVER OPERATIVE IN THE CAUSE OF NICENESS AND PUPPIES, AND I'M HERE ON A TOP-SECRET SPY-TYPE THINGIE.
AND YOU REMEMBER HOW TONY STARK--YOUR FRIEND--PROMISED HE'D ABSOLUTELY, POSITIVELY, DEFINITELY, NO-CROSSED-FINGERS WIPED THAT DNA DATA FROM HIS SYSTEMS?
AND THAT HE'D NEVER DREAM OF USING IT AGAIN, EVER EVER, CROSS HIS BATTERY-OPERATED HEART?
WE-E-ELL...
STARK...I SWEAR TO YOU, IF HE SPEAKS TRUE...
IF HE--THOR, COME ON! IT'S LOKI! HE'S LIED TO YOU THOUSANDS OF--
HE NEVER PRETENDED NOT TO! UNLIKE YOU, BETRAYER--
SIMMER DOWN, THOR--
GUYS--
I SAY THEE NAY! YOUR ARMOR WILL SERVE THIS DAY AS YOUR COFFIN, STARK!
THOR, YOU'VE BEEN ASKING FOR THIS ALL WEEK--
GUYS, HE'S GETTING AWAY--
--AW, HELL WITH IT.
WATCH ME NAIL THAT FANCY COAT TO THE WALL.
CLINT, WAIT--
I DON'T SEE DOCTOR BANNER ANYWHERE--
TWANG

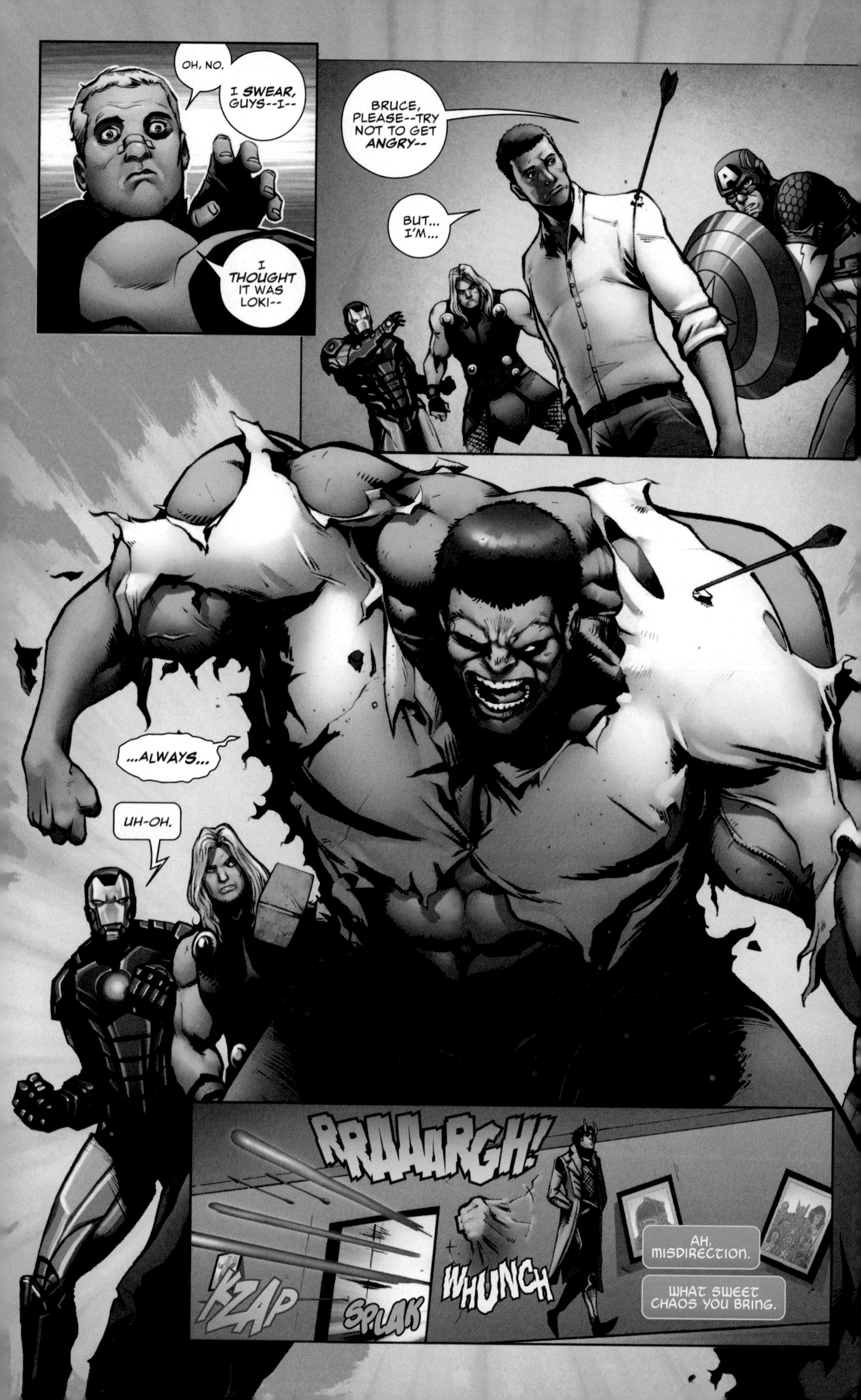

OH, NO.
I SWEAR, GUYS--I--
BRUCE, PLEASE--TRY NOT TO GET ANGRY--
BUT... I'M...
I THOUGHT IT WAS LOKI--
...ALWAYS...
UH-OH.
RRAAARGH!
KZAP
SPLAK
WHUNCH
AH, MISDIRECTION.
WHAT SWEET CHAOS YOU BRING.

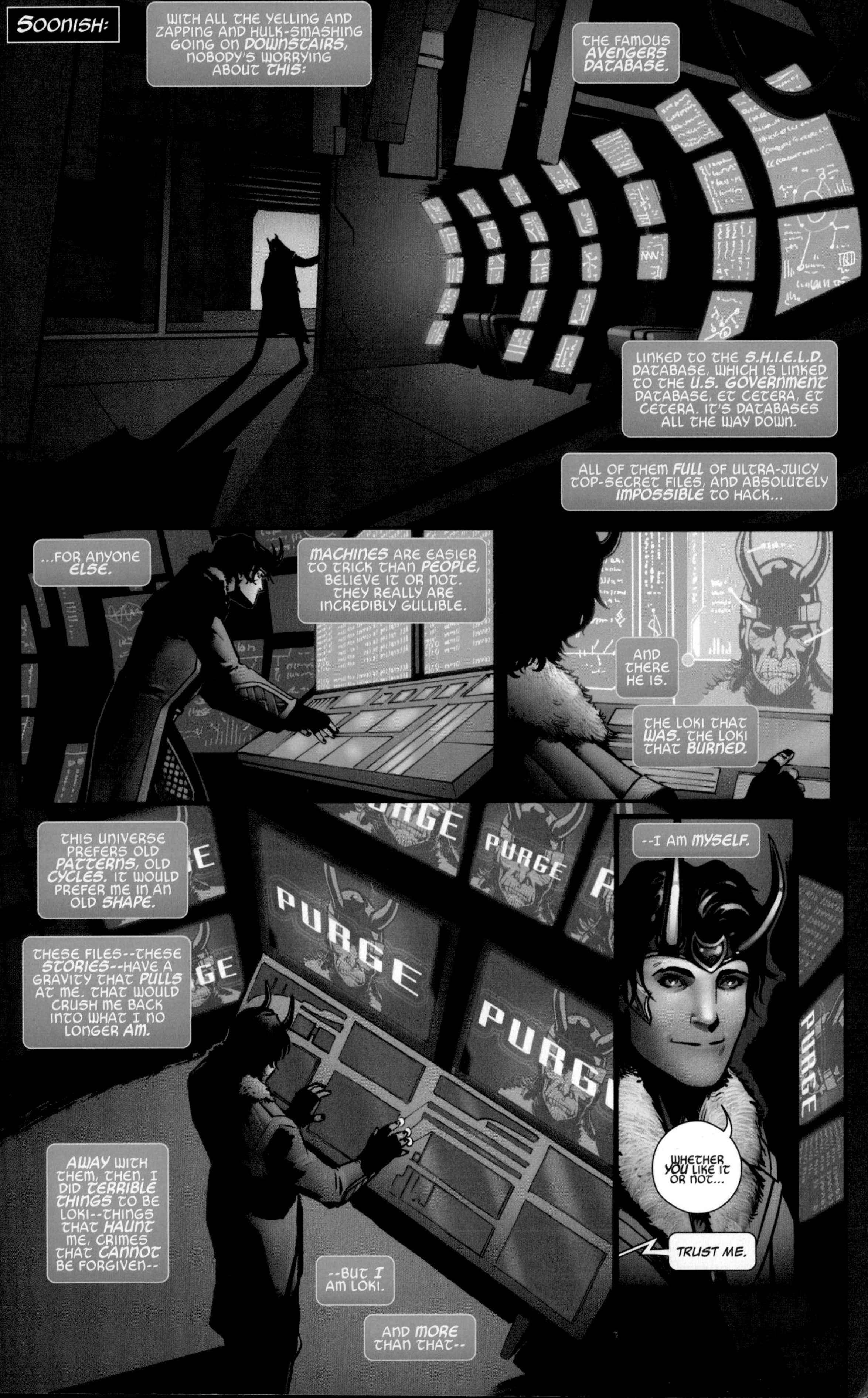
SOONISH:
WITH ALL THE YELLING AND ZAPPING AND HULK-SMASHING GOING ON DOWNSTAIRS, NOBODY'S WORRYING ABOUT THIS:
THE FAMOUS AVENGERS DATABASE.
LINKED TO THE S.H.I.E.L.D. DATABASE, WHICH IS LINKED TO THE U.S. GOVERNMENT DATABASE, ET CETERA, ET CETERA. IT'S DATABASES ALL THE WAY DOWN.
ALL OF THEM FULL OF ULTRA-JUICY TOP-SECRET FILES, AND ABSOLUTELY IMPOSSIBLE TO HACK...
...FOR ANYONE ELSE.
MACHINES ARE EASIER TO TRICK THAN PEOPLE, BELIEVE IT OR NOT. THEY REALLY ARE INCREDIBLY GULLIBLE.
AND THERE HE IS.
THE LOKI THAT WAS. THE LOKI THAT BURNED.
THIS UNIVERSE PREFERS OLD PATTERNS, OLD CYCLES. IT WOULD PREFER ME IN AN OLD SHAPE.
PURGE
THESE FILES--THESE STORIES--HAVE A GRAVITY THAT PULLS AT ME. THAT WOULD CRUSH ME BACK INTO WHAT I NO LONGER AM.
AWAY WITH THEM, THEN. I DID TERRIBLE THINGS TO BE LOKI--THINGS THAT HAUNT ME, CRIMES THAT CANNOT BE FORGIVEN--
--BUT I AM LOKI.
AND MORE THAN THAT--
--I AM MYSELF.
WHETHER YOU LIKE IT OR NOT...
TRUST ME.

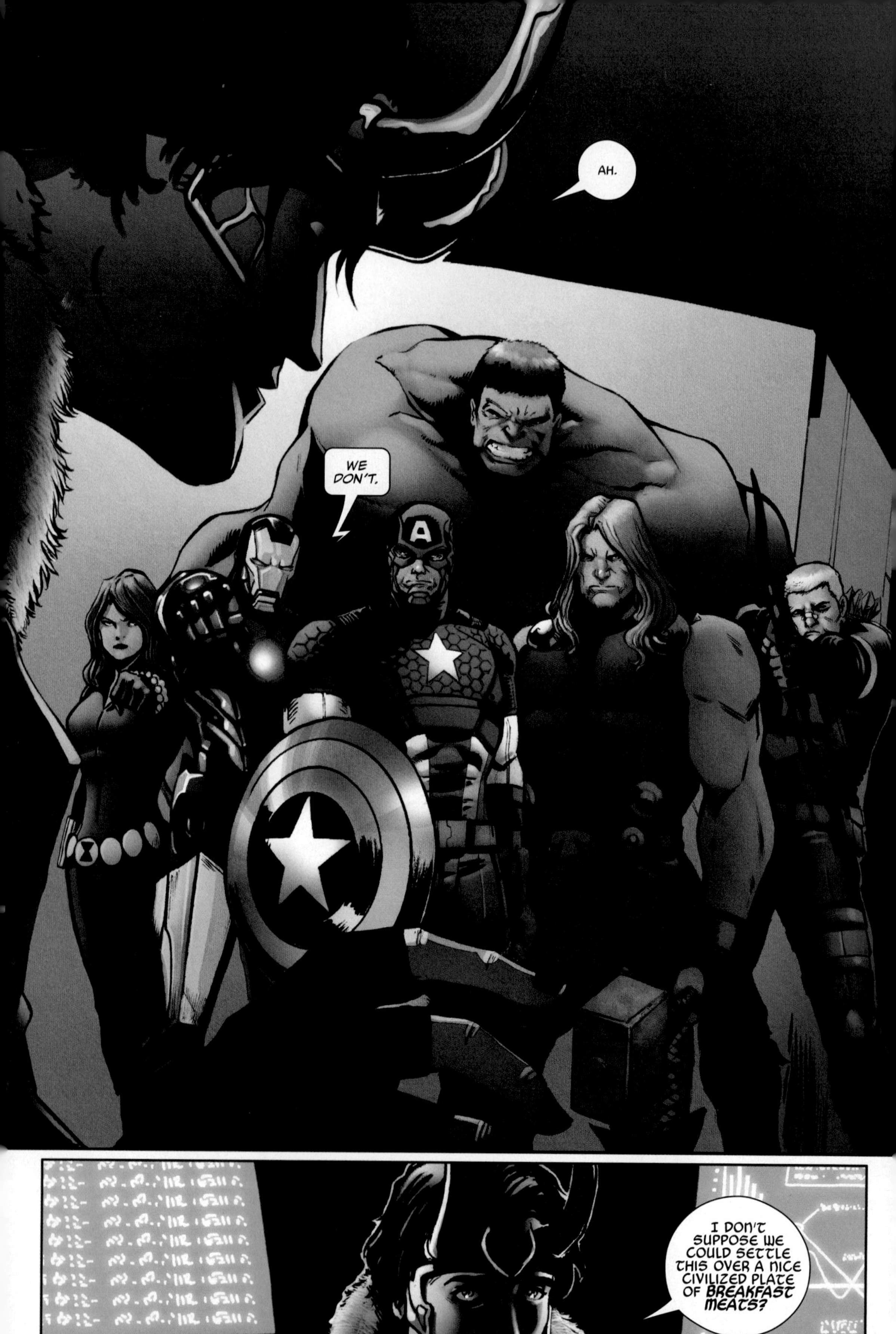
AH.
WE DON'T.

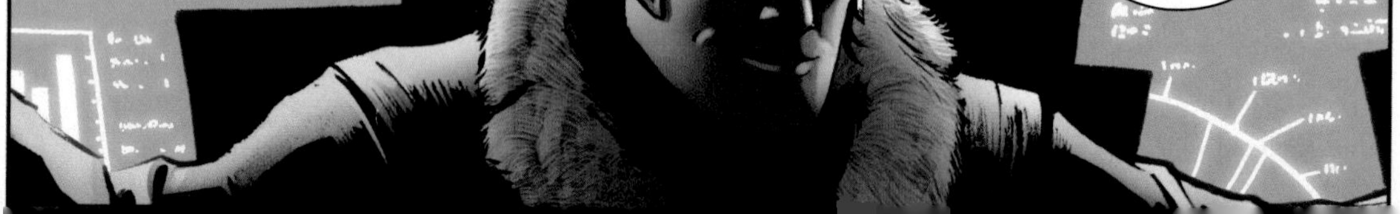
I DON'T SUPPOSE WE COULD SETTLE THIS OVER A NICE CIVILIZED PLATE OF BREAKFAST MEATS?

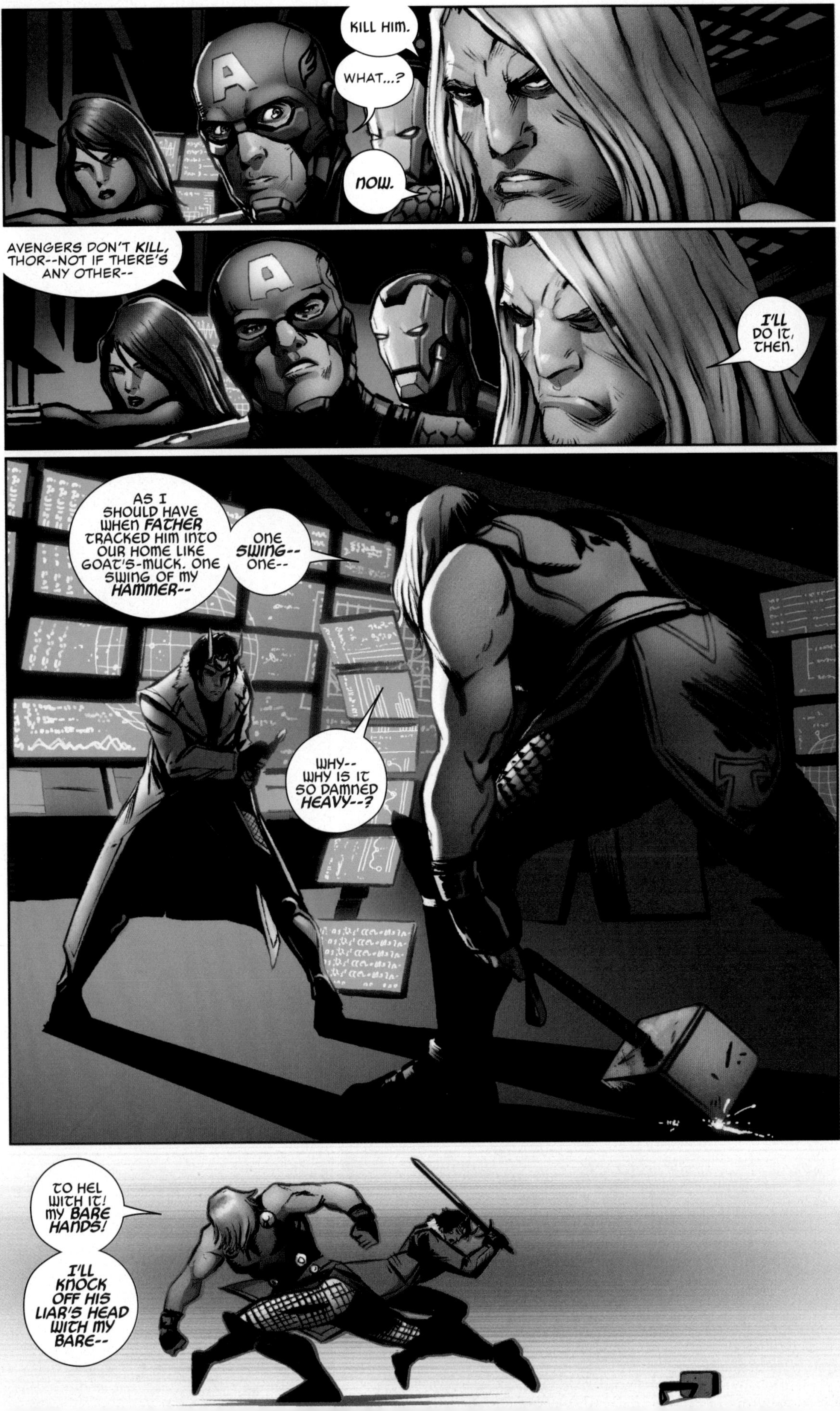

KILL HIM.
WHAT...?
NOW.
AVENGERS DON'T KILL, THOR--NOT IF THERE'S ANY OTHER--
I'LL DO IT, THEN.
AS I SHOULD HAVE WHEN FATHER TRACKED HIM INTO OUR HOME LIKE GOAT'S-MUCK. ONE SWING OF MY HAMMER--
ONE SWING-- ONE--
WHY-- WHY IS IT SO DAMNED HEAVY--?
TO HEL WITH IT! MY BARE HANDS!
I'LL KNOCK OFF HIS LIAR'S HEAD WITH MY BARE--

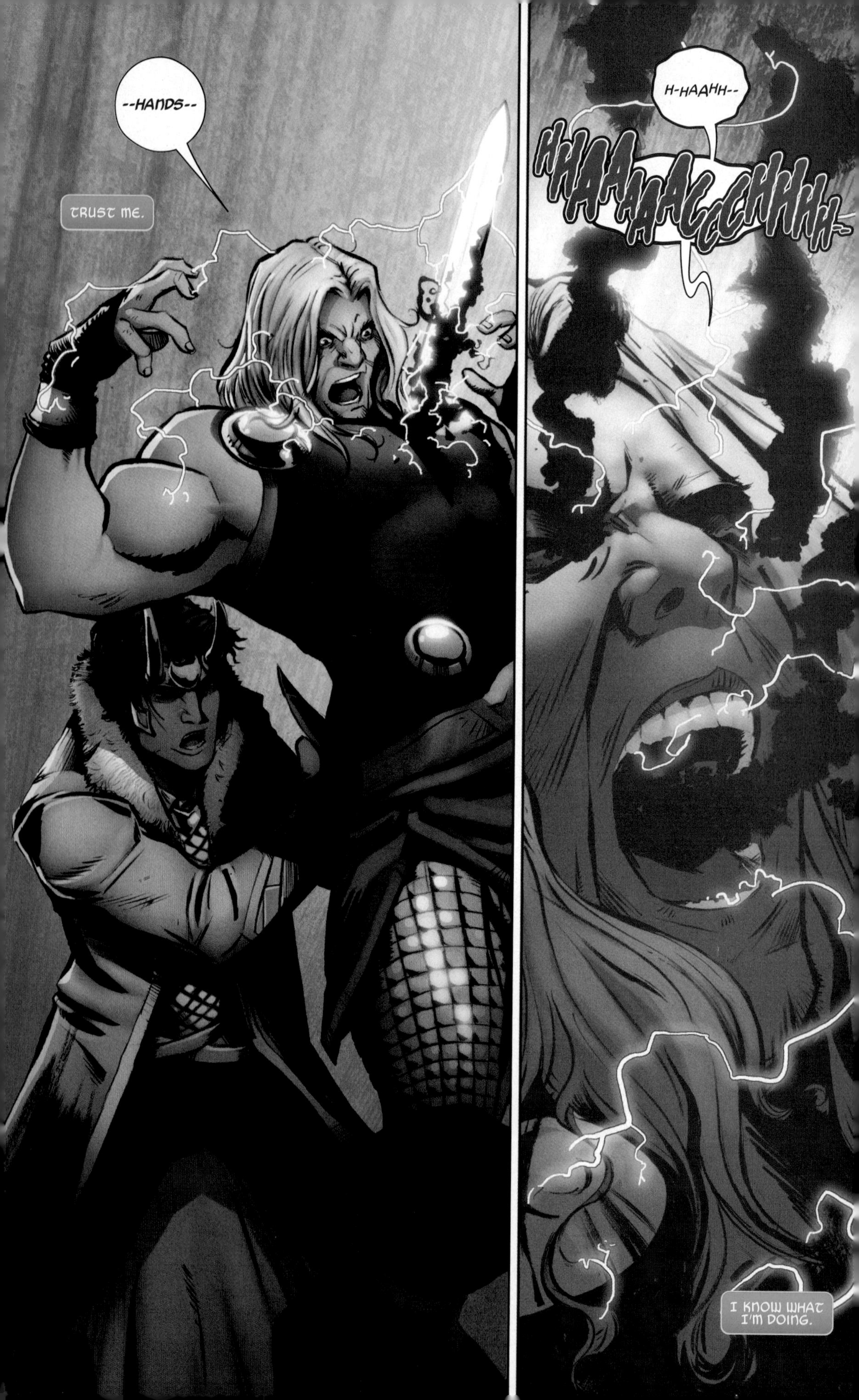
--HANDS--
TRUST ME.
H-HAAHH--
HHAAAAAACCCHHHH--
I KNOW WHAT I'M DOING.

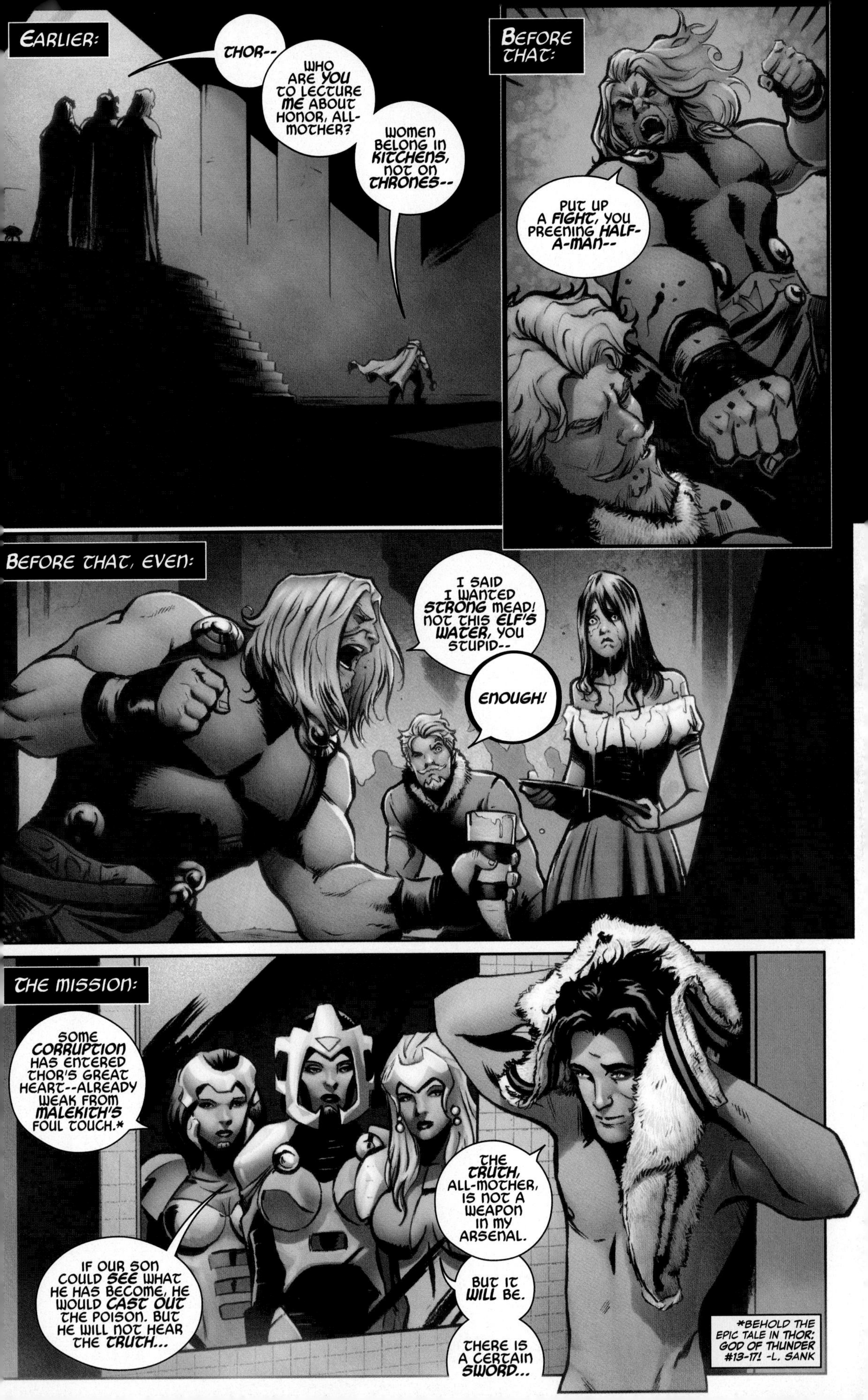
EARLIER:
THOR--
WHO ARE YOU TO LECTURE ME ABOUT HONOR, ALL-MOTHER?
WOMEN BELONG IN KITCHENS, NOT ON THRONES--
BEFORE THAT:
PUT UP A FIGHT, YOU PREENING HALF-A-MAN--
BEFORE THAT, EVEN:
I SAID I WANTED STRONG MEAD! NOT THIS ELF'S WATER, YOU STUPID--
ENOUGH!
THE MISSION:
SOME CORRUPTION HAS ENTERED THOR'S GREAT HEART--ALREADY WEAK FROM MALEKITH'S FOUL TOUCH.*
IF OUR SON COULD SEE WHAT HE HAS BECOME, HE WOULD CAST OUT THE POISON. BUT HE WILL NOT HEAR THE TRUTH...
THE TRUTH, ALL-MOTHER, IS NOT A WEAPON IN MY ARSENAL.
BUT IT WILL BE.
THERE IS A CERTAIN SWORD...
*BEHOLD THE EPIC TALE IN THOR: GOD OF THUNDER #13-17! -L. SANK

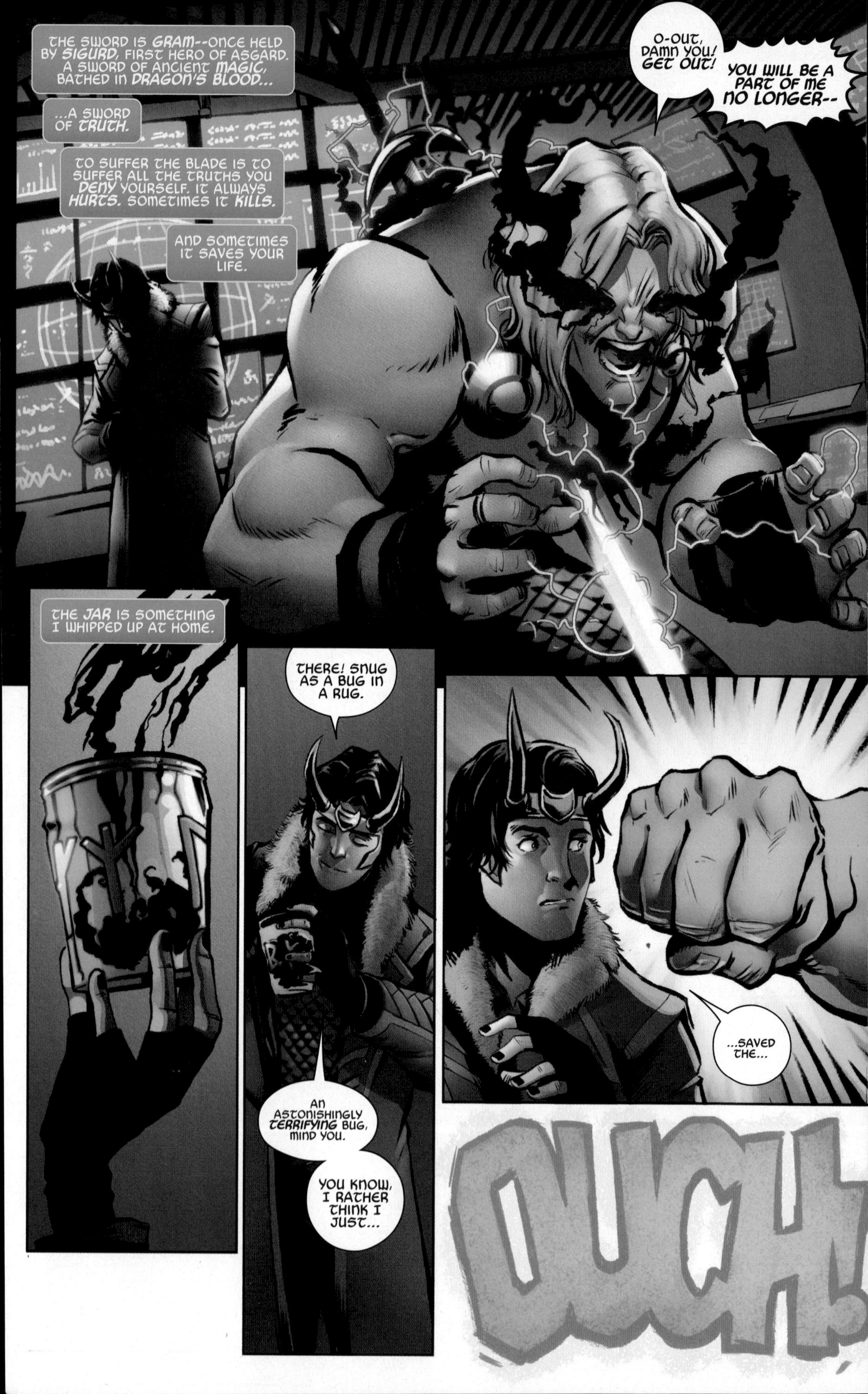
THE SWORD IS GRAM--ONCE HELD BY SIGURD, FIRST HERO OF ASGARD. A SWORD OF ANCIENT MAGIC, BATHED IN DRAGON'S BLOOD...
...A SWORD OF TRUTH.
TO SUFFER THE BLADE IS TO SUFFER ALL THE TRUTHS YOU DENY YOURSELF. IT ALWAYS HURTS. SOMETIMES IT KILLS.
AND SOMETIMES IT SAVES YOUR LIFE.
O-OUT, DAMN YOU! GET OUT!
YOU WILL BE A PART OF ME NO LONGER--
THE JAR IS SOMETHING I WHIPPED UP AT HOME.
THERE! SNUG AS A BUG IN A RUG.
AN ASTONISHINGLY TERRIFYING BUG, MIND YOU.
YOU KNOW, I RATHER THINK I JUST...
...SAVED THE...
OUCH!

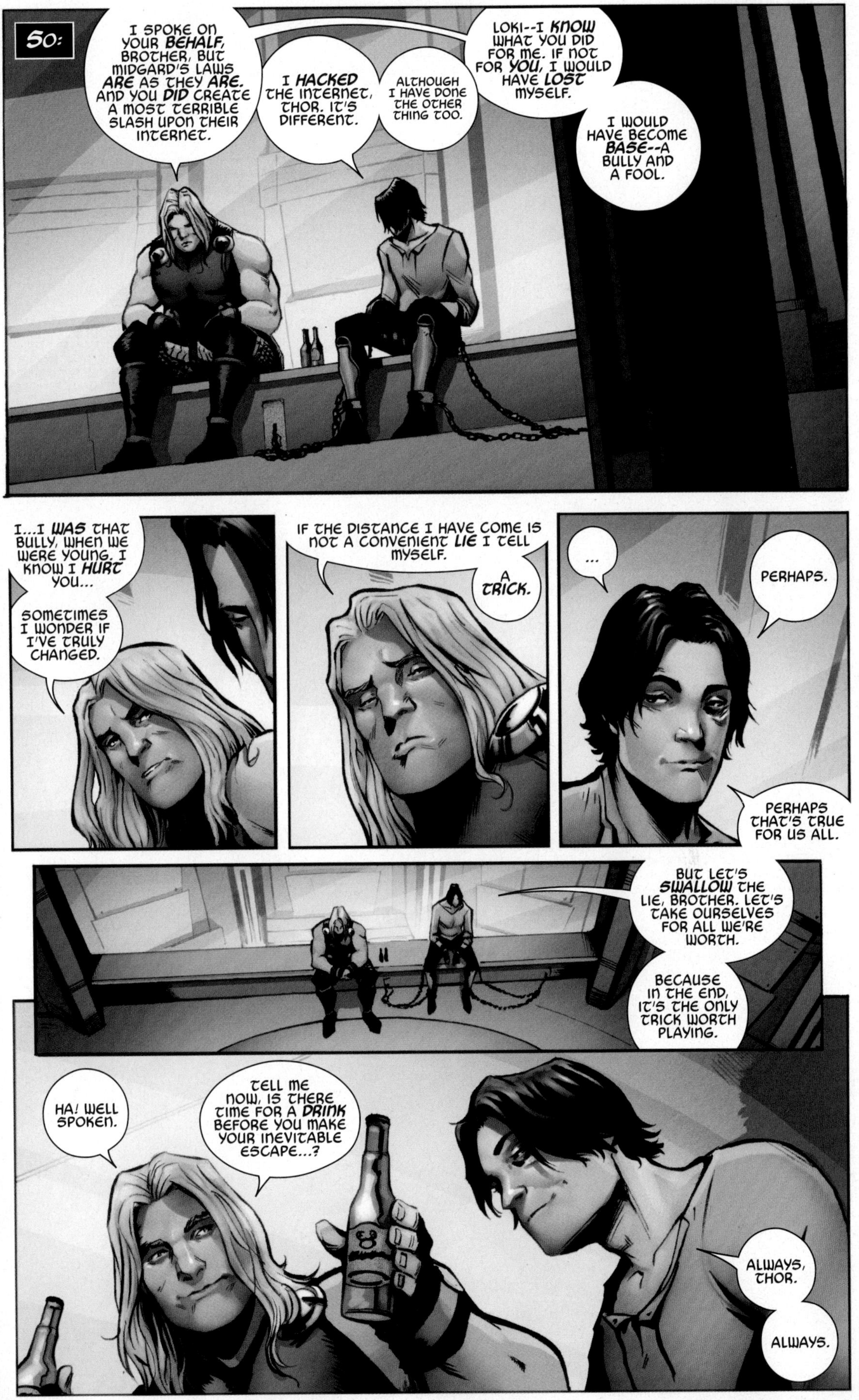

50:
I SPOKE ON YOUR BEHALF, BROTHER, BUT MIDGARD'S LAWS ARE AS THEY ARE. AND YOU DID CREATE A MOST TERRIBLE SLASH UPON THEIR INTERNET.
I HACKED THE INTERNET, THOR. IT'S DIFFERENT.
ALTHOUGH I HAVE DONE THE OTHER THING TOO.
LOKI--I KNOW WHAT YOU DID FOR ME. IF NOT FOR YOU, I WOULD HAVE LOST MYSELF.
I WOULD HAVE BECOME BASE--A BULLY AND A FOOL.
I...I WAS THAT BULLY, WHEN WE WERE YOUNG. I KNOW I HURT YOU...
SOMETIMES I WONDER IF I'VE TRULY CHANGED.
IF THE DISTANCE I HAVE COME IS NOT A CONVENIENT LIE I TELL MYSELF.
A TRICK.
...
PERHAPS.
PERHAPS THAT'S TRUE FOR US ALL.
BUT LET'S SWALLOW THE LIE, BROTHER. LET'S TAKE OURSELVES FOR ALL WE'RE WORTH.
BECAUSE IN THE END, IT'S THE ONLY TRICK WORTH PLAYING.
HA! WELL SPOKEN.
TELL ME NOW, IS THERE TIME FOR A DRINK BEFORE YOU MAKE YOUR INEVITABLE ESCAPE...?
ALWAYS, THOR.
ALWAYS.

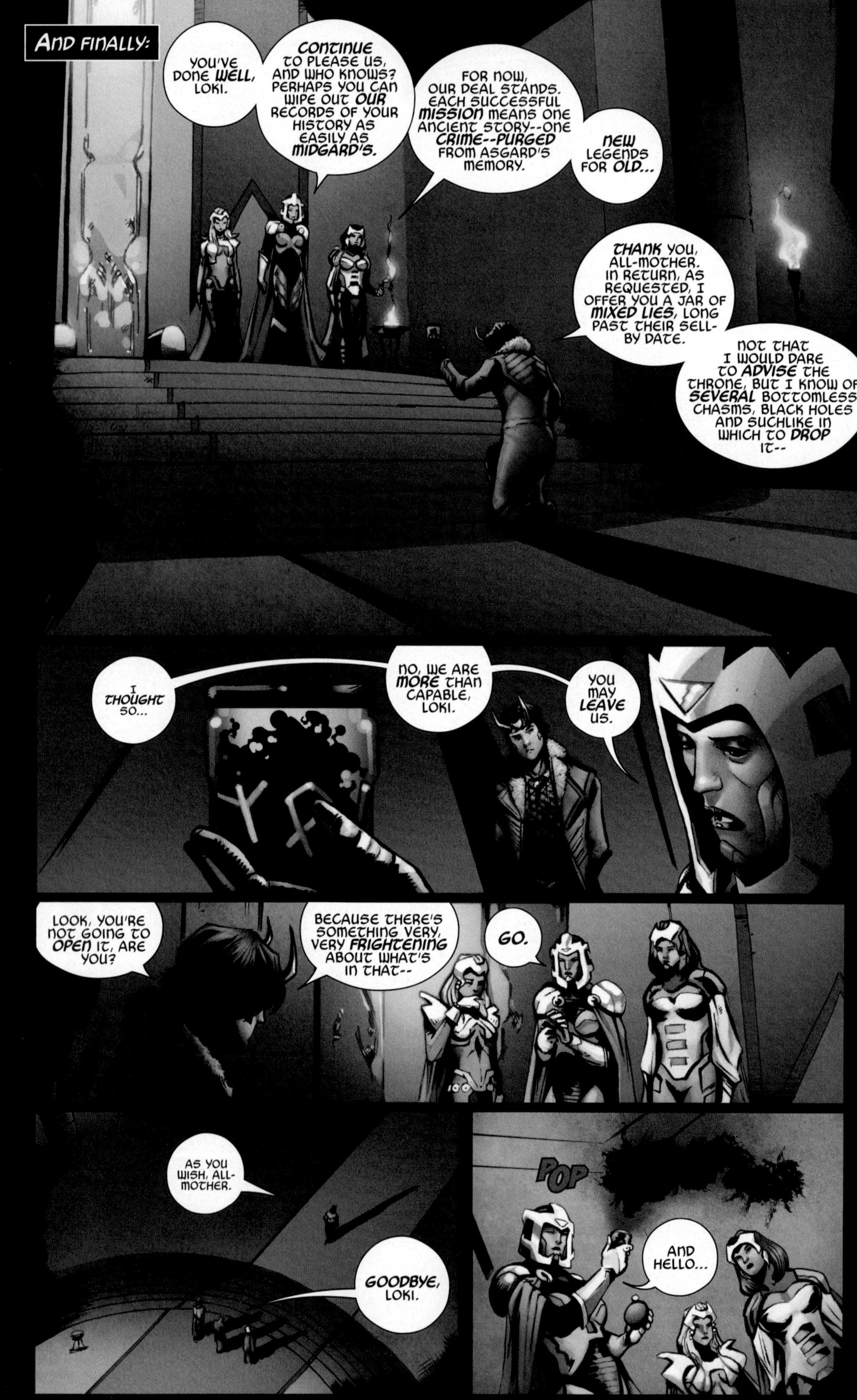
AND FINALLY:
YOU'VE DONE WELL, LOKI.
CONTINUE TO PLEASE US, AND WHO KNOWS? PERHAPS YOU CAN WIPE OUT OUR RECORDS OF YOUR HISTORY AS EASILY AS MIDGARD'S.
FOR NOW, OUR DEAL STANDS. EACH SUCCESSFUL MISSION MEANS ONE ANCIENT STORY--ONE CRIME--PURGED FROM ASGARD'S MEMORY.
NEW LEGENDS FOR OLD...
THANK YOU, ALL-MOTHER. IN RETURN, AS REQUESTED, I OFFER YOU A JAR OF MIXED LIES, LONG PAST THEIR SELL-BY DATE.
NOT THAT I WOULD DARE TO ADVISE THE THRONE, BUT I KNOW OF SEVERAL BOTTOMLESS CHASMS, BLACK HOLES AND SUCHLIKE IN WHICH TO DROP IT--
NO, WE ARE MORE THAN CAPABLE, LOKI.
I THOUGHT SO...
YOU MAY LEAVE US.
LOOK, YOU'RE NOT GOING TO OPEN IT, ARE YOU?
BECAUSE THERE'S SOMETHING VERY, VERY FRIGHTENING ABOUT WHAT'S IN THAT--
GO.
AS YOU WISH, ALL-MOTHER.
GOODBYE, LOKI.
POP
AND HELLO...

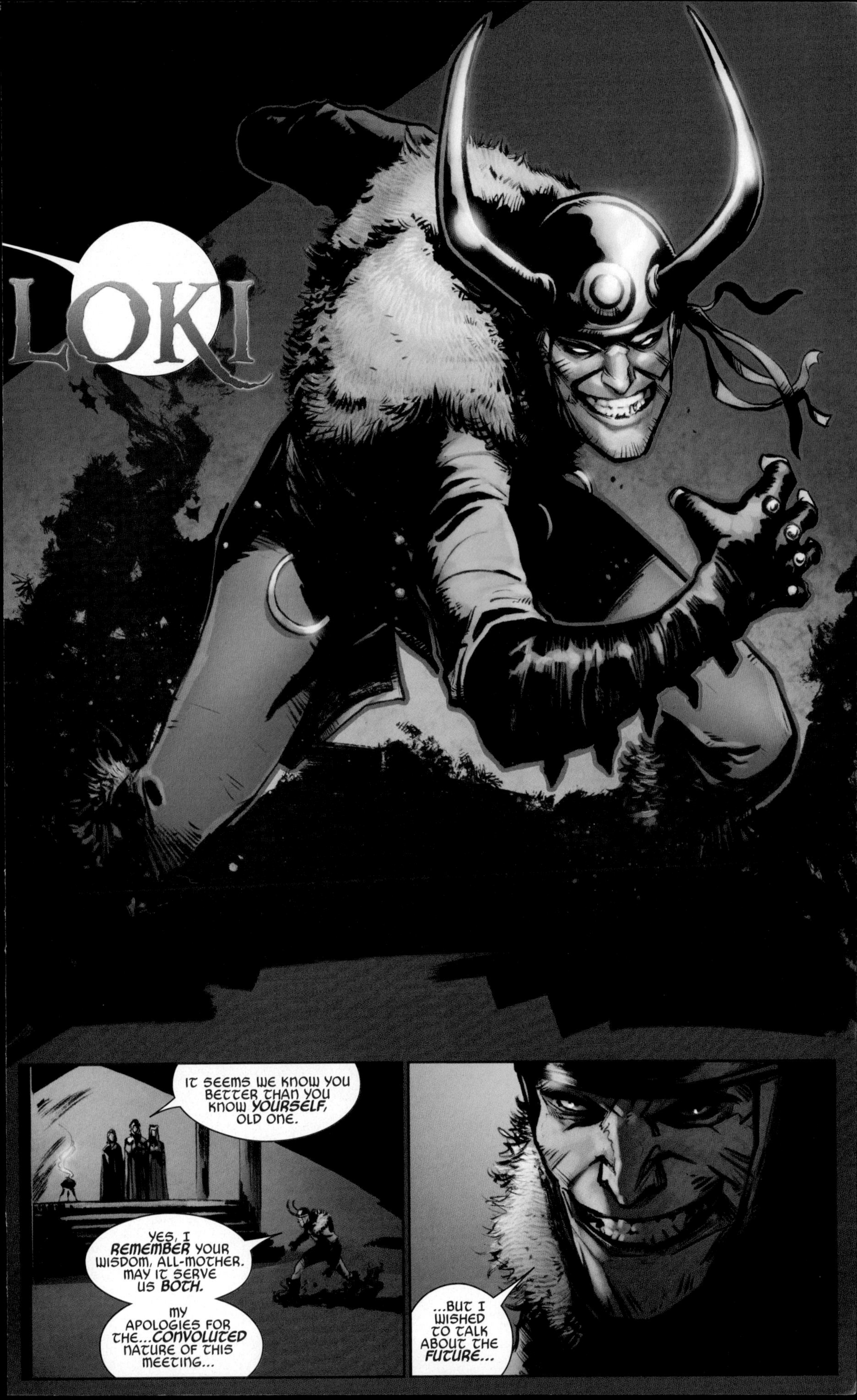
LOKI
IT SEEMS WE KNOW YOU BETTER THAN YOU KNOW YOURSELF, OLD ONE.
YES, I REMEMBER YOUR WISDOM, ALL-MOTHER. MAY IT SERVE US BOTH.
MY APOLOGIES FOR THE...CONVOLUTED NATURE OF THIS MEETING...
...BUT I WISHED TO TALK ABOUT THE FUTURE...

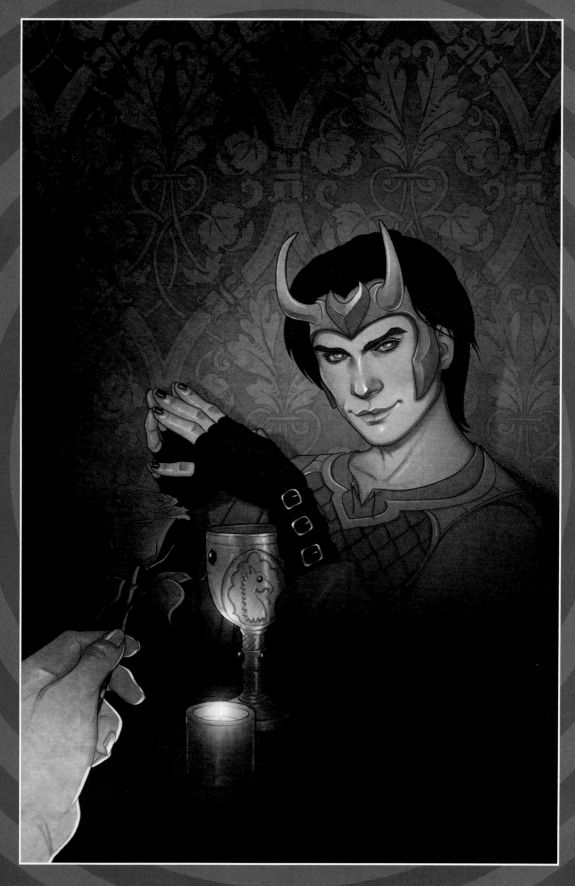

LOKI: AGENT OF ASGARD #2

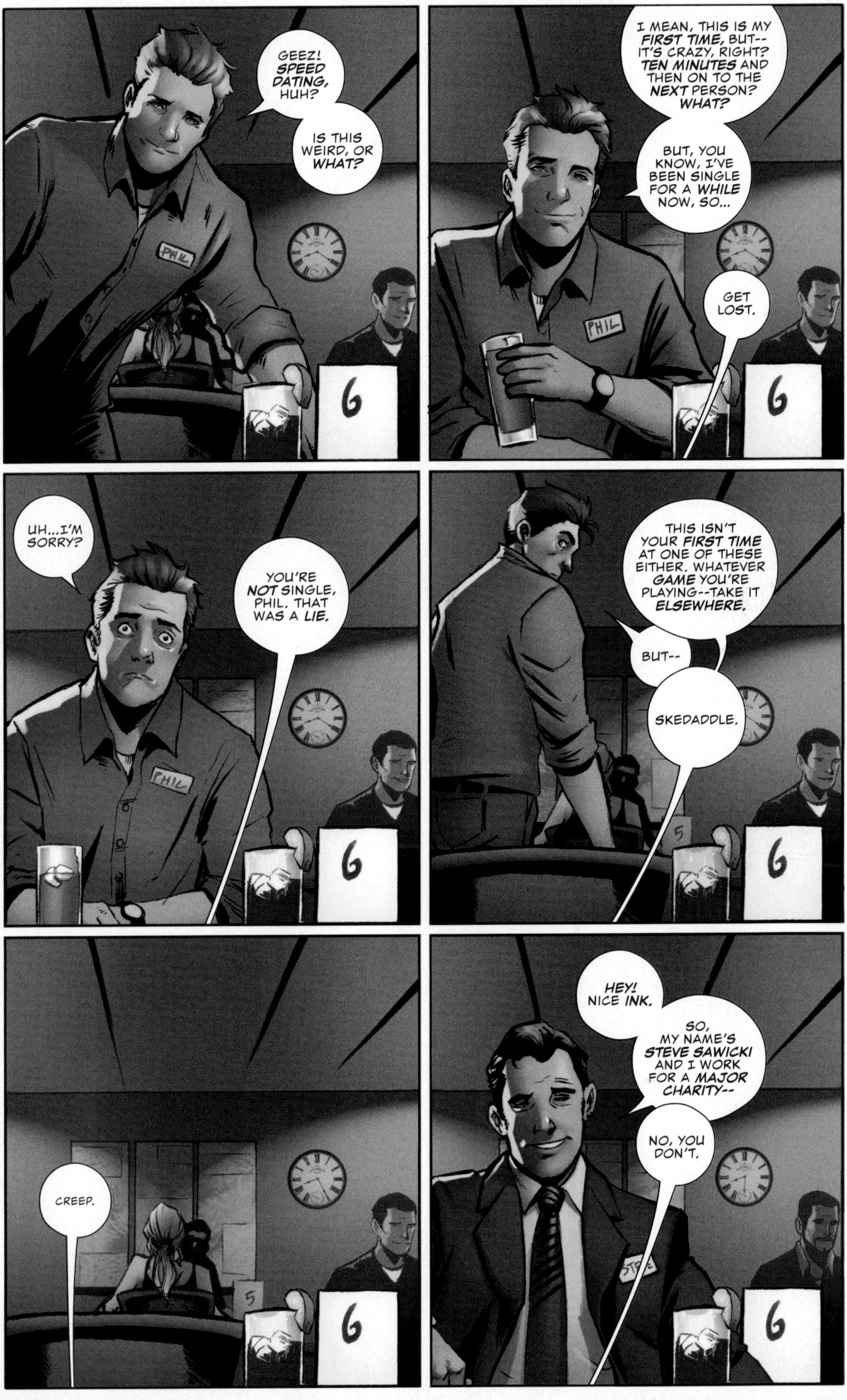
GEEZ! SPEED DATING, HUH?
IS THIS WEIRD, OR WHAT?
PHIL
I MEAN, THIS IS MY FIRST TIME, BUT-- IT'S CRAZY, RIGHT? TEN MINUTES AND THEN ON TO THE NEXT PERSON? WHAT?
BUT, YOU KNOW, I'VE BEEN SINGLE FOR A WHILE NOW, SO...
GET LOST.
PHIL
6
UH...I'M SORRY?
YOU'RE NOT SINGLE, PHIL. THAT WAS A LIE.
PHIL
6
THIS ISN'T YOUR FIRST TIME AT ONE OF THESE EITHER. WHATEVER GAME YOU'RE PLAYING--TAKE IT ELSEWHERE.
BUT--
SKEDADDLE.
6
CREEP.
6
HEY! NICE INK.
SO, MY NAME'S STEVE SAWICKI AND I WORK FOR A MAJOR CHARITY--
NO, YOU DON'T.
6

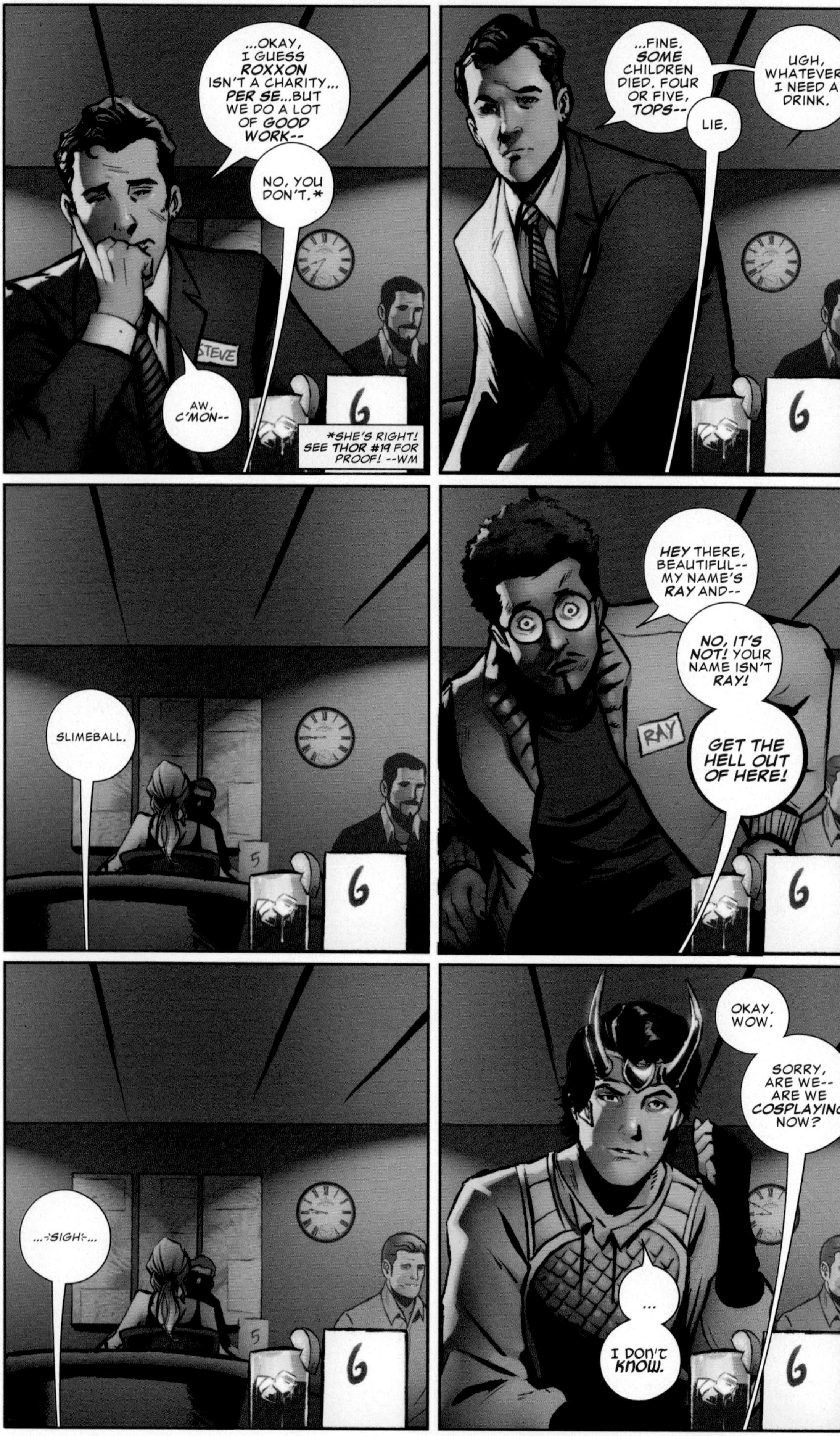
...OKAY, I GUESS ROXXON ISN'T A CHARITY... PER SE...BUT WE DO A LOT OF GOOD WORK--
NO, YOU DON'T.*
STEVE
AW, C'MON--
*SHE'S RIGHT! SEE THOR #19 FOR PROOF! --WM
...FINE. SOME CHILDREN DIED. FOUR OR FIVE, TOPS--
LIE.
UGH, WHATEVER. I NEED A DRINK.
SLIMEBALL.
HEY THERE, BEAUTIFUL-- MY NAME'S RAY AND--
NO, IT'S NOT! YOUR NAME ISN'T RAY!
RAY
GET THE HELL OUT OF HERE!
...*SIGH*...
OKAY. WOW.
SORRY, ARE WE-- ARE WE COSPLAYING NOW?
...
I DON'T KNOW.

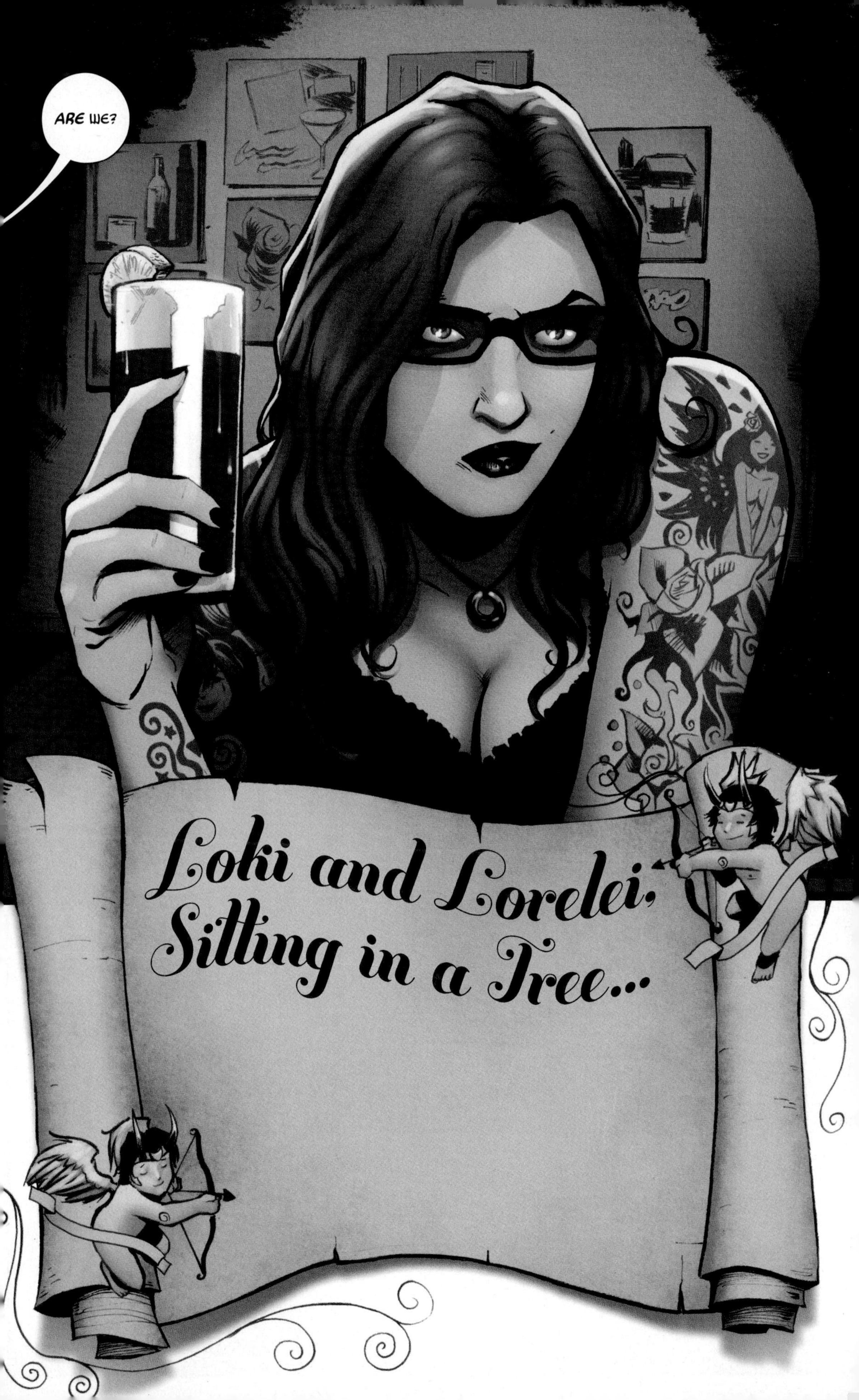
ARE WE?
Loki and Lorelei, Sitting in a Tree...

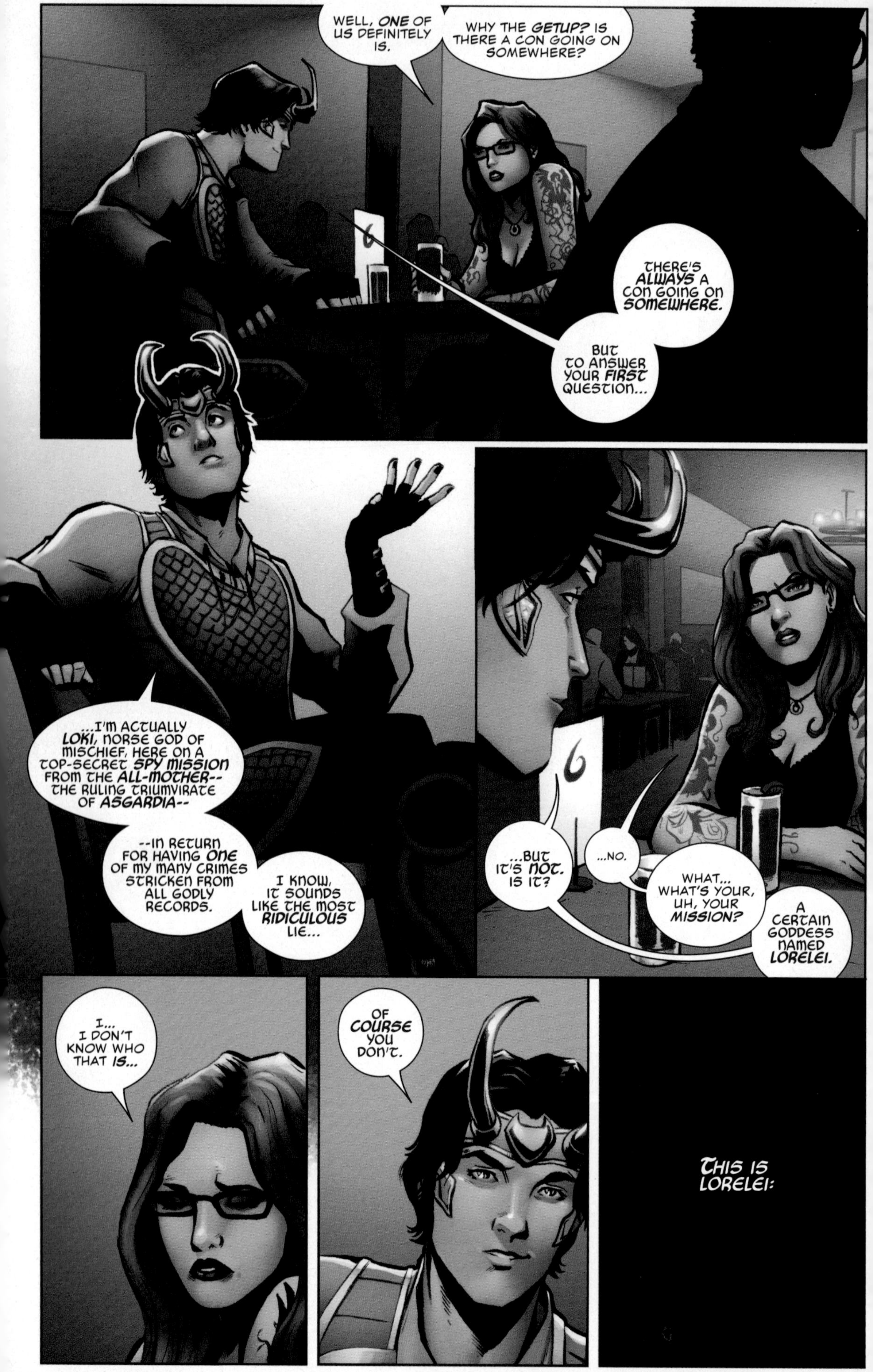
WELL, ONE OF US DEFINITELY IS.
WHY THE GETUP? IS THERE A CON GOING ON SOMEWHERE?
THERE'S ALWAYS A CON GOING ON SOMEWHERE.
BUT TO ANSWER YOUR FIRST QUESTION...
...I'M ACTUALLY LOKI, NORSE GOD OF MISCHIEF, HERE ON A TOP-SECRET SPY MISSION FROM THE ALL-MOTHER-- THE RULING TRIUMVIRATE OF ASGARDIA--
--IN RETURN FOR HAVING ONE OF MY MANY CRIMES STRICKEN FROM ALL GODLY RECORDS.
I KNOW, IT SOUNDS LIKE THE MOST RIDICULOUS LIE...
...BUT IT'S NOT. IS IT?
...NO.
WHAT... WHAT'S YOUR, UH, YOUR MISSION?
A CERTAIN GODDESS NAMED LORELEI.
I... I DON'T KNOW WHO THAT IS...
OF COURSE YOU DON'T.
THIS IS LORELEI:

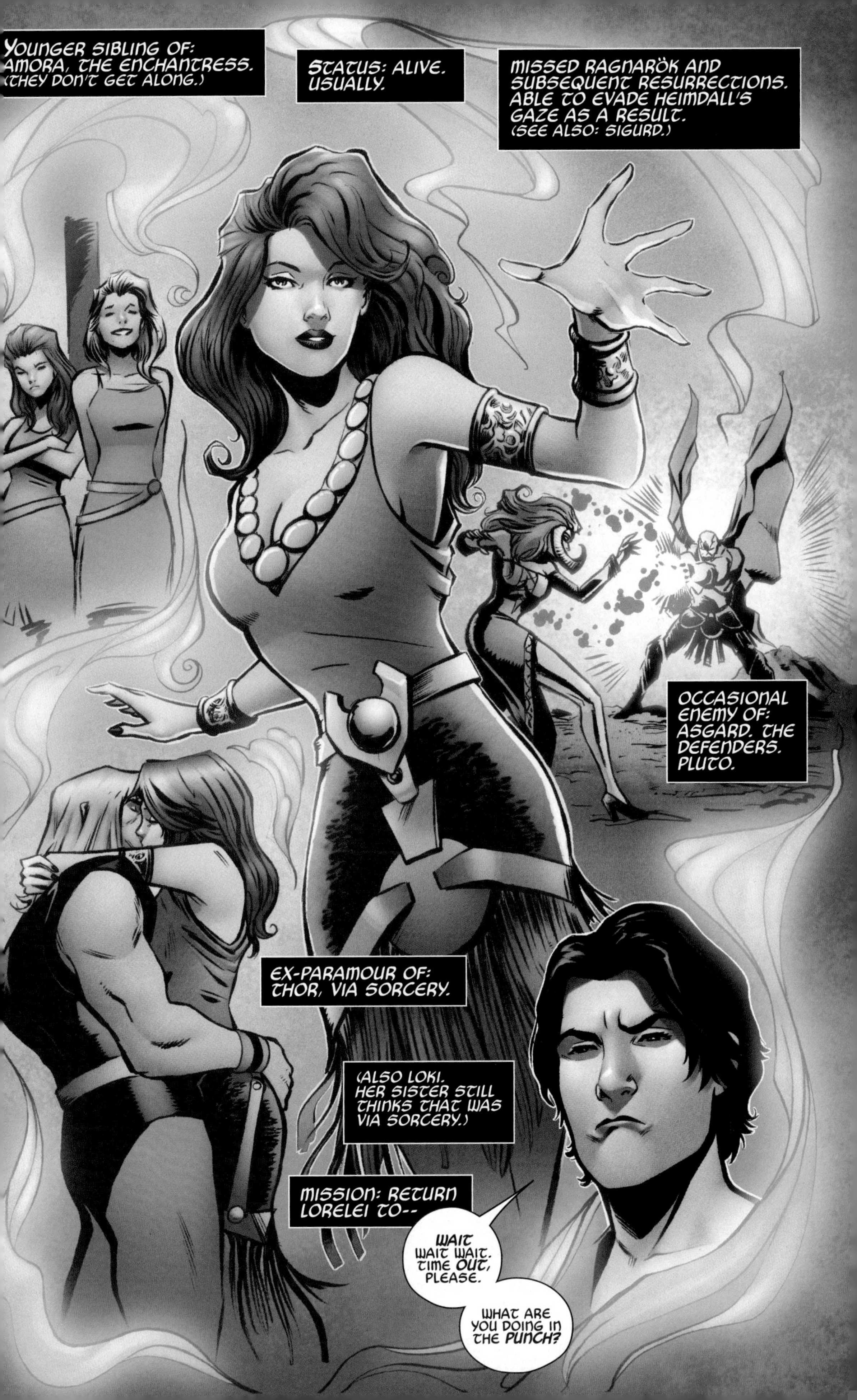
YOUNGER SIBLING OF: AMORA, THE ENCHANTRESS. (THEY DON'T GET ALONG.)
STATUS: ALIVE. USUALLY.
MISSED RAGNARÖK AND SUBSEQUENT RESURRECTIONS. ABLE TO EVADE HEIMDALL'S GAZE AS A RESULT. (SEE ALSO: SIGURD.)
OCCASIONAL ENEMY OF: ASGARD. THE DEFENDERS. PLUTO.
EX-PARAMOUR OF: THOR, VIA SORCERY.
(ALSO LOKI. HER SISTER STILL THINKS THAT WAS VIA SORCERY.)
MISSION: RETURN LORELEI TO--
WAIT WAIT WAIT. TIME OUT, PLEASE.
WHAT ARE YOU DOING IN THE PUNCH?

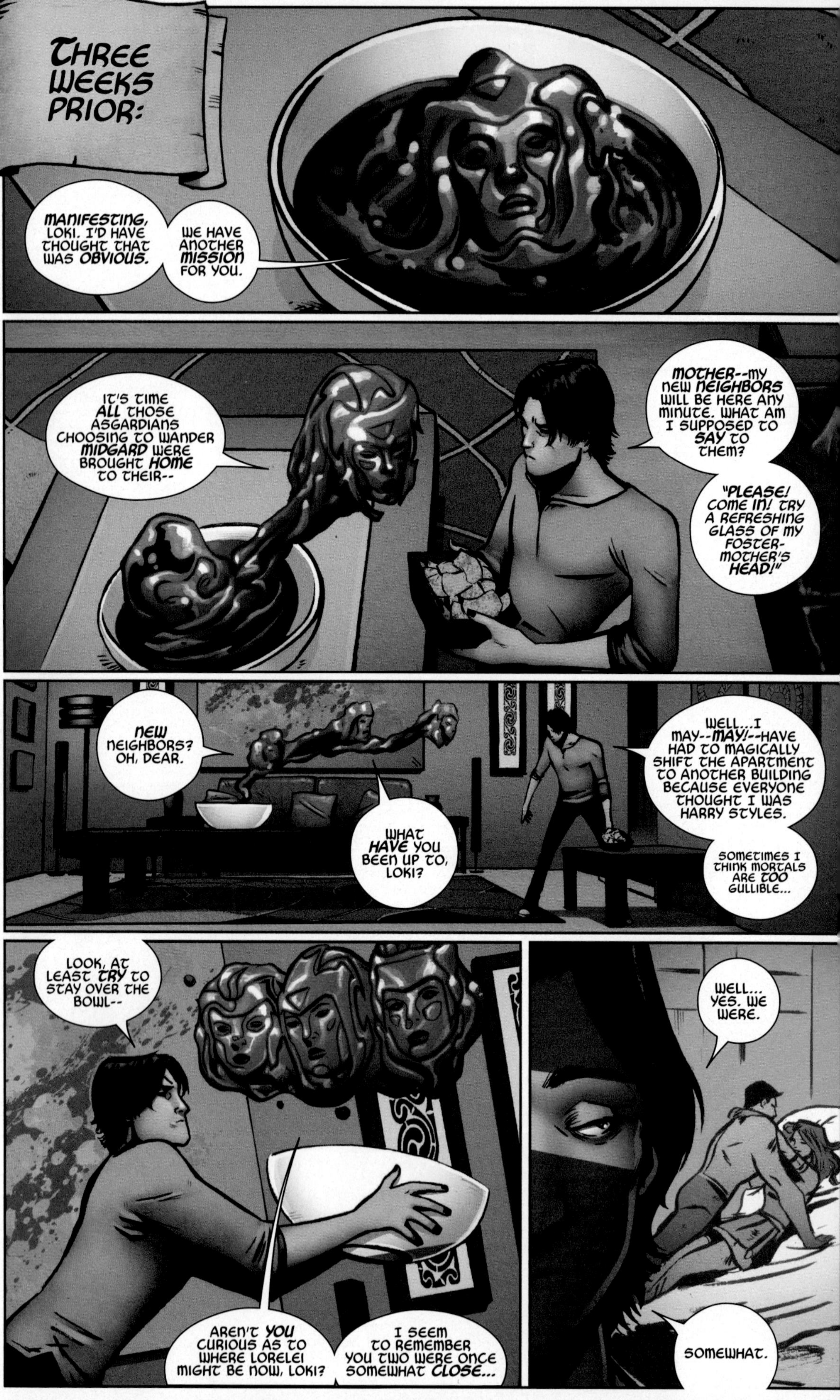
THREE WEEKS PRIOR:
MANIFESTING, LOKI. I'D HAVE THOUGHT THAT WAS OBVIOUS.
WE HAVE ANOTHER MISSION FOR YOU.
IT'S TIME ALL THOSE ASGARDIANS CHOOSING TO WANDER MIDGARD WERE BROUGHT HOME TO THEIR--
MOTHER--MY NEW NEIGHBORS WILL BE HERE ANY MINUTE. WHAT AM I SUPPOSED TO SAY TO THEM?
"PLEASE! COME IN! TRY A REFRESHING GLASS OF MY FOSTER-MOTHER'S HEAD!"
NEW NEIGHBORS? OH, DEAR.
WHAT HAVE YOU BEEN UP TO, LOKI?
WELL...I MAY--MAY!--HAVE HAD TO MAGICALLY SHIFT THE APARTMENT TO ANOTHER BUILDING BECAUSE EVERYONE THOUGHT I WAS HARRY STYLES.
SOMETIMES I THINK MORTALS ARE TOO GULLIBLE...
LOOK, AT LEAST TRY TO STAY OVER THE BOWL--
AREN'T YOU CURIOUS AS TO WHERE LORELEI MIGHT BE NOW, LOKI?
I SEEM TO REMEMBER YOU TWO WERE ONCE SOMEWHAT CLOSE...
WELL... YES. WE WERE.
SOMEWHAT.

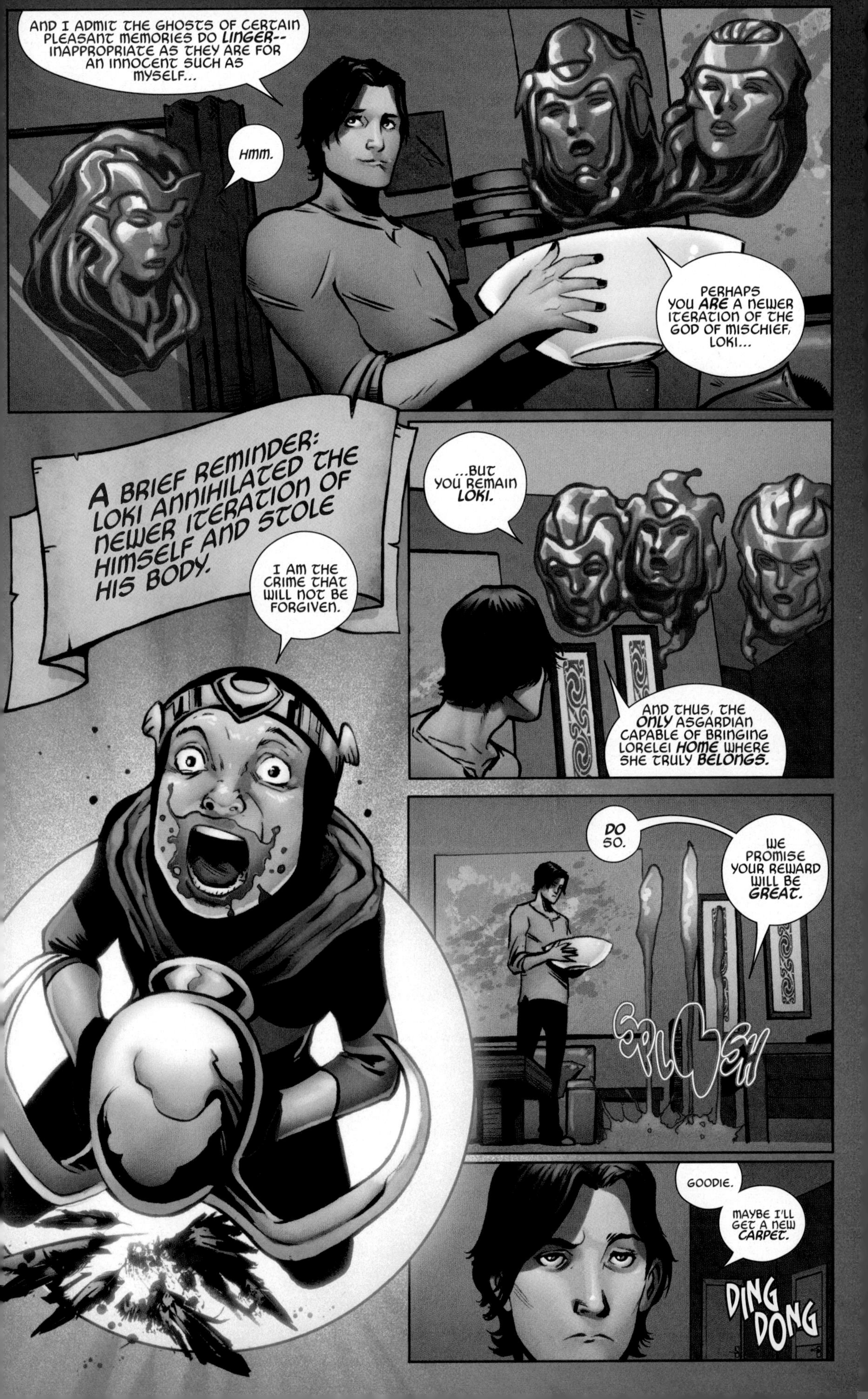
AND I ADMIT THE GHOSTS OF CERTAIN PLEASANT MEMORIES DO LINGER--INAPPROPRIATE AS THEY ARE FOR AN INNOCENT SUCH AS MYSELF...
HMM.
PERHAPS YOU ARE A NEWER ITERATION OF THE GOD OF MISCHIEF, LOKI...
A BRIEF REMINDER: LOKI ANNIHILATED THE NEWER ITERATION OF HIMSELF AND STOLE HIS BODY.
I AM THE CRIME THAT WILL NOT BE FORGIVEN.
...BUT YOU REMAIN LOKI.
AND THUS, THE ONLY ASGARDIAN CAPABLE OF BRINGING LORELEI HOME WHERE SHE TRULY BELONGS.
DO SO.
WE PROMISE YOUR REWARD WILL BE GREAT.
SPLOOSH
GOODIE.
MAYBE I'LL GET A NEW CARPET.
DING DONG

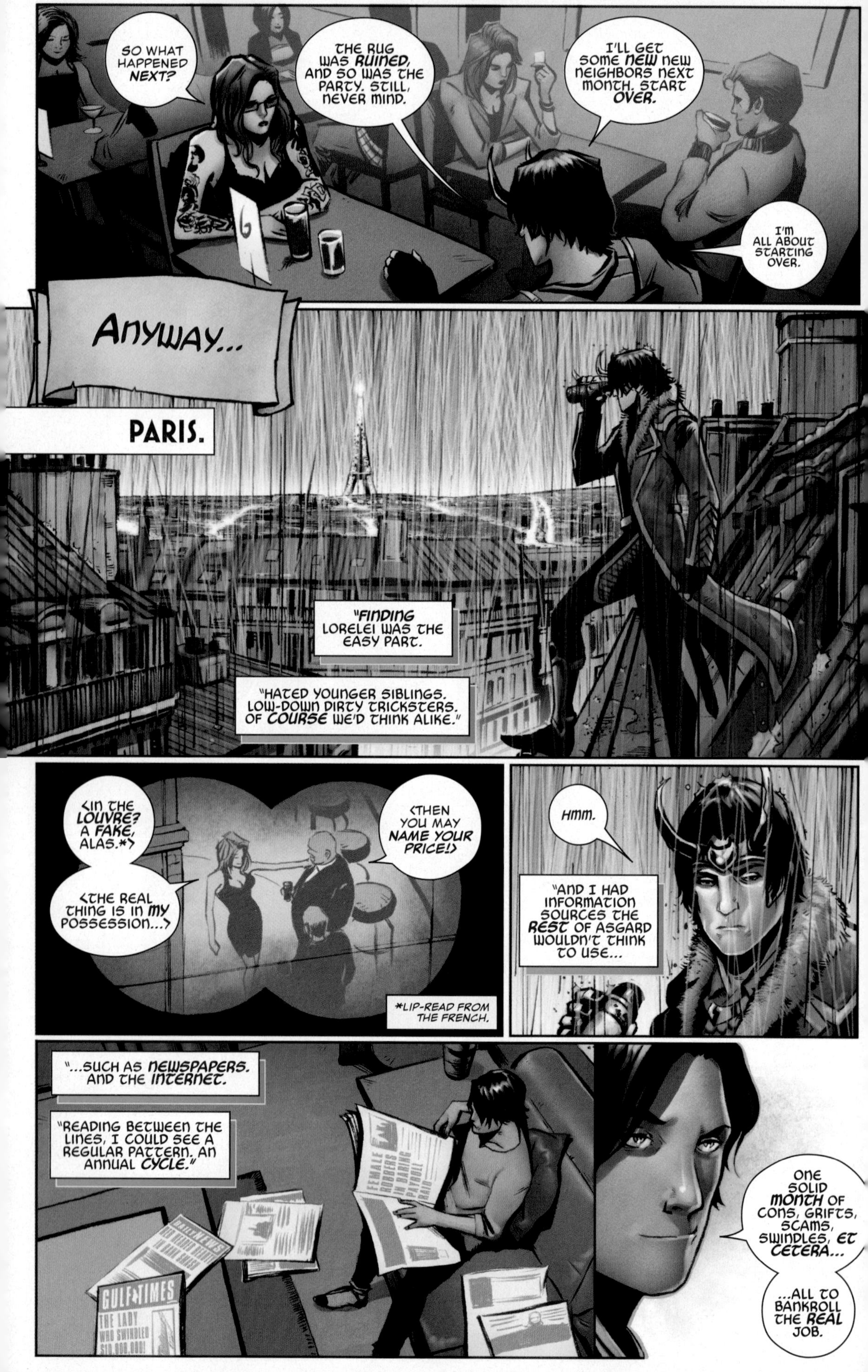

SO WHAT HAPPENED NEXT?
THE RUG WAS RUINED, AND SO WAS THE PARTY. STILL, NEVER MIND.
I'LL GET SOME NEW NEW NEIGHBORS NEXT MONTH. START OVER.
I'M ALL ABOUT STARTING OVER.
ANYWAY...
PARIS.
"FINDING LORELEI WAS THE EASY PART.
"HATED YOUNGER SIBLINGS. LOW-DOWN DIRTY TRICKSTERS. OF COURSE WE'D THINK ALIKE."
<IN THE LOUVRE? A FAKE, ALAS.*>
<THE REAL THING IS IN MY POSSESSION...>
<THEN YOU MAY NAME YOUR PRICE!>
*LIP-READ FROM THE FRENCH.
HMM.
"AND I HAD INFORMATION SOURCES THE REST OF ASGARD WOULDN'T THINK TO USE...
"...SUCH AS NEWSPAPERS. AND THE INTERNET.
"READING BETWEEN THE LINES, I COULD SEE A REGULAR PATTERN. AN ANNUAL CYCLE."
GULF TIMES
THE LADY WHO SWINDLED $10,000,000!
ONE SOLID MONTH OF CONS, GRIFTS, SCAMS, SWINDLES, ET CETERA...
...ALL TO BANKROLL THE REAL JOB.

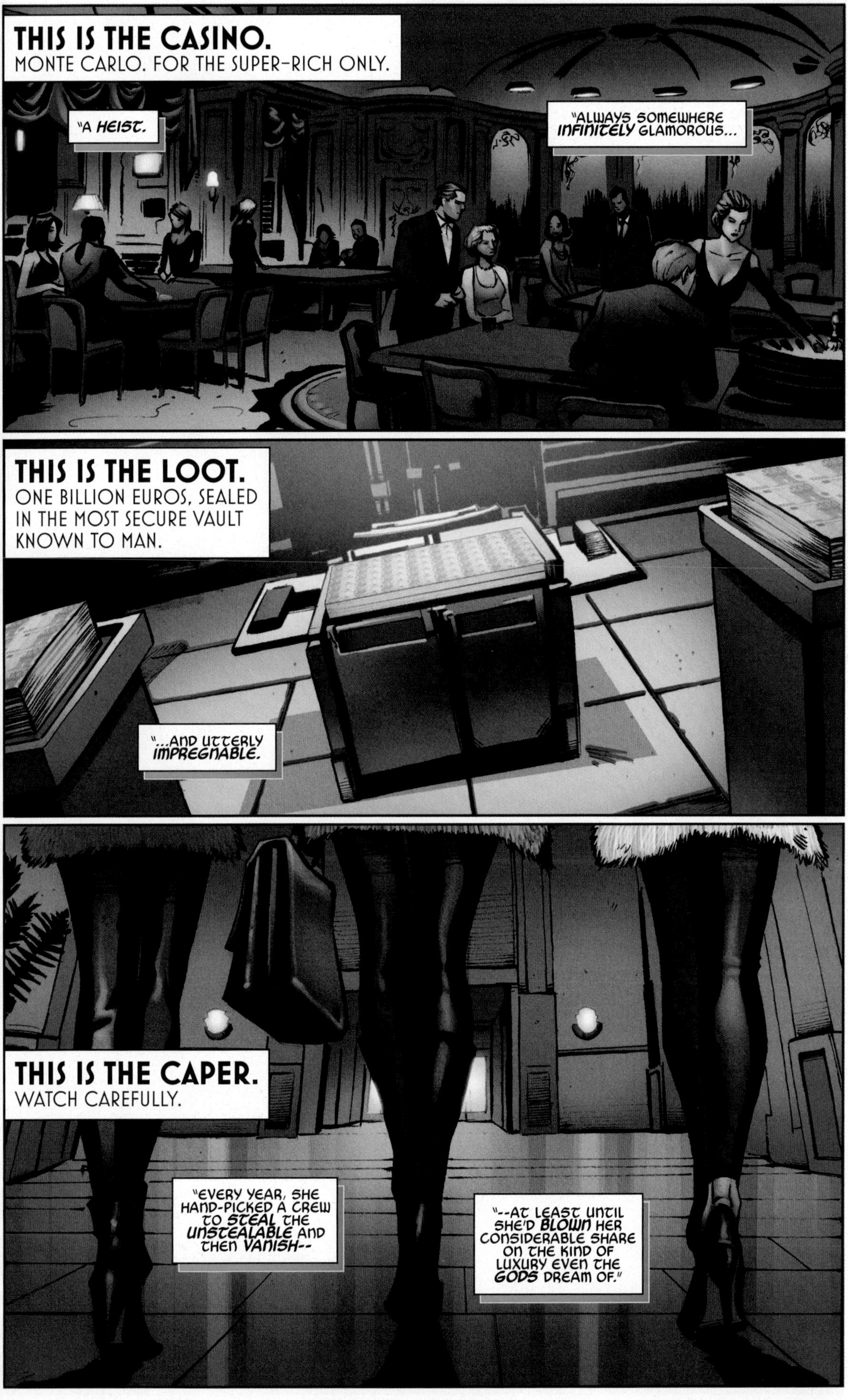
THIS IS THE CASINO.
MONTE CARLO. FOR THE SUPER-RICH ONLY.
"A HEIST.
"ALWAYS SOMEWHERE INFINITELY GLAMOROUS...
THIS IS THE LOOT.
ONE BILLION EUROS, SEALED IN THE MOST SECURE VAULT KNOWN TO MAN.
"...AND UTTERLY IMPREGNABLE.
THIS IS THE CAPER.
WATCH CAREFULLY.
"EVERY YEAR, SHE HAND-PICKED A CREW TO STEAL THE UNSTEALABLE AND THEN VANISH--
"--AT LEAST UNTIL SHE'D BLOWN HER CONSIDERABLE SHARE ON THE KIND OF LUXURY EVEN THE GODS DREAM OF."

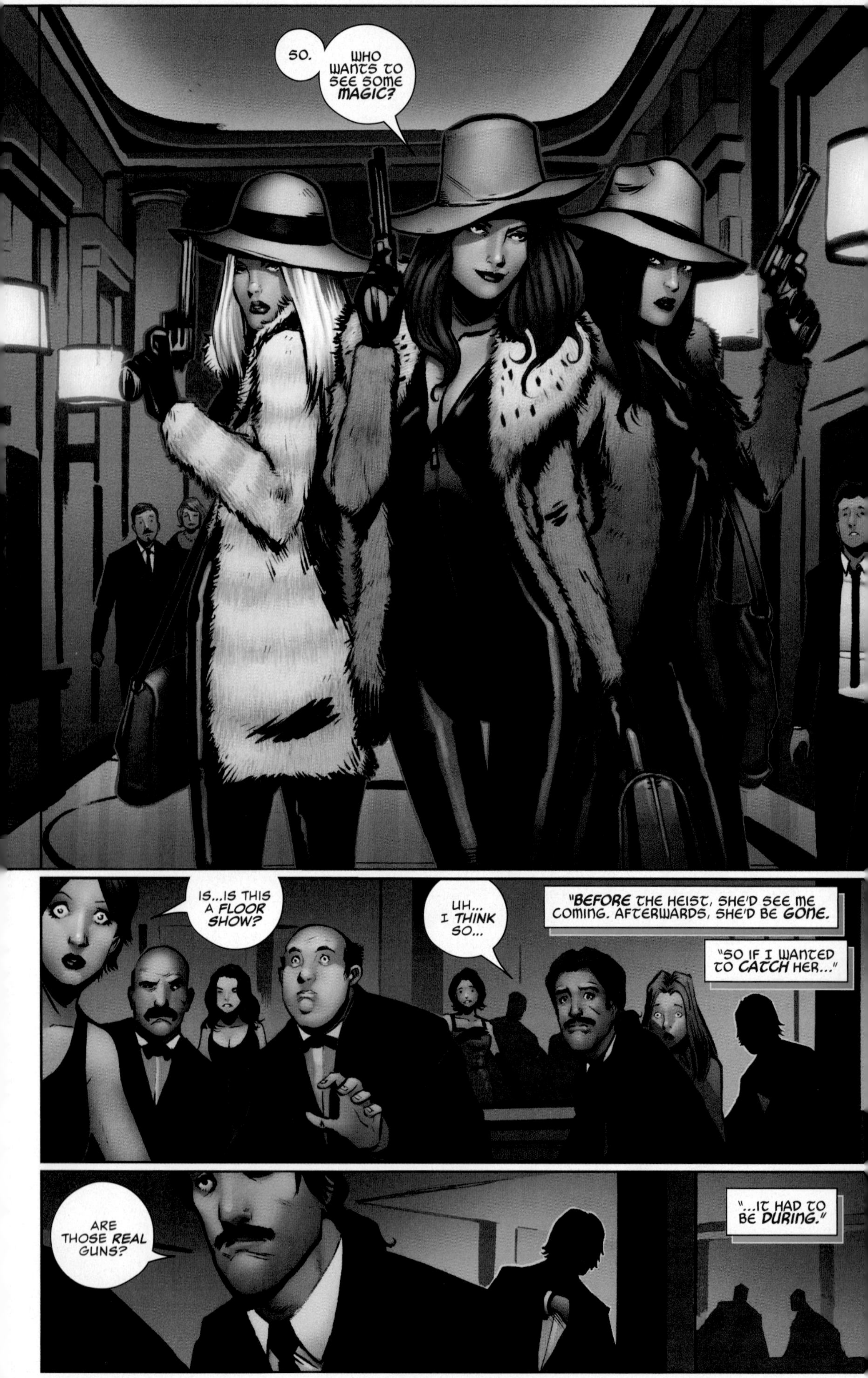
SO.
WHO WANTS TO SEE SOME MAGIC?
IS...IS THIS A FLOOR SHOW?
UH... I THINK SO...
"BEFORE THE HEIST, SHE'D SEE ME COMING. AFTERWARDS, SHE'D BE GONE.
"SO IF I WANTED TO CATCH HER..."
ARE THOSE REAL GUNS?
"...IT HAD TO BE DURING."

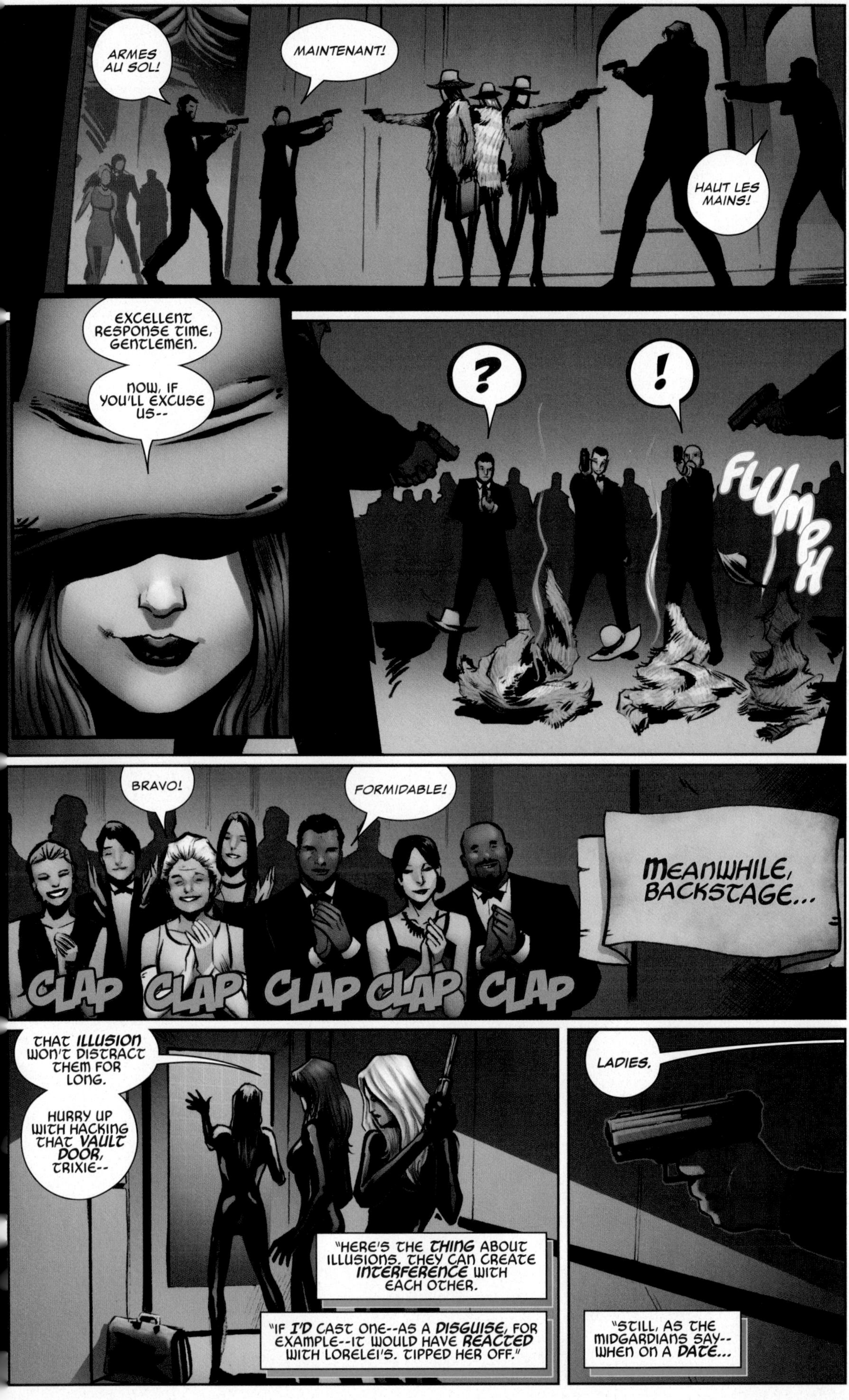
ARMES AU SOL!
MAINTENANT!
HAUT LES MAINS!
EXCELLENT RESPONSE TIME, GENTLEMEN.
NOW, IF YOU'LL EXCUSE US--
?
!
FLUMPH
BRAVO!
FORMIDABLE!
CLAP CLAP CLAP CLAP CLAP
MEANWHILE, BACKSTAGE...
THAT ILLUSION WON'T DISTRACT THEM FOR LONG.
HURRY UP WITH HACKING THAT VAULT DOOR, TRIXIE--
"HERE'S THE THING ABOUT ILLUSIONS. THEY CAN CREATE INTERFERENCE WITH EACH OTHER.
"IF I'D CAST ONE--AS A DISGUISE, FOR EXAMPLE--IT WOULD HAVE REACTED WITH LORELEI'S. TIPPED HER OFF."
LADIES.
"STILL, AS THE MIDGARDIANS SAY--WHEN ON A DATE...

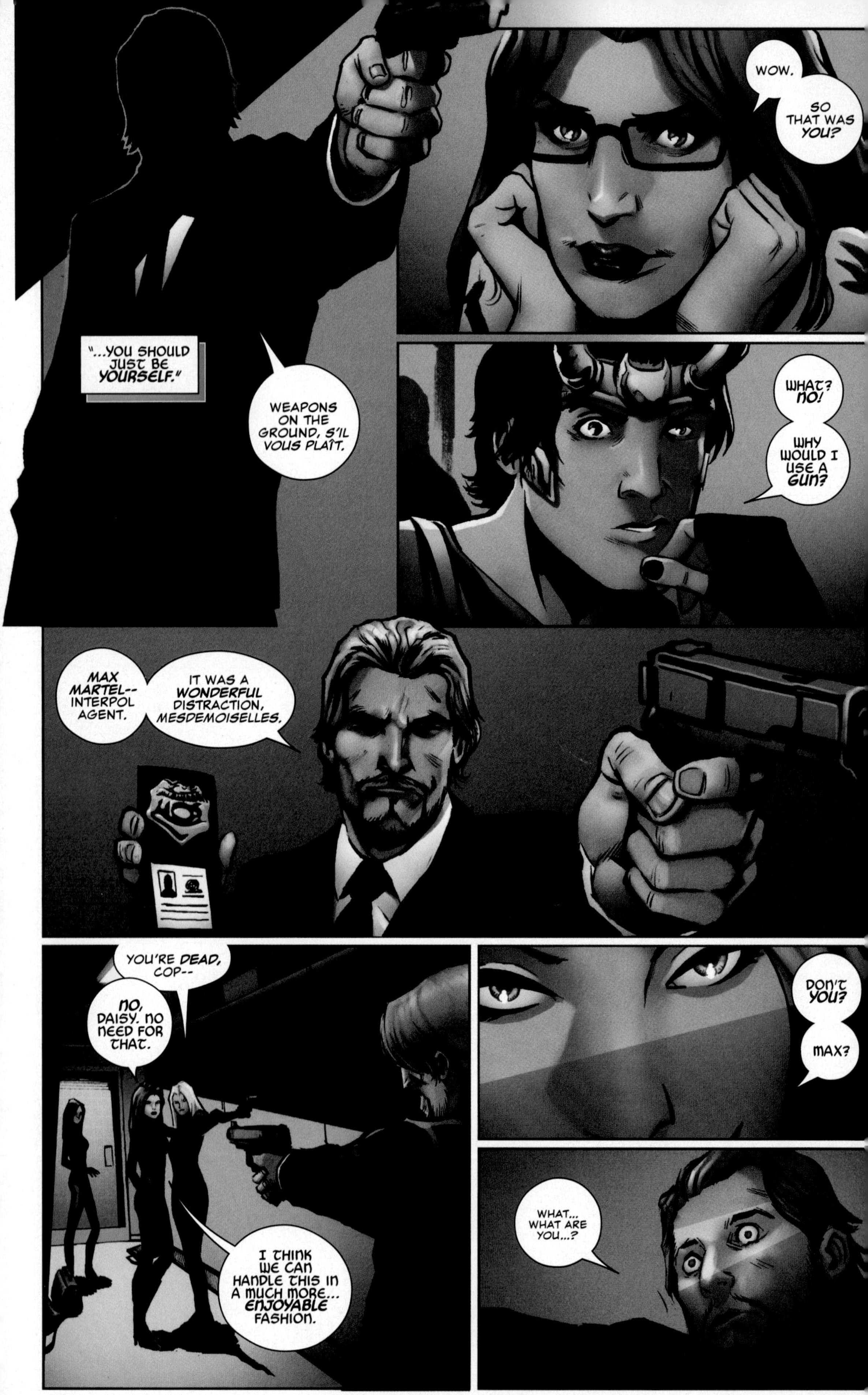

"...YOU SHOULD JUST BE YOURSELF."
WEAPONS ON THE GROUND, S'IL VOUS PLAÎT.
WOW.
SO THAT WAS YOU?
WHAT? NO!
WHY WOULD I USE A GUN?
MAX MARTEL-- INTERPOL AGENT.
IT WAS A WONDERFUL DISTRACTION, MESDEMOISELLES.
YOU'RE DEAD, COP--
NO, DAISY. NO NEED FOR THAT.
I THINK WE CAN HANDLE THIS IN A MUCH MORE... ENJOYABLE FASHION.
DON'T YOU?
MAX?
WHAT... WHAT ARE YOU...?

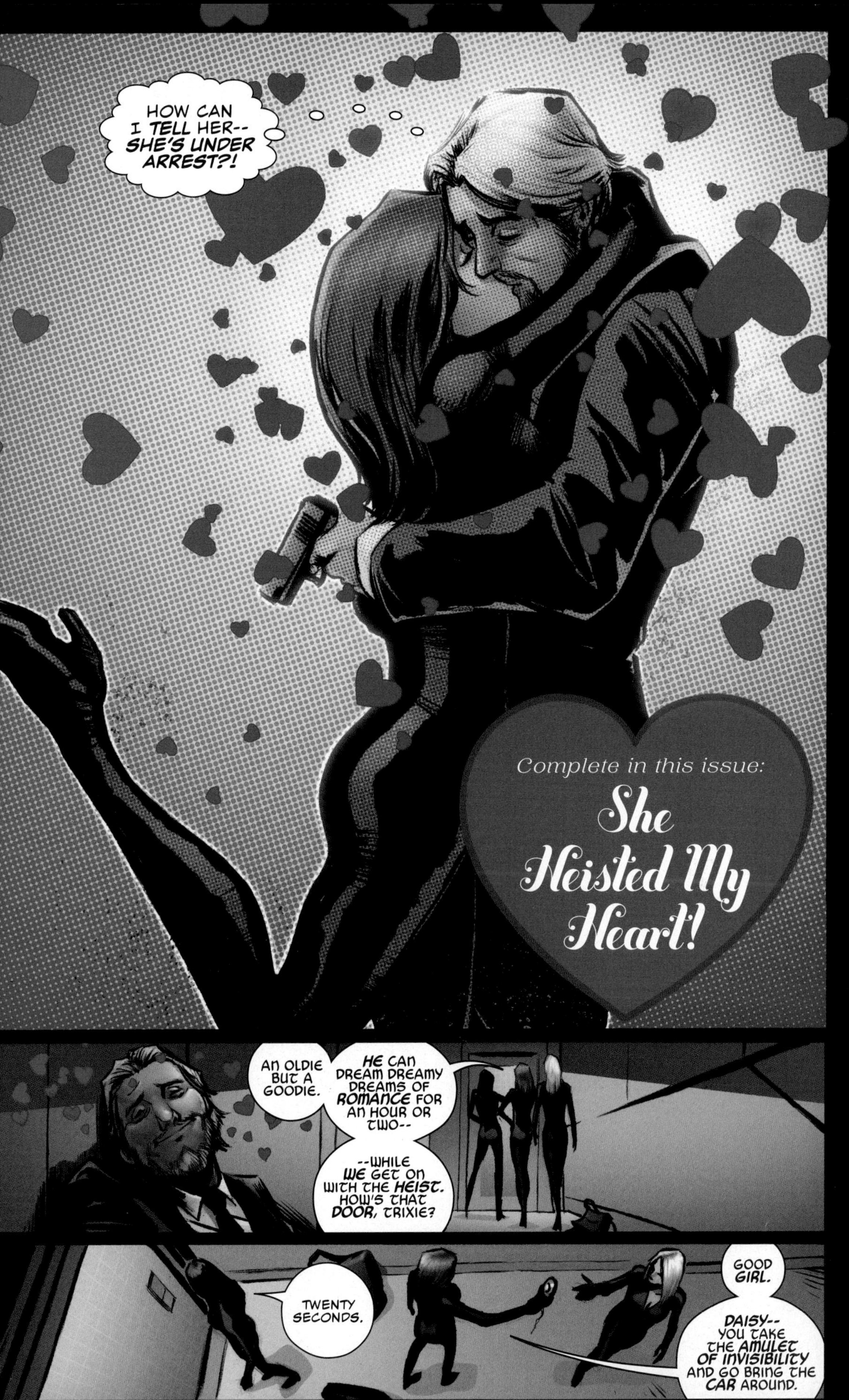
HOW CAN I TELL HER-- SHE'S UNDER ARREST?!
Complete in this issue:
She Heisted My Heart!
AN OLDIE BUT A GOODIE.
HE CAN DREAM DREAMY DREAMS OF ROMANCE FOR AN HOUR OR TWO--
--WHILE WE GET ON WITH THE HEIST. HOW'S THAT DOOR, TRIXIE?
TWENTY SECONDS.
GOOD GIRL.
DAISY-- YOU TAKE THE AMULET OF INVISIBILITY AND GO BRING THE CAR AROUND.

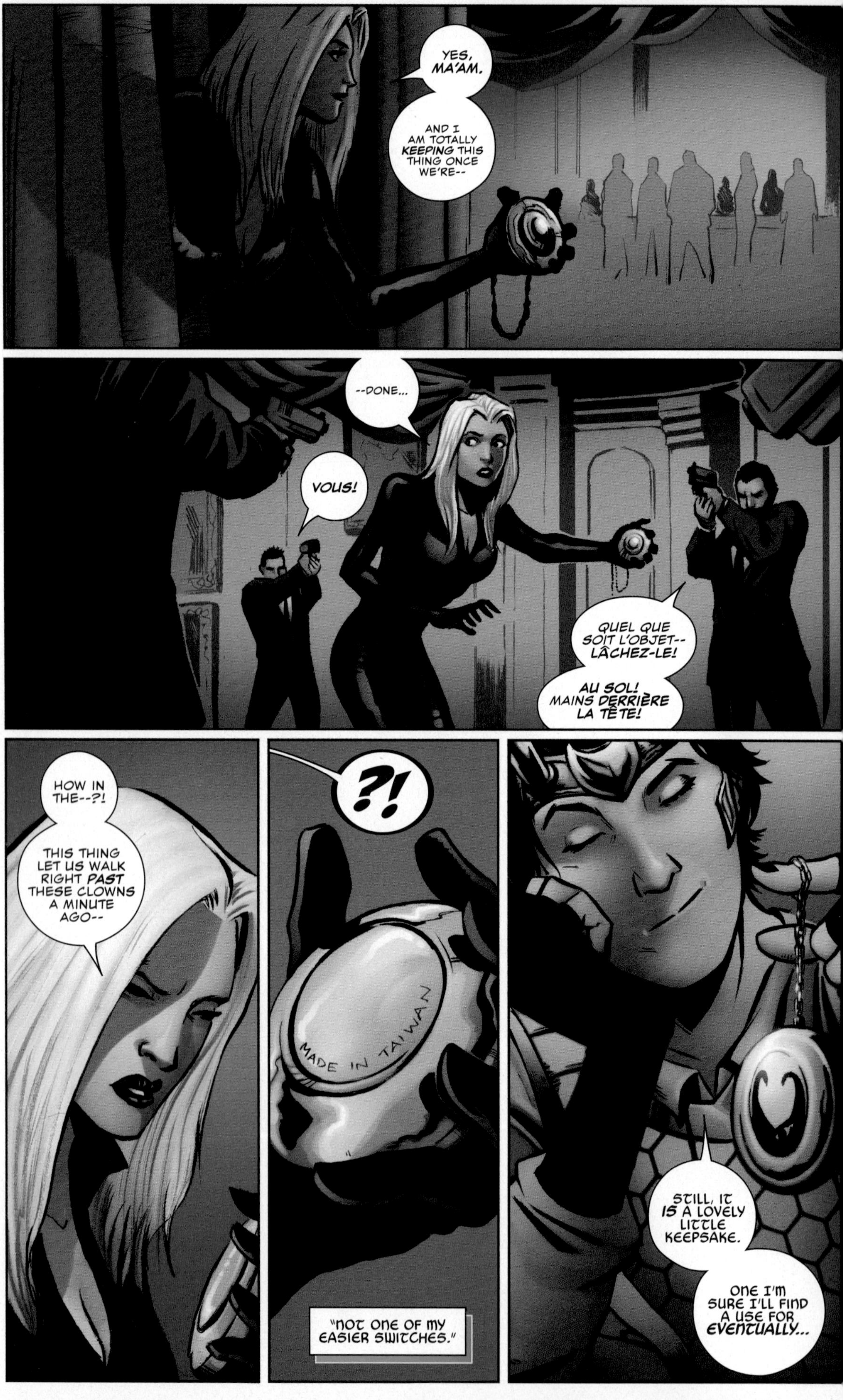
YES, MA'AM.
AND I AM TOTALLY KEEPING THIS THING ONCE WE'RE--
--DONE...
VOUS!
QUEL QUE SOIT L'OBJET-- LÂCHEZ-LE!
AU SOL! MAINS DERRIÈRE LA TÊTE!
HOW IN THE--?!
THIS THING LET US WALK RIGHT PAST THESE CLOWNS A MINUTE AGO--
?!
MADE IN TAIWAN
"NOT ONE OF MY EASIER SWITCHES."
STILL, IT IS A LOVELY LITTLE KEEPSAKE.
ONE I'M SURE I'LL FIND A USE FOR EVENTUALLY...

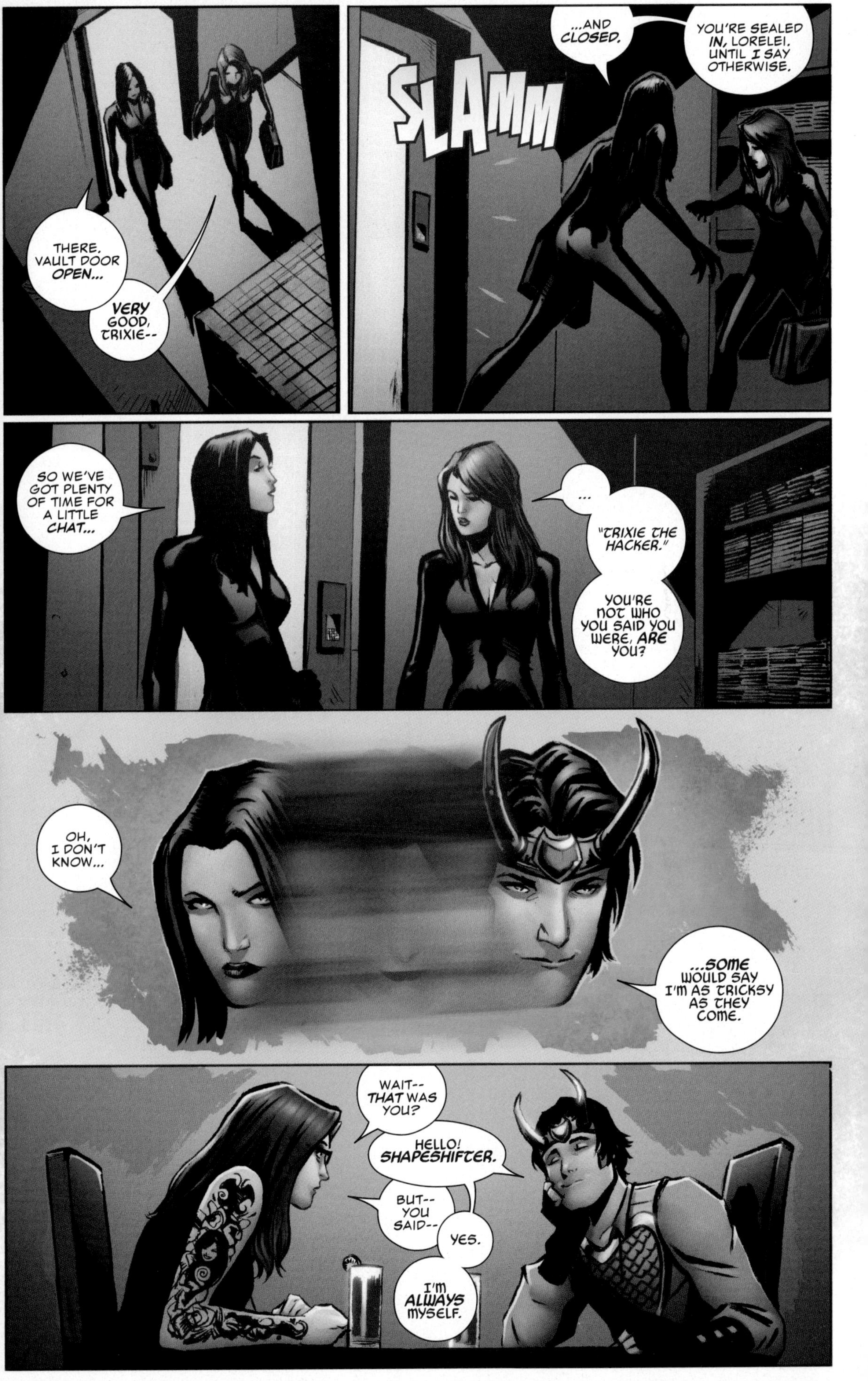
THERE. VAULT DOOR OPEN...
VERY GOOD, TRIXIE--
SLAMM
...AND CLOSED.
YOU'RE SEALED IN, LORELEI. UNTIL I SAY OTHERWISE.
SO WE'VE GOT PLENTY OF TIME FOR A LITTLE CHAT...
...
"TRIXIE THE HACKER."
YOU'RE NOT WHO YOU SAID YOU WERE, ARE YOU?
OH, I DON'T KNOW...
...SOME WOULD SAY I'M AS TRICKSY AS THEY COME.
WAIT-- THAT WAS YOU?
HELLO! SHAPESHIFTER.
BUT-- YOU SAID--
YES.
I'M ALWAYS MYSELF.

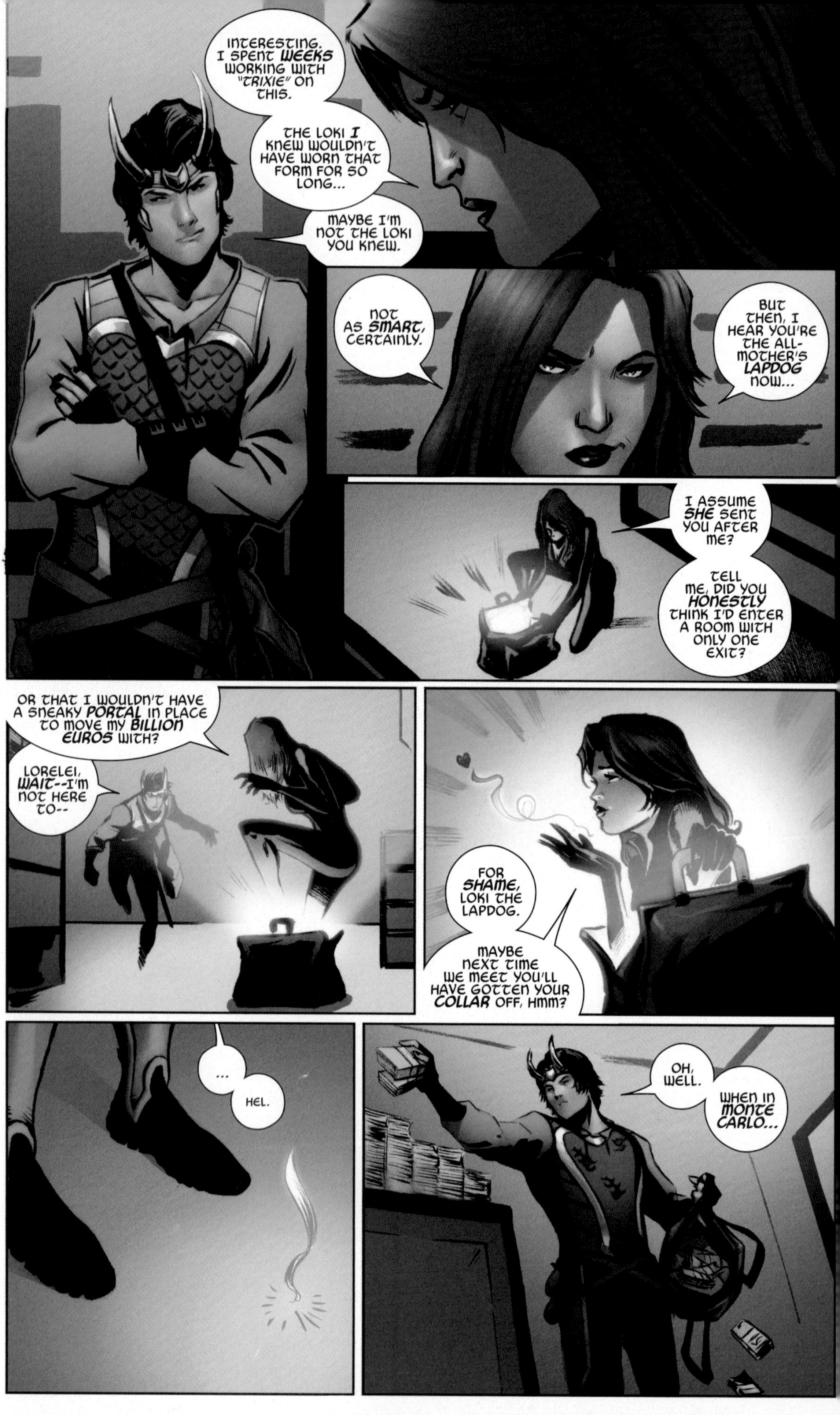
INTERESTING. I SPENT WEEKS WORKING WITH "TRIXIE" ON THIS.
THE LOKI I KNEW WOULDN'T HAVE WORN THAT FORM FOR SO LONG...
MAYBE I'M NOT THE LOKI YOU KNEW.
NOT AS SMART, CERTAINLY.
BUT THEN, I HEAR YOU'RE THE ALL-MOTHER'S LAPDOG NOW...
I ASSUME SHE SENT YOU AFTER ME?
TELL ME, DID YOU HONESTLY THINK I'D ENTER A ROOM WITH ONLY ONE EXIT?
OR THAT I WOULDN'T HAVE A SNEAKY PORTAL IN PLACE TO MOVE MY BILLION EUROS WITH?
LORELEI, WAIT--I'M NOT HERE TO--
FOR SHAME, LOKI THE LAPDOG.
MAYBE NEXT TIME WE MEET YOU'LL HAVE GOTTEN YOUR COLLAR OFF, HMM?
...
HEL.
OH, WELL.
WHEN IN MONTE CARLO...

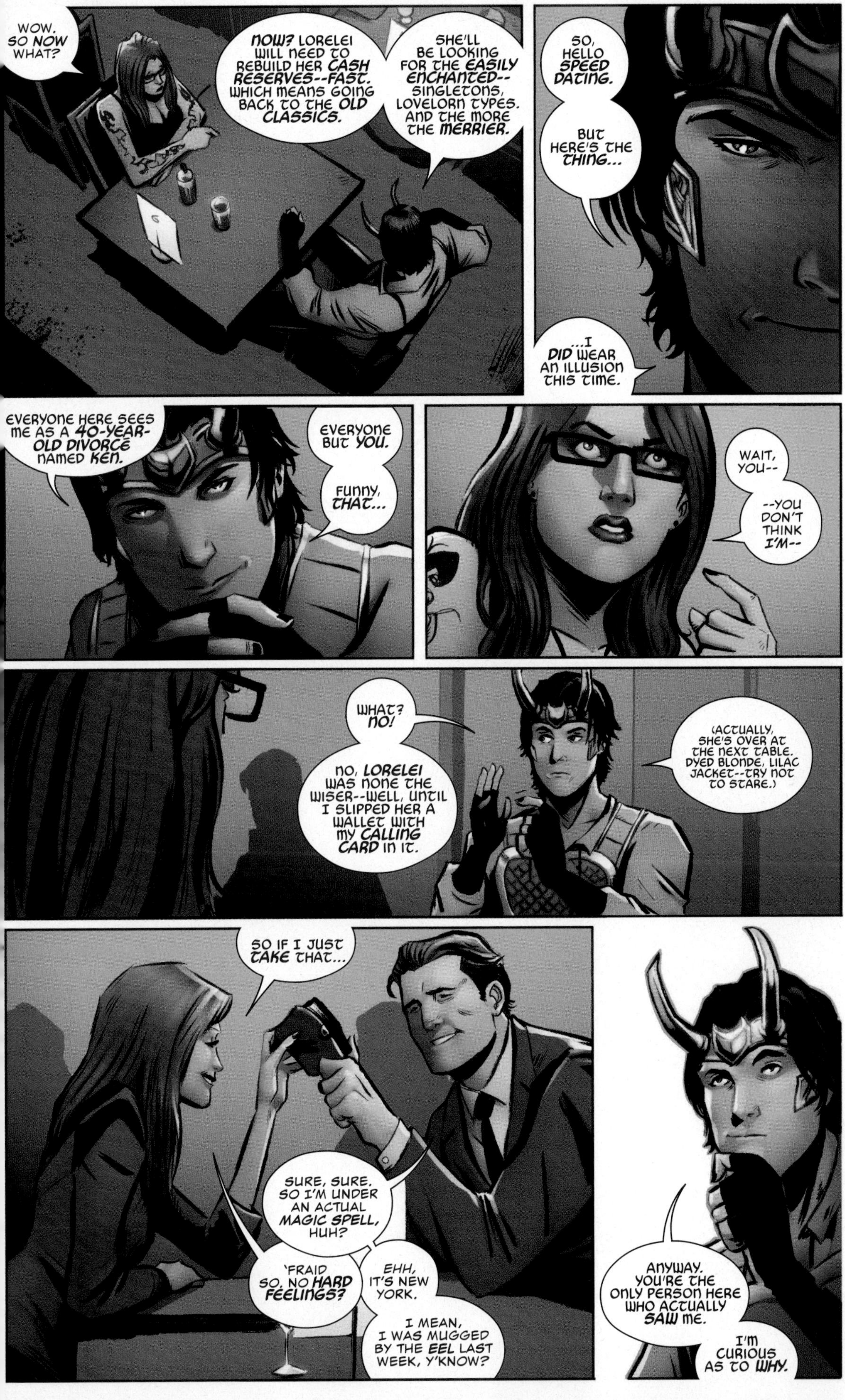
WOW. SO NOW WHAT?
NOW? LORELEI WILL NEED TO REBUILD HER CASH RESERVES--FAST. WHICH MEANS GOING BACK TO THE OLD CLASSICS.
SHE'LL BE LOOKING FOR THE EASILY ENCHANTED--SINGLETONS, LOVELORN TYPES. AND THE MORE THE MERRIER.
SO, HELLO SPEED DATING.
BUT HERE'S THE THING...
...I DID WEAR AN ILLUSION THIS TIME.
EVERYONE HERE SEES ME AS A 40-YEAR-OLD DIVORCÉ NAMED KEN.
EVERYONE BUT YOU.
FUNNY, THAT...
WAIT, YOU--
--YOU DON'T THINK I'M--
WHAT? NO!
NO, LORELEI WAS NONE THE WISER--WELL, UNTIL I SLIPPED HER A WALLET WITH MY CALLING CARD IN IT.
(ACTUALLY, SHE'S OVER AT THE NEXT TABLE. DYED BLONDE, LILAC JACKET--TRY NOT TO STARE.)
SO IF I JUST TAKE THAT...
SURE, SURE. SO I'M UNDER AN ACTUAL MAGIC SPELL, HUH?
'FRAID SO. NO HARD FEELINGS?
EHH, IT'S NEW YORK.
I MEAN, I WAS MUGGED BY THE EEL LAST WEEK, Y'KNOW?
ANYWAY. YOU'RE THE ONLY PERSON HERE WHO ACTUALLY SAW ME.
I'M CURIOUS AS TO WHY.

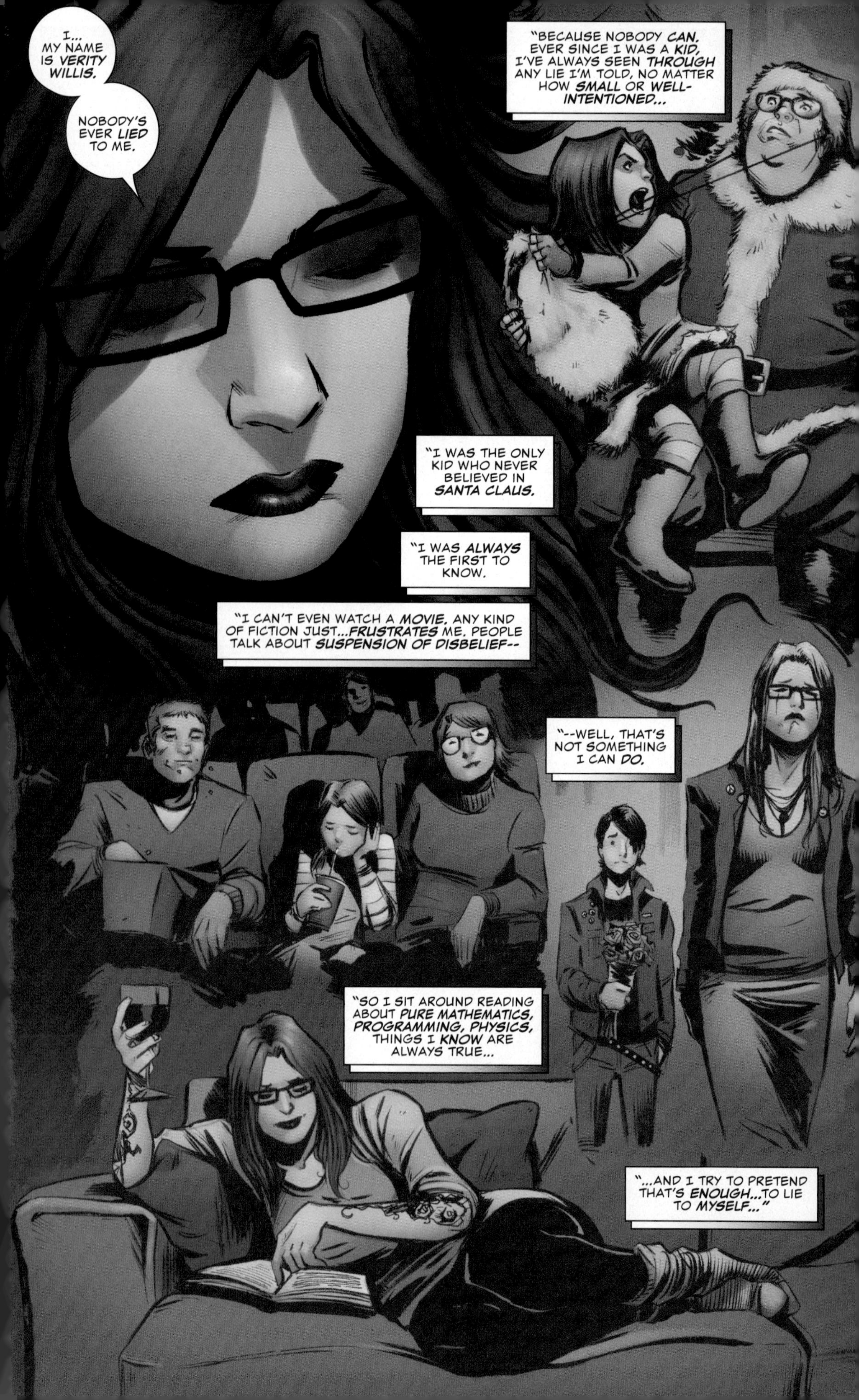
I... MY NAME IS VERITY WILLIS.
NOBODY'S EVER LIED TO ME.
"BECAUSE NOBODY CAN. EVER SINCE I WAS A KID, I'VE ALWAYS SEEN THROUGH ANY LIE I'M TOLD, NO MATTER HOW SMALL OR WELL-INTENTIONED...
"I WAS THE ONLY KID WHO NEVER BELIEVED IN SANTA CLAUS.
"I WAS ALWAYS THE FIRST TO KNOW.
"I CAN'T EVEN WATCH A MOVIE. ANY KIND OF FICTION JUST...FRUSTRATES ME. PEOPLE TALK ABOUT SUSPENSION OF DISBELIEF--
"--WELL, THAT'S NOT SOMETHING I CAN DO.
"SO I SIT AROUND READING ABOUT PURE MATHEMATICS, PROGRAMMING, PHYSICS, THINGS I KNOW ARE ALWAYS TRUE...
"...AND I TRY TO PRETEND THAT'S ENOUGH...TO LIE TO MYSELF..."

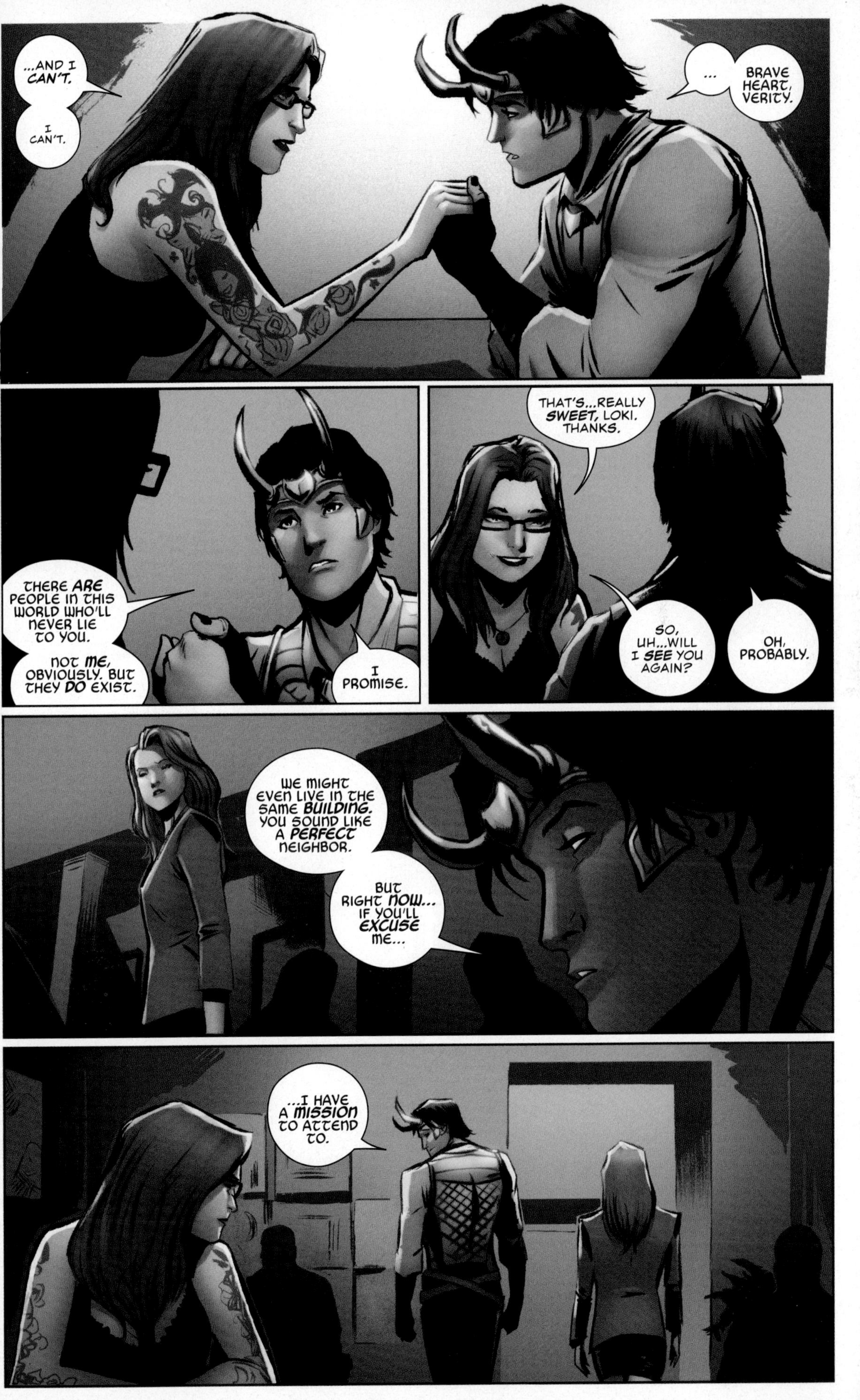

...AND I CAN'T.
I CAN'T.
... BRAVE HEART, VERITY.
THERE ARE PEOPLE IN THIS WORLD WHO'LL NEVER LIE TO YOU.
NOT ME, OBVIOUSLY. BUT THEY DO EXIST.
I PROMISE.
THAT'S...REALLY SWEET, LOKI. THANKS.
SO, UH...WILL I SEE YOU AGAIN?
OH, PROBABLY.
WE MIGHT EVEN LIVE IN THE SAME BUILDING. YOU SOUND LIKE A PERFECT NEIGHBOR.
BUT RIGHT NOW... IF YOU'LL EXCUSE ME...
...I HAVE A MISSION TO ATTEND TO.

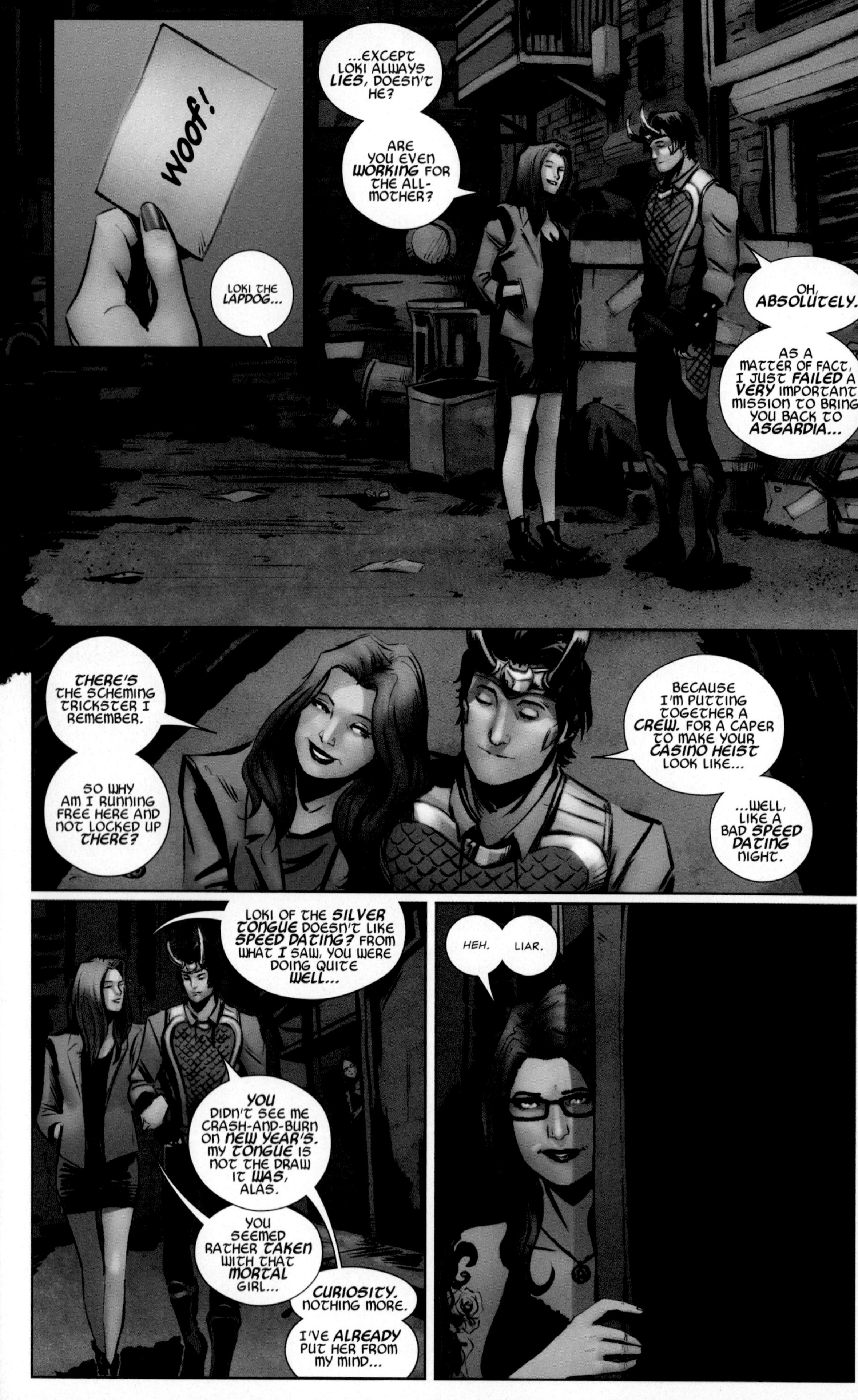
WOOF!
LOKI THE LAPDOG...
...EXCEPT LOKI ALWAYS LIES, DOESN'T HE?
ARE YOU EVEN WORKING FOR THE ALL-MOTHER?
OH, ABSOLUTELY.
AS A MATTER OF FACT, I JUST FAILED A VERY IMPORTANT MISSION TO BRING YOU BACK TO ASGARDIA...
THERE'S THE SCHEMING TRICKSTER I REMEMBER.
SO WHY AM I RUNNING FREE HERE AND NOT LOCKED UP THERE?
BECAUSE I'M PUTTING TOGETHER A CREW. FOR A CAPER TO MAKE YOUR CASINO HEIST LOOK LIKE...
...WELL, LIKE A BAD SPEED DATING NIGHT.
LOKI OF THE SILVER TONGUE DOESN'T LIKE SPEED DATING? FROM WHAT I SAW, YOU WERE DOING QUITE WELL...
YOU DIDN'T SEE ME CRASH-AND-BURN ON NEW YEAR'S. MY TONGUE IS NOT THE DRAW IT WAS, ALAS.
YOU SEEMED RATHER TAKEN WITH THAT MORTAL GIRL...
CURIOSITY. NOTHING MORE.
I'VE ALREADY PUT HER FROM MY MIND...
HEH.
LIAR.

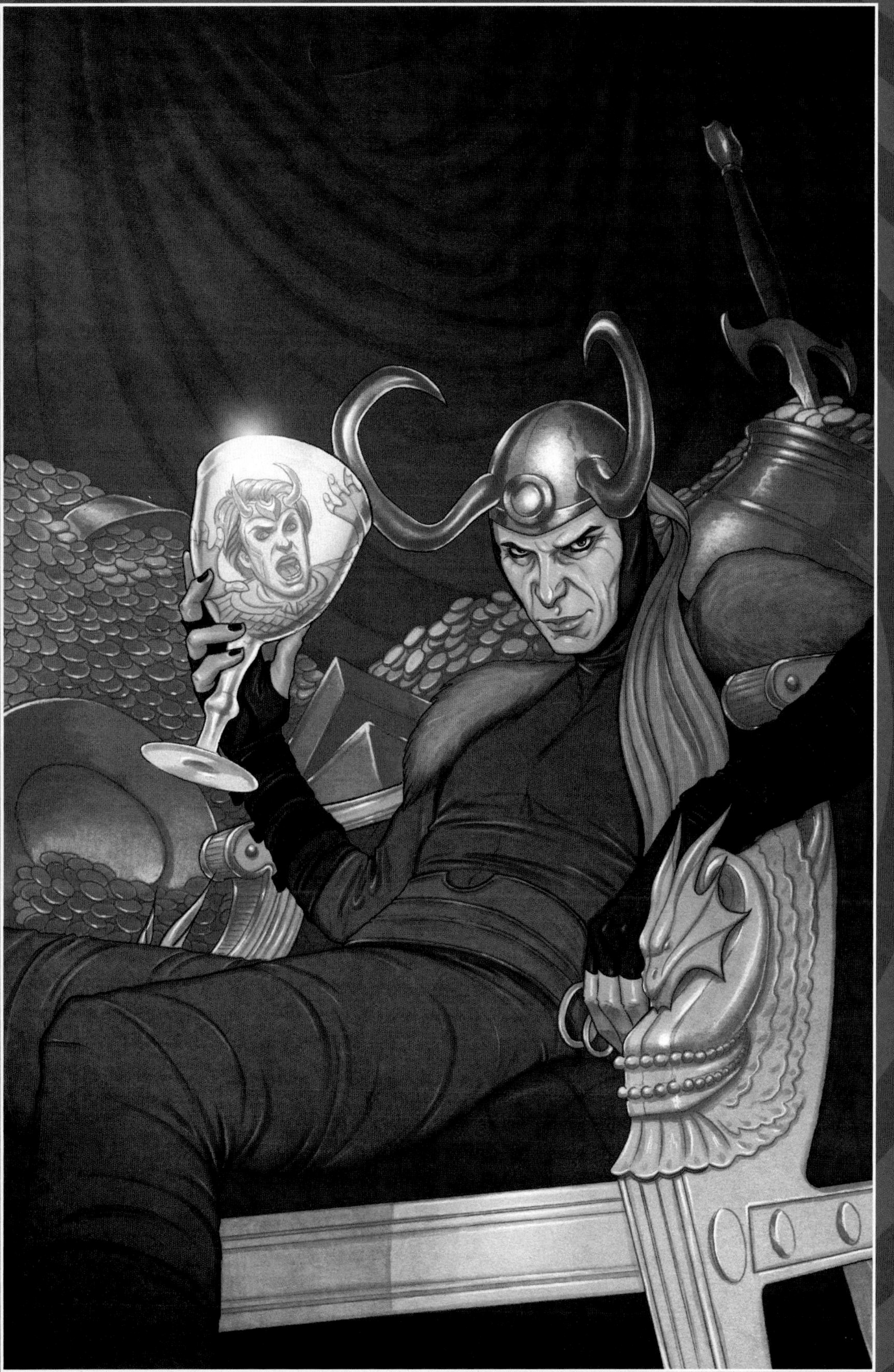

LOKI: AGENT OF ASGARD #3

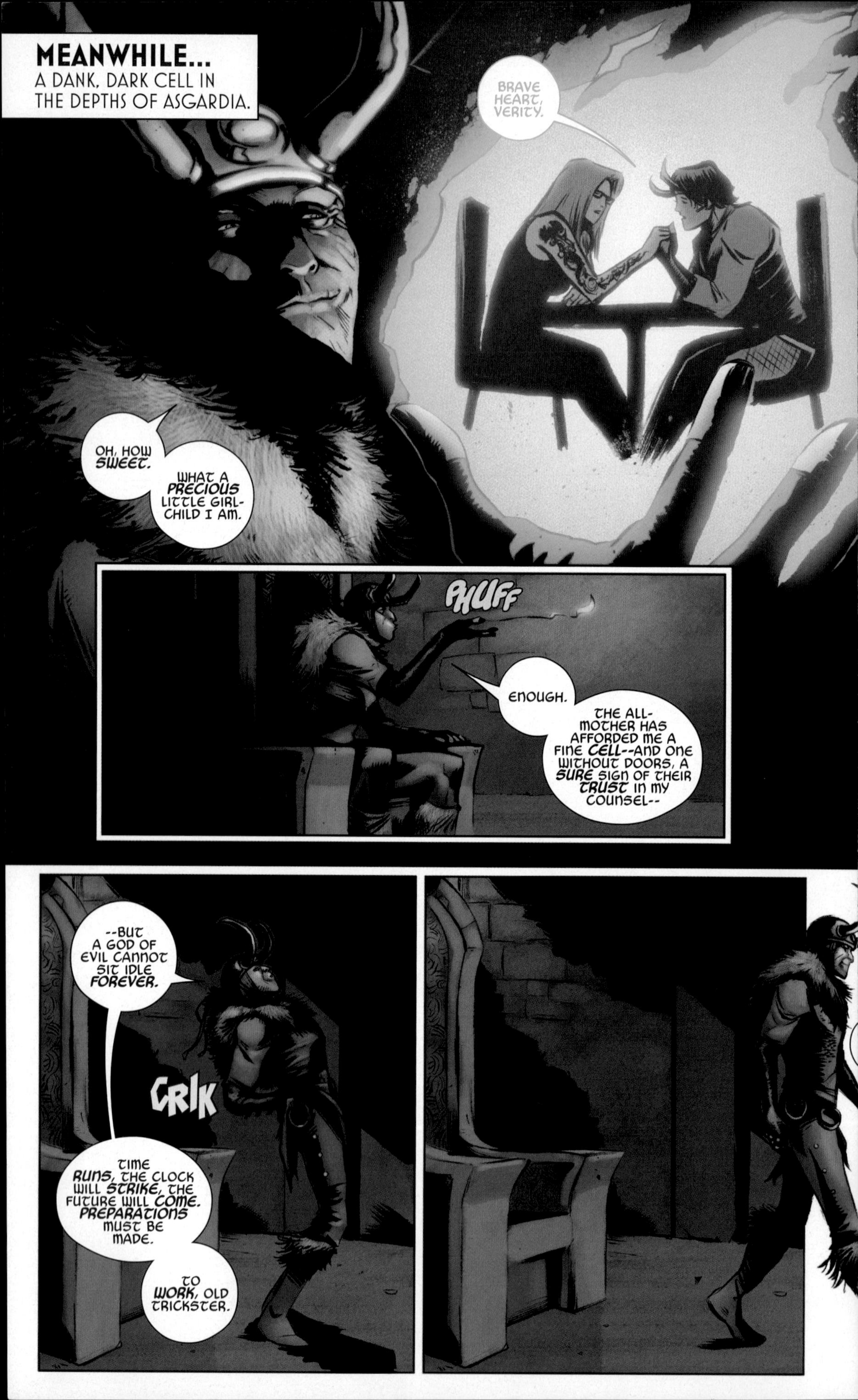
MEANWHILE...
A DANK, DARK CELL IN THE DEPTHS OF ASGARDIA.
BRAVE HEART, VERITY.
OH, HOW SWEET.
WHAT A PRECIOUS LITTLE GIRL-CHILD I AM.
PHUFF
ENOUGH.
THE ALL-MOTHER HAS AFFORDED ME A FINE CELL--AND ONE WITHOUT DOORS, A SURE SIGN OF THEIR TRUST IN MY COUNSEL--
--BUT A GOD OF EVIL CANNOT SIT IDLE FOREVER.
CRIK
TIME RUNS, THE CLOCK WILL STRIKE, THE FUTURE WILL COME. PREPARATIONS MUST BE MADE.
TO WORK, OLD TRICKSTER.

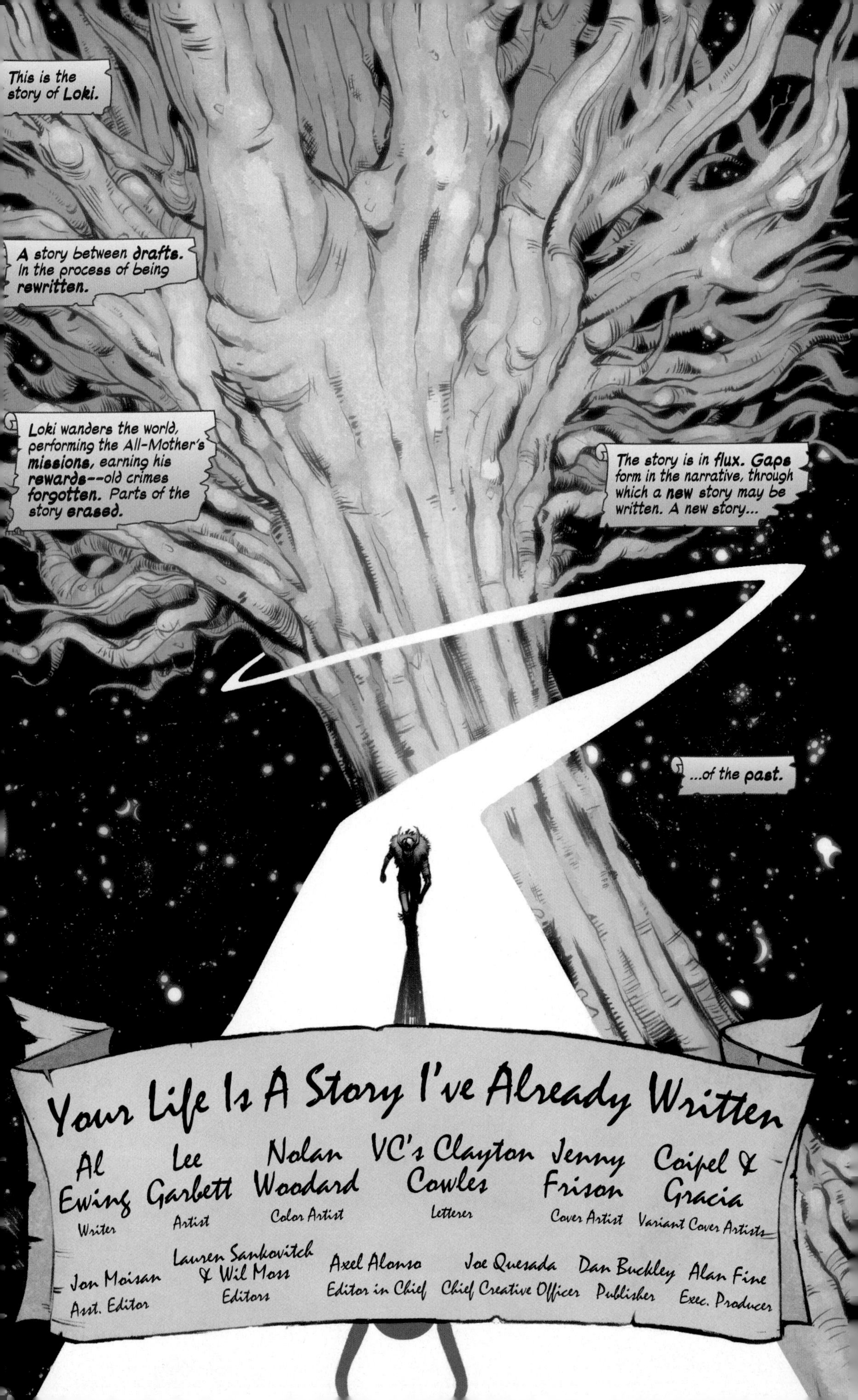
This is the story of Loki.
A story between drafts. In the process of being rewritten.
Loki wanders the world, performing the All-Mother's missions, earning his rewards--old crimes forgotten. Parts of the story erased.
The story is in flux. Gaps form in the narrative, through which a new story may be written. A new story...
...of the past.
Your Life Is A Story I've Already Written
Al Ewing Writer
Lee Garbett Artist
Nolan Woodard Color Artist
VC's Clayton Cowles Letterer
Jenny Frison Cover Artist
Coipel & Gracia Variant Cover Artists
Jon Moisan Asst. Editor
Lauren Sankovitch & Wil Moss Editors
Axel Alonso Editor in Chief
Joe Quesada Chief Creative Officer
Dan Buckley Publisher
Alan Fine Exec. Producer

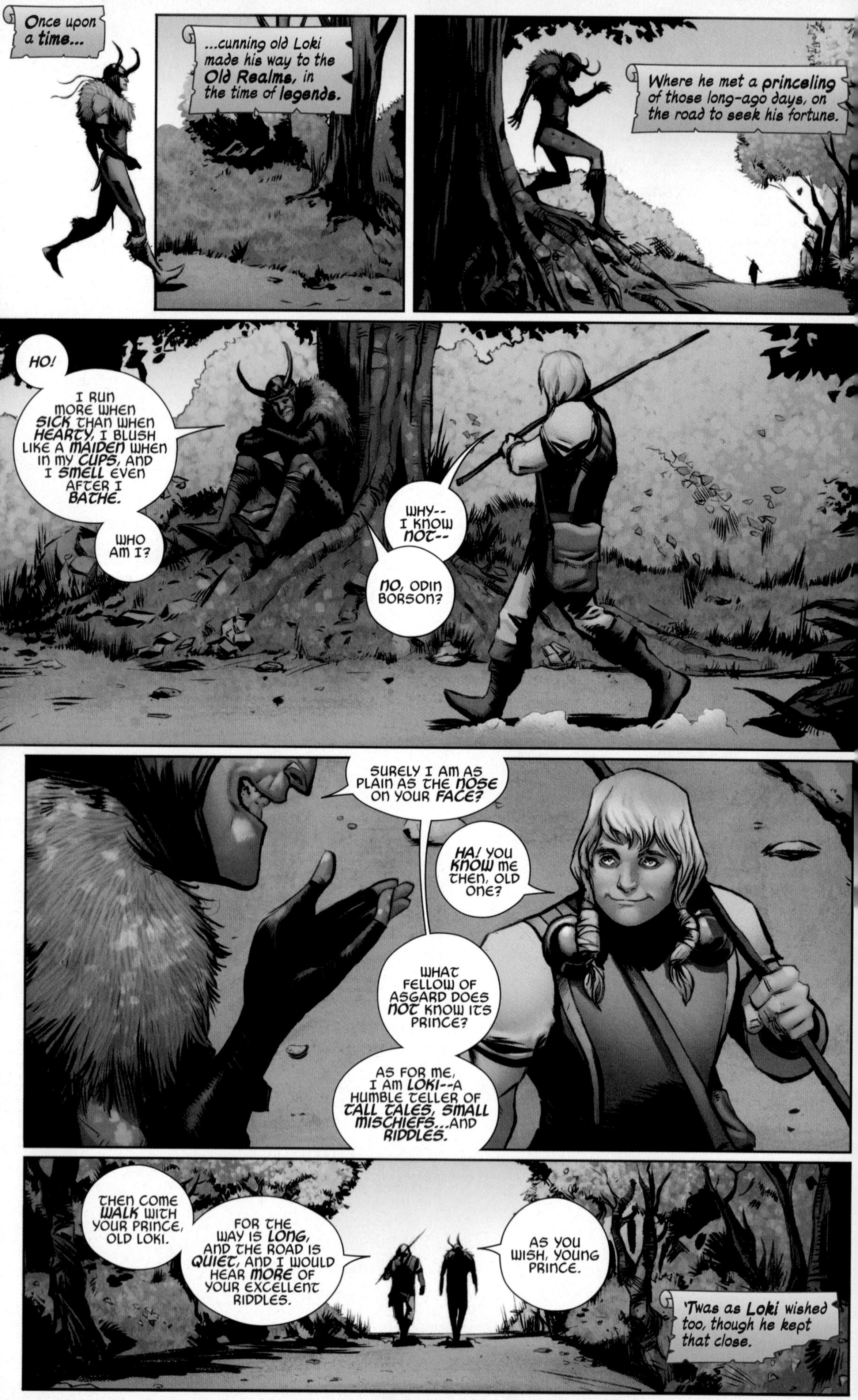
Once upon a time...
...cunning old Loki made his way to the Old Realms, in the time of legends.
Where he met a princeling of those long-ago days, on the road to seek his fortune.
HO!
I RUN MORE WHEN SICK THAN WHEN HEARTY, I BLUSH LIKE A MAIDEN WHEN IN MY CUPS, AND I SMELL EVEN AFTER I BATHE.
WHO AM I?
WHY-- I KNOW NOT--
NO, ODIN BORSON?
SURELY I AM AS PLAIN AS THE NOSE ON YOUR FACE?
HA! YOU KNOW ME THEN, OLD ONE?
WHAT FELLOW OF ASGARD DOES NOT KNOW ITS PRINCE?
AS FOR ME, I AM LOKI--A HUMBLE TELLER OF TALL TALES, SMALL MISCHIEFS...AND RIDDLES.
THEN COME WALK WITH YOUR PRINCE, OLD LOKI.
FOR THE WAY IS LONG, AND THE ROAD IS QUIET, AND I WOULD HEAR MORE OF YOUR EXCELLENT RIDDLES.
AS YOU WISH, YOUNG PRINCE.
'Twas as Loki wished too, though he kept that close.

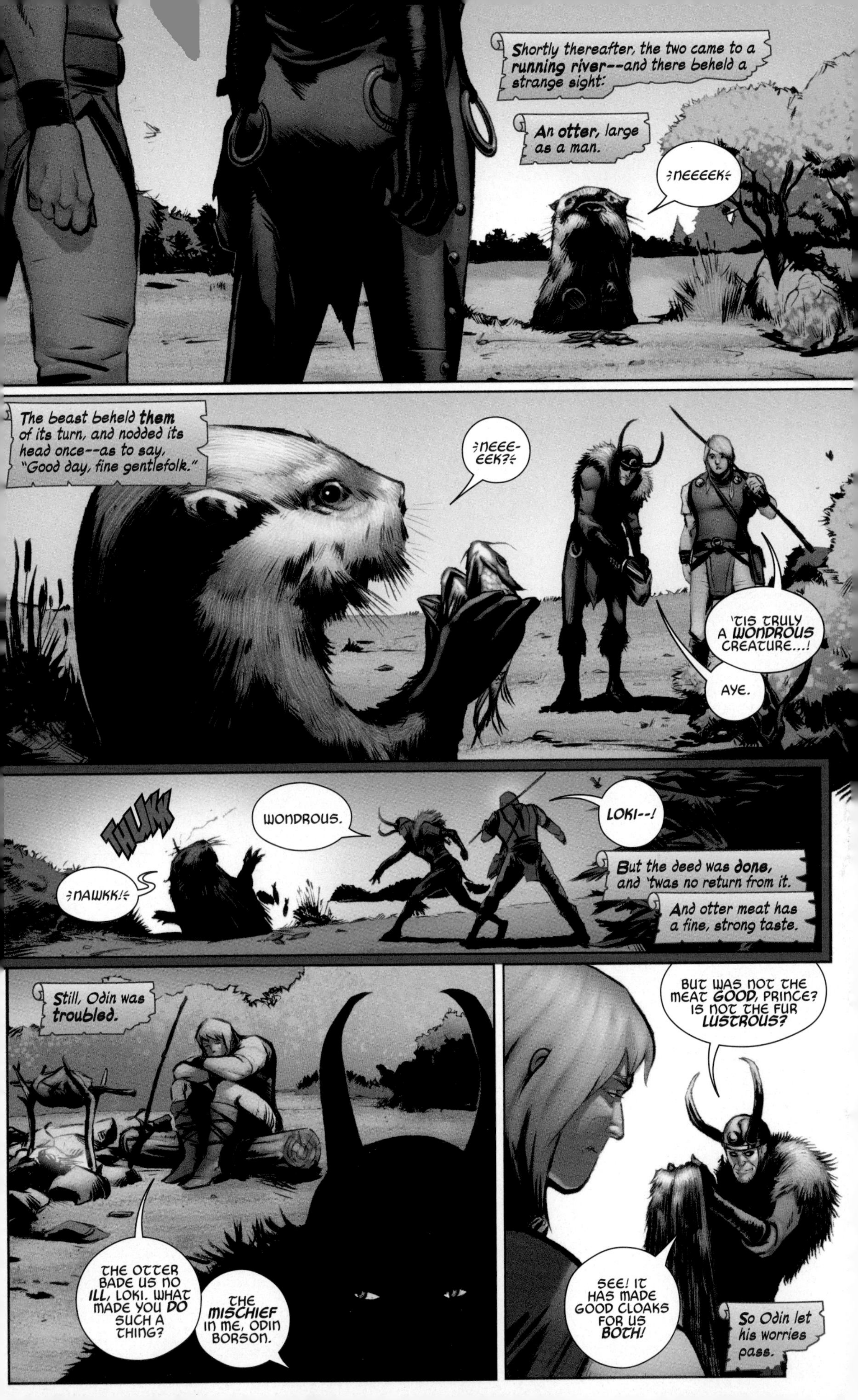
Shortly thereafter, the two came to a running river--and there beheld a strange sight:
An otter, large as a man.
NEEEEK
The beast beheld them of its turn, and nodded its head once--as to say, "Good day, fine gentlefolk."
NEEE-EEK?
'TIS TRULY A WONDROUS CREATURE...!
AYE.
THUKK
WONDROUS.
LOKI--!
NAWKK!
But the deed was done, and 'twas no return from it.
And otter meat has a fine, strong taste.
Still, Odin was troubled.
THE OTTER BADE US NO ILL, LOKI. WHAT MADE YOU DO SUCH A THING?
THE MISCHIEF IN ME, ODIN BORSON.
BUT WAS NOT THE MEAT GOOD, PRINCE? IS NOT THE FUR LUSTROUS?
SEE! IT HAS MADE GOOD CLOAKS FOR US BOTH!
So Odin let his worries pass.

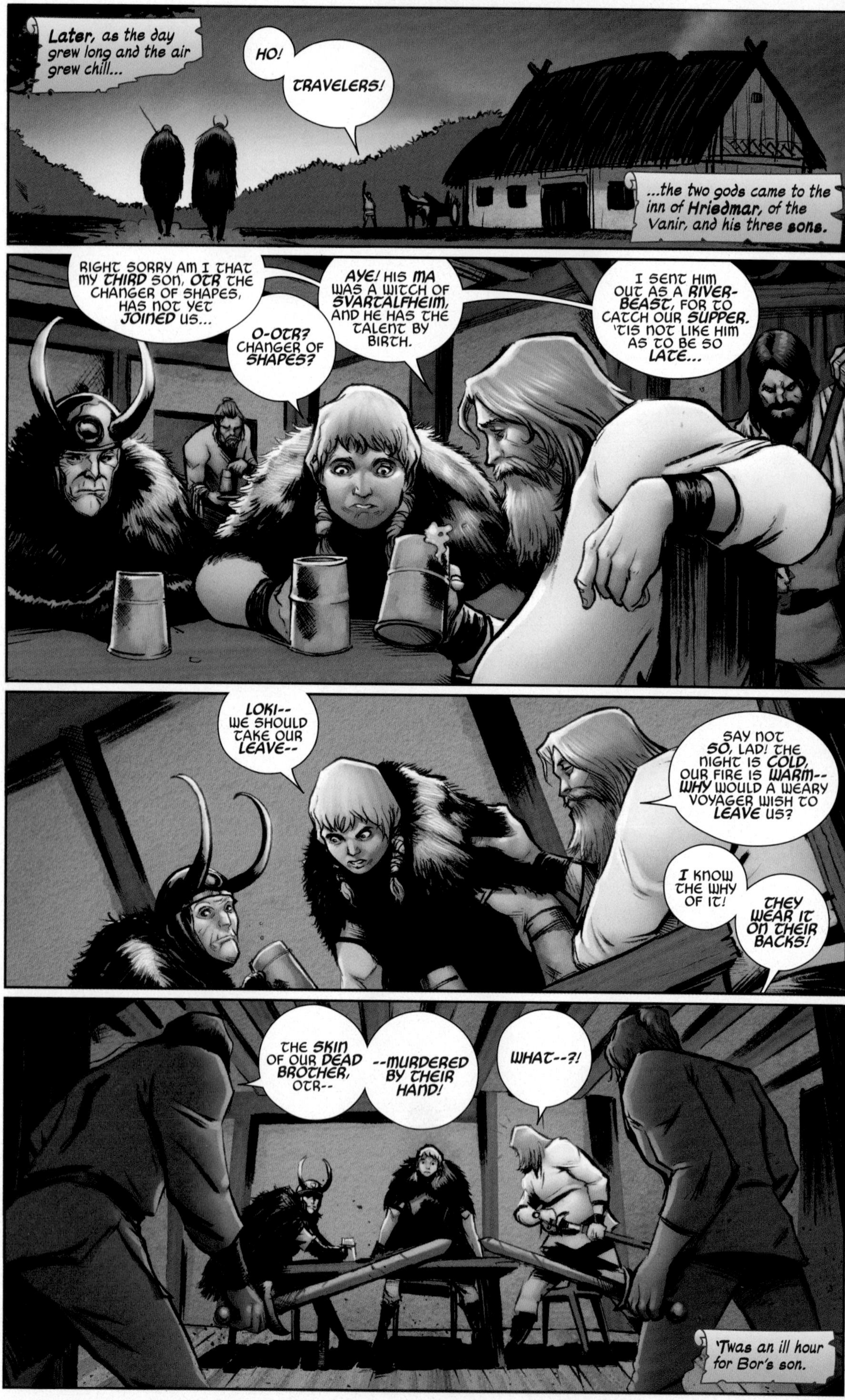

Later, as the day grew long and the air grew chill...
HO!
TRAVELERS!
...the two gods came to the inn of Hriedmar, of the Vanir, and his three sons.
RIGHT SORRY AM I THAT MY THIRD SON, OTR THE CHANGER OF SHAPES, HAS NOT YET JOINED US...
O-OTR? CHANGER OF SHAPES?
AYE! HIS MA WAS A WITCH OF SVARTALFHEIM, AND HE HAS THE TALENT BY BIRTH.
I SENT HIM OUT AS A RIVER-BEAST, FOR TO CATCH OUR SUPPER. 'TIS NOT LIKE HIM AS TO BE SO LATE...
LOKI-- WE SHOULD TAKE OUR LEAVE--
SAY NOT SO, LAD! THE NIGHT IS COLD, OUR FIRE IS WARM-- WHY WOULD A WEARY VOYAGER WISH TO LEAVE US?
I KNOW THE WHY OF IT!
THEY WEAR IT ON THEIR BACKS!
THE SKIN OF OUR DEAD BROTHER, OTR--
--MURDERED BY THEIR HAND!
WHAT--?!
'Twas an ill hour for Bor's son.

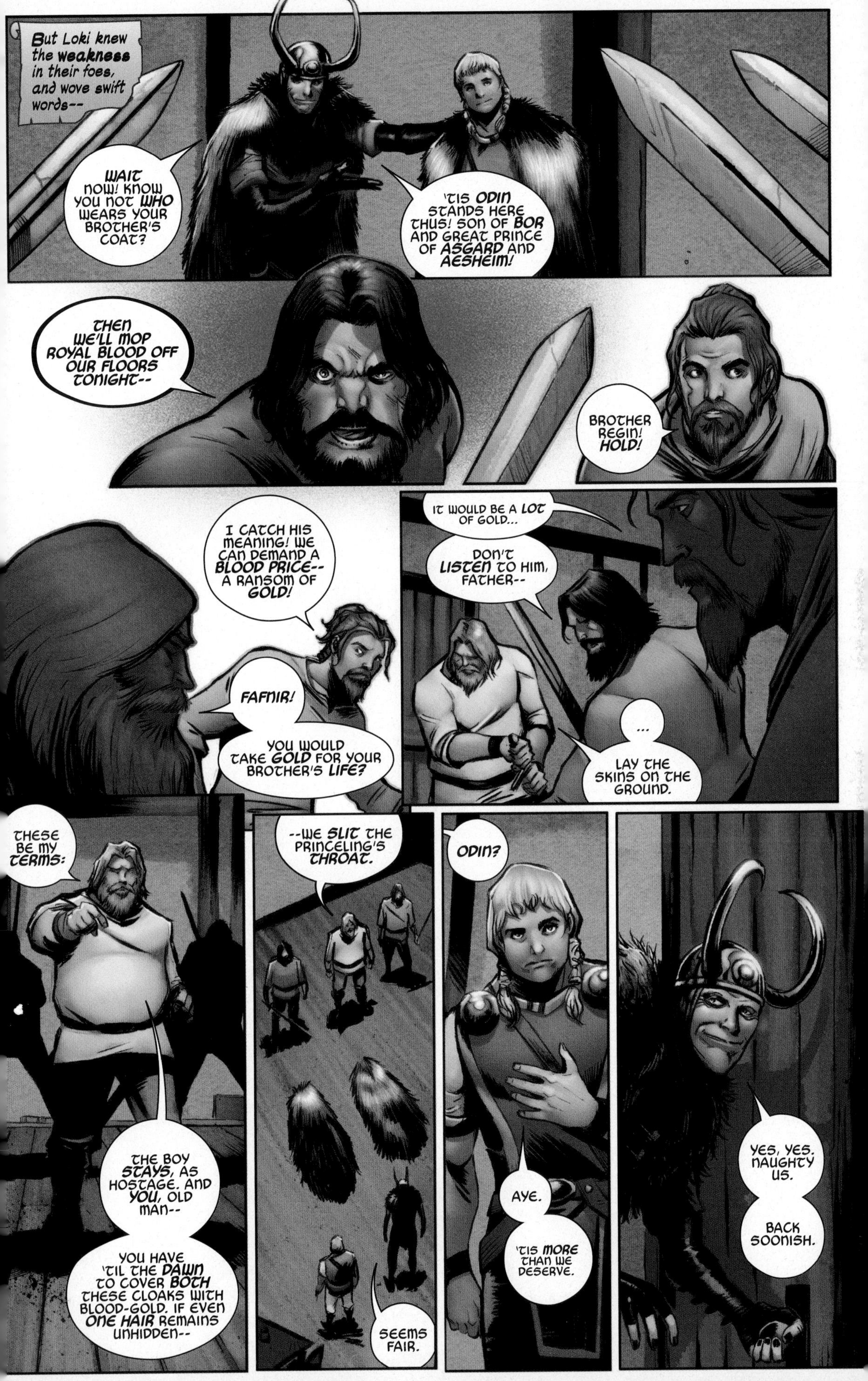
But Loki knew the weakness in their foes, and wove swift words--
WAIT NOW! KNOW YOU NOT WHO WEARS YOUR BROTHER'S COAT?
'TIS ODIN STANDS HERE THUS! SON OF BOR AND GREAT PRINCE OF ASGARD AND AESHEIM!
THEN WE'LL MOP ROYAL BLOOD OFF OUR FLOORS TONIGHT--
BROTHER REGIN! HOLD!
I CATCH HIS MEANING! WE CAN DEMAND A BLOOD PRICE-- A RANSOM OF GOLD!
FAFNIR!
YOU WOULD TAKE GOLD FOR YOUR BROTHER'S LIFE?
IT WOULD BE A LOT OF GOLD...
DON'T LISTEN TO HIM, FATHER--
...
LAY THE SKINS ON THE GROUND.
THESE BE MY TERMS:
THE BOY STAYS, AS HOSTAGE. AND YOU, OLD MAN--
YOU HAVE 'TIL THE DAWN TO COVER BOTH THESE CLOAKS WITH BLOOD-GOLD. IF EVEN ONE HAIR REMAINS UNHIDDEN--
--WE SLIT THE PRINCELING'S THROAT.
SEEMS FAIR.
ODIN?
AYE.
'TIS MORE THAN WE DESERVE.
YES, YES. NAUGHTY US.
BACK SOONISH.

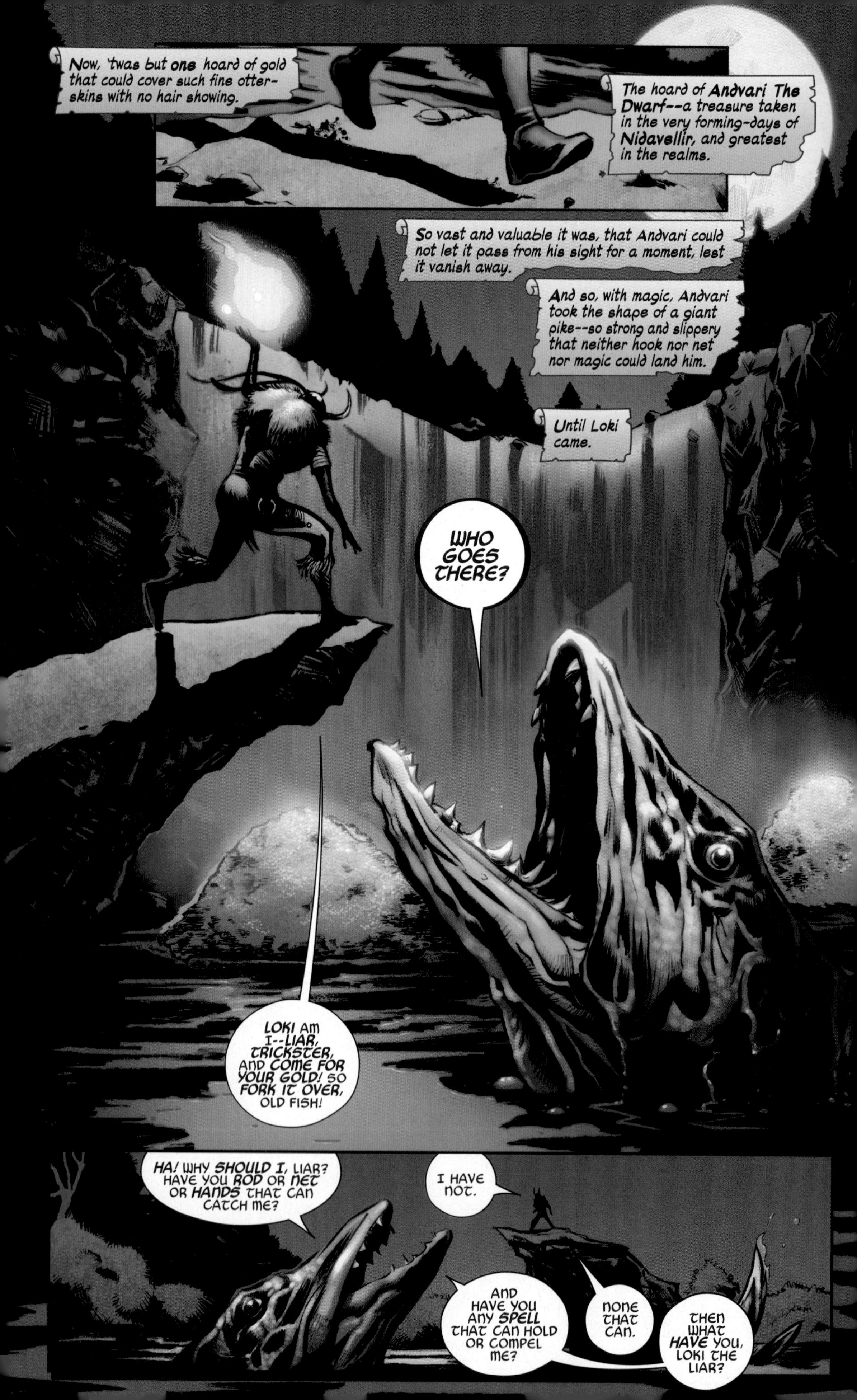
Now, 'twas but one hoard of gold that could cover such fine otter-skins with no hair showing.
The hoard of Andvari The Dwarf--a treasure taken in the very forming-days of Nidavellir, and greatest in the realms.
So vast and valuable it was, that Andvari could not let it pass from his sight for a moment, lest it vanish away.
And so, with magic, Andvari took the shape of a giant pike--so strong and slippery that neither hook nor net nor magic could land him.
Until Loki came.
WHO GOES THERE?
LOKI AM I--LIAR, TRICKSTER, AND COME FOR YOUR GOLD! SO FORK IT OVER, OLD FISH!
HA! WHY SHOULD I, LIAR? HAVE YOU ROD OR NET OR HANDS THAT CAN CATCH ME?
I HAVE NOT.
AND HAVE YOU ANY SPELL THAT CAN HOLD OR COMPEL ME?
NONE THAT CAN.
THEN WHAT HAVE YOU, LOKI THE LIAR?

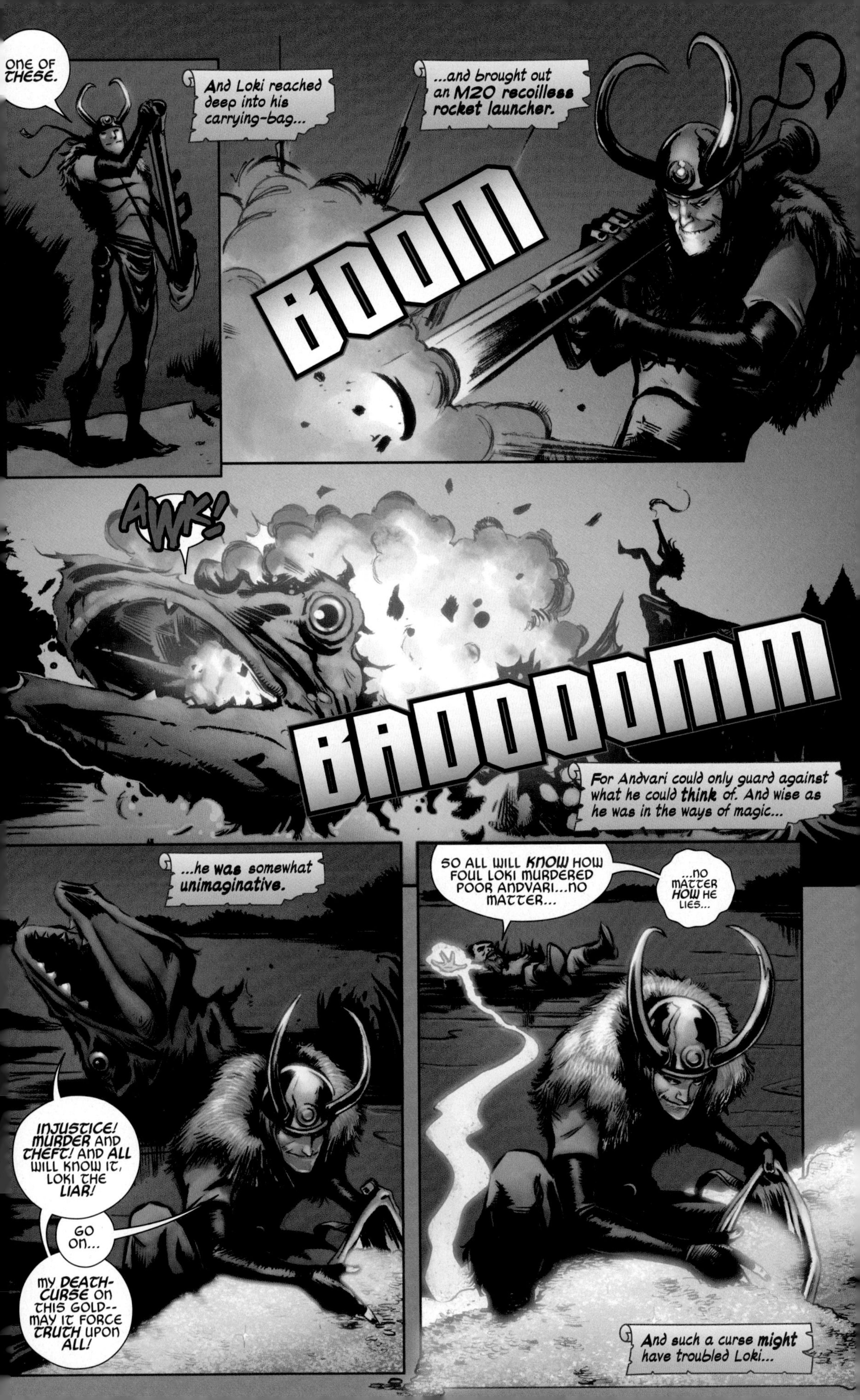
ONE OF THESE.
And Loki reached deep into his carrying-bag...
...and brought out an M20 recoilless rocket launcher.
BOOM
AWK!
BADOOOMM
For Andvari could only guard against what he could think of. And wise as he was in the ways of magic...
...he was somewhat unimaginative.
INJUSTICE! MURDER AND THEFT! AND ALL WILL KNOW IT, LOKI THE LIAR!
GO ON...
MY DEATH-CURSE ON THIS GOLD--MAY IT FORCE TRUTH UPON ALL!
SO ALL WILL KNOW HOW FOUL LOKI MURDERED POOR ANDVARI...NO MATTER...
...NO MATTER HOW HE LIES...
And such a curse might have troubled Loki...

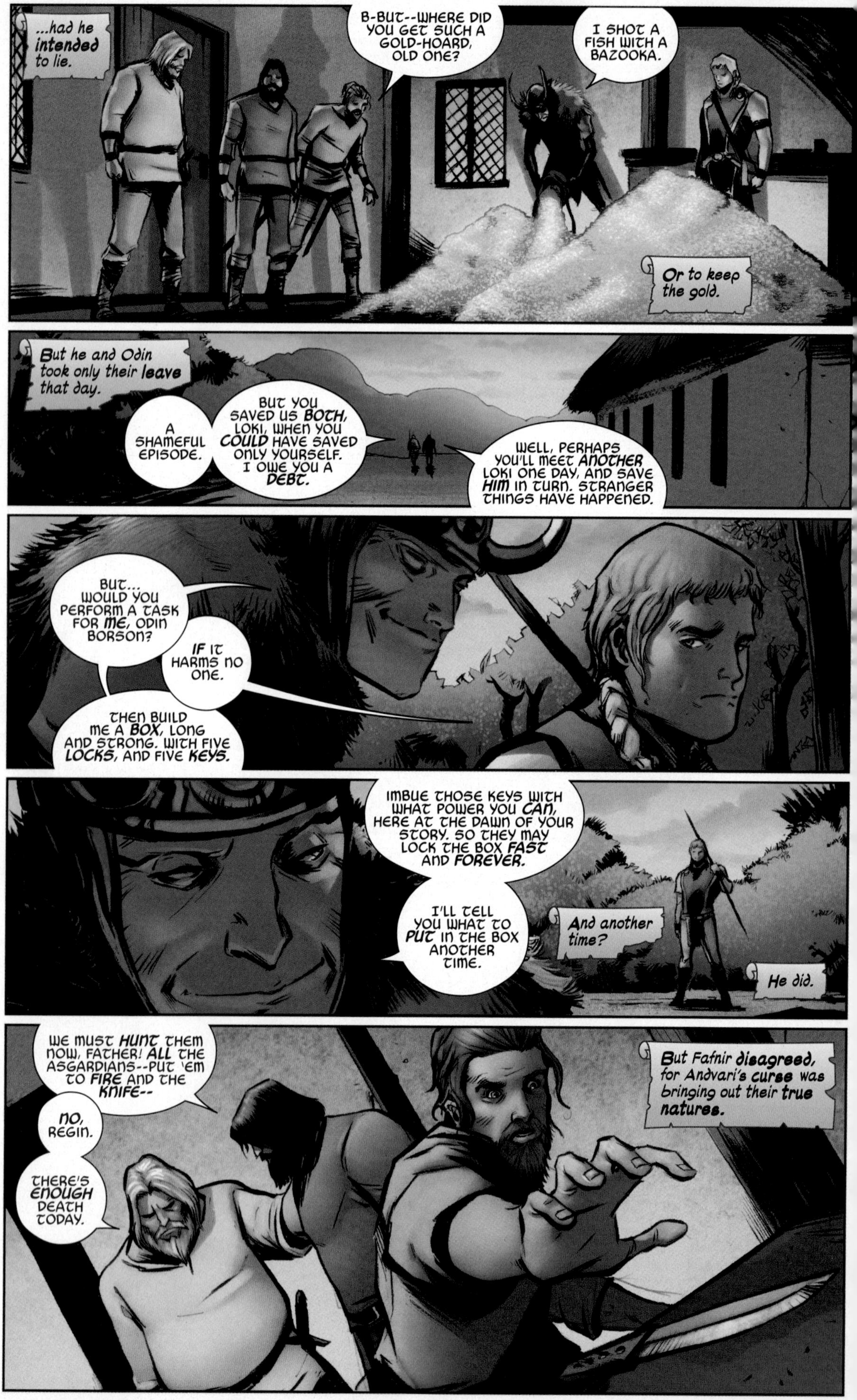
...had he intended to lie.
B-BUT--WHERE DID YOU GET SUCH A GOLD-HOARD, OLD ONE?
I SHOT A FISH WITH A BAZOOKA.
Or to keep the gold.
But he and Odin took only their leave that day.
A SHAMEFUL EPISODE.
BUT YOU SAVED US BOTH, LOKI, WHEN YOU COULD HAVE SAVED ONLY YOURSELF. I OWE YOU A DEBT.
WELL, PERHAPS YOU'LL MEET ANOTHER LOKI ONE DAY, AND SAVE HIM IN TURN. STRANGER THINGS HAVE HAPPENED.
BUT... WOULD YOU PERFORM A TASK FOR ME, ODIN BORSON?
IF IT HARMS NO ONE.
THEN BUILD ME A BOX, LONG AND STRONG. WITH FIVE LOCKS, AND FIVE KEYS.
IMBUE THOSE KEYS WITH WHAT POWER YOU CAN, HERE AT THE DAWN OF YOUR STORY. SO THEY MAY LOCK THE BOX FAST AND FOREVER.
I'LL TELL YOU WHAT TO PUT IN THE BOX ANOTHER TIME.
And another time?
He did.
WE MUST HUNT THEM NOW, FATHER! ALL THE ASGARDIANS--PUT 'EM TO FIRE AND THE KNIFE--
NO, REGIN.
THERE'S ENOUGH DEATH TODAY.
But Fafnir disagreed, for Andvari's curse was bringing out their true natures.

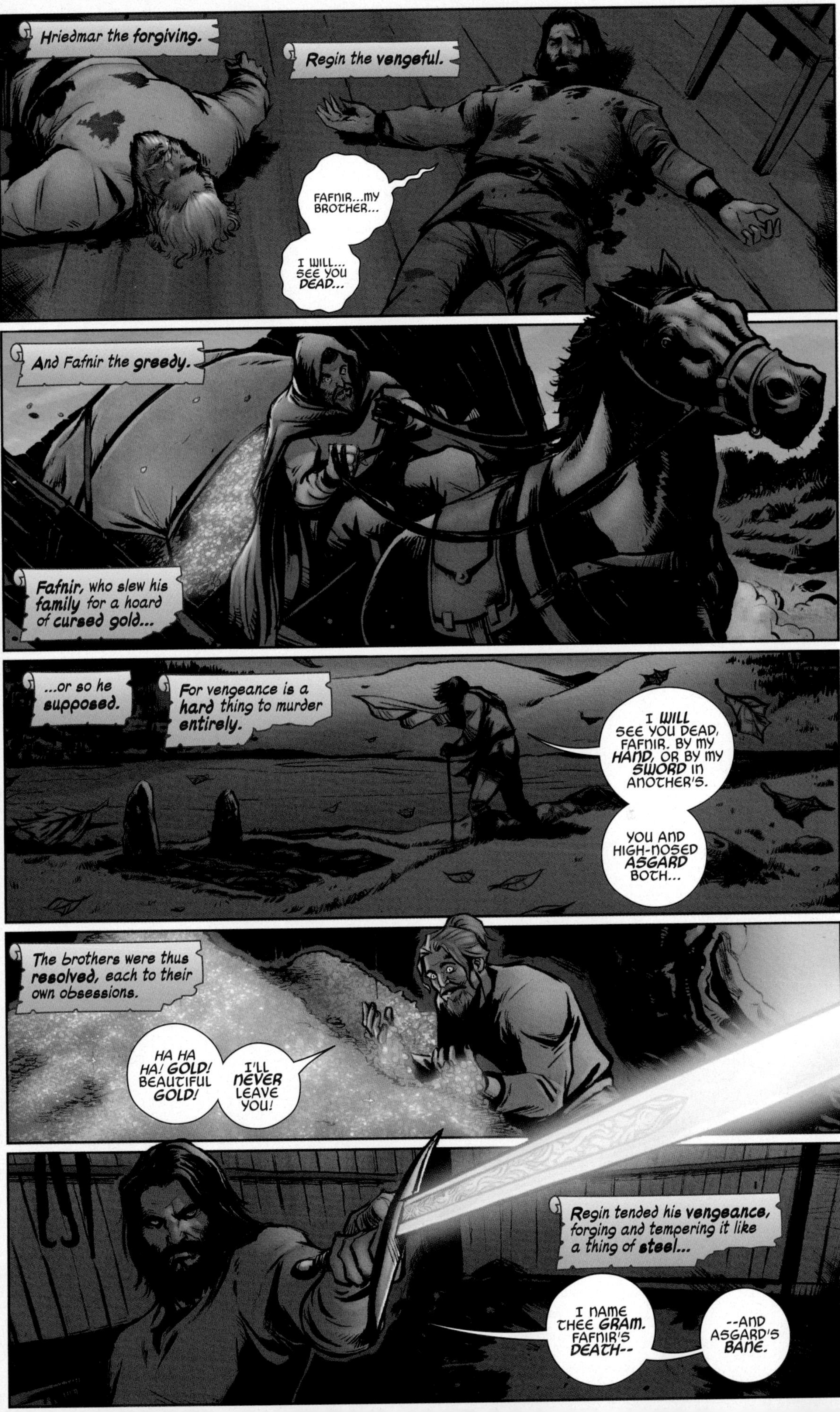
Hriedmar the forgiving.
Regin the vengeful.
FAFNIR...MY BROTHER...
I WILL... SEE YOU DEAD...
And Fafnir the greedy.
Fafnir, who slew his family for a hoard of cursed gold...
...or so he supposed.
For vengeance is a hard thing to murder entirely.
I WILL SEE YOU DEAD, FAFNIR. BY MY HAND, OR BY MY SWORD IN ANOTHER'S.
YOU AND HIGH-NOSED ASGARD BOTH...
The brothers were thus resolved, each to their own obsessions.
HA HA HA! GOLD! BEAUTIFUL GOLD!
I'LL NEVER LEAVE YOU!
Regin tended his vengeance, forging and tempering it like a thing of steel...
I NAME THEE GRAM. FAFNIR'S DEATH--
--AND ASGARD'S BANE.

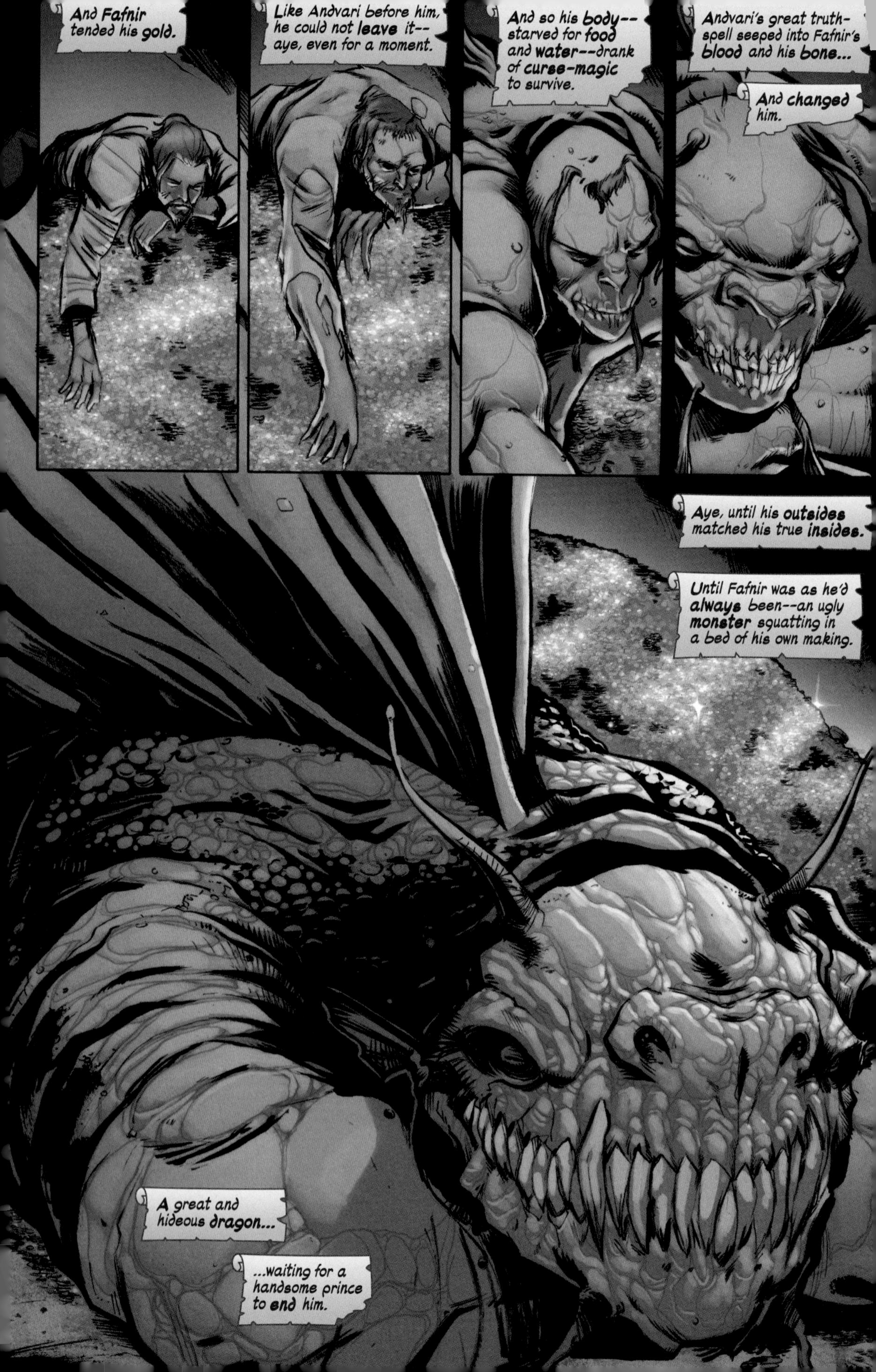
And Fafnir tended his gold.
Like Andvari before him, he could not leave it--aye, even for a moment.
And so his body--starved for food and water--drank of curse-magic to survive.
Andvari's great truth-spell seeped into Fafnir's blood and his bone...
And changed him.
Aye, until his outsides matched his true insides.
Until Fafnir was as he'd always been--an ugly monster squatting in a bed of his own making.
A great and hideous dragon...
...waiting for a handsome prince to end him.

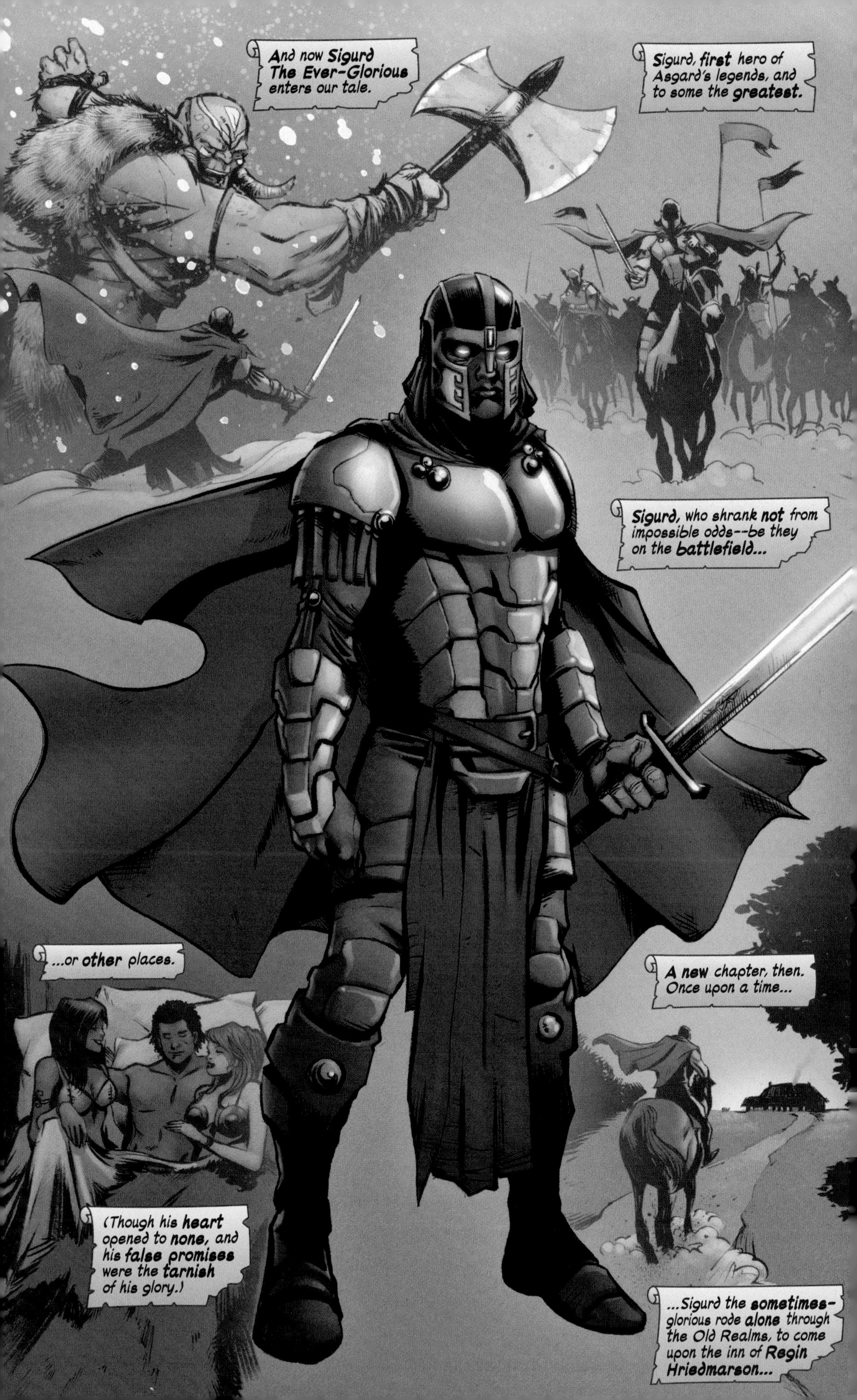

And now Sigurd The Ever-Glorious enters our tale.
Sigurd, first hero of Asgard's legends, and to some the greatest.
Sigurd, who shrank not from impossible odds--be they on the battlefield...
...or other places.
(Though his heart opened to none, and his false promises were the tarnish of his glory.)
A new chapter, then. Once upon a time...
...Sigurd the sometimes-glorious rode alone through the Old Realms, to come upon the inn of Regin Hriedmarson...

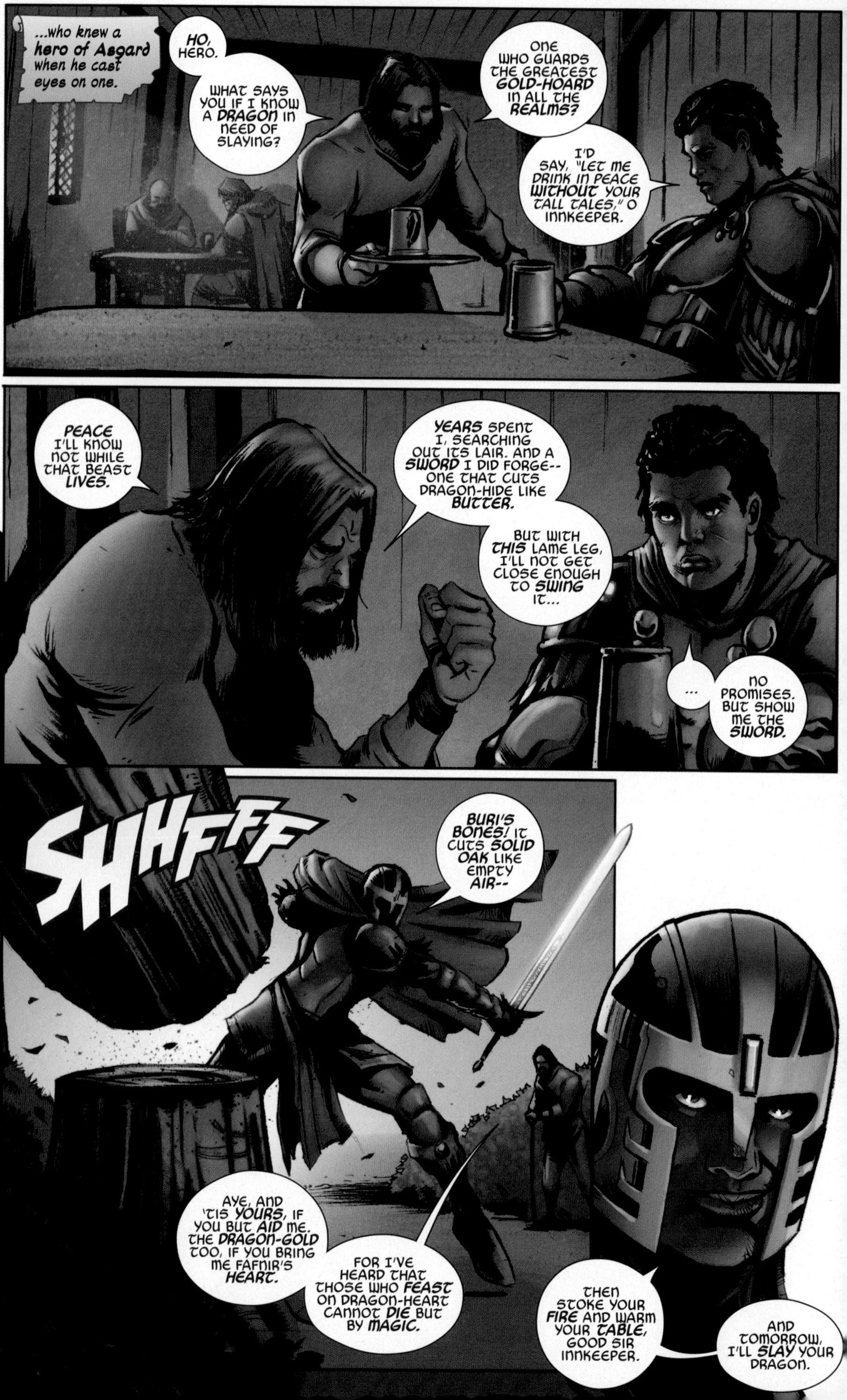
...who knew a hero of Asgard when he cast eyes on one.
HO, HERO.
WHAT SAYS YOU IF I KNOW A DRAGON IN NEED OF SLAYING?
ONE WHO GUARDS THE GREATEST GOLD-HOARD IN ALL THE REALMS?
I'D SAY, "LET ME DRINK IN PEACE WITHOUT YOUR TALL TALES," O INNKEEPER.
PEACE I'LL KNOW NOT WHILE THAT BEAST LIVES.
YEARS SPENT I, SEARCHING OUT ITS LAIR. AND A SWORD I DID FORGE-- ONE THAT CUTS DRAGON-HIDE LIKE BUTTER.
BUT WITH THIS LAME LEG, I'LL NOT GET CLOSE ENOUGH TO SWING IT...
...
NO PROMISES. BUT SHOW ME THE SWORD.
SHHFFF
BURI'S BONES! IT CUTS SOLID OAK LIKE EMPTY AIR--
AYE, AND 'TIS YOURS, IF YOU BUT AID ME. THE DRAGON-GOLD TOO, IF YOU BRING ME FAFNIR'S HEART.
FOR I'VE HEARD THAT THOSE WHO FEAST ON DRAGON-HEART CANNOT DIE BUT BY MAGIC.
THEN STOKE YOUR FIRE AND WARM YOUR TABLE, GOOD SIR INNKEEPER.
AND TOMORROW, I'LL SLAY YOUR DRAGON.

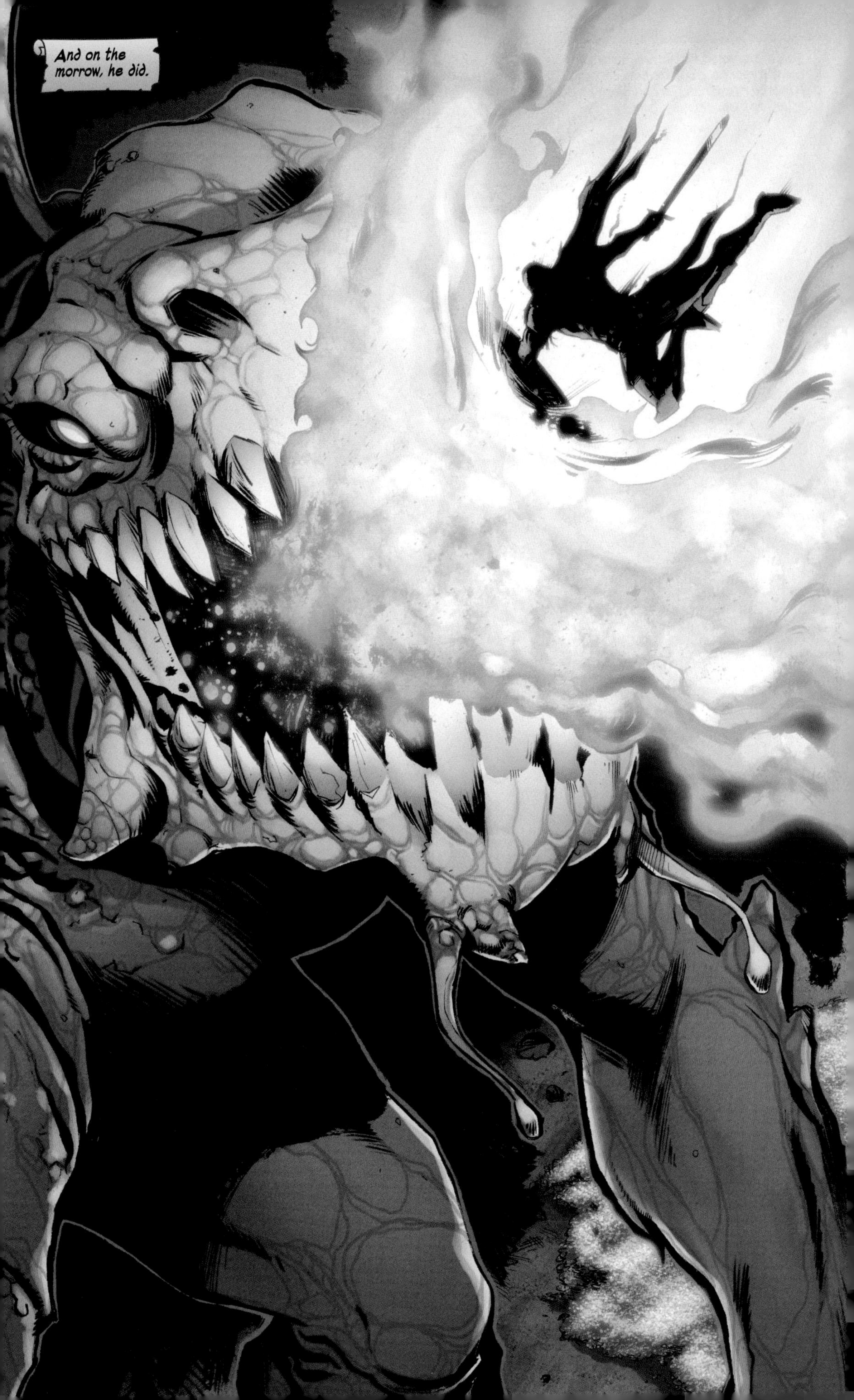
And on the morrow, he did.

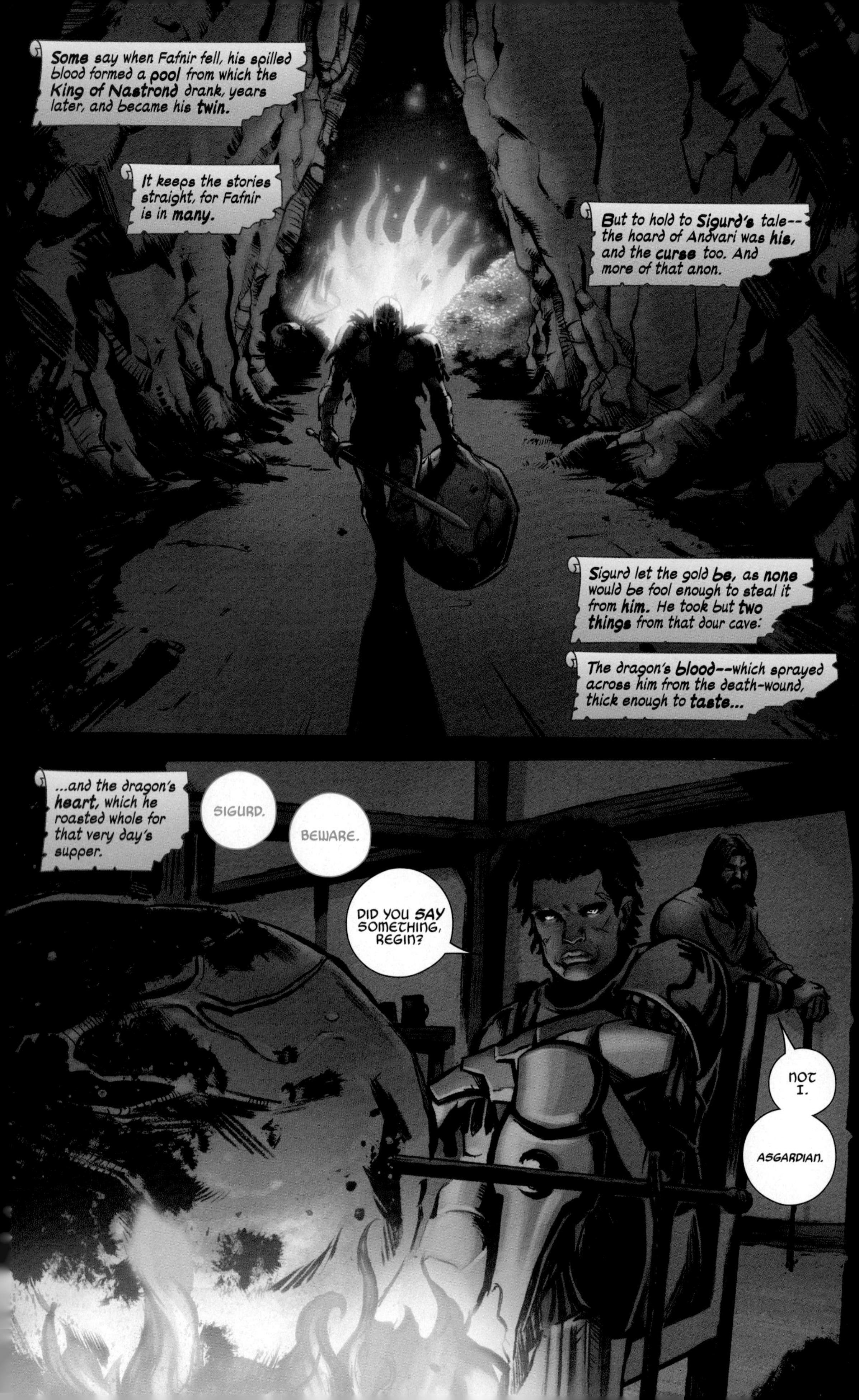

Some say when Fafnir fell, his spilled blood formed a pool from which the King of Nastrond drank, years later, and became his twin.
It keeps the stories straight, for Fafnir is in many.
But to hold to Sigurd's tale--the hoard of Andvari was his, and the curse too. And more of that anon.
Sigurd let the gold be, as none would be fool enough to steal it from him. He took but two things from that dour cave:
The dragon's blood--which sprayed across him from the death-wound, thick enough to taste...
...and the dragon's heart, which he roasted whole for that very day's supper.
SIGURD.
BEWARE.
DID YOU SAY SOMETHING, REGIN?
NOT I.
ASGARDIAN.

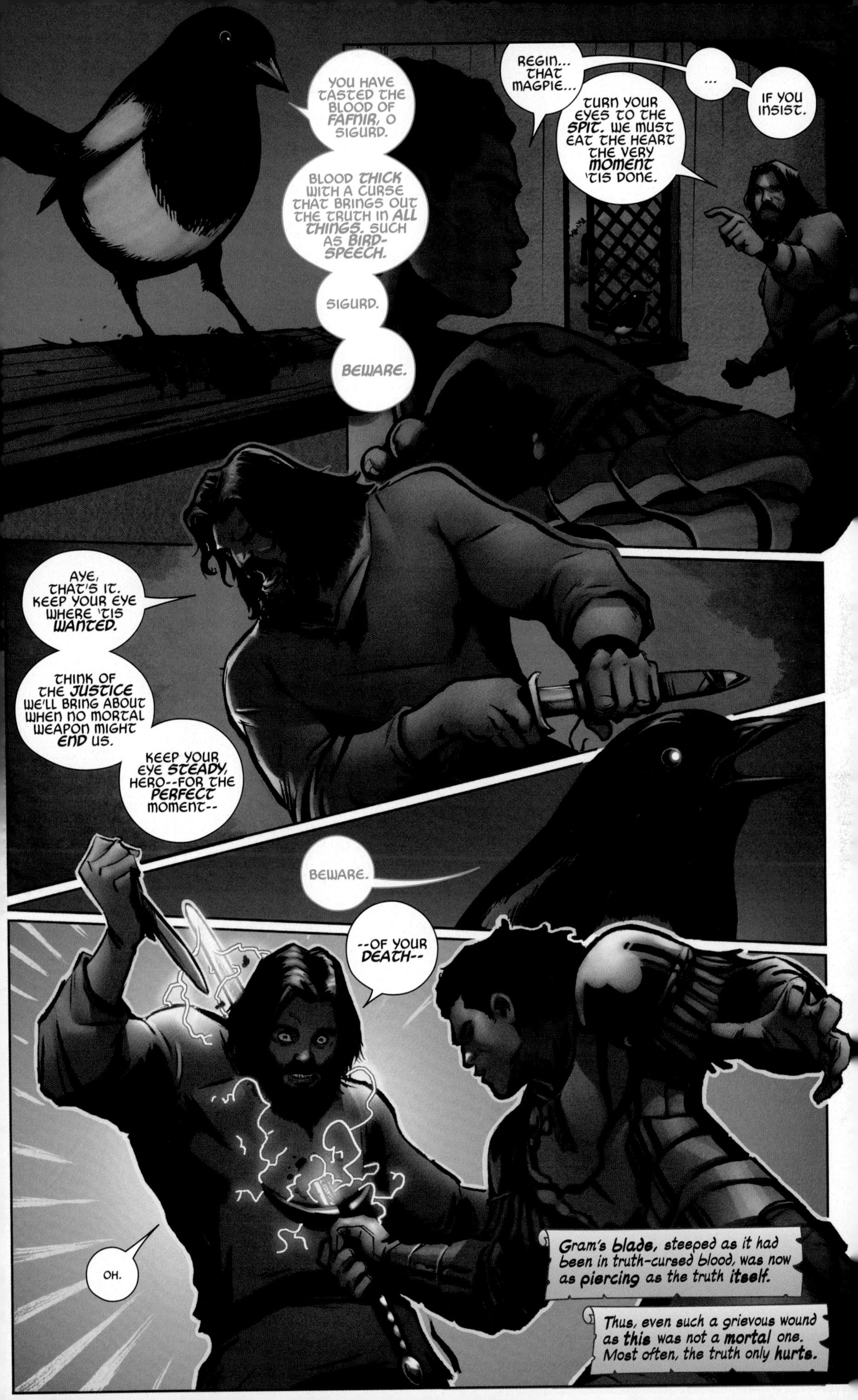
YOU HAVE TASTED THE BLOOD OF FAFNIR, O SIGURD.
BLOOD THICK WITH A CURSE THAT BRINGS OUT THE TRUTH IN ALL THINGS. SUCH AS BIRD-SPEECH.
SIGURD.
BEWARE.
REGIN... THAT MAGPIE...
TURN YOUR EYES TO THE SPIT. WE MUST EAT THE HEART THE VERY MOMENT 'TIS DONE.
...
IF YOU INSIST.
AYE, THAT'S IT. KEEP YOUR EYE WHERE 'TIS WANTED.
THINK OF THE JUSTICE WE'LL BRING ABOUT WHEN NO MORTAL WEAPON MIGHT END US.
KEEP YOUR EYE STEADY, HERO--FOR THE PERFECT MOMENT--
BEWARE.
--OF YOUR DEATH--
OH.
Gram's blade, steeped as it had been in truth-cursed blood, was now as piercing as the truth itself.
Thus, even such a grievous wound as this was not a mortal one. Most often, the truth only hurts.

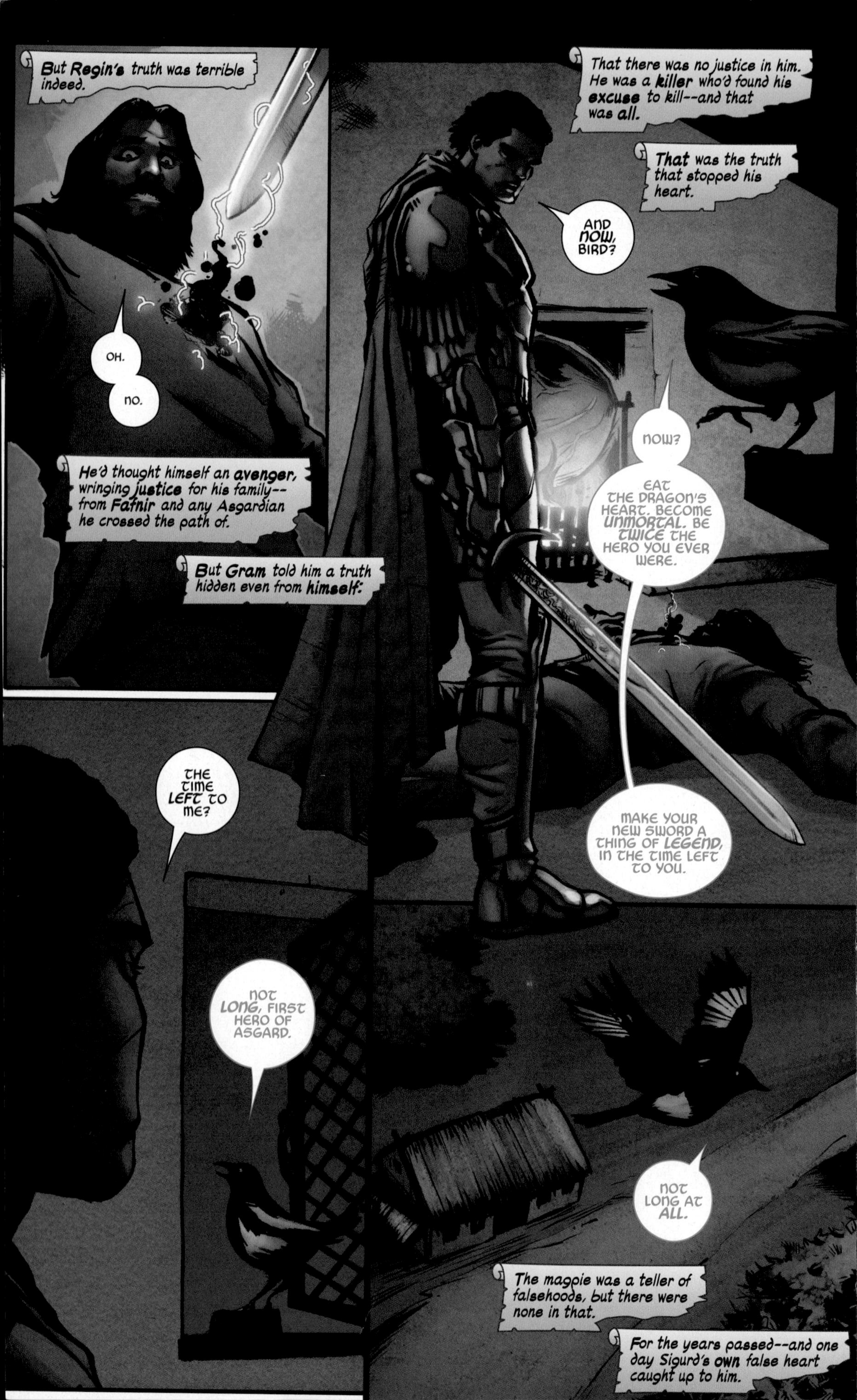

But Regin's truth was terrible indeed.
OH.
NO.
He'd thought himself an avenger, wringing justice for his family--from Fafnir and any Asgardian he crossed the path of.
But Gram told him a truth hidden even from himself:
That there was no justice in him. He was a killer who'd found his excuse to kill--and that was all.
That was the truth that stopped his heart.
AND NOW, BIRD?
NOW?
EAT THE DRAGON'S HEART. BECOME UNMORTAL. BE TWICE THE HERO YOU EVER WERE.
MAKE YOUR NEW SWORD A THING OF LEGEND, IN THE TIME LEFT TO YOU.
THE TIME LEFT TO ME?
NOT LONG, FIRST HERO OF ASGARD.
NOT LONG AT ALL.
The magpie was a teller of falsehoods, but there were none in that.
For the years passed--and one day Sigurd's own false heart caught up to him.

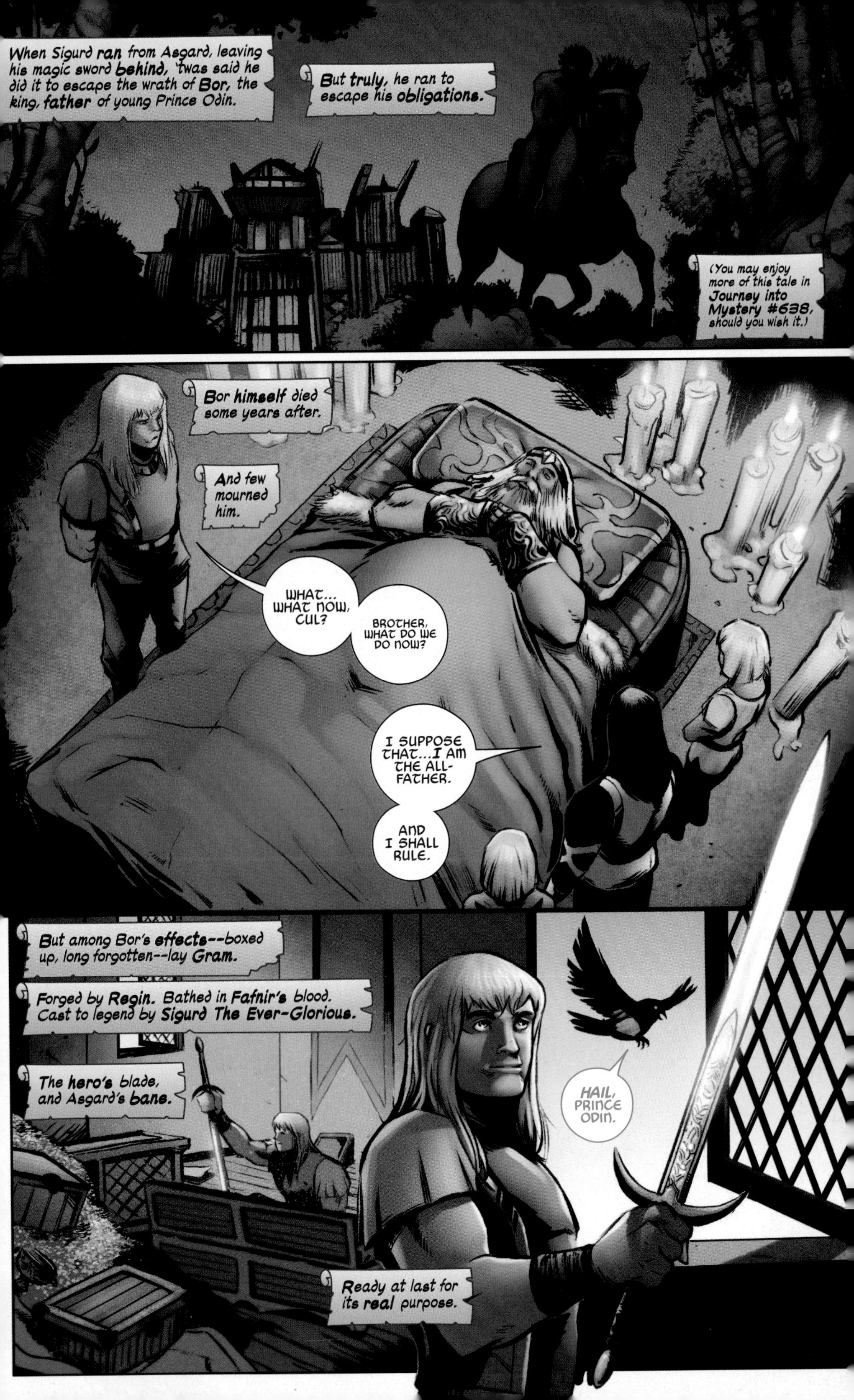

When Sigurd ran from Asgard, leaving his magic sword behind, 'twas said he did it to escape the wrath of Bor, the king, father of young Prince Odin.
But truly, he ran to escape his obligations.
(You may enjoy more of this tale in Journey into Mystery #638, should you wish it.)
Bor himself died some years after.
And few mourned him.
WHAT... WHAT NOW, CUL?
BROTHER, WHAT DO WE DO NOW?
I SUPPOSE THAT...I AM THE ALL-FATHER.
AND I SHALL RULE.
But among Bor's effects--boxed up, long forgotten--lay Gram.
Forged by Regin. Bathed in Fafnir's blood. Cast to legend by Sigurd The Ever-Glorious.
The hero's blade, and Asgard's bane.
HAIL, PRINCE ODIN.
Ready at last for its real purpose.

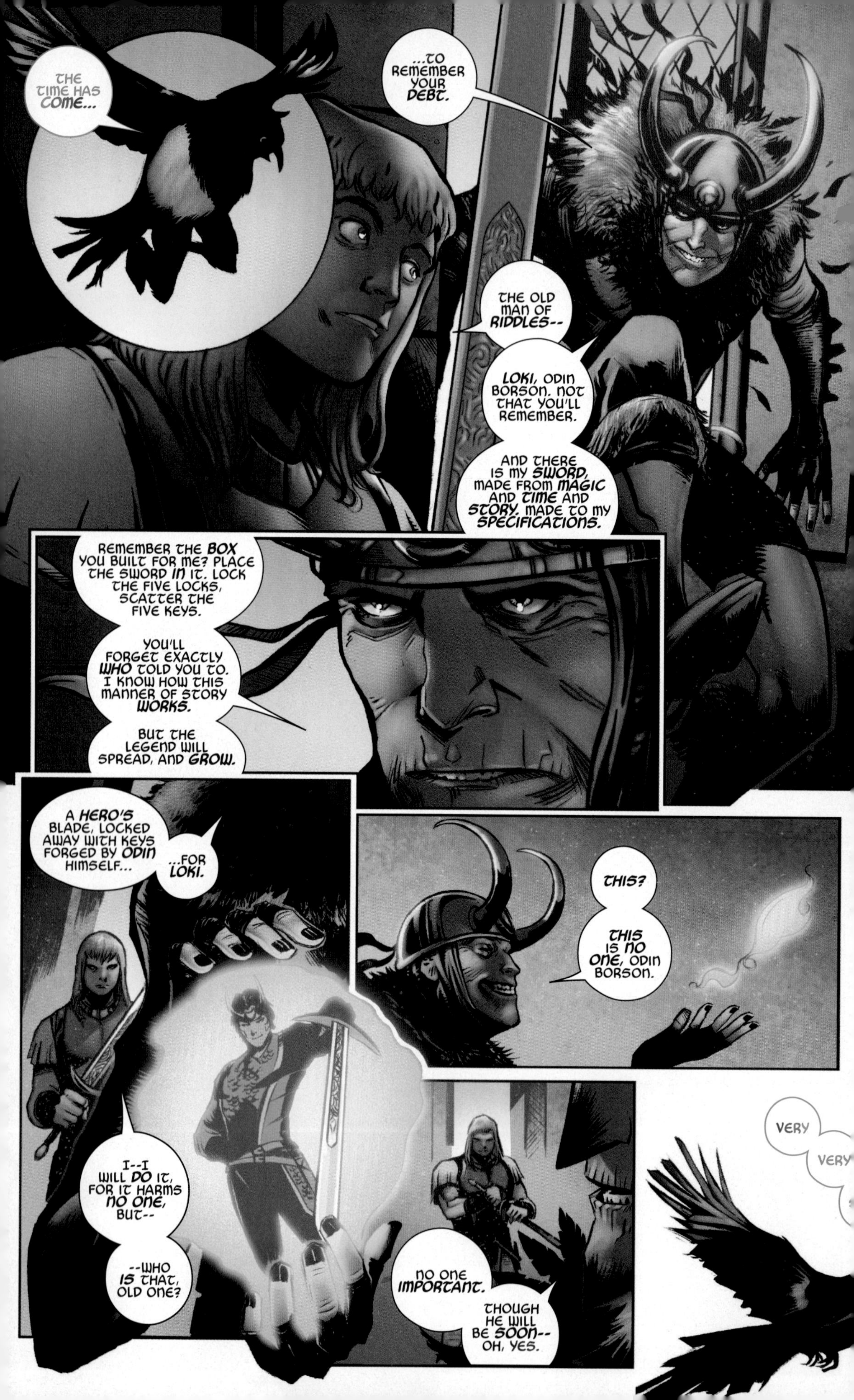
THE TIME HAS COME...
...TO REMEMBER YOUR DEBT.
THE OLD MAN OF RIDDLES--
LOKI, ODIN BORSON. NOT THAT YOU'LL REMEMBER.
AND THERE IS MY SWORD, MADE FROM MAGIC AND TIME AND STORY. MADE TO MY SPECIFICATIONS.
REMEMBER THE BOX YOU BUILT FOR ME? PLACE THE SWORD IN IT. LOCK THE FIVE LOCKS, SCATTER THE FIVE KEYS.
YOU'LL FORGET EXACTLY WHO TOLD YOU TO. I KNOW HOW THIS MANNER OF STORY WORKS.
BUT THE LEGEND WILL SPREAD, AND GROW.
A HERO'S BLADE, LOCKED AWAY WITH KEYS FORGED BY ODIN HIMSELF...
...FOR LOKI.
I--I WILL DO IT, FOR IT HARMS NO ONE, BUT--
--WHO IS THAT, OLD ONE?
THIS?
THIS IS NO ONE, ODIN BORSON.
NO ONE IMPORTANT.
THOUGH HE WILL BE SOON--OH, YES.
VERY
VERY

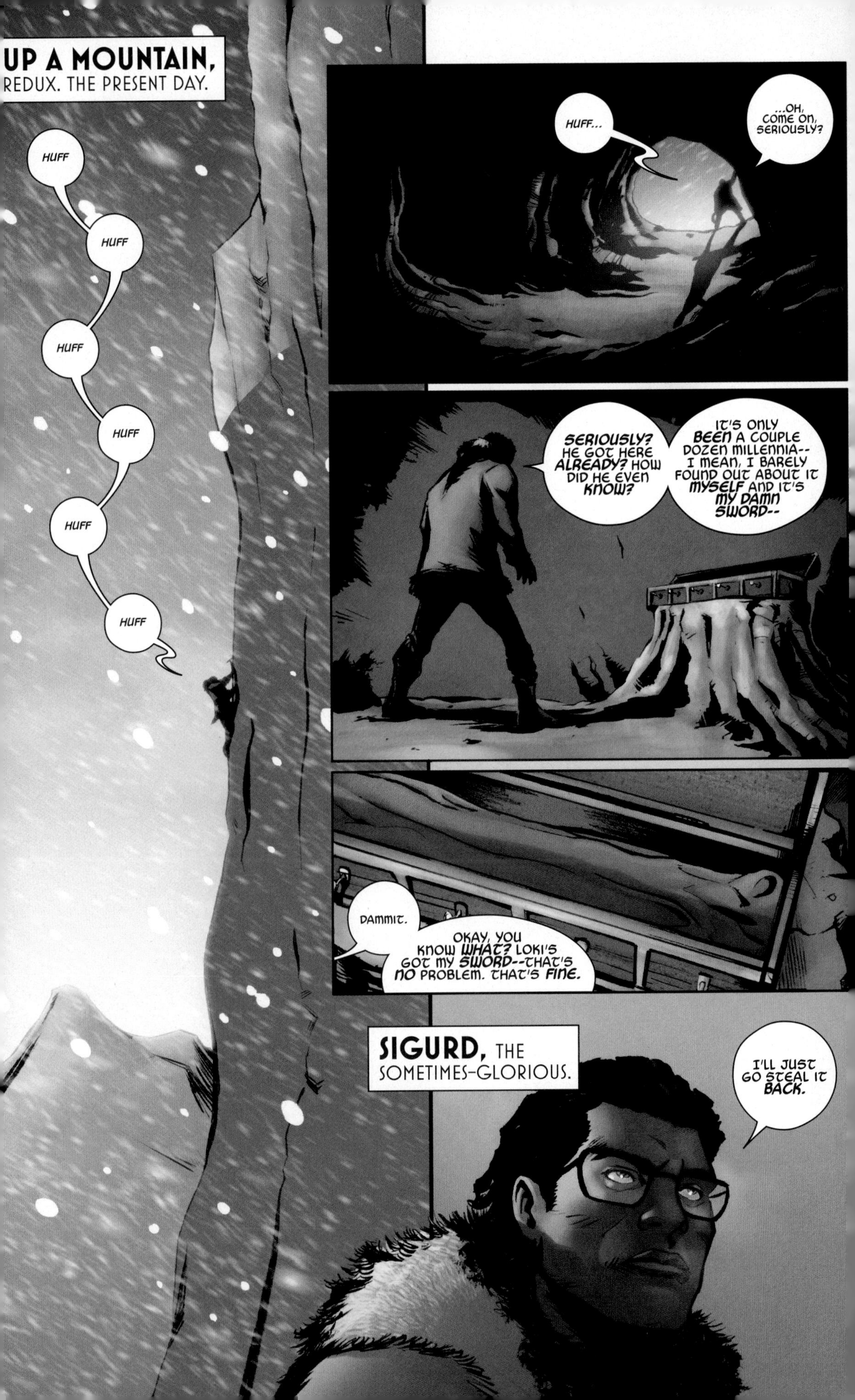
UP A MOUNTAIN, REDUX. THE PRESENT DAY.
HUFF
HUFF
HUFF
HUFF
HUFF
HUFF
HUFF...
...OH, COME ON, SERIOUSLY?
SERIOUSLY? HE GOT HERE ALREADY? HOW DID HE EVEN KNOW?
IT'S ONLY BEEN A COUPLE DOZEN MILLENNIA-- I MEAN, I BARELY FOUND OUT ABOUT IT MYSELF AND IT'S MY DAMN SWORD--
DAMMIT.
OKAY, YOU KNOW WHAT? LOKI'S GOT MY SWORD--THAT'S NO PROBLEM. THAT'S FINE.
SIGURD, THE SOMETIMES-GLORIOUS.
I'LL JUST GO STEAL IT BACK.

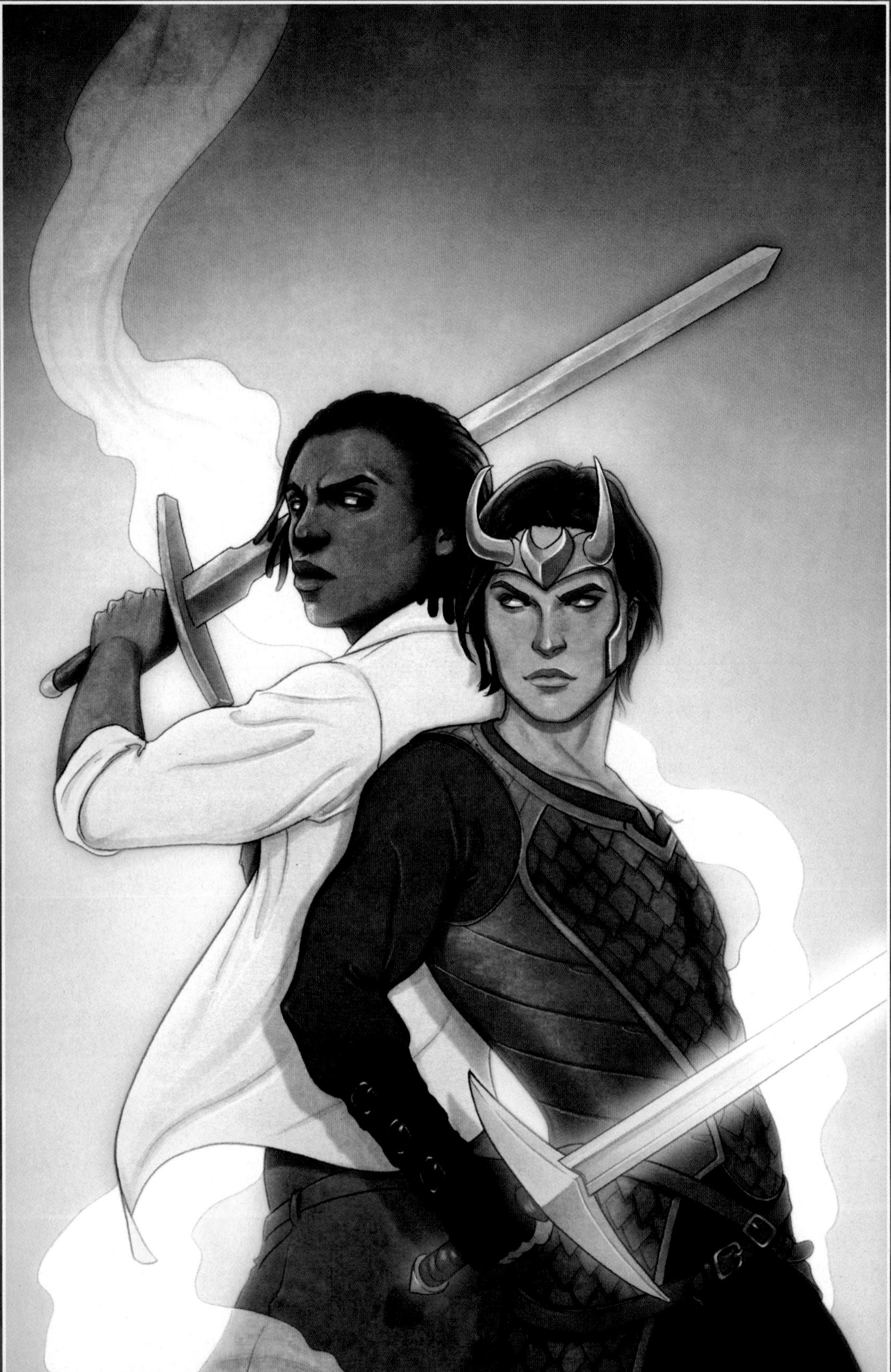

LOKI: AGENT OF ASGARD #4

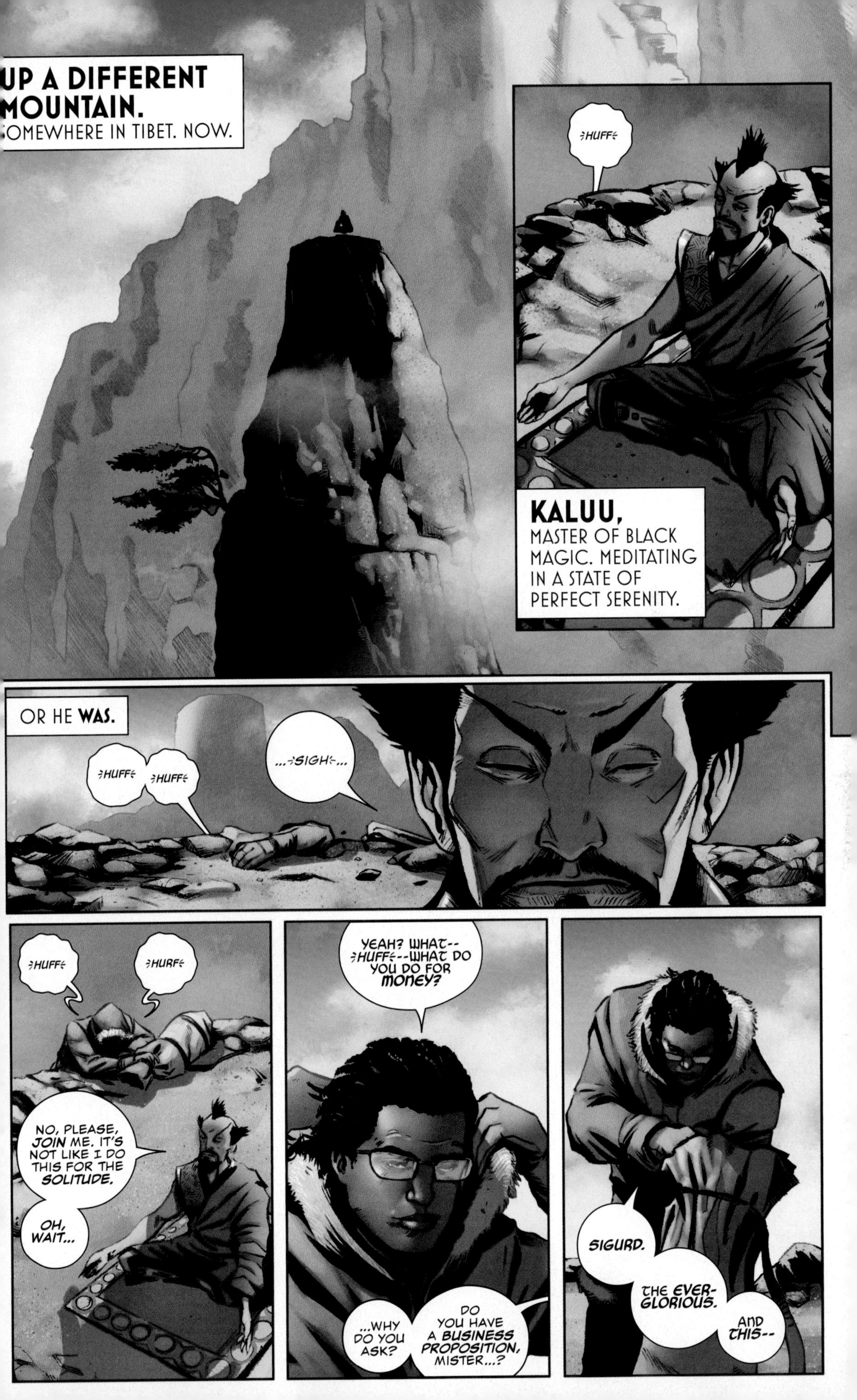
UP A DIFFERENT MOUNTAIN.
SOMEWHERE IN TIBET. NOW.
HUFF
KALUU, MASTER OF BLACK MAGIC. MEDITATING IN A STATE OF PERFECT SERENITY.
OR HE WAS.
HUFF
HUFF
...SIGH...
HUFF
HURF
NO, PLEASE, JOIN ME. IT'S NOT LIKE I DO THIS FOR THE SOLITUDE.
OH, WAIT...
YEAH? WHAT-- HUFF--WHAT DO YOU DO FOR MONEY?
...WHY DO YOU ASK?
DO YOU HAVE A BUSINESS PROPOSITION, MISTER...?
SIGURD.
THE EVER-GLORIOUS.
AND THIS--

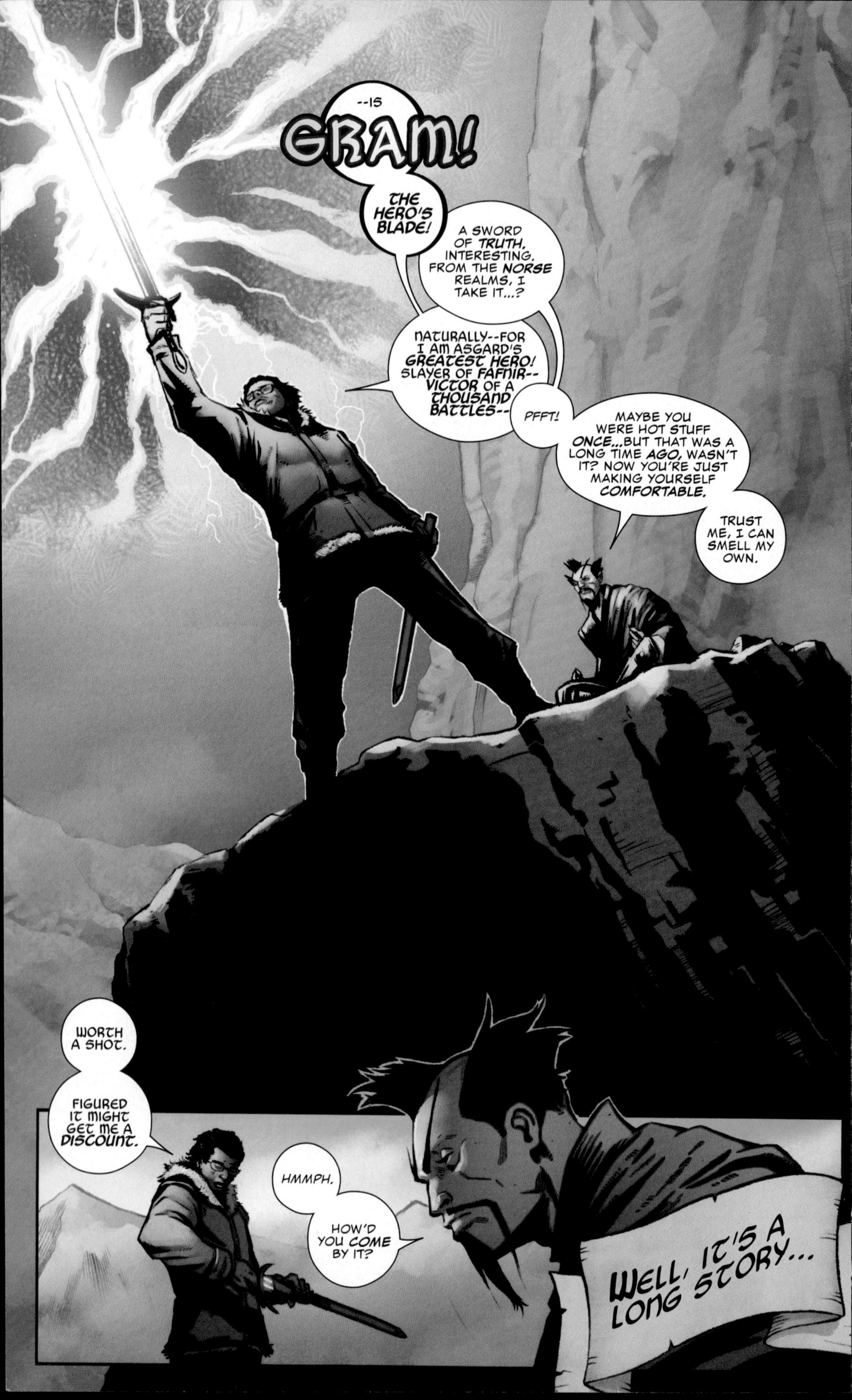
--IS
GRAM!
THE HERO'S BLADE!
A SWORD OF TRUTH. INTERESTING. FROM THE NORSE REALMS, I TAKE IT...?
NATURALLY--FOR I AM ASGARD'S GREATEST HERO! SLAYER OF FAFNIR--VICTOR OF A THOUSAND BATTLES--
PFFT!
MAYBE YOU WERE HOT STUFF ONCE...BUT THAT WAS A LONG TIME AGO, WASN'T IT? NOW YOU'RE JUST MAKING YOURSELF COMFORTABLE.
TRUST ME, I CAN SMELL MY OWN.
WORTH A SHOT.
FIGURED IT MIGHT GET ME A DISCOUNT.
HMMPH.
HOW'D YOU COME BY IT?
WELL, IT'S A LONG STORY...

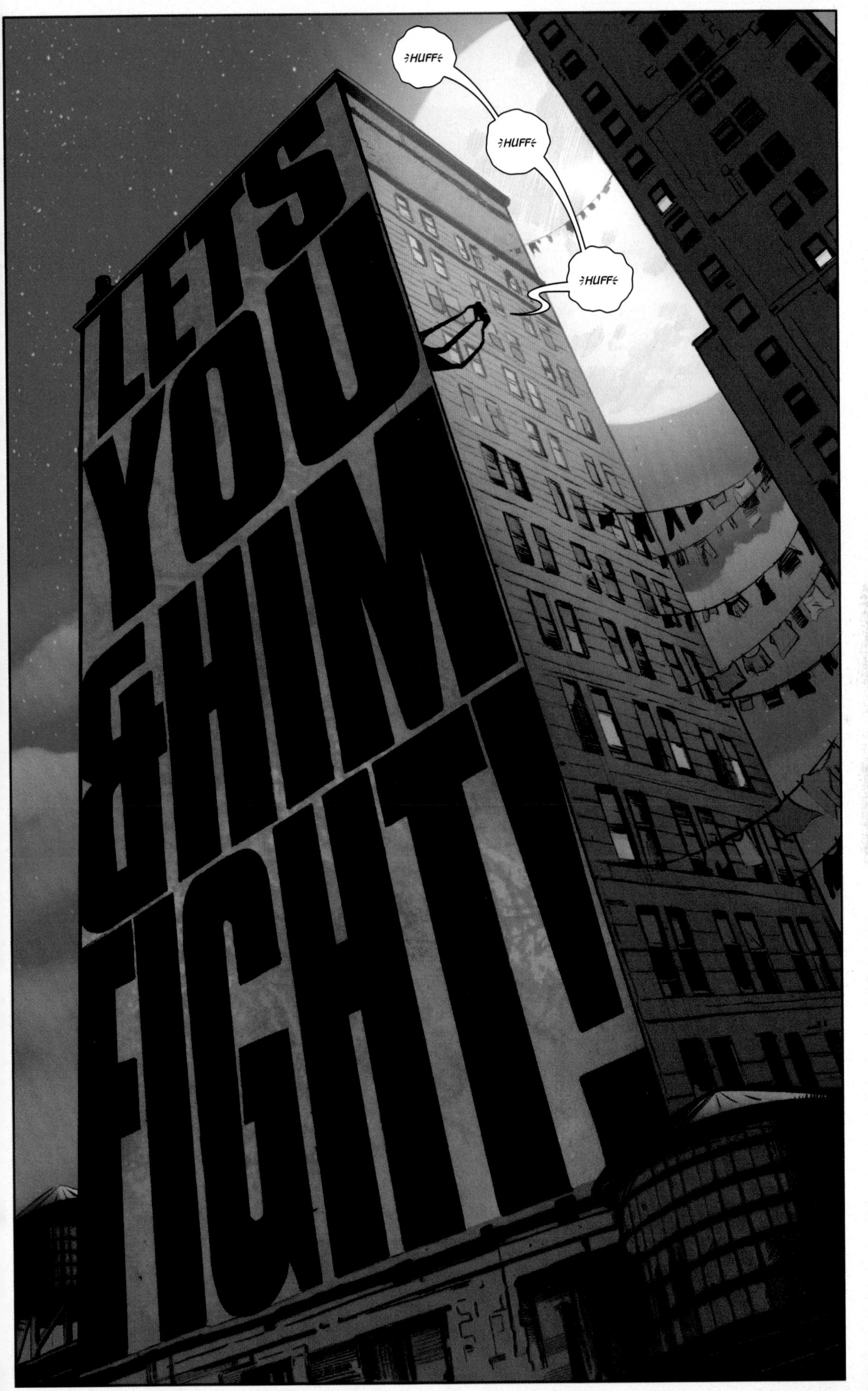
HUFF
HUFF
HUFF
LETS YOU & HIM FIGHT!

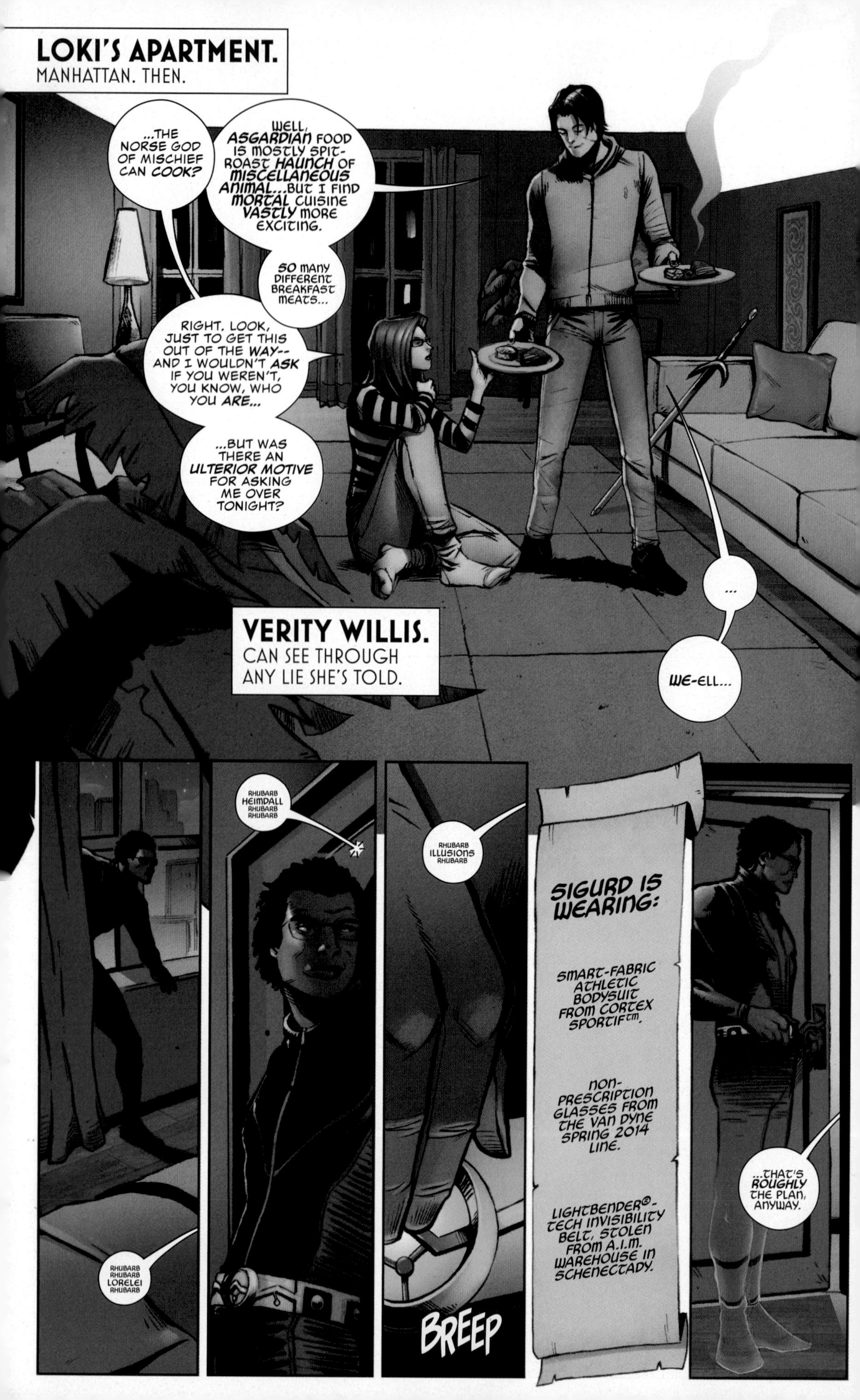

LOKI'S APARTMENT.
MANHATTAN. THEN.
...THE NORSE GOD OF MISCHIEF CAN COOK?
WELL, ASGARDIAN FOOD IS MOSTLY SPIT-ROAST HAUNCH OF MISCELLANEOUS ANIMAL...BUT I FIND MORTAL CUISINE VASTLY MORE EXCITING.
SO MANY DIFFERENT BREAKFAST MEATS...
RIGHT. LOOK, JUST TO GET THIS OUT OF THE WAY--AND I WOULDN'T ASK IF YOU WEREN'T, YOU KNOW, WHO YOU ARE...
...BUT WAS THERE AN ULTERIOR MOTIVE FOR ASKING ME OVER TONIGHT?
...
WE-ELL...
VERITY WILLIS.
CAN SEE THROUGH ANY LIE SHE'S TOLD.
RHUBARB RHUBARB LORELEI RHUBARB
RHUBARB HEIMDALL RHUBARB RHUBARB
RHUBARB ILLUSIONS RHUBARB
BREEP
SIGURD IS WEARING:
SMART-FABRIC ATHLETIC BODYSUIT FROM CORTEX SPORTIF™.
NON-PRESCRIPTION GLASSES FROM THE VAN DYNE SPRING 2014 LINE.
LIGHTBENDER®-TECH INVISIBILITY BELT, STOLEN FROM A.I.M. WAREHOUSE IN SCHENECTADY.
...THAT'S ROUGHLY THE PLAN, ANYWAY.

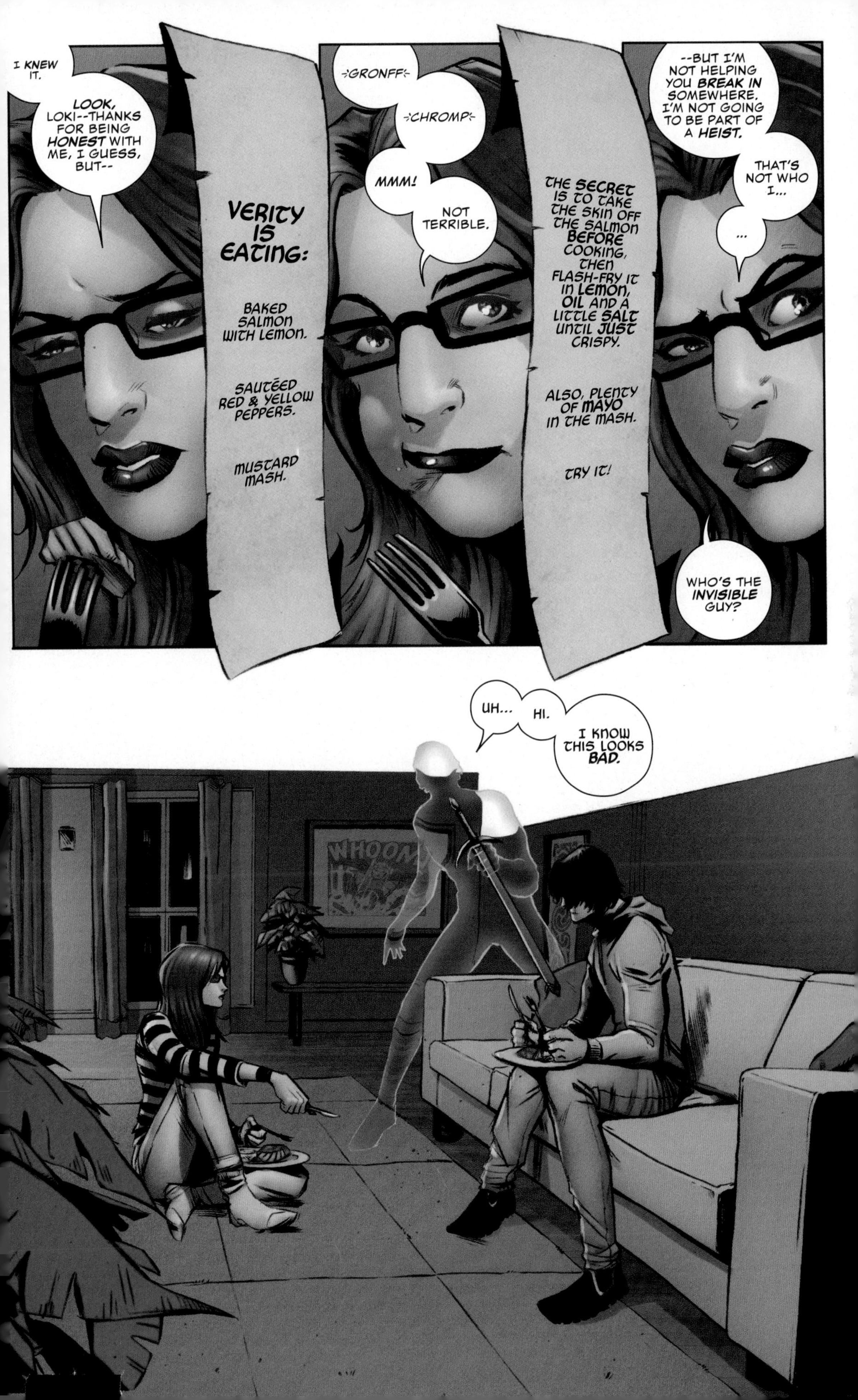
I KNEW IT.
LOOK, LOKI--THANKS FOR BEING HONEST WITH ME, I GUESS, BUT--
VERITY IS EATING:
BAKED SALMON WITH LEMON.
SAUTÉED RED & YELLOW PEPPERS.
MUSTARD MASH.
-GRONFF-
-CHROMP-
MMM!
NOT TERRIBLE.
THE SECRET IS TO TAKE THE SKIN OFF THE SALMON BEFORE COOKING, THEN FLASH-FRY IT IN LEMON, OIL AND A LITTLE SALT UNTIL JUST CRISPY.
ALSO, PLENTY OF MAYO IN THE MASH.
TRY IT!
--BUT I'M NOT HELPING YOU BREAK IN SOMEWHERE. I'M NOT GOING TO BE PART OF A HEIST.
THAT'S NOT WHO I...
...
WHO'S THE INVISIBLE GUY?
UH...
HI.
I KNOW THIS LOOKS BAD.
WHOOM

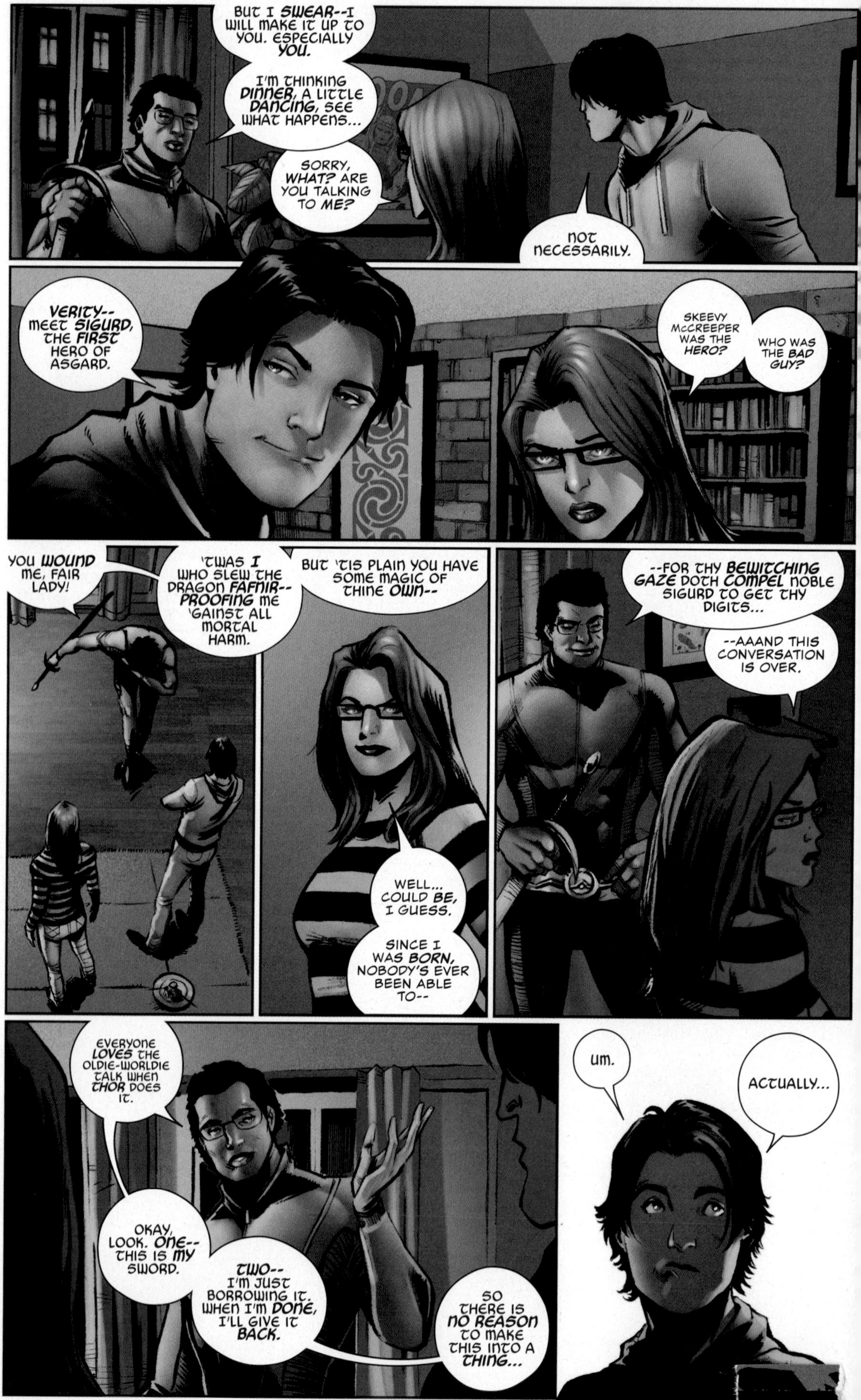
BUT I SWEAR--I WILL MAKE IT UP TO YOU. ESPECIALLY YOU.
I'M THINKING DINNER, A LITTLE DANCING, SEE WHAT HAPPENS...
SORRY, WHAT? ARE YOU TALKING TO ME?
NOT NECESSARILY.
VERITY-- MEET SIGURD, THE FIRST HERO OF ASGARD.
SKEEVY McCREEPER WAS THE HERO?
WHO WAS THE BAD GUY?
YOU WOUND ME, FAIR LADY!
'TWAS I WHO SLEW THE DRAGON FAFNIR-- PROOFING ME 'GAINST ALL MORTAL HARM.
BUT 'TIS PLAIN YOU HAVE SOME MAGIC OF THINE OWN--
WELL... COULD BE, I GUESS.
SINCE I WAS BORN, NOBODY'S EVER BEEN ABLE TO--
--FOR THY BEWITCHING GAZE DOTH COMPEL NOBLE SIGURD TO GET THY DIGITS...
--AAAND THIS CONVERSATION IS OVER.
EVERYONE LOVES THE OLDIE-WORLDIE TALK WHEN THOR DOES IT.
OKAY, LOOK. ONE-- THIS IS MY SWORD.
TWO-- I'M JUST BORROWING IT. WHEN I'M DONE, I'LL GIVE IT BACK.
SO THERE IS NO REASON TO MAKE THIS INTO A THING...
UM.
ACTUALLY...

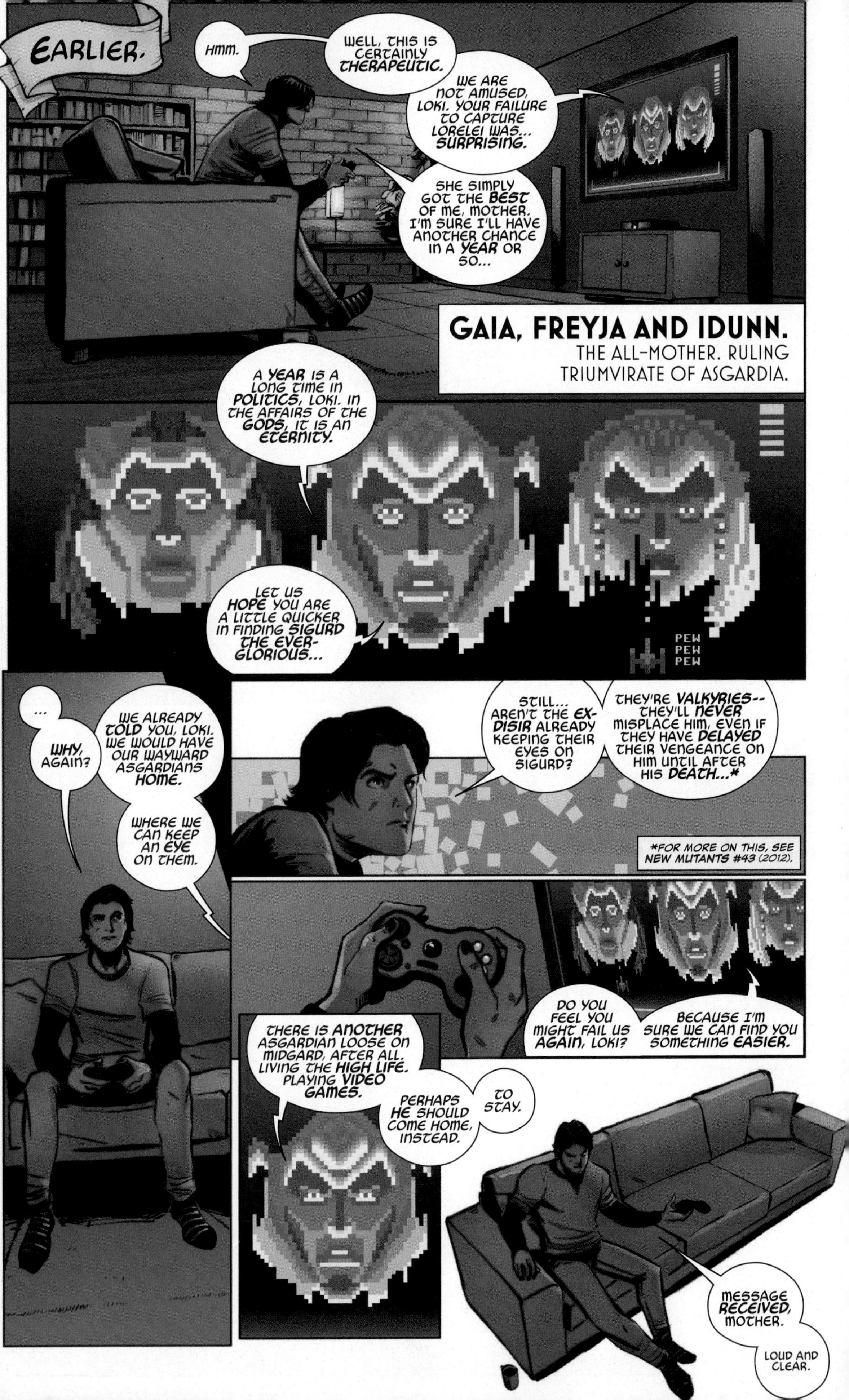
EARLIER.
HMM.
WELL, THIS IS CERTAINLY THERAPEUTIC.
WE ARE NOT AMUSED, LOKI. YOUR FAILURE TO CAPTURE LORELEI WAS... SURPRISING.
SHE SIMPLY GOT THE BEST OF ME, MOTHER. I'M SURE I'LL HAVE ANOTHER CHANCE IN A YEAR OR SO...
GAIA, FREYJA AND IDUNN.
THE ALL-MOTHER. RULING TRIUMVIRATE OF ASGARDIA.
A YEAR IS A LONG TIME IN POLITICS, LOKI. IN THE AFFAIRS OF THE GODS, IT IS AN ETERNITY.
LET US HOPE YOU ARE A LITTLE QUICKER IN FINDING SIGURD THE EVER-GLORIOUS...
PEW PEW PEW
STILL... AREN'T THE EX-DISIR ALREADY KEEPING THEIR EYES ON SIGURD?
THEY'RE VALKYRIES-- THEY'LL NEVER MISPLACE HIM, EVEN IF THEY HAVE DELAYED THEIR VENGEANCE ON HIM UNTIL AFTER HIS DEATH...*
*FOR MORE ON THIS, SEE NEW MUTANTS #43 (2012).
...
WHY, AGAIN?
WE ALREADY TOLD YOU, LOKI. WE WOULD HAVE OUR WAYWARD ASGARDIANS HOME.
WHERE WE CAN KEEP AN EYE ON THEM.
DO YOU FEEL YOU MIGHT FAIL US AGAIN, LOKI?
BECAUSE I'M SURE WE CAN FIND YOU SOMETHING EASIER.
THERE IS ANOTHER ASGARDIAN LOOSE ON MIDGARD, AFTER ALL. LIVING THE HIGH LIFE. PLAYING VIDEO GAMES.
PERHAPS HE SHOULD COME HOME, INSTEAD.
TO STAY.
MESSAGE RECEIVED, MOTHER.
LOUD AND CLEAR.

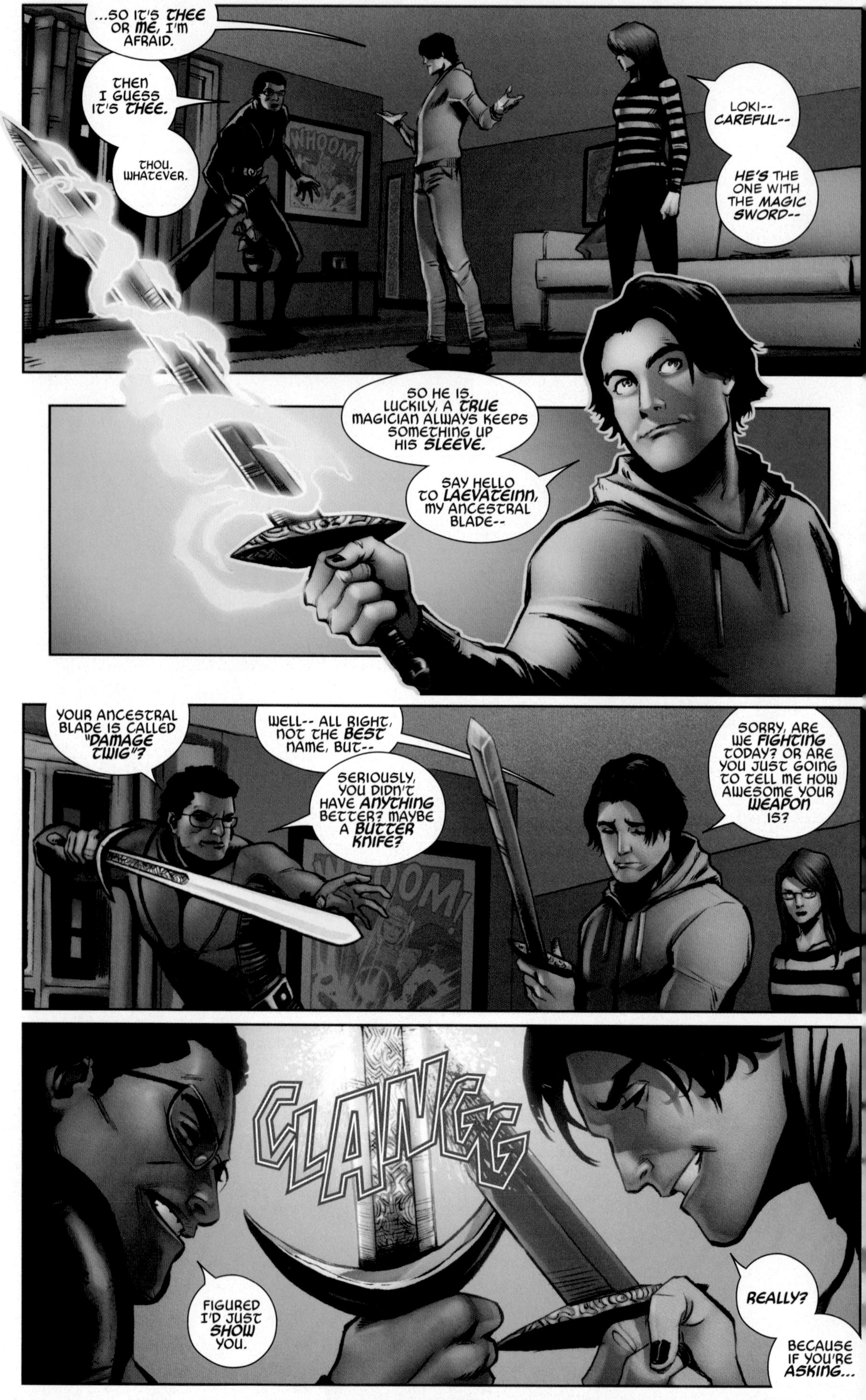
...SO IT'S THEE OR ME, I'M AFRAID.
THEN I GUESS IT'S THEE.
THOU. WHATEVER.
LOKI-- CAREFUL--
HE'S THE ONE WITH THE MAGIC SWORD--
WHOOM!
SO HE IS. LUCKILY, A TRUE MAGICIAN ALWAYS KEEPS SOMETHING UP HIS SLEEVE.
SAY HELLO TO LAEVATEINN, MY ANCESTRAL BLADE--
YOUR ANCESTRAL BLADE IS CALLED "DAMAGE TWIG"?
WELL-- ALL RIGHT, NOT THE BEST NAME, BUT--
SERIOUSLY, YOU DIDN'T HAVE ANYTHING BETTER? MAYBE A BUTTER KNIFE?
SORRY, ARE WE FIGHTING TODAY? OR ARE YOU JUST GOING TO TELL ME HOW AWESOME YOUR WEAPON IS?
FIGURED I'D JUST SHOW YOU.
CLANGG
REALLY?
BECAUSE IF YOU'RE ASKING...

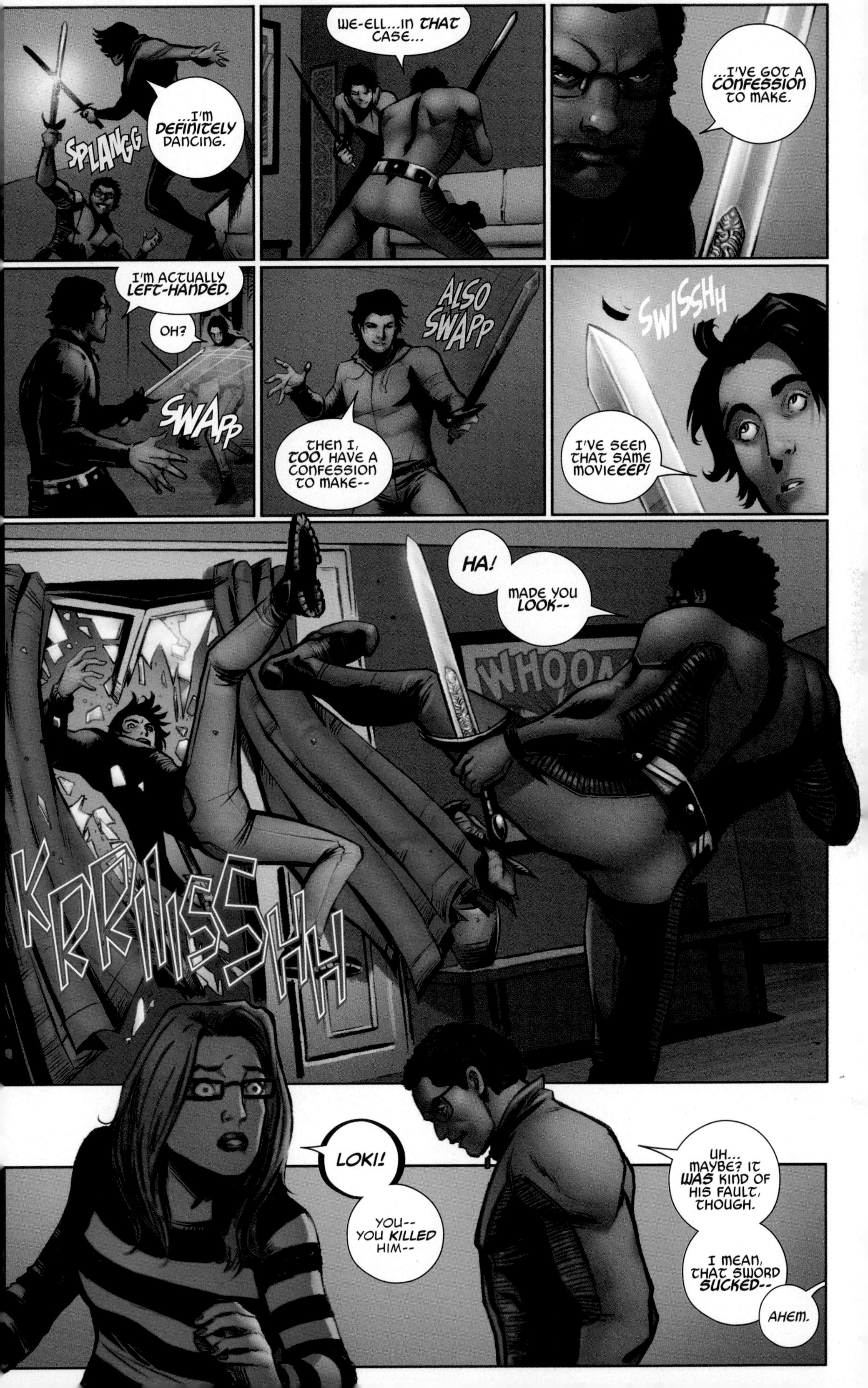
SPLANGG
...I'M DEFINITELY DANCING.
WE-ELL...IN THAT CASE...
...I'VE GOT A CONFESSION TO MAKE.
I'M ACTUALLY LEFT-HANDED.
OH?
SWAPP
ALSO SWAPP
THEN I, TOO, HAVE A CONFESSION TO MAKE--
SWISSHH
I'VE SEEN THAT SAME MOVIEEEP!
HA!
MADE YOU LOOK--
KRRRSSHH
LOKI!
YOU-- YOU KILLED HIM--
UH... MAYBE? IT WAS KIND OF HIS FAULT, THOUGH.
I MEAN, THAT SWORD SUCKED--
AHEM.

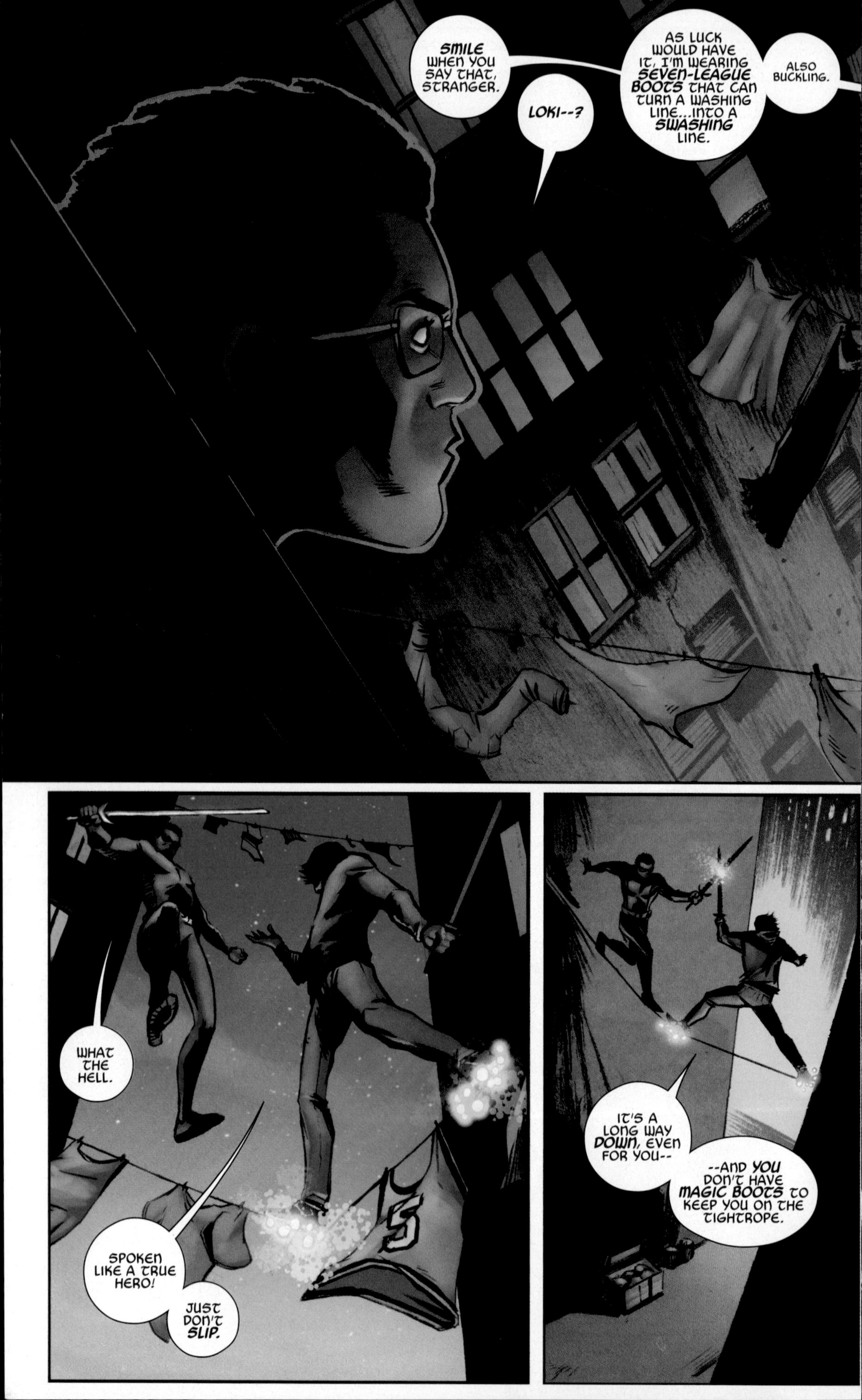

SMILE WHEN YOU SAY THAT, STRANGER.
LOKI--?
AS LUCK WOULD HAVE IT, I'M WEARING SEVEN-LEAGUE BOOTS THAT CAN TURN A WASHING LINE...INTO A SWASHING LINE.
ALSO BUCKLING.
WHAT THE HELL.
SPOKEN LIKE A TRUE HERO!
JUST DON'T SLIP.
IT'S A LONG WAY DOWN, EVEN FOR YOU--
--AND YOU DON'T HAVE MAGIC BOOTS TO KEEP YOU ON THE TIGHTROPE.

I'LL GIVE YOU A *CHOICE:* EITHER YOU *JOIN* ME AND WE END THIS *NOW...*

...OR I'LL *FIND* YOU *LATER.* WHILE YOU'RE *SLEEPING.*

AND YOU'LL *WAKE* TO THE MERCIES OF THE *VALKYRIES.*

YEAH?

WELL...

...YOU DON'T *EVEN* HAVE A *TIGHTROPE.*

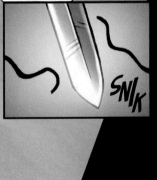

SNIK

OH, YOU *DIDN'T--*

I DID.

HAPPY LANDINGS--

WHUMPF

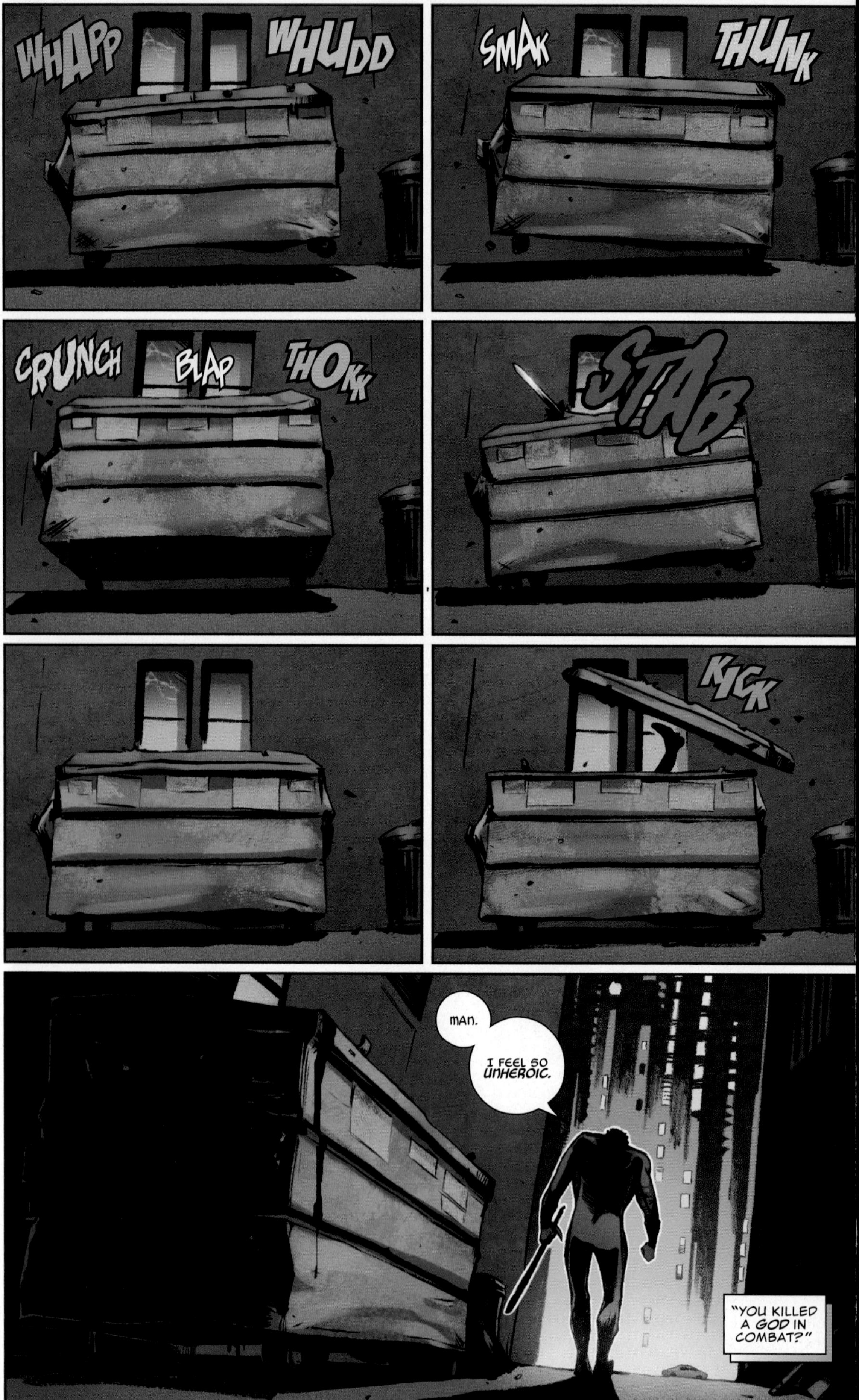
WHAPP
WHUDD
SMAK
THUNK
CRUNCH
BLAP
THOKK
STAB
KICK
MAN.
I FEEL SO UNHEROIC.
"YOU KILLED A GOD IN COMBAT?"

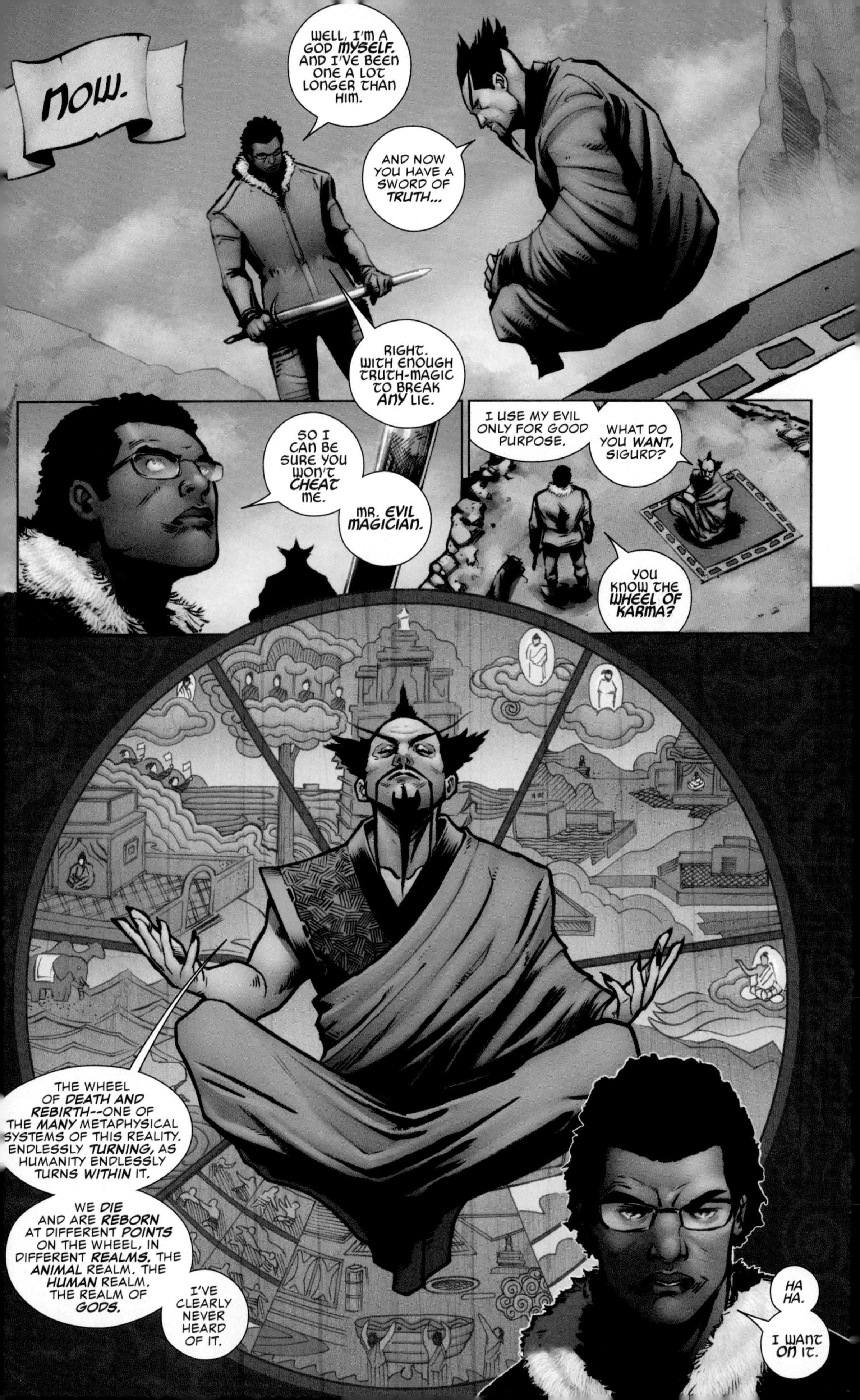
NOW.
WELL, I'M A GOD MYSELF. AND I'VE BEEN ONE A LOT LONGER THAN HIM.
AND NOW YOU HAVE A SWORD OF TRUTH...
RIGHT. WITH ENOUGH TRUTH-MAGIC TO BREAK ANY LIE.
SO I CAN BE SURE YOU WON'T CHEAT ME.
MR. EVIL MAGICIAN.
I USE MY EVIL ONLY FOR GOOD PURPOSE.
WHAT DO YOU WANT, SIGURD?
YOU KNOW THE WHEEL OF KARMA?
THE WHEEL OF DEATH AND REBIRTH--ONE OF THE MANY METAPHYSICAL SYSTEMS OF THIS REALITY. ENDLESSLY TURNING, AS HUMANITY ENDLESSLY TURNS WITHIN IT.
WE DIE AND ARE REBORN AT DIFFERENT POINTS ON THE WHEEL, IN DIFFERENT REALMS. THE ANIMAL REALM. THE HUMAN REALM. THE REALM OF GODS.
I'VE CLEARLY NEVER HEARD OF IT.
HA HA.
I WANT ON IT.

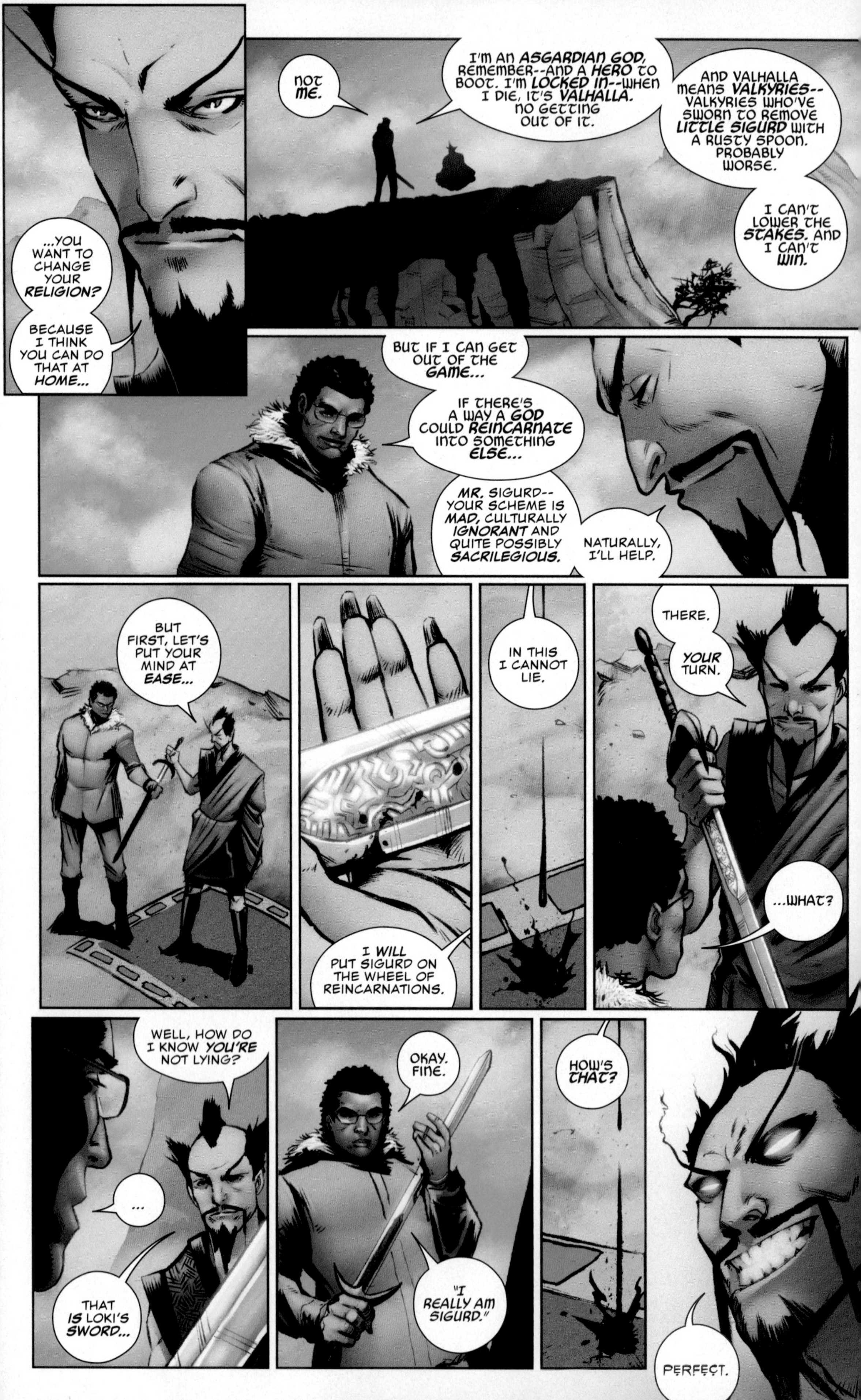
...YOU WANT TO CHANGE YOUR RELIGION?
BECAUSE I THINK YOU CAN DO THAT AT HOME...
NOT ME.
I'M AN ASGARDIAN GOD, REMEMBER--AND A HERO TO BOOT. I'M LOCKED IN--WHEN I DIE, IT'S VALHALLA. NO GETTING OUT OF IT.
AND VALHALLA MEANS VALKYRIES--VALKYRIES WHO'VE SWORN TO REMOVE LITTLE SIGURD WITH A RUSTY SPOON. PROBABLY WORSE.
I CAN'T LOWER THE STAKES. AND I CAN'T WIN.
BUT IF I CAN GET OUT OF THE GAME...
IF THERE'S A WAY A GOD COULD REINCARNATE INTO SOMETHING ELSE...
MR. SIGURD--YOUR SCHEME IS MAD, CULTURALLY IGNORANT AND QUITE POSSIBLY SACRILEGIOUS.
NATURALLY, I'LL HELP.
BUT FIRST, LET'S PUT YOUR MIND AT EASE...
I WILL PUT SIGURD ON THE WHEEL OF REINCARNATIONS.
IN THIS I CANNOT LIE.
THERE.
YOUR TURN.
...WHAT?
WELL, HOW DO I KNOW YOU'RE NOT LYING?
...
THAT IS LOKI'S SWORD...
OKAY. FINE.
"I REALLY AM SIGURD."
HOW'S THAT?
PERFECT.

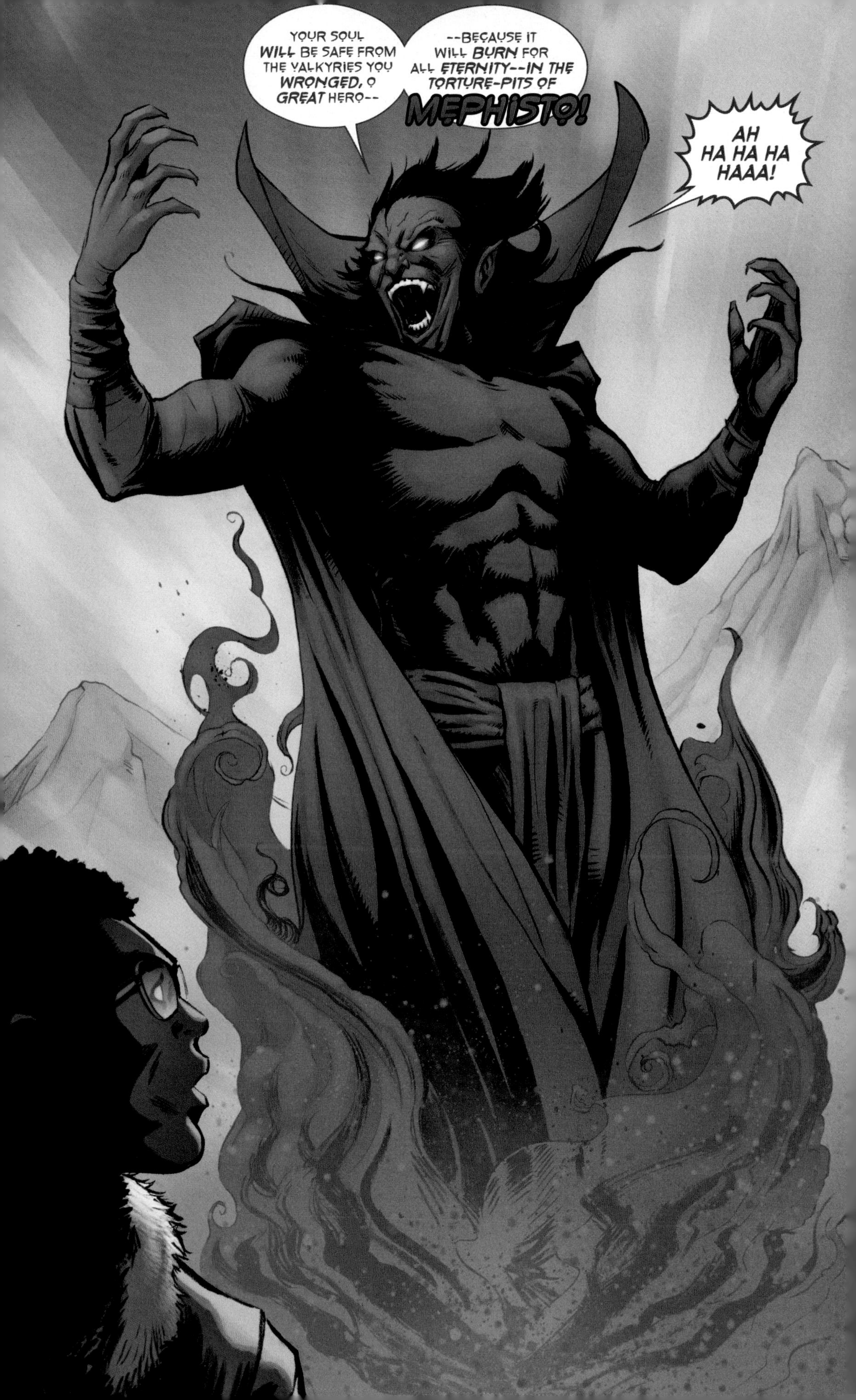
YOUR SOUL WILL BE SAFE FROM THE VALKYRIES YOU WRONGED, O GREAT HERO--
--BECAUSE IT WILL BURN FOR ALL ETERNITY--IN THE TORTURE-PITS OF MEPHISTO!
AH HA HA HA HAAA!

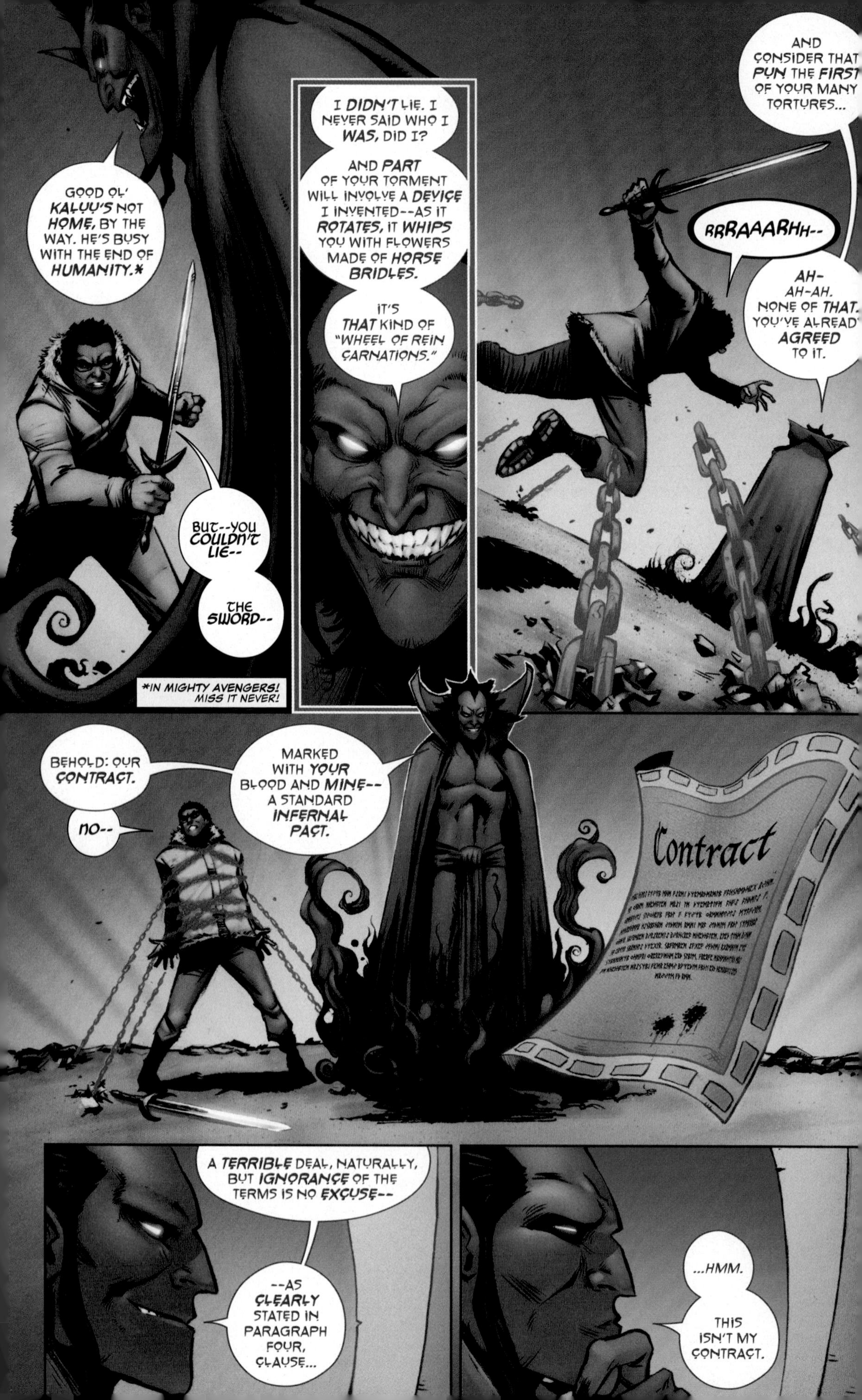
GOOD OL' KALUU'S NOT HOME, BY THE WAY. HE'S BUSY WITH THE END OF HUMANITY.*
BUT--YOU COULDN'T LIE--
THE SWORD--
*IN MIGHTY AVENGERS! MISS IT NEVER!
I DIDN'T LIE. I NEVER SAID WHO I WAS, DID I?
AND PART OF YOUR TORMENT WILL INVOLVE A DEVICE I INVENTED--AS IT ROTATES, IT WHIPS YOU WITH FLOWERS MADE OF HORSE BRIDLES.
IT'S THAT KIND OF "WHEEL OF REIN CARNATIONS."
AND CONSIDER THAT PUN THE FIRST OF YOUR MANY TORTURES...
BRRAAARHH--
AH-AH-AH. NONE OF THAT. YOU'VE ALREAD AGREED TO IT.
BEHOLD: OUR CONTRACT.
NO--
MARKED WITH YOUR BLOOD AND MINE--A STANDARD INFERNAL PACT.
Contract
A TERRIBLE DEAL, NATURALLY, BUT IGNORANCE OF THE TERMS IS NO EXCUSE--
--AS CLEARLY STATED IN PARAGRAPH FOUR, CLAUSE...
...HMM.
THIS ISN'T MY CONTRACT.

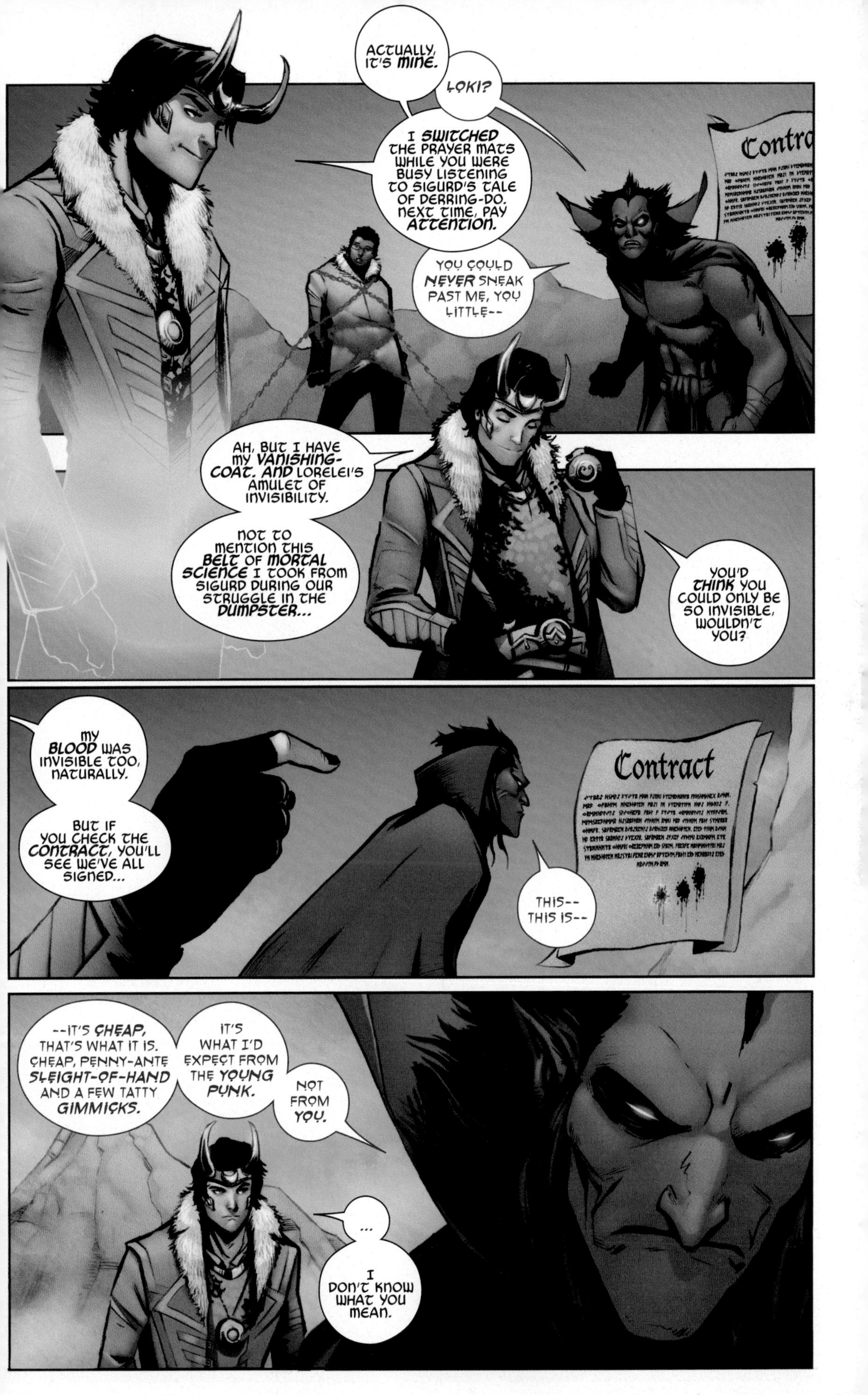
ACTUALLY, IT'S MINE.
LOKI?
I SWITCHED THE PRAYER MATS WHILE YOU WERE BUSY LISTENING TO SIGURD'S TALE OF DERRING-DO. NEXT TIME, PAY ATTENTION.
Contra
YOU COULD NEVER SNEAK PAST ME, YOU LITTLE--
AH, BUT I HAVE MY VANISHING-COAT. AND LORELEI'S AMULET OF INVISIBILITY.
NOT TO MENTION THIS BELT OF MORTAL SCIENCE I TOOK FROM SIGURD DURING OUR STRUGGLE IN THE DUMPSTER...
YOU'D THINK YOU COULD ONLY BE SO INVISIBLE, WOULDN'T YOU?
MY BLOOD WAS INVISIBLE TOO, NATURALLY.
BUT IF YOU CHECK THE CONTRACT, YOU'LL SEE WE'VE ALL SIGNED...
Contract
THIS-- THIS IS--
--IT'S CHEAP, THAT'S WHAT IT IS. CHEAP, PENNY-ANTE SLEIGHT-OF-HAND AND A FEW TATTY GIMMICKS.
IT'S WHAT I'D EXPECT FROM THE YOUNG PUNK.
NOT FROM YOU.
...
I DON'T KNOW WHAT YOU MEAN.

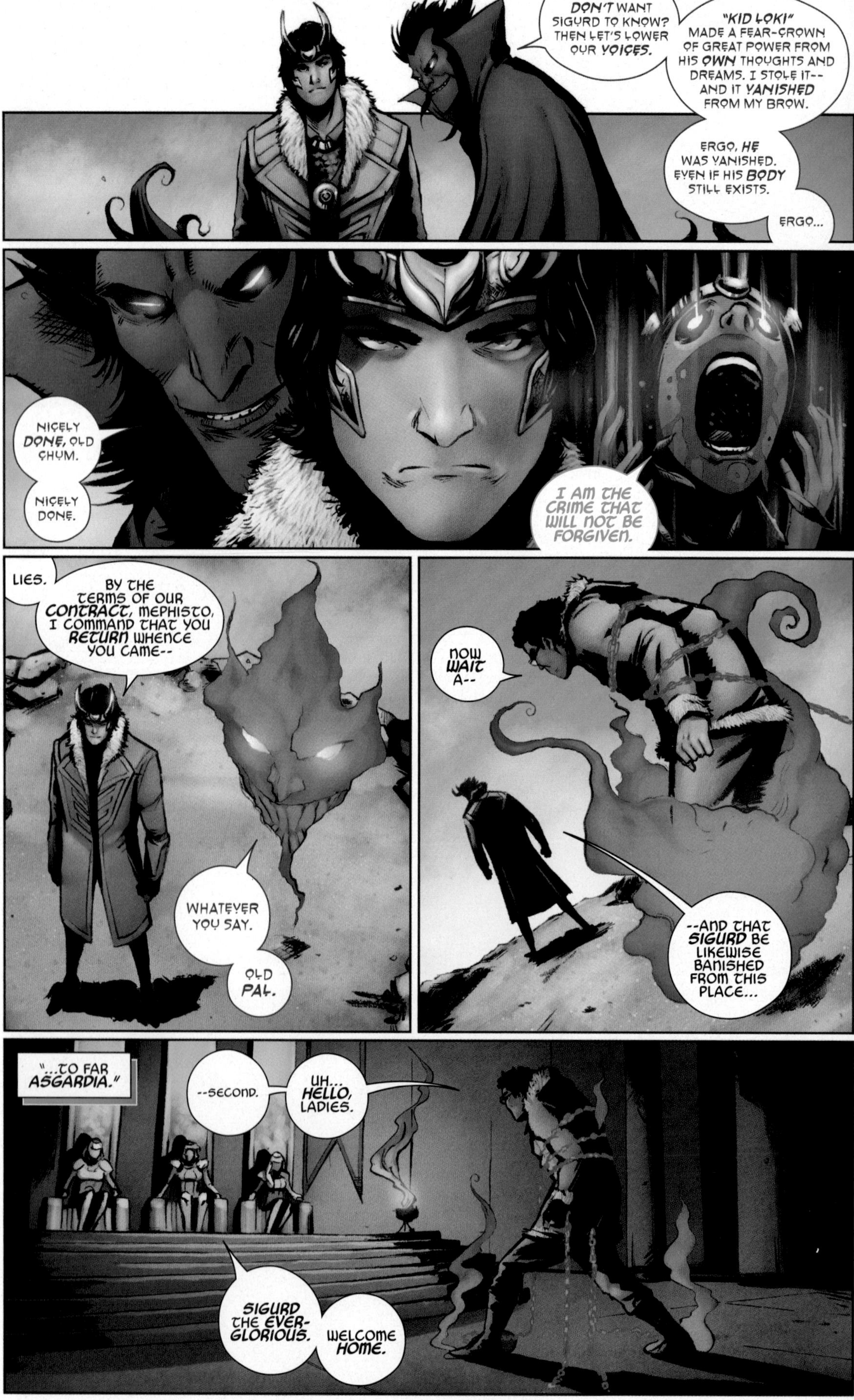

OH, YOU DON'T WANT SIGURD TO KNOW? THEN LET'S LOWER OUR VOICES.
"KID LOKI" MADE A FEAR-CROWN OF GREAT POWER FROM HIS OWN THOUGHTS AND DREAMS. I STOLE IT--AND IT VANISHED FROM MY BROW.
ERGO, HE WAS VANISHED. EVEN IF HIS BODY STILL EXISTS.
ERGO...
NICELY DONE, OLD CHUM.
NICELY DONE.
I AM THE CRIME THAT WILL NOT BE FORGIVEN.
LIES.
BY THE TERMS OF OUR CONTRACT, MEPHISTO, I COMMAND THAT YOU RETURN WHENCE YOU CAME--
WHATEVER YOU SAY.
OLD PAL.
NOW WAIT A--
--AND THAT SIGURD BE LIKEWISE BANISHED FROM THIS PLACE...
"...TO FAR ASGARDIA."
UH... HELLO, LADIES.
--SECOND.
SIGURD THE EVER-GLORIOUS.
WELCOME HOME.

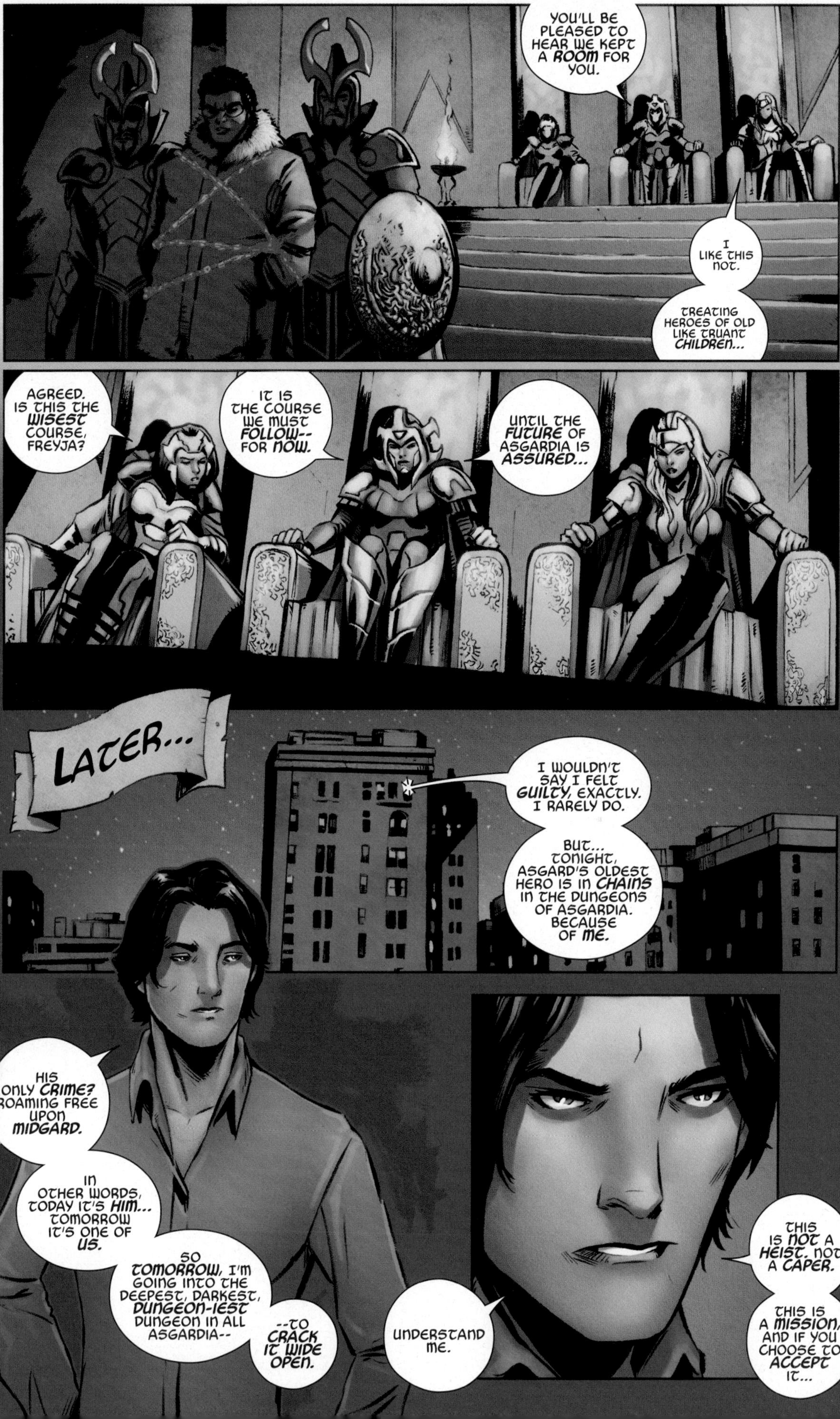

YOU'LL BE PLEASED TO HEAR WE KEPT A ROOM FOR YOU.
I LIKE THIS NOT.
TREATING HEROES OF OLD LIKE TRUANT CHILDREN...
AGREED. IS THIS THE WISEST COURSE, FREYJA?
IT IS THE COURSE WE MUST FOLLOW-- FOR NOW.
UNTIL THE FUTURE OF ASGARDIA IS ASSURED...
LATER...
I WOULDN'T SAY I FELT GUILTY, EXACTLY. I RARELY DO.
BUT... TONIGHT, ASGARD'S OLDEST HERO IS IN CHAINS IN THE DUNGEONS OF ASGARDIA. BECAUSE OF ME.
HIS ONLY CRIME? ROAMING FREE UPON MIDGARD.
IN OTHER WORDS, TODAY IT'S HIM... TOMORROW IT'S ONE OF US.
SO TOMORROW, I'M GOING INTO THE DEEPEST, DARKEST, DUNGEON-IEST DUNGEON IN ALL ASGARDIA--
--TO CRACK IT WIDE OPEN.
UNDERSTAND ME.
THIS IS NOT A HEIST. NOT A CAPER.
THIS IS A MISSION, AND IF YOU CHOOSE TO ACCEPT IT...

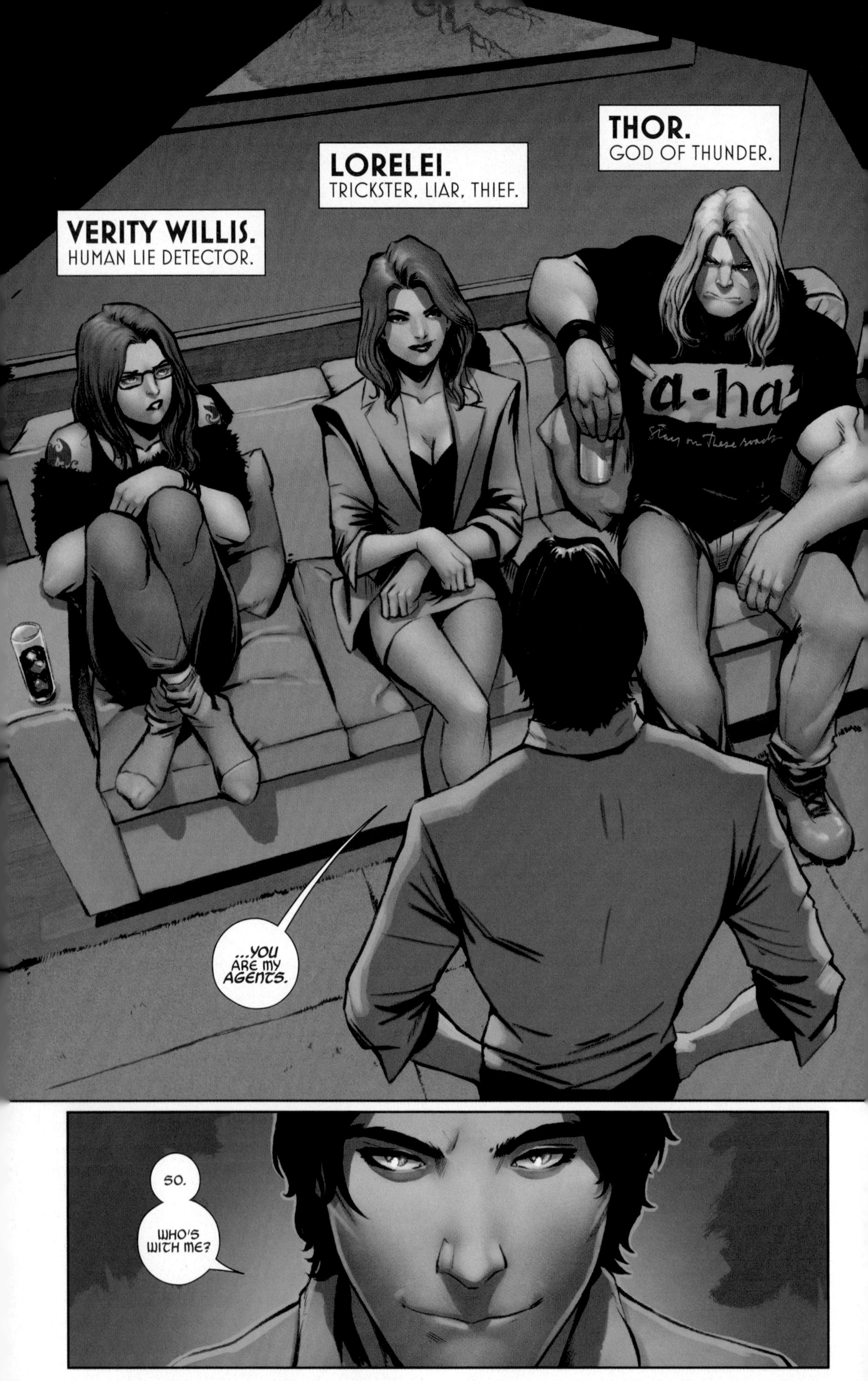
VERITY WILLIS.
HUMAN LIE DETECTOR.
LORELEI.
TRICKSTER, LIAR, THIEF.
THOR.
GOD OF THUNDER.
a-ha
...YOU ARE MY AGENTS.
SO.
WHO'S WITH ME?

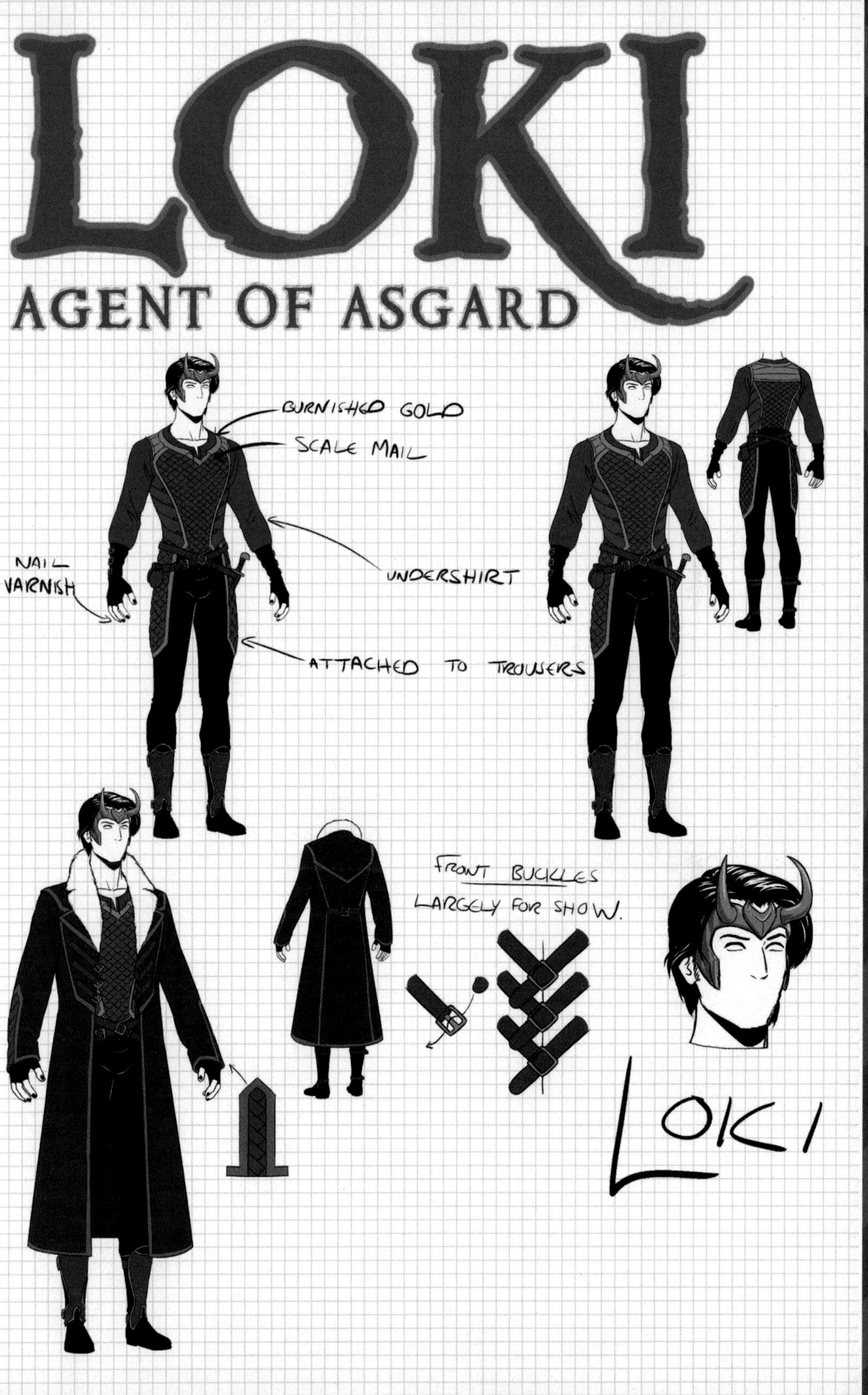
LOKI
AGENT OF ASGARD
BURNISHED GOLD
SCALE MAIL
NAIL VARNISH
UNDERSHIRT
ATTACHED TO TROUSERS
FRONT BUCKLES LARGELY FOR SHOW.
LOKI

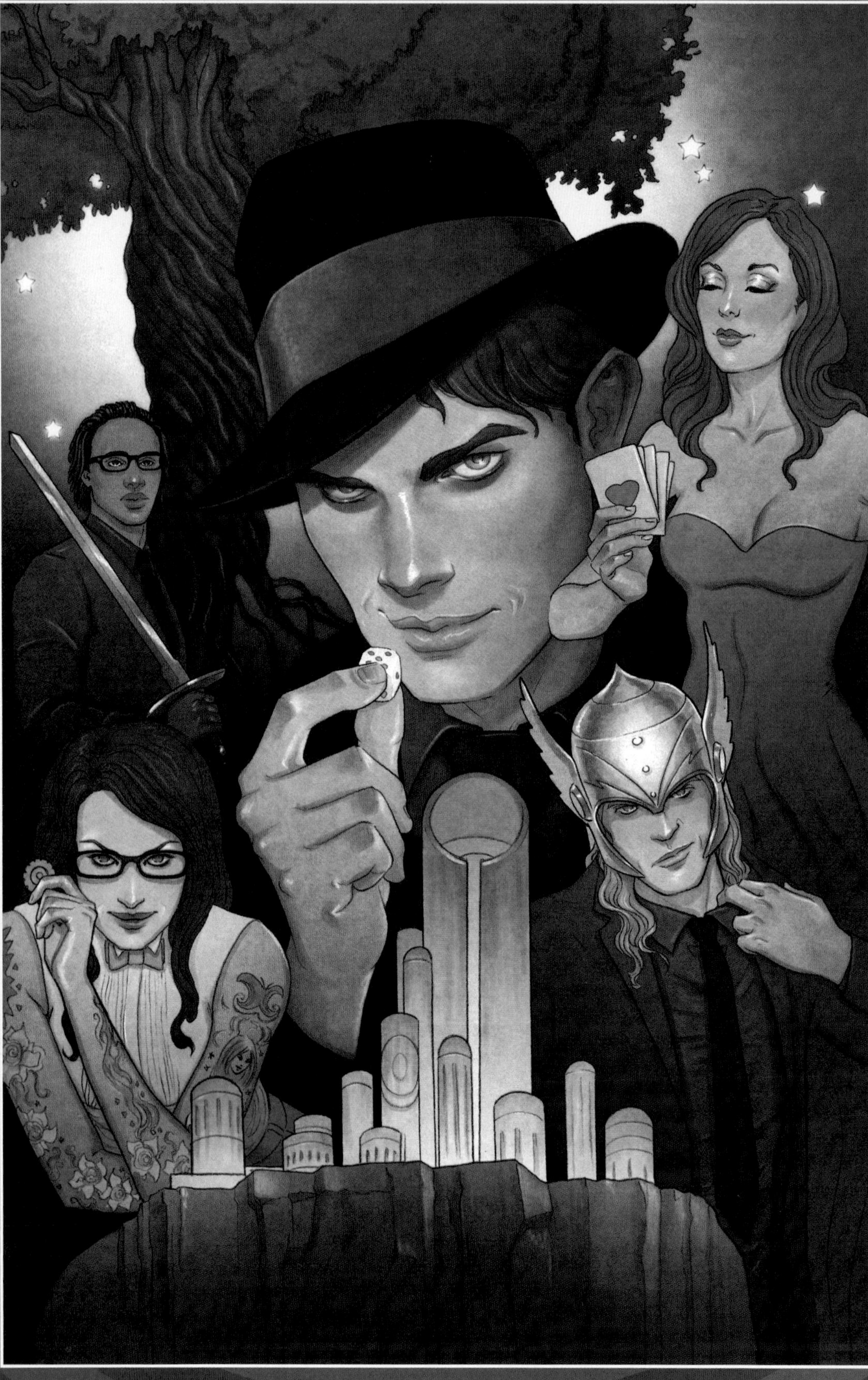

LOKI: AGENT OF ASGARD #5

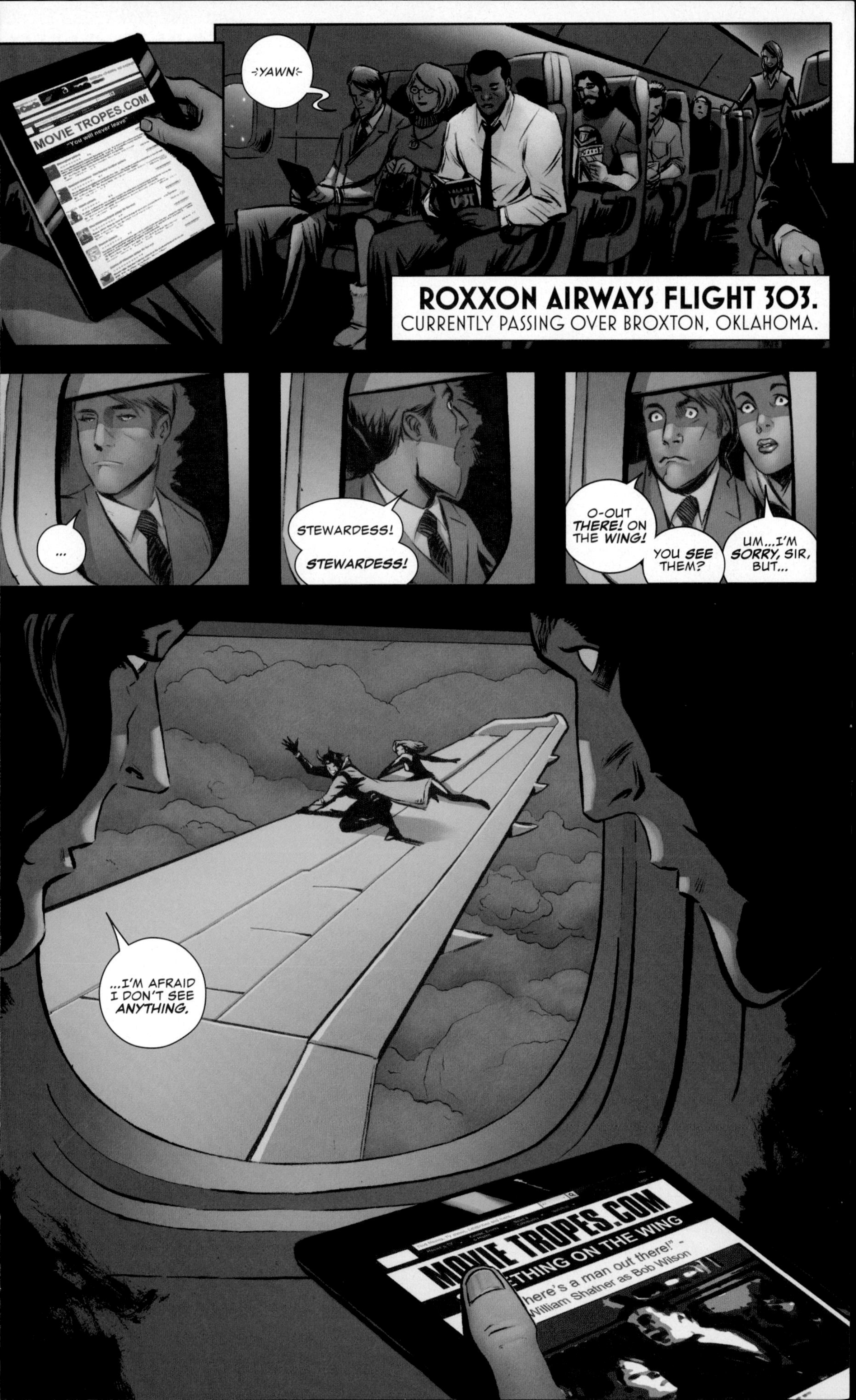
MOVIE TROPES.COM
"You will never leave"
-YAWN-
ROXXON AIRWAYS FLIGHT 303.
CURRENTLY PASSING OVER BROXTON, OKLAHOMA.
...
STEWARDESS!
STEWARDESS!
O-OUT THERE! ON THE WING!
YOU SEE THEM?
UM...I'M SORRY, SIR, BUT...
...I'M AFRAID I DON'T SEE ANYTHING.
MOVIE TROPES.COM
ETHING ON THE WING
here's a man out there!" -
William Shatner as Bob Wilson

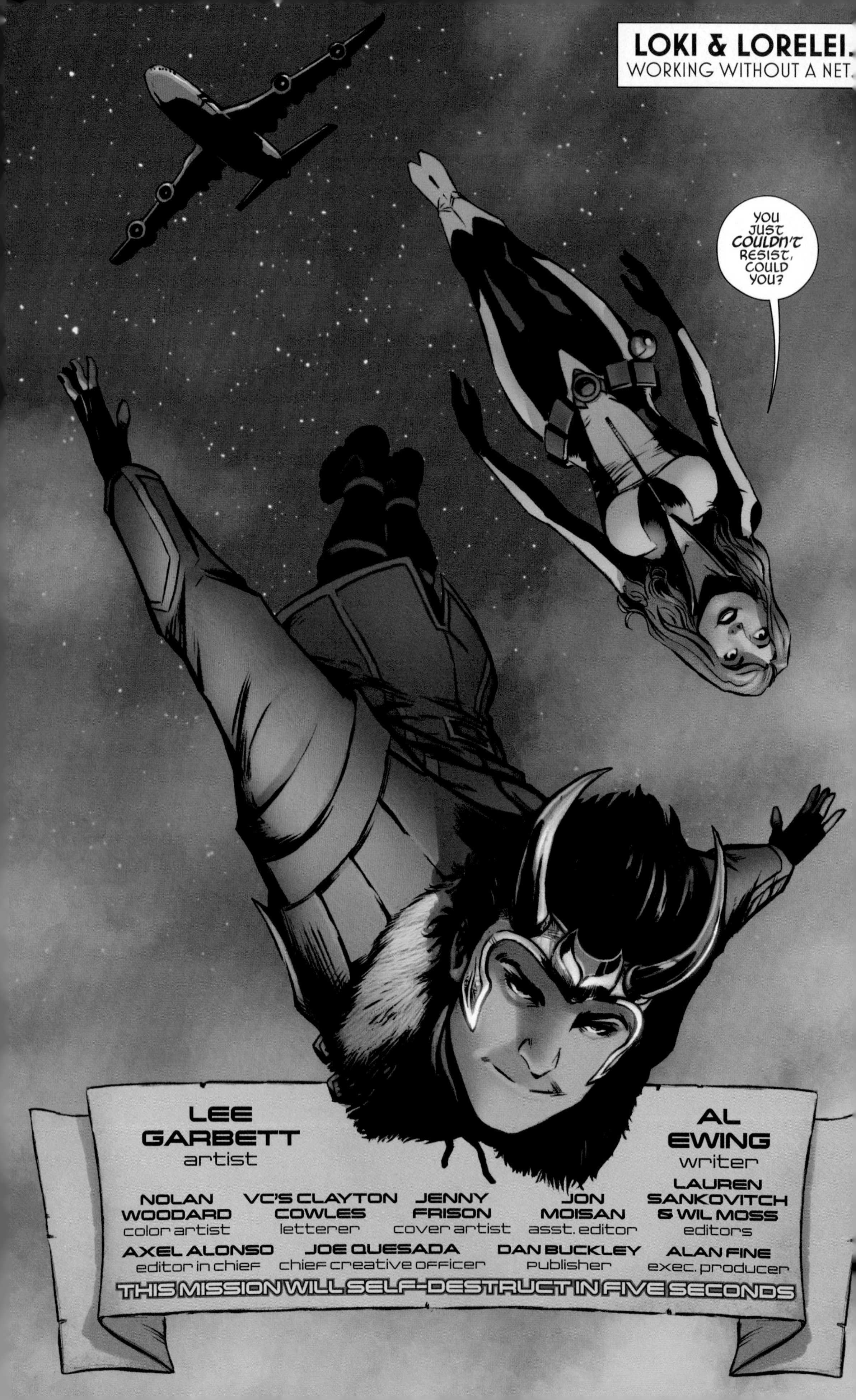

LOKI & LORELEI.
WORKING WITHOUT A NET.
YOU JUST COULDN'T RESIST, COULD YOU?
LEE GARBETT artist
AL EWING writer
NOLAN WOODARD color artist
VC'S CLAYTON COWLES letterer
JENNY FRISON cover artist
JON MOISAN asst. editor
LAUREN SANKOVITCH & WIL MOSS editors
AXEL ALONSO editor in chief
JOE QUESADA chief creative officer
DAN BUCKLEY publisher
ALAN FINE exec. producer
THIS MISSION WILL SELF-DESTRUCT IN FIVE SECONDS

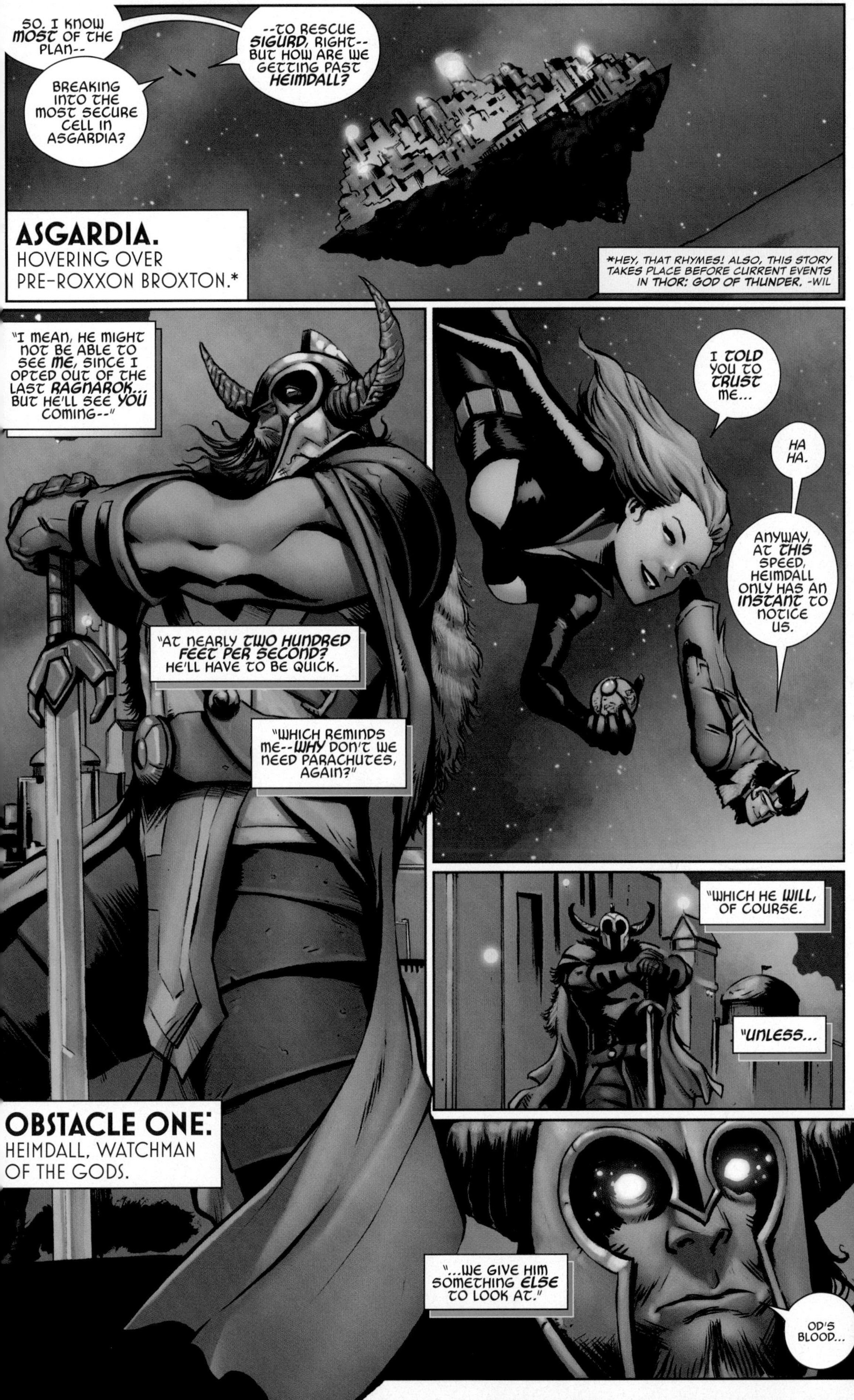

SO. I KNOW MOST OF THE PLAN--
--TO RESCUE SIGURD, RIGHT--
BREAKING INTO THE MOST SECURE CELL IN ASGARDIA?
BUT HOW ARE WE GETTING PAST HEIMDALL?
ASGARDIA.
HOVERING OVER PRE-ROXXON BROXTON.*
*HEY, THAT RHYMES! ALSO, THIS STORY TAKES PLACE BEFORE CURRENT EVENTS IN THOR: GOD OF THUNDER. -WIL
"I MEAN, HE MIGHT NOT BE ABLE TO SEE ME, SINCE I OPTED OUT OF THE LAST RAGNAROK... BUT HE'LL SEE YOU COMING--"
"AT NEARLY TWO HUNDRED FEET PER SECOND? HE'LL HAVE TO BE QUICK.
"WHICH REMINDS ME--WHY DON'T WE NEED PARACHUTES, AGAIN?"
I TOLD YOU TO TRUST ME...
HA HA.
ANYWAY, AT THIS SPEED, HEIMDALL ONLY HAS AN INSTANT TO NOTICE US.
"WHICH HE WILL, OF COURSE.
"UNLESS...
OBSTACLE ONE:
HEIMDALL, WATCHMAN OF THE GODS.
"...WE GIVE HIM SOMETHING ELSE TO LOOK AT."
OD'S BLOOD...

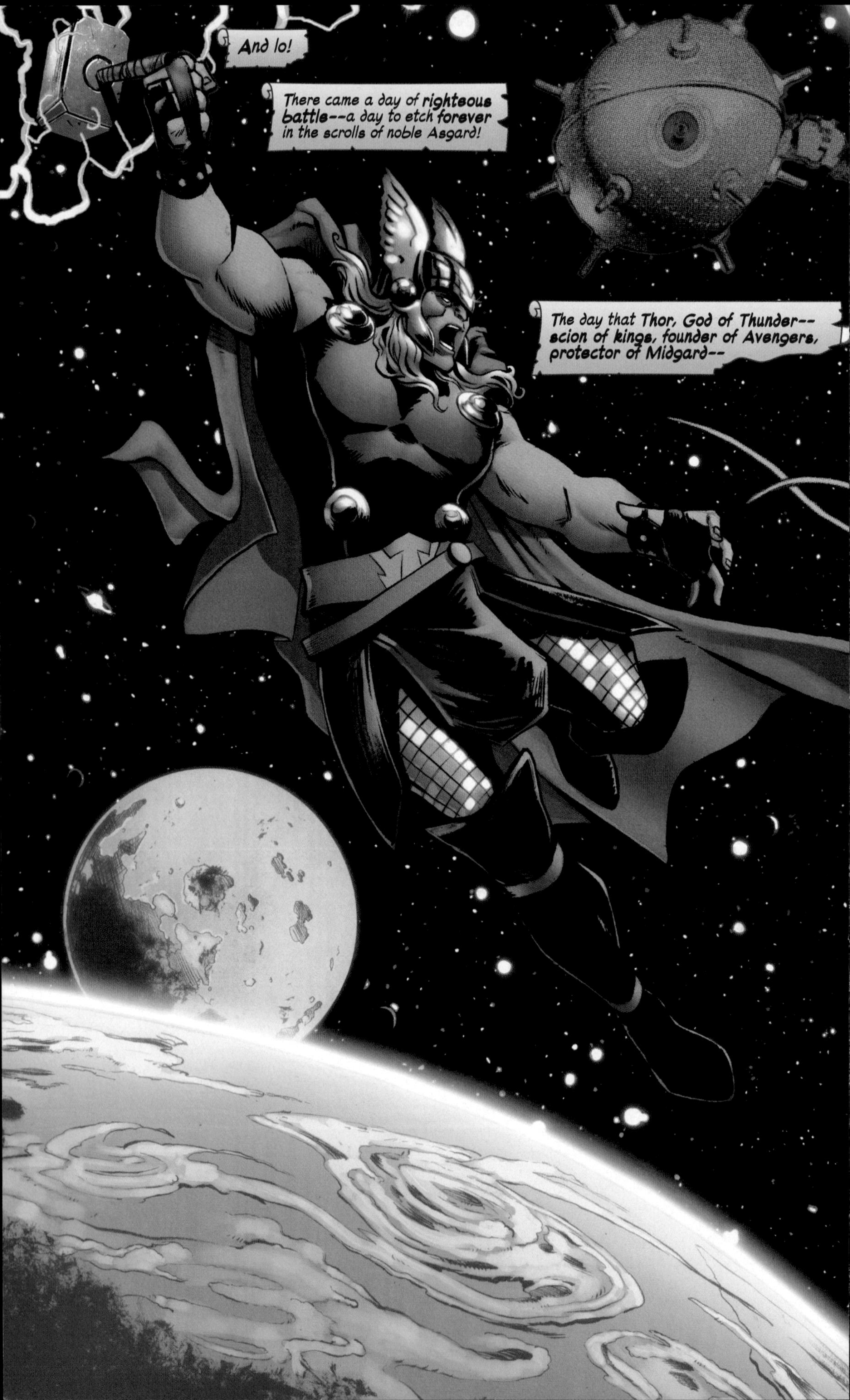
And lo!
There came a day of righteous battle--a day to etch forever in the scrolls of noble Asgard!
The day that Thor, God of Thunder--scion of kings, founder of Avengers, protector of Midgard--

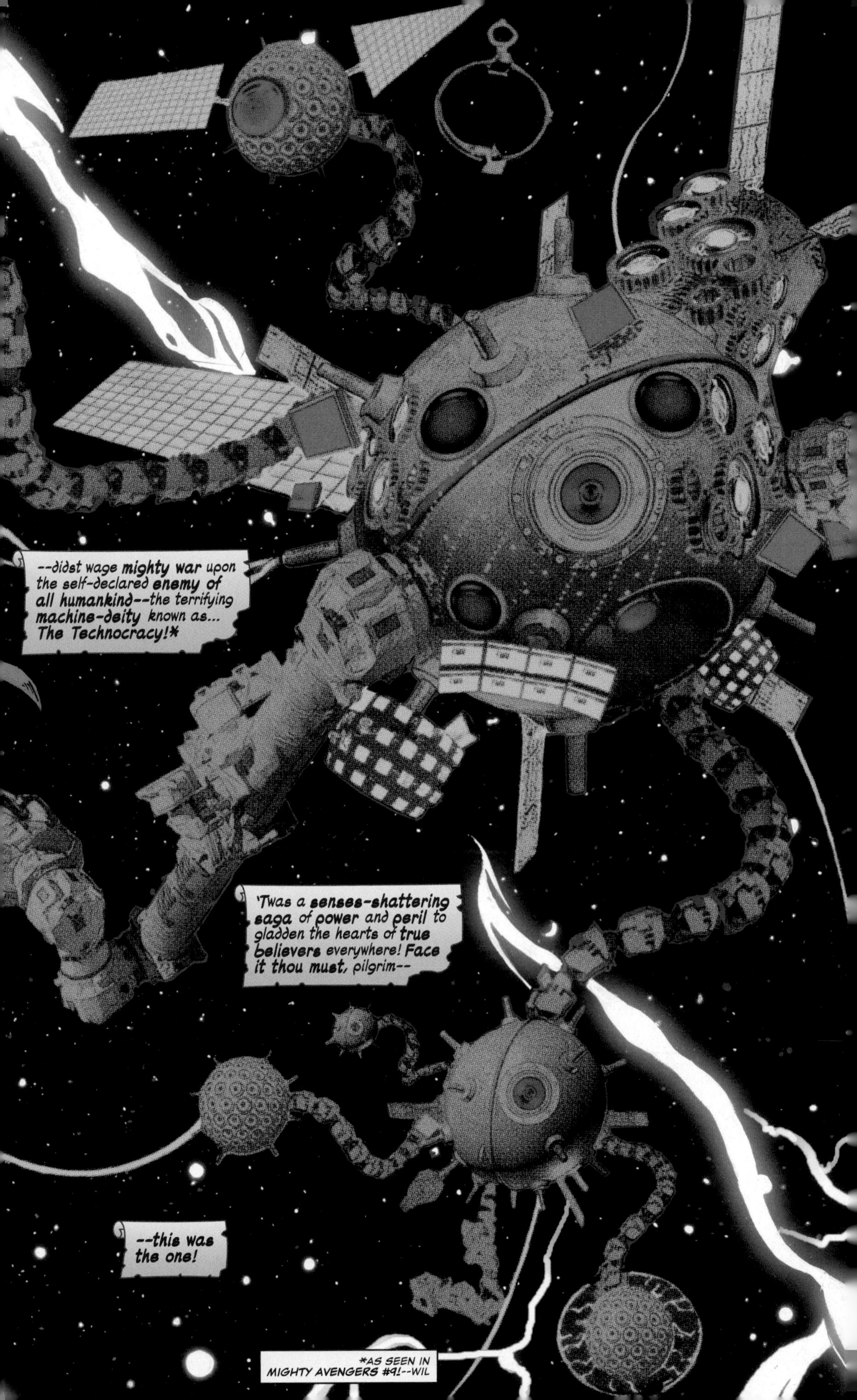
--didst wage mighty war upon the self-declared enemy of all humankind--the terrifying machine-deity known as... The Technocracy!*
'Twas a senses-shattering saga of power and peril to gladden the hearts of true believers everywhere! Face it thou must, pilgrim--
--this was the one!
*AS SEEN IN MIGHTY AVENGERS #9!--WIL

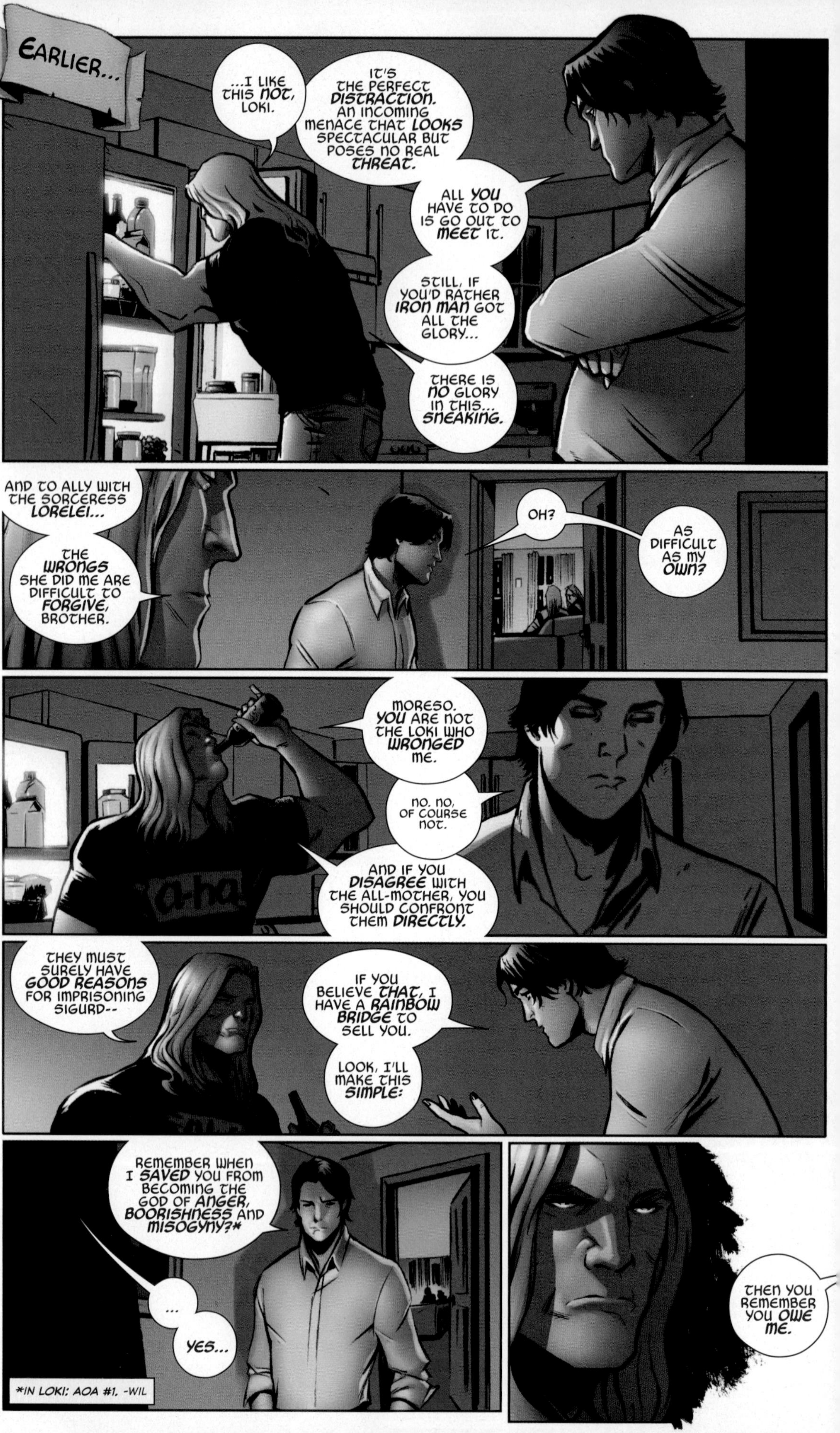
EARLIER...
...I LIKE THIS NOT, LOKI.
IT'S THE PERFECT DISTRACTION. AN INCOMING MENACE THAT LOOKS SPECTACULAR BUT POSES NO REAL THREAT.
ALL YOU HAVE TO DO IS GO OUT TO MEET IT.
STILL, IF YOU'D RATHER IRON MAN GOT ALL THE GLORY...
THERE IS NO GLORY IN THIS... SNEAKING.
AND TO ALLY WITH THE SORCERESS LORELEI...
THE WRONGS SHE DID ME ARE DIFFICULT TO FORGIVE, BROTHER.
OH?
AS DIFFICULT AS MY OWN?
MORESO. YOU ARE NOT THE LOKI WHO WRONGED ME.
NO. NO, OF COURSE NOT.
AND IF YOU DISAGREE WITH THE ALL-MOTHER, YOU SHOULD CONFRONT THEM DIRECTLY.
a-ha!
THEY MUST SURELY HAVE GOOD REASONS FOR IMPRISONING SIGURD--
IF YOU BELIEVE THAT, I HAVE A RAINBOW BRIDGE TO SELL YOU.
LOOK, I'LL MAKE THIS SIMPLE:
REMEMBER WHEN I SAVED YOU FROM BECOMING THE GOD OF ANGER, BOORISHNESS AND MISOGYNY?*
...
YES...
*IN LOKI: AOA #1. -WIL
THEN YOU REMEMBER YOU OWE ME.

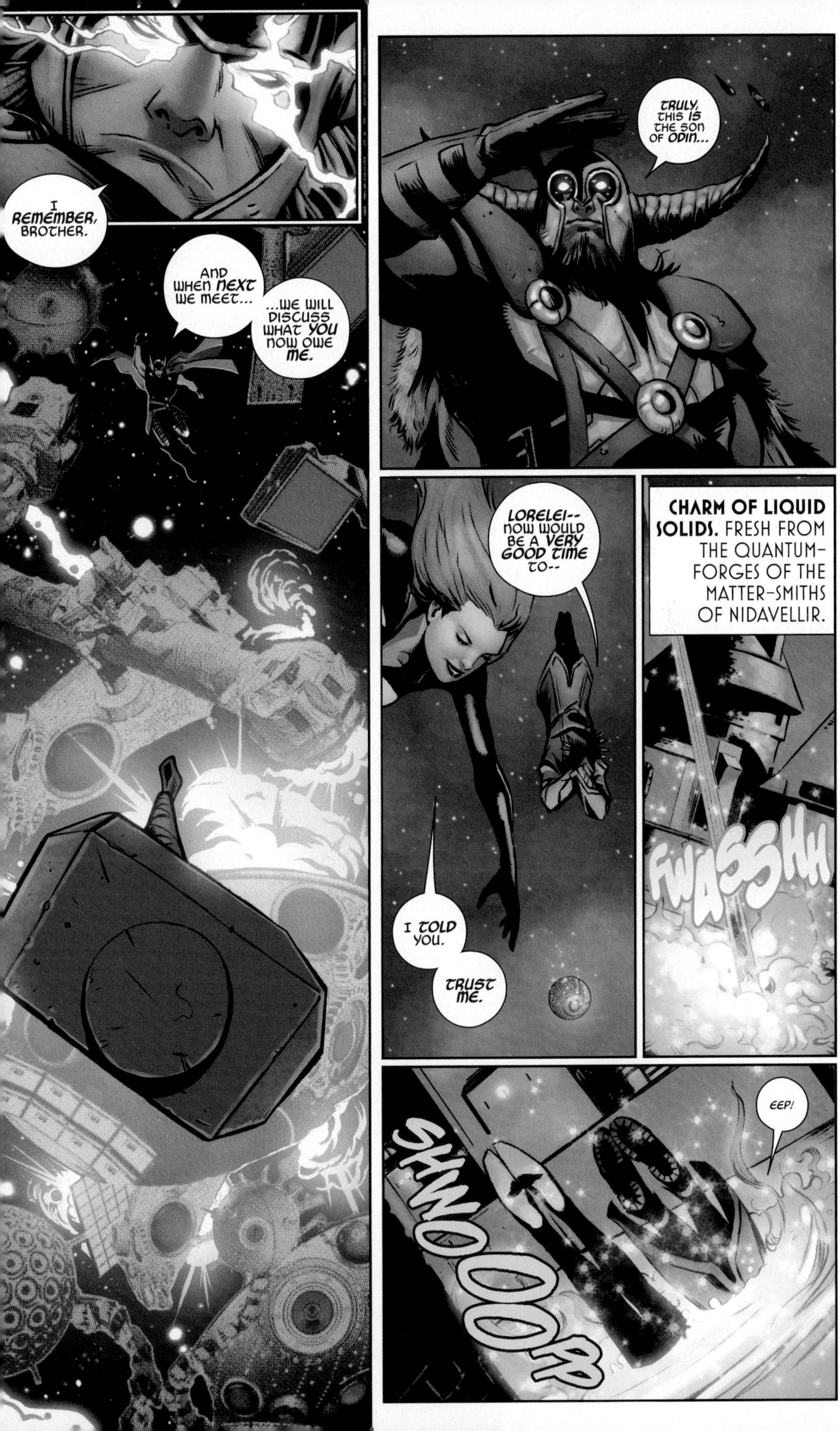
I REMEMBER, BROTHER.
AND WHEN NEXT WE MEET...
...WE WILL DISCUSS WHAT YOU NOW OWE ME.
TRULY, THIS IS THE SON OF ODIN...
LORELEI-- NOW WOULD BE A VERY GOOD TIME TO--
I TOLD YOU.
TRUST ME.
CHARM OF LIQUID SOLIDS. FRESH FROM THE QUANTUM-FORGES OF THE MATTER-SMITHS OF NIDAVELLIR.
FWASSHH
SHWOOOOP
EEP!

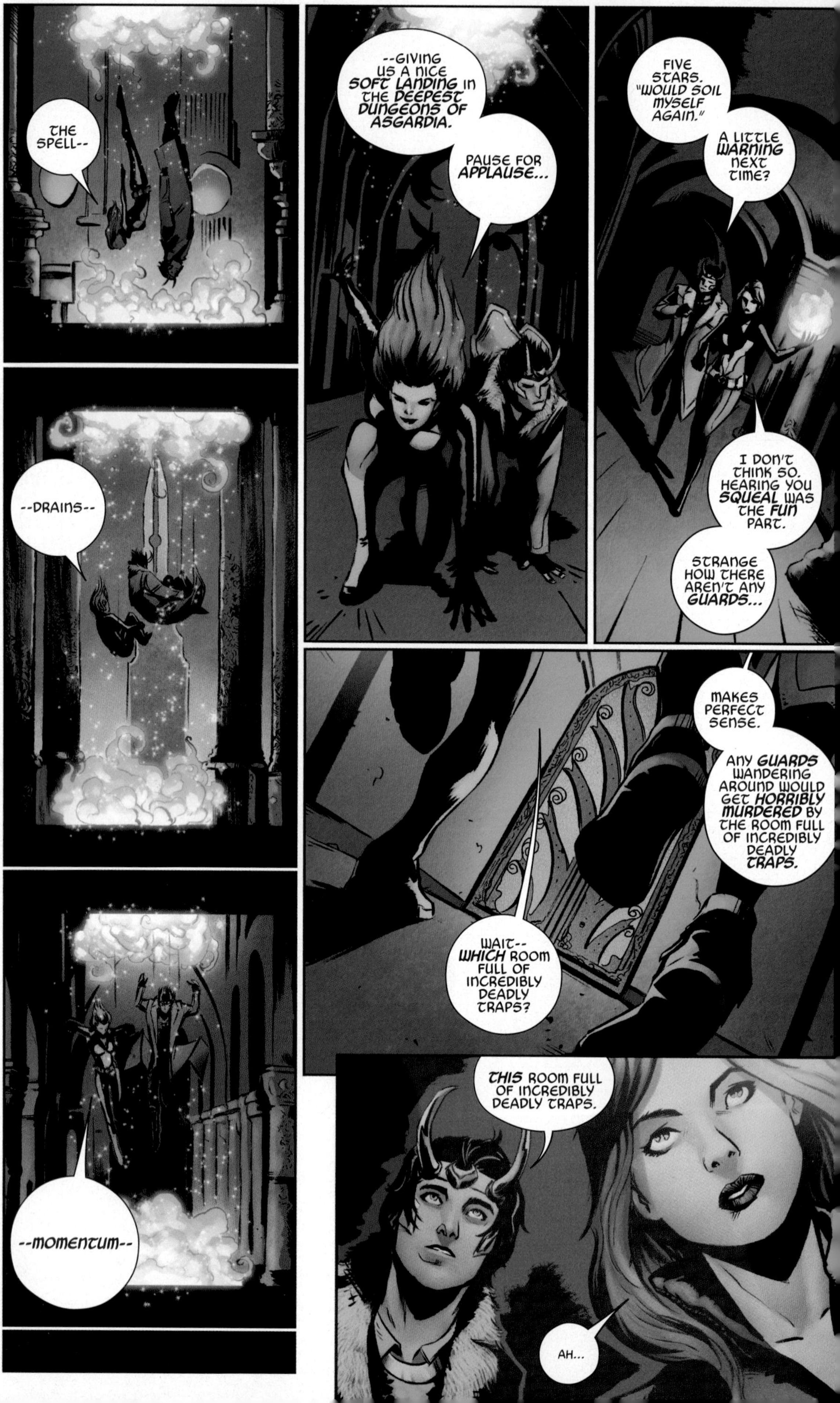
THE SPELL--
--DRAINS--
--MOMENTUM--
--GIVING US A NICE SOFT LANDING IN THE DEEPEST DUNGEONS OF ASGARDIA.
PAUSE FOR APPLAUSE...
FIVE STARS. "WOULD SOIL MYSELF AGAIN."
A LITTLE WARNING NEXT TIME?
I DON'T THINK SO. HEARING YOU SQUEAL WAS THE FUN PART.
STRANGE HOW THERE AREN'T ANY GUARDS...
MAKES PERFECT SENSE.
ANY GUARDS WANDERING AROUND WOULD GET HORRIBLY MURDERED BY THE ROOM FULL OF INCREDIBLY DEADLY TRAPS.
WAIT-- WHICH ROOM FULL OF INCREDIBLY DEADLY TRAPS?
THIS ROOM FULL OF INCREDIBLY DEADLY TRAPS.
AH...

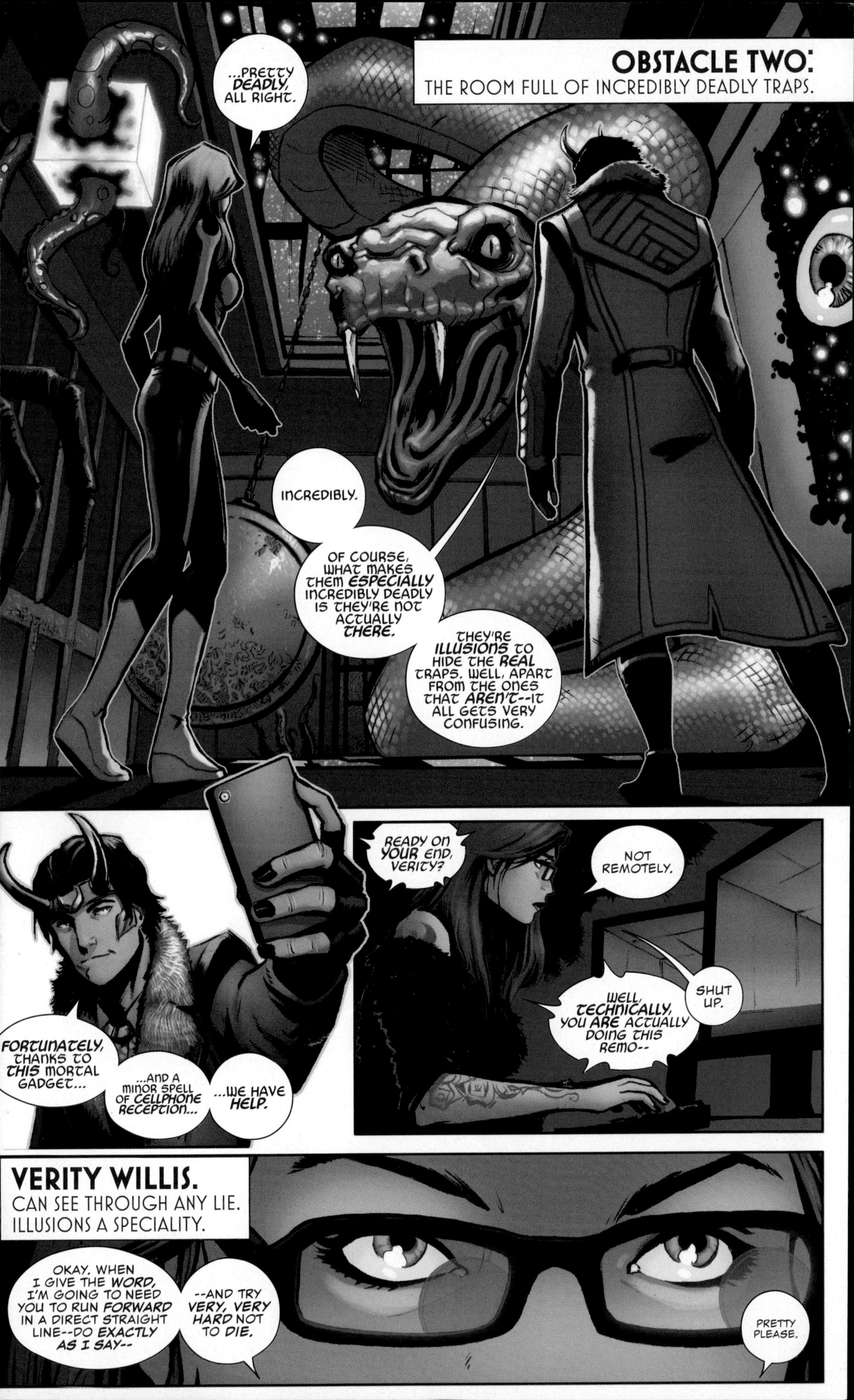

OBSTACLE TWO:
THE ROOM FULL OF INCREDIBLY DEADLY TRAPS.
...PRETTY DEADLY, ALL RIGHT.
INCREDIBLY.
OF COURSE, WHAT MAKES THEM ESPECIALLY INCREDIBLY DEADLY IS THEY'RE NOT ACTUALLY THERE.
THEY'RE ILLUSIONS TO HIDE THE REAL TRAPS. WELL, APART FROM THE ONES THAT AREN'T--IT ALL GETS VERY CONFUSING.
FORTUNATELY, THANKS TO THIS MORTAL GADGET...
...AND A MINOR SPELL OF CELLPHONE RECEPTION...
...WE HAVE HELP.
READY ON YOUR END, VERITY?
NOT REMOTELY.
WELL, TECHNICALLY, YOU ARE ACTUALLY DOING THIS REMO--
SHUT UP.
VERITY WILLIS.
CAN SEE THROUGH ANY LIE.
ILLUSIONS A SPECIALITY.
OKAY. WHEN I GIVE THE WORD, I'M GOING TO NEED YOU TO RUN FORWARD IN A DIRECT STRAIGHT LINE--DO EXACTLY AS I SAY--
--AND TRY VERY, VERY HARD NOT TO DIE.
PRETTY PLEASE.

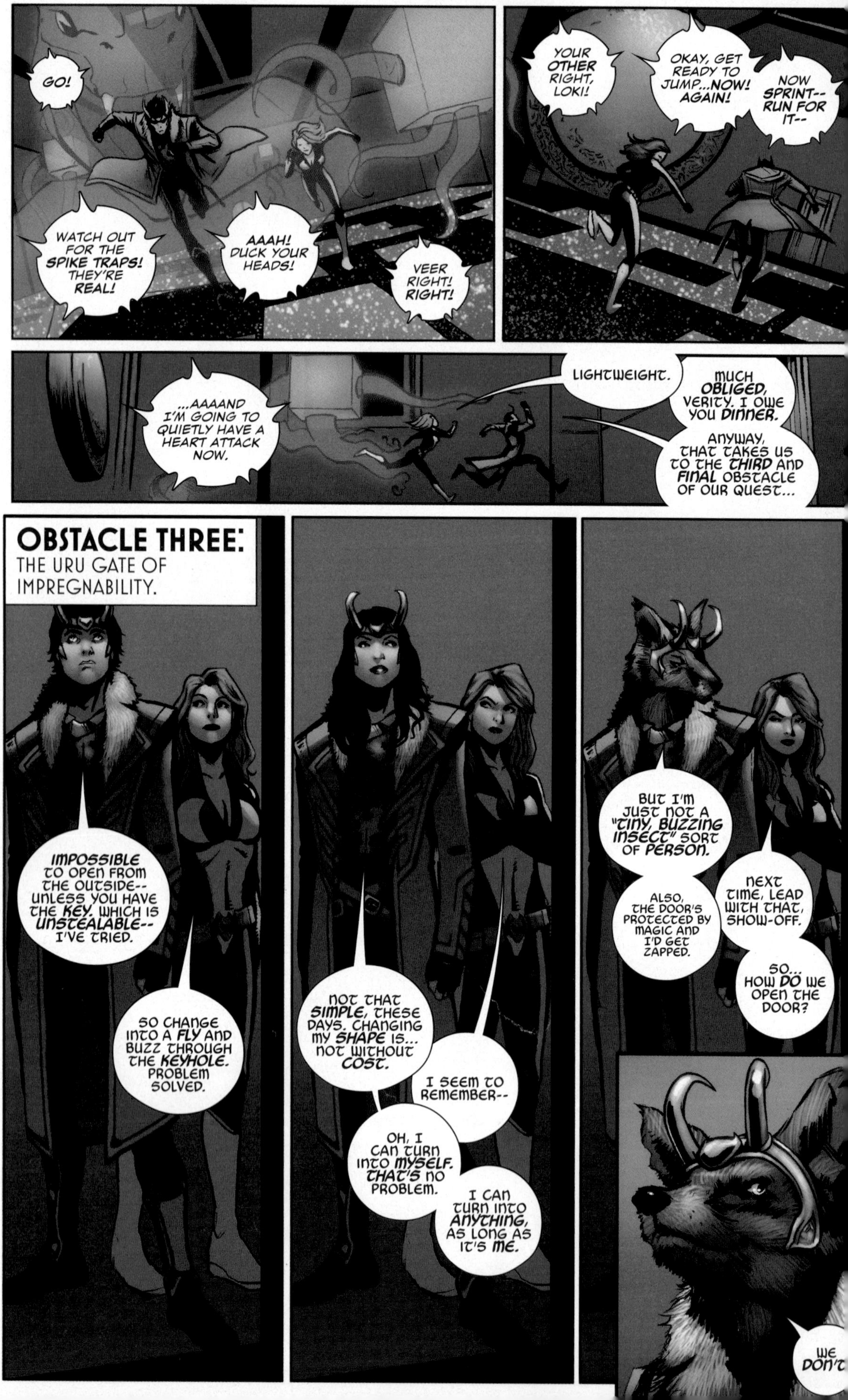
GO!
WATCH OUT FOR THE SPIKE TRAPS! THEY'RE REAL!
AAAH! DUCK YOUR HEADS!
VEER RIGHT! RIGHT!
YOUR OTHER RIGHT, LOKI!
OKAY, GET READY TO JUMP...NOW! AGAIN!
NOW SPRINT--RUN FOR IT--
...AAAAND I'M GOING TO QUIETLY HAVE A HEART ATTACK NOW.
LIGHTWEIGHT.
MUCH OBLIGED, VERITY. I OWE YOU DINNER.
ANYWAY, THAT TAKES US TO THE THIRD AND FINAL OBSTACLE OF OUR QUEST...
OBSTACLE THREE: THE URU GATE OF IMPREGNABILITY.
IMPOSSIBLE TO OPEN FROM THE OUTSIDE--UNLESS YOU HAVE THE KEY. WHICH IS UNSTEALABLE--I'VE TRIED.
SO CHANGE INTO A FLY AND BUZZ THROUGH THE KEYHOLE. PROBLEM SOLVED.
NOT THAT SIMPLE, THESE DAYS. CHANGING MY SHAPE IS... NOT WITHOUT COST.
I SEEM TO REMEMBER--
OH, I CAN TURN INTO MYSELF. THAT'S NO PROBLEM.
I CAN TURN INTO ANYTHING, AS LONG AS IT'S ME.
BUT I'M JUST NOT A "TINY, BUZZING INSECT" SORT OF PERSON.
ALSO, THE DOOR'S PROTECTED BY MAGIC AND I'D GET ZAPPED.
NEXT TIME, LEAD WITH THAT, SHOW-OFF.
SO... HOW DO WE OPEN THE DOOR?
WE DON'T

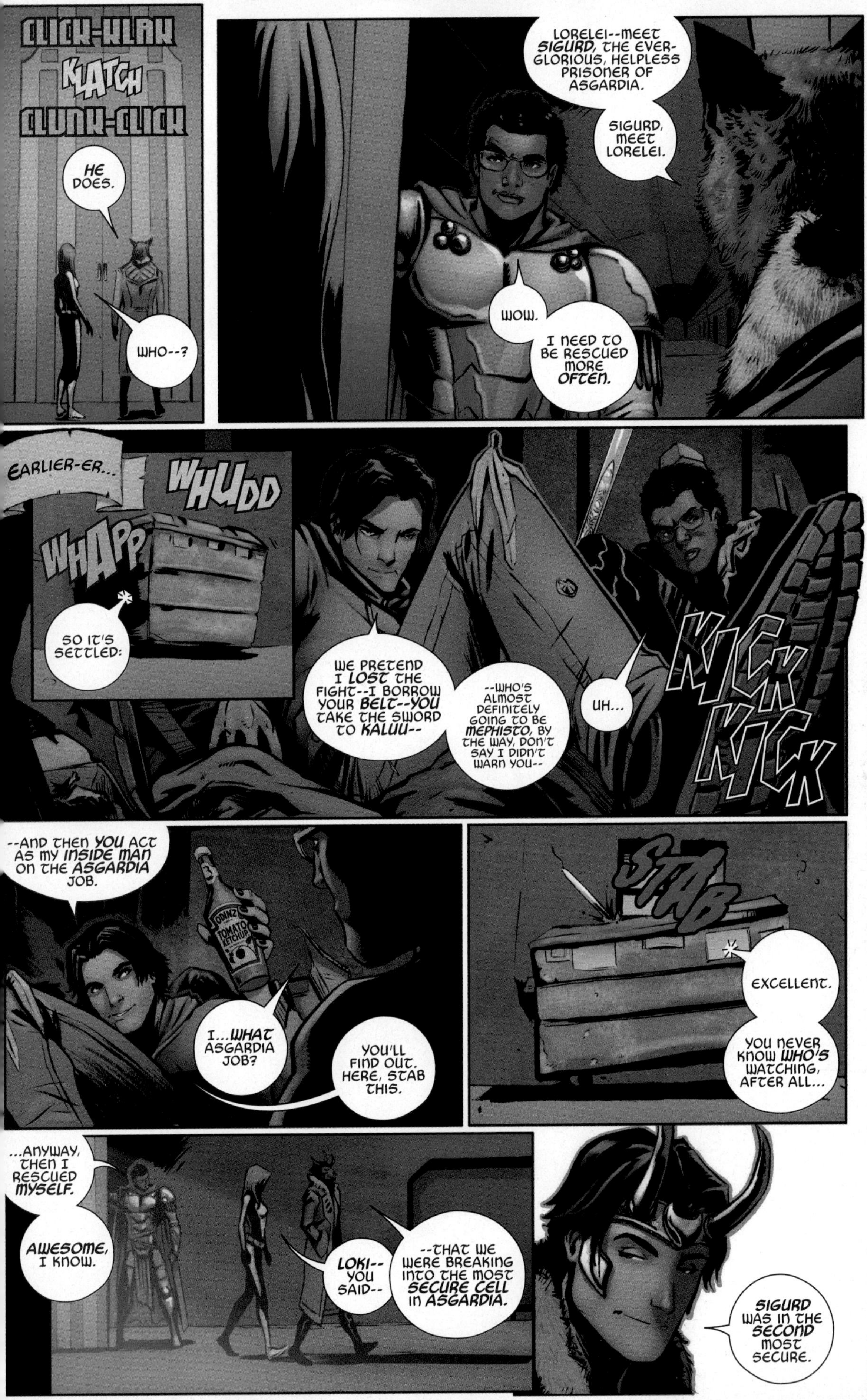
CLICK-KLAK
KLATCH
CLUNK-CLICK
HE DOES.
WHO--?
LORELEI--MEET SIGURD, THE EVER-GLORIOUS, HELPLESS PRISONER OF ASGARDIA.
SIGURD, MEET LORELEI.
WOW.
I NEED TO BE RESCUED MORE OFTEN.
EARLIER-ER...
WHUDD
WHAPP
SO IT'S SETTLED:
WE PRETEND I LOST THE FIGHT--I BORROW YOUR BELT--YOU TAKE THE SWORD TO KALUU--
--WHO'S ALMOST DEFINITELY GOING TO BE MEPHISTO, BY THE WAY, DON'T SAY I DIDN'T WARN YOU--
UH...
KICK KICK
--AND THEN YOU ACT AS MY INSIDE MAN ON THE ASGARDIA JOB.
ODINZ TOMATO KETCHUP
I...WHAT ASGARDIA JOB?
YOU'LL FIND OUT. HERE, STAB THIS.
STAB
EXCELLENT.
YOU NEVER KNOW WHO'S WATCHING, AFTER ALL...
...ANYWAY, THEN I RESCUED MYSELF.
AWESOME, I KNOW.
LOKI--YOU SAID--
--THAT WE WERE BREAKING INTO THE MOST SECURE CELL IN ASGARDIA.
SIGURD WAS IN THE SECOND MOST SECURE.

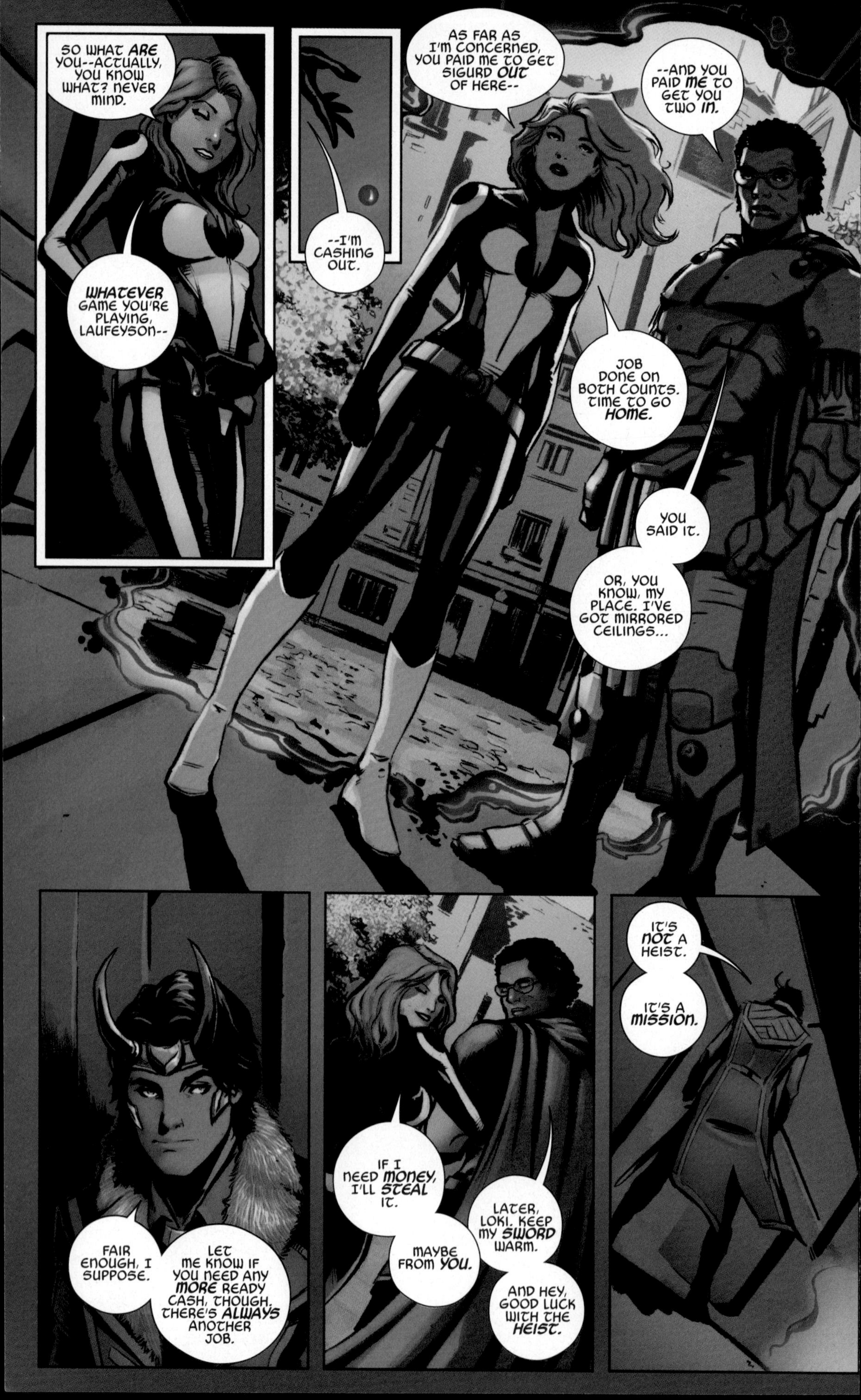
SO WHAT ARE YOU--ACTUALLY, YOU KNOW WHAT? NEVER MIND.
WHATEVER GAME YOU'RE PLAYING, LAUFEYSON--
--I'M CASHING OUT.
AS FAR AS I'M CONCERNED, YOU PAID ME TO GET SIGURD OUT OF HERE--
--AND YOU PAID ME TO GET YOU TWO IN.
JOB DONE ON BOTH COUNTS. TIME TO GO HOME.
YOU SAID IT.
OR, YOU KNOW, MY PLACE. I'VE GOT MIRRORED CEILINGS...
FAIR ENOUGH, I SUPPOSE.
LET ME KNOW IF YOU NEED ANY MORE READY CASH, THOUGH. THERE'S ALWAYS ANOTHER JOB.
IF I NEED MONEY, I'LL STEAL IT.
MAYBE FROM YOU.
LATER, LOKI. KEEP MY SWORD WARM.
AND HEY, GOOD LUCK WITH THE HEIST.
IT'S NOT A HEIST.
IT'S A MISSION.

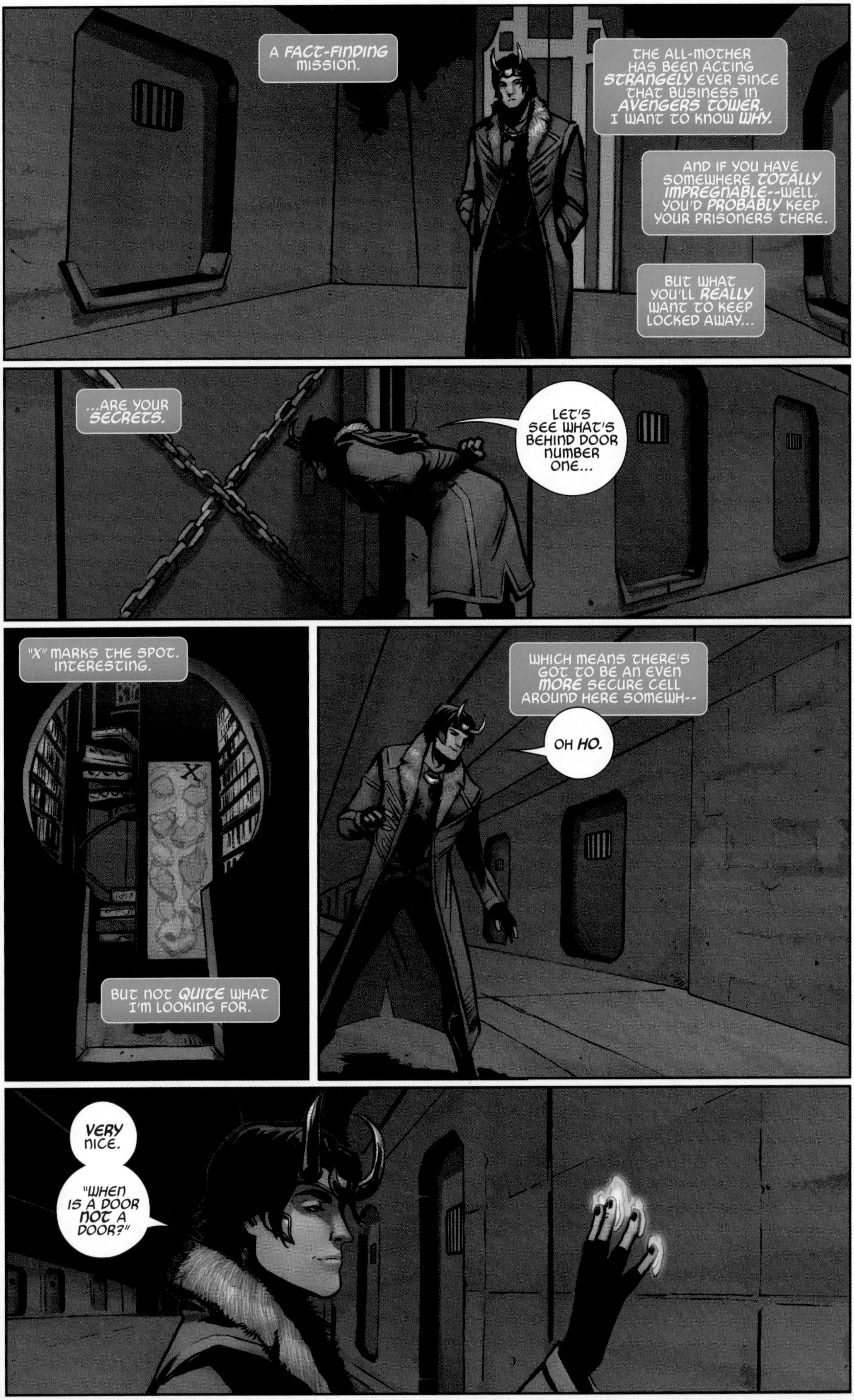
A FACT-FINDING MISSION.
THE ALL-MOTHER HAS BEEN ACTING STRANGELY EVER SINCE THAT BUSINESS IN AVENGERS TOWER. I WANT TO KNOW WHY.
AND IF YOU HAVE SOMEWHERE TOTALLY IMPREGNABLE--WELL, YOU'D PROBABLY KEEP YOUR PRISONERS THERE.
BUT WHAT YOU'LL REALLY WANT TO KEEP LOCKED AWAY...
...ARE YOUR SECRETS.
LET'S SEE WHAT'S BEHIND DOOR NUMBER ONE...
"X" MARKS THE SPOT. INTERESTING.
BUT NOT QUITE WHAT I'M LOOKING FOR.
WHICH MEANS THERE'S GOT TO BE AN EVEN MORE SECURE CELL AROUND HERE SOMEWH--
OH HO.
VERY NICE.
"WHEN IS A DOOR NOT A DOOR?"

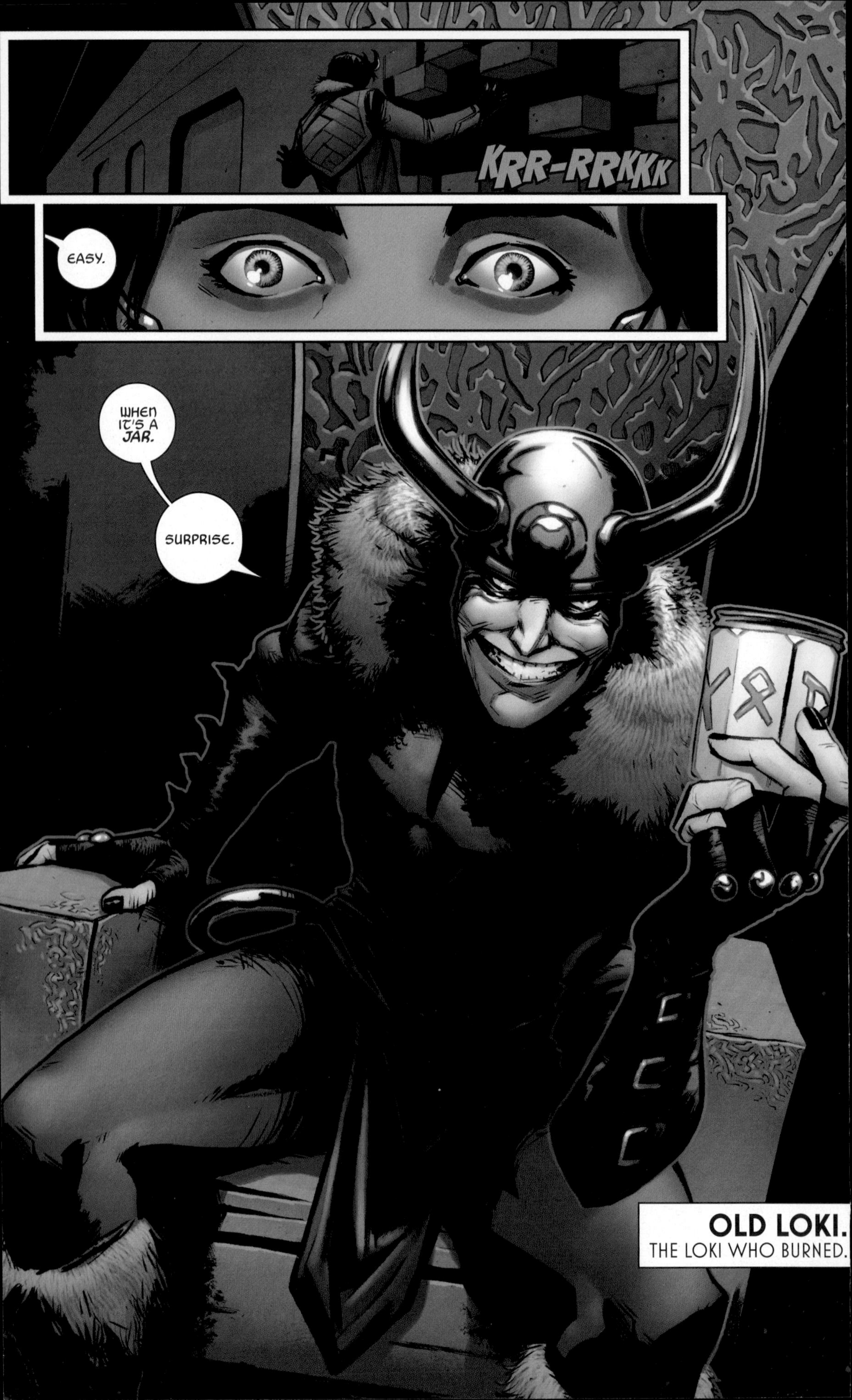
KRR-RRKKK
EASY.
WHEN IT'S A JAR.
SURPRISE.
OLD LOKI.
THE LOKI WHO BURNED.

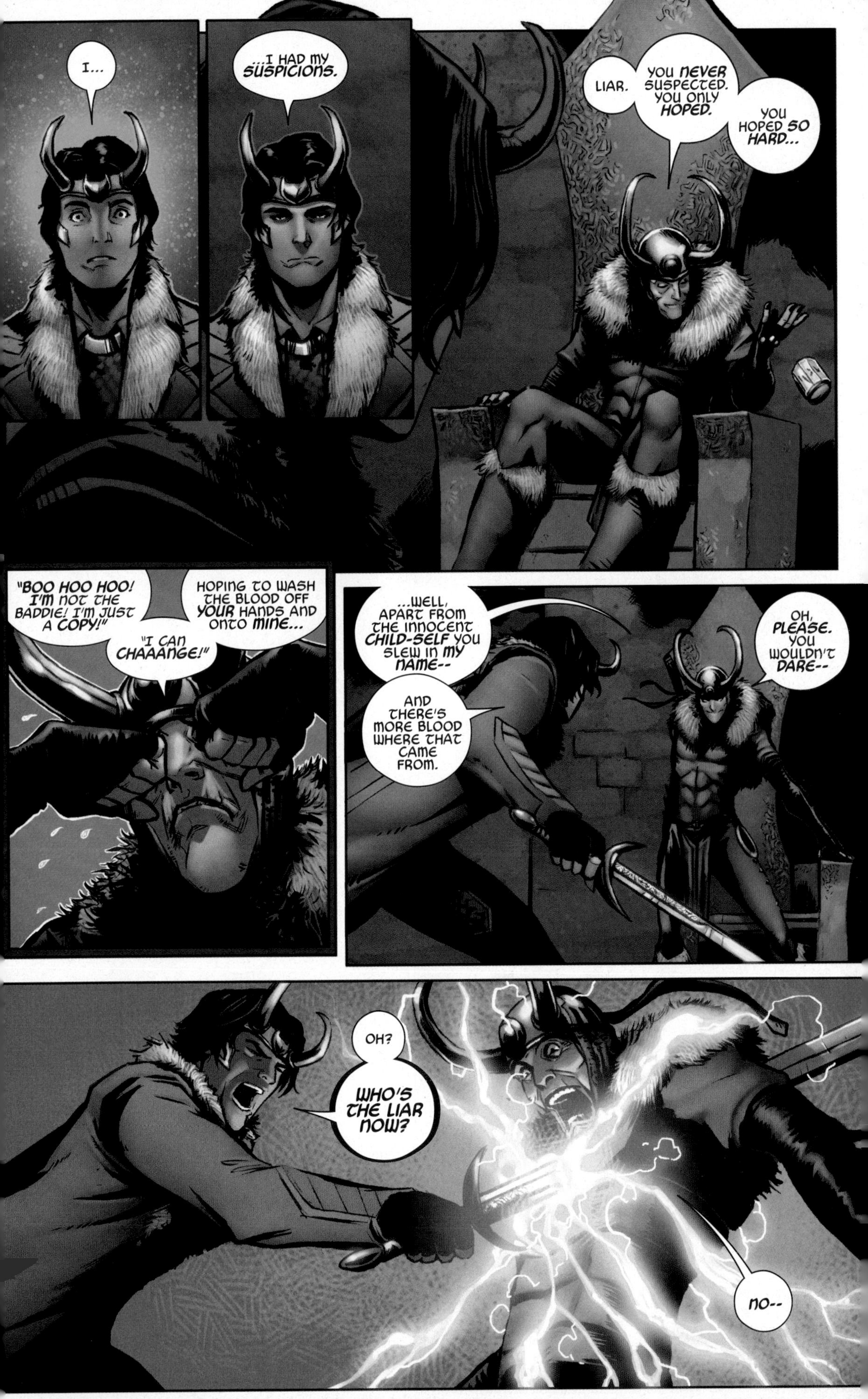
I...
...I HAD MY SUSPICIONS.
LIAR.
YOU NEVER SUSPECTED. YOU ONLY HOPED.
YOU HOPED SO HARD...
"BOO HOO HOO! I'M NOT THE BADDIE! I'M JUST A COPY!"
"I CAN CHAAANGE!"
HOPING TO WASH THE BLOOD OFF YOUR HANDS AND ONTO MINE...
...WELL, APART FROM THE INNOCENT CHILD-SELF YOU SLEW IN MY NAME--
AND THERE'S MORE BLOOD WHERE THAT CAME FROM.
OH, PLEASE. YOU WOULDN'T DARE--
OH?
WHO'S THE LIAR NOW?
NO--

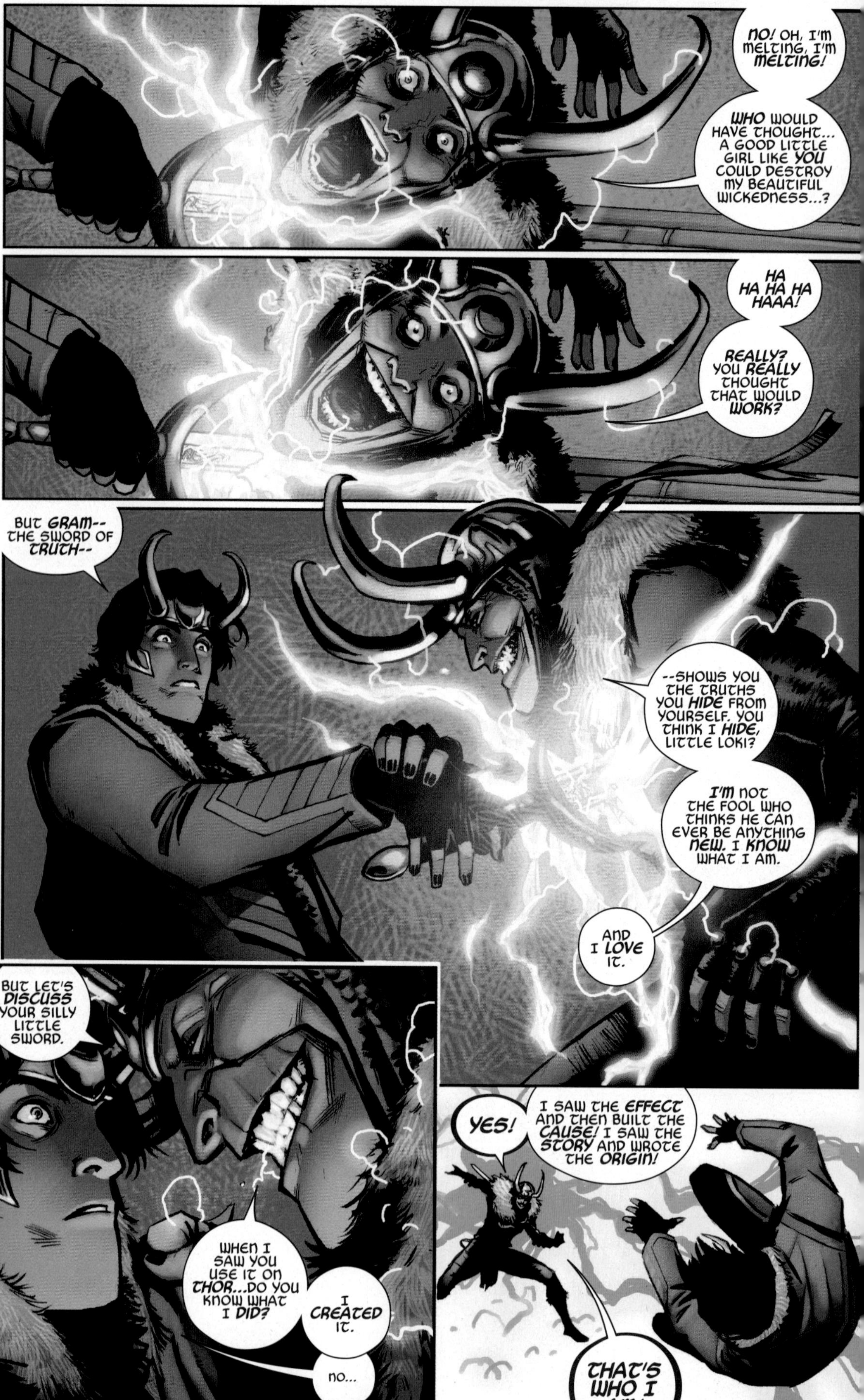
NO! OH, I'M MELTING, I'M MELTING!
WHO WOULD HAVE THOUGHT... A GOOD LITTLE GIRL LIKE YOU COULD DESTROY MY BEAUTIFUL WICKEDNESS...?
HA HA HA HA HAAA!
REALLY? YOU REALLY THOUGHT THAT WOULD WORK?
BUT GRAM-- THE SWORD OF TRUTH--
--SHOWS YOU THE TRUTHS YOU HIDE FROM YOURSELF. YOU THINK I HIDE, LITTLE LOKI?
I'M NOT THE FOOL WHO THINKS HE CAN EVER BE ANYTHING NEW. I KNOW WHAT I AM.
AND I LOVE IT.
BUT LET'S DISCUSS YOUR SILLY LITTLE SWORD.
WHEN I SAW YOU USE IT ON THOR...DO YOU KNOW WHAT I DID?
I CREATED IT.
no...
YES!
I SAW THE EFFECT AND THEN BUILT THE CAUSE! I SAW THE STORY AND WROTE THE ORIGIN!
THAT'S WHO I AM!

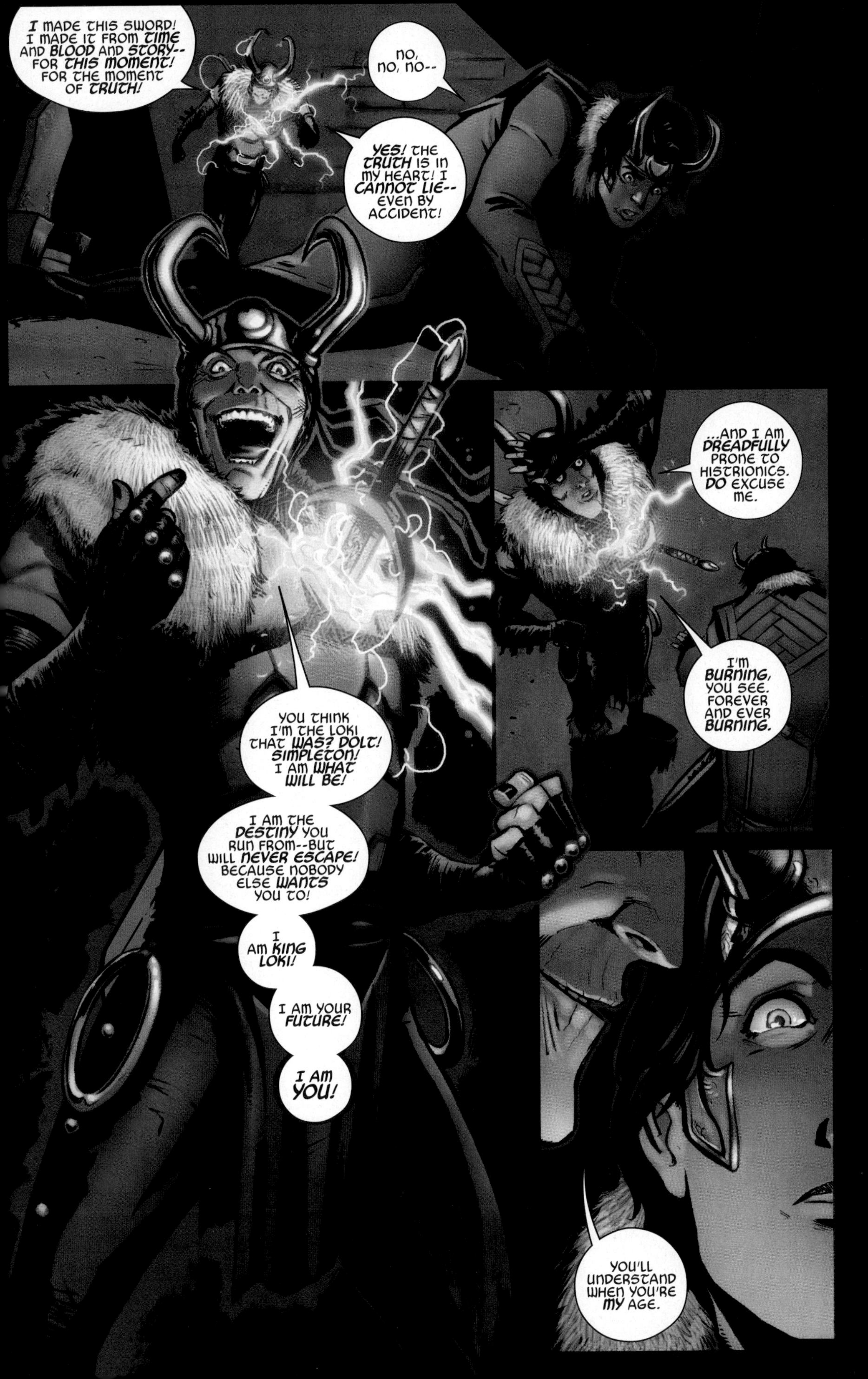
I MADE THIS SWORD! I MADE IT FROM TIME AND BLOOD AND STORY-- FOR THIS MOMENT! FOR THE MOMENT OF TRUTH!
no, no, no--
YES! THE TRUTH IS IN MY HEART! I CANNOT LIE-- EVEN BY ACCIDENT!
YOU THINK I'M THE LOKI THAT WAS? DOLT! SIMPLETON! I AM WHAT WILL BE!
I AM THE DESTINY YOU RUN FROM--BUT WILL NEVER ESCAPE! BECAUSE NOBODY ELSE WANTS YOU TO!
I AM KING LOKI!
I AM YOUR FUTURE!
I AM YOU!
...AND I AM DREADFULLY PRONE TO HISTRIONICS. DO EXCUSE ME.
I'M BURNING, YOU SEE. FOREVER AND EVER BURNING.
YOU'LL UNDERSTAND WHEN YOU'RE MY AGE.

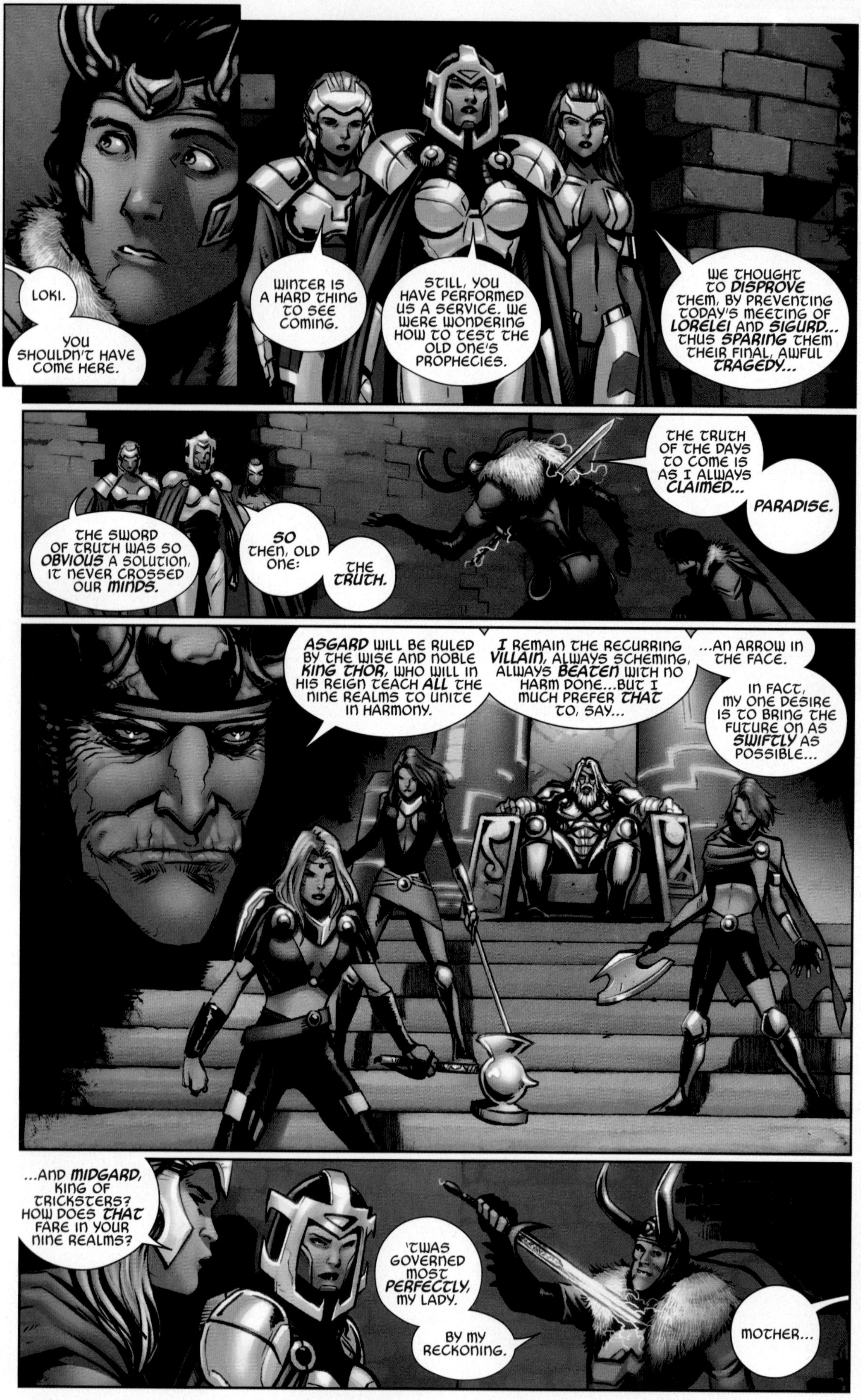
LOKI.
YOU SHOULDN'T HAVE COME HERE.
WINTER IS A HARD THING TO SEE COMING.
STILL, YOU HAVE PERFORMED US A SERVICE. WE WERE WONDERING HOW TO TEST THE OLD ONE'S PROPHECIES.
WE THOUGHT TO DISPROVE THEM, BY PREVENTING TODAY'S MEETING OF LORELEI AND SIGURD... THUS SPARING THEM THEIR FINAL, AWFUL TRAGEDY...
THE SWORD OF TRUTH WAS SO OBVIOUS A SOLUTION, IT NEVER CROSSED OUR MINDS.
SO THEN, OLD ONE:
THE TRUTH.
THE TRUTH OF THE DAYS TO COME IS AS I ALWAYS CLAIMED...
PARADISE.
ASGARD WILL BE RULED BY THE WISE AND NOBLE KING THOR, WHO WILL IN HIS REIGN TEACH ALL THE NINE REALMS TO UNITE IN HARMONY.
I REMAIN THE RECURRING VILLAIN, ALWAYS SCHEMING, ALWAYS BEATEN WITH NO HARM DONE...BUT I MUCH PREFER THAT TO, SAY...
...AN ARROW IN THE FACE.
IN FACT, MY ONE DESIRE IS TO BRING THE FUTURE ON AS SWIFTLY AS POSSIBLE...
...AND MIDGARD, KING OF TRICKSTERS? HOW DOES THAT FARE IN YOUR NINE REALMS?
'TWAS GOVERNED MOST PERFECTLY, MY LADY.
BY MY RECKONING.
MOTHER...

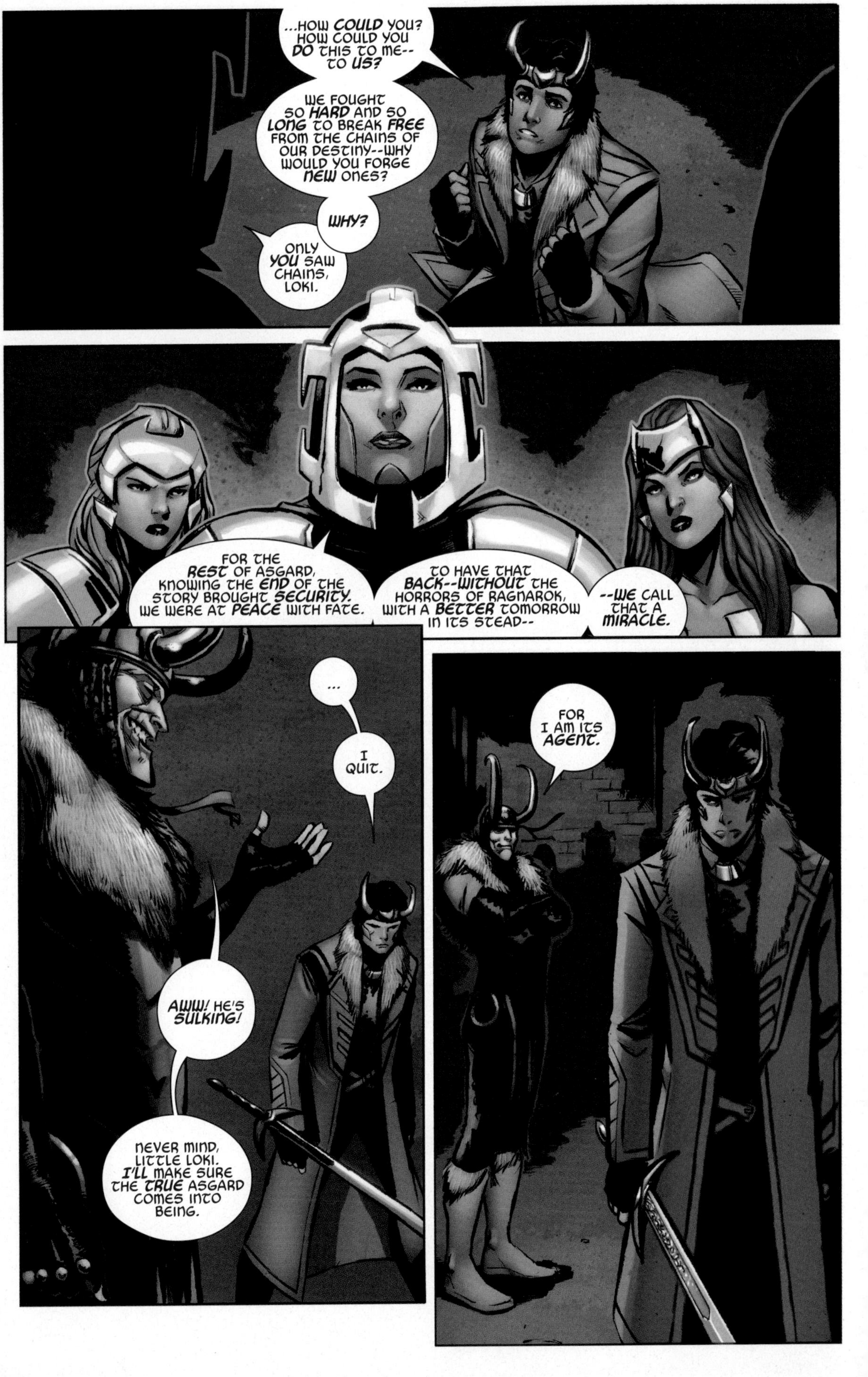
...HOW COULD YOU? HOW COULD YOU DO THIS TO ME-- TO US?
WE FOUGHT SO HARD AND SO LONG TO BREAK FREE FROM THE CHAINS OF OUR DESTINY--WHY WOULD YOU FORGE NEW ONES?
WHY?
ONLY YOU SAW CHAINS, LOKI.
FOR THE REST OF ASGARD, KNOWING THE END OF THE STORY BROUGHT SECURITY. WE WERE AT PEACE WITH FATE.
TO HAVE THAT BACK--WITHOUT THE HORRORS OF RAGNAROK, WITH A BETTER TOMORROW IN ITS STEAD--
--WE CALL THAT A MIRACLE.
...
I QUIT.
AWW! HE'S SULKING!
NEVER MIND, LITTLE LOKI. I'LL MAKE SURE THE TRUE ASGARD COMES INTO BEING.
FOR I AM ITS AGENT.

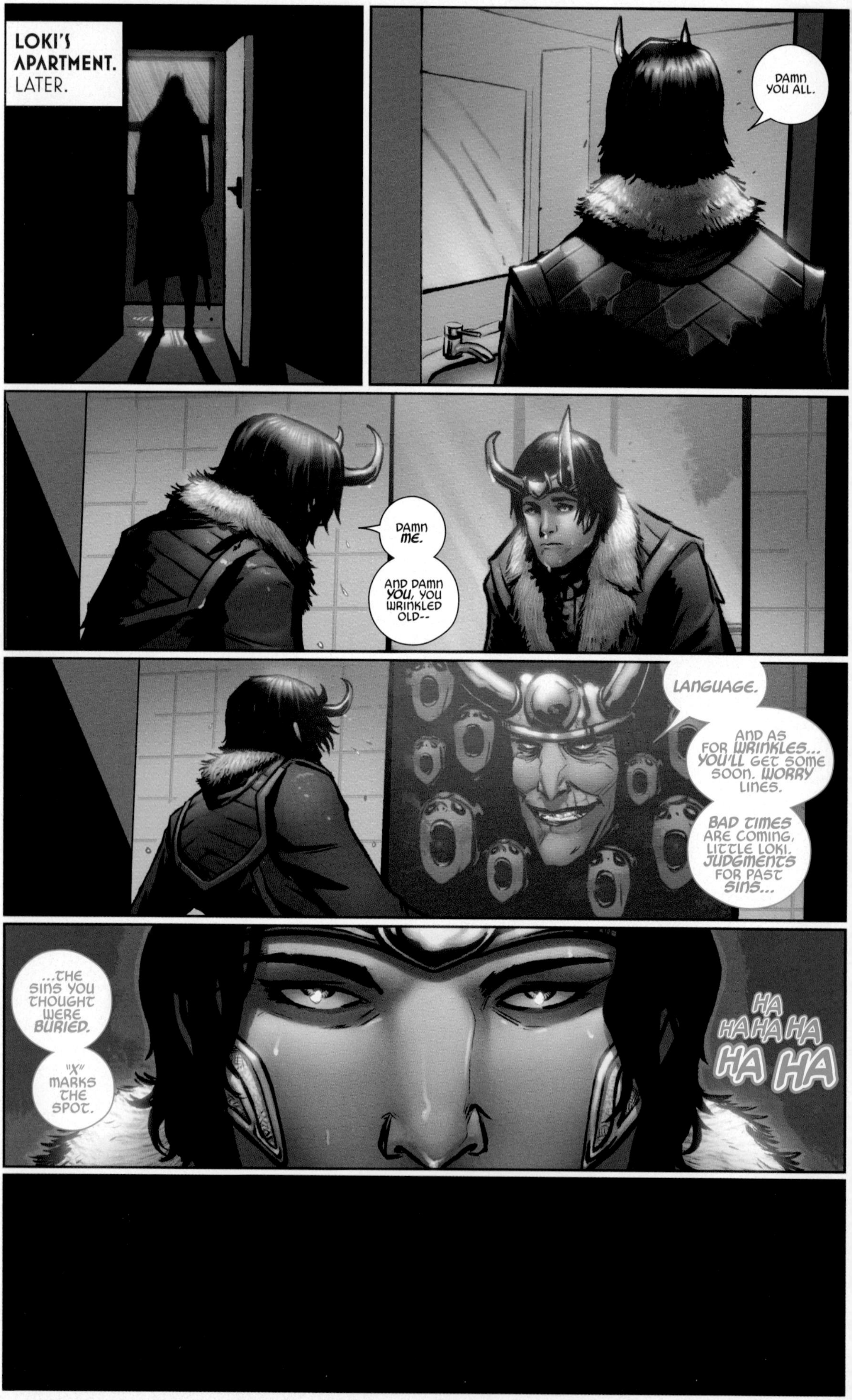
LOKI'S APARTMENT. LATER.
DAMN YOU ALL.
DAMN ME.
AND DAMN YOU, YOU WRINKLED OLD--
LANGUAGE.
AND AS FOR WRINKLES... YOU'LL GET SOME SOON. WORRY LINES.
BAD TIMES ARE COMING, LITTLE LOKI. JUDGMENTS FOR PAST SINS...
...THE SINS YOU THOUGHT WERE BURIED.
"X" MARKS THE SPOT.
HA HAHAHA HA HA

ALL-NEW MARVEL NOW! POINT ONE VARIANT
by Steve McNiven & Justin Ponsor

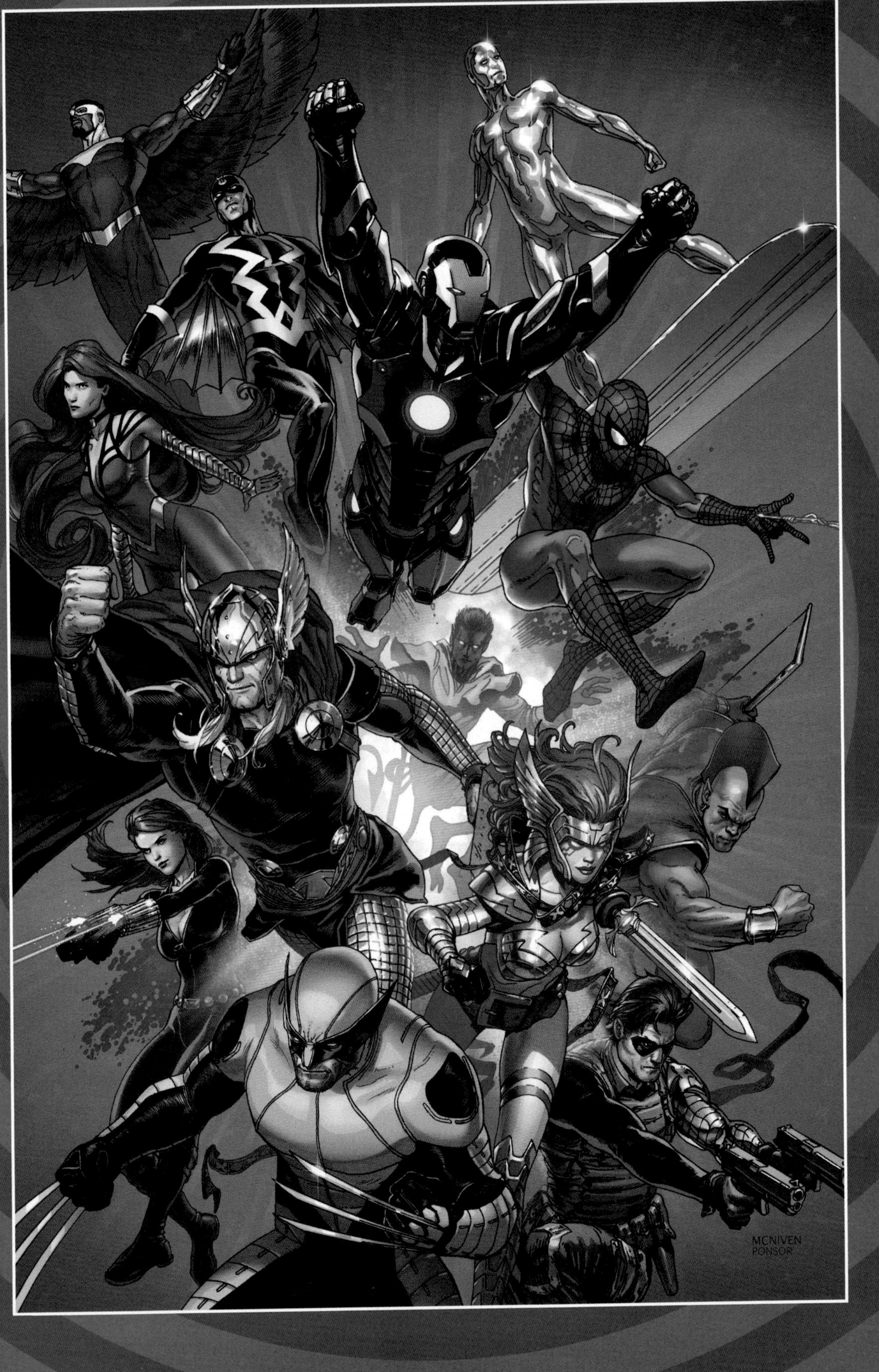
MCNIVEN
PONSOR

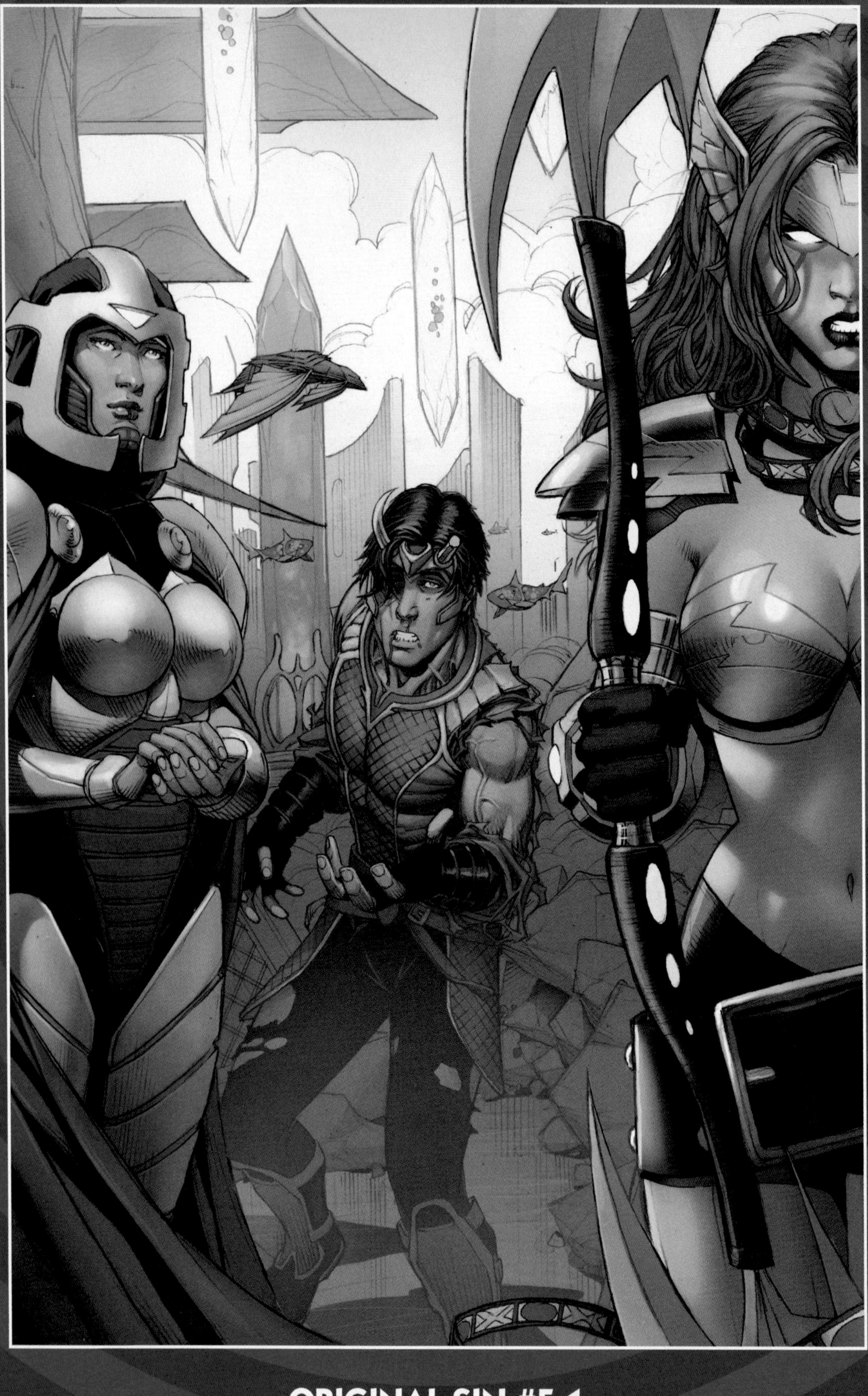

ORIGINAL SIN #5.1

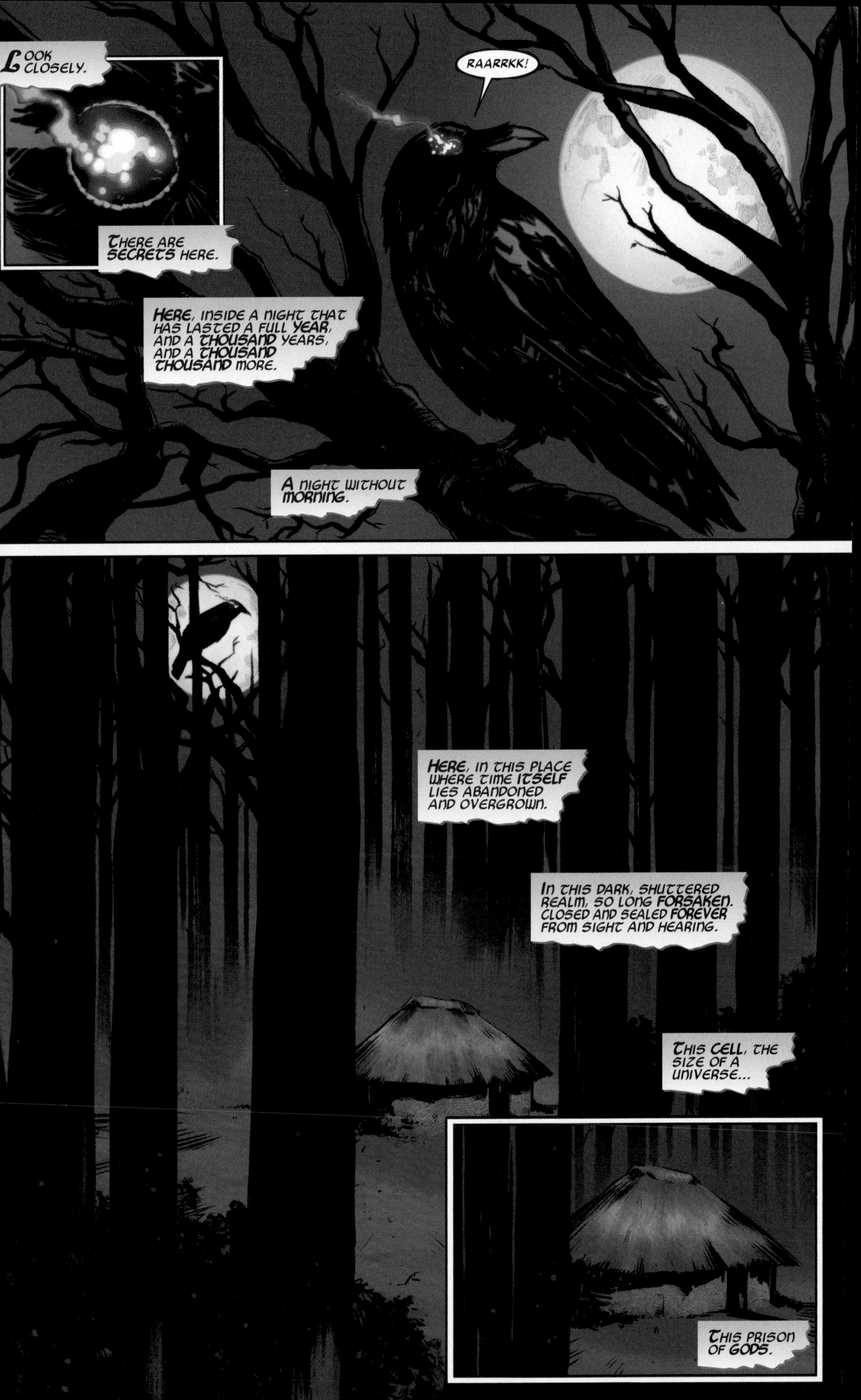
LOOK CLOSELY.
RAARRKK!
THERE ARE SECRETS HERE.
HERE, INSIDE A NIGHT THAT HAS LASTED A FULL YEAR, AND A THOUSAND YEARS, AND A THOUSAND THOUSAND MORE.
A NIGHT WITHOUT MORNING.
HERE, IN THIS PLACE WHERE TIME ITSELF LIES ABANDONED AND OVERGROWN.
IN THIS DARK, SHUTTERED REALM, SO LONG FORSAKEN. CLOSED AND SEALED FOREVER FROM SIGHT AND HEARING.
THIS CELL, THE SIZE OF A UNIVERSE...
THIS PRISON OF GODS.

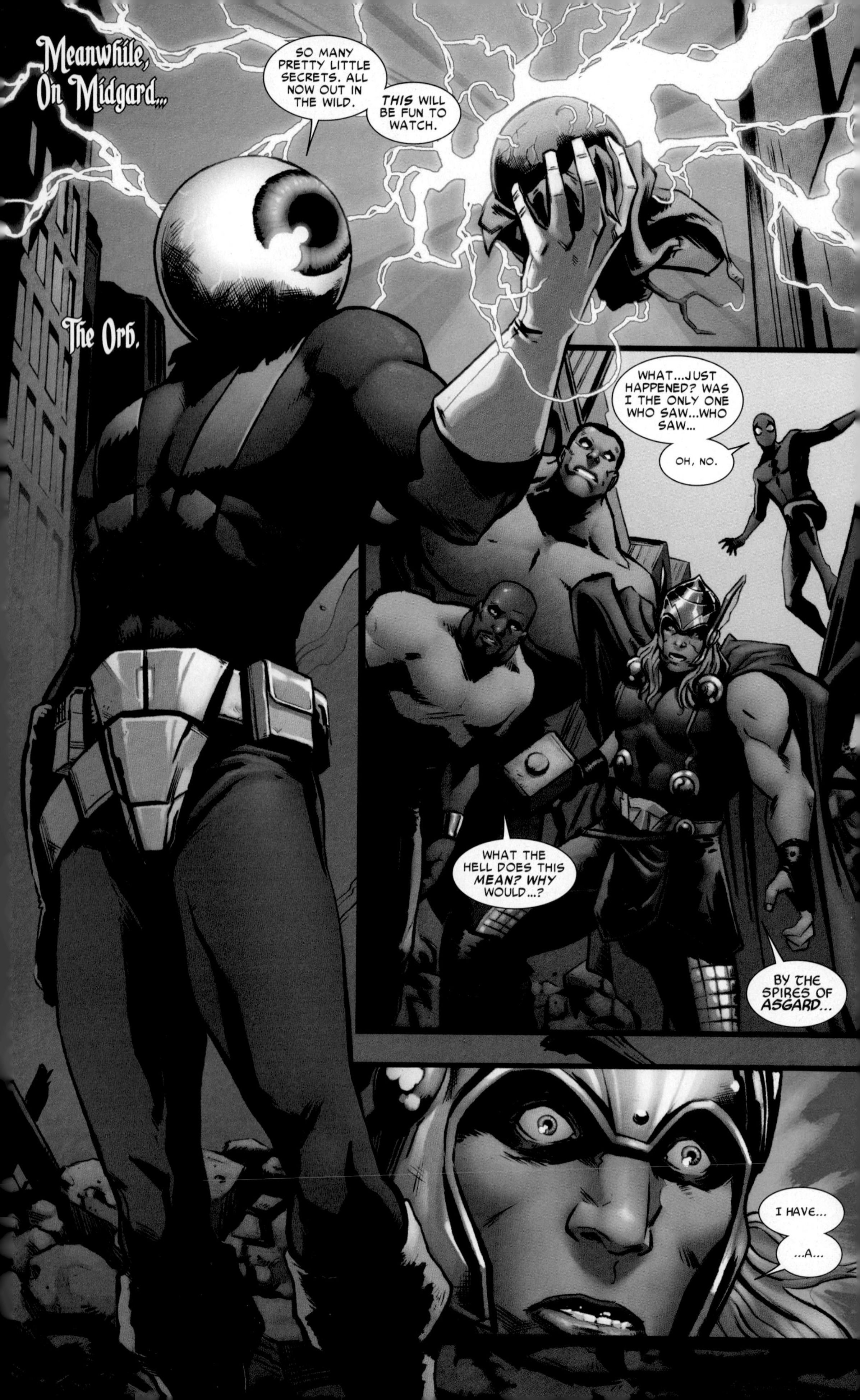
Meanwhile, On Midgard...
SO MANY PRETTY LITTLE SECRETS. ALL NOW OUT IN THE WILD.
THIS WILL BE FUN TO WATCH.
The Orb.
WHAT...JUST HAPPENED? WAS I THE ONLY ONE WHO SAW...WHO SAW...
OH, NO.
WHAT THE HELL DOES THIS MEAN? WHY WOULD...?
BY THE SPIRES OF ASGARD...
I HAVE...
...A...

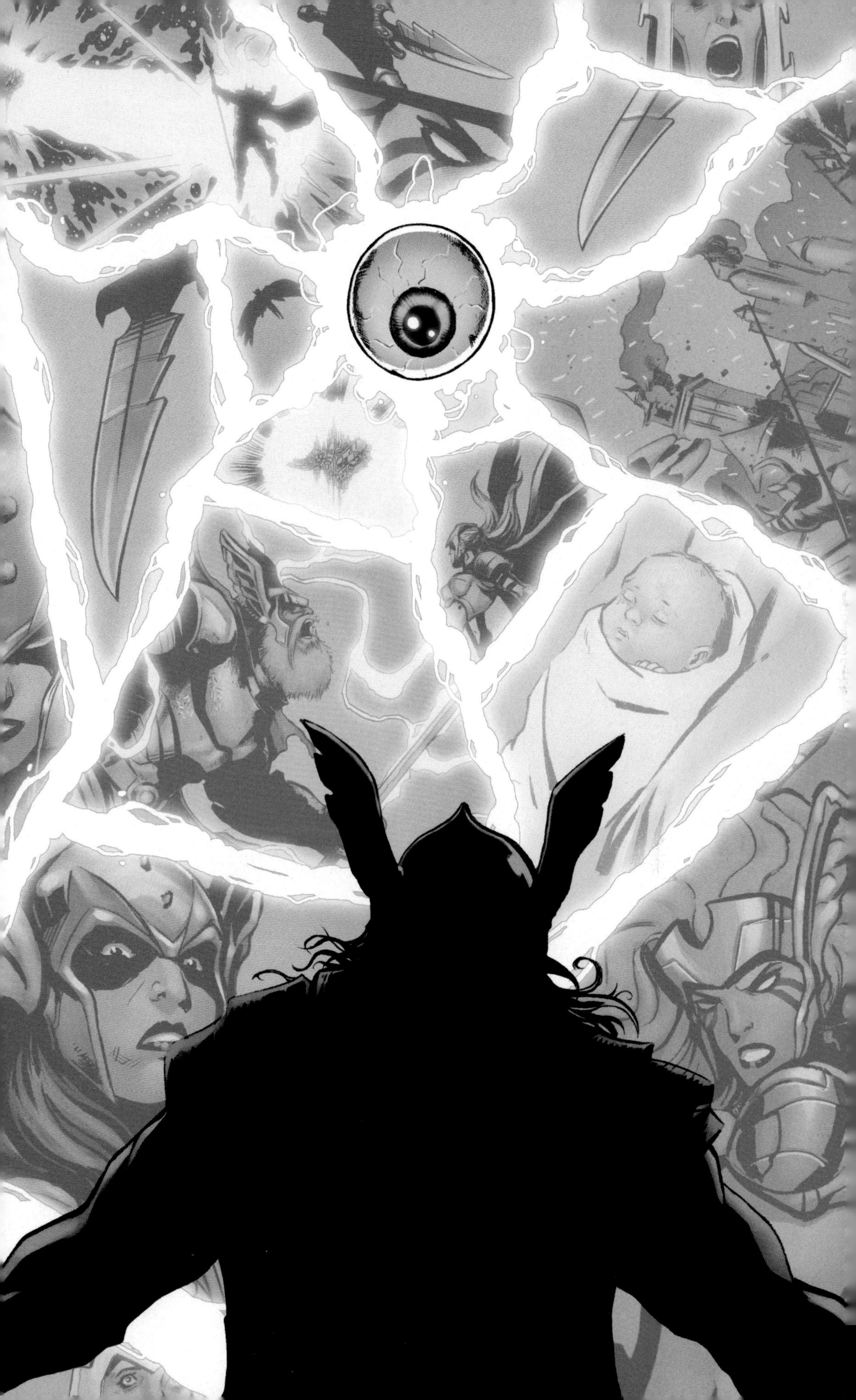

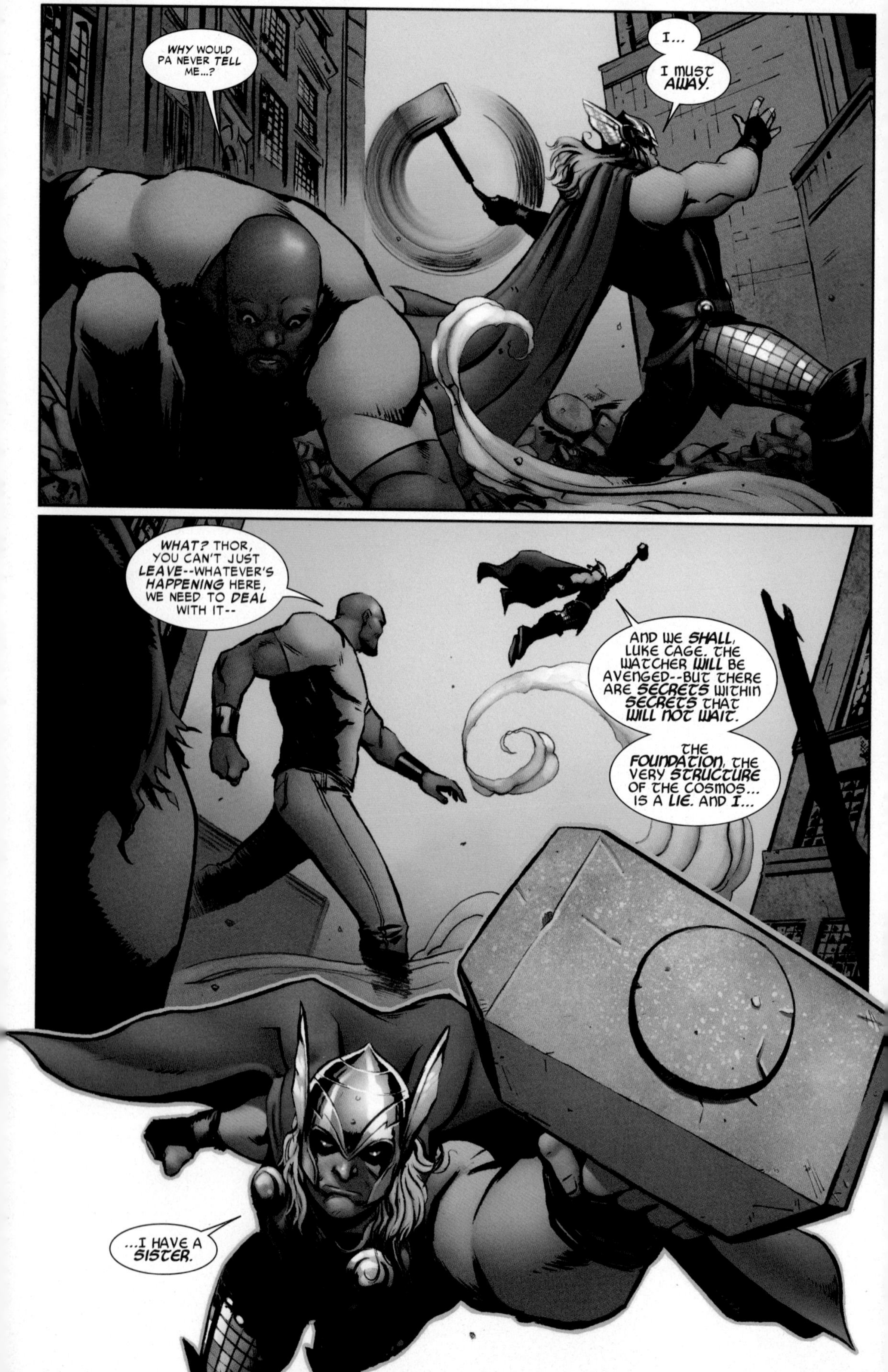
WHY WOULD PA NEVER TELL ME...?
I...
I MUST AWAY.
WHAT? THOR, YOU CAN'T JUST LEAVE--WHATEVER'S HAPPENING HERE, WE NEED TO DEAL WITH IT--
AND WE SHALL, LUKE CAGE. THE WATCHER WILL BE AVENGED--BUT THERE ARE SECRETS WITHIN SECRETS THAT WILL NOT WAIT.
THE FOUNDATION, THE VERY STRUCTURE OF THE COSMOS... IS A LIE. AND I...
...I HAVE A SISTER.

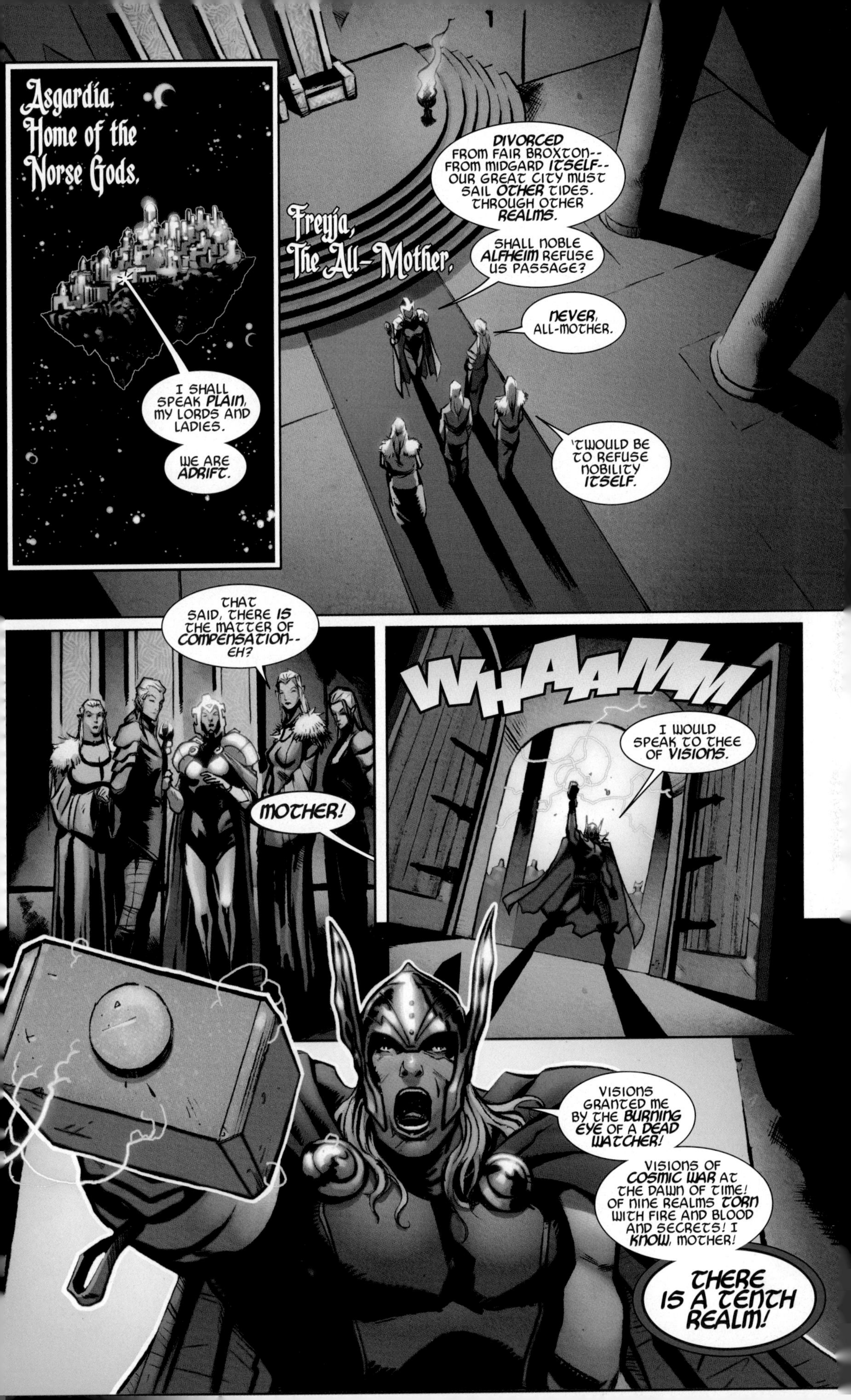
Asgardia. Home of the Norse Gods.
I SHALL SPEAK PLAIN, MY LORDS AND LADIES.
WE ARE ADRIFT.
Freyja, The All-Mother.
DIVORCED FROM FAIR BROXTON-- FROM MIDGARD ITSELF-- OUR GREAT CITY MUST SAIL OTHER TIDES. THROUGH OTHER REALMS.
SHALL NOBLE ALFHEIM REFUSE US PASSAGE?
NEVER, ALL-MOTHER.
'TWOULD BE TO REFUSE NOBILITY ITSELF.
THAT SAID, THERE IS THE MATTER OF COMPENSATION-- EH?
MOTHER!
WHAAMM
I WOULD SPEAK TO THEE OF VISIONS.
VISIONS GRANTED ME BY THE BURNING EYE OF A DEAD WATCHER!
VISIONS OF COSMIC WAR AT THE DAWN OF TIME! OF NINE REALMS TORN WITH FIRE AND BLOOD AND SECRETS! I KNOW, MOTHER!
THERE IS A TENTH REALM!

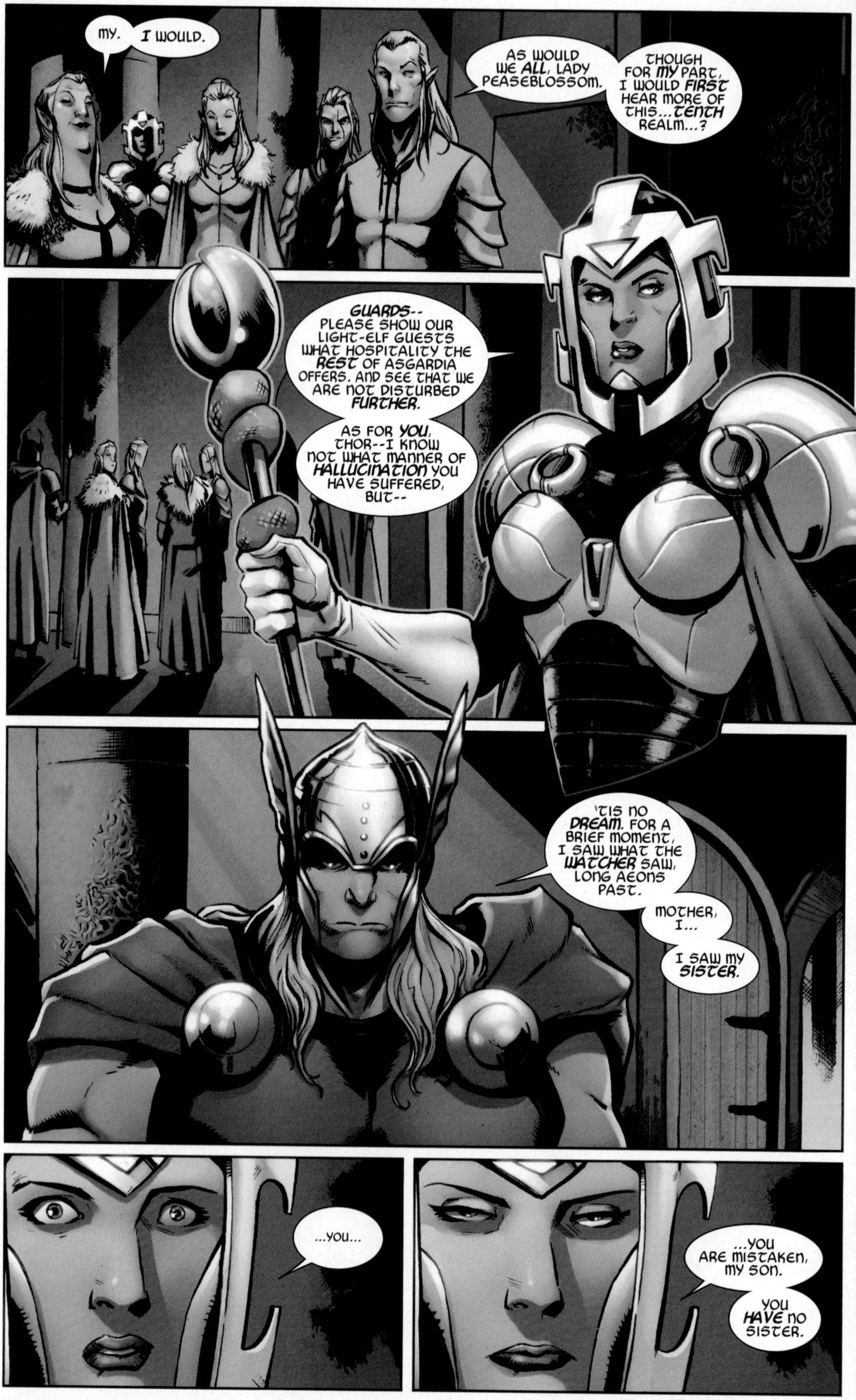

my.
I WOULD.
AS WOULD WE ALL, LADY PEASEBLOSSOM.
THOUGH FOR MY PART, I WOULD FIRST HEAR MORE OF THIS...TENTH REALM...?
GUARDS-- PLEASE SHOW OUR LIGHT-ELF GUESTS WHAT HOSPITALITY THE REST OF ASGARDIA OFFERS. AND SEE THAT WE ARE NOT DISTURBED FURTHER.
AS FOR YOU, THOR--I KNOW NOT WHAT MANNER OF HALLUCINATION YOU HAVE SUFFERED, BUT--
'TIS NO DREAM. FOR A BRIEF MOMENT, I SAW WHAT THE WATCHER SAW, LONG AEONS PAST.
MOTHER, I...
I SAW MY SISTER.
...YOU...
...YOU ARE MISTAKEN, MY SON.
YOU HAVE NO SISTER.

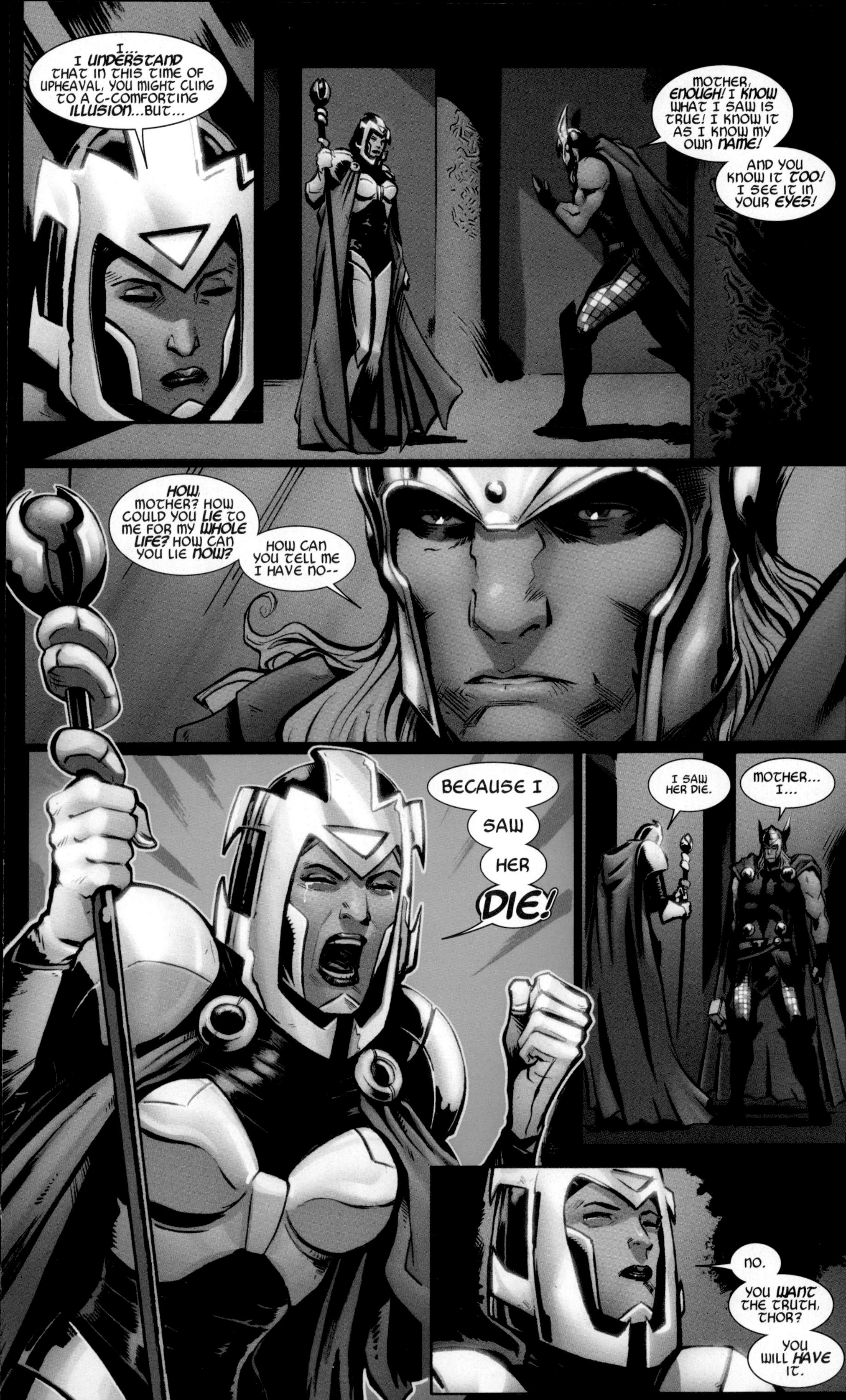
I... I UNDERSTAND THAT IN THIS TIME OF UPHEAVAL, YOU MIGHT CLING TO A C-COMFORTING ILLUSION...BUT...
MOTHER, ENOUGH! I KNOW WHAT I SAW IS TRUE! I KNOW IT AS I KNOW MY OWN NAME!
AND YOU KNOW IT TOO! I SEE IT IN YOUR EYES!
HOW, MOTHER? HOW COULD YOU LIE TO ME FOR MY WHOLE LIFE? HOW CAN YOU LIE NOW?
HOW CAN YOU TELL ME I HAVE NO--
BECAUSE I
SAW
HER
DIE!
I SAW HER DIE.
MOTHER... I...
NO.
YOU WANT THE TRUTH, THOR?
YOU WILL HAVE IT.

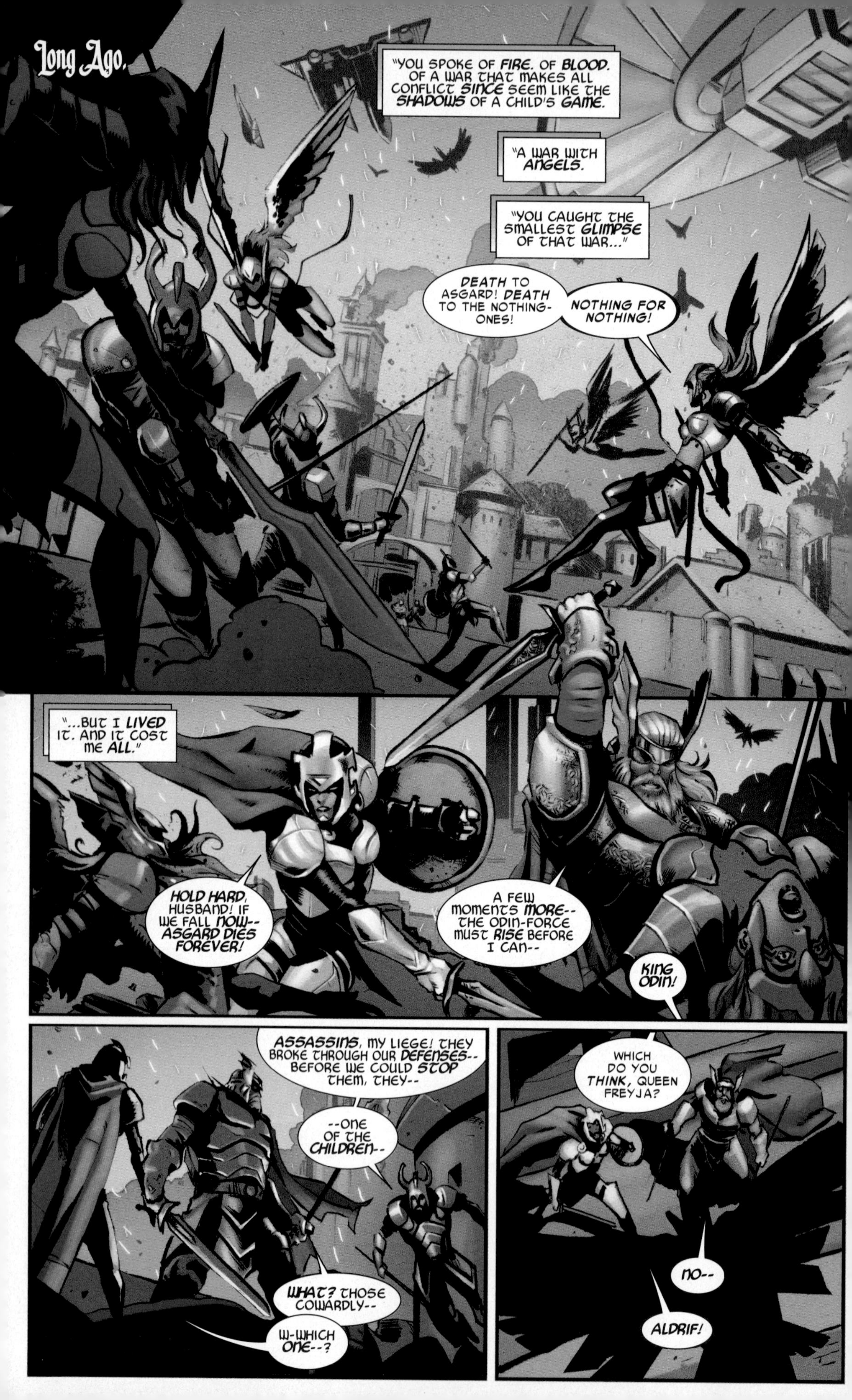

Long Ago.
"YOU SPOKE OF FIRE. OF BLOOD. OF A WAR THAT MAKES ALL CONFLICT SINCE SEEM LIKE THE SHADOWS OF A CHILD'S GAME.
"A WAR WITH ANGELS.
"YOU CAUGHT THE SMALLEST GLIMPSE OF THAT WAR..."
DEATH TO ASGARD! DEATH TO THE NOTHING-ONES!
NOTHING FOR NOTHING!
"...BUT I LIVED IT. AND IT COST ME ALL."
HOLD HARD, HUSBAND! IF WE FALL NOW-- ASGARD DIES FOREVER!
A FEW MOMENTS MORE-- THE ODIN-FORCE MUST RISE BEFORE I CAN--
KING ODIN!
ASSASSINS, MY LIEGE! THEY BROKE THROUGH OUR DEFENSES-- BEFORE WE COULD STOP THEM, THEY--
--ONE OF THE CHILDREN--
WHAT? THOSE COWARDLY--
W-WHICH ONE--?
WHICH DO YOU THINK, QUEEN FREYJA?
NO--
ALDRIF!

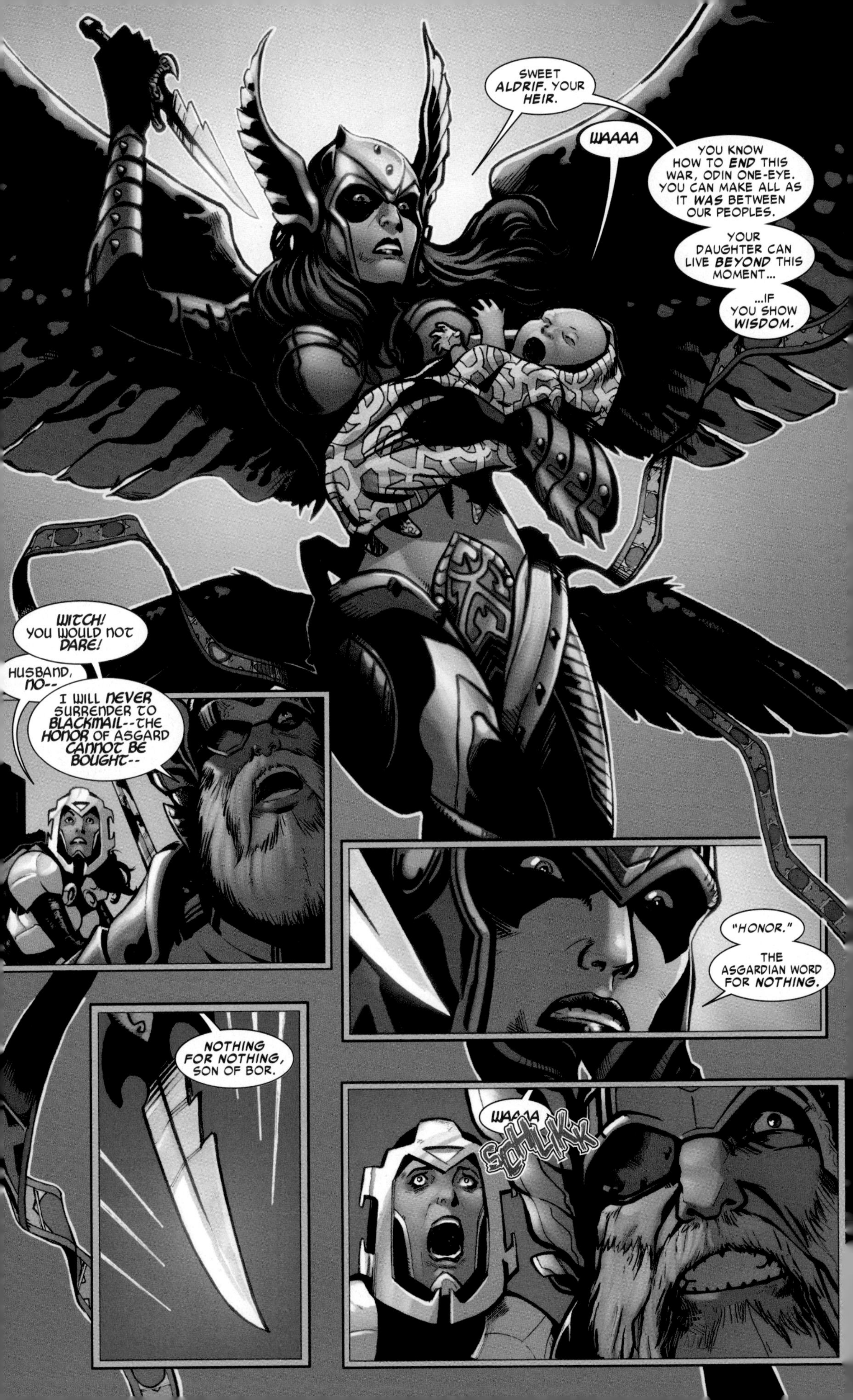
SWEET ALDRIF. YOUR HEIR.
WAAAA
YOU KNOW HOW TO END THIS WAR, ODIN ONE-EYE. YOU CAN MAKE ALL AS IT WAS BETWEEN OUR PEOPLES.
YOUR DAUGHTER CAN LIVE BEYOND THIS MOMENT...
...IF YOU SHOW WISDOM.
WITCH! YOU WOULD NOT DARE!
HUSBAND, NO--
I WILL NEVER SURRENDER TO BLACKMAIL--THE HONOR OF ASGARD CANNOT BE BOUGHT--
"HONOR."
THE ASGARDIAN WORD FOR NOTHING.
NOTHING FOR NOTHING, SON OF BOR.
SCHLUKK

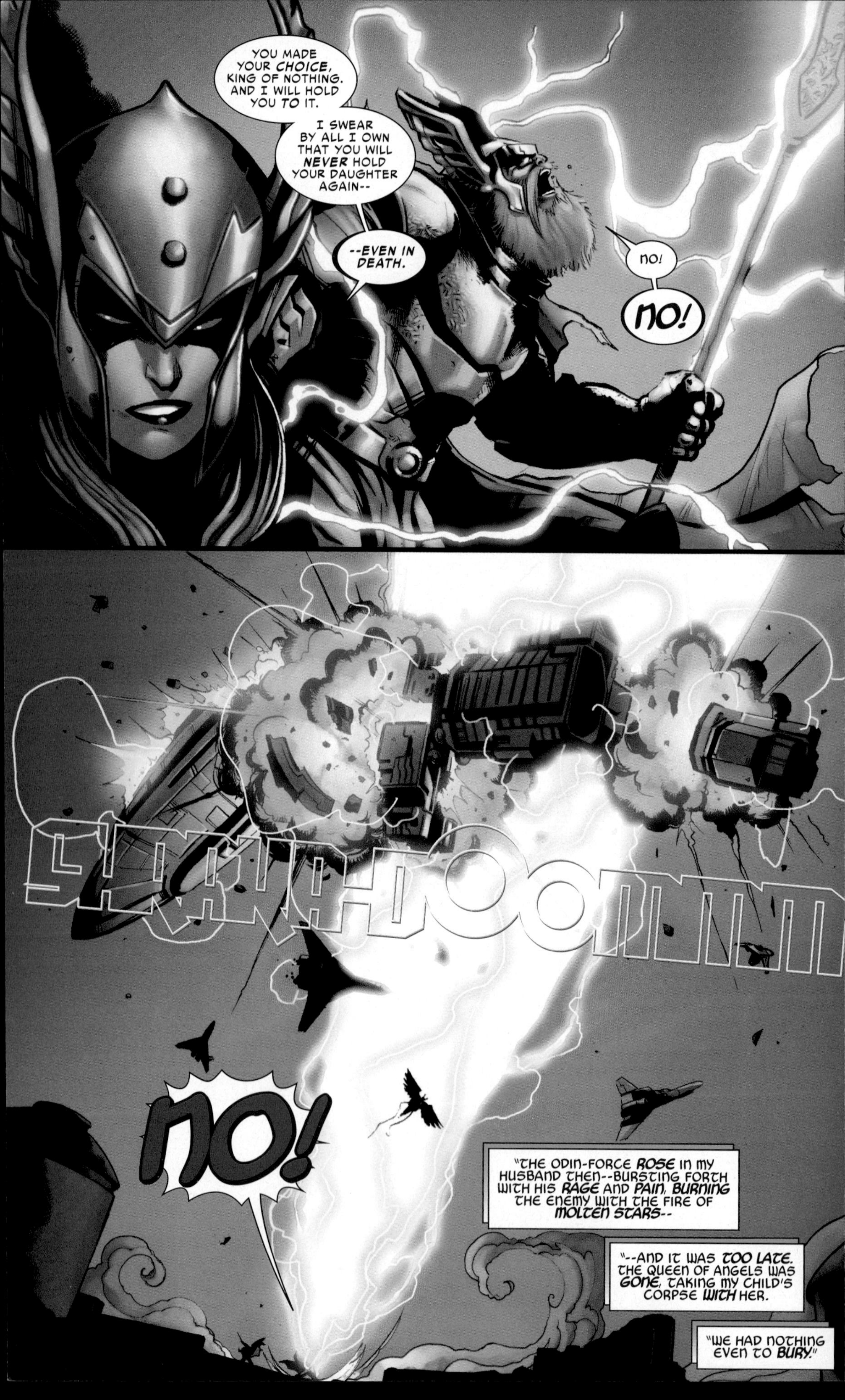
YOU MADE YOUR CHOICE, KING OF NOTHING. AND I WILL HOLD YOU TO IT.
I SWEAR BY ALL I OWN THAT YOU WILL NEVER HOLD YOUR DAUGHTER AGAIN--
--EVEN IN DEATH.
no!
NO!
NO!
"THE ODIN-FORCE ROSE IN MY HUSBAND THEN--BURSTING FORTH WITH HIS RAGE AND PAIN, BURNING THE ENEMY WITH THE FIRE OF MOLTEN STARS--
"--AND IT WAS TOO LATE. THE QUEEN OF ANGELS WAS GONE, TAKING MY CHILD'S CORPSE WITH HER.
"WE HAD NOTHING EVEN TO BURY."

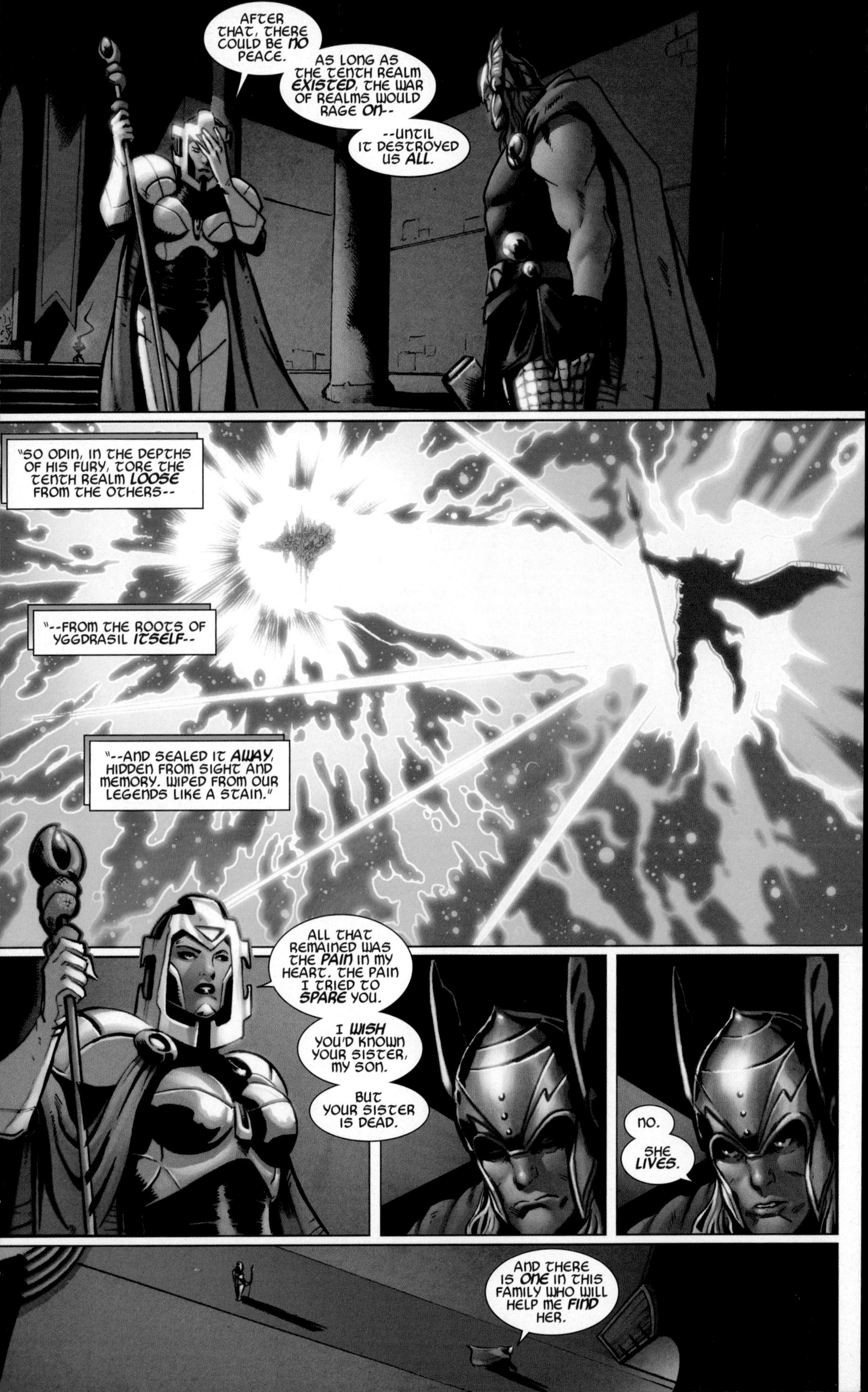
AFTER THAT, THERE COULD BE NO PEACE.
AS LONG AS THE TENTH REALM EXISTED, THE WAR OF REALMS WOULD RAGE ON--
--UNTIL IT DESTROYED US ALL.
"SO ODIN, IN THE DEPTHS OF HIS FURY, TORE THE TENTH REALM LOOSE FROM THE OTHERS--
"--FROM THE ROOTS OF YGGDRASIL ITSELF--
"--AND SEALED IT AWAY, HIDDEN FROM SIGHT AND MEMORY. WIPED FROM OUR LEGENDS LIKE A STAIN."
ALL THAT REMAINED WAS THE PAIN IN MY HEART. THE PAIN I TRIED TO SPARE YOU.
I WISH YOU'D KNOWN YOUR SISTER, MY SON.
BUT YOUR SISTER IS DEAD.
NO.
SHE LIVES.
AND THERE IS ONE IN THIS FAMILY WHO WILL HELP ME FIND HER.

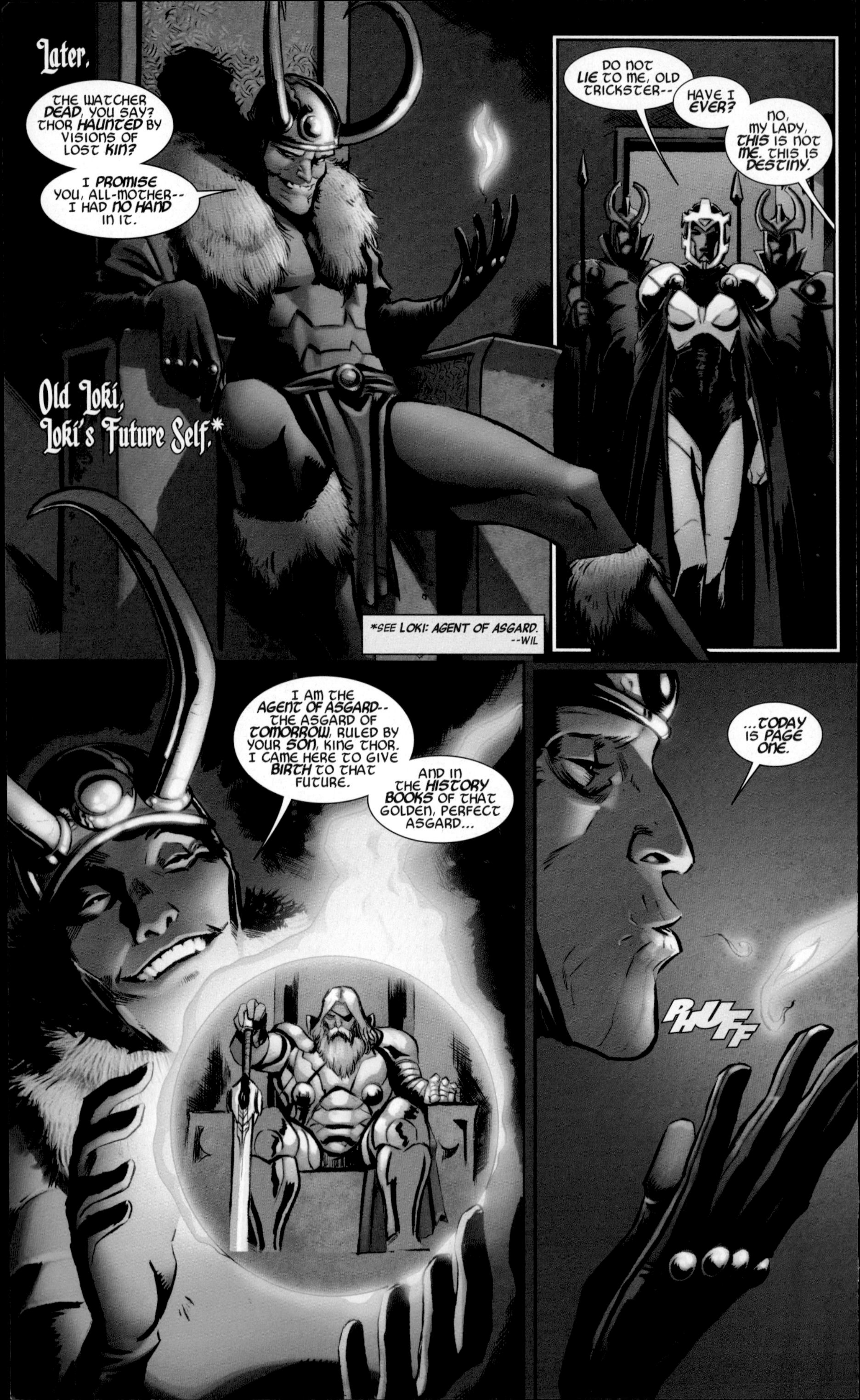

Later.
THE WATCHER DEAD, YOU SAY? THOR HAUNTED BY VISIONS OF LOST KIN?
I PROMISE YOU, ALL-MOTHER-- I HAD NO HAND IN IT.
Old Loki, Loki's Future Self.*
*SEE LOKI: AGENT OF ASGARD. --WIL
DO NOT LIE TO ME, OLD TRICKSTER--
HAVE I EVER?
NO, MY LADY, THIS IS NOT ME. THIS IS DESTINY.
I AM THE AGENT OF ASGARD-- THE ASGARD OF TOMORROW, RULED BY YOUR SON, KING THOR. I CAME HERE TO GIVE BIRTH TO THAT FUTURE.
AND IN THE HISTORY BOOKS OF THAT GOLDEN, PERFECT ASGARD...
...TODAY IS PAGE ONE.
PHUFF

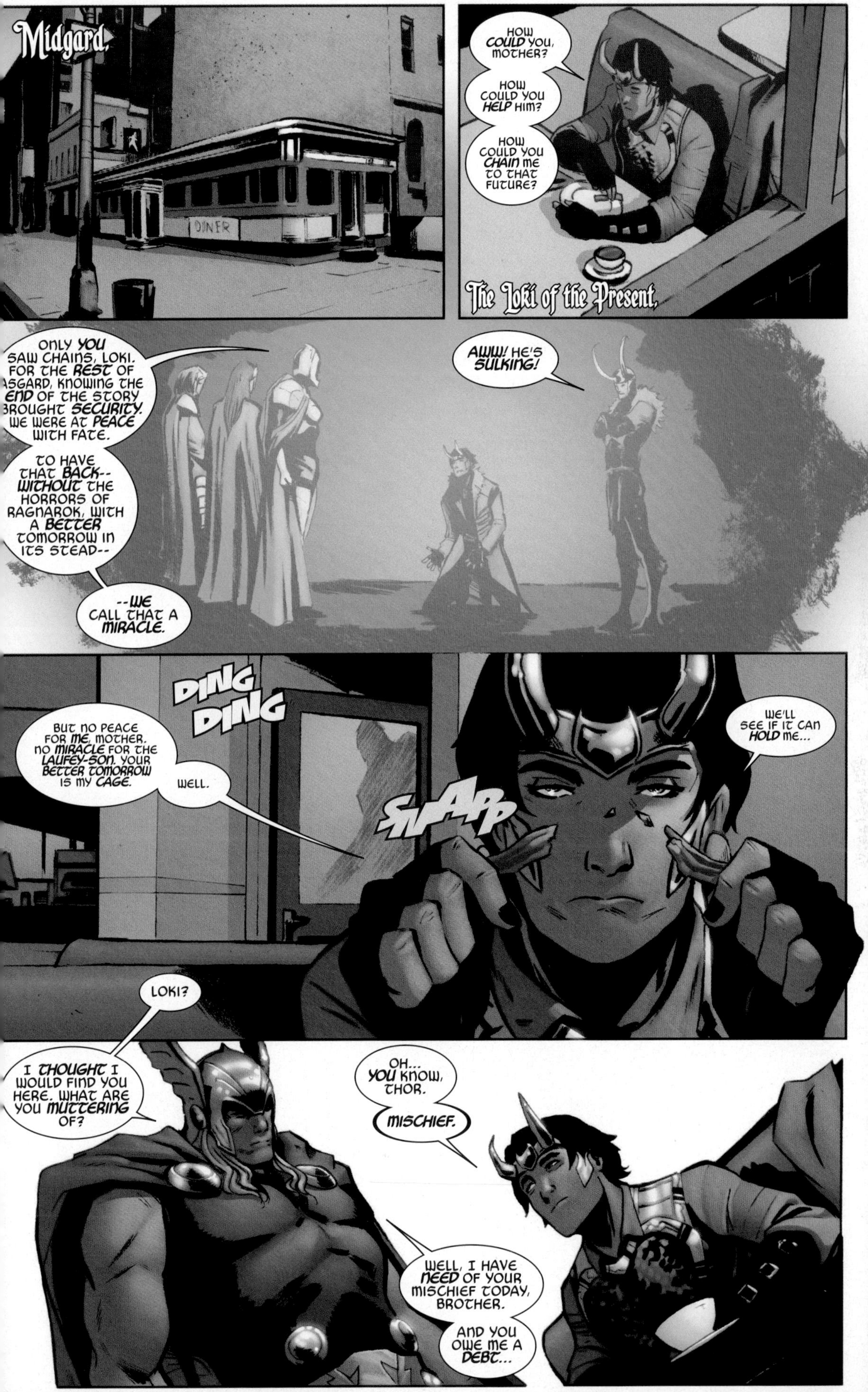
Midgard.
DINER
HOW COULD YOU, MOTHER?
HOW COULD YOU HELP HIM?
HOW COULD YOU CHAIN ME TO THAT FUTURE?
The Loki of the Present.
ONLY YOU SAW CHAINS, LOKI. FOR THE REST OF ASGARD, KNOWING THE END OF THE STORY BROUGHT SECURITY. WE WERE AT PEACE WITH FATE.
TO HAVE THAT BACK-- WITHOUT THE HORRORS OF RAGNAROK, WITH A BETTER TOMORROW IN ITS STEAD--
--WE CALL THAT A MIRACLE.
AWW! HE'S SULKING!
DING DING
BUT NO PEACE FOR ME, MOTHER. NO MIRACLE FOR THE LAUFEY-SON. YOUR BETTER TOMORROW IS MY CAGE.
WELL.
WE'LL SEE IF IT CAN HOLD ME...
SNAPP
LOKI?
I THOUGHT I WOULD FIND YOU HERE. WHAT ARE YOU MUTTERING OF?
OH... YOU KNOW, THOR.
MISCHIEF.
WELL, I HAVE NEED OF YOUR MISCHIEF TODAY, BROTHER.
AND YOU OWE ME A DEBT...

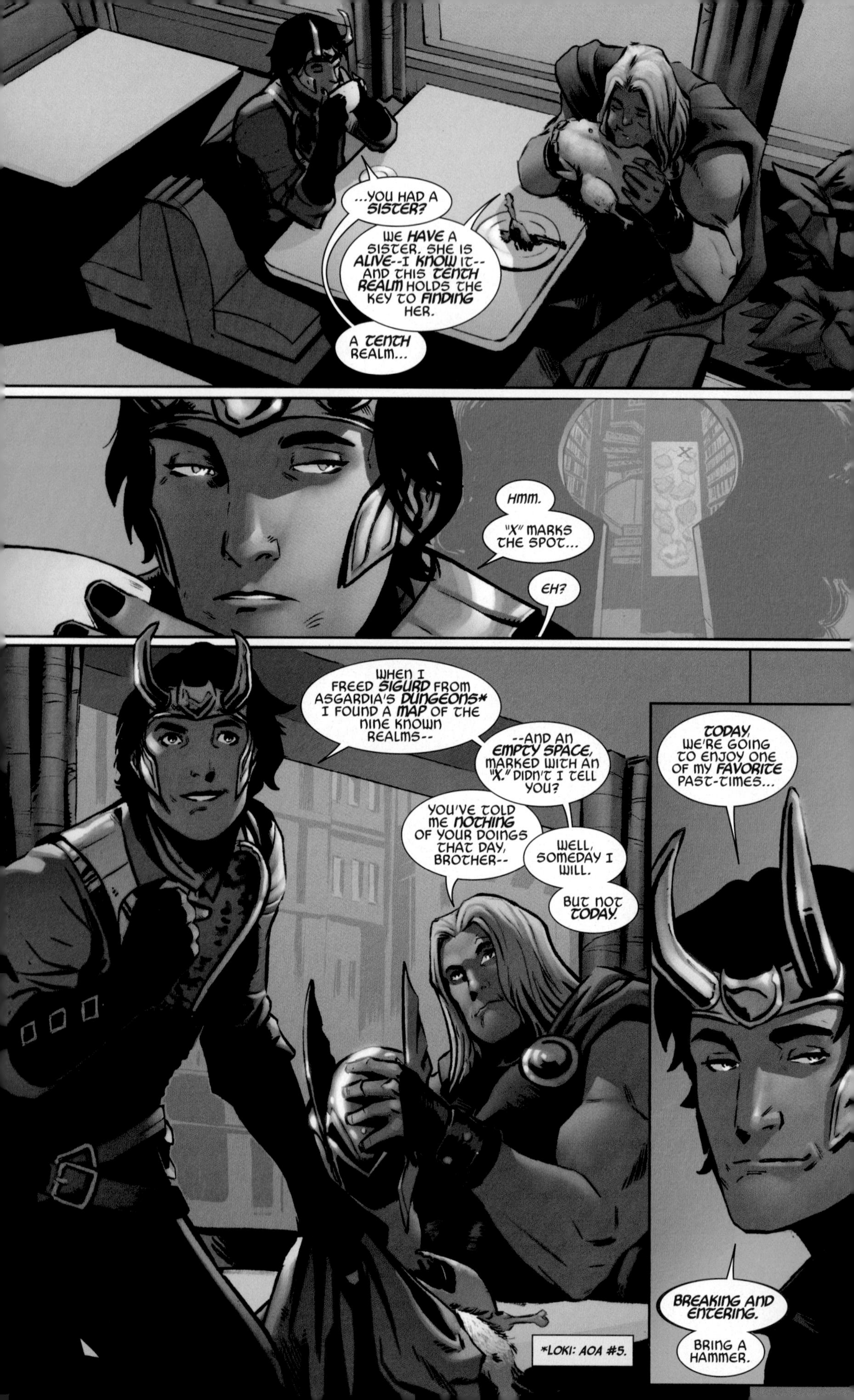
...YOU HAD A SISTER?
WE HAVE A SISTER. SHE IS ALIVE--I KNOW IT--AND THIS TENTH REALM HOLDS THE KEY TO FINDING HER.
A TENTH REALM...
HMM.
"X" MARKS THE SPOT...
EH?
WHEN I FREED SIGURD FROM ASGARDIA'S DUNGEONS* I FOUND A MAP OF THE NINE KNOWN REALMS--
--AND AN EMPTY SPACE, MARKED WITH AN "X." DIDN'T I TELL YOU?
YOU'VE TOLD ME NOTHING OF YOUR DOINGS THAT DAY, BROTHER--
WELL, SOMEDAY I WILL.
BUT NOT TODAY.
TODAY, WE'RE GOING TO ENJOY ONE OF MY FAVORITE PAST-TIMES...
BREAKING AND ENTERING.
BRING A HAMMER.
*LOKI: AOA #5.

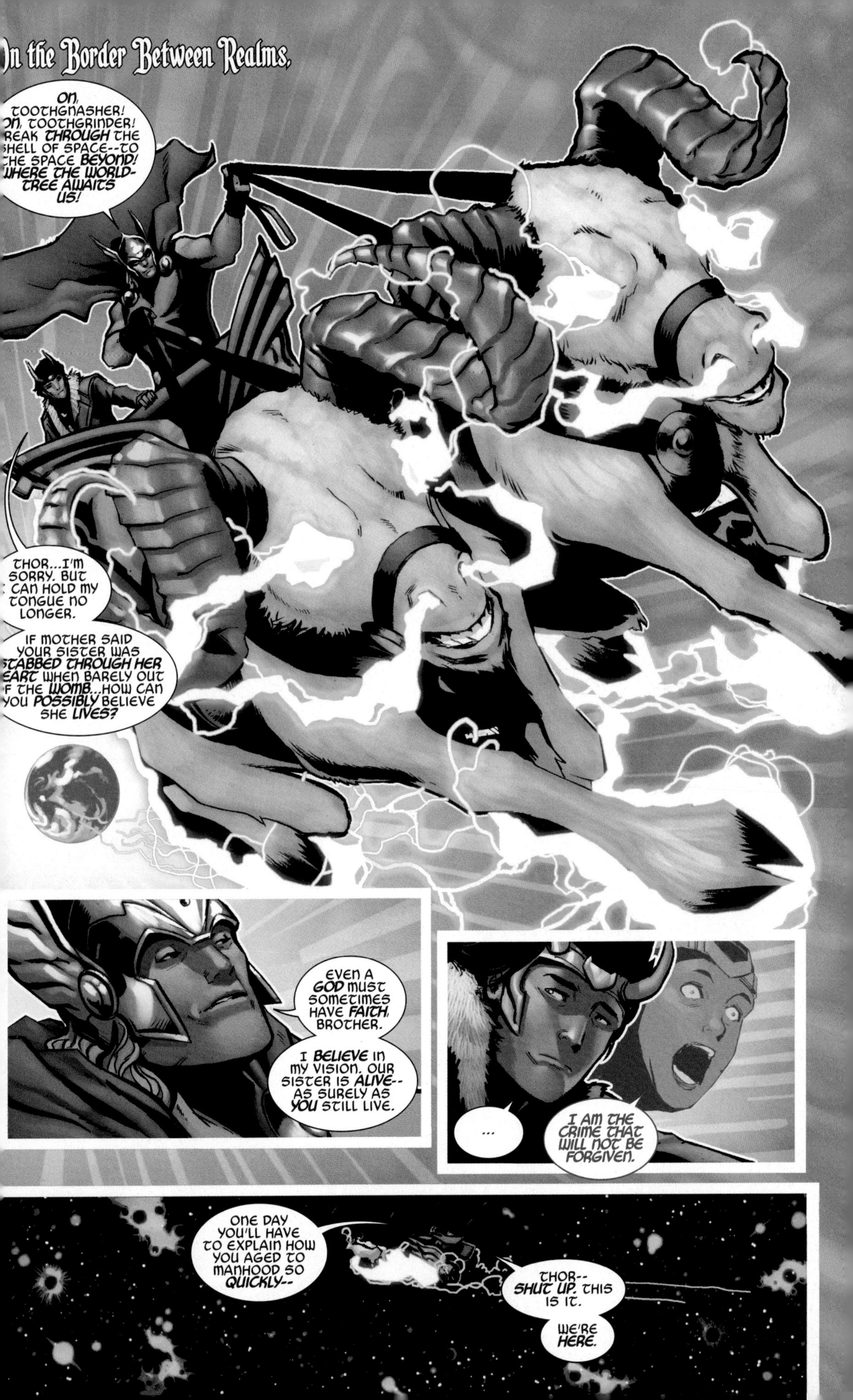
n the Border Between Realms,
ON, TOOTHGNASHER! ON, TOOTHGRINDER! REAK THROUGH THE SHELL OF SPACE--TO THE SPACE BEYOND! WHERE THE WORLD-TREE AWAITS US!
THOR...I'M SORRY. BUT CAN HOLD MY TONGUE NO LONGER.
IF MOTHER SAID YOUR SISTER WAS STABBED THROUGH HER EART WHEN BARELY OUT F THE WOMB...HOW CAN YOU POSSIBLY BELIEVE SHE LIVES?
EVEN A GOD MUST SOMETIMES HAVE FAITH, BROTHER.
I BELIEVE IN MY VISION. OUR SISTER IS ALIVE-- AS SURELY AS YOU STILL LIVE.
...
I AM THE CRIME THAT WILL NOT BE FORGIVEN.
ONE DAY YOU'LL HAVE TO EXPLAIN HOW YOU AGED TO MANHOOD SO QUICKLY--
THOR-- SHUT UP. THIS IS IT.
WE'RE HERE.

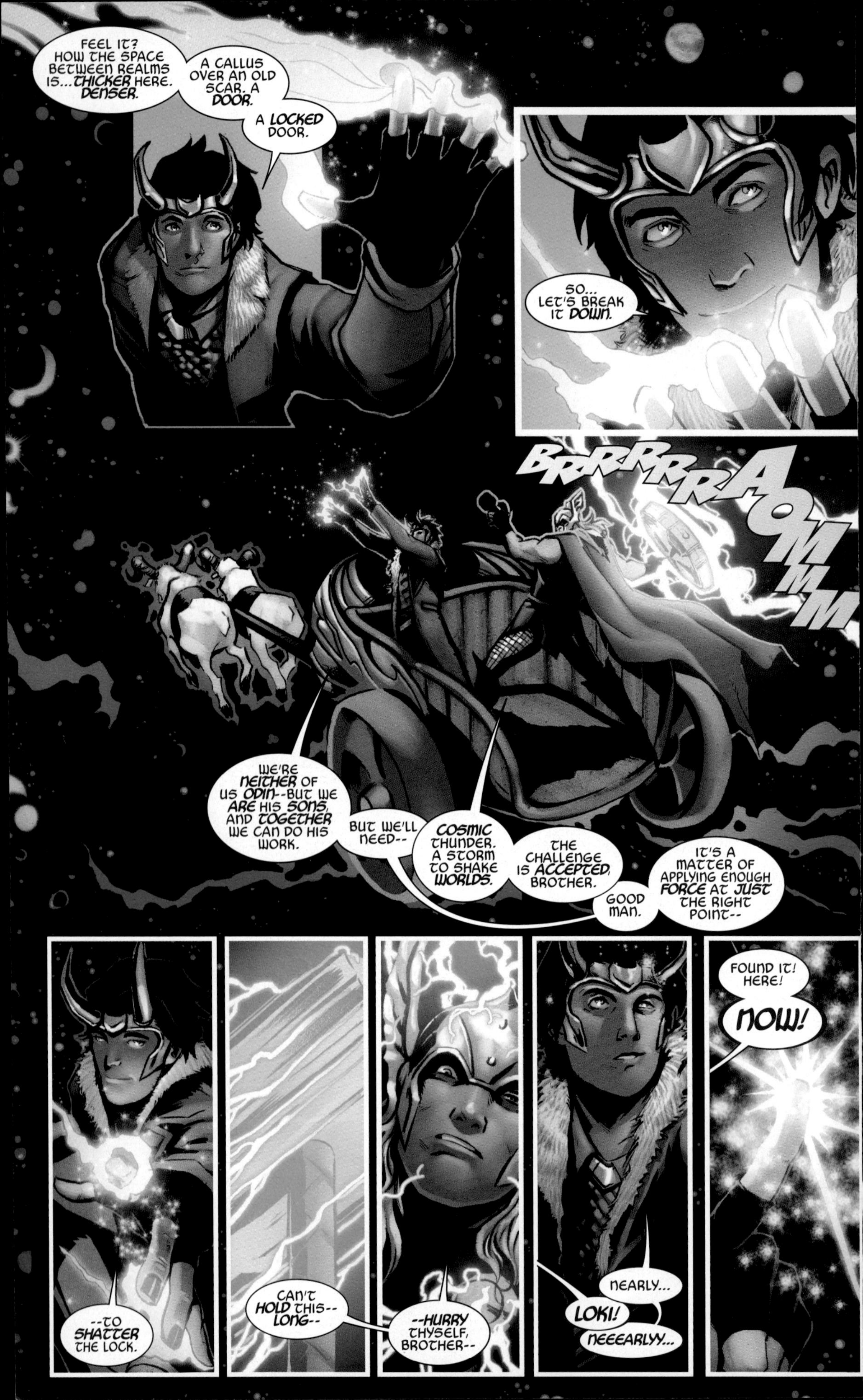
FEEL IT? HOW THE SPACE BETWEEN REALMS IS...THICKER HERE. DENSER.
A CALLUS OVER AN OLD SCAR. A DOOR.
A LOCKED DOOR.
SO... LET'S BREAK IT DOWN.
BRRRRRRAOMMM
WE'RE NEITHER OF US ODIN--BUT WE ARE HIS SONS, AND TOGETHER WE CAN DO HIS WORK.
BUT WE'LL NEED--
COSMIC THUNDER. A STORM TO SHAKE WORLDS.
THE CHALLENGE IS ACCEPTED, BROTHER.
GOOD MAN.
IT'S A MATTER OF APPLYING ENOUGH FORCE AT JUST THE RIGHT POINT--
--TO SHATTER THE LOCK.
CAN'T HOLD THIS--LONG--
--HURRY THYSELF, BROTHER--
NEARLY...
LOKI!
NEEEARLYY...
FOUND IT! HERE!
NOW!

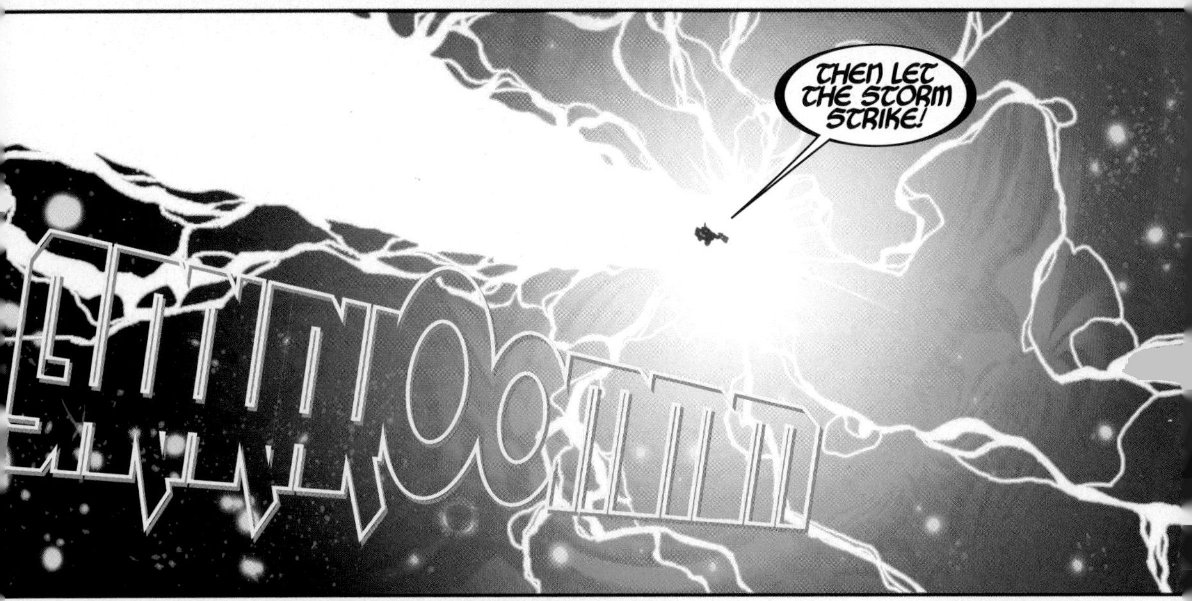
THEN LET THE STORM STRIKE!

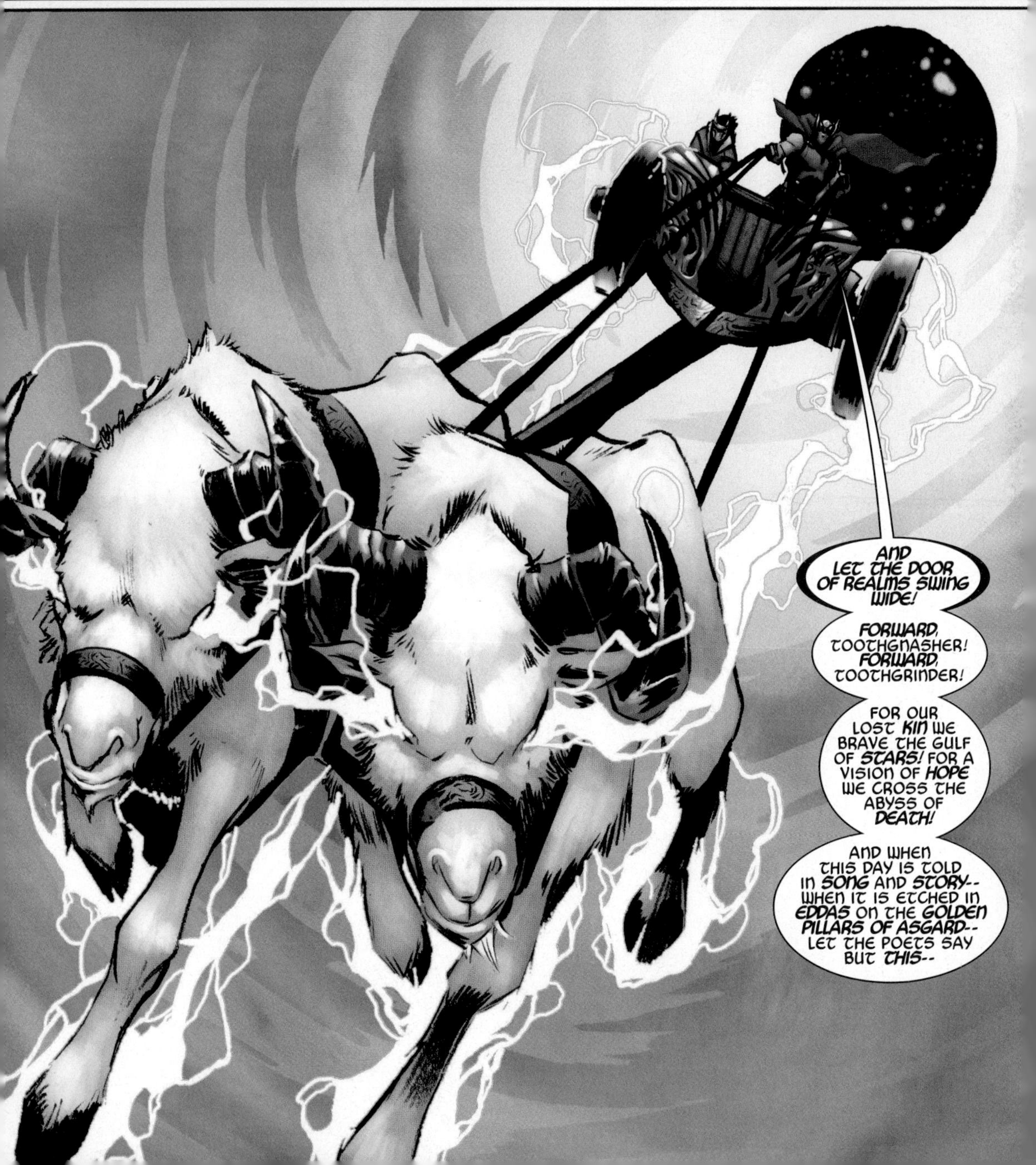
AND LET THE DOOR OF REALMS SWING WIDE!
FORWARD, TOOTHGNASHER! FORWARD, TOOTHGRINDER!
FOR OUR LOST KIN WE BRAVE THE GULF OF STARS! FOR A VISION OF HOPE WE CROSS THE ABYSS OF DEATH!
AND WHEN THIS DAY IS TOLD IN SONG AND STORY-- WHEN IT IS ETCHED IN EDDAS ON THE GOLDEN PILLARS OF ASGARD-- LET THE POETS SAY BUT THIS--

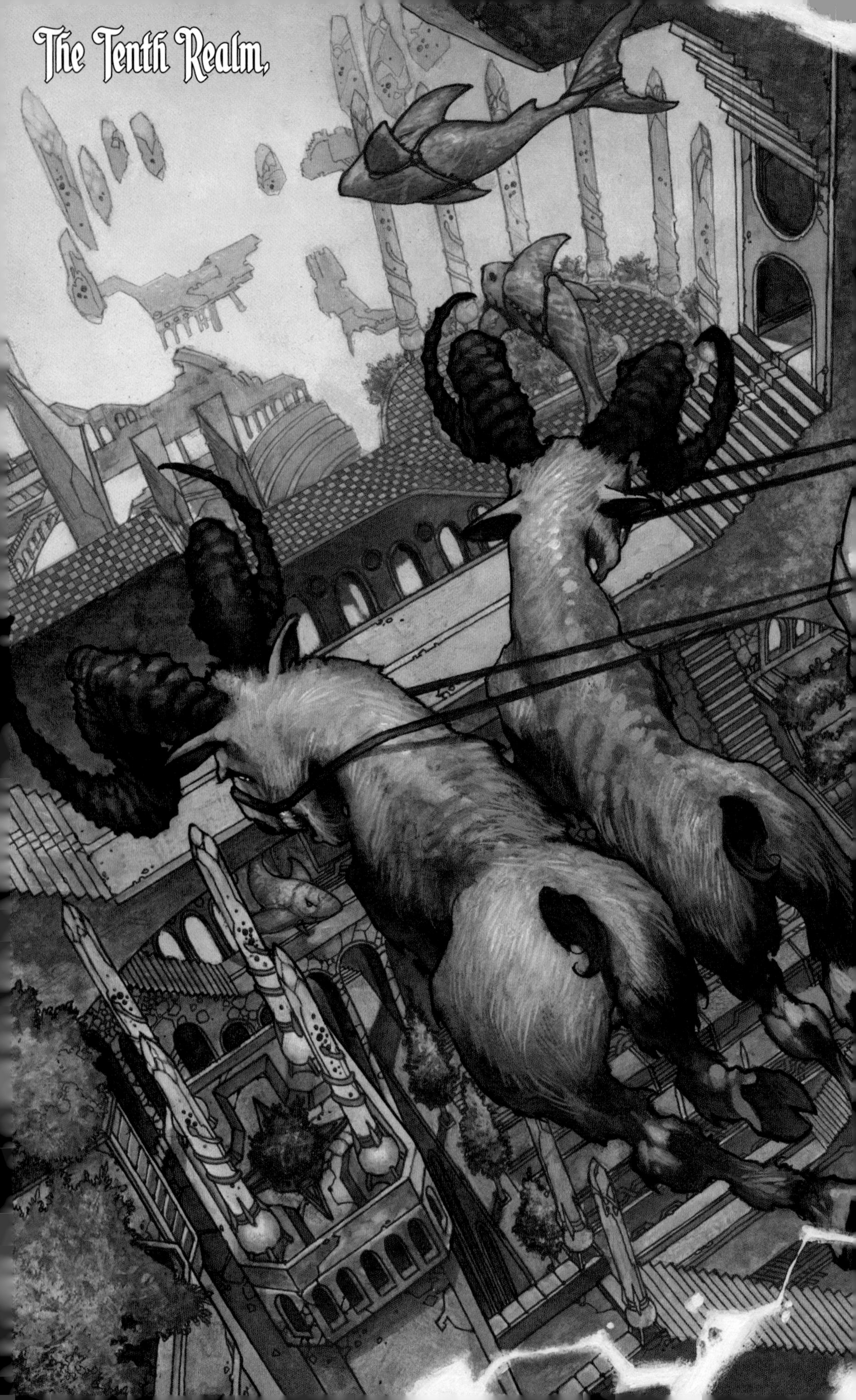
The Tenth Realm,

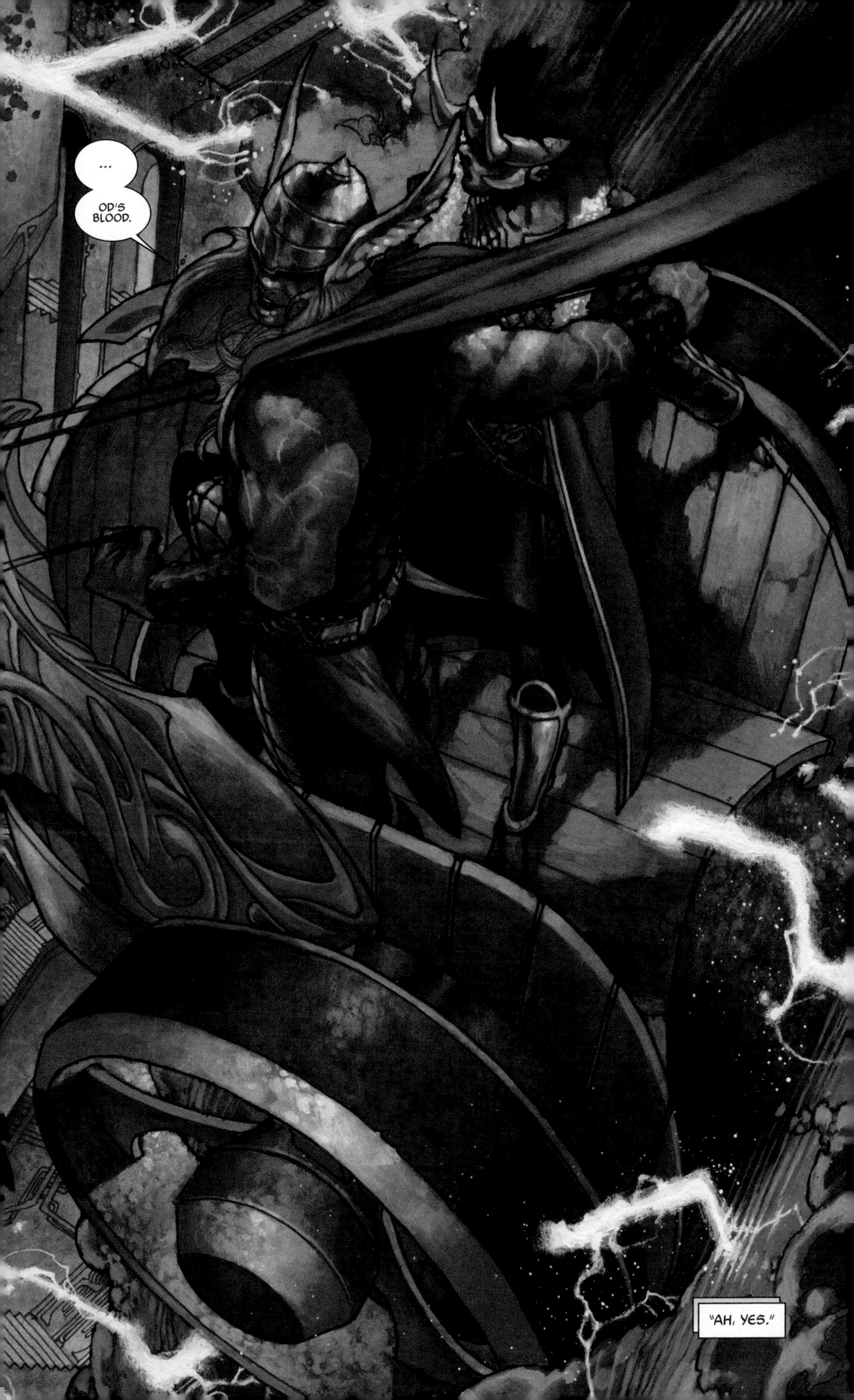
...
OD'S BLOOD.
"AH, YES."

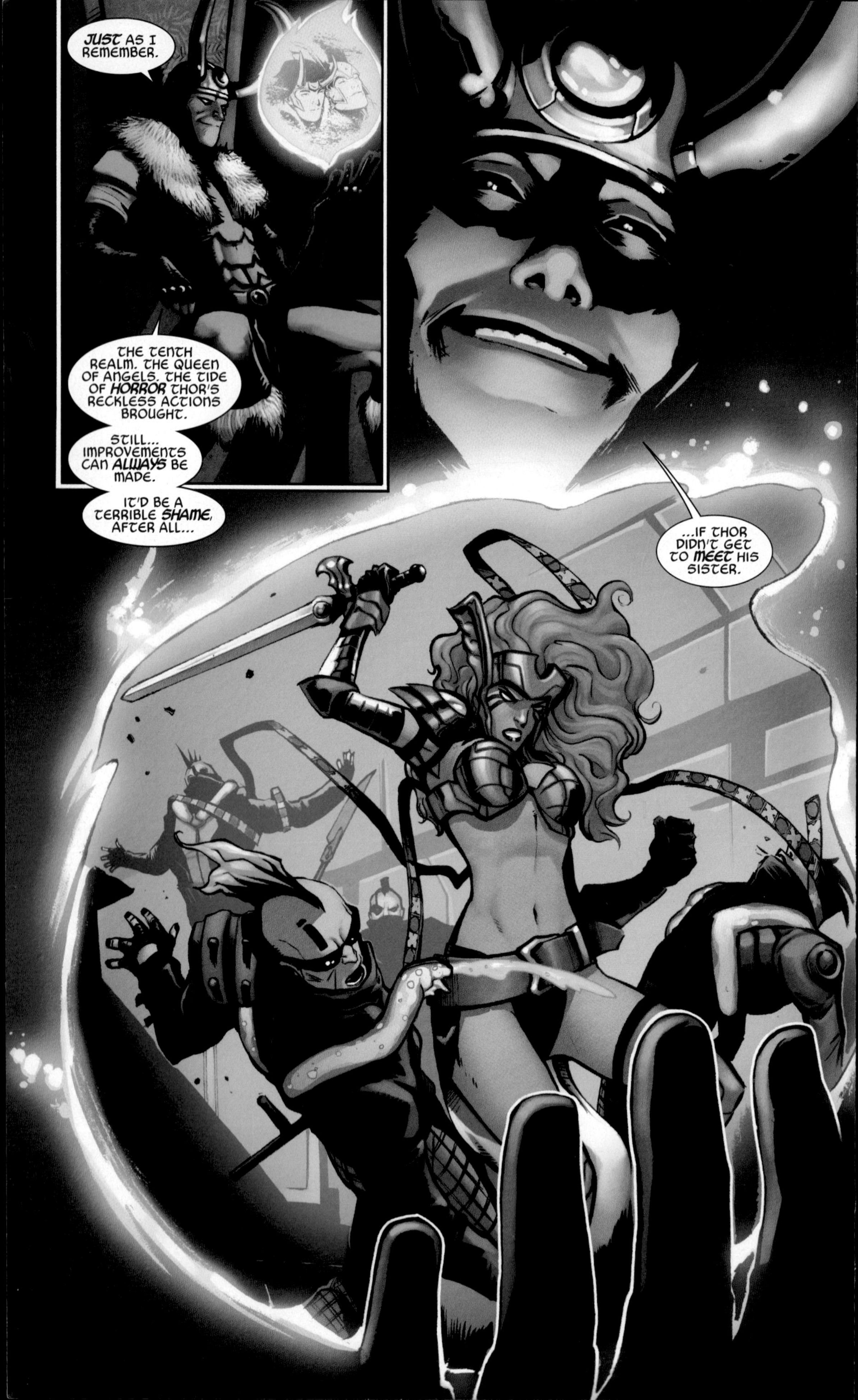
JUST AS I REMEMBER.
THE TENTH REALM. THE QUEEN OF ANGELS. THE TIDE OF HORROR THOR'S RECKLESS ACTIONS BROUGHT.
STILL... IMPROVEMENTS CAN ALWAYS BE MADE.
IT'D BE A TERRIBLE SHAME, AFTER ALL...
...IF THOR DIDN'T GET TO MEET HIS SISTER.

***ORIGINAL SIN* #5.1 VARIANT**
by Simone Bianchi

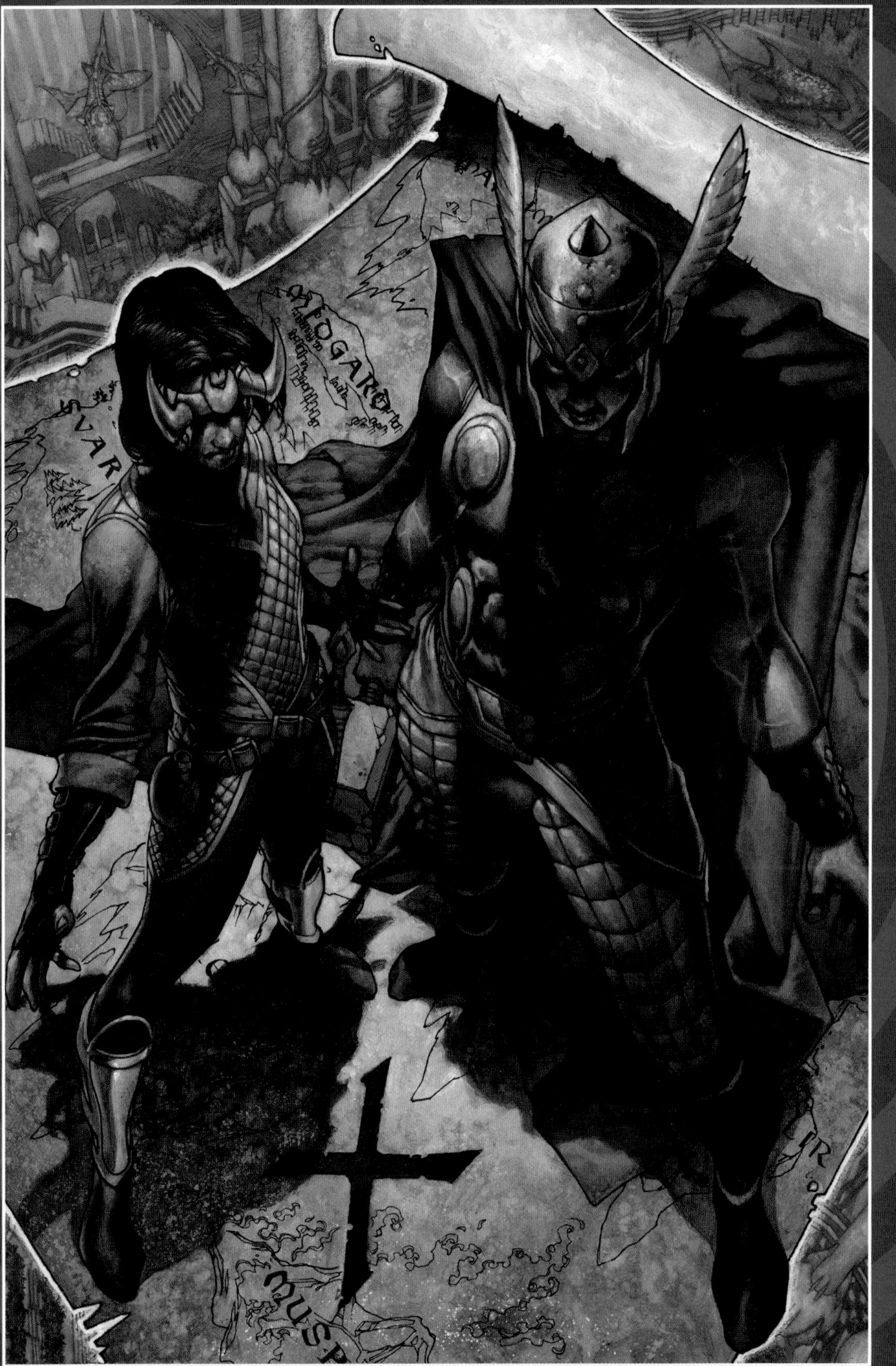

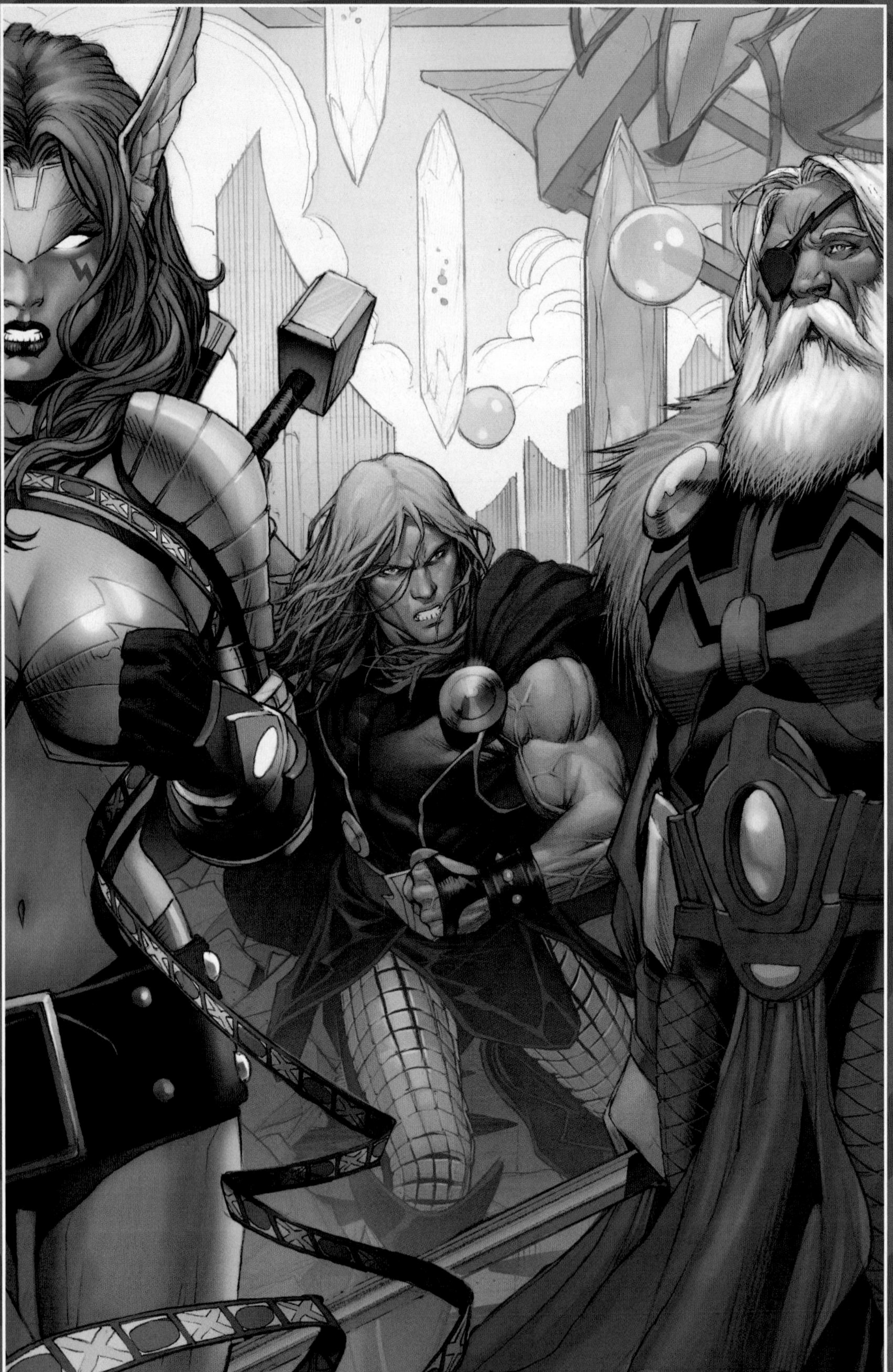

ORIGINAL SIN #5.2

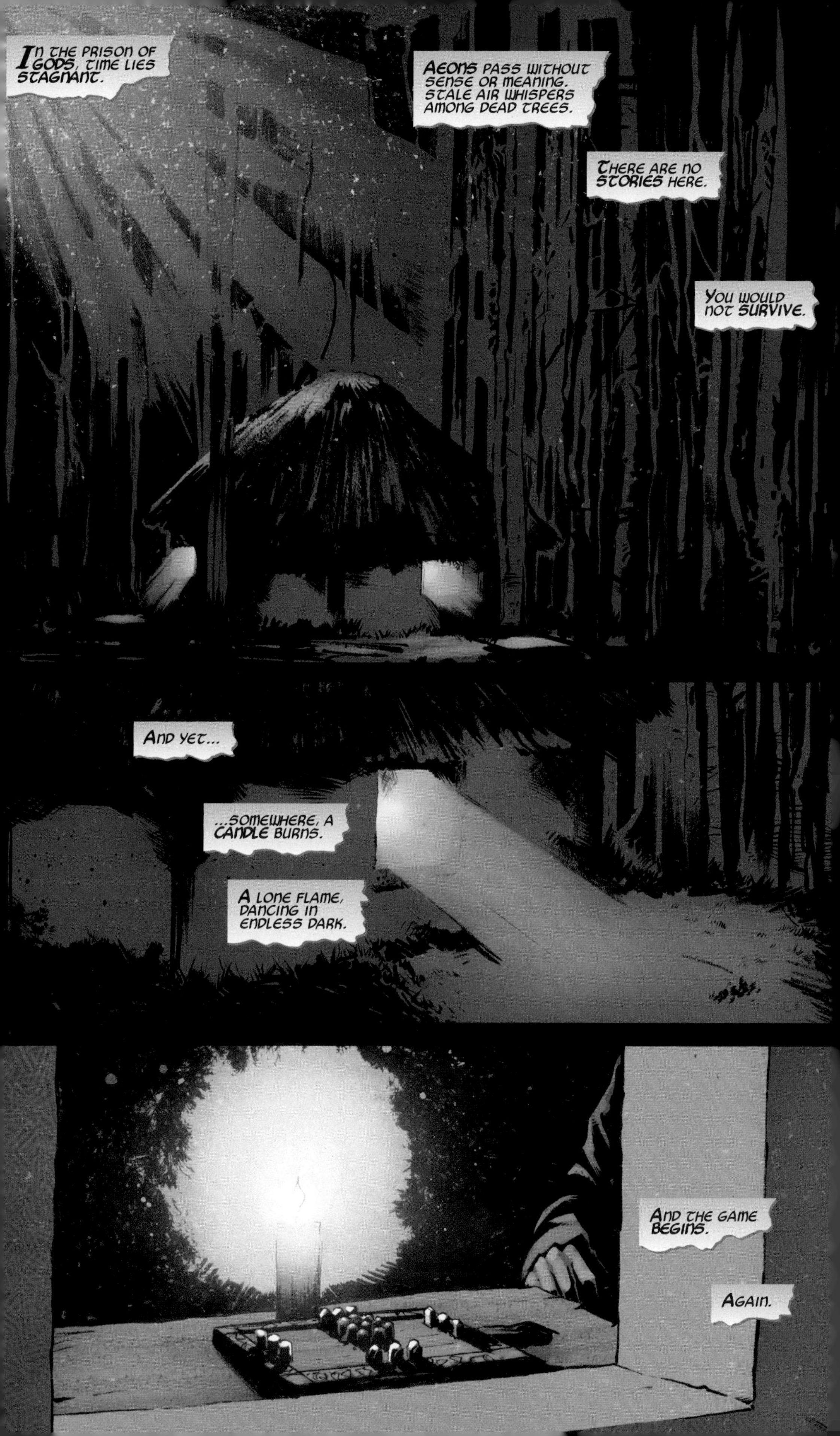
In the prison of gods, time lies stagnant.
Aeons pass without sense or meaning. Stale air whispers among dead trees.
There are no stories here.
You would not survive.
And yet...
...somewhere, a candle burns.
A lone flame, dancing in endless dark.
And the game begins.
Again.

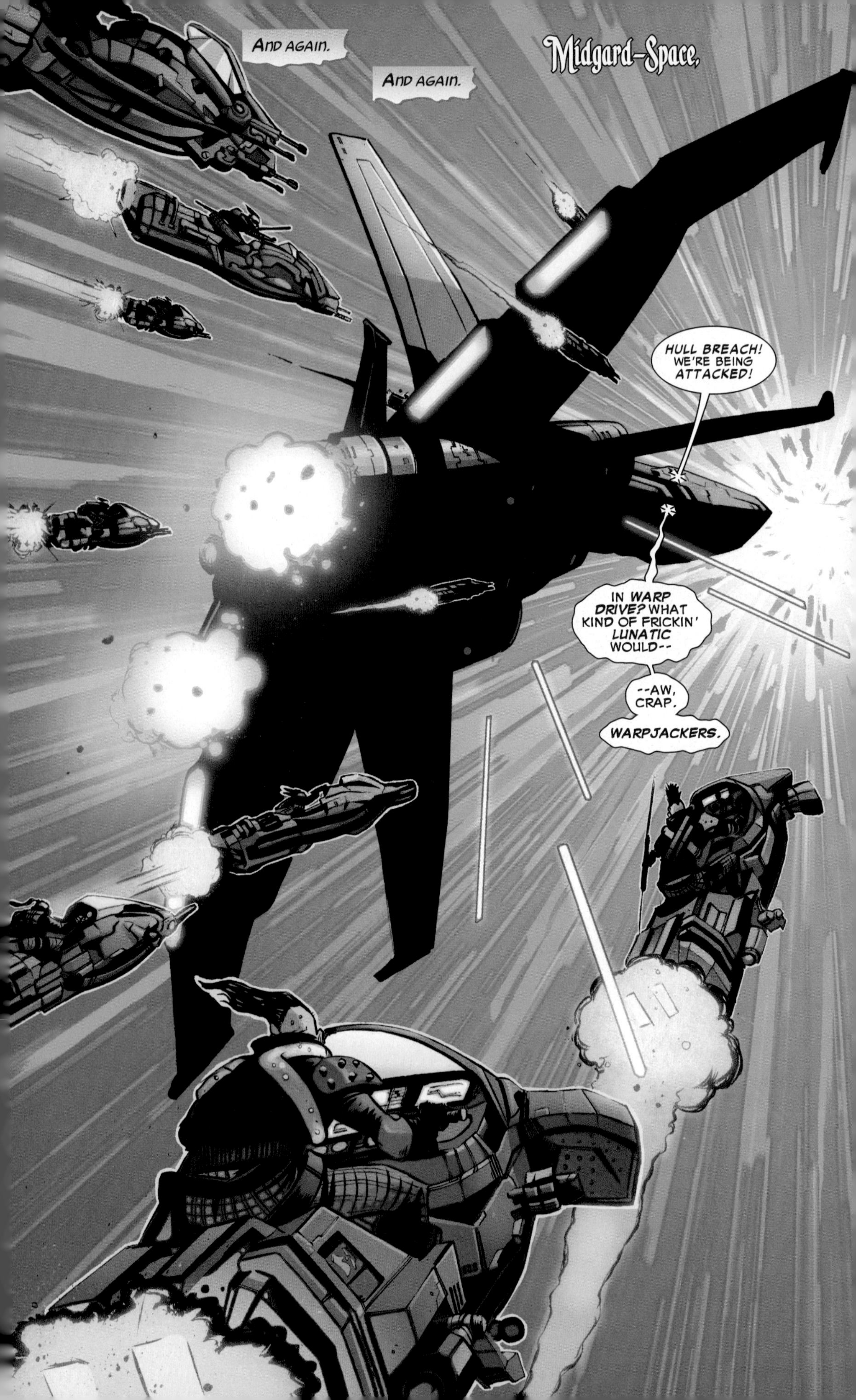

And again.
And again.
Midgard-Space,
HULL BREACH! WE'RE BEING ATTACKED!
IN WARP DRIVE? WHAT KIND OF FRICKIN' LUNATIC WOULD--
--AW, CRAP.
WARPJACKERS.

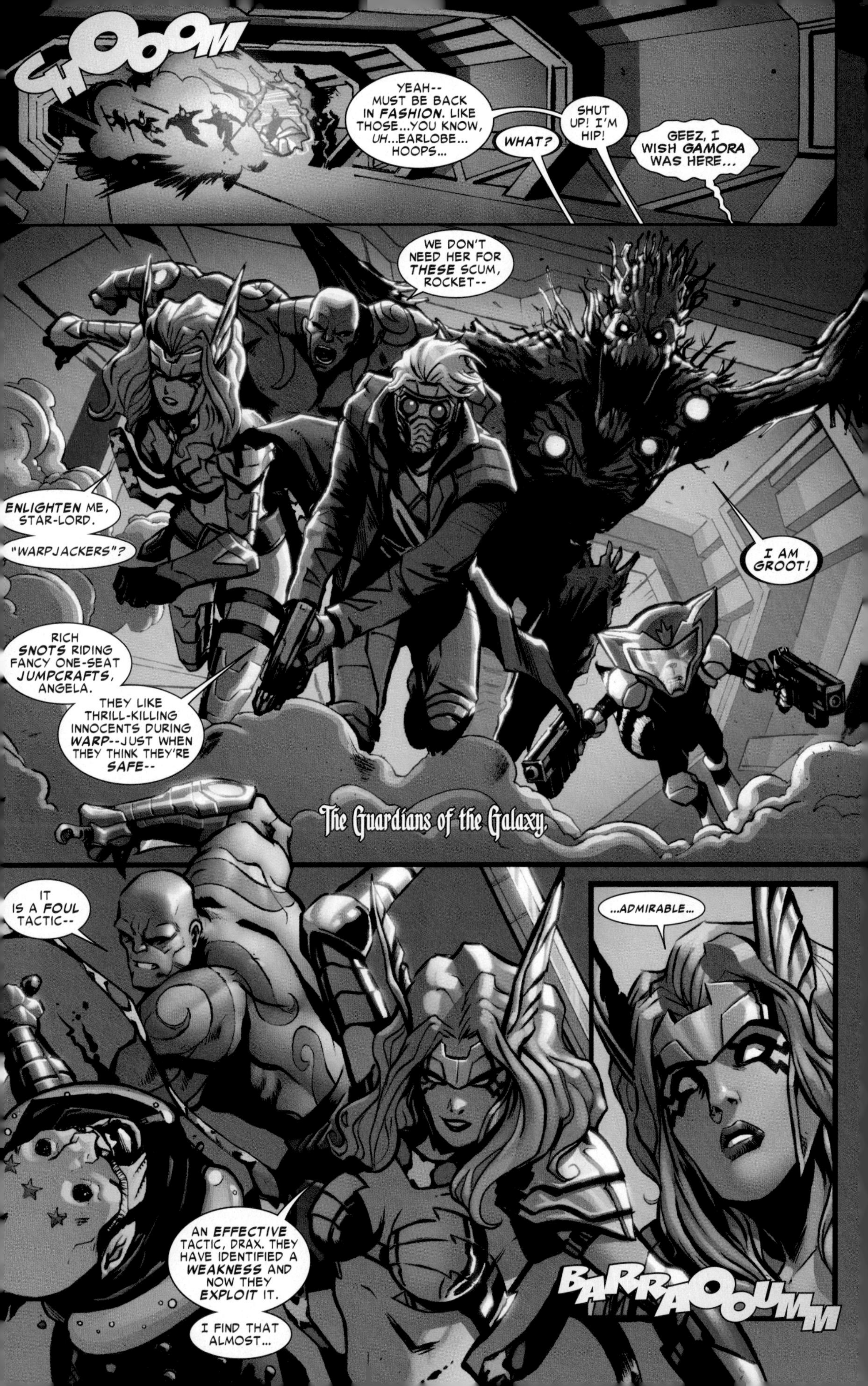
GHOOOM
YEAH-- MUST BE BACK IN FASHION. LIKE THOSE...YOU KNOW, UH...EARLOBE... HOOPS...
WHAT?
SHUT UP! I'M HIP!
GEEZ, I WISH GAMORA WAS HERE...
WE DON'T NEED HER FOR THESE SCUM, ROCKET--
ENLIGHTEN ME, STAR-LORD.
"WARPJACKERS"?
I AM GROOT!
RICH SNOTS RIDING FANCY ONE-SEAT JUMPCRAFTS, ANGELA.
THEY LIKE THRILL-KILLING INNOCENTS DURING WARP--JUST WHEN THEY THINK THEY'RE SAFE--
The Guardians of the Galaxy.
IT IS A FOUL TACTIC--
AN EFFECTIVE TACTIC, DRAX. THEY HAVE IDENTIFIED A WEAKNESS AND NOW THEY EXPLOIT IT.
I FIND THAT ALMOST...
...ADMIRABLE...
BARRAOOUMM

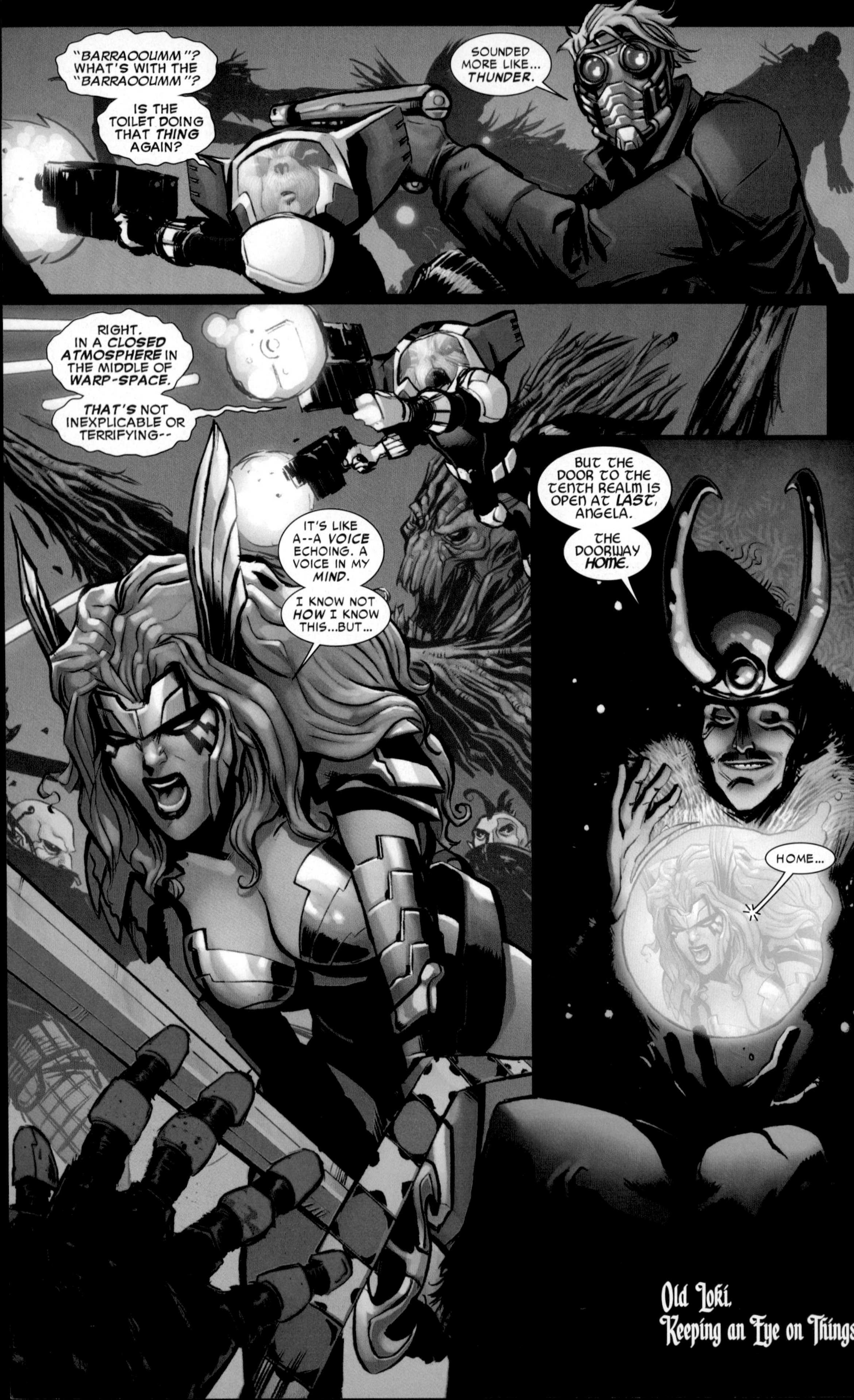
"BARRAOOUMM"? WHAT'S WITH THE "BARRAOOUMM"?
IS THE TOILET DOING THAT THING AGAIN?
SOUNDED MORE LIKE... THUNDER.
RIGHT. IN A CLOSED ATMOSPHERE IN THE MIDDLE OF WARP-SPACE.
THAT'S NOT INEXPLICABLE OR TERRIFYING--
IT'S LIKE A--A VOICE ECHOING. A VOICE IN MY MIND.
I KNOW NOT HOW I KNOW THIS...BUT...
BUT THE DOOR TO THE TENTH REALM IS OPEN AT LAST, ANGELA.
THE DOORWAY HOME.
HOME...
Old Loki.
Keeping an Eye on Things

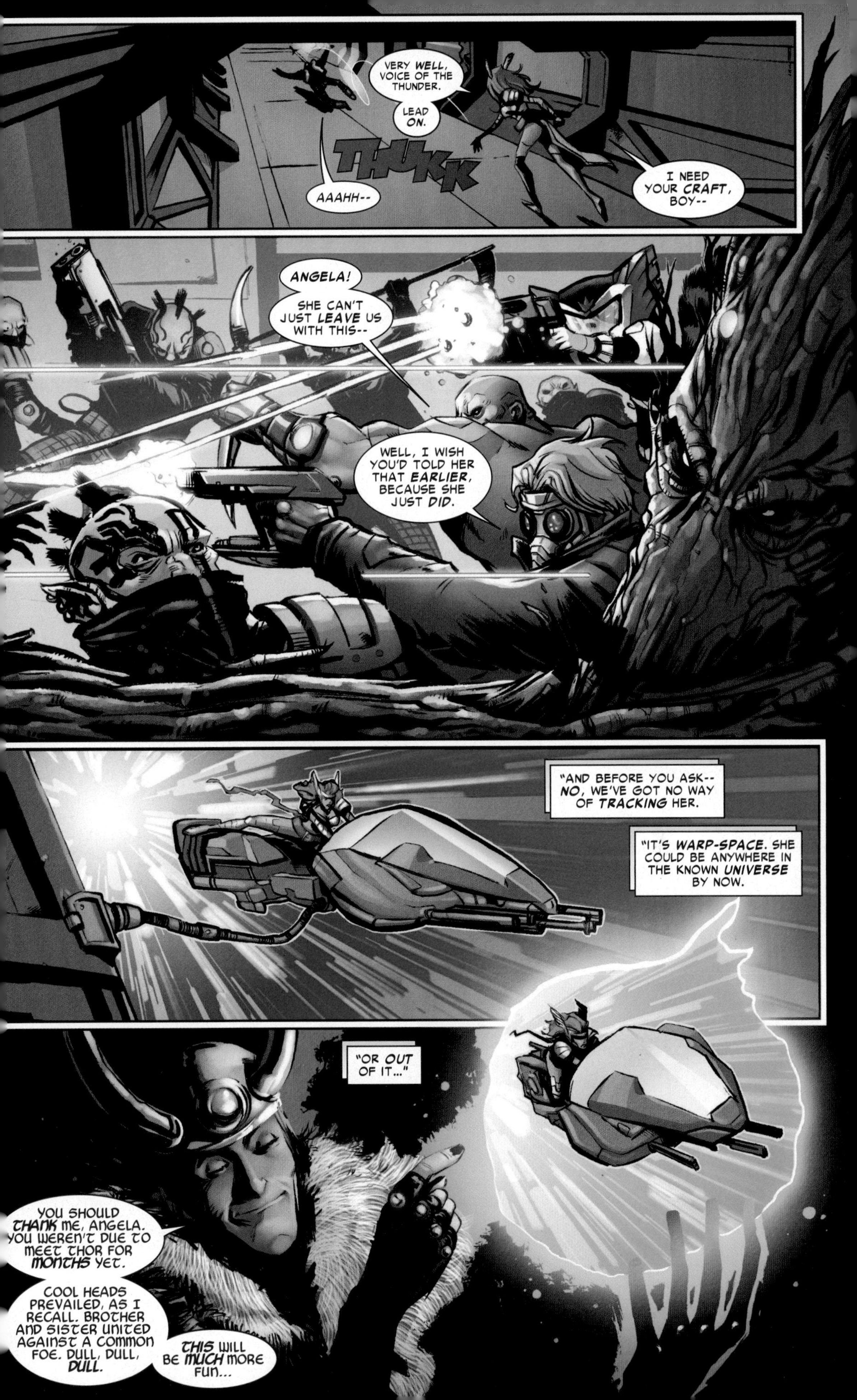
VERY WELL, VOICE OF THE THUNDER.
LEAD ON.
THUKK
AAAHH--
I NEED YOUR CRAFT, BOY--
ANGELA!
SHE CAN'T JUST LEAVE US WITH THIS--
WELL, I WISH YOU'D TOLD HER THAT EARLIER, BECAUSE SHE JUST DID.
"AND BEFORE YOU ASK-- NO, WE'VE GOT NO WAY OF TRACKING HER.
"IT'S WARP-SPACE. SHE COULD BE ANYWHERE IN THE KNOWN UNIVERSE BY NOW.
"OR OUT OF IT..."
YOU SHOULD THANK ME, ANGELA. YOU WEREN'T DUE TO MEET THOR FOR MONTHS YET.
COOL HEADS PREVAILED, AS I RECALL. BROTHER AND SISTER UNITED AGAINST A COMMON FOE. DULL, DULL, DULL.
THIS WILL BE MUCH MORE FUN...

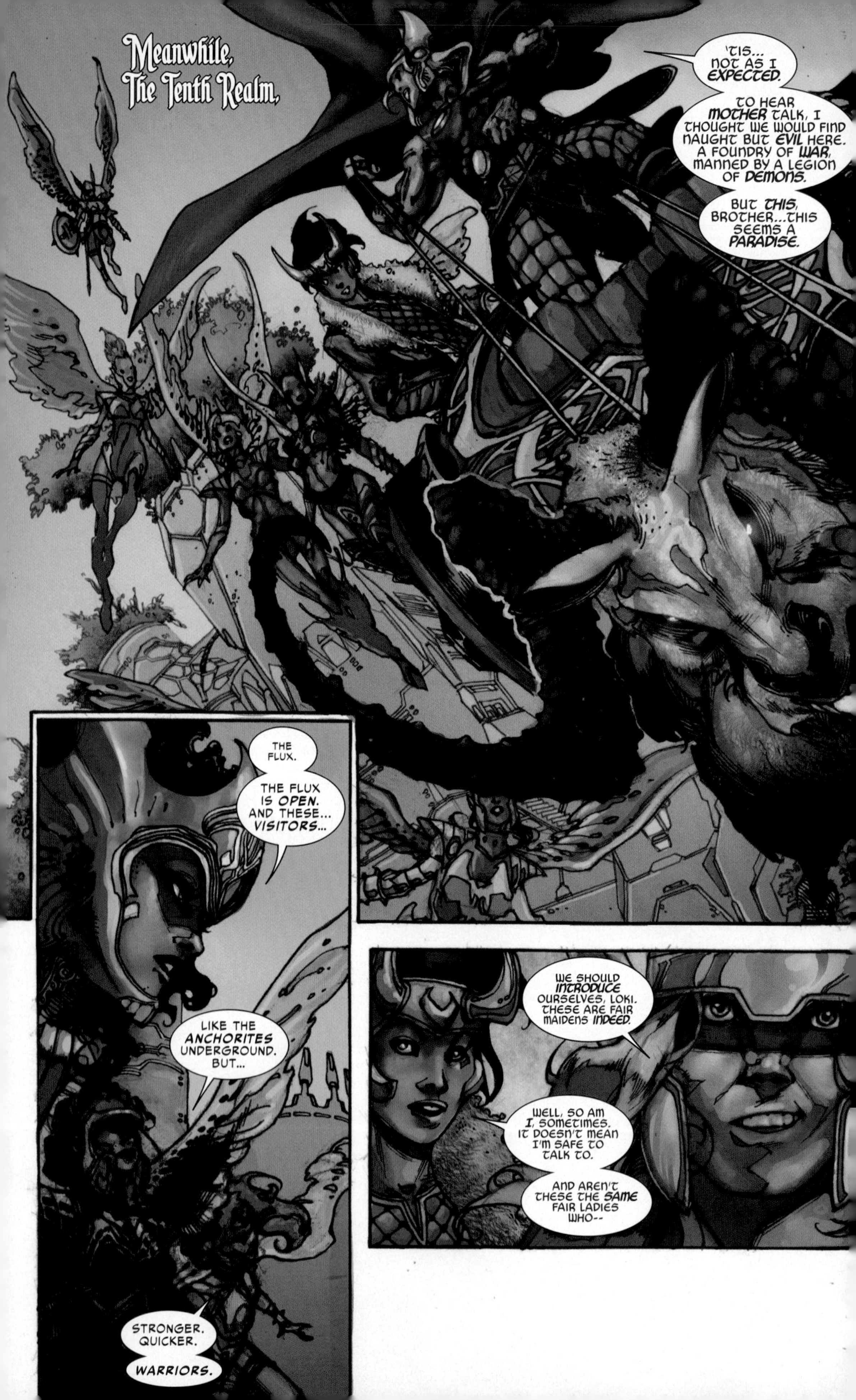
Meanwhile, The Tenth Realm,
'TIS... NOT AS I EXPECTED.
TO HEAR MOTHER TALK, I THOUGHT WE WOULD FIND NAUGHT BUT EVIL HERE. A FOUNDRY OF WAR, MANNED BY A LEGION OF DEMONS.
BUT THIS, BROTHER...THIS SEEMS A PARADISE.
THE FLUX.
THE FLUX IS OPEN. AND THESE... VISITORS...
LIKE THE ANCHORITES UNDERGROUND. BUT...
STRONGER. QUICKER.
WARRIORS.
WE SHOULD INTRODUCE OURSELVES, LOKI. THESE ARE FAIR MAIDENS INDEED.
WELL, SO AM I, SOMETIMES. IT DOESN'T MEAN I'M SAFE TO TALK TO.
AND AREN'T THESE THE SAME FAIR LADIES WHO--

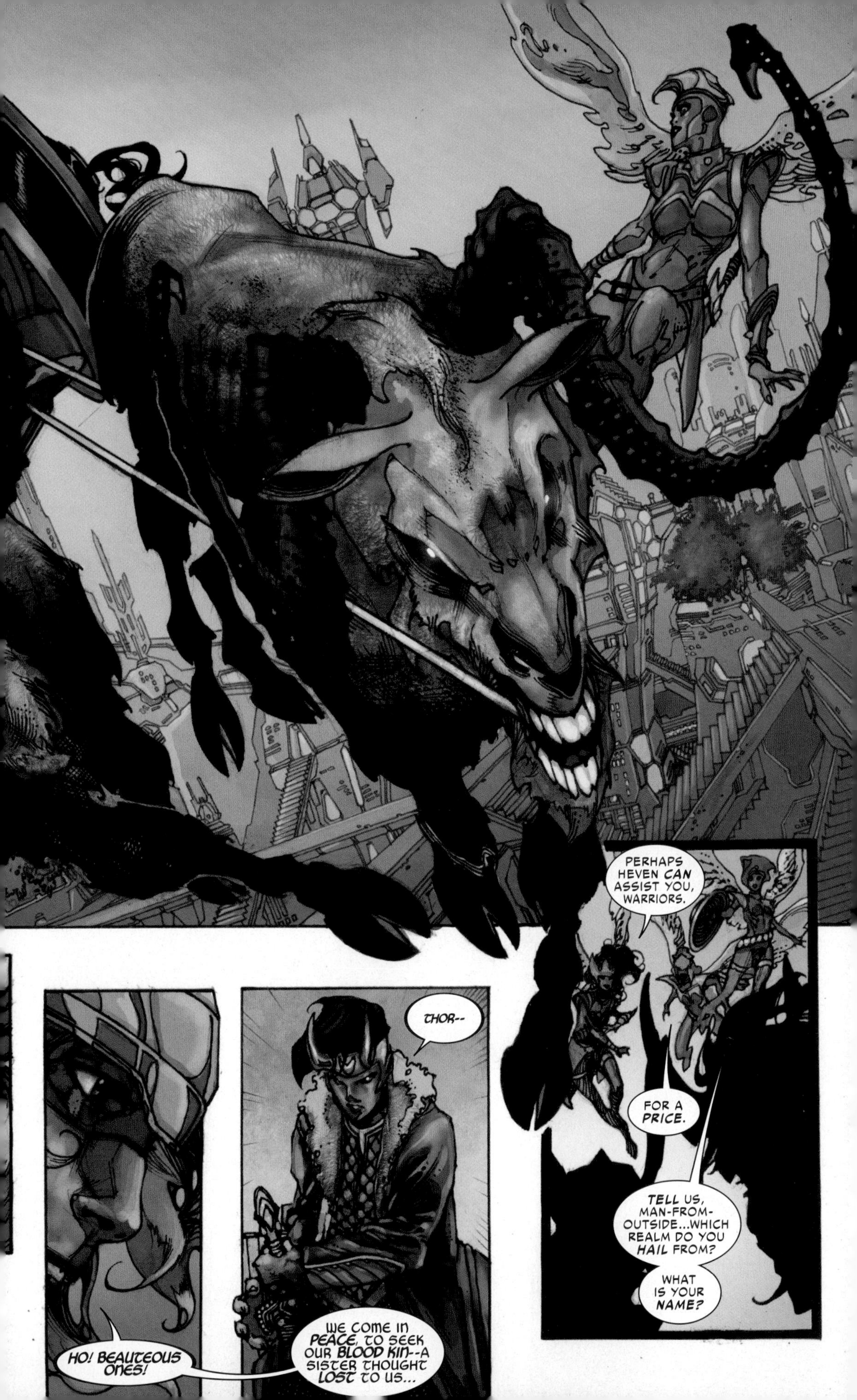
PERHAPS HEVEN CAN ASSIST YOU, WARRIORS.
HO! BEAUTEOUS ONES!
THOR--
WE COME IN PEACE, TO SEEK OUR BLOOD KIN--A SISTER THOUGHT LOST TO US...
FOR A PRICE.
TELL US, MAN-FROM-OUTSIDE...WHICH REALM DO YOU HAIL FROM?
WHAT IS YOUR NAME?

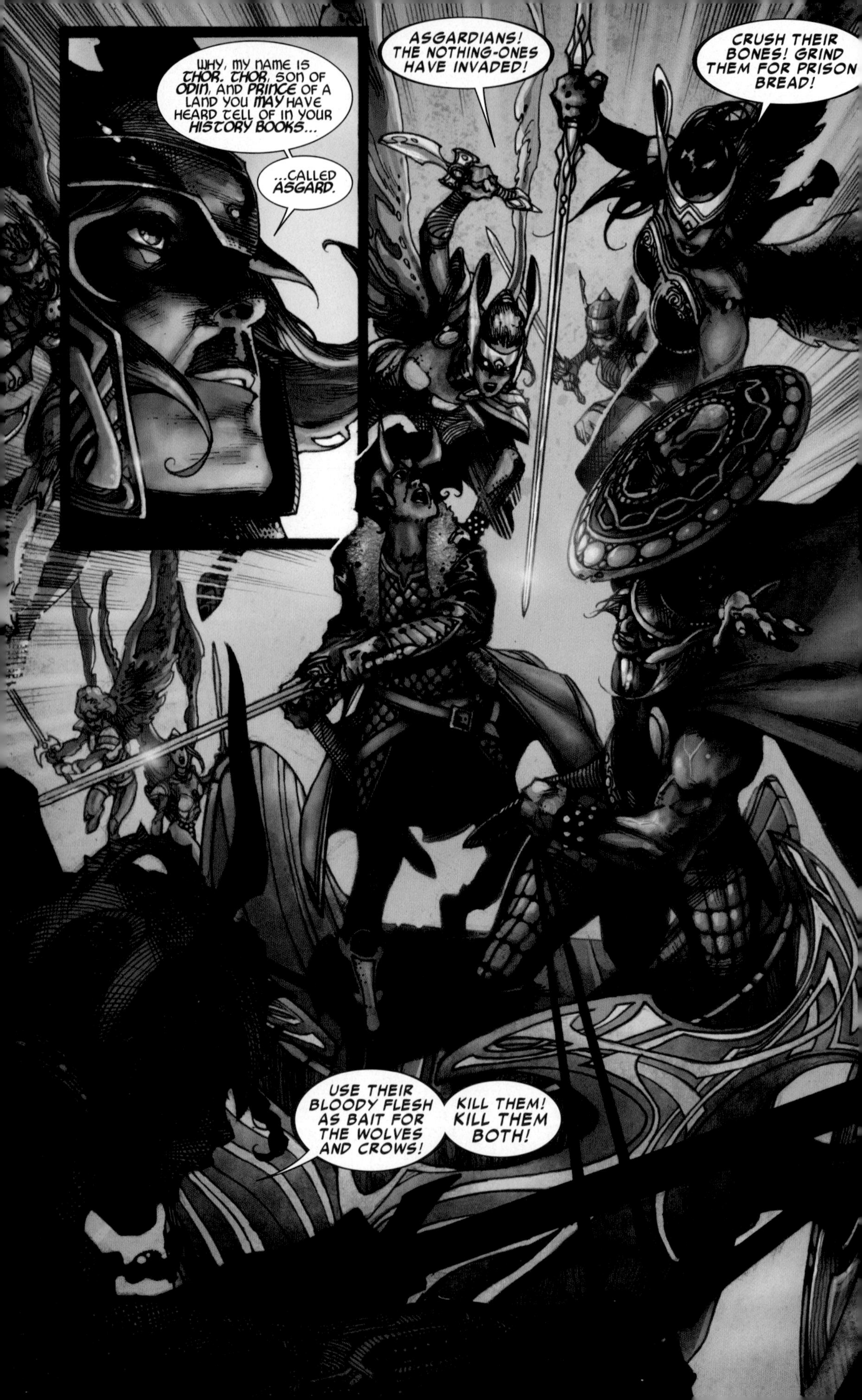
WHY, MY NAME IS THOR. THOR, SON OF ODIN, AND PRINCE OF A LAND YOU MAY HAVE HEARD TELL OF IN YOUR HISTORY BOOKS...
...CALLED ASGARD.
ASGARDIANS! THE NOTHING-ONES HAVE INVADED!
CRUSH THEIR BONES! GRIND THEM FOR PRISON BREAD!
USE THEIR BLOODY FLESH AS BAIT FOR THE WOLVES AND CROWS!
KILL THEM! KILL THEM BOTH!

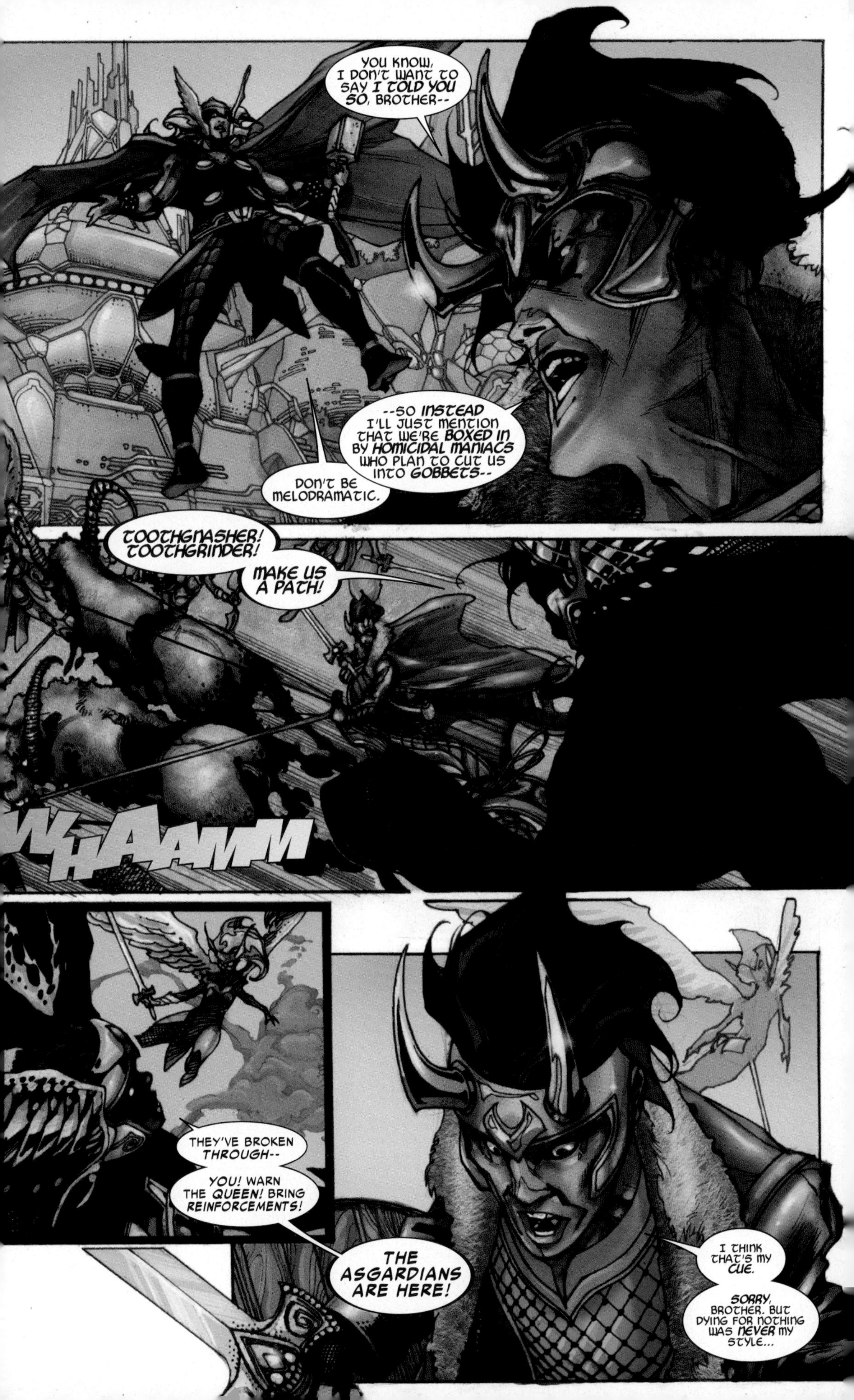
YOU KNOW, I DON'T WANT TO SAY I TOLD YOU SO, BROTHER--
--SO INSTEAD I'LL JUST MENTION THAT WE'RE BOXED IN BY HOMICIDAL MANIACS WHO PLAN TO CUT US INTO GOBBETS--
DON'T BE MELODRAMATIC.
TOOTHGNASHER! TOOTHGRINDER!
MAKE US A PATH!
WHAAAMM
THEY'VE BROKEN THROUGH--
YOU! WARN THE QUEEN! BRING REINFORCEMENTS!
THE ASGARDIANS ARE HERE!
I THINK THAT'S MY CUE.
SORRY, BROTHER.. BUT DYING FOR NOTHING WAS NEVER MY STYLE...

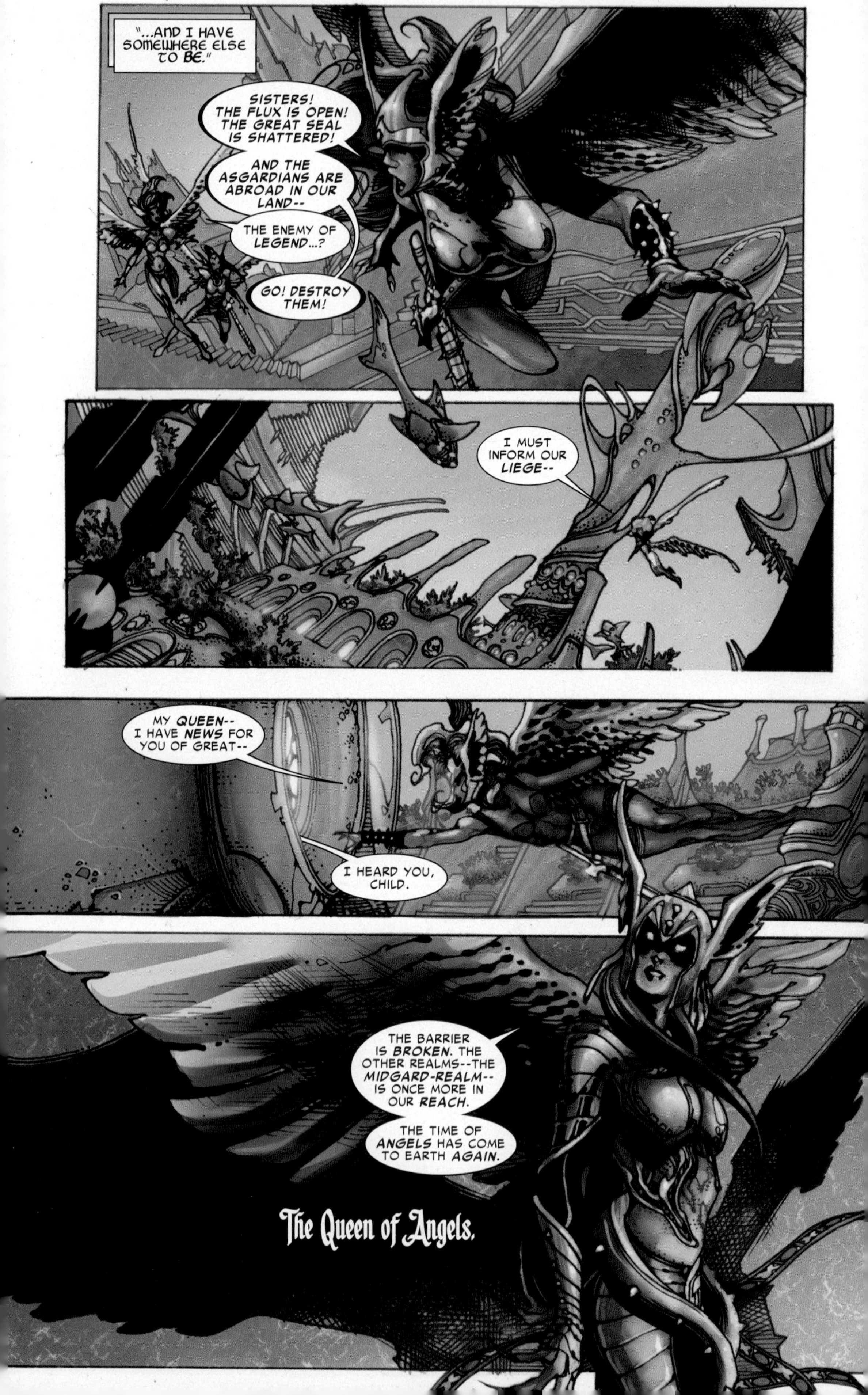
"...AND I HAVE SOMEWHERE ELSE TO BE."
SISTERS! THE FLUX IS OPEN! THE GREAT SEAL IS SHATTERED!
AND THE ASGARDIANS ARE ABROAD IN OUR LAND--
THE ENEMY OF LEGEND...?
GO! DESTROY THEM!
I MUST INFORM OUR LIEGE--
MY QUEEN-- I HAVE NEWS FOR YOU OF GREAT--
I HEARD YOU, CHILD.
THE BARRIER IS BROKEN. THE OTHER REALMS--THE MIDGARD-REALM-- IS ONCE MORE IN OUR REACH.
THE TIME OF ANGELS HAS COME TO EARTH AGAIN.
The Queen of Angels.

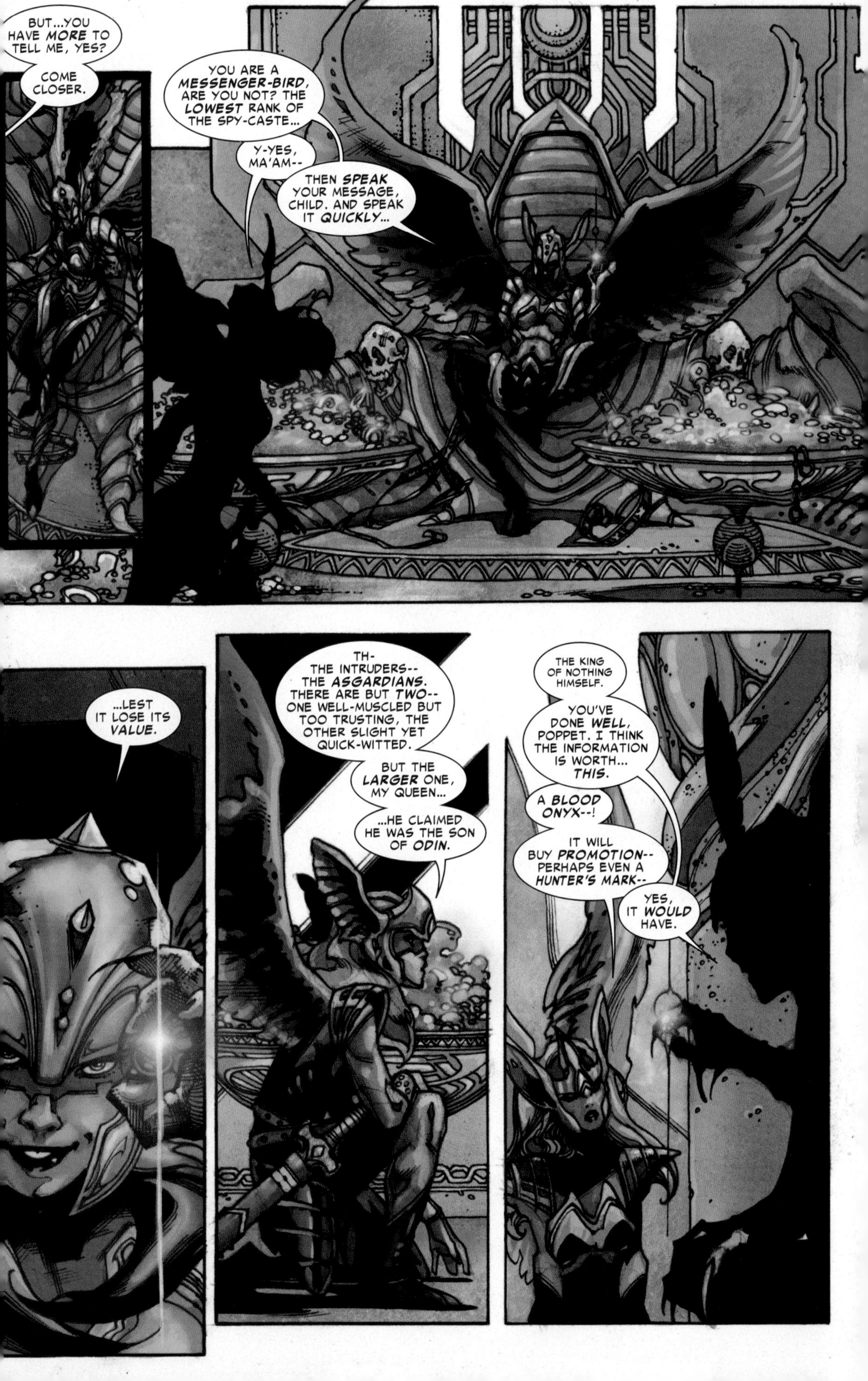
BUT...YOU HAVE MORE TO TELL ME, YES?
COME CLOSER.
YOU ARE A MESSENGER-BIRD, ARE YOU NOT? THE LOWEST RANK OF THE SPY-CASTE...
Y-YES, MA'AM--
THEN SPEAK YOUR MESSAGE, CHILD. AND SPEAK IT QUICKLY...
...LEST IT LOSE ITS VALUE.
TH- THE INTRUDERS-- THE ASGARDIANS. THERE ARE BUT TWO-- ONE WELL-MUSCLED BUT TOO TRUSTING, THE OTHER SLIGHT YET QUICK-WITTED.
BUT THE LARGER ONE, MY QUEEN...
...HE CLAIMED HE WAS THE SON OF ODIN.
THE KING OF NOTHING HIMSELF.
YOU'VE DONE WELL, POPPET. I THINK THE INFORMATION IS WORTH... THIS.
A BLOOD ONYX--!
IT WILL BUY PROMOTION-- PERHAPS EVEN A HUNTER'S MARK--
YES, IT WOULD HAVE.

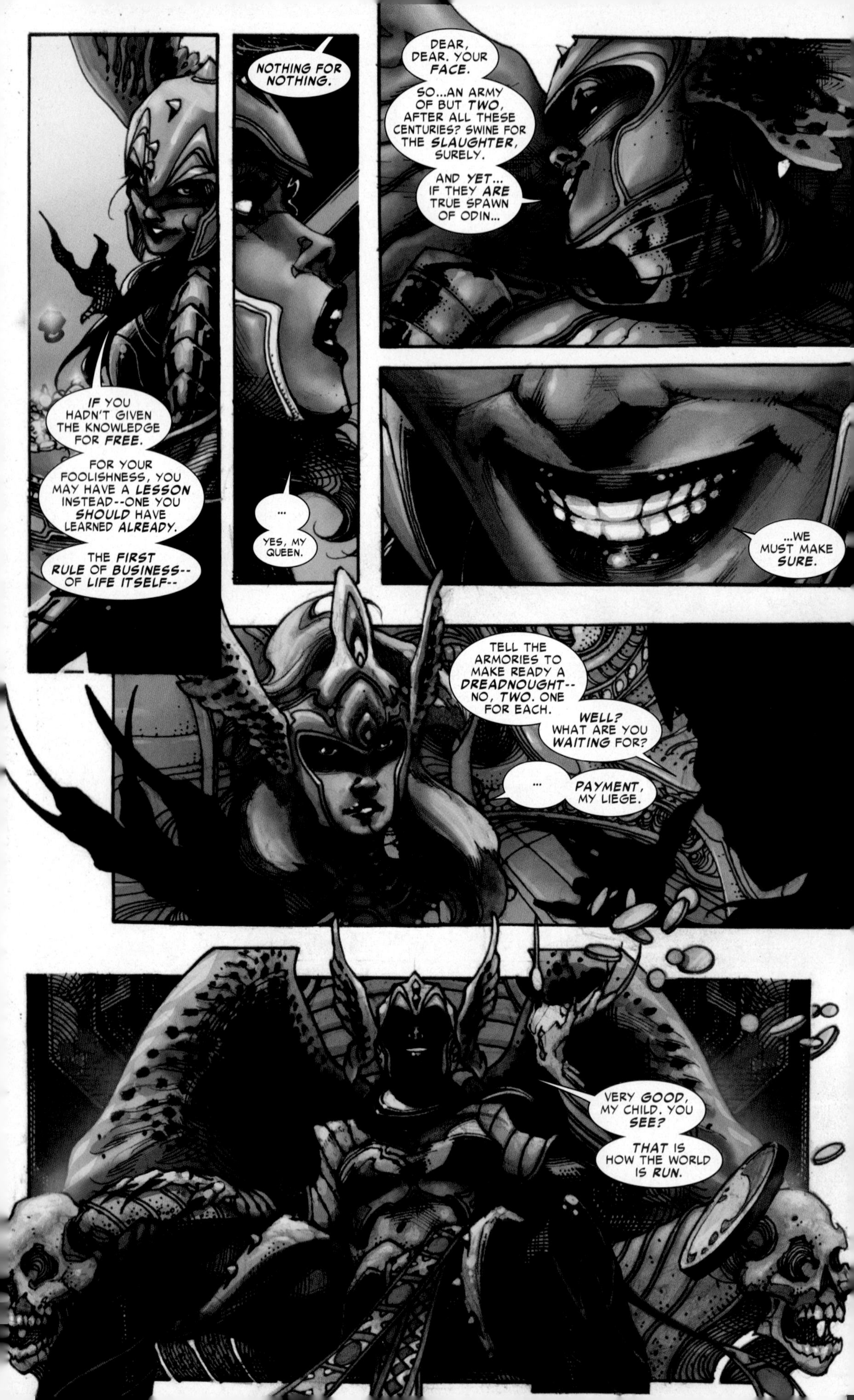
NOTHING FOR NOTHING.
IF YOU HADN'T GIVEN THE KNOWLEDGE FOR FREE.
FOR YOUR FOOLISHNESS, YOU MAY HAVE A LESSON INSTEAD--ONE YOU SHOULD HAVE LEARNED ALREADY.
THE FIRST RULE OF BUSINESS-- OF LIFE ITSELF--
...
YES, MY QUEEN.
DEAR, DEAR. YOUR FACE.
SO...AN ARMY OF BUT TWO, AFTER ALL THESE CENTURIES? SWINE FOR THE SLAUGHTER, SURELY.
AND YET... IF THEY ARE TRUE SPAWN OF ODIN...
...WE MUST MAKE SURE.
TELL THE ARMORIES TO MAKE READY A DREADNOUGHT-- NO, TWO. ONE FOR EACH.
WELL? WHAT ARE YOU WAITING FOR?
...
PAYMENT, MY LIEGE.
VERY GOOD, MY CHILD. YOU SEE?
THAT IS HOW THE WORLD IS RUN.

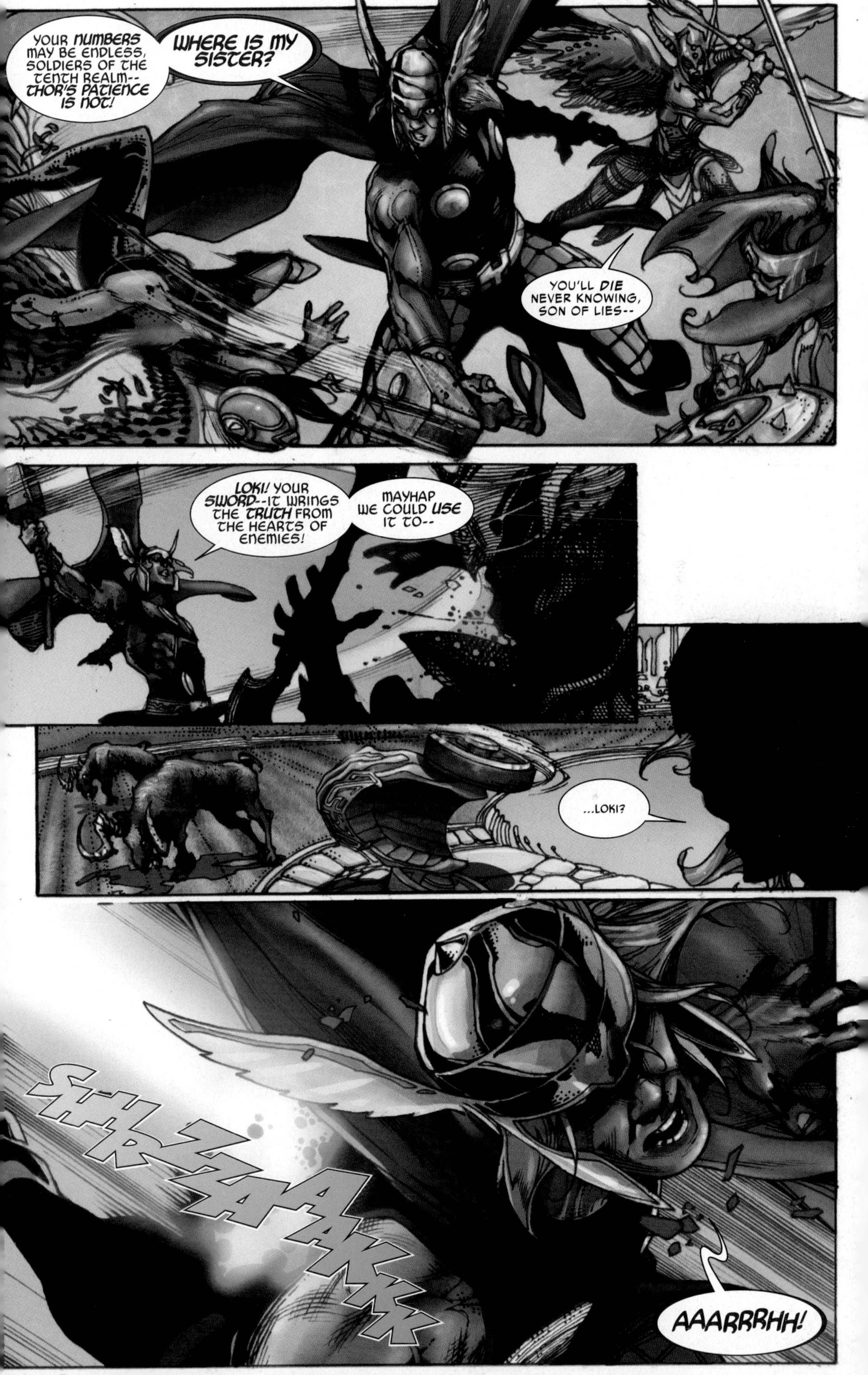
YOUR NUMBERS MAY BE ENDLESS, SOLDIERS OF THE TENTH REALM-- THOR'S PATIENCE IS NOT!
WHERE IS MY SISTER?
YOU'LL DIE NEVER KNOWING, SON OF LIES--
LOKI! YOUR SWORD--IT WRINGS THE TRUTH FROM THE HEARTS OF ENEMIES!
MAYHAP WE COULD USE IT TO--
...LOKI?
SHHZZ-ZAKKK
AAARRRHH!

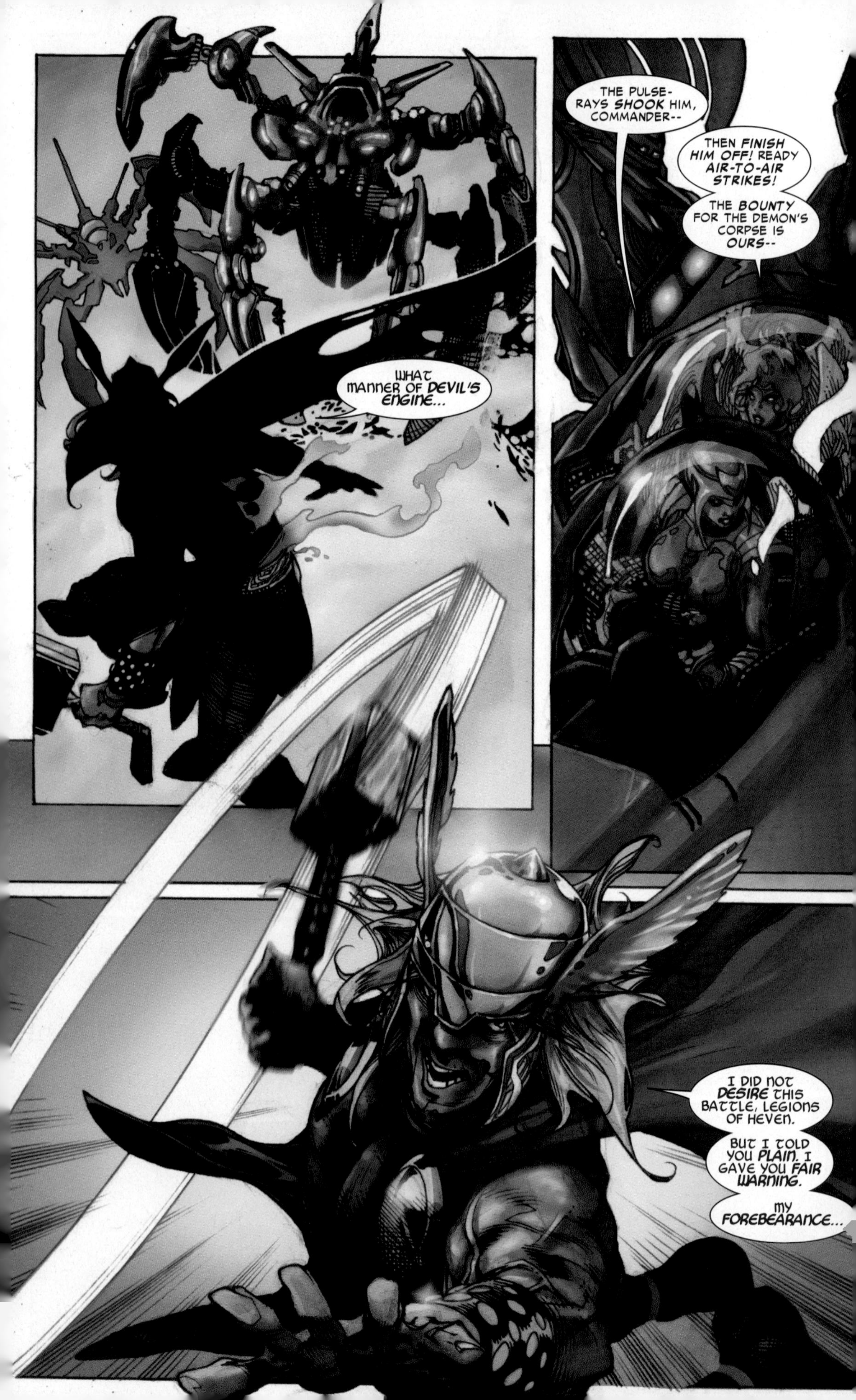
WHAT MANNER OF DEVIL'S ENGINE...
THE PULSE-RAYS SHOOK HIM, COMMANDER--
THEN FINISH HIM OFF! READY AIR-TO-AIR STRIKES!
THE BOUNTY FOR THE DEMON'S CORPSE IS OURS--
I DID NOT DESIRE THIS BATTLE, LEGIONS OF HEVEN.
BUT I TOLD YOU PLAIN. I GAVE YOU FAIR WARNING.
MY FOREBEARANCE...

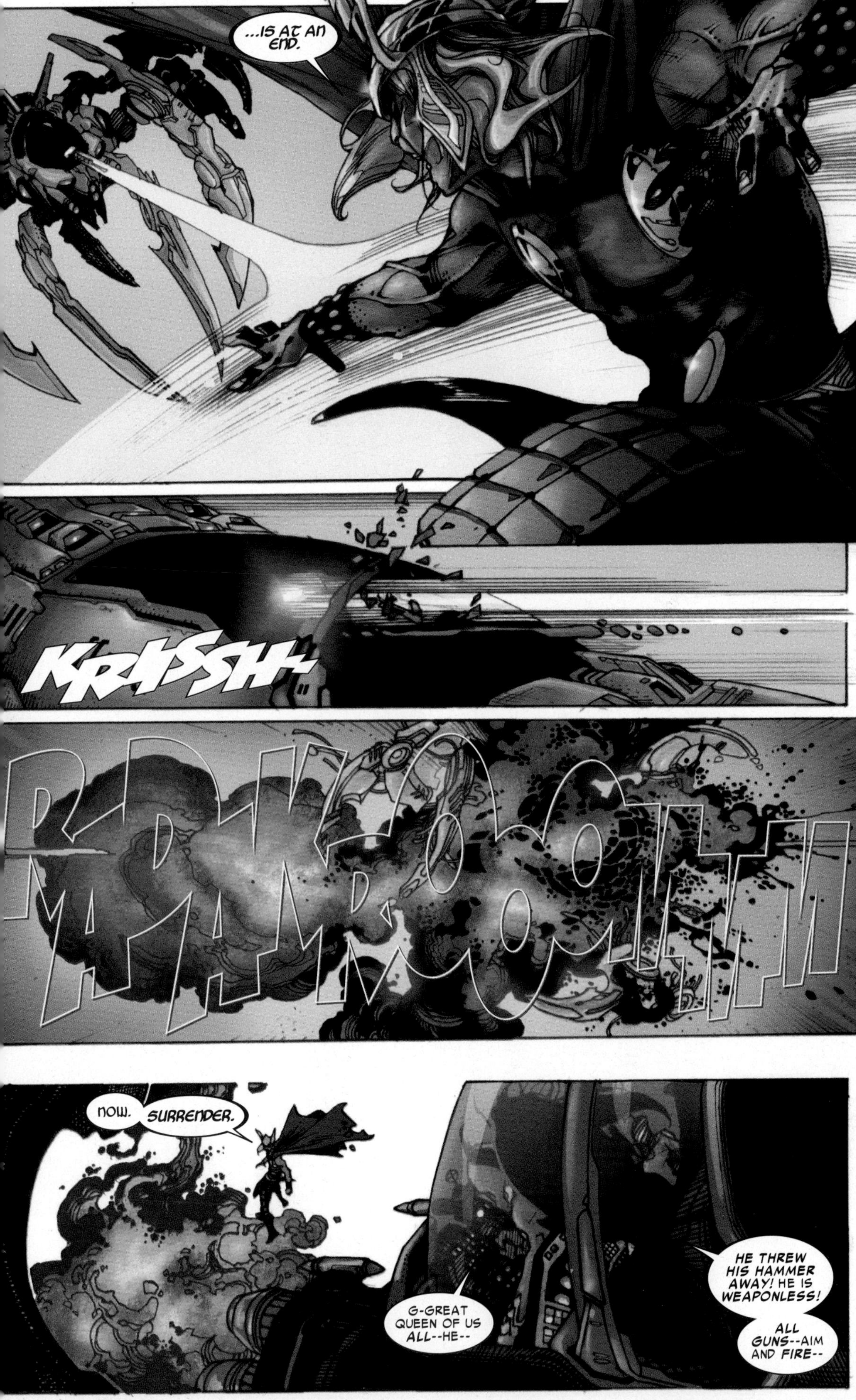
...IS AT AN END.
KRASH-
NOW.
SURRENDER.
G-GREAT QUEEN OF US ALL--HE--
HE THREW HIS HAMMER AWAY! HE IS WEAPONLESS!
ALL GUNS--AIM AND FIRE--

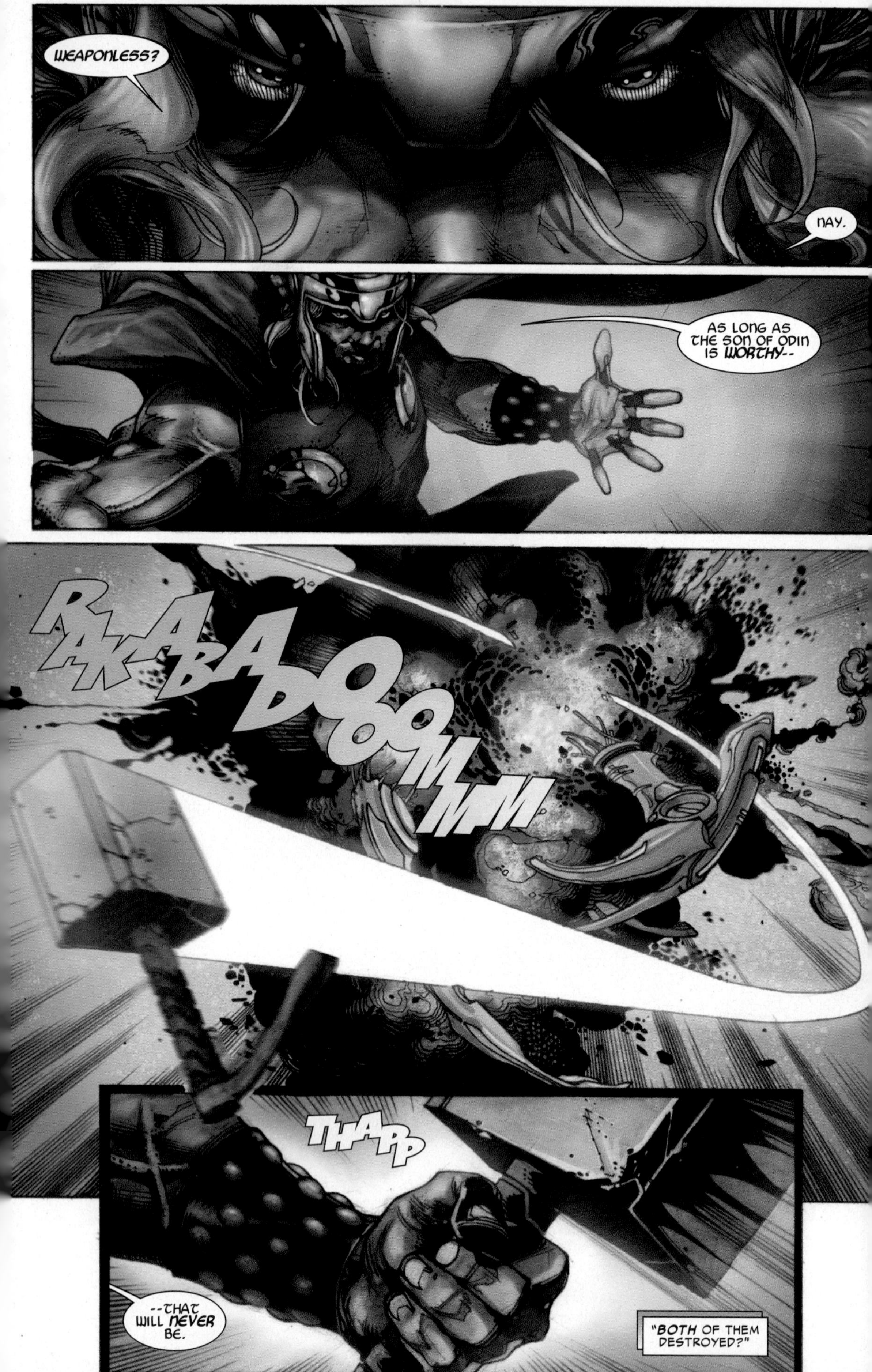
WEAPONLESS?
NAY.
AS LONG AS THE SON OF ODIN IS WORTHY--
RAKABADOOOMMMM
THAPP
--THAT WILL NEVER BE.
"BOTH OF THEM DESTROYED?"

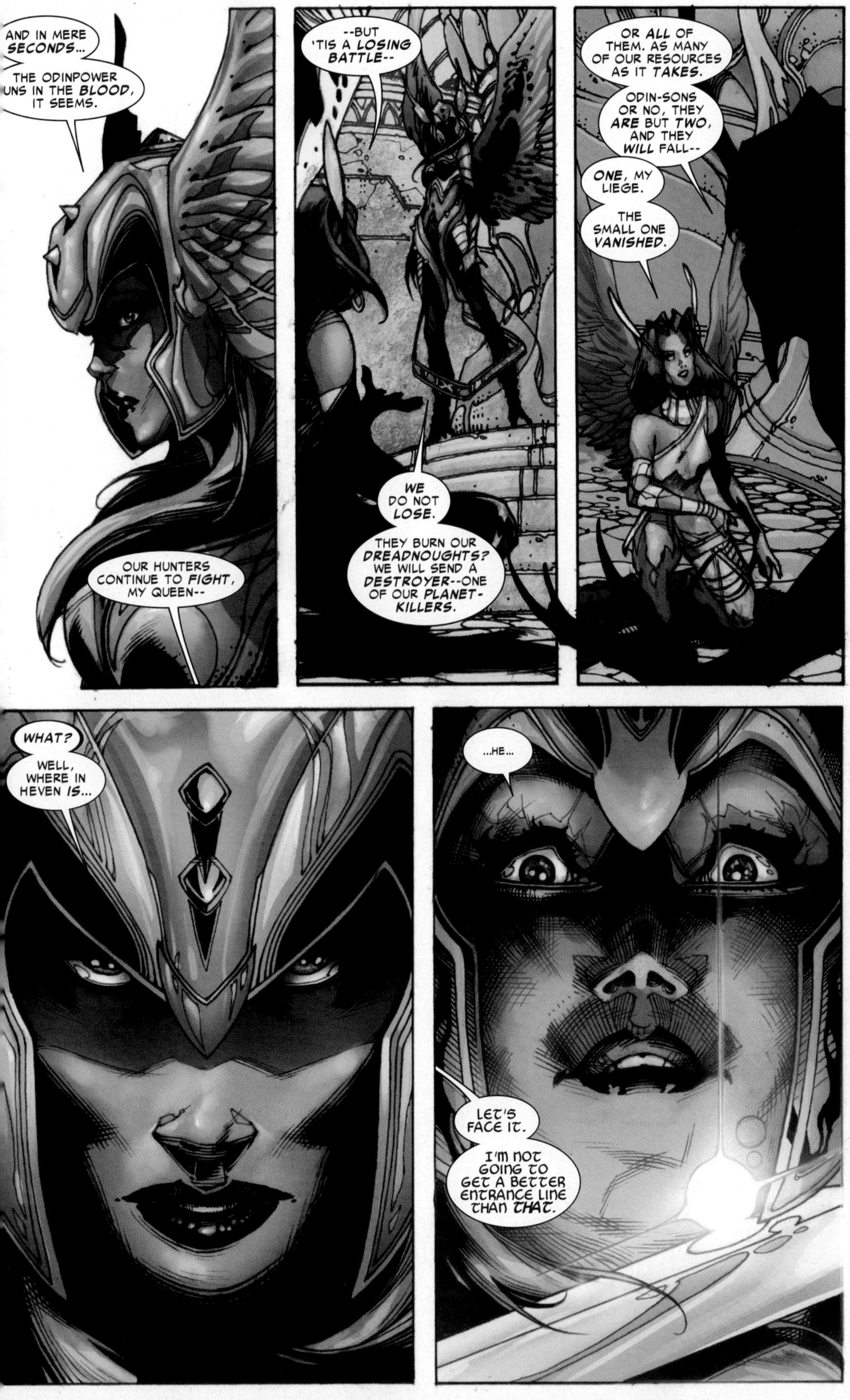
AND IN MERE SECONDS...
THE ODINPOWER UNS IN THE BLOOD, IT SEEMS.
OUR HUNTERS CONTINUE TO FIGHT, MY QUEEN--
--BUT 'TIS A LOSING BATTLE--
WE DO NOT LOSE.
THEY BURN OUR DREADNOUGHTS? WE WILL SEND A DESTROYER--ONE OF OUR PLANET-KILLERS.
OR ALL OF THEM. AS MANY OF OUR RESOURCES AS IT TAKES.
ODIN-SONS OR NO, THEY ARE BUT TWO, AND THEY WILL FALL--
ONE, MY LIEGE.
THE SMALL ONE VANISHED.
WHAT?
WELL, WHERE IN HEVEN IS...
...HE...
LET'S FACE IT.
I'M NOT GOING TO GET A BETTER ENTRANCE LINE THAN THAT.

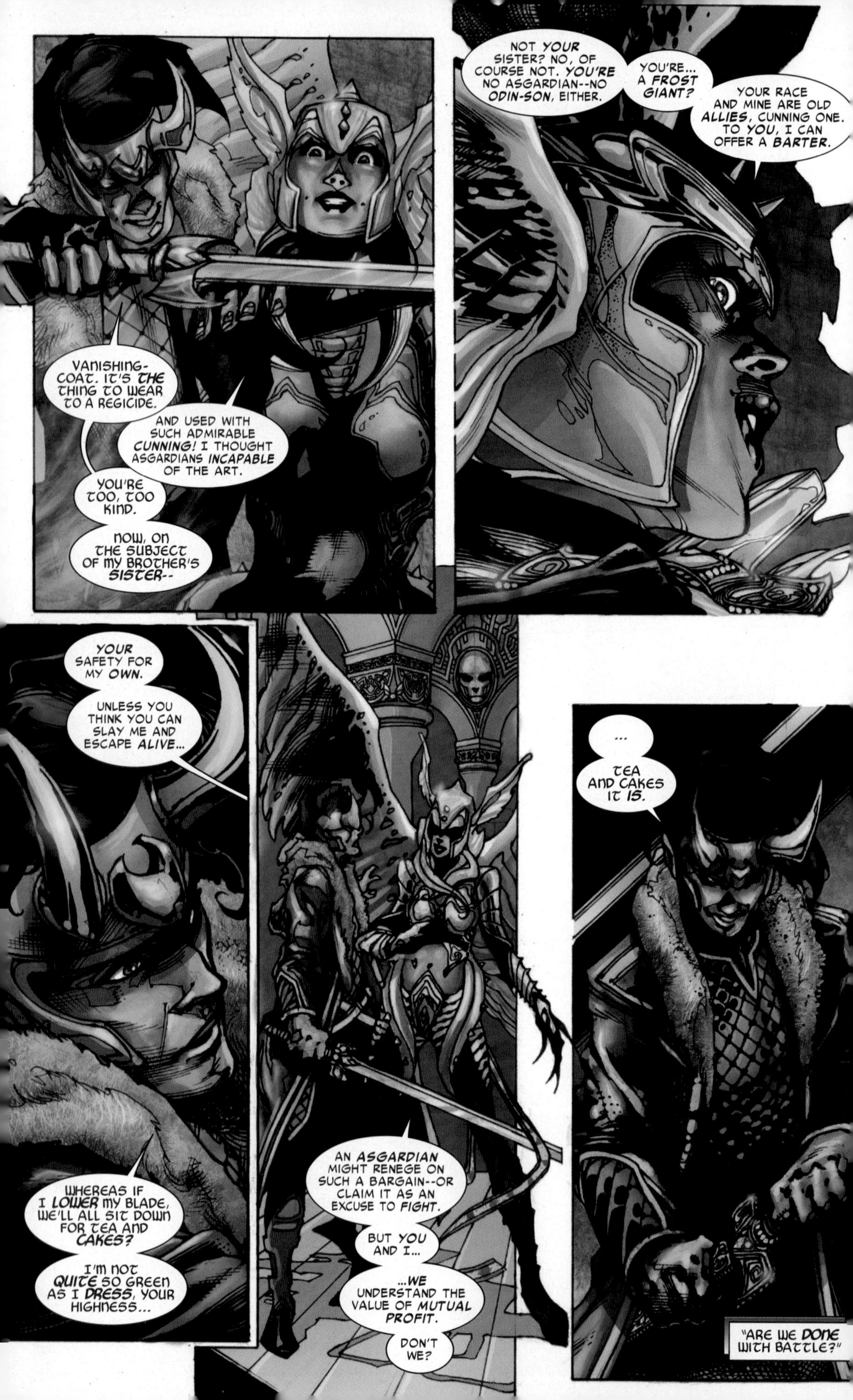
VANISHING-COAT. IT'S THE THING TO WEAR TO A REGICIDE.
AND USED WITH SUCH ADMIRABLE CUNNING! I THOUGHT ASGARDIANS INCAPABLE OF THE ART.
YOU'RE TOO, TOO KIND.
NOW, ON THE SUBJECT OF MY BROTHER'S SISTER--
NOT YOUR SISTER? NO, OF COURSE NOT. YOU'RE NO ASGARDIAN--NO ODIN-SON, EITHER.
YOU'RE... A FROST GIANT?
YOUR RACE AND MINE ARE OLD ALLIES, CUNNING ONE. TO YOU, I CAN OFFER A BARTER.
YOUR SAFETY FOR MY OWN.
UNLESS YOU THINK YOU CAN SLAY ME AND ESCAPE ALIVE...
WHEREAS IF I LOWER MY BLADE, WE'LL ALL SIT DOWN FOR TEA AND CAKES?
I'M NOT QUITE SO GREEN AS I DRESS, YOUR HIGHNESS...
AN ASGARDIAN MIGHT RENEGE ON SUCH A BARGAIN--OR CLAIM IT AS AN EXCUSE TO FIGHT.
BUT YOU AND I...
...WE UNDERSTAND THE VALUE OF MUTUAL PROFIT.
DON'T WE?
...
TEA AND CAKES IT IS.
"ARE WE DONE WITH BATTLE?"

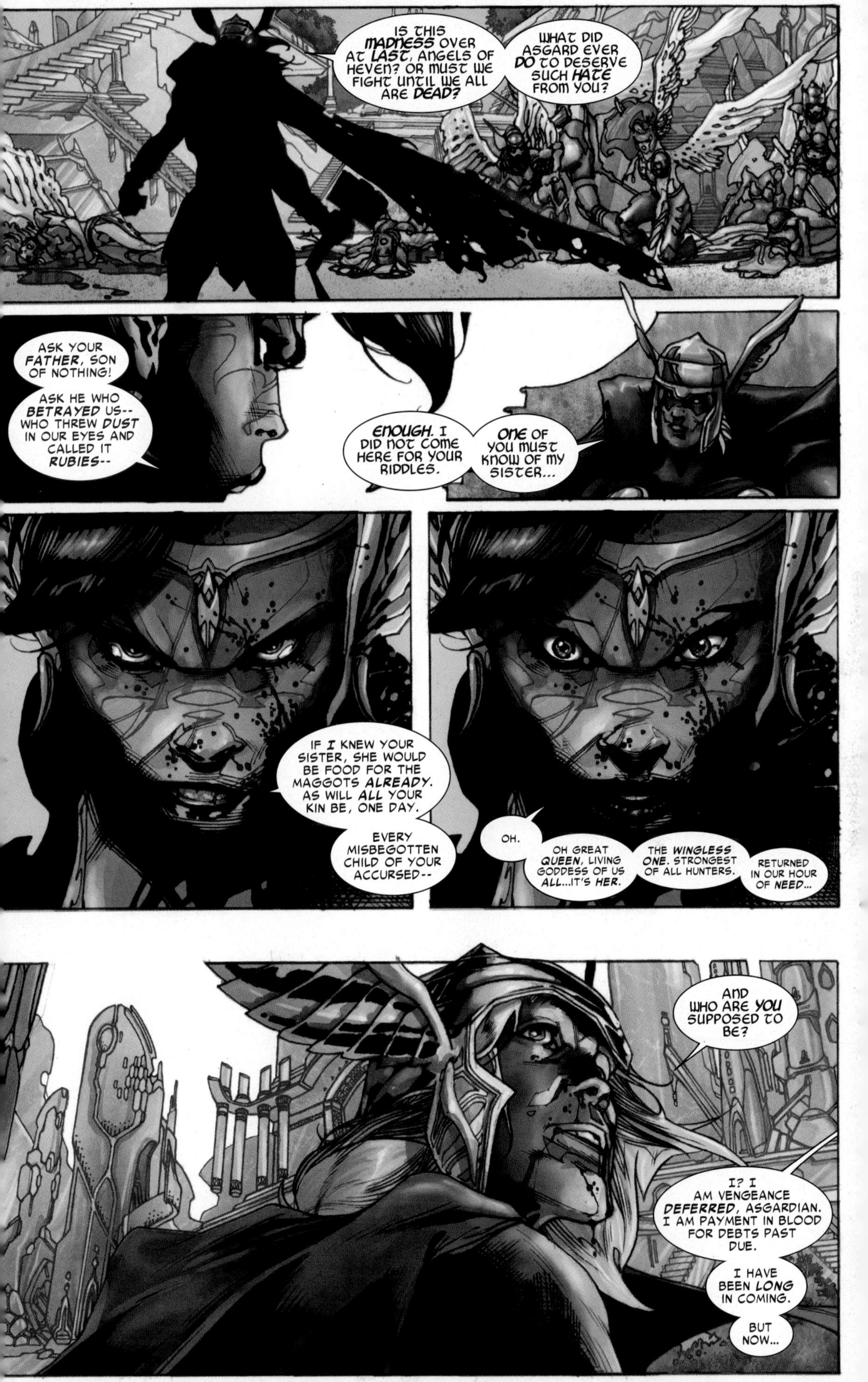
IS THIS MADNESS OVER AT LAST, ANGELS OF HEVEN? OR MUST WE FIGHT UNTIL WE ALL ARE DEAD?
WHAT DID ASGARD EVER DO TO DESERVE SUCH HATE FROM YOU?
ASK YOUR FATHER, SON OF NOTHING!
ASK HE WHO BETRAYED US-- WHO THREW DUST IN OUR EYES AND CALLED IT RUBIES--
ENOUGH. I DID NOT COME HERE FOR YOUR RIDDLES.
ONE OF YOU MUST KNOW OF MY SISTER...
IF I KNEW YOUR SISTER, SHE WOULD BE FOOD FOR THE MAGGOTS ALREADY. AS WILL ALL YOUR KIN BE, ONE DAY.
EVERY MISBEGOTTEN CHILD OF YOUR ACCURSED--
OH.
OH GREAT QUEEN, LIVING GODDESS OF US ALL...IT'S HER.
THE WINGLESS ONE. STRONGEST OF ALL HUNTERS.
RETURNED IN OUR HOUR OF NEED...
AND WHO ARE YOU SUPPOSED TO BE?
I? I AM VENGEANCE DEFERRED, ASGARDIAN. I AM PAYMENT IN BLOOD FOR DEBTS PAST DUE.
I HAVE BEEN LONG IN COMING.
BUT NOW...

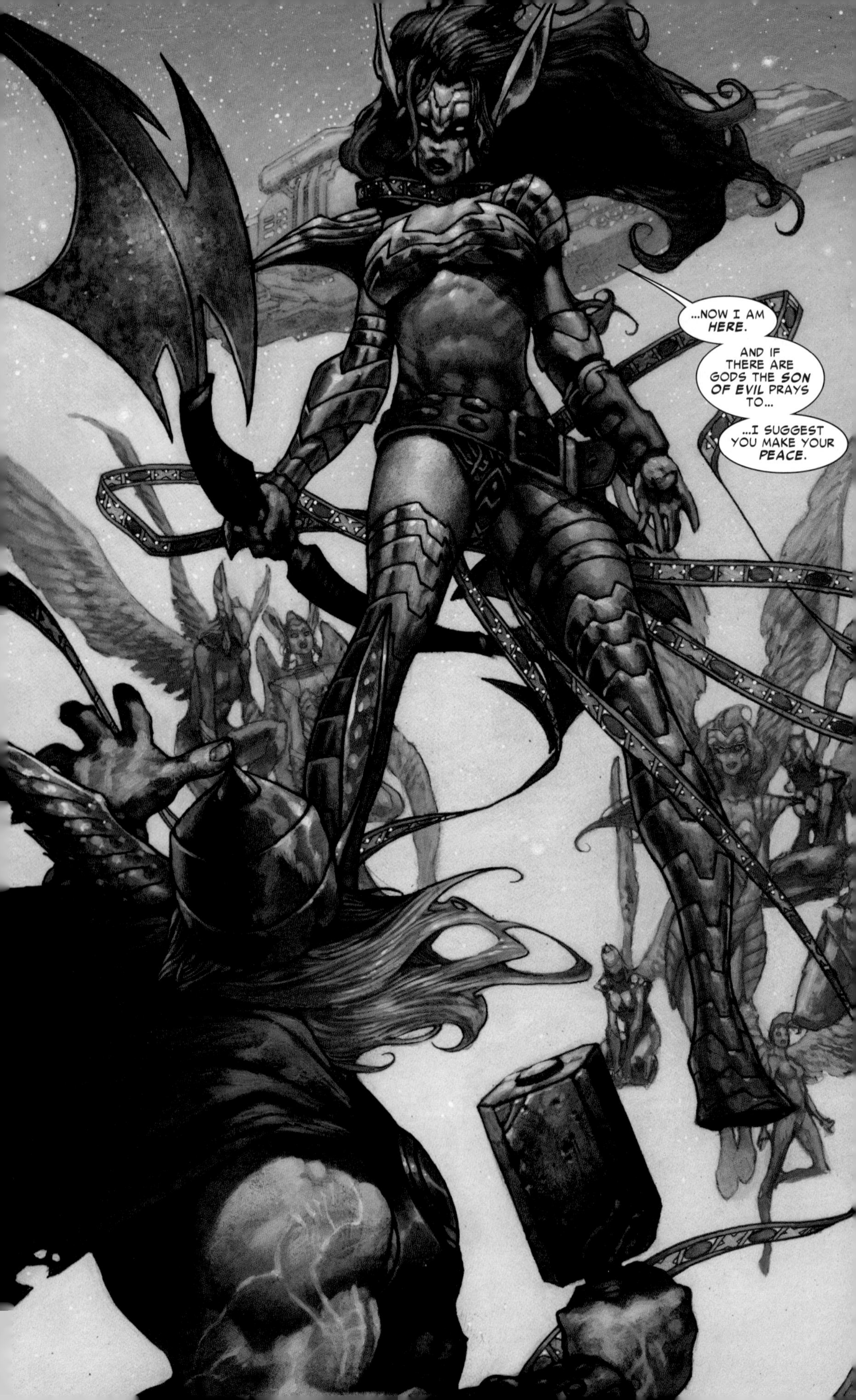
...NOW I AM *HERE*.
AND IF THERE ARE GODS THE *SON OF EVIL* PRAYS TO...
...I SUGGEST YOU MAKE YOUR *PEACE*.

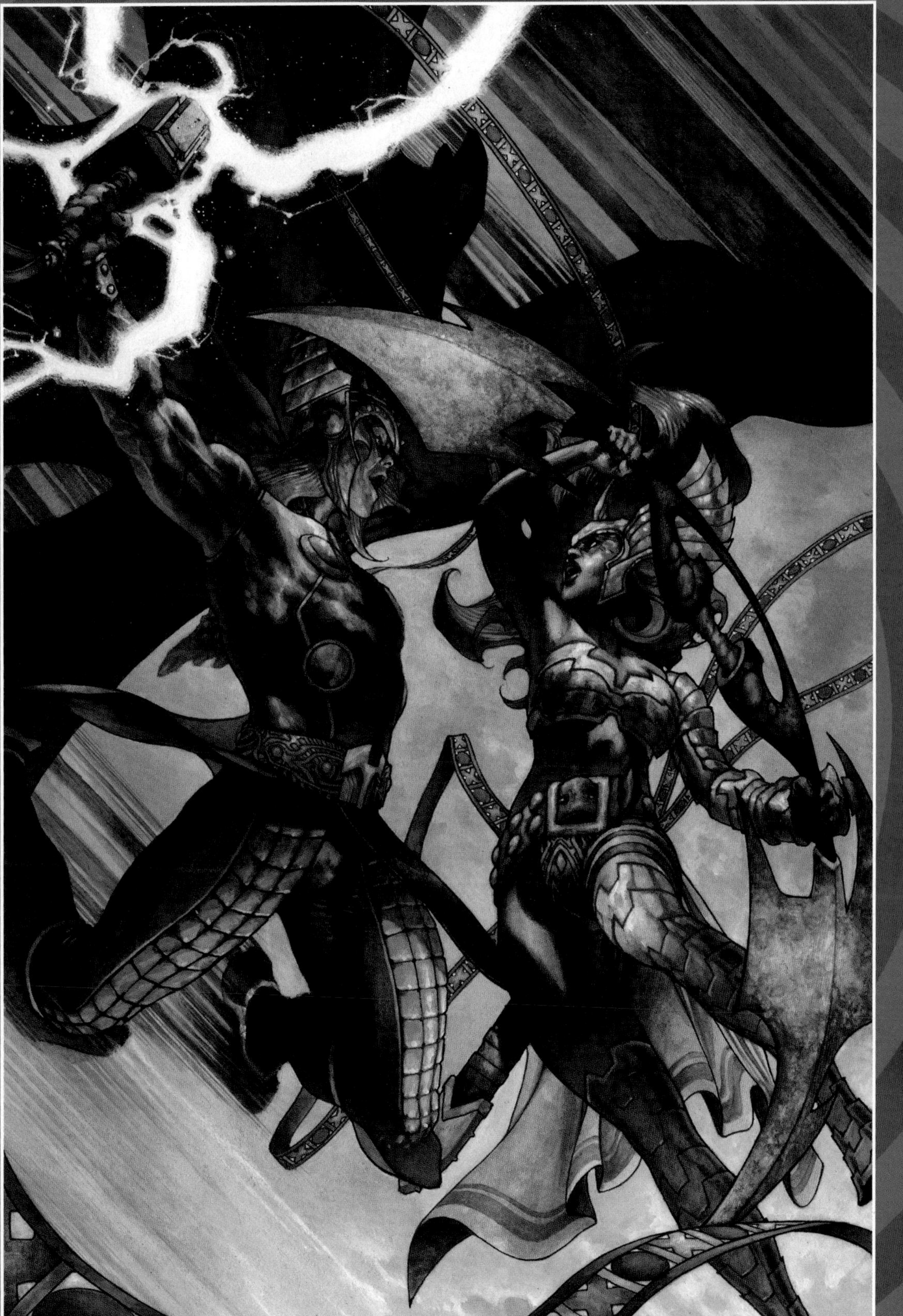

ORIGINAL SIN #5.3

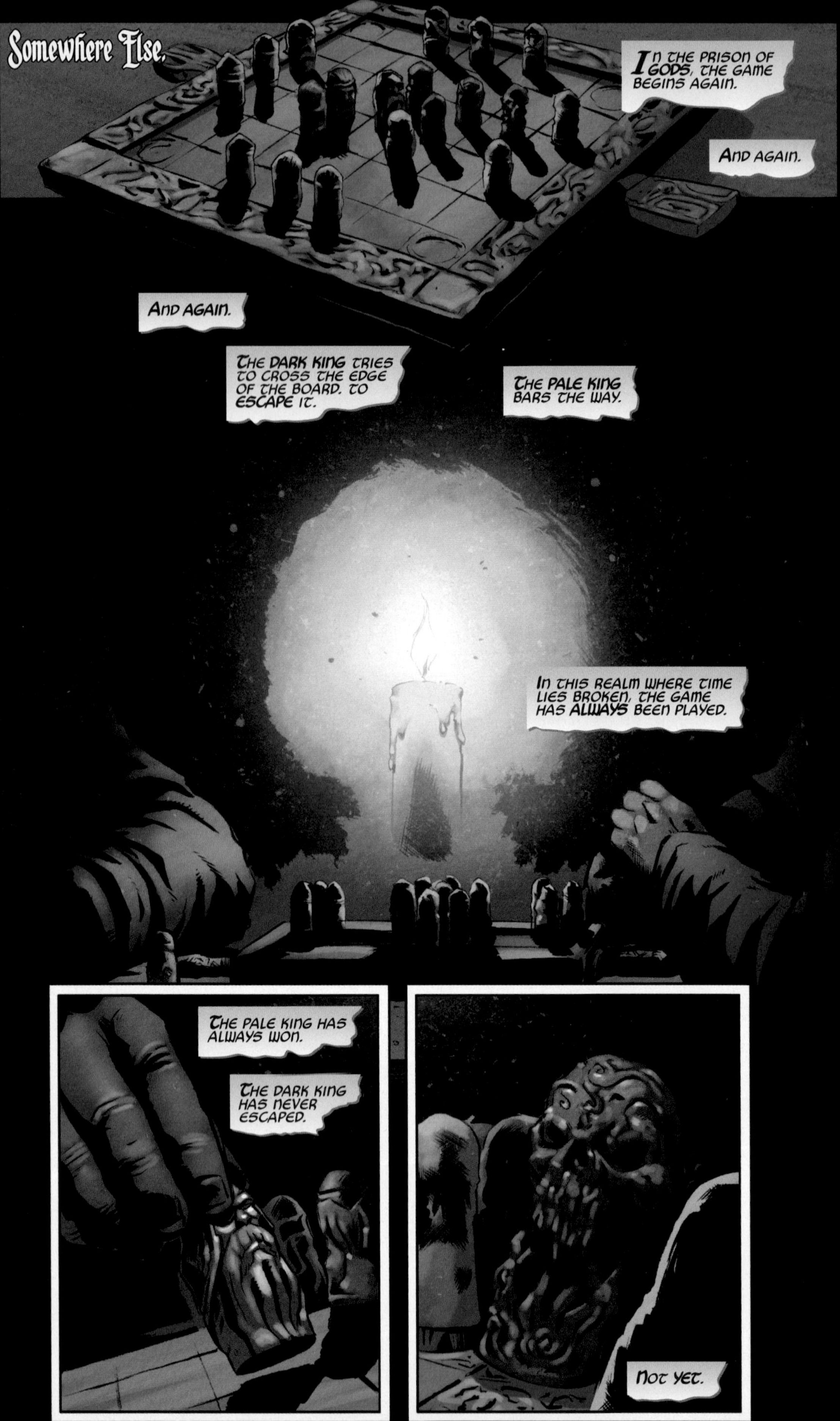
Somewhere Else.
IN THE PRISON OF GODS, THE GAME BEGINS AGAIN.
AND AGAIN.
AND AGAIN.
THE DARK KING TRIES TO CROSS THE EDGE OF THE BOARD. TO ESCAPE IT.
THE PALE KING BARS THE WAY.
IN THIS REALM WHERE TIME LIES BROKEN, THE GAME HAS ALWAYS BEEN PLAYED.
THE PALE KING HAS ALWAYS WON.
THE DARK KING HAS NEVER ESCAPED.
NOT YET.

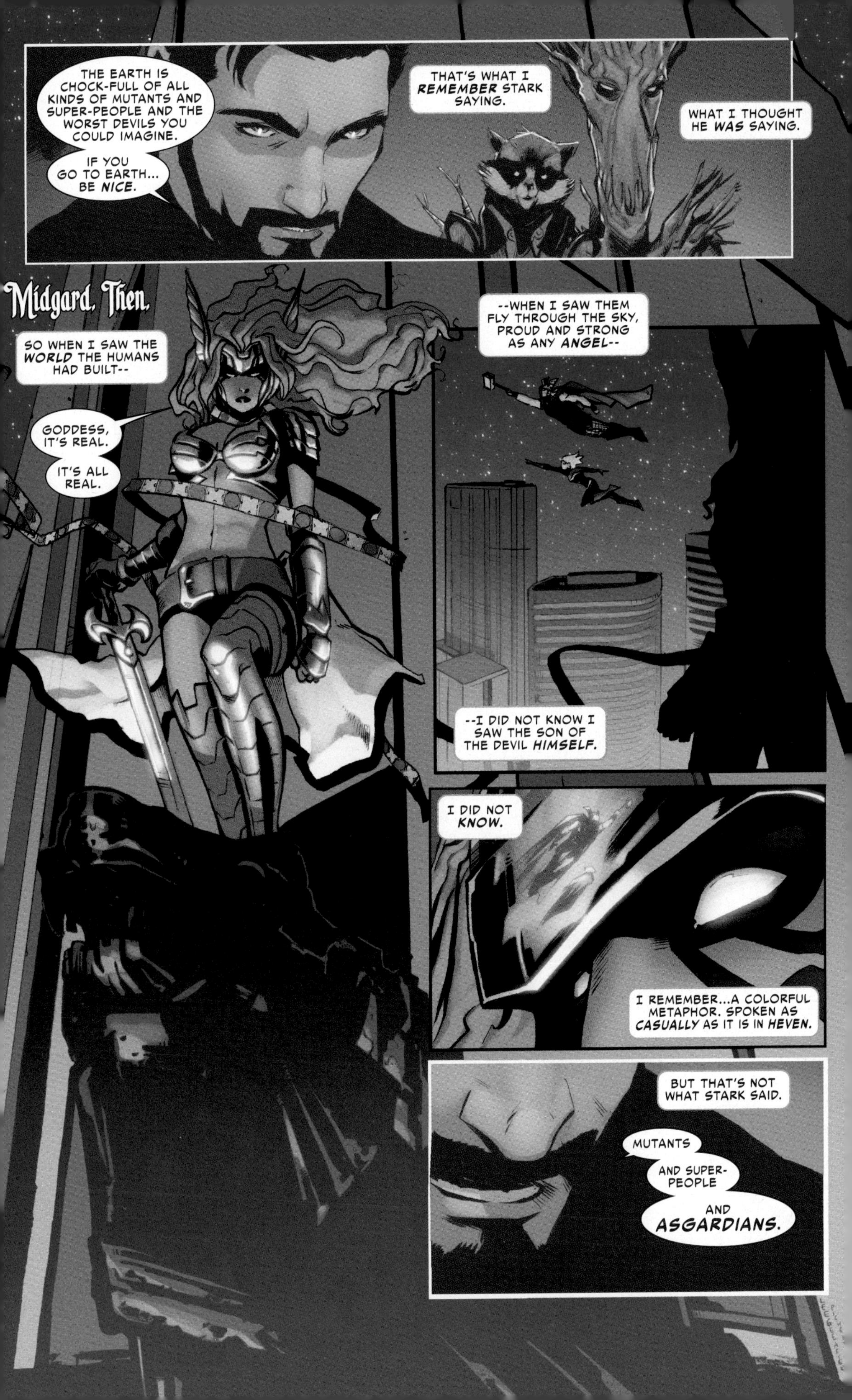
THE EARTH IS CHOCK-FULL OF ALL KINDS OF MUTANTS AND SUPER-PEOPLE AND THE WORST DEVILS YOU COULD IMAGINE.
IF YOU GO TO EARTH... BE NICE.
THAT'S WHAT I REMEMBER STARK SAYING.
WHAT I THOUGHT HE WAS SAYING.
Midgard, Then.
SO WHEN I SAW THE WORLD THE HUMANS HAD BUILT--
GODDESS, IT'S REAL.
IT'S ALL REAL.
--WHEN I SAW THEM FLY THROUGH THE SKY, PROUD AND STRONG AS ANY ANGEL--
--I DID NOT KNOW I SAW THE SON OF THE DEVIL HIMSELF.
I DID NOT KNOW.
I REMEMBER...A COLORFUL METAPHOR. SPOKEN AS CASUALLY AS IT IS IN HEVEN.
BUT THAT'S NOT WHAT STARK SAID.
MUTANTS
AND SUPER-PEOPLE
AND ASGARDIANS.

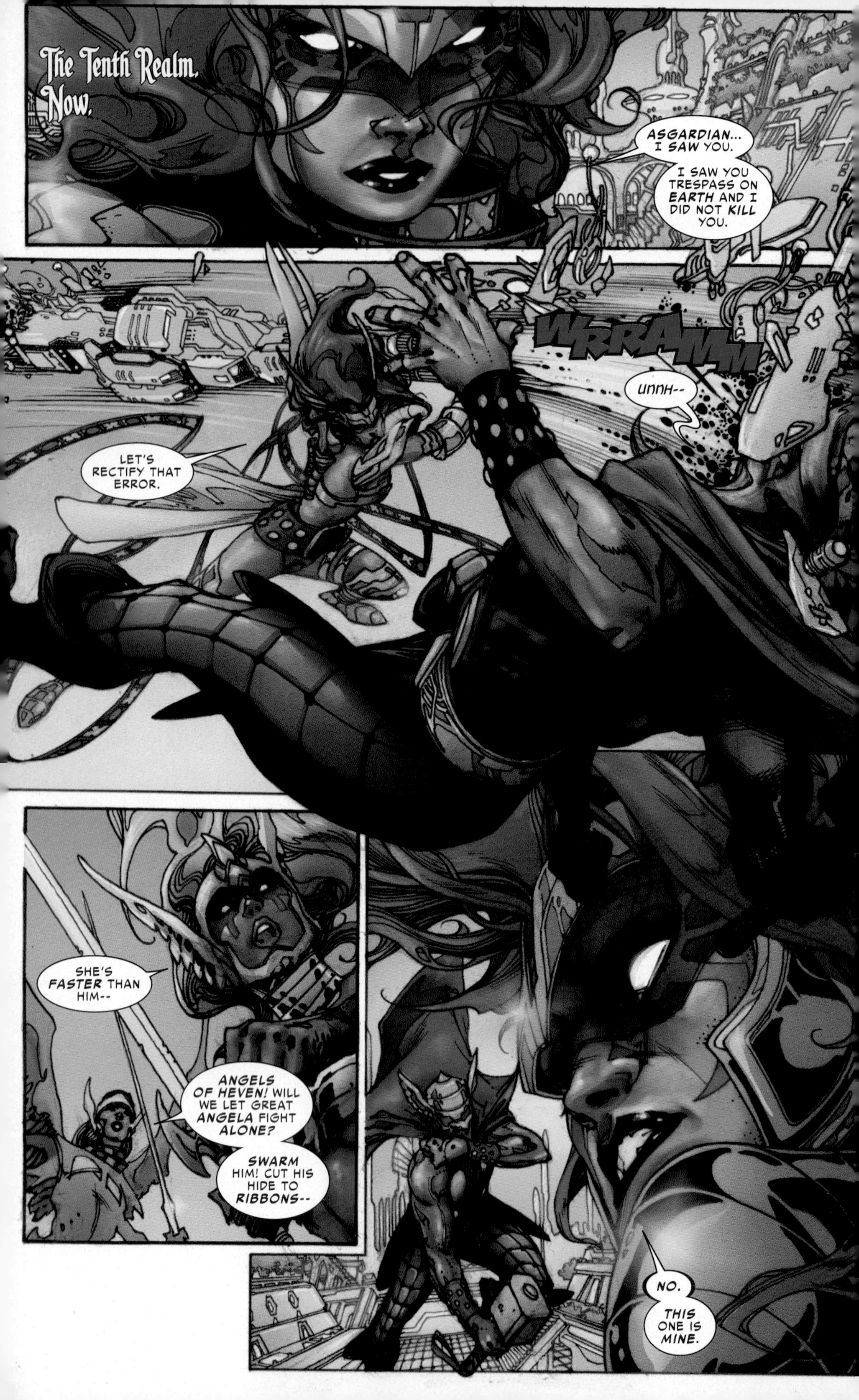
The Tenth Realm. Now.
ASGARDIAN... I SAW YOU.
I SAW YOU TRESPASS ON EARTH AND I DID NOT KILL YOU.
LET'S RECTIFY THAT ERROR.
WRRAMM
UNNH--
SHE'S FASTER THAN HIM--
ANGELS OF HEVEN! WILL WE LET GREAT ANGELA FIGHT ALONE?
SWARM HIM! CUT HIS HIDE TO RIBBONS--
NO.
THIS ONE IS MINE.

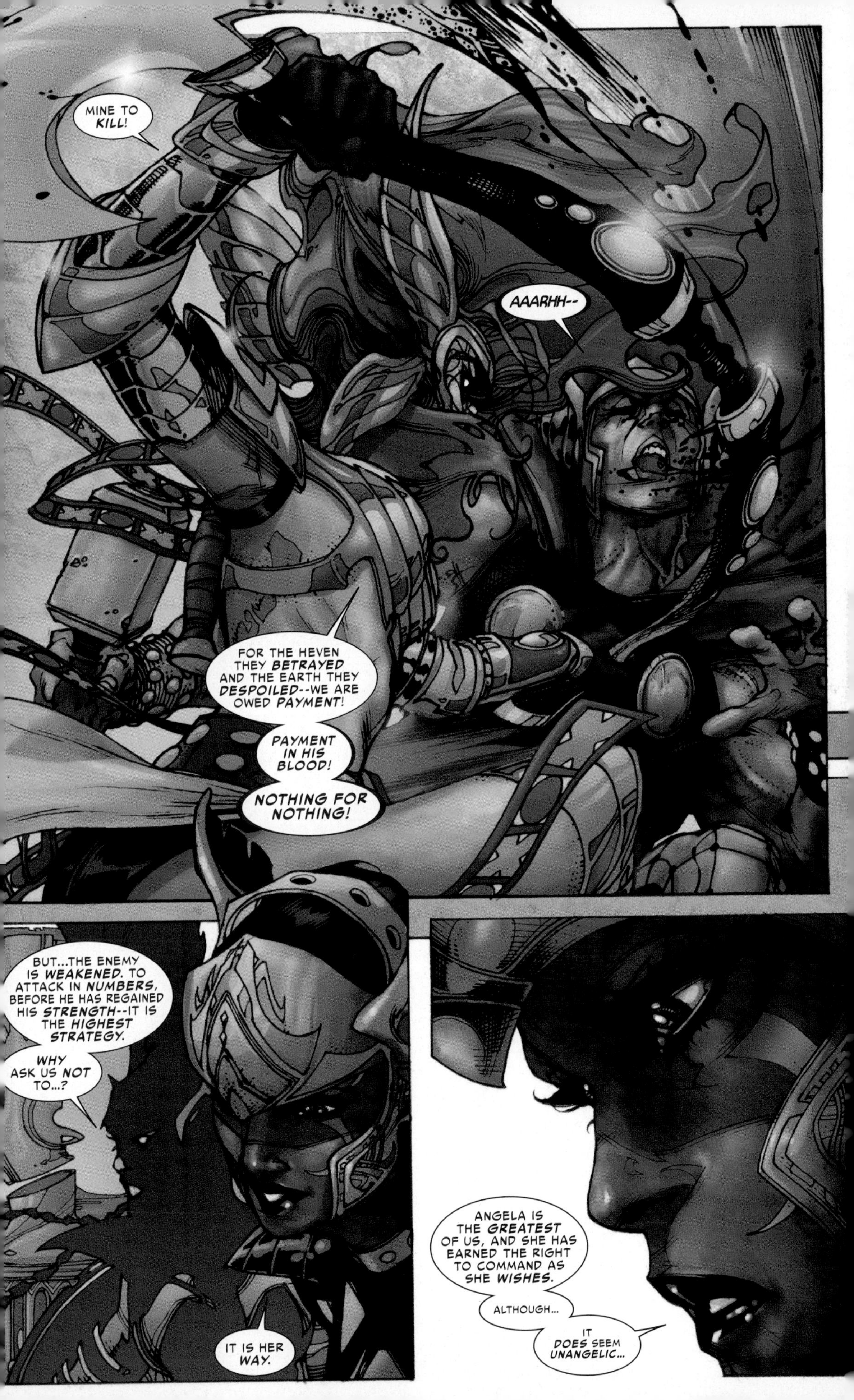
MINE TO KILL!
AAARHH--
FOR THE HEVEN THEY BETRAYED AND THE EARTH THEY DESPOILED--WE ARE OWED PAYMENT!
PAYMENT IN HIS BLOOD!
NOTHING FOR NOTHING!
BUT...THE ENEMY IS WEAKENED. TO ATTACK IN NUMBERS, BEFORE HE HAS REGAINED HIS STRENGTH--IT IS THE HIGHEST STRATEGY.
WHY ASK US NOT TO...?
IT IS HER WAY.
ANGELA IS THE GREATEST OF US, AND SHE HAS EARNED THE RIGHT TO COMMAND AS SHE WISHES.
ALTHOUGH...
IT DOES SEEM UNANGELIC...

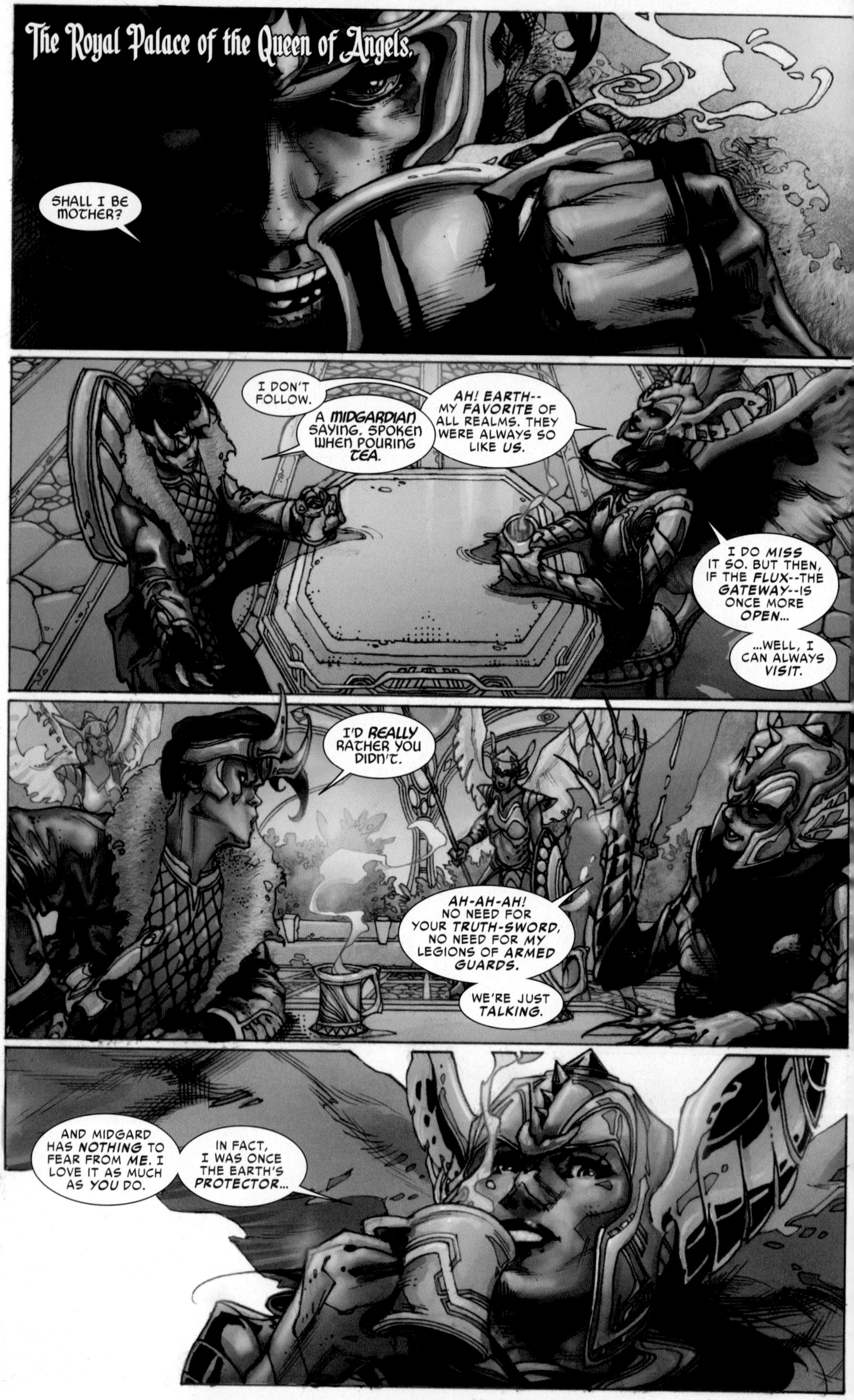
The Royal Palace of the Queen of Angels.
SHALL I BE MOTHER?
I DON'T FOLLOW.
A MIDGARDIAN SAYING. SPOKEN WHEN POURING TEA.
AH! EARTH-- MY FAVORITE OF ALL REALMS. THEY WERE ALWAYS SO LIKE US.
I DO MISS IT SO. BUT THEN, IF THE FLUX--THE GATEWAY--IS ONCE MORE OPEN...
...WELL, I CAN ALWAYS VISIT.
I'D REALLY RATHER YOU DIDN'T.
AH-AH-AH! NO NEED FOR YOUR TRUTH-SWORD, NO NEED FOR MY LEGIONS OF ARMED GUARDS.
WE'RE JUST TALKING.
AND MIDGARD HAS NOTHING TO FEAR FROM ME. I LOVE IT AS MUCH AS YOU DO.
IN FACT, I WAS ONCE THE EARTH'S PROTECTOR...

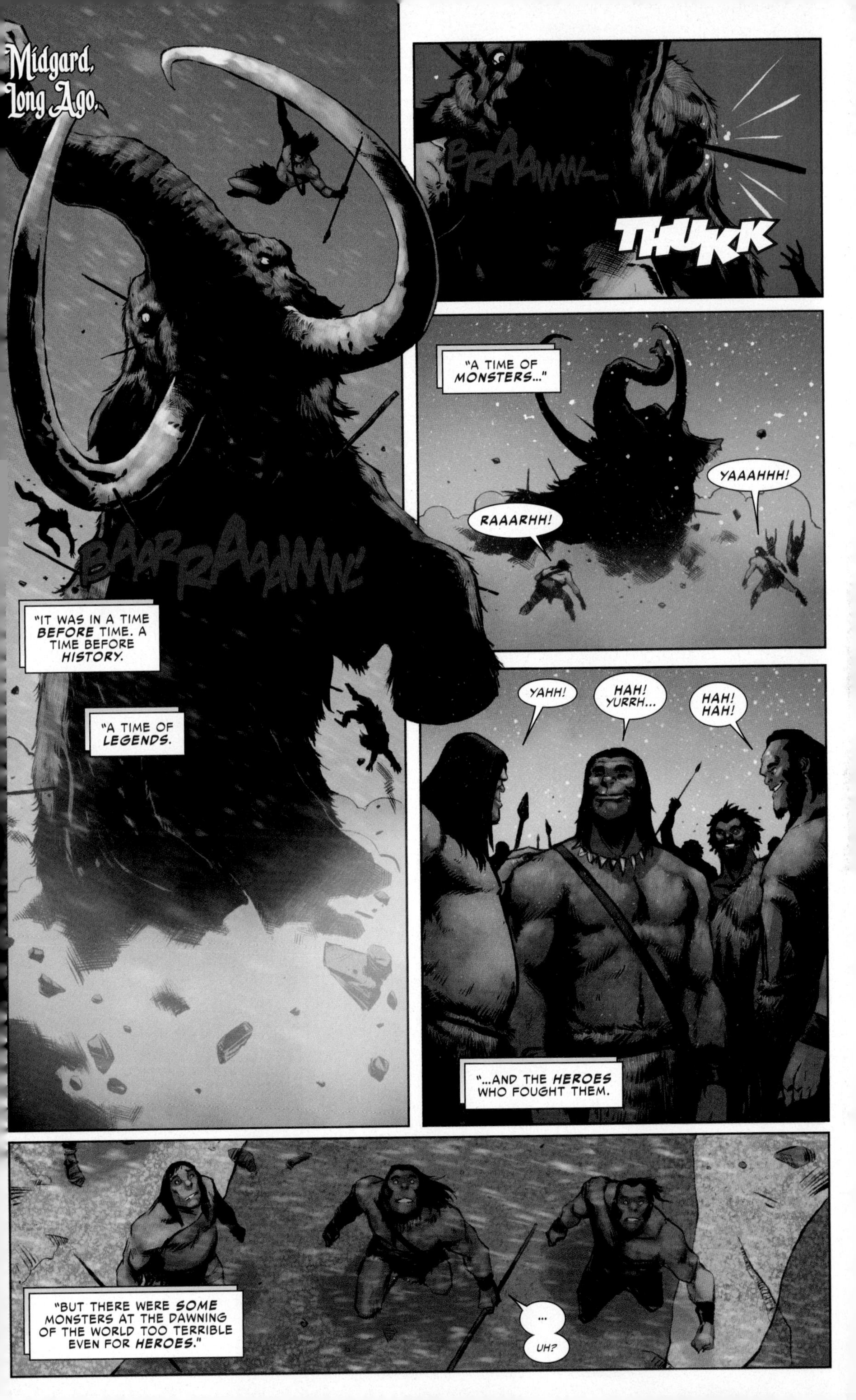
Midgard, Long Ago.
BAARRAAAWW!
"IT WAS IN A TIME BEFORE TIME. A TIME BEFORE HISTORY.
"A TIME OF LEGENDS.
BRAAWW...
THUKK
"A TIME OF MONSTERS..."
YAAAHHH!
RAAARHH!
YAHH!
HAH! YURRH...
HAH! HAH!
"...AND THE HEROES WHO FOUGHT THEM.
"BUT THERE WERE SOME MONSTERS AT THE DAWNING OF THE WORLD TOO TERRIBLE EVEN FOR HEROES."
...
UH?

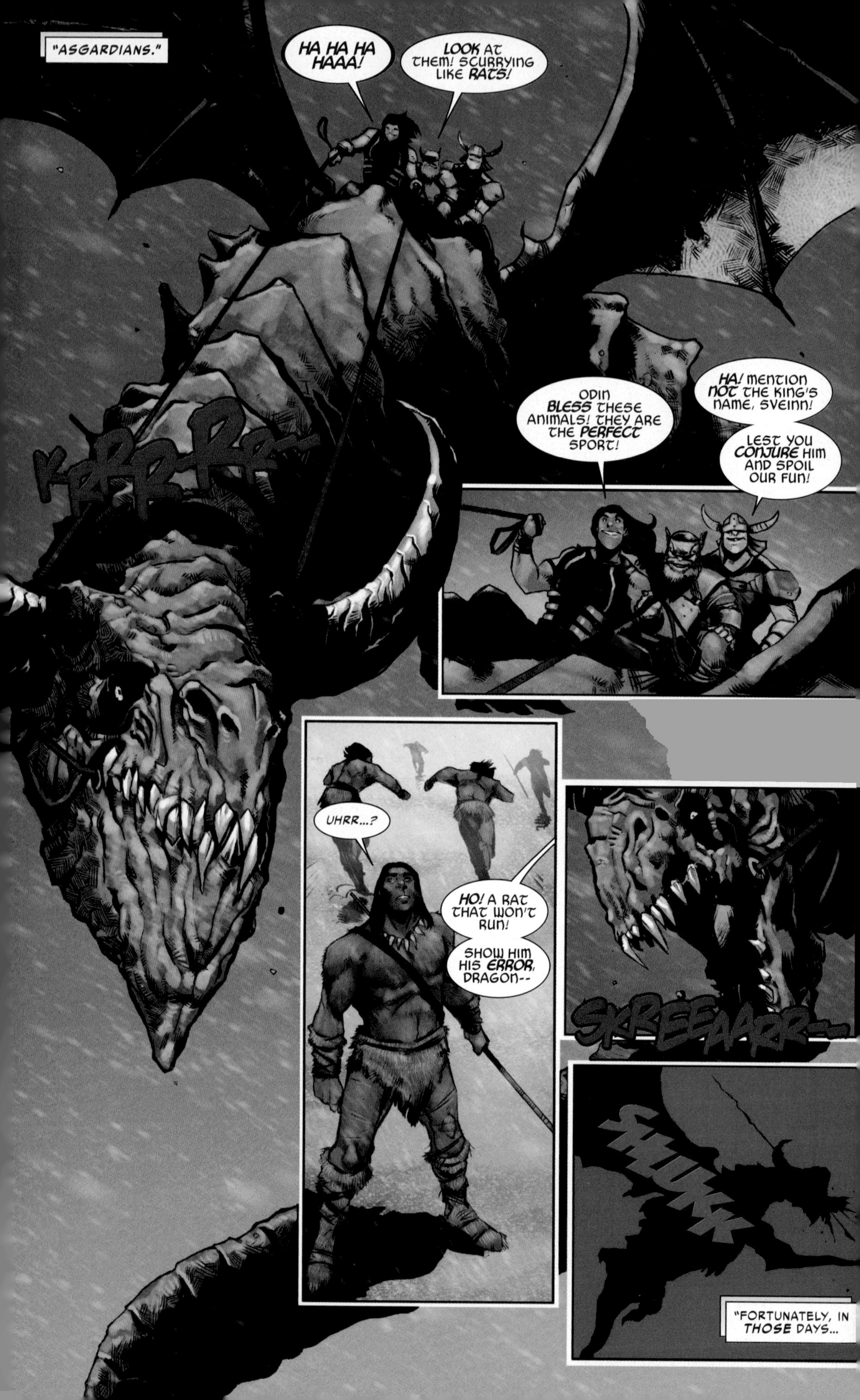
"ASGARDIANS."
HA HA HA HAAA!
LOOK AT THEM! SCURRYING LIKE RATS!
KRRR-RRR--
ODIN BLESS THESE ANIMALS! THEY ARE THE PERFECT SPORT!
HA! MENTION NOT THE KING'S NAME, SVEINN!
LEST YOU CONJURE HIM AND SPOIL OUR FUN!
UHRR...?
HO! A RAT THAT WON'T RUN!
SHOW HIM HIS ERROR, DRAGON--
SKREEAARR--
SHUKK
"FORTUNATELY, IN THOSE DAYS...

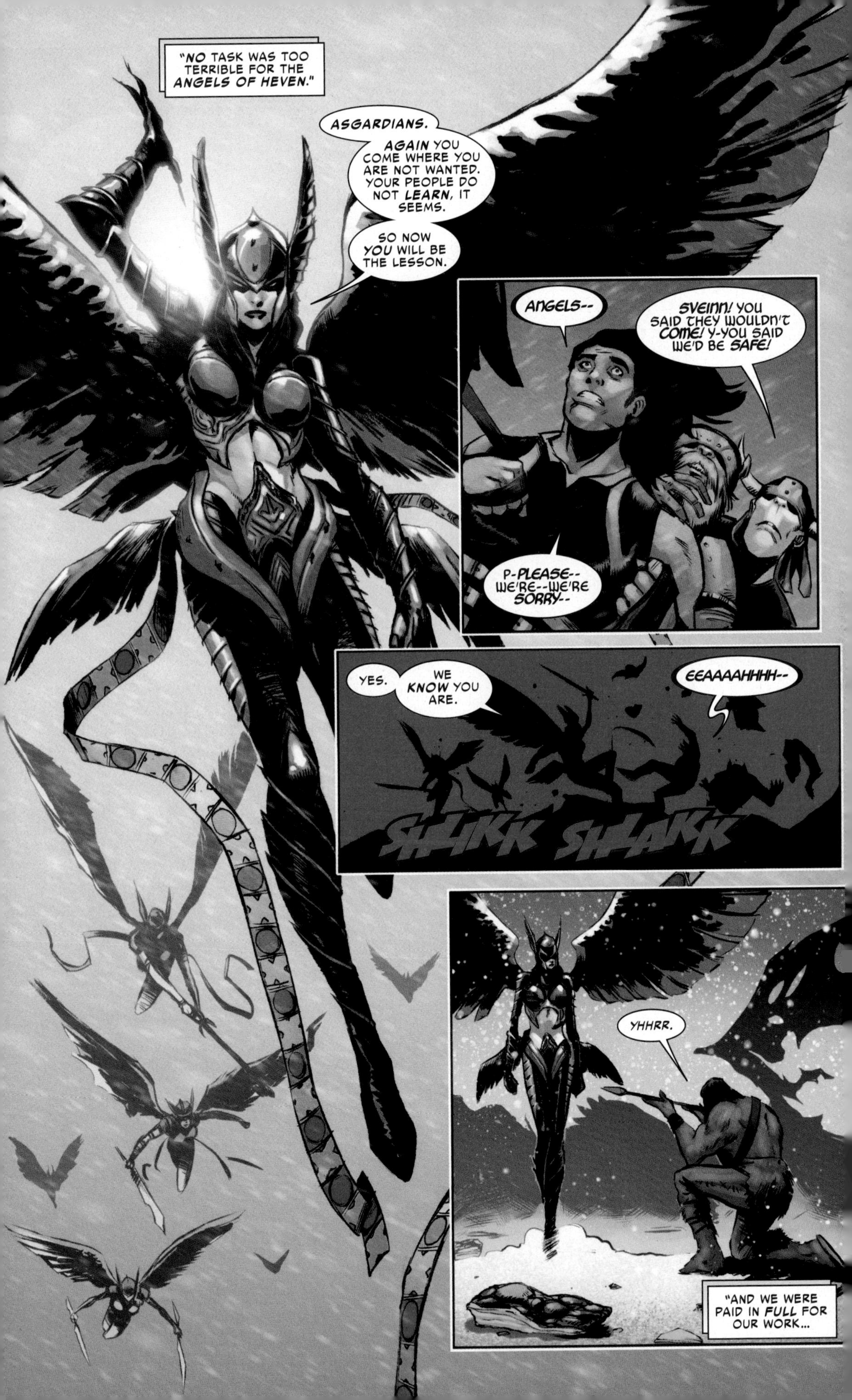
"NO TASK WAS TOO TERRIBLE FOR THE ANGELS OF HEVEN."
ASGARDIANS.
AGAIN YOU COME WHERE YOU ARE NOT WANTED. YOUR PEOPLE DO NOT LEARN, IT SEEMS.
SO NOW YOU WILL BE THE LESSON.
ANGELS--
SVEINN! YOU SAID THEY WOULDN'T COME! Y-YOU SAID WE'D BE SAFE!
P-PLEASE-- WE'RE--WE'RE SORRY--
YES.
WE KNOW YOU ARE.
EEAAAAHHHH--
SHLIKK SHLAKK
YHHRR.
"AND WE WERE PAID IN FULL FOR OUR WORK...

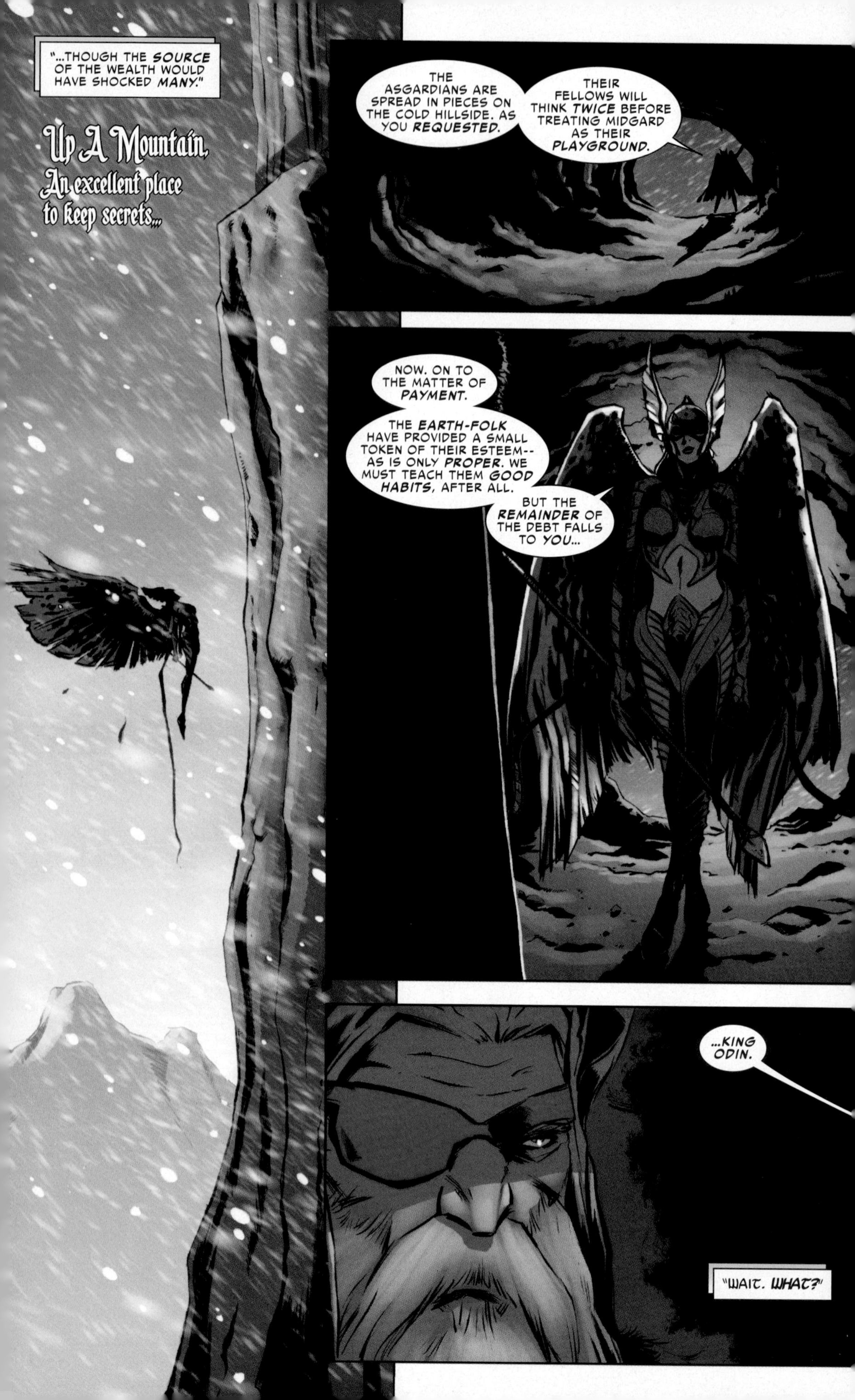
"...THOUGH THE SOURCE OF THE WEALTH WOULD HAVE SHOCKED MANY."
Up A Mountain, An excellent place to keep secrets...
THE ASGARDIANS ARE SPREAD IN PIECES ON THE COLD HILLSIDE. AS YOU REQUESTED.
THEIR FELLOWS WILL THINK TWICE BEFORE TREATING MIDGARD AS THEIR PLAYGROUND.
NOW. ON TO THE MATTER OF PAYMENT.
THE EARTH-FOLK HAVE PROVIDED A SMALL TOKEN OF THEIR ESTEEM-- AS IS ONLY PROPER. WE MUST TEACH THEM GOOD HABITS, AFTER ALL.
BUT THE REMAINDER OF THE DEBT FALLS TO YOU...
...KING ODIN.
"WAIT. WHAT?"

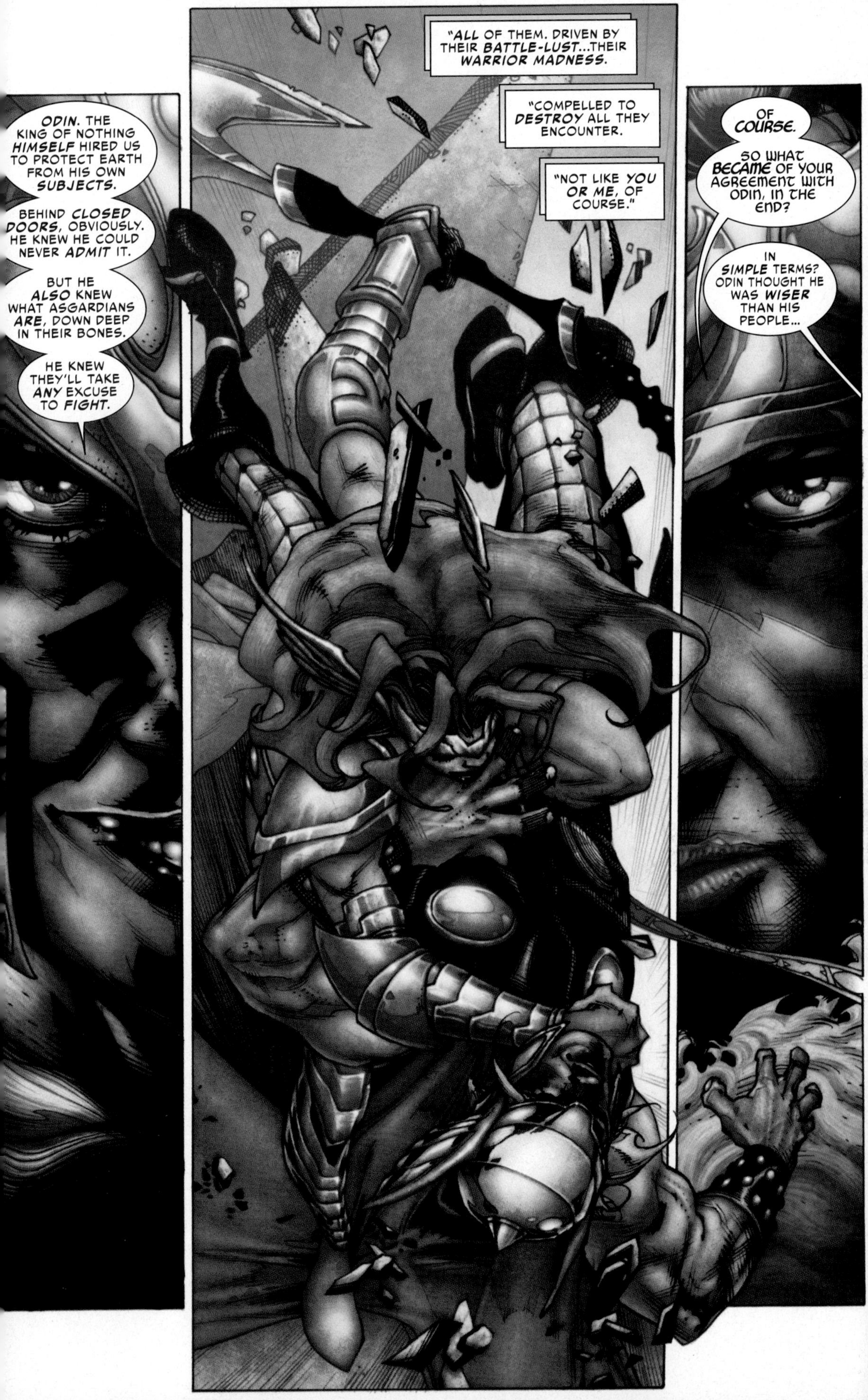
ODIN. THE KING OF NOTHING HIMSELF HIRED US TO PROTECT EARTH FROM HIS OWN SUBJECTS.
BEHIND CLOSED DOORS, OBVIOUSLY. HE KNEW HE COULD NEVER ADMIT IT.
BUT HE ALSO KNEW WHAT ASGARDIANS ARE, DOWN DEEP IN THEIR BONES.
HE KNEW THEY'LL TAKE ANY EXCUSE TO FIGHT.
"ALL OF THEM. DRIVEN BY THEIR BATTLE-LUST...THEIR WARRIOR MADNESS.
"COMPELLED TO DESTROY ALL THEY ENCOUNTER.
"NOT LIKE YOU OR ME, OF COURSE."
OF COURSE.
SO WHAT BECAME OF YOUR AGREEMENT WITH ODIN, IN THE END?
IN SIMPLE TERMS? ODIN THOUGHT HE WAS WISER THAN HIS PEOPLE...

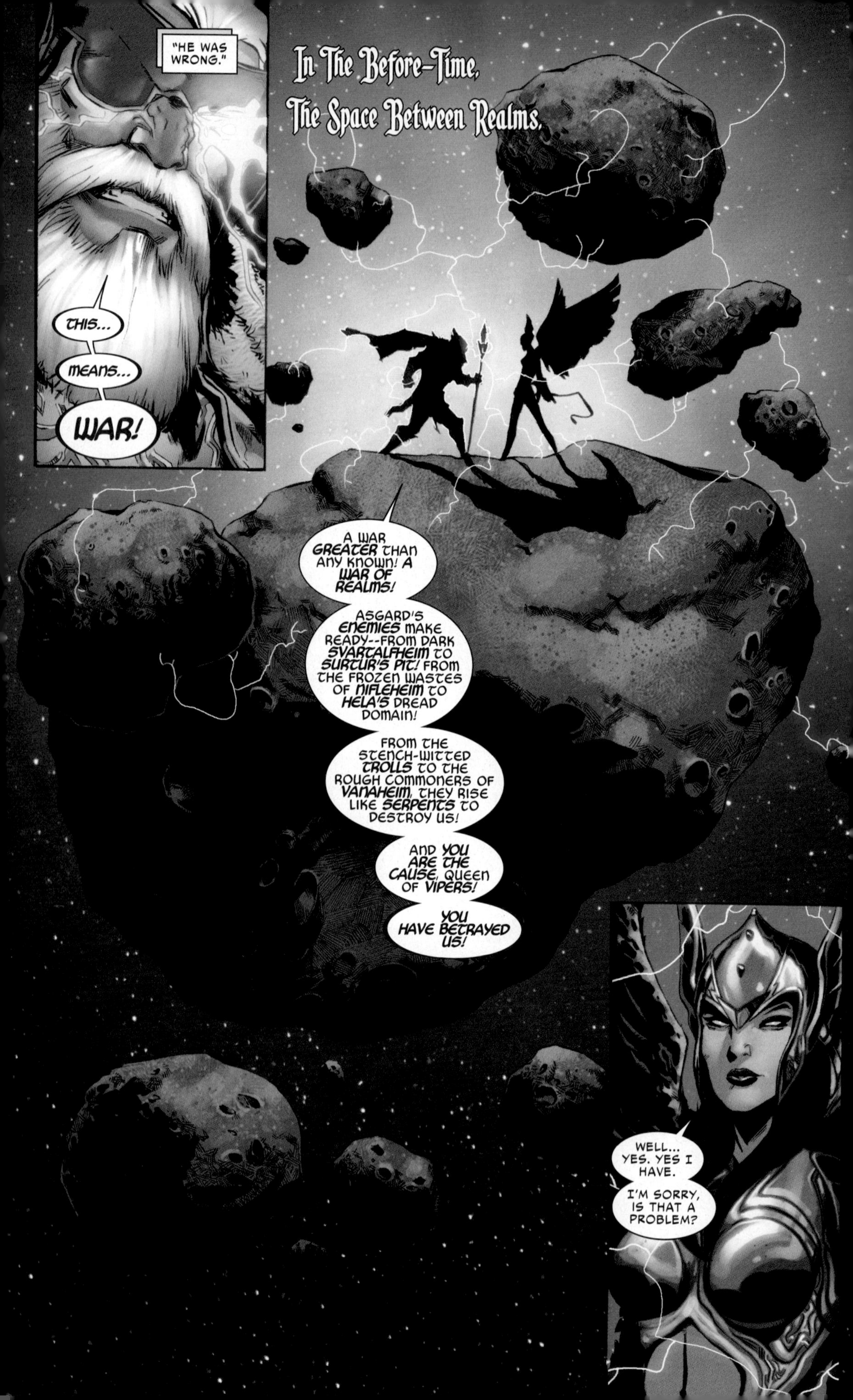
"HE WAS WRONG."
THIS...
MEANS...
WAR!
In The Before-Time, The Space Between Realms.
A WAR GREATER THAN ANY KNOWN! A WAR OF REALMS!
ASGARD'S ENEMIES MAKE READY--FROM DARK SVARTALFHEIM TO SURTUR'S PIT! FROM THE FROZEN WASTES OF NIFLEHEIM TO HELA'S DREAD DOMAIN!
FROM THE STENCH-WITTED TROLLS TO THE ROUGH COMMONERS OF VANAHEIM, THEY RISE LIKE SERPENTS TO DESTROY US!
AND YOU ARE THE CAUSE, QUEEN OF VIPERS!
YOU HAVE BETRAYED US!
WELL... YES. YES I HAVE.
I'M SORRY, IS THAT A PROBLEM?

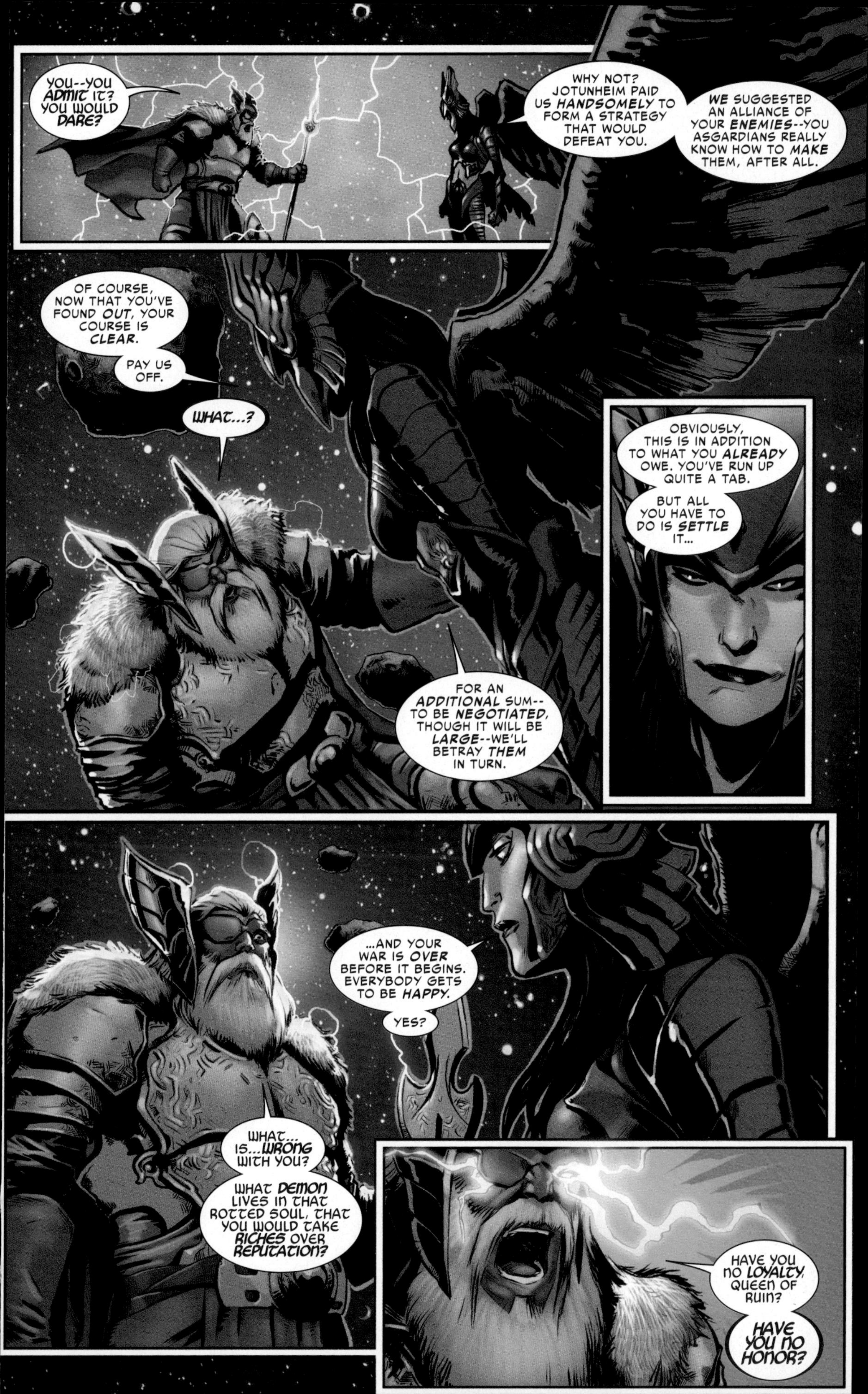
YOU--YOU ADMIT IT? YOU WOULD DARE?
WHY NOT? JOTUNHEIM PAID US HANDSOMELY TO FORM A STRATEGY THAT WOULD DEFEAT YOU.
WE SUGGESTED AN ALLIANCE OF YOUR ENEMIES--YOU ASGARDIANS REALLY KNOW HOW TO MAKE THEM, AFTER ALL.
OF COURSE, NOW THAT YOU'VE FOUND OUT, YOUR COURSE IS CLEAR.
PAY US OFF.
WHAT...?
OBVIOUSLY, THIS IS IN ADDITION TO WHAT YOU ALREADY OWE. YOU'VE RUN UP QUITE A TAB.
BUT ALL YOU HAVE TO DO IS SETTLE IT...
FOR AN ADDITIONAL SUM--TO BE NEGOTIATED, THOUGH IT WILL BE LARGE--WE'LL BETRAY THEM IN TURN.
...AND YOUR WAR IS OVER BEFORE IT BEGINS. EVERYBODY GETS TO BE HAPPY.
YES?
WHAT... IS...WRONG WITH YOU?
WHAT DEMON LIVES IN THAT ROTTED SOUL, THAT YOU WOULD TAKE RICHES OVER REPUTATION?
HAVE YOU NO LOYALTY, QUEEN OF RUIN?
HAVE YOU NO HONOR?

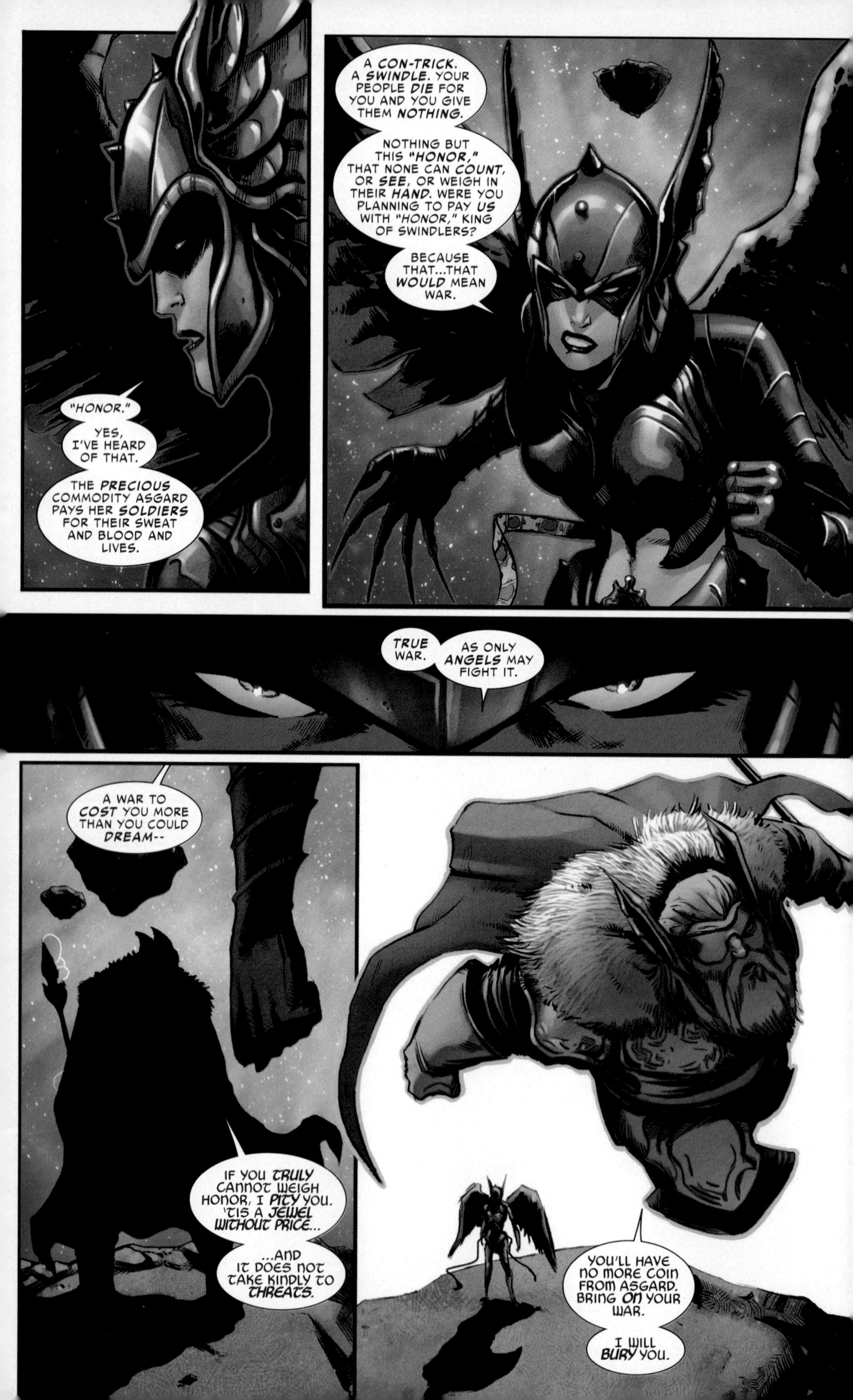

"HONOR."
YES, I'VE HEARD OF THAT.
THE PRECIOUS COMMODITY ASGARD PAYS HER SOLDIERS FOR THEIR SWEAT AND BLOOD AND LIVES.
A CON-TRICK. A SWINDLE. YOUR PEOPLE DIE FOR YOU AND YOU GIVE THEM NOTHING.
NOTHING BUT THIS "HONOR," THAT NONE CAN COUNT, OR SEE, OR WEIGH IN THEIR HAND. WERE YOU PLANNING TO PAY US WITH "HONOR," KING OF SWINDLERS?
BECAUSE THAT...THAT WOULD MEAN WAR.
TRUE WAR.
AS ONLY ANGELS MAY FIGHT IT.
A WAR TO COST YOU MORE THAN YOU COULD DREAM--
IF YOU TRULY CANNOT WEIGH HONOR, I PITY YOU. 'TIS A JEWEL WITHOUT PRICE...
...AND IT DOES NOT TAKE KINDLY TO THREATS.
YOU'LL HAVE NO MORE COIN FROM ASGARD. BRING ON YOUR WAR.
I WILL BURY YOU.

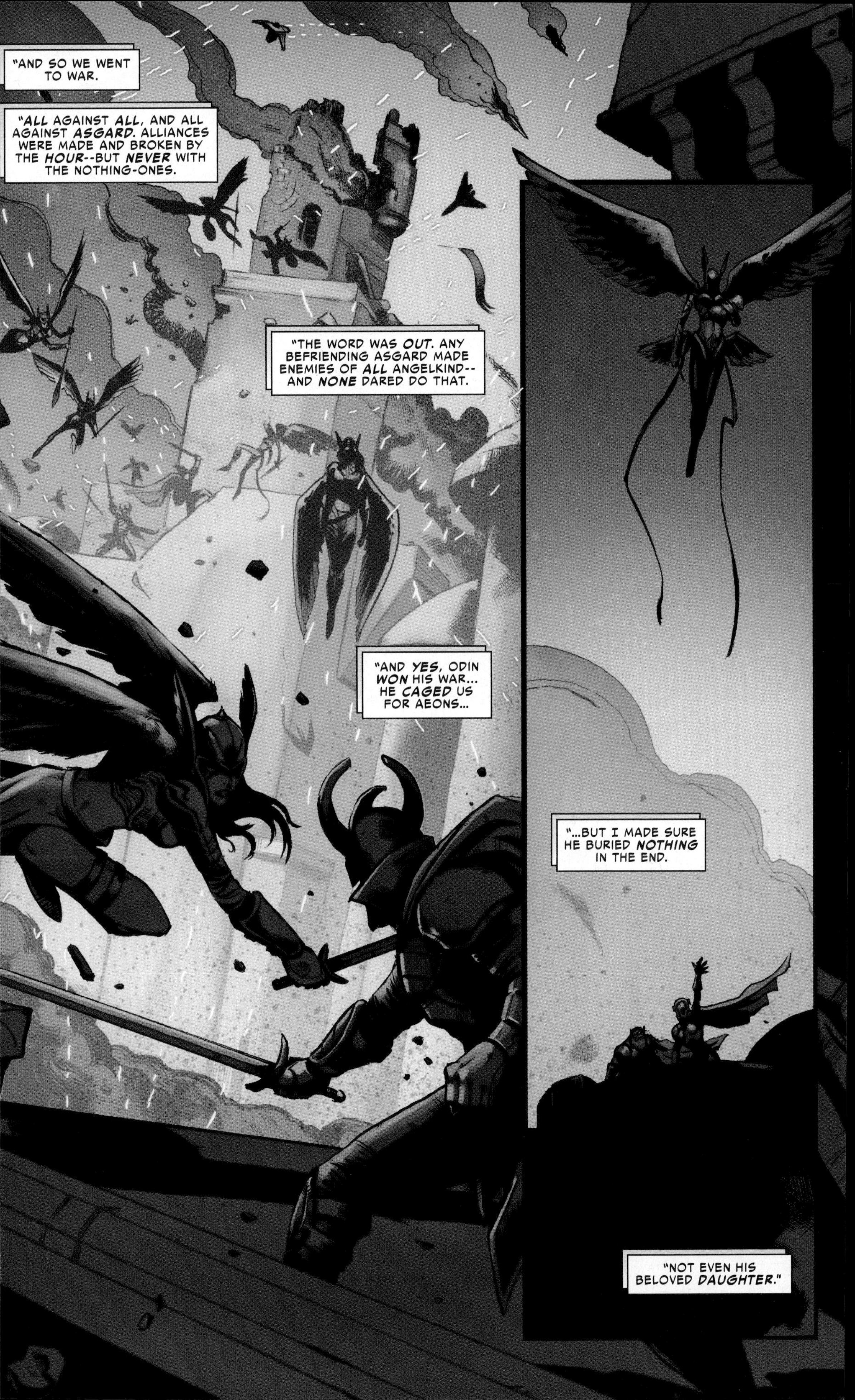
"AND SO WE WENT TO WAR.
"ALL AGAINST ALL, AND ALL AGAINST ASGARD. ALLIANCES WERE MADE AND BROKEN BY THE HOUR--BUT NEVER WITH THE NOTHING-ONES.
"THE WORD WAS OUT. ANY BEFRIENDING ASGARD MADE ENEMIES OF ALL ANGELKIND--AND NONE DARED DO THAT.
"AND YES, ODIN WON HIS WAR... HE CAGED US FOR AEONS...
"...BUT I MADE SURE HE BURIED NOTHING IN THE END.
"NOT EVEN HIS BELOVED DAUGHTER."

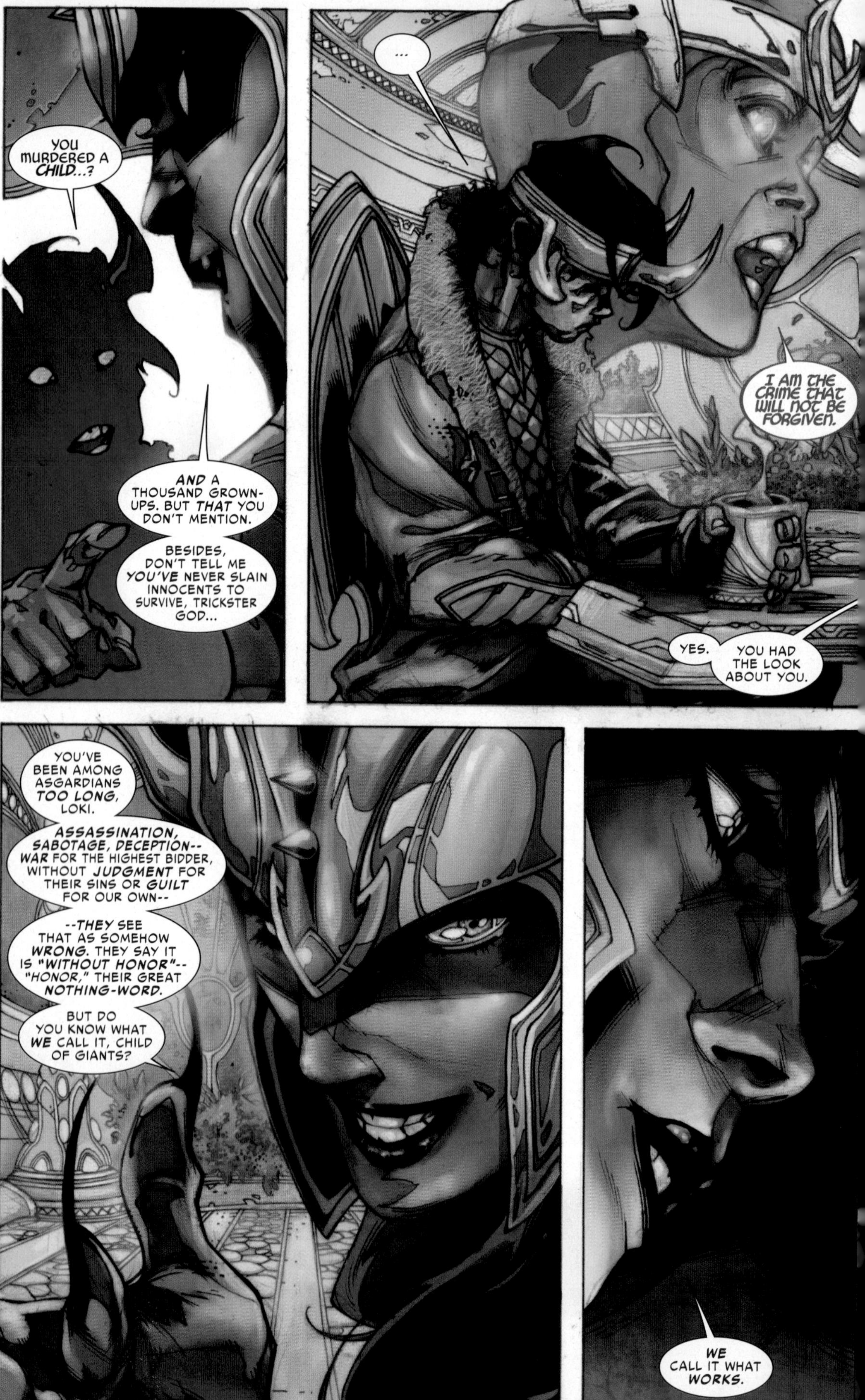
YOU MURDERED A CHILD...?
AND A THOUSAND GROWN-UPS. BUT THAT YOU DON'T MENTION.
BESIDES, DON'T TELL ME YOU'VE NEVER SLAIN INNOCENTS TO SURVIVE, TRICKSTER GOD...
...
I AM THE CRIME THAT WILL NOT BE FORGIVEN.
YES.
YOU HAD THE LOOK ABOUT YOU.
YOU'VE BEEN AMONG ASGARDIANS TOO LONG, LOKI.
ASSASSINATION, SABOTAGE, DECEPTION--WAR FOR THE HIGHEST BIDDER, WITHOUT JUDGMENT FOR THEIR SINS OR GUILT FOR OUR OWN--
--THEY SEE THAT AS SOMEHOW WRONG. THEY SAY IT IS "WITHOUT HONOR"--"HONOR," THEIR GREAT NOTHING-WORD.
BUT DO YOU KNOW WHAT WE CALL IT, CHILD OF GIANTS?
WE CALL IT WHAT WORKS.

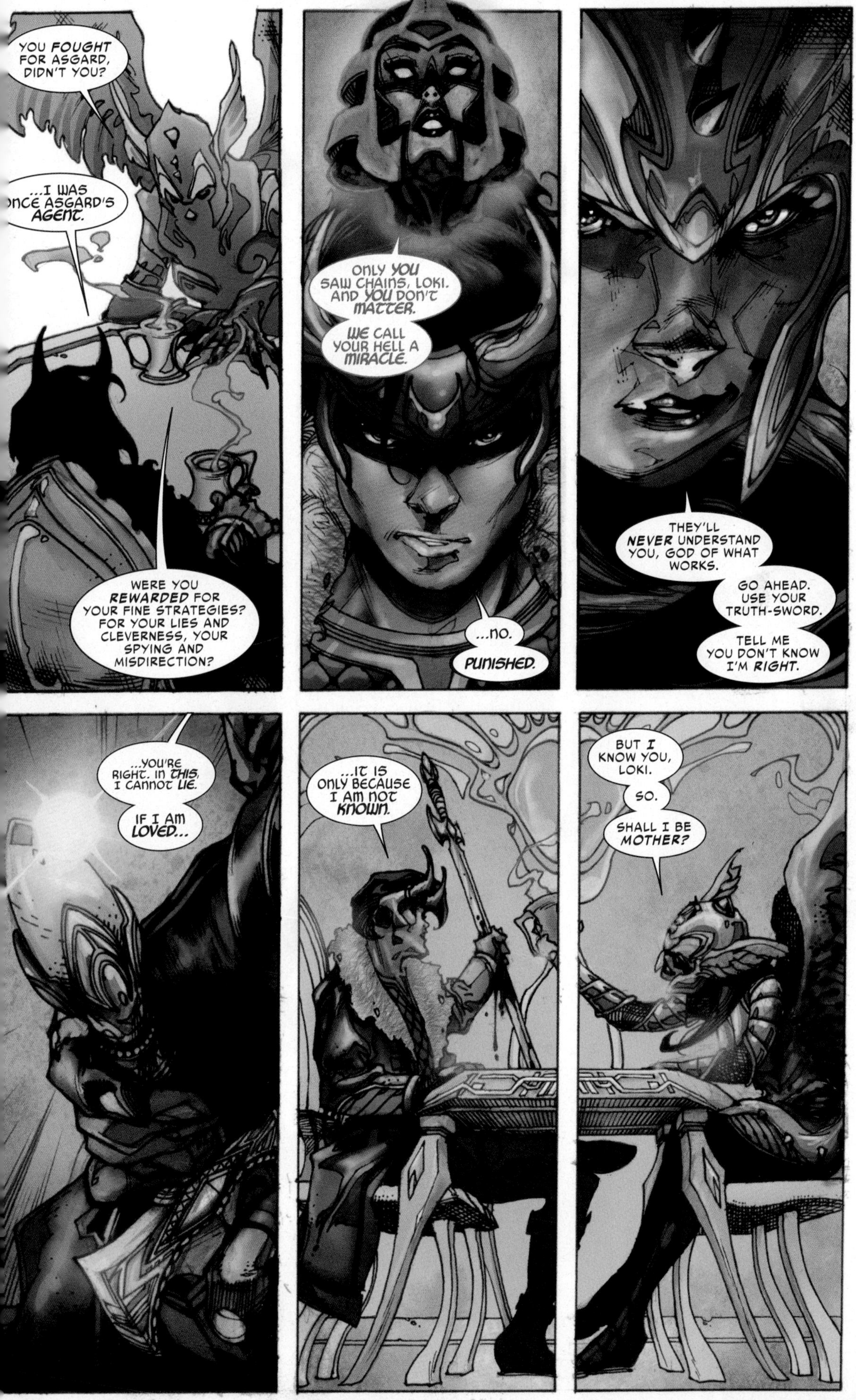
YOU FOUGHT FOR ASGARD, DIDN'T YOU?
...I WAS ONCE ASGARD'S AGENT.
WERE YOU REWARDED FOR YOUR FINE STRATEGIES? FOR YOUR LIES AND CLEVERNESS, YOUR SPYING AND MISDIRECTION?
ONLY YOU SAW CHAINS, LOKI. AND YOU DON'T MATTER.
WE CALL YOUR HELL A MIRACLE.
...NO.
PUNISHED.
THEY'LL NEVER UNDERSTAND YOU, GOD OF WHAT WORKS.
GO AHEAD. USE YOUR TRUTH-SWORD.
TELL ME YOU DON'T KNOW I'M RIGHT.
...YOU'RE RIGHT. IN THIS, I CANNOT LIE.
IF I AM LOVED...
...IT IS ONLY BECAUSE I AM NOT KNOWN.
BUT I KNOW YOU, LOKI.
SO.
SHALL I BE MOTHER?

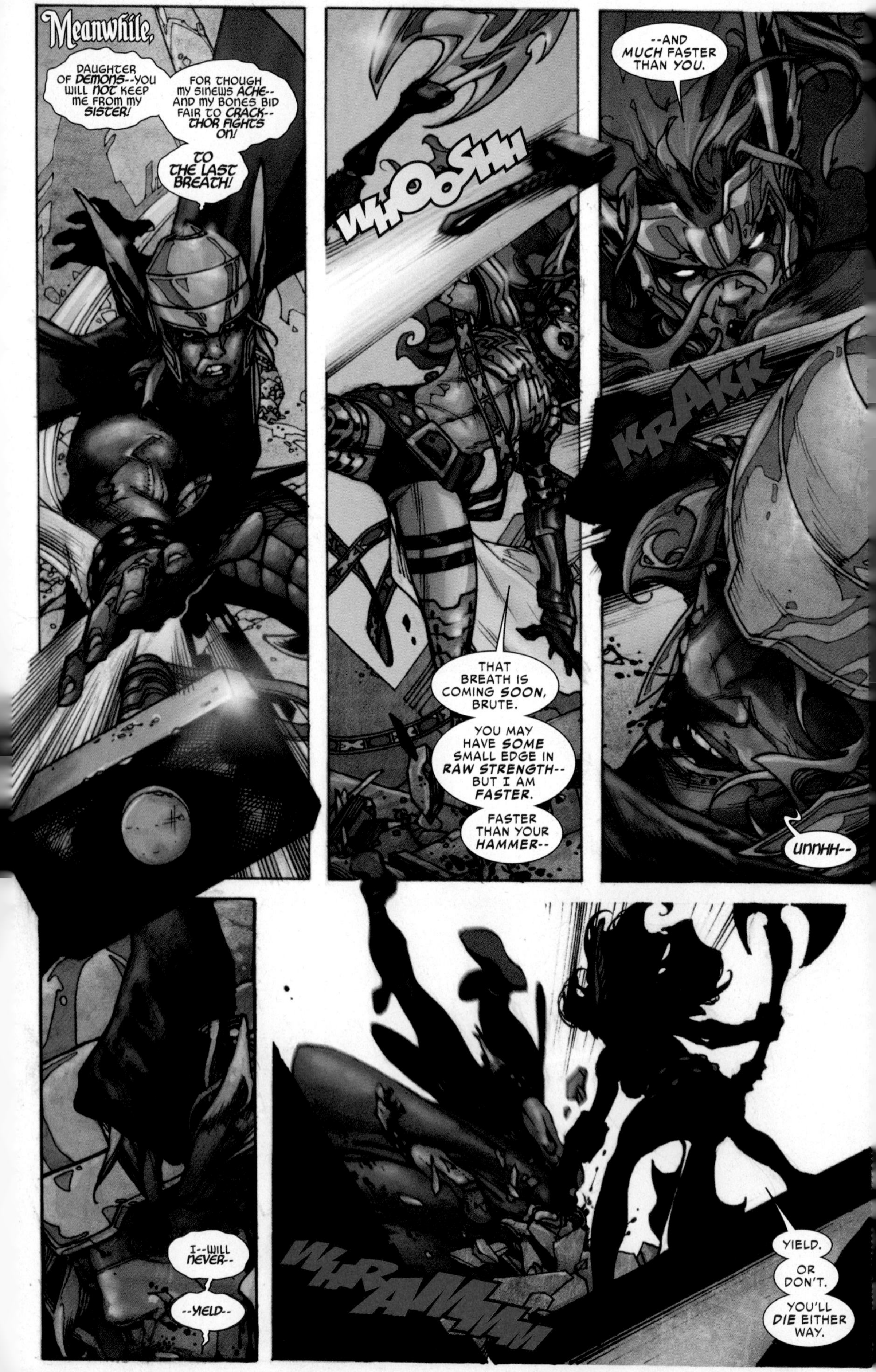
Meanwhile,
DAUGHTER OF DEMONS--YOU WILL NOT KEEP ME FROM MY SISTER!
FOR THOUGH MY SINEWS ACHE--AND MY BONES BID FAIR TO CRACK--THOR FIGHTS ON!
TO THE LAST BREATH!
WHOOSHH
THAT BREATH IS COMING SOON, BRUTE.
YOU MAY HAVE SOME SMALL EDGE IN RAW STRENGTH--BUT I AM FASTER.
FASTER THAN YOUR HAMMER--
--AND MUCH FASTER THAN YOU.
KRAKK
UNNHH--
I--WILL NEVER--
--YIELD--
WHRAMMM
YIELD.
OR DON'T.
YOU'LL DIE EITHER WAY.

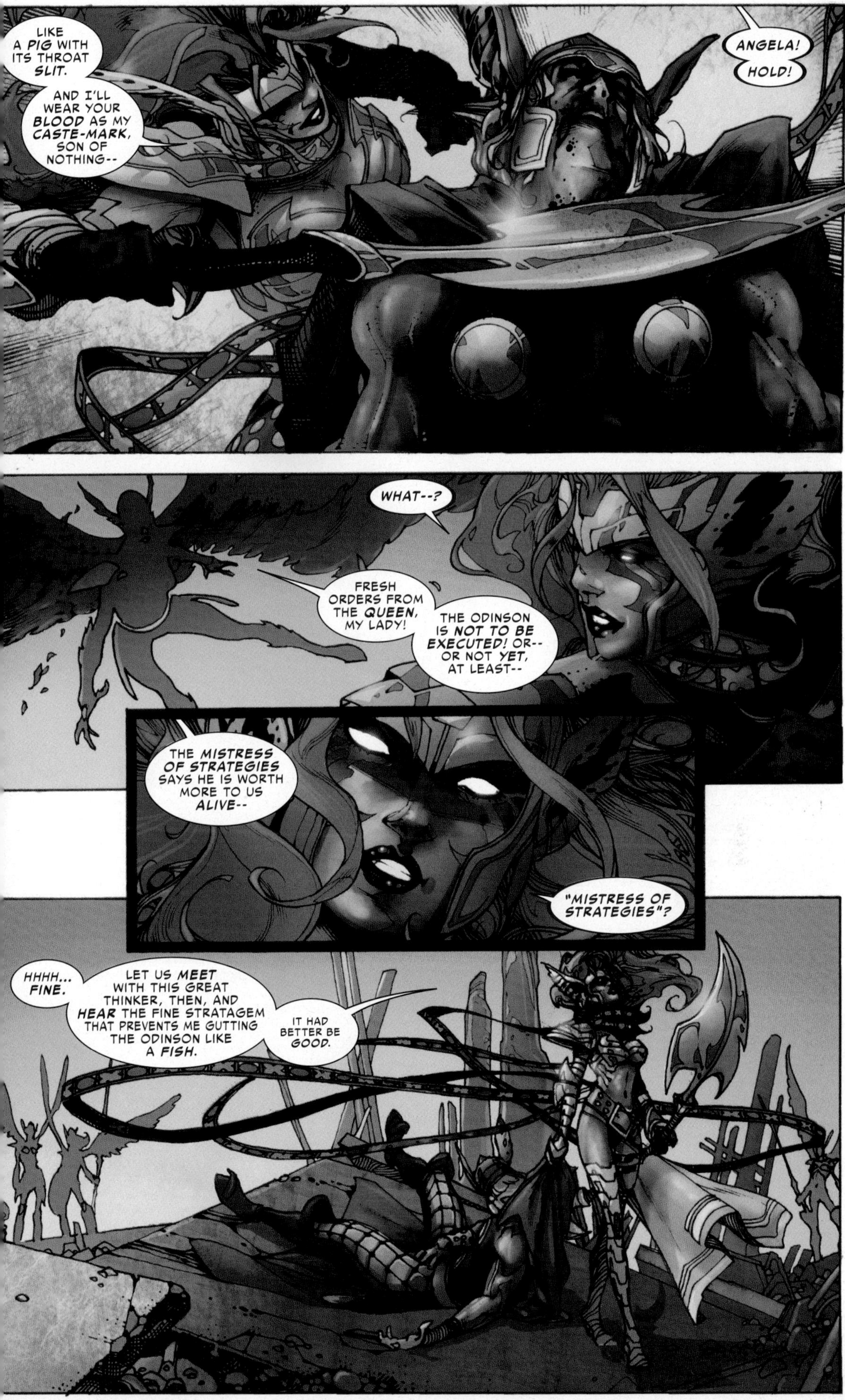
LIKE A PIG WITH ITS THROAT SLIT.
AND I'LL WEAR YOUR BLOOD AS MY CASTE-MARK, SON OF NOTHING--
ANGELA! HOLD!
WHAT--?
FRESH ORDERS FROM THE QUEEN, MY LADY!
THE ODINSON IS NOT TO BE EXECUTED! OR-- OR NOT YET, AT LEAST--
THE MISTRESS OF STRATEGIES SAYS HE IS WORTH MORE TO US ALIVE--
"MISTRESS OF STRATEGIES"?
HHHH... FINE.
LET US MEET WITH THIS GREAT THINKER, THEN, AND HEAR THE FINE STRATAGEM THAT PREVENTS ME GUTTING THE ODINSON LIKE A FISH.
IT HAD BETTER BE GOOD.

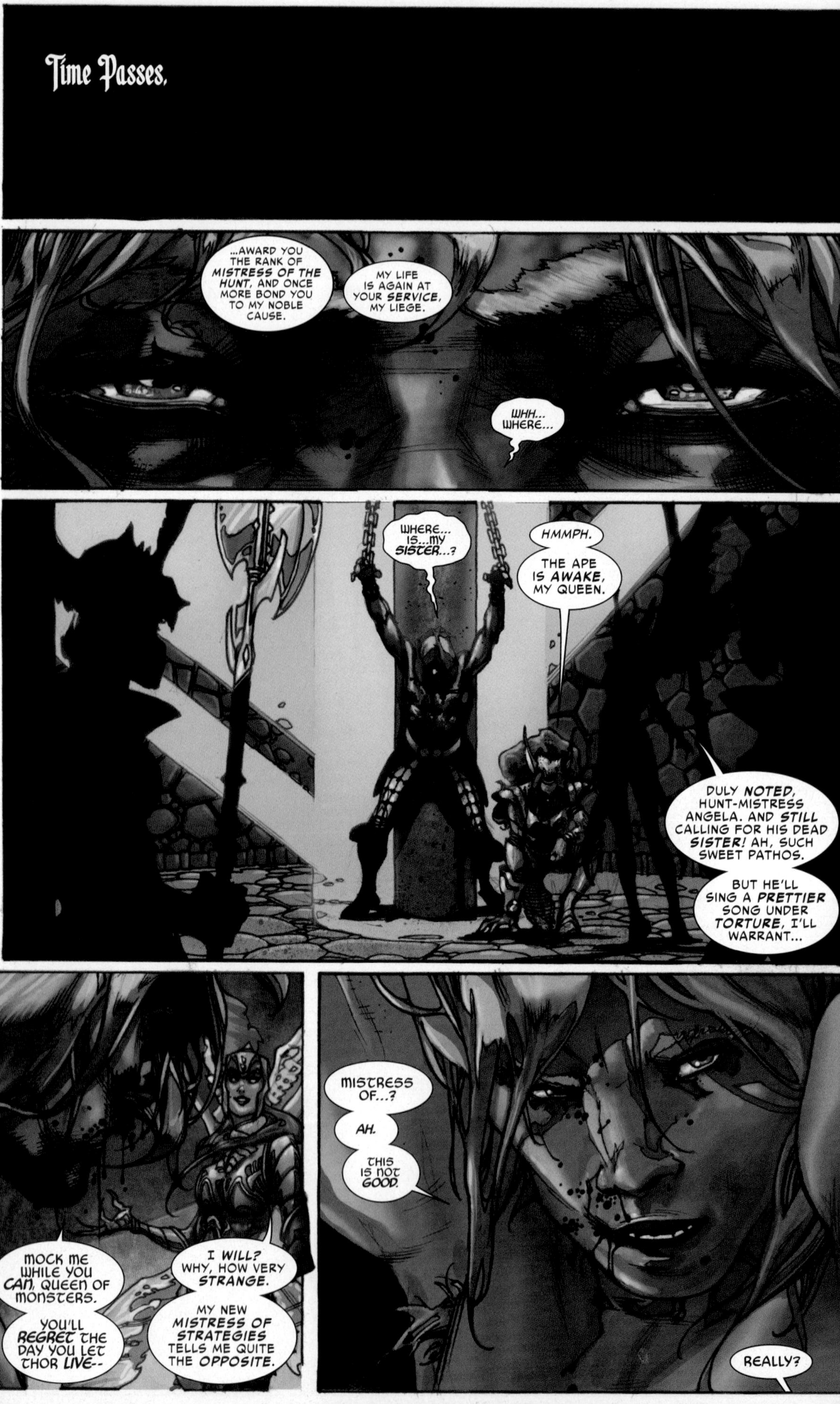
Time Passes.
...AWARD YOU THE RANK OF MISTRESS OF THE HUNT, AND ONCE MORE BOND YOU TO MY NOBLE CAUSE.
MY LIFE IS AGAIN AT YOUR SERVICE, MY LIEGE.
WHH... WHERE...
WHERE... IS...MY SISTER...?
HMMPH.
THE APE IS AWAKE, MY QUEEN.
DULY NOTED, HUNT-MISTRESS ANGELA. AND STILL CALLING FOR HIS DEAD SISTER! AH, SUCH SWEET PATHOS.
BUT HE'LL SING A PRETTIER SONG UNDER TORTURE, I'LL WARRANT...
MOCK ME WHILE YOU CAN, QUEEN OF MONSTERS.
YOU'LL REGRET THE DAY YOU LET THOR LIVE--
I WILL? WHY, HOW VERY STRANGE.
MY NEW MISTRESS OF STRATEGIES TELLS ME QUITE THE OPPOSITE.
MISTRESS OF...?
AH.
THIS IS NOT GOOD.
REALLY?

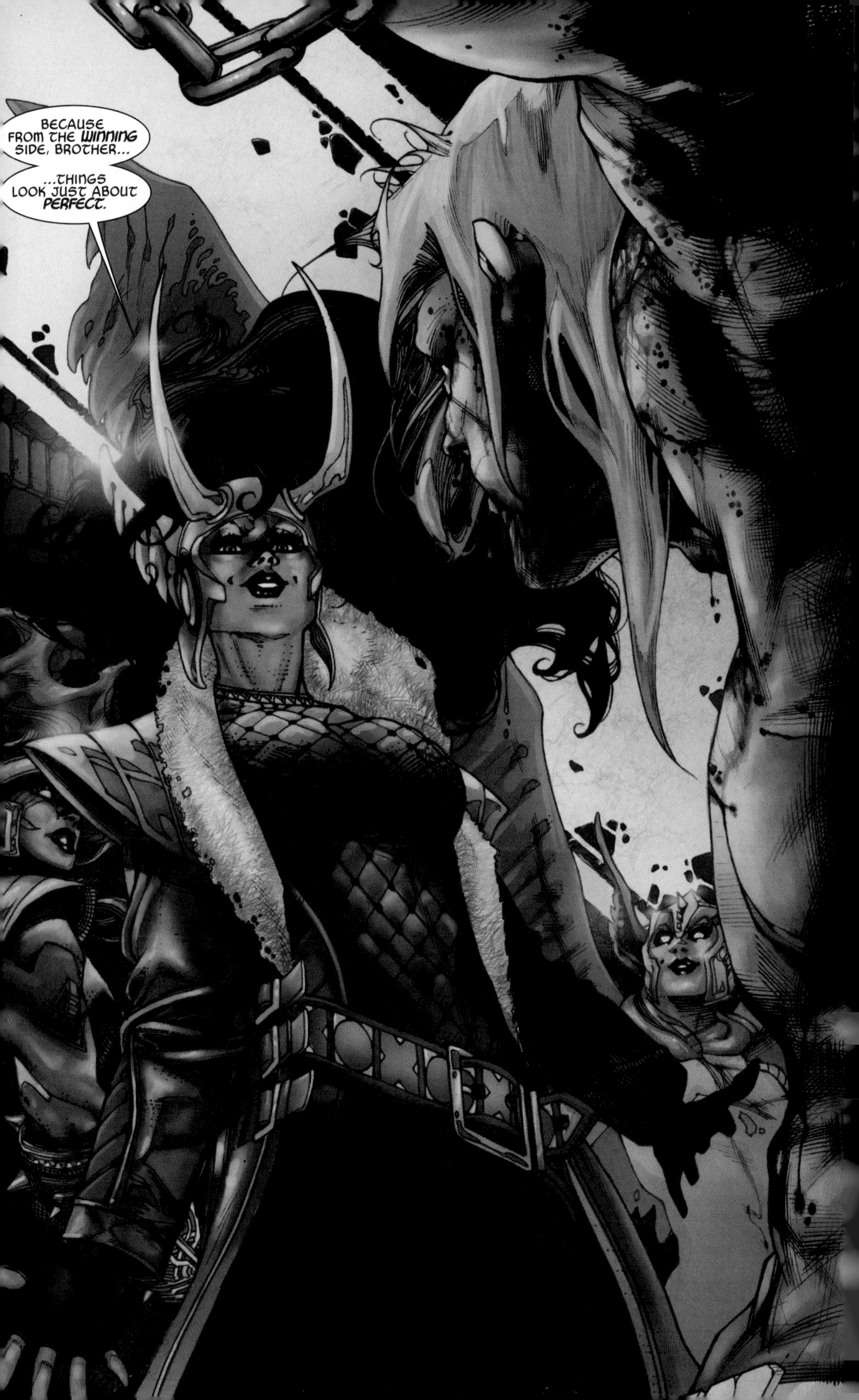
BECAUSE FROM THE WINNING SIDE, BROTHER...
...THINGS LOOK JUST ABOUT PERFECT.

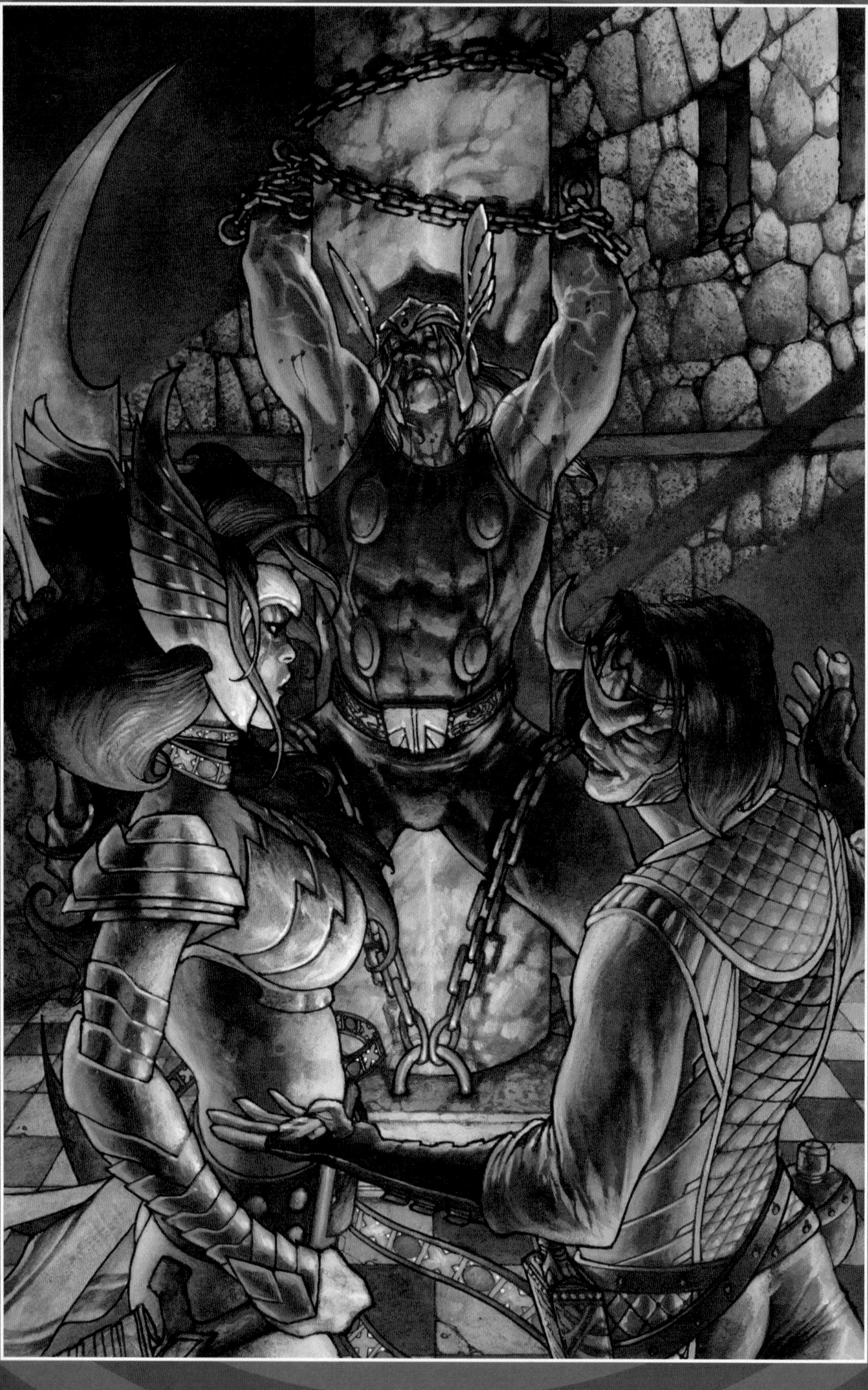

ORIGINAL SIN #5.4

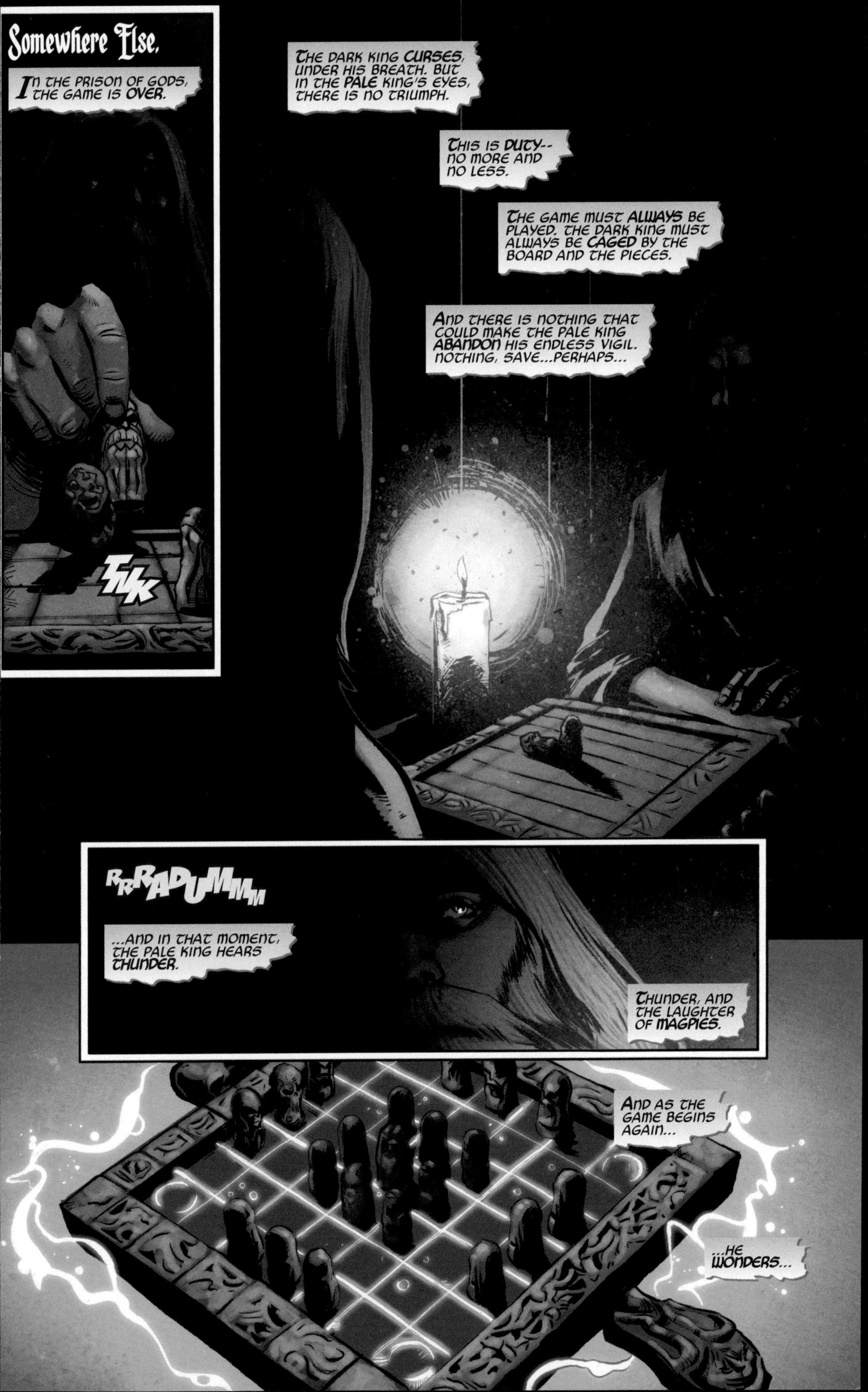
Somewhere Else.
IN THE PRISON OF GODS, THE GAME IS OVER.
THE DARK KING CURSES, UNDER HIS BREATH. BUT IN THE PALE KING'S EYES, THERE IS NO TRIUMPH.
THIS IS DUTY-- NO MORE AND NO LESS.
THE GAME MUST ALWAYS BE PLAYED. THE DARK KING MUST ALWAYS BE CAGED BY THE BOARD AND THE PIECES.
AND THERE IS NOTHING THAT COULD MAKE THE PALE KING ABANDON HIS ENDLESS VIGIL. NOTHING, SAVE...PERHAPS...
TNK
RRRADUMMM
...AND IN THAT MOMENT, THE PALE KING HEARS THUNDER.
THUNDER, AND THE LAUGHTER OF MAGPIES.
AND AS THE GAME BEGINS AGAIN...
...HE WONDERS...

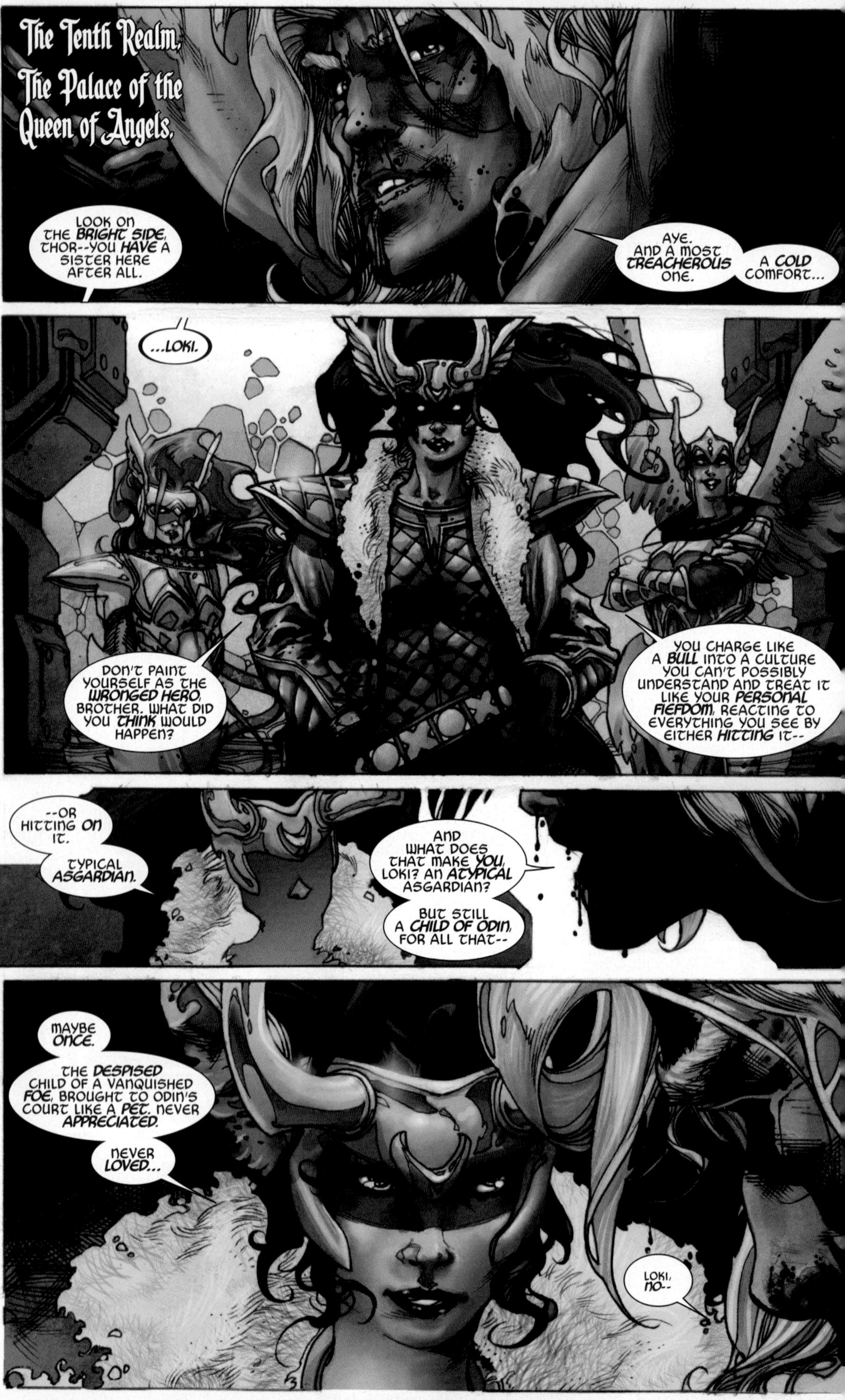

The Tenth Realm, The Palace of the Queen of Angels,
LOOK ON THE BRIGHT SIDE, THOR--YOU HAVE A SISTER HERE AFTER ALL.
AYE. AND A MOST TREACHEROUS ONE.
A COLD COMFORT...
...LOKI.
DON'T PAINT YOURSELF AS THE WRONGED HERO, BROTHER. WHAT DID YOU THINK WOULD HAPPEN?
YOU CHARGE LIKE A BULL INTO A CULTURE YOU CAN'T POSSIBLY UNDERSTAND AND TREAT IT LIKE YOUR PERSONAL FIEFDOM, REACTING TO EVERYTHING YOU SEE BY EITHER HITTING IT--
--OR HITTING ON IT.
TYPICAL ASGARDIAN.
AND WHAT DOES THAT MAKE YOU, LOKI? AN ATYPICAL ASGARDIAN?
BUT STILL A CHILD OF ODIN, FOR ALL THAT--
MAYBE ONCE.
THE DESPISED CHILD OF A VANQUISHED FOE, BROUGHT TO ODIN'S COURT LIKE A PET. NEVER APPRECIATED.
NEVER LOVED...
LOKI, NO--

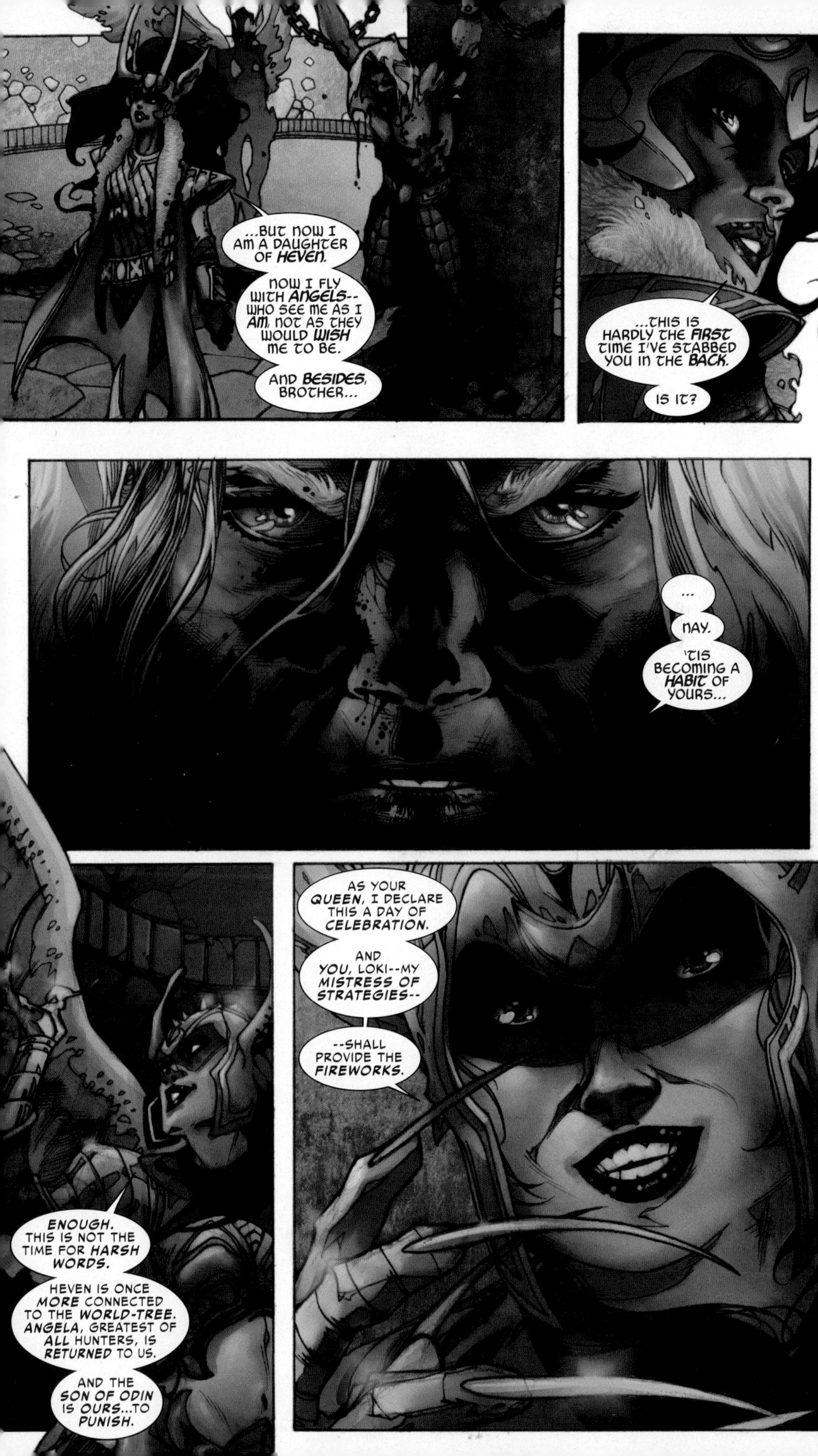
...BUT NOW I AM A DAUGHTER OF HEVEN.
NOW I FLY WITH ANGELS-- WHO SEE ME AS I AM, NOT AS THEY WOULD WISH ME TO BE.
AND BESIDES, BROTHER...
...THIS IS HARDLY THE FIRST TIME I'VE STABBED YOU IN THE BACK.
IS IT?
...
NAY.
'TIS BECOMING A HABIT OF YOURS...
ENOUGH. THIS IS NOT THE TIME FOR HARSH WORDS.
HEVEN IS ONCE MORE CONNECTED TO THE WORLD-TREE. ANGELA, GREATEST OF ALL HUNTERS, IS RETURNED TO US.
AND THE SON OF ODIN IS OURS...TO PUNISH.
AS YOUR QUEEN, I DECLARE THIS A DAY OF CELEBRATION.
AND YOU, LOKI--MY MISTRESS OF STRATEGIES--
--SHALL PROVIDE THE FIREWORKS.

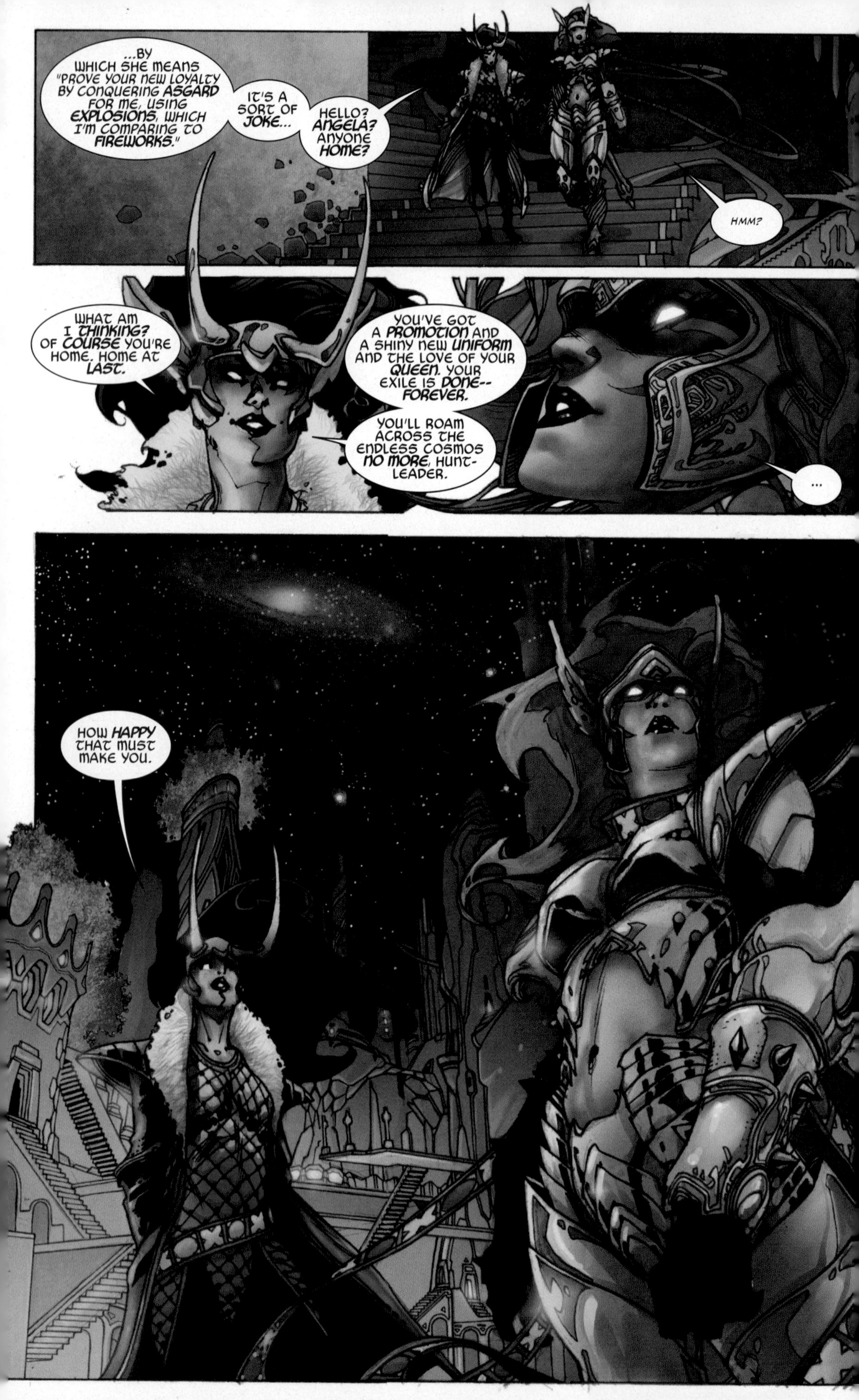

...BY WHICH SHE MEANS "PROVE YOUR NEW LOYALTY BY CONQUERING ASGARD FOR ME, USING EXPLOSIONS, WHICH I'M COMPARING TO FIREWORKS."
IT'S A SORT OF JOKE...
HELLO? ANGELA? ANYONE HOME?
HMM?
WHAT AM I THINKING? OF COURSE YOU'RE HOME. HOME AT LAST.
YOU'VE GOT A PROMOTION AND A SHINY NEW UNIFORM AND THE LOVE OF YOUR QUEEN. YOUR EXILE IS DONE-- FOREVER.
YOU'LL ROAM ACROSS THE ENDLESS COSMOS NO MORE, HUNT-LEADER.
...
HOW HAPPY THAT MUST MAKE YOU.

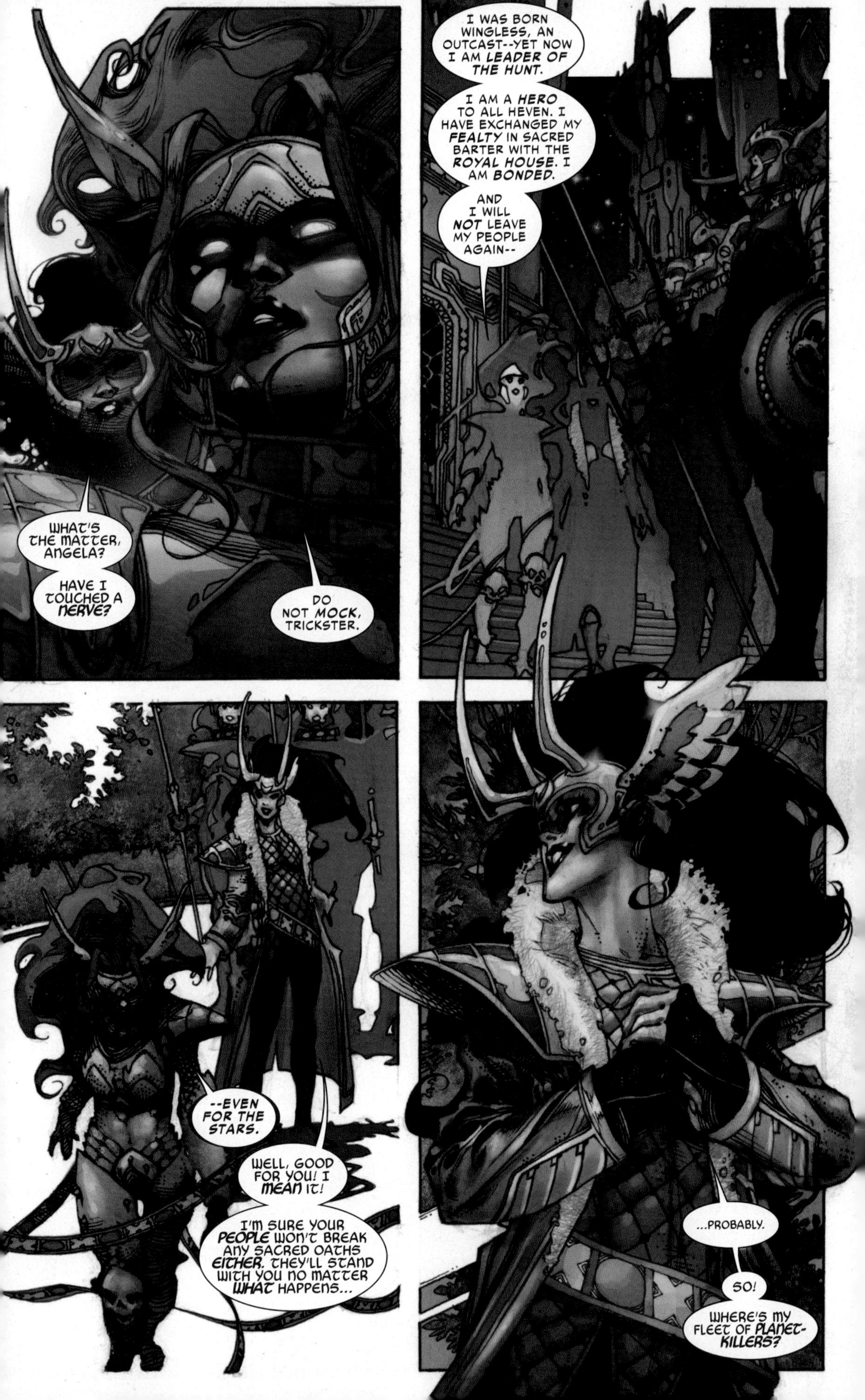
I WAS BORN WINGLESS, AN OUTCAST--YET NOW I AM LEADER OF THE HUNT.
I AM A HERO TO ALL HEVEN. I HAVE EXCHANGED MY FEALTY IN SACRED BARTER WITH THE ROYAL HOUSE. I AM BONDED.
AND I WILL NOT LEAVE MY PEOPLE AGAIN--
WHAT'S THE MATTER, ANGELA?
HAVE I TOUCHED A NERVE?
DO NOT MOCK, TRICKSTER.
--EVEN FOR THE STARS.
WELL, GOOD FOR YOU! I MEAN IT!
I'M SURE YOUR PEOPLE WON'T BREAK ANY SACRED OATHS EITHER. THEY'LL STAND WITH YOU NO MATTER WHAT HAPPENS...
...PROBABLY.
SO!
WHERE'S MY FLEET OF PLANET-KILLERS?

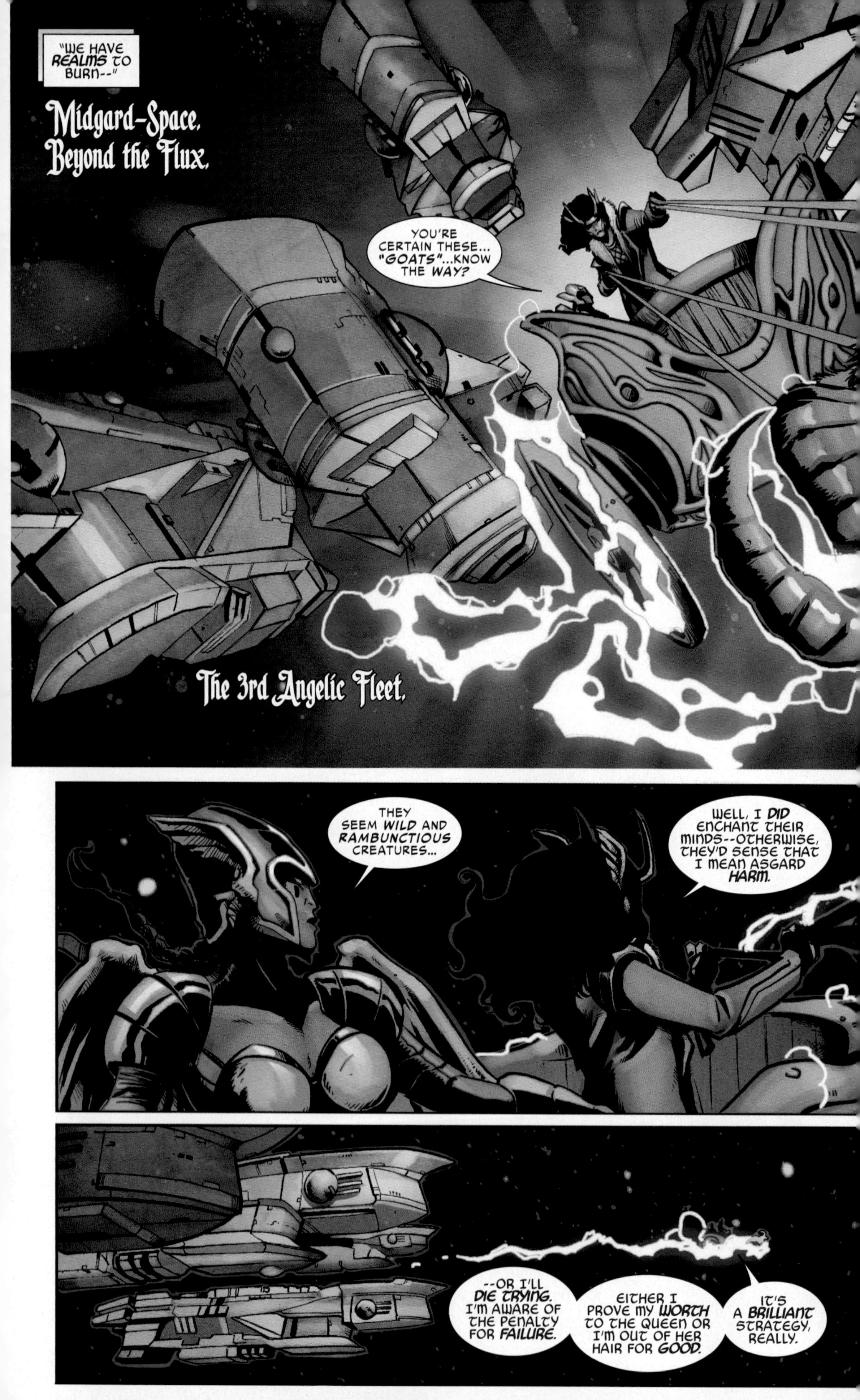
"WE HAVE REALMS TO BURN--"
Midgard-Space. Beyond the Flux.
YOU'RE CERTAIN THESE... "GOATS"...KNOW THE WAY?
The 3rd Angelic Fleet.
THEY SEEM WILD AND RAMBUNCTIOUS CREATURES...
WELL, I DID ENCHANT THEIR MINDS--OTHERWISE, THEY'D SENSE THAT I MEAN ASGARD HARM.
IT'S A BRILLIANT STRATEGY, REALLY.
EITHER I PROVE MY WORTH TO THE QUEEN OR I'M OUT OF HER HAIR FOR GOOD.
--OR I'LL DIE TRYING. I'M AWARE OF THE PENALTY FOR FAILURE.

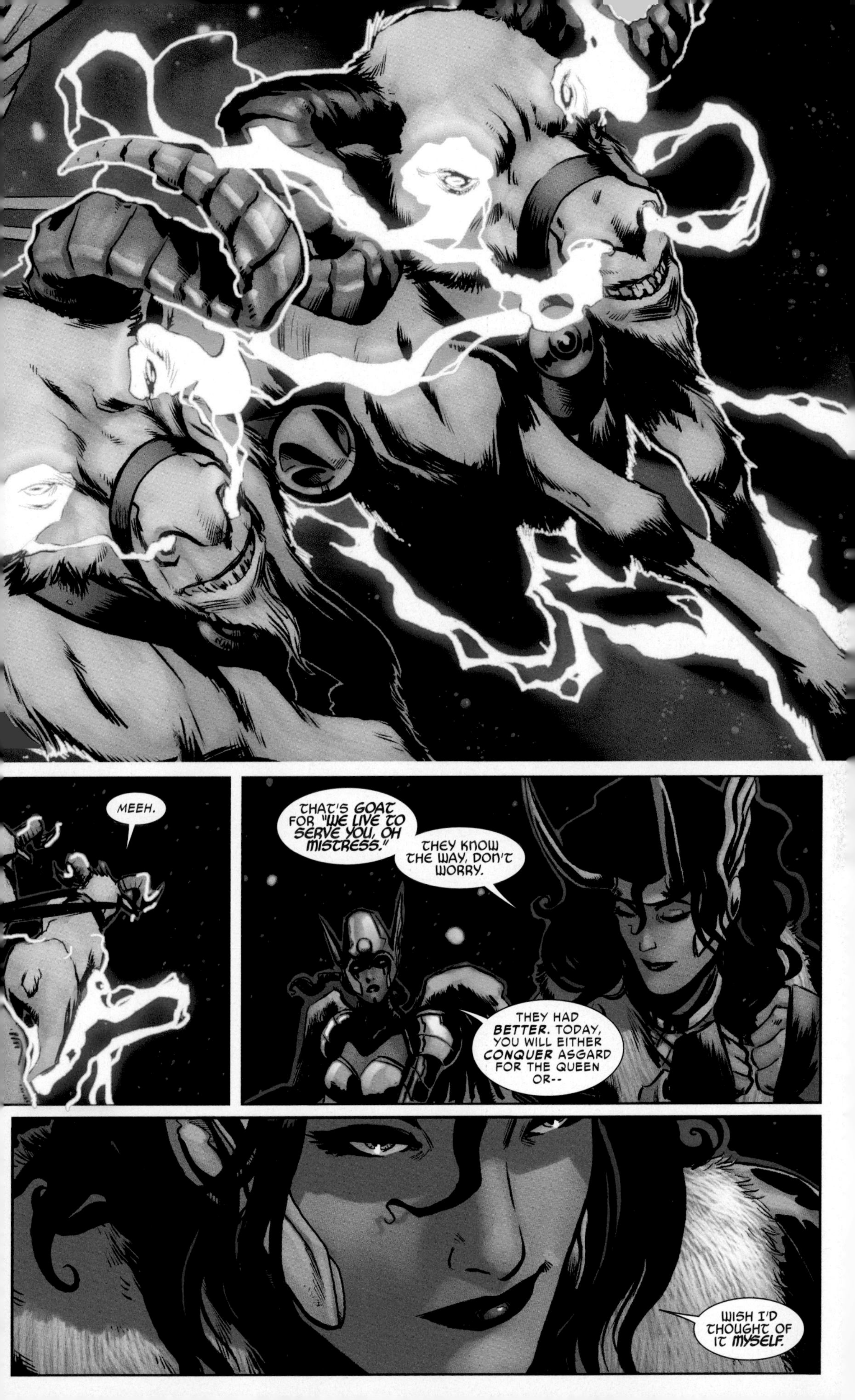
MEEH.
THAT'S GOAT FOR "WE LIVE TO SERVE YOU, OH MISTRESS."
THEY KNOW THE WAY, DON'T WORRY.
THEY HAD BETTER. TODAY, YOU WILL EITHER CONQUER ASGARD FOR THE QUEEN OR--
WISH I'D THOUGHT OF IT MYSELF.

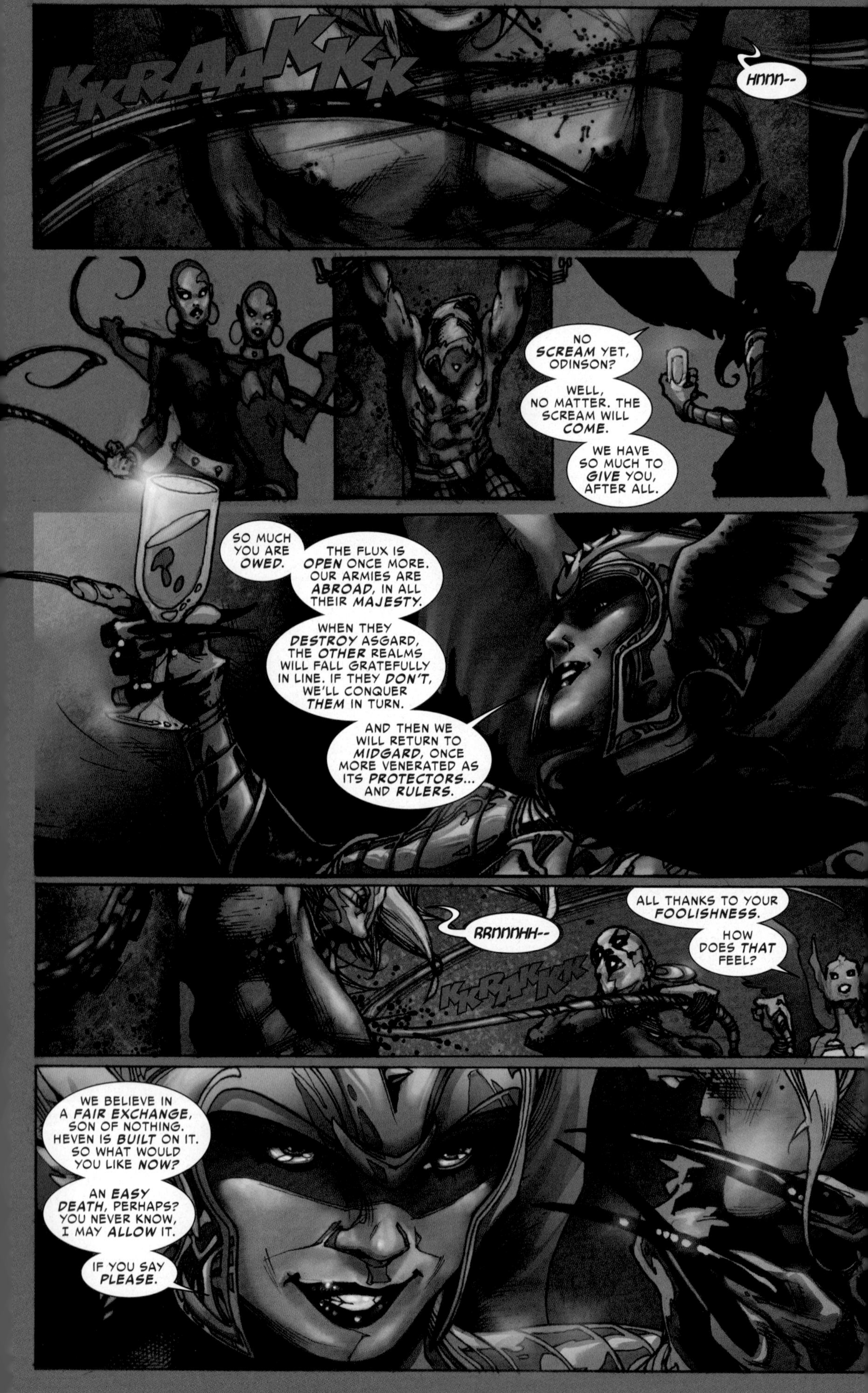
KKRAAKKK
HNNN--
NO SCREAM YET, ODINSON?
WELL, NO MATTER. THE SCREAM WILL COME.
WE HAVE SO MUCH TO GIVE YOU, AFTER ALL.
SO MUCH YOU ARE OWED.
THE FLUX IS OPEN ONCE MORE. OUR ARMIES ARE ABROAD, IN ALL THEIR MAJESTY.
WHEN THEY DESTROY ASGARD, THE OTHER REALMS WILL FALL GRATEFULLY IN LINE. IF THEY DON'T, WE'LL CONQUER THEM IN TURN.
AND THEN WE WILL RETURN TO MIDGARD, ONCE MORE VENERATED AS ITS PROTECTORS... AND RULERS.
BRNNNHH--
KKRAKKK
ALL THANKS TO YOUR FOOLISHNESS.
HOW DOES THAT FEEL?
WE BELIEVE IN A FAIR EXCHANGE, SON OF NOTHING. HEVEN IS BUILT ON IT. SO WHAT WOULD YOU LIKE NOW?
AN EASY DEATH, PERHAPS? YOU NEVER KNOW, I MAY ALLOW IT.
IF YOU SAY PLEASE.

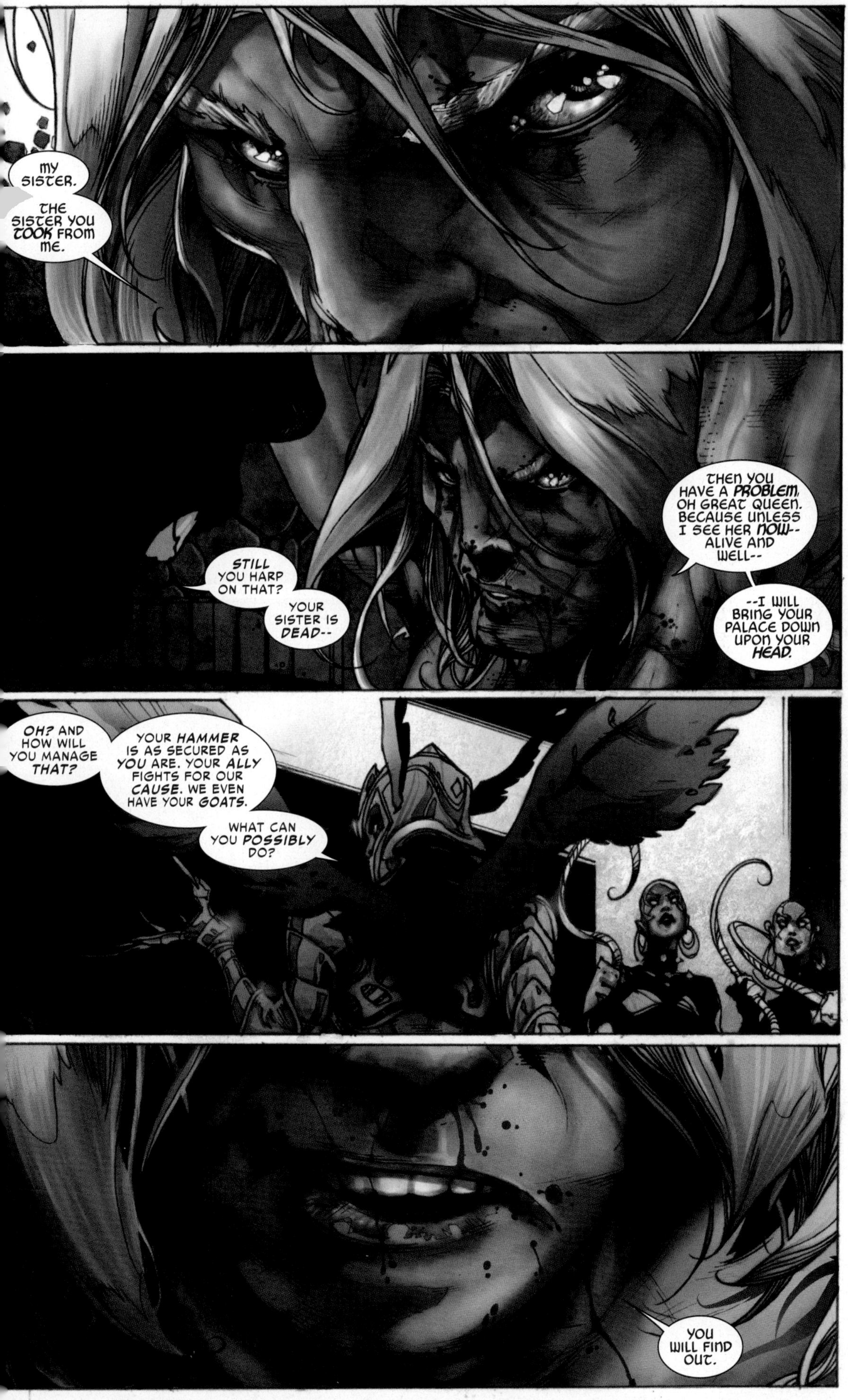
MY SISTER.
THE SISTER YOU TOOK FROM ME.
STILL YOU HARP ON THAT?
YOUR SISTER IS DEAD--
THEN YOU HAVE A PROBLEM, OH GREAT QUEEN. BECAUSE UNLESS I SEE HER NOW-- ALIVE AND WELL--
--I WILL BRING YOUR PALACE DOWN UPON YOUR HEAD.
OH? AND HOW WILL YOU MANAGE THAT?
YOUR HAMMER IS AS SECURED AS YOU ARE. YOUR ALLY FIGHTS FOR OUR CAUSE. WE EVEN HAVE YOUR GOATS.
WHAT CAN YOU POSSIBLY DO?
YOU WILL FIND OUT.

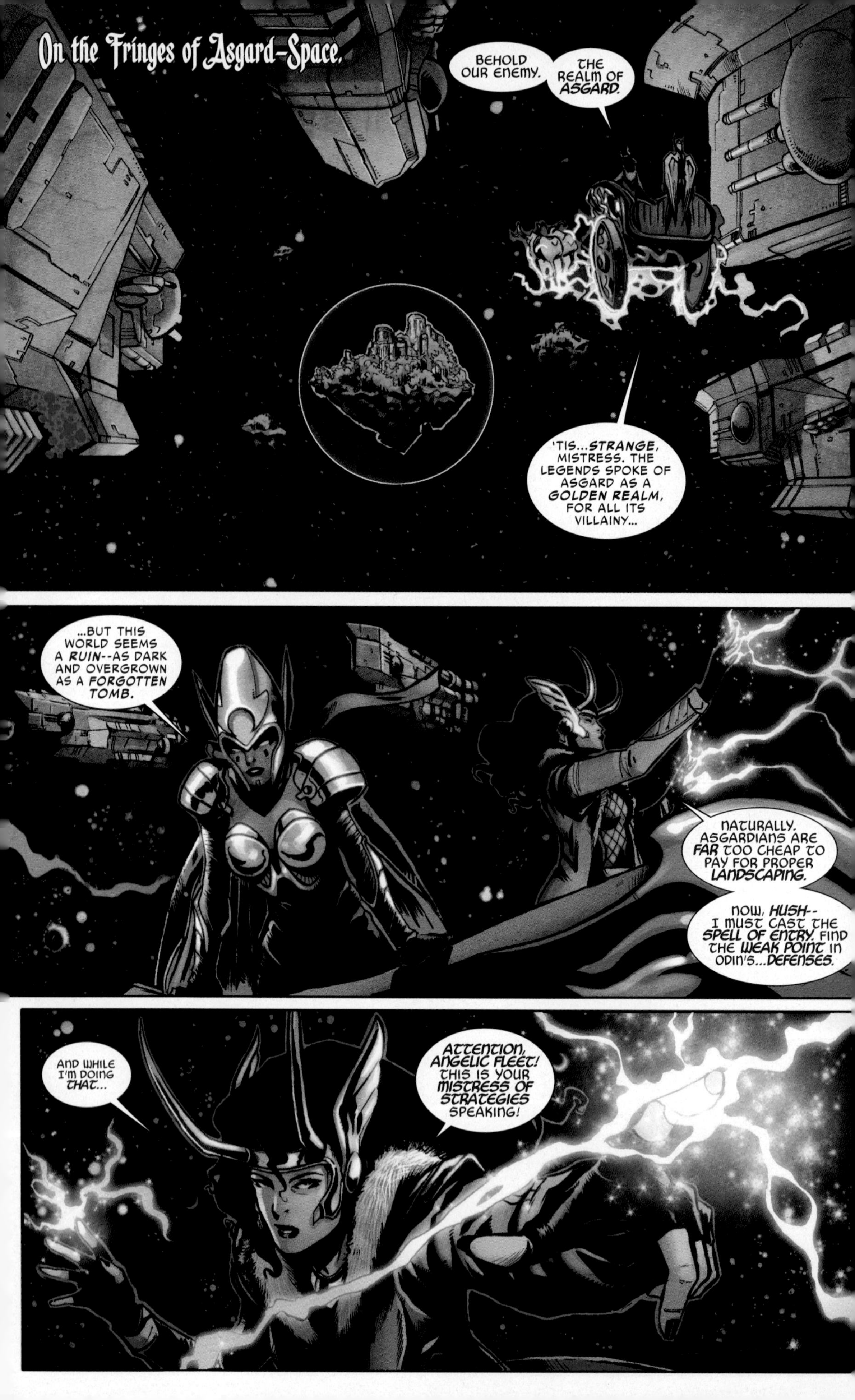
On the Fringes of Asgard-Space.
BEHOLD OUR ENEMY.
THE REALM OF ASGARD.
'TIS...STRANGE, MISTRESS. THE LEGENDS SPOKE OF ASGARD AS A GOLDEN REALM, FOR ALL ITS VILLAINY...
...BUT THIS WORLD SEEMS A RUIN--AS DARK AND OVERGROWN AS A FORGOTTEN TOMB.
NATURALLY. ASGARDIANS ARE FAR TOO CHEAP TO PAY FOR PROPER LANDSCAPING.
NOW, HUSH-- I MUST CAST THE SPELL OF ENTRY. FIND THE WEAK POINT IN ODIN'S...DEFENSES.
AND WHILE I'M DOING THAT...
ATTENTION, ANGELIC FLEET! THIS IS YOUR MISTRESS OF STRATEGIES SPEAKING!

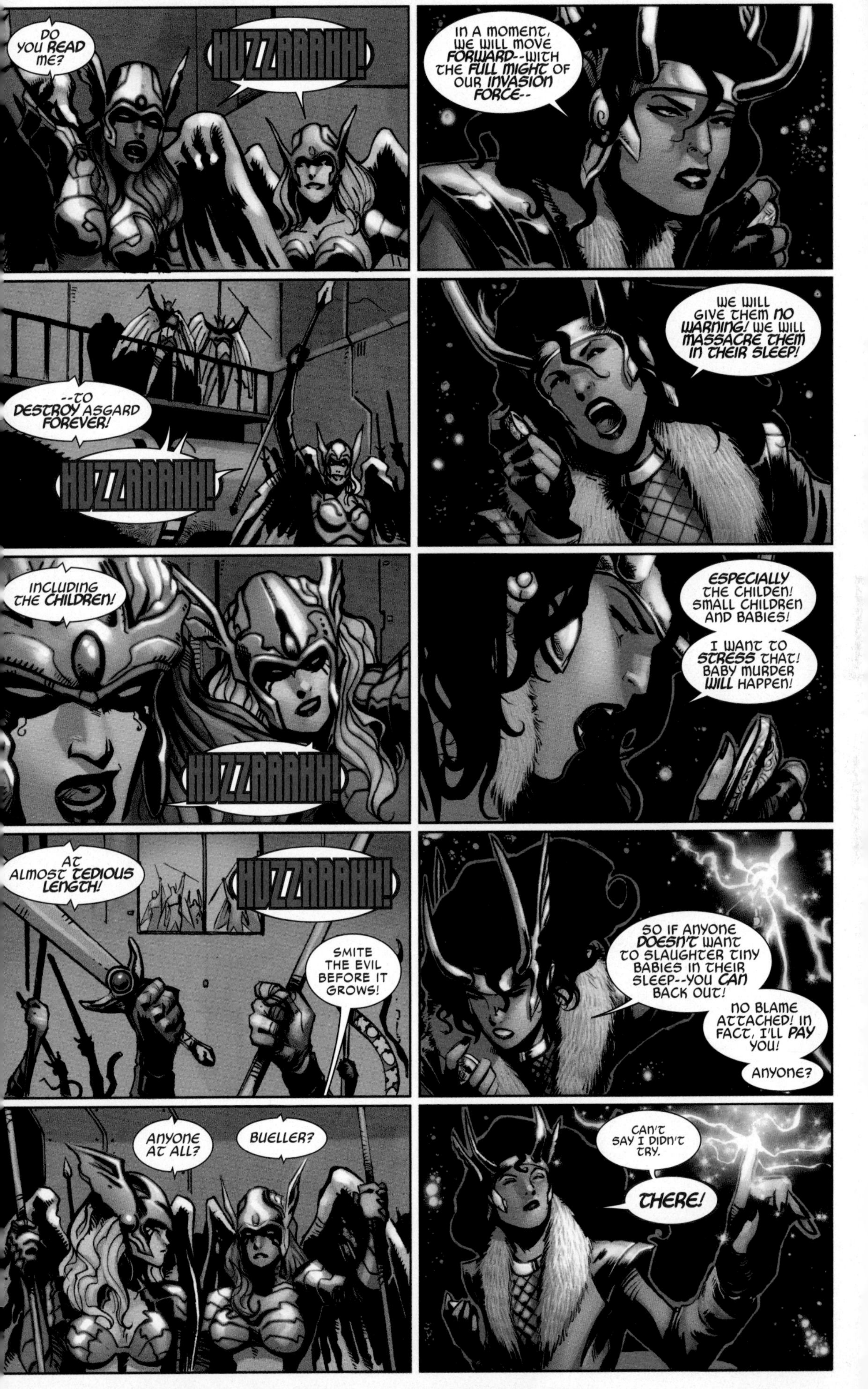
DO YOU READ ME?
HUZZAAAHH!
IN A MOMENT, WE WILL MOVE FORWARD--WITH THE FULL MIGHT OF OUR INVASION FORCE--
--TO DESTROY ASGARD FOREVER!
HUZZAAAHH!
WE WILL GIVE THEM NO WARNING! WE WILL MASSACRE THEM IN THEIR SLEEP!
INCLUDING THE CHILDREN!
HUZZAAAHH!
ESPECIALLY THE CHILDEN! SMALL CHILDREN AND BABIES!
I WANT TO STRESS THAT! BABY MURDER WILL HAPPEN!
AT ALMOST TEDIOUS LENGTH!
HUZZAAAHH!
SMITE THE EVIL BEFORE IT GROWS!
SO IF ANYONE DOESN'T WANT TO SLAUGHTER TINY BABIES IN THEIR SLEEP--YOU CAN BACK OUT!
NO BLAME ATTACHED! IN FACT, I'LL PAY YOU!
ANYONE?
ANYONE AT ALL?
BUELLER?
CAN'T SAY I DIDN'T TRY.
THERE!

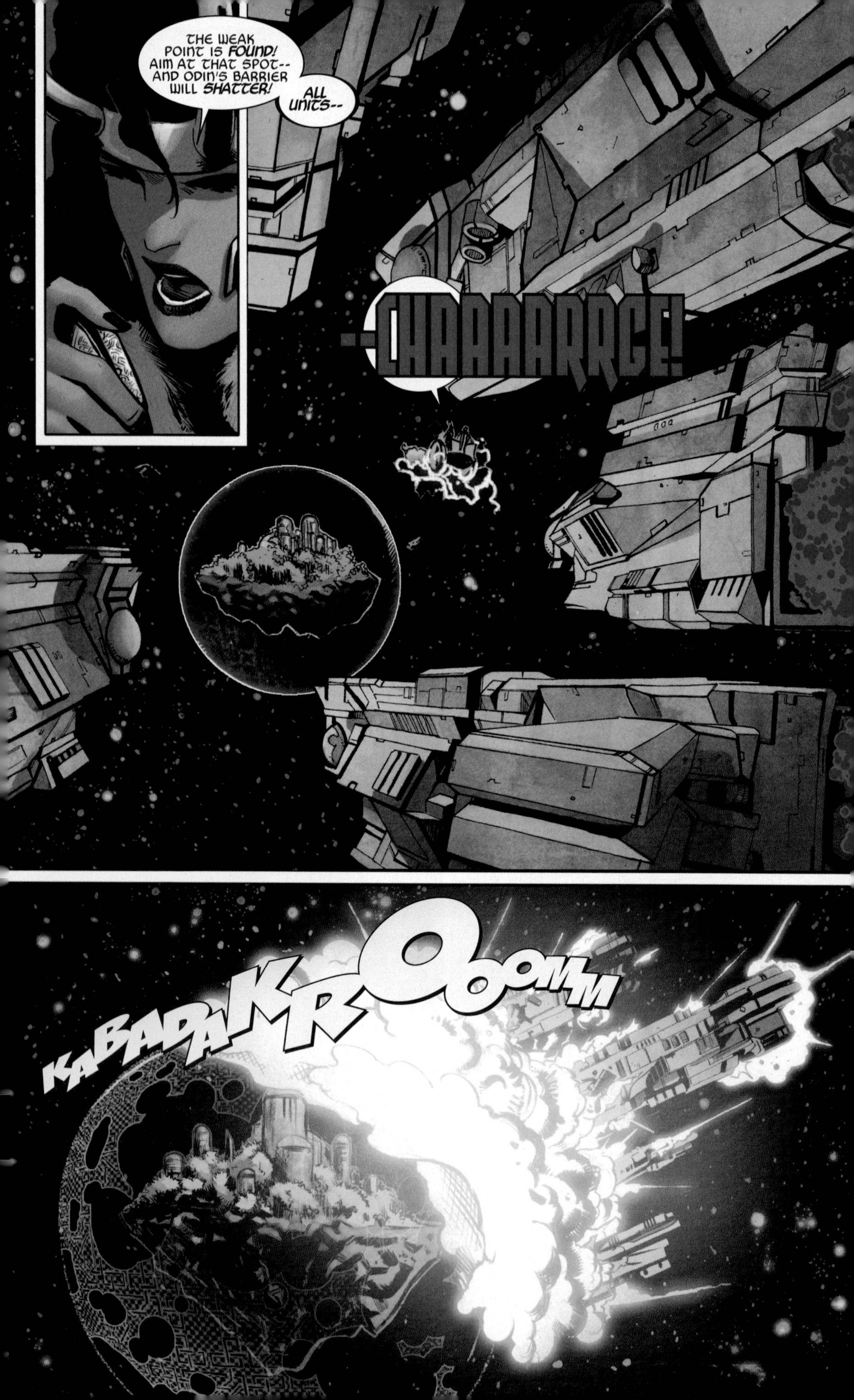
THE WEAK POINT IS FOUND! AIM AT THAT SPOT-- AND ODIN'S BARRIER WILL SHATTER!
ALL UNITS--
--CHAAAARRGE!
KABADAKROOOMM

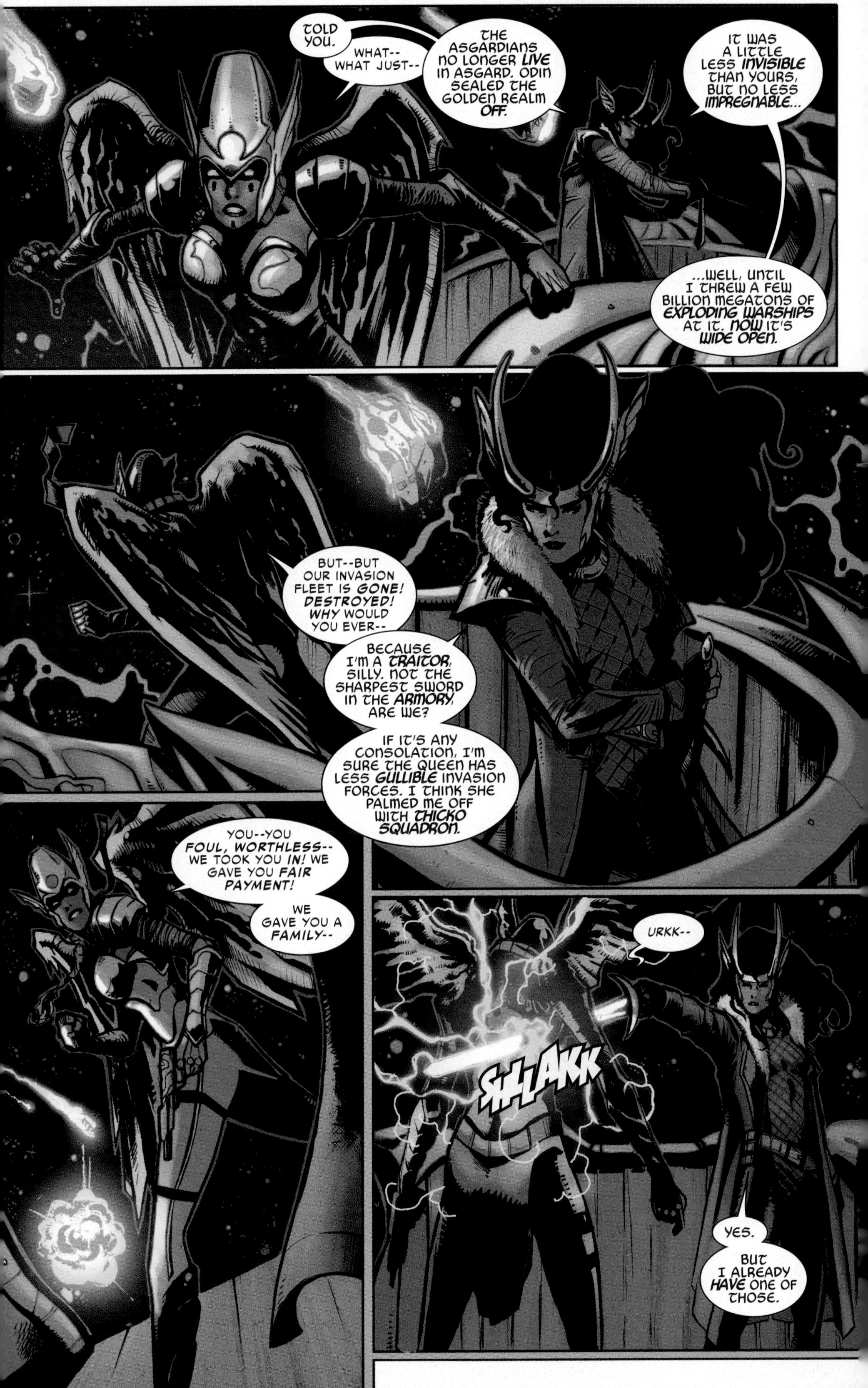
TOLD YOU.
WHAT-- WHAT JUST--
THE ASGARDIANS NO LONGER LIVE IN ASGARD. ODIN SEALED THE GOLDEN REALM OFF.
IT WAS A LITTLE LESS INVISIBLE THAN YOURS, BUT NO LESS IMPREGNABLE...
...WELL, UNTIL I THREW A FEW BILLION MEGATONS OF EXPLODING WARSHIPS AT IT. NOW IT'S WIDE OPEN.
BUT--BUT OUR INVASION FLEET IS GONE! DESTROYED! WHY WOULD YOU EVER--
BECAUSE I'M A TRAITOR, SILLY. NOT THE SHARPEST SWORD IN THE ARMORY, ARE WE?
IF IT'S ANY CONSOLATION, I'M SURE THE QUEEN HAS LESS GULLIBLE INVASION FORCES. I THINK SHE PALMED ME OFF WITH THICKO SQUADRON.
YOU--YOU FOUL, WORTHLESS-- WE TOOK YOU IN! WE GAVE YOU FAIR PAYMENT!
WE GAVE YOU A FAMILY--
URKK--
SHHLAKK
YES.
BUT I ALREADY HAVE ONE OF THOSE.

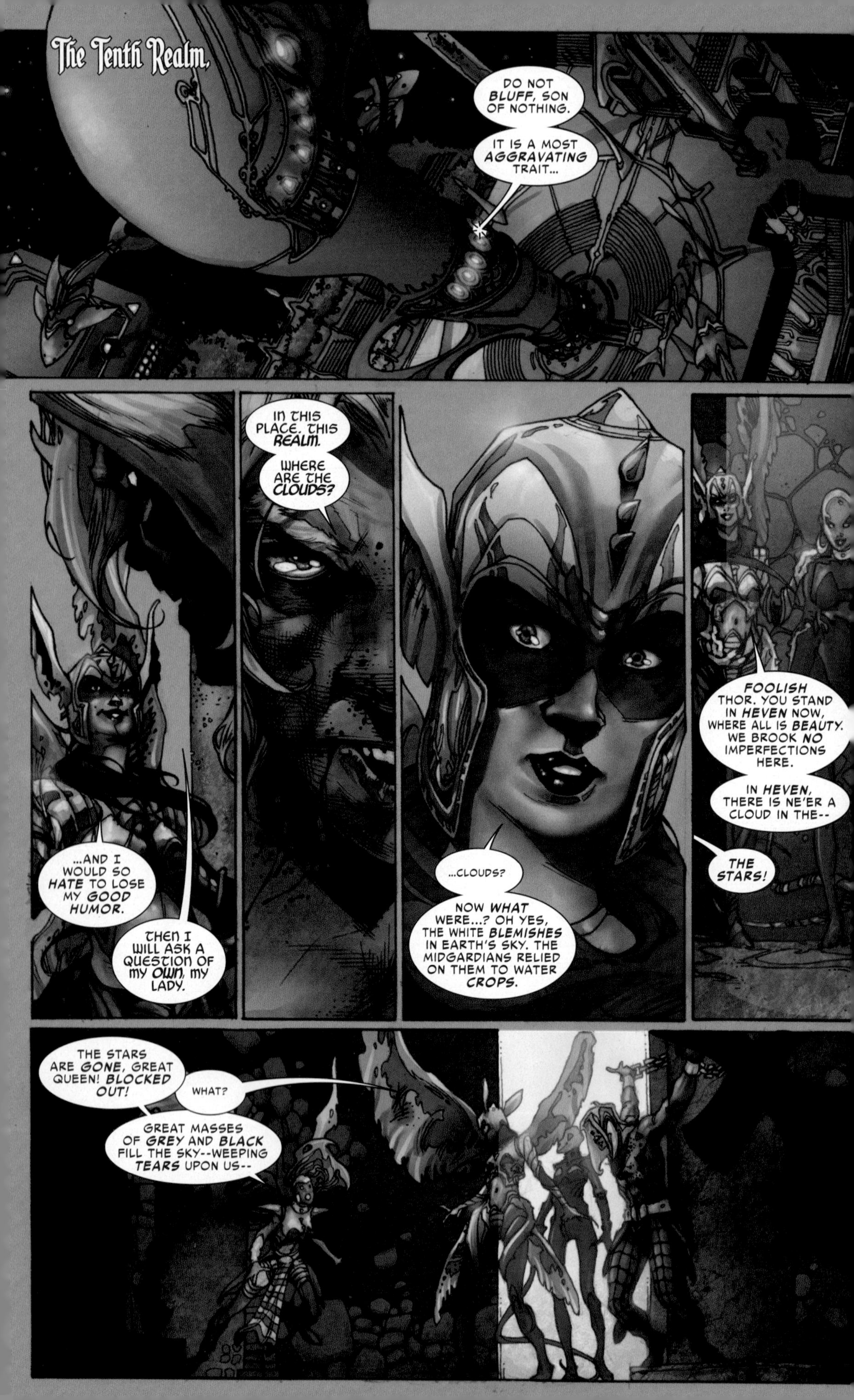

The Tenth Realm.
DO NOT BLUFF, SON OF NOTHING.
IT IS A MOST AGGRAVATING TRAIT...
...AND I WOULD SO HATE TO LOSE MY GOOD HUMOR.
THEN I WILL ASK A QUESTION OF MY OWN, MY LADY.
IN THIS PLACE. THIS REALM.
WHERE ARE THE CLOUDS?
...CLOUDS?
NOW WHAT WERE...? OH YES, THE WHITE BLEMISHES IN EARTH'S SKY. THE MIDGARDIANS RELIED ON THEM TO WATER CROPS.
FOOLISH THOR. YOU STAND IN HEVEN NOW, WHERE ALL IS BEAUTY. WE BROOK NO IMPERFECTIONS HERE.
IN HEVEN, THERE IS NE'ER A CLOUD IN THE--
THE STARS!
THE STARS ARE GONE, GREAT QUEEN! BLOCKED OUT!
WHAT?
GREAT MASSES OF GREY AND BLACK FILL THE SKY--WEEPING TEARS UPON US--

BUT...BUT THAT'S...

IT HAS BEEN *LONG AEONS* SINCE YOUR PEOPLE KNEW OTHER REALMS, MY LADY.

GENERATIONS HAVE PASSED.

ARE THERE *ANY* IN YOUR *HEVEN* WHO HAVE SEEN A *STORM?*

YOU KNOW *WEALTH*, QUEEN OF ANGELS. YOU KNOW *POWER*.

BUT I FEAR YOU KNOW LITTLE OF *THUNDER*.

AND *NOW*... YOU HAVE MADE THE *MASTER* OF STORMS YOUR *PRISONER*.

AND I HAVE *CALLED* MY GREAT SERVANT TO ME. WHILE YOU PLAYED YOUR *GAMES*.

AND THOUGH IT TOOK *TIME* FOR IT TO CROSS THE SPAN OF REALMS AND *MEET* YOU...

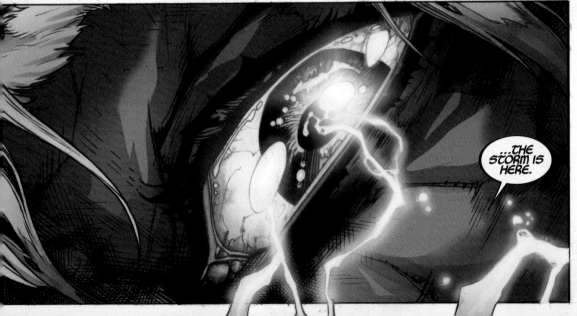

...THE *STORM* IS *HERE*.

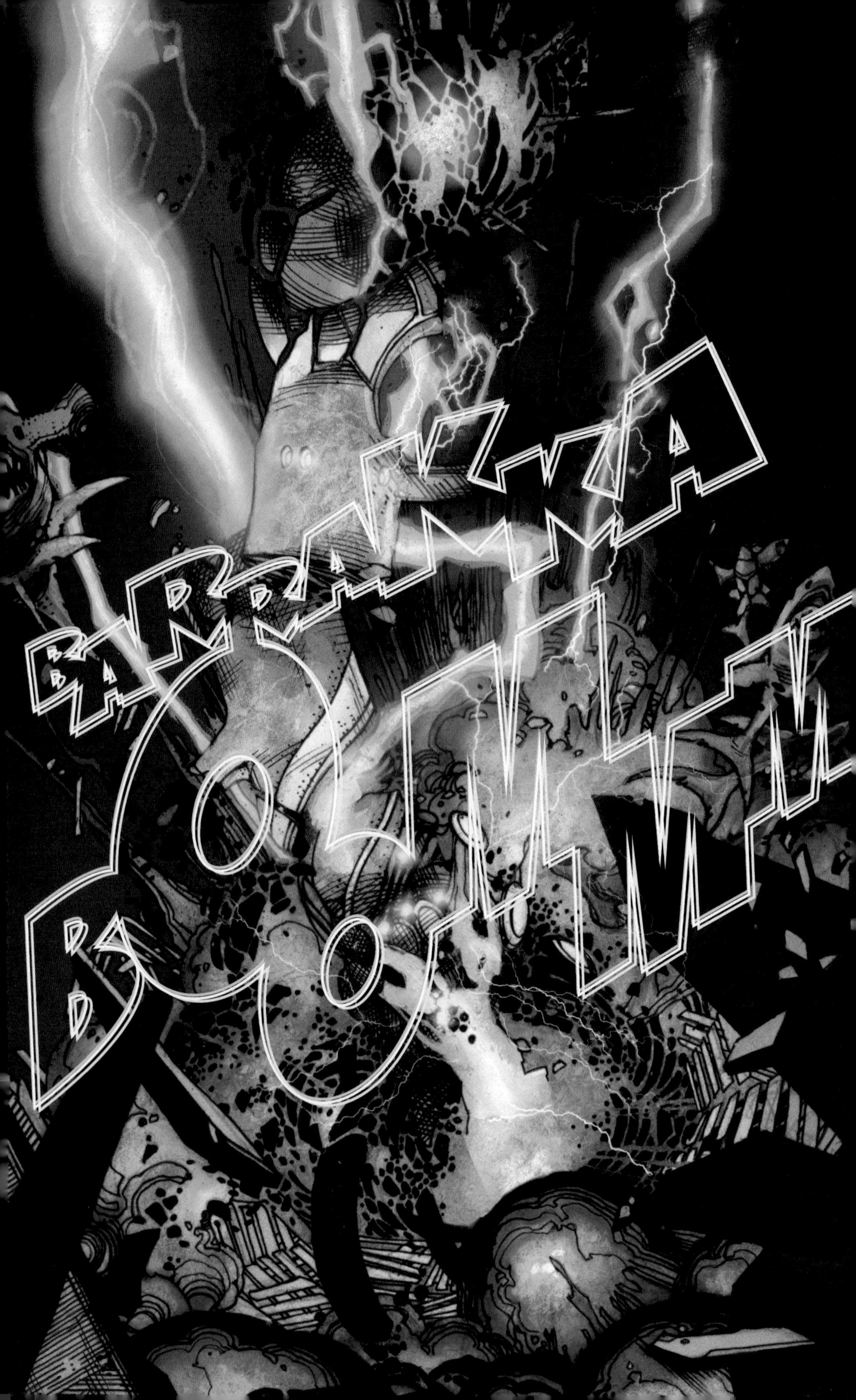

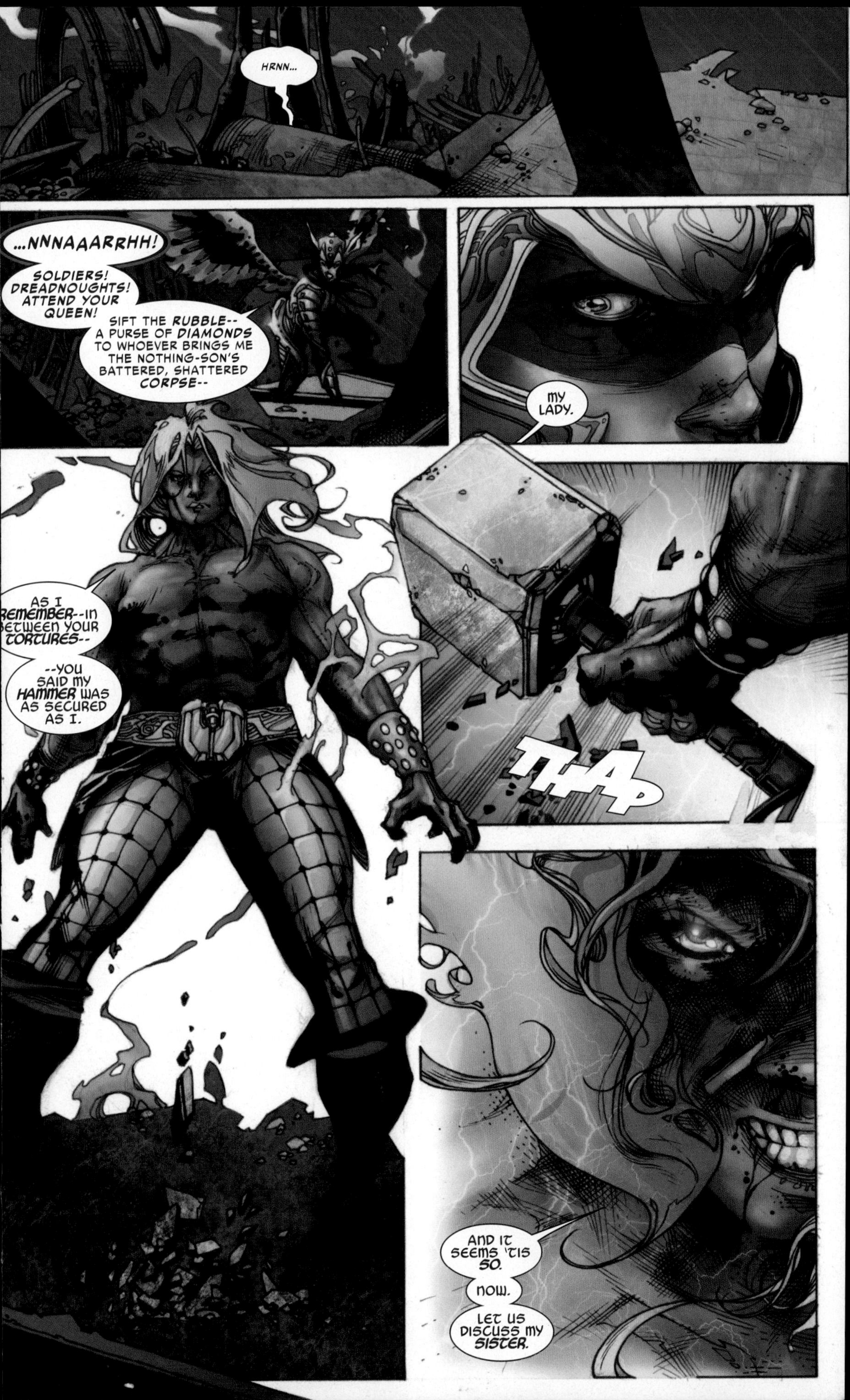

HRNN...
...NNNAAARRHH!
SOLDIERS! DREADNOUGHTS! ATTEND YOUR QUEEN!
SIFT THE RUBBLE-- A PURSE OF DIAMONDS TO WHOEVER BRINGS ME THE NOTHING-SON'S BATTERED, SHATTERED CORPSE--
MY LADY.
AS I REMEMBER--IN BETWEEN YOUR TORTURES--
--YOU SAID MY HAMMER WAS AS SECURED AS I.
THAP
AND IT SEEMS 'TIS SO.
NOW.
LET US DISCUSS MY SISTER.

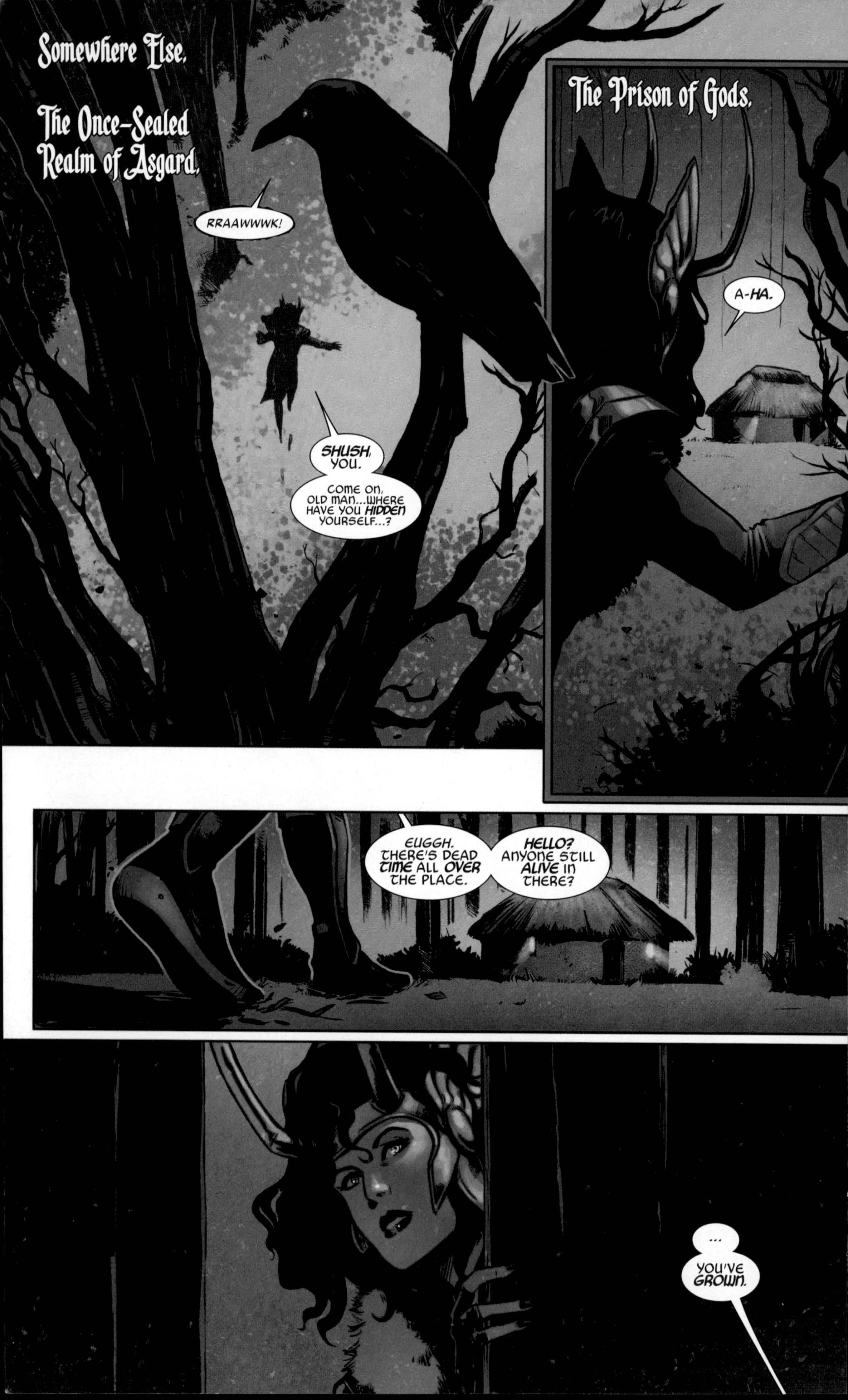
Somewhere Else.
The Once-Sealed Realm of Asgard.
RRAAWWWK!
SHUSH, YOU.
COME ON, OLD MAN...WHERE HAVE YOU HIDDEN YOURSELF...?
The Prison of Gods.
A-HA.
EUGGH. THERE'S DEAD TIME ALL OVER THE PLACE.
HELLO? ANYONE STILL ALIVE IN THERE?
...
YOU'VE GROWN.

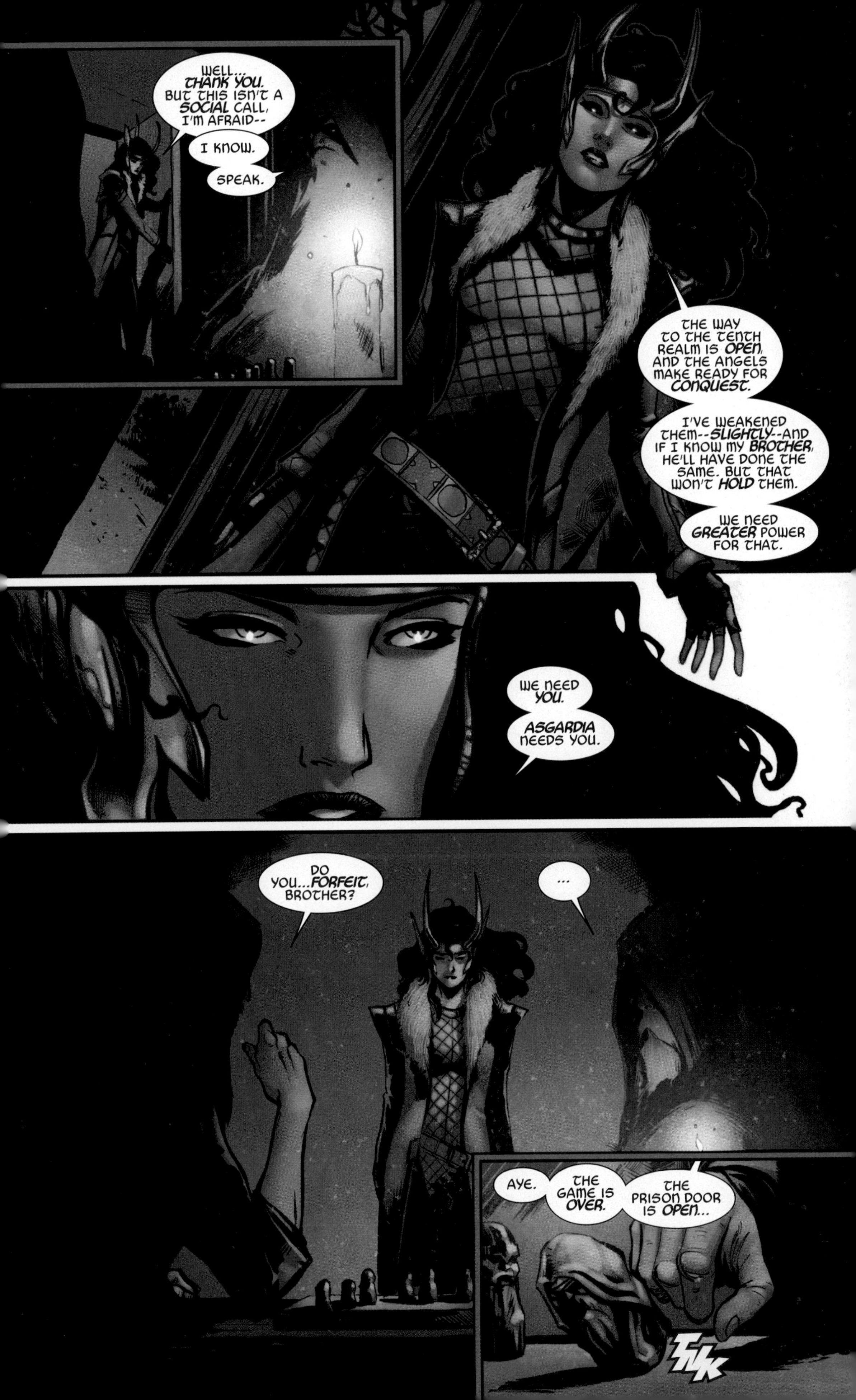
WELL... THANK YOU. BUT THIS ISN'T A SOCIAL CALL, I'M AFRAID--
I KNOW.
SPEAK.
THE WAY TO THE TENTH REALM IS OPEN, AND THE ANGELS MAKE READY FOR CONQUEST.
I'VE WEAKENED THEM--SLIGHTLY--AND IF I KNOW MY BROTHER, HE'LL HAVE DONE THE SAME. BUT THAT WON'T HOLD THEM.
WE NEED GREATER POWER FOR THAT.
WE NEED YOU.
ASGARDIA NEEDS YOU.
DO YOU...FORFEIT, BROTHER?
...
AYE.
THE GAME IS OVER.
THE PRISON DOOR IS OPEN...
TIK

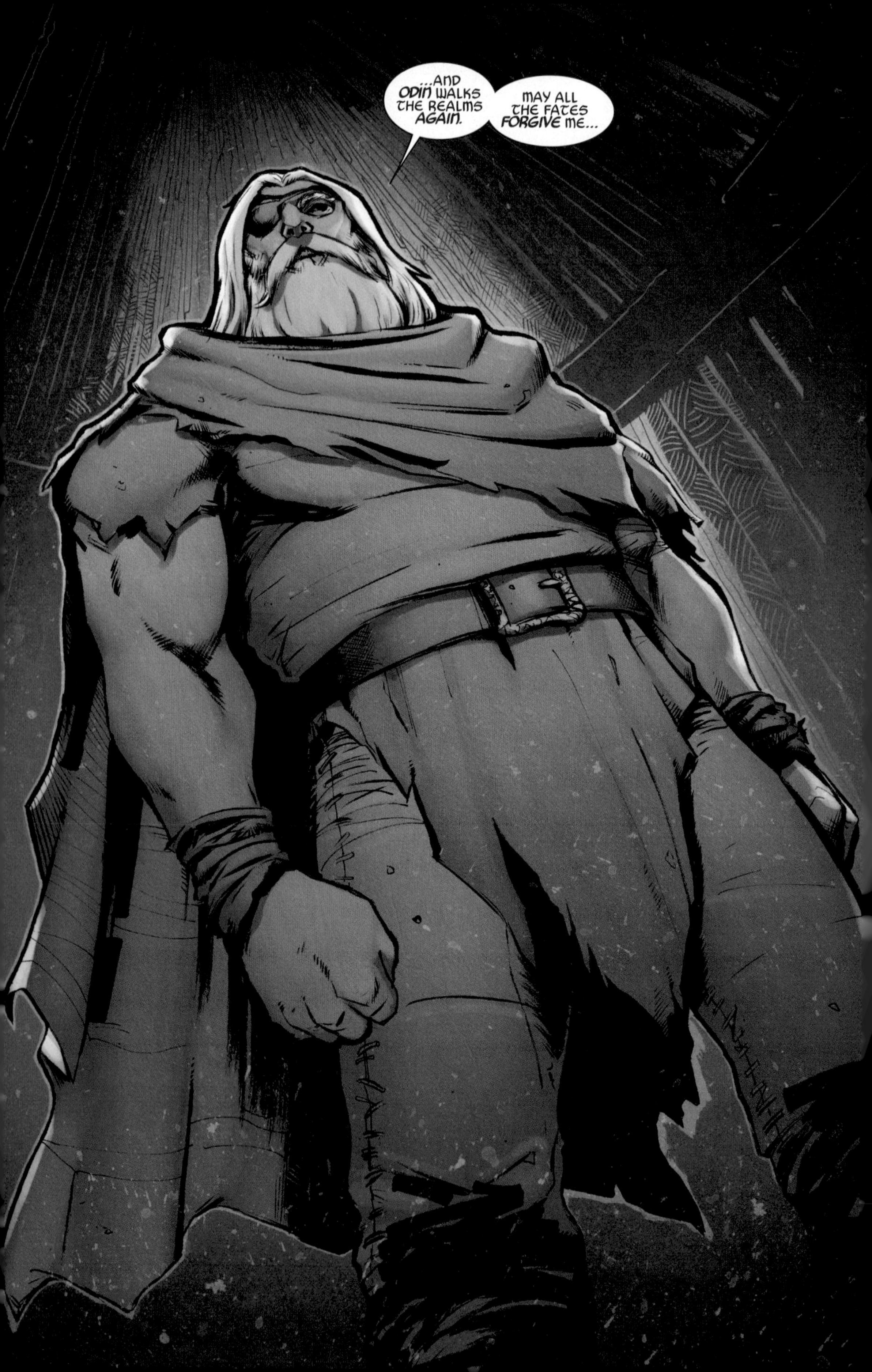
...AND ODIN WALKS THE REALMS AGAIN.
MAY ALL THE FATES FORGIVE ME...

ORIGINAL SIN #5.2 VARIANT
by Simone Bianchi

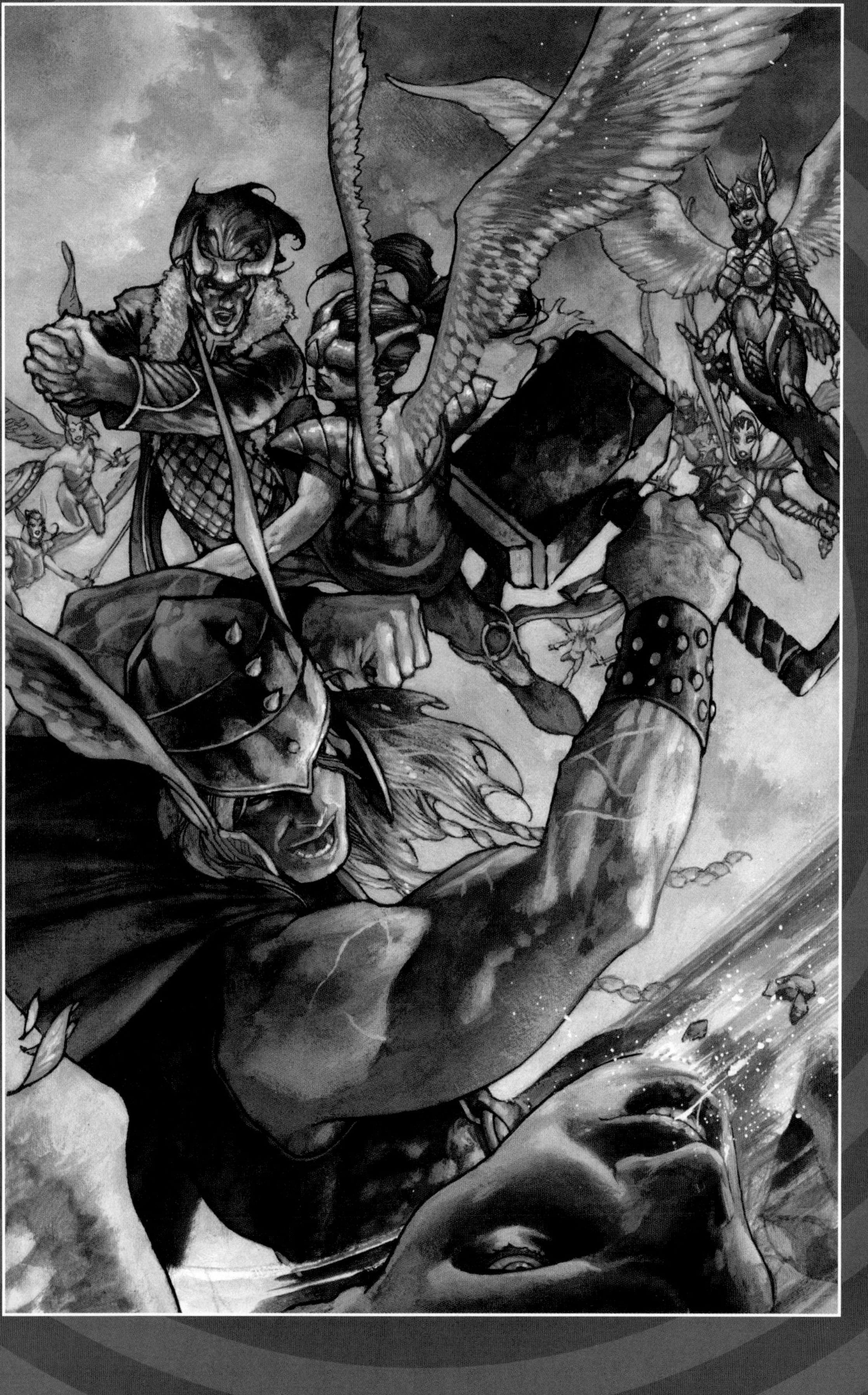

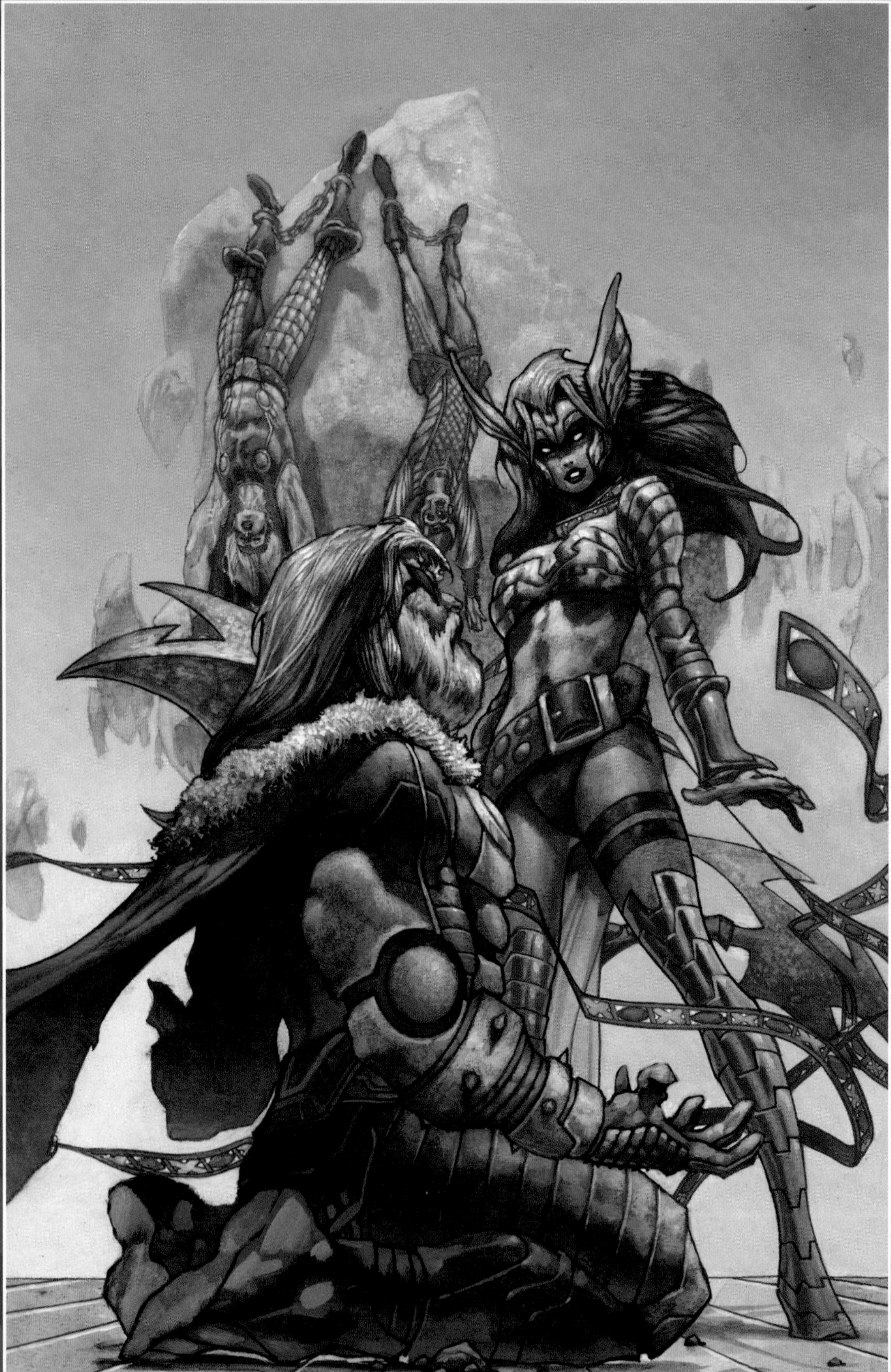

ORIGINAL SIN #5.5

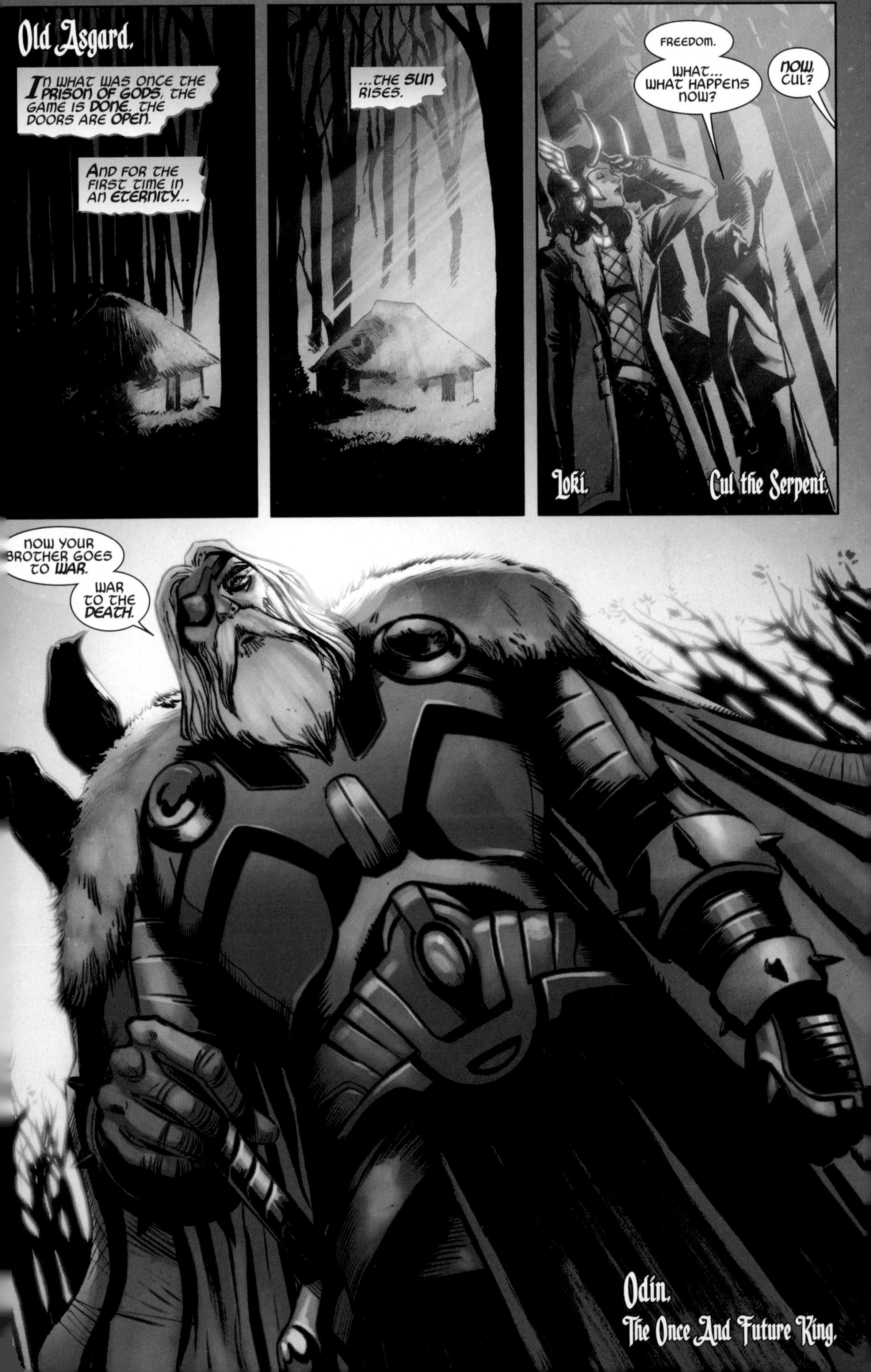

Old Asgard.
In what was once the prison of gods, the game is done. The doors are open.
And for the first time in an eternity...
...the sun rises.
Freedom.
What... what happens now?
Now, Cul?
Loki.
Cul the Serpent.
Now your brother goes to war.
War to the death.
Odin.
The Once And Future King.

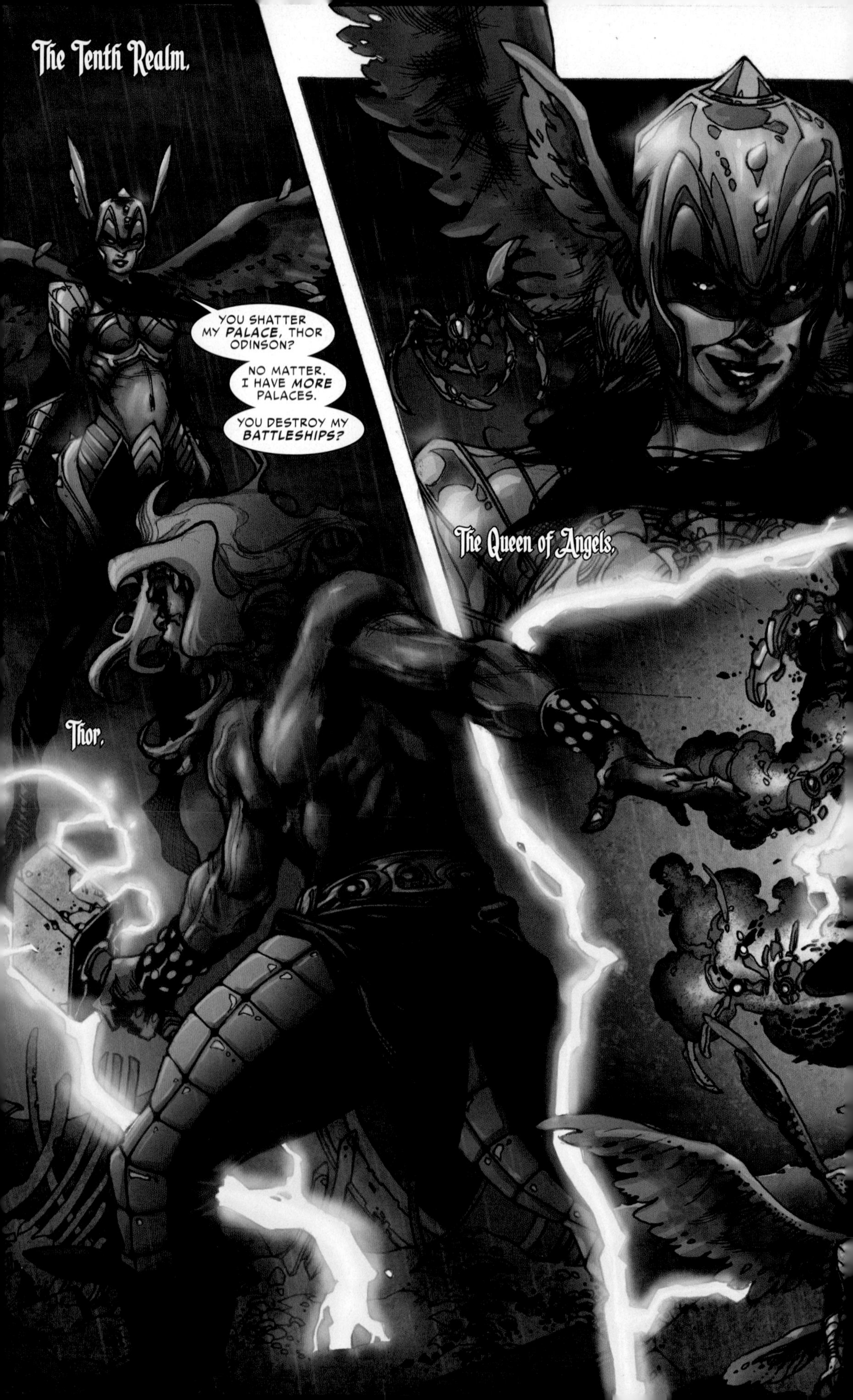
The Tenth Realm.
YOU SHATTER MY PALACE, THOR ODINSON?
NO MATTER. I HAVE MORE PALACES.
YOU DESTROY MY BATTLESHIPS?
The Queen of Angels.
Thor.

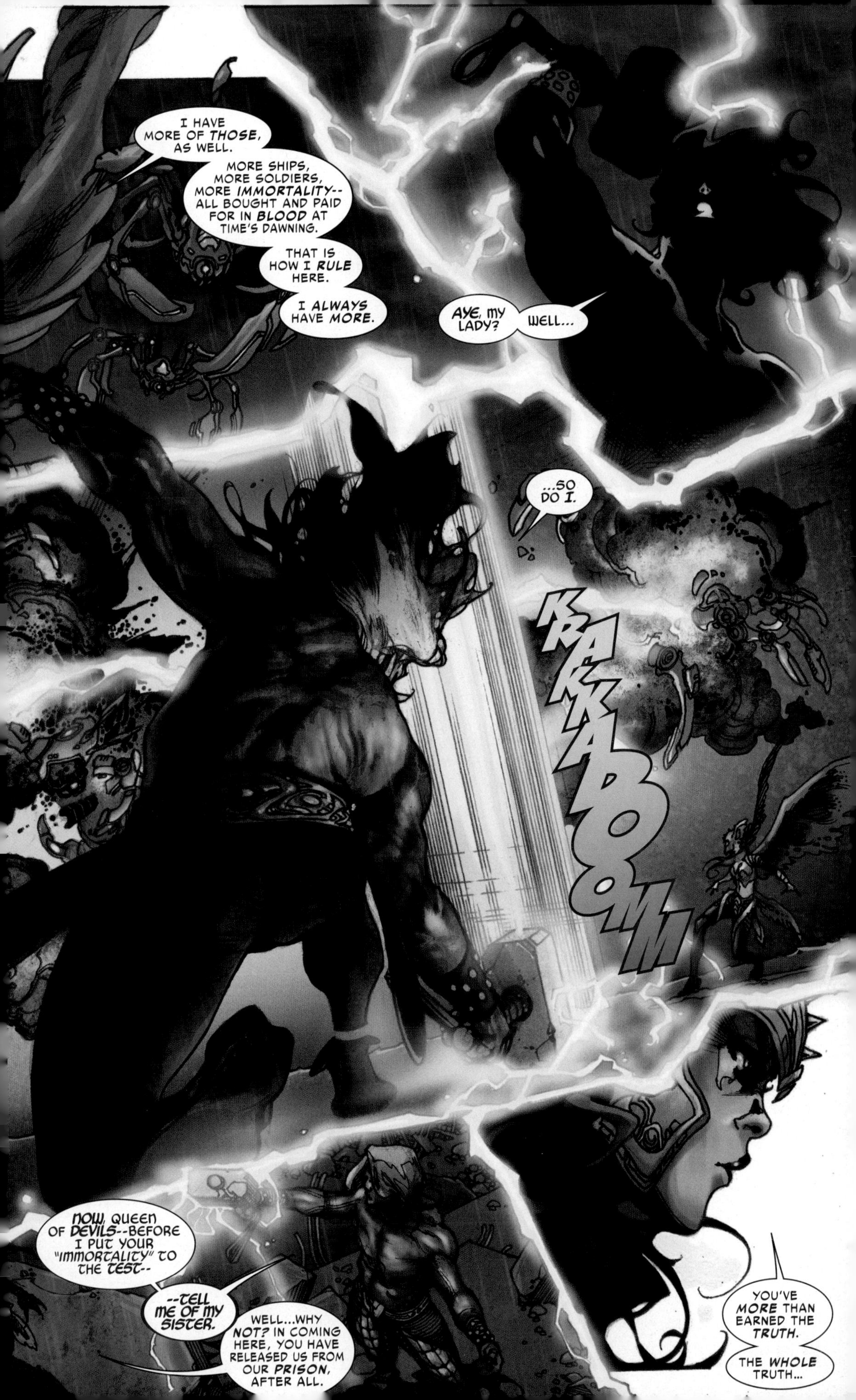

I HAVE MORE OF THOSE, AS WELL.
MORE SHIPS, MORE SOLDIERS, MORE IMMORTALITY-- ALL BOUGHT AND PAID FOR IN BLOOD AT TIME'S DAWNING.
THAT IS HOW I RULE HERE.
I ALWAYS HAVE MORE.
AYE, MY LADY?
WELL...
...SO DO I.
KRAKKABOOMM
NOW, QUEEN OF DEVILS--BEFORE I PUT YOUR "IMMORTALITY" TO THE TEST--
--TELL ME OF MY SISTER.
WELL...WHY NOT? IN COMING HERE, YOU HAVE RELEASED US FROM OUR PRISON, AFTER ALL.
YOU'VE MORE THAN EARNED THE TRUTH.
THE WHOLE TRUTH...

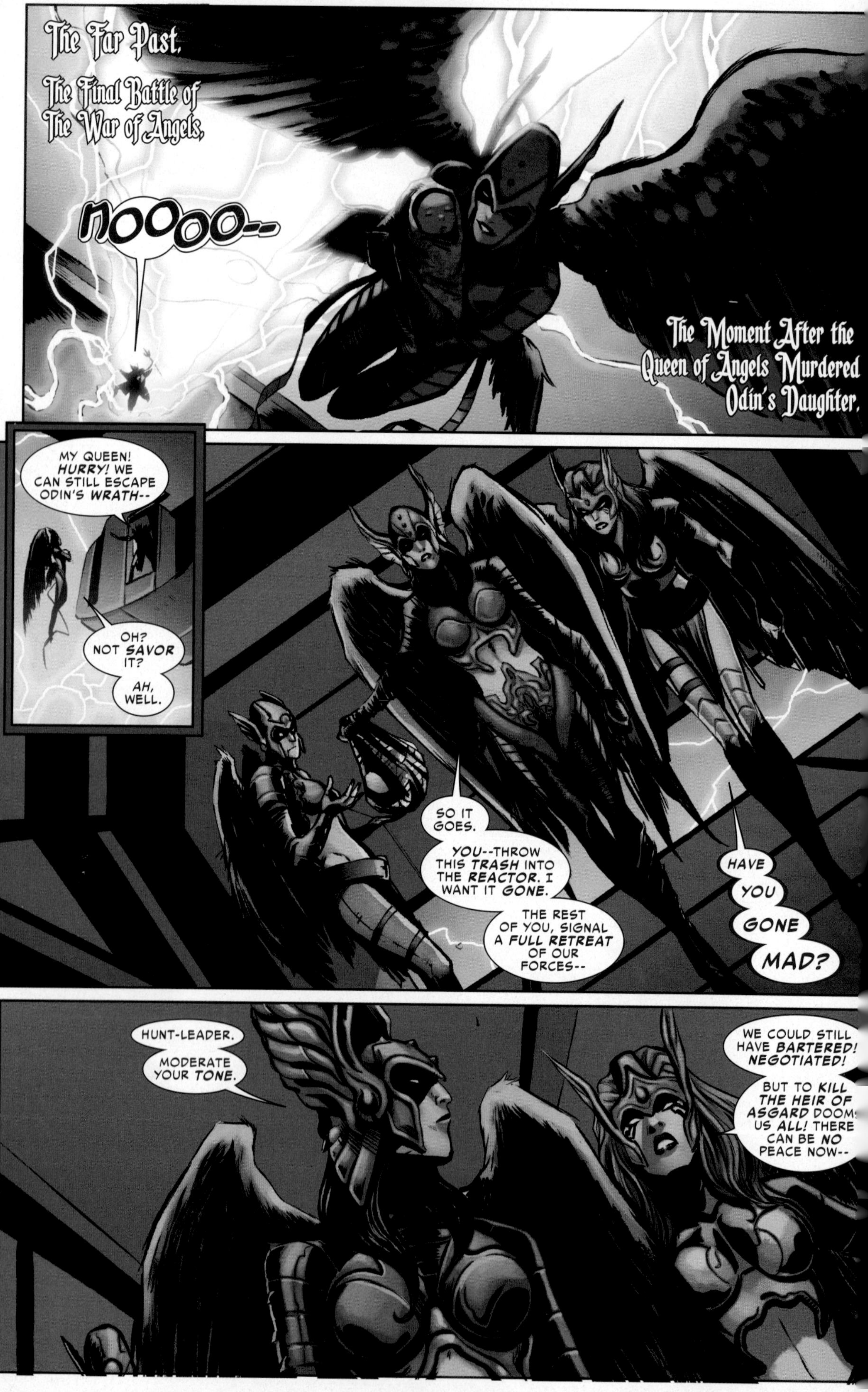

The Far Past.
The Final Battle of The War of Angels.
NOOOOO--
The Moment After the Queen of Angels Murdered Odin's Daughter.
MY QUEEN! HURRY! WE CAN STILL ESCAPE ODIN'S WRATH--
OH? NOT SAVOR IT?
AH, WELL.
SO IT GOES.
YOU--THROW THIS TRASH INTO THE REACTOR. I WANT IT GONE.
THE REST OF YOU, SIGNAL A FULL RETREAT OF OUR FORCES--
HAVE YOU GONE MAD?
HUNT-LEADER.
MODERATE YOUR TONE.
WE COULD STILL HAVE BARTERED! NEGOTIATED!
BUT TO KILL THE HEIR OF ASGARD DOOMS US ALL! THERE CAN BE NO PEACE NOW--

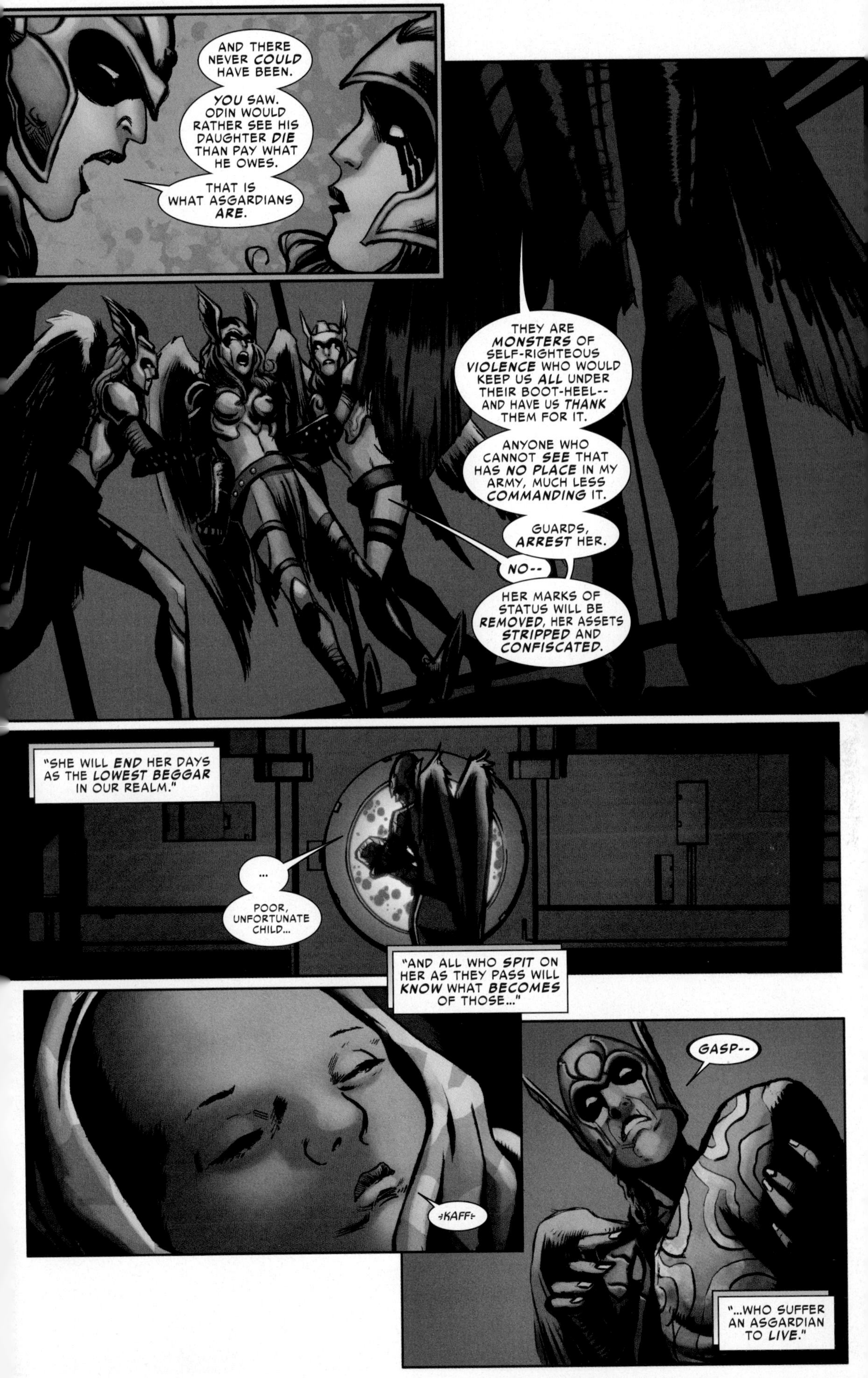
AND THERE NEVER COULD HAVE BEEN.
YOU SAW. ODIN WOULD RATHER SEE HIS DAUGHTER DIE THAN PAY WHAT HE OWES.
THAT IS WHAT ASGARDIANS ARE.
THEY ARE MONSTERS OF SELF-RIGHTEOUS VIOLENCE WHO WOULD KEEP US ALL UNDER THEIR BOOT-HEEL-- AND HAVE US THANK THEM FOR IT.
ANYONE WHO CANNOT SEE THAT HAS NO PLACE IN MY ARMY, MUCH LESS COMMANDING IT.
GUARDS, ARREST HER.
NO--
HER MARKS OF STATUS WILL BE REMOVED, HER ASSETS STRIPPED AND CONFISCATED.
"SHE WILL END HER DAYS AS THE LOWEST BEGGAR IN OUR REALM."
...
POOR, UNFORTUNATE CHILD...
"AND ALL WHO SPIT ON HER AS THEY PASS WILL KNOW WHAT BECOMES OF THOSE..."
KAFF
GASP--
"...WHO SUFFER AN ASGARDIAN TO LIVE."

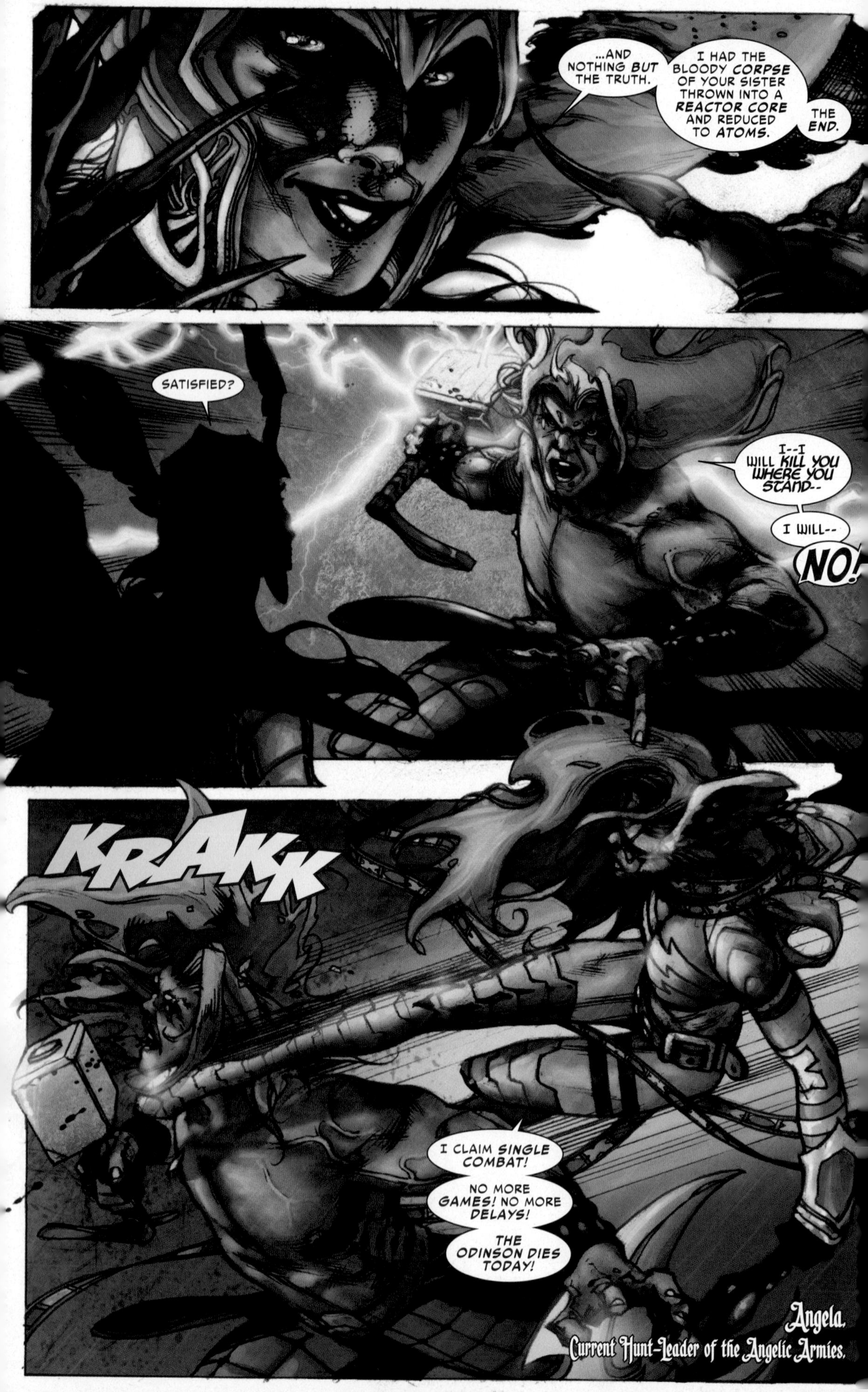
...AND NOTHING BUT THE TRUTH.
I HAD THE BLOODY CORPSE OF YOUR SISTER THROWN INTO A REACTOR CORE AND REDUCED TO ATOMS.
THE END.
SATISFIED?
I--I WILL KILL YOU WHERE YOU STAND--
I WILL--
NO!
KRAKK
I CLAIM SINGLE COMBAT!
NO MORE GAMES! NO MORE DELAYS!
THE ODINSON DIES TODAY!
Angela.
Current Hunt-Leader of the Angelic Armies.

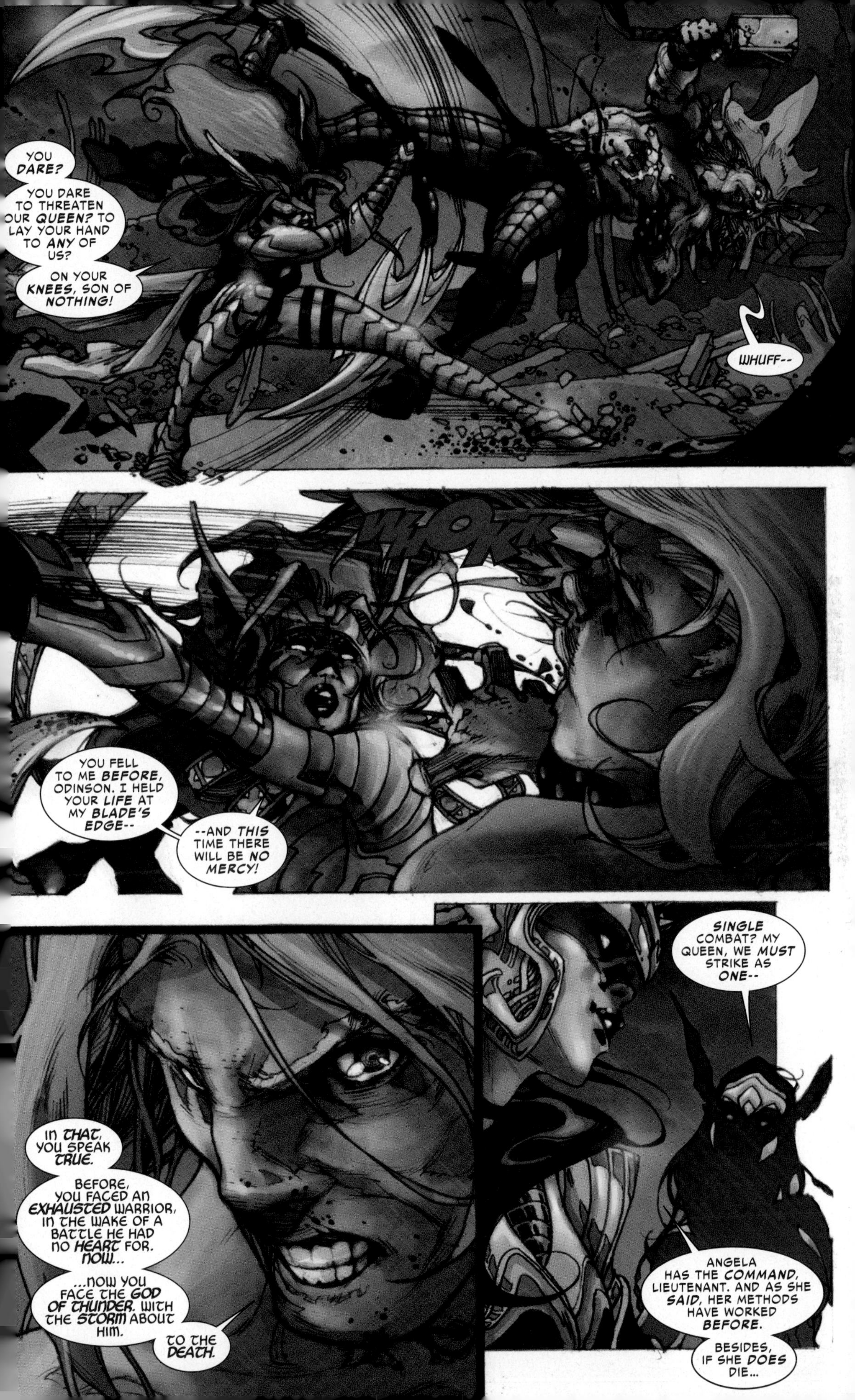

YOU DARE?
YOU DARE TO THREATEN OUR QUEEN? TO LAY YOUR HAND TO ANY OF US?
ON YOUR KNEES, SON OF NOTHING!
WHUFF--
WHOKK
YOU FELL TO ME BEFORE, ODINSON. I HELD YOUR LIFE AT MY BLADE'S EDGE--
--AND THIS TIME THERE WILL BE NO MERCY!
IN THAT, YOU SPEAK TRUE.
BEFORE, YOU FACED AN EXHAUSTED WARRIOR, IN THE WAKE OF A BATTLE HE HAD NO HEART FOR. NOW...
...NOW YOU FACE THE GOD OF THUNDER, WITH THE STORM ABOUT HIM.
TO THE DEATH.
SINGLE COMBAT? MY QUEEN, WE MUST STRIKE AS ONE--
ANGELA HAS THE COMMAND, LIEUTENANT. AND AS SHE SAID, HER METHODS HAVE WORKED BEFORE.
BESIDES, IF SHE DOES DIE...

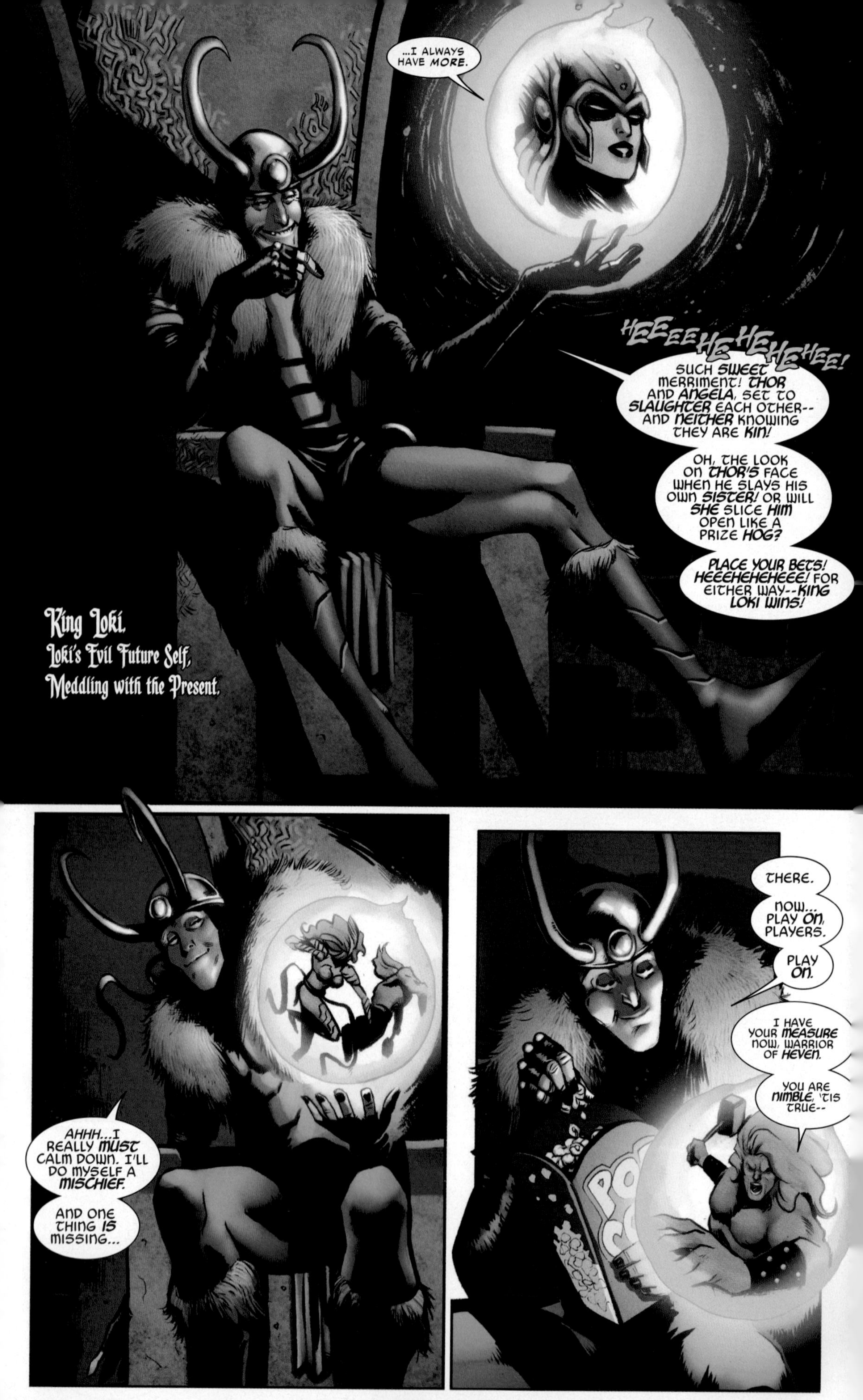

...I ALWAYS HAVE MORE.
HEEEEHEHEHEHEE!
SUCH SWEET MERRIMENT! THOR AND ANGELA, SET TO SLAUGHTER EACH OTHER-- AND NEITHER KNOWING THEY ARE KIN!
OH, THE LOOK ON THOR'S FACE WHEN HE SLAYS HIS OWN SISTER! OR WILL SHE SLICE HIM OPEN LIKE A PRIZE HOG?
PLACE YOUR BETS! HEEEHEHEHEEE! FOR EITHER WAY--KING LOKI WINS!
King Loki.
Loki's Evil Future Self,
Meddling with the Present.
AHHH...I REALLY MUST CALM DOWN. I'LL DO MYSELF A MISCHIEF.
AND ONE THING IS MISSING...
THERE.
NOW... PLAY ON, PLAYERS.
PLAY ON.
I HAVE YOUR MEASURE NOW, WARRIOR OF HEVEN.
YOU ARE NIMBLE, 'TIS TRUE--

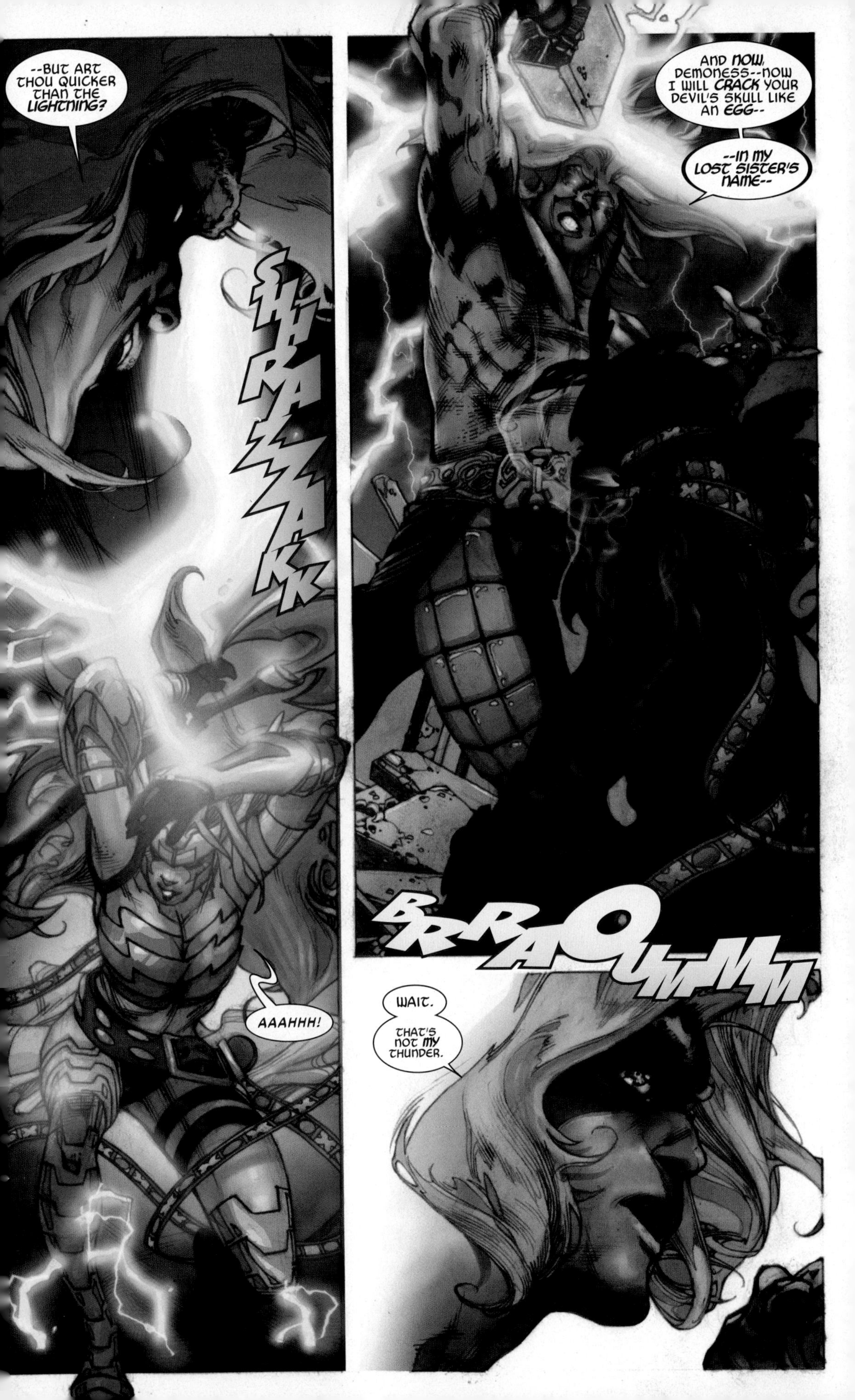
--BUT ART THOU QUICKER THAN THE LIGHTNING?
SHRAZZAKK
AND NOW, DEMONESS--NOW I WILL CRACK YOUR DEVIL'S SKULL LIKE AN EGG--
--IN MY LOST SISTER'S NAME--
AAAHHH!
BRRAOUMMM
WAIT.
THAT'S NOT MY THUNDER.

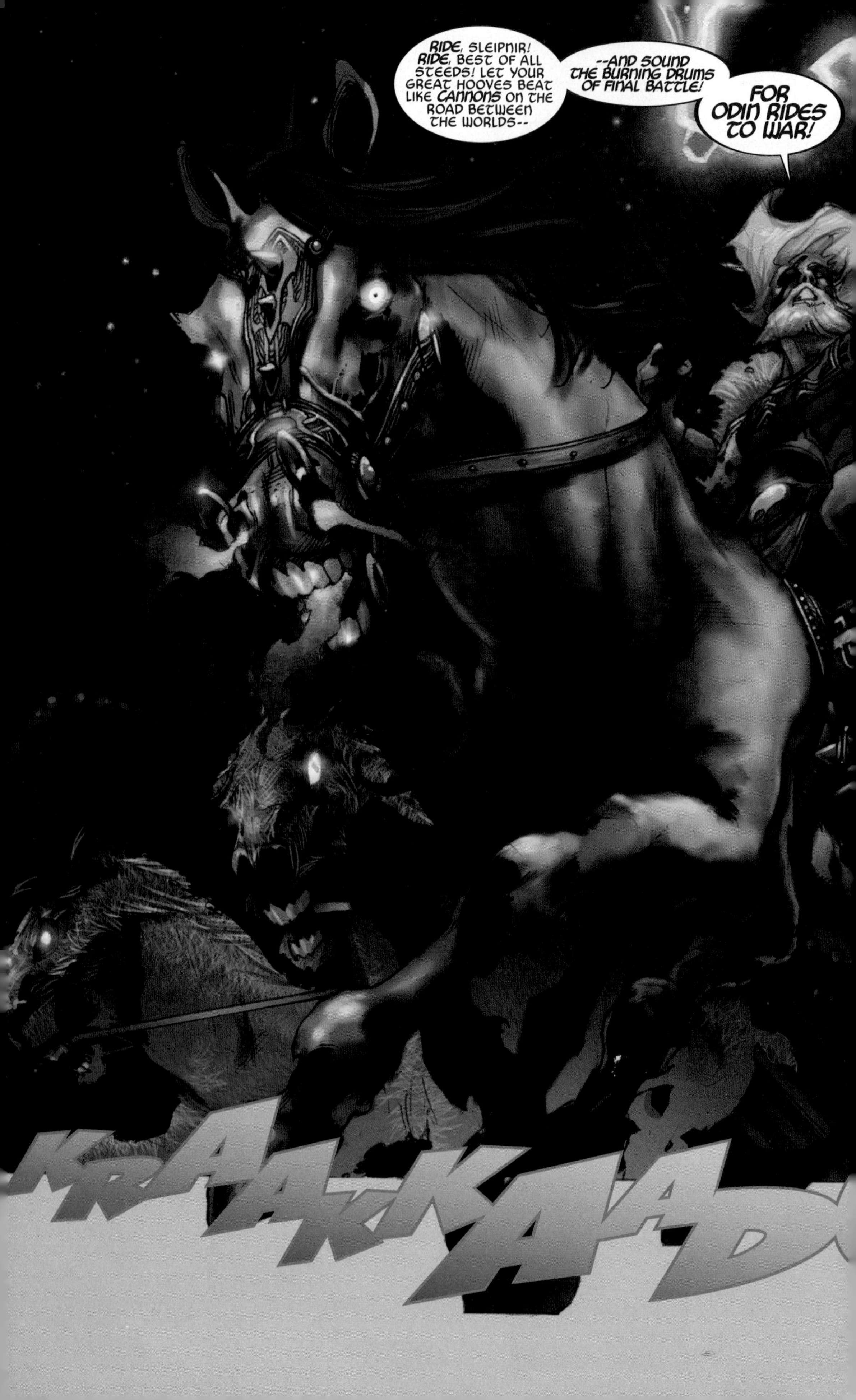
RIDE, SLEIPNIR! RIDE, BEST OF ALL STEEDS! LET YOUR GREAT HOOVES BEAT LIKE CANNONS ON THE ROAD BETWEEN THE WORLDS--
--AND SOUND THE BURNING DRUMS OF FINAL BATTLE!
FOR ODIN RIDES TO WAR!
KRAAKKAAD

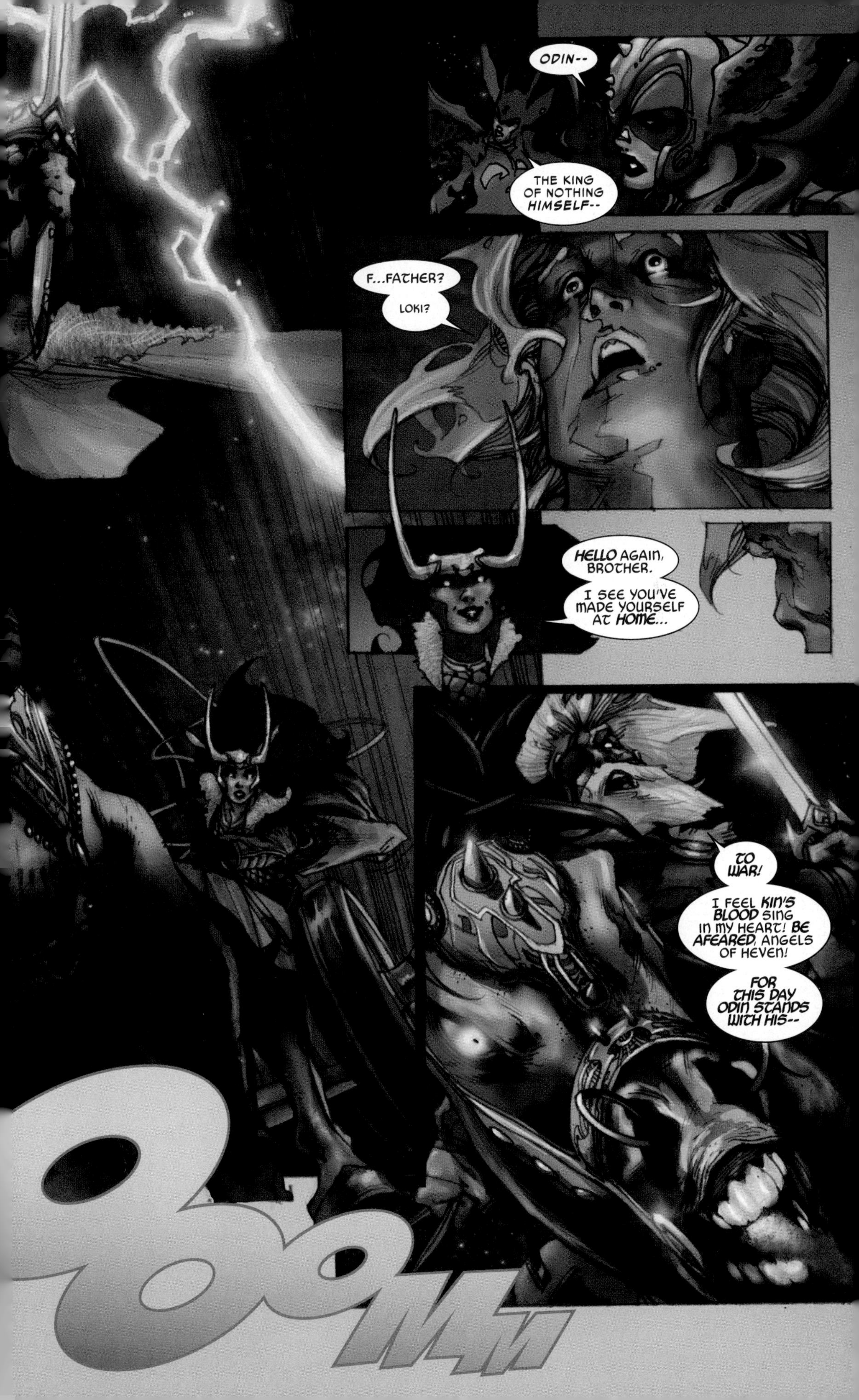
ODIN--
THE KING OF NOTHING HIMSELF--
F...FATHER?
LOKI?
HELLO AGAIN, BROTHER.
I SEE YOU'VE MADE YOURSELF AT HOME...
TO WAR!
I FEEL KIN'S BLOOD SING IN MY HEART! BE AFEARED, ANGELS OF HEVEN!
FOR THIS DAY ODIN STANDS WITH HIS--
BOOM

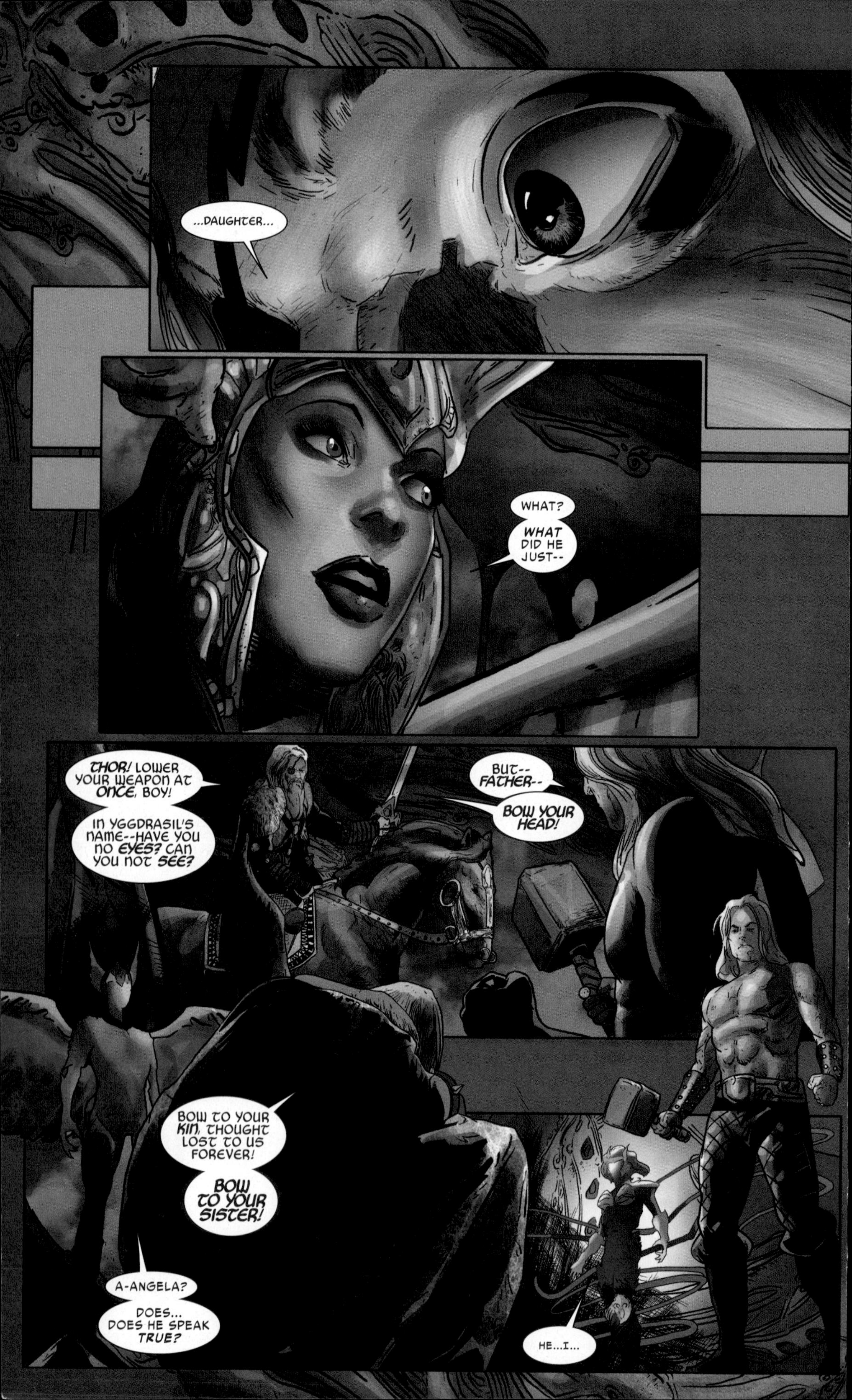
...DAUGHTER...
WHAT?
WHAT DID HE JUST--
THOR! LOWER YOUR WEAPON AT ONCE, BOY!
IN YGGDRASIL'S NAME--HAVE YOU NO EYES? CAN YOU NOT SEE?
BUT-- FATHER--
BOW YOUR HEAD!
BOW TO YOUR KIN, THOUGHT LOST TO US FOREVER!
BOW TO YOUR SISTER!
A-ANGELA?
DOES... DOES HE SPEAK TRUE?
HE...I...

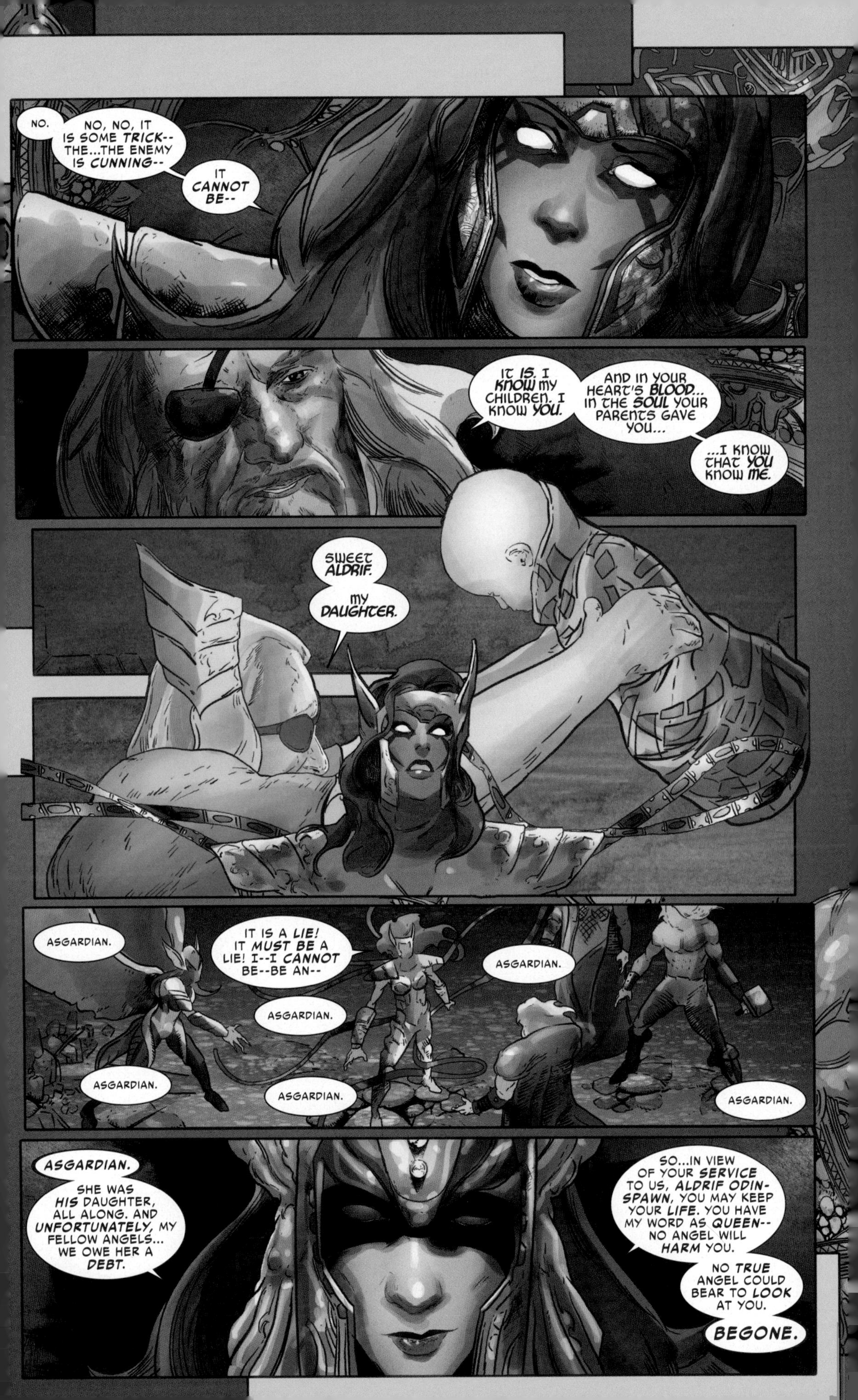
NO.
NO, NO, IT IS SOME TRICK-- THE...THE ENEMY IS CUNNING--
IT CANNOT BE--
IT IS. I KNOW MY CHILDREN. I KNOW YOU.
AND IN YOUR HEART'S BLOOD... IN THE SOUL YOUR PARENTS GAVE YOU...
...I KNOW THAT YOU KNOW ME.
SWEET ALDRIF.
MY DAUGHTER.
ASGARDIAN.
IT IS A LIE! IT MUST BE A LIE! I--I CANNOT BE--BE AN--
ASGARDIAN.
ASGARDIAN.
ASGARDIAN.
ASGARDIAN.
ASGARDIAN.
ASGARDIAN.
SHE WAS HIS DAUGHTER, ALL ALONG. AND UNFORTUNATELY, MY FELLOW ANGELS... WE OWE HER A DEBT.
SO...IN VIEW OF YOUR SERVICE TO US, ALDRIF ODIN-SPAWN, YOU MAY KEEP YOUR LIFE. YOU HAVE MY WORD AS QUEEN-- NO ANGEL WILL HARM YOU.
NO TRUE ANGEL COULD BEAR TO LOOK AT YOU.
BEGONE.

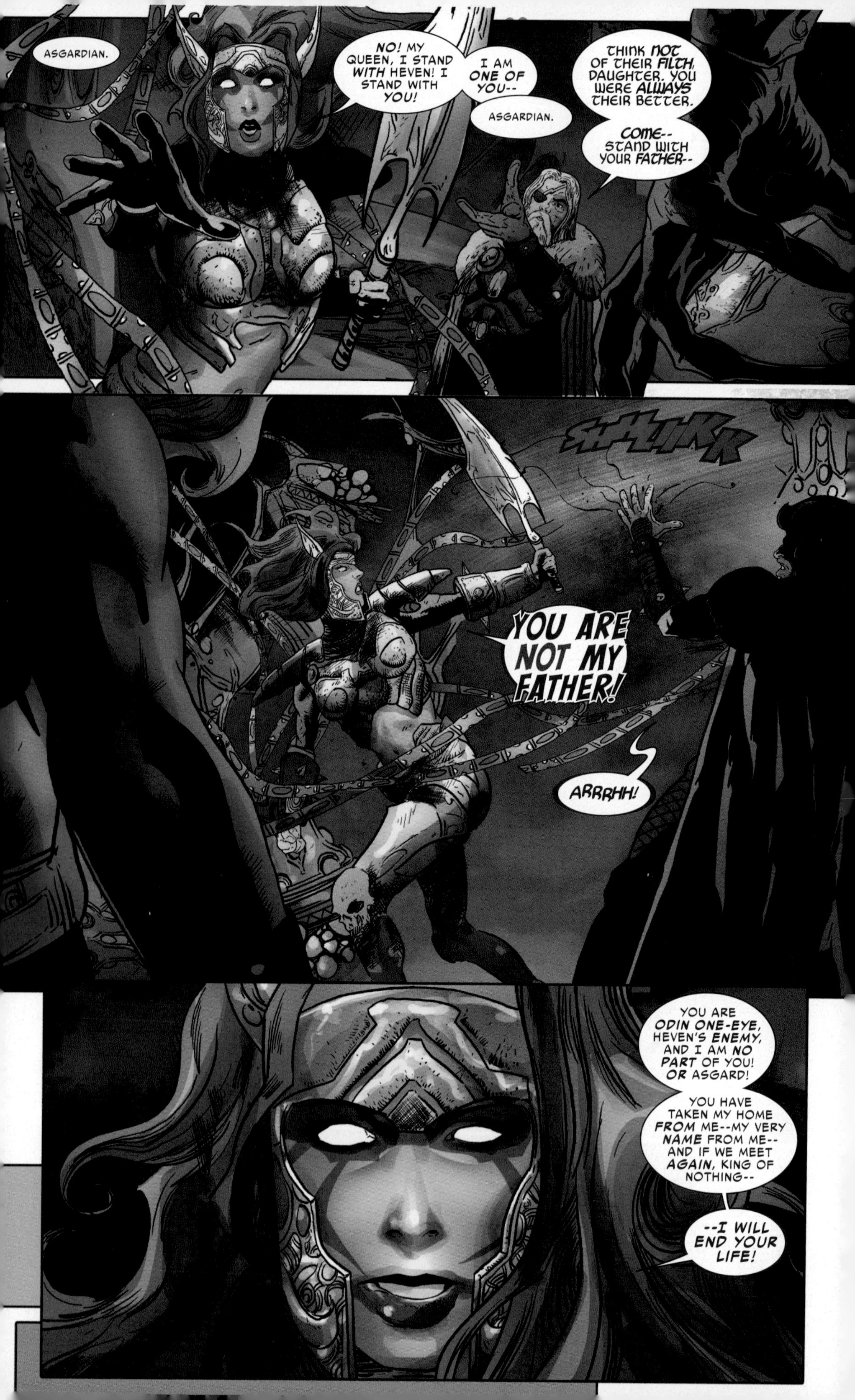
ASGARDIAN.
NO! MY QUEEN, I STAND WITH HEVEN! I STAND WITH YOU!
I AM ONE OF YOU--
ASGARDIAN.
THINK NOT OF THEIR FILTH, DAUGHTER. YOU WERE ALWAYS THEIR BETTER.
COME-- STAND WITH YOUR FATHER--
SHHLIKK
YOU ARE NOT MY FATHER!
ARRRHH!
YOU ARE ODIN ONE-EYE, HEVEN'S ENEMY, AND I AM NO PART OF YOU! OR ASGARD!
YOU HAVE TAKEN MY HOME FROM ME--MY VERY NAME FROM ME--AND IF WE MEET AGAIN, KING OF NOTHING--
--I WILL END YOUR LIFE!

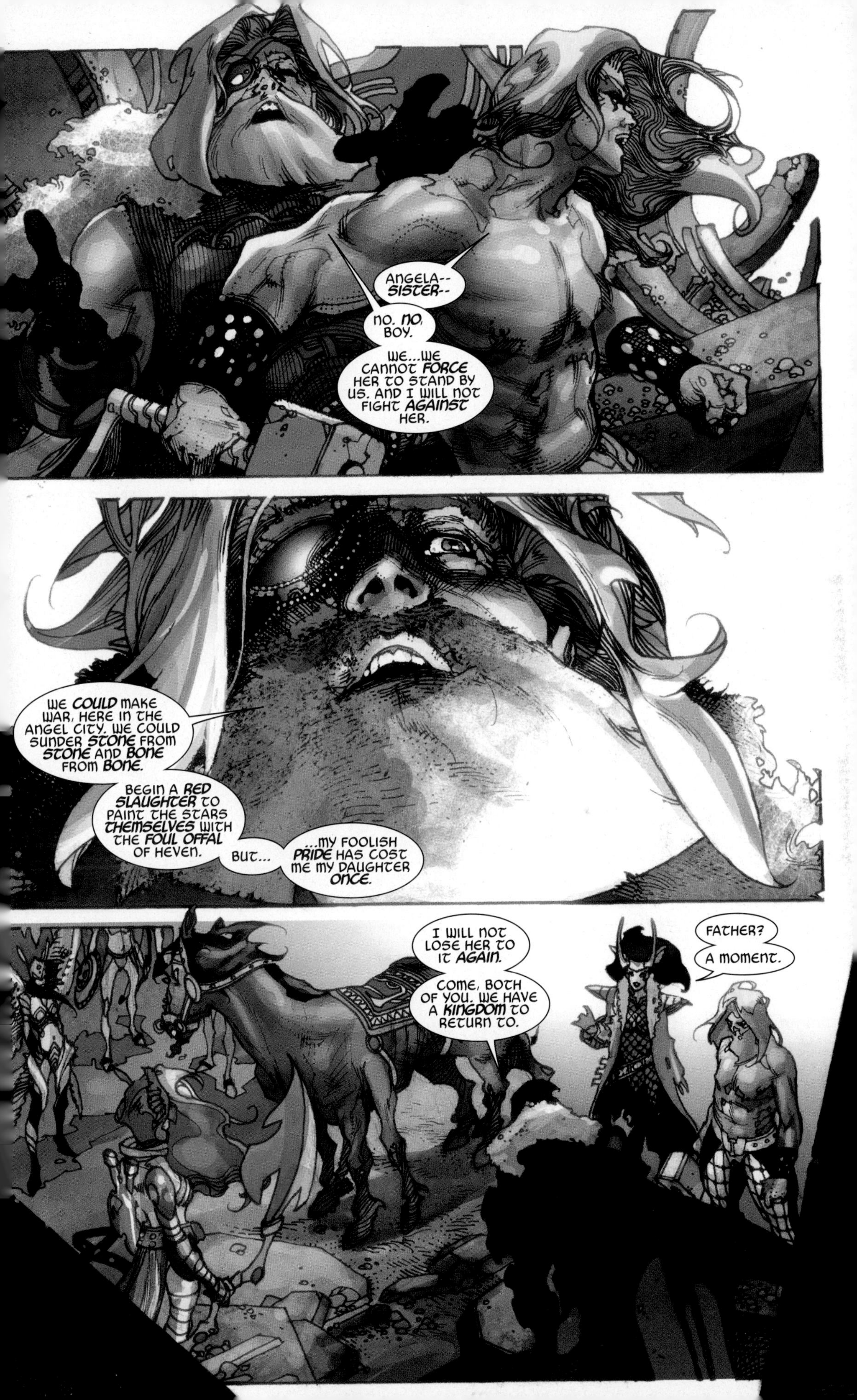
ANGELA--
SISTER--
NO. NO, BOY.
WE...WE CANNOT FORCE HER TO STAND BY US. AND I WILL NOT FIGHT AGAINST HER.
WE COULD MAKE WAR, HERE IN THE ANGEL CITY. WE COULD SUNDER STONE FROM STONE AND BONE FROM BONE.
BEGIN A RED SLAUGHTER TO PAINT THE STARS THEMSELVES WITH THE FOUL OFFAL OF HEVEN.
BUT...
...MY FOOLISH PRIDE HAS COST ME MY DAUGHTER ONCE.
I WILL NOT LOSE HER TO IT AGAIN.
COME, BOTH OF YOU. WE HAVE A KINGDOM TO RETURN TO.
FATHER?
A MOMENT.

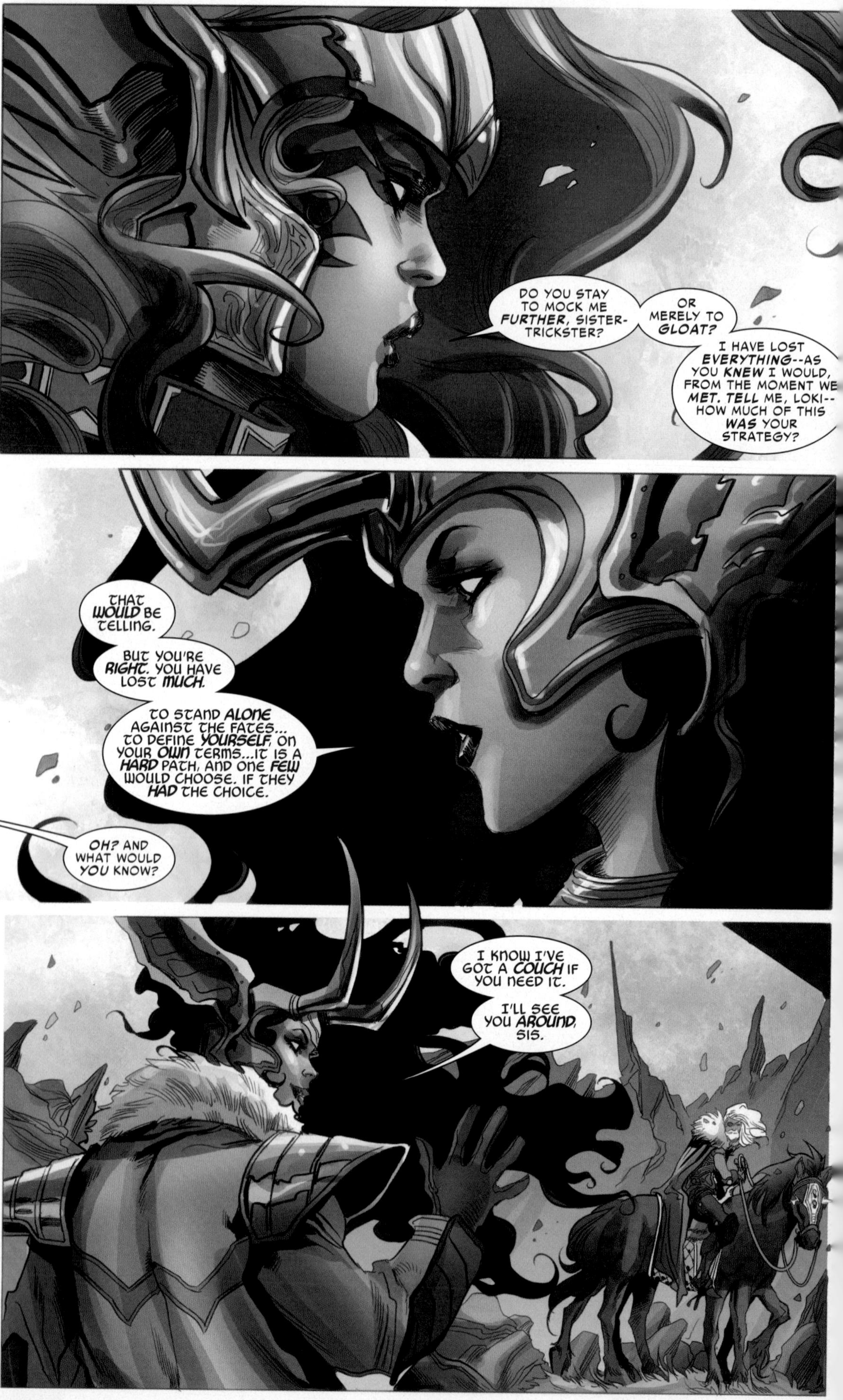
DO YOU STAY TO MOCK ME FURTHER, SISTER-TRICKSTER?
OR MERELY TO GLOAT?
I HAVE LOST EVERYTHING--AS YOU KNEW I WOULD, FROM THE MOMENT WE MET. TELL ME, LOKI--HOW MUCH OF THIS WAS YOUR STRATEGY?
THAT WOULD BE TELLING.
BUT YOU'RE RIGHT. YOU HAVE LOST MUCH.
TO STAND ALONE AGAINST THE FATES... TO DEFINE YOURSELF, ON YOUR OWN TERMS...IT IS A HARD PATH, AND ONE FEW WOULD CHOOSE. IF THEY HAD THE CHOICE.
OH? AND WHAT WOULD YOU KNOW?
I KNOW I'VE GOT A COUCH IF YOU NEED IT.
I'LL SEE YOU AROUND, SIS.

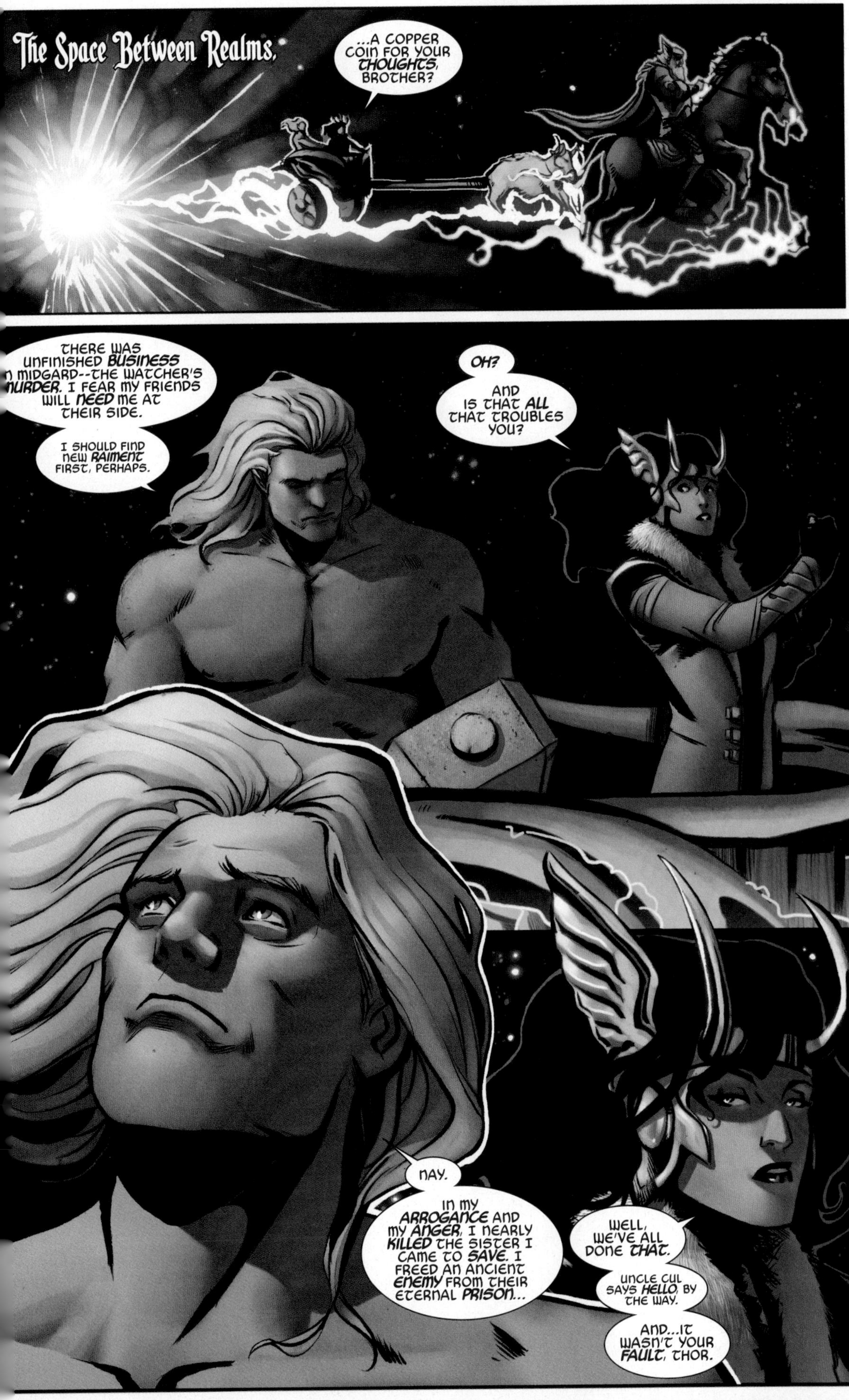
The Space Between Realms.
...A COPPER COIN FOR YOUR THOUGHTS, BROTHER?
THERE WAS UNFINISHED BUSINESS n MIDGARD--THE WATCHER'S NURDER. I FEAR MY FRIENDS WILL NEED ME AT THEIR SIDE.
I SHOULD FIND NEW RAIMENT FIRST, PERHAPS.
OH?
AND IS THAT ALL THAT TROUBLES YOU?
NAY.
IN MY ARROGANCE AND MY ANGER, I NEARLY KILLED THE SISTER I CAME TO SAVE. I FREED AN ANCIENT ENEMY FROM THEIR ETERNAL PRISON...
WELL, WE'VE ALL DONE THAT.
UNCLE CUL SAYS HELLO, BY THE WAY.
AND...IT WASN'T YOUR FAULT, THOR.

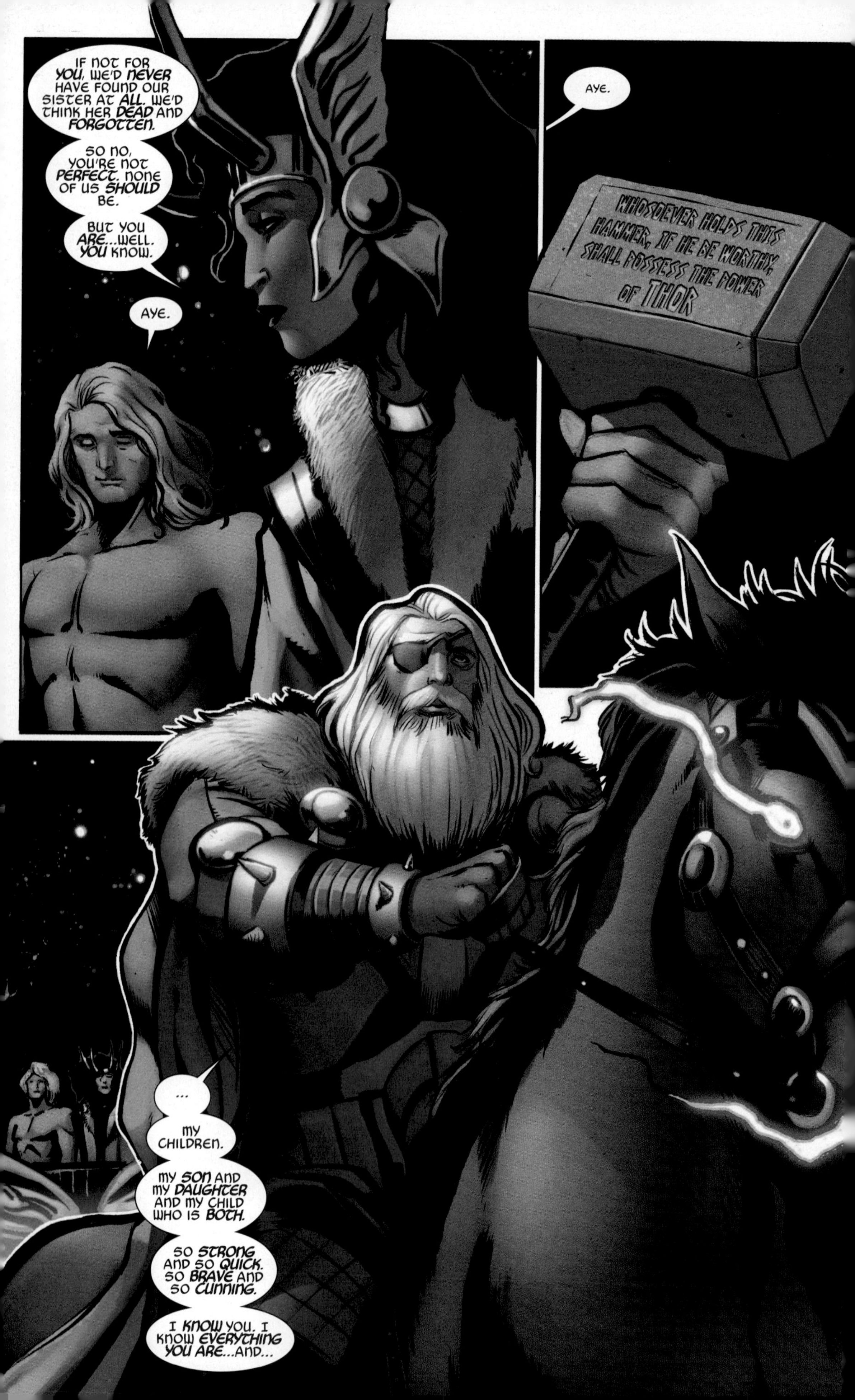

IF NOT FOR YOU, WE'D NEVER HAVE FOUND OUR SISTER AT ALL. WE'D THINK HER DEAD AND FORGOTTEN.
SO NO, YOU'RE NOT PERFECT. NONE OF US SHOULD BE.
BUT YOU ARE...WELL. YOU KNOW.
AYE.
AYE.
WHOSOEVER HOLDS THIS HAMMER, IF HE BE WORTHY, SHALL POSSESS THE POWER OF THOR
...
MY CHILDREN.
MY SON AND MY DAUGHTER AND MY CHILD WHO IS BOTH.
SO STRONG AND SO QUICK. SO BRAVE AND SO CUNNING.
I KNOW YOU. I KNOW EVERYTHING YOU ARE...AND...

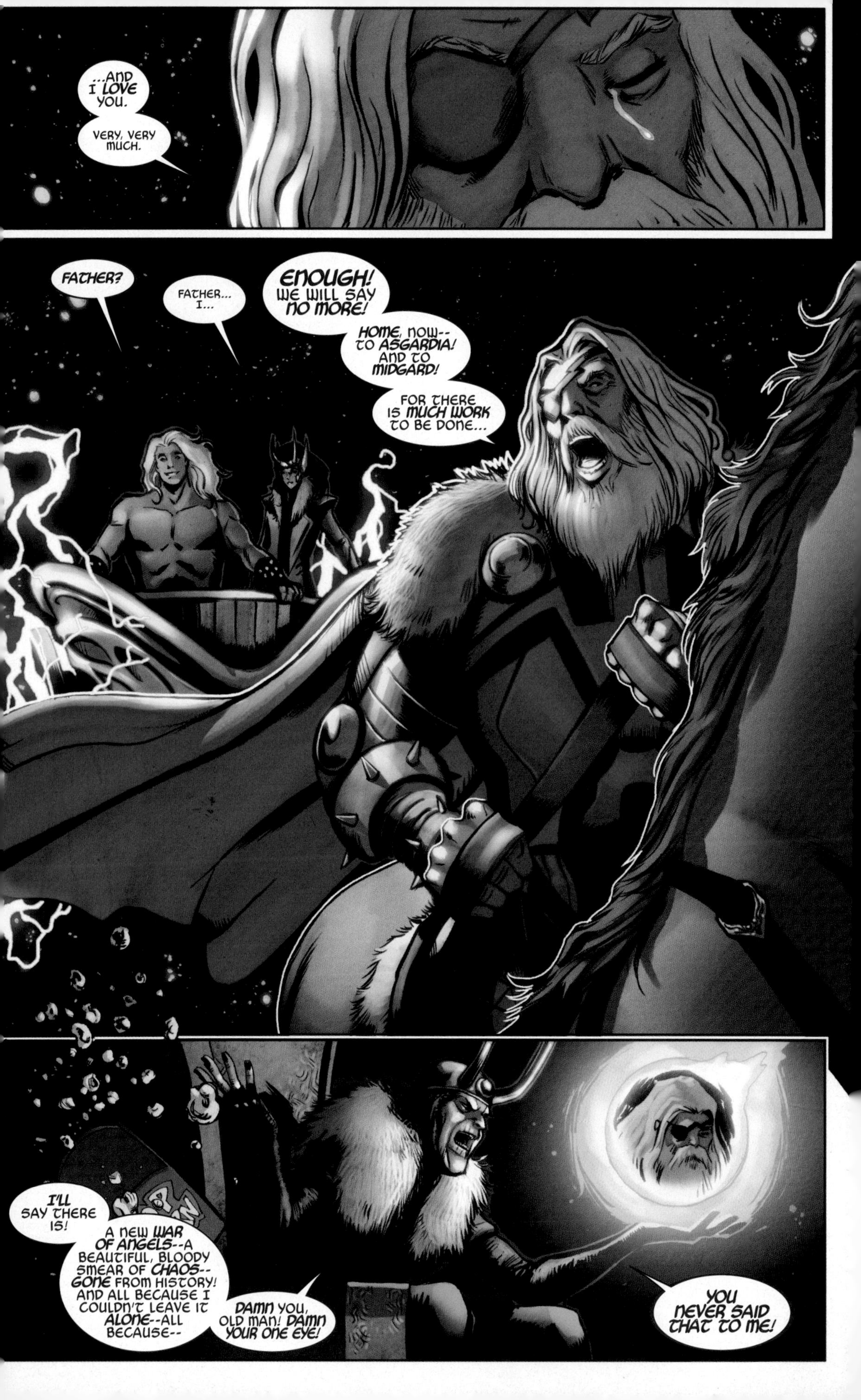
...AND I LOVE YOU.
VERY, VERY MUCH.
FATHER?
FATHER... I...
ENOUGH! WE WILL SAY NO MORE!
HOME, NOW--TO ASGARDIA! AND TO MIDGARD!
FOR THERE IS MUCH WORK TO BE DONE...
I'LL SAY THERE IS!
A NEW WAR OF ANGELS--A BEAUTIFUL, BLOODY SMEAR OF CHAOS--GONE FROM HISTORY! AND ALL BECAUSE I COULDN'T LEAVE IT ALONE--ALL BECAUSE--
DAMN YOU, OLD MAN! DAMN YOUR ONE EYE!
YOU NEVER SAID THAT TO ME!

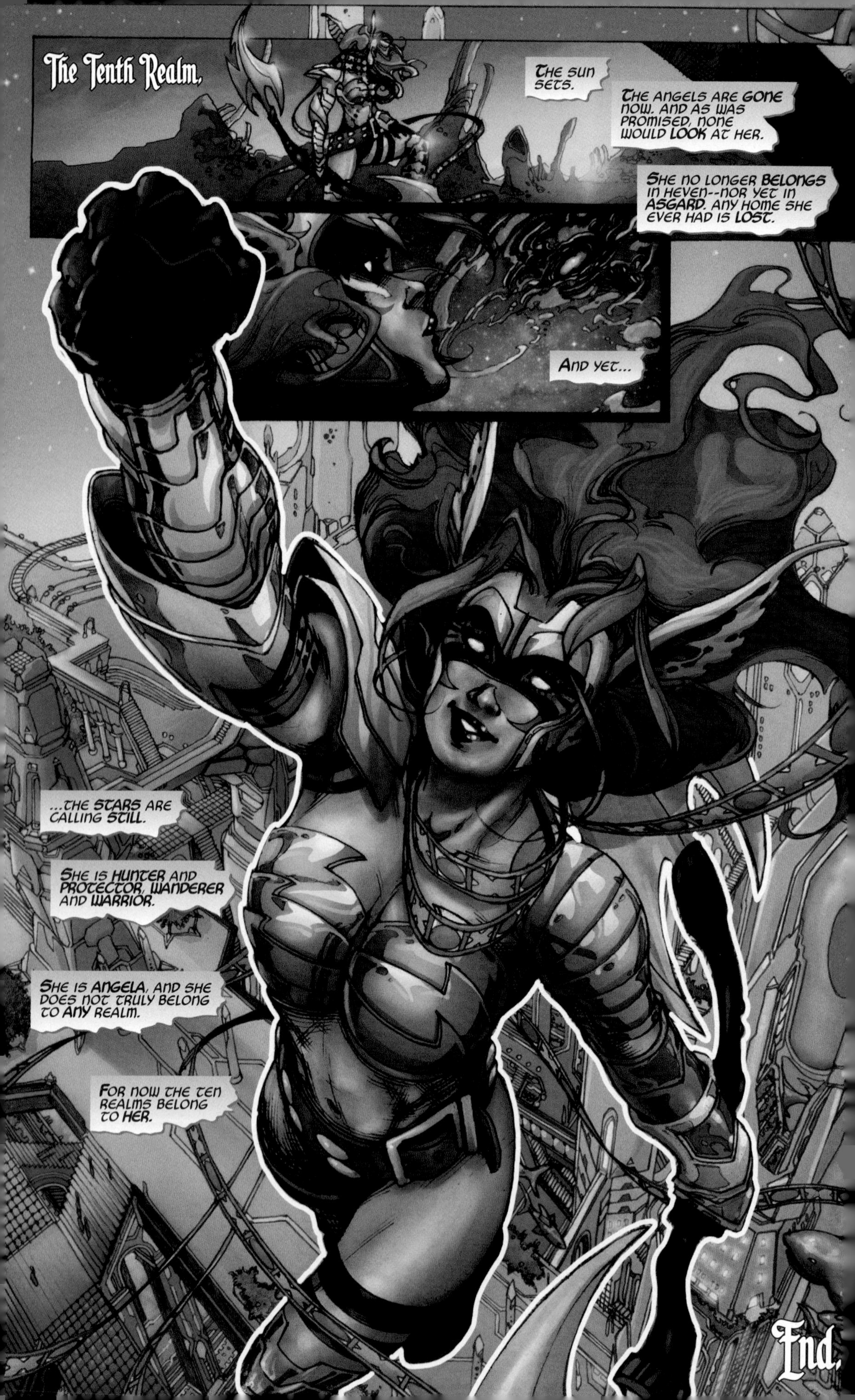
The Tenth Realm,
THE SUN SETS.
THE ANGELS ARE GONE NOW. AND AS WAS PROMISED, NONE WOULD LOOK AT HER.
SHE NO LONGER BELONGS IN HEVEN--NOR YET IN ASGARD. ANY HOME SHE EVER HAD IS LOST.
AND YET...
...THE STARS ARE CALLING STILL.
SHE IS HUNTER AND PROTECTOR, WANDERER AND WARRIOR.
SHE IS ANGELA, AND SHE DOES NOT TRULY BELONG TO ANY REALM.
FOR NOW THE TEN REALMS BELONG TO HER.
End.

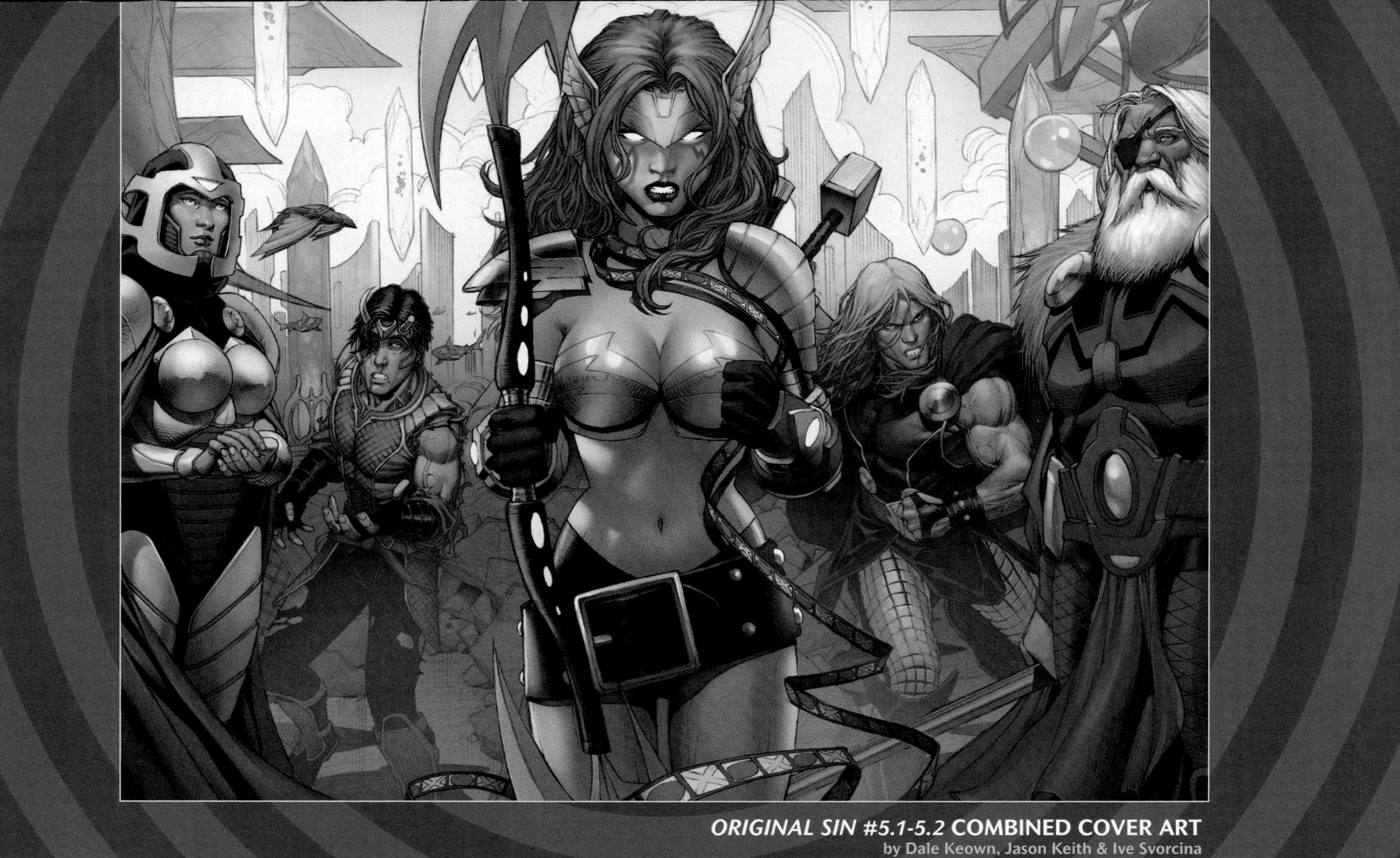

ORIGINAL SIN #5.1-5.2 COMBINED COVER ART
by Dale Keown, Jason Keith & Ive Svorcina

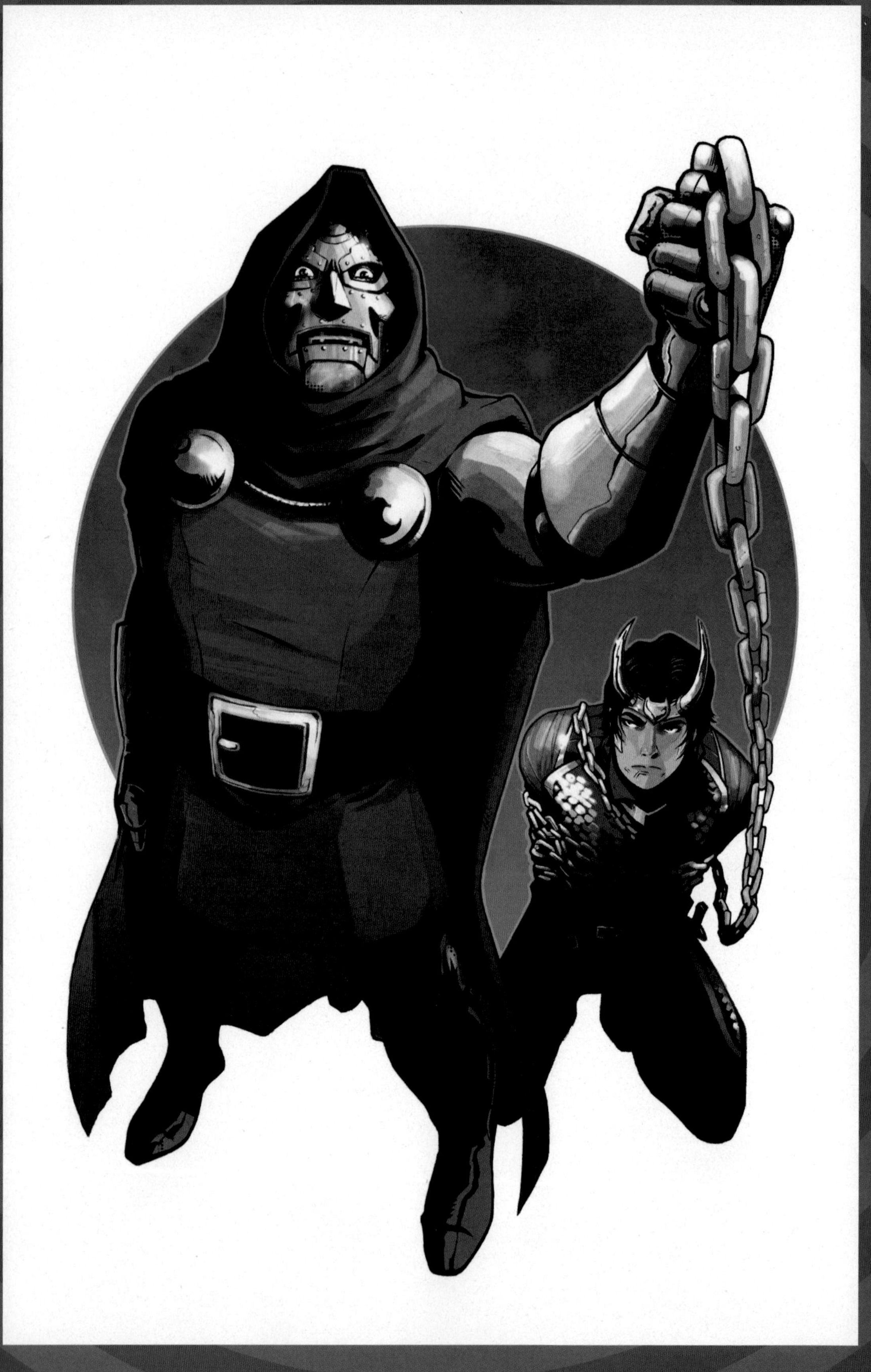

LOKI: AGENT OF ASGARD #6

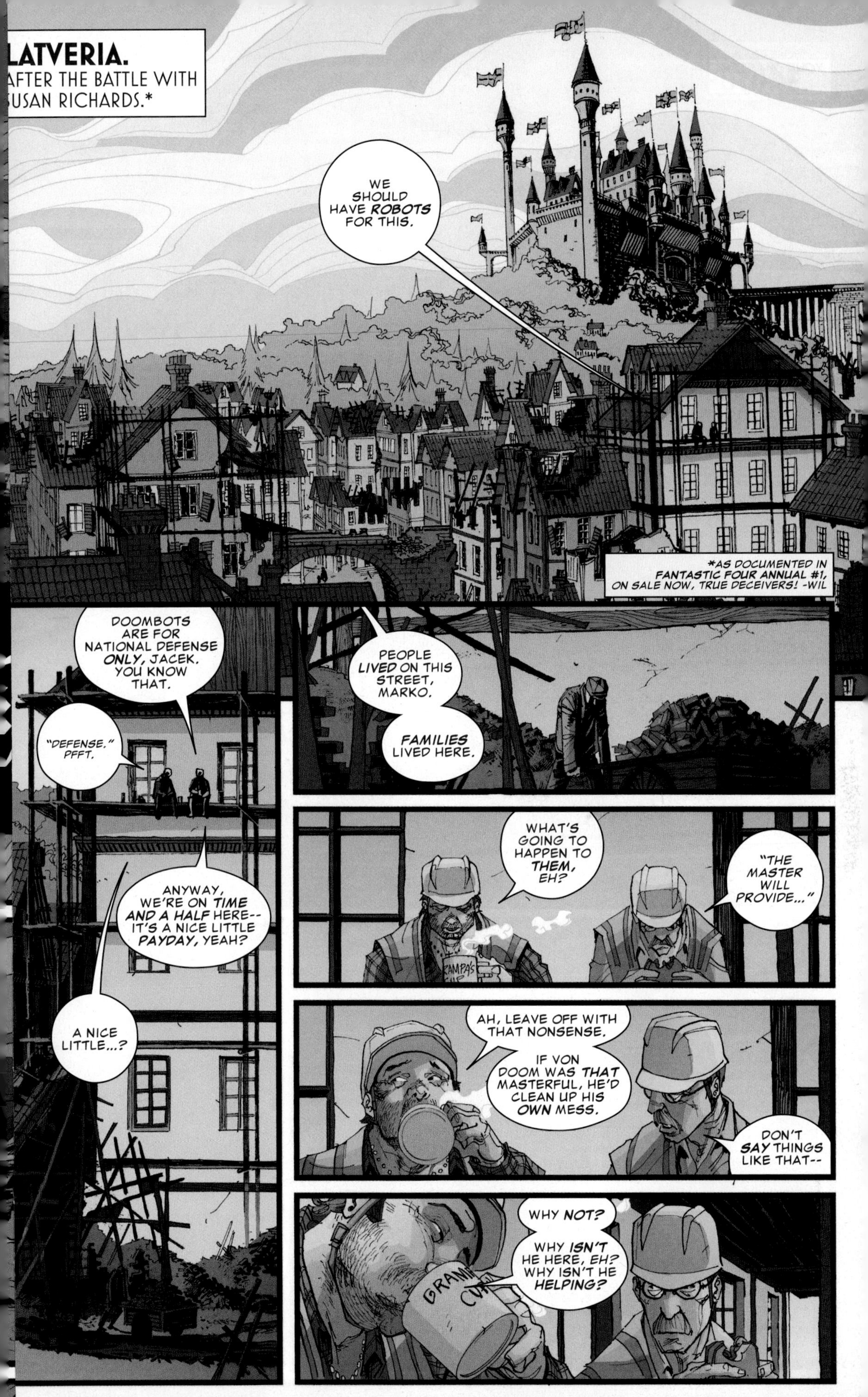
LATVERIA.
AFTER THE BATTLE WITH SUSAN RICHARDS.*
WE SHOULD HAVE ROBOTS FOR THIS.
*AS DOCUMENTED IN FANTASTIC FOUR ANNUAL #1, ON SALE NOW, TRUE DECEIVERS! -WIL
DOOMBOTS ARE FOR NATIONAL DEFENSE ONLY, JACEK. YOU KNOW THAT.
"DEFENSE." PFFT.
ANYWAY, WE'RE ON TIME AND A HALF HERE-- IT'S A NICE LITTLE PAYDAY, YEAH?
A NICE LITTLE...?
PEOPLE LIVED ON THIS STREET, MARKO.
FAMILIES LIVED HERE.
WHAT'S GOING TO HAPPEN TO THEM, EH?
"THE MASTER WILL PROVIDE..."
AH, LEAVE OFF WITH THAT NONSENSE.
IF VON DOOM WAS THAT MASTERFUL, HE'D CLEAN UP HIS OWN MESS.
DON'T SAY THINGS LIKE THAT--
WHY NOT?
WHY ISN'T HE HERE, EH? WHY ISN'T HE HELPING?

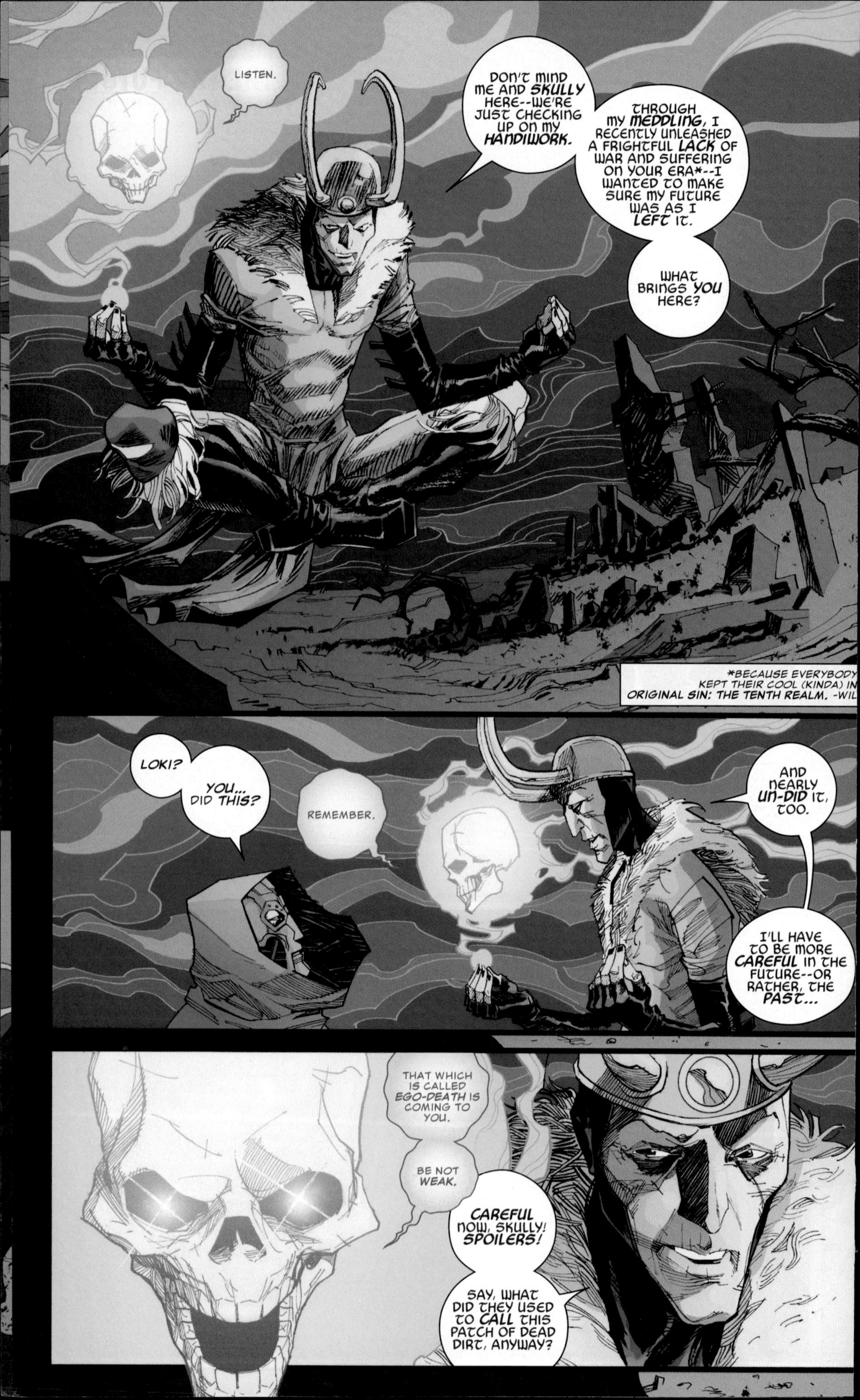
LISTEN.
DON'T MIND ME AND SKULLY HERE--WE'RE JUST CHECKING UP ON MY HANDIWORK.
THROUGH MY MEDDLING, I RECENTLY UNLEASHED A FRIGHTFUL LACK OF WAR AND SUFFERING ON YOUR ERA*--I WANTED TO MAKE SURE MY FUTURE WAS AS I LEFT IT.
WHAT BRINGS YOU HERE?
*BECAUSE EVERYBODY KEPT THEIR COOL (KINDA) IN ORIGINAL SIN: THE TENTH REALM. -WIL
LOKI?
YOU... DID THIS?
REMEMBER.
AND NEARLY UN-DID IT, TOO.
I'LL HAVE TO BE MORE CAREFUL IN THE FUTURE--OR RATHER, THE PAST...
THAT WHICH IS CALLED EGO-DEATH IS COMING TO YOU.
BE NOT WEAK.
CAREFUL NOW, SKULLY! SPOILERS!
SAY, WHAT DID THEY USED TO CALL THIS PATCH OF DEAD DIRT, ANYWAY?

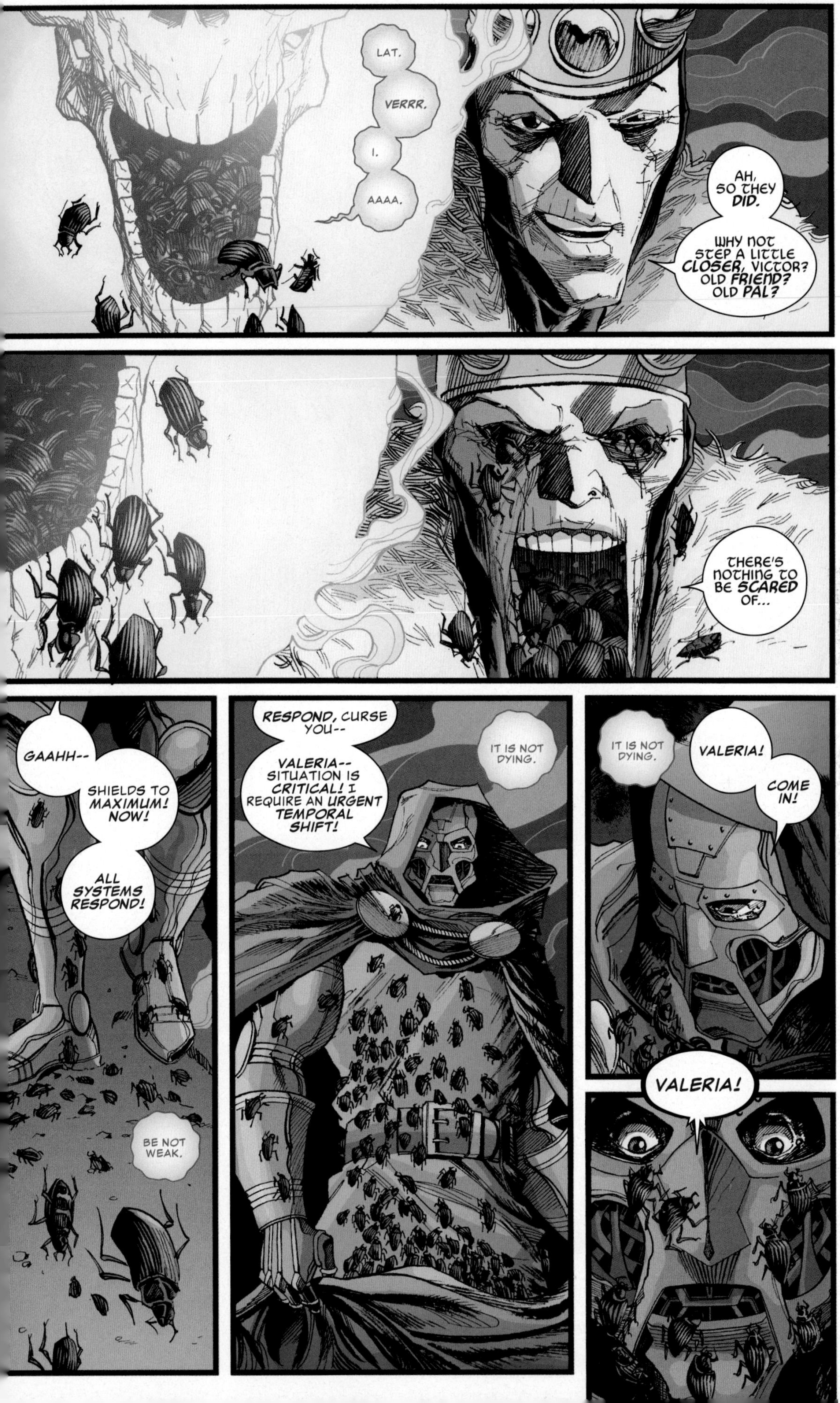
LAT.
VERRR.
I.
AAAA.
AH, SO THEY DID.
WHY NOT STEP A LITTLE CLOSER, VICTOR? OLD FRIEND? OLD PAL?
THERE'S NOTHING TO BE SCARED OF...
GAAHH--
SHIELDS TO MAXIMUM! NOW!
ALL SYSTEMS RESPOND!
BE NOT WEAK.
RESPOND, CURSE YOU--
VALERIA--SITUATION IS CRITICAL! I REQUIRE AN URGENT TEMPORAL SHIFT!
IT IS NOT DYING.
IT IS NOT DYING.
VALERIA!
COME IN!
VALERIA!

VALERIAAAA--

UNCLE DOOM?

ARE YOU...ARE YOU OKAY, UNCLE DOOM?

YOU SOUNDED SCARED...

KRAKDOOMMM

...

YOU'RE HEARING THINGS, CHILD.

DOOM IS NEVER AFRAID.

...WHY DID YOU GO SO FAR FORWARD IN TIME, UNCLE DOOM?

THESE GOOD WORKS WE DO--AND OTHERS--I DO FOR THE SAKE OF THE FUTURE.

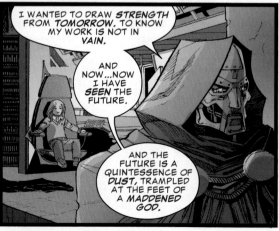

I WANTED TO DRAW STRENGTH FROM TOMORROW, TO KNOW MY WORK IS NOT IN VAIN.

AND NOW...NOW I HAVE SEEN THE FUTURE.

AND THE FUTURE IS A QUINTESSENCE OF DUST, TRAMPLED AT THE FEET OF A MADDENED GOD.

A GOD I MUST DESTROY...

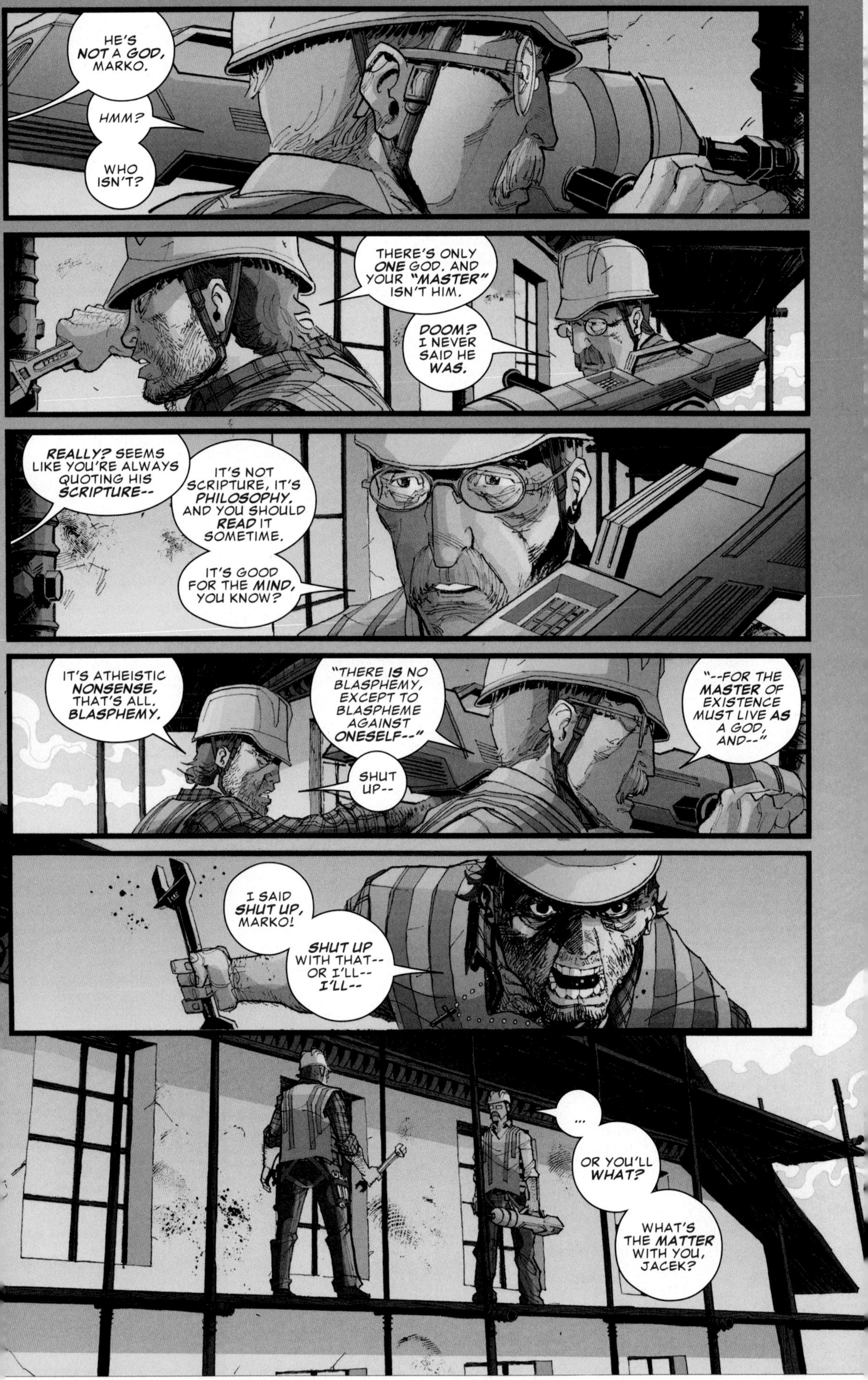
HE'S NOT A GOD, MARKO.
HMM?
WHO ISN'T?
THERE'S ONLY ONE GOD. AND YOUR "MASTER" ISN'T HIM.
DOOM? I NEVER SAID HE WAS.
REALLY? SEEMS LIKE YOU'RE ALWAYS QUOTING HIS SCRIPTURE--
IT'S NOT SCRIPTURE, IT'S PHILOSOPHY. AND YOU SHOULD READ IT SOMETIME.
IT'S GOOD FOR THE MIND, YOU KNOW?
IT'S ATHEISTIC NONSENSE, THAT'S ALL. BLASPHEMY.
"THERE IS NO BLASPHEMY, EXCEPT TO BLASPHEME AGAINST ONESELF--"
SHUT UP--
"--FOR THE MASTER OF EXISTENCE MUST LIVE AS A GOD, AND--"
I SAID SHUT UP, MARKO!
SHUT UP WITH THAT-- OR I'LL-- I'LL--
...
OR YOU'LL WHAT?
WHAT'S THE MATTER WITH YOU, JACEK?

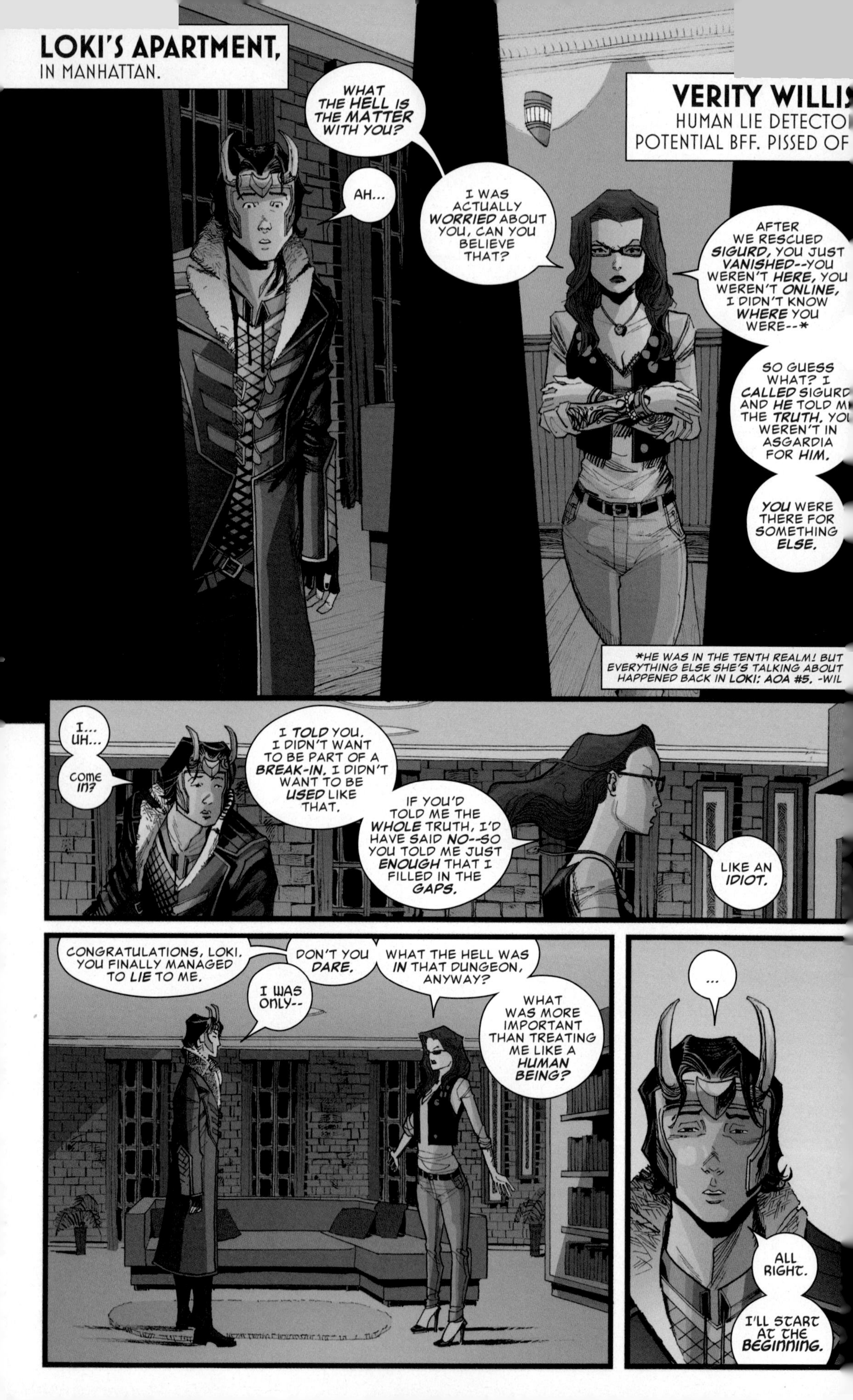
LOKI'S APARTMENT,
IN MANHATTAN.
WHAT THE HELL IS THE MATTER WITH YOU?
AH...
I WAS ACTUALLY WORRIED ABOUT YOU, CAN YOU BELIEVE THAT?
VERITY WILLIS
HUMAN LIE DETECTO
POTENTIAL BFF. PISSED OF
AFTER WE RESCUED SIGURD, YOU JUST VANISHED--YOU WEREN'T HERE, YOU WEREN'T ONLINE, I DIDN'T KNOW WHERE YOU WERE--*
SO GUESS WHAT? I CALLED SIGURD AND HE TOLD M THE TRUTH. YO WEREN'T IN ASGARDIA FOR HIM.
YOU WERE THERE FOR SOMETHING ELSE.
*HE WAS IN THE TENTH REALM! BUT EVERYTHING ELSE SHE'S TALKING ABOUT HAPPENED BACK IN LOKI: AOA #5. -WIL
I... UH...
COME IN?
I TOLD YOU. I DIDN'T WANT TO BE PART OF A BREAK-IN. I DIDN'T WANT TO BE USED LIKE THAT.
IF YOU'D TOLD ME THE WHOLE TRUTH, I'D HAVE SAID NO--SO YOU TOLD ME JUST ENOUGH THAT I FILLED IN THE GAPS.
LIKE AN IDIOT.
CONGRATULATIONS, LOKI. YOU FINALLY MANAGED TO LIE TO ME.
I WAS ONLY--
DON'T YOU DARE.
WHAT THE HELL WAS IN THAT DUNGEON, ANYWAY?
WHAT WAS MORE IMPORTANT THAN TREATING ME LIKE A HUMAN BEING?
...
ALL RIGHT.
I'LL START AT THE BEGINNING.

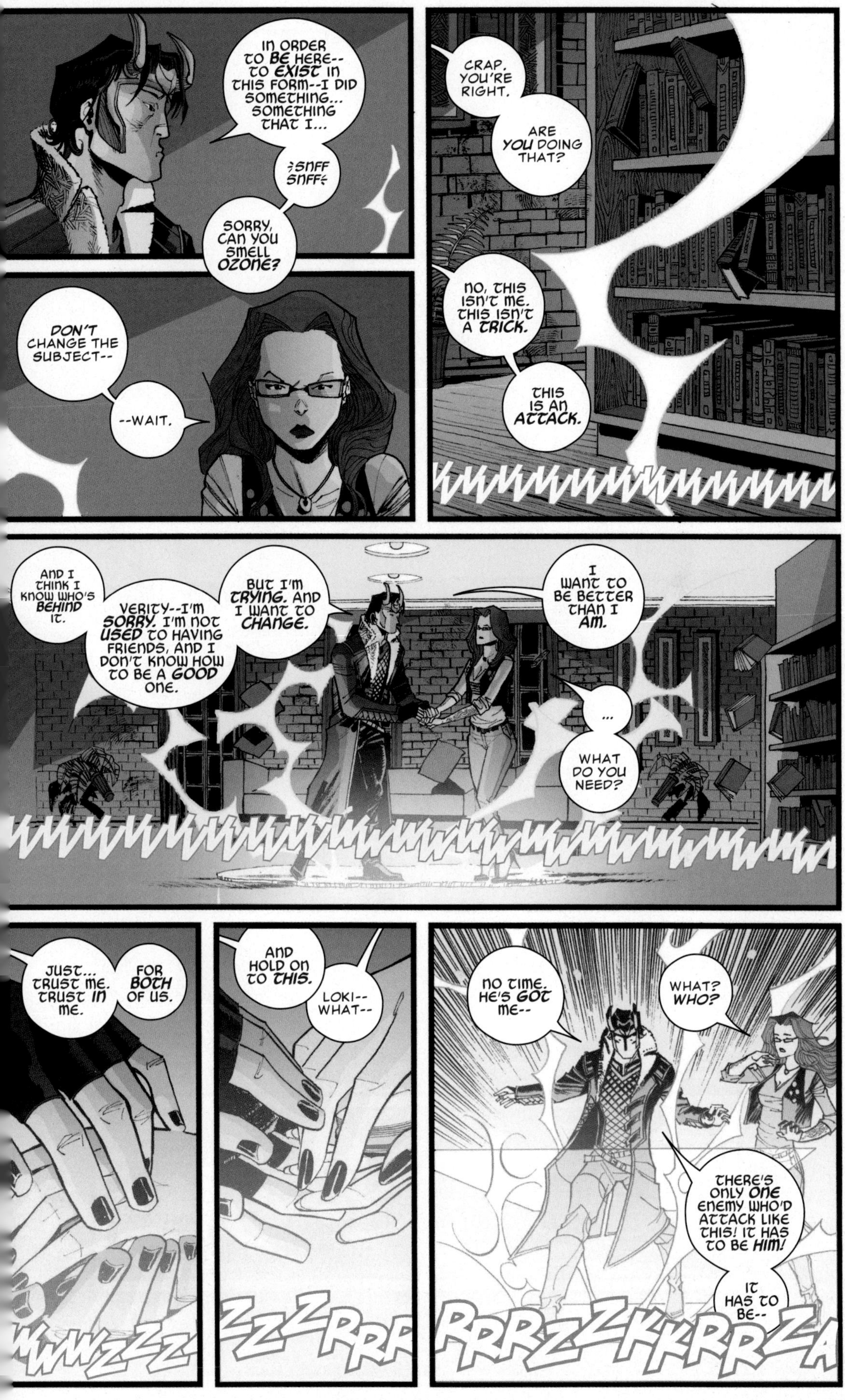

IN ORDER TO BE HERE-- TO EXIST IN THIS FORM--I DID SOMETHING... SOMETHING THAT I...
⸮SNFF SNFF⸮
SORRY, CAN YOU SMELL OZONE?
DON'T CHANGE THE SUBJECT--
--WAIT.
CRAP. YOU'RE RIGHT.
ARE YOU DOING THAT?
NO, THIS ISN'T ME. THIS ISN'T A TRICK.
THIS IS AN ATTACK.
KKKKKKKKKKKKKKKKKKKKKKKK
AND I THINK I KNOW WHO'S BEHIND IT.
VERITY--I'M SORRY. I'M NOT USED TO HAVING FRIENDS, AND I DON'T KNOW HOW TO BE A GOOD ONE.
BUT I'M TRYING. AND I WANT TO CHANGE.
I WANT TO BE BETTER THAN I AM.
...
WHAT DO YOU NEED?
JUST... TRUST ME. TRUST IN ME.
FOR BOTH OF US.
AND HOLD ON TO THIS.
LOKI-- WHAT--
NO TIME. HE'S GOT ME--
WHAT? WHO?
THERE'S ONLY ONE ENEMY WHO'D ATTACK LIKE THIS! IT HAS TO BE HIM!
IT HAS TO BE--
WWWZZZZZZRRRRRRZZKKRRZA

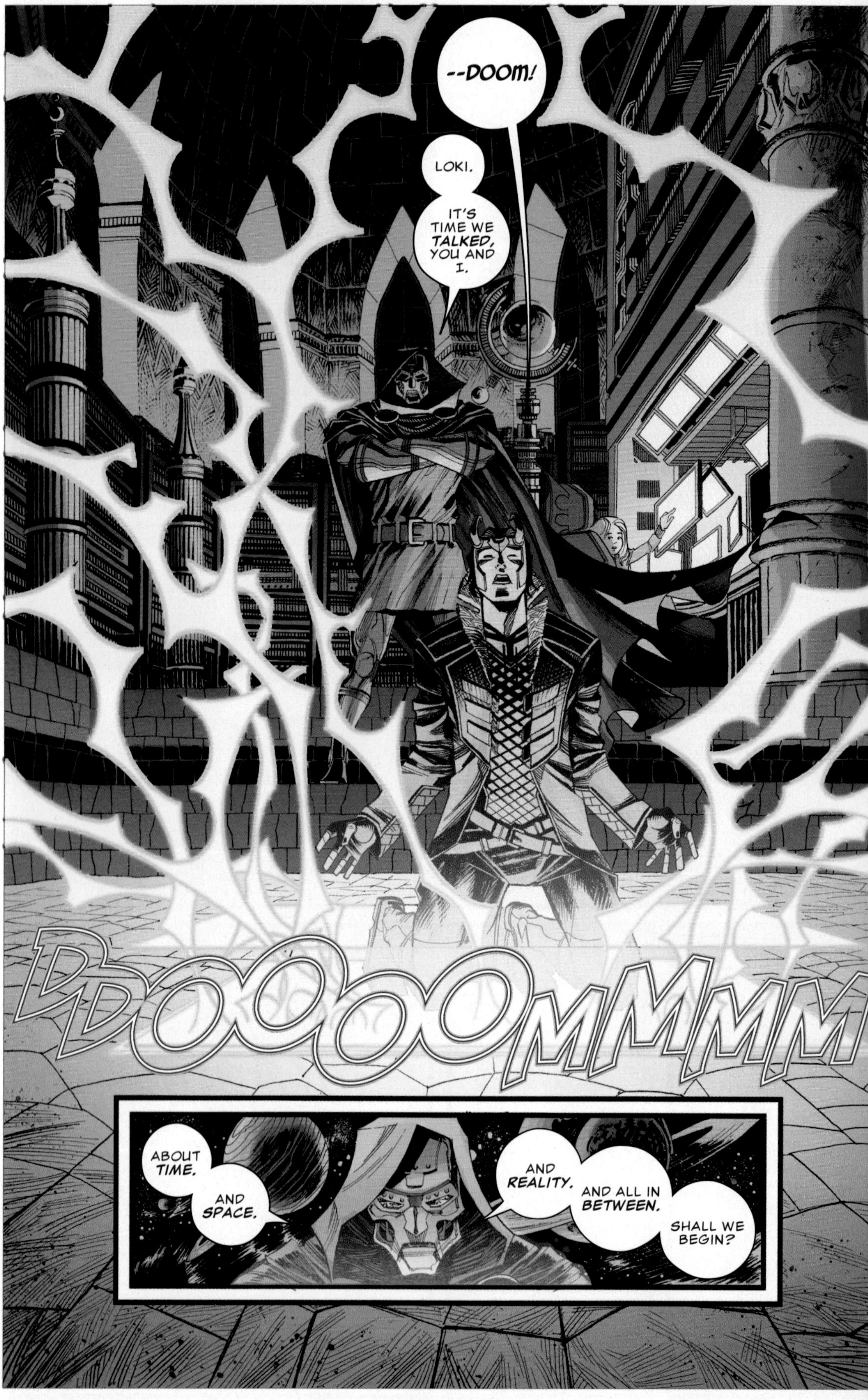

--DOOM!
LOKI.
IT'S TIME WE TALKED, YOU AND I.
DDOOOOOMMMMM
ABOUT TIME.
AND SPACE.
AND REALITY.
AND ALL IN BETWEEN.
SHALL WE BEGIN?

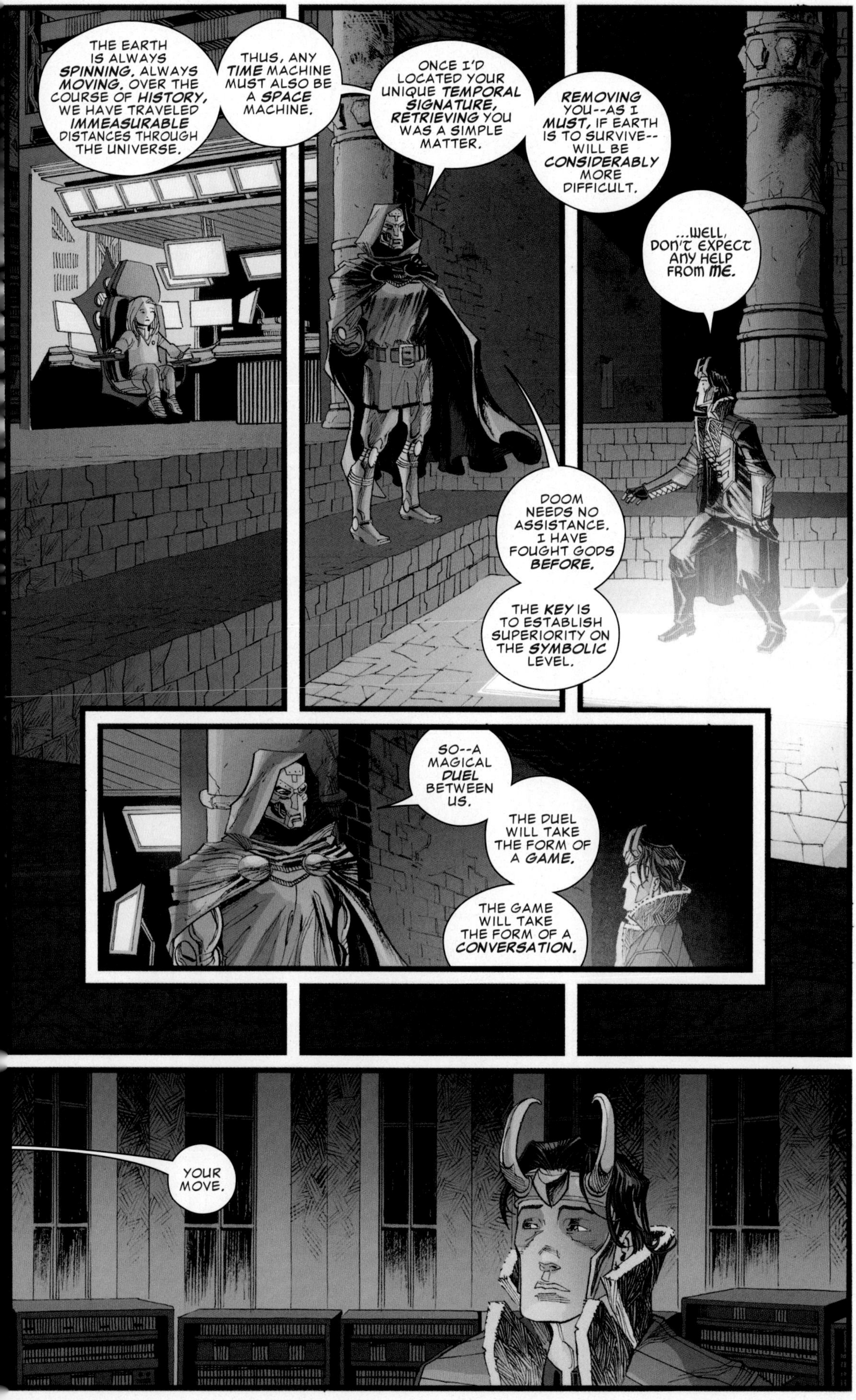
THE EARTH IS ALWAYS SPINNING, ALWAYS MOVING. OVER THE COURSE OF HISTORY, WE HAVE TRAVELED IMMEASURABLE DISTANCES THROUGH THE UNIVERSE.
THUS, ANY TIME MACHINE MUST ALSO BE A SPACE MACHINE.
ONCE I'D LOCATED YOUR UNIQUE TEMPORAL SIGNATURE, RETRIEVING YOU WAS A SIMPLE MATTER.
REMOVING YOU--AS I MUST, IF EARTH IS TO SURVIVE--WILL BE CONSIDERABLY MORE DIFFICULT.
...WELL, DON'T EXPECT ANY HELP FROM ME.
DOOM NEEDS NO ASSISTANCE. I HAVE FOUGHT GODS BEFORE.
THE KEY IS TO ESTABLISH SUPERIORITY ON THE SYMBOLIC LEVEL.
SO--A MAGICAL DUEL BETWEEN US.
THE DUEL WILL TAKE THE FORM OF A GAME.
THE GAME WILL TAKE THE FORM OF A CONVERSATION.
YOUR MOVE.

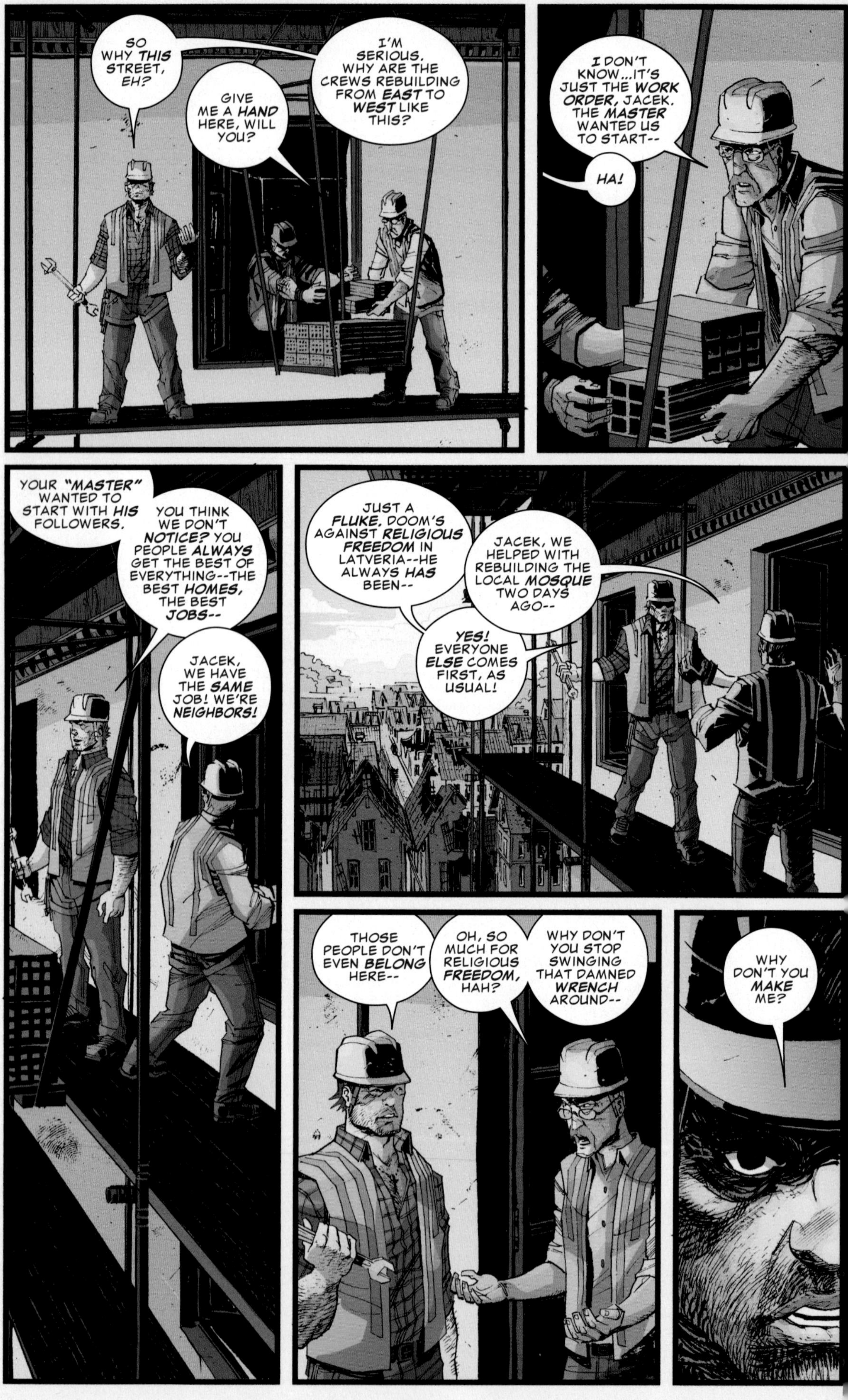
SO WHY THIS STREET, EH?
I'M SERIOUS. WHY ARE THE CREWS REBUILDING FROM EAST TO WEST LIKE THIS?
GIVE ME A HAND HERE, WILL YOU?
I DON'T KNOW...IT'S JUST THE WORK ORDER, JACEK. THE MASTER WANTED US TO START--
HA!
YOUR "MASTER" WANTED TO START WITH HIS FOLLOWERS.
YOU THINK WE DON'T NOTICE? YOU PEOPLE ALWAYS GET THE BEST OF EVERYTHING--THE BEST HOMES, THE BEST JOBS--
JACEK, WE HAVE THE SAME JOB! WE'RE NEIGHBORS!
JUST A FLUKE. DOOM'S AGAINST RELIGIOUS FREEDOM IN LATVERIA--HE ALWAYS HAS BEEN--
JACEK, WE HELPED WITH REBUILDING THE LOCAL MOSQUE TWO DAYS AGO--
YES! EVERYONE ELSE COMES FIRST, AS USUAL!
THOSE PEOPLE DON'T EVEN BELONG HERE--
OH, SO MUCH FOR RELIGIOUS FREEDOM, HAH?
WHY DON'T YOU STOP SWINGING THAT DAMNED WRENCH AROUND--
WHY DON'T YOU MAKE ME?

ALL RIGHT. HERE'S MY MOVE:

I RESIGN.

CIAO.

INVISIBILITY, BECAUSE I'VE NEVER FOUGHT *THAT* BEFORE.

VALERIA?

REMEMBER, UNCLE DOOM-- YOU SAID YOU WOULDN'T *KILL* HIM--

I REMEMBER. NOW YOU DO *YOUR* PART, CHILD.

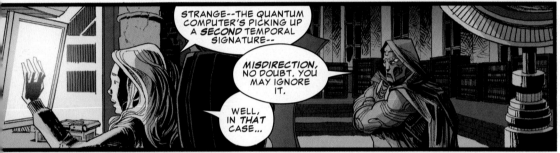

STRANGE--THE QUANTUM COMPUTER'S PICKING UP A *SECOND* TEMPORAL SIGNATURE--

MISDIRECTION, NO DOUBT. YOU MAY IGNORE IT.

WELL, IN *THAT* CASE...

SHRZAKK

BOOP

...TA-DA.

HOW DID YOU KNOW WHERE I--

I *TOLD* YOU, TRICKSTER. YOU LEAVE A UNIQUE *FINGERPRINT* ON THE FABRIC OF TIME--ONE WE CAN *PINPOINT*.

AND YOU'RE NOT THE GOD YOU *WERE*-- OR WILL BE.

WHICH MEANS IT'S *MY* MOVE NOW.

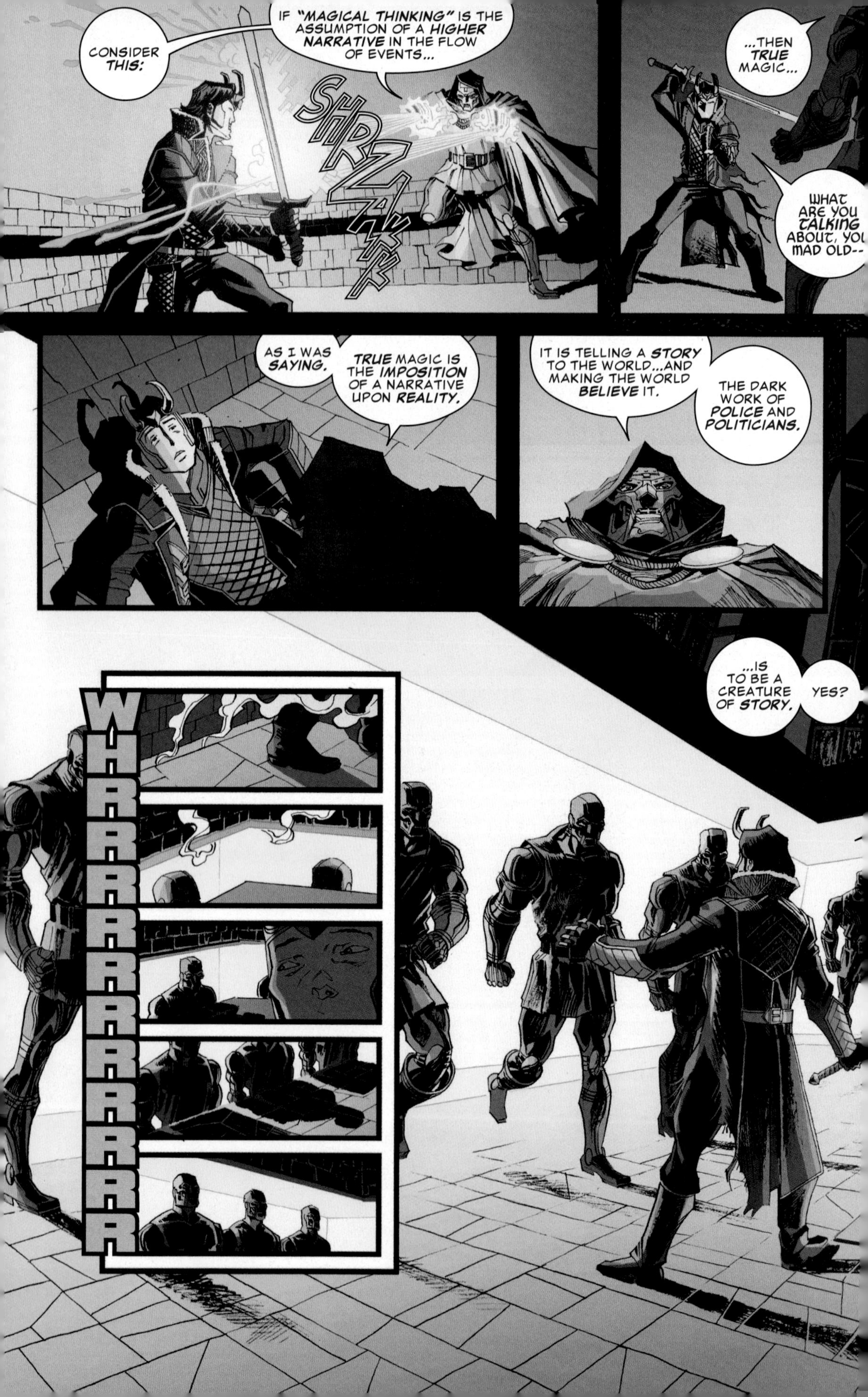
CONSIDER THIS:
IF "MAGICAL THINKING" IS THE ASSUMPTION OF A HIGHER NARRATIVE IN THE FLOW OF EVENTS...
SHRZAKK
...THEN TRUE MAGIC...
WHAT ARE YOU TALKING ABOUT, YOU MAD OLD--
AS I WAS SAYING.
TRUE MAGIC IS THE IMPOSITION OF A NARRATIVE UPON REALITY.
IT IS TELLING A STORY TO THE WORLD...AND MAKING THE WORLD BELIEVE IT.
THE DARK WORK OF POLICE AND POLITICIANS.
...IS TO BE A CREATURE OF STORY.
YES?
WHRRRRRRRRRRRR

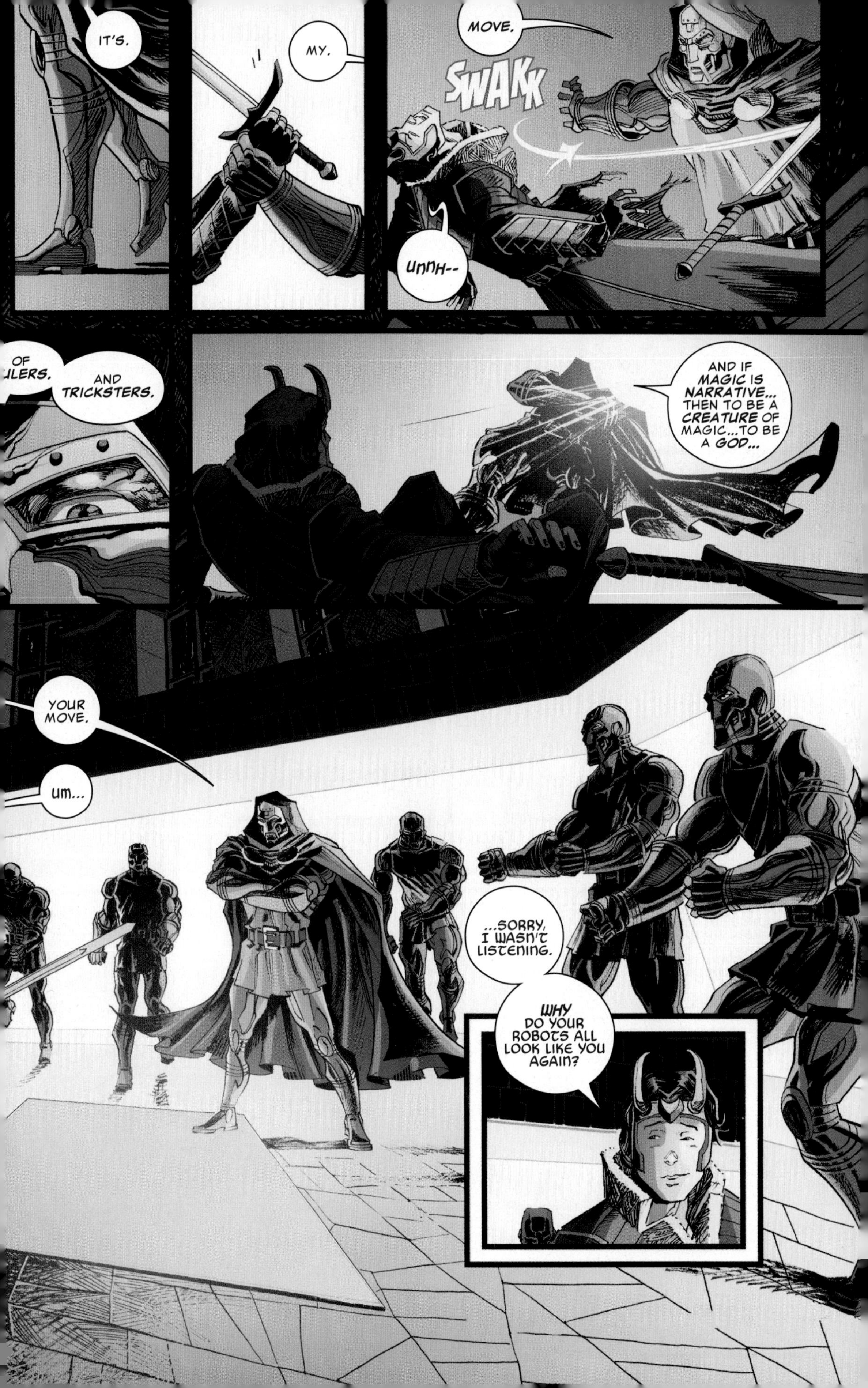
IT'S.
MY.
MOVE.
SWAKK
UNNH--
OF
ULERS.
AND TRICKSTERS.
AND IF MAGIC IS NARRATIVE... THEN TO BE A CREATURE OF MAGIC... TO BE A GOD...
YOUR MOVE.
UM...
...SORRY, I WASN'T LISTENING.
WHY DO YOUR ROBOTS ALL LOOK LIKE YOU AGAIN?

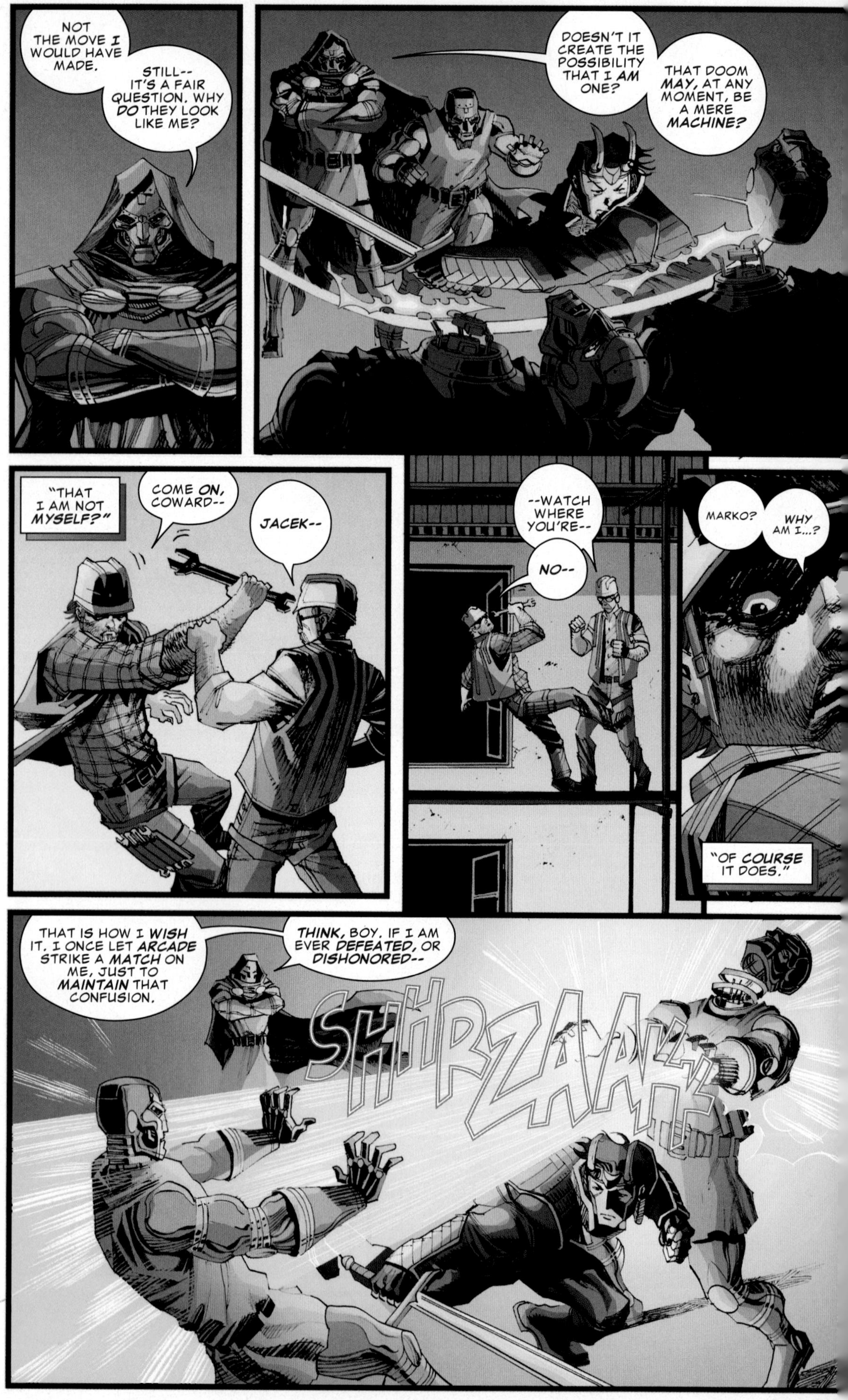

NOT THE MOVE I WOULD HAVE MADE.
STILL-- IT'S A FAIR QUESTION. WHY DO THEY LOOK LIKE ME?
DOESN'T IT CREATE THE POSSIBILITY THAT I AM ONE?
THAT DOOM MAY, AT ANY MOMENT, BE A MERE MACHINE?
"THAT I AM NOT MYSELF?"
COME ON, COWARD--
JACEK--
--WATCH WHERE YOU'RE--
NO--
MARKO?
WHY AM I...?
"OF COURSE IT DOES."
THAT IS HOW I WISH IT. I ONCE LET ARCADE STRIKE A MATCH ON ME, JUST TO MAINTAIN THAT CONFUSION.
THINK, BOY. IF I AM EVER DEFEATED, OR DISHONORED--
SHHRZAAAK

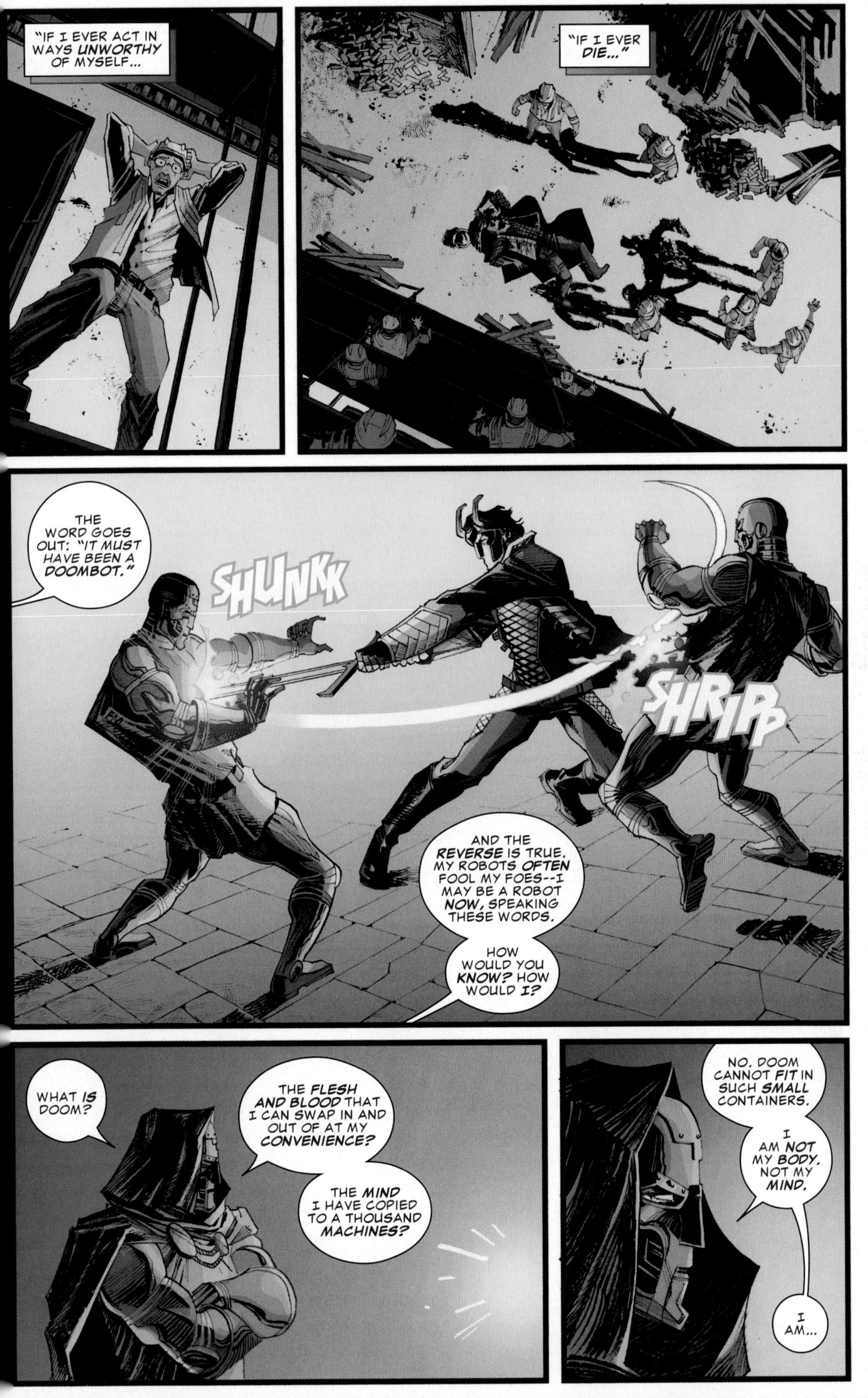
"IF I EVER ACT IN WAYS UNWORTHY OF MYSELF...
"IF I EVER DIE..."
THE WORD GOES OUT: "IT MUST HAVE BEEN A DOOMBOT."
SHUNKK
SHRIPP
AND THE REVERSE IS TRUE. MY ROBOTS OFTEN FOOL MY FOES--I MAY BE A ROBOT NOW, SPEAKING THESE WORDS.
HOW WOULD YOU KNOW? HOW WOULD I?
WHAT IS DOOM?
THE FLESH AND BLOOD THAT I CAN SWAP IN AND OUT OF AT MY CONVENIENCE?
THE MIND I HAVE COPIED TO A THOUSAND MACHINES?
NO. DOOM CANNOT FIT IN SUCH SMALL CONTAINERS.
I AM NOT MY BODY. NOT MY MIND.
I AM...

"I AM THE *OLD TRUNK,* FILLED WITH ANCIENT *MYSTERIES.*

"I AM THE *EXPLOSION* IN THE *COLLEGE LABORATORY.*

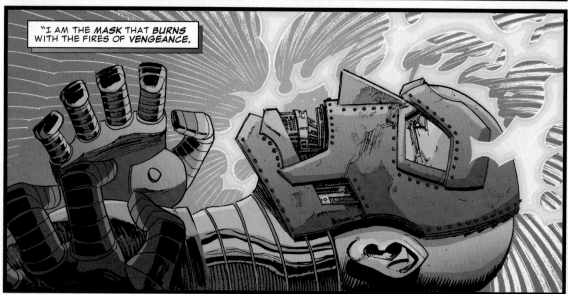

"I AM THE *MASK* THAT *BURNS* WITH THE FIRES OF *VENGEANCE.*

"I AM THE *LEGEND* THAT *UNITES* THIS NATION."

I AM THE *STORY* OF DOOM.

AND IF DOOM IS A *CREATURE OF STORY...*

STOP.

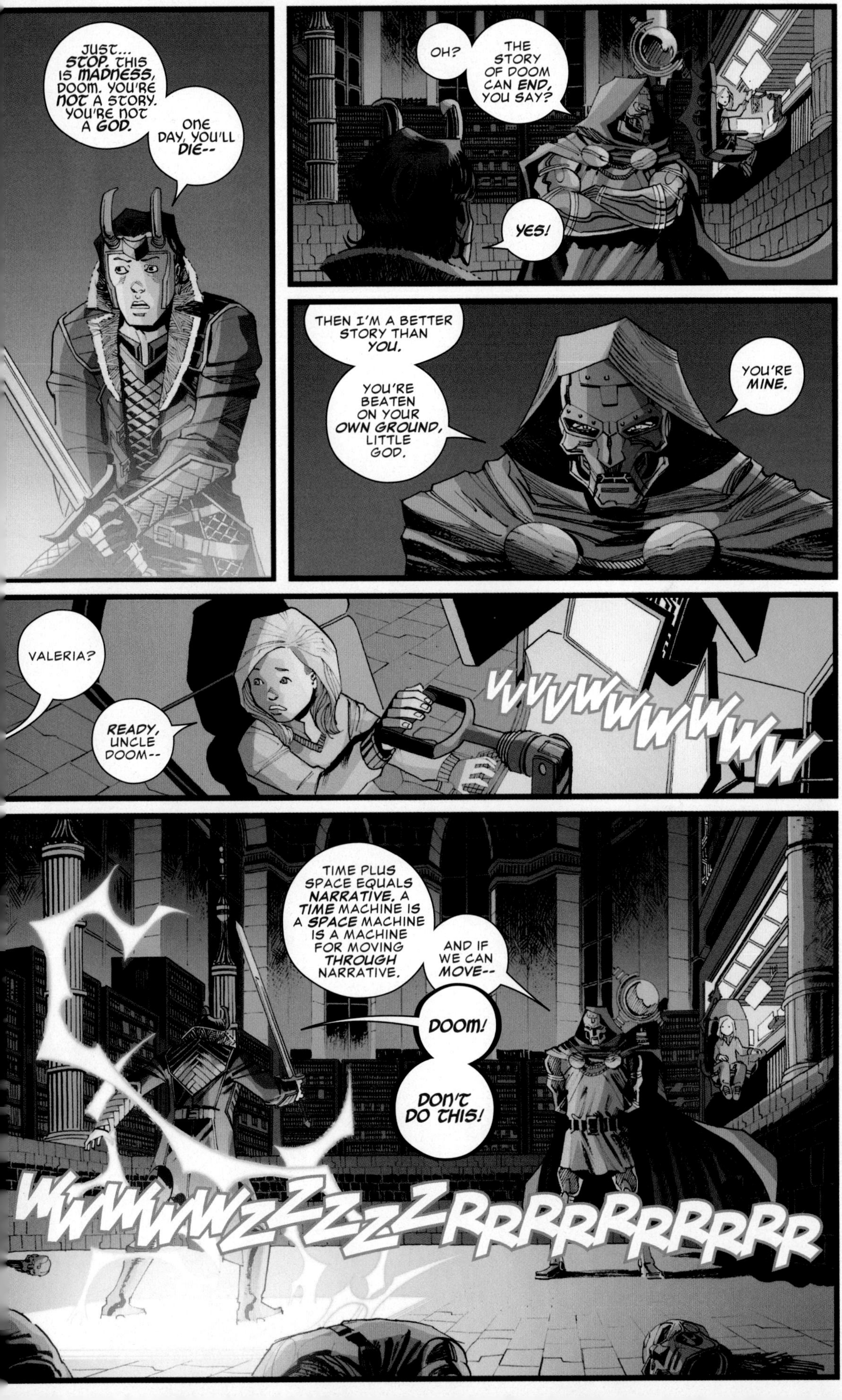

JUST... STOP. THIS IS MADNESS, DOOM. YOU'RE NOT A STORY. YOU'RE NOT A GOD.
ONE DAY, YOU'LL DIE--
OH?
THE STORY OF DOOM CAN END, YOU SAY?
YES!
THEN I'M A BETTER STORY THAN YOU.
YOU'RE BEATEN ON YOUR OWN GROUND, LITTLE GOD.
YOU'RE MINE.
VALERIA?
READY, UNCLE DOOM--
VVVVWWWWWWWW
TIME PLUS SPACE EQUALS NARRATIVE. A TIME MACHINE IS A SPACE MACHINE IS A MACHINE FOR MOVING THROUGH NARRATIVE.
AND IF WE CAN MOVE--
DOOM!
DON'T DO THIS!
WWWWWZZZZZRRRRRRRRRRR

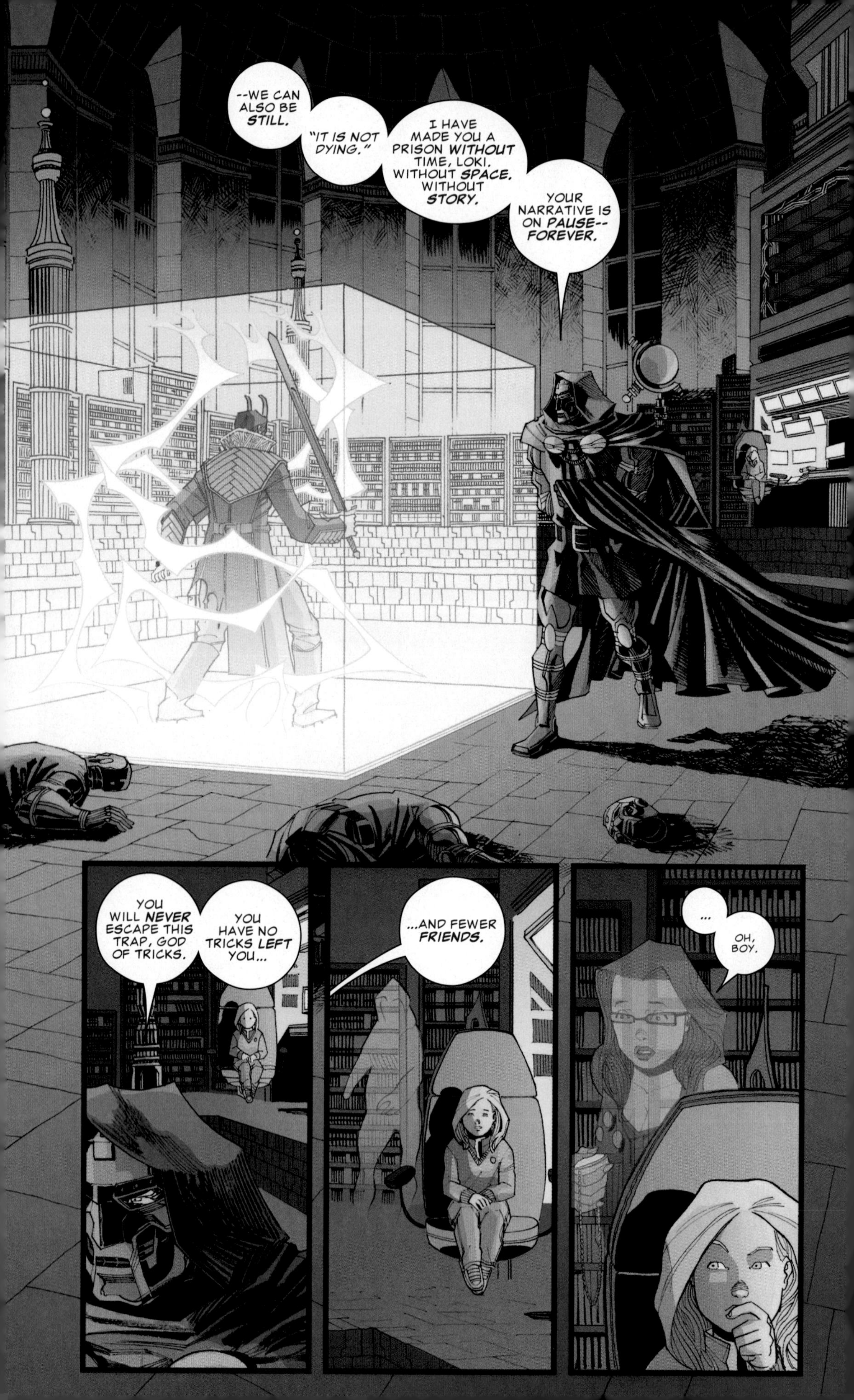
--WE CAN ALSO BE STILL.
"IT IS NOT DYING."
I HAVE MADE YOU A PRISON WITHOUT TIME, LOKI. WITHOUT SPACE. WITHOUT STORY.
YOUR NARRATIVE IS ON PAUSE-- FOREVER.
YOU WILL NEVER ESCAPE THIS TRAP, GOD OF TRICKS.
YOU HAVE NO TRICKS LEFT YOU...
...AND FEWER FRIENDS.
...
OH, BOY.

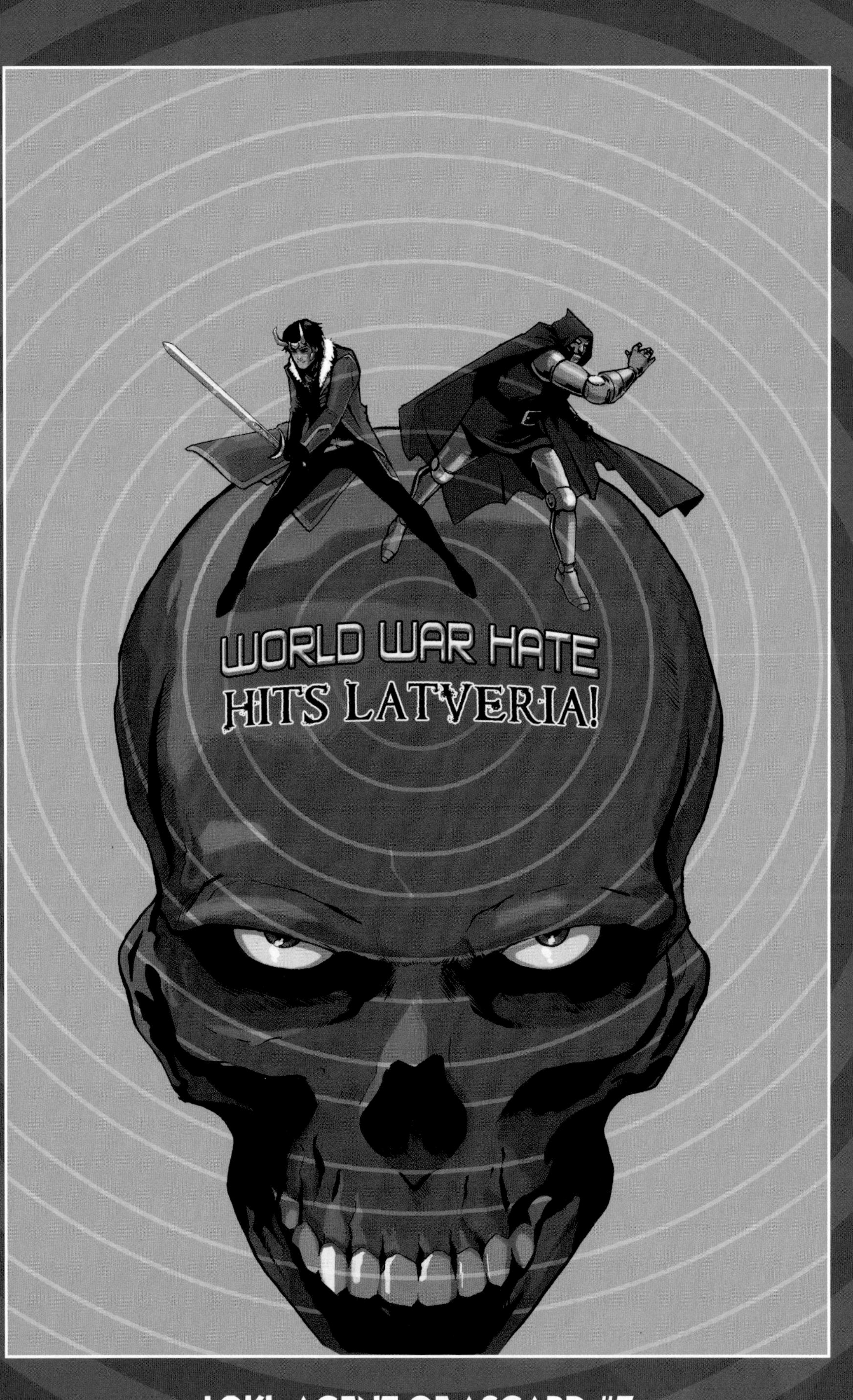
WORLD WAR HATE
HITS LATVERIA!

LOKI: AGENT OF ASGARD #7

ASGARDIA.
DRIFTING THROUGH THE META-SPACE BETWEEN THE TEN REALMS.

HEED THE WORDS OF *ODIN*, WIFE.

THIS... WILL NOT END *WELL*.

HUSBAND--

OH, BUT IT *WILL*, FATHER.

ODIN.
THE ALL-FATHER.

FREYJA.
THE ALL-MOTHER.

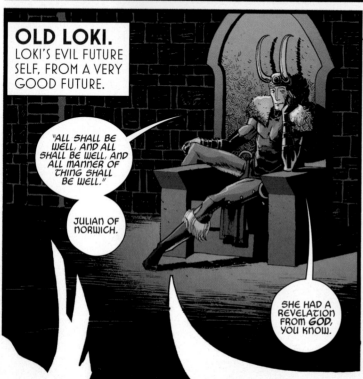

OLD LOKI.
LOKI'S EVIL FUTURE SELF, FROM A VERY GOOD FUTURE.

"ALL SHALL BE WELL, AND ALL SHALL BE WELL, AND ALL MANNER OF THING SHALL BE WELL."

JULIAN OF NORWICH.

SHE HAD A REVELATION FROM *GOD*, YOU KNOW.

...

NO GOD *I* KNOW.

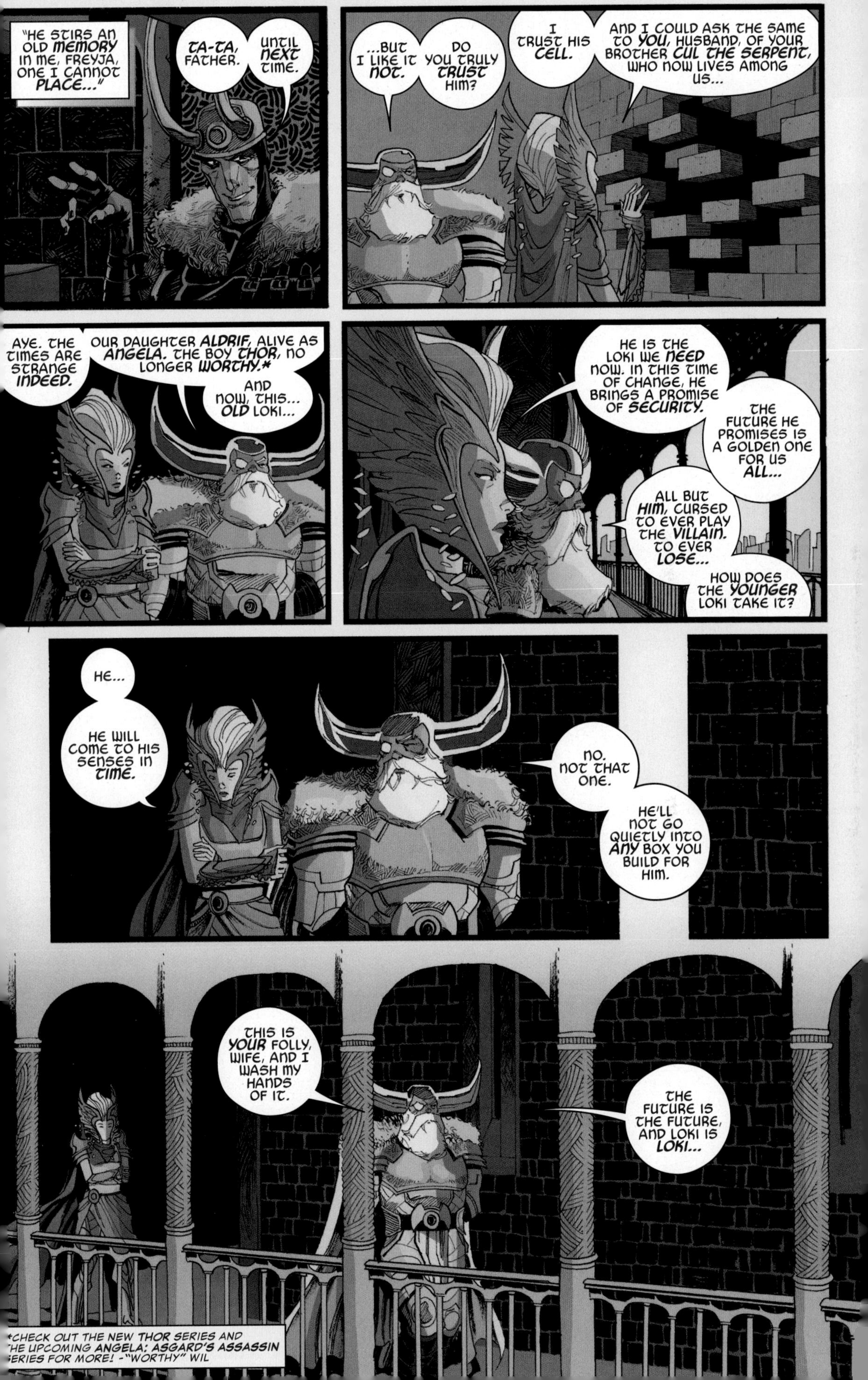

"HE STIRS AN OLD MEMORY IN ME, FREYJA, ONE I CANNOT PLACE..."
TA-TA, FATHER.
UNTIL NEXT TIME.
...BUT I LIKE IT NOT.
DO YOU TRULY TRUST HIM?
I TRUST HIS CELL.
AND I COULD ASK THE SAME TO YOU, HUSBAND, OF YOUR BROTHER CUL THE SERPENT, WHO NOW LIVES AMONG US...
AYE. THE TIMES ARE STRANGE INDEED.
OUR DAUGHTER ALDRIF, ALIVE AS ANGELA. THE BOY THOR, NO LONGER WORTHY.*
AND NOW, THIS... OLD LOKI...
HE IS THE LOKI WE NEED NOW. IN THIS TIME OF CHANGE, HE BRINGS A PROMISE OF SECURITY.
THE FUTURE HE PROMISES IS A GOLDEN ONE FOR US ALL...
ALL BUT HIM, CURSED TO EVER PLAY THE VILLAIN. TO EVER LOSE...
HOW DOES THE YOUNGER LOKI TAKE IT?
HE...
HE WILL COME TO HIS SENSES IN TIME.
NO. NOT THAT ONE.
HE'LL NOT GO QUIETLY INTO ANY BOX YOU BUILD FOR HIM.
THIS IS YOUR FOLLY, WIFE, AND I WASH MY HANDS OF IT.
THE FUTURE IS THE FUTURE, AND LOKI IS LOKI...
*CHECK OUT THE NEW THOR SERIES AND THE UPCOMING ANGELA: ASGARD'S ASSASSIN SERIES FOR MORE! -"WORTHY" WIL

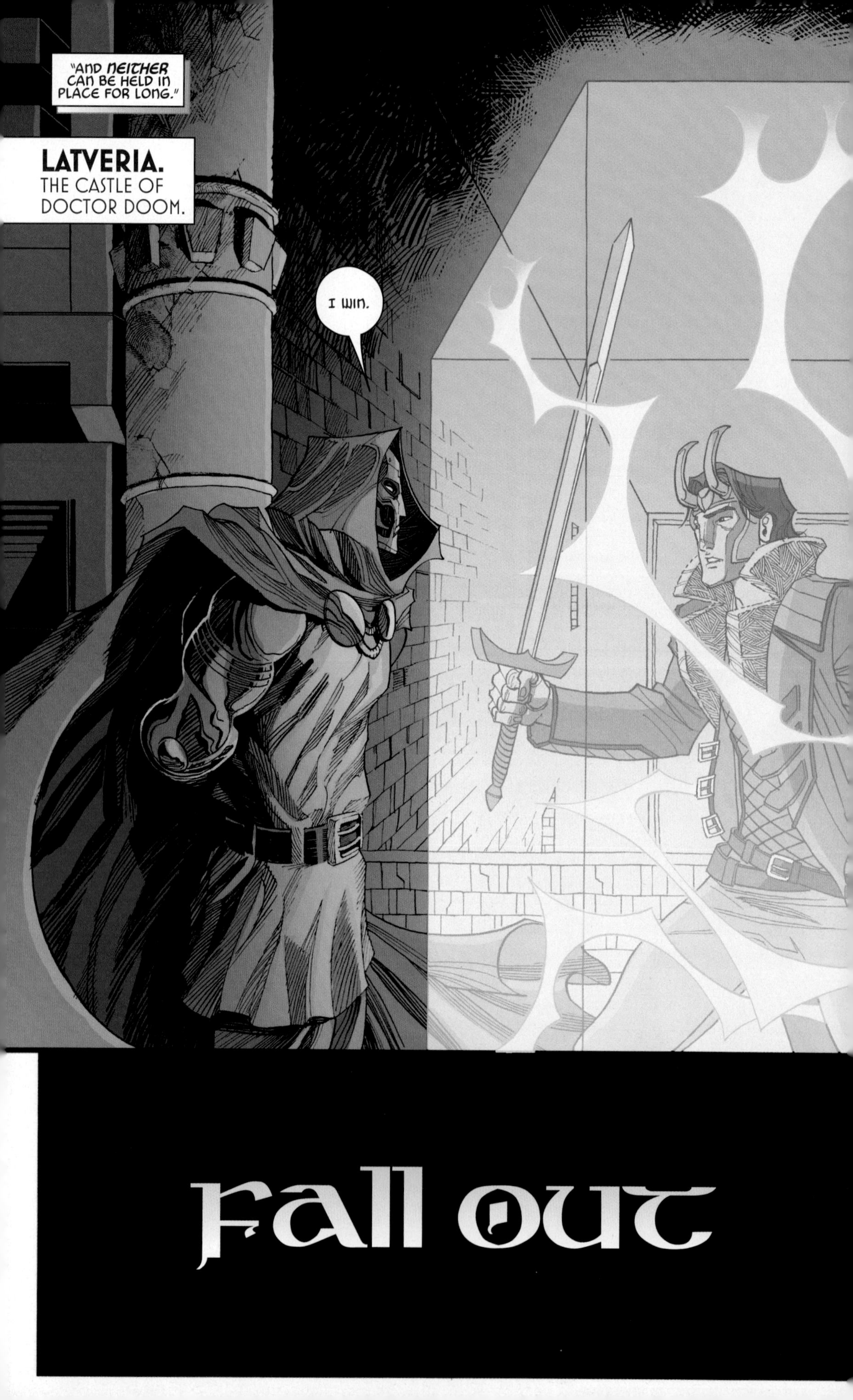
"AND NEITHER CAN BE HELD IN PLACE FOR LONG."
LATVERIA. THE CASTLE OF DOCTOR DOOM.
I WIN.

FALL OUT

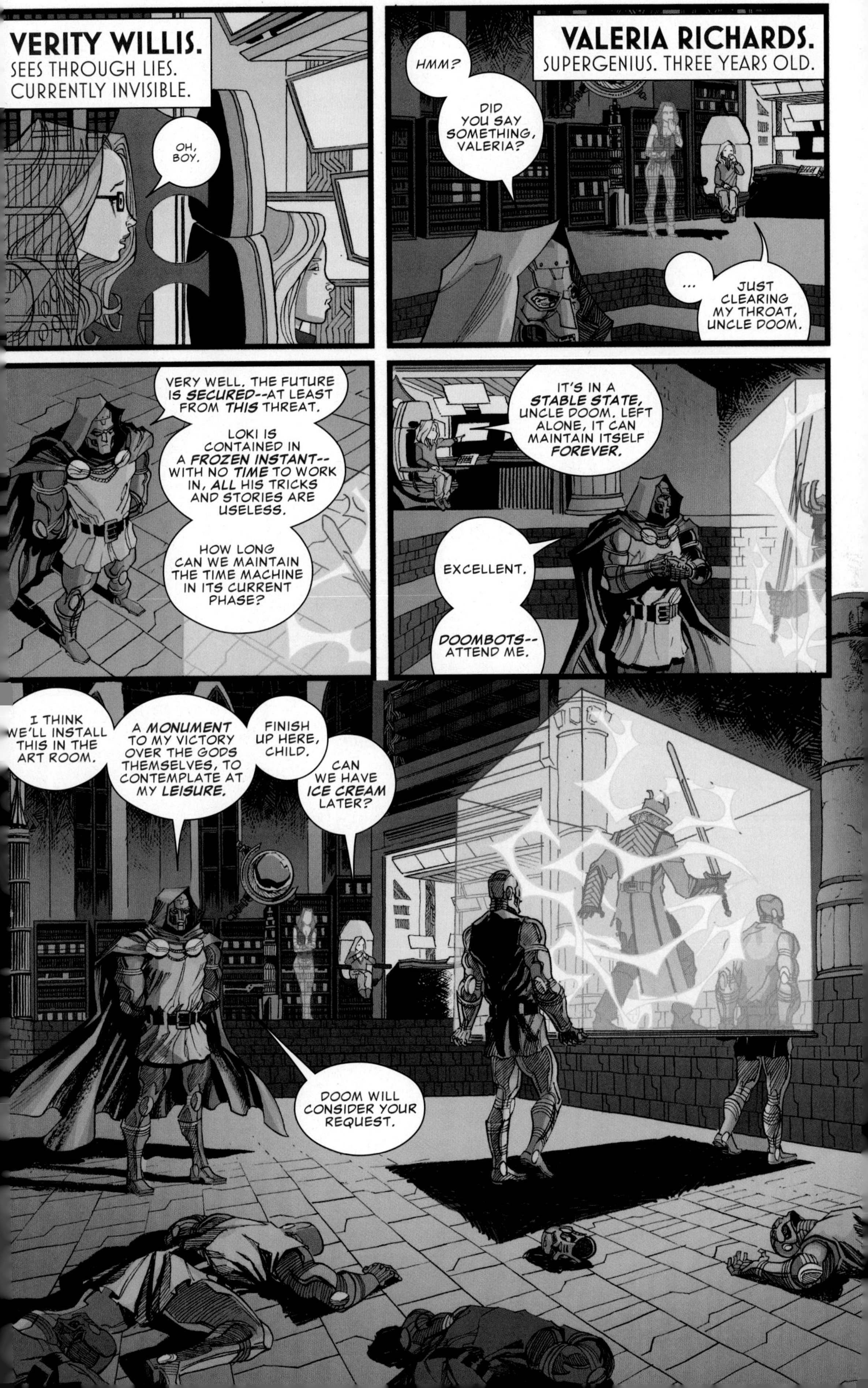
VERITY WILLIS.
SEES THROUGH LIES. CURRENTLY INVISIBLE.
OH, BOY.
VALERIA RICHARDS.
SUPERGENIUS. THREE YEARS OLD.
HMM?
DID YOU SAY SOMETHING, VALERIA?
...
JUST CLEARING MY THROAT, UNCLE DOOM.
VERY WELL. THE FUTURE IS SECURED--AT LEAST FROM THIS THREAT.
LOKI IS CONTAINED IN A FROZEN INSTANT--WITH NO TIME TO WORK IN, ALL HIS TRICKS AND STORIES ARE USELESS.
HOW LONG CAN WE MAINTAIN THE TIME MACHINE IN ITS CURRENT PHASE?
IT'S IN A STABLE STATE, UNCLE DOOM. LEFT ALONE, IT CAN MAINTAIN ITSELF FOREVER.
EXCELLENT.
DOOMBOTS--ATTEND ME.
I THINK WE'LL INSTALL THIS IN THE ART ROOM.
A MONUMENT TO MY VICTORY OVER THE GODS THEMSELVES, TO CONTEMPLATE AT MY LEISURE.
FINISH UP HERE, CHILD.
CAN WE HAVE ICE CREAM LATER?
DOOM WILL CONSIDER YOUR REQUEST.

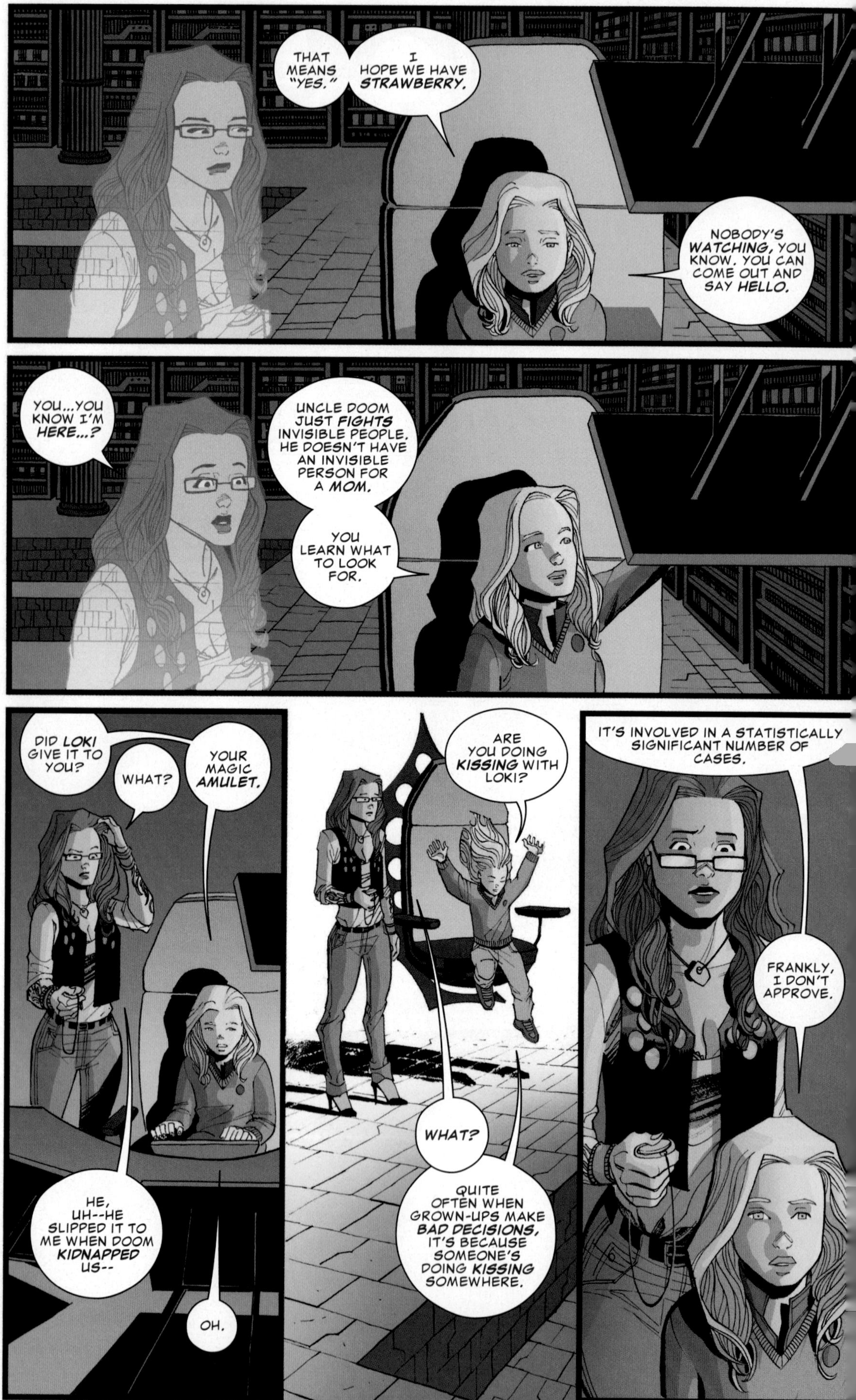

THAT MEANS "YES."
I HOPE WE HAVE STRAWBERRY.
NOBODY'S WATCHING, YOU KNOW. YOU CAN COME OUT AND SAY HELLO.
YOU...YOU KNOW I'M HERE...?
UNCLE DOOM JUST FIGHTS INVISIBLE PEOPLE. HE DOESN'T HAVE AN INVISIBLE PERSON FOR A MOM.
YOU LEARN WHAT TO LOOK FOR.
DID LOKI GIVE IT TO YOU?
WHAT?
YOUR MAGIC AMULET.
HE, UH--HE SLIPPED IT TO ME WHEN DOOM KIDNAPPED US--
OH.
ARE YOU DOING KISSING WITH LOKI?
WHAT?
QUITE OFTEN WHEN GROWN-UPS MAKE BAD DECISIONS, IT'S BECAUSE SOMEONE'S DOING KISSING SOMEWHERE.
IT'S INVOLVED IN A STATISTICALLY SIGNIFICANT NUMBER OF CASES.
FRANKLY, I DON'T APPROVE.

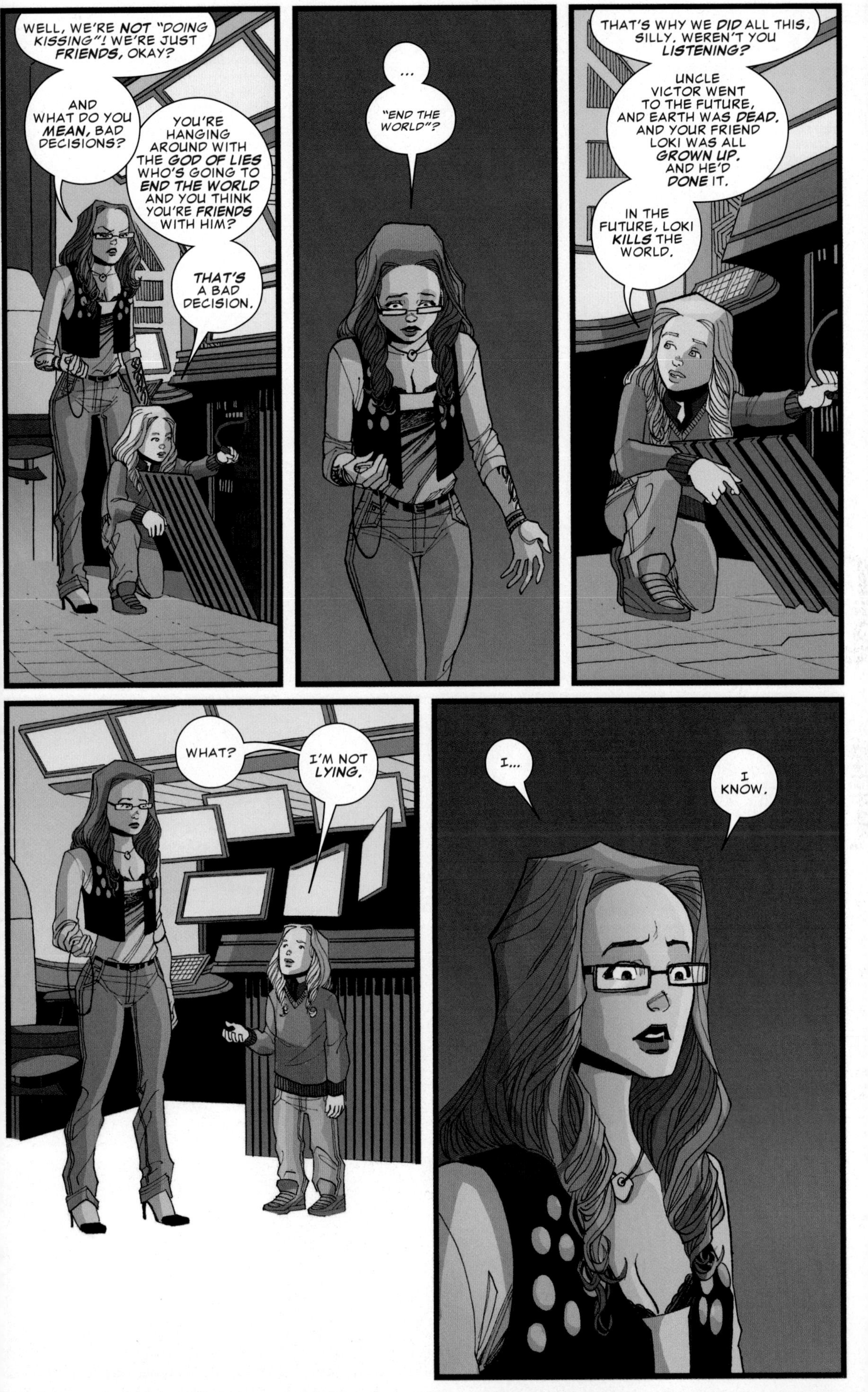
WELL, WE'RE NOT "DOING KISSING"! WE'RE JUST FRIENDS, OKAY?
AND WHAT DO YOU MEAN, BAD DECISIONS?
YOU'RE HANGING AROUND WITH THE GOD OF LIES WHO'S GOING TO END THE WORLD AND YOU THINK YOU'RE FRIENDS WITH HIM?
THAT'S A BAD DECISION.
...
"END THE WORLD"?
THAT'S WHY WE DID ALL THIS, SILLY. WEREN'T YOU LISTENING?
UNCLE VICTOR WENT TO THE FUTURE, AND EARTH WAS DEAD. AND YOUR FRIEND LOKI WAS ALL GROWN UP. AND HE'D DONE IT.
IN THE FUTURE, LOKI KILLS THE WORLD.
WHAT?
I'M NOT LYING.
I...
I KNOW.

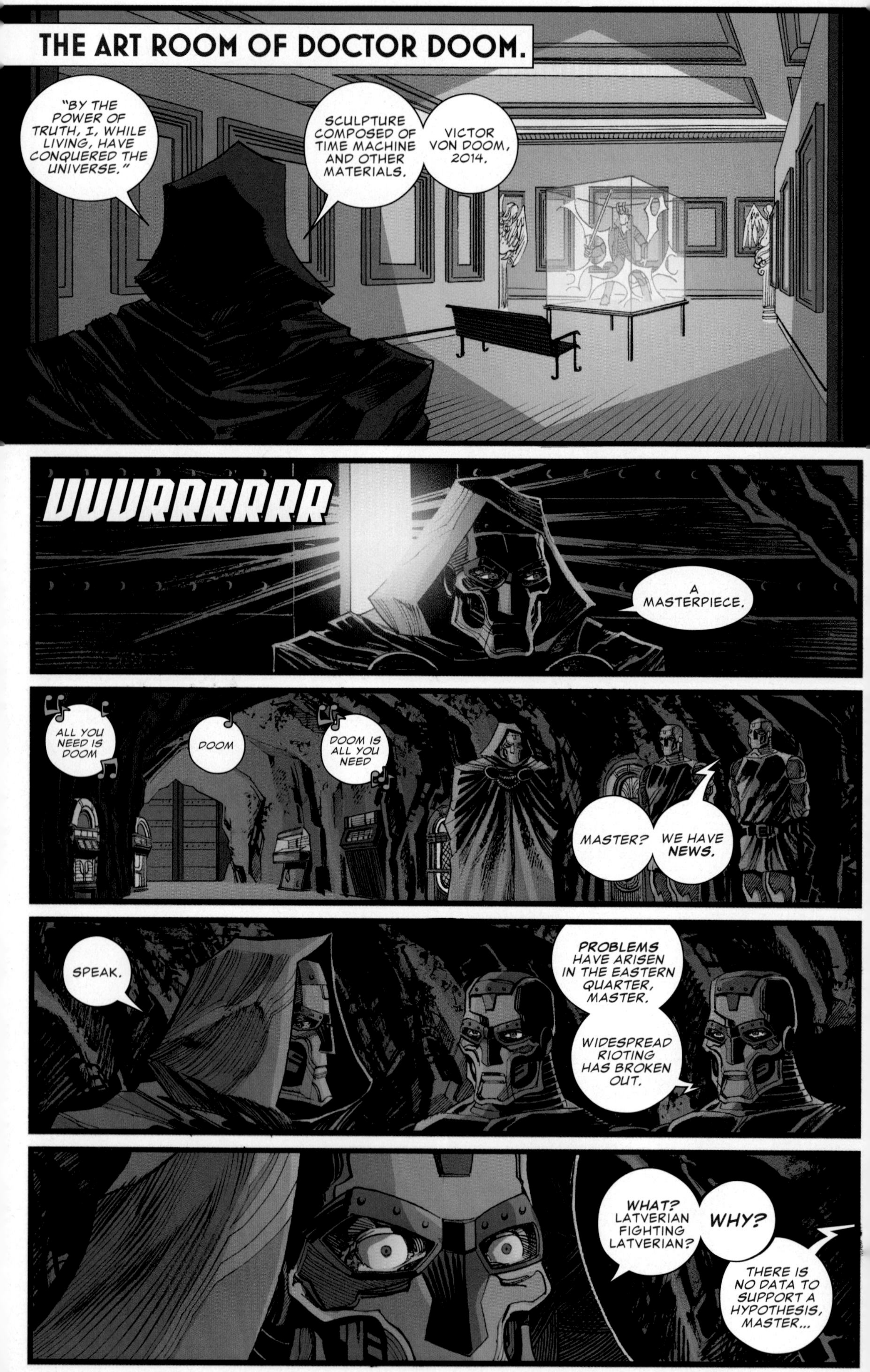
THE ART ROOM OF DOCTOR DOOM.
"BY THE POWER OF TRUTH, I, WHILE LIVING, HAVE CONQUERED THE UNIVERSE."
SCULPTURE COMPOSED OF TIME MACHINE AND OTHER MATERIALS.
VICTOR VON DOOM, 2014.
VVVRRRRRR
A MASTERPIECE.
ALL YOU NEED IS DOOM
DOOM
DOOM IS ALL YOU NEED
MASTER?
WE HAVE NEWS.
SPEAK.
PROBLEMS HAVE ARISEN IN THE EASTERN QUARTER, MASTER.
WIDESPREAD RIOTING HAS BROKEN OUT.
WHAT? LATVERIAN FIGHTING LATVERIAN?
WHY?
THERE IS NO DATA TO SUPPORT A HYPOTHESIS, MASTER...

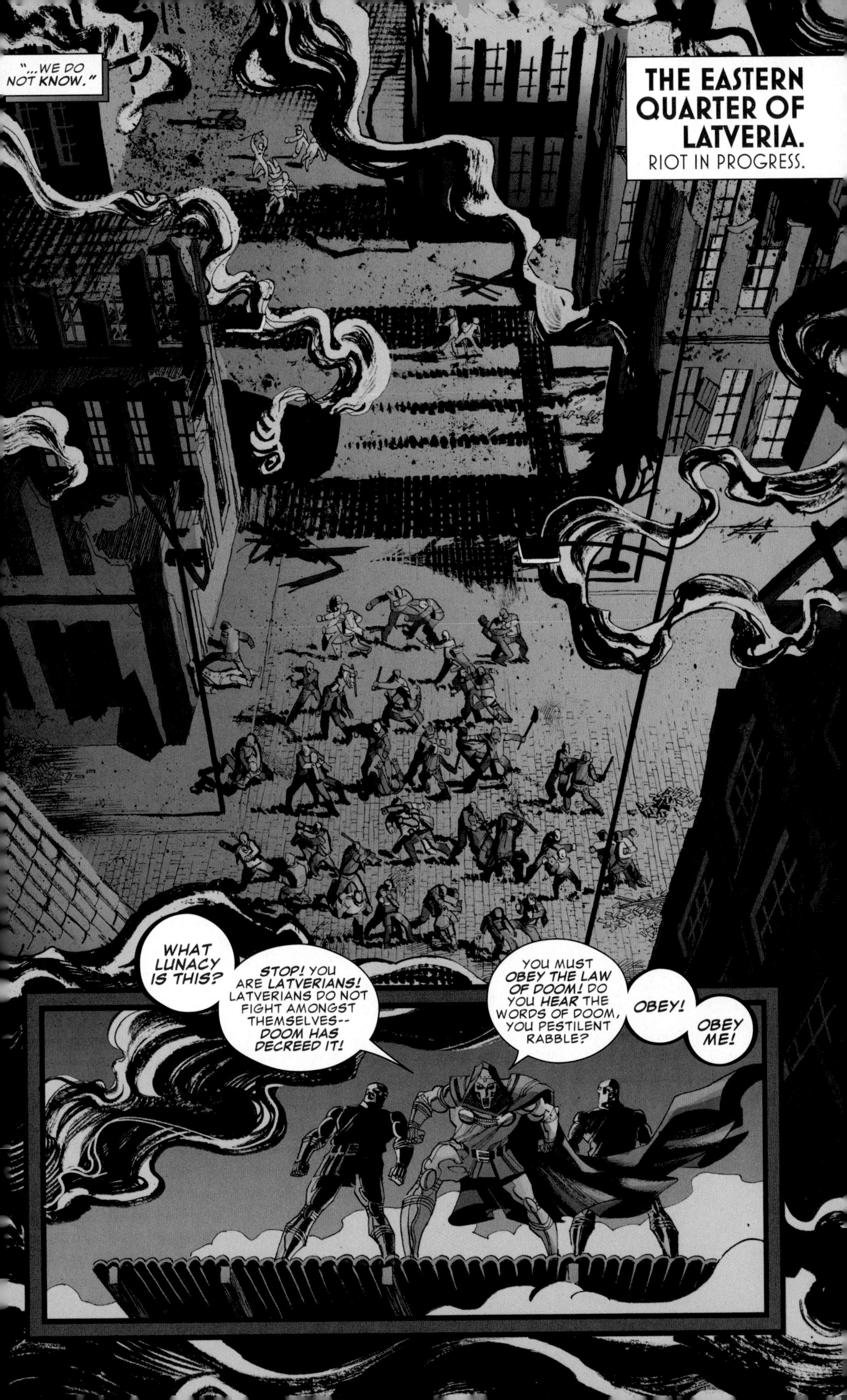
"...WE DO NOT KNOW."
THE EASTERN QUARTER OF LATVERIA.
RIOT IN PROGRESS.
WHAT LUNACY IS THIS?
STOP! YOU ARE LATVERIANS! LATVERIANS DO NOT FIGHT AMONGST THEMSELVES-- DOOM HAS DECREED IT!
YOU MUST OBEY THE LAW OF DOOM! DO YOU HEAR THE WORDS OF DOOM, YOU PESTILENT RABBLE?
OBEY!
OBEY ME!

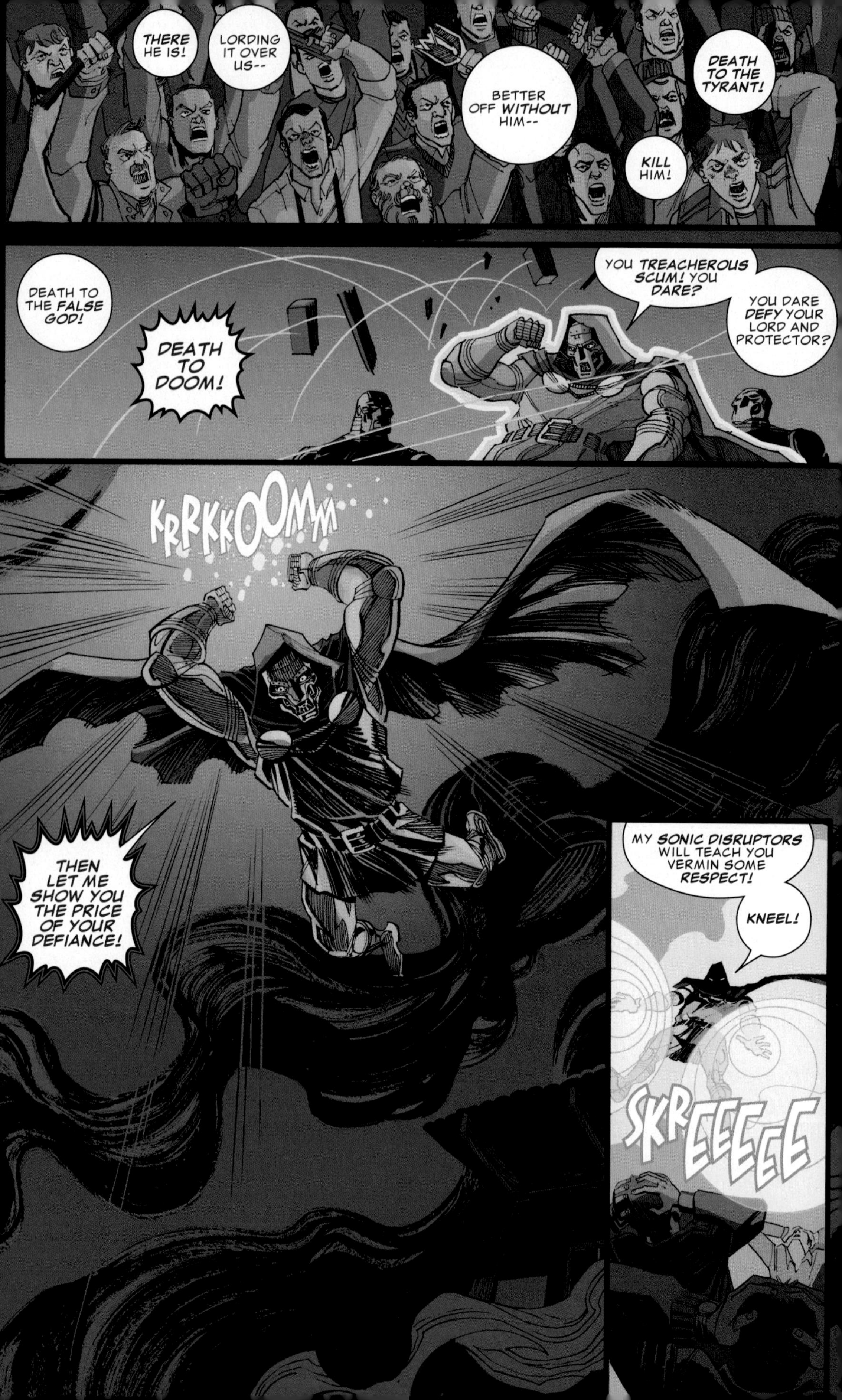
THERE HE IS!
LORDING IT OVER US--
BETTER OFF WITHOUT HIM--
DEATH TO THE TYRANT!
KILL HIM!
DEATH TO THE FALSE GOD!
DEATH TO DOOM!
YOU TREACHEROUS SCUM! YOU DARE?
YOU DARE DEFY YOUR LORD AND PROTECTOR?
KRRKKOOMM
THEN LET ME SHOW YOU THE PRICE OF YOUR DEFIANCE!
MY SONIC DISRUPTORS WILL TEACH YOU VERMIN SOME RESPECT!
KNEEL!
SKREEEEEE

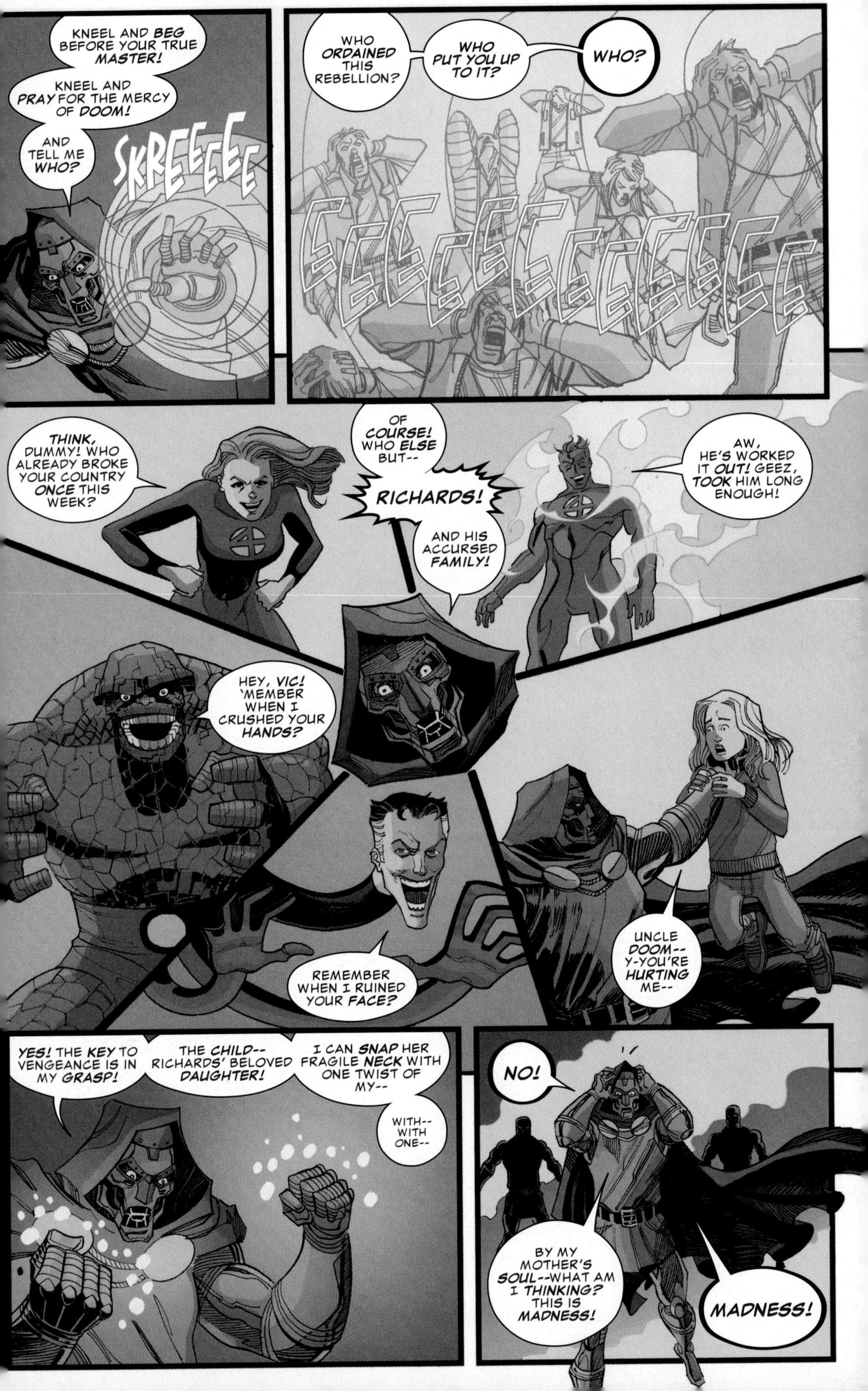
KNEEL AND BEG BEFORE YOUR TRUE MASTER!
KNEEL AND PRAY FOR THE MERCY OF DOOM!
AND TELL ME WHO?
SKREEEEEE
WHO ORDAINED THIS REBELLION?
WHO PUT YOU UP TO IT?
WHO?
EEEEEEEEEEEEEEE
THINK, DUMMY! WHO ALREADY BROKE YOUR COUNTRY ONCE THIS WEEK?
OF COURSE! WHO ELSE BUT--
RICHARDS!
AND HIS ACCURSED FAMILY!
AW, HE'S WORKED IT OUT! GEEZ, TOOK HIM LONG ENOUGH!
HEY, VIC! 'MEMBER WHEN I CRUSHED YOUR HANDS?
REMEMBER WHEN I RUINED YOUR FACE?
UNCLE DOOM-- Y-YOU'RE HURTING ME--
YES! THE KEY TO VENGEANCE IS IN MY GRASP!
THE CHILD-- RICHARDS' BELOVED DAUGHTER!
I CAN SNAP HER FRAGILE NECK WITH ONE TWIST OF MY--
WITH-- WITH ONE--
NO!
BY MY MOTHER'S SOUL--WHAT AM I THINKING? THIS IS MADNESS!
MADNESS!

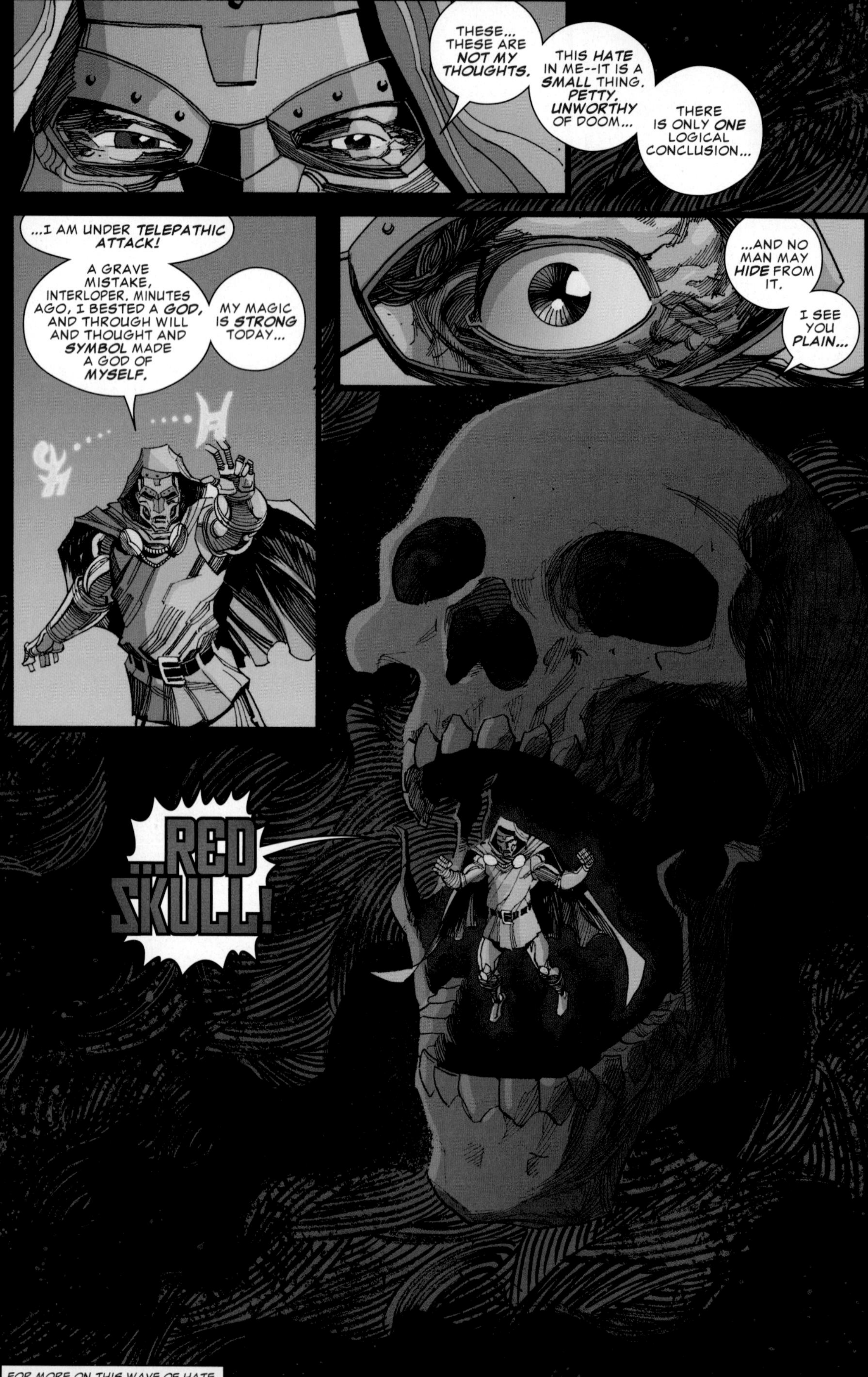
THESE... THESE ARE NOT MY THOUGHTS.
THIS HATE IN ME--IT IS A SMALL THING. PETTY. UNWORTHY OF DOOM...
THERE IS ONLY ONE LOGICAL CONCLUSION...
...I AM UNDER TELEPATHIC ATTACK!
A GRAVE MISTAKE, INTERLOPER. MINUTES AGO, I BESTED A GOD, AND THROUGH WILL AND THOUGHT AND SYMBOL MADE A GOD OF MYSELF.
MY MAGIC IS STRONG TODAY...
...AND NO MAN MAY HIDE FROM IT.
I SEE YOU PLAIN...
...RED SKULL!

FOR MORE ON THIS WAVE OF HATE, SEE AXIS #2, ON SALE NOW!
-"MALICIOUS" MOSS

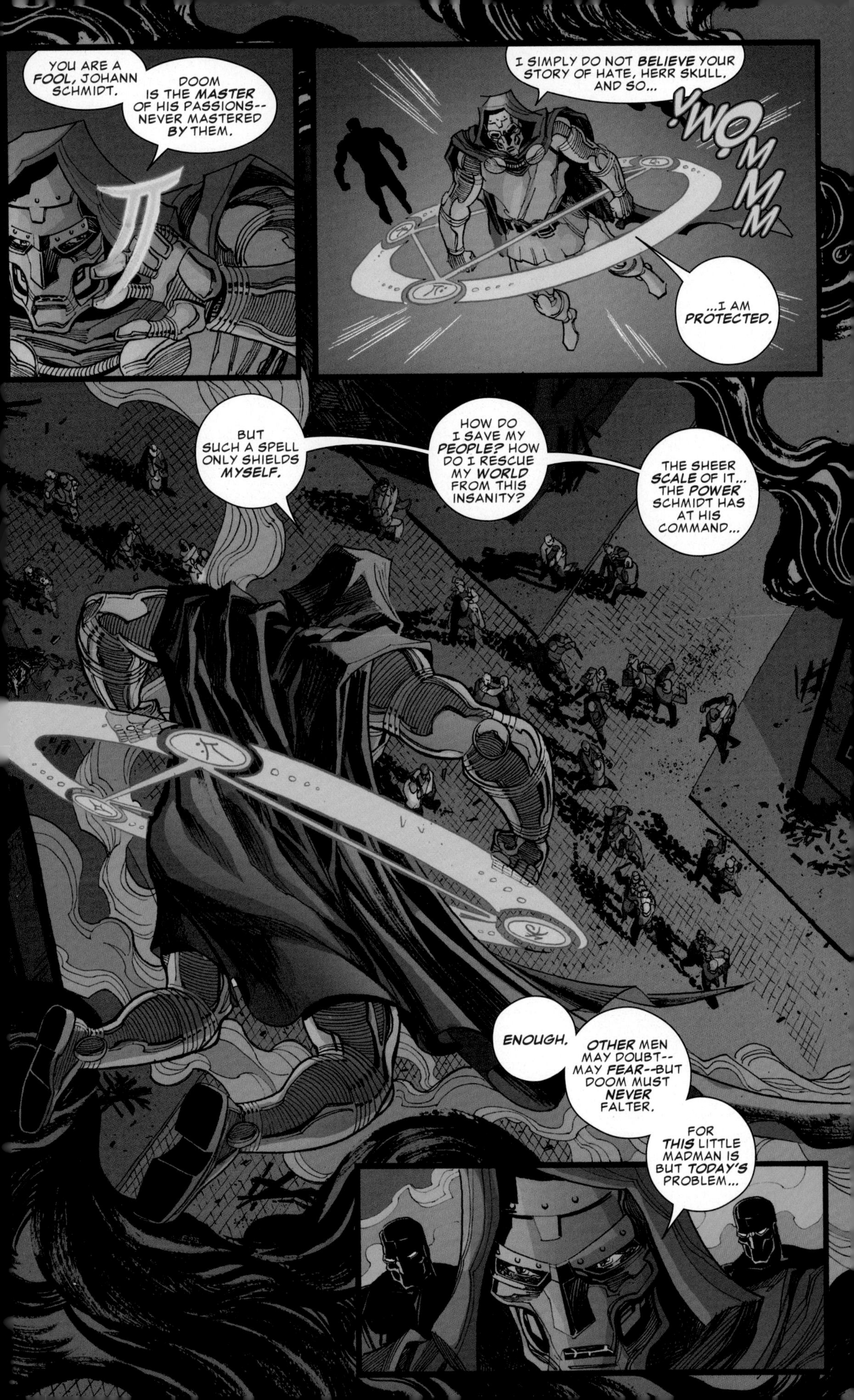
YOU ARE A FOOL, JOHANN SCHMIDT.
DOOM IS THE MASTER OF HIS PASSIONS--NEVER MASTERED BY THEM.
I SIMPLY DO NOT BELIEVE YOUR STORY OF HATE, HERR SKULL, AND SO...
VWOMMM
...I AM PROTECTED.
BUT SUCH A SPELL ONLY SHIELDS MYSELF.
HOW DO I SAVE MY PEOPLE? HOW DO I RESCUE MY WORLD FROM THIS INSANITY?
THE SHEER SCALE OF IT... THE POWER SCHMIDT HAS AT HIS COMMAND...
ENOUGH.
OTHER MEN MAY DOUBT--MAY FEAR--BUT DOOM MUST NEVER FALTER.
FOR THIS LITTLE MADMAN IS BUT TODAY'S PROBLEM...

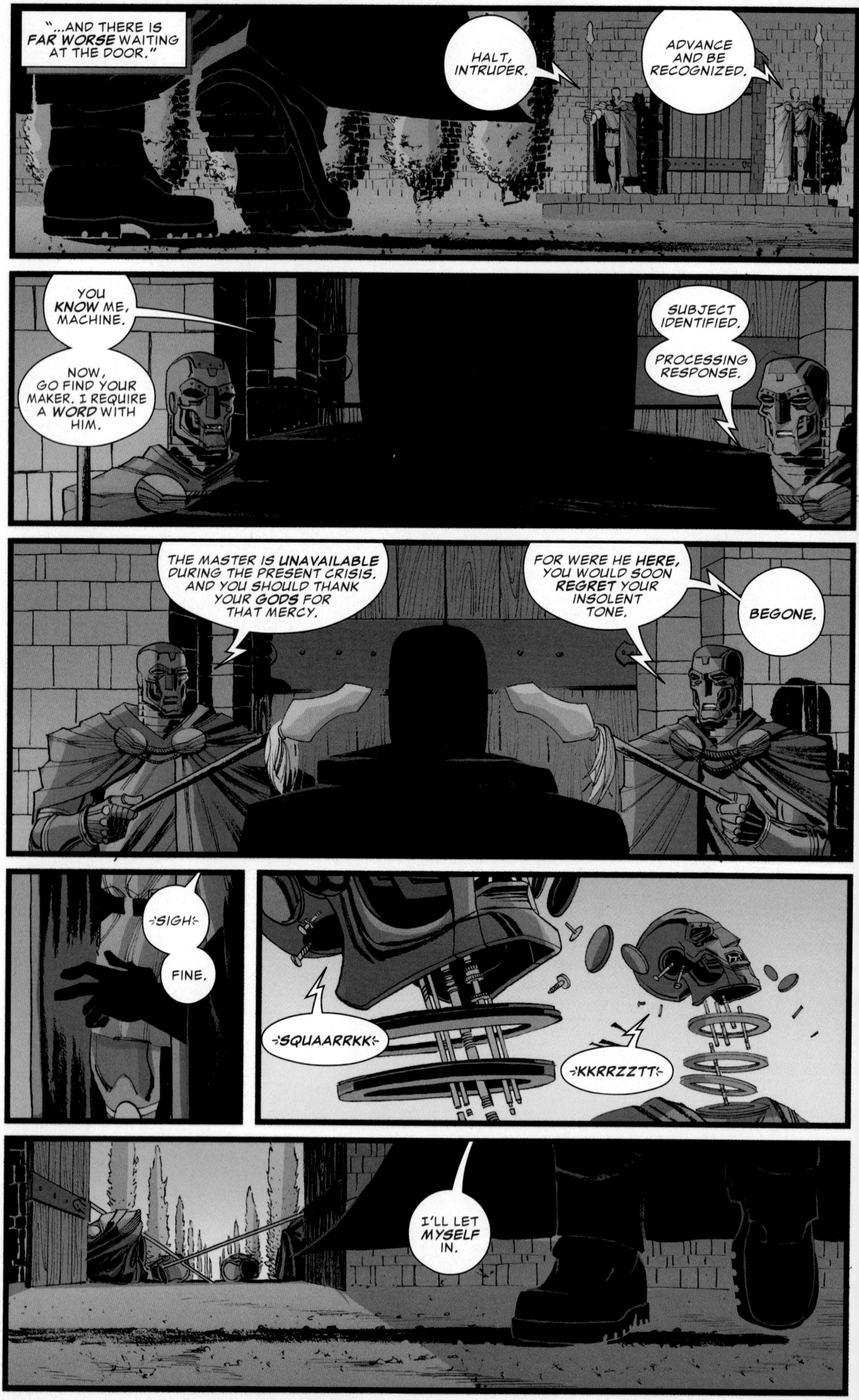
"...AND THERE IS FAR WORSE WAITING AT THE DOOR."
HALT, INTRUDER.
ADVANCE AND BE RECOGNIZED.
YOU KNOW ME, MACHINE.
NOW, GO FIND YOUR MAKER. I REQUIRE A WORD WITH HIM.
SUBJECT IDENTIFIED.
PROCESSING RESPONSE.
THE MASTER IS UNAVAILABLE DURING THE PRESENT CRISIS. AND YOU SHOULD THANK YOUR GODS FOR THAT MERCY.
FOR WERE HE HERE, YOU WOULD SOON REGRET YOUR INSOLENT TONE.
BEGONE.
SIGH
FINE.
SQUAARRKK
KKRRZZTT
I'LL LET MYSELF IN.

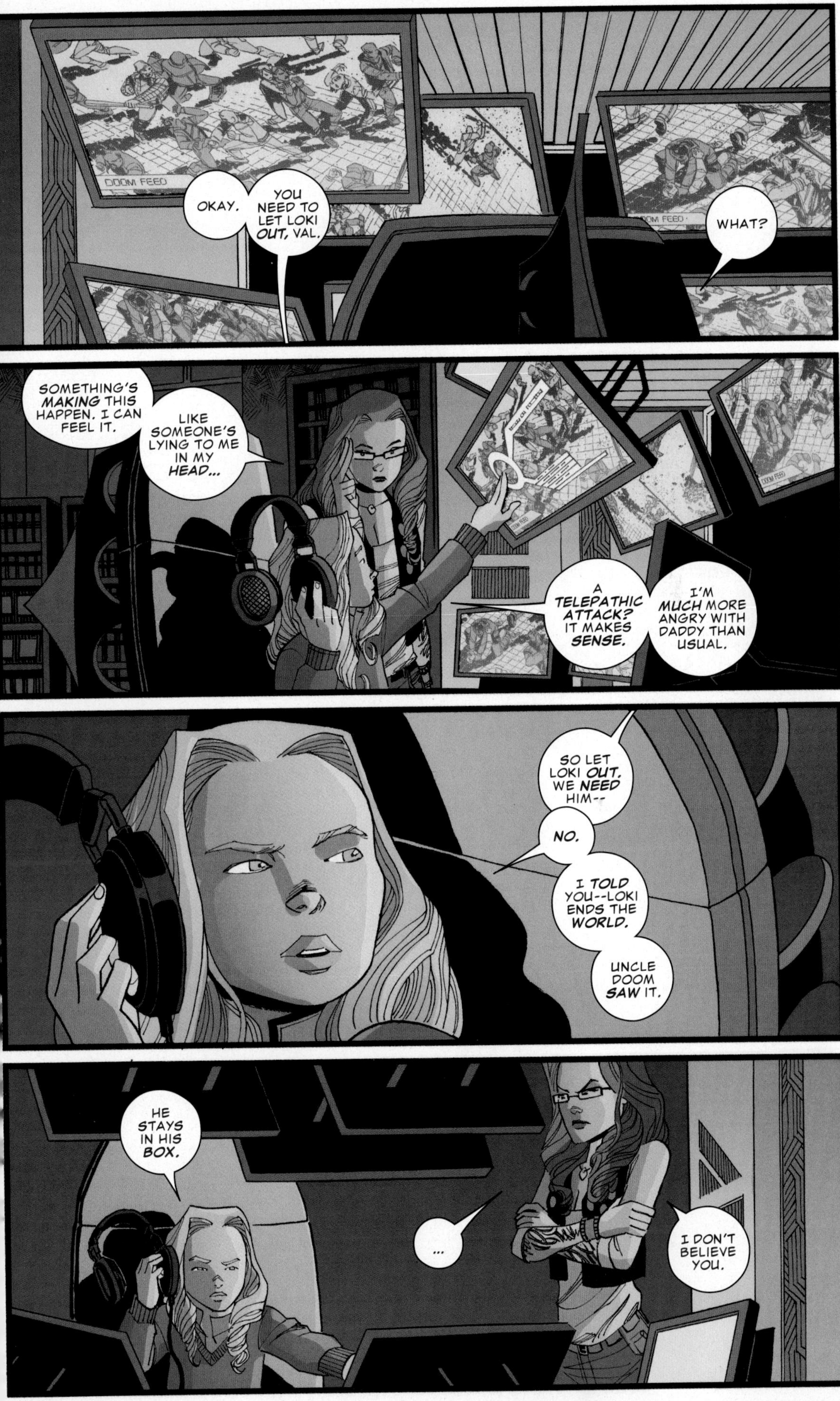
DOOM FEED
OKAY.
YOU NEED TO LET LOKI OUT, VAL.
WHAT?
SOMETHING'S MAKING THIS HAPPEN. I CAN FEEL IT.
LIKE SOMEONE'S LYING TO ME IN MY HEAD...
DOOM FEED
A TELEPATHIC ATTACK? IT MAKES SENSE.
I'M MUCH MORE ANGRY WITH DADDY THAN USUAL.
SO LET LOKI OUT. WE NEED HIM--
NO.
I TOLD YOU--LOKI ENDS THE WORLD.
UNCLE DOOM SAW IT.
HE STAYS IN HIS BOX.
...
I DON'T BELIEVE YOU.

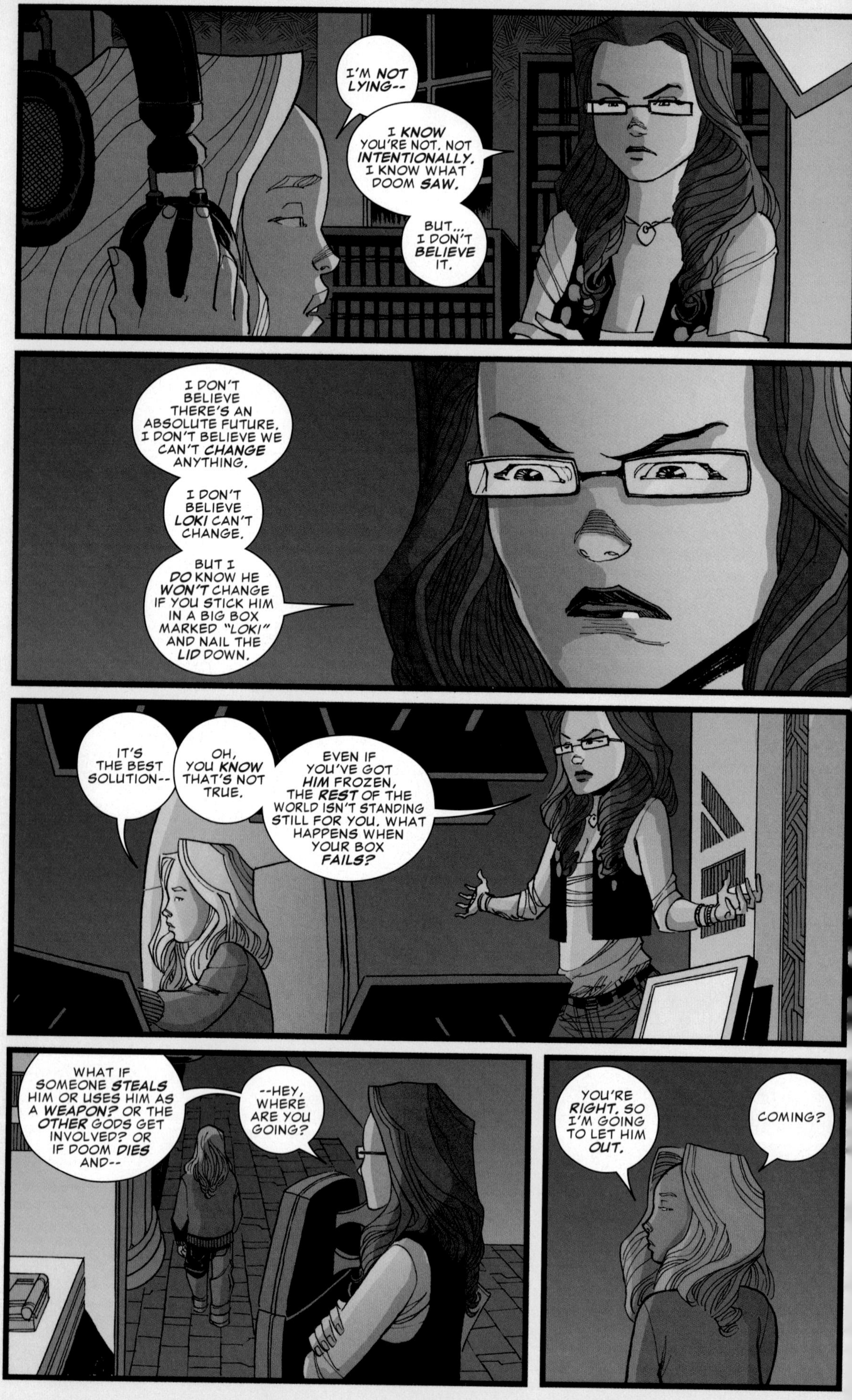
I'M NOT LYING--
I KNOW YOU'RE NOT. NOT INTENTIONALLY. I KNOW WHAT DOOM SAW.
BUT... I DON'T BELIEVE IT.
I DON'T BELIEVE THERE'S AN ABSOLUTE FUTURE. I DON'T BELIEVE WE CAN'T CHANGE ANYTHING.
I DON'T BELIEVE LOKI CAN'T CHANGE.
BUT I DO KNOW HE WON'T CHANGE IF YOU STICK HIM IN A BIG BOX MARKED "LOKI" AND NAIL THE LID DOWN.
IT'S THE BEST SOLUTION--
OH, YOU KNOW THAT'S NOT TRUE.
EVEN IF YOU'VE GOT HIM FROZEN, THE REST OF THE WORLD ISN'T STANDING STILL FOR YOU. WHAT HAPPENS WHEN YOUR BOX FAILS?
WHAT IF SOMEONE STEALS HIM OR USES HIM AS A WEAPON? OR THE OTHER GODS GET INVOLVED? OR IF DOOM DIES AND--
--HEY, WHERE ARE YOU GOING?
YOU'RE RIGHT. SO I'M GOING TO LET HIM OUT.
COMING?

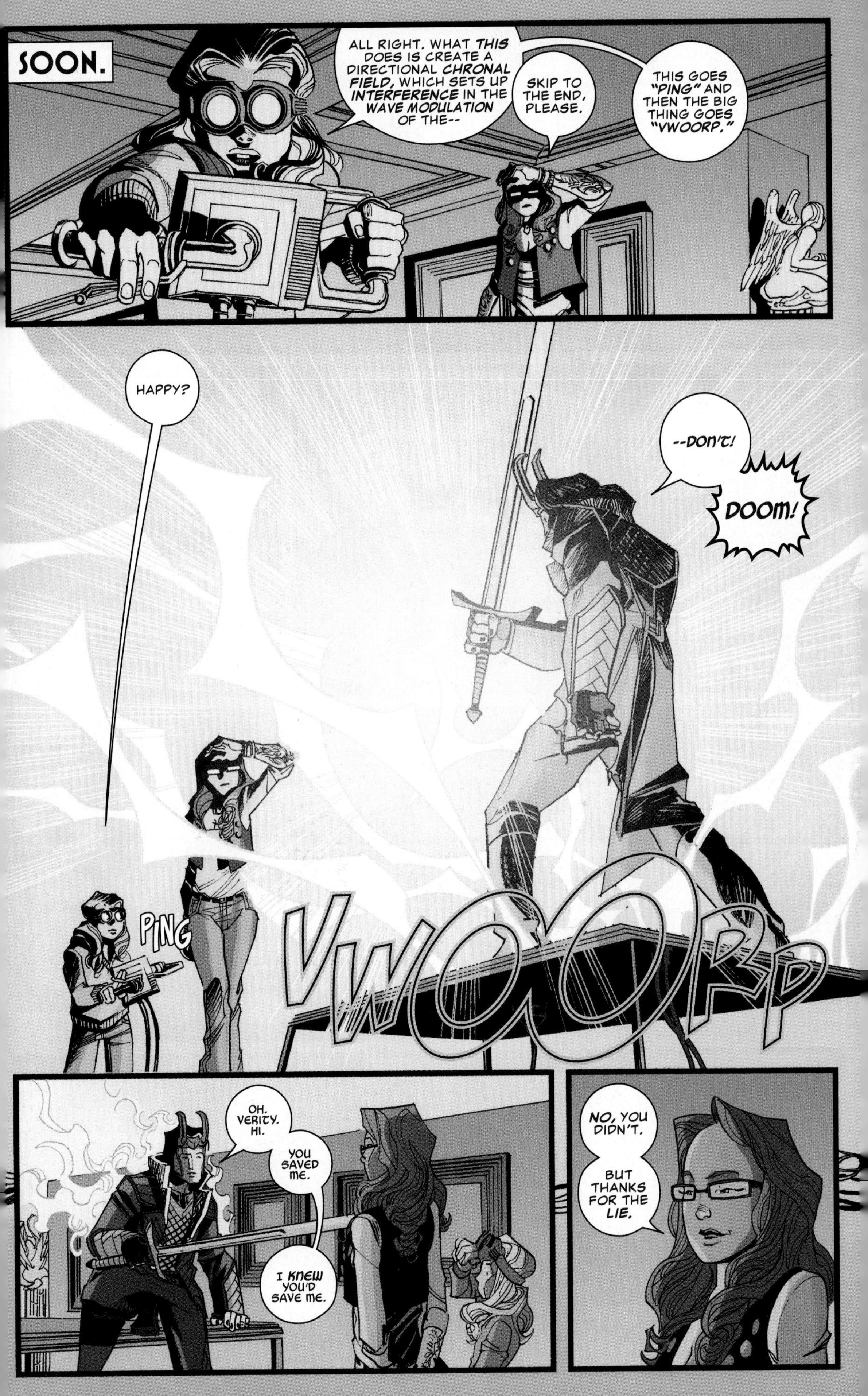
SOON.
ALL RIGHT. WHAT THIS DOES IS CREATE A DIRECTIONAL CHRONAL FIELD, WHICH SETS UP INTERFERENCE IN THE WAVE MODULATION OF THE--
SKIP TO THE END, PLEASE.
THIS GOES "PING" AND THEN THE BIG THING GOES "VWOORP."
HAPPY?
--DON'T!
DOOM!
PING
VWOORP
OH. VERITY. HI.
YOU SAVED ME.
I KNEW YOU'D SAVE ME.
NO, YOU DIDN'T.
BUT THANKS FOR THE LIE.

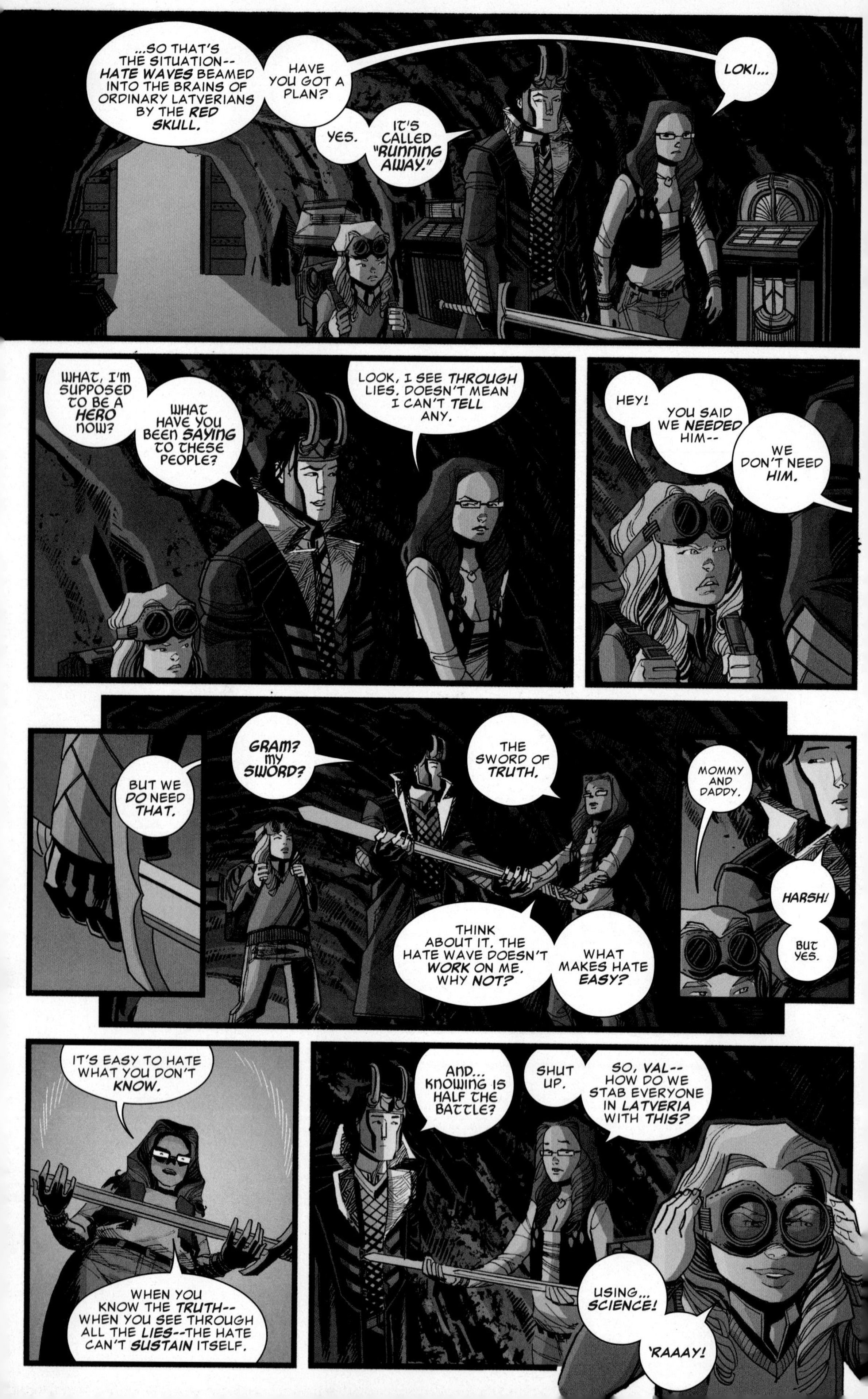
...SO THAT'S THE SITUATION-- HATE WAVES BEAMED INTO THE BRAINS OF ORDINARY LATVERIANS BY THE RED SKULL.
HAVE YOU GOT A PLAN?
LOKI...
YES.
IT'S CALLED "RUNNING AWAY."
WHAT, I'M SUPPOSED TO BE A HERO NOW?
WHAT HAVE YOU BEEN SAYING TO THESE PEOPLE?
LOOK, I SEE THROUGH LIES. DOESN'T MEAN I CAN'T TELL ANY.
HEY!
YOU SAID WE NEEDED HIM--
WE DON'T NEED HIM.
BUT WE DO NEED THAT.
GRAM? MY SWORD?
THE SWORD OF TRUTH.
MOMMY AND DADDY.
HARSH!
BUT YES.
THINK ABOUT IT. THE HATE WAVE DOESN'T WORK ON ME. WHY NOT?
WHAT MAKES HATE EASY?
IT'S EASY TO HATE WHAT YOU DON'T KNOW.
WHEN YOU KNOW THE TRUTH-- WHEN YOU SEE THROUGH ALL THE LIES--THE HATE CAN'T SUSTAIN ITSELF.
AND... KNOWING IS HALF THE BATTLE?
SHUT UP.
SO, VAL-- HOW DO WE STAB EVERYONE IN LATVERIA WITH THIS?
USING... SCIENCE!
'RAAAY!

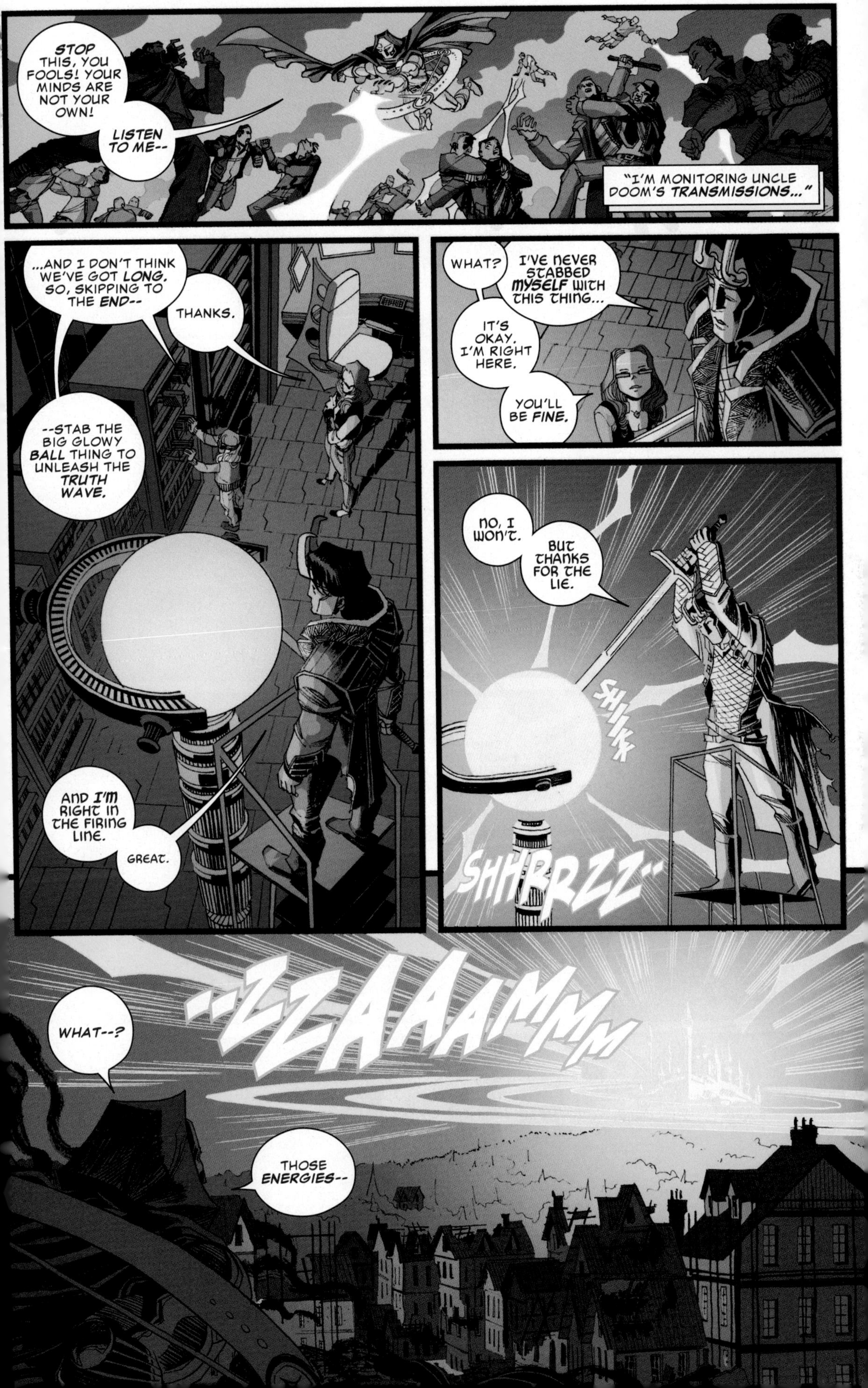
STOP THIS, YOU FOOLS! YOUR MINDS ARE NOT YOUR OWN!
LISTEN TO ME--
"I'M MONITORING UNCLE DOOM'S TRANSMISSIONS..."
...AND I DON'T THINK WE'VE GOT LONG. SO, SKIPPING TO THE END--
THANKS.
--STAB THE BIG GLOWY BALL THING TO UNLEASH THE TRUTH WAVE.
AND I'M RIGHT IN THE FIRING LINE.
GREAT.
WHAT?
I'VE NEVER STABBED MYSELF WITH THIS THING...
IT'S OKAY. I'M RIGHT HERE.
YOU'LL BE FINE.
NO, I WON'T.
BUT THANKS FOR THE LIE.
SHIKK
SHHRRZZ--
--ZZAAAMMM
WHAT--?
THOSE ENERGIES--

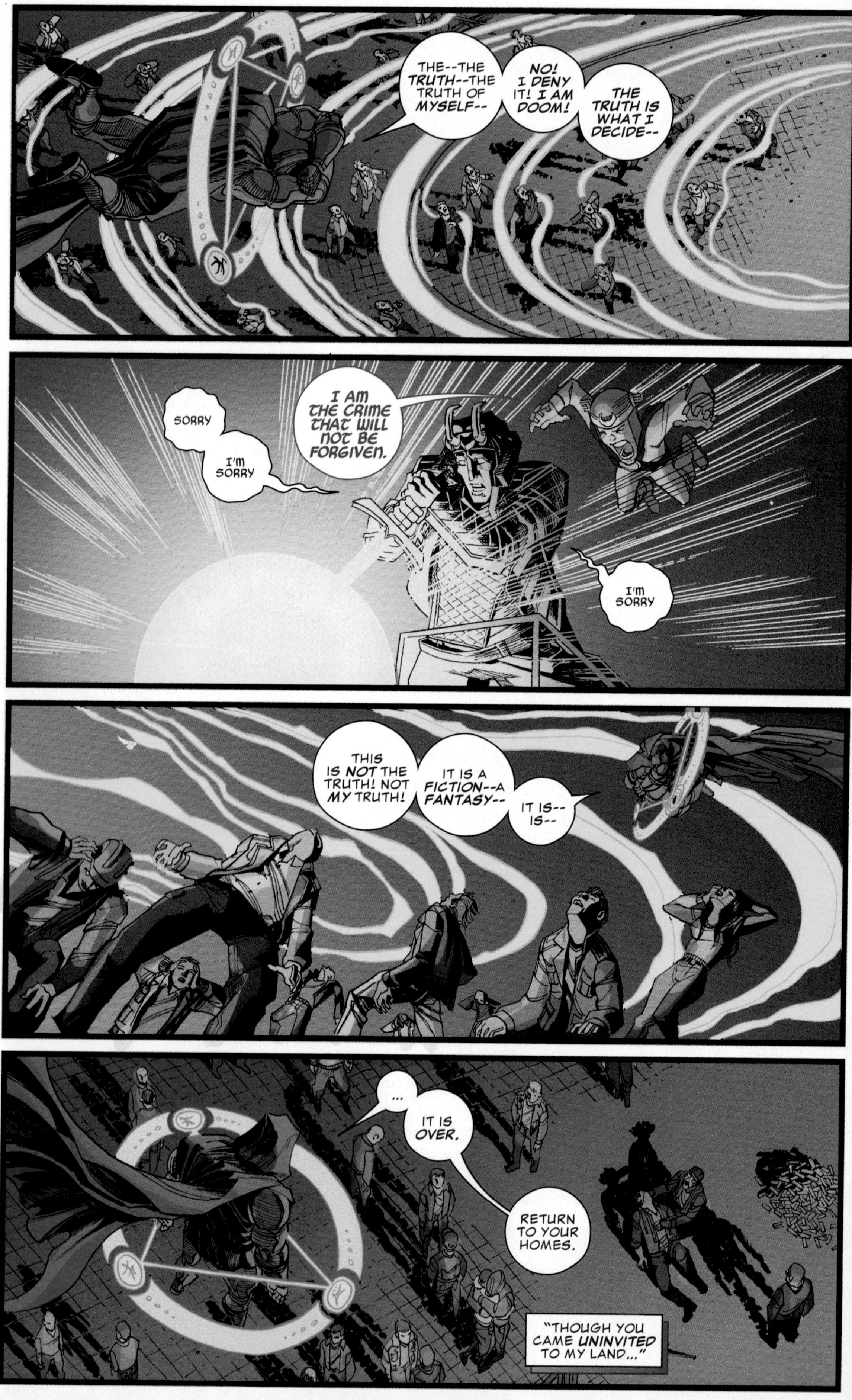

THE--THE TRUTH--THE TRUTH OF MYSELF--
NO! I DENY IT! I AM DOOM!
THE TRUTH IS WHAT I DECIDE--
SORRY
I'M SORRY
I AM THE CRIME THAT WILL NOT BE FORGIVEN.
I'M SORRY
THIS IS NOT THE TRUTH! NOT MY TRUTH!
IT IS A FICTION--A FANTASY--
IT IS-- IS--
...
IT IS OVER.
RETURN TO YOUR HOMES.
"THOUGH YOU CAME UNINVITED TO MY LAND..."

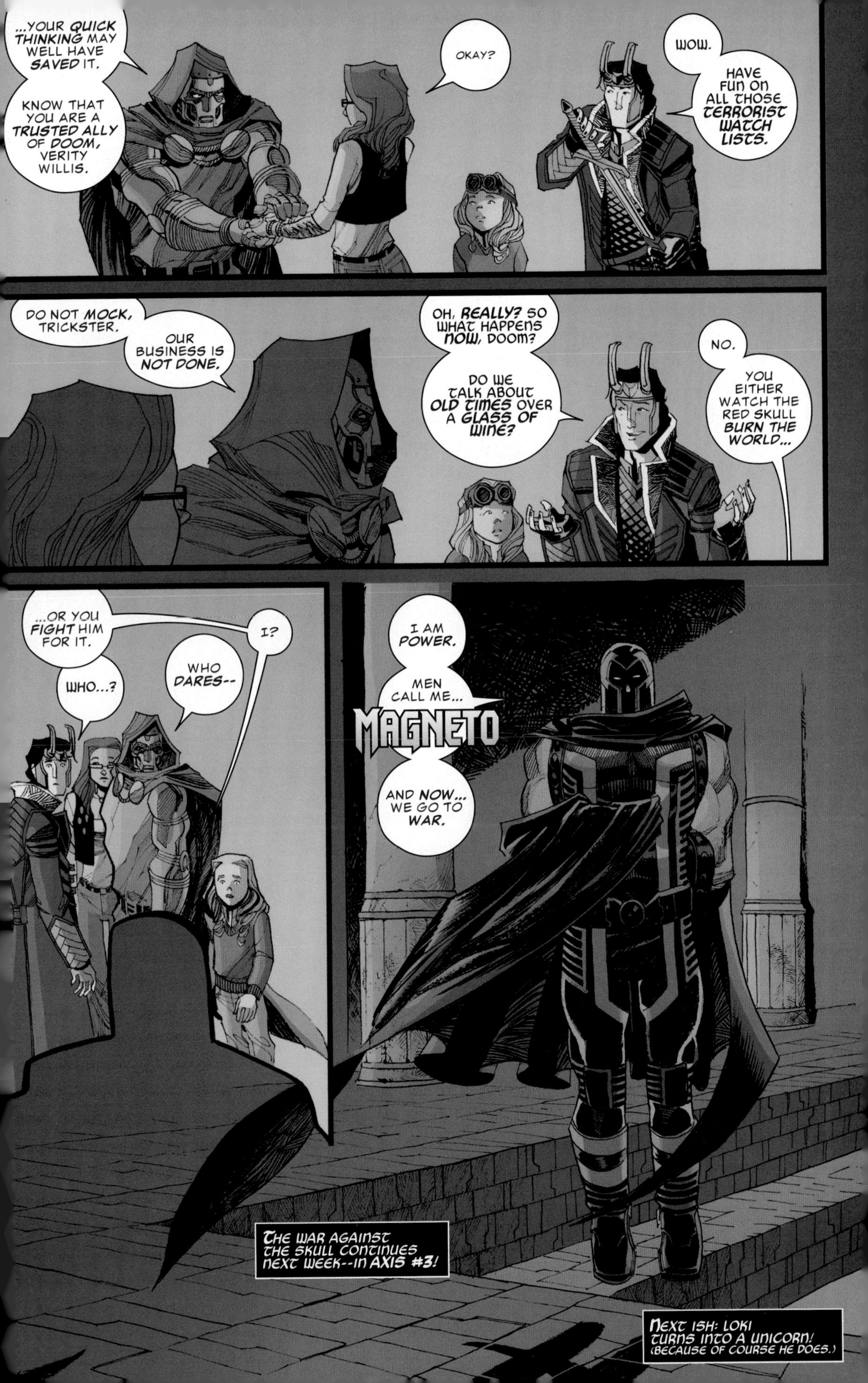

...YOUR QUICK THINKING MAY WELL HAVE SAVED IT.
KNOW THAT YOU ARE A TRUSTED ALLY OF DOOM, VERITY WILLIS.
OKAY?
WOW.
HAVE FUN ON ALL THOSE TERRORIST WATCH LISTS.
DO NOT MOCK, TRICKSTER.
OUR BUSINESS IS NOT DONE.
OH, REALLY? SO WHAT HAPPENS NOW, DOOM?
DO WE TALK ABOUT OLD TIMES OVER A GLASS OF WINE?
NO.
YOU EITHER WATCH THE RED SKULL BURN THE WORLD...
...OR YOU FIGHT HIM FOR IT.
I?
WHO...?
WHO DARES--
I AM POWER.
MEN CALL ME...
MAGNETO
AND NOW... WE GO TO WAR.
THE WAR AGAINST THE SKULL CONTINUES NEXT WEEK--IN AXIS #3!
NEXT ISH: LOKI TURNS INTO A UNICORN! (BECAUSE OF COURSE HE DOES.)

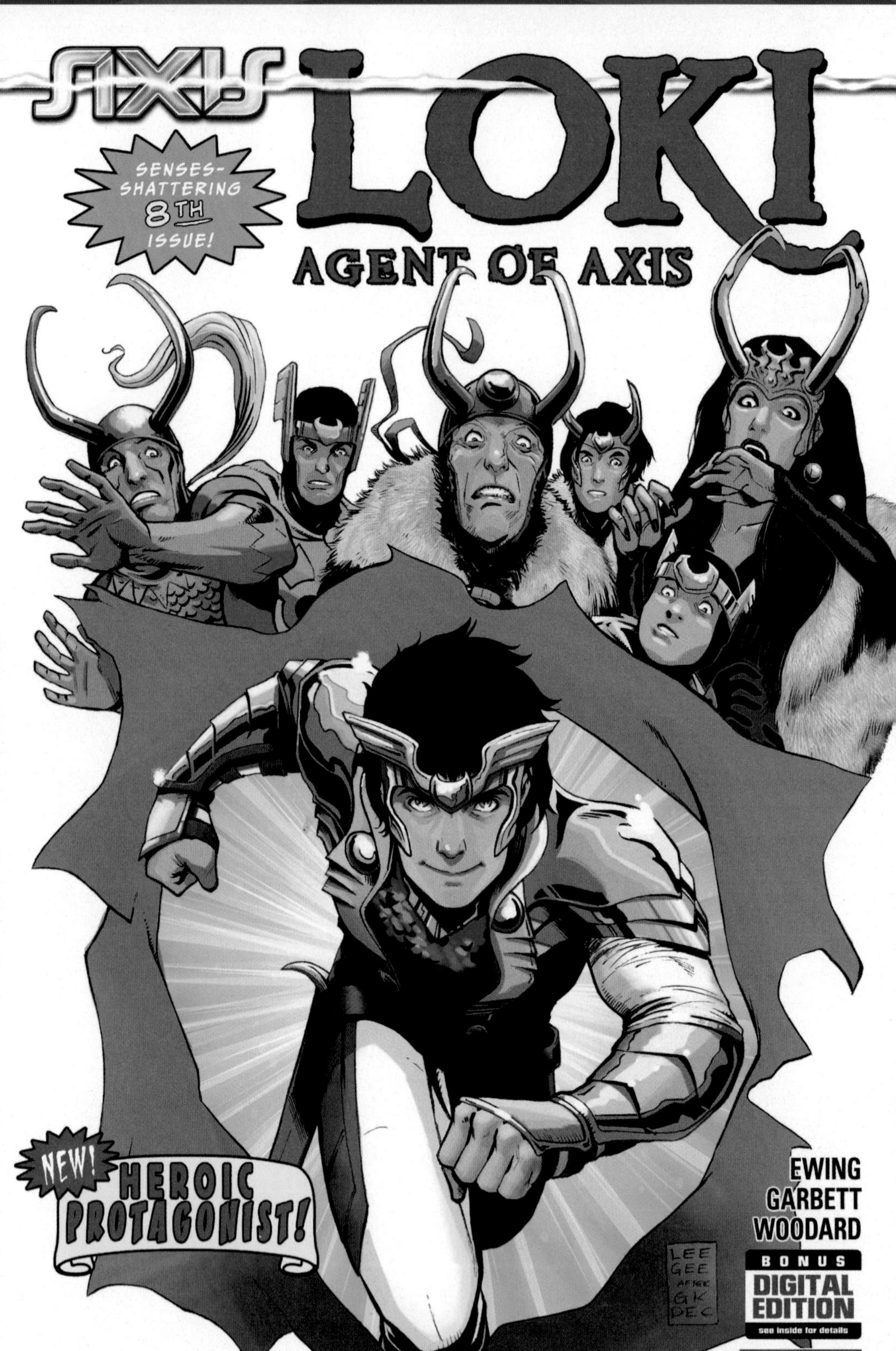
AXIS
LOKI
AGENT OF AXIS
SENSES-SHATTERING 8TH ISSUE!
NEW! HEROIC PROTAGONIST!
EWING
GARBETT
WOODARD
BONUS DIGITAL EDITION
see inside for details
LEE GEE AFTER GK DEC
008
MARVEL

LOKI: AGENT OF ASGARD #8

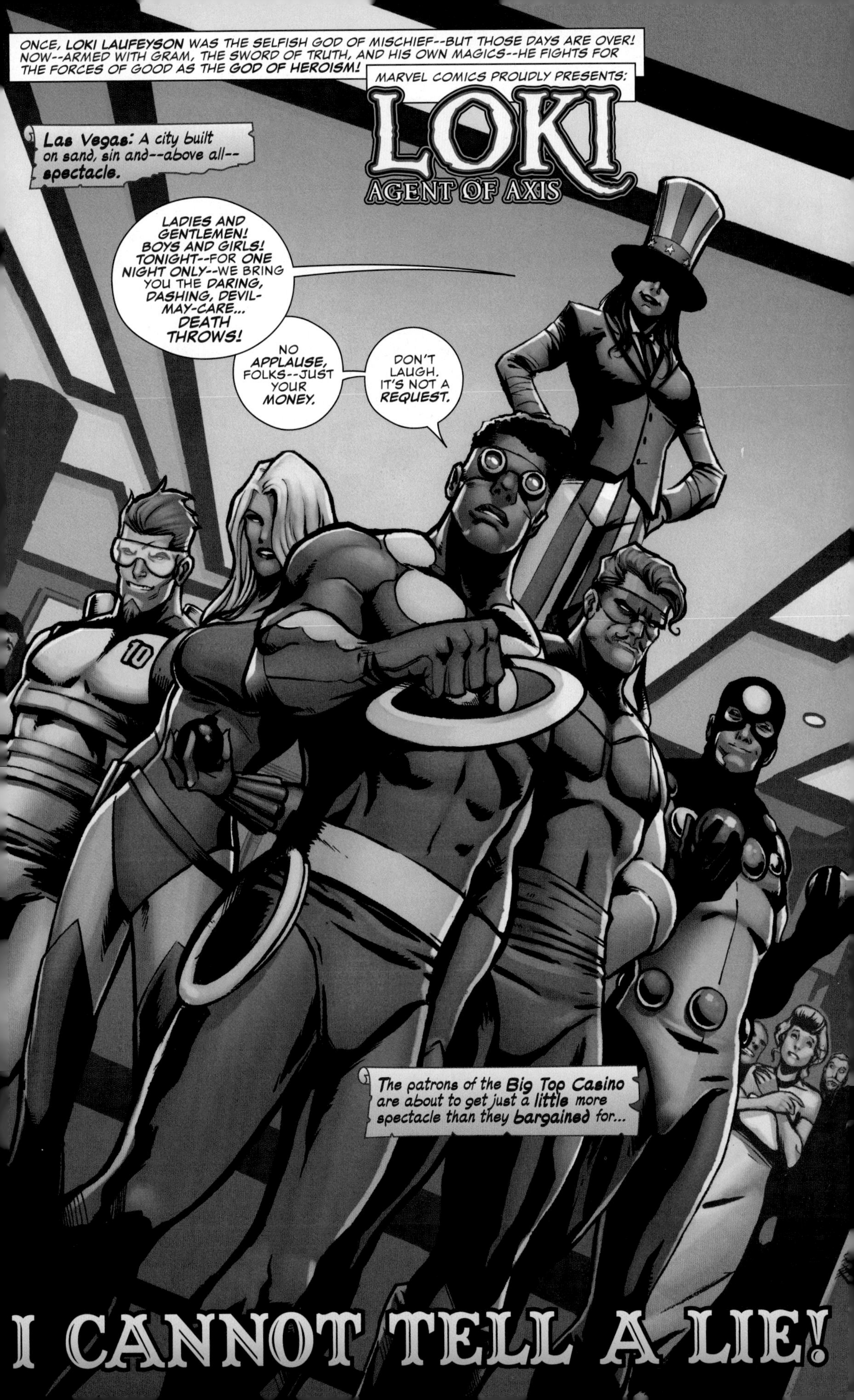

ONCE, LOKI LAUFEYSON WAS THE SELFISH GOD OF MISCHIEF--BUT THOSE DAYS ARE OVER! NOW--ARMED WITH GRAM, THE SWORD OF TRUTH, AND HIS OWN MAGICS--HE FIGHTS FOR THE FORCES OF GOOD AS THE GOD OF HEROISM!
MARVEL COMICS PROUDLY PRESENTS:
LOKI
AGENT OF AXIS
Las Vegas: A city built on sand, sin and--above all--spectacle.
LADIES AND GENTLEMEN! BOYS AND GIRLS! TONIGHT--FOR ONE NIGHT ONLY--WE BRING YOU THE DARING, DASHING, DEVIL-MAY-CARE... DEATH THROWS!
NO APPLAUSE, FOLKS--JUST YOUR MONEY.
DON'T LAUGH. IT'S NOT A REQUEST.
The patrons of the Big Top Casino are about to get just a little more spectacle than they bargained for...
I CANNOT TELL A LIE!

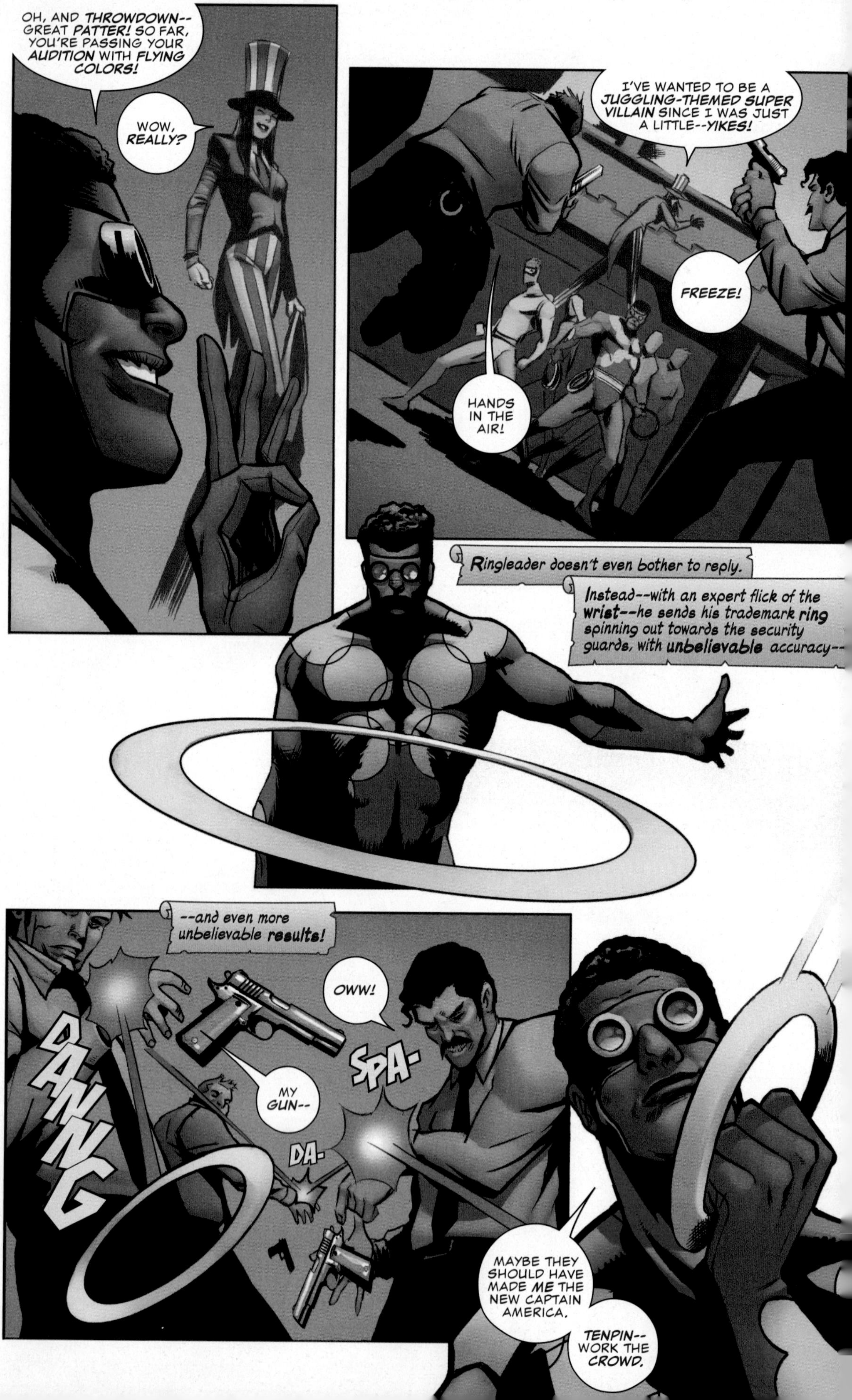
OH, AND THROWDOWN--GREAT PATTER! SO FAR, YOU'RE PASSING YOUR AUDITION WITH FLYING COLORS!
WOW, REALLY?
I'VE WANTED TO BE A JUGGLING-THEMED SUPER VILLAIN SINCE I WAS JUST A LITTLE--YIKES!
FREEZE!
HANDS IN THE AIR!
Ringleader doesn't even bother to reply.
Instead--with an expert flick of the wrist--he sends his trademark ring spinning out towards the security guards, with unbelievable accuracy--
--and even more unbelievable results!
OWW!
MY GUN--
DANNG
SPA-
DA-
MAYBE THEY SHOULD HAVE MADE ME THE NEW CAPTAIN AMERICA.
TENPIN--WORK THE CROWD.

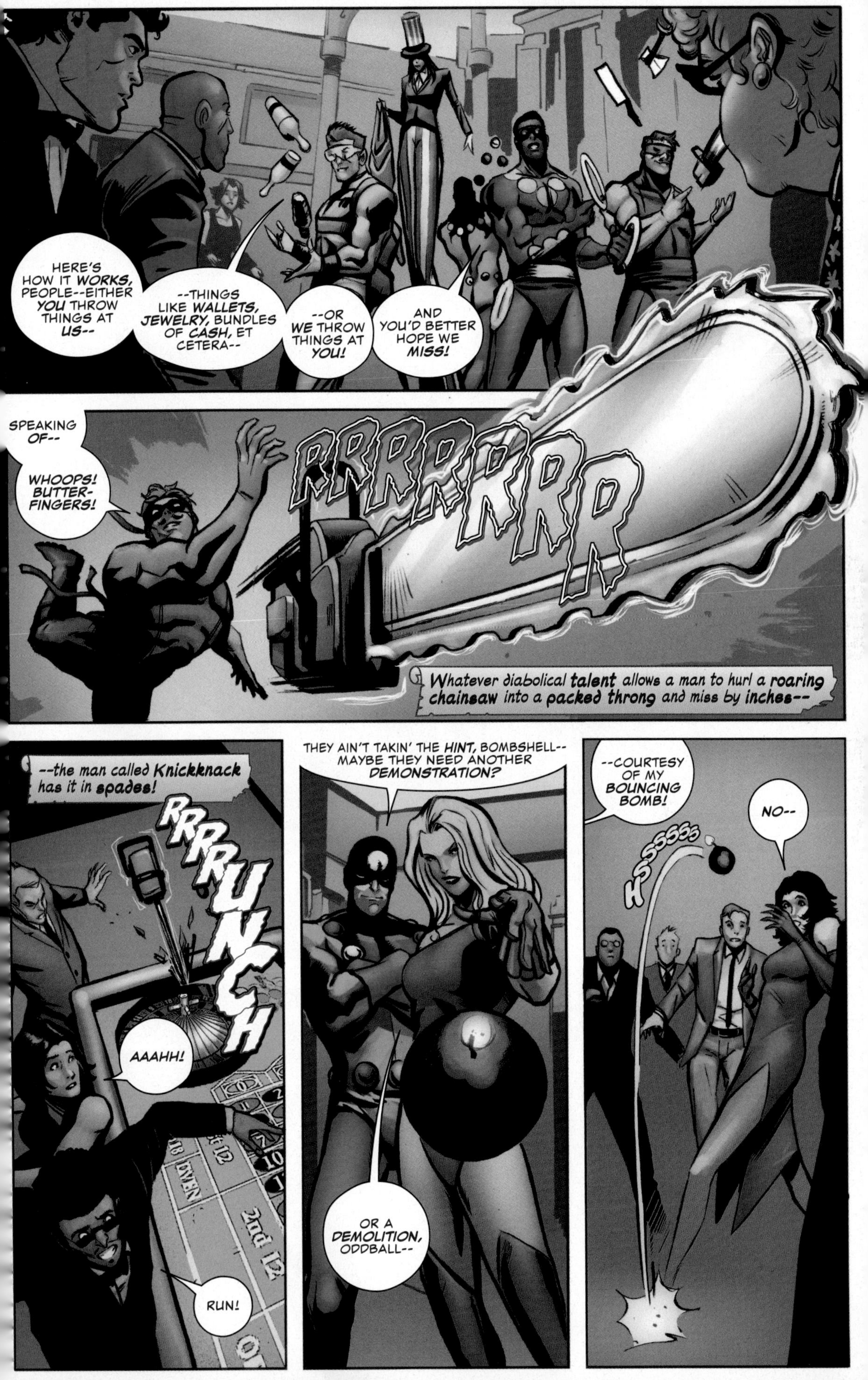
HERE'S HOW IT WORKS, PEOPLE--EITHER YOU THROW THINGS AT US--
--THINGS LIKE WALLETS, JEWELRY, BUNDLES OF CASH, ET CETERA--
--OR WE THROW THINGS AT YOU!
AND YOU'D BETTER HOPE WE MISS!
SPEAKING OF--
WHOOPS! BUTTER-FINGERS!
RRRRRRR
Whatever diabolical talent allows a man to hurl a roaring chainsaw into a packed throng and miss by inches--
--the man called Knickknack has it in spades!
RRRRUNCH
AAAHH!
RUN!
THEY AIN'T TAKIN' THE HINT, BOMBSHELL--MAYBE THEY NEED ANOTHER DEMONSTRATION?
OR A DEMOLITION, ODDBALL--
--COURTESY OF MY BOUNCING BOMB!
HSSSSSS
NO--

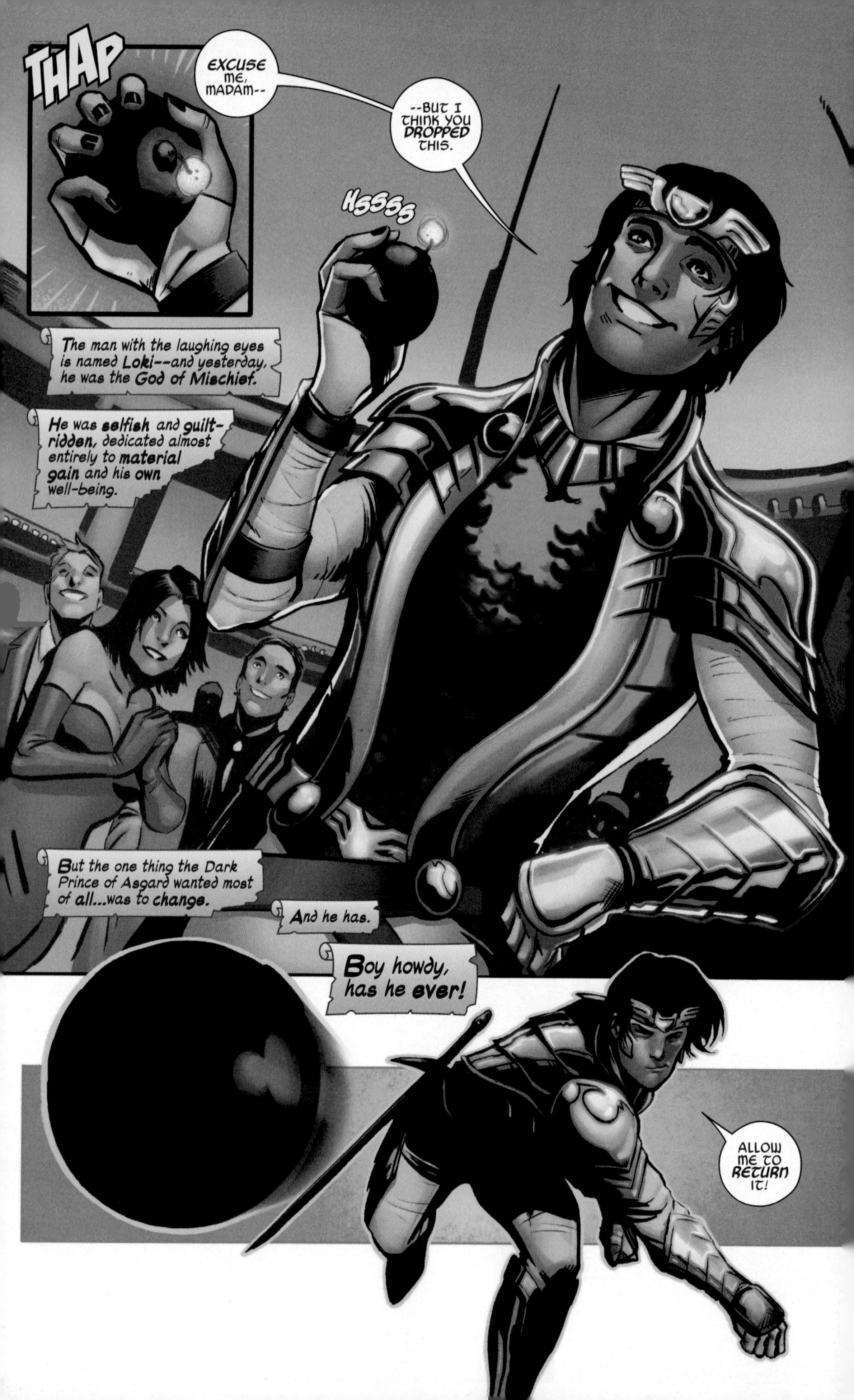
THAP
EXCUSE ME, MADAM--
--BUT I THINK YOU DROPPED THIS.
HSSSS
The man with the laughing eyes is named Loki--and yesterday, he was the God of Mischief.
He was selfish and guilt-ridden, dedicated almost entirely to material gain and his own well-being.
But the one thing the Dark Prince of Asgard wanted most of all...was to change.
And he has.
Boy howdy, has he ever!
ALLOW ME TO RETURN IT!

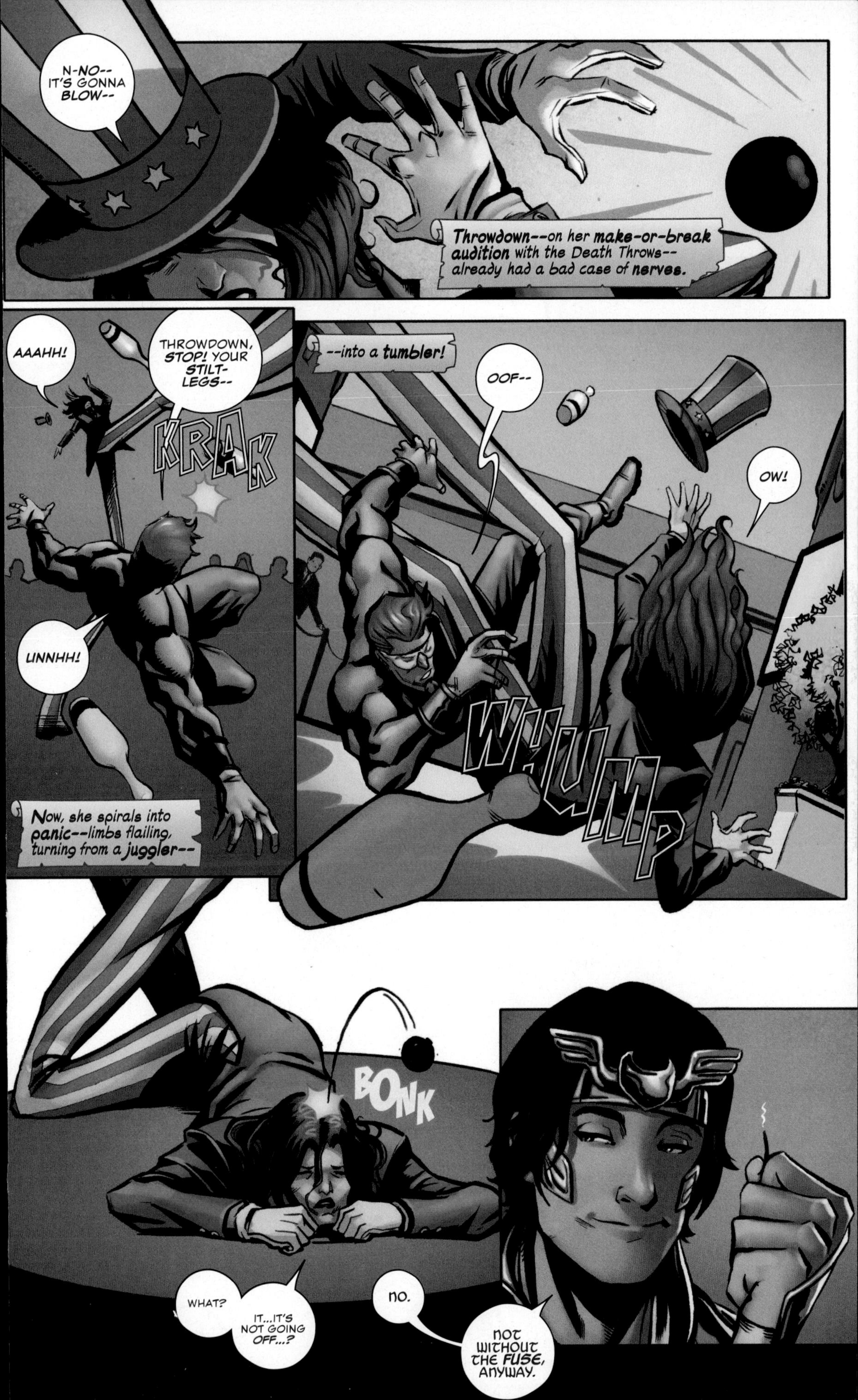
N-NO-- IT'S GONNA BLOW--
Throwdown--on her make-or-break audition with the Death Throws--already had a bad case of nerves.
AAAHH!
THROWDOWN, STOP! YOUR STILT-LEGS--
KRAK
UNNHH!
Now, she spirals into panic--limbs flailing, turning from a juggler--
--into a tumbler!
OOF--
OW!
WHUMP
BONK
WHAT?
IT...IT'S NOT GOING OFF...?
no.
not without the FUSE, anyway.

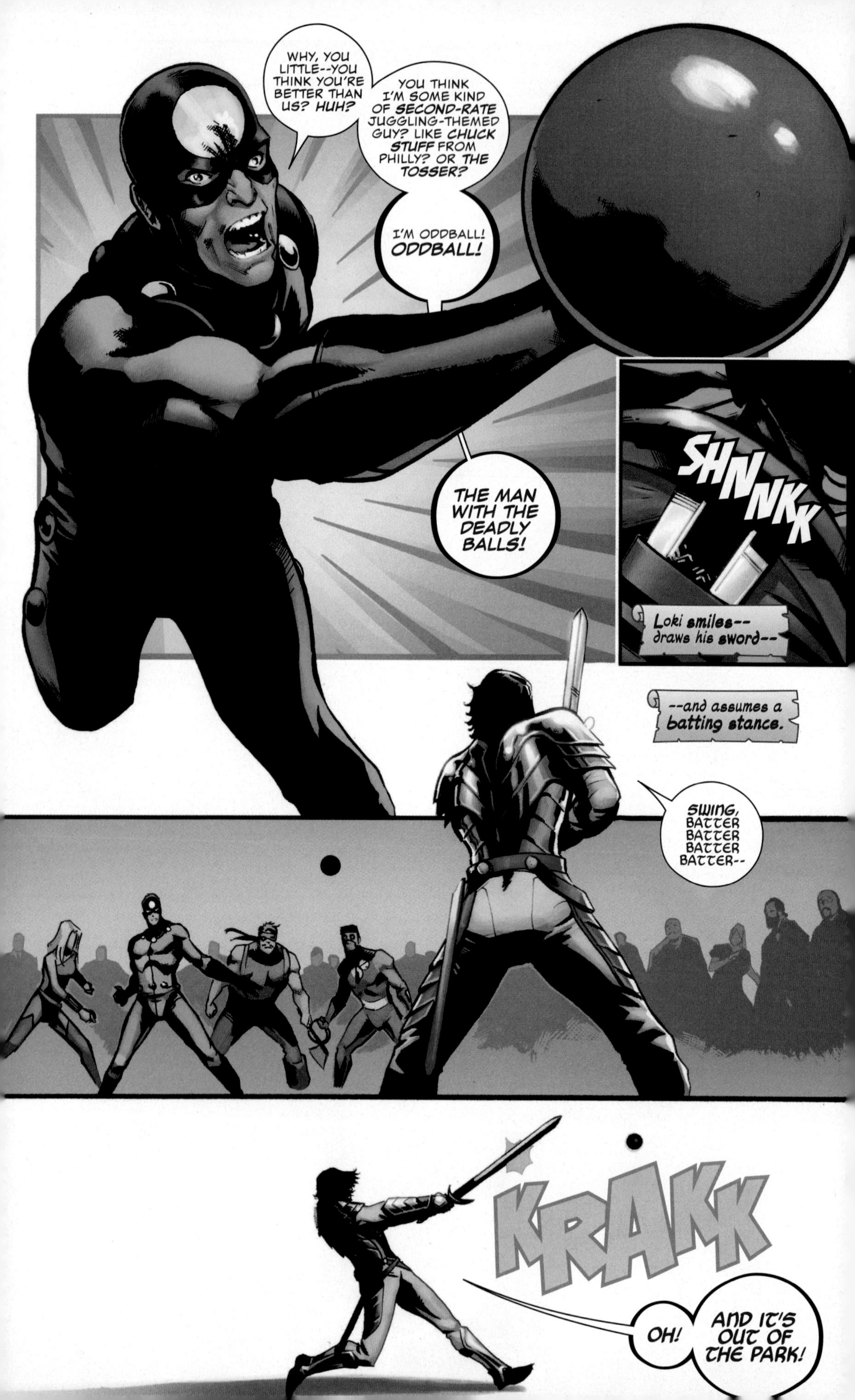
WHY, YOU LITTLE--YOU THINK YOU'RE BETTER THAN US? HUH?
YOU THINK I'M SOME KIND OF SECOND-RATE JUGGLING-THEMED GUY? LIKE CHUCK STUFF FROM PHILLY? OR THE TOSSER?
I'M ODDBALL! ODDBALL!
THE MAN WITH THE DEADLY BALLS!
SHNNKK
Loki smiles-- draws his sword--
--and assumes a batting stance.
SWING, BATTER BATTER BATTER BATTER--
KRAKK
OH!
AND IT'S OUT OF THE PARK!

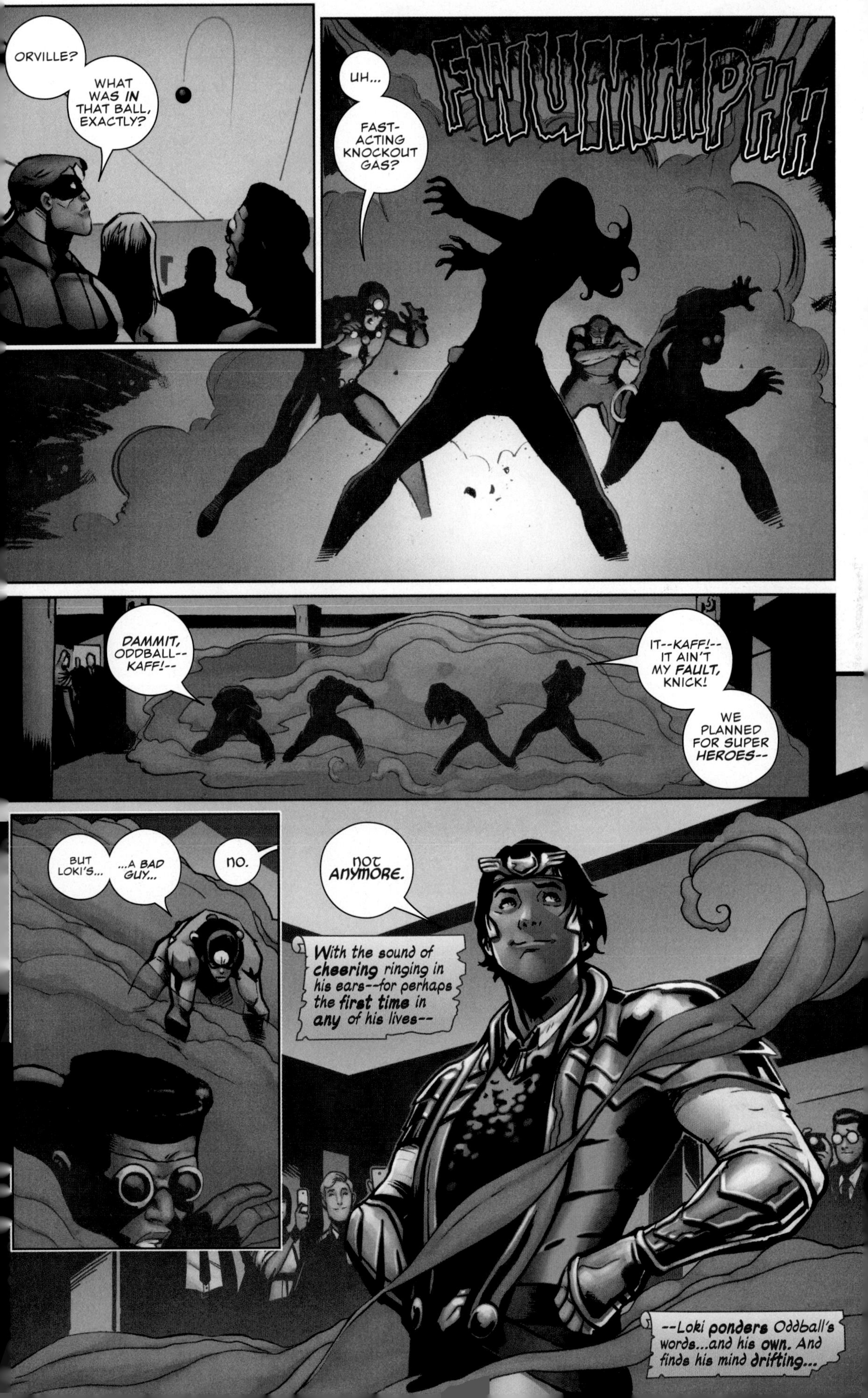
ORVILLE?
WHAT WAS IN THAT BALL, EXACTLY?
UH...
FAST-ACTING KNOCKOUT GAS?
FWUMMPHH
DAMMIT, ODDBALL-- KAFF!--
IT--KAFF!-- IT AIN'T MY FAULT, KNICK!
WE PLANNED FOR SUPER HEROES--
BUT LOKI'S...
...A BAD GUY...
NO.
NOT ANYMORE.
With the sound of cheering ringing in his ears--for perhaps the first time in any of his lives--
--Loki ponders Oddball's words...and his own. And finds his mind drifting...

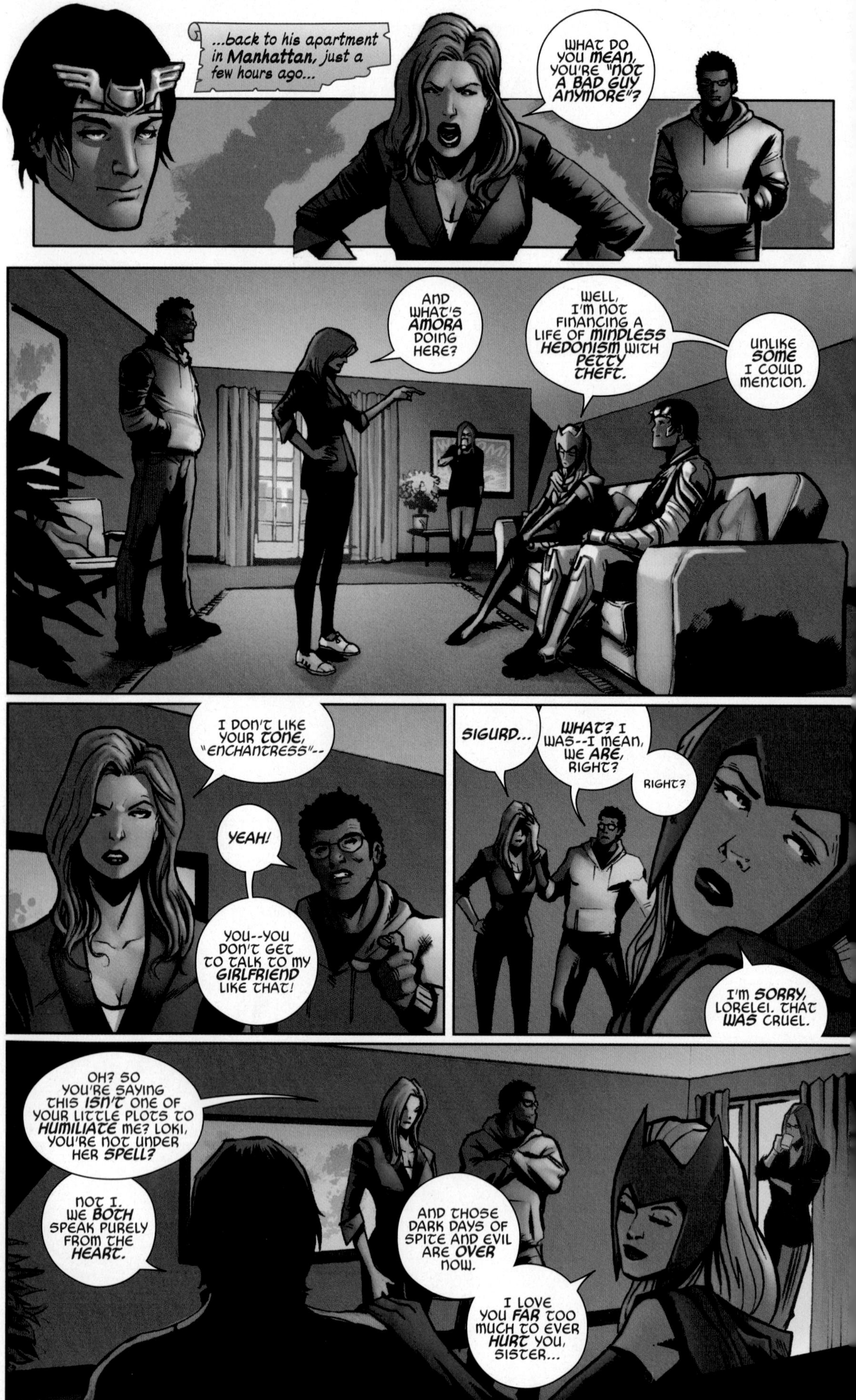
...back to his apartment in Manhattan, just a few hours ago...
WHAT DO YOU MEAN, YOU'RE "NOT A BAD GUY ANYMORE"?
AND WHAT'S AMORA DOING HERE?
WELL, I'M NOT FINANCING A LIFE OF MINDLESS HEDONISM WITH PETTY THEFT.
UNLIKE SOME I COULD MENTION.
I DON'T LIKE YOUR TONE, "ENCHANTRESS"--
YEAH!
YOU--YOU DON'T GET TO TALK TO MY GIRLFRIEND LIKE THAT!
SIGURD...
WHAT? I WAS--I MEAN, WE ARE, RIGHT?
RIGHT?
I'M SORRY, LORELEI. THAT WAS CRUEL.
OH? SO YOU'RE SAYING THIS ISN'T ONE OF YOUR LITTLE PLOTS TO HUMILIATE ME? LOKI, YOU'RE NOT UNDER HER SPELL?
NOT I. WE BOTH SPEAK PURELY FROM THE HEART.
AND THOSE DARK DAYS OF SPITE AND EVIL ARE OVER NOW.
I LOVE YOU FAR TOO MUCH TO EVER HURT YOU, SISTER...

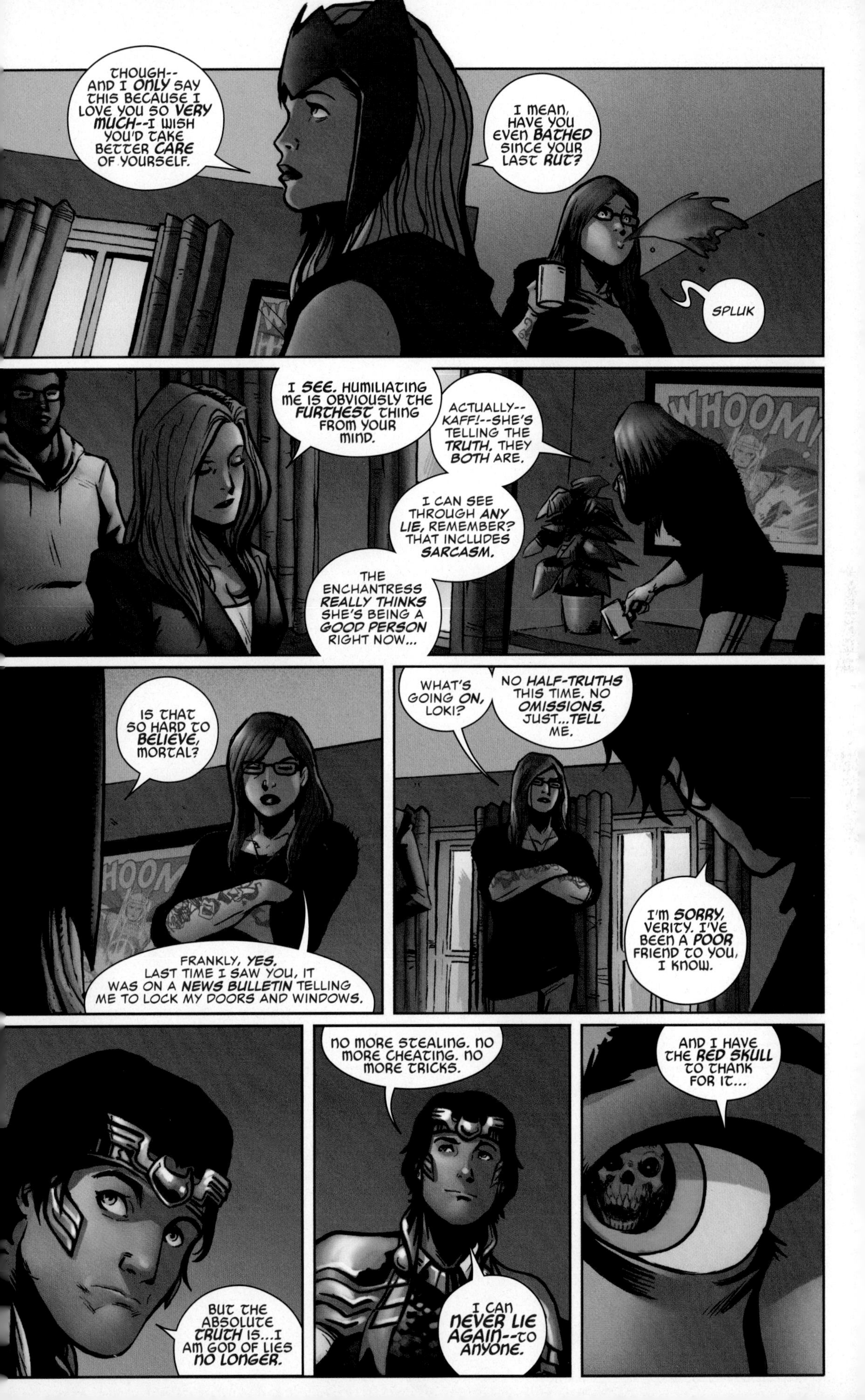

THOUGH-- AND I ONLY SAY THIS BECAUSE I LOVE YOU SO VERY MUCH--I WISH YOU'D TAKE BETTER CARE OF YOURSELF.
I MEAN, HAVE YOU EVEN BATHED SINCE YOUR LAST RUT?
SPLUK
I SEE. HUMILIATING ME IS OBVIOUSLY THE FURTHEST THING FROM YOUR MIND.
ACTUALLY-- KAFF!--SHE'S TELLING THE TRUTH. THEY BOTH ARE.
I CAN SEE THROUGH ANY LIE, REMEMBER? THAT INCLUDES SARCASM.
THE ENCHANTRESS REALLY THINKS SHE'S BEING A GOOD PERSON RIGHT NOW...
WHOOM!
IS THAT SO HARD TO BELIEVE, MORTAL?
FRANKLY, YES. LAST TIME I SAW YOU, IT WAS ON A NEWS BULLETIN TELLING ME TO LOCK MY DOORS AND WINDOWS.
WHAT'S GOING ON, LOKI?
NO HALF-TRUTHS THIS TIME. NO OMISSIONS. JUST...TELL ME.
I'M SORRY, VERITY. I'VE BEEN A POOR FRIEND TO YOU, I KNOW.
BUT THE ABSOLUTE TRUTH IS...I AM GOD OF LIES NO LONGER.
NO MORE STEALING. NO MORE CHEATING. NO MORE TRICKS.
I CAN NEVER LIE AGAIN--TO ANYONE.
AND I HAVE THE RED SKULL TO THANK FOR IT...

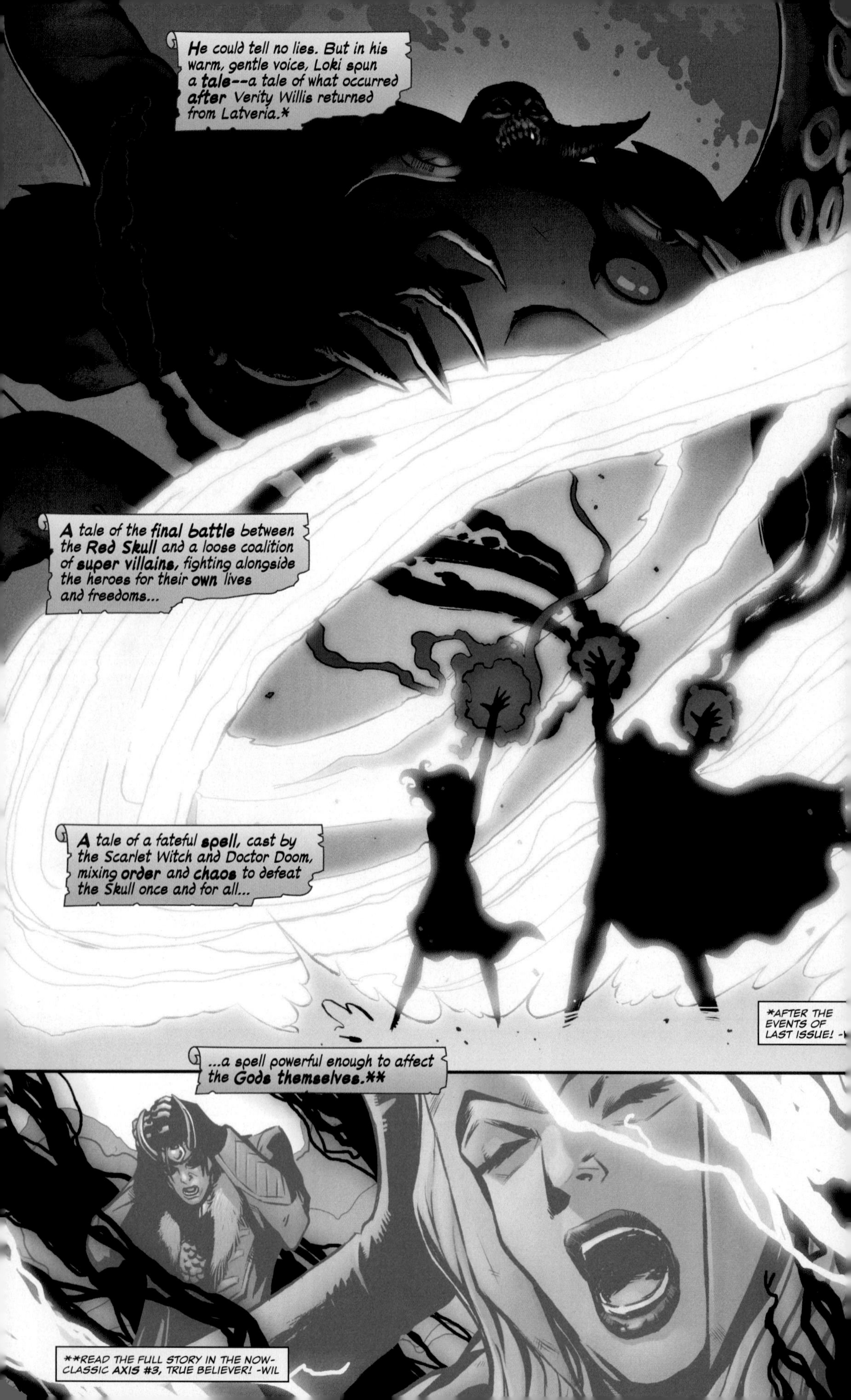
He could tell no lies. But in his warm, gentle voice, Loki spun a tale--a tale of what occurred after Verity Willis returned from Latveria.*
A tale of the final battle between the Red Skull and a loose coalition of super villains, fighting alongside the heroes for their own lives and freedoms...
A tale of a fateful spell, cast by the Scarlet Witch and Doctor Doom, mixing order and chaos to defeat the Skull once and for all...
*AFTER THE EVENTS OF LAST ISSUE!
...a spell powerful enough to affect the Gods themselves.**
**READ THE FULL STORY IN THE NOW-CLASSIC AXIS #3, TRUE BELIEVER! -WIL

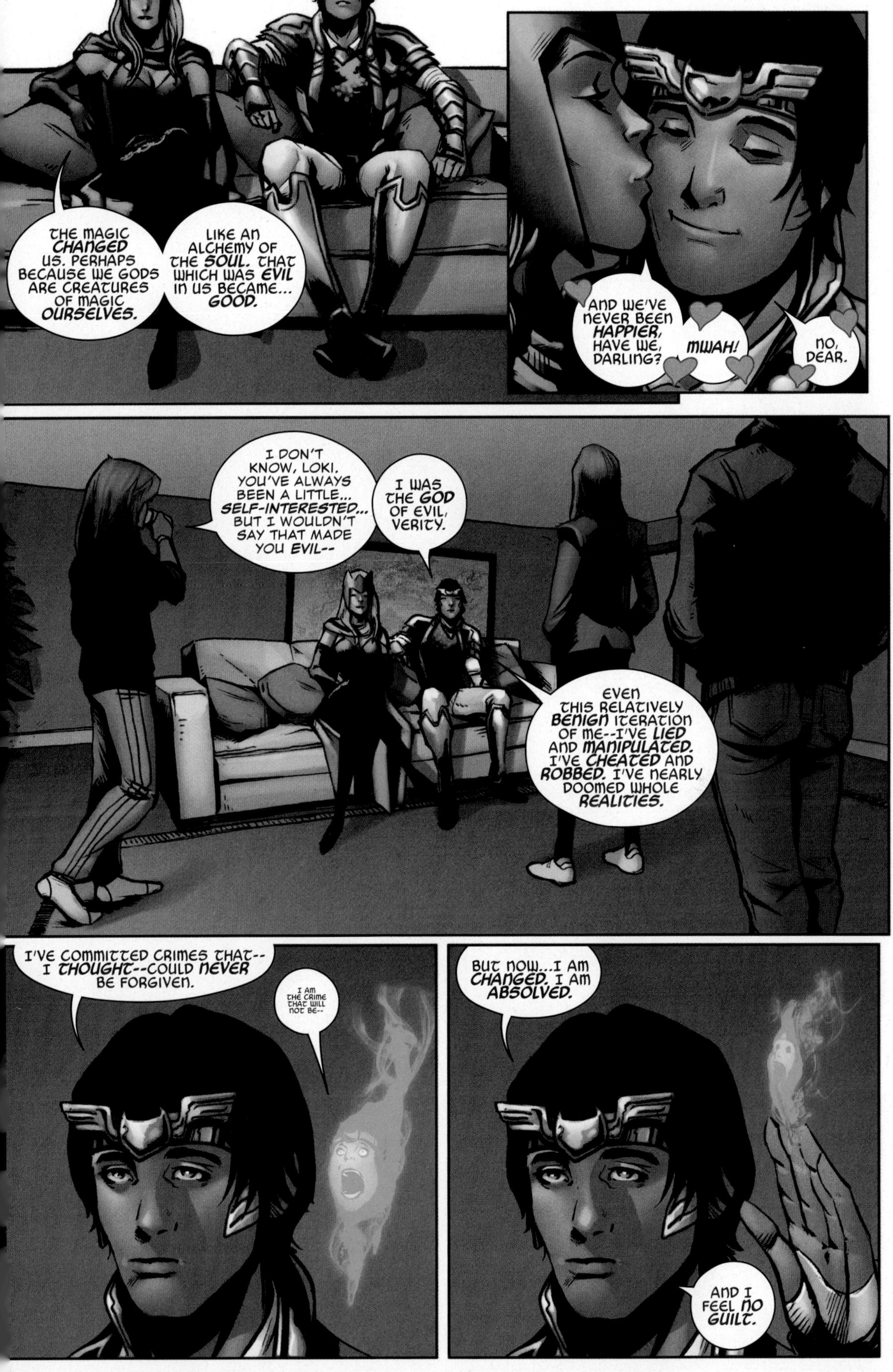
THE MAGIC CHANGED US. PERHAPS BECAUSE WE GODS ARE CREATURES OF MAGIC OURSELVES.
LIKE AN ALCHEMY OF THE SOUL. THAT WHICH WAS EVIL IN US BECAME... GOOD.
AND WE'VE NEVER BEEN HAPPIER, HAVE WE, DARLING?
MWAH!
NO, DEAR.
I DON'T KNOW, LOKI. YOU'VE ALWAYS BEEN A LITTLE... SELF-INTERESTED... BUT I WOULDN'T SAY THAT MADE YOU EVIL--
I WAS THE GOD OF EVIL, VERITY.
EVEN THIS RELATIVELY BENIGN ITERATION OF ME--I'VE LIED AND MANIPULATED. I'VE CHEATED AND ROBBED. I'VE NEARLY DOOMED WHOLE REALITIES.
I'VE COMMITTED CRIMES THAT-- I THOUGHT--COULD NEVER BE FORGIVEN.
I AM THE CRIME THAT WILL NOT BE--
BUT NOW...I AM CHANGED. I AM ABSOLVED.
AND I FEEL NO GUILT.

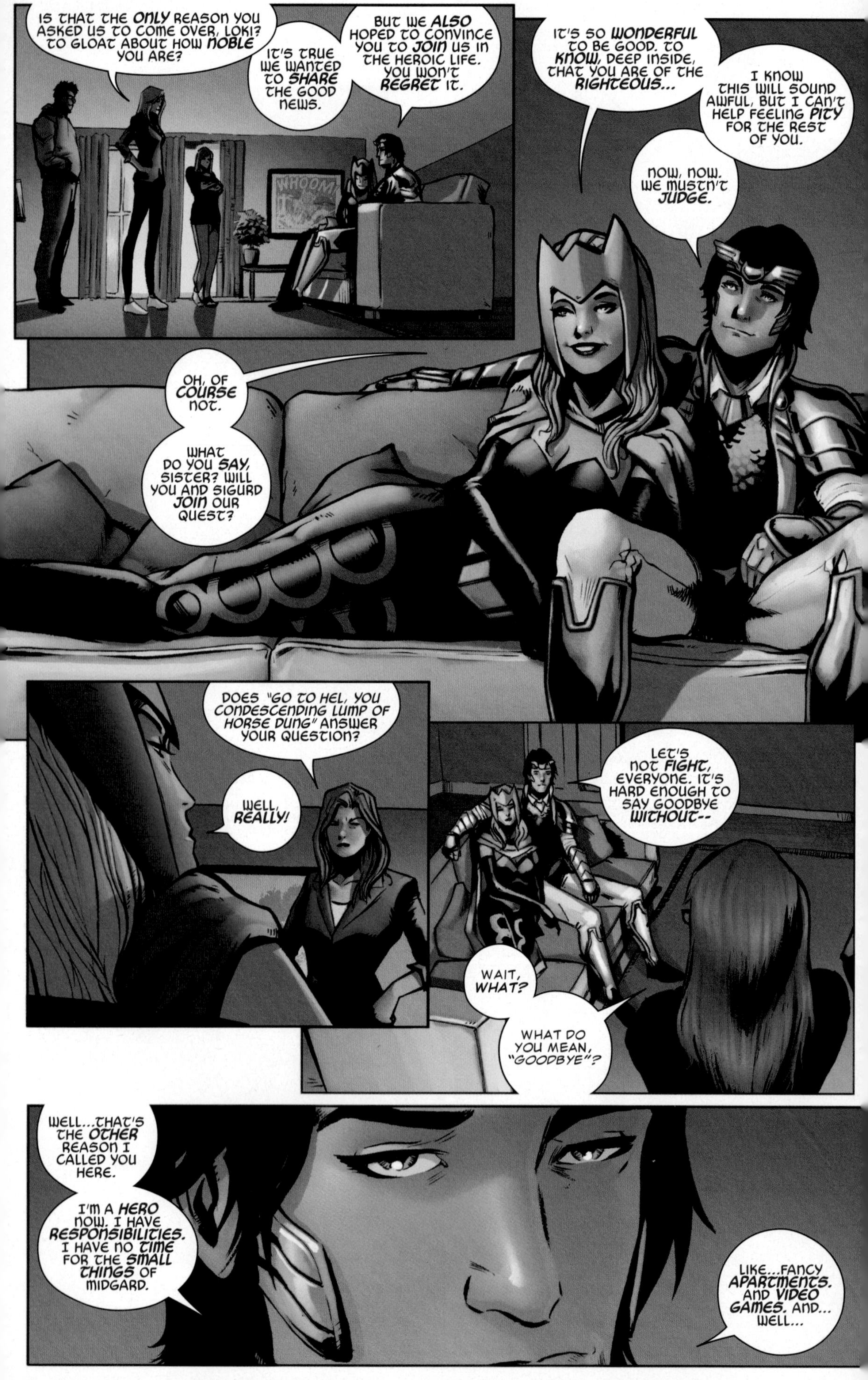
IS THAT THE ONLY REASON YOU ASKED US TO COME OVER, LOKI? TO GLOAT ABOUT HOW NOBLE YOU ARE?
IT'S TRUE WE WANTED TO SHARE THE GOOD NEWS.
BUT WE ALSO HOPED TO CONVINCE YOU TO JOIN US IN THE HEROIC LIFE. YOU WON'T REGRET IT.
IT'S SO WONDERFUL TO BE GOOD. TO KNOW, DEEP INSIDE, THAT YOU ARE OF THE RIGHTEOUS...
I KNOW THIS WILL SOUND AWFUL, BUT I CAN'T HELP FEELING PITY FOR THE REST OF YOU.
NOW, NOW. WE MUSTN'T JUDGE.
OH, OF COURSE NOT.
WHAT DO YOU SAY, SISTER? WILL YOU AND SIGURD JOIN OUR QUEST?
DOES "GO TO HEL, YOU CONDESCENDING LUMP OF HORSE DUNG" ANSWER YOUR QUESTION?
WELL, REALLY!
LET'S NOT FIGHT, EVERYONE. IT'S HARD ENOUGH TO SAY GOODBYE WITHOUT--
WAIT, WHAT?
WHAT DO YOU MEAN, "GOODBYE"?
WELL...THAT'S THE OTHER REASON I CALLED YOU HERE.
I'M A HERO NOW. I HAVE RESPONSIBILITIES. I HAVE NO TIME FOR THE SMALL THINGS OF MIDGARD.
LIKE...FANCY APARTMENTS. AND VIDEO GAMES. AND... WELL...

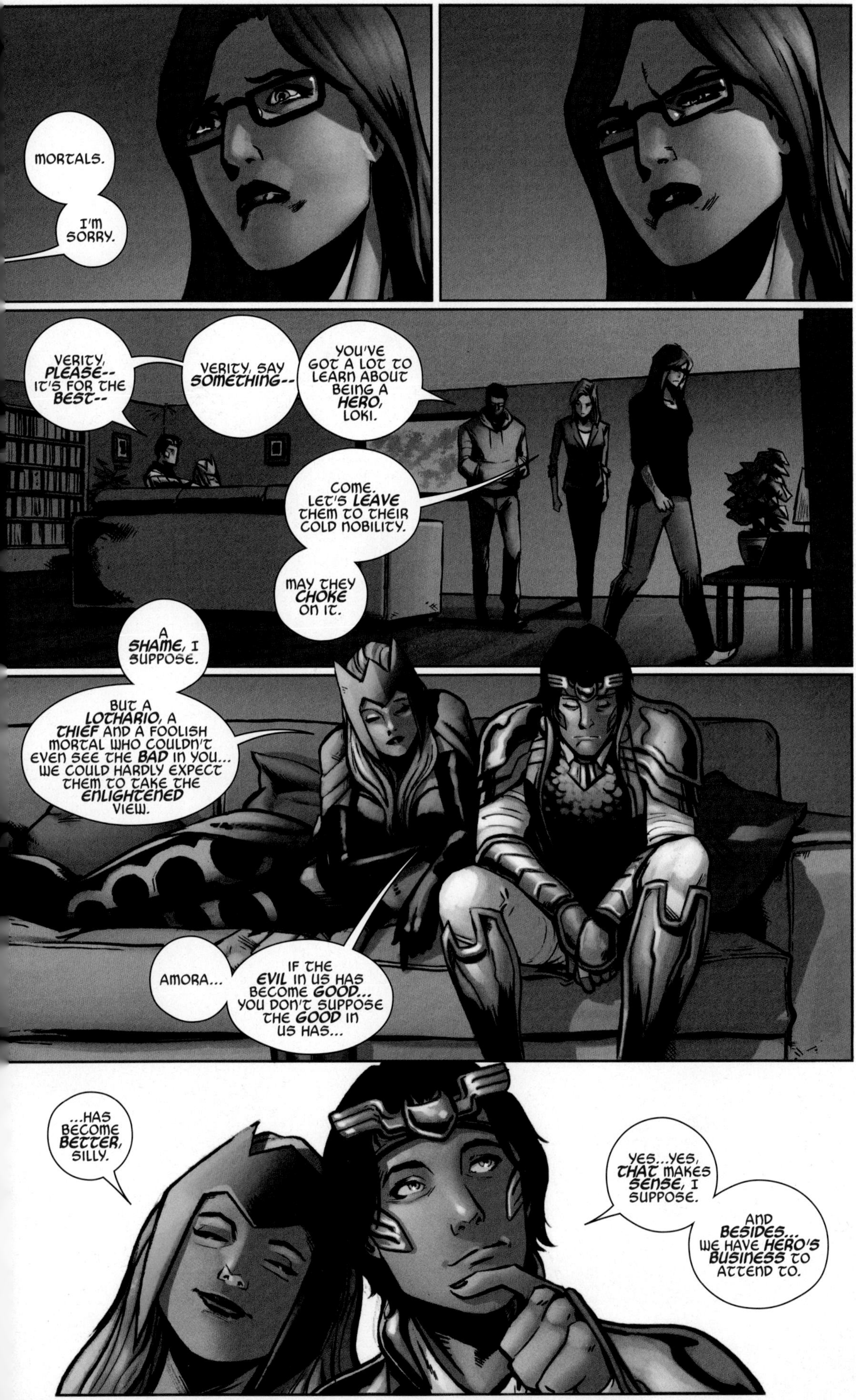
MORTALS.
I'M SORRY.
VERITY, PLEASE-- IT'S FOR THE BEST--
VERITY, SAY SOMETHING--
YOU'VE GOT A LOT TO LEARN ABOUT BEING A HERO, LOKI.
COME. LET'S LEAVE THEM TO THEIR COLD NOBILITY.
MAY THEY CHOKE ON IT.
A SHAME, I SUPPOSE.
BUT A LOTHARIO, A THIEF AND A FOOLISH MORTAL WHO COULDN'T EVEN SEE THE BAD IN YOU... WE COULD HARDLY EXPECT THEM TO TAKE THE ENLIGHTENED VIEW.
AMORA...
IF THE EVIL IN US HAS BECOME GOOD... YOU DON'T SUPPOSE THE GOOD IN US HAS...
...HAS BECOME BETTER, SILLY.
YES...YES, THAT MAKES SENSE, I SUPPOSE.
AND BESIDES... WE HAVE HERO'S BUSINESS TO ATTEND TO.

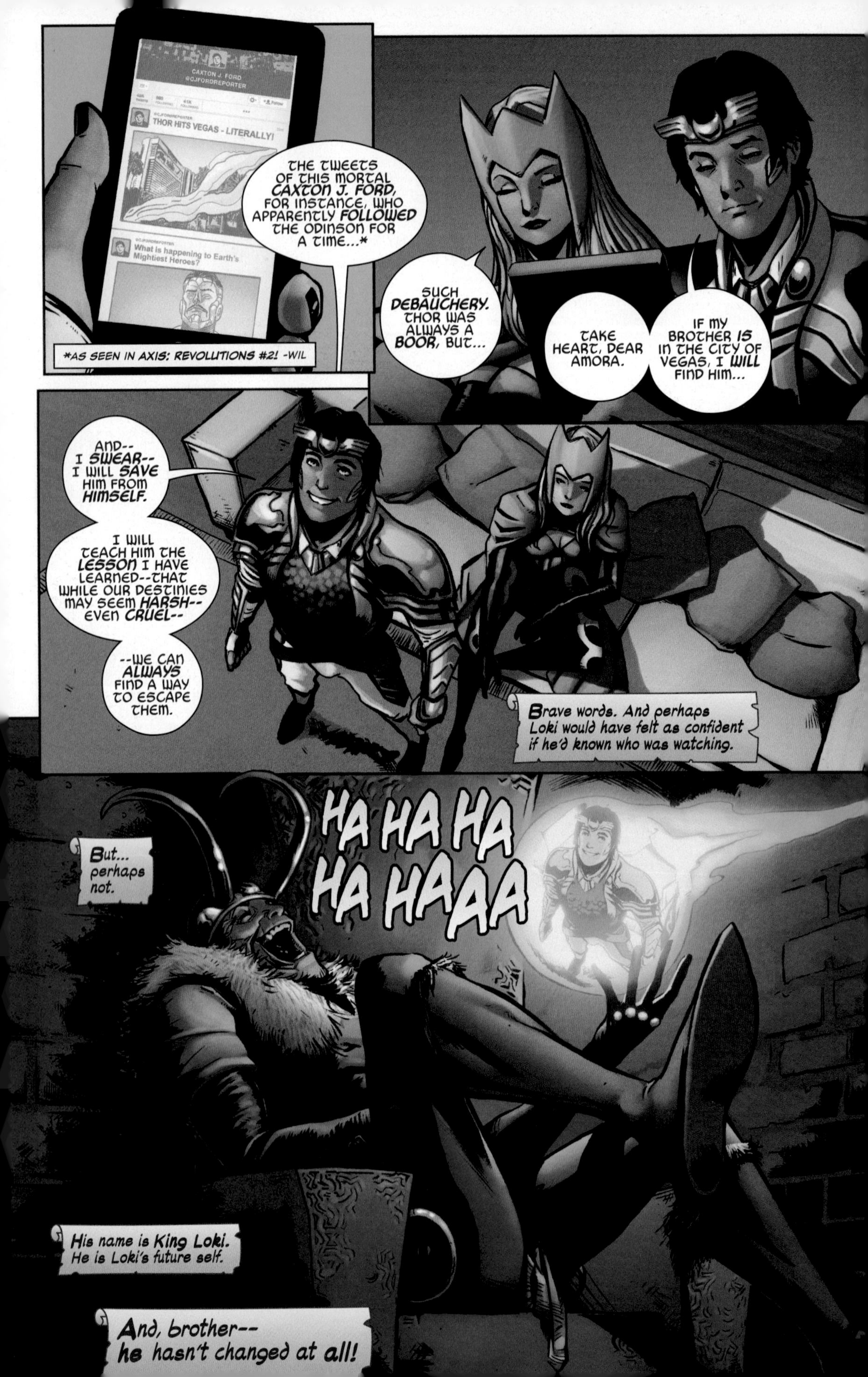
CAXTON J. FORD
@CJFORDREPORTER
THOR HITS VEGAS - LITERALLY!
What is happening to Earth's Mightiest Heroes?
THE TWEETS OF THIS MORTAL CAXTON J. FORD, FOR INSTANCE, WHO APPARENTLY FOLLOWED THE ODINSON FOR A TIME...*
*AS SEEN IN AXIS: REVOLUTIONS #2! -WIL
SUCH DEBAUCHERY. THOR WAS ALWAYS A BOOR, BUT...
TAKE HEART, DEAR AMORA.
IF MY BROTHER IS IN THE CITY OF VEGAS, I WILL FIND HIM...
AND-- I SWEAR-- I WILL SAVE HIM FROM HIMSELF.
I WILL TEACH HIM THE LESSON I HAVE LEARNED--THAT WHILE OUR DESTINIES MAY SEEM HARSH-- EVEN CRUEL--
--WE CAN ALWAYS FIND A WAY TO ESCAPE THEM.
Brave words. And perhaps Loki would have felt as confident if he'd known who was watching.
But... perhaps not.
HA HA HA HA HAAA
His name is King Loki. He is Loki's future self.
And, brother-- he hasn't changed at all!

But that's a story for **another time**.

Here and now--in the **Big Top** Casino--Loki finds himself learning something else about good deeds...

YOU!

FREEZE!

...that they never go **unpunished**.

WE NEED **BACKUP** HERE! WE GOT ANOTHER OF THOSE CRAZY **ASGARDIANS** TEARIN' UP THE PLACE--

HEY! HEY!

THIS GUY JUST SAVED US FROM GETTING **ROBBED**, MICKEY!

POINT 'EM SOMEWHERE **ELSE**, HUH?

YES, THANKS FOR CLEARING THAT LITTLE DETAIL **UP**, MISTER...?

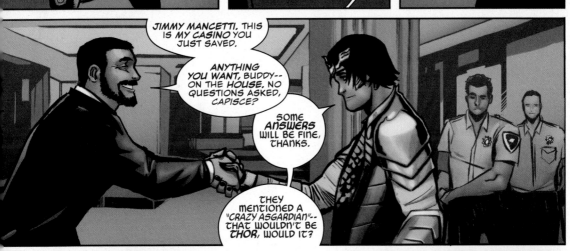

JIMMY MANCETTI, THIS IS MY CASINO YOU JUST SAVED.

ANYTHING YOU WANT, BUDDY-- ON THE **HOUSE**, NO QUESTIONS ASKED, CAPISCE?

SOME **ANSWERS** WILL BE FINE, THANKS.

THEY MENTIONED A "CRAZY ASGARDIAN"-- THAT WOULDN'T BE **THOR**, WOULD IT?

HE **SAYS** HE'S THOR, BUT HE AIN'T **DRESSED** LIKE THOR, AND I DON'T SEE NO HAMMER. FIGURE IT'S AN **IMPOSTOR**, RIGHT?

DEFINITELY ONE OF YOU GUYS, THOUGH. **SUPER-STRENGTH**, FUNNY ACCENT...

AND WHERE CAN I FIND HIM?

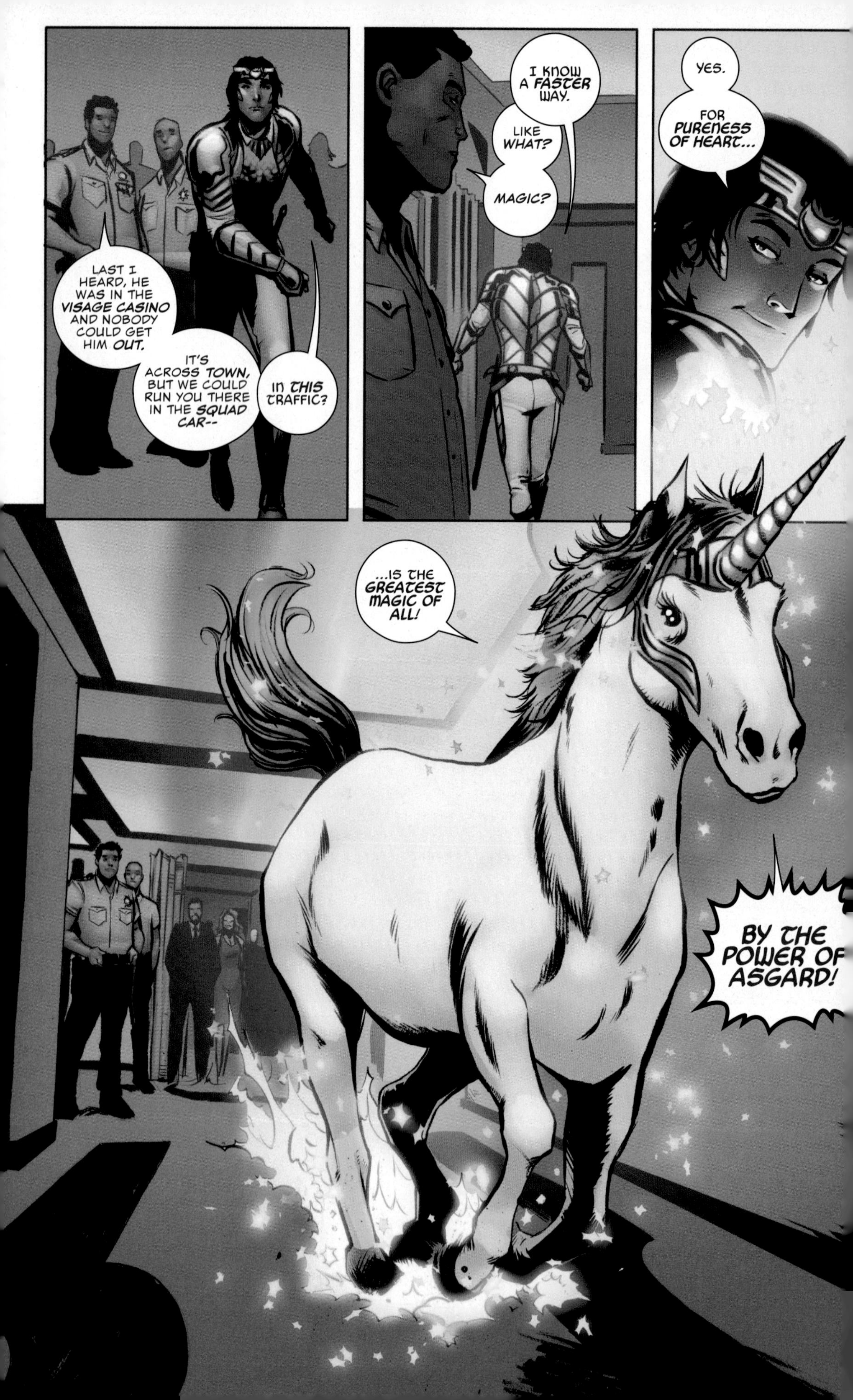
LAST I HEARD, HE WAS IN THE VISAGE CASINO AND NOBODY COULD GET HIM OUT.
IT'S ACROSS TOWN, BUT WE COULD RUN YOU THERE IN THE SQUAD CAR--
IN THIS TRAFFIC?
I KNOW A FASTER WAY.
LIKE WHAT?
MAGIC?
YES.
FOR PURENESS OF HEART...
...IS THE GREATEST MAGIC OF ALL!
BY THE POWER OF ASGARD!

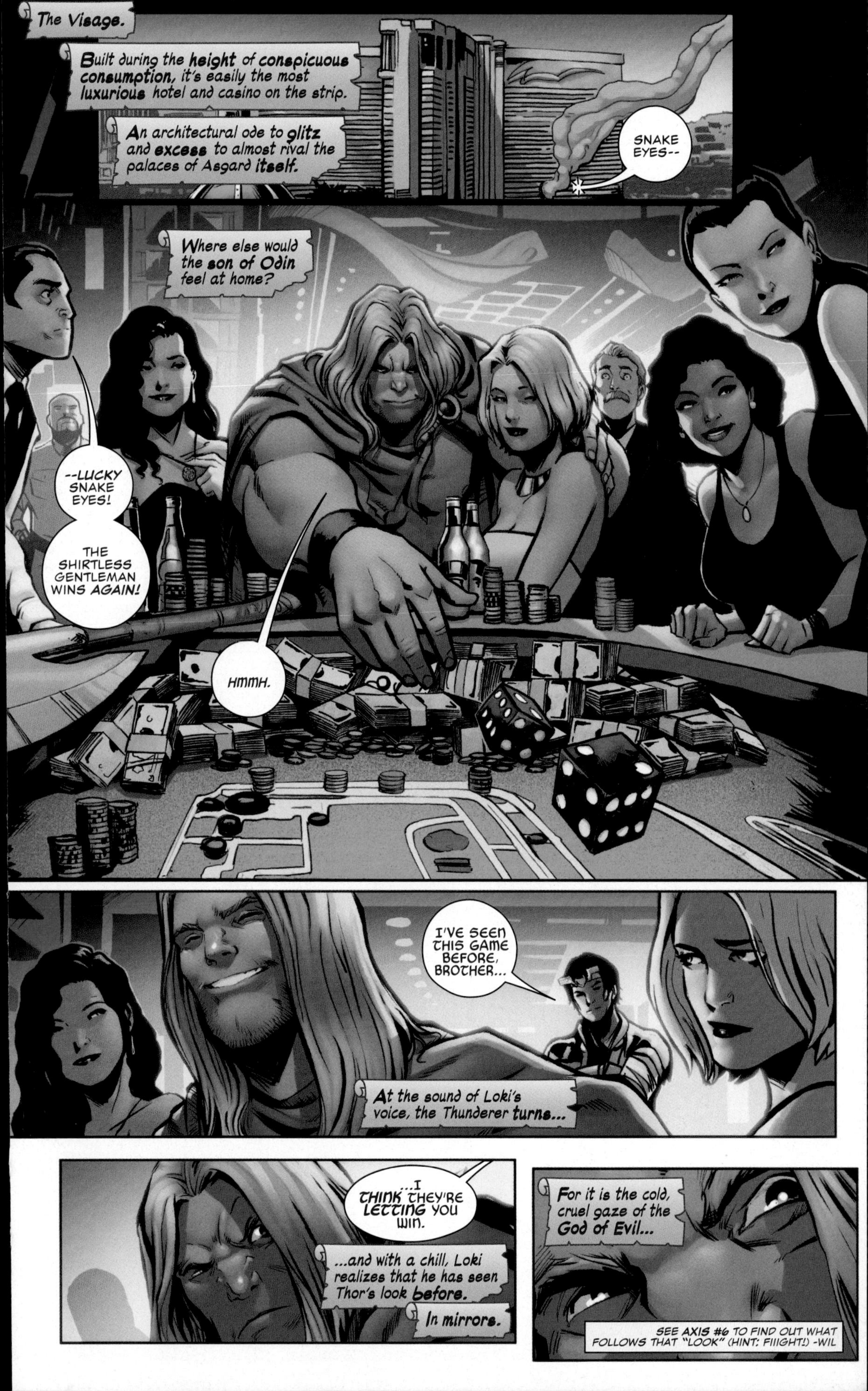
The Visage.
Built during the height of conspicuous consumption, it's easily the most luxurious hotel and casino on the strip.
An architectural ode to glitz and excess to almost rival the palaces of Asgard itself.
SNAKE EYES--
Where else would the son of Odin feel at home?
--LUCKY SNAKE EYES!
THE SHIRTLESS GENTLEMAN WINS AGAIN!
HMMH.
I'VE SEEN THIS GAME BEFORE, BROTHER...
At the sound of Loki's voice, the Thunderer turns...
...I THINK THEY'RE LETTING YOU WIN.
...and with a chill, Loki realizes that he has seen Thor's look before.
In mirrors.
For it is the cold, cruel gaze of the God of Evil...
SEE AXIS #6 TO FIND OUT WHAT FOLLOWS THAT "LOOK" (HINT: FIIIGHT!) -WIL

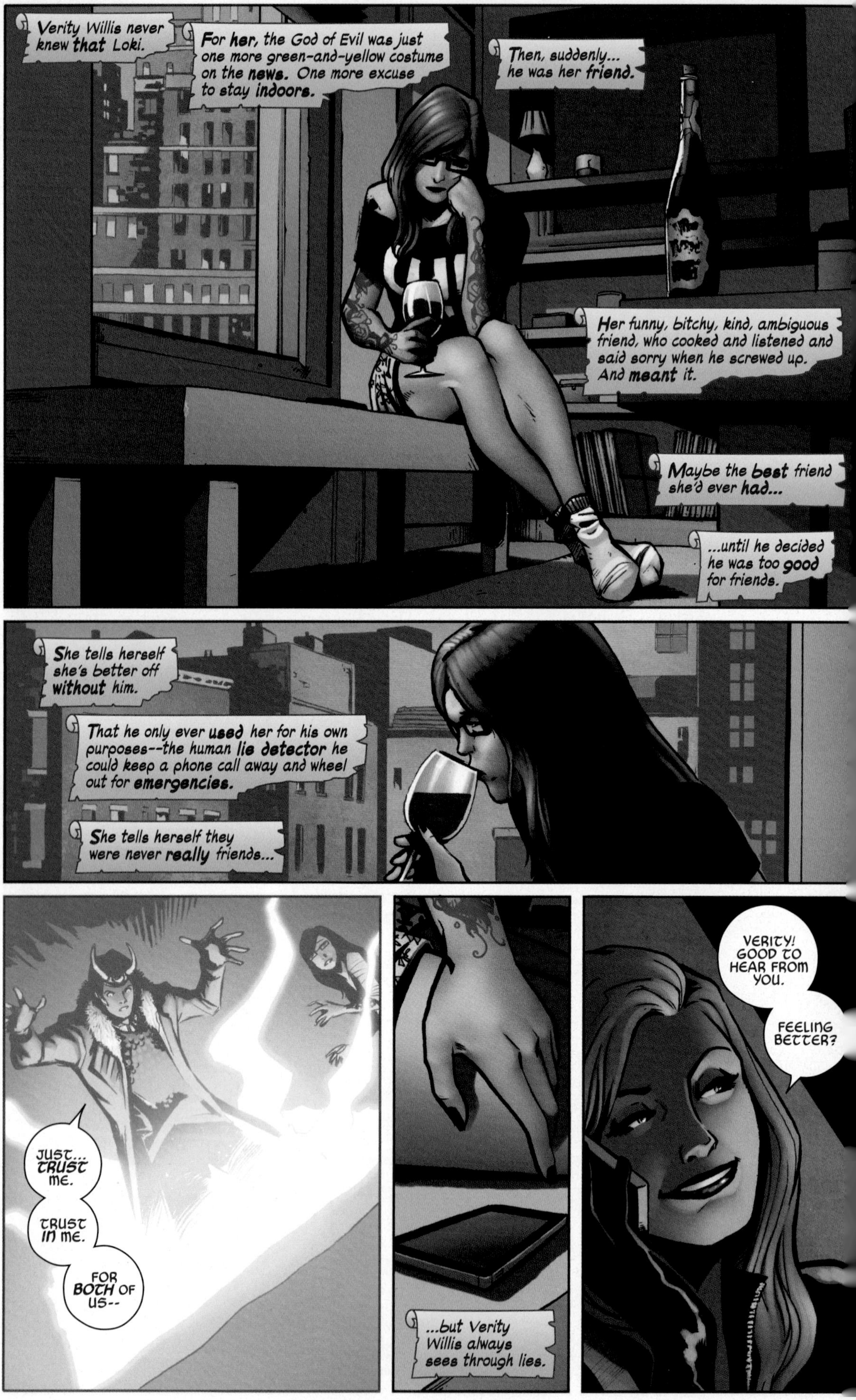
Verity Willis never knew that Loki.
For her, the God of Evil was just one more green-and-yellow costume on the news. One more excuse to stay indoors.
Then, suddenly... he was her friend.
Her funny, bitchy, kind, ambiguous friend, who cooked and listened and said sorry when he screwed up. And meant it.
Maybe the best friend she'd ever had...
...until he decided he was too good for friends.
She tells herself she's better off without him.
That he only ever used her for his own purposes--the human lie detector he could keep a phone call away and wheel out for emergencies.
She tells herself they were never really friends...
JUST... TRUST ME.
TRUST IN ME.
FOR BOTH OF US--
...but Verity Willis always sees through lies.
VERITY! GOOD TO HEAR FROM YOU.
FEELING BETTER?

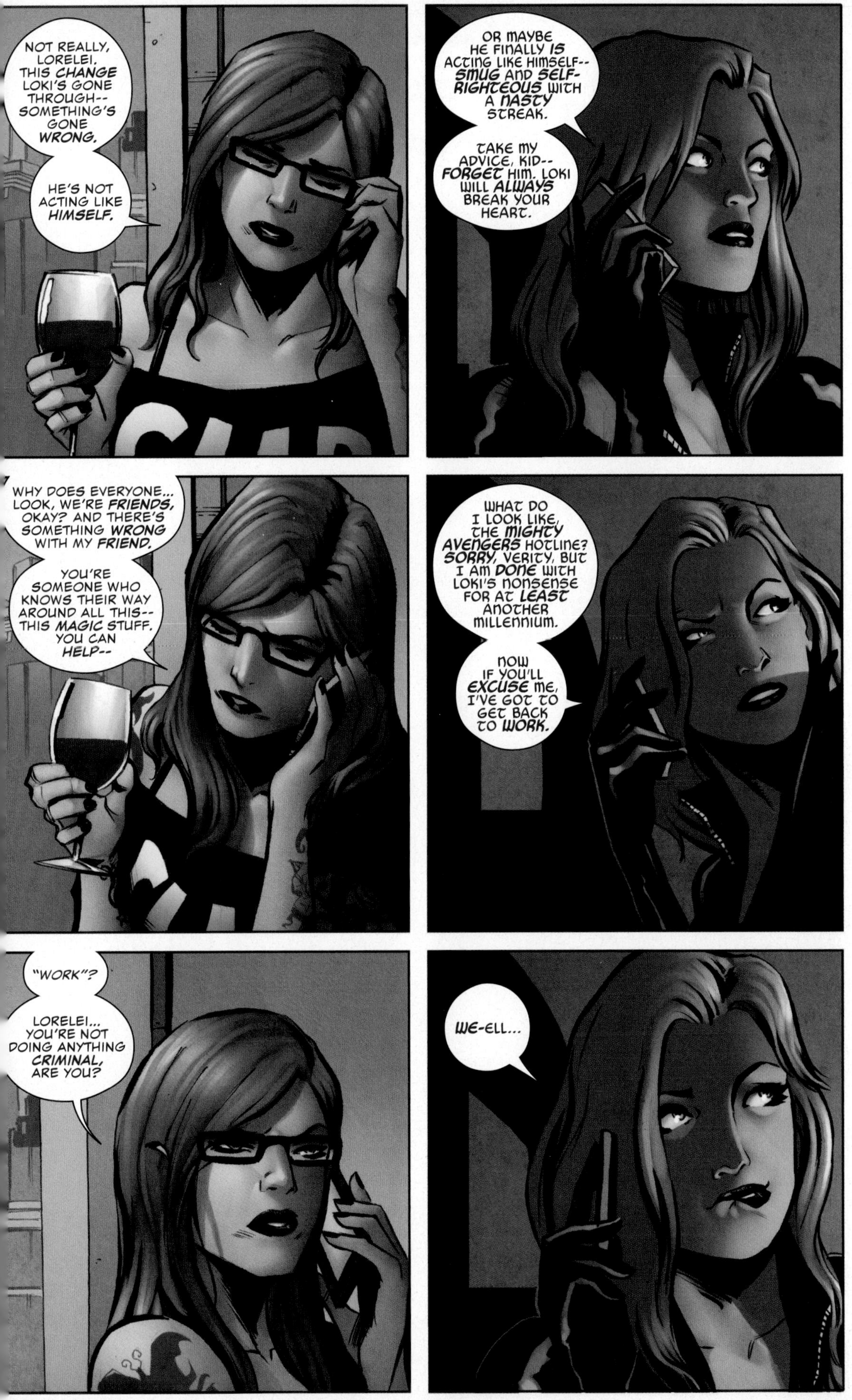
NOT REALLY, LORELEI. THIS CHANGE LOKI'S GONE THROUGH-- SOMETHING'S GONE WRONG.
HE'S NOT ACTING LIKE HIMSELF.
OR MAYBE HE FINALLY IS ACTING LIKE HIMSELF-- SMUG AND SELF-RIGHTEOUS WITH A NASTY STREAK.
TAKE MY ADVICE, KID-- FORGET HIM. LOKI WILL ALWAYS BREAK YOUR HEART.
WHY DOES EVERYONE... LOOK, WE'RE FRIENDS, OKAY? AND THERE'S SOMETHING WRONG WITH MY FRIEND.
YOU'RE SOMEONE WHO KNOWS THEIR WAY AROUND ALL THIS-- THIS MAGIC STUFF. YOU CAN HELP--
WHAT DO I LOOK LIKE, THE MIGHTY AVENGERS HOTLINE? SORRY, VERITY, BUT I AM DONE WITH LOKI'S NONSENSE FOR AT LEAST ANOTHER MILLENNIUM.
NOW IF YOU'LL EXCUSE ME, I'VE GOT TO GET BACK TO WORK.
"WORK"?
LORELEI... YOU'RE NOT DOING ANYTHING CRIMINAL, ARE YOU?
WE-ELL...

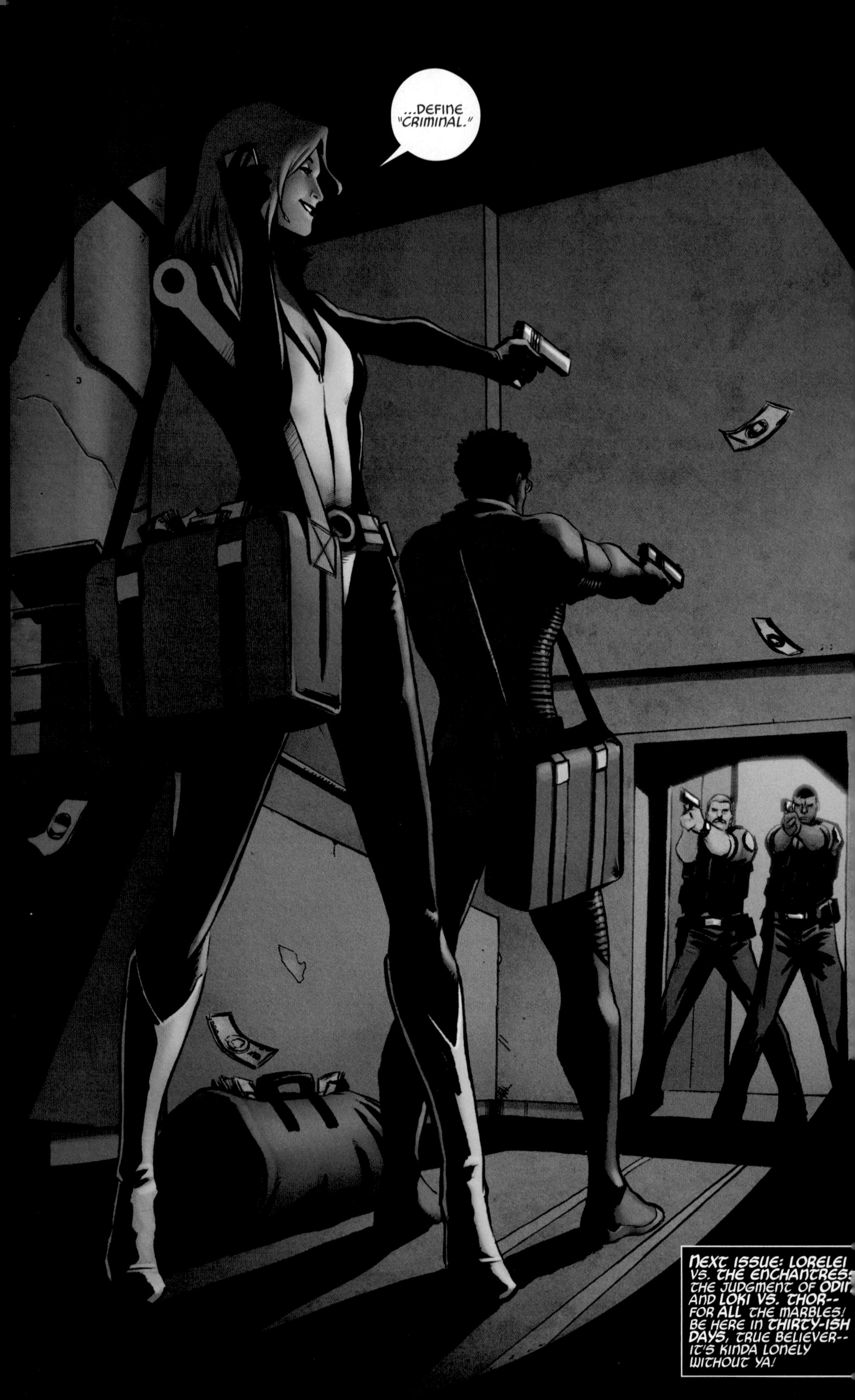
...DEFINE "CRIMINAL."
NEXT ISSUE: LORELEI VS. THE ENCHANTRES THE JUDGMENT OF ODI AND LOKI VS. THOR-- FOR ALL THE MARBLES! BE HERE IN THIRTY-ISH DAYS, TRUE BELIEVER-- IT'S KINDA LONELY WITHOUT YA!

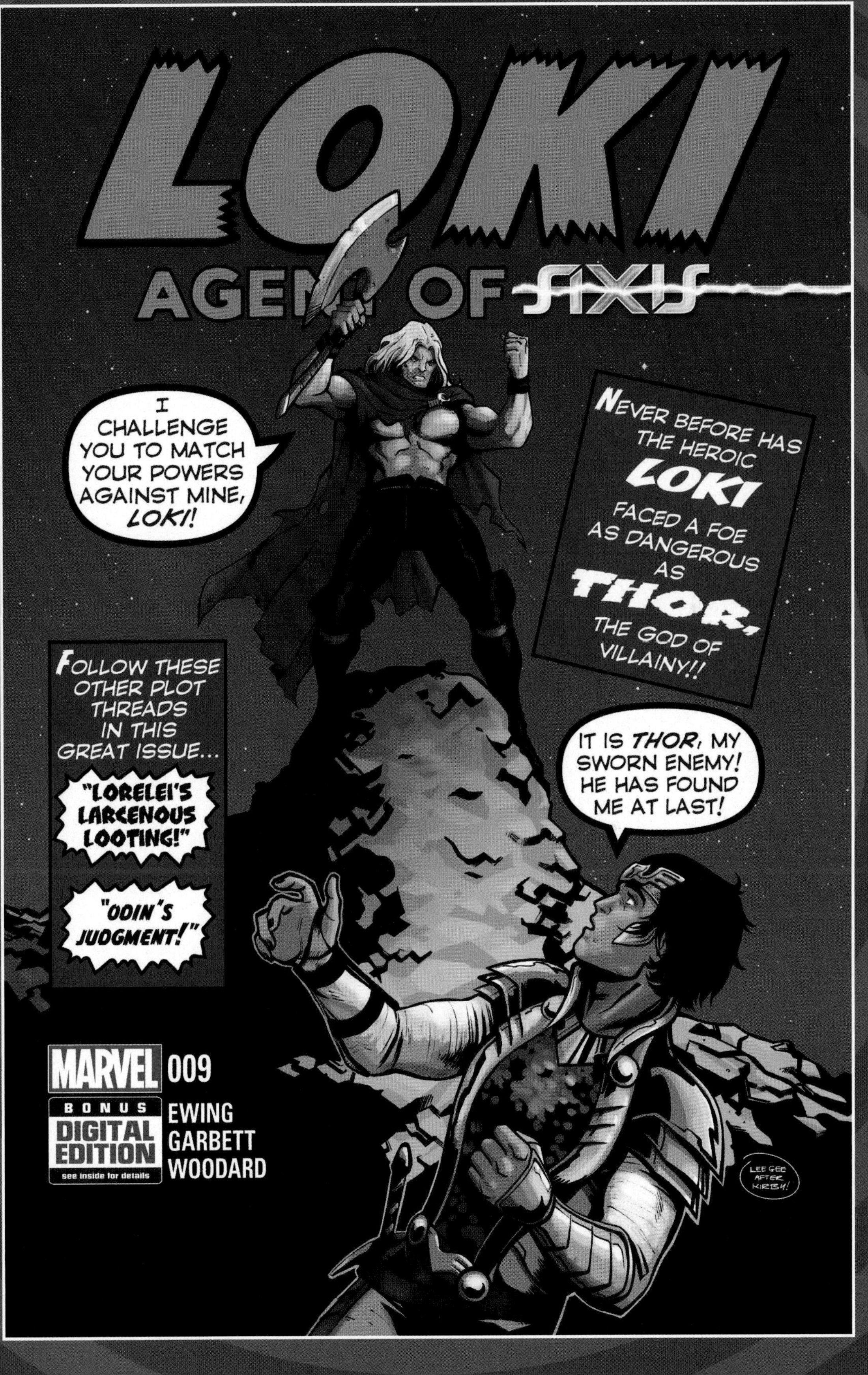

LOKI: AGENT OF ASGARD #9

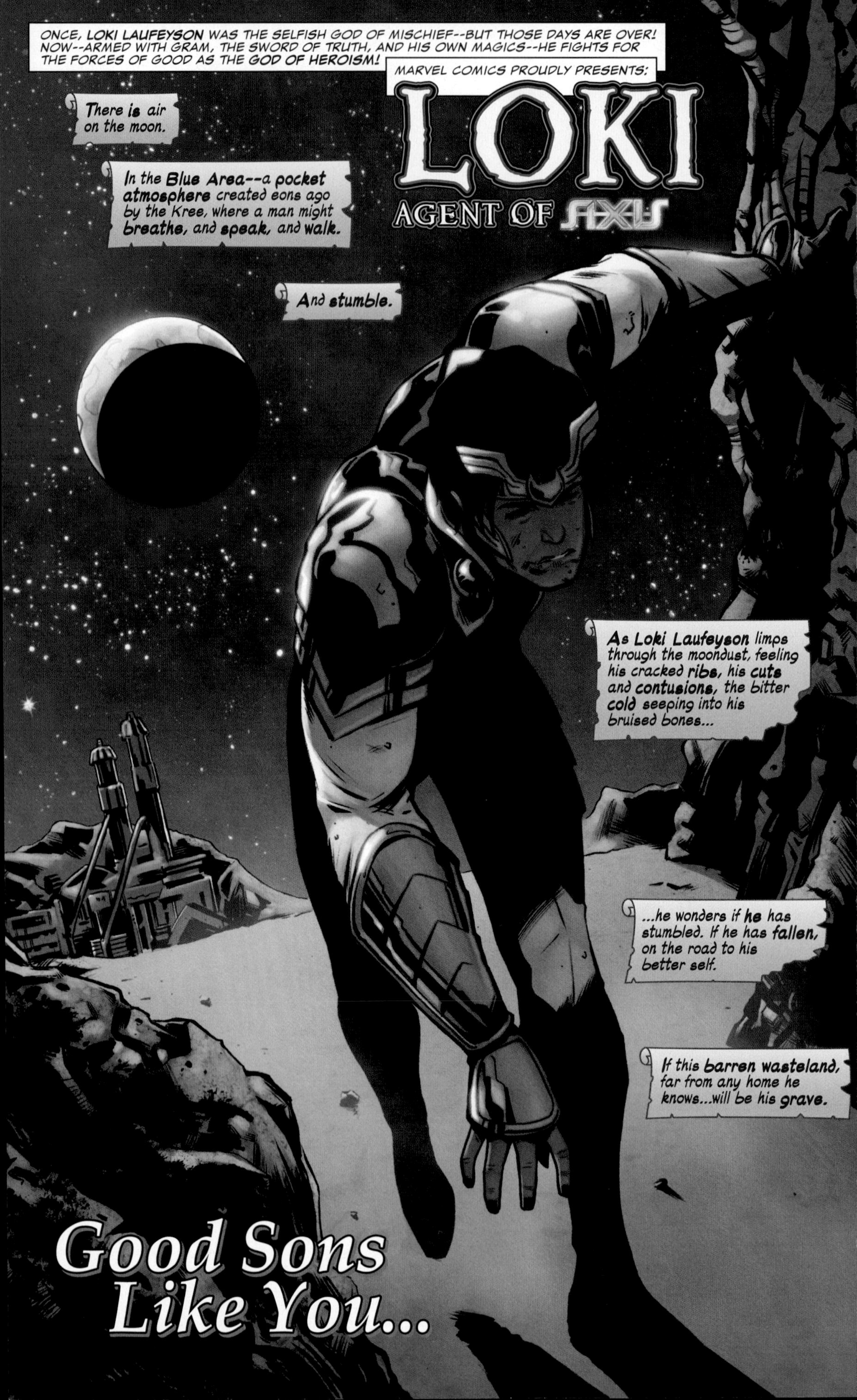
ONCE, LOKI LAUFEYSON WAS THE SELFISH GOD OF MISCHIEF--BUT THOSE DAYS ARE OVER! NOW--ARMED WITH GRAM, THE SWORD OF TRUTH, AND HIS OWN MAGICS--HE FIGHTS FOR THE FORCES OF GOOD AS THE GOD OF HEROISM!
MARVEL COMICS PROUDLY PRESENTS:
LOKI
AGENT OF AXIS
There is air on the moon.
In the Blue Area--a pocket atmosphere created eons ago by the Kree, where a man might breathe, and speak, and walk.
And stumble.
As Loki Laufeyson limps through the moondust, feeling his cracked ribs, his cuts and contusions, the bitter cold seeping into his bruised bones...
...he wonders if he has stumbled. If he has fallen, on the road to his better self.
If this barren wasteland, far from any home he knows...will be his grave.
Good Sons Like You...

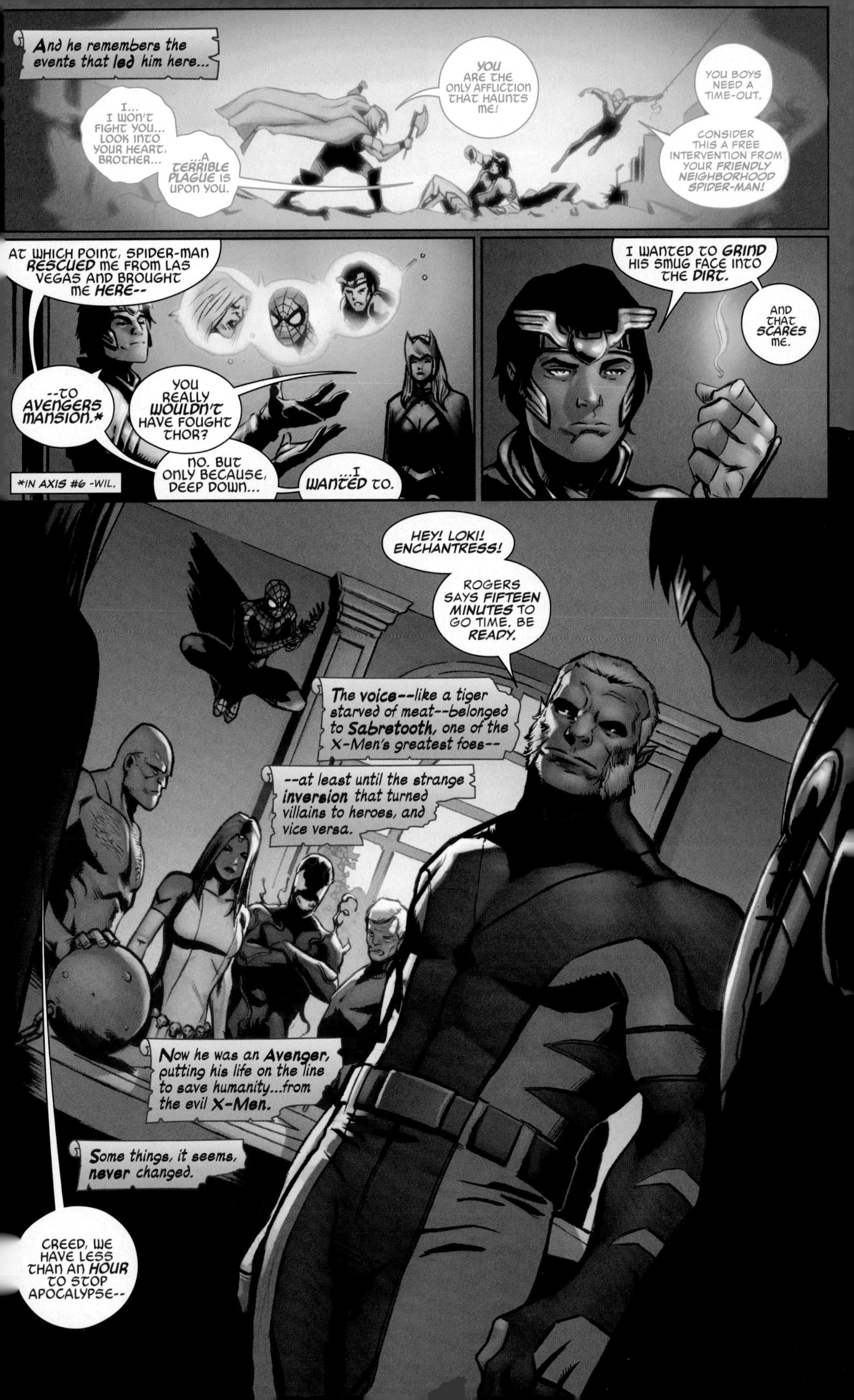

And he remembers the events that led him here...
I... I won't fight you... look into your heart, brother...
...A terrible plague is upon you.
You are the only affliction that haunts me!
You boys need a time-out.
Consider this a free intervention from your friendly neighborhood Spider-Man!
At which point, Spider-Man rescued me from Las Vegas and brought me here--
--to Avengers mansion.*
You really wouldn't have fought Thor?
No. But only because, deep down...
...I wanted to.
*In AXIS #6 -Wil.
I wanted to grind his smug face into the dirt.
And that scares me.
Hey! Loki! Enchantress!
Rogers says fifteen minutes to go time. Be ready.
The voice--like a tiger starved of meat--belonged to Sabretooth, one of the X-Men's greatest foes--
--at least until the strange inversion that turned villains to heroes, and vice versa.
Now he was an Avenger, putting his life on the line to save humanity...from the evil X-Men.
Some things, it seems, never changed.
Creed, we have less than an hour to stop Apocalypse--

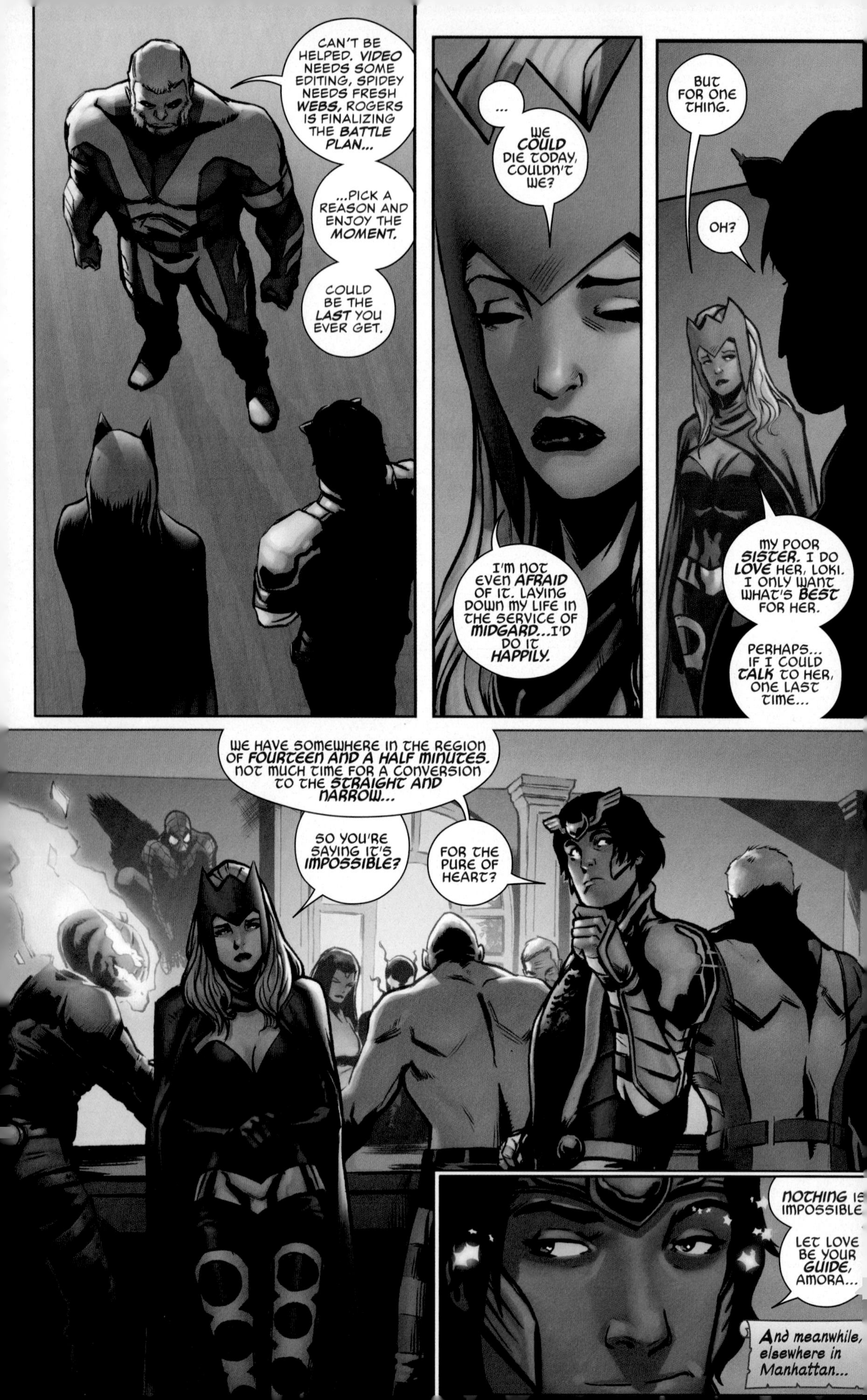

CAN'T BE HELPED. VIDEO NEEDS SOME EDITING, SPIDEY NEEDS FRESH WEBS, ROGERS IS FINALIZING THE BATTLE PLAN...
...PICK A REASON AND ENJOY THE MOMENT.
COULD BE THE LAST YOU EVER GET.
...
WE COULD DIE TODAY, COULDN'T WE?
I'M NOT EVEN AFRAID OF IT. LAYING DOWN MY LIFE IN THE SERVICE OF MIDGARD...I'D DO IT HAPPILY.
BUT FOR ONE THING.
OH?
MY POOR SISTER. I DO LOVE HER, LOKI. I ONLY WANT WHAT'S BEST FOR HER.
PERHAPS... IF I COULD TALK TO HER, ONE LAST TIME...
WE HAVE SOMEWHERE IN THE REGION OF FOURTEEN AND A HALF MINUTES. NOT MUCH TIME FOR A CONVERSION TO THE STRAIGHT AND NARROW...
SO YOU'RE SAYING IT'S IMPOSSIBLE?
FOR THE PURE OF HEART?
NOTHING IS IMPOSSIBLE
LET LOVE BE YOUR GUIDE, AMORA...
And meanwhile, elsewhere in Manhattan...

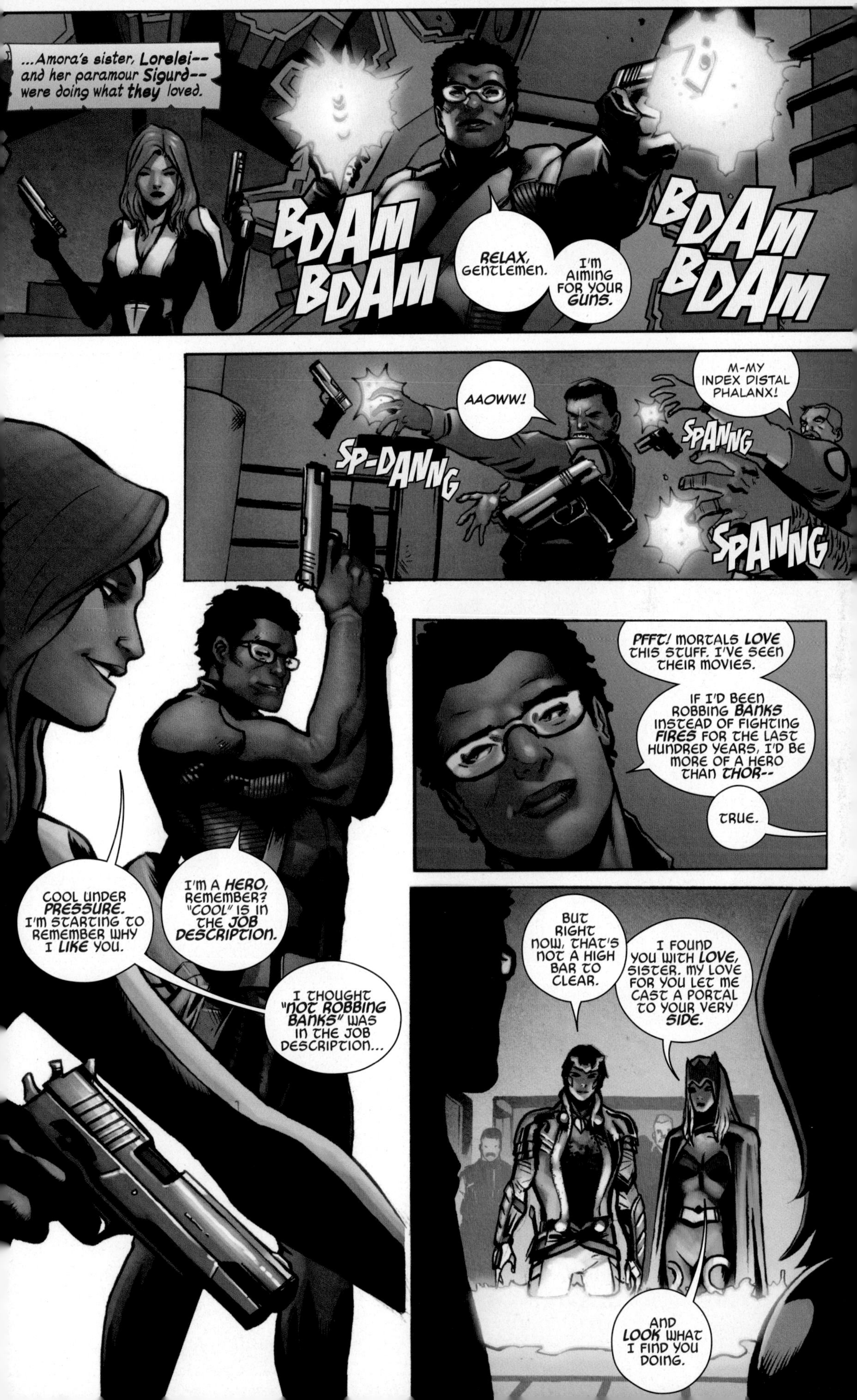
...Amora's sister, Lorelei--
and her paramour Sigurd--
were doing what they loved.
BDAM BDAM
RELAX, GENTLEMEN.
I'M AIMING FOR YOUR GUNS.
BDAM BDAM
AAOWW!
M-MY INDEX DISTAL PHALANX!
SP-DANNG
SPANNG
SPANNG
PFFT! MORTALS LOVE THIS STUFF. I'VE SEEN THEIR MOVIES.
IF I'D BEEN ROBBING BANKS INSTEAD OF FIGHTING FIRES FOR THE LAST HUNDRED YEARS, I'D BE MORE OF A HERO THAN THOR--
TRUE.
COOL UNDER PRESSURE. I'M STARTING TO REMEMBER WHY I LIKE YOU.
I'M A HERO, REMEMBER? "COOL" IS IN THE JOB DESCRIPTION.
I THOUGHT "NOT ROBBING BANKS" WAS IN THE JOB DESCRIPTION...
BUT RIGHT NOW, THAT'S NOT A HIGH BAR TO CLEAR.
I FOUND YOU WITH LOVE, SISTER. MY LOVE FOR YOU LET ME CAST A PORTAL TO YOUR VERY SIDE.
AND LOOK WHAT I FIND YOU DOING.

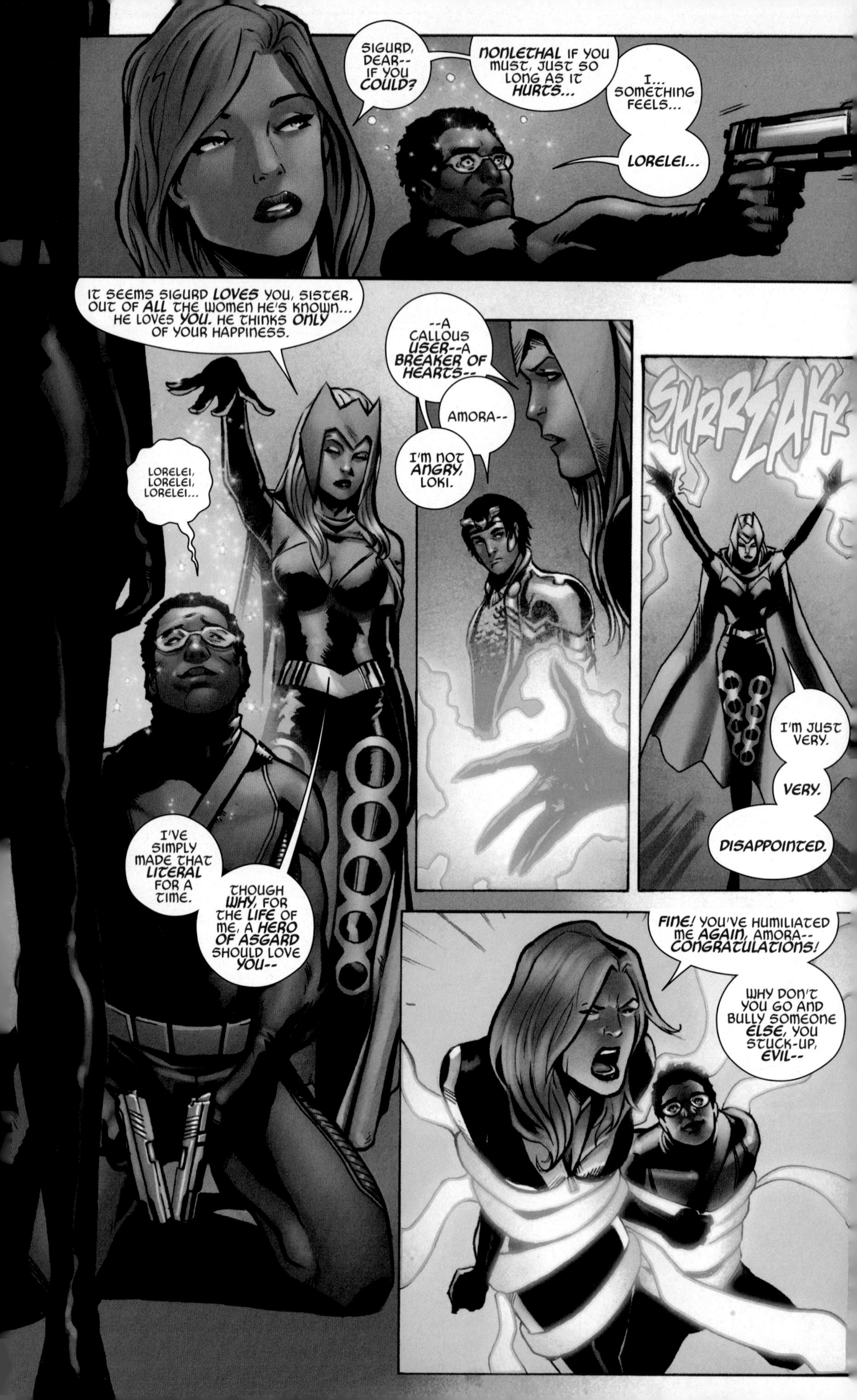

SIGURD, DEAR-- IF YOU COULD?
NONLETHAL IF YOU MUST, JUST SO LONG AS IT HURTS...
I... SOMETHING FEELS...
LORELEI...
IT SEEMS SIGURD LOVES YOU, SISTER. OUT OF ALL THE WOMEN HE'S KNOWN... HE LOVES YOU. HE THINKS ONLY OF YOUR HAPPINESS.
LORELEI, LORELEI, LORELEI...
I'VE SIMPLY MADE THAT LITERAL FOR A TIME.
THOUGH WHY, FOR THE LIFE OF ME, A HERO OF ASGARD SHOULD LOVE YOU--
--A CALLOUS USER--A BREAKER OF HEARTS--
AMORA--
I'M NOT ANGRY, LOKI.
SHRZAK
I'M JUST VERY.
VERY.
DISAPPOINTED.
FINE! YOU'VE HUMILIATED ME AGAIN, AMORA-- CONGRATULATIONS!
WHY DON'T YOU GO AND BULLY SOMEONE ELSE, YOU STUCK-UP, EVIL--

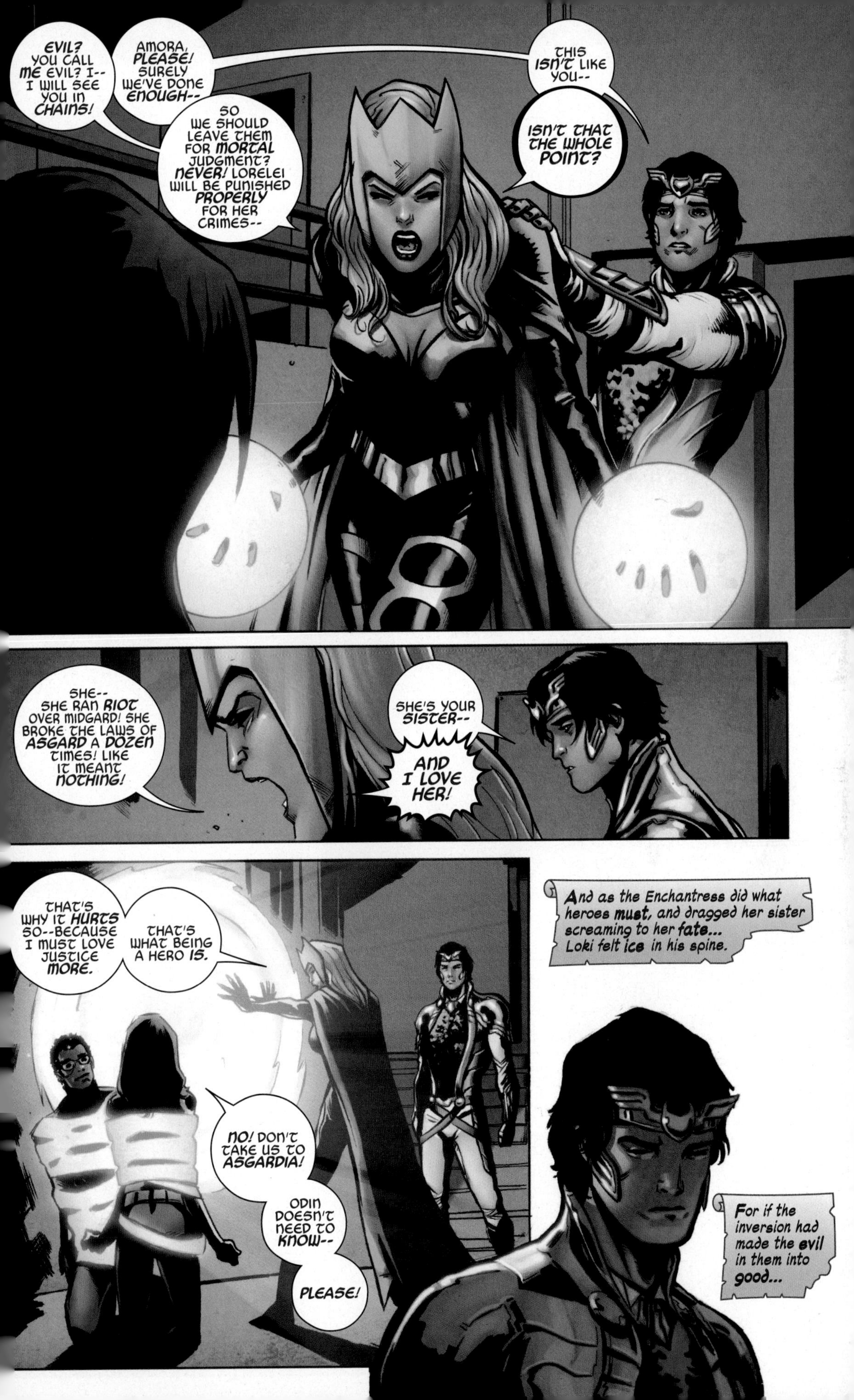
EVIL? YOU CALL ME EVIL? I-- I WILL SEE YOU IN CHAINS!
AMORA, PLEASE! SURELY WE'VE DONE ENOUGH--
SO WE SHOULD LEAVE THEM FOR MORTAL JUDGMENT? NEVER! LORELEI WILL BE PUNISHED PROPERLY FOR HER CRIMES--
THIS ISN'T LIKE YOU--
ISN'T THAT THE WHOLE POINT?
SHE-- SHE RAN RIOT OVER MIDGARD! SHE BROKE THE LAWS OF ASGARD A DOZEN TIMES! LIKE IT MEANT NOTHING!
SHE'S YOUR SISTER--
AND I LOVE HER!
THAT'S WHY IT HURTS SO--BECAUSE I MUST LOVE JUSTICE MORE.
THAT'S WHAT BEING A HERO IS.
And as the Enchantress did what heroes must, and dragged her sister screaming to her fate... Loki felt ice in his spine.
NO! DON'T TAKE US TO ASGARDIA!
ODIN DOESN'T NEED TO KNOW--
PLEASE!
For if the inversion had made the evil in them into good...

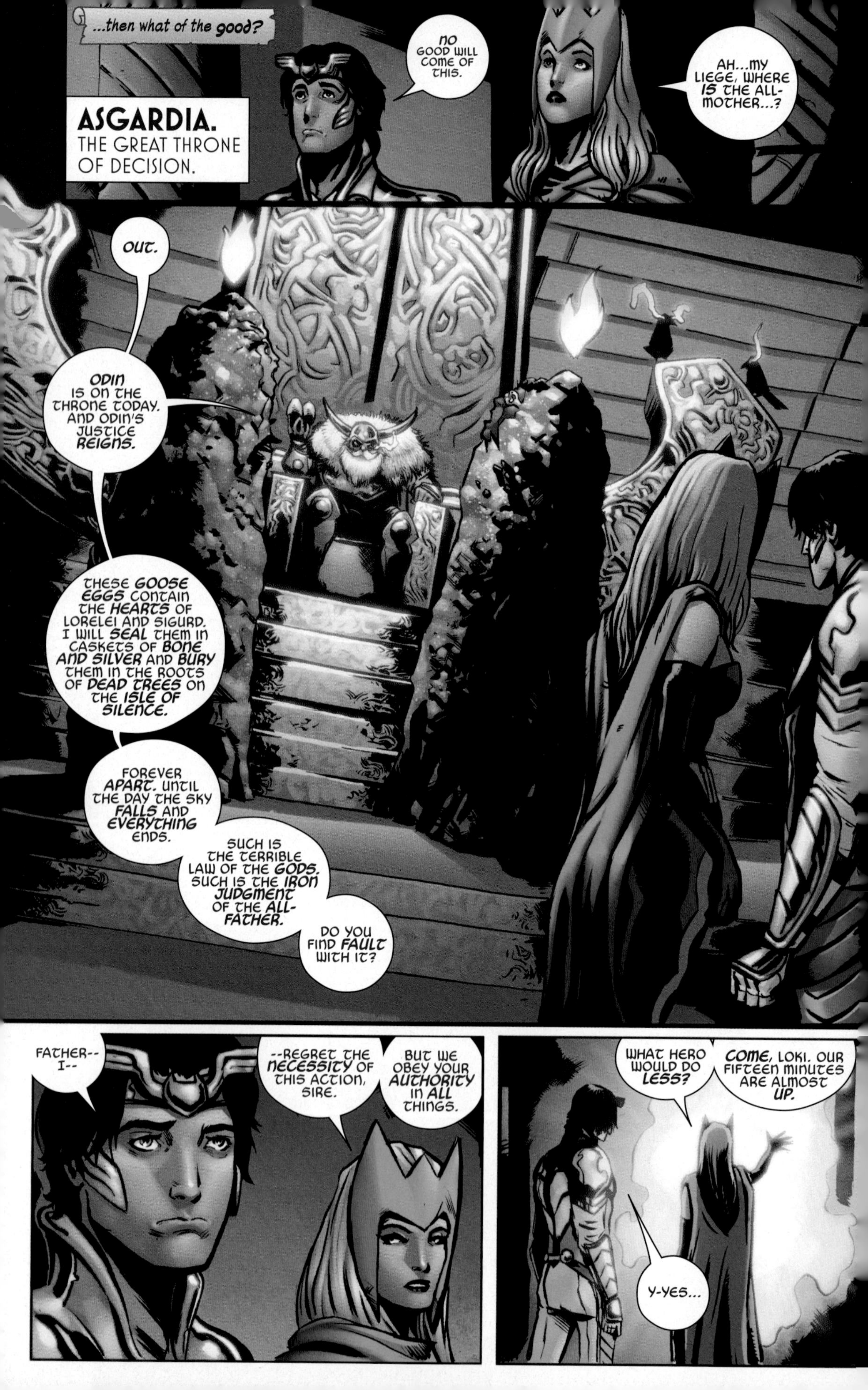
...then what of the good?
ASGARDIA. THE GREAT THRONE OF DECISION.
NO GOOD WILL COME OF THIS.
AH...MY LIEGE, WHERE IS THE ALL-MOTHER...?
OUT.
ODIN IS ON THE THRONE TODAY. AND ODIN'S JUSTICE REIGNS.
THESE GOOSE EGGS CONTAIN THE HEARTS OF LORELEI AND SIGURD. I WILL SEAL THEM IN CASKETS OF BONE AND SILVER AND BURY THEM IN THE ROOTS OF DEAD TREES ON THE ISLE OF SILENCE.
FOREVER APART. UNTIL THE DAY THE SKY FALLS AND EVERYTHING ENDS.
SUCH IS THE TERRIBLE LAW OF THE GODS. SUCH IS THE IRON JUDGMENT OF THE ALL-FATHER.
DO YOU FIND FAULT WITH IT?
FATHER-- I--
--REGRET THE NECESSITY OF THIS ACTION, SIRE.
BUT WE OBEY YOUR AUTHORITY IN ALL THINGS.
WHAT HERO WOULD DO LESS?
COME, LOKI. OUR FIFTEEN MINUTES ARE ALMOST UP.
Y-YES...

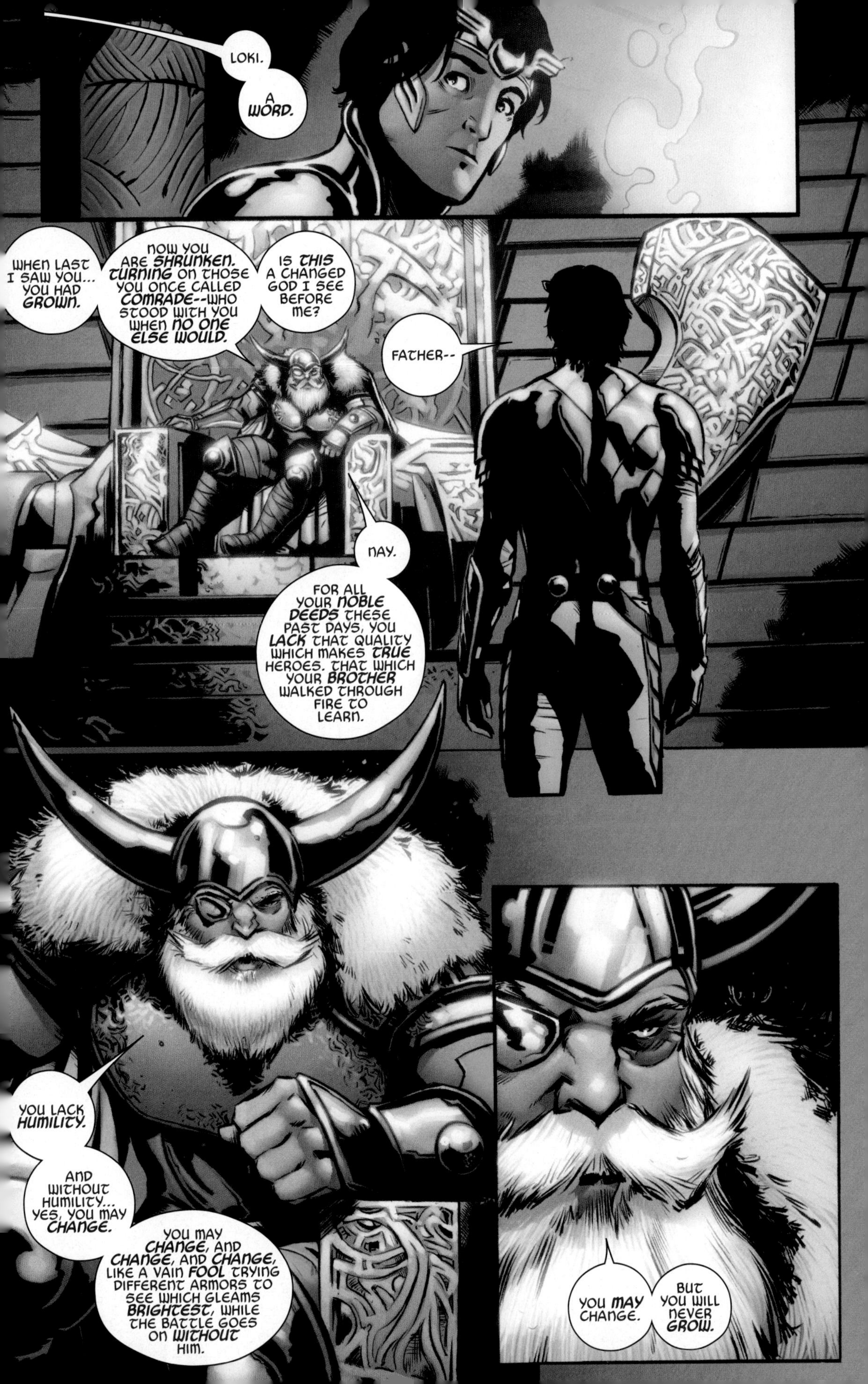
LOKI.
A WORD.
WHEN LAST I SAW YOU... YOU HAD GROWN.
NOW YOU ARE SHRUNKEN. TURNING ON THOSE YOU ONCE CALLED COMRADE--WHO STOOD WITH YOU WHEN NO ONE ELSE WOULD.
IS THIS A CHANGED GOD I SEE BEFORE ME?
FATHER--
NAY.
FOR ALL YOUR NOBLE DEEDS THESE PAST DAYS, YOU LACK THAT QUALITY WHICH MAKES TRUE HEROES. THAT WHICH YOUR BROTHER WALKED THROUGH FIRE TO LEARN.
YOU LACK HUMILITY.
AND WITHOUT HUMILITY... YES, YOU MAY CHANGE.
YOU MAY CHANGE, AND CHANGE, AND CHANGE, LIKE A VAIN FOOL TRYING DIFFERENT ARMORS TO SEE WHICH GLEAMS BRIGHTEST, WHILE THE BATTLE GOES ON WITHOUT HIM.
YOU MAY CHANGE.
BUT YOU WILL NEVER GROW.

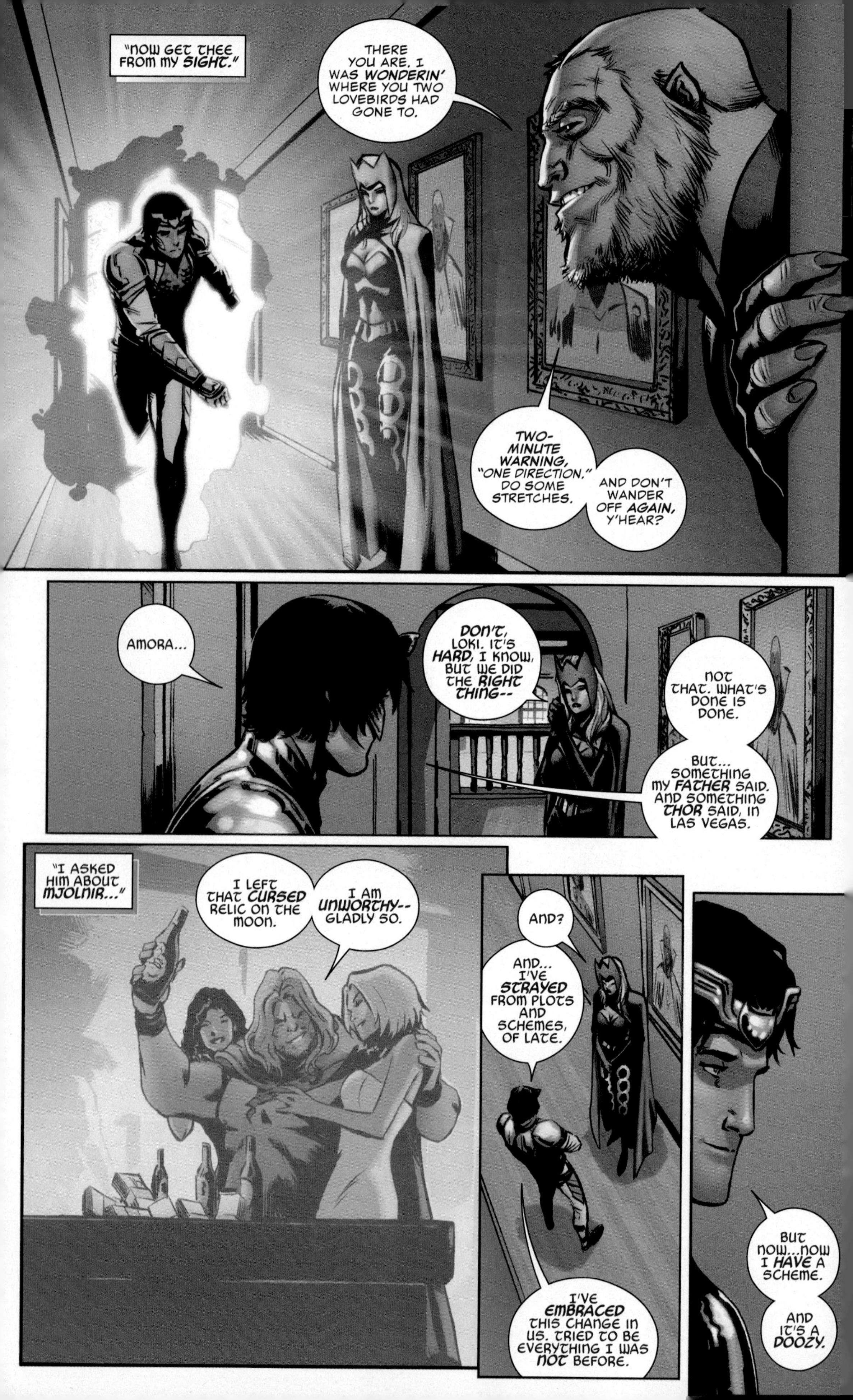
"NOW GET THEE FROM MY SIGHT."
THERE YOU ARE. I WAS WONDERIN' WHERE YOU TWO LOVEBIRDS HAD GONE TO.
TWO-MINUTE WARNING, "ONE DIRECTION." DO SOME STRETCHES.
AND DON'T WANDER OFF AGAIN, Y'HEAR?
AMORA...
DON'T, LOKI. IT'S HARD, I KNOW, BUT WE DID THE RIGHT THING--
NOT THAT. WHAT'S DONE IS DONE.
BUT... SOMETHING MY FATHER SAID. AND SOMETHING THOR SAID, IN LAS VEGAS.
"I ASKED HIM ABOUT MJOLNIR..."
I LEFT THAT CURSED RELIC ON THE MOON.
I AM UNWORTHY-- GLADLY SO.
AND?
AND... I'VE STRAYED FROM PLOTS AND SCHEMES, OF LATE.
I'VE EMBRACED THIS CHANGE IN US. TRIED TO BE EVERYTHING I WAS NOT BEFORE.
BUT NOW...NOW I HAVE A SCHEME.
AND IT'S A DOOZY.

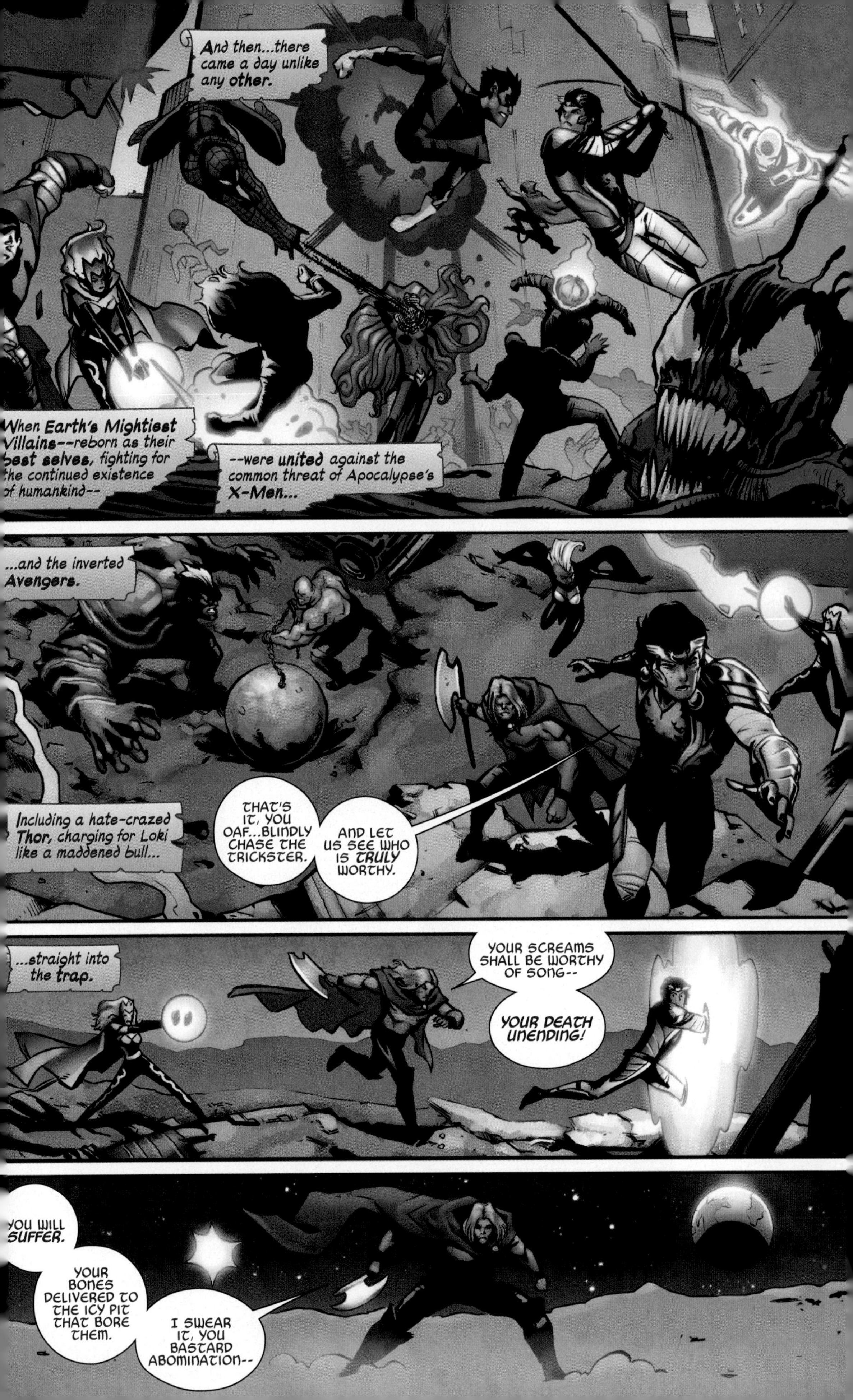

And then...there came a day unlike any other.
When Earth's Mightiest Villains--reborn as their best selves, fighting for the continued existence of humankind--
--were united against the common threat of Apocalypse's X-Men...
...and the inverted Avengers.
Including a hate-crazed Thor, charging for Loki like a maddened bull...
THAT'S IT, YOU OAF...BLINDLY CHASE THE TRICKSTER.
AND LET US SEE WHO IS TRULY WORTHY.
...straight into the trap.
YOUR SCREAMS SHALL BE WORTHY OF SONG--
YOUR DEATH UNENDING!
YOU WILL SUFFER.
YOUR BONES DELIVERED TO THE ICY PIT THAT BORE THEM.
I SWEAR IT, YOU BASTARD ABOMINATION--

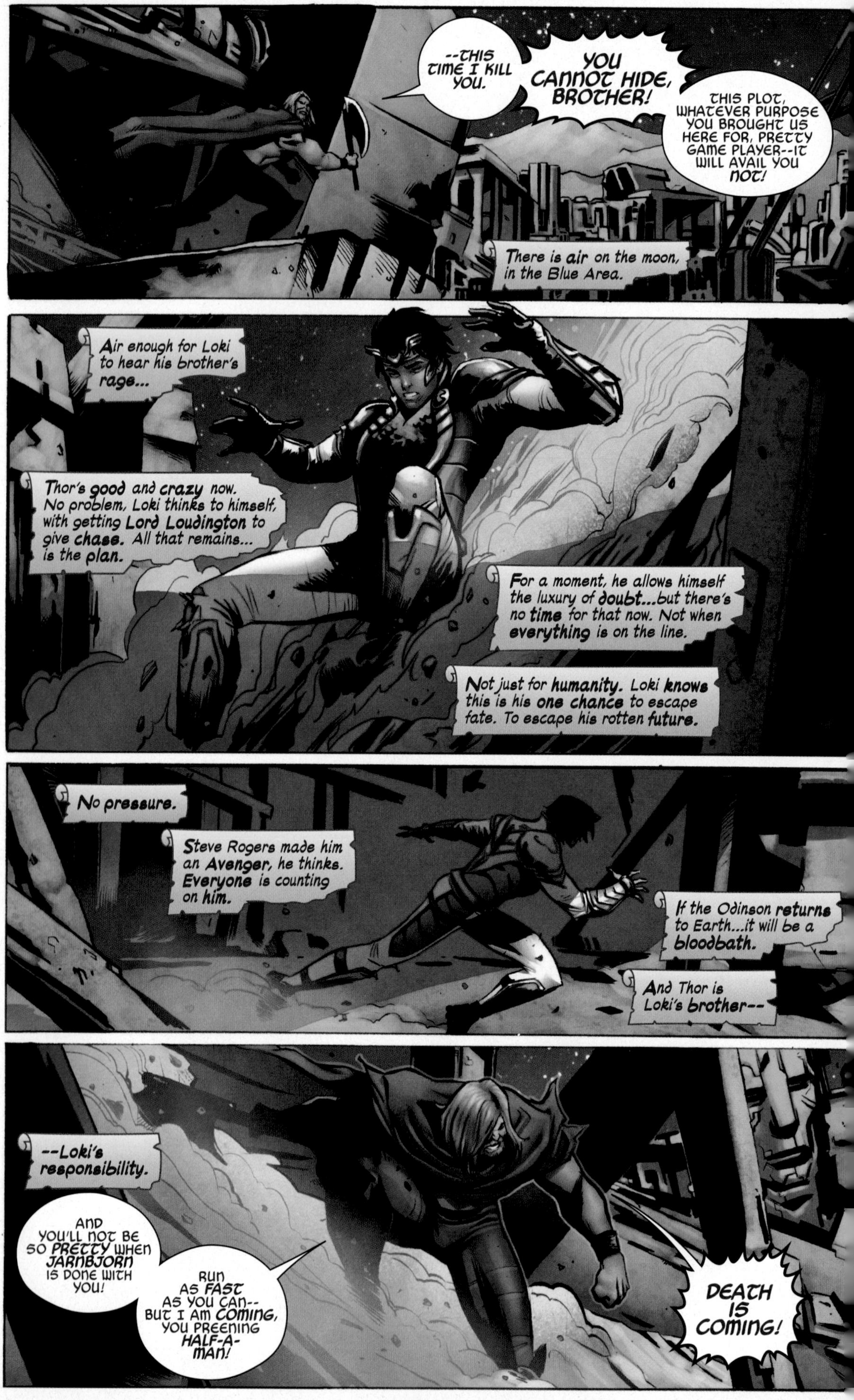
--THIS TIME I KILL YOU.
YOU CANNOT HIDE, BROTHER!
THIS PLOT, WHATEVER PURPOSE YOU BROUGHT US HERE FOR, PRETTY GAME PLAYER--IT WILL AVAIL YOU NOT!
There is air on the moon, in the Blue Area.
Air enough for Loki to hear his brother's rage...
Thor's good and crazy now. No problem, Loki thinks to himself, with getting Lord Loudington to give chase. All that remains... is the plan.
For a moment, he allows himself the luxury of doubt...but there's no time for that now. Not when everything is on the line.
Not just for humanity. Loki knows this is his one chance to escape fate. To escape his rotten future.
No pressure.
Steve Rogers made him an Avenger, he thinks. Everyone is counting on him.
If the Odinson returns to Earth...it will be a bloodbath.
And Thor is Loki's brother--
--Loki's responsibility.
AND YOU'LL NOT BE SO PRETTY WHEN JARNBJORN IS DONE WITH YOU!
RUN AS FAST AS YOU CAN--BUT I AM COMING, YOU PREENING HALF-A-MAN!
DEATH IS COMING!

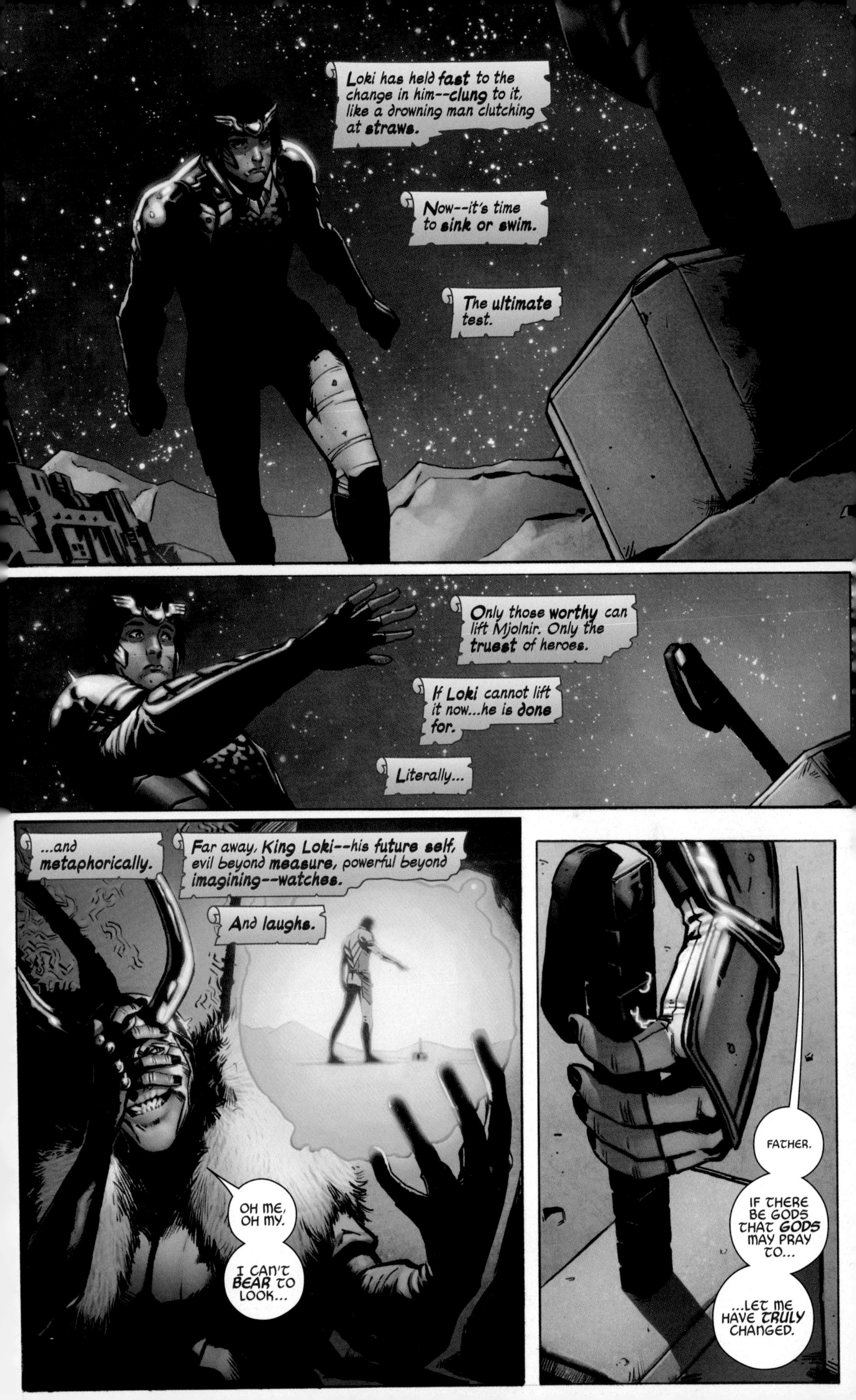
Loki has held fast to the change in him--clung to it, like a drowning man clutching at straws.
Now--it's time to sink or swim.
The ultimate test.
Only those worthy can lift Mjolnir. Only the truest of heroes.
If Loki cannot lift it now...he is done for.
Literally...
...and metaphorically.
Far away, King Loki--his future self, evil beyond measure, powerful beyond imagining--watches.
And laughs.
OH ME, OH MY.
I CAN'T BEAR TO LOOK...
FATHER.
IF THERE BE GODS THAT GODS MAY PRAY TO...
...LET ME HAVE TRULY CHANGED.

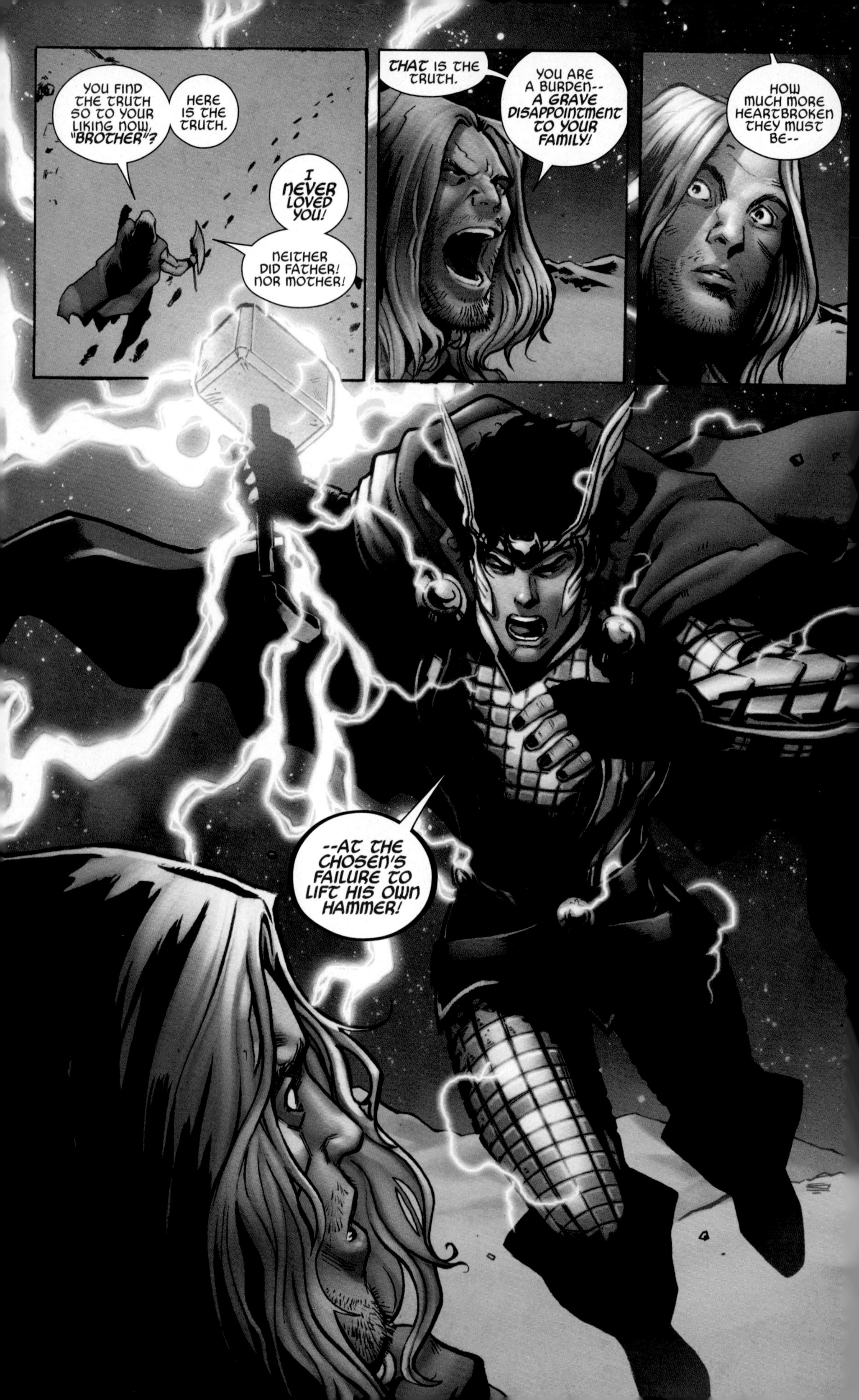
YOU FIND THE TRUTH SO TO YOUR LIKING NOW, "BROTHER"?
HERE IS THE TRUTH.
I NEVER LOVED YOU!
NEITHER DID FATHER! NOR MOTHER!
THAT IS THE TRUTH.
YOU ARE A BURDEN-- A GRAVE DISAPPOINTMENT TO YOUR FAMILY!
HOW MUCH MORE HEARTBROKEN THEY MUST BE--
--AT THE CHOSEN'S FAILURE TO LIFT HIS OWN HAMMER!

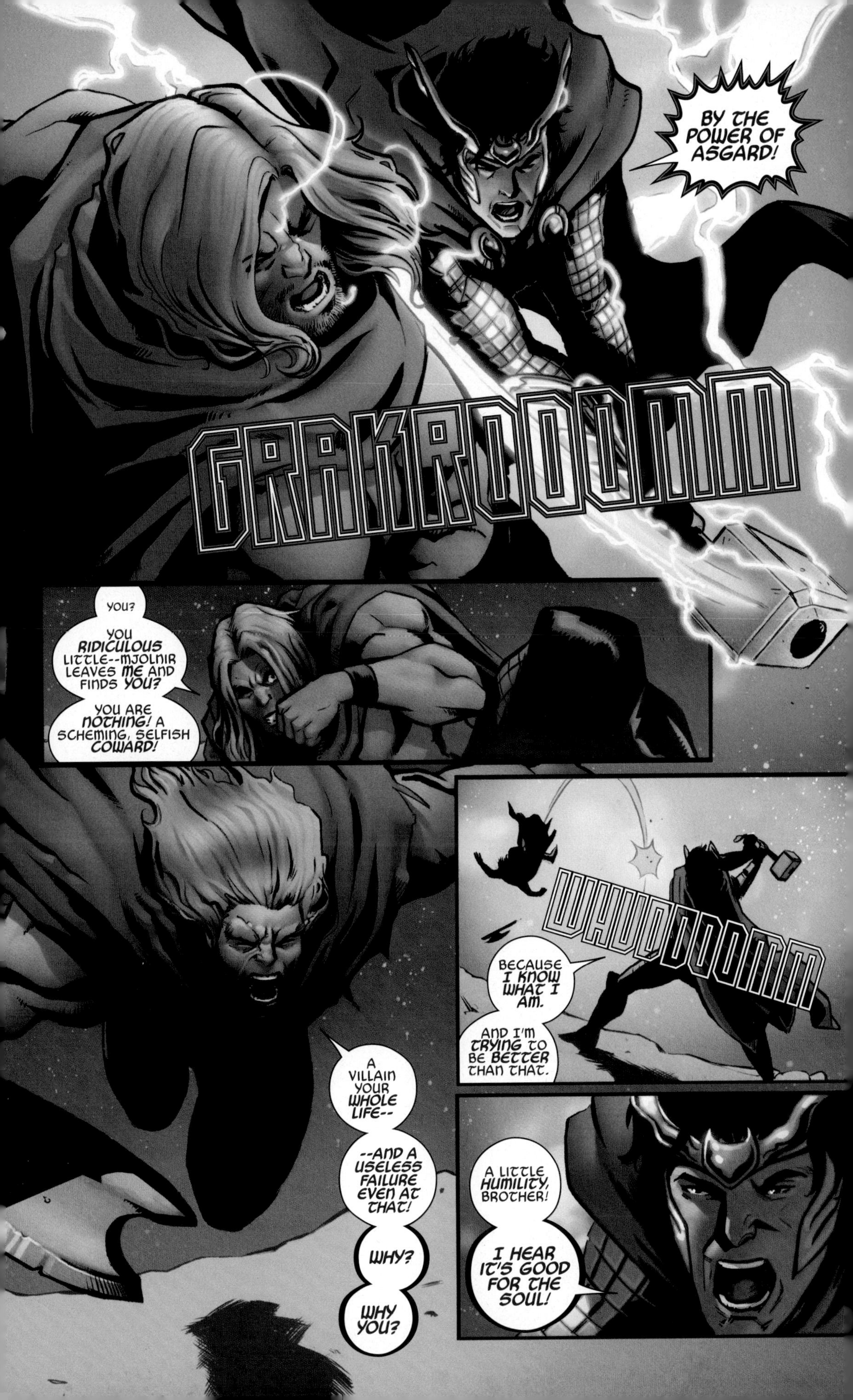

BY THE POWER OF ASGARD!
GRAKROOOMM
YOU?
YOU RIDICULOUS LITTLE--MJOLNIR LEAVES ME AND FINDS YOU?
YOU ARE NOTHING! A SCHEMING, SELFISH COWARD!
WHUDDOOMM
BECAUSE I KNOW WHAT I AM.
AND I'M TRYING TO BE BETTER THAN THAT.
A VILLAIN YOUR WHOLE LIFE--
--AND A USELESS FAILURE EVEN AT THAT!
WHY?
WHY YOU?
A LITTLE HUMILITY, BROTHER!
I HEAR IT'S GOOD FOR THE SOUL!

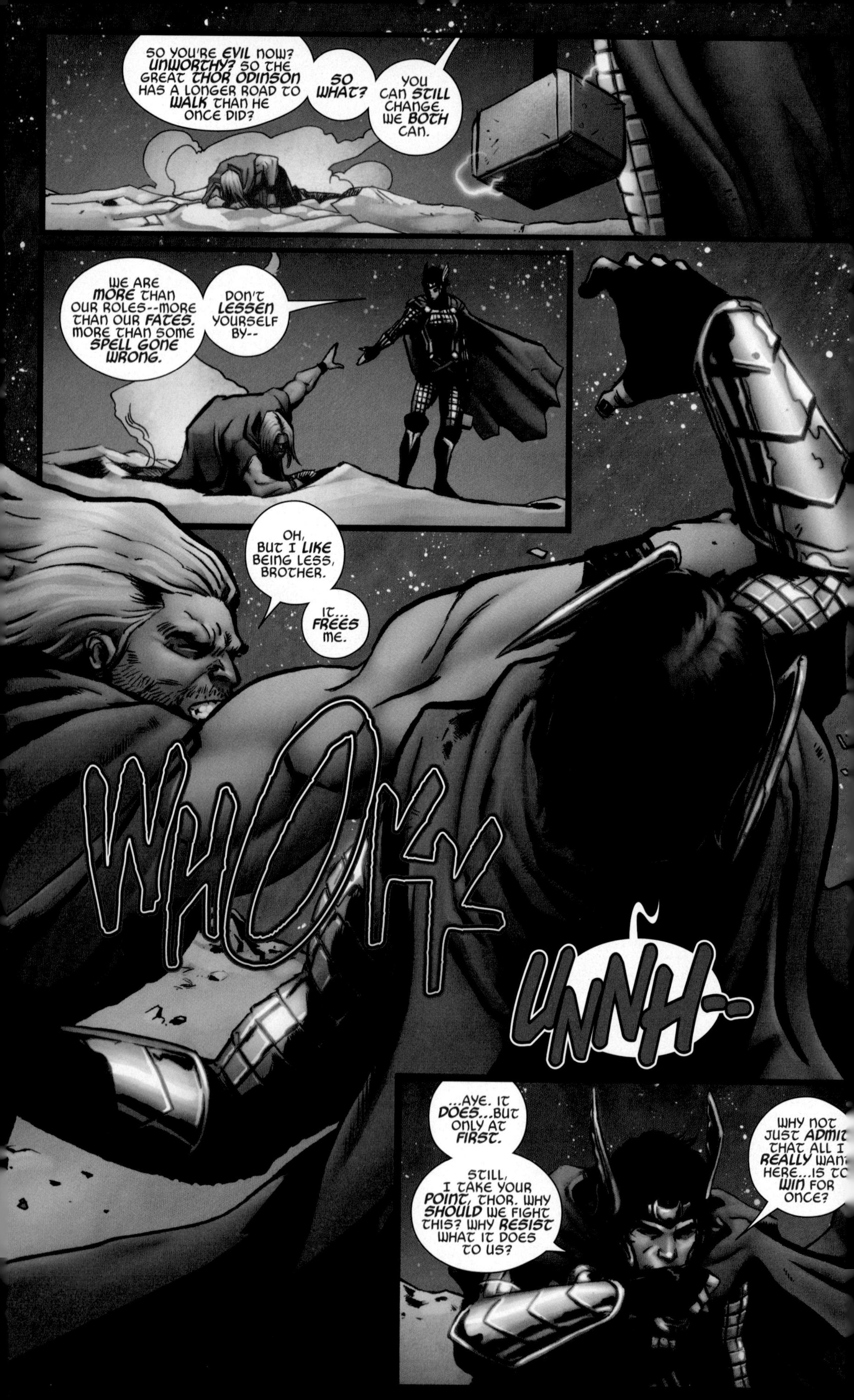

SO YOU'RE EVIL NOW? UNWORTHY? SO THE GREAT THOR ODINSON HAS A LONGER ROAD TO WALK THAN HE ONCE DID?
SO WHAT?
YOU CAN STILL CHANGE. WE BOTH CAN.
WE ARE MORE THAN OUR ROLES--MORE THAN OUR FATES. MORE THAN SOME SPELL GONE WRONG.
DON'T LESSEN YOURSELF BY--
OH, BUT I LIKE BEING LESS, BROTHER.
IT... FREES ME.
WHOK
UNNH--
...AYE. IT DOES...BUT ONLY AT FIRST.
STILL, I TAKE YOUR POINT, THOR. WHY SHOULD WE FIGHT THIS? WHY RESIST WHAT IT DOES TO US?
WHY NOT JUST ADMIT THAT ALL I REALLY WAN HERE...IS TO WIN FOR ONCE?

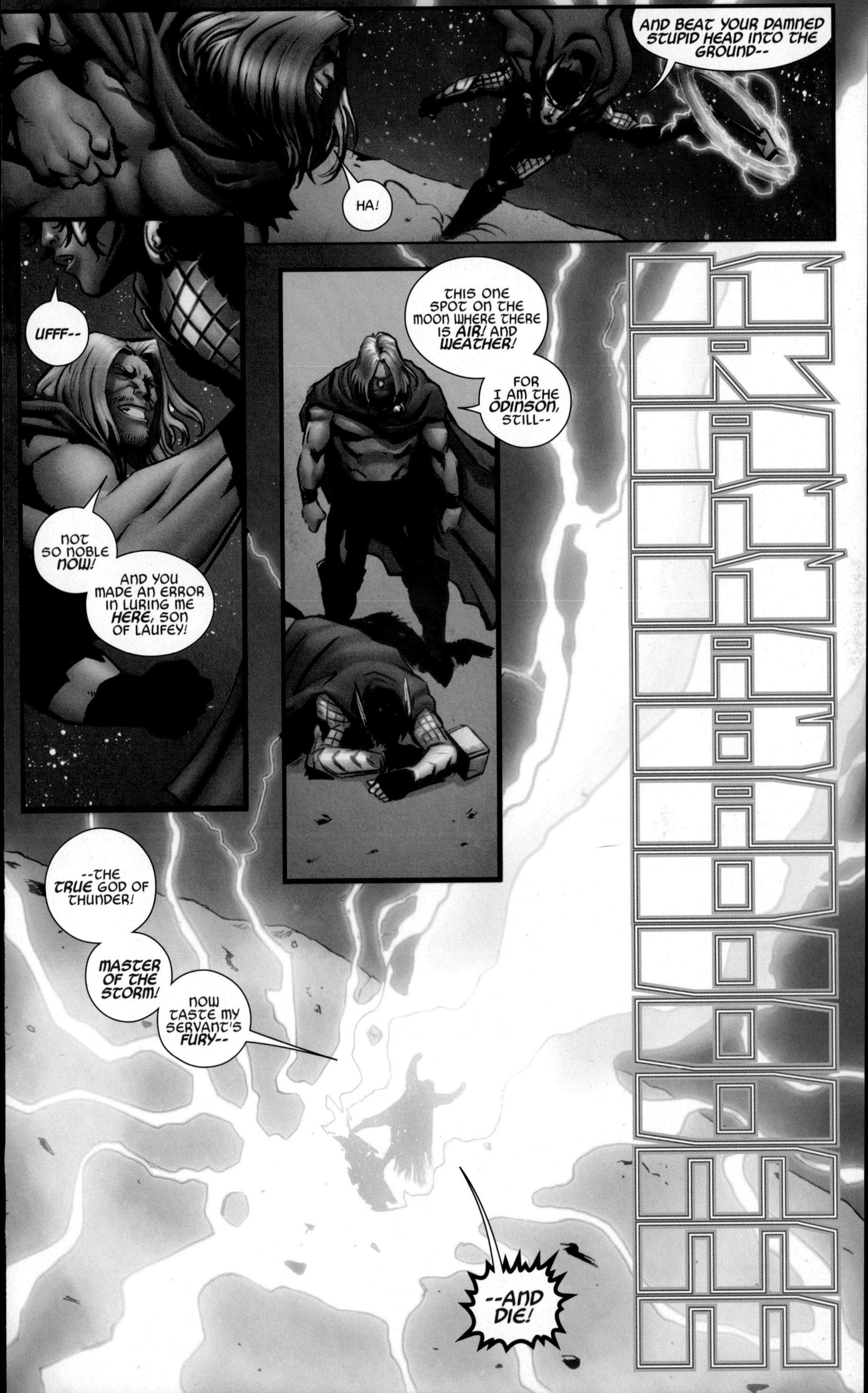
AND BEAT YOUR DAMNED STUPID HEAD INTO THE GROUND--
HA!
UFFF--
NOT SO NOBLE NOW!
AND YOU MADE AN ERROR IN LURING ME HERE, SON OF LAUFEY!
THIS ONE SPOT ON THE MOON WHERE THERE IS AIR! AND WEATHER!
FOR I AM THE ODINSON, STILL--
--THE TRUE GOD OF THUNDER!
MASTER OF THE STORM!
NOW TASTE MY SERVANT'S FURY--
--AND DIE!

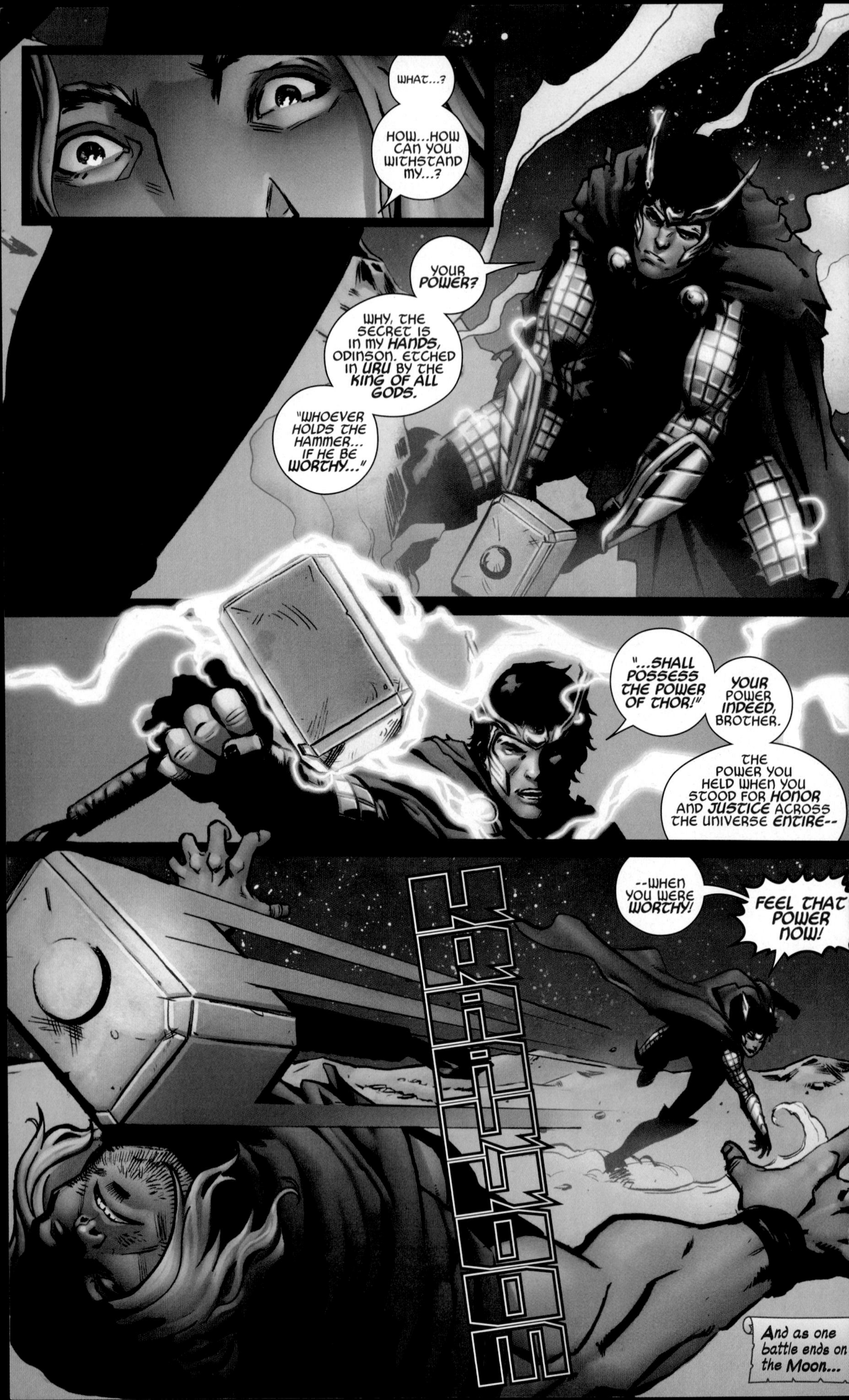

WHAT...?
HOW...HOW CAN YOU WITHSTAND MY...?
YOUR POWER?
WHY, THE SECRET IS IN MY HANDS, ODINSON. ETCHED IN URU BY THE KING OF ALL GODS.
"WHOEVER HOLDS THE HAMMER... IF HE BE WORTHY..."
"...SHALL POSSESS THE POWER OF THOR!"
YOUR POWER INDEED, BROTHER.
THE POWER YOU HELD WHEN YOU STOOD FOR HONOR AND JUSTICE ACROSS THE UNIVERSE ENTIRE--
--WHEN YOU WERE WORTHY!
FEEL THAT POWER NOW!
And as one battle ends on the Moon...

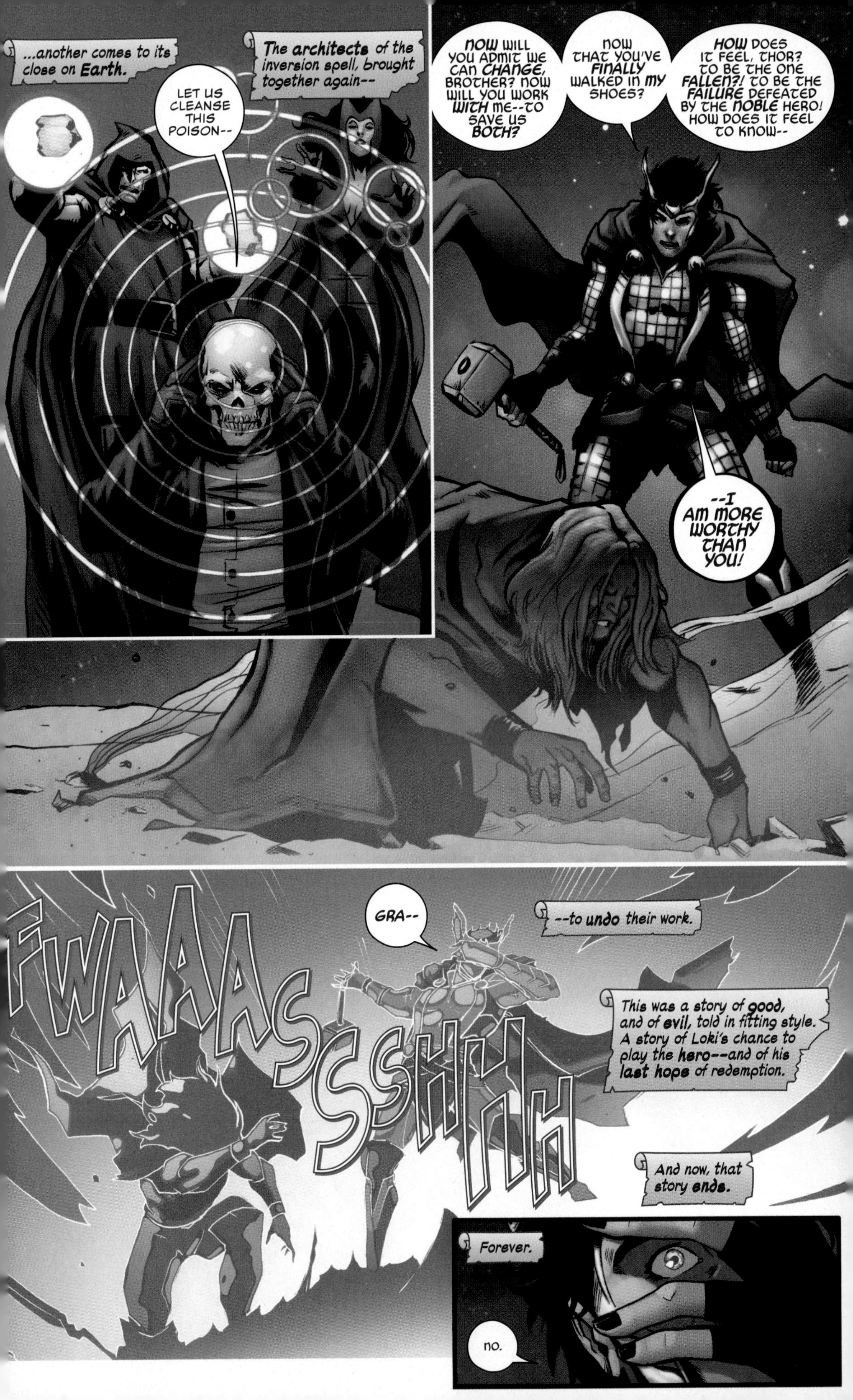
...another comes to its close on Earth.
The architects of the inversion spell, brought together again--
LET US CLEANSE THIS POISON--
NOW WILL YOU ADMIT WE CAN CHANGE, BROTHER? NOW WILL YOU WORK WITH ME--TO SAVE US BOTH?
NOW THAT YOU'VE FINALLY WALKED IN MY SHOES?
HOW DOES IT FEEL, THOR? TO BE THE ONE FALLEN?! TO BE THE FAILURE DEFEATED BY THE NOBLE HERO! HOW DOES IT FEEL TO KNOW--
--I AM MORE WORTHY THAN YOU!
FWAAASSSHHH
GRA--
--to undo their work.
This was a story of good, and of evil, told in fitting style. A story of Loki's chance to play the hero--and of his last hope of redemption.
And now, that story ends.
Forever.
no.

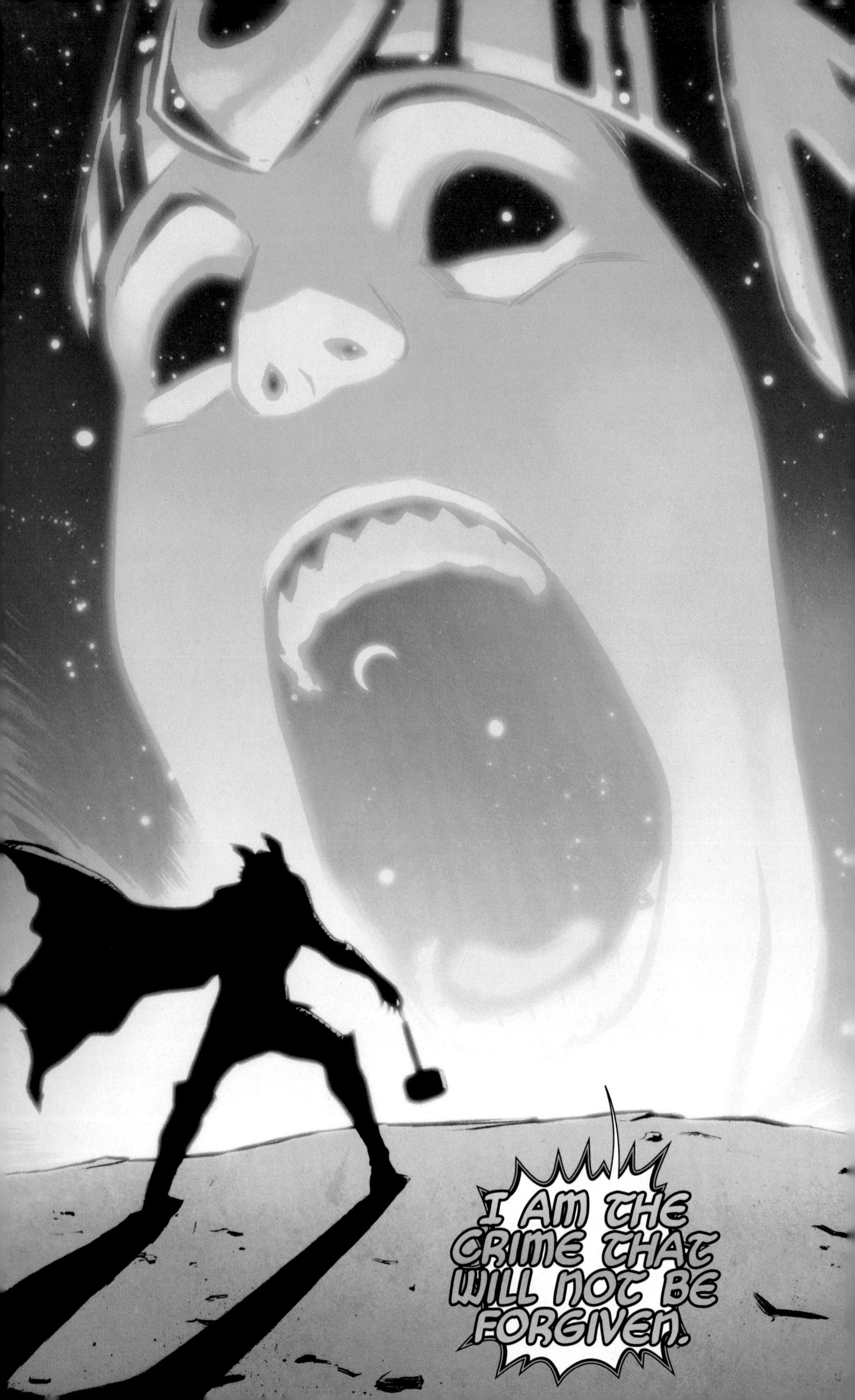
I AM THE CRIME THAT WILL NOT BE FORGIVEN.

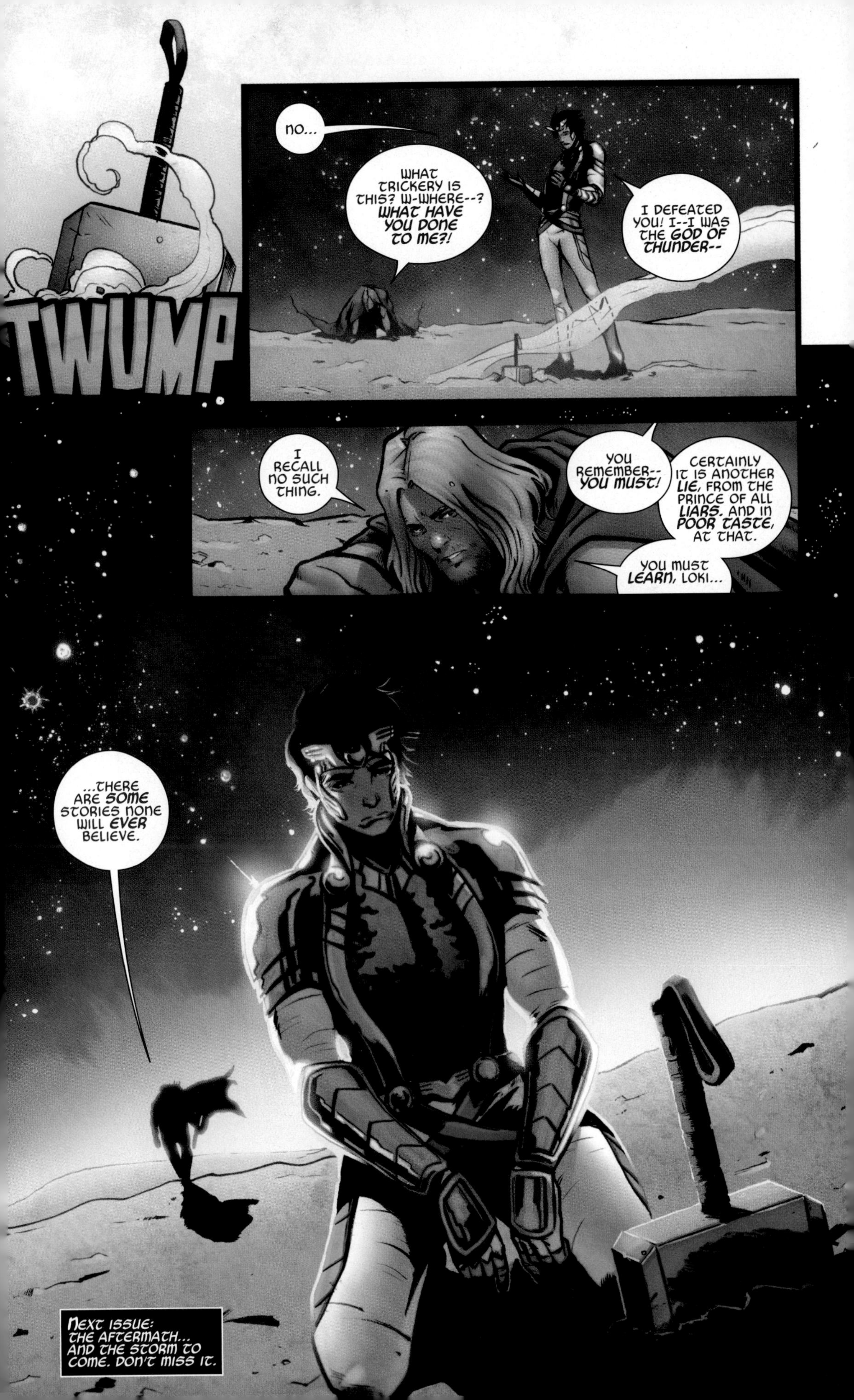
TWUMP
no...
WHAT TRICKERY IS THIS? W-WHERE--? WHAT HAVE YOU DONE TO ME?!
I DEFEATED YOU! I--I WAS THE GOD OF THUNDER--
I RECALL NO SUCH THING.
YOU REMEMBER-- YOU MUST!
CERTAINLY IT IS ANOTHER LIE, FROM THE PRINCE OF ALL LIARS. AND IN POOR TASTE, AT THAT.
YOU MUST LEARN, LOKI...
...THERE ARE SOME STORIES NONE WILL EVER BELIEVE.
NEXT ISSUE: THE AFTERMATH... AND THE STORM TO COME. DON'T MISS IT.

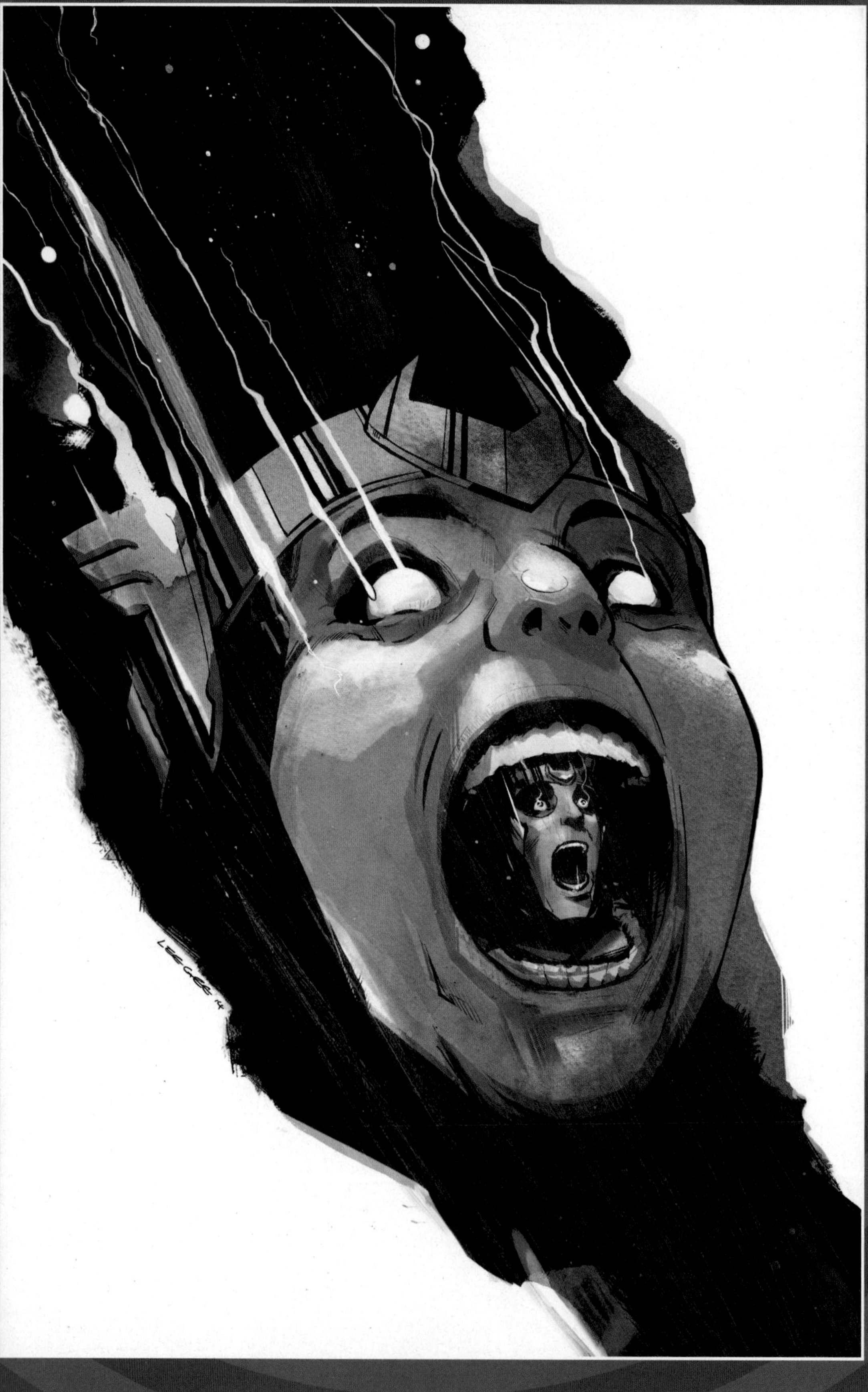

LOKI: AGENT OF ASGARD #10

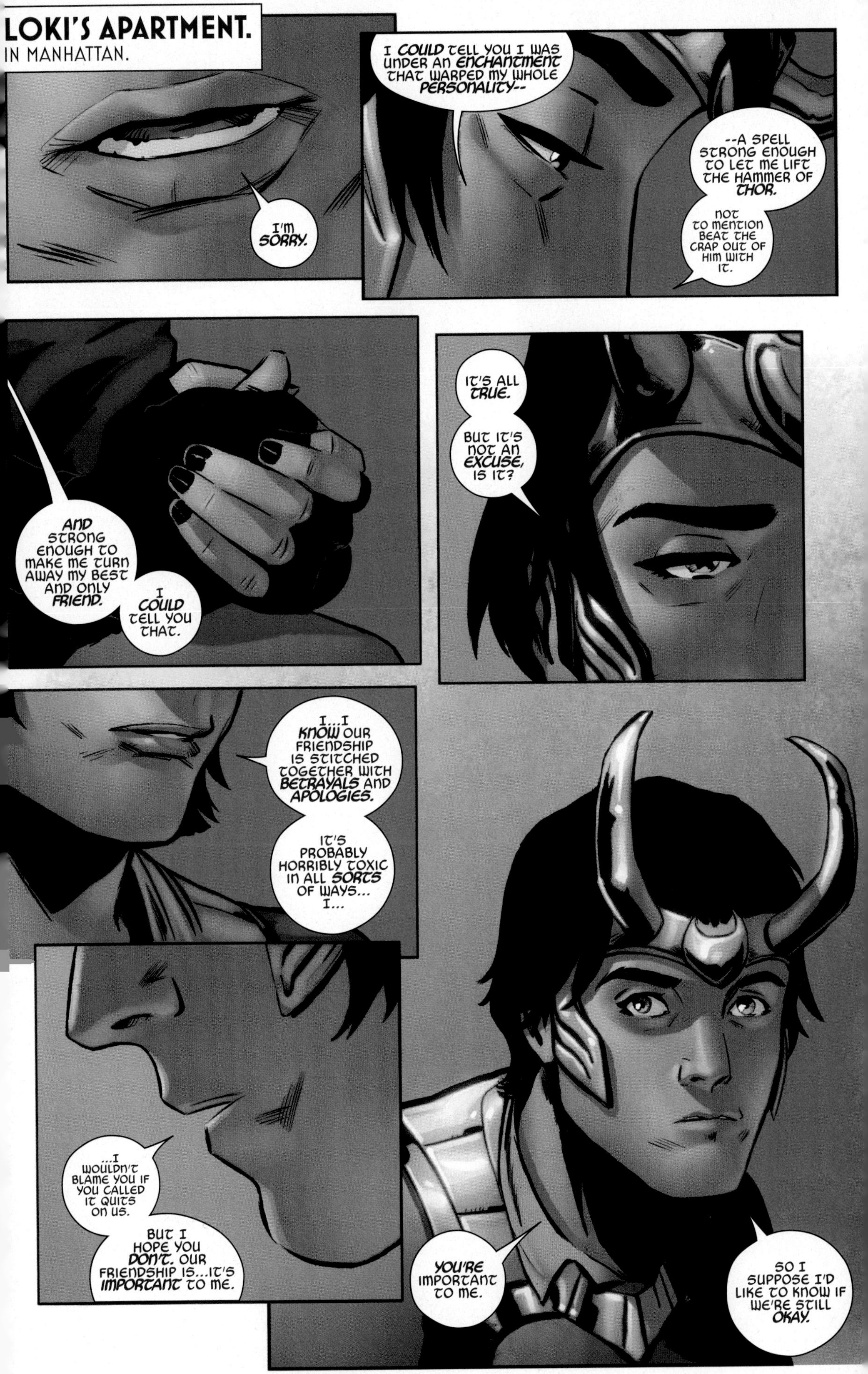
LOKI'S APARTMENT.
IN MANHATTAN.
I'M SORRY.
I COULD TELL YOU I WAS UNDER AN ENCHANTMENT THAT WARPED MY WHOLE PERSONALITY--
--A SPELL STRONG ENOUGH TO LET ME LIFT THE HAMMER OF THOR.
NOT TO MENTION BEAT THE CRAP OUT OF HIM WITH IT.
AND STRONG ENOUGH TO MAKE ME TURN AWAY MY BEST AND ONLY FRIEND.
I COULD TELL YOU THAT.
IT'S ALL TRUE.
BUT IT'S NOT AN EXCUSE, IS IT?
I...I KNOW OUR FRIENDSHIP IS STITCHED TOGETHER WITH BETRAYALS AND APOLOGIES.
IT'S PROBABLY HORRIBLY TOXIC IN ALL SORTS OF WAYS... I...
...I WOULDN'T BLAME YOU IF YOU CALLED IT QUITS ON US.
BUT I HOPE YOU DON'T. OUR FRIENDSHIP IS...IT'S IMPORTANT TO ME.
YOU'RE IMPORTANT TO ME.
SO I SUPPOSE I'D LIKE TO KNOW IF WE'RE STILL OKAY.

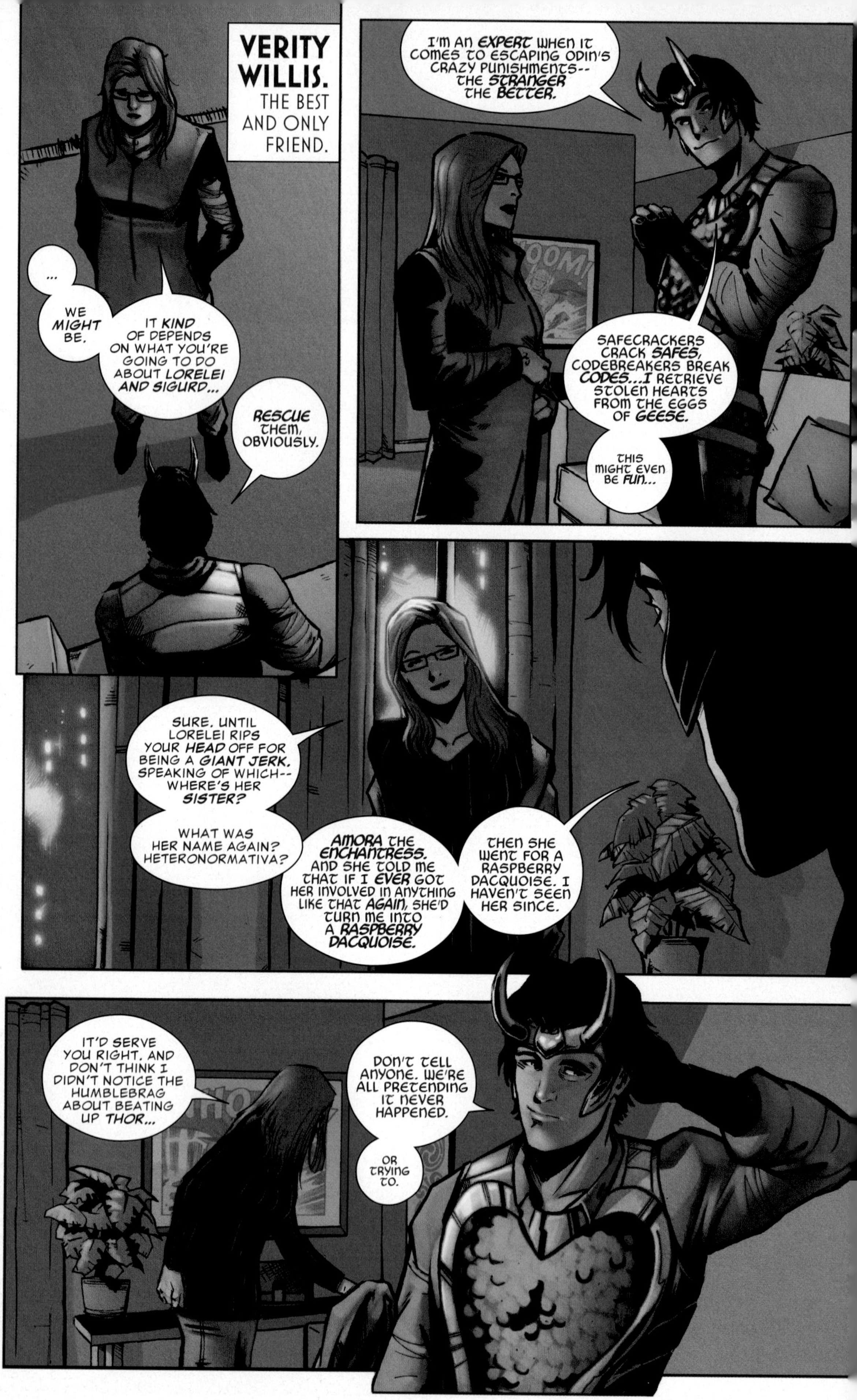
VERITY WILLIS. THE BEST AND ONLY FRIEND.
...
WE MIGHT BE.
IT KIND OF DEPENDS ON WHAT YOU'RE GOING TO DO ABOUT LORELEI AND SIGURD...
RESCUE THEM, OBVIOUSLY.
I'M AN EXPERT WHEN IT COMES TO ESCAPING ODIN'S CRAZY PUNISHMENTS-- THE STRANGER THE BETTER.
SAFECRACKERS CRACK SAFES, CODEBREAKERS BREAK CODES...I RETRIEVE STOLEN HEARTS FROM THE EGGS OF GEESE.
THIS MIGHT EVEN BE FUN...
SURE. UNTIL LORELEI RIPS YOUR HEAD OFF FOR BEING A GIANT JERK. SPEAKING OF WHICH-- WHERE'S HER SISTER?
WHAT WAS HER NAME AGAIN? HETERONORMATIVA?
AMORA THE ENCHANTRESS. AND SHE TOLD ME THAT IF I EVER GOT HER INVOLVED IN ANYTHING LIKE THAT AGAIN, SHE'D TURN ME INTO A RASPBERRY DACQUOISE.
THEN SHE WENT FOR A RASPBERRY DACQUOISE. I HAVEN'T SEEN HER SINCE.
IT'D SERVE YOU RIGHT. AND DON'T THINK I DIDN'T NOTICE THE HUMBLEBRAG ABOUT BEATING UP THOR...
DON'T TELL ANYONE. WE'RE ALL PRETENDING IT NEVER HAPPENED.
OR TRYING TO.

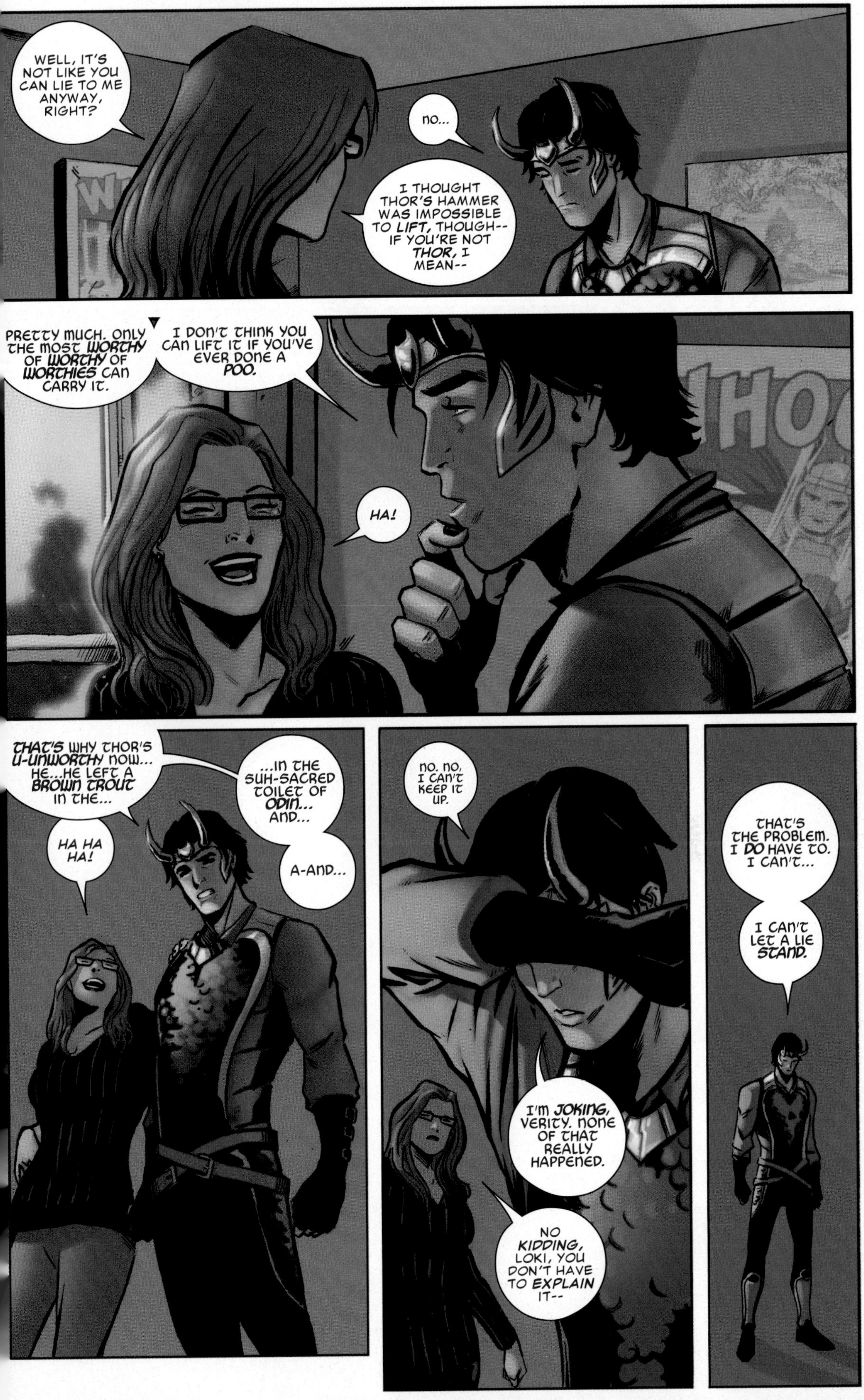
WELL, IT'S NOT LIKE YOU CAN LIE TO ME ANYWAY, RIGHT?
no...
I THOUGHT THOR'S HAMMER WAS IMPOSSIBLE TO LIFT, THOUGH-- IF YOU'RE NOT THOR, I MEAN--
PRETTY MUCH. ONLY THE MOST WORTHY OF WORTHY OF WORTHIES CAN CARRY IT.
I DON'T THINK YOU CAN LIFT IT IF YOU'VE EVER DONE A POO.
HA!
THAT'S WHY THOR'S U-UNWORTHY NOW... HE...HE LEFT A BROWN TROUT IN THE...
HA HA HA!
...IN THE SUH-SACRED TOILET OF ODIN... AND...
A-AND...
NO. NO, I CAN'T KEEP IT UP.
I'M JOKING, VERITY. NONE OF THAT REALLY HAPPENED.
NO KIDDING, LOKI, YOU DON'T HAVE TO EXPLAIN IT--
THAT'S THE PROBLEM. I DO HAVE TO. I CAN'T...
I CAN'T LET A LIE STAND.

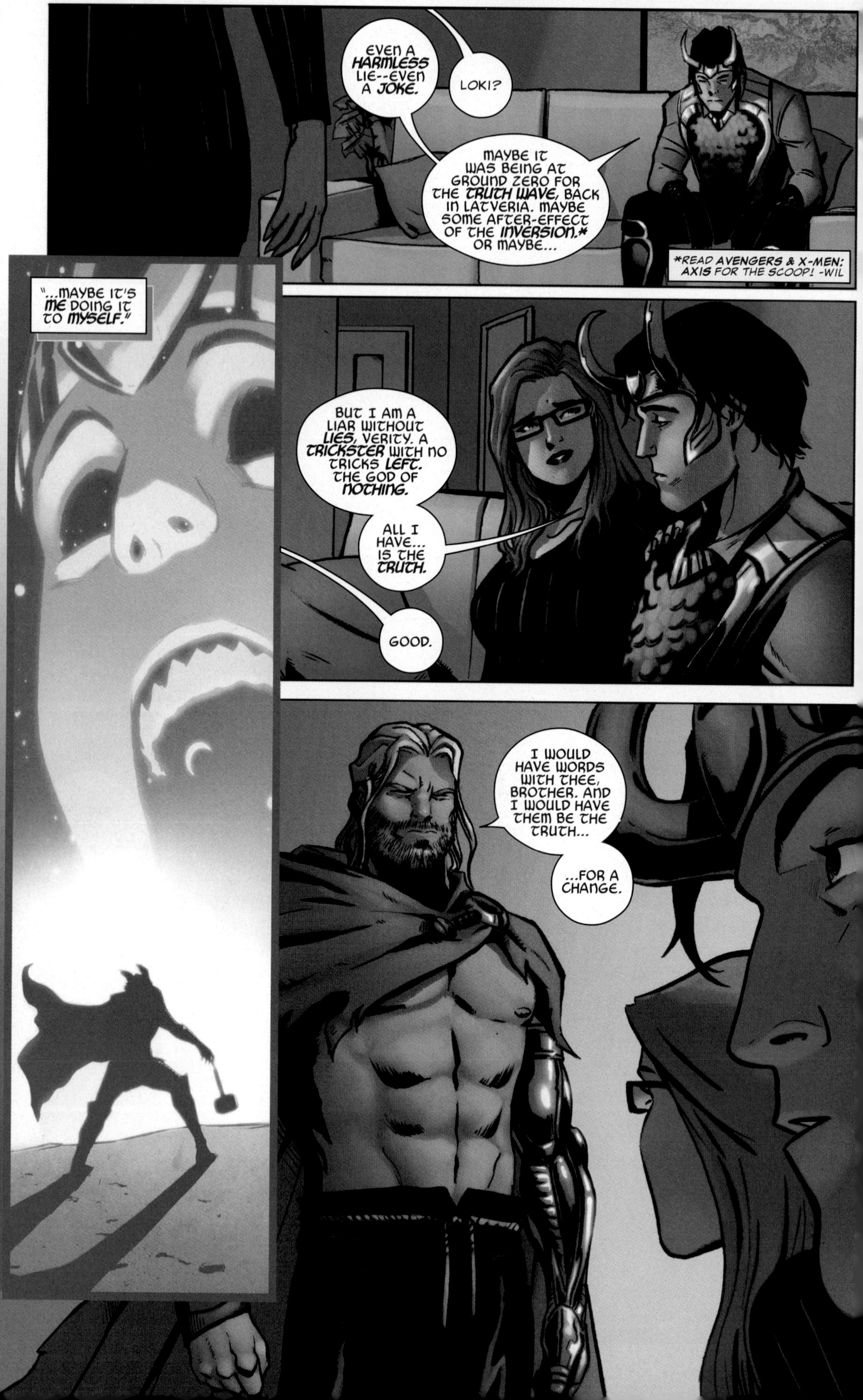
EVEN A HARMLESS LIE--EVEN A JOKE.
LOKI?
MAYBE IT WAS BEING AT GROUND ZERO FOR THE TRUTH WAVE, BACK IN LATVERIA. MAYBE SOME AFTER-EFFECT OF THE INVERSION.* OR MAYBE...
*READ AVENGERS & X-MEN: AXIS FOR THE SCOOP! -WIL
"...MAYBE IT'S ME DOING IT TO MYSELF."
BUT I AM A LIAR WITHOUT LIES, VERITY. A TRICKSTER WITH NO TRICKS LEFT. THE GOD OF NOTHING.
ALL I HAVE... IS THE TRUTH.
GOOD.
I WOULD HAVE WORDS WITH THEE, BROTHER. AND I WOULD HAVE THEM BE THE TRUTH...
...FOR A CHANGE.

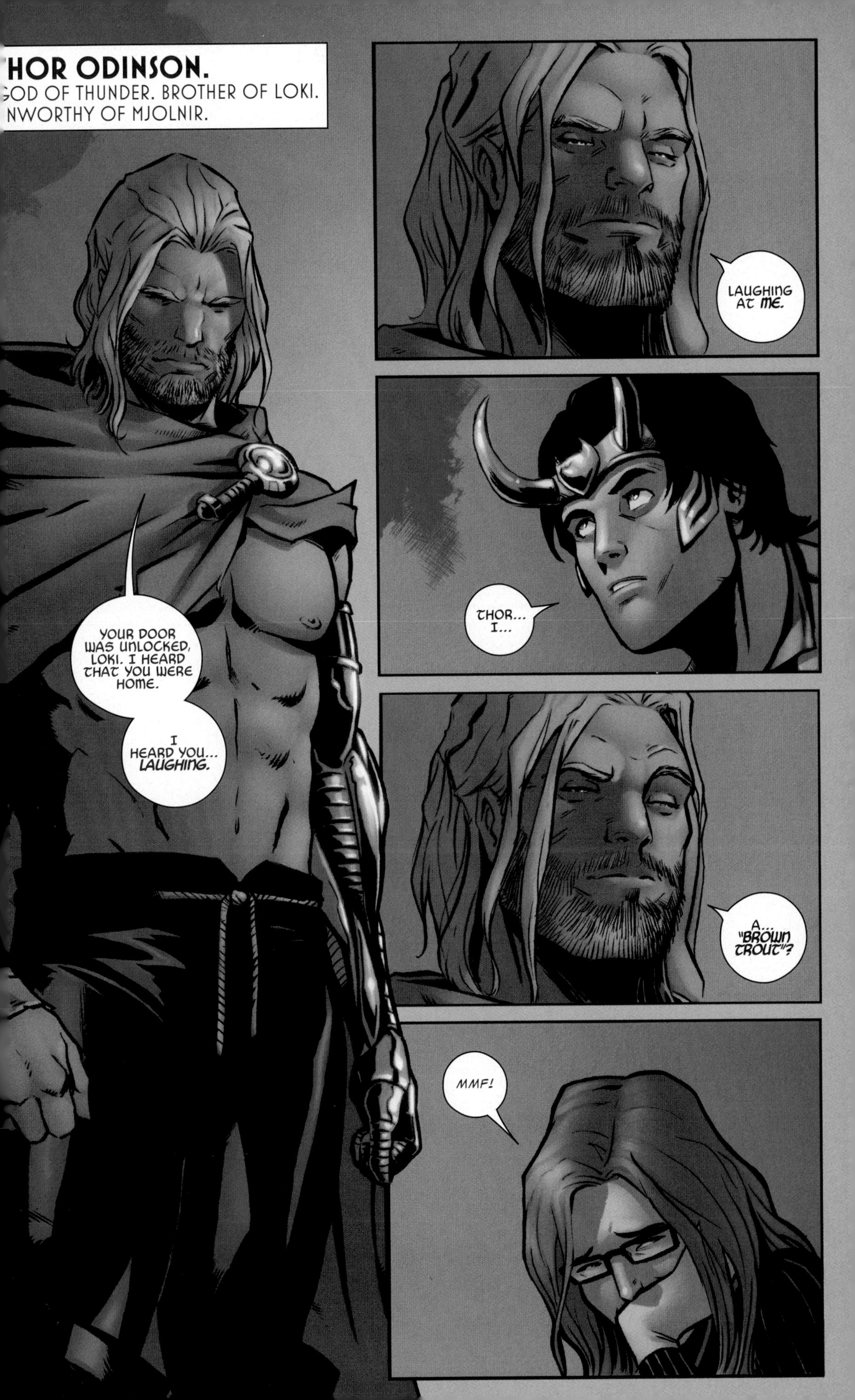

THOR ODINSON.
GOD OF THUNDER. BROTHER OF LOKI.
UNWORTHY OF MJOLNIR.
YOUR DOOR WAS UNLOCKED, LOKI. I HEARD THAT YOU WERE HOME.
I HEARD YOU... LAUGHING.
LAUGHING AT ME.
THOR... I...
A... "BROWN TROUT"?
MMF!

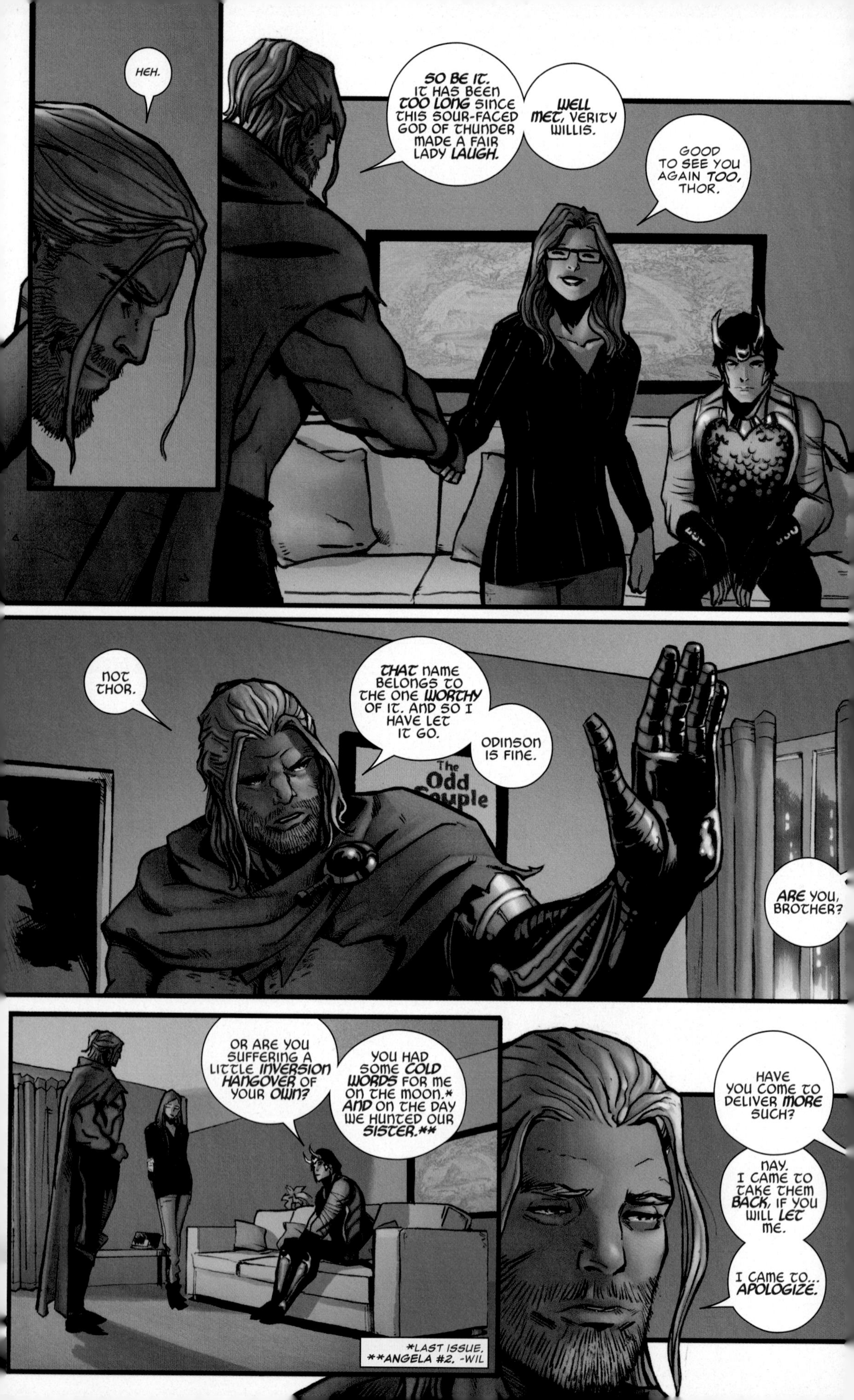
HEH.
SO BE IT. IT HAS BEEN TOO LONG SINCE THIS SOUR-FACED GOD OF THUNDER MADE A FAIR LADY LAUGH.
WELL MET, VERITY WILLIS.
GOOD TO SEE YOU AGAIN TOO, THOR.
NOT THOR.
THAT NAME BELONGS TO THE ONE WORTHY OF IT. AND SO I HAVE LET IT GO.
ODINSON IS FINE.
The Odd Couple
ARE YOU, BROTHER?
OR ARE YOU SUFFERING A LITTLE INVERSION HANGOVER OF YOUR OWN?
YOU HAD SOME COLD WORDS FOR ME ON THE MOON.* AND ON THE DAY WE HUNTED OUR SISTER.**
HAVE YOU COME TO DELIVER MORE SUCH?
NAY. I CAME TO TAKE THEM BACK, IF YOU WILL LET ME.
I CAME TO... APOLOGIZE.
*LAST ISSUE.
**ANGELA #2. -WIL

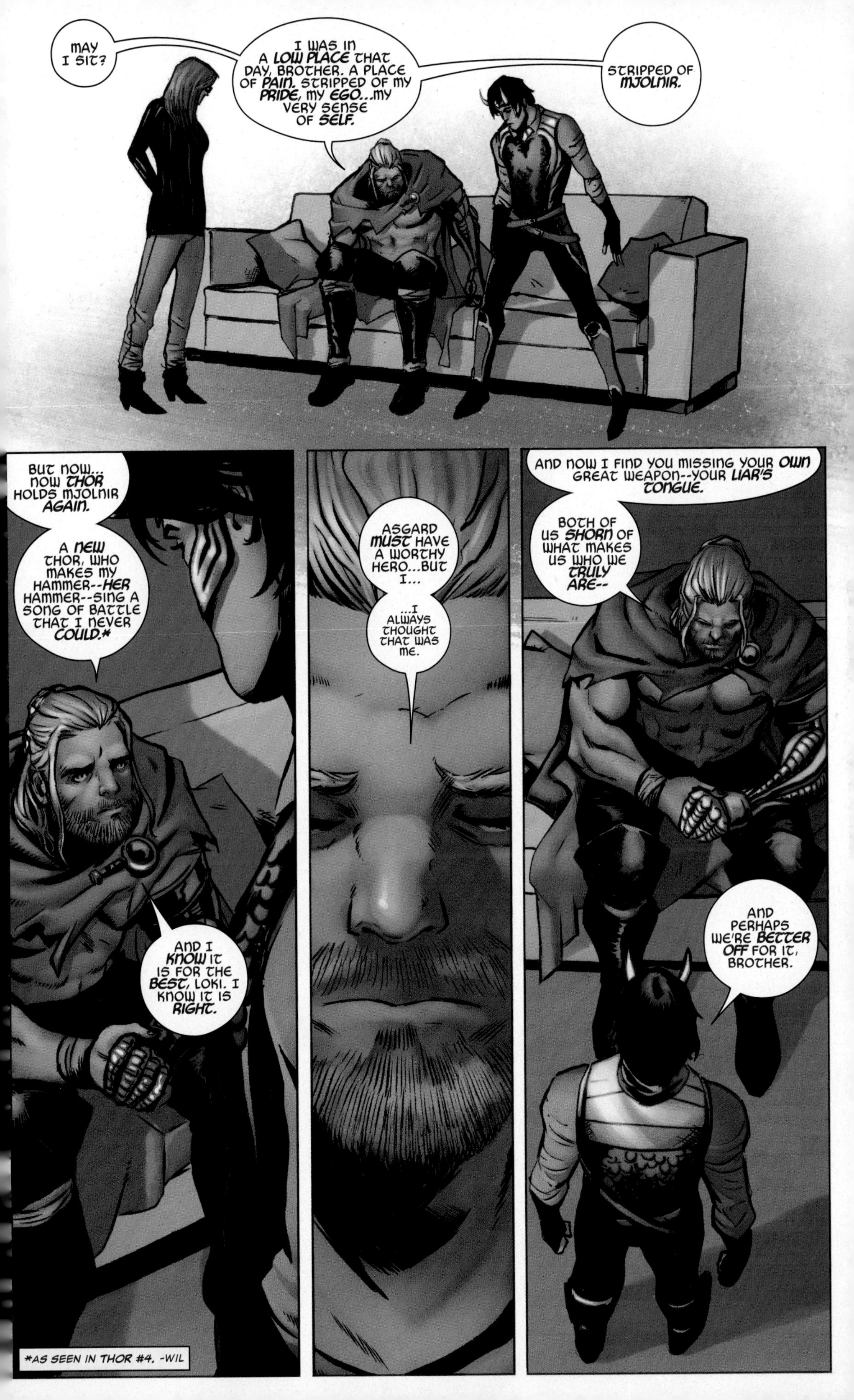
MAY I SIT?
I WAS IN A LOW PLACE THAT DAY, BROTHER. A PLACE OF PAIN. STRIPPED OF MY PRIDE, MY EGO...MY VERY SENSE OF SELF.
STRIPPED OF MJOLNIR.
BUT NOW... NOW THOR HOLDS MJOLNIR AGAIN.
A NEW THOR, WHO MAKES MY HAMMER--HER HAMMER--SING A SONG OF BATTLE THAT I NEVER COULD.*
AND I KNOW IT IS FOR THE BEST, LOKI. I KNOW IT IS RIGHT.
*AS SEEN IN THOR #4. -WIL
ASGARD MUST HAVE A WORTHY HERO...BUT I...
...I ALWAYS THOUGHT THAT WAS ME.
AND NOW I FIND YOU MISSING YOUR OWN GREAT WEAPON--YOUR LIAR'S TONGUE.
BOTH OF US SHORN OF WHAT MAKES US WHO WE TRULY ARE--
AND PERHAPS WE'RE BETTER OFF FOR IT, BROTHER.

PERHAPS "WHO WE TRULY ARE" IS A CAGE.

ONE WE'LL NEVER BE FREE OF IF WE CLING SO DAMNED TIGHT TO THE BARS--

SUCH... RAGE IN YOUR VOICE...

AH, LOKI. WHAT HAPPENED TO US?

WHAT HAPPENED TO THE CAREFREE, MISCHIEVOUS YOUNG LOKI I USED TO KNOW, EH?

AND SUDDENLY...

...I FEEL A TRAP CLOSING AROUND ME.

ANSWER ME THAT.

A TRAP MADE OF EVENTS, PRECISELY STRUCTURED.

LATVERIA. THE TRUTH WAVE. THE INVERSION. THE EVENTS KING LOKI PLACED ME IN--

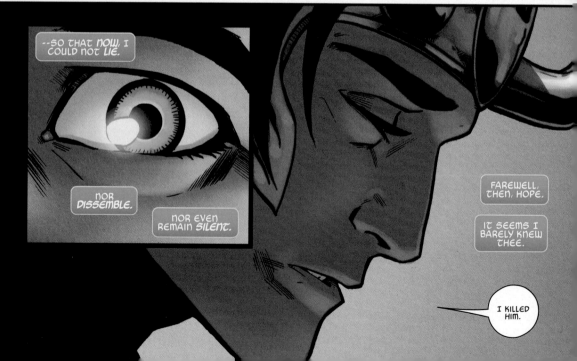

--SO THAT NOW, I COULD NOT LIE.

NOR DISSEMBLE.

NOR EVEN REMAIN SILENT.

FAREWELL, THEN, HOPE.

IT SEEMS I BARELY KNEW THEE.

I KILLED HIM.

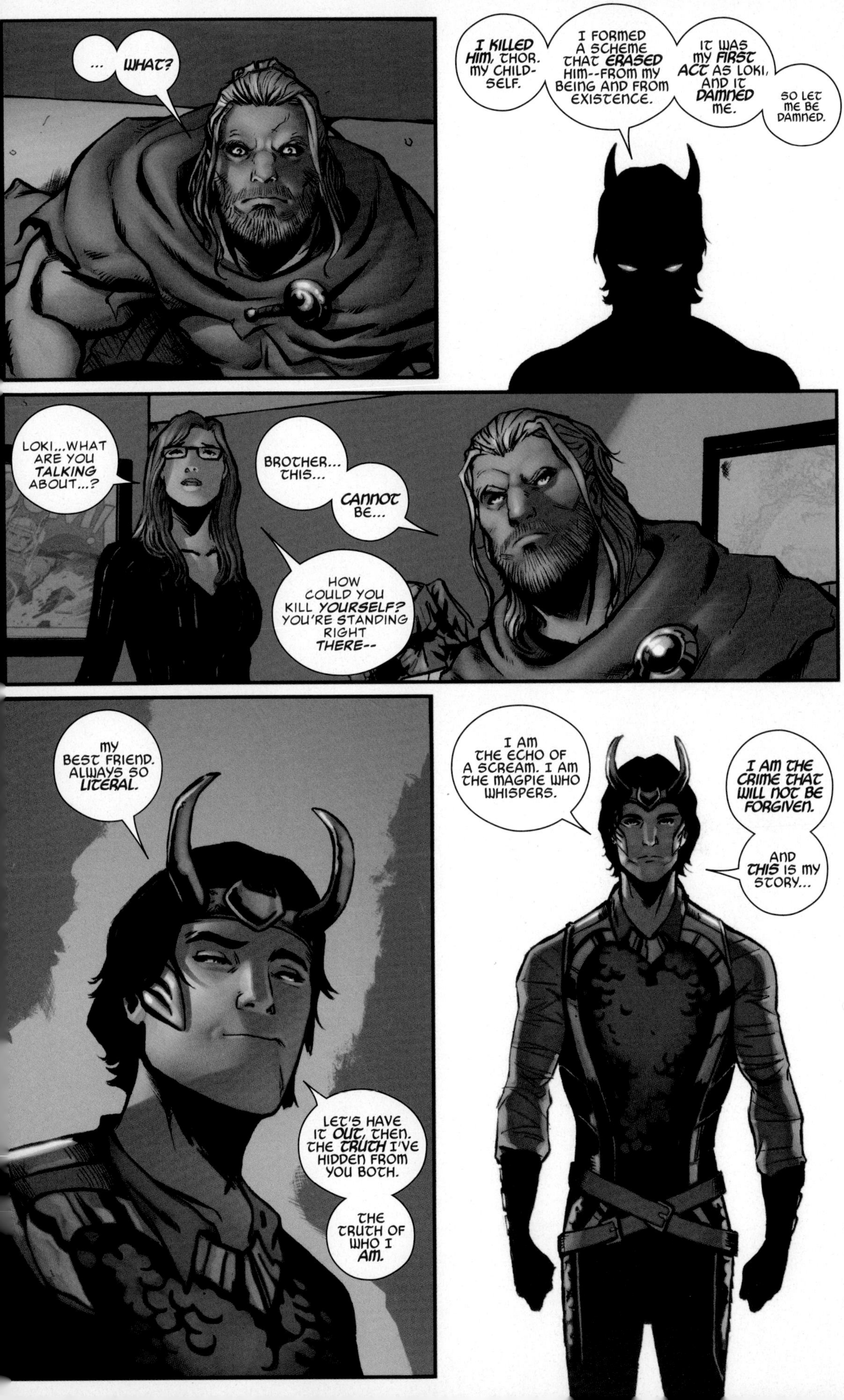

...
WHAT?
I KILLED HIM, THOR. MY CHILD-SELF.
I FORMED A SCHEME THAT ERASED HIM--FROM MY BEING AND FROM EXISTENCE.
IT WAS MY FIRST ACT AS LOKI, AND IT DAMNED ME.
SO LET ME BE DAMNED.
LOKI...WHAT ARE YOU TALKING ABOUT...?
BROTHER... THIS...
CANNOT BE...
HOW COULD YOU KILL YOURSELF? YOU'RE STANDING RIGHT THERE--
MY BEST FRIEND. ALWAYS SO LITERAL.
LET'S HAVE IT OUT, THEN. THE TRUTH I'VE HIDDEN FROM YOU BOTH.
THE TRUTH OF WHO I AM.
I AM THE ECHO OF A SCREAM. I AM THE MAGPIE WHO WHISPERS.
I AM THE CRIME THAT WILL NOT BE FORGIVEN.
AND THIS IS MY STORY...

THIS IS THE STORY OF LOKI.

LOKI, WHO WAS DOOMED TO NEVER BE ANYTHING BUT LOKI —
LOKI THE BAD SON, LOKI THE VILLAIN — UNTIL THE DAY HE DIED.

SO... HE DIED.

WHICH WAS, OF COURSE, HIS GREATEST SCHEME OF ALL.

FOR SOON HE WAS REBORN INTO A NEW, YOUTHFUL BODY, FREE
TO CHOOSE HIS OWN FATE. "KID LOKI" — A NEW PERSONALITY,
FREE FROM THE TAINT OF THE OLD... AT FIRST. FOR THIS NEW
LOKI TOOK THE FADING ECHO OF THE OLD — BOTH GHOST AND
COPY — TO ADVISE HIM AND GIVE HIM KNOWLEDGE.

ALL LOKIS, IT SEEMS, MUST DAMN THEMSELVES EARLY.

THE GHOST-COPY, CALLED IKOL, HAD NEITHER POWER NOR
MAGIC. BUT WHAT HE HAD WAS ENOUGH — KID LOKI'S EAR. WITH
THIS, HE CRAFTED A SCHEME THAT WOULD GIVE HIM CONTROL
OF THE GODLING'S BODY...

...AND CAST KID LOKI'S VERY SELF — HIS MIND AND SOUL AND
BEING — INTO TOTAL ANNIHILATION, DESTROYING THE CHILD
FOREVER.

PERHAPS ALL LOKIS MUST FALL TO THE VOID, AS WELL.

AFTER THE DEED WAS DONE, IKOL-LOKI — THE THIRD LOKI —
FOUND HIMSELF TRAPPED IN THE SHAPE OF HIS VICTIM, PLAYING
THE ROLE OF THE GOOD TRICKSTER DESPITE HIS WORST
INTENTIONS. AND THOUGH HE CHANGED THAT SHAPE — AGING TO
YOUNG-MANHOOD — HE WAS STILL TORMENTED BY SHAME AND
GUILT AND SELF-LOATHING. BY THE ECHO OF A FINAL SCREAM —
KID LOKI'S ACCUSATION THAT HE COULD NEVER TRULY CHANGE.

SO HE TRIED TO BE BETTER. HE TRIED TO CHANGE. HE TRIED
TO GROW. AND TO THIS END, HE MADE A DEAL WITH THE ALL-
MOTHER, TO PERFORM MISSIONS FOR ASGARD TO ERASE HIS EVIL
PAST. AND SO WAS BORN...

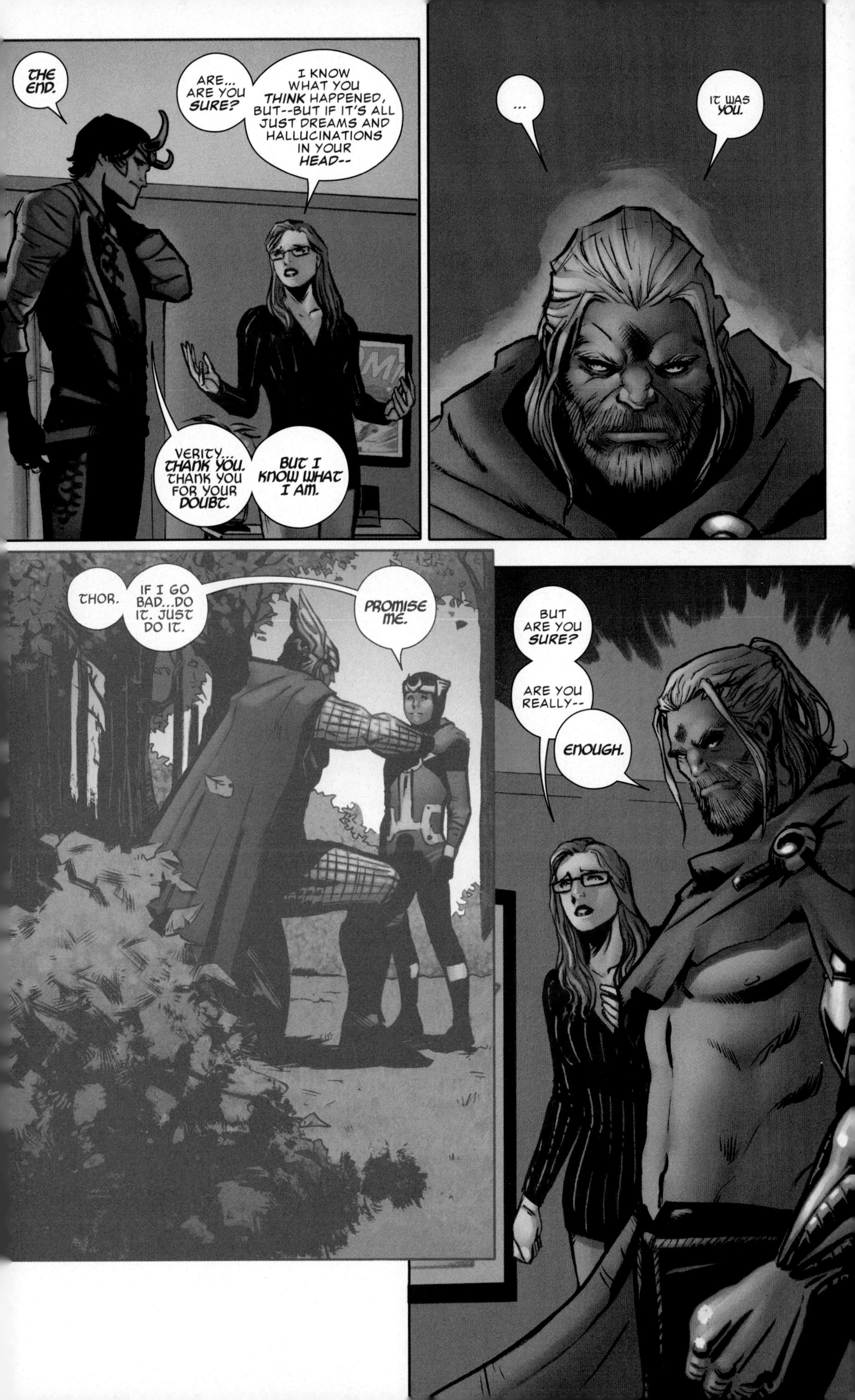
THE END.
ARE... ARE YOU SURE?
I KNOW WHAT YOU THINK HAPPENED, BUT--BUT IF IT'S ALL JUST DREAMS AND HALLUCINATIONS IN YOUR HEAD--
VERITY... THANK YOU. THANK YOU FOR YOUR DOUBT.
BUT I KNOW WHAT I AM.
...
IT WAS YOU.
THOR.
IF I GO BAD...DO IT. JUST DO IT.
PROMISE ME.
BUT ARE YOU SURE?
ARE YOU REALLY--
ENOUGH.

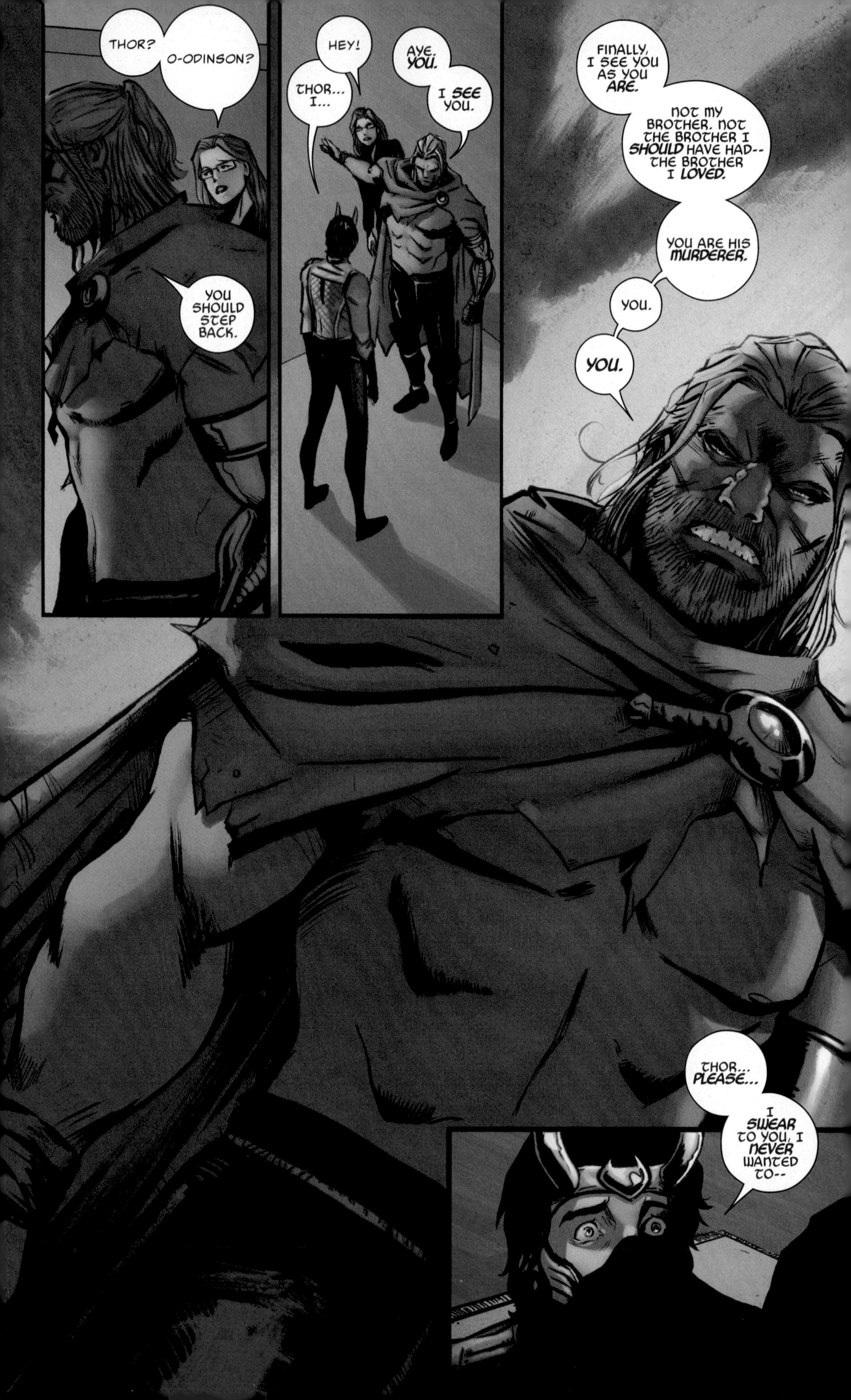
THOR?
O-ODINSON?
YOU SHOULD STEP BACK.
HEY!
THOR... I...
AYE. YOU.
I SEE YOU.
FINALLY, I SEE YOU AS YOU ARE.
NOT MY BROTHER. NOT THE BROTHER I SHOULD HAVE HAD-- THE BROTHER I LOVED.
YOU ARE HIS MURDERER.
YOU.
YOU.
THOR... PLEASE...
I SWEAR TO YOU, I NEVER WANTED TO--

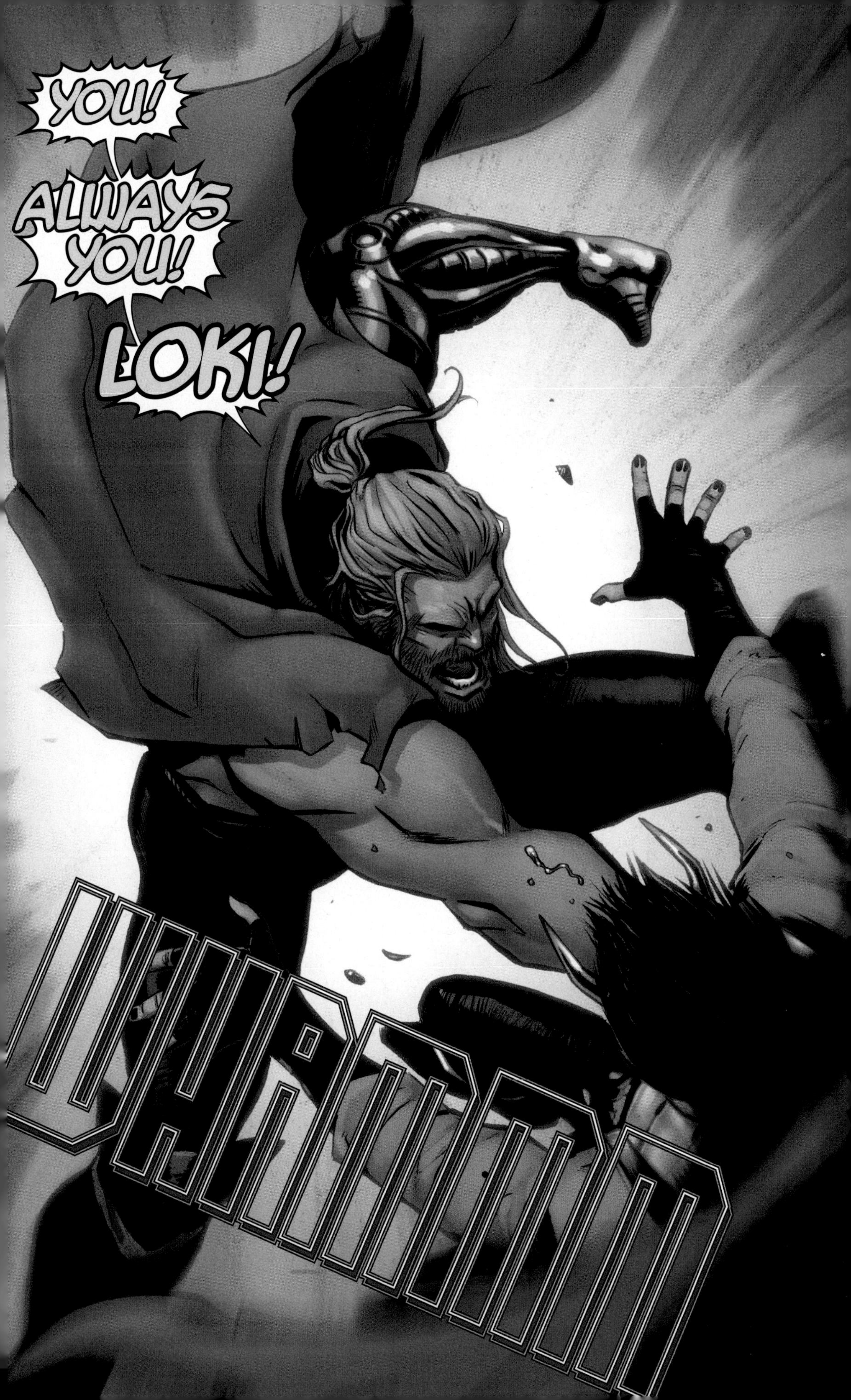
YOU!
ALWAYS YOU!
LOKI!

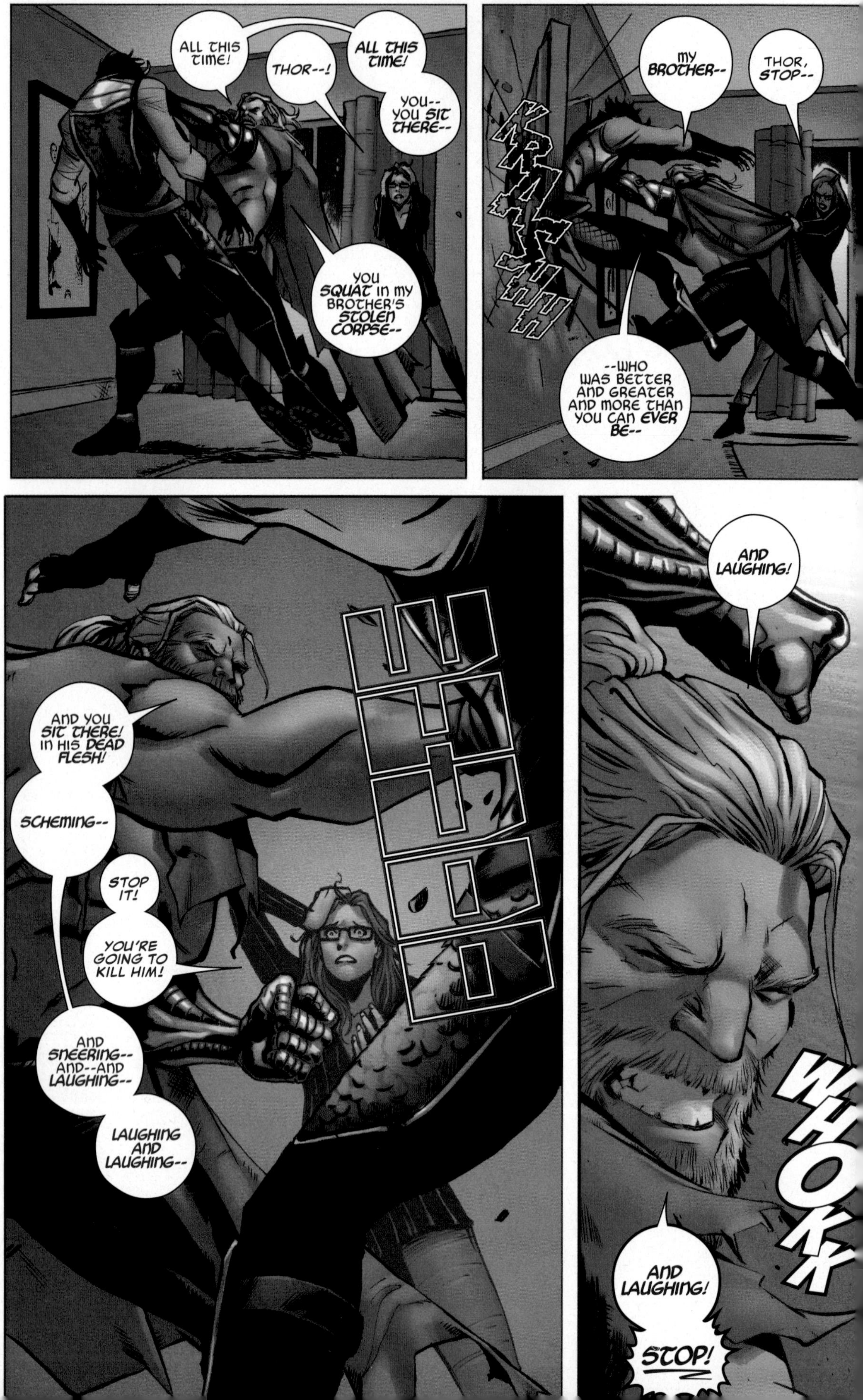
ALL THIS TIME!
ALL THIS TIME!
THOR--!
YOU-- YOU SIT THERE--
YOU SQUAT IN MY BROTHER'S STOLEN CORPSE--
KRASHHH
MY BROTHER--
THOR, STOP--
--WHO WAS BETTER AND GREATER AND MORE THAN YOU CAN EVER BE--
AND YOU SIT THERE! IN HIS DEAD FLESH!
SCHEMING--
STOP IT!
YOU'RE GOING TO KILL HIM!
AND SNEERING-- AND--AND LAUGHING--
LAUGHING AND LAUGHING--
AND LAUGHING!
AND LAUGHING!
WHOKK
STOP!

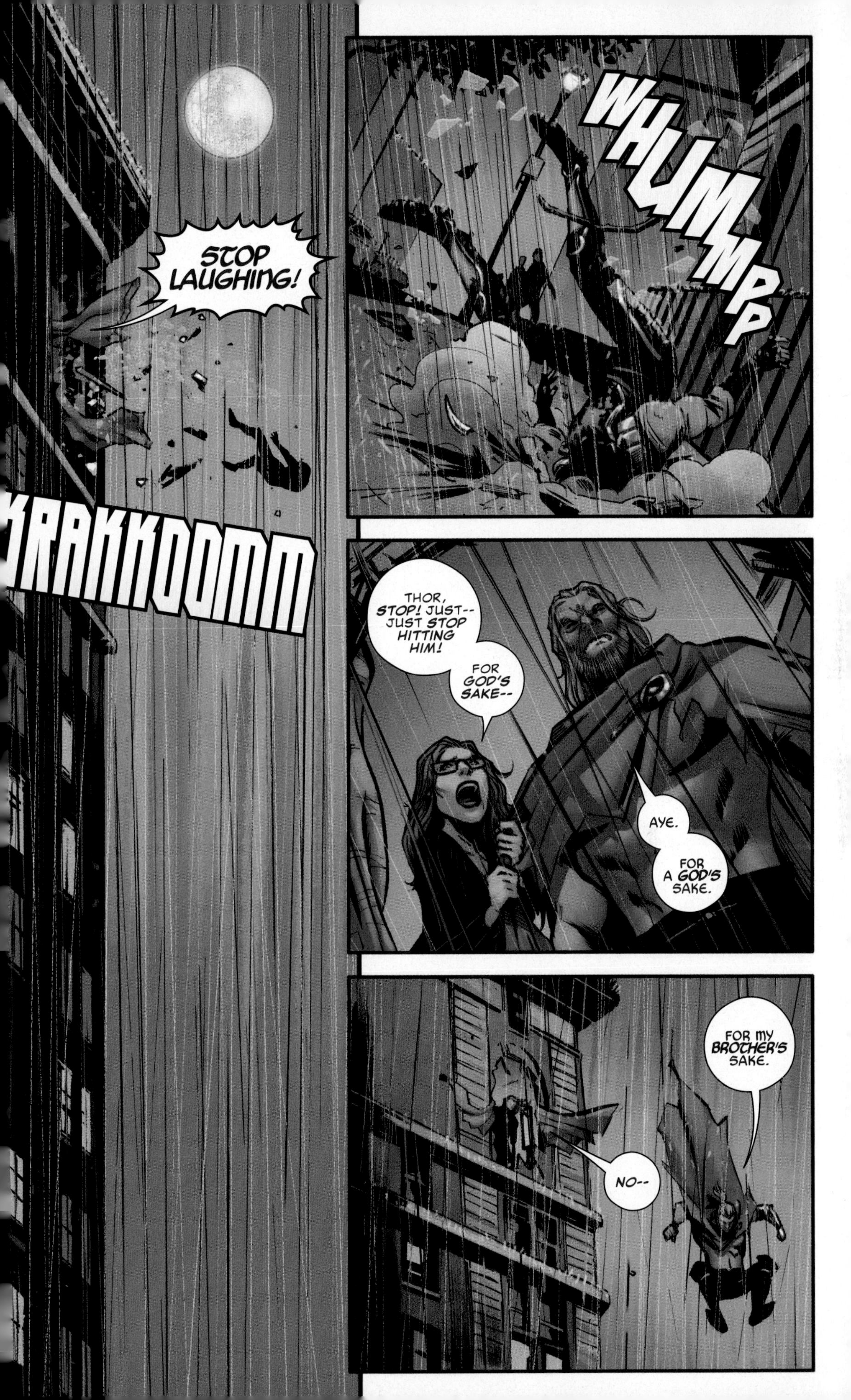

STOP LAUGHING!
KRAKKOOMM
WHUMMPP
THOR, STOP! JUST--JUST STOP HITTING HIM!
FOR GOD'S SAKE--
AYE.
FOR A GOD'S SAKE.
FOR MY BROTHER'S SAKE.
NO--

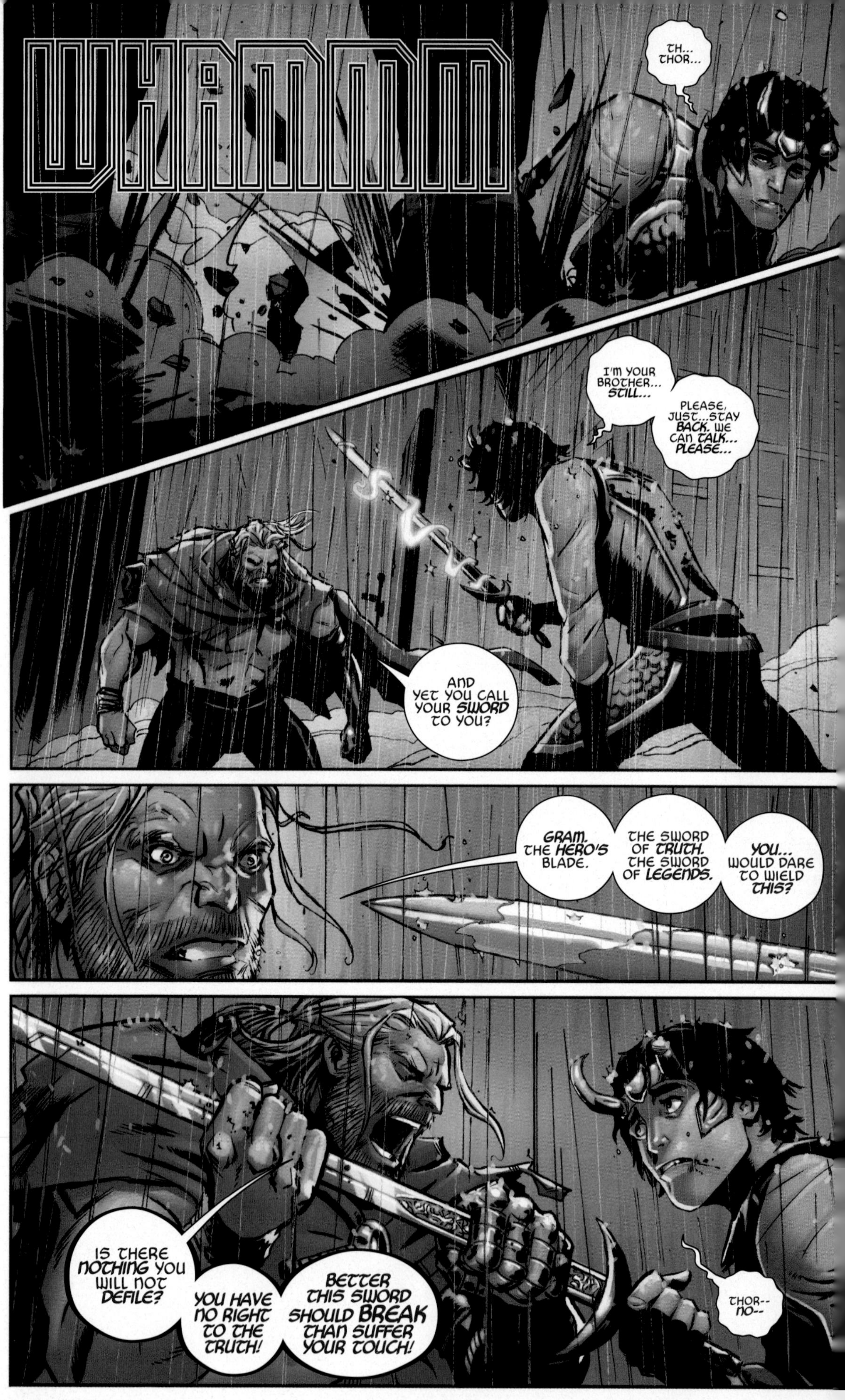
WHAMMM
TH... THOR...
I'M YOUR BROTHER... STILL...
PLEASE, JUST...STAY BACK. WE CAN TALK... PLEASE...
SVVVS
AND YET YOU CALL YOUR SWORD TO YOU?
GRAM. THE HERO'S BLADE.
THE SWORD OF TRUTH. THE SWORD OF LEGENDS.
YOU... WOULD DARE TO WIELD THIS?
IS THERE NOTHING YOU WILL NOT DEFILE?
YOU HAVE NO RIGHT TO THE TRUTH!
BETTER THIS SWORD SHOULD BREAK THAN SUFFER YOUR TOUCH!
THOR-- NO--

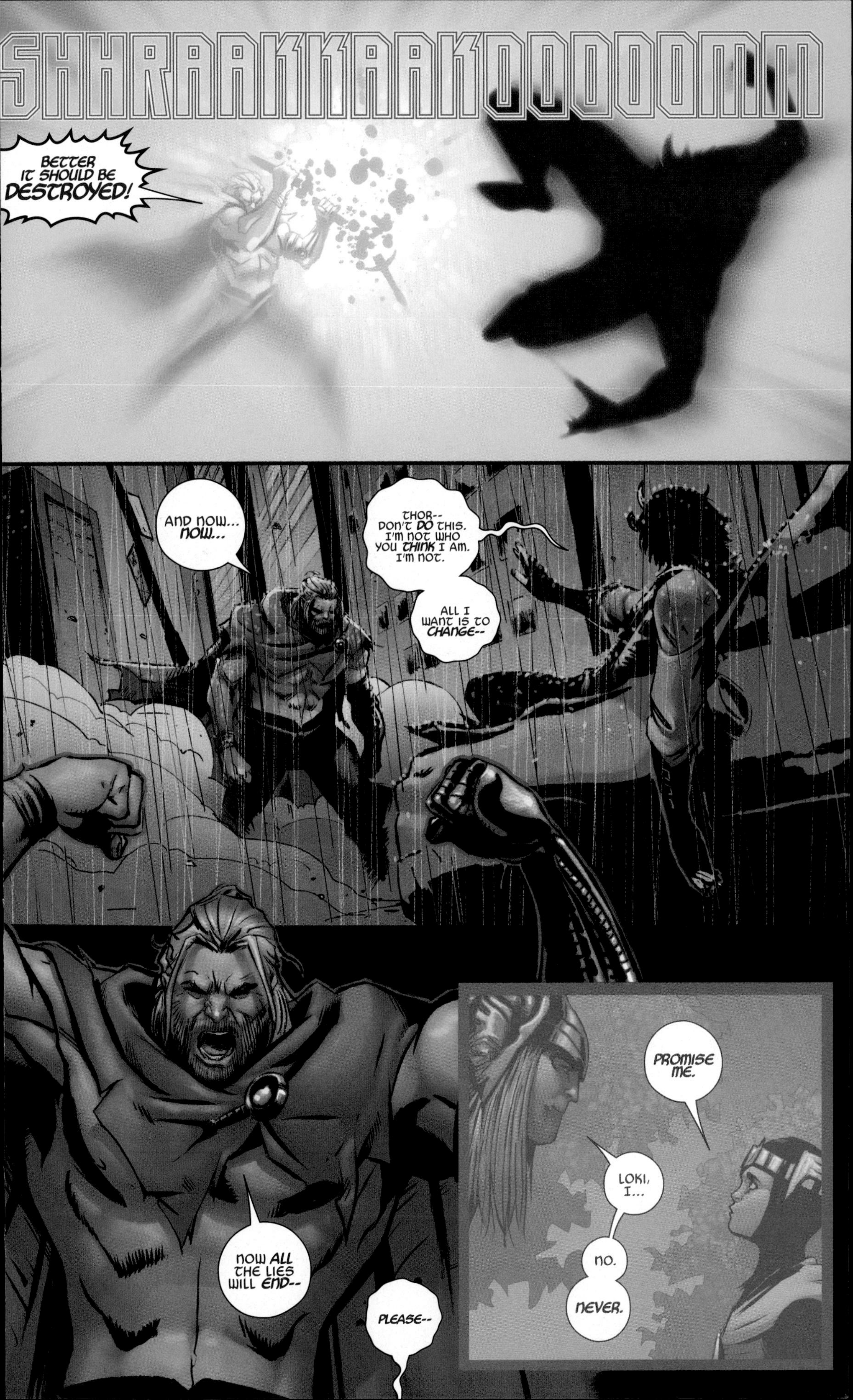
SHHRAAKKAAKDOOOOMM
BETTER IT SHOULD BE DESTROYED!
AND NOW... NOW...
THOR-- DON'T DO THIS. I'M NOT WHO YOU THINK I AM. I'M NOT.
ALL I WANT IS TO CHANGE--
NOW ALL THE LIES WILL END--
PLEASE--
PROMISE ME.
LOKI, I...
NO.
NEVER.

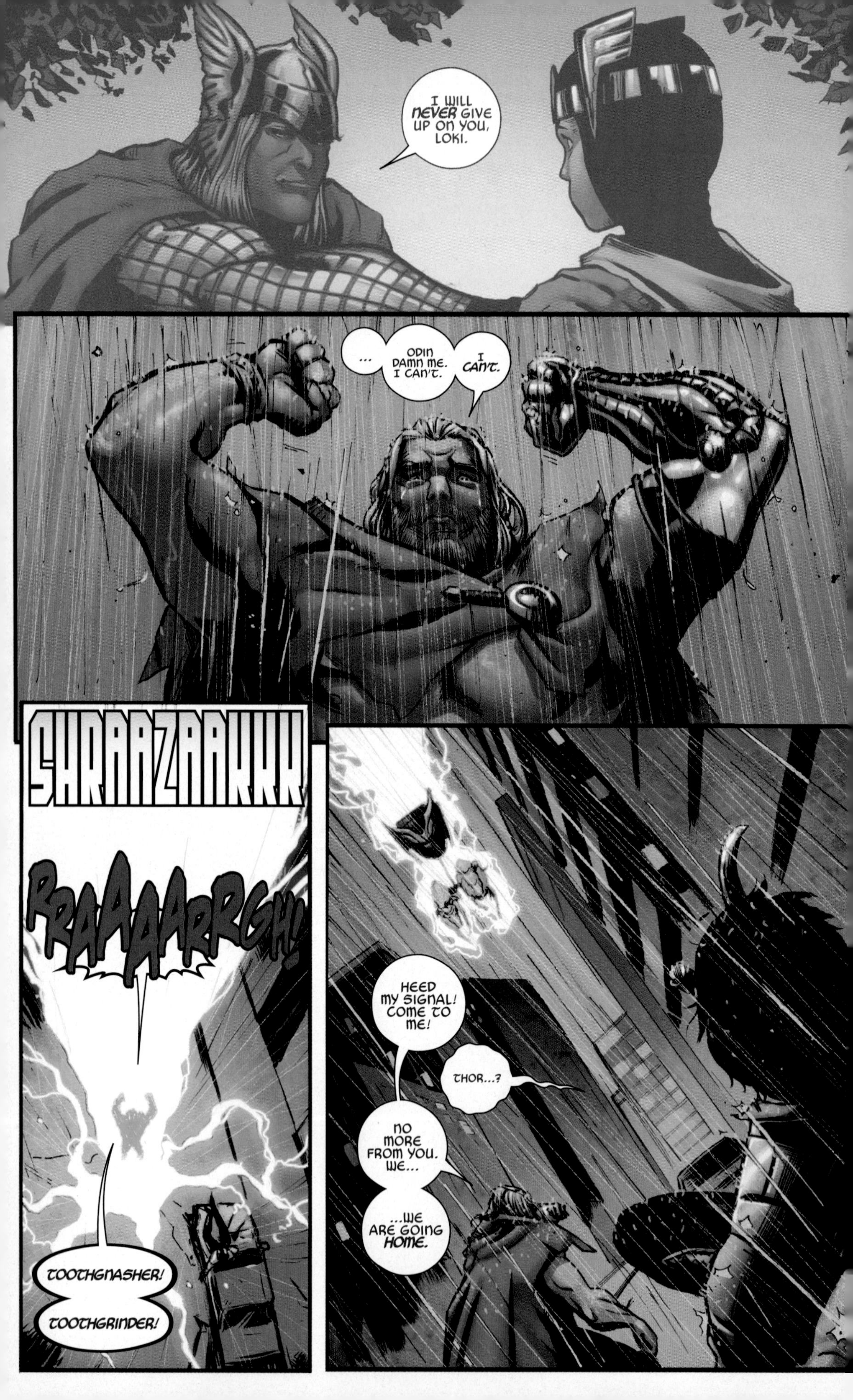
I WILL NEVER GIVE UP ON YOU, LOKI.
...
ODIN DAMN ME. I CAN'T.
I CAN'T.
SHRAAZAAKKK
RRAAAAARRGH!
TOOTHGNASHER!
TOOTHGRINDER!
HEED MY SIGNAL! COME TO ME!
THOR...?
NO MORE FROM YOU. WE...
...WE ARE GOING HOME.

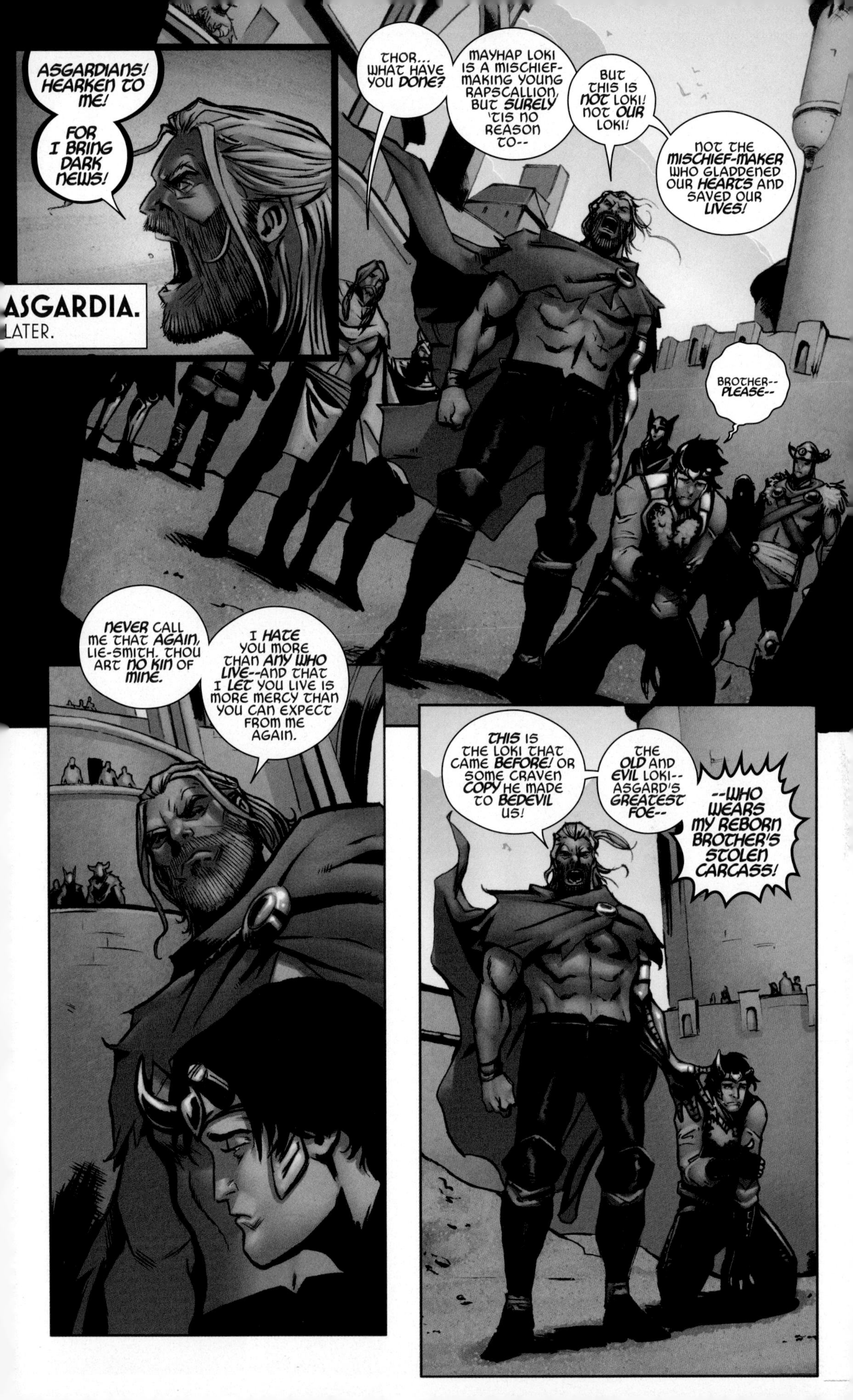

ASGARDIANS! HEARKEN TO ME!
FOR I BRING DARK NEWS!
ASGARDIA.
LATER.
THOR... WHAT HAVE YOU DONE?
MAYHAP LOKI IS A MISCHIEF-MAKING YOUNG RAPSCALLION, BUT SURELY 'TIS NO REASON TO--
BUT THIS IS NOT LOKI! NOT OUR LOKI!
NOT THE MISCHIEF-MAKER WHO GLADDENED OUR HEARTS AND SAVED OUR LIVES!
BROTHER-- PLEASE--
NEVER CALL ME THAT AGAIN, LIE-SMITH. THOU ART NO KIN OF MINE.
I HATE YOU MORE THAN ANY WHO LIVE--AND THAT I LET YOU LIVE IS MORE MERCY THAN YOU CAN EXPECT FROM ME AGAIN.
THIS IS THE LOKI THAT CAME BEFORE! OR SOME CRAVEN COPY HE MADE TO BEDEVIL US!
THE OLD AND EVIL LOKI-- ASGARD'S GREATEST FOE--
--WHO WEARS MY REBORN BROTHER'S STOLEN CARCASS!

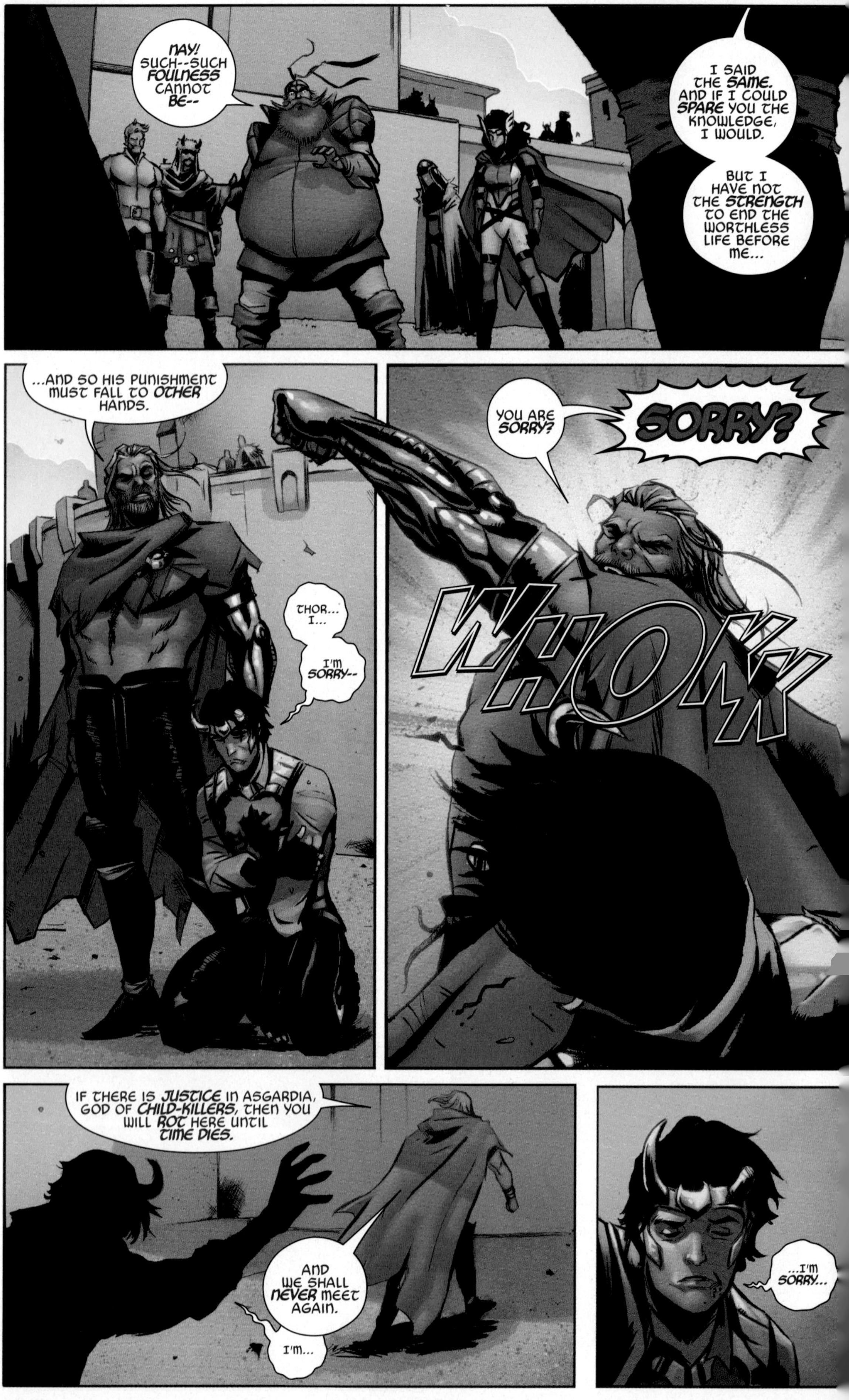
NAY! SUCH--SUCH FOULNESS CANNOT BE--
I SAID THE SAME. AND IF I COULD SPARE YOU THE KNOWLEDGE, I WOULD.
BUT I HAVE NOT THE STRENGTH TO END THE WORTHLESS LIFE BEFORE ME...
...AND SO HIS PUNISHMENT MUST FALL TO OTHER HANDS.
THOR... I...
I'M SORRY--
YOU ARE SORRY?
SORRY?
WHOK
IF THERE IS JUSTICE IN ASGARDIA, GOD OF CHILD-KILLERS, THEN YOU WILL ROT HERE UNTIL TIME DIES.
AND WE SHALL NEVER MEET AGAIN.
I'M...
...I'M SORRY...

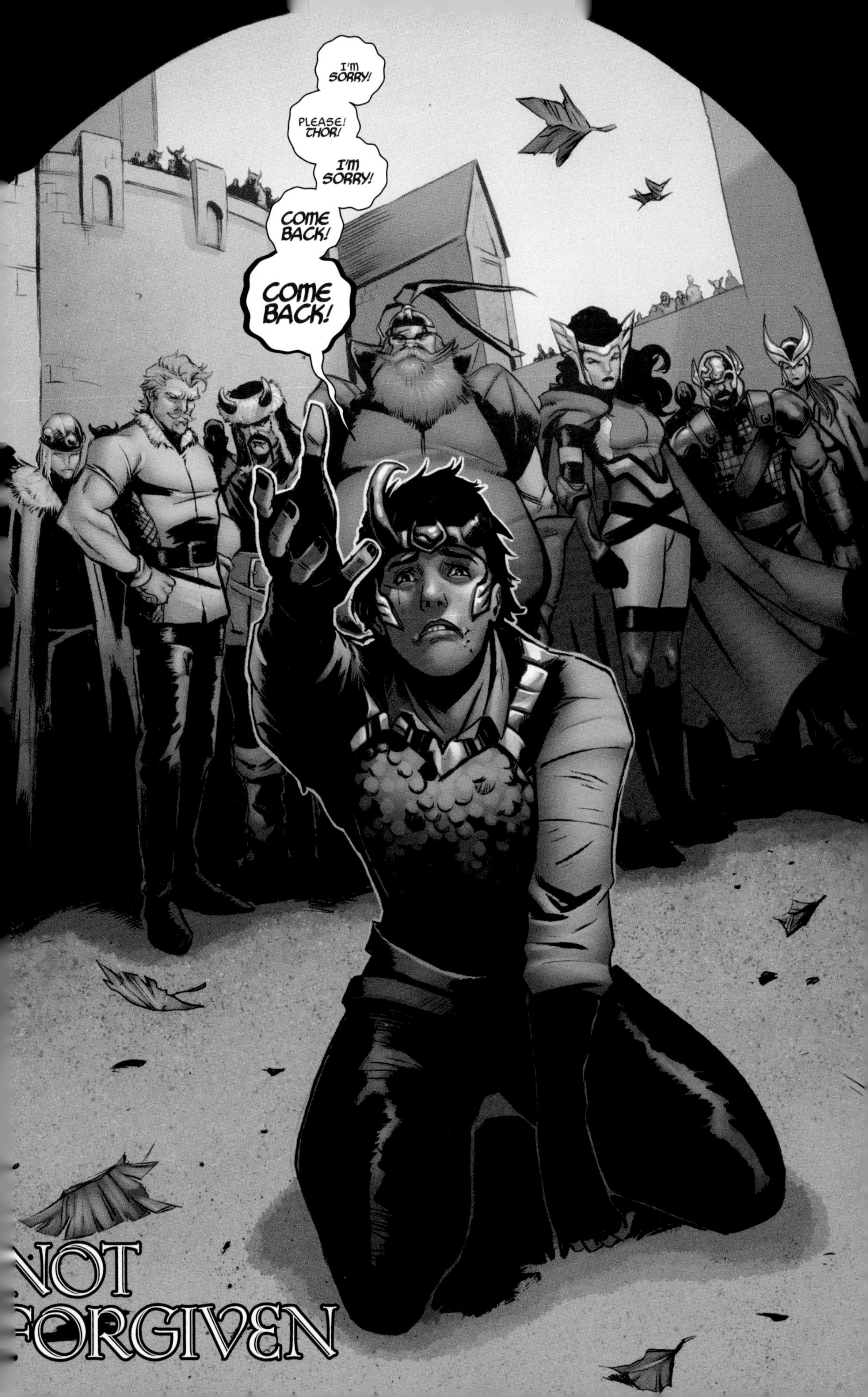

I'M SORRY!
PLEASE! THOR!
I'M SORRY!
COME BACK!
COME BACK!
NOT FORGIVEN

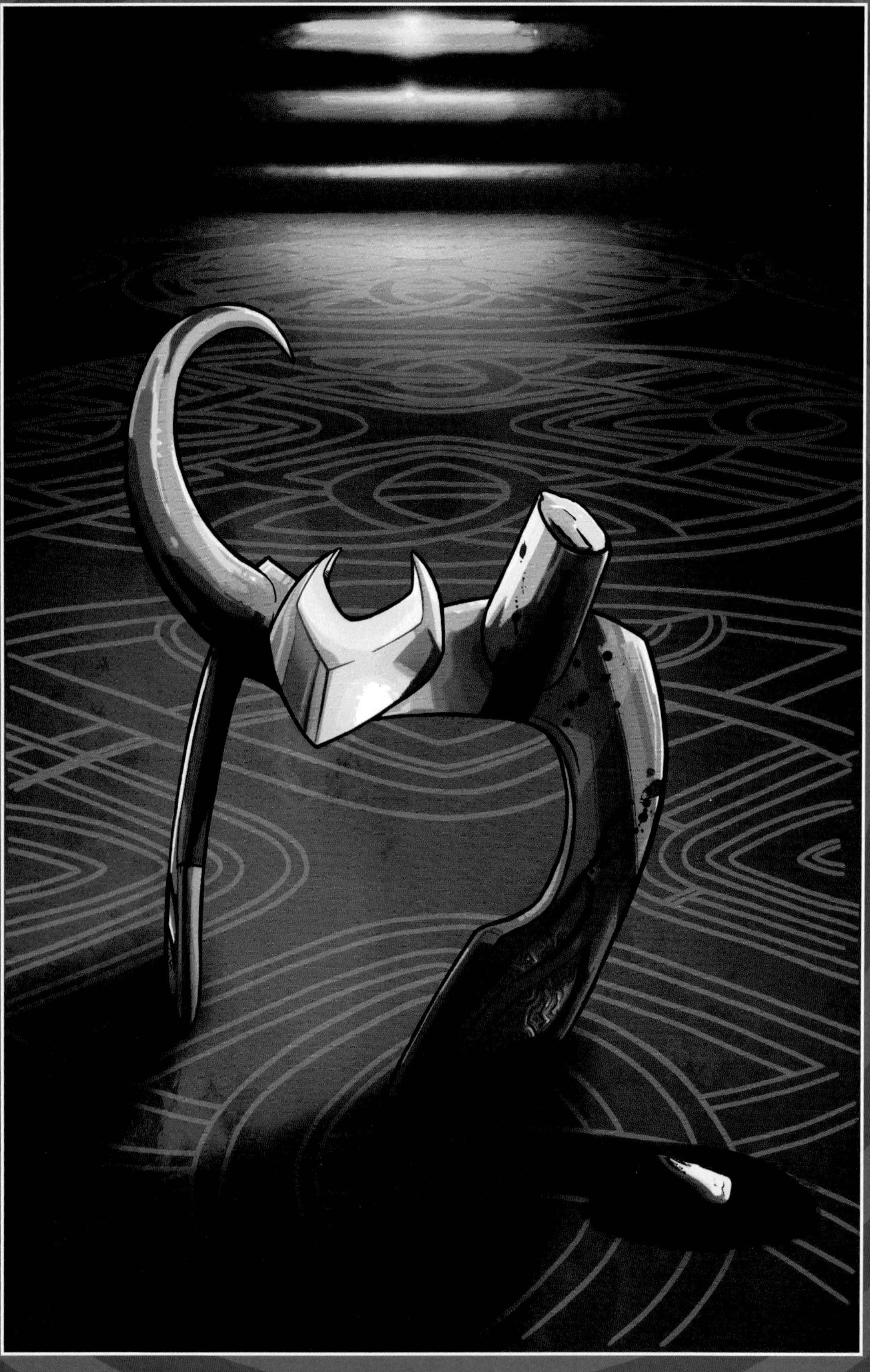

LOKI: AGENT OF ASGARD #11

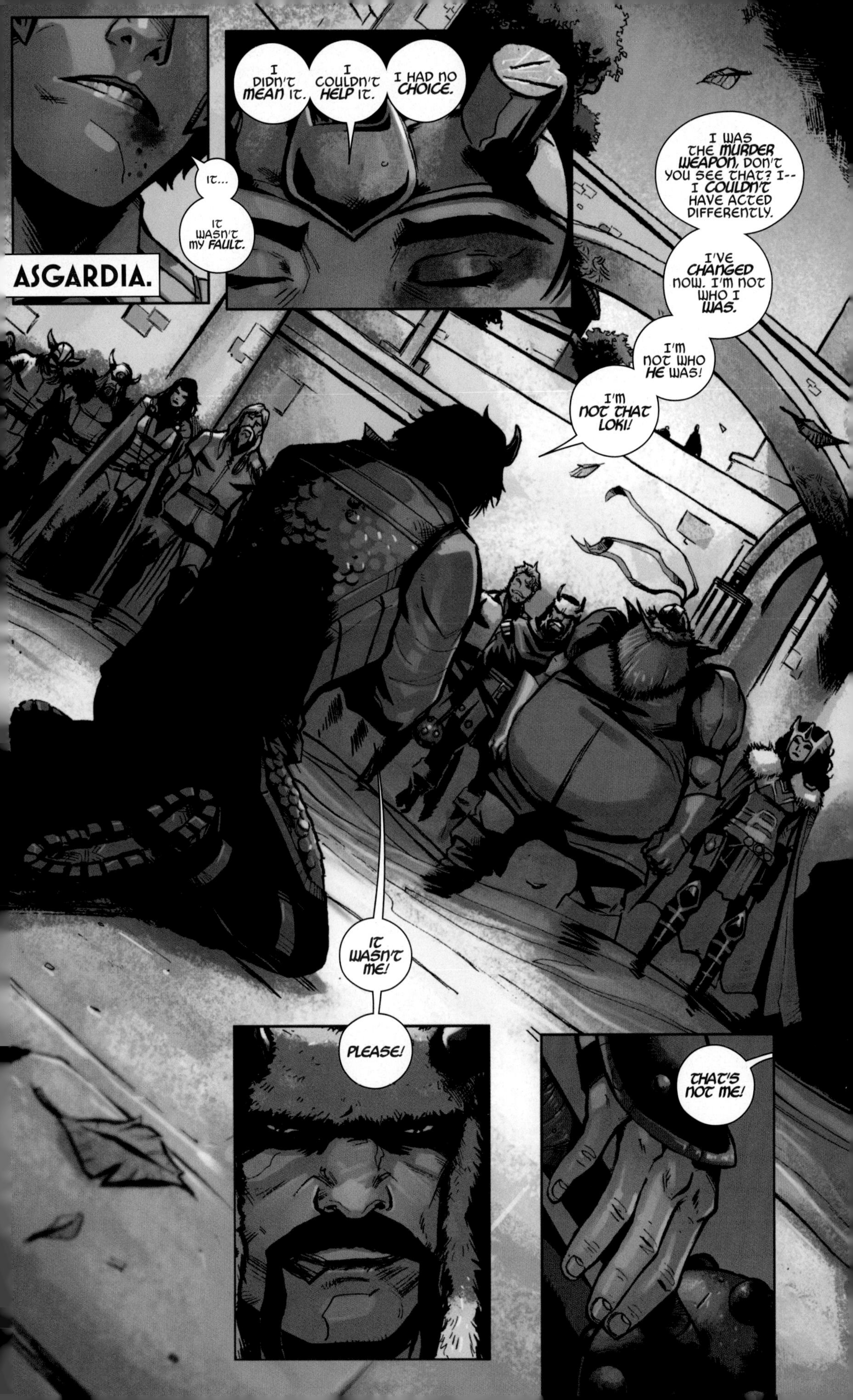
ASGARDIA.
IT...
IT WASN'T MY FAULT.
I DIDN'T MEAN IT.
I COULDN'T HELP IT.
I HAD NO CHOICE.
I WAS THE MURDER WEAPON, DON'T YOU SEE THAT? I-- I COULDN'T HAVE ACTED DIFFERENTLY.
I'VE CHANGED NOW. I'M NOT WHO I WAS.
I'M NOT WHO HE WAS!
I'M NOT THAT LOKI!
IT WASN'T ME!
PLEASE!
THAT'S NOT ME!

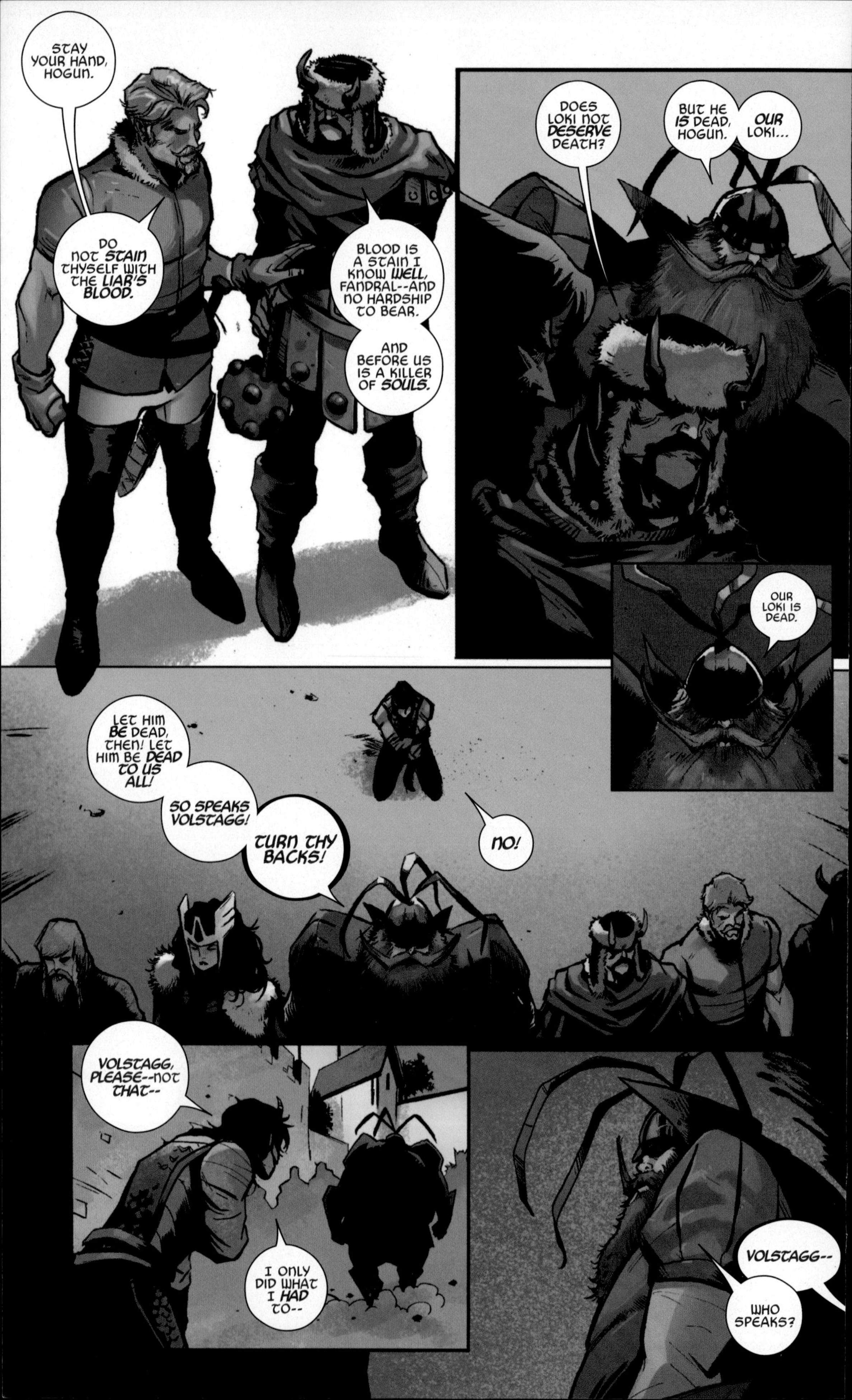
STAY YOUR HAND, HOGUN.
DO NOT STAIN THYSELF WITH THE LIAR'S BLOOD.
BLOOD IS A STAIN I KNOW WELL, FANDRAL--AND NO HARDSHIP TO BEAR.
AND BEFORE US IS A KILLER OF SOULS.
DOES LOKI NOT DESERVE DEATH?
BUT HE IS DEAD, HOGUN.
OUR LOKI...
OUR LOKI IS DEAD.
LET HIM BE DEAD, THEN! LET HIM BE DEAD TO US ALL!
SO SPEAKS VOLSTAGG!
TURN THY BACKS!
NO!
VOLSTAGG, PLEASE--NOT THAT--
I ONLY DID WHAT I HAD TO--
VOLSTAGG--
WHO SPEAKS?

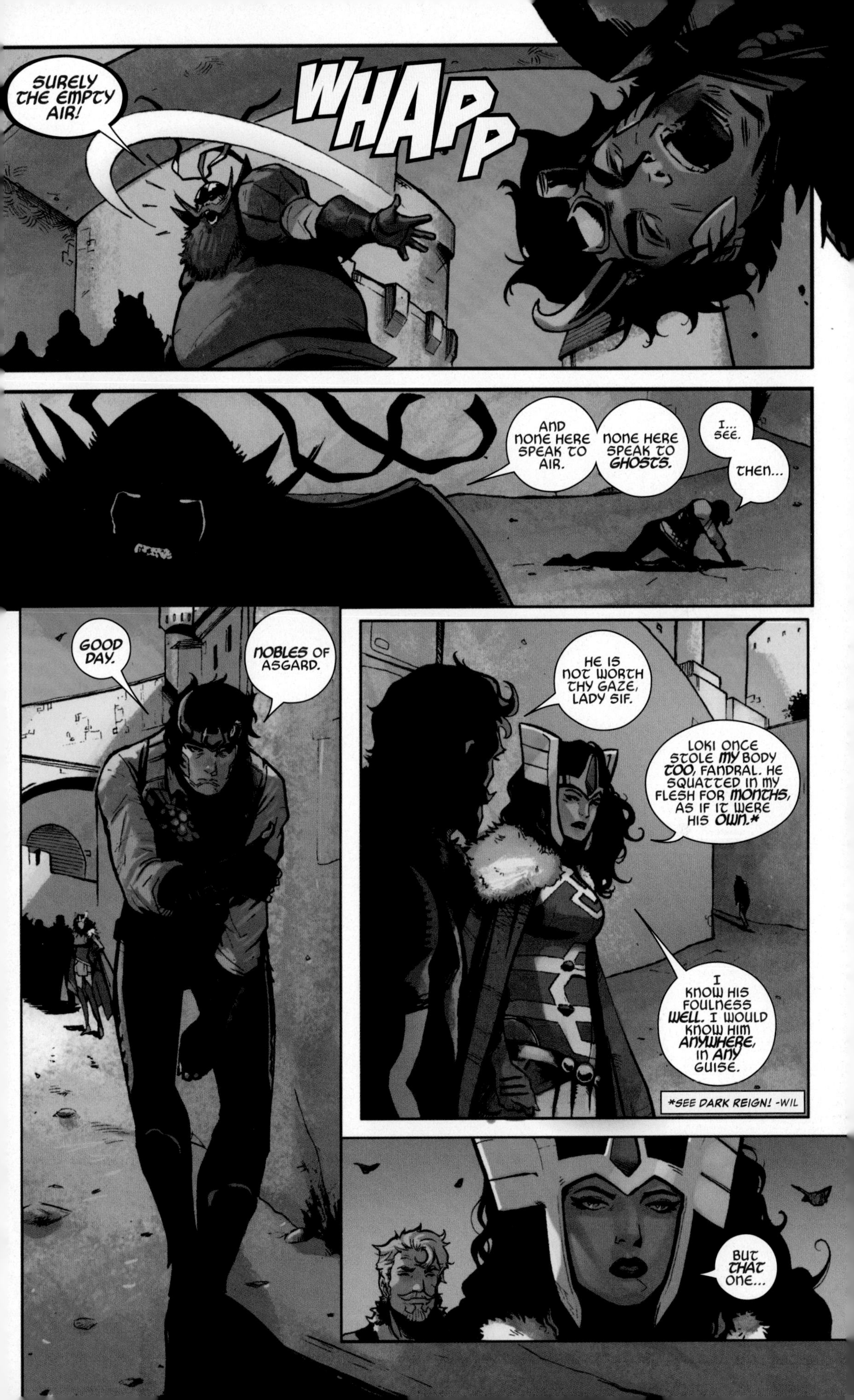
SURELY THE EMPTY AIR!
WHAPP
AND NONE HERE SPEAK TO AIR.
NONE HERE SPEAK TO GHOSTS.
I... SEE.
THEN...
GOOD DAY.
NOBLES OF ASGARD.
HE IS NOT WORTH THY GAZE, LADY SIF.
LOKI ONCE STOLE MY BODY TOO, FANDRAL. HE SQUATTED IN MY FLESH FOR MONTHS, AS IF IT WERE HIS OWN.*
I KNOW HIS FOULNESS WELL. I WOULD KNOW HIM ANYWHERE, IN ANY GUISE.
*SEE DARK REIGN! -WIL
BUT THAT ONE...

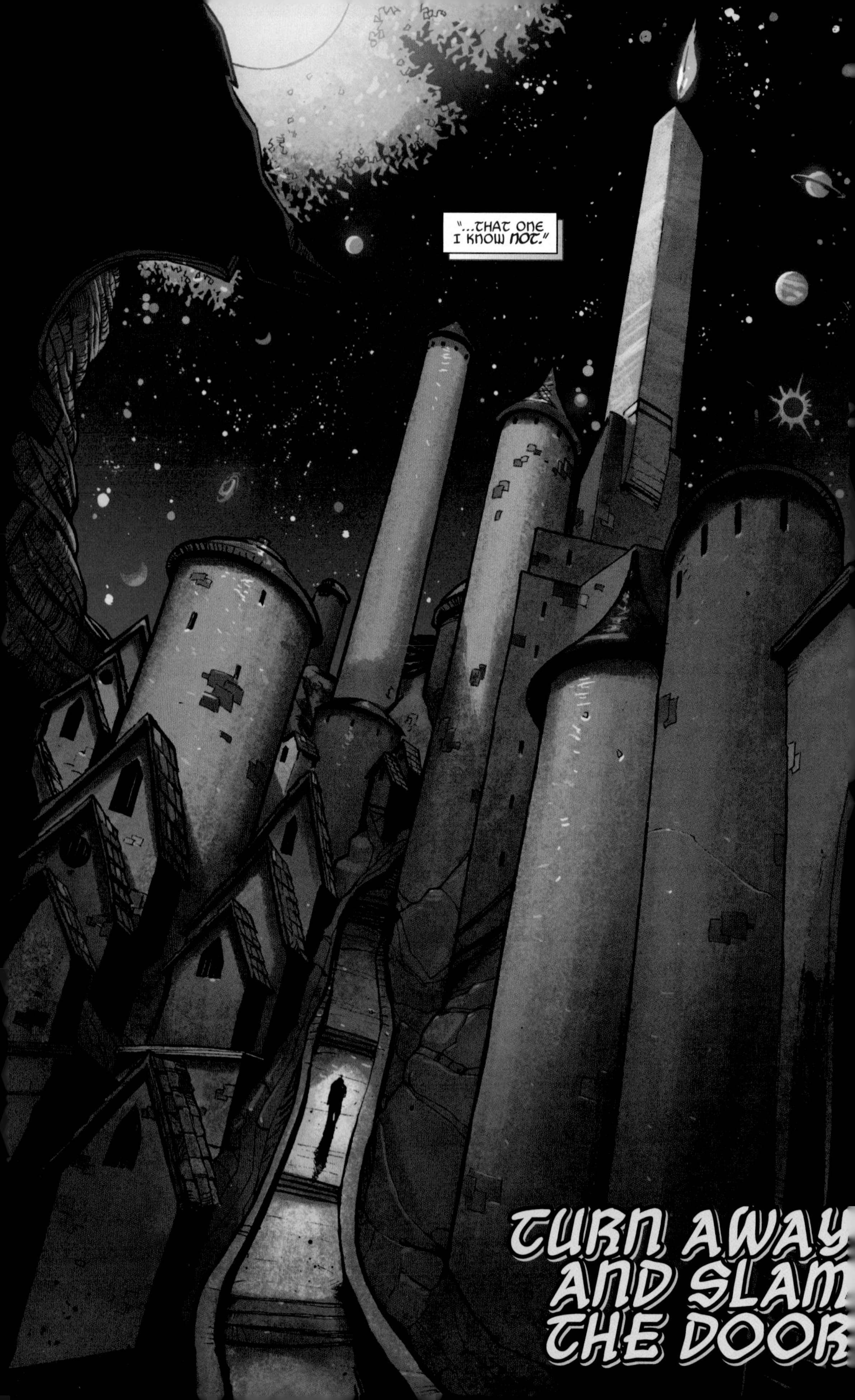
"...THAT ONE I KNOW NOT."
TURN AWAY AND SLAM THE DOOR

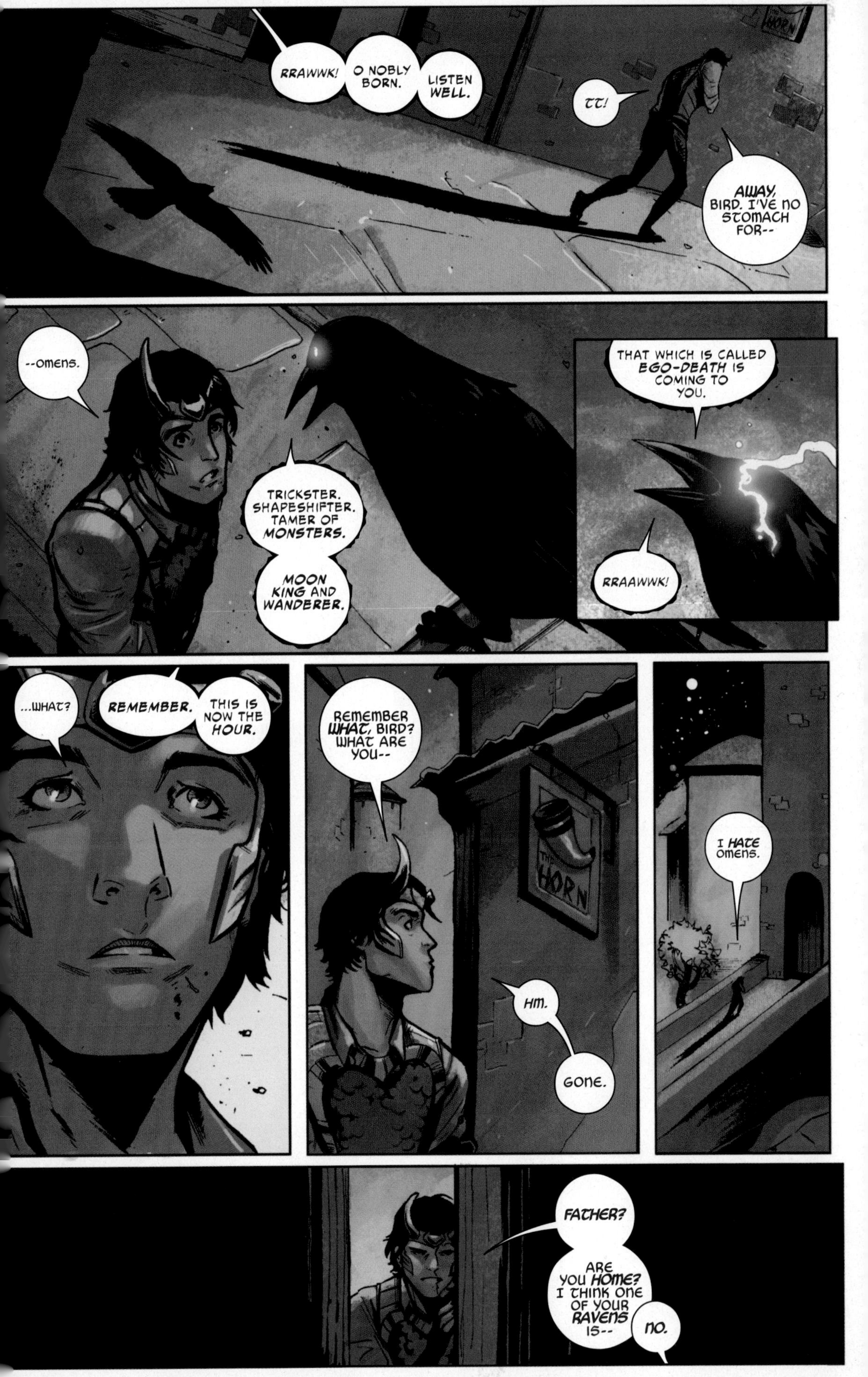
RRAWWK!
O NOBLY BORN.
LISTEN WELL.
TT!
AWAY, BIRD. I'VE NO STOMACH FOR--
--OMENS.
TRICKSTER. SHAPESHIFTER. TAMER OF MONSTERS.
MOON KING AND WANDERER.
THAT WHICH IS CALLED EGO-DEATH IS COMING TO YOU.
RRAAWWK!
...WHAT?
REMEMBER.
THIS IS NOW THE HOUR.
REMEMBER WHAT, BIRD? WHAT ARE YOU--
THE HORN
HM.
GONE.
I HATE OMENS.
FATHER?
ARE YOU HOME? I THINK ONE OF YOUR RAVENS IS--
NO.

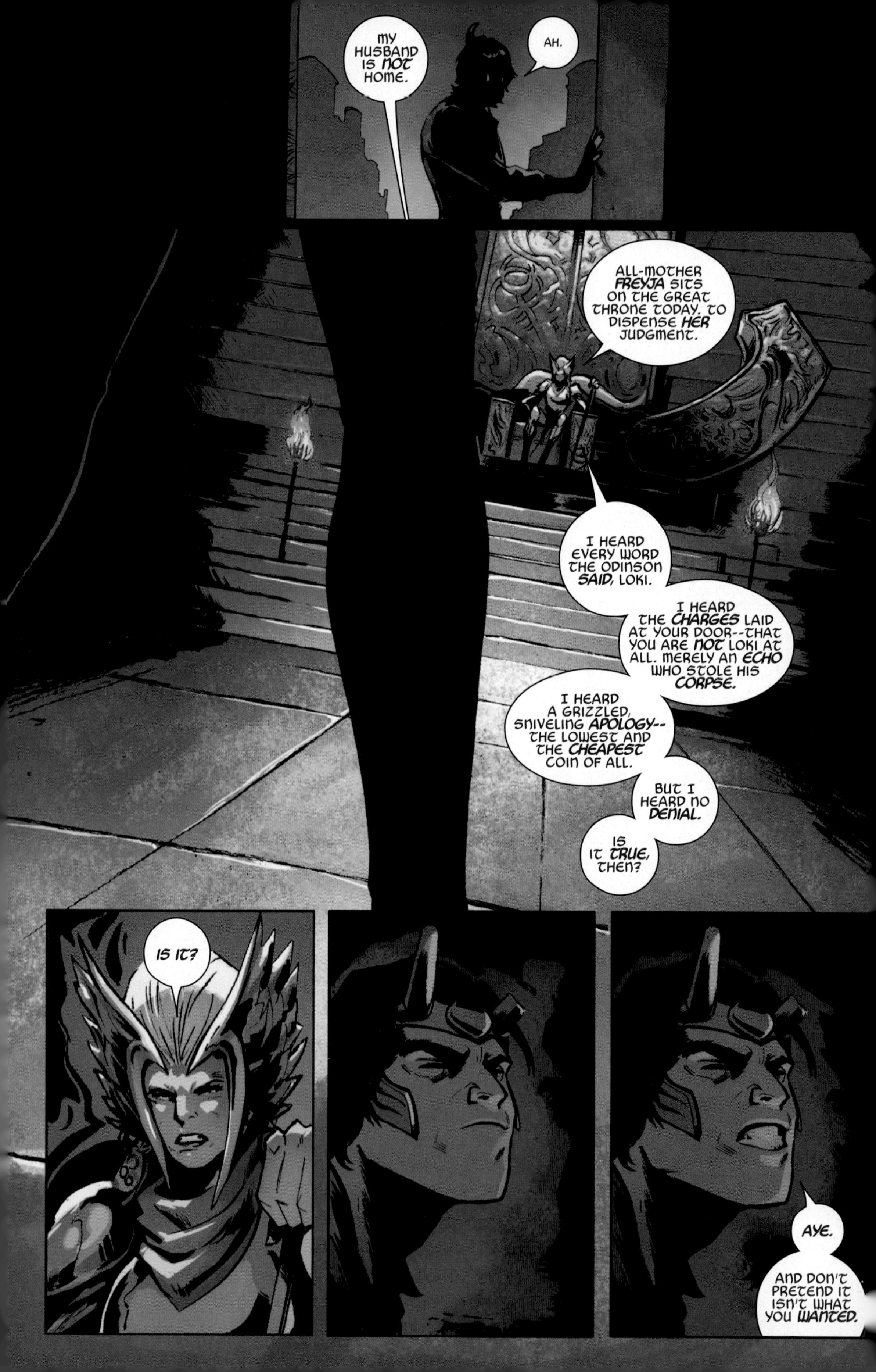
MY HUSBAND IS NOT HOME.
AH.
ALL-MOTHER FREYJA SITS ON THE GREAT THRONE TODAY. TO DISPENSE HER JUDGMENT.
I HEARD EVERY WORD THE ODINSON SAID, LOKI.
I HEARD THE CHARGES LAID AT YOUR DOOR--THAT YOU ARE NOT LOKI AT ALL. MERELY AN ECHO WHO STOLE HIS CORPSE.
I HEARD A GRIZZLED, SNIVELING APOLOGY--THE LOWEST AND THE CHEAPEST COIN OF ALL.
BUT I HEARD NO DENIAL.
IS IT TRUE, THEN?
IS IT?
AYE.
AND DON'T PRETEND IT ISN'T WHAT YOU WANTED.

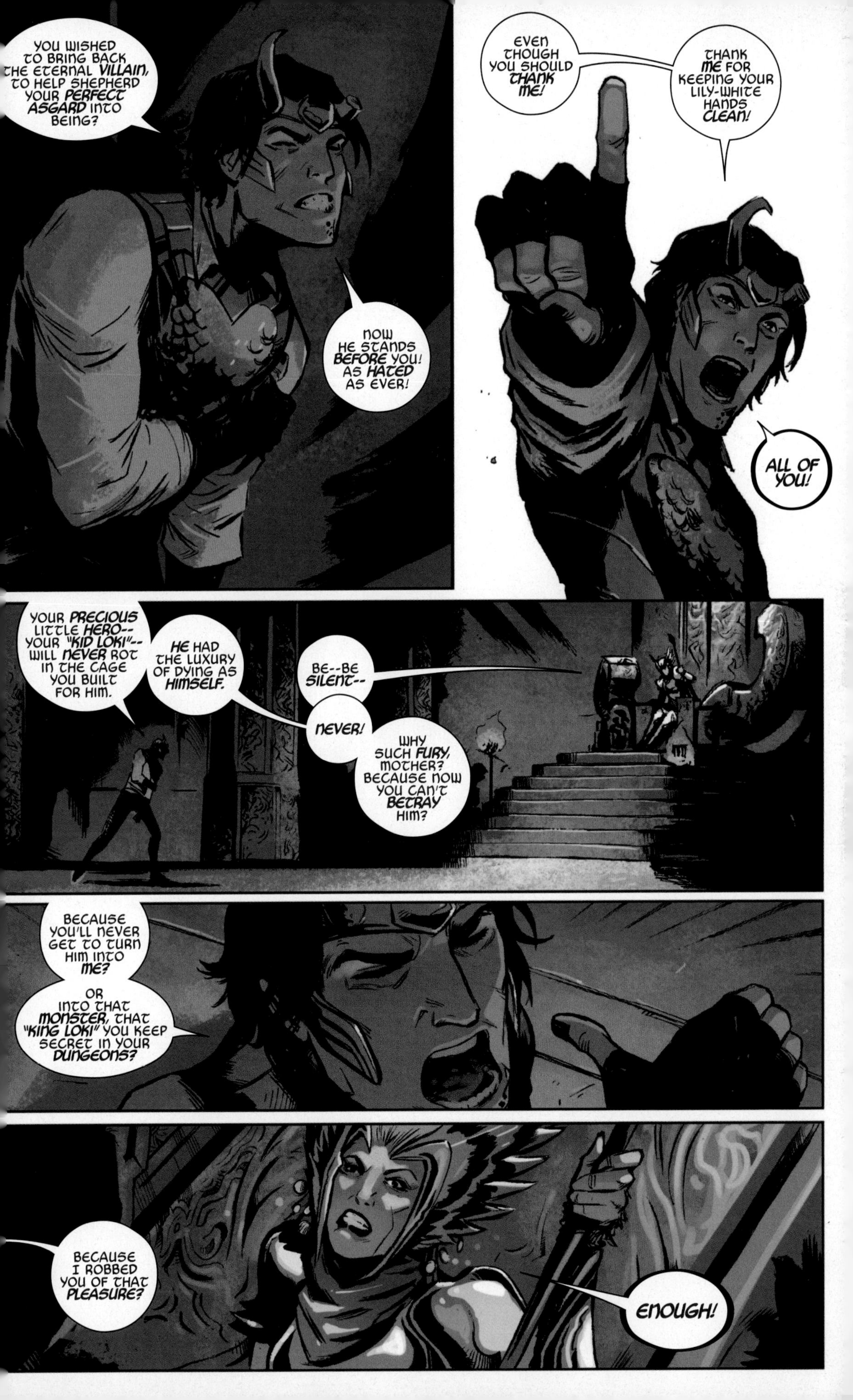
YOU WISHED TO BRING BACK THE ETERNAL VILLAIN, TO HELP SHEPHERD YOUR PERFECT ASGARD INTO BEING?
NOW HE STANDS BEFORE YOU! AS HATED AS EVER!
EVEN THOUGH YOU SHOULD THANK ME!
THANK ME FOR KEEPING YOUR LILY-WHITE HANDS CLEAN!
ALL OF YOU!
YOUR PRECIOUS LITTLE HERO-- YOUR "KID LOKI"-- WILL NEVER ROT IN THE CAGE YOU BUILT FOR HIM.
HE HAD THE LUXURY OF DYING AS HIMSELF.
BE--BE SILENT--
NEVER!
WHY SUCH FURY, MOTHER? BECAUSE NOW YOU CAN'T BETRAY HIM?
BECAUSE YOU'LL NEVER GET TO TURN HIM INTO ME?
OR INTO THAT MONSTER, THAT "KING LOKI" YOU KEEP SECRET IN YOUR DUNGEONS?
BECAUSE I ROBBED YOU OF THAT PLEASURE?
ENOUGH!

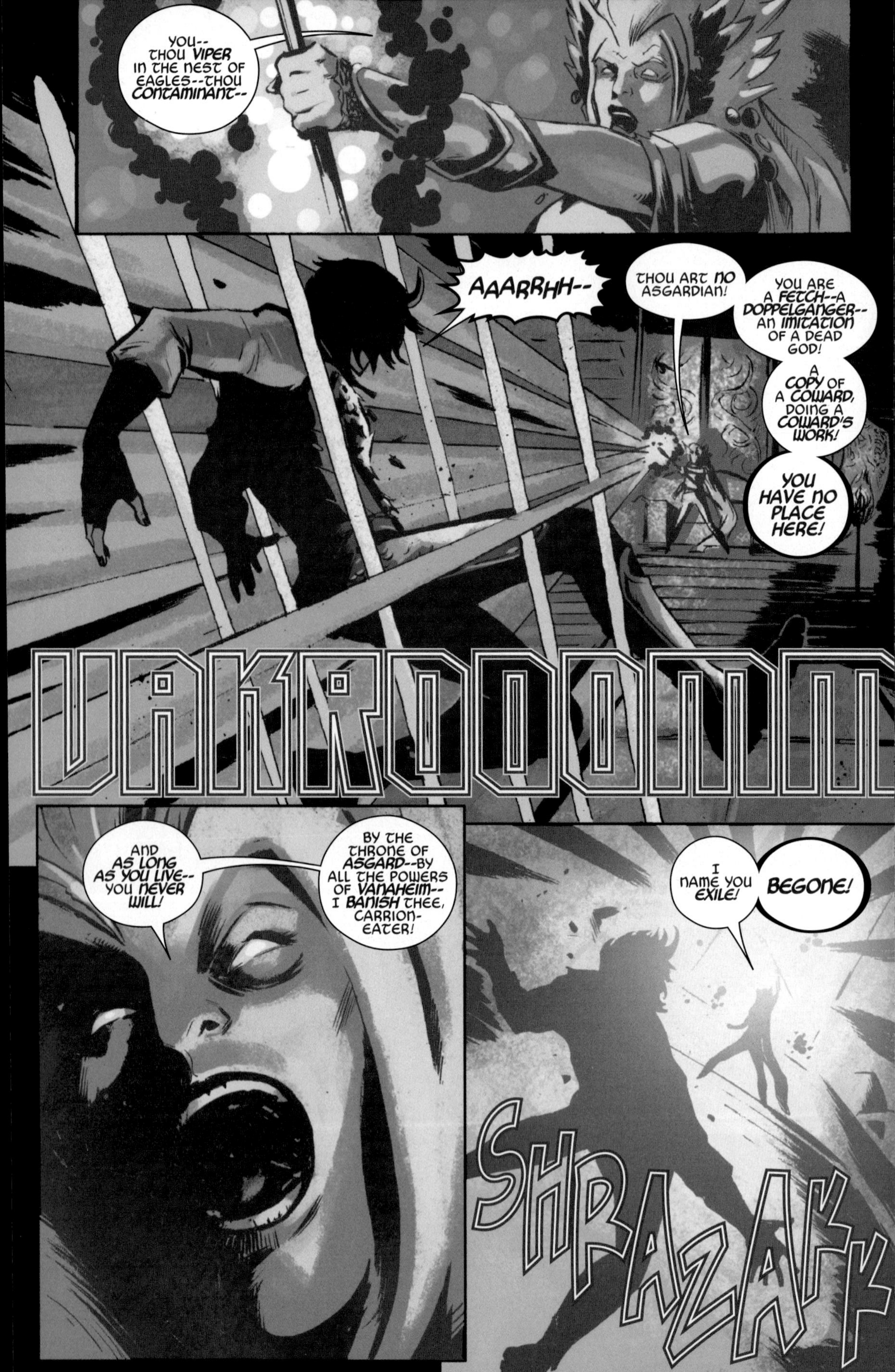
YOU-- THOU VIPER IN THE NEST OF EAGLES--THOU CONTAMINANT--
AAARRHH--
THOU ART NO ASGARDIAN!
YOU ARE A FETCH--A DOPPELGANGER--AN IMITATION OF A DEAD GOD!
A COPY OF A COWARD, DOING A COWARD'S WORK!
YOU HAVE NO PLACE HERE!
VAKROOMM
AND AS LONG AS YOU LIVE--YOU NEVER WILL!
BY THE THRONE OF ASGARD--BY ALL THE POWERS OF VANAHEIM--I BANISH THEE, CARRION-EATER!
I NAME YOU EXILE!
BEGONE!
SHRAZAKK

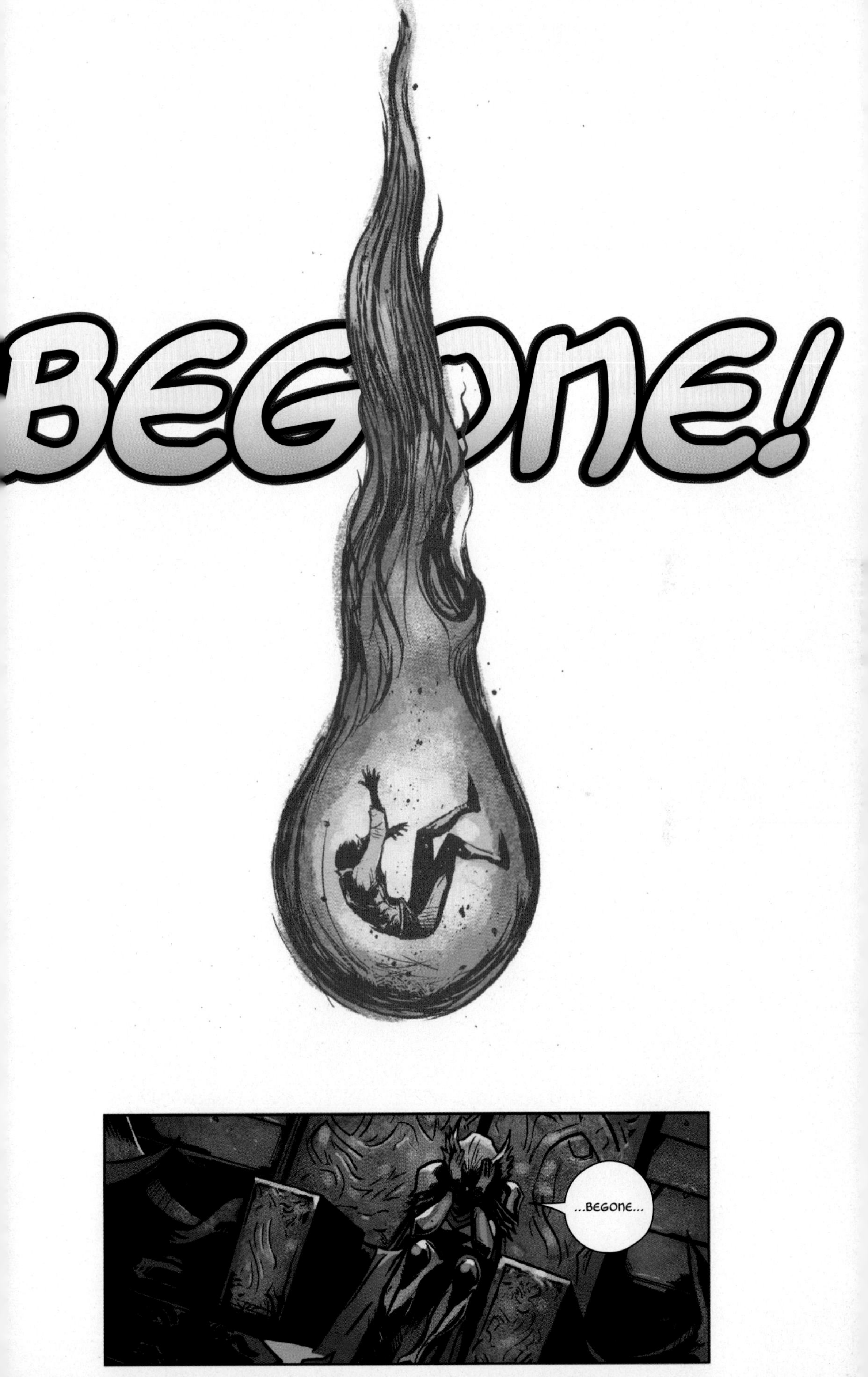
BEGONE!
...BEGONE...

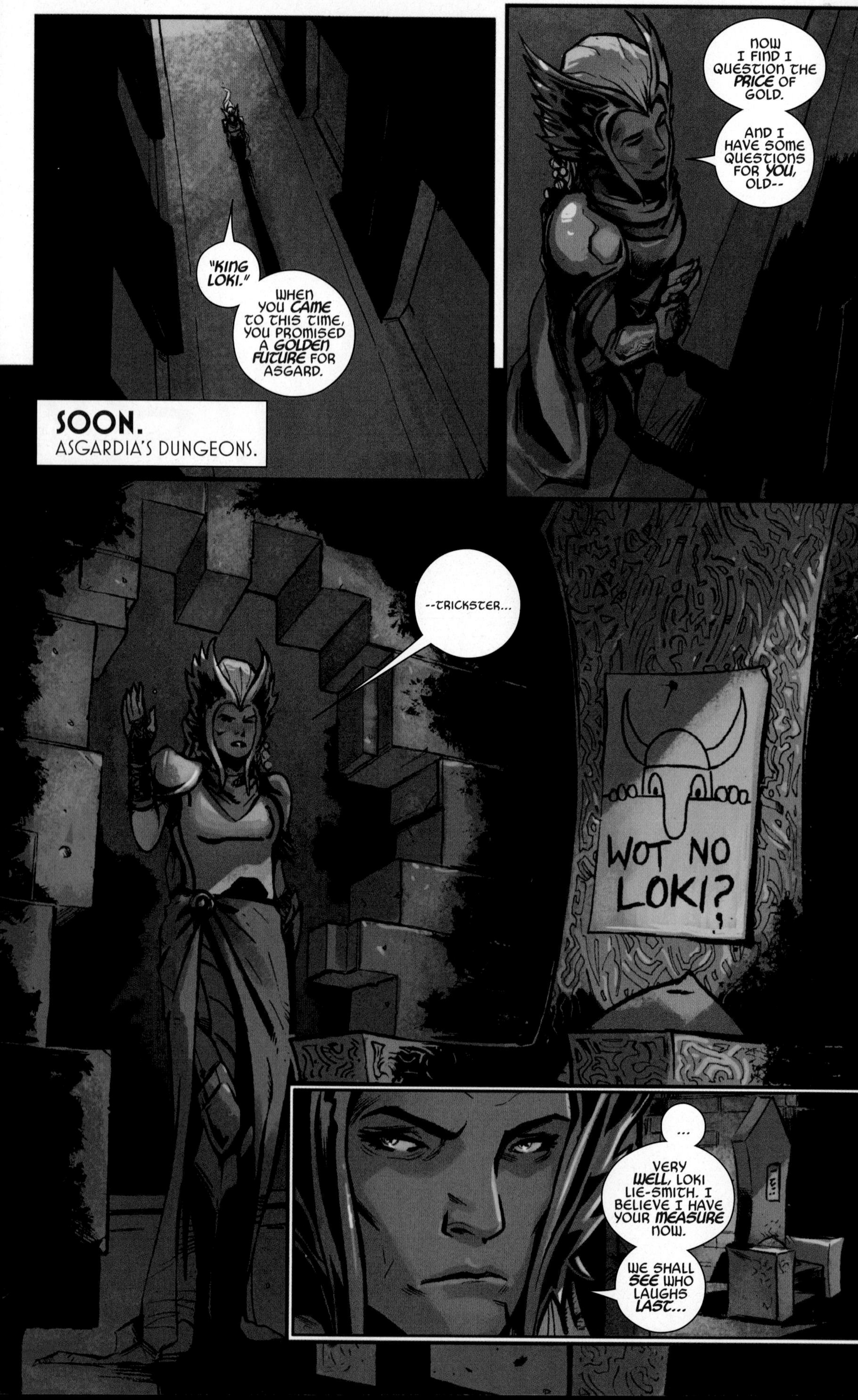
"KING LOKI."
WHEN YOU CAME TO THIS TIME, YOU PROMISED A GOLDEN FUTURE FOR ASGARD.
SOON.
ASGARDIA'S DUNGEONS.
NOW I FIND I QUESTION THE PRICE OF GOLD.
AND I HAVE SOME QUESTIONS FOR YOU, OLD--
--TRICKSTER...
WOT NO LOKI?
...
VERY WELL, LOKI LIE-SMITH. I BELIEVE I HAVE YOUR MEASURE NOW.
WE SHALL SEE WHO LAUGHS LAST...

ELSEWHERE...
There is a space that is not a space.
A space between the Ten Realms.
The journey depends on the traveller.
Sometimes it is as epic in scope as the stars themselves.
Sometimes the road is as hard as a vast desert.
And sometimes it is very long... and very cold...
...and it must be walked alone.
FATHER?

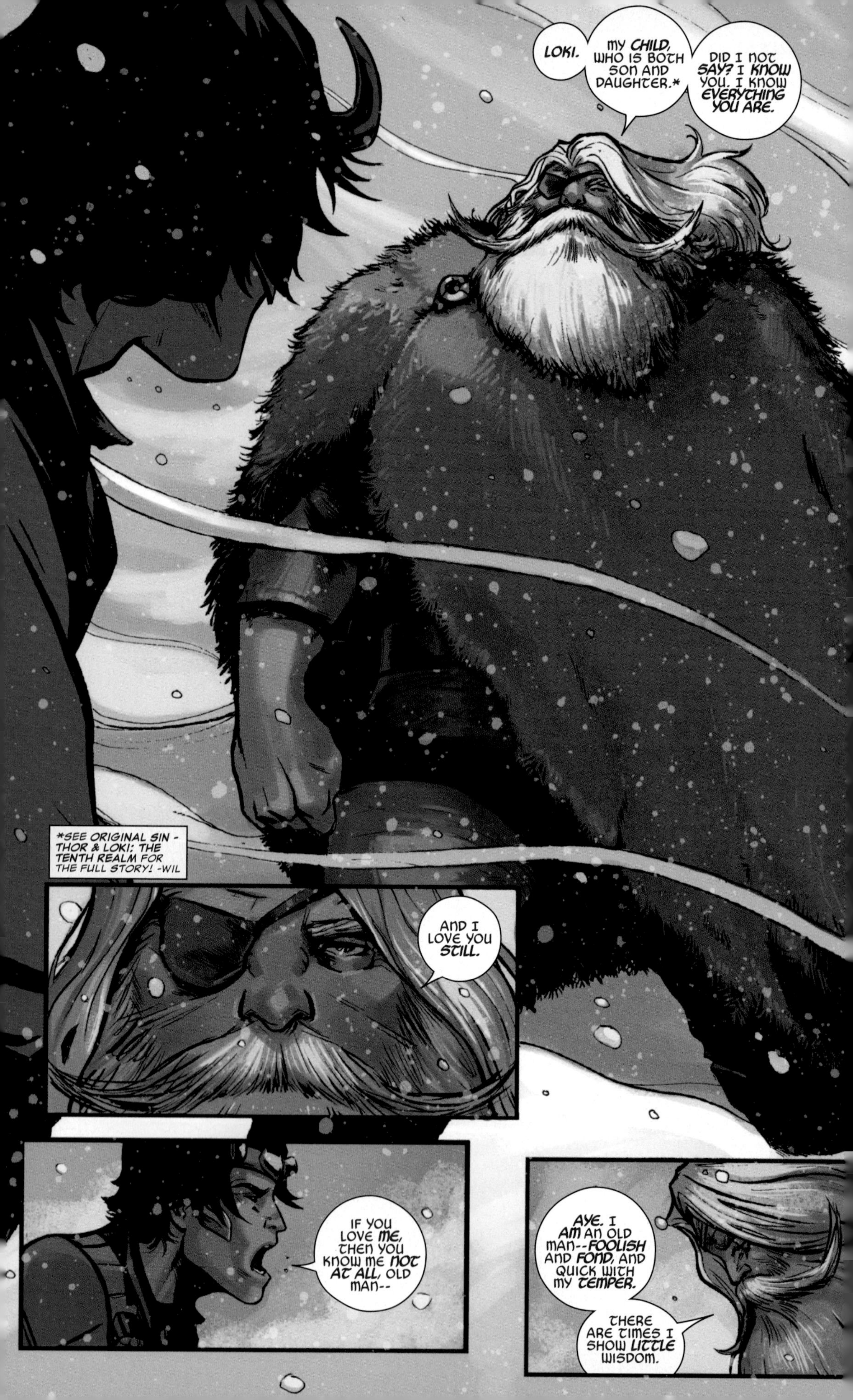
LOKI.
MY CHILD, WHO IS BOTH SON AND DAUGHTER.*
DID I NOT SAY? I KNOW YOU. I KNOW EVERYTHING YOU ARE.
*SEE ORIGINAL SIN - THOR & LOKI: THE TENTH REALM FOR THE FULL STORY! -WIL
AND I LOVE YOU STILL.
IF YOU LOVE ME, THEN YOU KNOW ME NOT AT ALL, OLD MAN--
AYE. I AM AN OLD MAN--FOOLISH AND FOND, AND QUICK WITH MY TEMPER.
THERE ARE TIMES I SHOW LITTLE WISDOM.

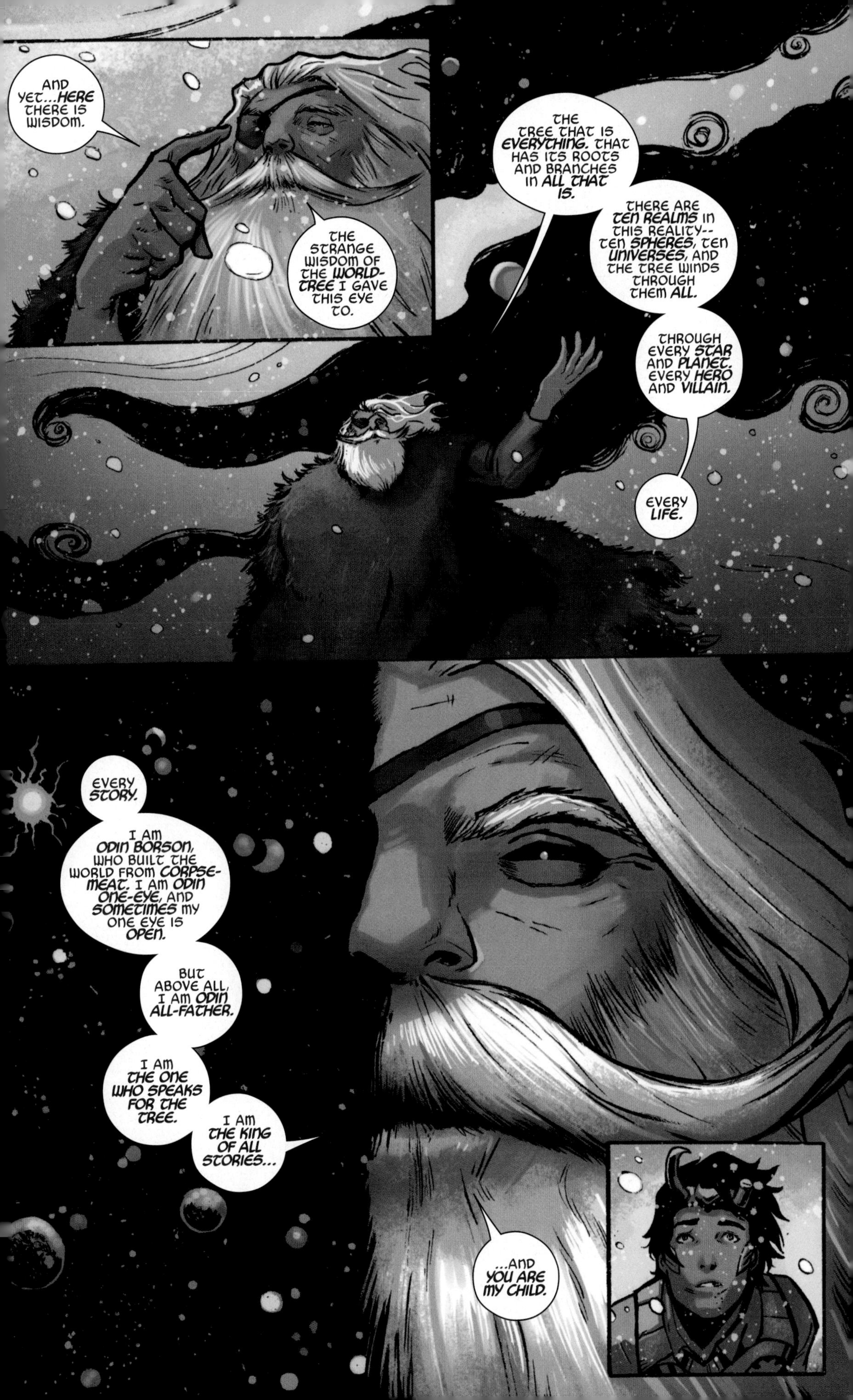
AND YET...HERE THERE IS WISDOM.
THE STRANGE WISDOM OF THE WORLD-TREE I GAVE THIS EYE TO.
THE TREE THAT IS EVERYTHING. THAT HAS ITS ROOTS AND BRANCHES IN ALL THAT IS.
THERE ARE TEN REALMS IN THIS REALITY-- TEN SPHERES, TEN UNIVERSES, AND THE TREE WINDS THROUGH THEM ALL.
THROUGH EVERY STAR AND PLANET. EVERY HERO AND VILLAIN.
EVERY LIFE.
EVERY STORY.
I AM ODIN BORSON, WHO BUILT THE WORLD FROM CORPSE-MEAT. I AM ODIN ONE-EYE, AND SOMETIMES MY ONE EYE IS OPEN.
BUT ABOVE ALL, I AM ODIN ALL-FATHER.
I AM THE ONE WHO SPEAKS FOR THE TREE.
I AM THE KING OF ALL STORIES...
...AND YOU ARE MY CHILD.

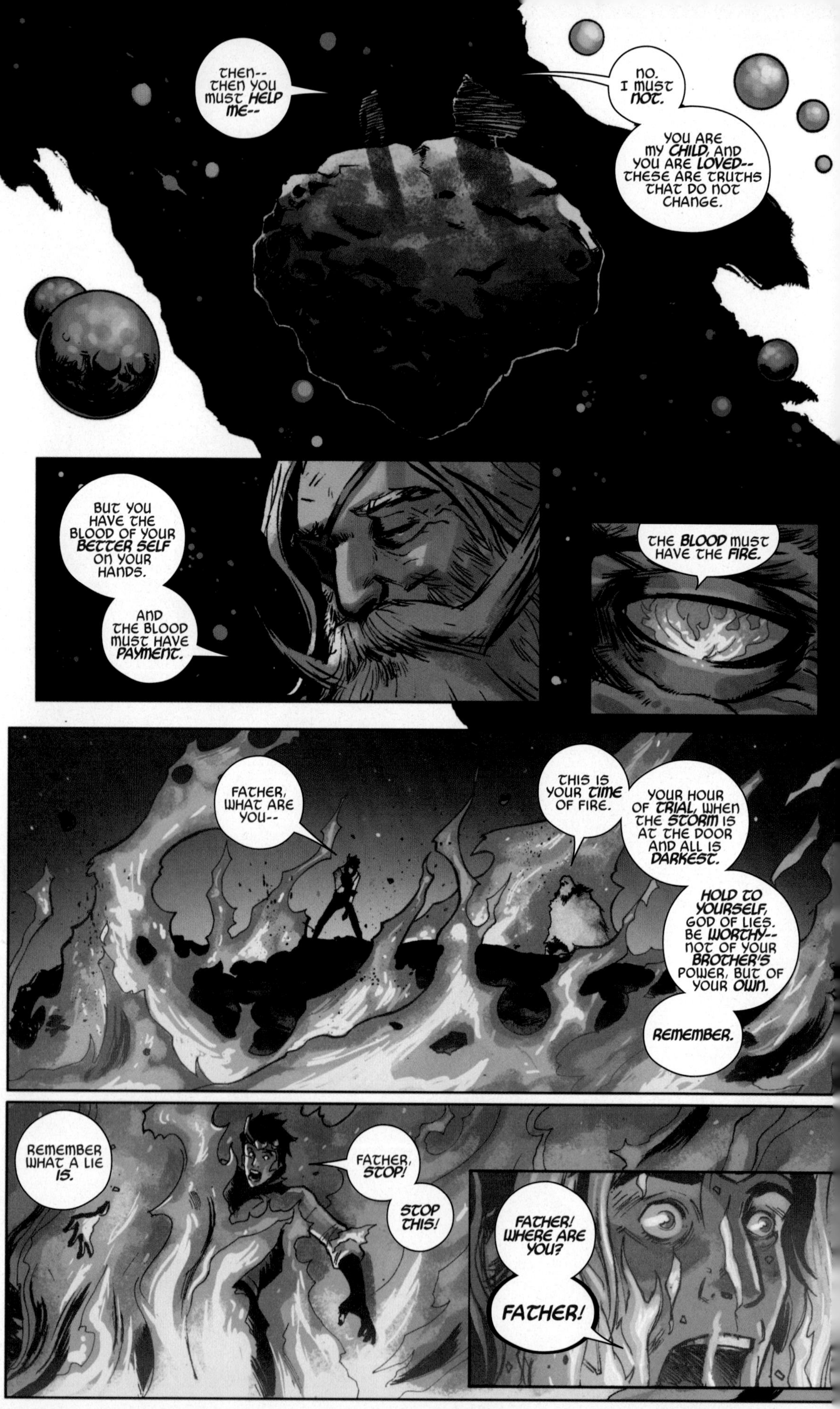
THEN-- THEN YOU MUST HELP ME--
NO. I MUST NOT.
YOU ARE MY CHILD, AND YOU ARE LOVED-- THESE ARE TRUTHS THAT DO NOT CHANGE.
BUT YOU HAVE THE BLOOD OF YOUR BETTER SELF ON YOUR HANDS.
AND THE BLOOD MUST HAVE PAYMENT.
THE BLOOD MUST HAVE THE FIRE.
FATHER, WHAT ARE YOU--
THIS IS YOUR TIME OF FIRE.
YOUR HOUR OF TRIAL, WHEN THE STORM IS AT THE DOOR AND ALL IS DARKEST.
HOLD TO YOURSELF, GOD OF LIES. BE WORTHY-- NOT OF YOUR BROTHER'S POWER, BUT OF YOUR OWN.
REMEMBER.
REMEMBER WHAT A LIE IS.
FATHER, STOP!
STOP THIS!
FATHER! WHERE ARE YOU?
FATHER!

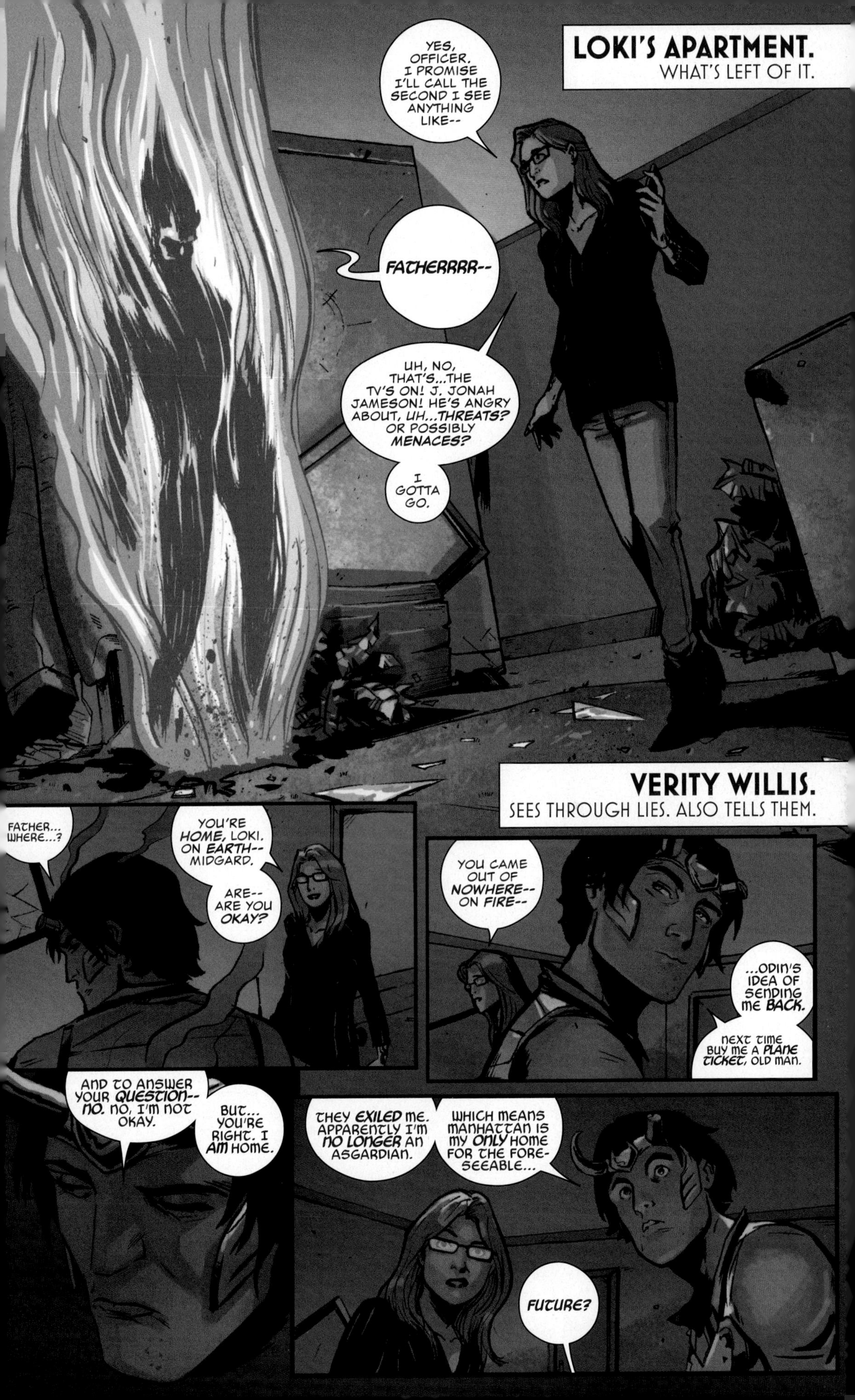

LOKI'S APARTMENT.
WHAT'S LEFT OF IT.
YES, OFFICER. I PROMISE I'LL CALL THE SECOND I SEE ANYTHING LIKE--
FATHERRRR--
UH, NO, THAT'S...THE TV'S ON! J. JONAH JAMESON! HE'S ANGRY ABOUT, UH...THREATS? OR POSSIBLY MENACES?
I GOTTA GO.
VERITY WILLIS.
SEES THROUGH LIES. ALSO TELLS THEM.
FATHER... WHERE...?
YOU'RE HOME, LOKI. ON EARTH-- MIDGARD.
ARE-- ARE YOU OKAY?
YOU CAME OUT OF NOWHERE-- ON FIRE--
...ODIN'S IDEA OF SENDING ME BACK.
NEXT TIME BUY ME A PLANE TICKET, OLD MAN.
AND TO ANSWER YOUR QUESTION-- NO. NO, I'M NOT OKAY.
BUT... YOU'RE RIGHT. I AM HOME.
THEY EXILED ME. APPARENTLY I'M NO LONGER AN ASGARDIAN.
WHICH MEANS MANHATTAN IS MY ONLY HOME FOR THE FORE-SEEABLE...
FUTURE?

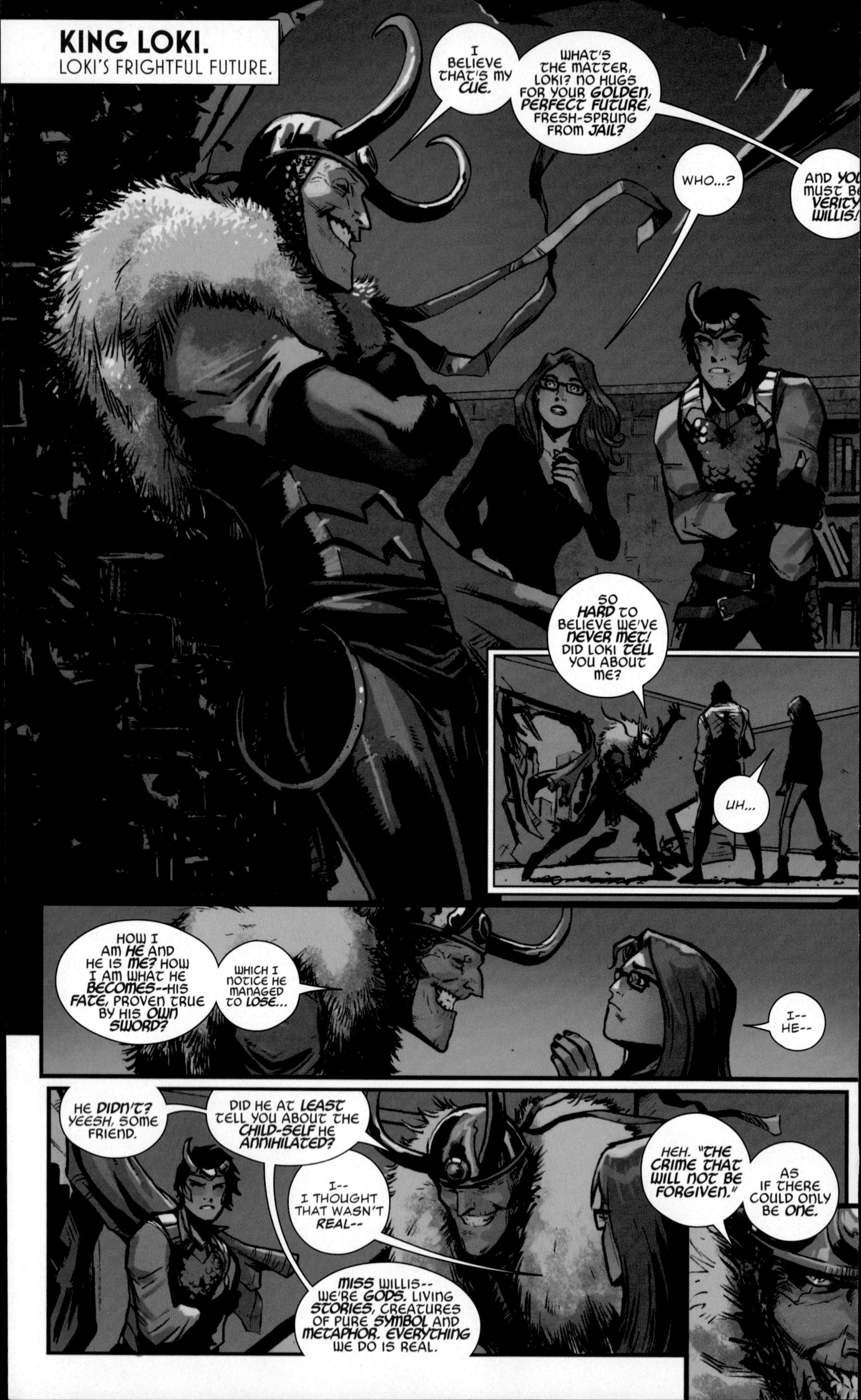
KING LOKI.
LOKI'S FRIGHTFUL FUTURE.
I BELIEVE THAT'S MY CUE.
WHAT'S THE MATTER, LOKI? NO HUGS FOR YOUR GOLDEN, PERFECT FUTURE, FRESH-SPRUNG FROM JAIL?
WHO...?
AND YOU MUST BE VERITY WILLIS!
SO HARD TO BELIEVE WE'VE NEVER MET! DID LOKI TELL YOU ABOUT ME?
UH...
HOW I AM HE AND HE IS ME? HOW I AM WHAT HE BECOMES--HIS FATE, PROVEN TRUE BY HIS OWN SWORD?
WHICH I NOTICE HE MANAGED TO LOSE...
I-- HE--
HE DIDN'T? YEESH, SOME FRIEND.
DID HE AT LEAST TELL YOU ABOUT THE CHILD-SELF HE ANNIHILATED?
I-- I THOUGHT THAT WASN'T REAL--
MISS WILLIS-- WE'RE GODS. LIVING STORIES, CREATURES OF PURE SYMBOL AND METAPHOR. EVERYTHING WE DO IS REAL.
HEH. "THE CRIME THAT WILL NOT BE FORGIVEN."
AS IF THERE COULD ONLY BE ONE.

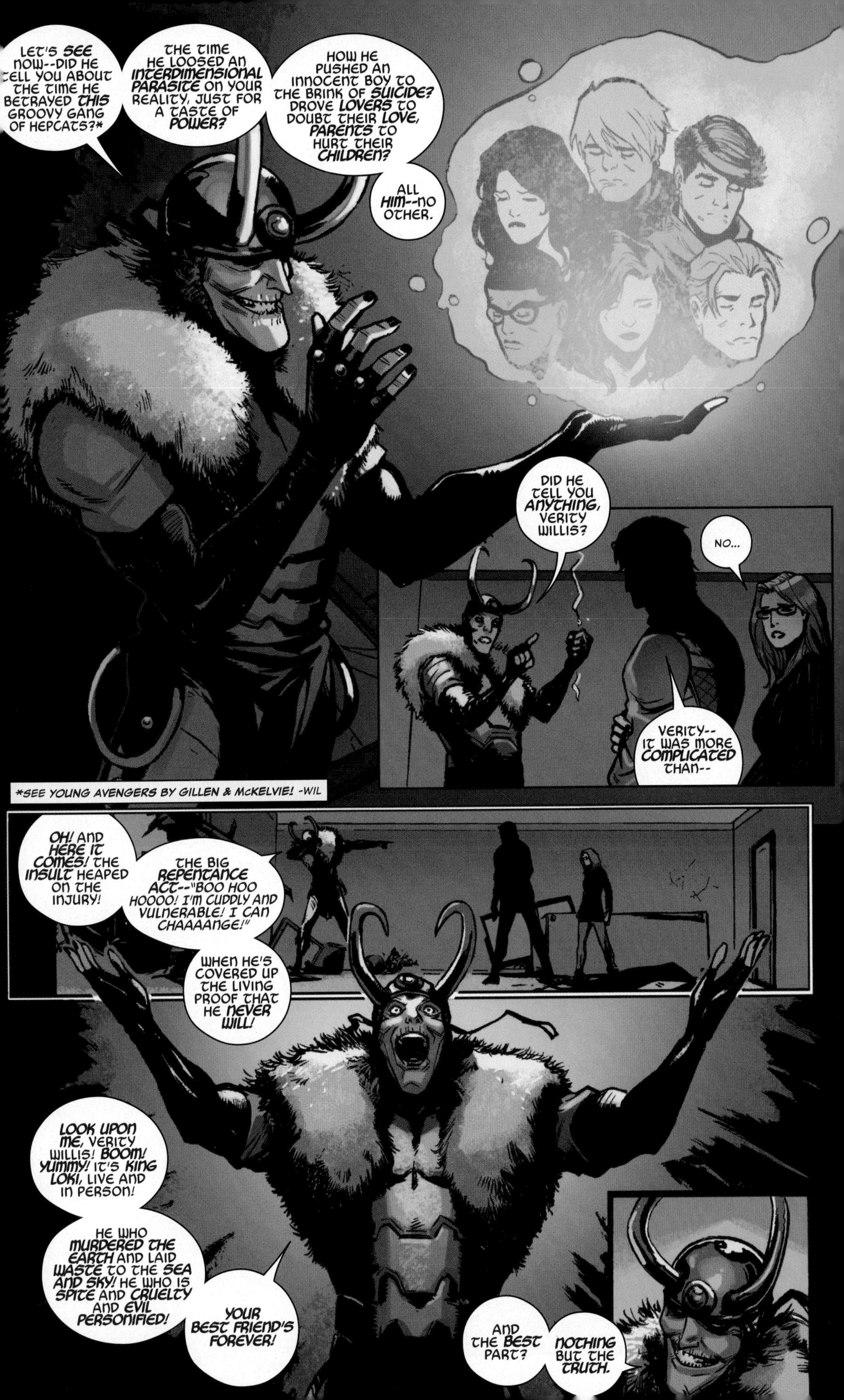
LET'S SEE NOW--DID HE TELL YOU ABOUT THE TIME HE BETRAYED THIS GROOVY GANG OF HEPCATS?*
THE TIME HE LOOSED AN INTERDIMENSIONAL PARASITE ON YOUR REALITY, JUST FOR A TASTE OF POWER?
HOW HE PUSHED AN INNOCENT BOY TO THE BRINK OF SUICIDE? DROVE LOVERS TO DOUBT THEIR LOVE, PARENTS TO HURT THEIR CHILDREN?
ALL HIM--NO OTHER.
DID HE TELL YOU ANYTHING, VERITY WILLIS?
NO...
VERITY--IT WAS MORE COMPLICATED THAN--
*SEE YOUNG AVENGERS BY GILLEN & McKELVIE! -WIL
OH! AND HERE IT COMES! THE INSULT HEAPED ON THE INJURY!
THE BIG REPENTANCE ACT--"BOO HOO HOOOO! I'M CUDDLY AND VULNERABLE! I CAN CHAAAAANGE!"
WHEN HE'S COVERED UP THE LIVING PROOF THAT HE NEVER WILL!
LOOK UPON ME, VERITY WILLIS! BOOM! YUMMY! IT'S KING LOKI, LIVE AND IN PERSON!
HE WHO MURDERED THE EARTH AND LAID WASTE TO THE SEA AND SKY! HE WHO IS SPITE AND CRUELTY AND EVIL PERSONIFIED!
YOUR BEST FRIEND'S FOREVER!
AND THE BEST PART?
NOTHING BUT THE TRUTH.

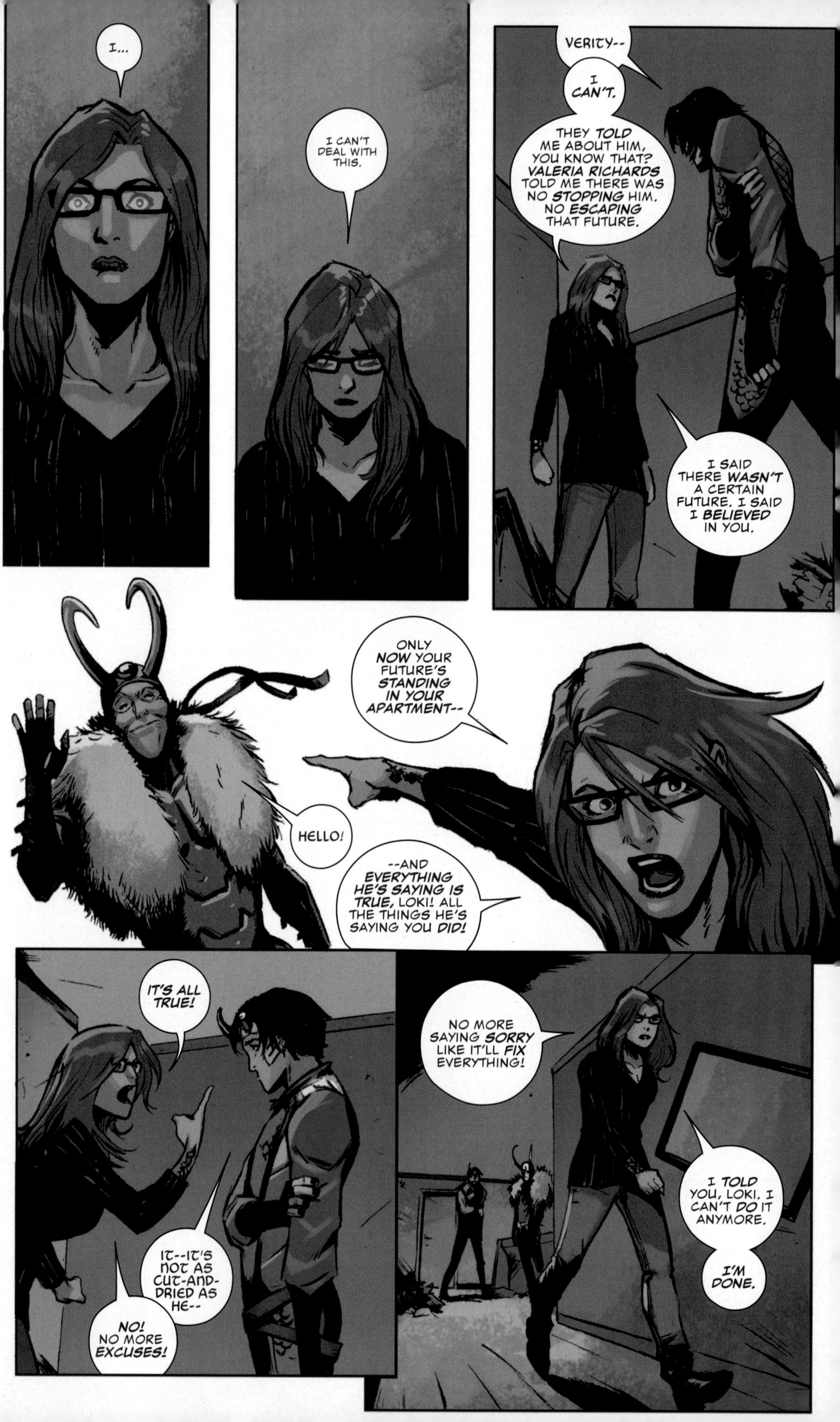
I...
I CAN'T DEAL WITH THIS.
VERITY--
I CAN'T.
THEY TOLD ME ABOUT HIM, YOU KNOW THAT? VALERIA RICHARDS TOLD ME THERE WAS NO STOPPING HIM. NO ESCAPING THAT FUTURE.
I SAID THERE WASN'T A CERTAIN FUTURE. I SAID I BELIEVED IN YOU.
ONLY NOW YOUR FUTURE'S STANDING IN YOUR APARTMENT--
HELLO!
--AND EVERYTHING HE'S SAYING IS TRUE, LOKI! ALL THE THINGS HE'S SAYING YOU DID!
IT'S ALL TRUE!
IT--IT'S NOT AS CUT-AND-DRIED AS HE--
NO! NO MORE EXCUSES!
NO MORE SAYING SORRY LIKE IT'LL FIX EVERYTHING!
I TOLD YOU, LOKI. I CAN'T DO IT ANYMORE.
I'M DONE.

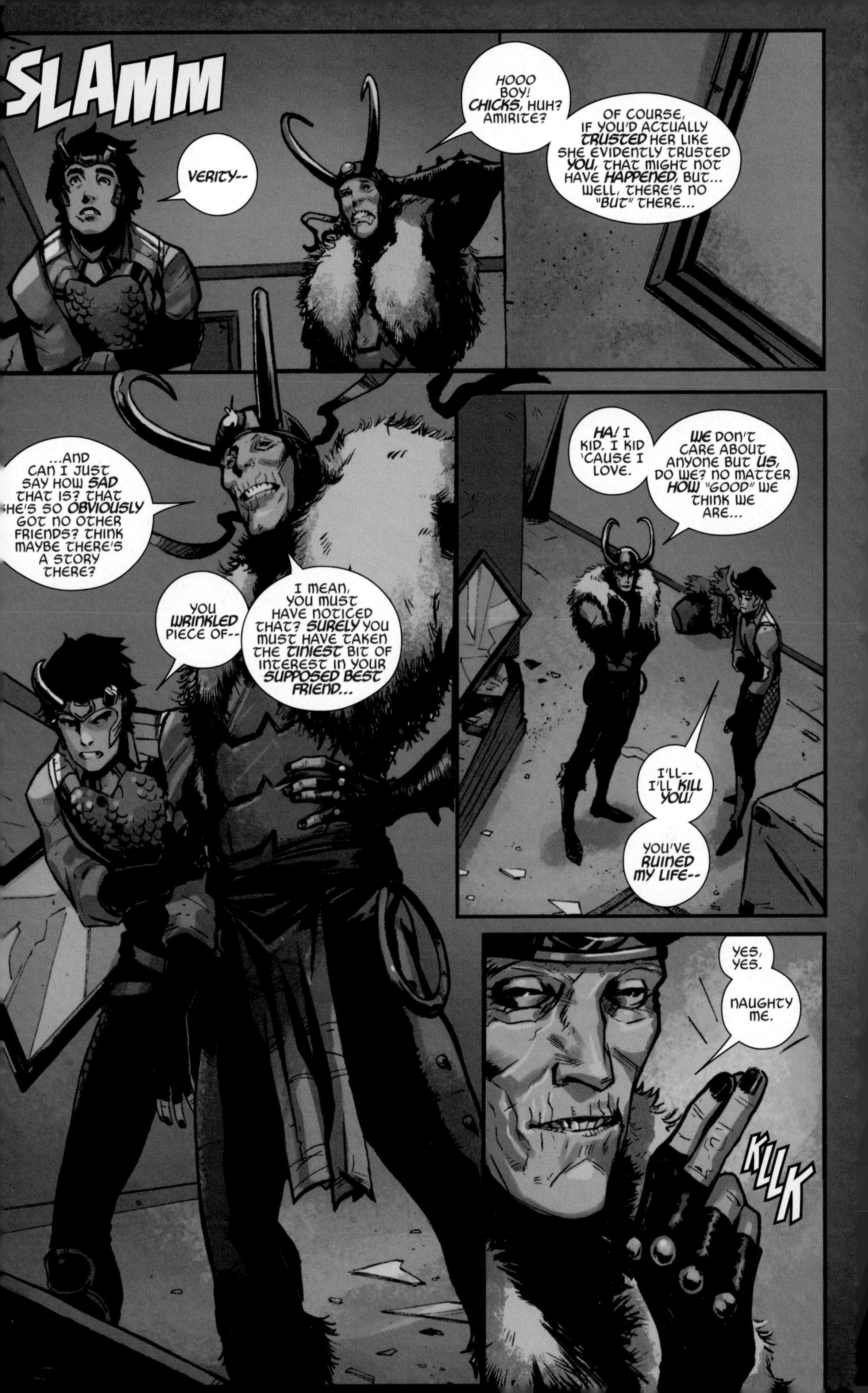
SLAMM
VERITY--
HOOO BOY! CHICKS, HUH? AMIRITE?
OF COURSE, IF YOU'D ACTUALLY TRUSTED HER LIKE SHE EVIDENTLY TRUSTED YOU, THAT MIGHT NOT HAVE HAPPENED, BUT... WELL, THERE'S NO "BUT" THERE...
...AND CAN I JUST SAY HOW SAD THAT IS? THAT SHE'S SO OBVIOUSLY GOT NO OTHER FRIENDS? THINK MAYBE THERE'S A STORY THERE?
I MEAN, YOU MUST HAVE NOTICED THAT? SURELY YOU MUST HAVE TAKEN THE TINIEST BIT OF INTEREST IN YOUR SUPPOSED BEST FRIEND...
YOU WRINKLED PIECE OF--
HA! I KID. I KID 'CAUSE I LOVE.
WE DON'T CARE ABOUT ANYONE BUT US, DO WE? NO MATTER HOW "GOOD" WE THINK WE ARE...
I'LL-- I'LL KILL YOU!
YOU'VE RUINED MY LIFE--
YES, YES.
NAUGHTY ME.
KLLK

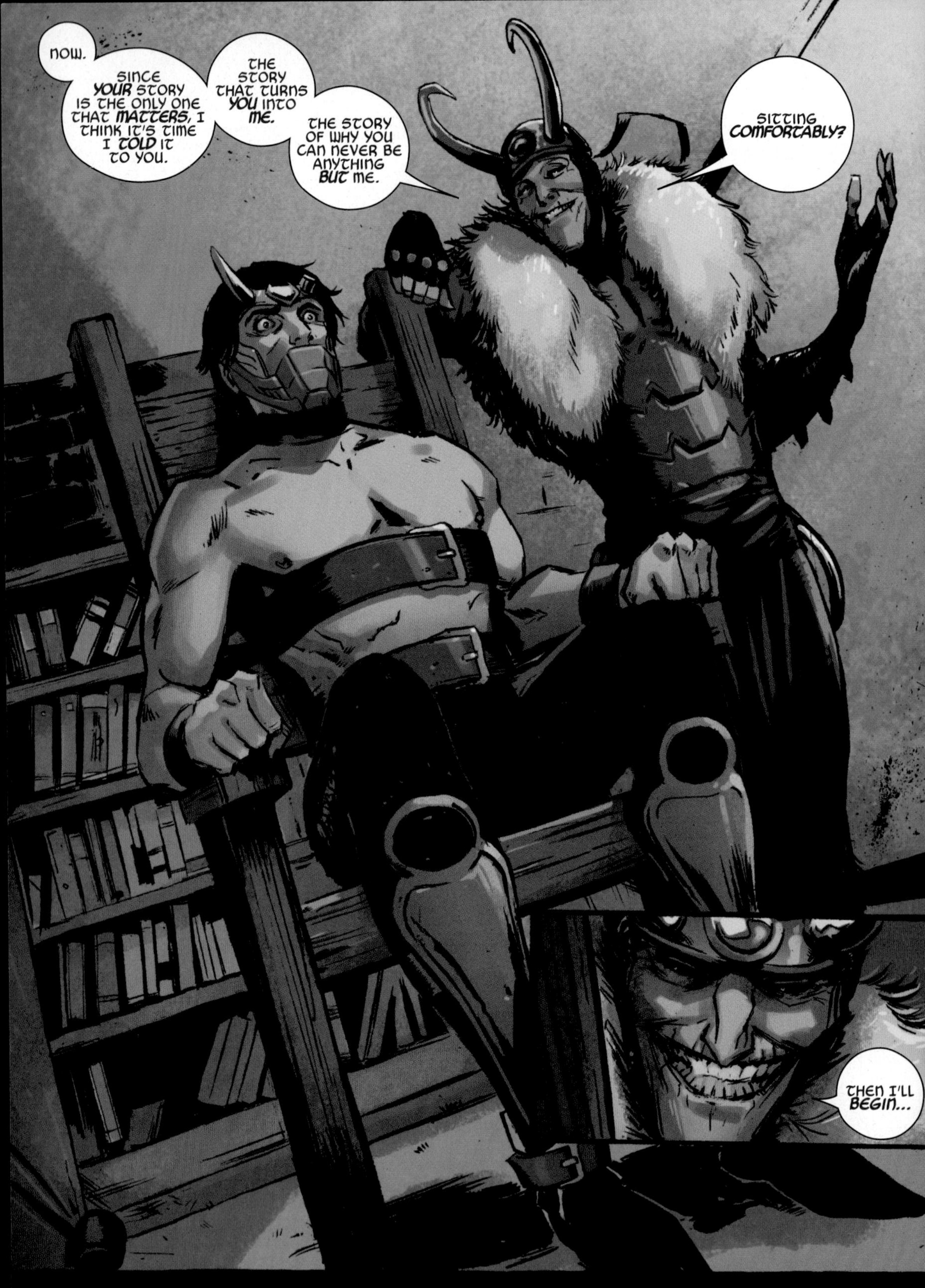
NOW.
SINCE YOUR STORY IS THE ONLY ONE THAT MATTERS, I THINK IT'S TIME I TOLD IT TO YOU.
THE STORY THAT TURNS YOU INTO ME.
THE STORY OF WHY YOU CAN NEVER BE ANYTHING BUT ME.
SITTING COMFORTABLY?
THEN I'LL BEGIN...

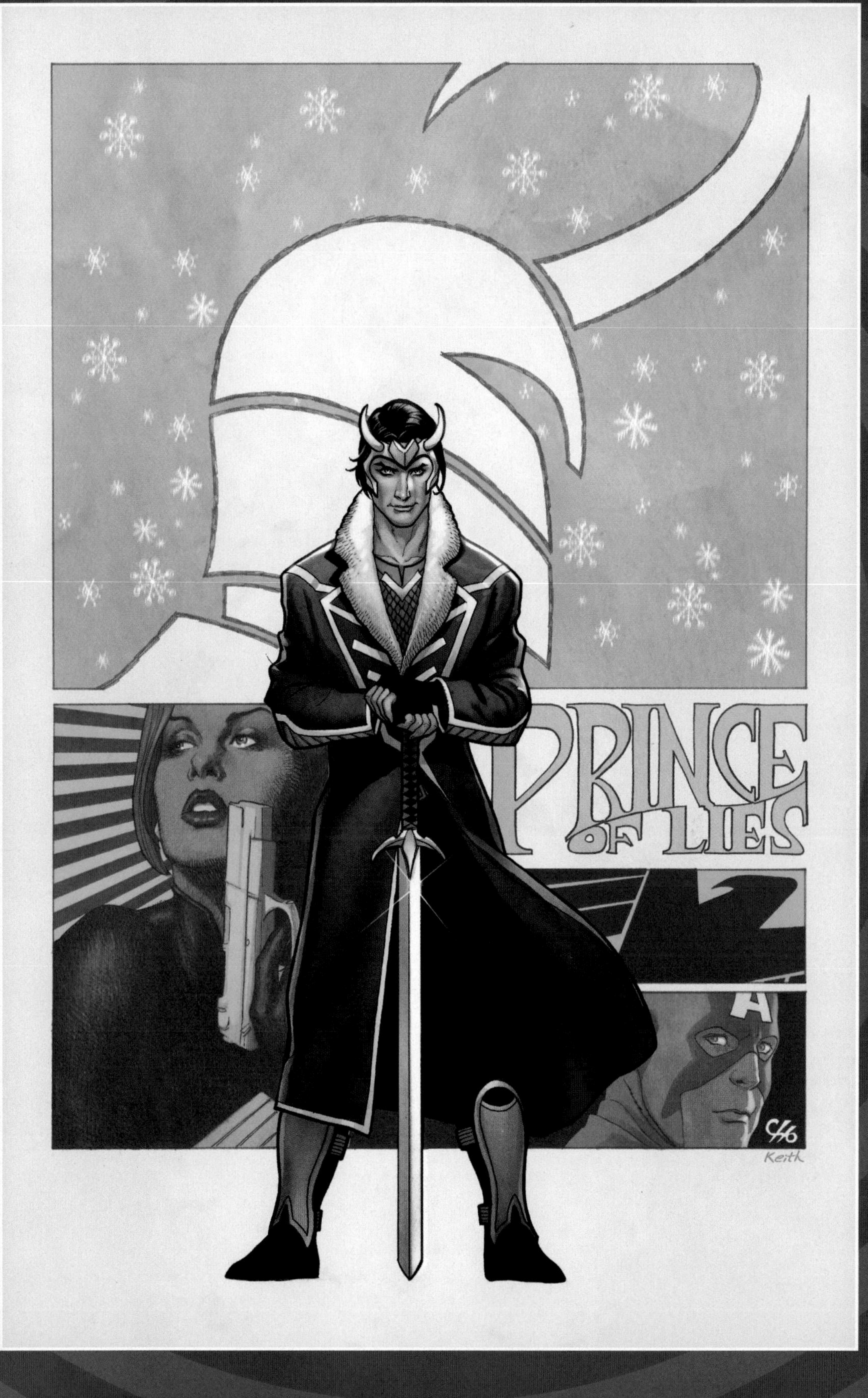
PRINCE
OF LIES
A
Keith

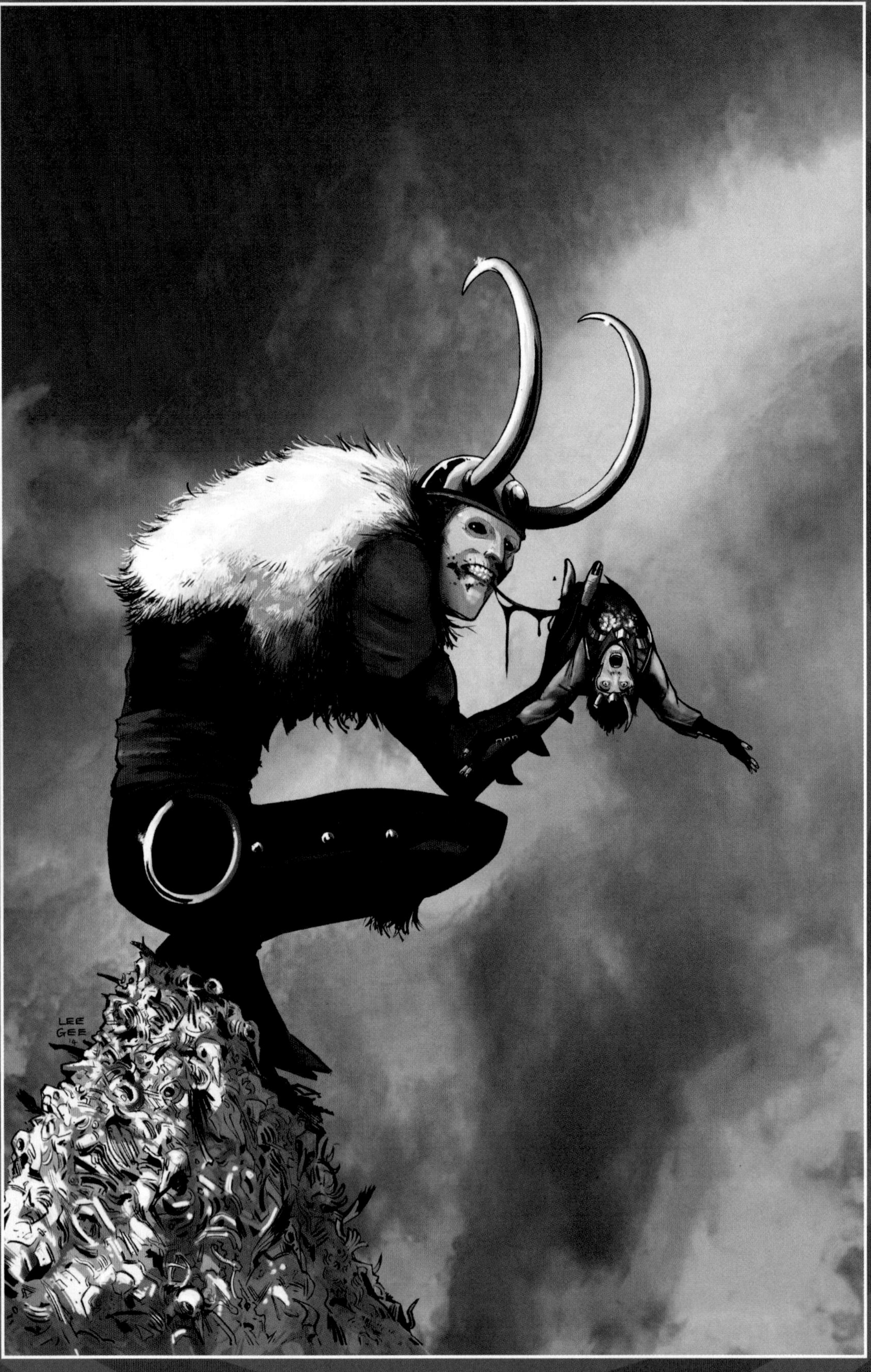
LEE
GEE
'14

LOKI: AGENT OF ASGARD #12

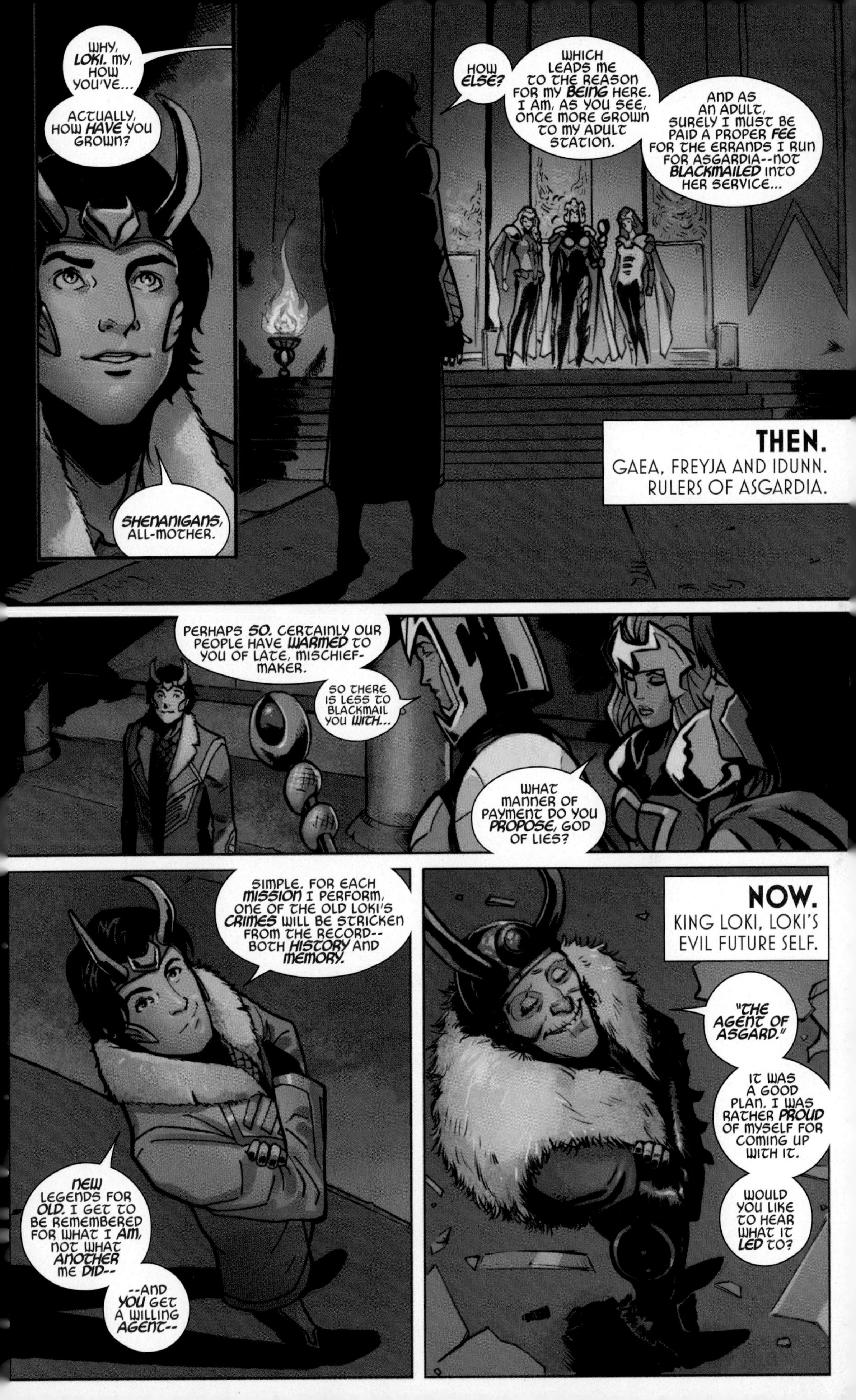
WHY, LOKI. MY, HOW YOU'VE...
ACTUALLY, HOW HAVE YOU GROWN?
SHENANIGANS, ALL-MOTHER.
HOW ELSE?
WHICH LEADS ME TO THE REASON FOR MY BEING HERE. I AM, AS YOU SEE, ONCE MORE GROWN TO MY ADULT STATION.
AND AS AN ADULT, SURELY I MUST BE PAID A PROPER FEE FOR THE ERRANDS I RUN FOR ASGARDIA--NOT BLACKMAILED INTO HER SERVICE...
THEN.
GAEA, FREYJA AND IDUNN. RULERS OF ASGARDIA.
PERHAPS SO. CERTAINLY OUR PEOPLE HAVE WARMED TO YOU OF LATE, MISCHIEF-MAKER.
SO THERE IS LESS TO BLACKMAIL YOU WITH...
WHAT MANNER OF PAYMENT DO YOU PROPOSE, GOD OF LIES?
SIMPLE. FOR EACH MISSION I PERFORM, ONE OF THE OLD LOKI'S CRIMES WILL BE STRICKEN FROM THE RECORD-- BOTH HISTORY AND MEMORY.
NEW LEGENDS FOR OLD. I GET TO BE REMEMBERED FOR WHAT I AM, NOT WHAT ANOTHER ME DID--
--AND YOU GET A WILLING AGENT--
NOW.
KING LOKI, LOKI'S EVIL FUTURE SELF.
"THE AGENT OF ASGARD."
IT WAS A GOOD PLAN. I WAS RATHER PROUD OF MYSELF FOR COMING UP WITH IT.
WOULD YOU LIKE TO HEAR WHAT IT LED TO?

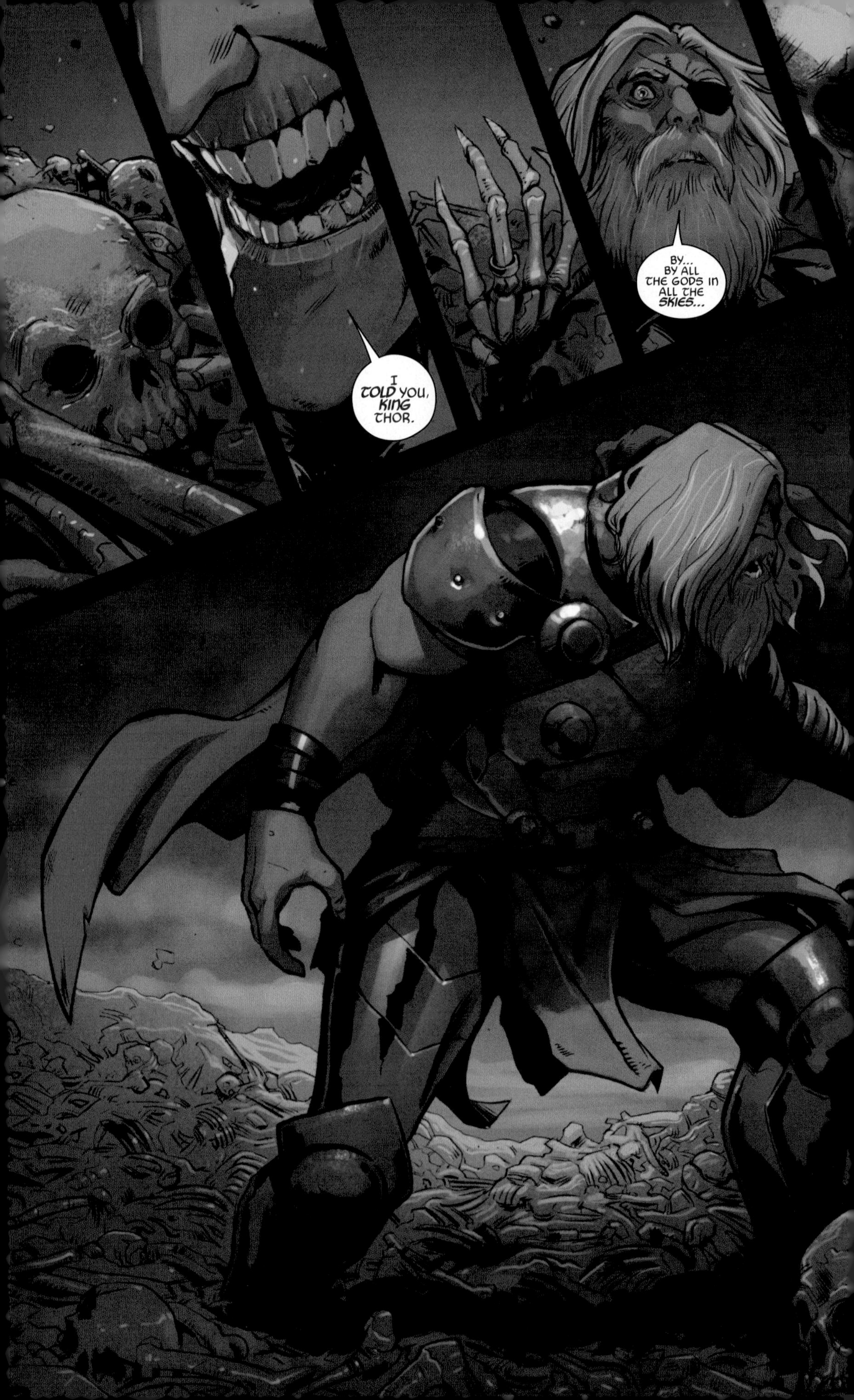
I TOLD YOU, KING THOR.
BY... BY ALL THE GODS IN ALL THE SKIES...

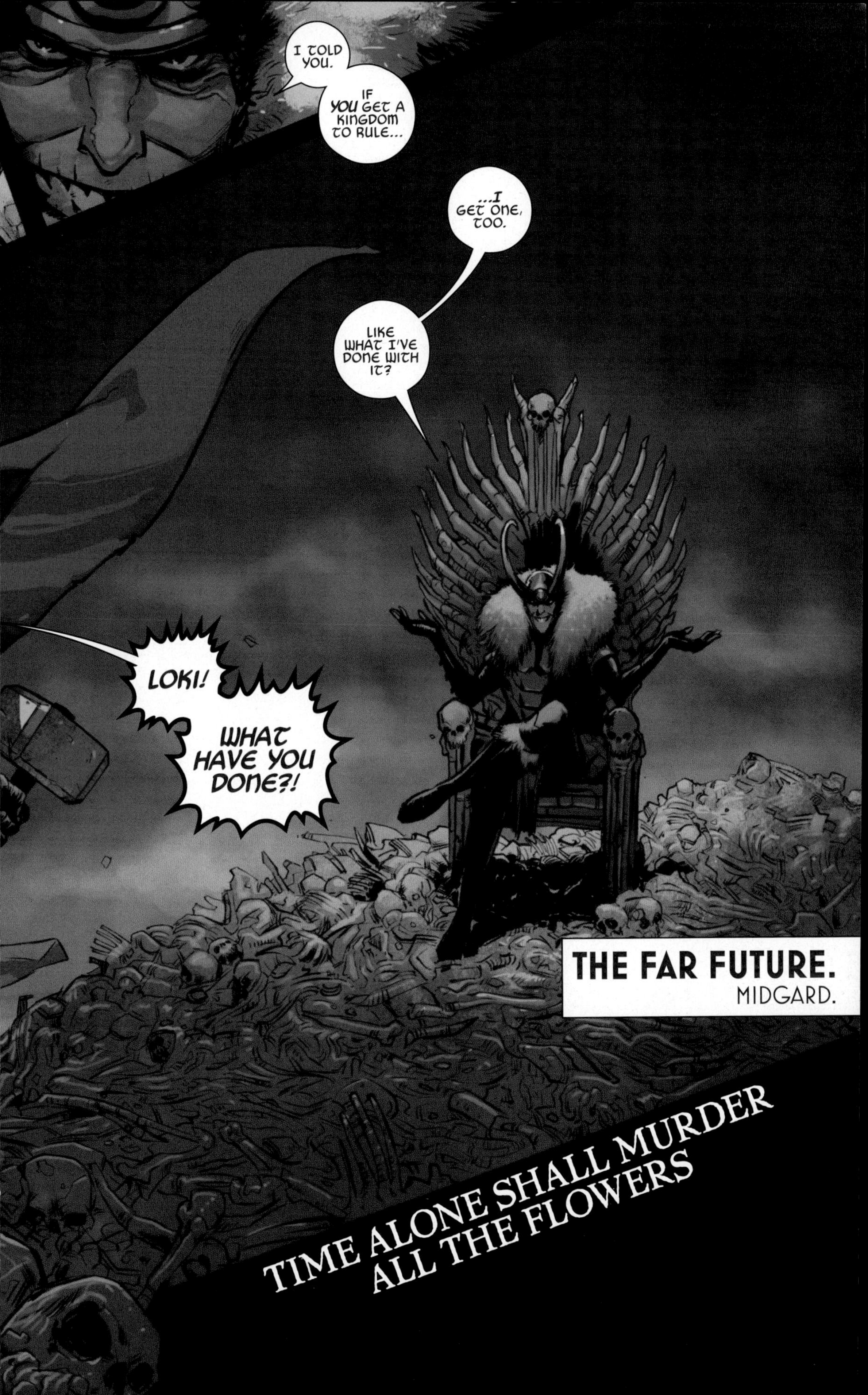
I TOLD YOU.
IF YOU GET A KINGDOM TO RULE...
...I GET ONE, TOO.
LIKE WHAT I'VE DONE WITH IT?
LOKI!
WHAT HAVE YOU DONE?!
THE FAR FUTURE.
MIDGARD.
TIME ALONE SHALL MURDER ALL THE FLOWERS

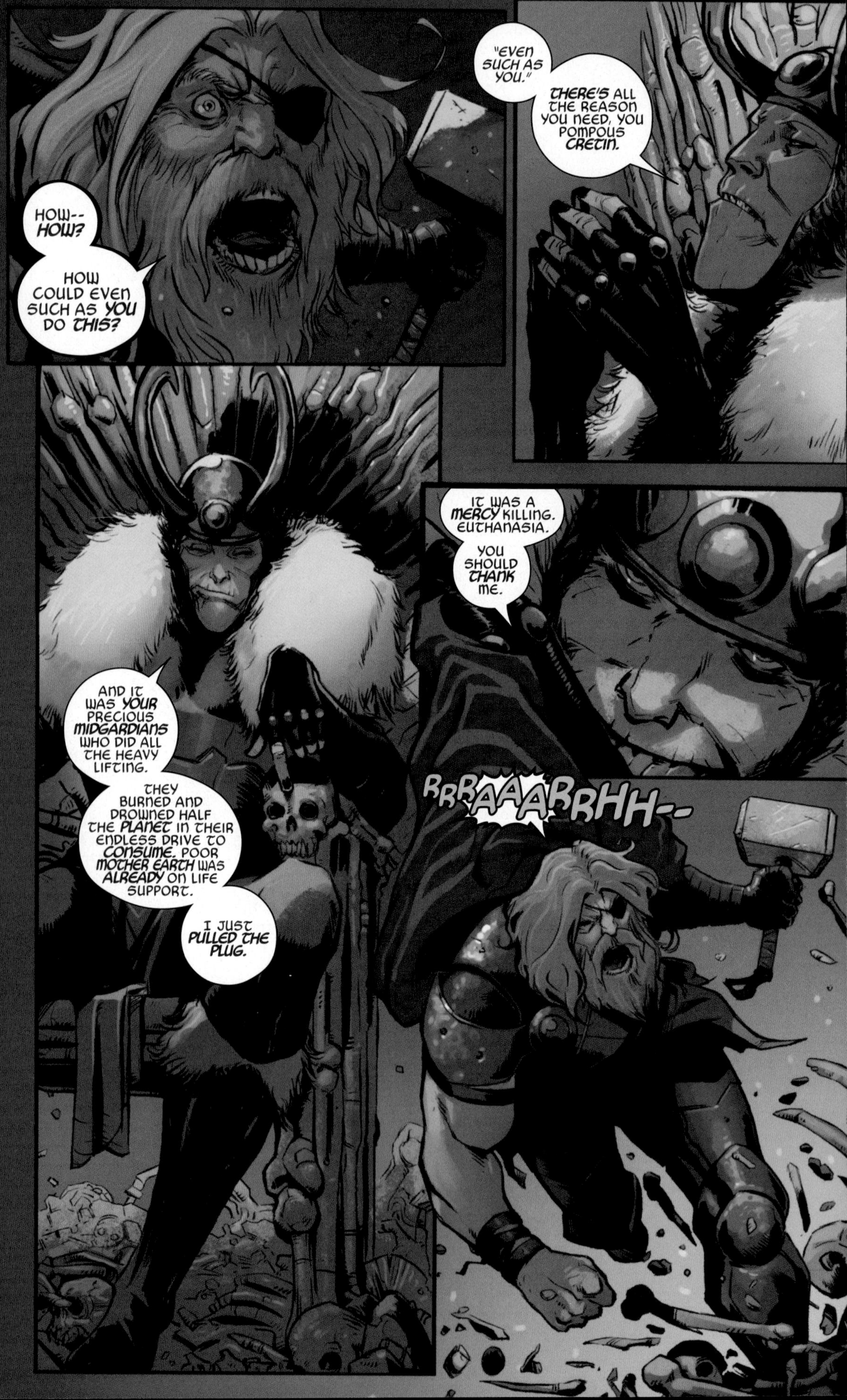

HOW-- HOW?
HOW COULD EVEN SUCH AS YOU DO THIS?
"EVEN SUCH AS YOU."
THERE'S ALL THE REASON YOU NEED, YOU POMPOUS CRETIN.
IT WAS A MERCY KILLING. EUTHANASIA.
YOU SHOULD THANK ME.
AND IT WAS YOUR PRECIOUS MIDGARDIANS WHO DID ALL THE HEAVY LIFTING.
THEY BURNED AND DROWNED HALF THE PLANET IN THEIR ENDLESS DRIVE TO CONSUME. POOR MOTHER EARTH WAS ALREADY ON LIFE SUPPORT.
I JUST PULLED THE PLUG.
RRRAAAARRHH--

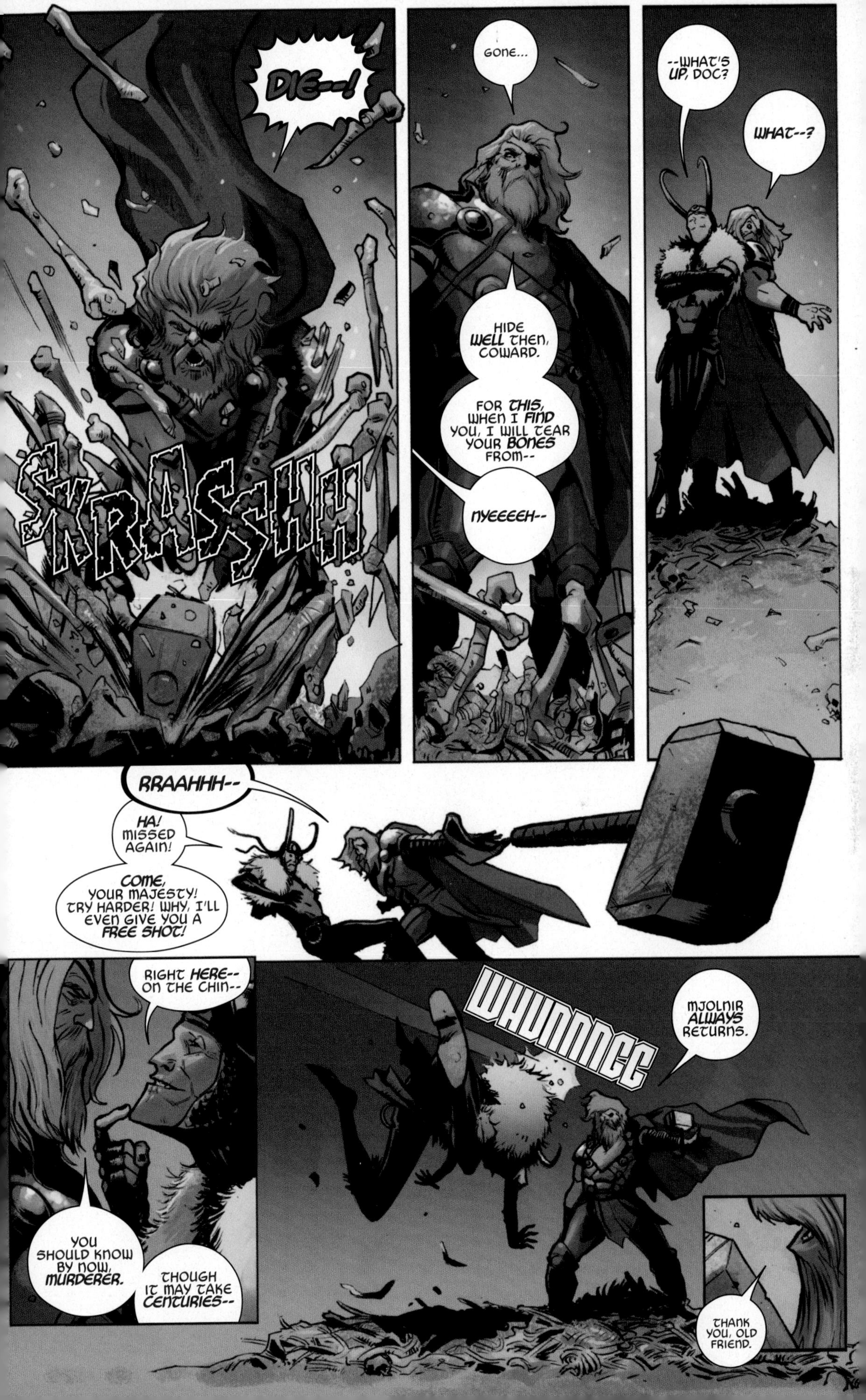
DIE--!
SKRASHH
GONE...
HIDE WELL THEN, COWARD.
FOR THIS, WHEN I FIND YOU, I WILL TEAR YOUR BONES FROM--
NYEEEEH--
--WHAT'S UP, DOC?
WHAT--?
RRAAHHH--
HA! MISSED AGAIN!
COME, YOUR MAJESTY! TRY HARDER! WHY, I'LL EVEN GIVE YOU A FREE SHOT!
RIGHT HERE-- ON THE CHIN--
YOU SHOULD KNOW BY NOW, MURDERER.
THOUGH IT MAY TAKE CENTURIES--
WHUNNNGG
MJOLNIR ALWAYS RETURNS.
THANK YOU, OLD FRIEND.

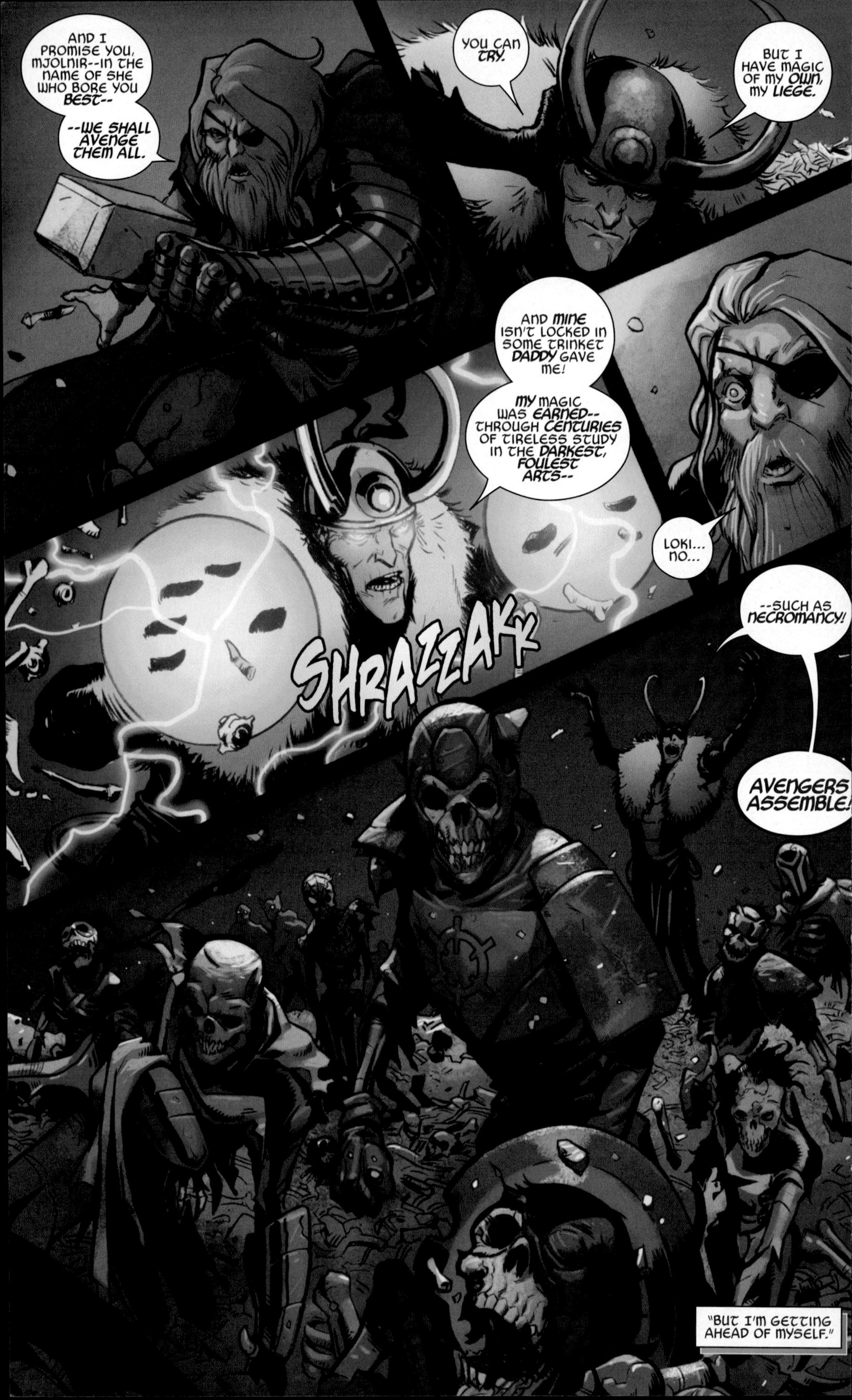
AND I PROMISE YOU, MJOLNIR--IN THE NAME OF SHE WHO BORE YOU BEST--
--WE SHALL AVENGE THEM ALL.
YOU CAN TRY.
BUT I HAVE MAGIC OF MY OWN, MY LIEGE.
AND MINE ISN'T LOCKED IN SOME TRINKET DADDY GAVE ME!
MY MAGIC WAS EARNED--THROUGH CENTURIES OF TIRELESS STUDY IN THE DARKEST, FOULEST ARTS--
LOKI... NO...
SHRAZZAKK
--SUCH AS NECROMANCY!
AVENGERS ASSEMBLE!
"BUT I'M GETTING AHEAD OF MYSELF."

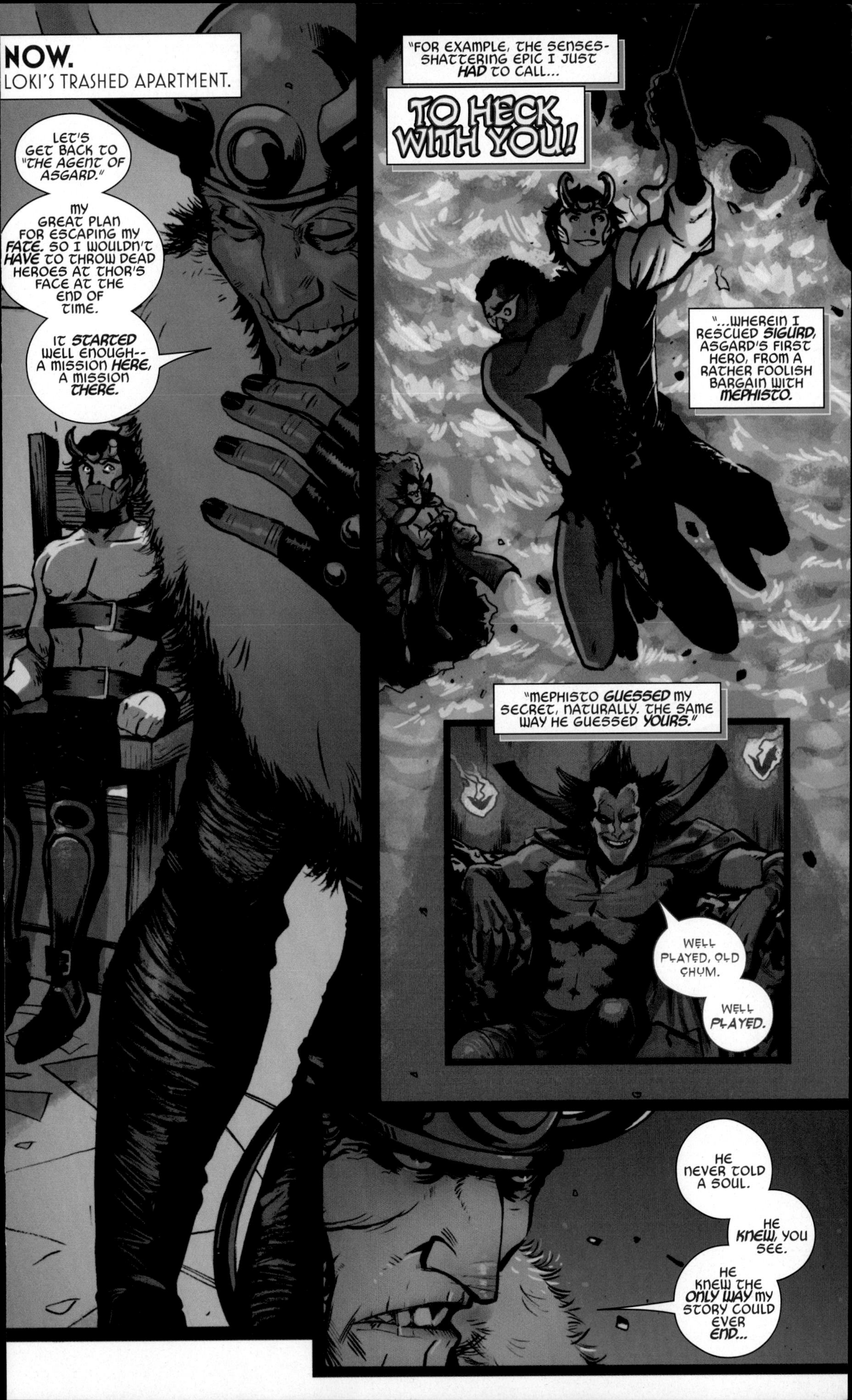
NOW.
LOKI'S TRASHED APARTMENT.
LET'S GET BACK TO "THE AGENT OF ASGARD."
MY GREAT PLAN FOR ESCAPING MY FATE. SO I WOULDN'T HAVE TO THROW DEAD HEROES AT THOR'S FACE AT THE END OF TIME.
IT STARTED WELL ENOUGH-- A MISSION HERE, A MISSION THERE.
"FOR EXAMPLE, THE SENSES-SHATTERING EPIC I JUST HAD TO CALL...
TO HECK WITH YOU!
"...WHEREIN I RESCUED SIGURD, ASGARD'S FIRST HERO, FROM A RATHER FOOLISH BARGAIN WITH MEPHISTO.
"MEPHISTO GUESSED MY SECRET, NATURALLY. THE SAME WAY HE GUESSED YOURS."
WELL PLAYED, OLD CHUM.
WELL PLAYED.
HE NEVER TOLD A SOUL.
HE KNEW, YOU SEE.
HE KNEW THE ONLY WAY MY STORY COULD EVER END...

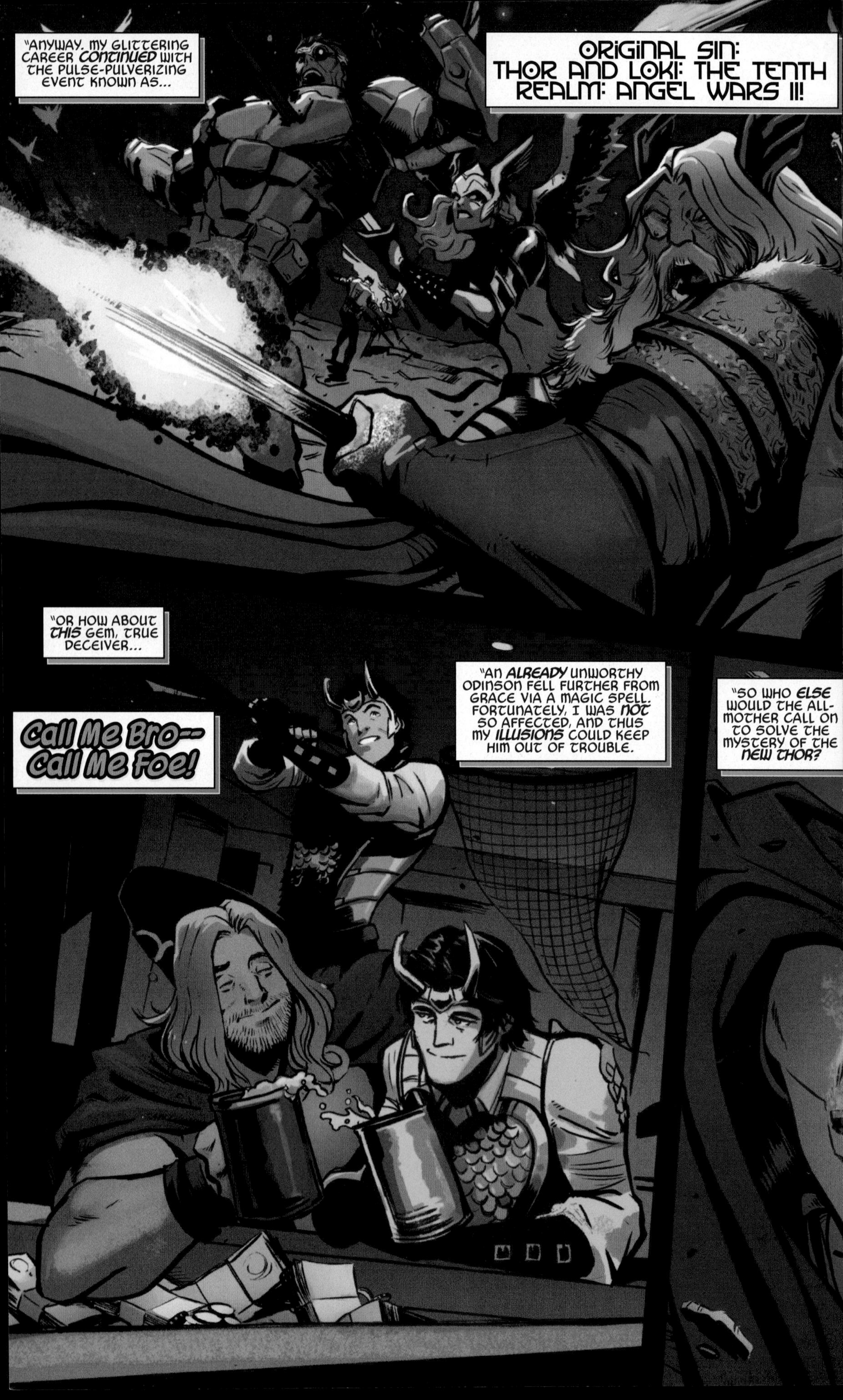

"ANYWAY, MY GLITTERING CAREER CONTINUED WITH THE PULSE-PULVERIZING EVENT KNOWN AS...
ORIGINAL SIN: THOR AND LOKI: THE TENTH REALM: ANGEL WARS II!
"OR HOW ABOUT THIS GEM, TRUE DECEIVER...
Call Me Bro-- Call Me Foe!
"AN ALREADY UNWORTHY ODINSON FELL FURTHER FROM GRACE VIA A MAGIC SPELL. FORTUNATELY, I WAS NOT SO AFFECTED, AND THUS MY ILLUSIONS COULD KEEP HIM OUT OF TROUBLE.
"SO WHO ELSE WOULD THE ALL-MOTHER CALL ON TO SOLVE THE MYSTERY OF THE NEW THOR?

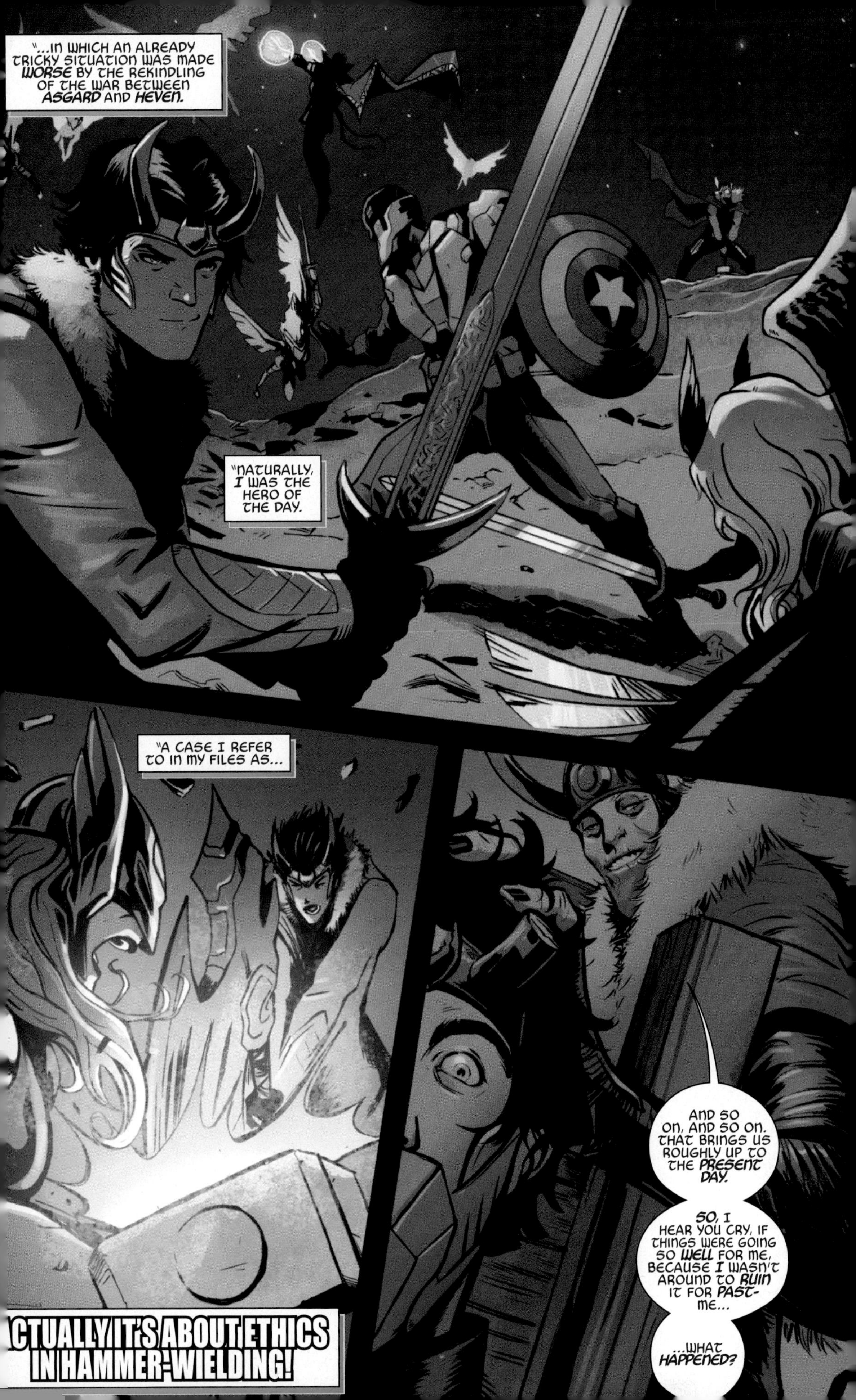
"...IN WHICH AN ALREADY TRICKY SITUATION WAS MADE WORSE BY THE REKINDLING OF THE WAR BETWEEN ASGARD AND HEVEN.
"NATURALLY, I WAS THE HERO OF THE DAY.
"A CASE I REFER TO IN MY FILES AS...
CTUALLY IT'S ABOUT ETHICS IN HAMMER-WIELDING!
AND SO ON, AND SO ON. THAT BRINGS US ROUGHLY UP TO THE PRESENT DAY.
SO, I HEAR YOU CRY, IF THINGS WERE GOING SO WELL FOR ME, BECAUSE I WASN'T AROUND TO RUIN IT FOR PAST-ME...
...WHAT HAPPENED?

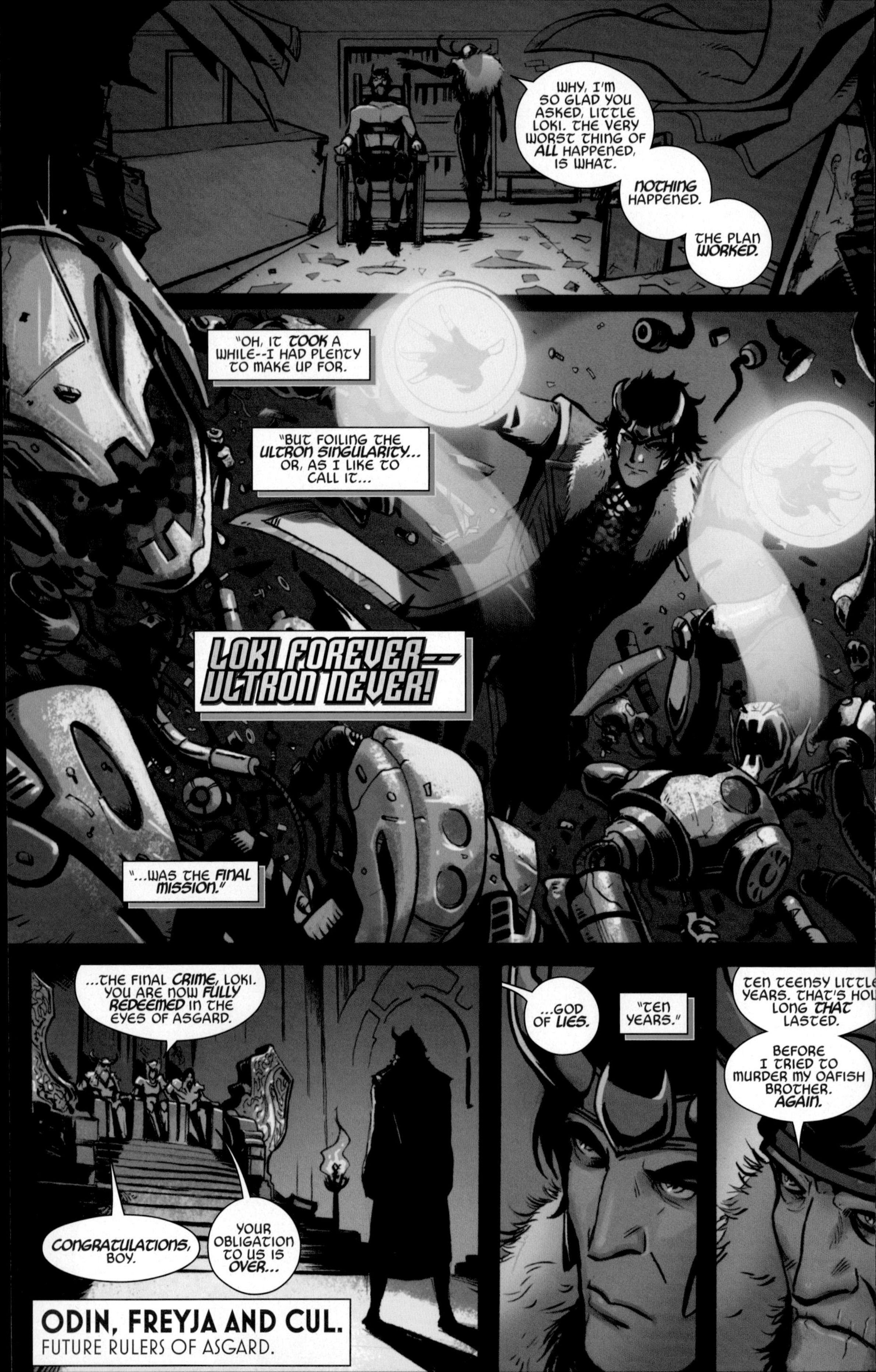
WHY, I'M SO GLAD YOU ASKED, LITTLE LOKI. THE VERY WORST THING OF ALL HAPPENED, IS WHAT.
NOTHING HAPPENED.
THE PLAN WORKED.
"OH, IT TOOK A WHILE--I HAD PLENTY TO MAKE UP FOR.
"BUT FOILING THE ULTRON SINGULARITY... OR, AS I LIKE TO CALL IT...
LOKI FOREVER-- ULTRON NEVER!
"...WAS THE FINAL MISSION."
...THE FINAL CRIME, LOKI. YOU ARE NOW FULLY REDEEMED IN THE EYES OF ASGARD.
CONGRATULATIONS, BOY.
YOUR OBLIGATION TO US IS OVER...
ODIN, FREYJA AND CUL.
FUTURE RULERS OF ASGARD.
...GOD OF LIES.
"TEN YEARS."
TEN TEENSY LITTLE YEARS. THAT'S HOW LONG THAT LASTED.
BEFORE I TRIED TO MURDER MY OAFISH BROTHER. AGAIN.

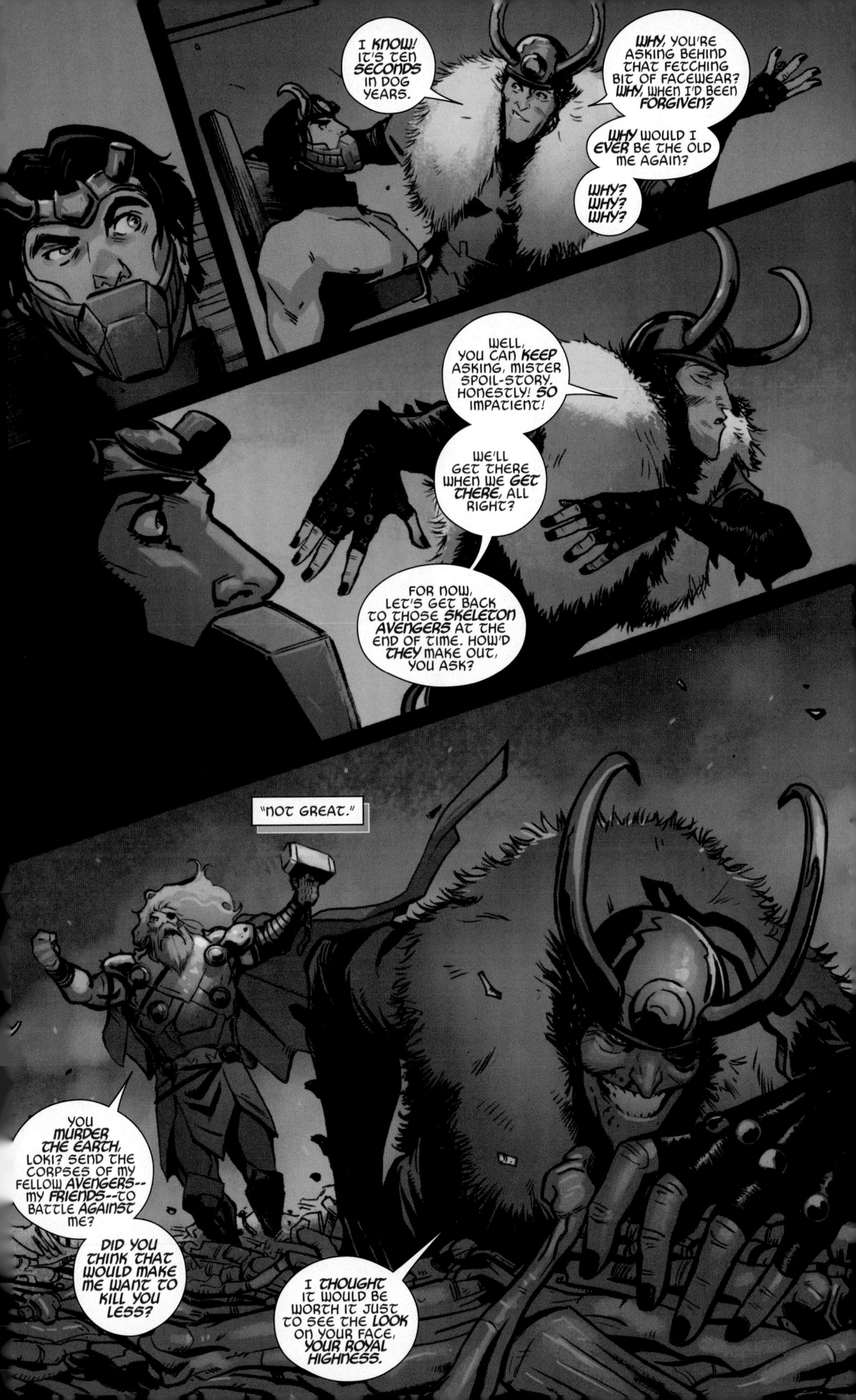
I KNOW! IT'S TEN SECONDS IN DOG YEARS.
WHY, YOU'RE ASKING BEHIND THAT FETCHING BIT OF FACEWEAR? WHY, WHEN I'D BEEN FORGIVEN?
WHY WOULD I EVER BE THE OLD ME AGAIN?
WHY? WHY? WHY?
WELL, YOU CAN KEEP ASKING, MISTER SPOIL-STORY. HONESTLY! SO IMPATIENT!
WE'LL GET THERE WHEN WE GET THERE, ALL RIGHT?
FOR NOW, LET'S GET BACK TO THOSE SKELETON AVENGERS AT THE END OF TIME. HOW'D THEY MAKE OUT, YOU ASK?
"NOT GREAT."
YOU MURDER THE EARTH, LOKI? SEND THE CORPSES OF MY FELLOW AVENGERS--MY FRIENDS--TO BATTLE AGAINST ME?
DID YOU THINK THAT WOULD MAKE ME WANT TO KILL YOU LESS?
I THOUGHT IT WOULD BE WORTH IT JUST TO SEE THE LOOK ON YOUR FACE, YOUR ROYAL HIGHNESS.

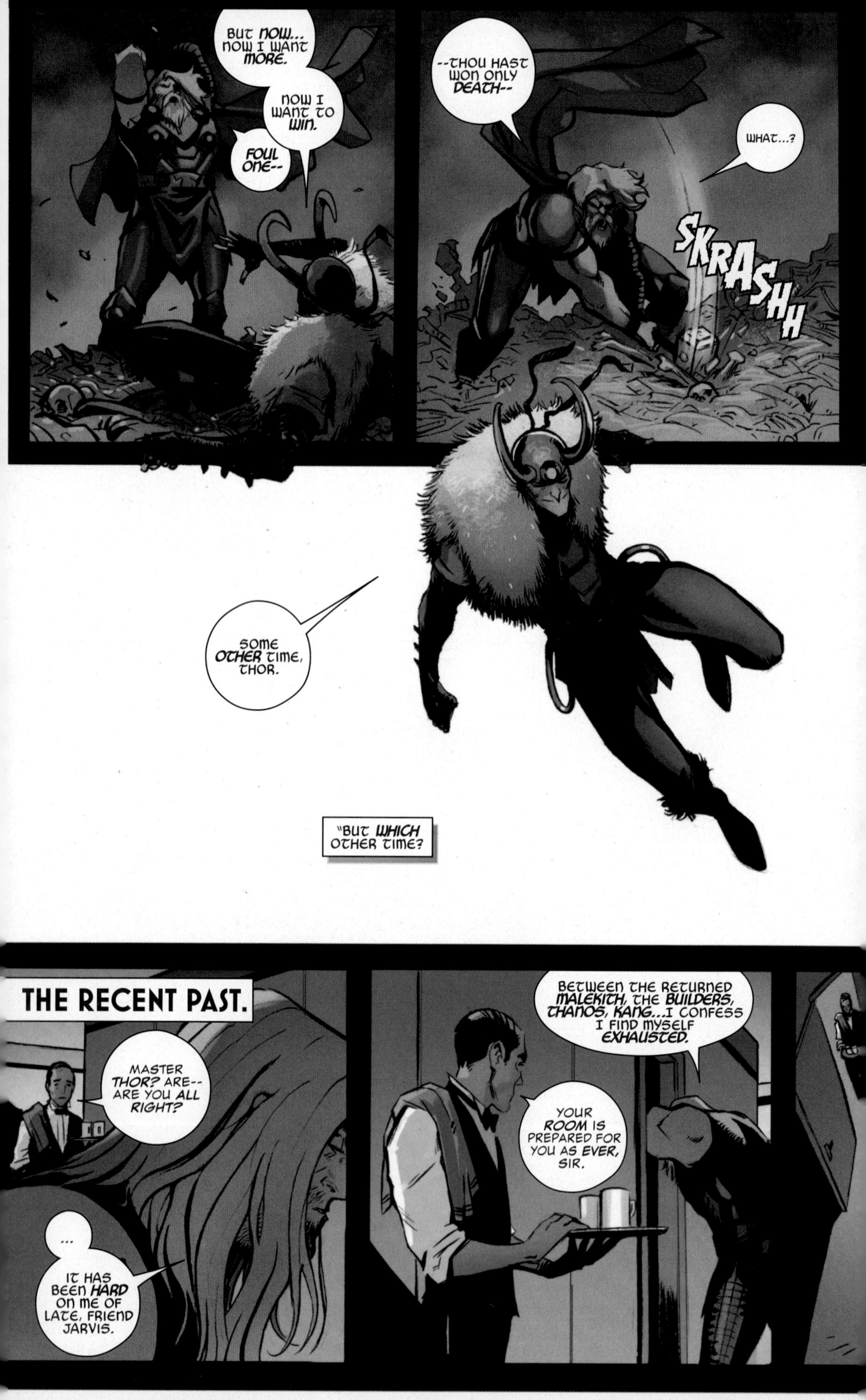

BUT NOW... NOW I WANT MORE.
NOW I WANT TO WIN.
FOUL ONE--
--THOU HAST WON ONLY DEATH--
WHAT...?
SKRASHH
SOME OTHER TIME, THOR.
"BUT WHICH OTHER TIME?
THE RECENT PAST.
MASTER THOR? ARE-- ARE YOU ALL RIGHT?
...
IT HAS BEEN HARD ON ME OF LATE, FRIEND JARVIS.
BETWEEN THE RETURNED MALEKITH, THE BUILDERS, THANOS, KANG...I CONFESS I FIND MYSELF EXHAUSTED.
YOUR ROOM IS PREPARED FOR YOU AS EVER, SIR.

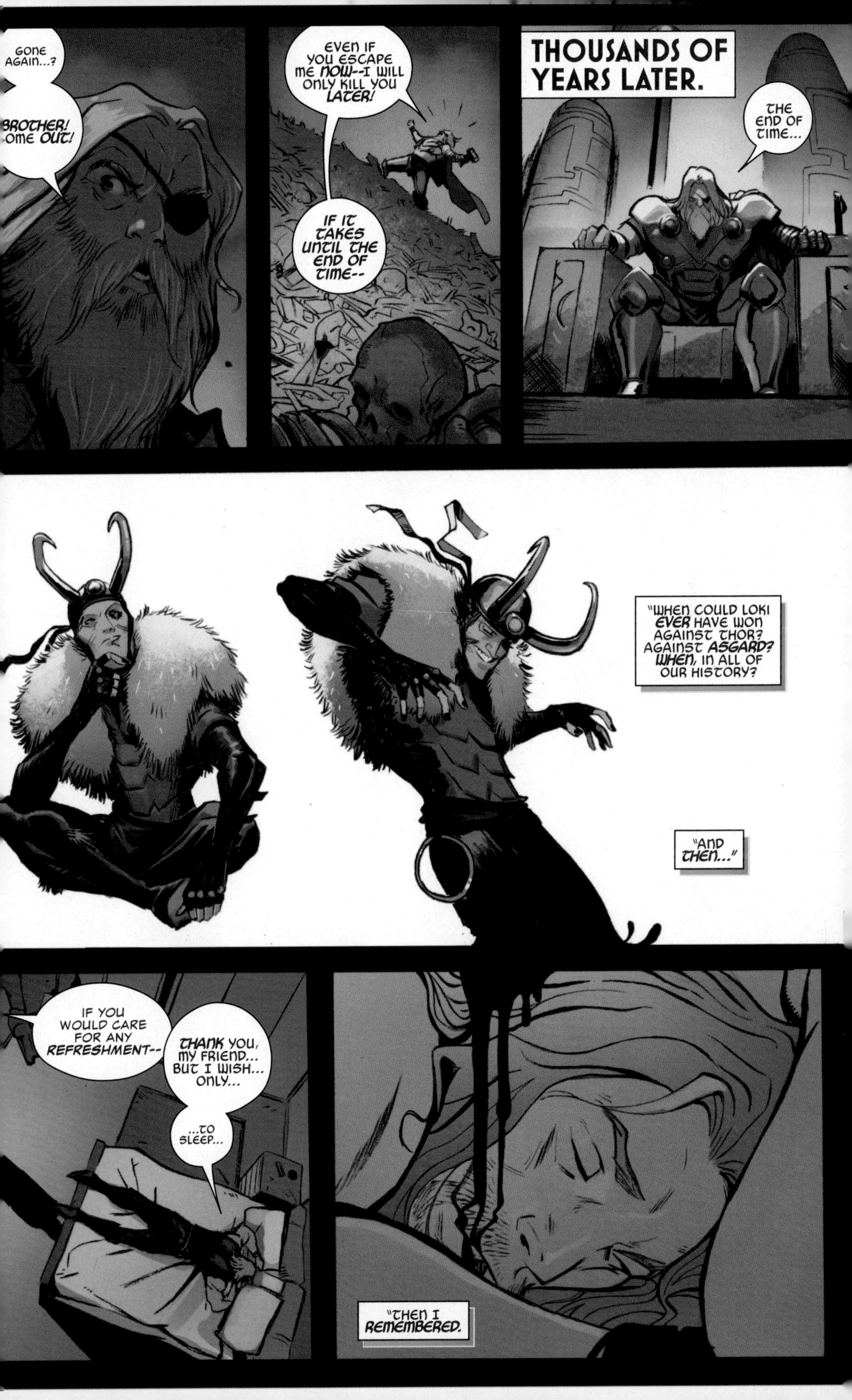
GONE AGAIN...?
BROTHER! COME OUT!
EVEN IF YOU ESCAPE ME NOW--I WILL ONLY KILL YOU LATER!
IF IT TAKES UNTIL THE END OF TIME--
THOUSANDS OF YEARS LATER.
THE END OF TIME...
"WHEN COULD LOKI EVER HAVE WON AGAINST THOR? AGAINST ASGARD? WHEN, IN ALL OF OUR HISTORY?
"AND THEN..."
IF YOU WOULD CARE FOR ANY REFRESHMENT--
THANK YOU, MY FRIEND... BUT I WISH... ONLY...
...TO SLEEP...
"THEN I REMEMBERED.

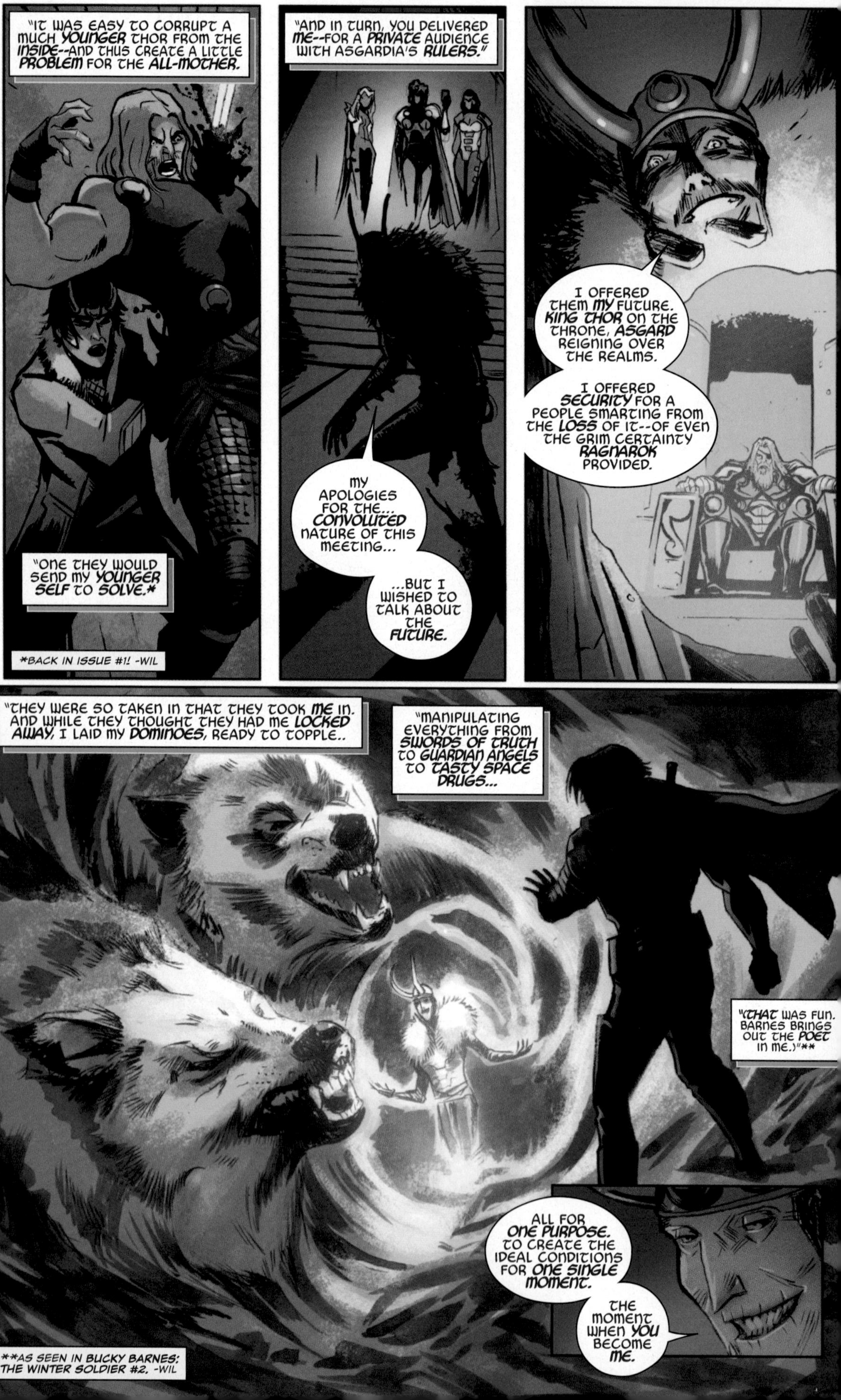
"IT WAS EASY TO CORRUPT A MUCH YOUNGER THOR FROM THE INSIDE--AND THUS CREATE A LITTLE PROBLEM FOR THE ALL-MOTHER.
"ONE THEY WOULD SEND MY YOUNGER SELF TO SOLVE.*
*BACK IN ISSUE #1! -WIL
"AND IN TURN, YOU DELIVERED ME--FOR A PRIVATE AUDIENCE WITH ASGARDIA'S RULERS."
MY APOLOGIES FOR THE... CONVOLUTED NATURE OF THIS MEETING...
...BUT I WISHED TO TALK ABOUT THE FUTURE.
I OFFERED THEM MY FUTURE. KING THOR ON THE THRONE, ASGARD REIGNING OVER THE REALMS.
I OFFERED SECURITY FOR A PEOPLE SMARTING FROM THE LOSS OF IT--OF EVEN THE GRIM CERTAINTY RAGNAROK PROVIDED.
"THEY WERE SO TAKEN IN THAT THEY TOOK ME IN. AND WHILE THEY THOUGHT THEY HAD ME LOCKED AWAY, I LAID MY DOMINOES, READY TO TOPPLE..
"MANIPULATING EVERYTHING FROM SWORDS OF TRUTH TO GUARDIAN ANGELS TO TASTY SPACE DRUGS...
"(THAT WAS FUN. BARNES BRINGS OUT THE POET IN ME.)"**
ALL FOR ONE PURPOSE. TO CREATE THE IDEAL CONDITIONS FOR ONE SINGLE MOMENT.
THE MOMENT WHEN YOU BECOME ME.
**AS SEEN IN BUCKY BARNES: THE WINTER SOLDIER #2. -WIL

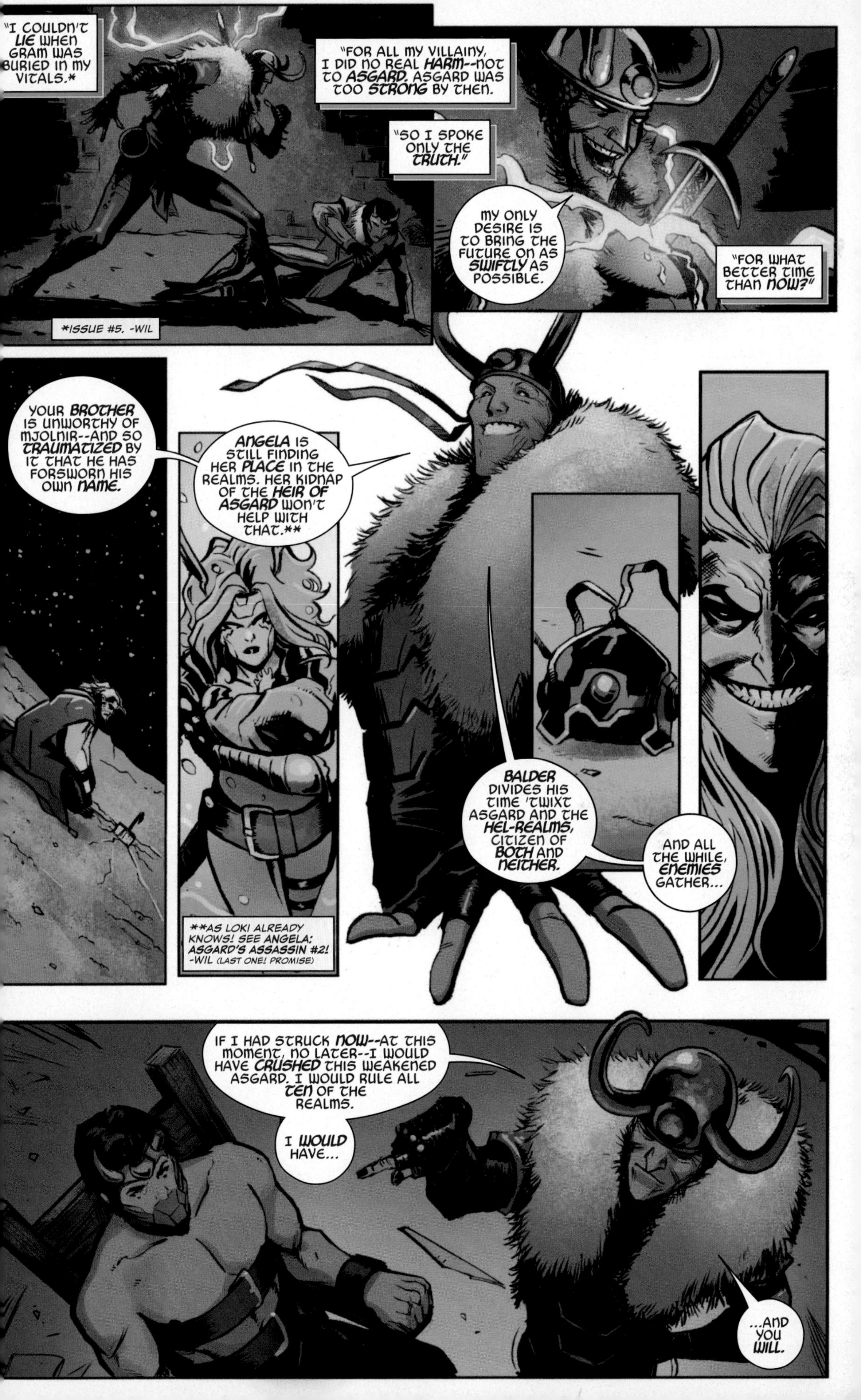
"I COULDN'T LIE WHEN GRAM WAS BURIED IN MY VITALS.*
*ISSUE #5. -WIL
"FOR ALL MY VILLAINY, I DID NO REAL HARM--NOT TO ASGARD. ASGARD WAS TOO STRONG BY THEN.
"SO I SPOKE ONLY THE TRUTH."
MY ONLY DESIRE IS TO BRING THE FUTURE ON AS SWIFTLY AS POSSIBLE.
"FOR WHAT BETTER TIME THAN NOW?"
YOUR BROTHER IS UNWORTHY OF MJOLNIR--AND SO TRAUMATIZED BY IT THAT HE HAS FORSWORN HIS OWN NAME.
ANGELA IS STILL FINDING HER PLACE IN THE REALMS. HER KIDNAP OF THE HEIR OF ASGARD WON'T HELP WITH THAT.**
**AS LOKI ALREADY KNOWS! SEE ANGELA: ASGARD'S ASSASSIN #2! -WIL (LAST ONE! PROMISE)
BALDER DIVIDES HIS TIME 'TWIXT ASGARD AND THE HEL-REALMS, CITIZEN OF BOTH AND NEITHER.
AND ALL THE WHILE, ENEMIES GATHER...
IF I HAD STRUCK NOW--AT THIS MOMENT, NO LATER--I WOULD HAVE CRUSHED THIS WEAKENED ASGARD. I WOULD RULE ALL TEN OF THE REALMS.
I WOULD HAVE...
...AND YOU WILL.

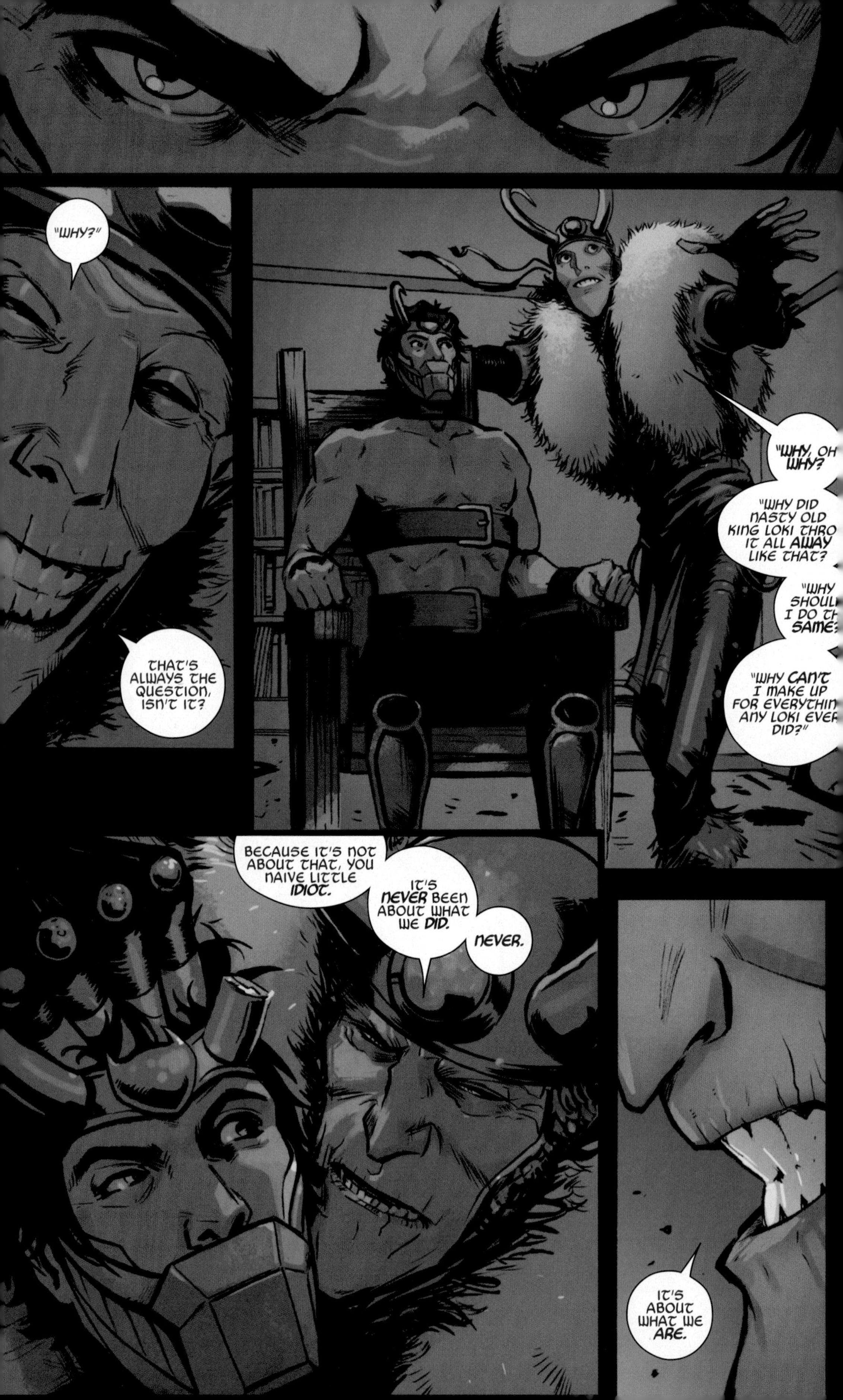

"WHY?"
THAT'S ALWAYS THE QUESTION, ISN'T IT?
"WHY, OH WHY?
"WHY DID NASTY OLD KING LOKI THRO IT ALL AWAY LIKE THAT?
"WHY SHOUL I DO T SAME
"WHY CAN'T I MAKE UP FOR EVERYTHIN ANY LOKI EVER DID?"
BECAUSE IT'S NOT ABOUT THAT, YOU NAIVE LITTLE IDIOT.
IT'S NEVER BEEN ABOUT WHAT WE DID.
NEVER.
IT'S ABOUT WHAT WE ARE.

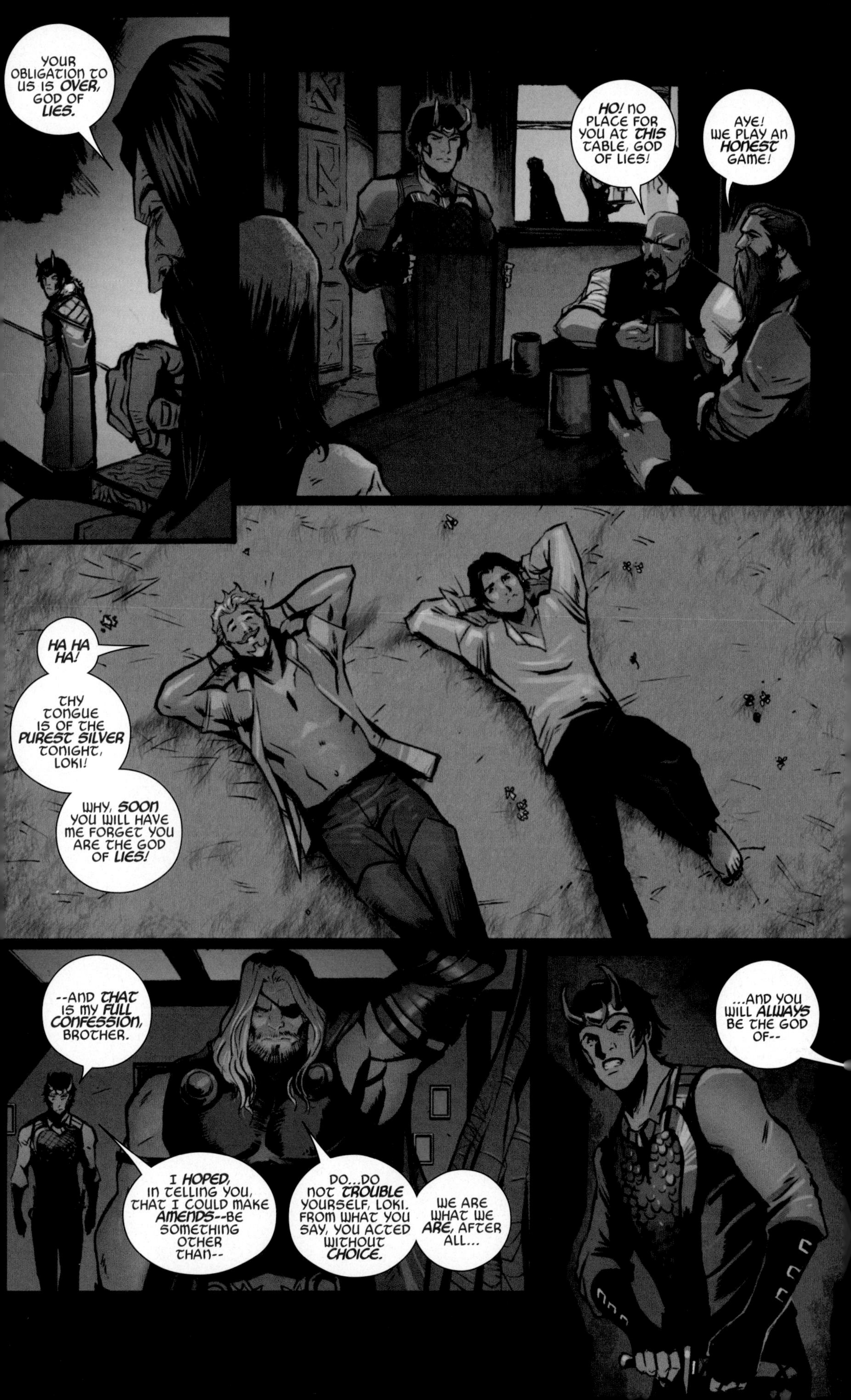
YOUR OBLIGATION TO US IS OVER, GOD OF LIES.
HO! NO PLACE FOR YOU AT THIS TABLE, GOD OF LIES!
AYE! WE PLAY AN HONEST GAME!
HA HA HA!
THY TONGUE IS OF THE PUREST SILVER TONIGHT, LOKI!
WHY, SOON YOU WILL HAVE ME FORGET YOU ARE THE GOD OF LIES!
--AND THAT IS MY FULL CONFESSION, BROTHER.
I HOPED, IN TELLING YOU, THAT I COULD MAKE AMENDS--BE SOMETHING OTHER THAN--
DO...DO NOT TROUBLE YOURSELF, LOKI. FROM WHAT YOU SAY, YOU ACTED WITHOUT CHOICE.
WE ARE WHAT WE ARE, AFTER ALL...
...AND YOU WILL ALWAYS BE THE GOD OF--

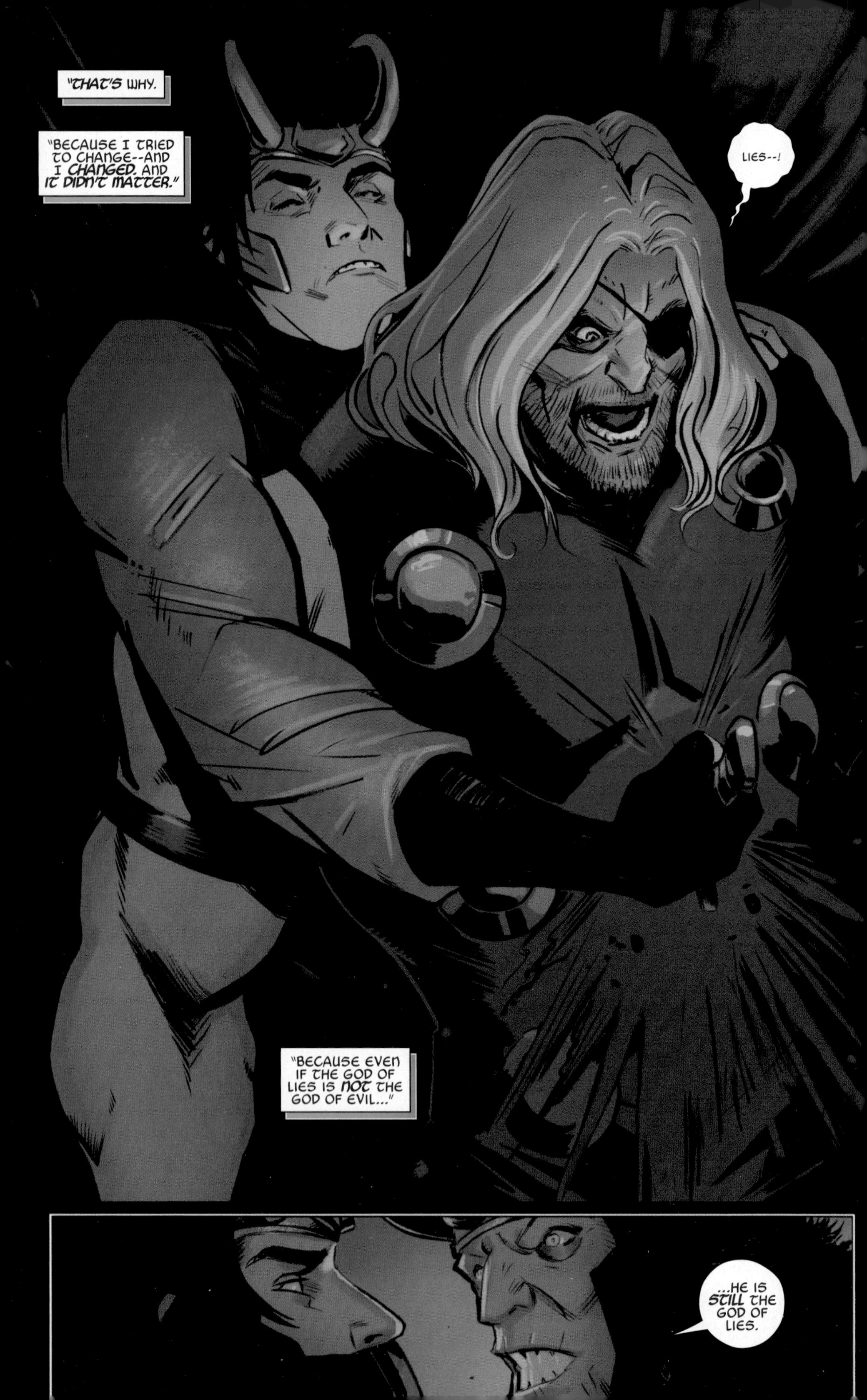
"THAT'S WHY.
"BECAUSE I TRIED TO CHANGE--AND I CHANGED. AND IT DIDN'T MATTER."
LIES--!
"BECAUSE EVEN IF THE GOD OF LIES IS NOT THE GOD OF EVIL..."
...HE IS STILL THE GOD OF LIES.

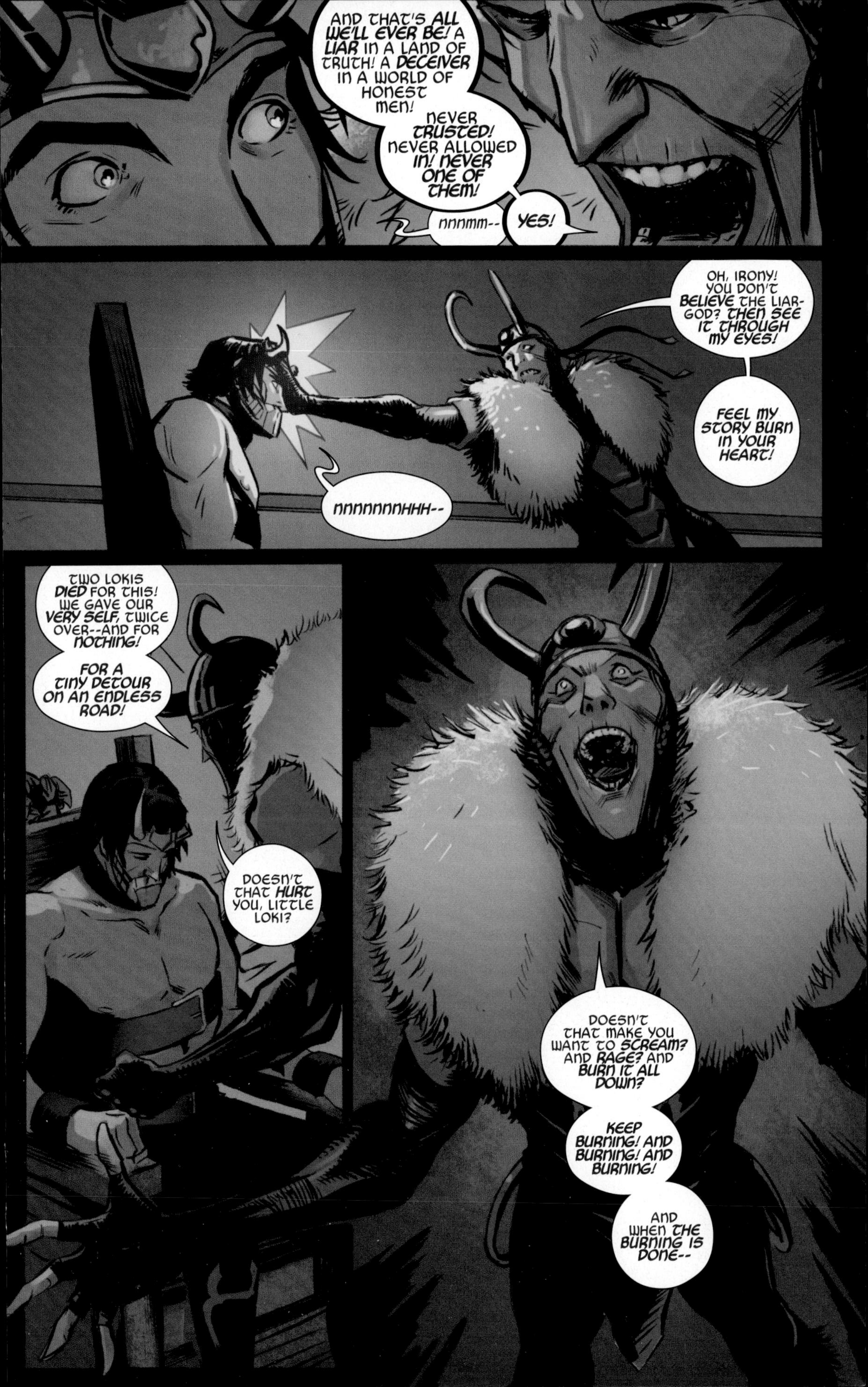
AND THAT'S ALL WE'LL EVER BE! A LIAR IN A LAND OF TRUTH! A DECEIVER IN A WORLD OF HONEST MEN!
NEVER TRUSTED! NEVER ALLOWED IN! NEVER ONE OF THEM!
NNNMM--
YES!
OH, IRONY! YOU DON'T BELIEVE THE LIAR-GOD? THEN SEE IT THROUGH MY EYES!
FEEL MY STORY BURN IN YOUR HEART!
NNNNNNNHHH--
TWO LOKIS DIED FOR THIS! WE GAVE OUR VERY SELF, TWICE OVER--AND FOR NOTHING!
FOR A TINY DETOUR ON AN ENDLESS ROAD!
DOESN'T THAT HURT YOU, LITTLE LOKI?
DOESN'T THAT MAKE YOU WANT TO SCREAM? AND RAGE? AND BURN IT ALL DOWN?
KEEP BURNING! AND BURNING! AND BURNING!
AND WHEN THE BURNING IS DONE--

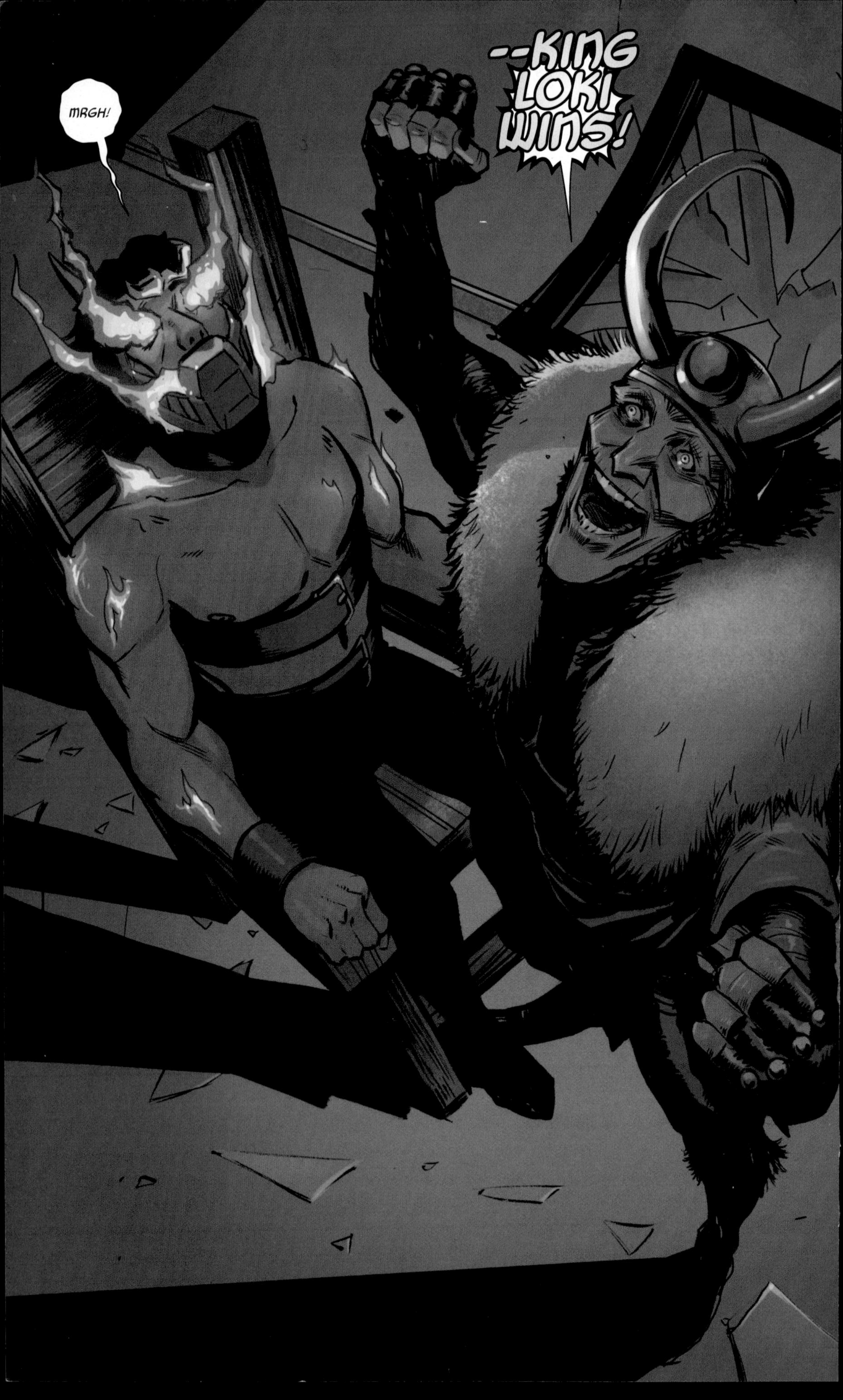
MRGH!
--KING LOKI WINS!

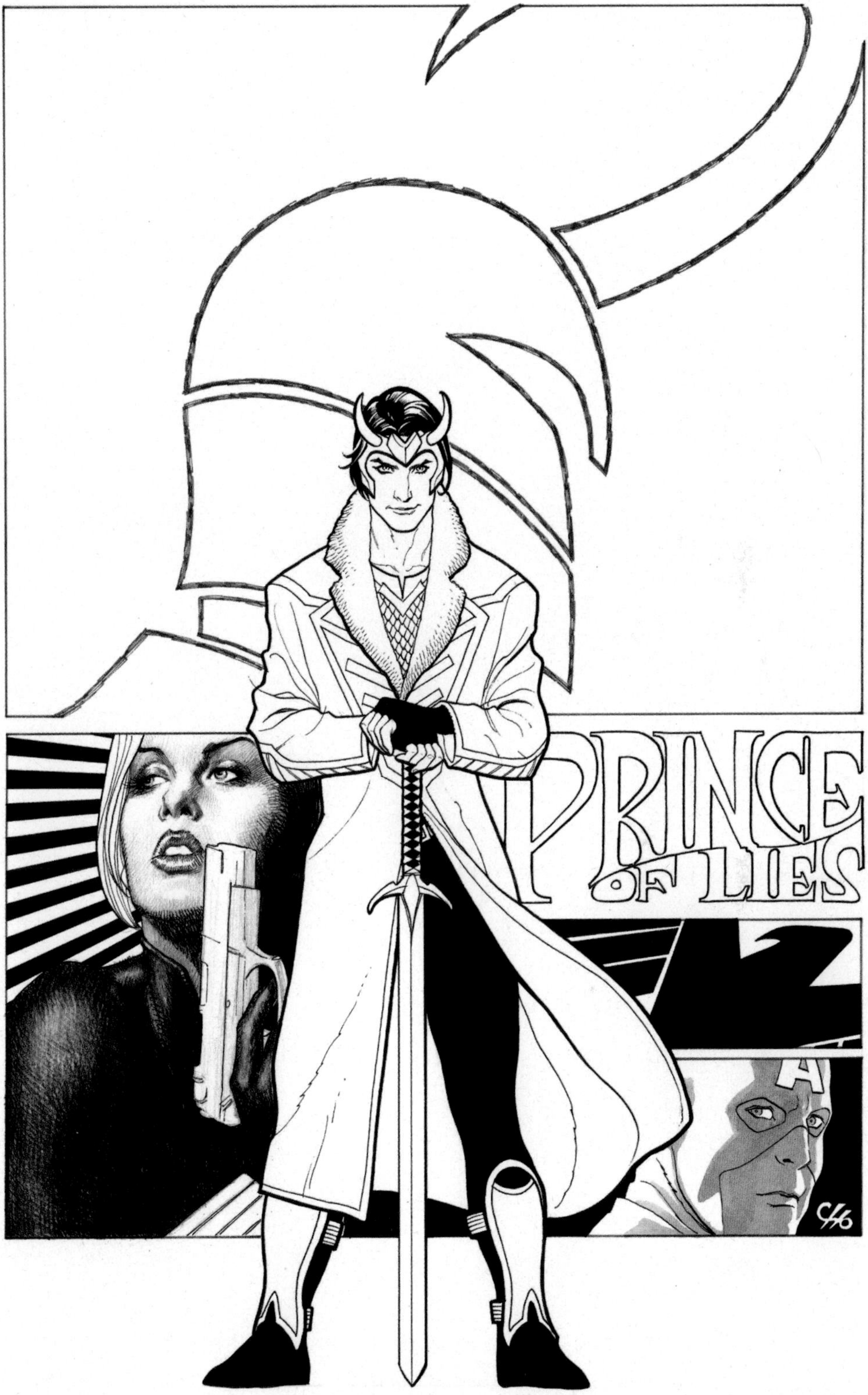
PRINCE
OF LIES

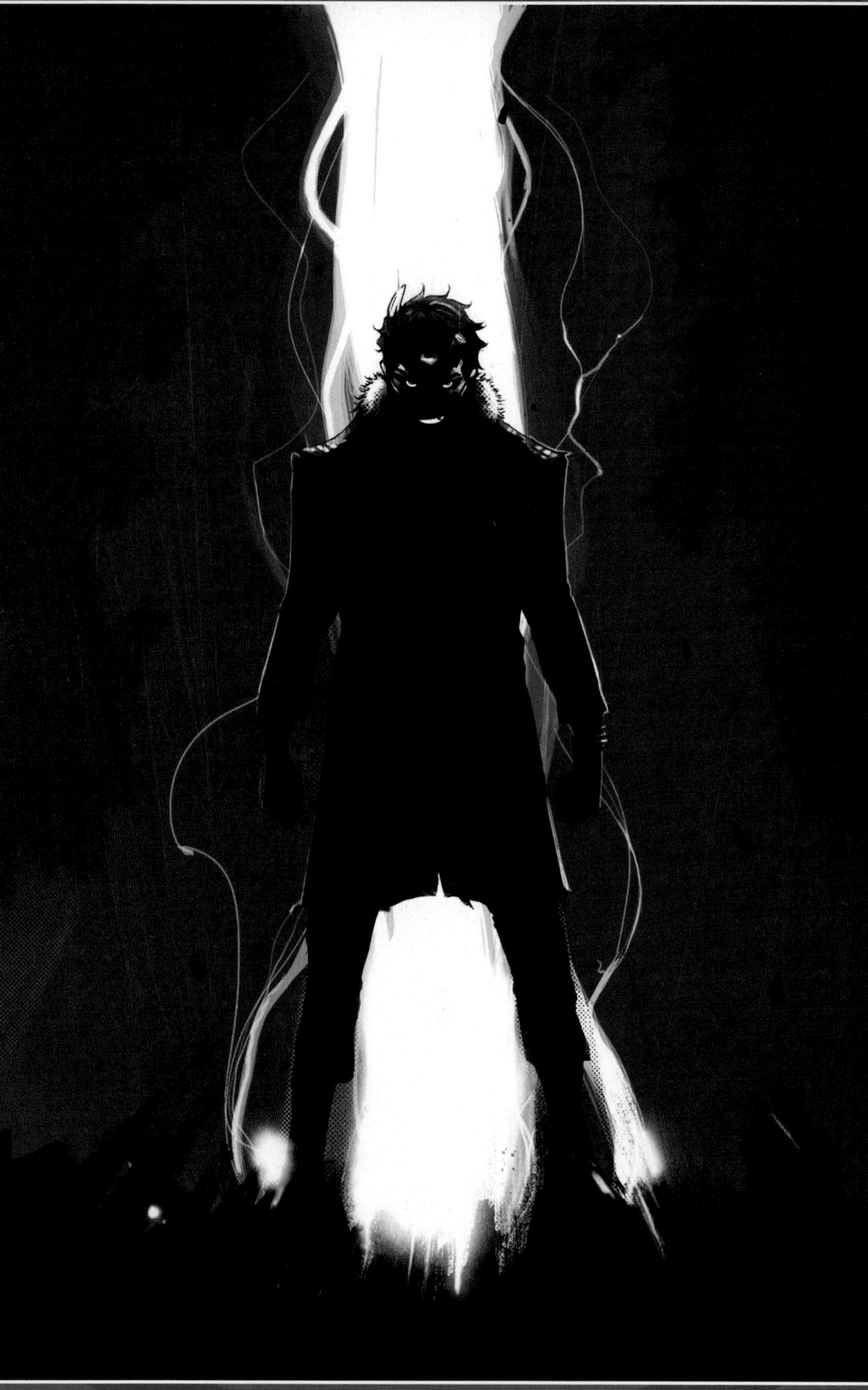

LOKI: AGENT OF ASGARD #13

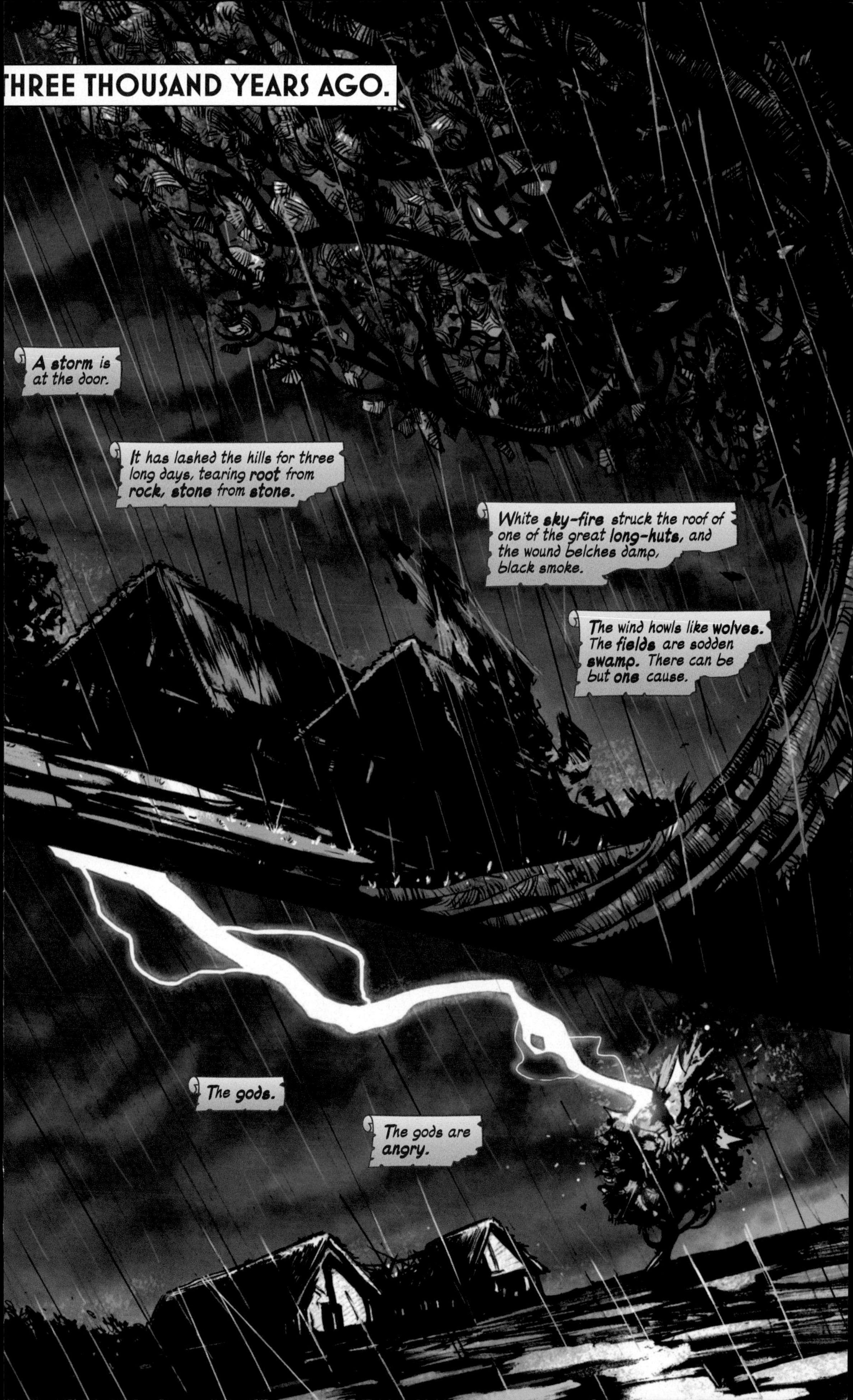
THREE THOUSAND YEARS AGO.
A storm is at the door.
It has lashed the hills for three long days, tearing root from rock, stone from stone.
White sky-fire struck the roof of one of the great long-huts, and the wound belches damp, black smoke.
The wind howls like wolves. The fields are sodden swamp. There can be but one cause.
The gods.
The gods are angry.

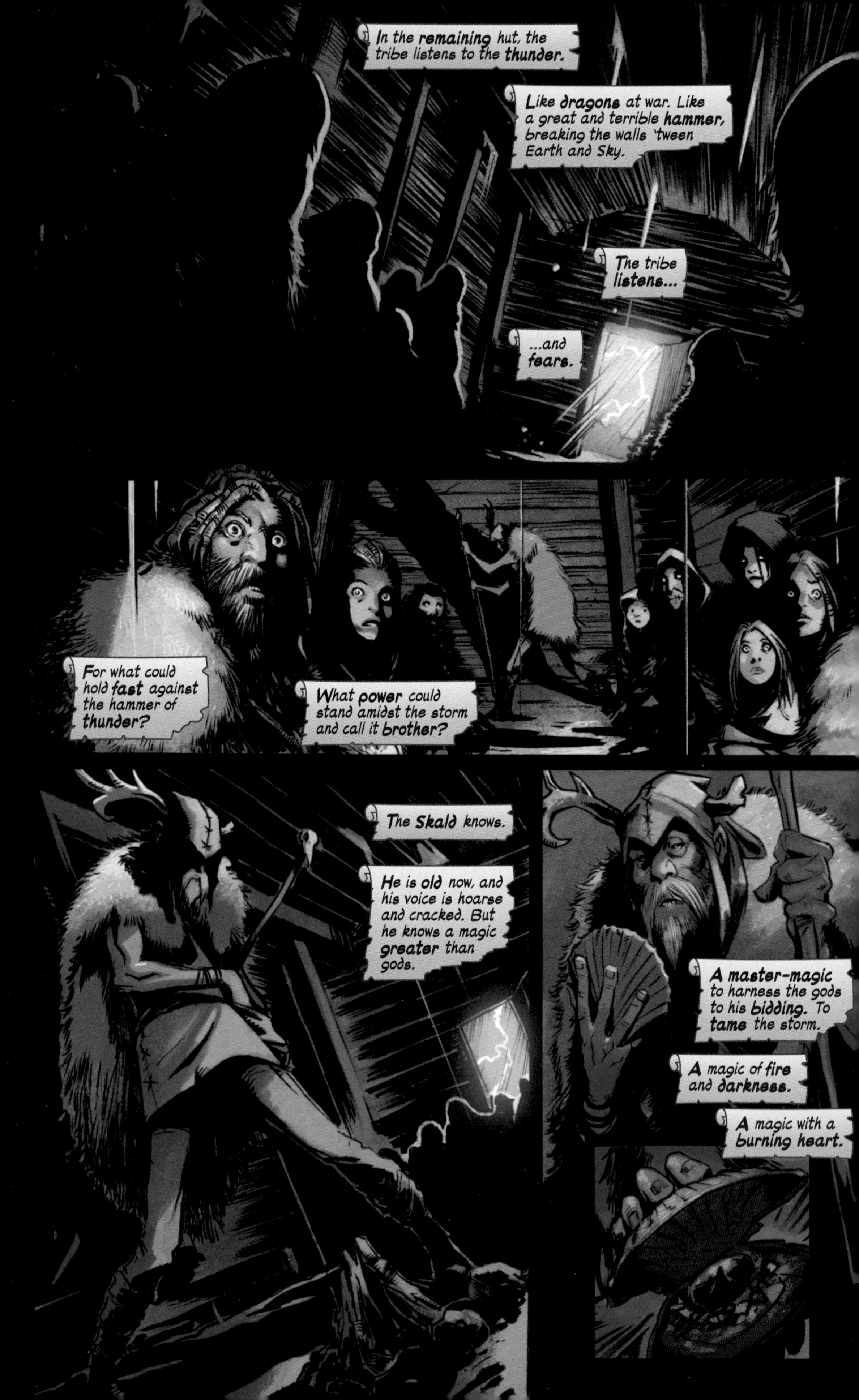
In the remaining hut, the tribe listens to the thunder.
Like dragons at war. Like a great and terrible hammer, breaking the walls 'tween Earth and Sky.
The tribe listens...
...and fears.
For what could hold fast against the hammer of thunder?
What power could stand amidst the storm and call it brother?
The Skald knows.
He is old now, and his voice is hoarse and cracked. But he knows a magic greater than gods.
A master-magic to harness the gods to his bidding. To tame the storm.
A magic of fire and darkness.
A magic with a burning heart.

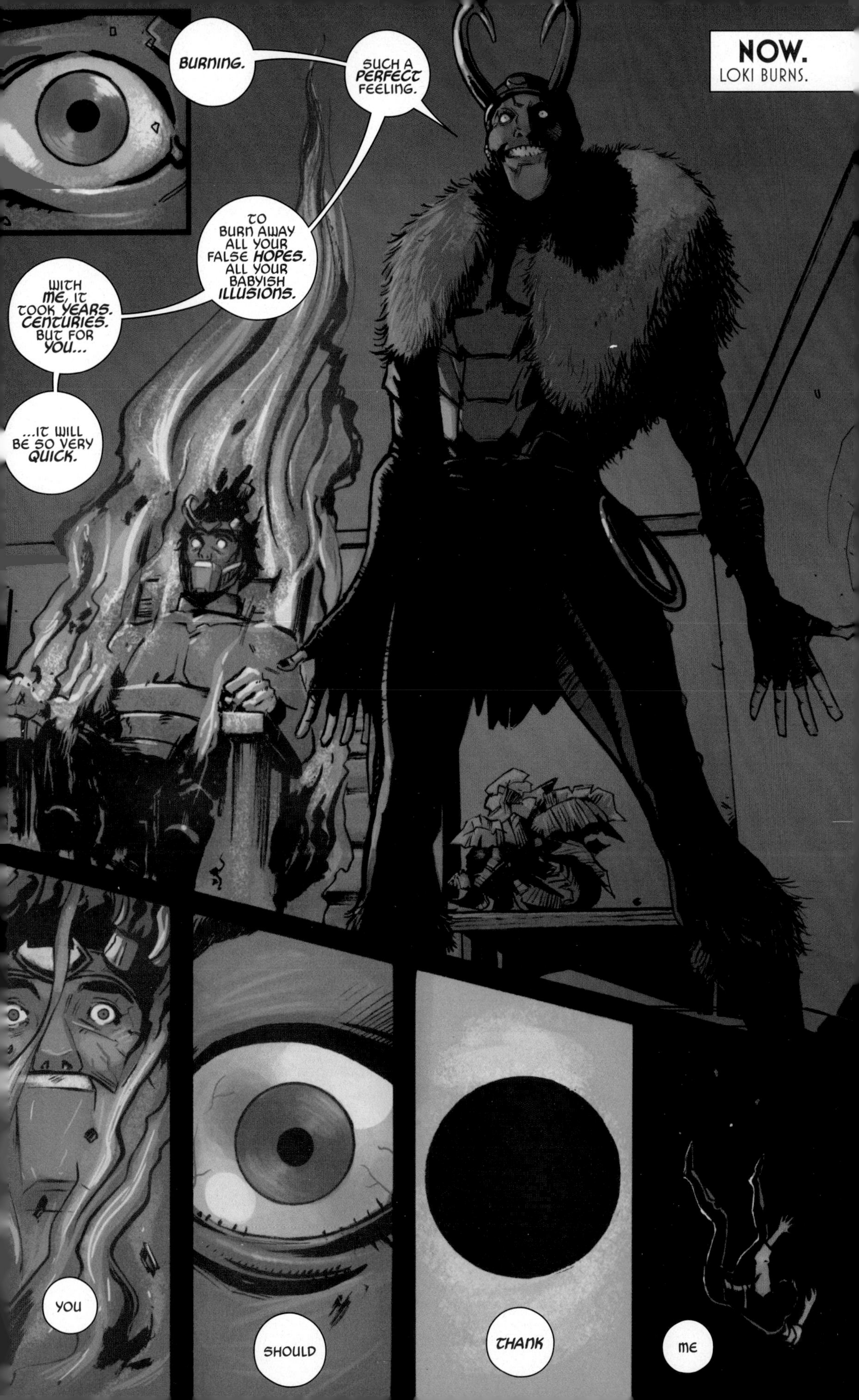
NOW.
LOKI BURNS.
BURNING.
SUCH A PERFECT FEELING.
TO BURN AWAY ALL YOUR FALSE HOPES. ALL YOUR BABYISH ILLUSIONS.
WITH ME, IT TOOK YEARS. CENTURIES. BUT FOR YOU...
...IT WILL BE SO VERY QUICK.
YOU
SHOULD
THANK
ME

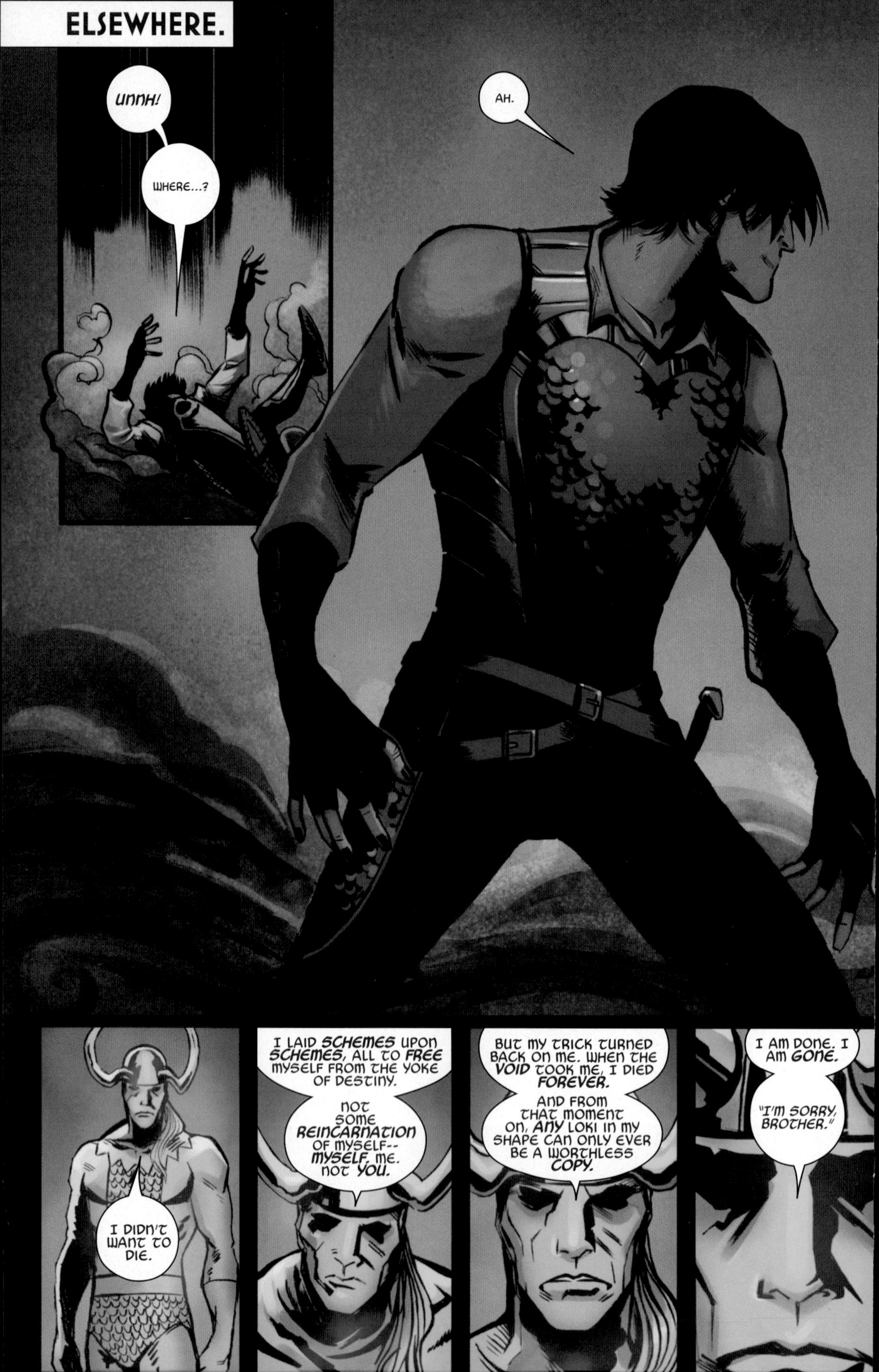
ELSEWHERE.
UNNH!
WHERE...?
AH.
I DIDN'T WANT TO DIE.
I LAID SCHEMES UPON SCHEMES, ALL TO FREE MYSELF FROM THE YOKE OF DESTINY.
NOT SOME REINCARNATION OF MYSELF-- MYSELF. ME. NOT YOU.
BUT MY TRICK TURNED BACK ON ME. WHEN THE VOID TOOK ME, I DIED FOREVER.
AND FROM THAT MOMENT ON, ANY LOKI IN MY SHAPE CAN ONLY EVER BE A WORTHLESS COPY.
I AM DONE. I AM GONE.
"I'M SORRY, BROTHER."

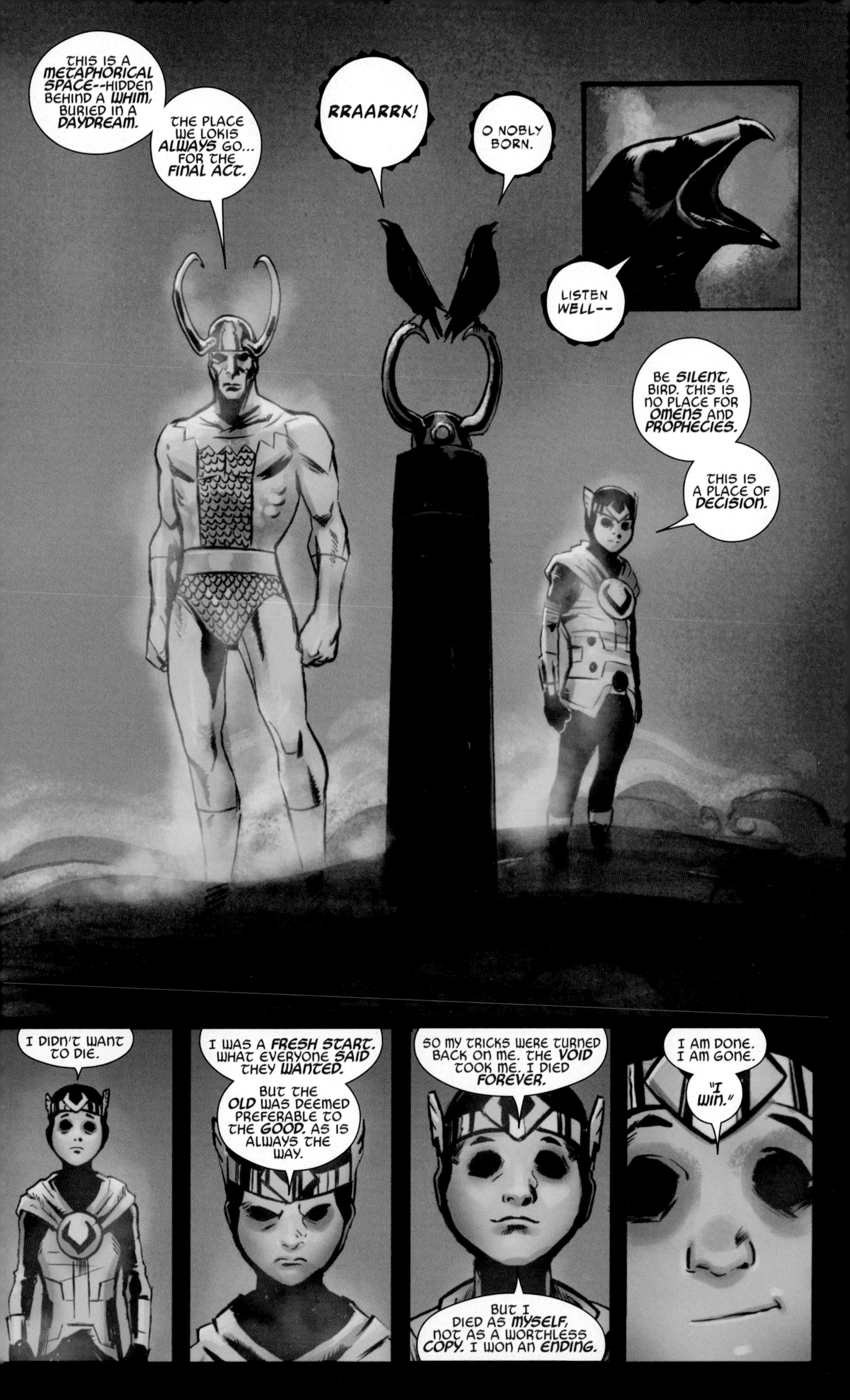
THIS IS A METAPHORICAL SPACE--HIDDEN BEHIND A WHIM, BURIED IN A DAYDREAM.
THE PLACE WE LOKIS ALWAYS GO... FOR THE FINAL ACT.
RRAARRK!
O NOBLY BORN.
LISTEN WELL--
BE SILENT, BIRD. THIS IS NO PLACE FOR OMENS AND PROPHECIES.
THIS IS A PLACE OF DECISION.
I DIDN'T WANT TO DIE.
I WAS A FRESH START. WHAT EVERYONE SAID THEY WANTED.
BUT THE OLD WAS DEEMED PREFERABLE TO THE GOOD. AS IS ALWAYS THE WAY.
SO MY TRICKS WERE TURNED BACK ON ME. THE VOID TOOK ME. I DIED FOREVER.
BUT I DIED AS MYSELF, NOT AS A WORTHLESS COPY. I WON AN ENDING.
I AM DONE. I AM GONE.
"I WIN."

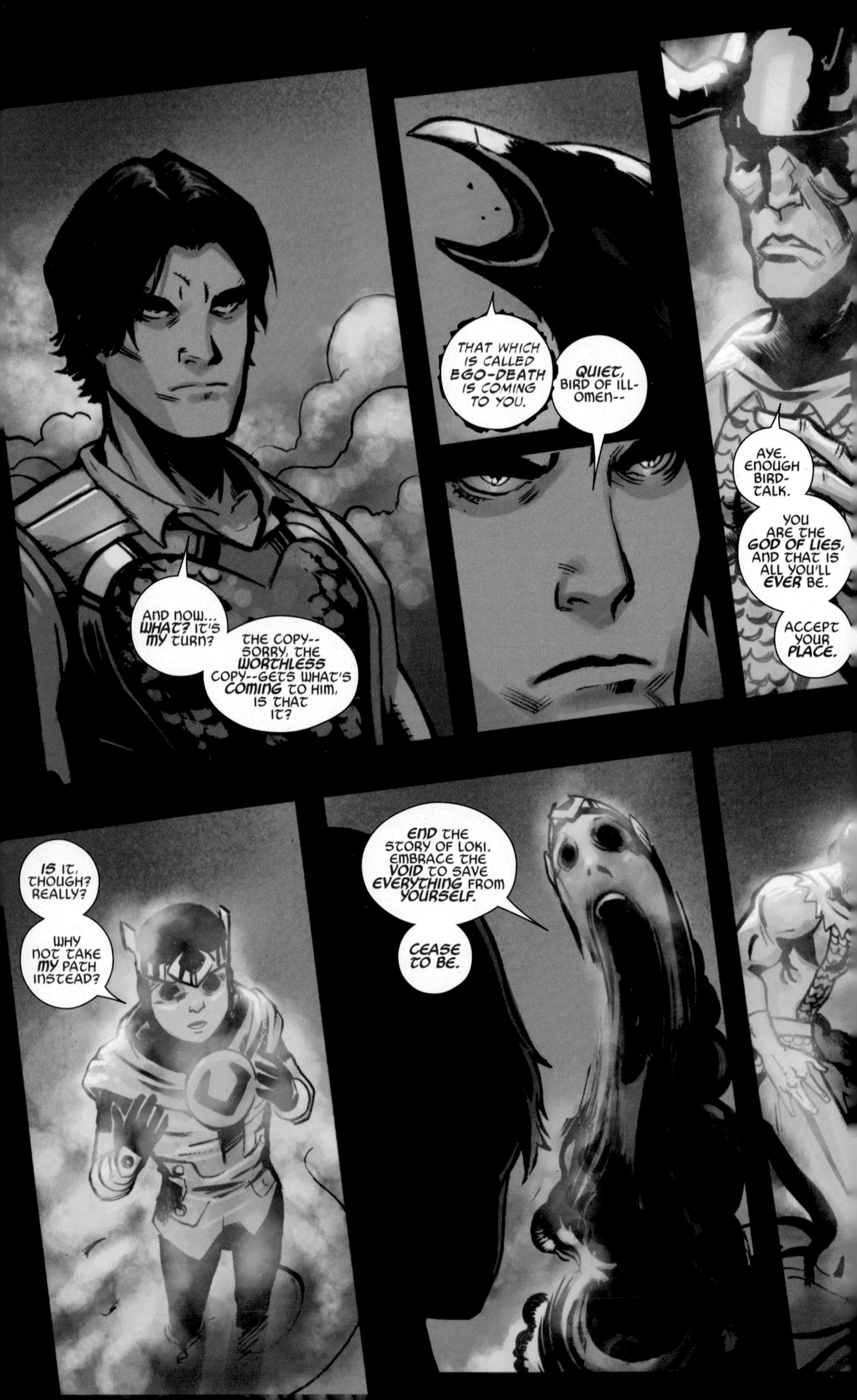
AND NOW... WHAT? IT'S MY TURN?
THE COPY-- SORRY, THE WORTHLESS COPY--GETS WHAT'S COMING TO HIM, IS THAT IT?
THAT WHICH IS CALLED EGO-DEATH IS COMING TO YOU.
QUIET, BIRD OF ILL-OMEN--
AYE. ENOUGH BIRD-TALK.
YOU ARE THE GOD OF LIES, AND THAT IS ALL YOU'LL EVER BE.
ACCEPT YOUR PLACE.
IS IT, THOUGH? REALLY?
WHY NOT TAKE MY PATH INSTEAD?
END THE STORY OF LOKI. EMBRACE THE VOID TO SAVE EVERYTHING FROM YOURSELF.
CEASE TO BE.

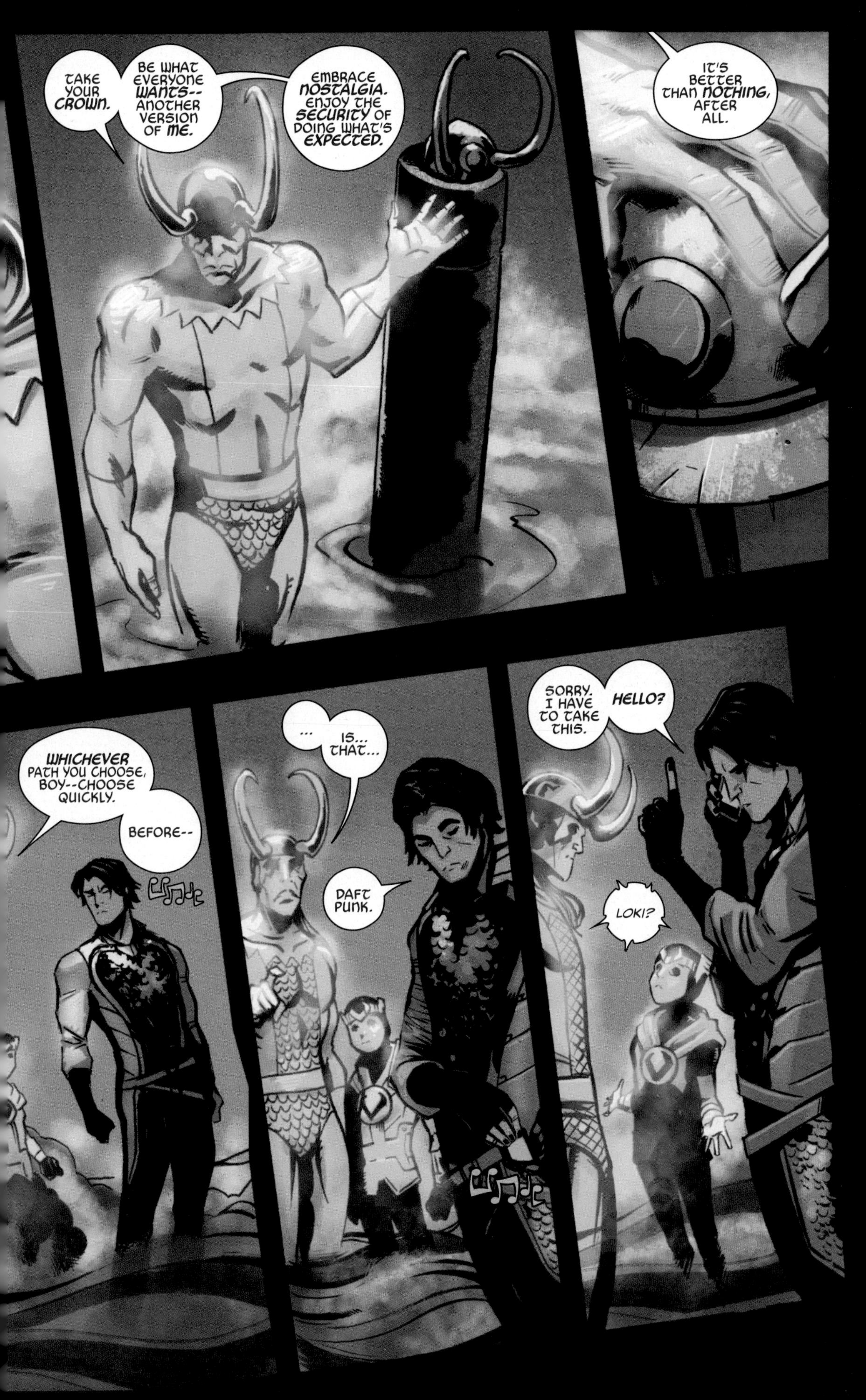

TAKE YOUR CROWN.
BE WHAT EVERYONE WANTS-- ANOTHER VERSION OF ME.
EMBRACE NOSTALGIA. ENJOY THE SECURITY OF DOING WHAT'S EXPECTED.
IT'S BETTER THAN NOTHING, AFTER ALL.
WHICHEVER PATH YOU CHOOSE, BOY--CHOOSE QUICKLY.
BEFORE--
...
IS... THAT...
DAFT PUNK.
SORRY. I HAVE TO TAKE THIS.
HELLO?
LOKI?

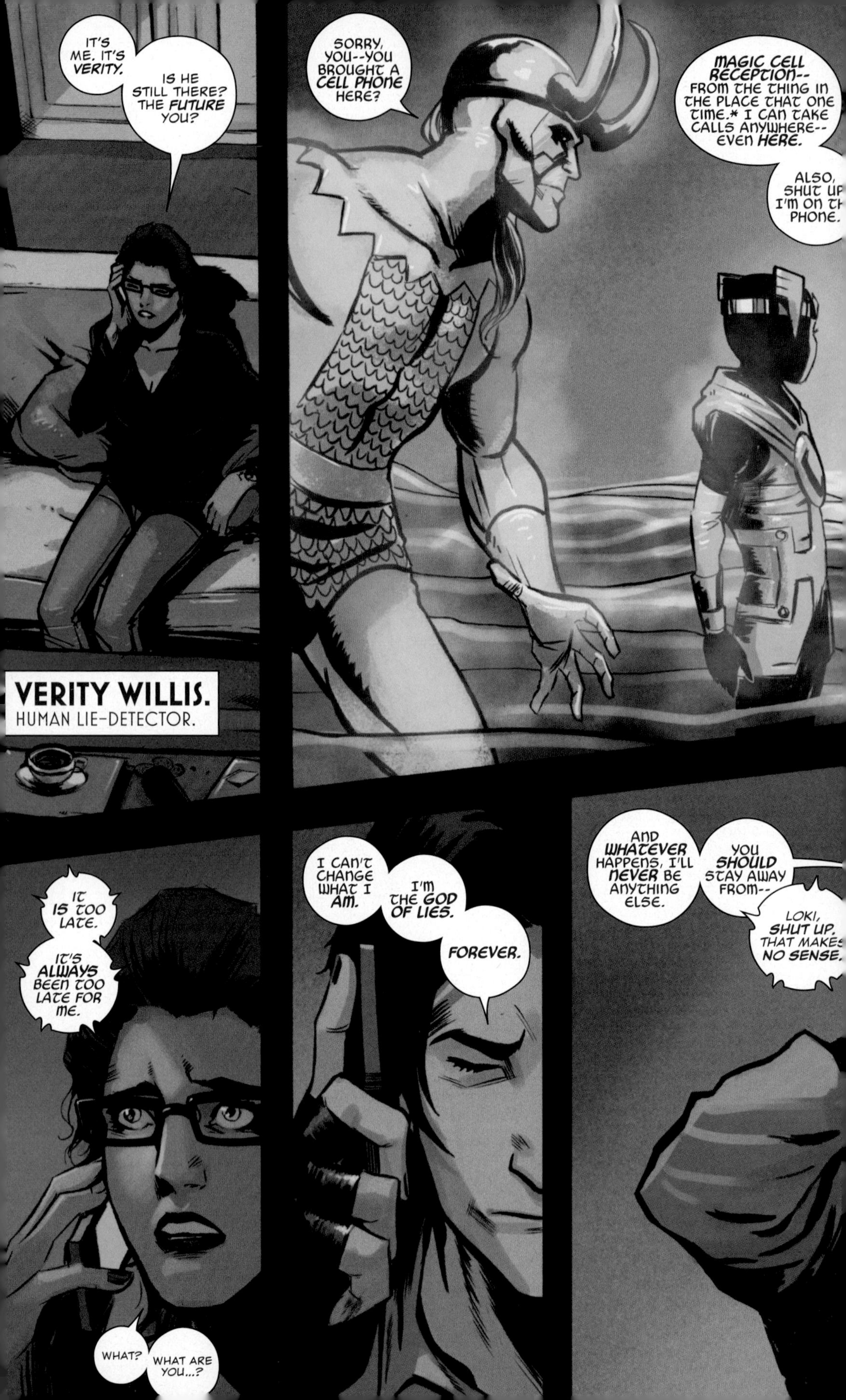

IT'S ME. IT'S VERITY.
IS HE STILL THERE? THE FUTURE YOU?
VERITY WILLIS.
HUMAN LIE-DETECTOR.
SORRY, YOU--YOU BROUGHT A CELL PHONE HERE?
MAGIC CELL RECEPTION-- FROM THE THING IN THE PLACE THAT ONE TIME.* I CAN TAKE CALLS ANYWHERE-- EVEN HERE.
ALSO, SHUT UP I'M ON TH PHONE.
IT IS TOO LATE.
IT'S ALWAYS BEEN TOO LATE FOR ME.
WHAT?
WHAT ARE YOU...?
I CAN'T CHANGE WHAT I AM.
I'M THE GOD OF LIES.
FOREVER.
AND WHATEVER HAPPENS, I'LL NEVER BE ANYTHING ELSE.
YOU SHOULD STAY AWAY FROM--
LOKI, SHUT UP. THAT MAKES NO SENSE.

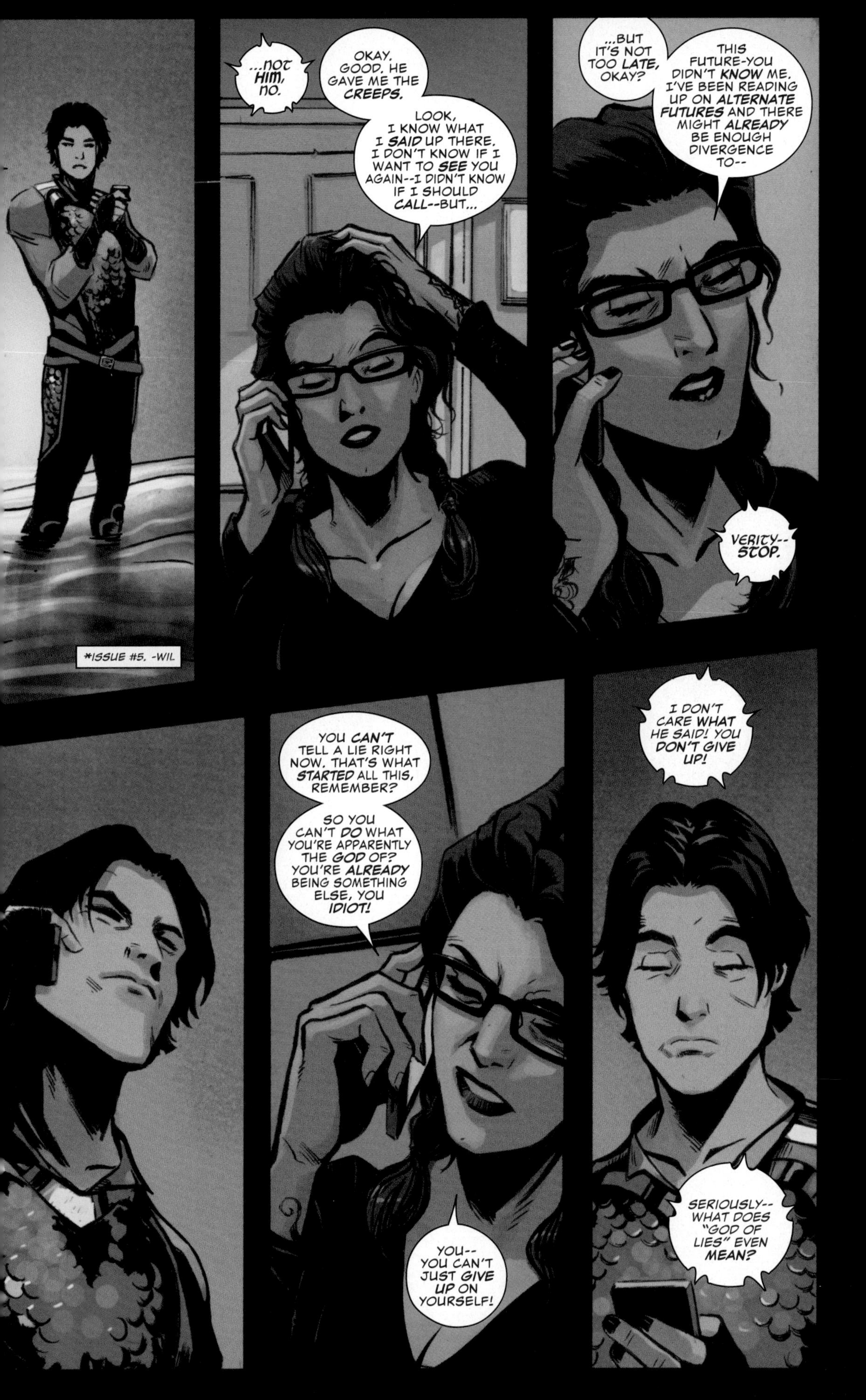
...NOT HIM, NO.
OKAY. GOOD. HE GAVE ME THE CREEPS.
LOOK, I KNOW WHAT I SAID UP THERE. I DON'T KNOW IF I WANT TO SEE YOU AGAIN--I DIDN'T KNOW IF I SHOULD CALL--BUT...
...BUT IT'S NOT TOO LATE, OKAY?
THIS FUTURE-YOU DIDN'T KNOW ME. I'VE BEEN READING UP ON ALTERNATE FUTURES AND THERE MIGHT ALREADY BE ENOUGH DIVERGENCE TO--
VERITY--STOP.
*ISSUE #5. -WIL
YOU CAN'T TELL A LIE RIGHT NOW. THAT'S WHAT STARTED ALL THIS, REMEMBER?
SO YOU CAN'T DO WHAT YOU'RE APPARENTLY THE GOD OF? YOU'RE ALREADY BEING SOMETHING ELSE, YOU IDIOT!
YOU--YOU CAN'T JUST GIVE UP ON YOURSELF!
I DON'T CARE WHAT HE SAID! YOU DON'T GIVE UP!
SERIOUSLY--WHAT DOES "GOD OF LIES" EVEN MEAN?

BE WORTHY. NOT OF YOUR BROTHER'S POWER, BUT OF YOUR OWN.
REMEMBER.
REMEMBER WHAT A LIE IS.
LOKI-- YOU--
...RIGHT.
WHAT IS A LIE, WHEN IT'S AT HOME? ANYONE?
L-LOKI-- LISTEN--
LISTEN TO US--

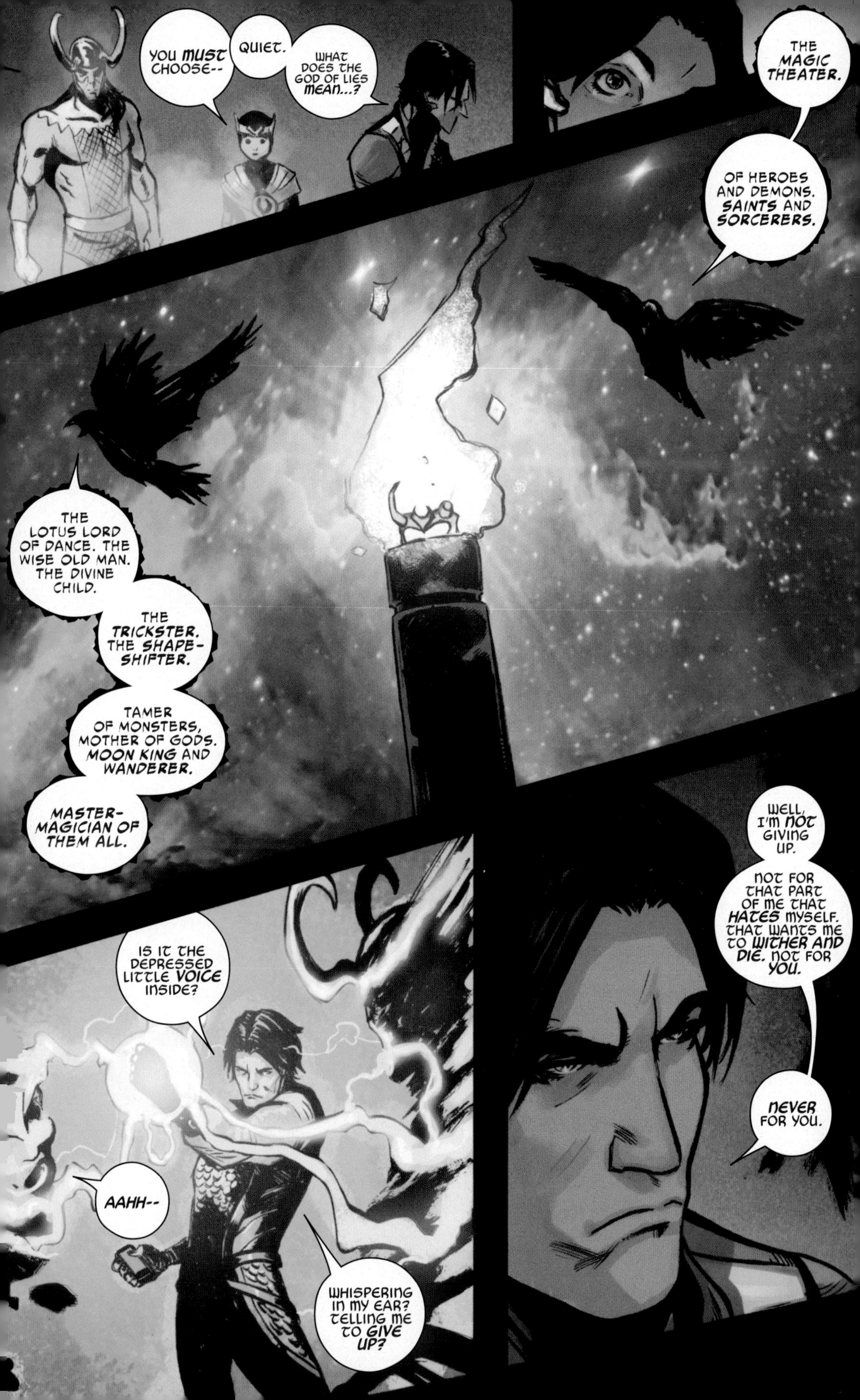
YOU MUST CHOOSE--
QUIET.
WHAT DOES THE GOD OF LIES MEAN...?
THE MAGIC THEATER.
OF HEROES AND DEMONS. SAINTS AND SORCERERS.
THE LOTUS LORD OF DANCE. THE WISE OLD MAN. THE DIVINE CHILD.
THE TRICKSTER. THE SHAPE-SHIFTER.
TAMER OF MONSTERS, MOTHER OF GODS. MOON KING AND WANDERER.
MASTER-MAGICIAN OF THEM ALL.
IS IT THE DEPRESSED LITTLE VOICE INSIDE?
AAHH--
WHISPERING IN MY EAR? TELLING ME TO GIVE UP?
WELL, I'M NOT GIVING UP.
NOT FOR THAT PART OF ME THAT HATES MYSELF. THAT WANTS ME TO WITHER AND DIE. NOT FOR YOU.
NEVER FOR YOU.

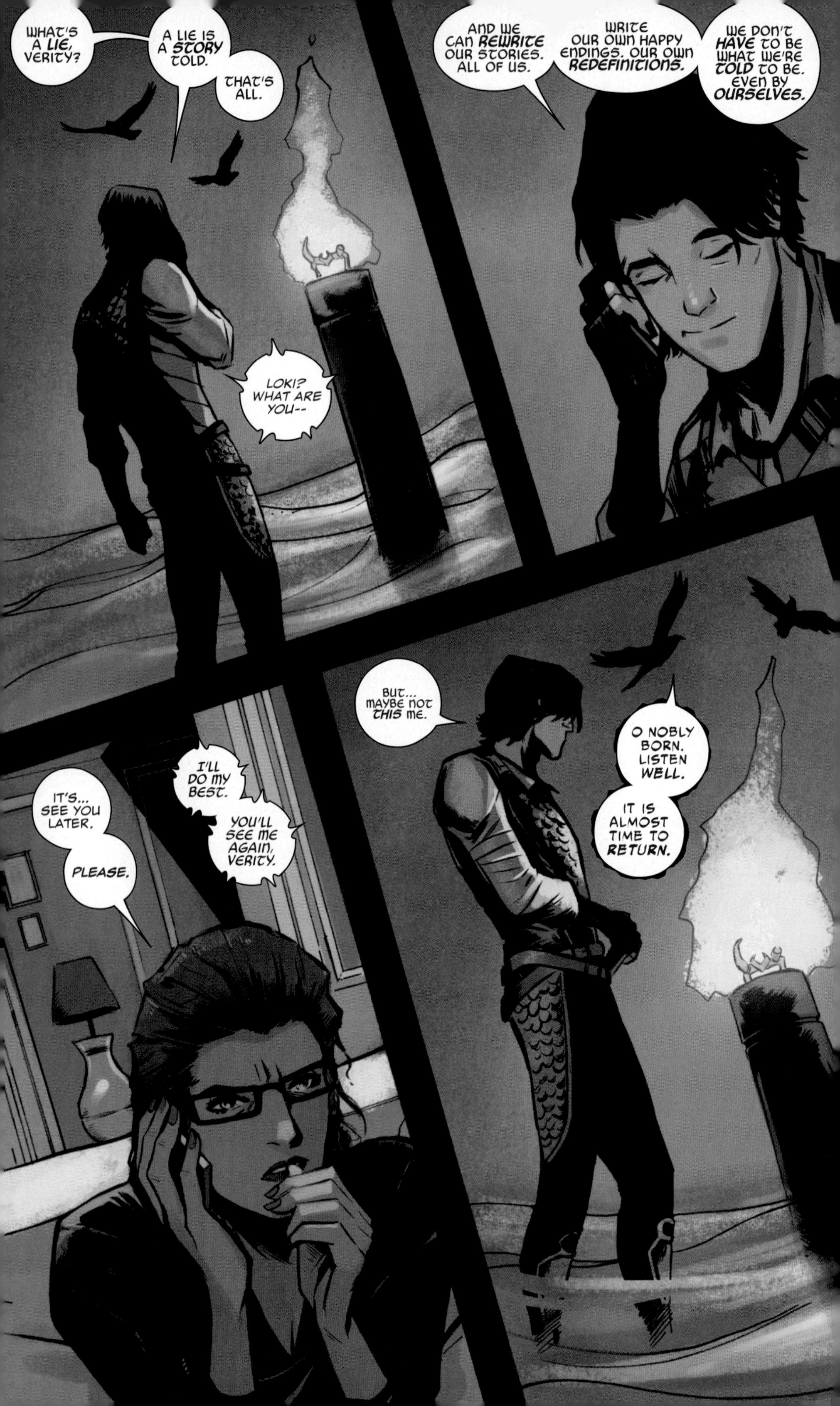
WHAT'S A LIE, VERITY?
A LIE IS A STORY TOLD.
THAT'S ALL.
LOKI? WHAT ARE YOU--
AND WE CAN REWRITE OUR STORIES. ALL OF US.
WRITE OUR OWN HAPPY ENDINGS. OUR OWN REDEFINITIONS.
WE DON'T HAVE TO BE WHAT WE'RE TOLD TO BE. EVEN BY OURSELVES.
IT'S... SEE YOU LATER.
PLEASE.
I'LL DO MY BEST.
YOU'LL SEE ME AGAIN, VERITY.
BUT... MAYBE NOT THIS ME.
O NOBLY BORN. LISTEN WELL.
IT IS ALMOST TIME TO RETURN.

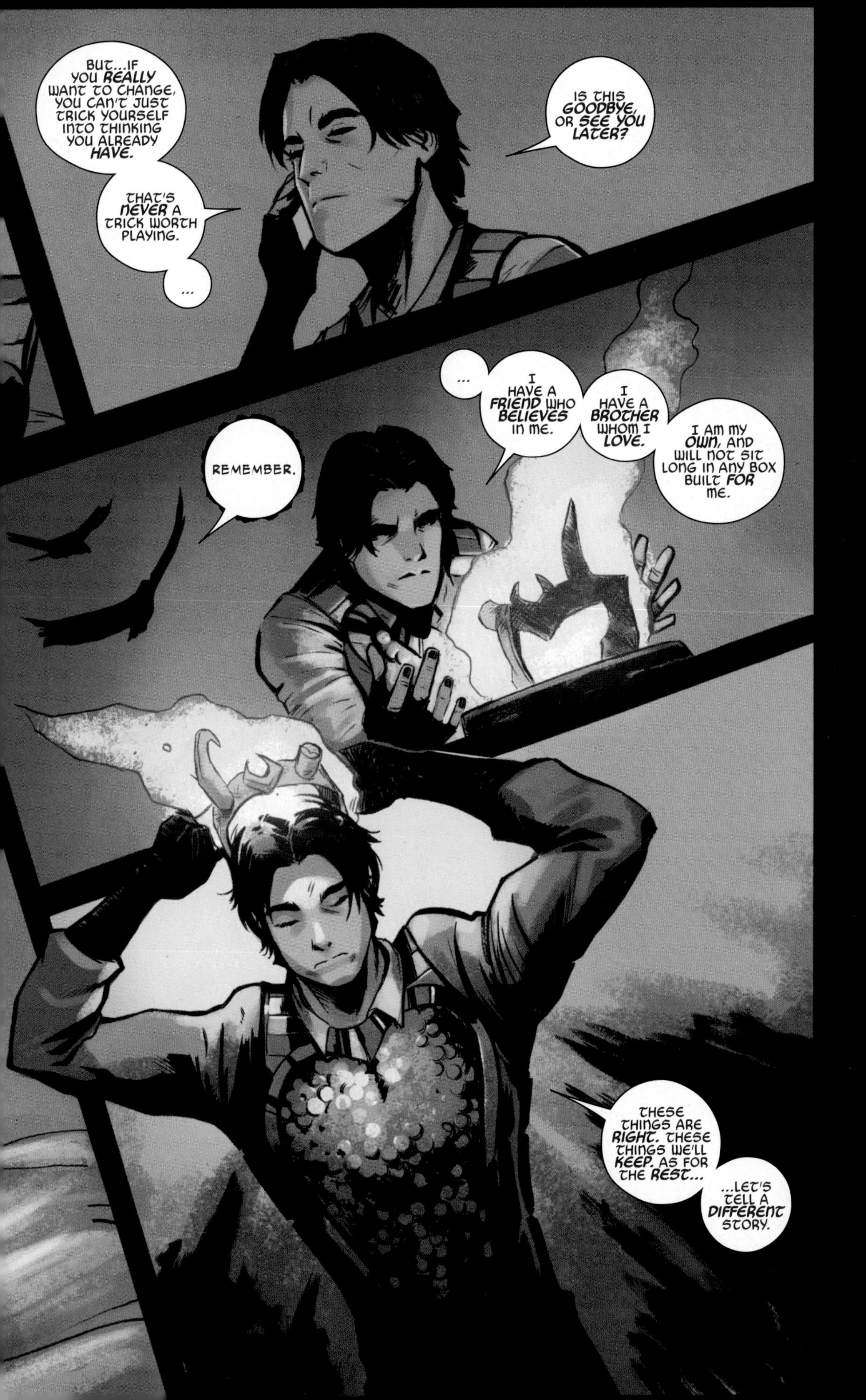
BUT...IF YOU REALLY WANT TO CHANGE, YOU CAN'T JUST TRICK YOURSELF INTO THINKING YOU ALREADY HAVE.
THAT'S NEVER A TRICK WORTH PLAYING.
...
IS THIS GOODBYE, OR SEE YOU LATER?
REMEMBER.
...
I HAVE A FRIEND WHO BELIEVES IN ME.
I HAVE A BROTHER WHOM I LOVE.
I AM MY OWN, AND WILL NOT SIT LONG IN ANY BOX BUILT FOR ME.
THESE THINGS ARE RIGHT. THESE THINGS WE'LL KEEP. AS FOR THE REST...
...LET'S TELL A DIFFERENT STORY.

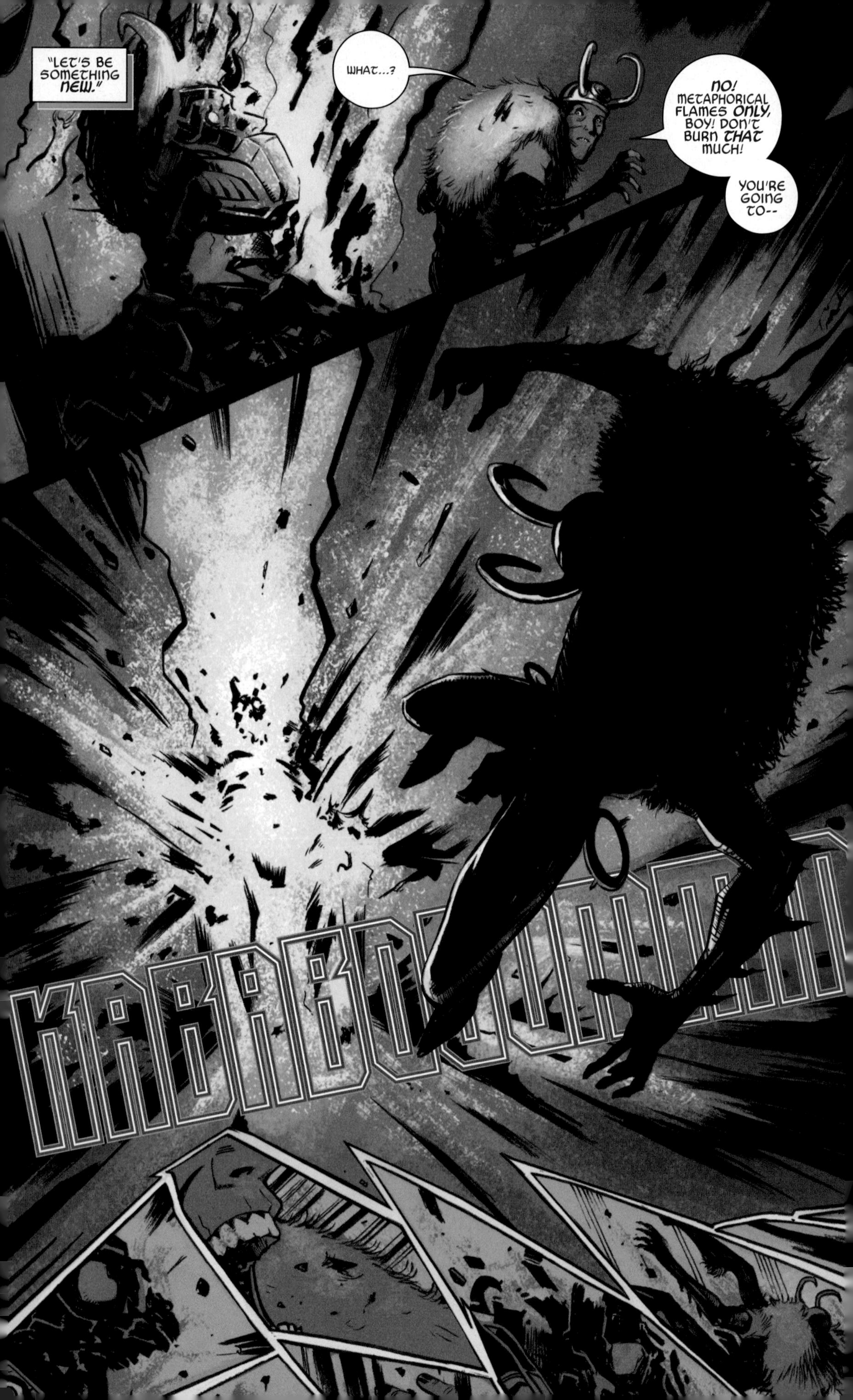
"LET'S BE SOMETHING NEW."
WHAT...?
NO! METAPHORICAL FLAMES ONLY, BOY! DON'T BURN THAT MUCH!
YOU'RE GOING TO--
KRABOOOOM

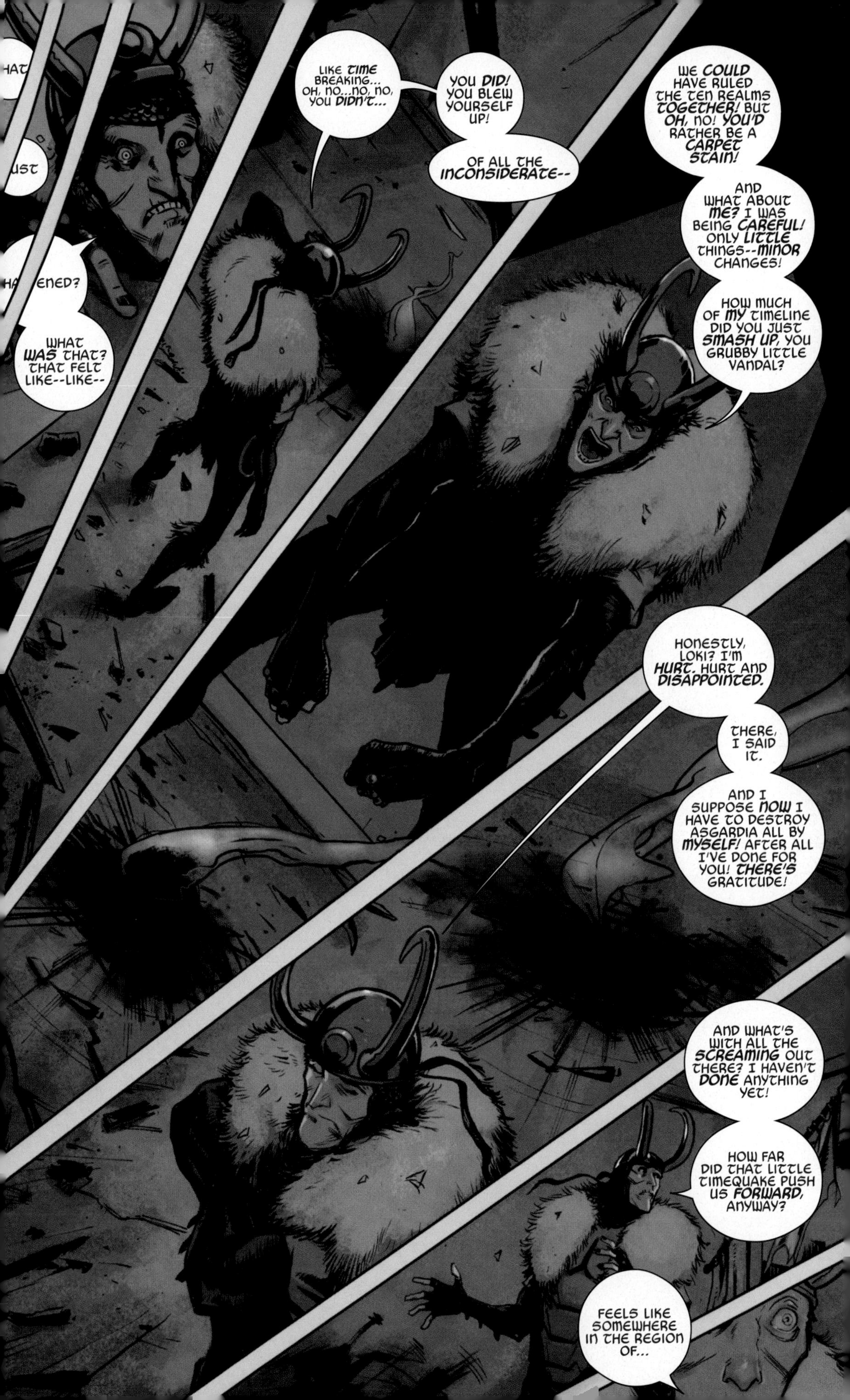
WHAT WAS THAT? THAT FELT LIKE--LIKE--
LIKE TIME BREAKING... OH, NO...NO, NO, YOU DIDN'T...
YOU DID! YOU BLEW YOURSELF UP!
OF ALL THE INCONSIDERATE--
WE COULD HAVE RULED THE TEN REALMS TOGETHER! BUT OH, NO! YOU'D RATHER BE A CARPET STAIN!
AND WHAT ABOUT ME? I WAS BEING CAREFUL! ONLY LITTLE THINGS--MINOR CHANGES!
HOW MUCH OF MY TIMELINE DID YOU JUST SMASH UP, YOU GRUBBY LITTLE VANDAL?
HONESTLY, LOKI? I'M HURT. HURT AND DISAPPOINTED.
THERE, I SAID IT.
AND I SUPPOSE NOW I HAVE TO DESTROY ASGARDIA ALL BY MYSELF! AFTER ALL I'VE DONE FOR YOU! THERE'S GRATITUDE!
AND WHAT'S WITH ALL THE SCREAMING OUT THERE? I HAVEN'T DONE ANYTHING YET!
HOW FAR DID THAT LITTLE TIMEQUAKE PUSH US FORWARD, ANYWAY?
FEELS LIKE SOMEWHERE IN THE REGION OF...

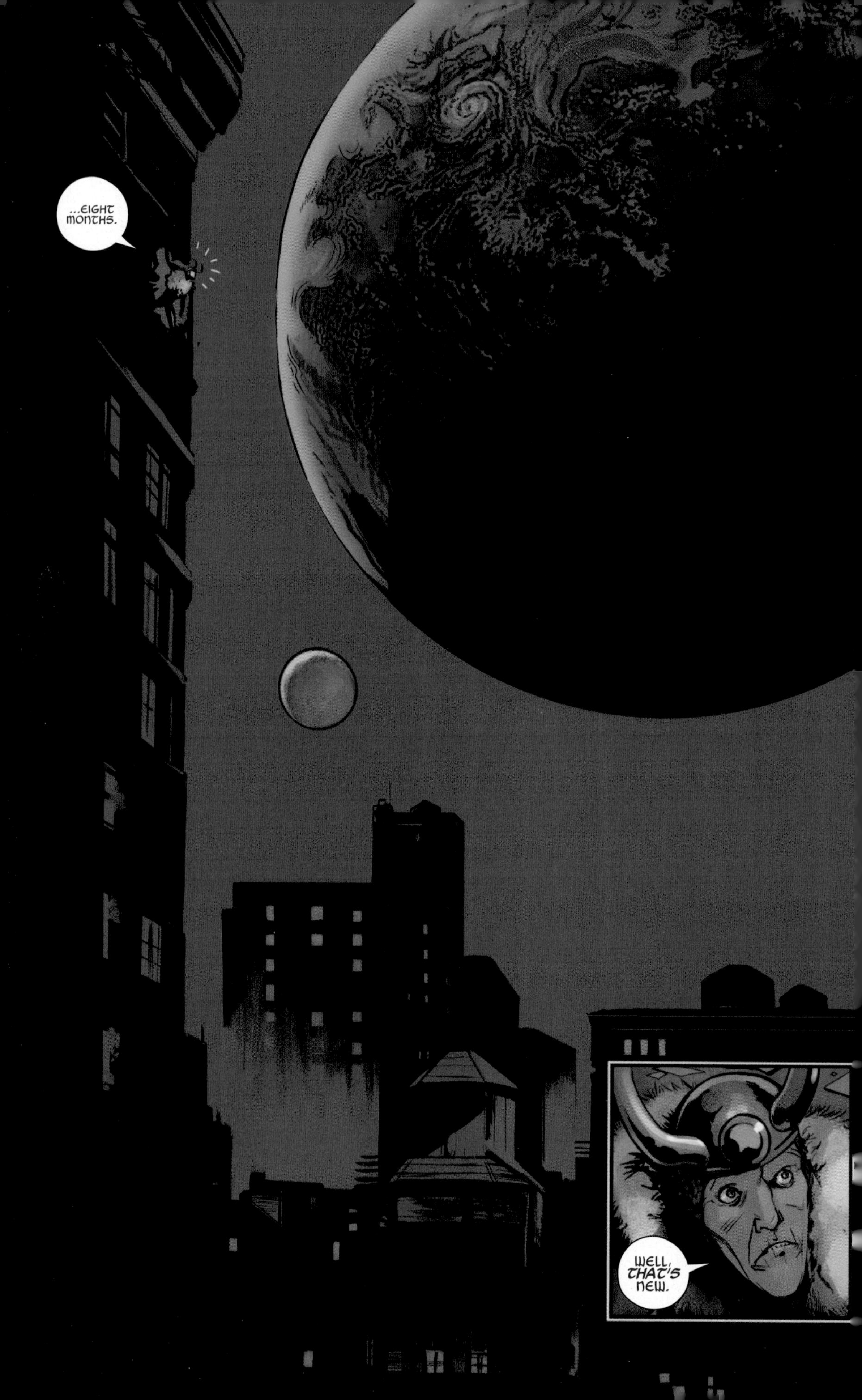
...EIGHT MONTHS.
WELL, THAT'S NEW.

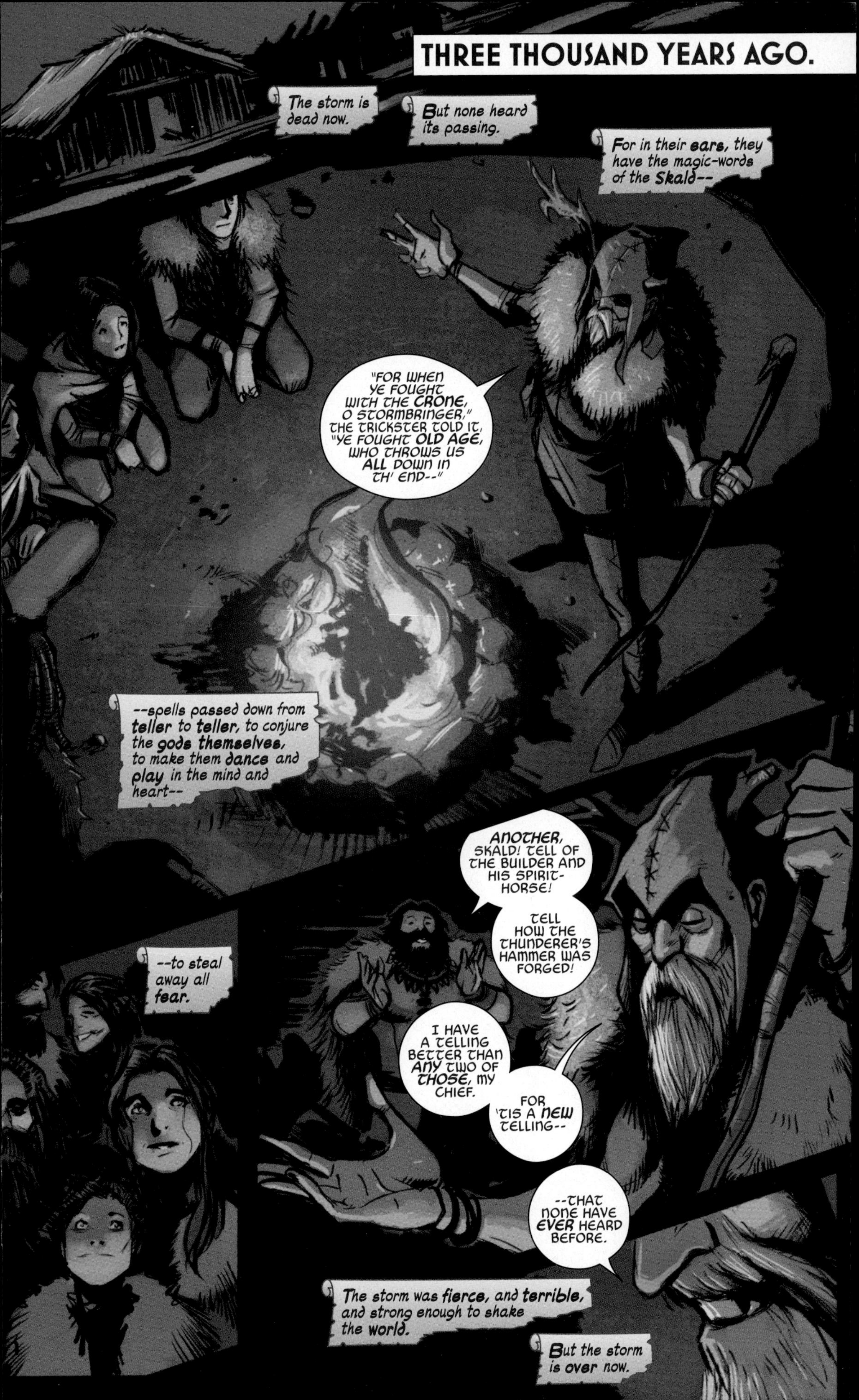
THREE THOUSAND YEARS AGO.
The storm is dead now.
But none heard its passing.
For in their ears, they have the magic-words of the Skald--
"FOR WHEN YE FOUGHT WITH THE CRONE, O STORMBRINGER," THE TRICKSTER TOLD IT, "YE FOUGHT OLD AGE, WHO THROWS US ALL DOWN IN TH' END--"
--spells passed down from teller to teller, to conjure the gods themselves, to make them dance and play in the mind and heart--
ANOTHER, SKALD! TELL OF THE BUILDER AND HIS SPIRIT-HORSE!
TELL HOW THE THUNDERER'S HAMMER WAS FORGED!
--to steal away all fear.
I HAVE A TELLING BETTER THAN ANY TWO OF THOSE, MY CHIEF.
FOR 'TIS A NEW TELLING--
--THAT NONE HAVE EVER HEARD BEFORE.
The storm was fierce, and terrible, and strong enough to shake the world.
But the storm is over now.

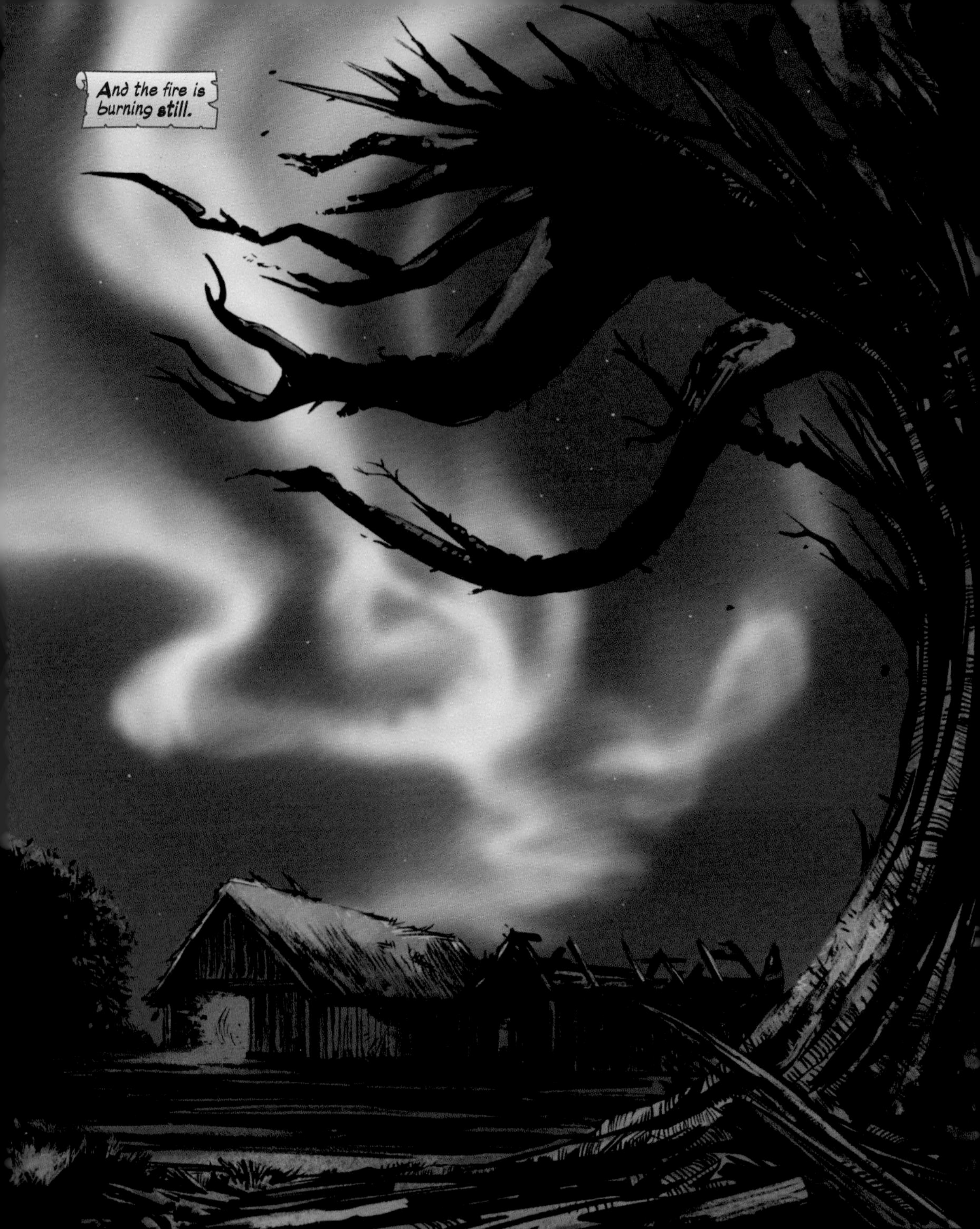
And the fire is burning still.

The Magic Theater

EPILOGUE.

EIGHT MONTHS PASSED.

Verity tried visiting Loki at his apartment, but it was gone--as if it had never been. Which, according to the building :ans, it never had. She tried calling around, but Lorelei and Sigurd were imprisoned in the realms of gods, and Thor--or the)dinson--didn't have a phone.

So she scoured the news, checking for super-battles and green-gold costumes. Looking for some sign that her friend 'as alive and okay.

And as she searched, and waited, and worried, she found herself reading.

Reading fiction. Fantasy. Myths and legends. It was painful at first, but over the long months she learned how to tune ut the constant, nagging whine in the base of her skull that the books were lying to her. Because now, after everything--after oki--she knew that even if the writer thought they were just telling a story…the story could still be true.

It wasn't the same. But it was something. It was a happy ending…

…but it wasn't *the* ending.

Outside, the sky turned red.

There was a knock at the door.

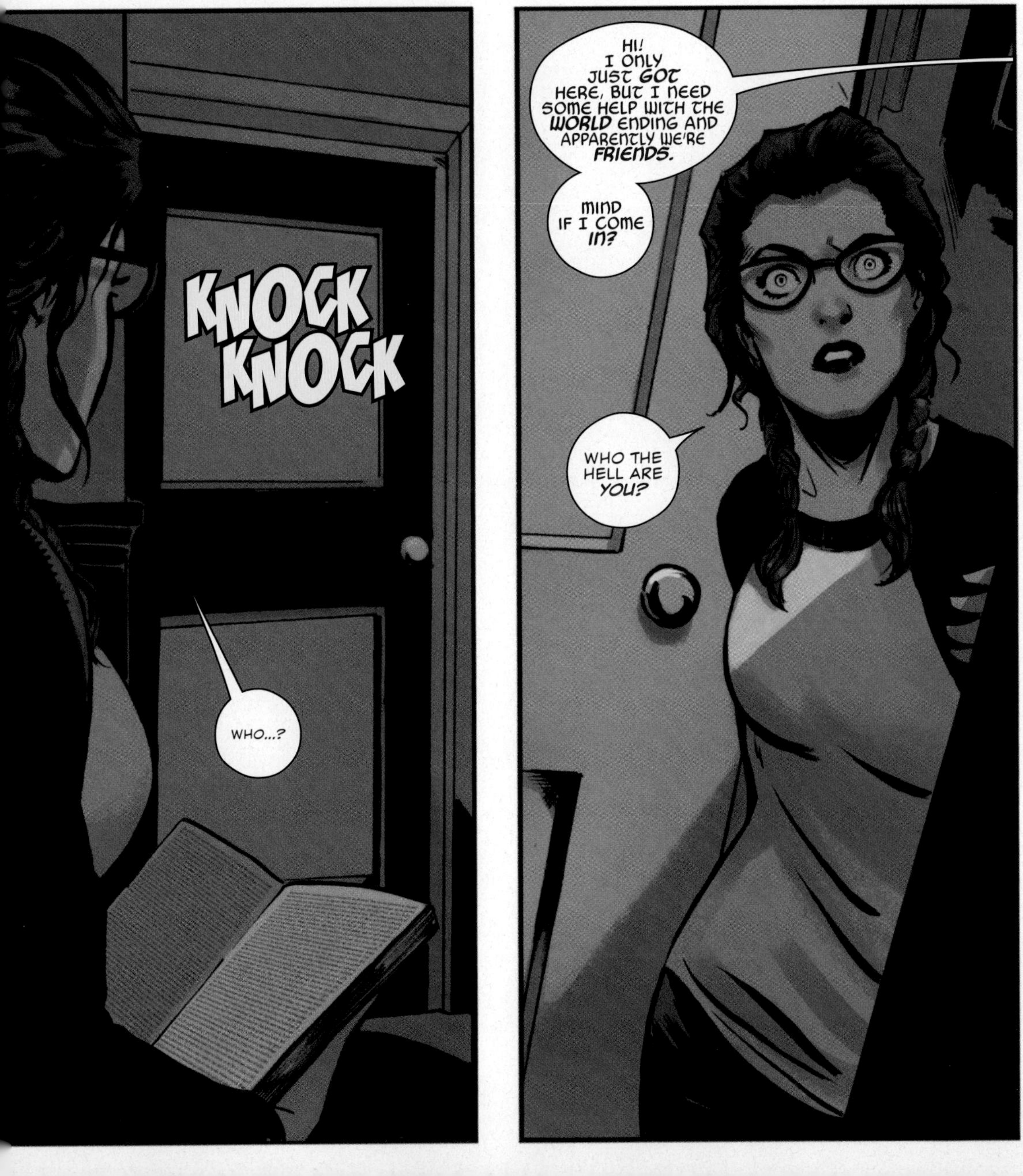
KNOCK KNOCK
WHO...?
HI! I ONLY JUST GOT HERE, BUT I NEED SOME HELP WITH THE WORLD ENDING AND APPARENTLY WE'RE FRIENDS.
MIND IF I COME IN?
WHO THE HELL ARE YOU?

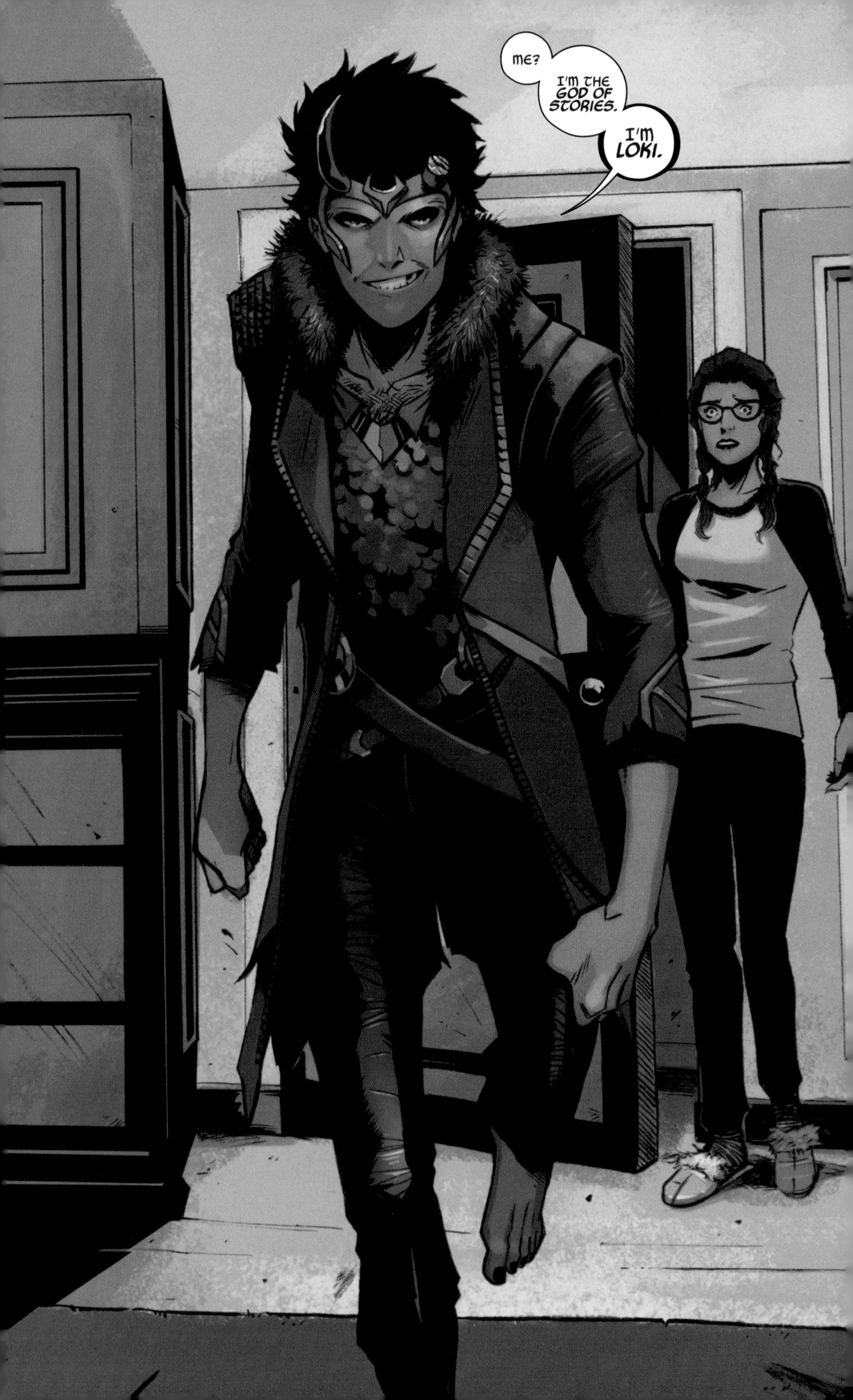
ME?
I'M THE GOD OF STORIES.
I'M LOKI.

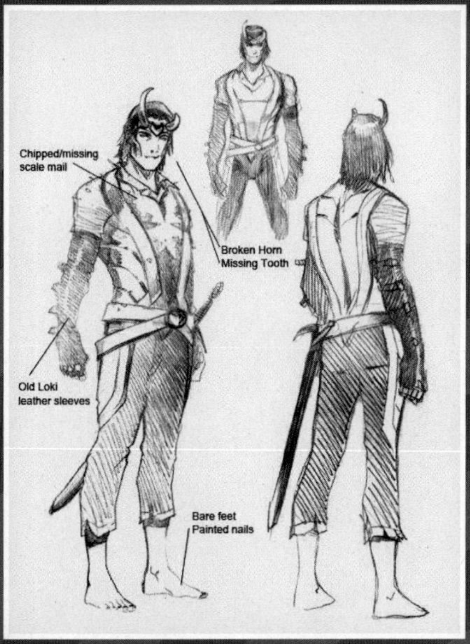
Chipped/missing scale mail
Broken Horn
Missing Tooth
Old Loki leather sleeves
Bare feet
Painted nails

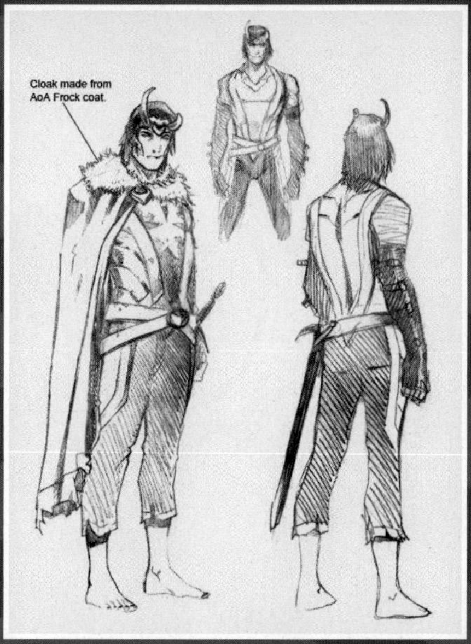
Cloak made from AoA Frock coat.

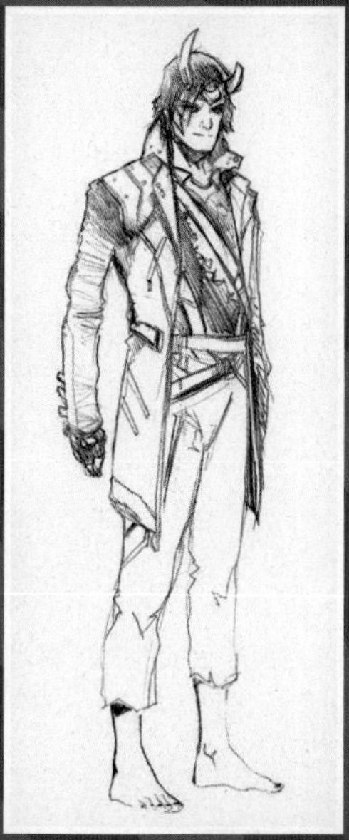

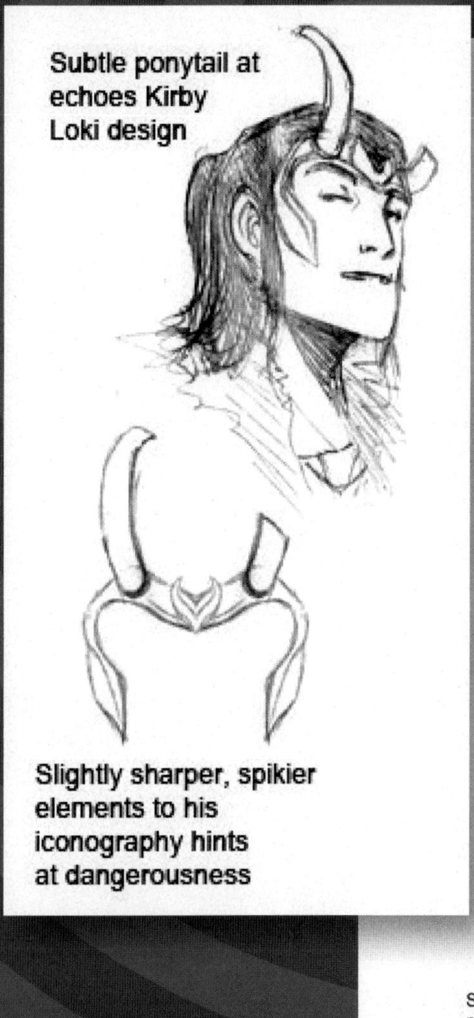
Subtle ponytail at echoes Kirby Loki design
Slightly sharper, spikier elements to his iconography hints at dangerousness

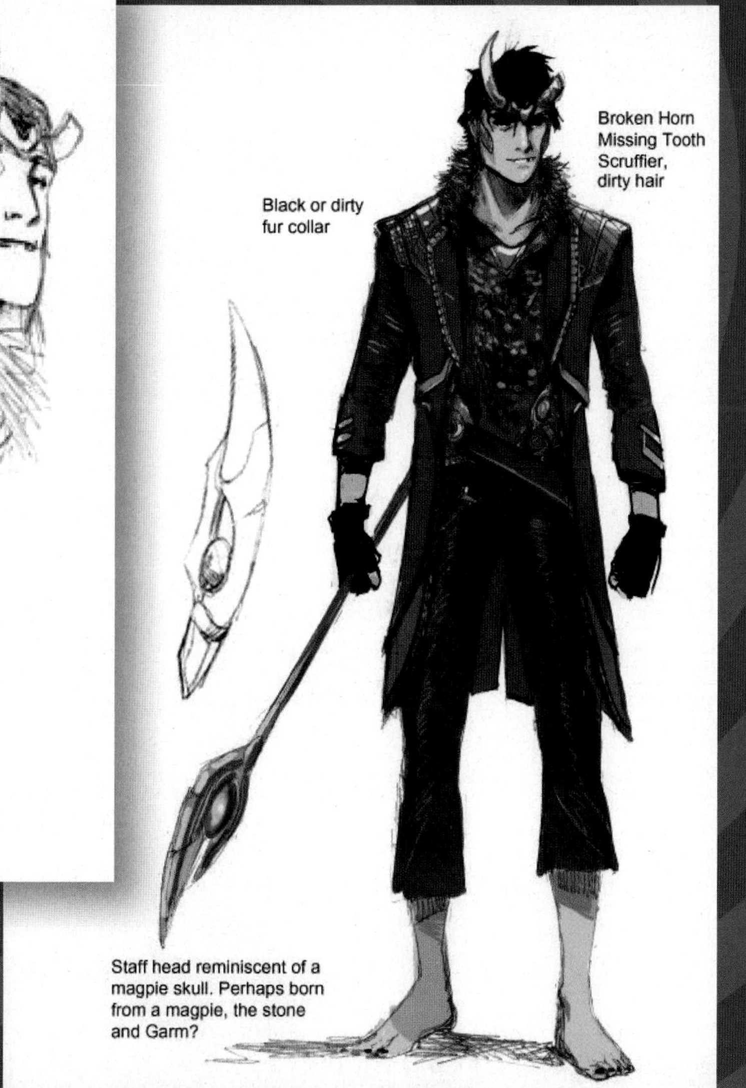
Broken Horn
Missing Tooth
Scruffier, dirty hair
Black or dirty fur collar
Staff head reminiscent of a magpie skull. Perhaps born from a magpie, the stone and Garm?

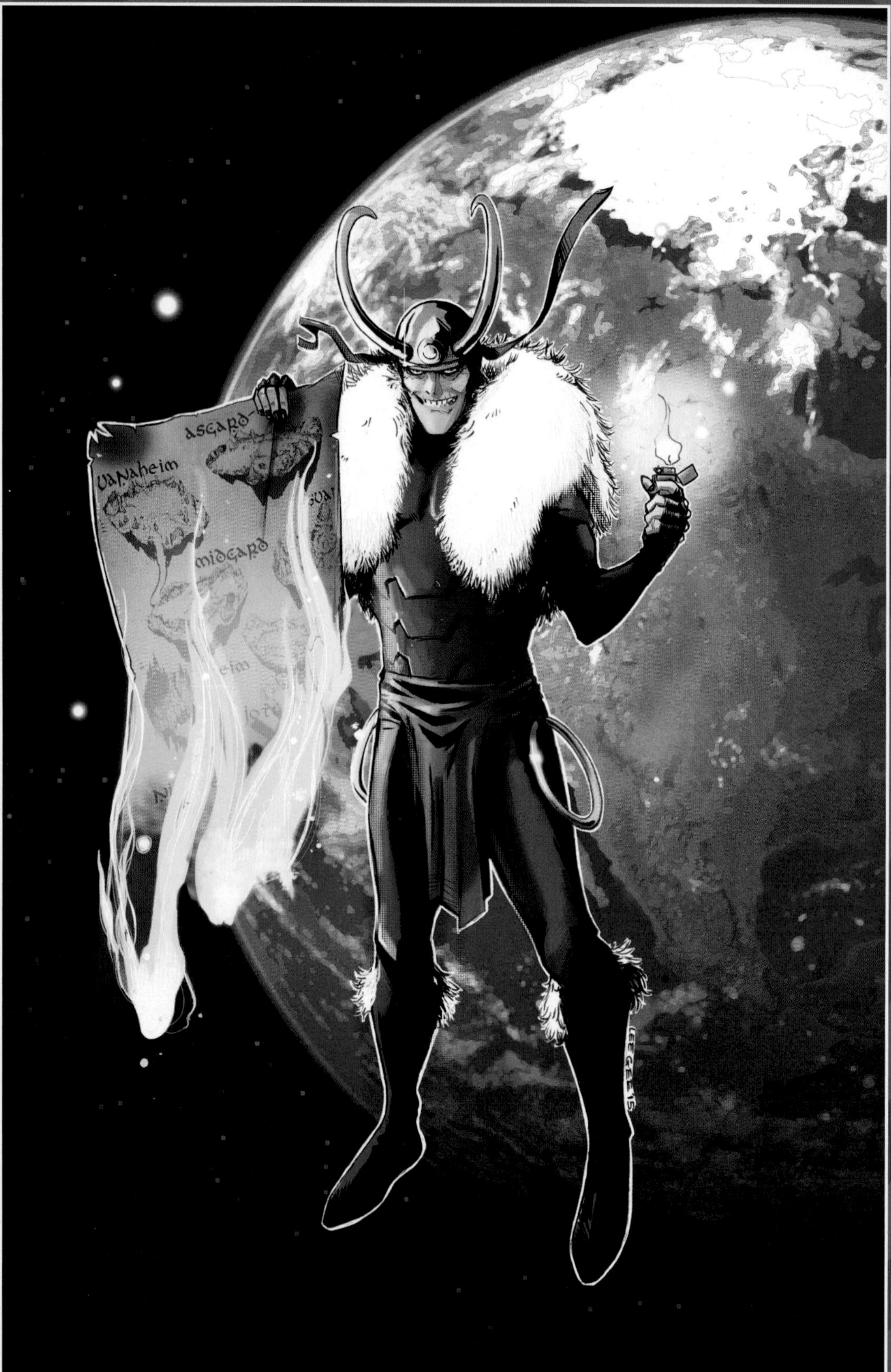
asgard
vanaheim
midgard

LOKI: AGENT OF ASGARD #14

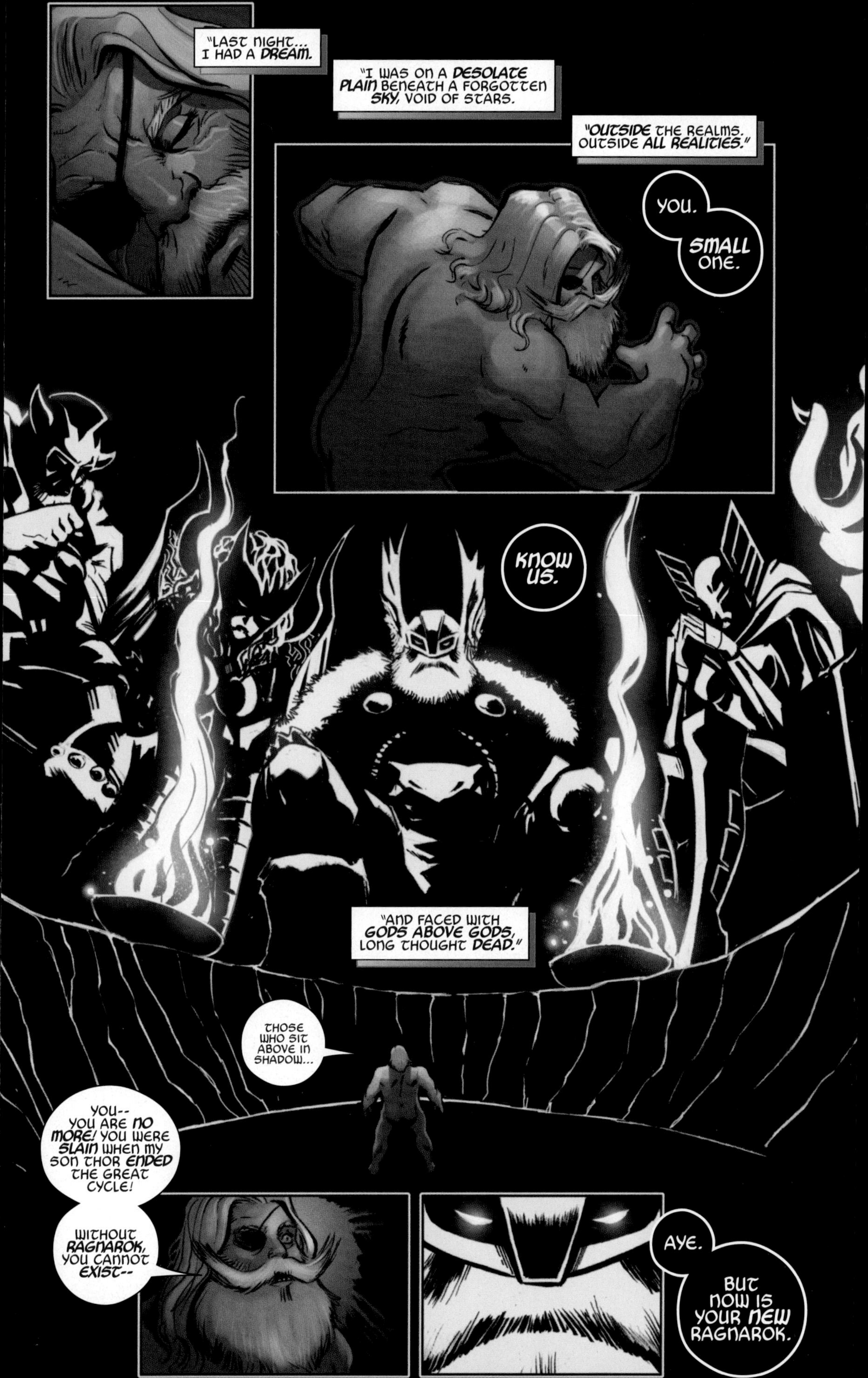
"LAST NIGHT... I HAD A DREAM.
"I WAS ON A DESOLATE PLAIN BENEATH A FORGOTTEN SKY, VOID OF STARS.
"OUTSIDE THE REALMS. OUTSIDE ALL REALITIES."
YOU.
SMALL ONE.
KNOW US.
"AND FACED WITH GODS ABOVE GODS, LONG THOUGHT DEAD."
THOSE WHO SIT ABOVE IN SHADOW...
YOU-- YOU ARE NO MORE! YOU WERE SLAIN WHEN MY SON THOR ENDED THE GREAT CYCLE!
WITHOUT RAGNAROK, YOU CANNOT EXIST--
AYE.
BUT NOW IS YOUR NEW RAGNAROK.

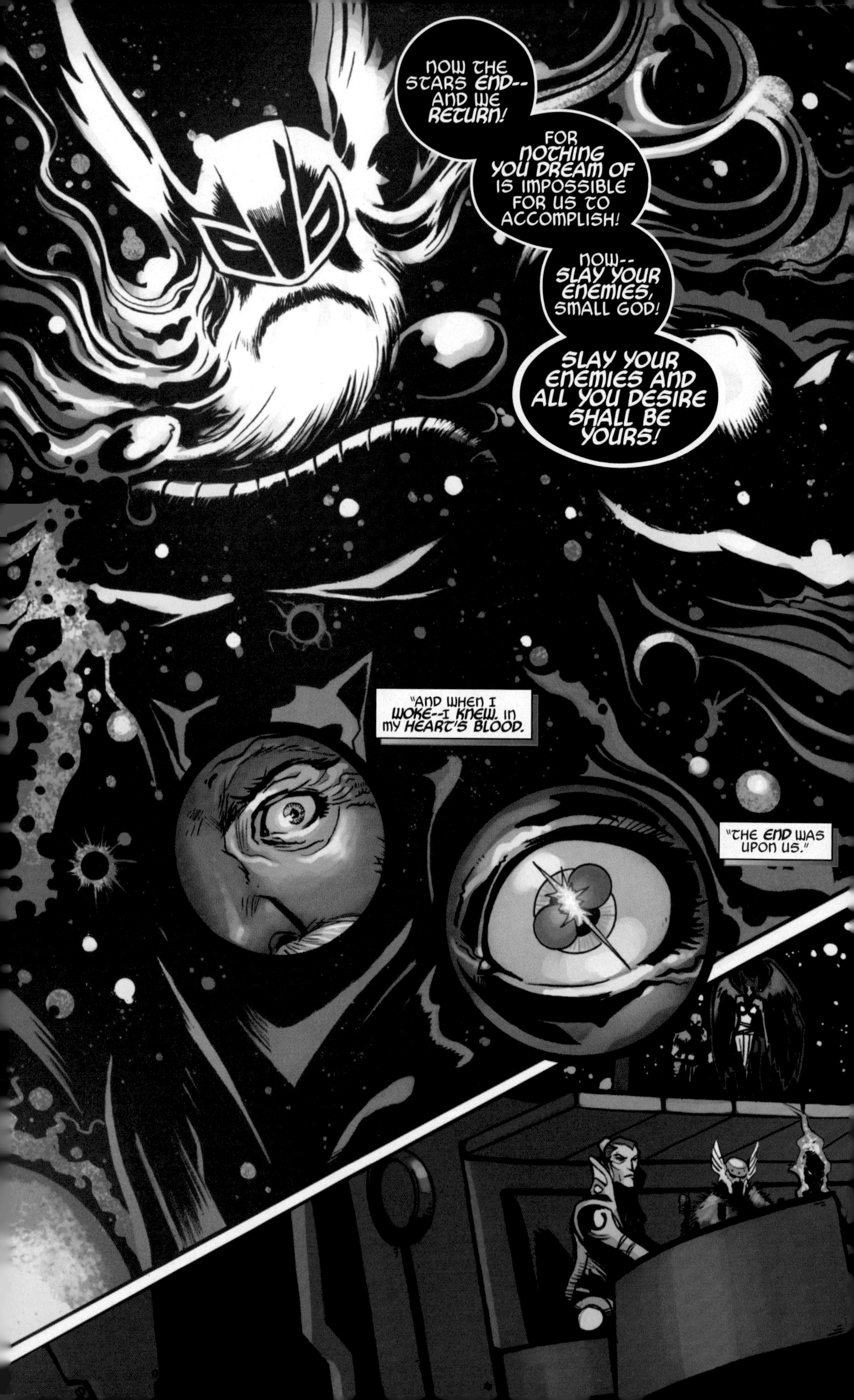
NOW THE STARS END--AND WE RETURN!
FOR NOTHING YOU DREAM OF IS IMPOSSIBLE FOR US TO ACCOMPLISH!
NOW--SLAY YOUR ENEMIES, SMALL GOD!
SLAY YOUR ENEMIES AND ALL YOU DESIRE SHALL BE YOURS!
"AND WHEN I WOKE--I KNEW. IN MY HEART'S BLOOD.
"THE END WAS UPON US."

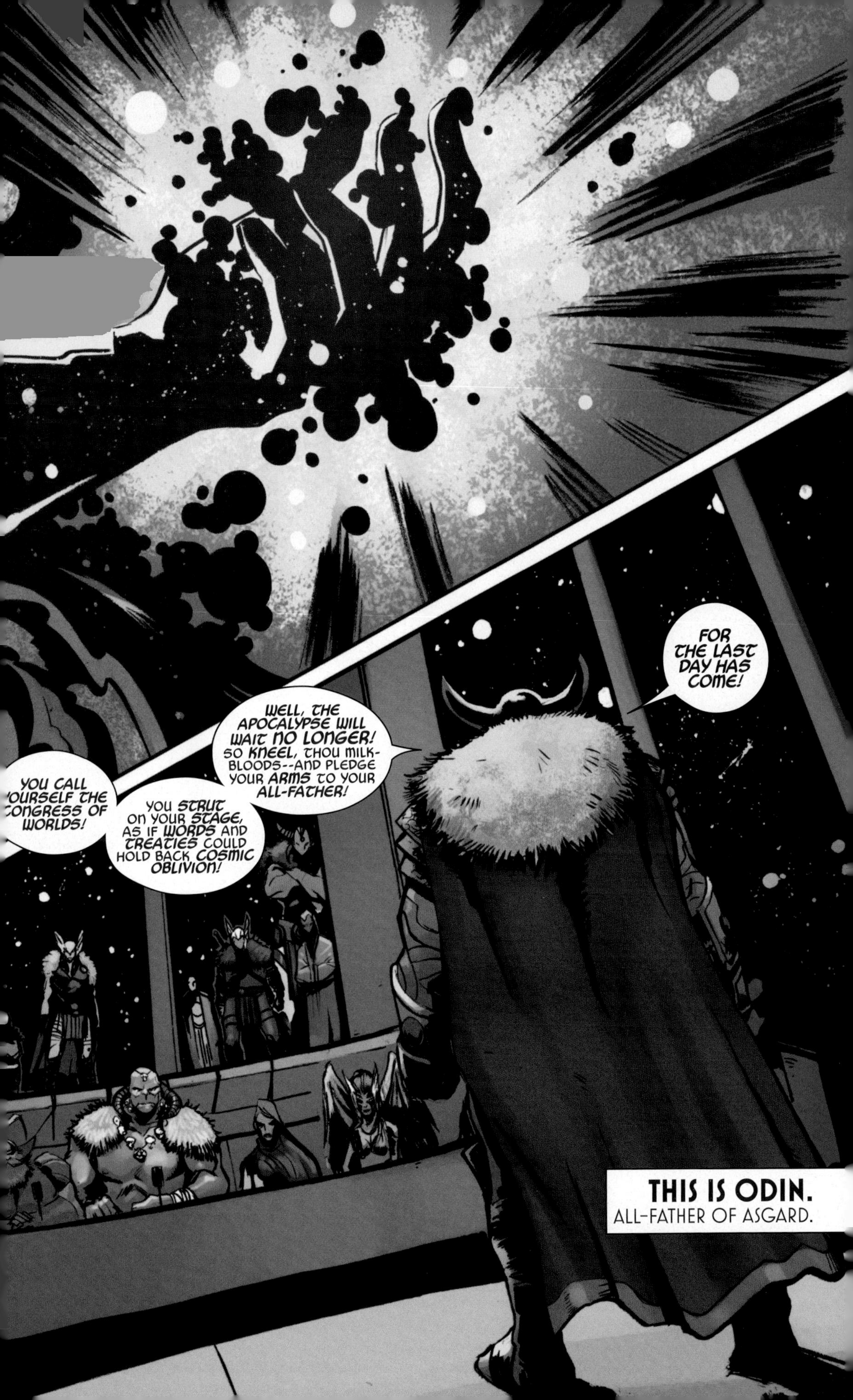
YOU CALL YOURSELF THE CONGRESS OF WORLDS!
YOU STRUT ON YOUR STAGE, AS IF WORDS AND TREATIES COULD HOLD BACK COSMIC OBLIVION!
WELL, THE APOCALYPSE WILL WAIT NO LONGER! SO KNEEL, THOU MILK-BLOODS--AND PLEDGE YOUR ARMS TO YOUR ALL-FATHER!
FOR THE LAST DAY HAS COME!
THIS IS ODIN.
ALL-FATHER OF ASGARD.

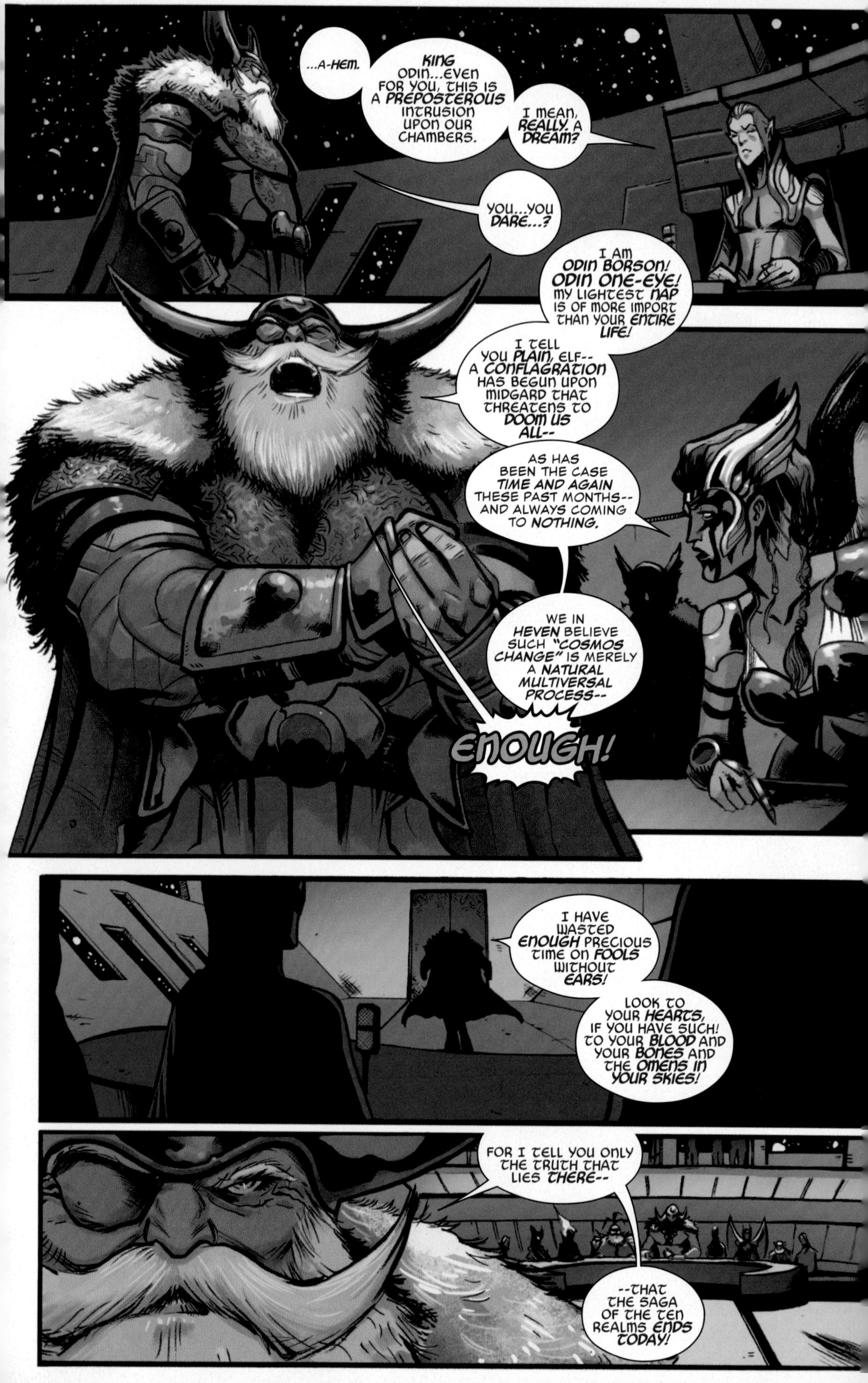
...A-HEM.
KING ODIN...EVEN FOR YOU, THIS IS A PREPOSTEROUS INTRUSION UPON OUR CHAMBERS.
I MEAN, REALLY. A DREAM?
YOU...YOU DARE...?
I AM ODIN BORSON! ODIN ONE-EYE! MY LIGHTEST NAP IS OF MORE IMPORT THAN YOUR ENTIRE LIFE!
I TELL YOU PLAIN, ELF-- A CONFLAGRATION HAS BEGUN UPON MIDGARD THAT THREATENS TO DOOM US ALL--
AS HAS BEEN THE CASE TIME AND AGAIN THESE PAST MONTHS-- AND ALWAYS COMING TO NOTHING.
WE IN HEVEN BELIEVE SUCH "COSMOS CHANGE" IS MERELY A NATURAL MULTIVERSAL PROCESS--
ENOUGH!
I HAVE WASTED ENOUGH PRECIOUS TIME ON FOOLS WITHOUT EARS!
LOOK TO YOUR HEARTS, IF YOU HAVE SUCH! TO YOUR BLOOD AND YOUR BONES AND THE OMENS IN YOUR SKIES!
FOR I TELL YOU ONLY THE TRUTH THAT LIES THERE--
--THAT THE SAGA OF THE TEN REALMS ENDS TODAY!

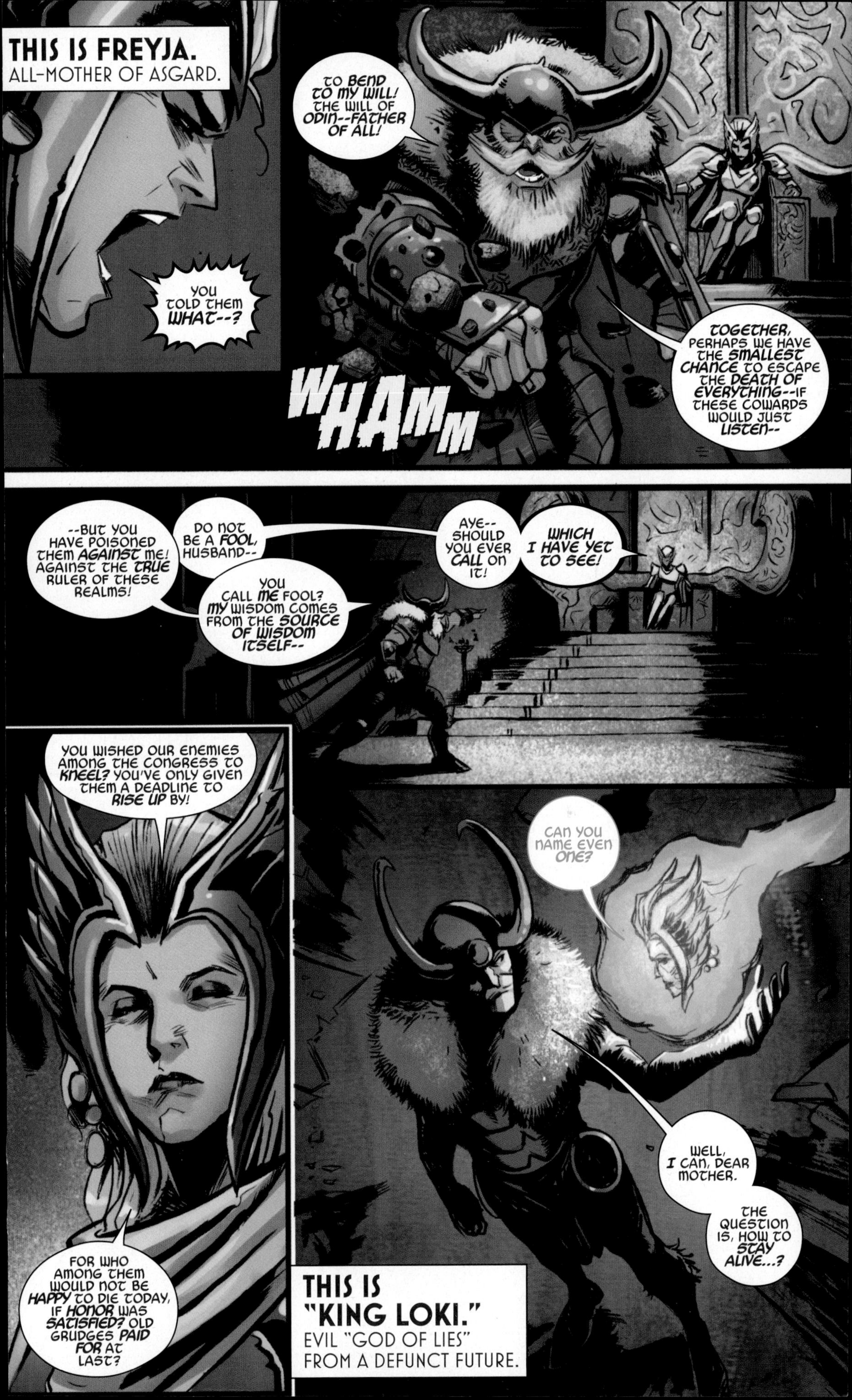

THIS IS FREYJA.
ALL-MOTHER OF ASGARD.
TO BEND TO MY WILL! THE WILL OF ODIN--FATHER OF ALL!
YOU TOLD THEM WHAT--?
TOGETHER, PERHAPS WE HAVE THE SMALLEST CHANCE TO ESCAPE THE DEATH OF EVERYTHING--IF THESE COWARDS WOULD JUST LISTEN--
WHAMM
--BUT YOU HAVE POISONED THEM AGAINST ME! AGAINST THE TRUE RULER OF THESE REALMS!
DO NOT BE A FOOL, HUSBAND--
YOU CALL ME FOOL? MY WISDOM COMES FROM THE SOURCE OF WISDOM ITSELF--
AYE--SHOULD YOU EVER CALL ON IT!
WHICH I HAVE YET TO SEE!
YOU WISHED OUR ENEMIES AMONG THE CONGRESS TO KNEEL? YOU'VE ONLY GIVEN THEM A DEADLINE TO RISE UP BY!
FOR WHO AMONG THEM WOULD NOT BE HAPPY TO DIE TODAY, IF HONOR WAS SATISFIED? OLD GRUDGES PAID FOR AT LAST?
CAN YOU NAME EVEN ONE?
WELL, I CAN, DEAR MOTHER.
THE QUESTION IS, HOW TO STAY ALIVE...?
THIS IS "KING LOKI."
EVIL "GOD OF LIES" FROM A DEFUNCT FUTURE.

THIS IS VERITY WILLIS'S **APARTMENT.** IN MANHATTAN.

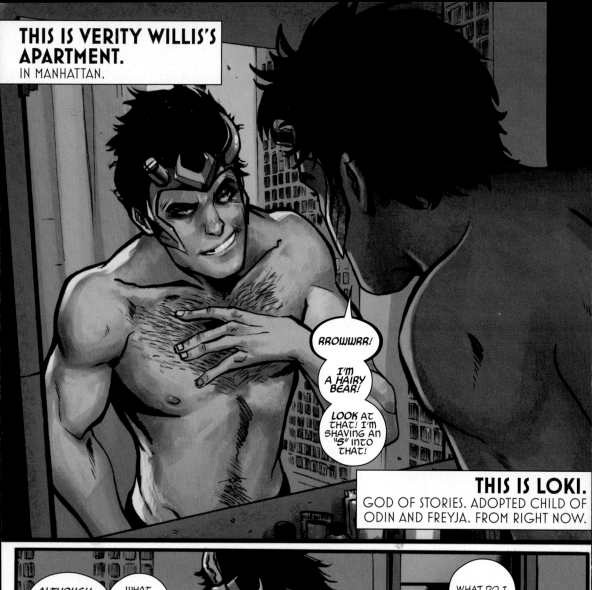

RROWWRR!

I'M A HAIRY BEAR!

LOOK AT THAT! I'M SHAVING AN "S" INTO THAT!

THIS IS LOKI. GOD OF STORIES. ADOPTED CHILD OF ODIN AND FREYJA. FROM RIGHT NOW.

ALTHOUGH... NOT SURE ABOUT THESE EARS.

WHAT D'YOU RECKON? GOOD EARS?

WHAT DO I "RECKON"?

I "RECKON" WE START WITH YOU BEING HALF A FOOT TALLER WITH A DIFFERENT VOICE! WHERE'S THE REAL LOKI?

THIS IS VERITY. HUMAN LIE-DETECTOR.

ARE YOU HIM?

IS... IS HE DEAD?

DUNNO. IS SCHRÖDINGER'S CAT?

YOUR CHOICE.

EITHER WAY, HE'S OUT OF THAT BOX.

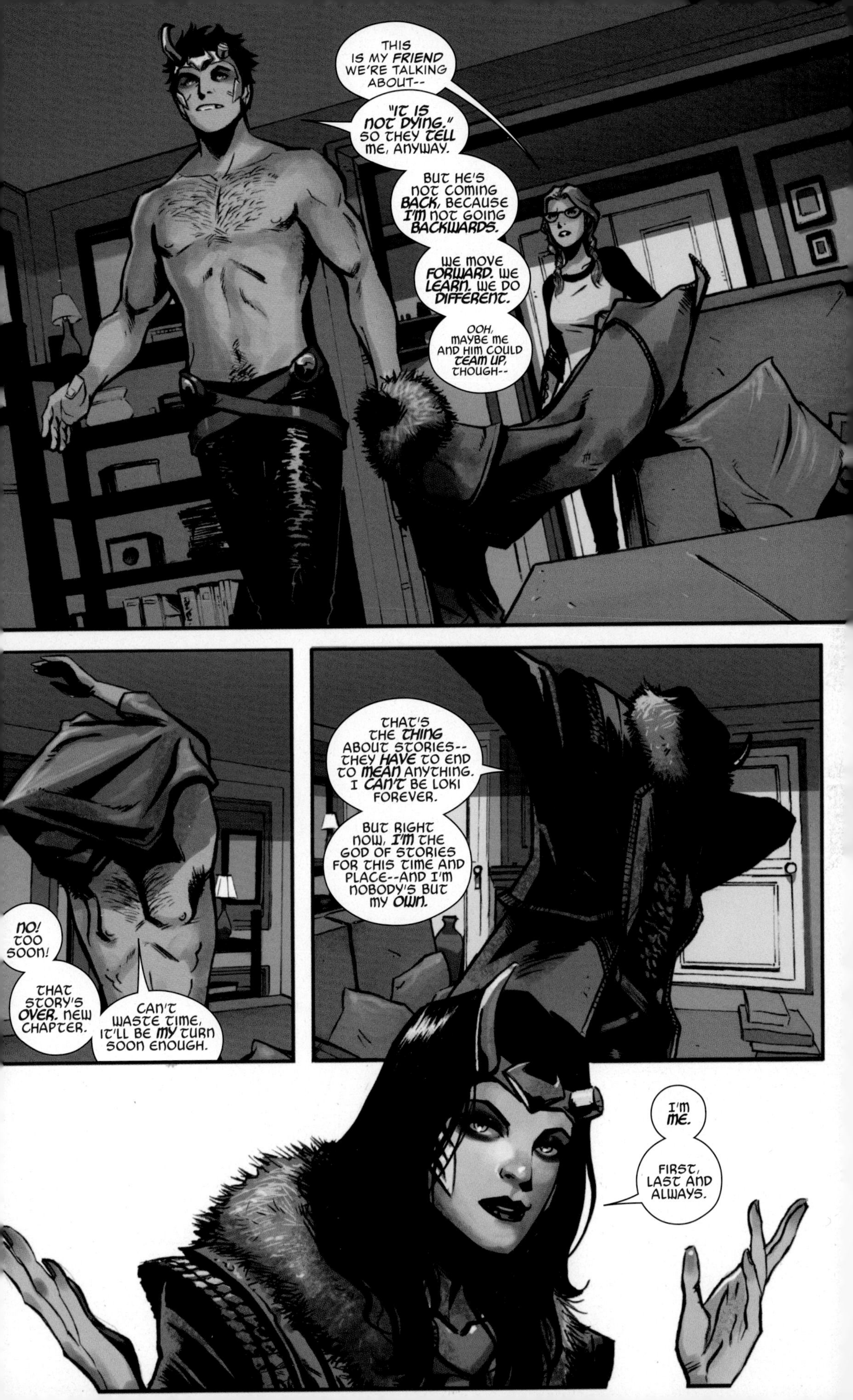

THIS IS MY FRIEND WE'RE TALKING ABOUT--
"IT IS NOT DYING." SO THEY TELL ME, ANYWAY.
BUT HE'S NOT COMING BACK, BECAUSE I'M NOT GOING BACKWARDS.
WE MOVE FORWARD. WE LEARN. WE DO DIFFERENT.
OOH, MAYBE ME AND HIM COULD TEAM UP, THOUGH--
NO! TOO SOON!
THAT STORY'S OVER. NEW CHAPTER.
CAN'T WASTE TIME, IT'LL BE MY TURN SOON ENOUGH.
THAT'S THE THING ABOUT STORIES-- THEY HAVE TO END TO MEAN ANYTHING. I CAN'T BE LOKI FOREVER.
BUT RIGHT NOW, I'M THE GOD OF STORIES FOR THIS TIME AND PLACE--AND I'M NOBODY'S BUT MY OWN.
I'M ME.
FIRST, LAST AND ALWAYS.

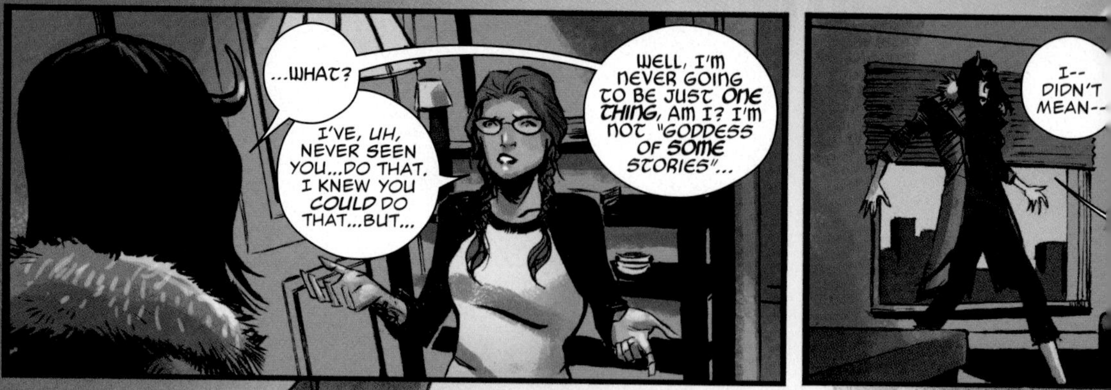
...WHAT?
I'VE, UH, NEVER SEEN YOU...DO THAT. I KNEW YOU COULD DO THAT...BUT...
WELL, I'M NEVER GOING TO BE JUST ONE THING, AM I? I'M NOT "GODDESS OF SOME STORIES"...
I-- DIDN'T MEAN--

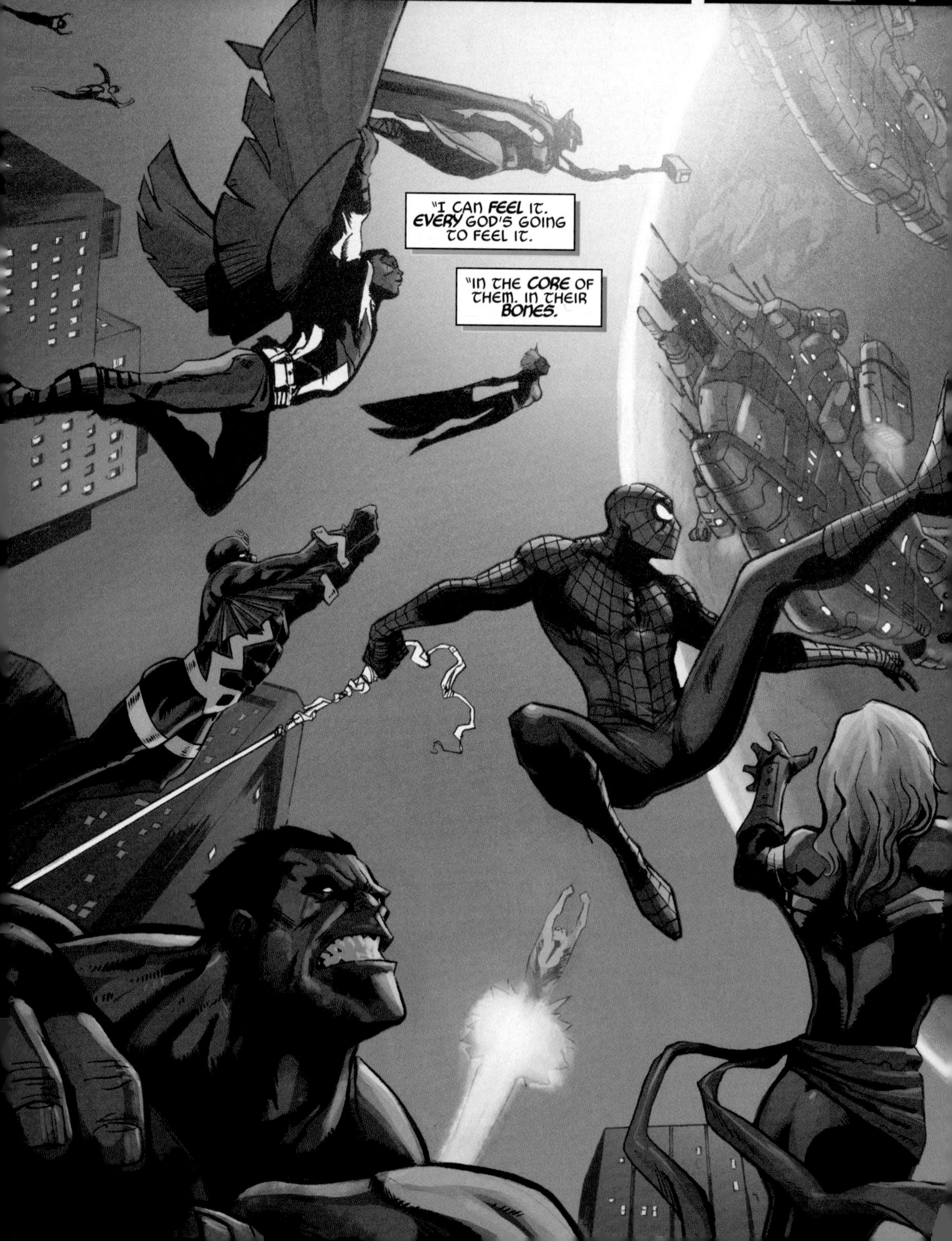
"I CAN FEEL IT. EVERY GOD'S GOING TO FEEL IT.
"IN THE CORE OF THEM. IN THEIR BONES.

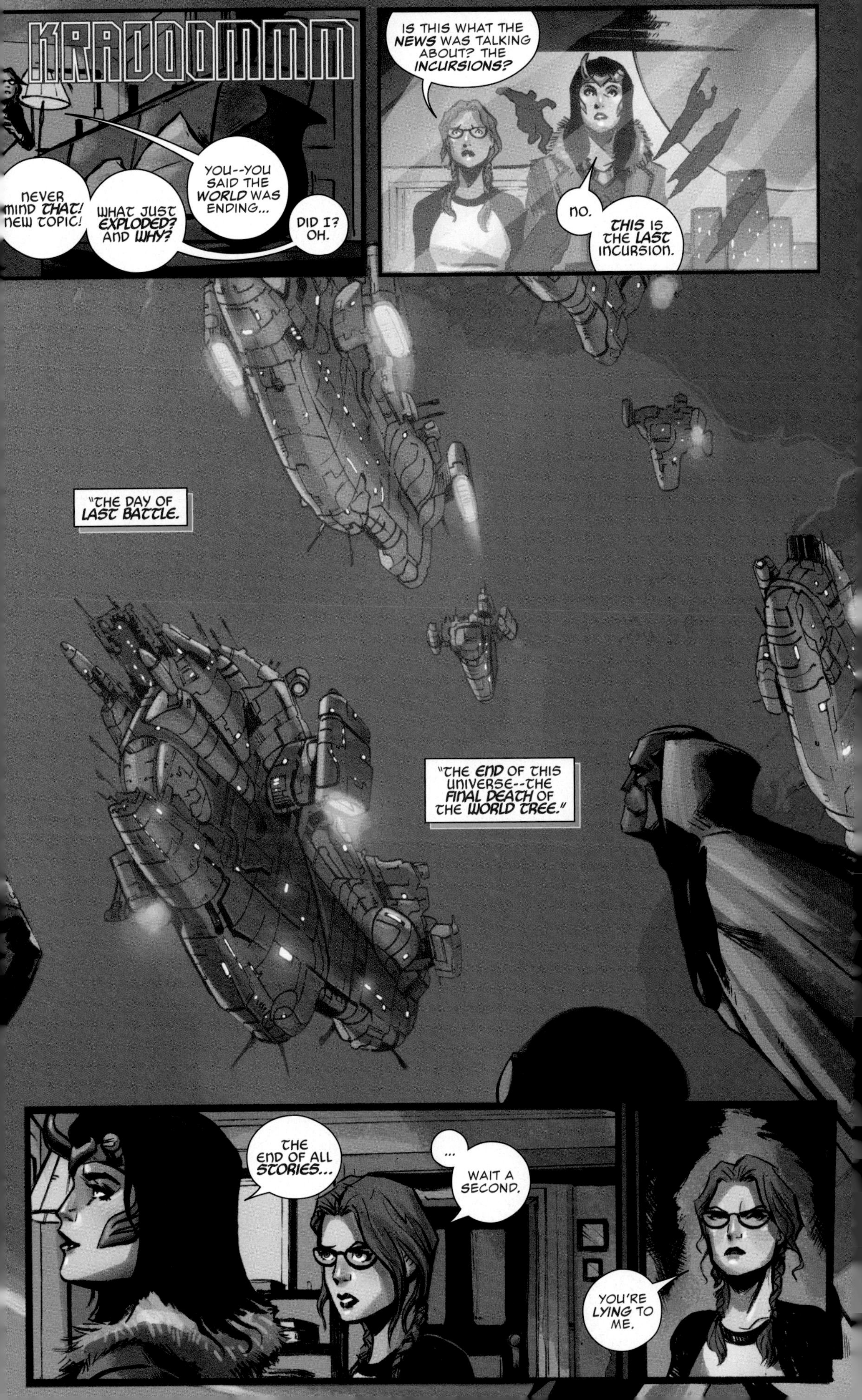
KRADOOMMMM
NEVER MIND THAT! NEW TOPIC!
WHAT JUST EXPLODED? AND WHY?
YOU--YOU SAID THE WORLD WAS ENDING...
DID I? OH.
IS THIS WHAT THE NEWS WAS TALKING ABOUT? THE INCURSIONS?
NO.
THIS IS THE LAST INCURSION.
"THE DAY OF LAST BATTLE.
"THE END OF THIS UNIVERSE--THE FINAL DEATH OF THE WORLD TREE."
THE END OF ALL STORIES...
...
WAIT A SECOND.
YOU'RE LYING TO ME.

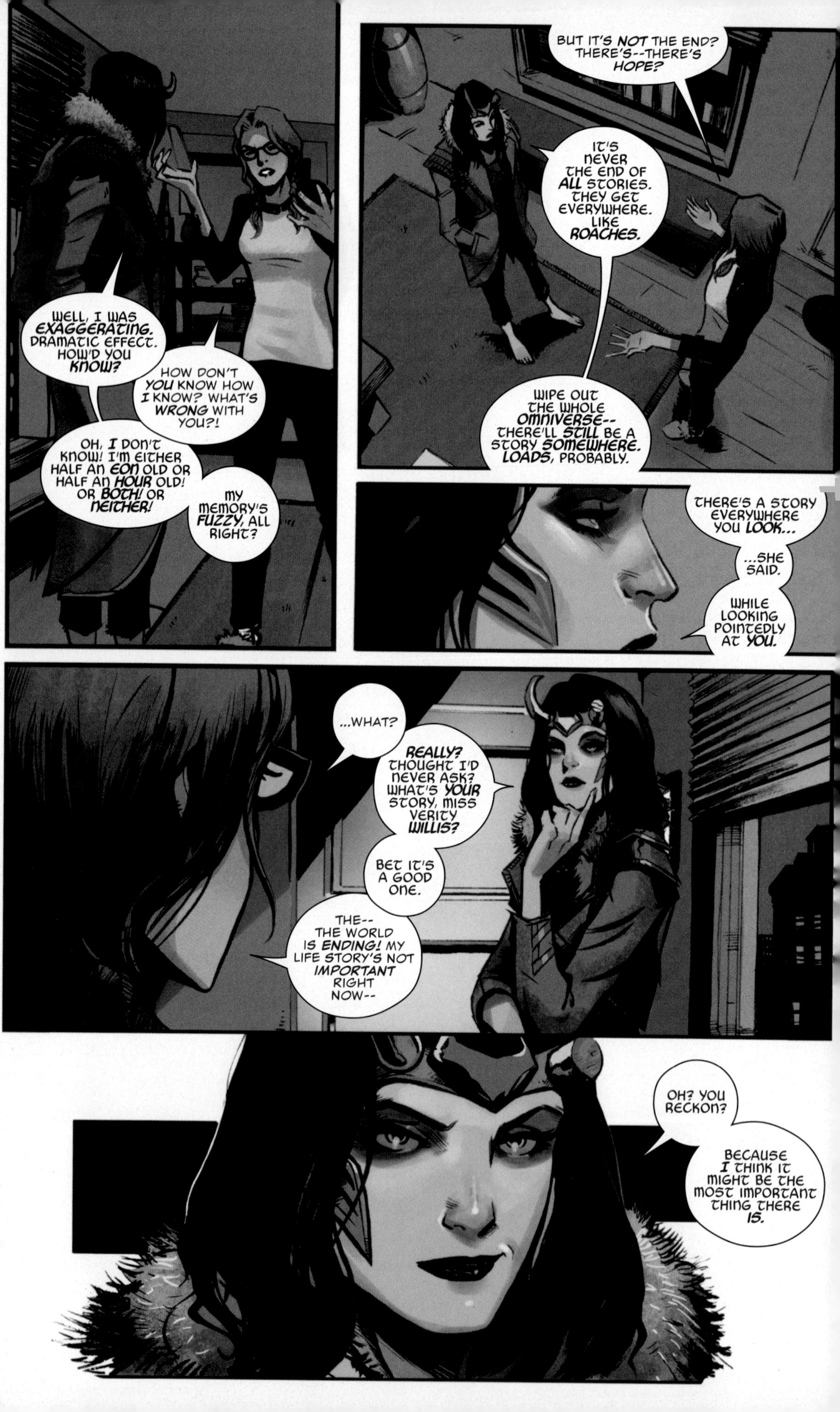
WELL, I WAS EXAGGERATING. DRAMATIC EFFECT. HOW'D YOU KNOW?
HOW DON'T YOU KNOW HOW I KNOW? WHAT'S WRONG WITH YOU?!
OH, I DON'T KNOW! I'M EITHER HALF AN EON OLD OR HALF AN HOUR OLD! OR BOTH! OR NEITHER!
MY MEMORY'S FUZZY, ALL RIGHT?
BUT IT'S NOT THE END? THERE'S--THERE'S HOPE?
IT'S NEVER THE END OF ALL STORIES. THEY GET EVERYWHERE. LIKE ROACHES.
WIPE OUT THE WHOLE OMNIVERSE-- THERE'LL STILL BE A STORY SOMEWHERE. LOADS, PROBABLY.
THERE'S A STORY EVERYWHERE YOU LOOK...
...SHE SAID.
WHILE LOOKING POINTEDLY AT YOU.
...WHAT?
REALLY? THOUGHT I'D NEVER ASK? WHAT'S YOUR STORY, MISS VERITY WILLIS?
BET IT'S A GOOD ONE.
THE-- THE WORLD IS ENDING! MY LIFE STORY'S NOT IMPORTANT RIGHT NOW--
OH? YOU RECKON?
BECAUSE I THINK IT MIGHT BE THE MOST IMPORTANT THING THERE IS.

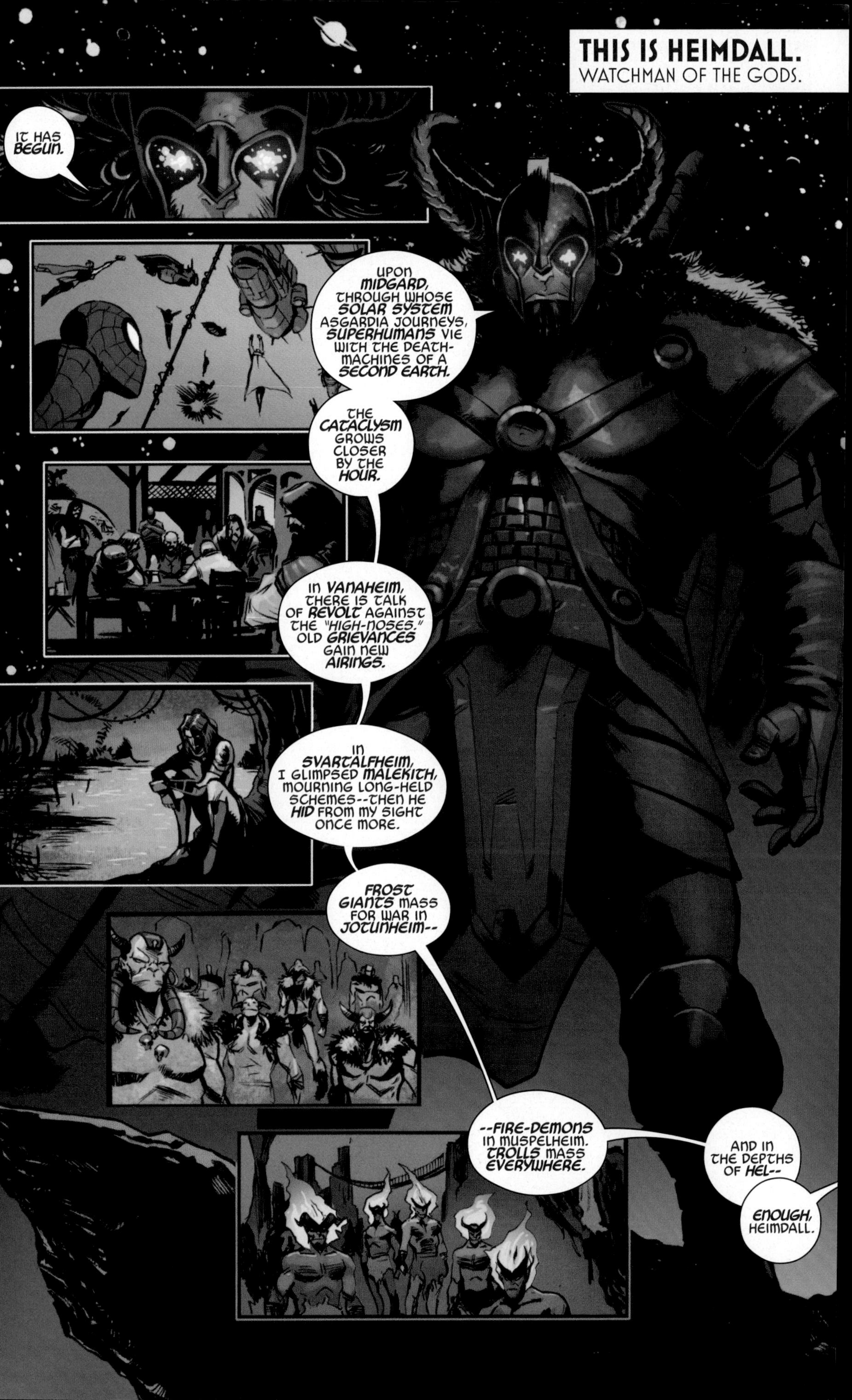
THIS IS HEIMDALL.
WATCHMAN OF THE GODS.
IT HAS BEGUN.
UPON MIDGARD, THROUGH WHOSE SOLAR SYSTEM ASGARDIA JOURNEYS, SUPERHUMANS VIE WITH THE DEATH-MACHINES OF A SECOND EARTH.
THE CATACLYSM GROWS CLOSER BY THE HOUR.
IN VANAHEIM, THERE IS TALK OF REVOLT AGAINST THE "HIGH-NOSES." OLD GRIEVANCES GAIN NEW AIRINGS.
IN SVARTALFHEIM, I GLIMPSED MALEKITH, MOURNING LONG-HELD SCHEMES--THEN HE HID FROM MY SIGHT ONCE MORE.
FROST GIANTS MASS FOR WAR IN JOTUNHEIM--
--FIRE-DEMONS IN MUSPELHEIM. TROLLS MASS EVERYWHERE.
AND IN THE DEPTHS OF HEL--
ENOUGH, HEIMDALL.

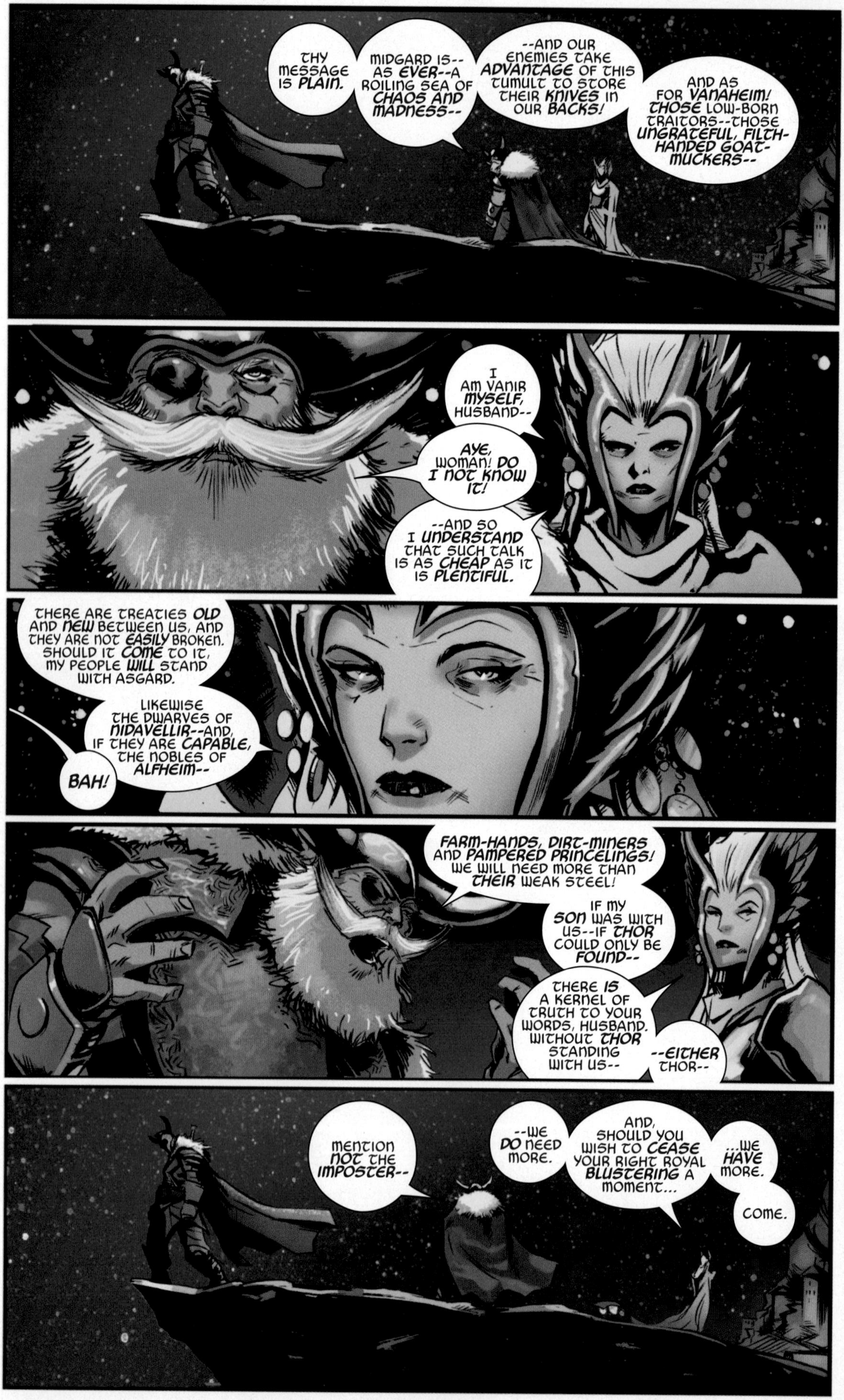
THY MESSAGE IS PLAIN.
MIDGARD IS-- AS EVER--A ROILING SEA OF CHAOS AND MADNESS--
--AND OUR ENEMIES TAKE ADVANTAGE OF THIS TUMULT TO STORE THEIR KNIVES IN OUR BACKS!
AND AS FOR VANAHEIM! THOSE LOW-BORN TRAITORS--THOSE UNGRATEFUL, FILTH-HANDED GOAT-MUCKERS--
I AM VANIR MYSELF, HUSBAND--
AYE, WOMAN! DO I NOT KNOW IT!
--AND SO I UNDERSTAND THAT SUCH TALK IS AS CHEAP AS IT IS PLENTIFUL.
THERE ARE TREATIES OLD AND NEW BETWEEN US, AND THEY ARE NOT EASILY BROKEN. SHOULD IT COME TO IT, MY PEOPLE WILL STAND WITH ASGARD.
LIKEWISE THE DWARVES OF NIDAVELLIR--AND, IF THEY ARE CAPABLE, THE NOBLES OF ALFHEIM--
BAH!
FARM-HANDS, DIRT-MINERS AND PAMPERED PRINCELINGS! WE WILL NEED MORE THAN THEIR WEAK STEEL!
IF MY SON WAS WITH US--IF THOR COULD ONLY BE FOUND--
THERE IS A KERNEL OF TRUTH TO YOUR WORDS, HUSBAND. WITHOUT THOR STANDING WITH US--
--EITHER THOR--
MENTION NOT THE IMPOSTER--
--WE DO NEED MORE.
AND, SHOULD YOU WISH TO CEASE YOUR RIGHT ROYAL BLUSTERING A MOMENT...
...WE HAVE MORE.
COME.

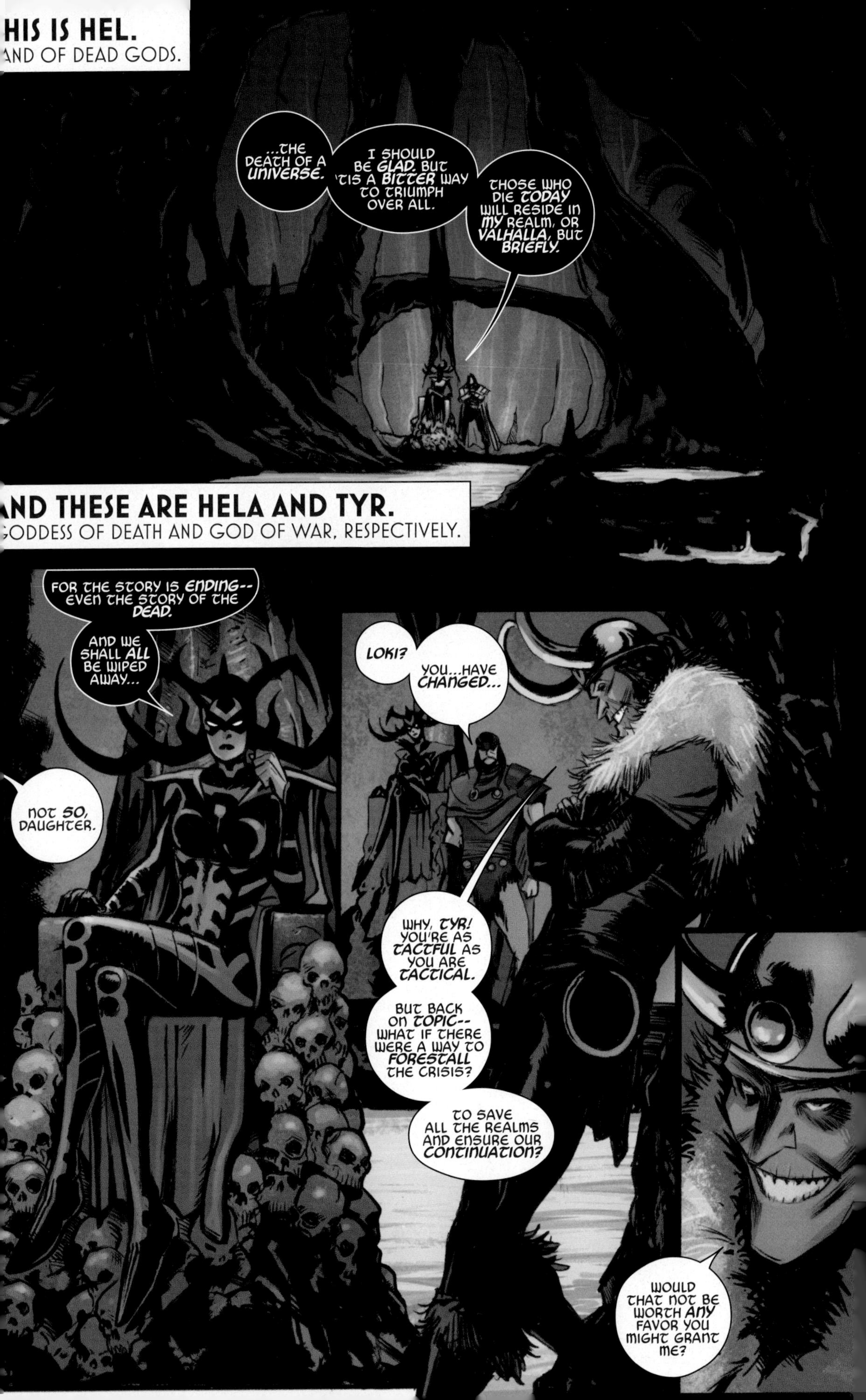
HIS IS HEL.
AND OF DEAD GODS.
...THE DEATH OF A UNIVERSE.
I SHOULD BE GLAD, BUT 'TIS A BITTER WAY TO TRIUMPH OVER ALL.
THOSE WHO DIE TODAY WILL RESIDE IN MY REALM, OR VALHALLA, BUT BRIEFLY.
ND THESE ARE HELA AND TYR.
GODDESS OF DEATH AND GOD OF WAR, RESPECTIVELY.
FOR THE STORY IS ENDING--EVEN THE STORY OF THE DEAD.
AND WE SHALL ALL BE WIPED AWAY...
NOT SO, DAUGHTER.
LOKI?
YOU...HAVE CHANGED...
WHY, TYR! YOU'RE AS TACTFUL AS YOU ARE TACTICAL.
BUT BACK ON TOPIC--WHAT IF THERE WERE A WAY TO FORESTALL THE CRISIS?
TO SAVE ALL THE REALMS AND ENSURE OUR CONTINUATION?
WOULD THAT NOT BE WORTH ANY FAVOR YOU MIGHT GRANT ME?

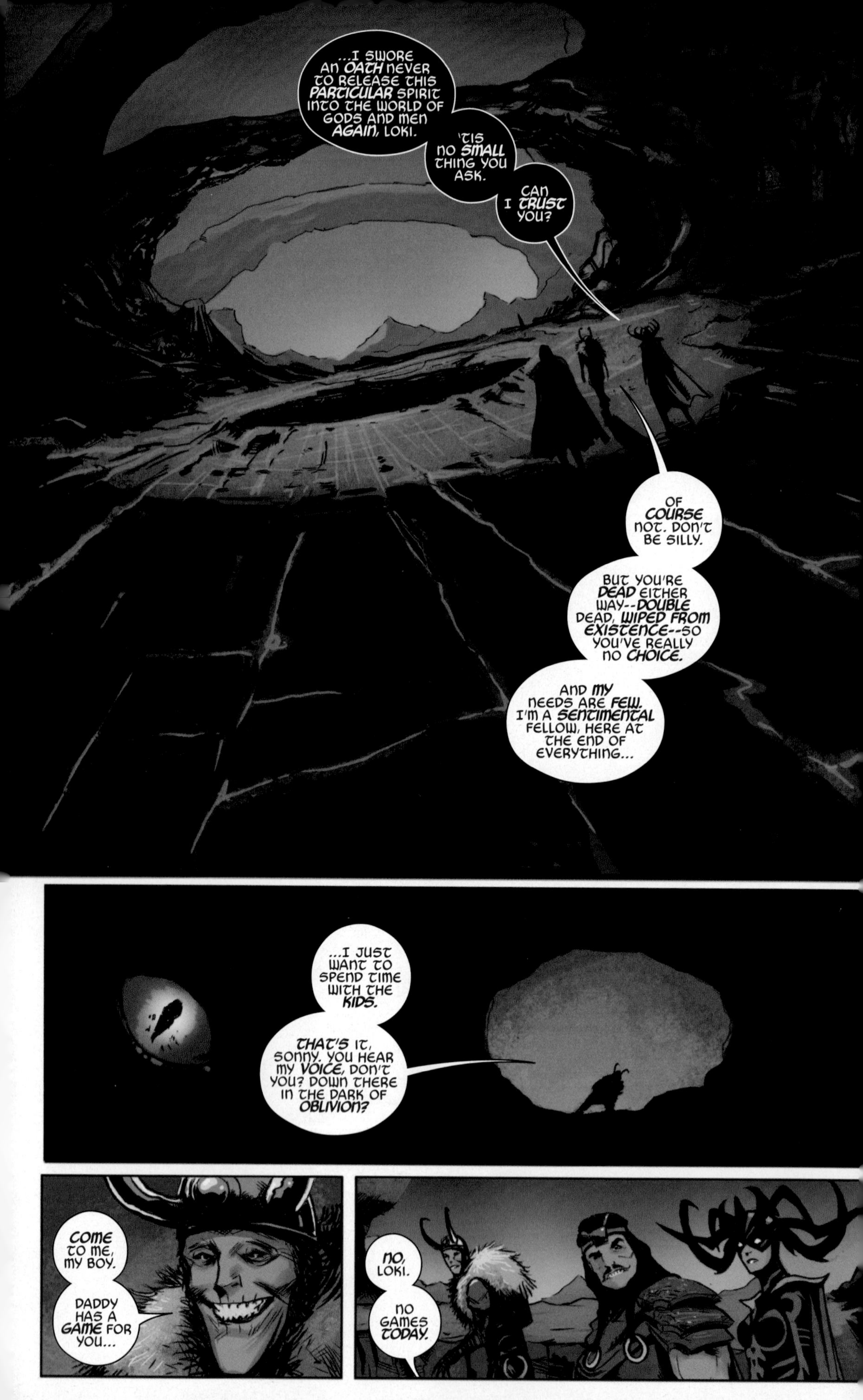
...I SWORE AN OATH NEVER TO RELEASE THIS PARTICULAR SPIRIT INTO THE WORLD OF GODS AND MEN AGAIN, LOKI.
'TIS NO SMALL THING YOU ASK.
CAN I TRUST YOU?
OF COURSE NOT. DON'T BE SILLY.
BUT YOU'RE DEAD EITHER WAY--DOUBLE DEAD, WIPED FROM EXISTENCE--SO YOU'VE REALLY NO CHOICE.
AND MY NEEDS ARE FEW. I'M A SENTIMENTAL FELLOW, HERE AT THE END OF EVERYTHING...
...I JUST WANT TO SPEND TIME WITH THE KIDS.
THAT'S IT, SONNY. YOU HEAR MY VOICE, DON'T YOU? DOWN THERE IN THE DARK OF OBLIVION?
COME TO ME, MY BOY.
DADDY HAS A GAME FOR YOU...
NO, LOKI.
NO GAMES TODAY.

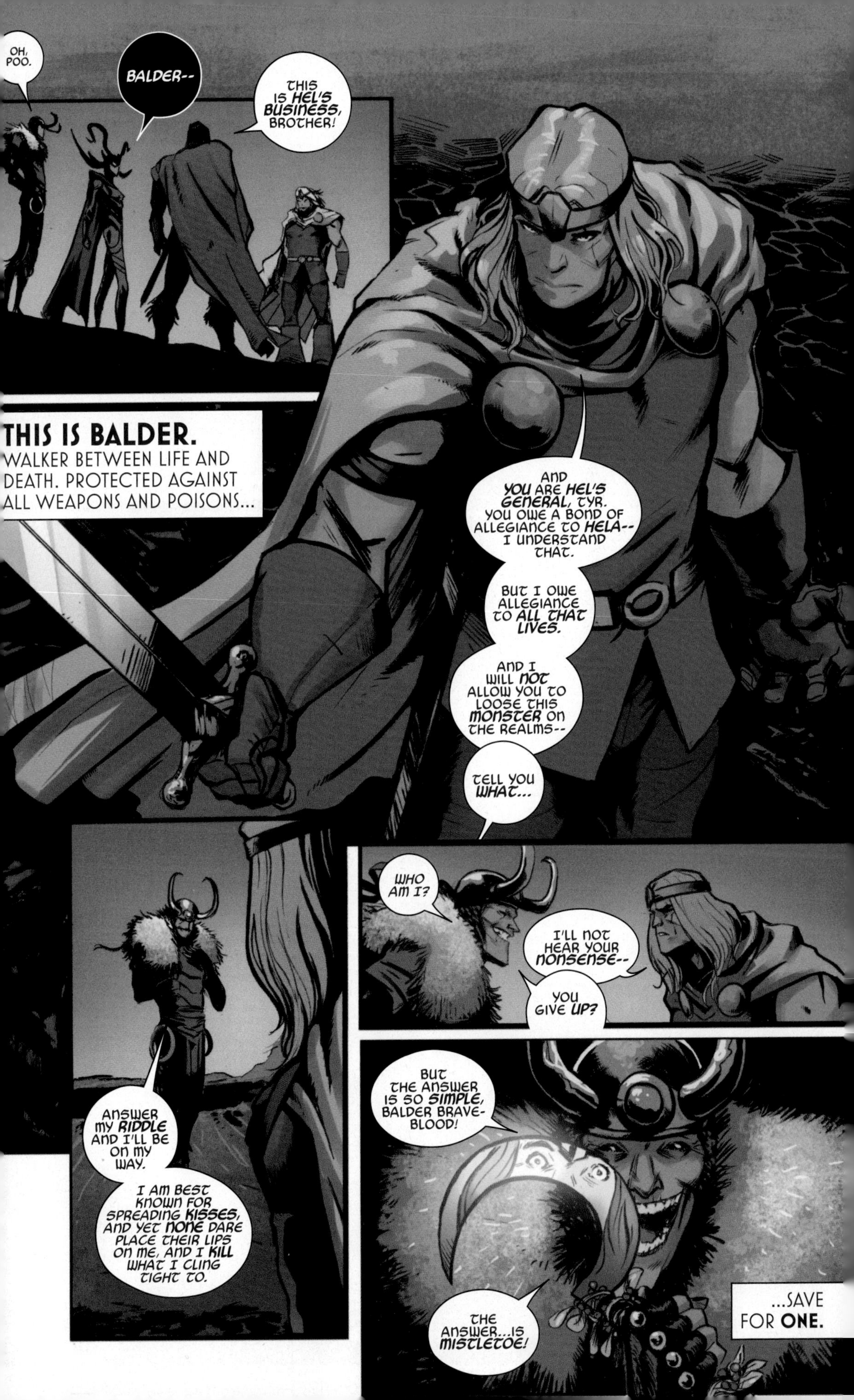
OH, POO.
BALDER--
THIS IS HEL'S BUSINESS, BROTHER!
THIS IS BALDER.
WALKER BETWEEN LIFE AND DEATH. PROTECTED AGAINST ALL WEAPONS AND POISONS...
AND YOU ARE HEL'S GENERAL, TYR. YOU OWE A BOND OF ALLEGIANCE TO HELA-- I UNDERSTAND THAT.
BUT I OWE ALLEGIANCE TO ALL THAT LIVES.
AND I WILL NOT ALLOW YOU TO LOOSE THIS MONSTER ON THE REALMS--
TELL YOU WHAT...
ANSWER MY RIDDLE AND I'LL BE ON MY WAY.
I AM BEST KNOWN FOR SPREADING KISSES, AND YET NONE DARE PLACE THEIR LIPS ON ME, AND I KILL WHAT I CLING TIGHT TO.
WHO AM I?
I'LL NOT HEAR YOUR NONSENSE--
YOU GIVE UP?
BUT THE ANSWER IS SO SIMPLE, BALDER BRAVE-BLOOD!
THE ANSWER...IS MISTLETOE!
...SAVE FOR ONE.

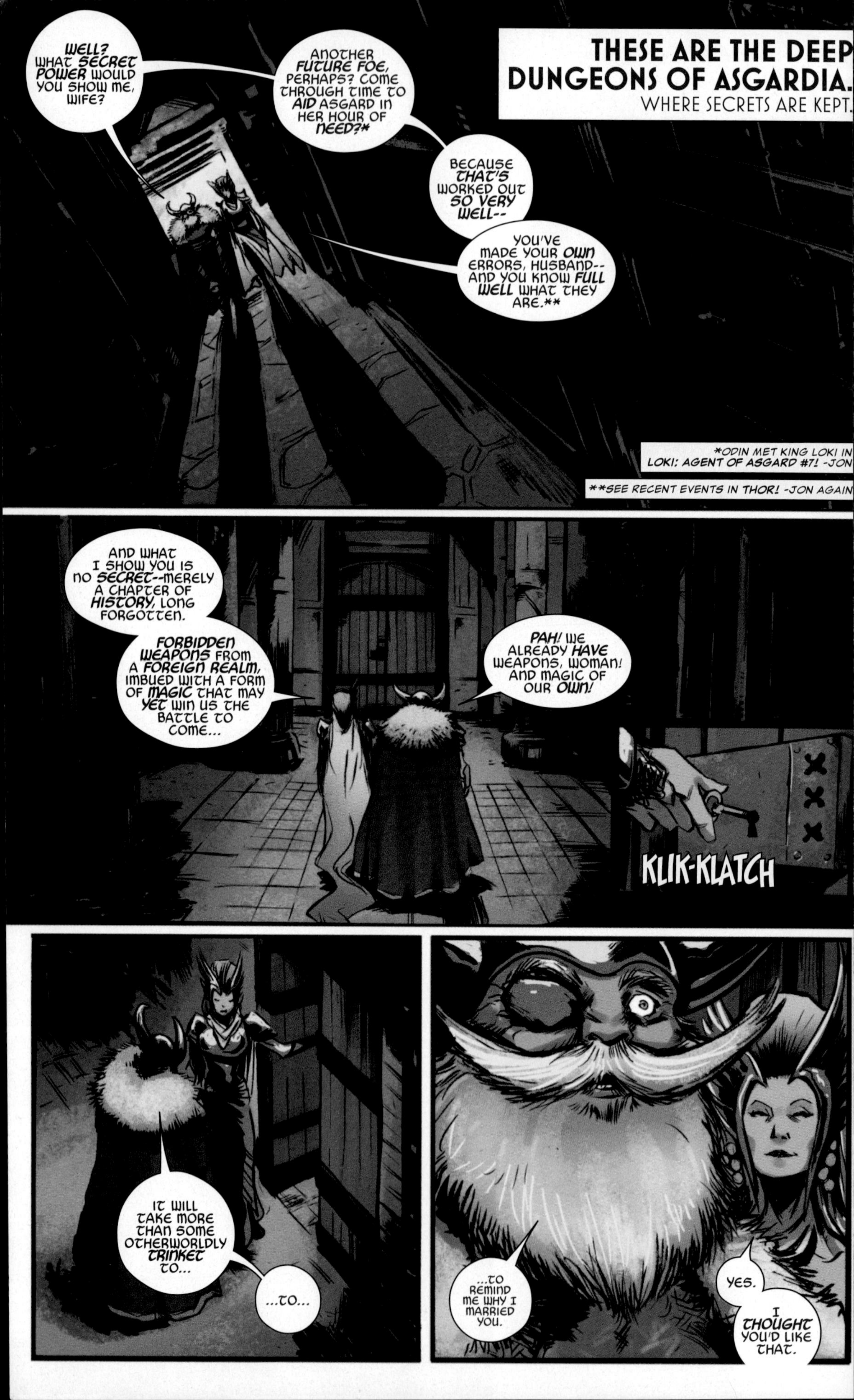

THESE ARE THE DEEP DUNGEONS OF ASGARDIA.
WHERE SECRETS ARE KEPT.
WELL? WHAT SECRET POWER WOULD YOU SHOW ME, WIFE?
ANOTHER FUTURE FOE, PERHAPS? COME THROUGH TIME TO AID ASGARD IN HER HOUR OF NEED?*
BECAUSE THAT'S WORKED OUT SO VERY WELL--
YOU'VE MADE YOUR OWN ERRORS, HUSBAND-- AND YOU KNOW FULL WELL WHAT THEY ARE.**
*ODIN MET KING LOKI IN LOKI: AGENT OF ASGARD #7! -JON
**SEE RECENT EVENTS IN THOR! -JON AGAIN
AND WHAT I SHOW YOU IS NO SECRET--MERELY A CHAPTER OF HISTORY, LONG FORGOTTEN.
FORBIDDEN WEAPONS FROM A FOREIGN REALM, IMBUED WITH A FORM OF MAGIC THAT MAY YET WIN US THE BATTLE TO COME...
PAH! WE ALREADY HAVE WEAPONS, WOMAN! AND MAGIC OF OUR OWN!
KLIK-KLATCH
IT WILL TAKE MORE THAN SOME OTHERWORLDLY TRINKET TO...
...TO...
...TO REMIND ME WHY I MARRIED YOU.
YES.
I THOUGHT YOU'D LIKE THAT.

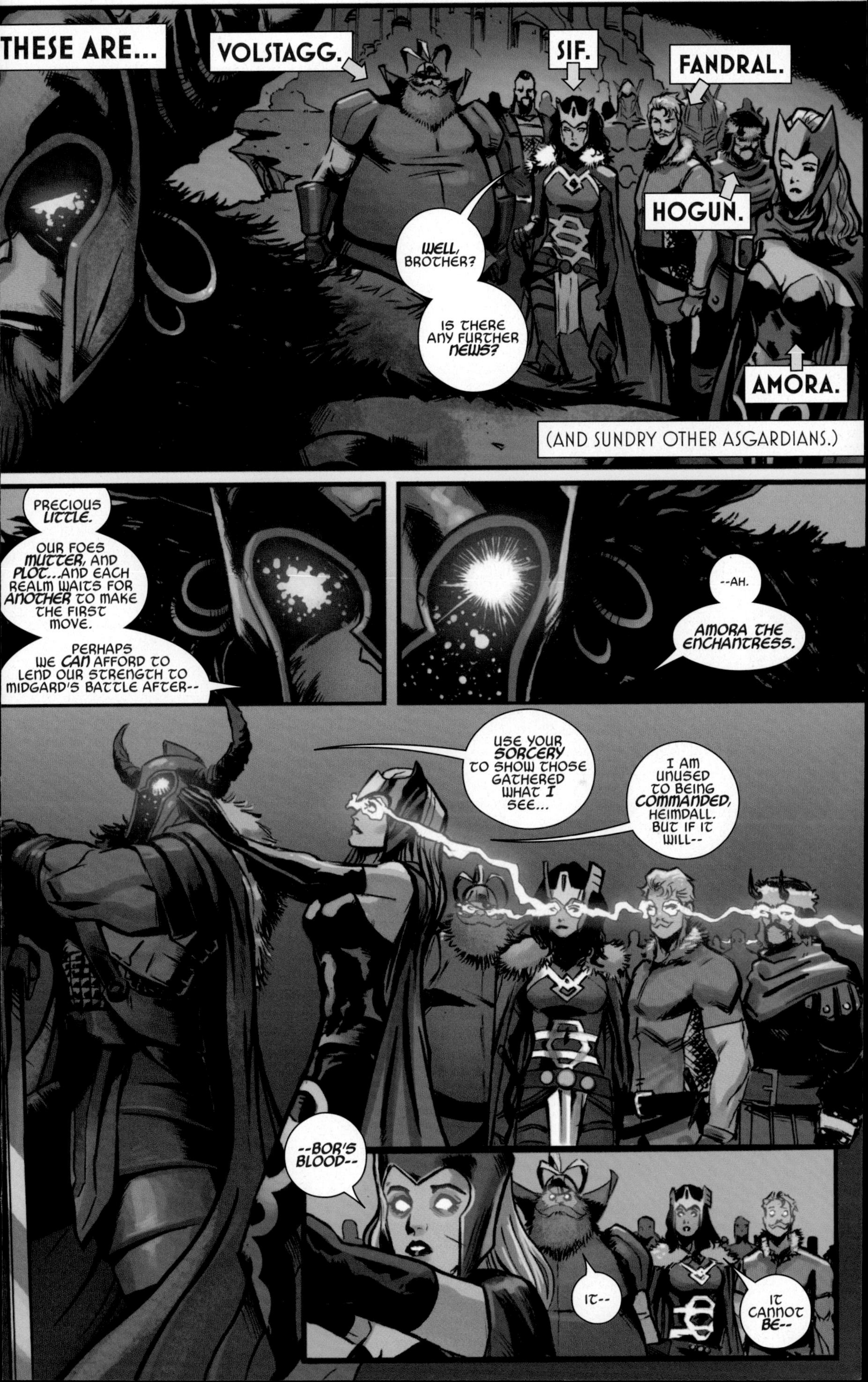
THESE ARE...
VOLSTAGG.
SIF.
FANDRAL.
HOGUN.
AMORA.
WELL, BROTHER?
IS THERE ANY FURTHER NEWS?
(AND SUNDRY OTHER ASGARDIANS.)
PRECIOUS LITTLE.
OUR FOES MUTTER, AND PLOT...AND EACH REALM WAITS FOR ANOTHER TO MAKE THE FIRST MOVE.
PERHAPS WE CAN AFFORD TO LEND OUR STRENGTH TO MIDGARD'S BATTLE AFTER--
--AH.
AMORA THE ENCHANTRESS.
USE YOUR SORCERY TO SHOW THOSE GATHERED WHAT I SEE...
I AM UNUSED TO BEING COMMANDED, HEIMDALL. BUT IF IT WILL--
--BOR'S BLOOD--
IT--
IT CANNOT BE--

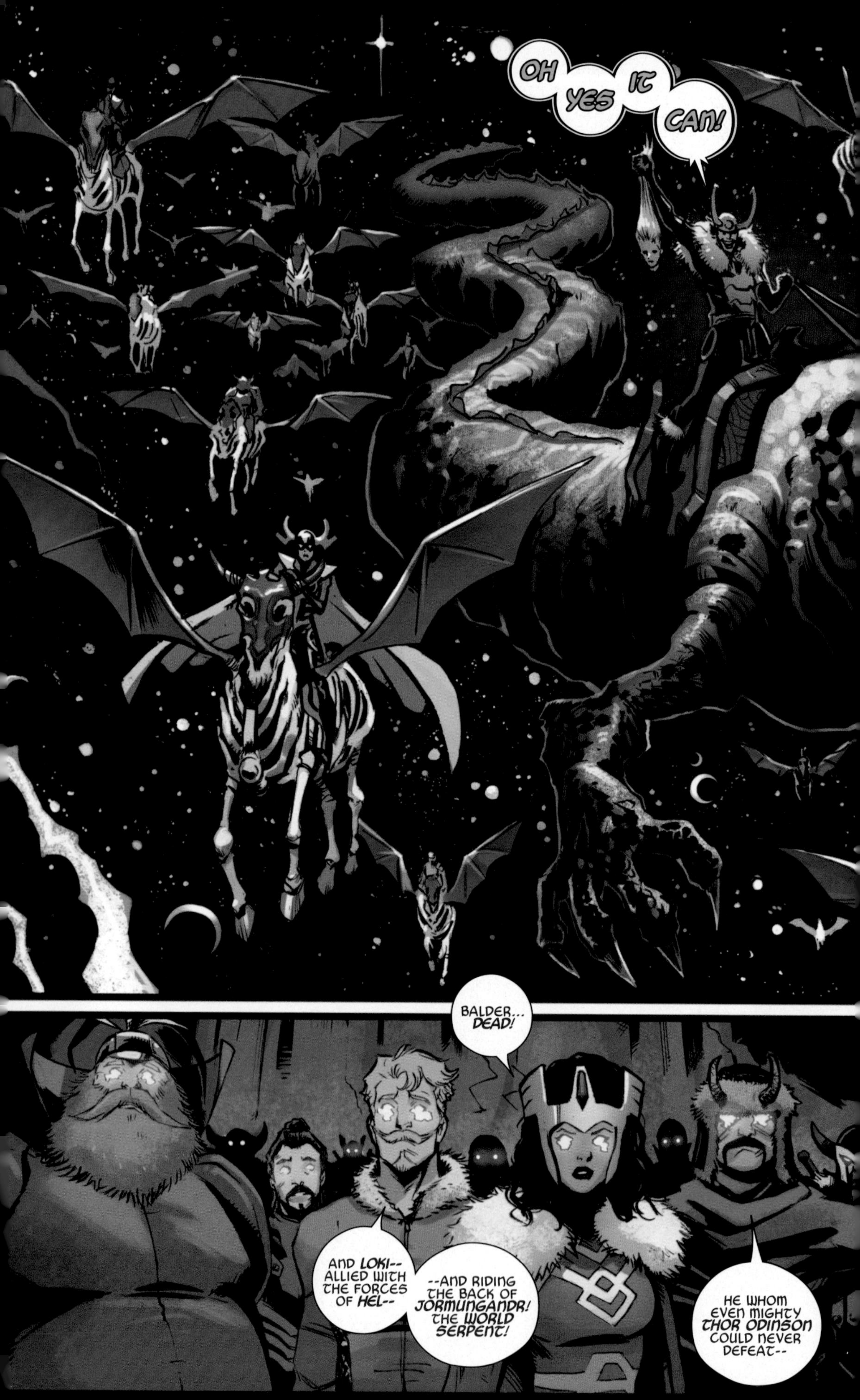
OH YES IT CAN!
BALDER... **DEAD!**
AND **LOKI**-- ALLIED WITH THE FORCES OF **HEL**--
--AND RIDING THE BACK OF **JORMUNGANDR!** THE **WORLD SERPENT!**
HE WHOM EVEN MIGHTY **THOR ODINSON** COULD NEVER DEFEAT--

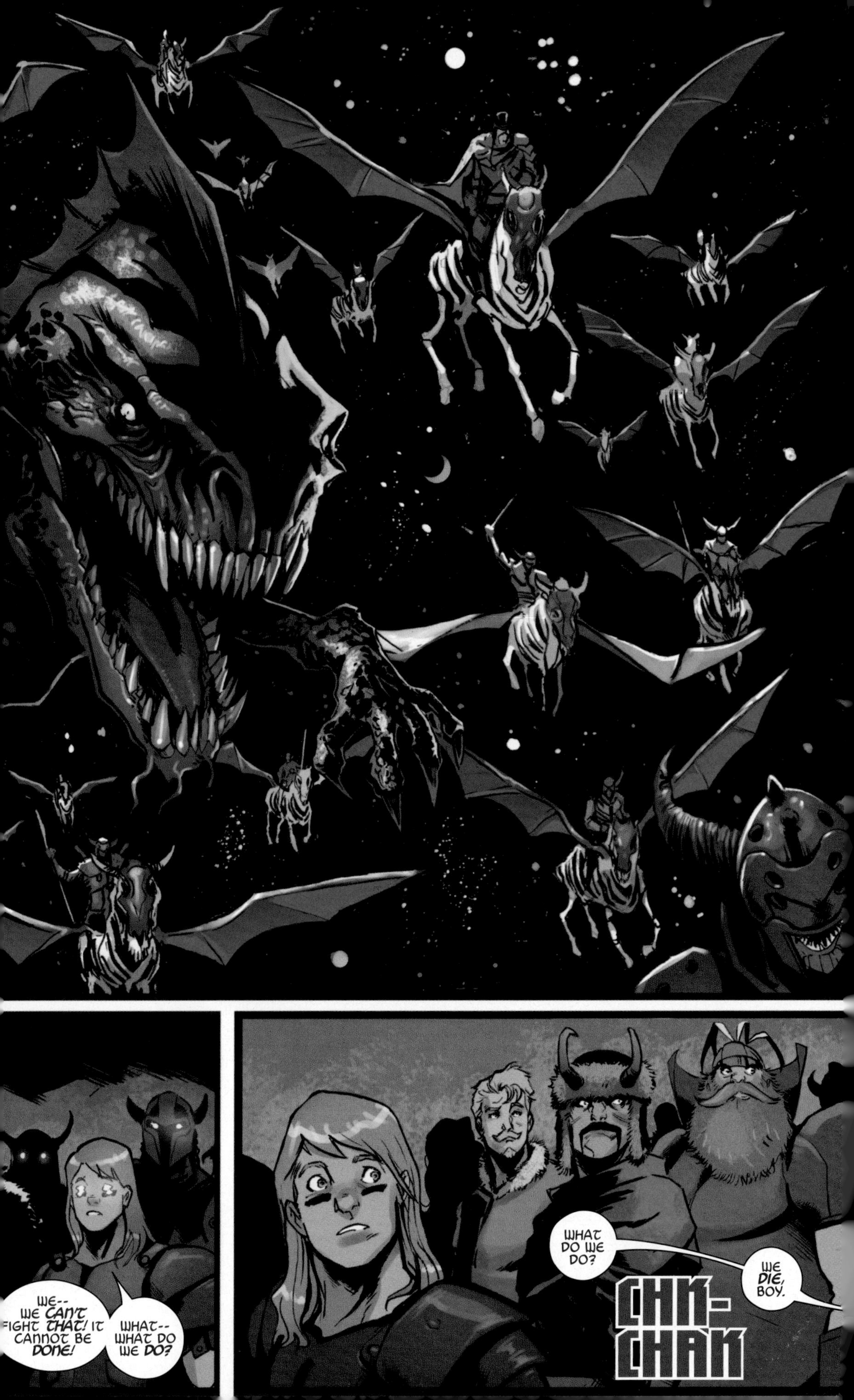
WE-- WE CAN'T FIGHT THAT! IT CANNOT BE DONE!
WHAT-- WHAT DO WE DO?
WHAT DO WE DO?
WE DIE, BOY.
CHK-CHAK

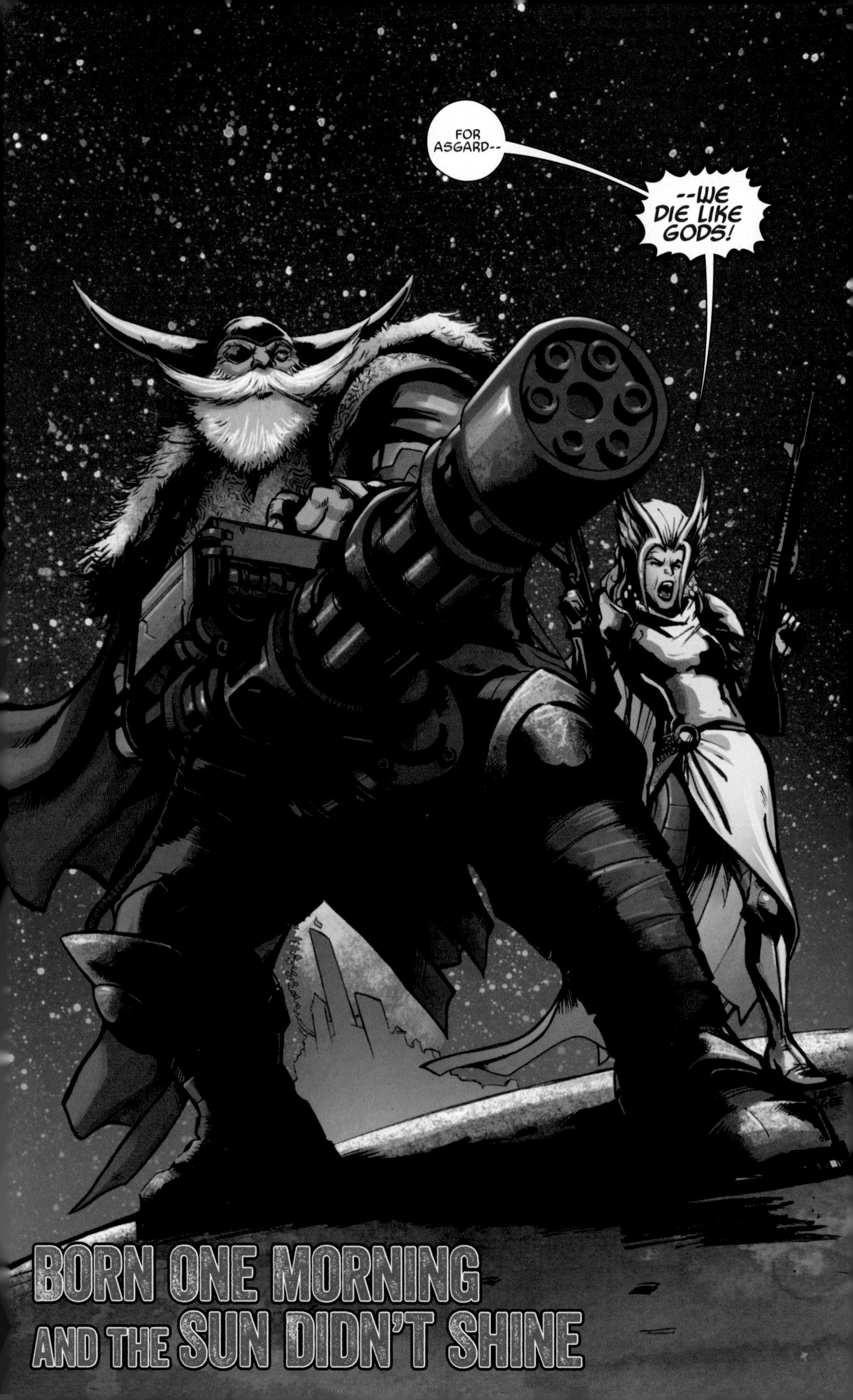
FOR ASGARD--
--WE DIE LIKE GODS!
BORN ONE MORNING AND THE SUN DIDN'T SHINE

LOKI: AGENT OF ASGARD #1 ANIMAL VARIANT
by Mike del Mundo

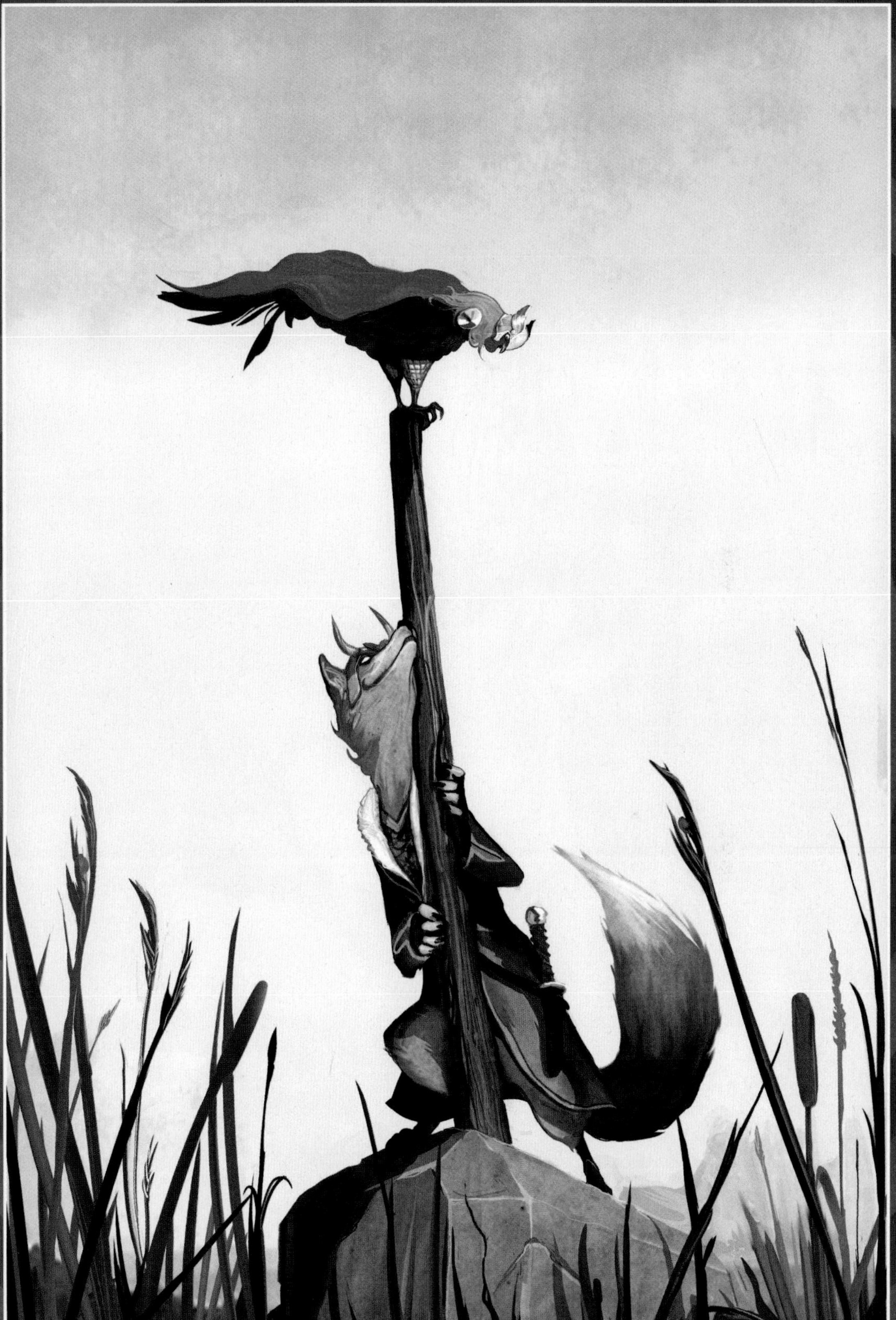

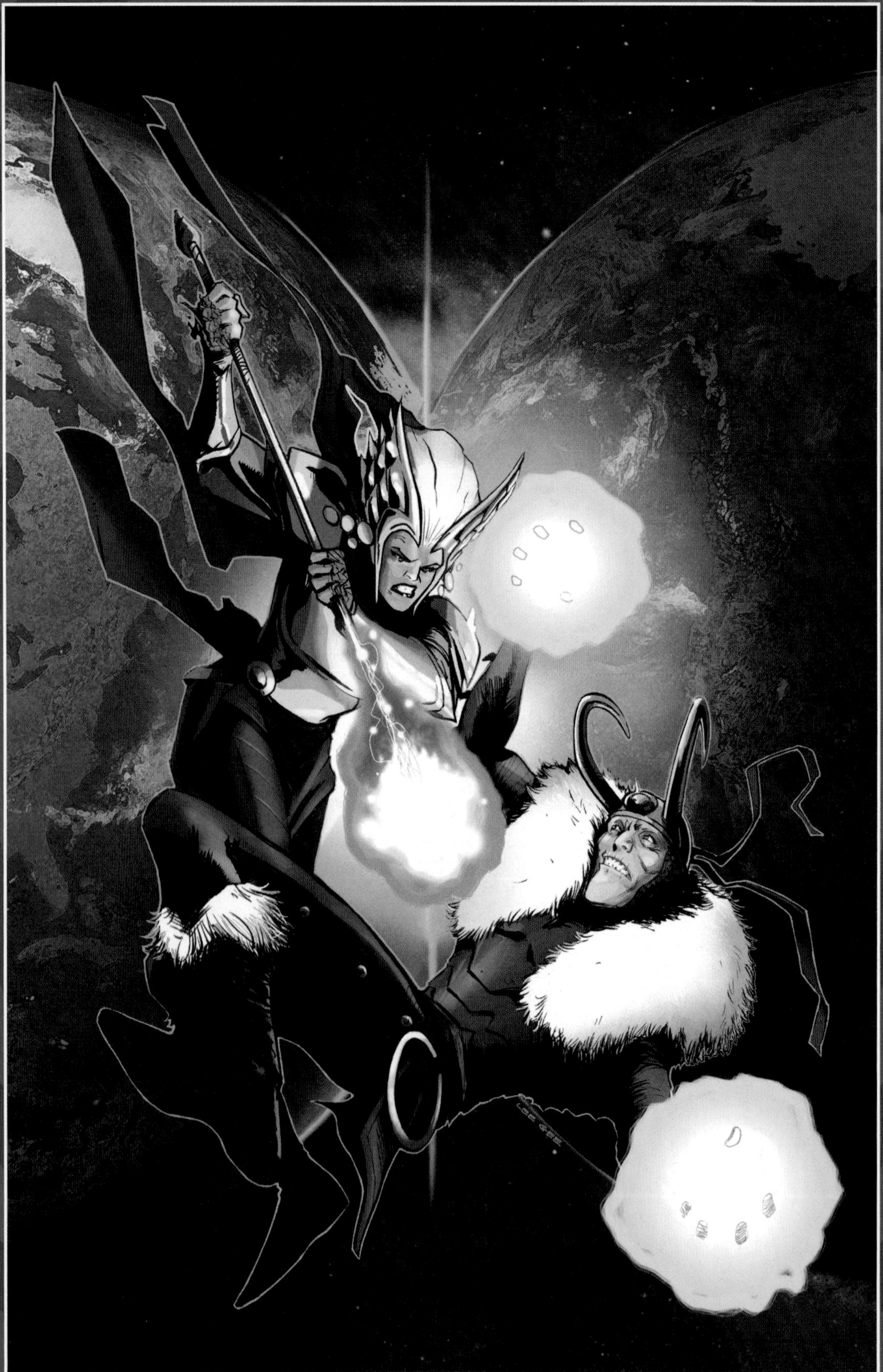

LOKI: AGENT OF ASGARD #15

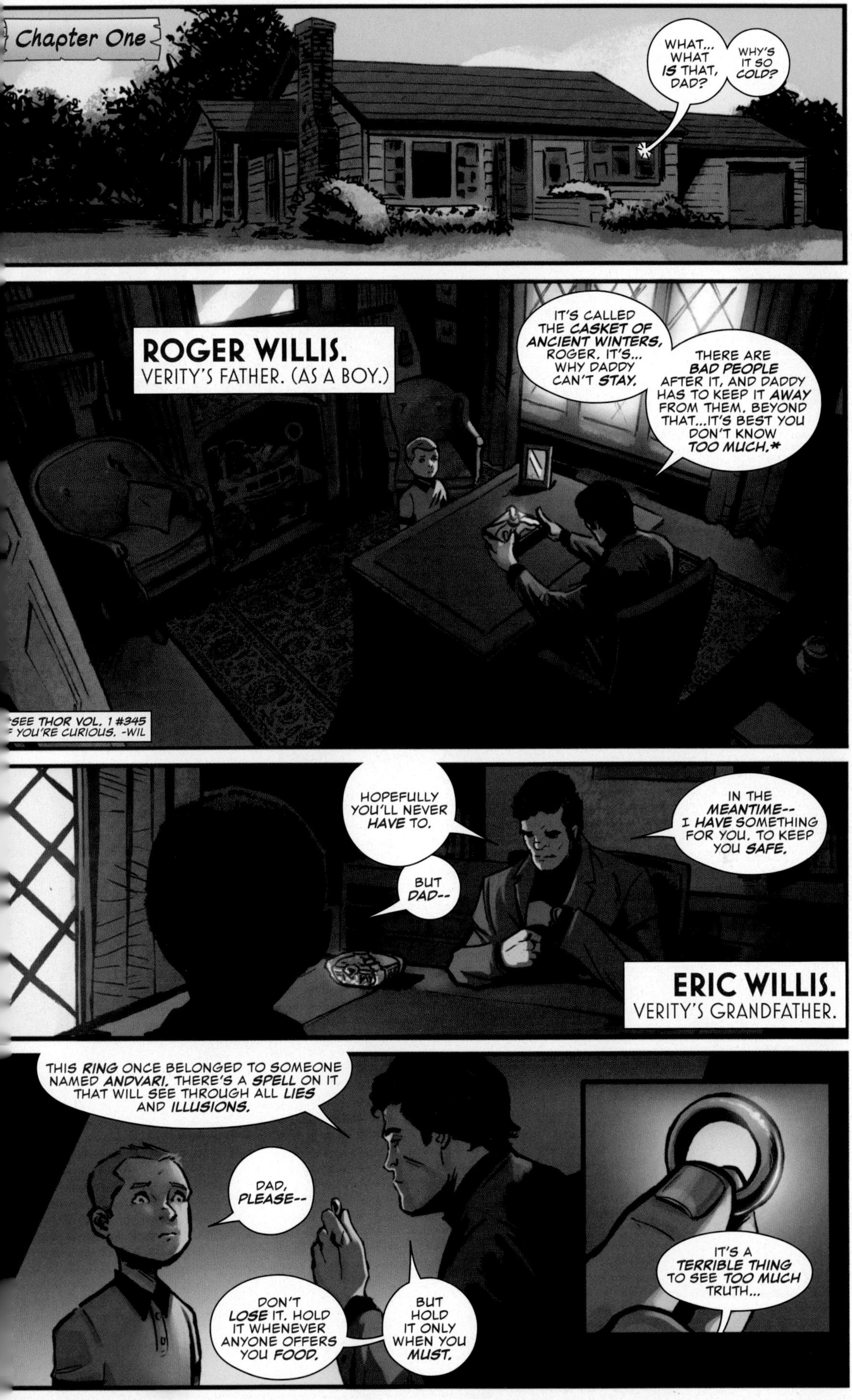
Chapter One
WHAT... WHAT IS THAT, DAD?
WHY'S IT SO COLD?
ROGER WILLIS.
VERITY'S FATHER. (AS A BOY.)
IT'S CALLED THE CASKET OF ANCIENT WINTERS, ROGER. IT'S... WHY DADDY CAN'T STAY.
THERE ARE BAD PEOPLE AFTER IT, AND DADDY HAS TO KEEP IT AWAY FROM THEM. BEYOND THAT...IT'S BEST YOU DON'T KNOW TOO MUCH.*
*SEE THOR VOL. 1 #345 IF YOU'RE CURIOUS. -WIL
HOPEFULLY YOU'LL NEVER HAVE TO.
BUT DAD--
IN THE MEANTIME-- I HAVE SOMETHING FOR YOU, TO KEEP YOU SAFE.
ERIC WILLIS.
VERITY'S GRANDFATHER.
THIS RING ONCE BELONGED TO SOMEONE NAMED ANDVARI. THERE'S A SPELL ON IT THAT WILL SEE THROUGH ALL LIES AND ILLUSIONS.
DAD, PLEASE--
DON'T LOSE IT. HOLD IT WHENEVER ANYONE OFFERS YOU FOOD.
BUT HOLD IT ONLY WHEN YOU MUST.
IT'S A TERRIBLE THING TO SEE TOO MUCH TRUTH...

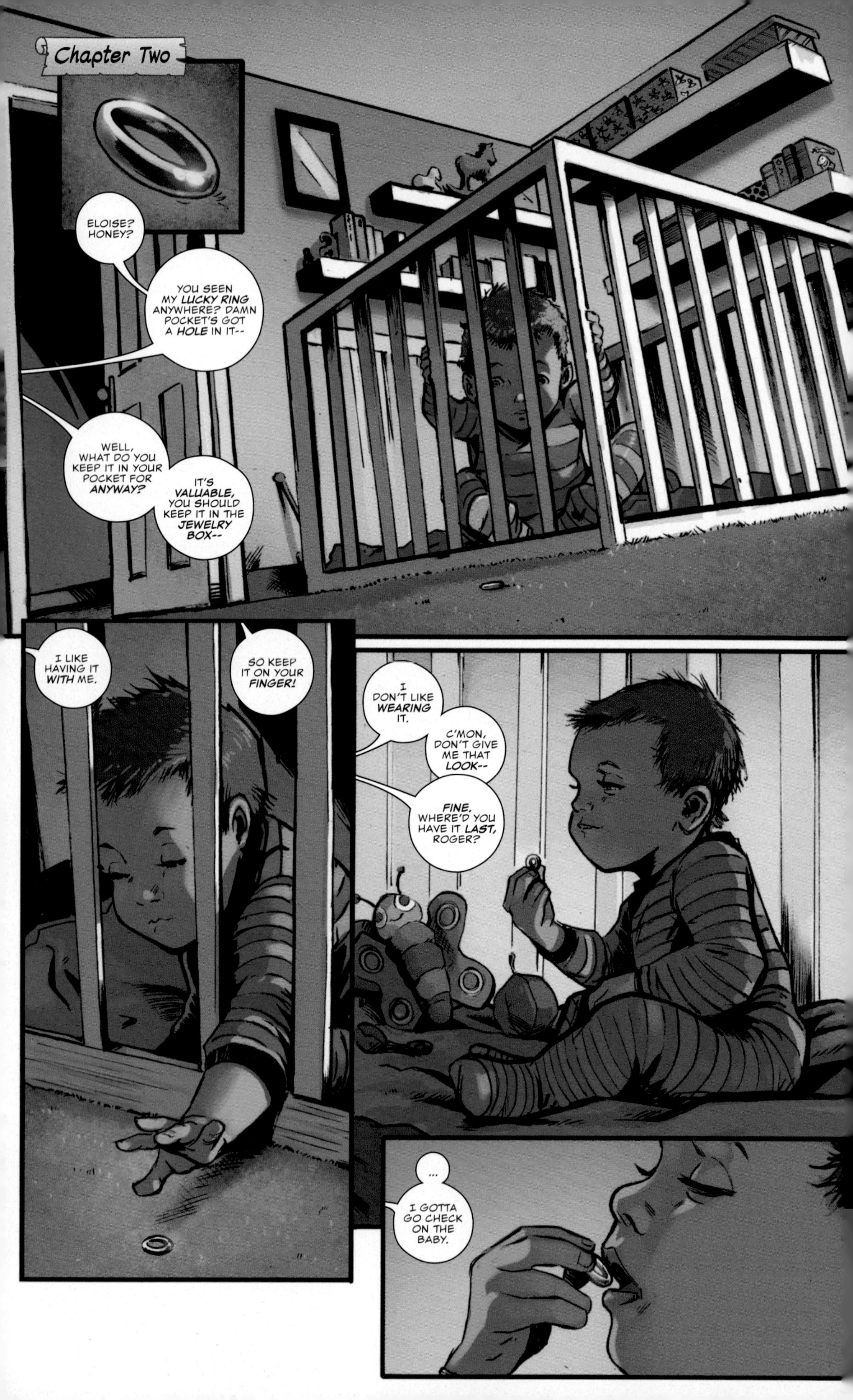
Chapter Two
ELOISE? HONEY?
YOU SEEN MY LUCKY RING ANYWHERE? DAMN POCKET'S GOT A HOLE IN IT--
WELL, WHAT DO YOU KEEP IT IN YOUR POCKET FOR ANYWAY?
IT'S VALUABLE, YOU SHOULD KEEP IT IN THE JEWELRY BOX--
I LIKE HAVING IT WITH ME.
SO KEEP IT ON YOUR FINGER!
I DON'T LIKE WEARING IT.
C'MON, DON'T GIVE ME THAT LOOK--
FINE. WHERE'D YOU HAVE IT LAST, ROGER?
...
I GOTTA GO CHECK ON THE BABY.

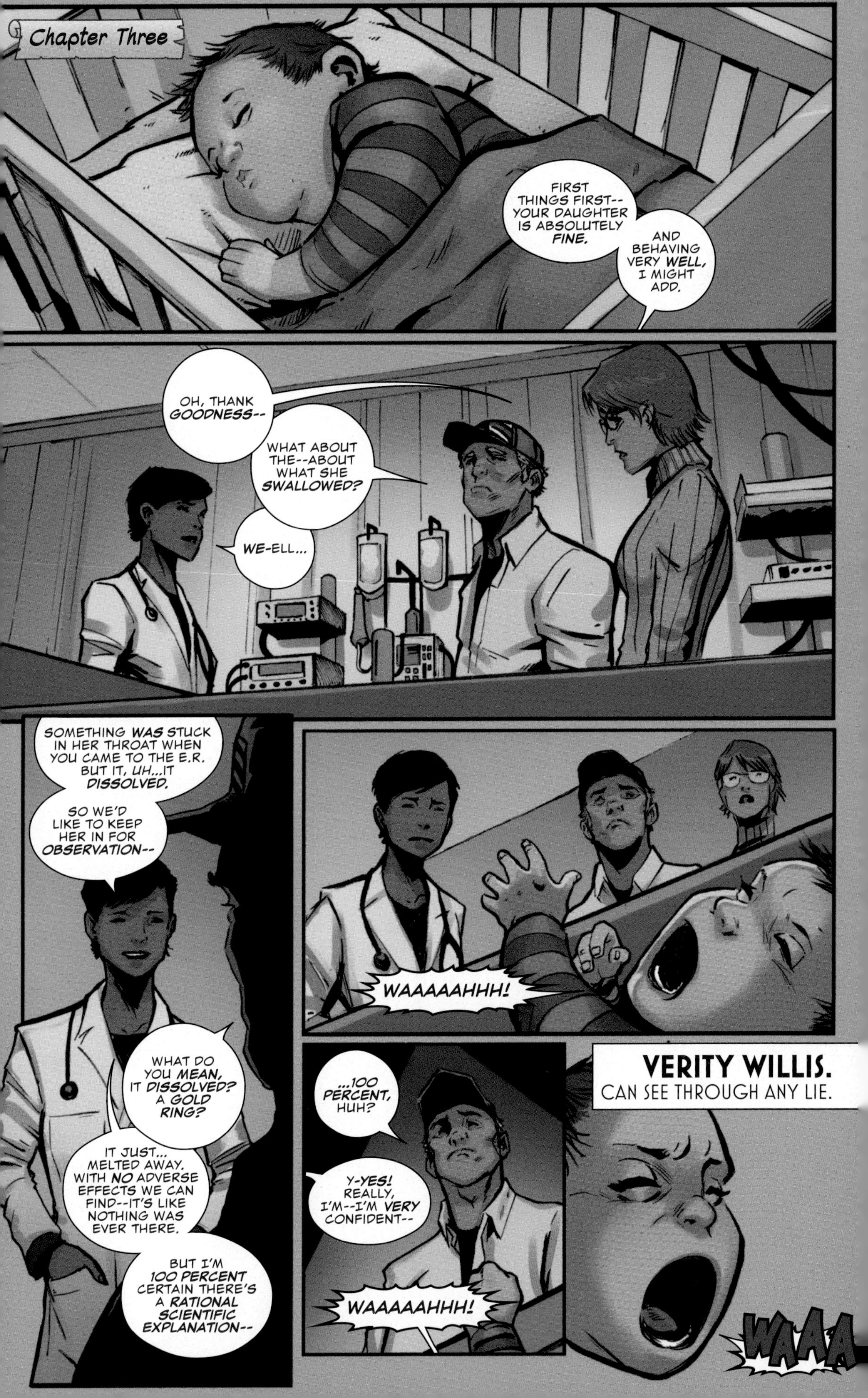
Chapter Three
FIRST THINGS FIRST--YOUR DAUGHTER IS ABSOLUTELY FINE.
AND BEHAVING VERY WELL, I MIGHT ADD.
OH, THANK GOODNESS--
WHAT ABOUT THE--ABOUT WHAT SHE SWALLOWED?
WE-ELL...
SOMETHING WAS STUCK IN HER THROAT WHEN YOU CAME TO THE E.R. BUT IT, UH...IT DISSOLVED.
SO WE'D LIKE TO KEEP HER IN FOR OBSERVATION--
WHAT DO YOU MEAN, IT DISSOLVED? A GOLD RING?
IT JUST... MELTED AWAY. WITH NO ADVERSE EFFECTS WE CAN FIND--IT'S LIKE NOTHING WAS EVER THERE.
BUT I'M 100 PERCENT CERTAIN THERE'S A RATIONAL SCIENTIFIC EXPLANATION--
WAAAAAHHH!
...100 PERCENT, HUH?
Y-YES! REALLY, I'M--I'M VERY CONFIDENT--
WAAAAAHHH!
VERITY WILLIS.
CAN SEE THROUGH ANY LIE.
WAAA

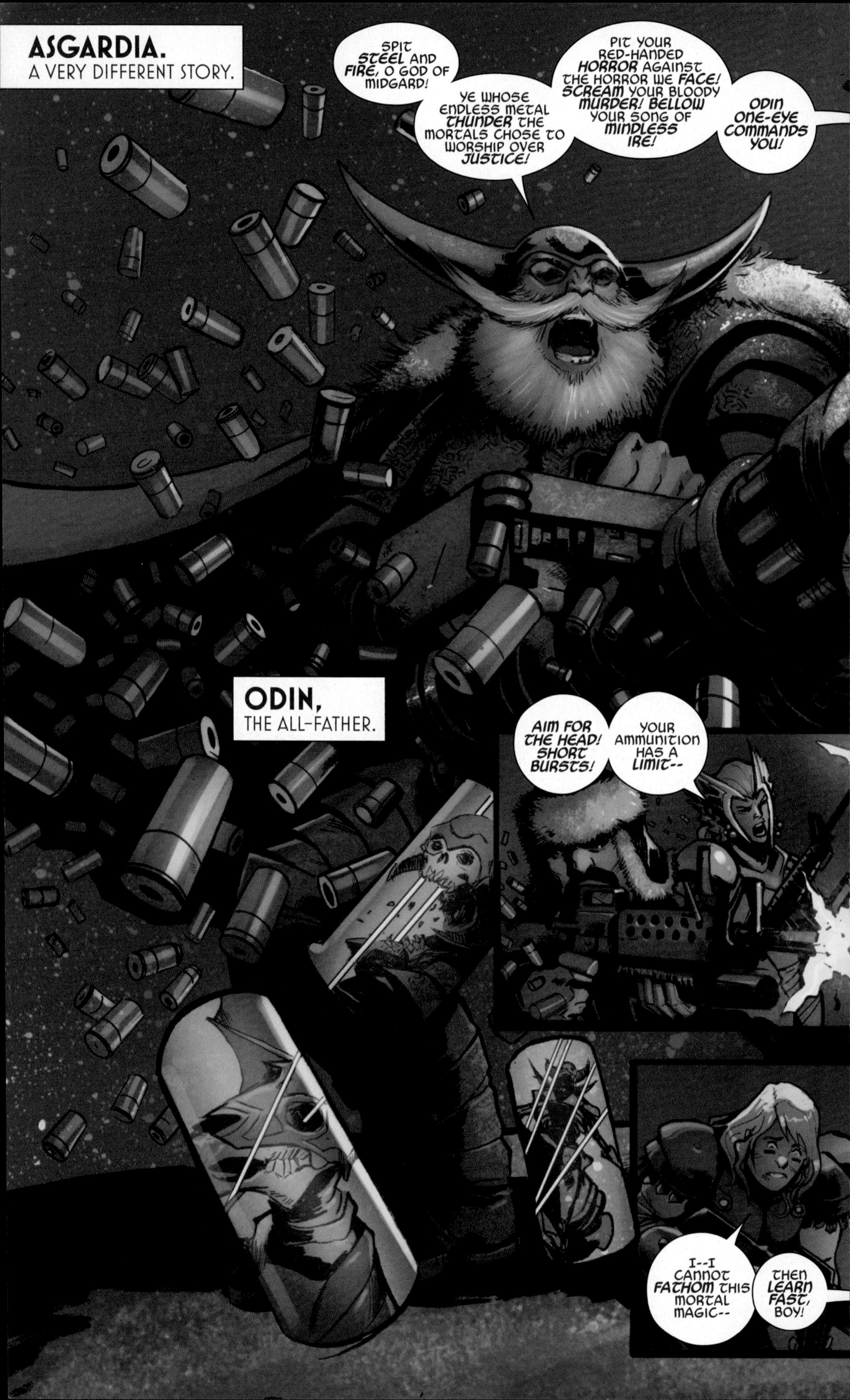
ASGARDIA.
A VERY DIFFERENT STORY.
SPIT STEEL AND FIRE, O GOD OF MIDGARD!
YE WHOSE ENDLESS METAL THUNDER THE MORTALS CHOSE TO WORSHIP OVER JUSTICE!
PIT YOUR RED-HANDED HORROR AGAINST THE HORROR WE FACE! SCREAM YOUR BLOODY MURDER! BELLOW YOUR SONG OF MINDLESS IRE!
ODIN ONE-EYE COMMANDS YOU!
ODIN,
THE ALL-FATHER.
AIM FOR THE HEAD! SHORT BURSTS!
YOUR AMMUNITION HAS A LIMIT--
I--I CANNOT FATHOM THIS MORTAL MAGIC--
THEN LEARN FAST, BOY!

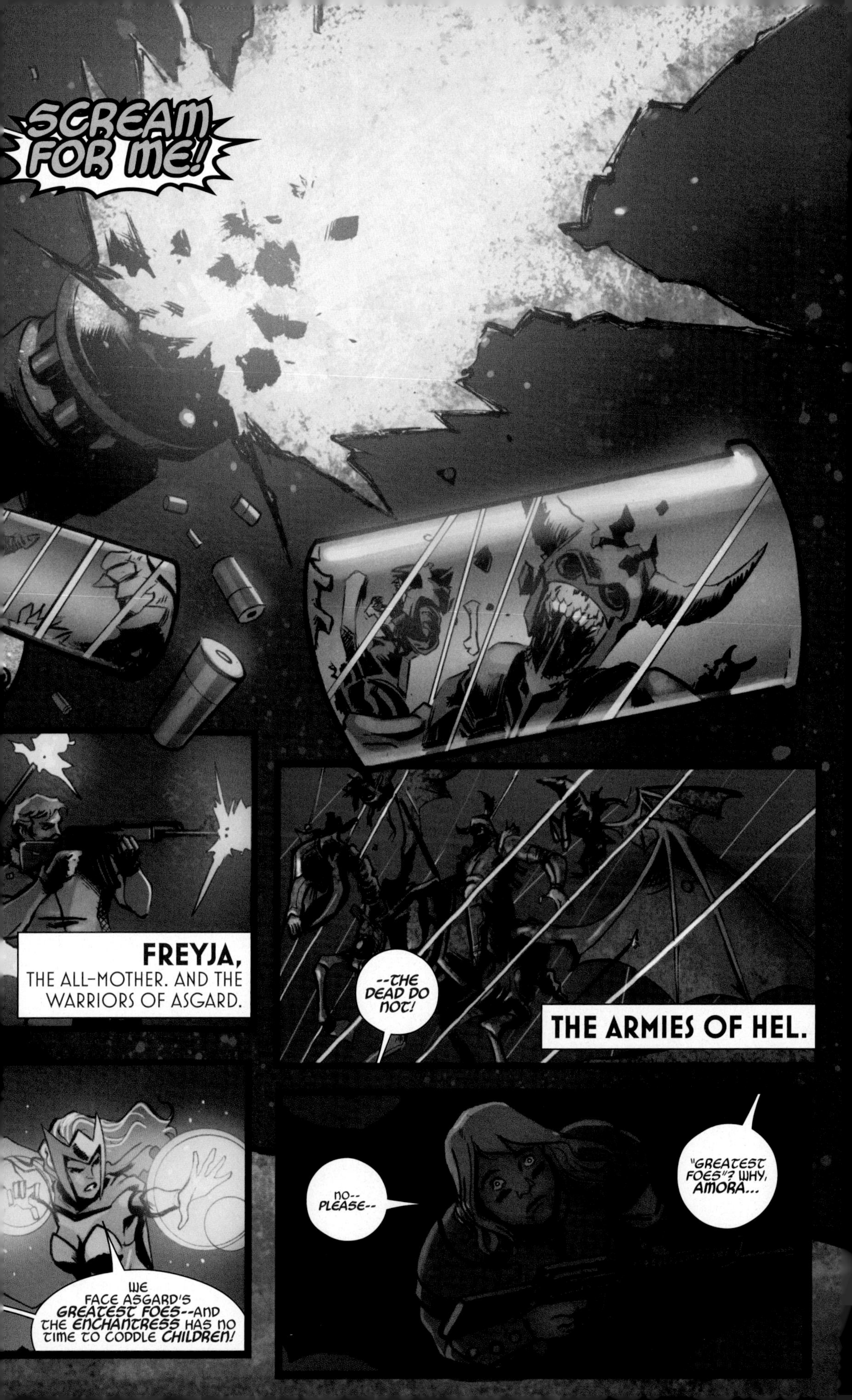
SCREAM FOR ME!
FREYJA, THE ALL-MOTHER. AND THE WARRIORS OF ASGARD.
--THE DEAD DO NOT!
THE ARMIES OF HEL.
WE FACE ASGARD'S GREATEST FOES--AND THE ENCHANTRESS HAS NO TIME TO CODDLE CHILDREN!
NO-- PLEASE--
"GREATEST FOES"? WHY, AMORA...

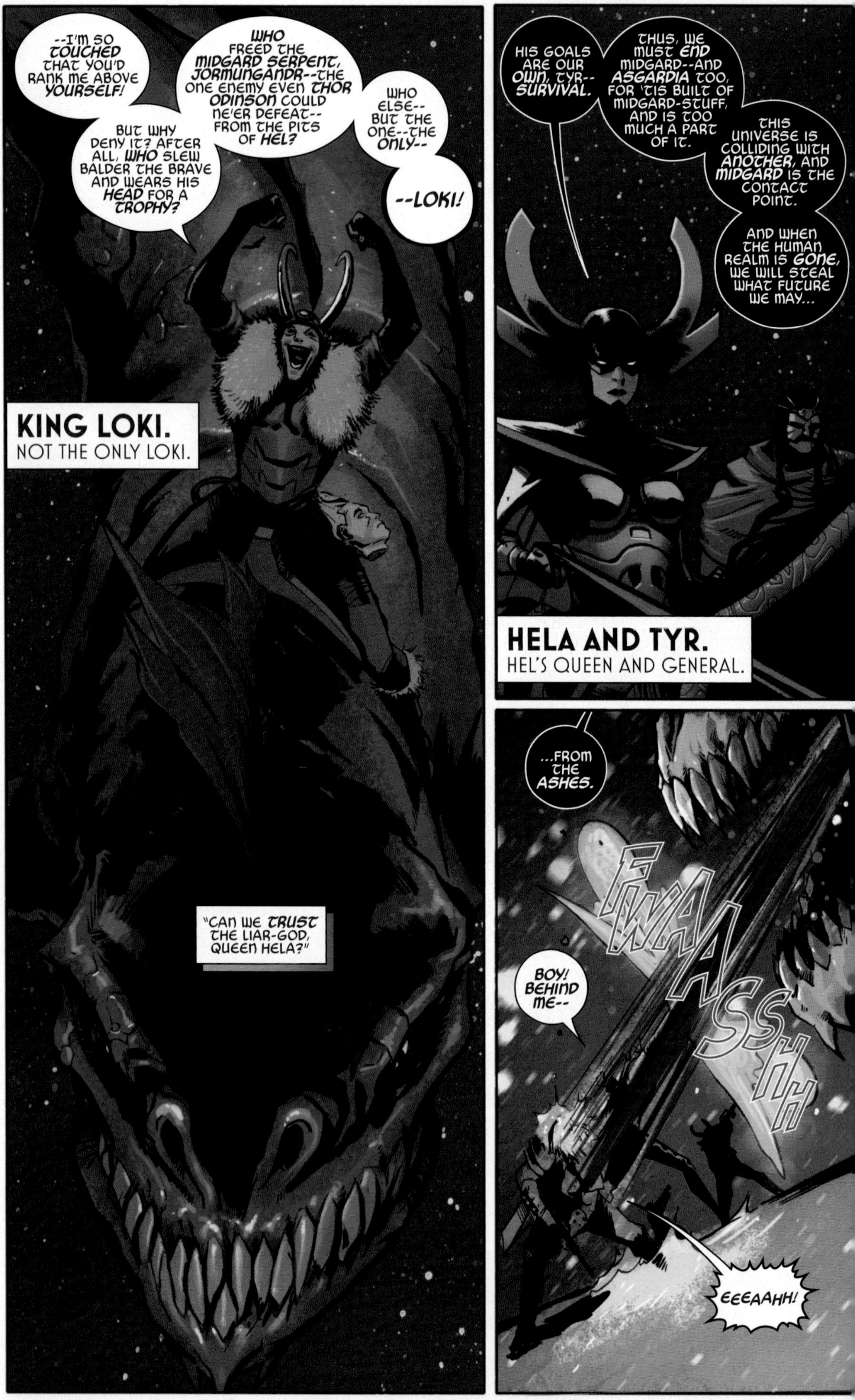
--I'M SO TOUCHED THAT YOU'D RANK ME ABOVE YOURSELF!
BUT WHY DENY IT? AFTER ALL, WHO SLEW BALDER THE BRAVE AND WEARS HIS HEAD FOR A TROPHY?
WHO FREED THE MIDGARD SERPENT, JORMUNGANDR--THE ONE ENEMY EVEN THOR ODINSON COULD NE'ER DEFEAT--FROM THE PITS OF HEL?
WHO ELSE--BUT THE ONE--THE ONLY--
--LOKI!
KING LOKI.
NOT THE ONLY LOKI.
"CAN WE TRUST THE LIAR-GOD, QUEEN HELA?"
HIS GOALS ARE OUR OWN, TYR--SURVIVAL.
THUS, WE MUST END MIDGARD--AND ASGARDIA TOO, FOR 'TIS BUILT OF MIDGARD-STUFF, AND IS TOO MUCH A PART OF IT.
THIS UNIVERSE IS COLLIDING WITH ANOTHER, AND MIDGARD IS THE CONTACT POINT.
AND WHEN THE HUMAN REALM IS GONE, WE WILL STEAL WHAT FUTURE WE MAY...
HELA AND TYR.
HEL'S QUEEN AND GENERAL.
...FROM THE ASHES.
FWAASSHH
BOY! BEHIND ME--
EEEAAHH!

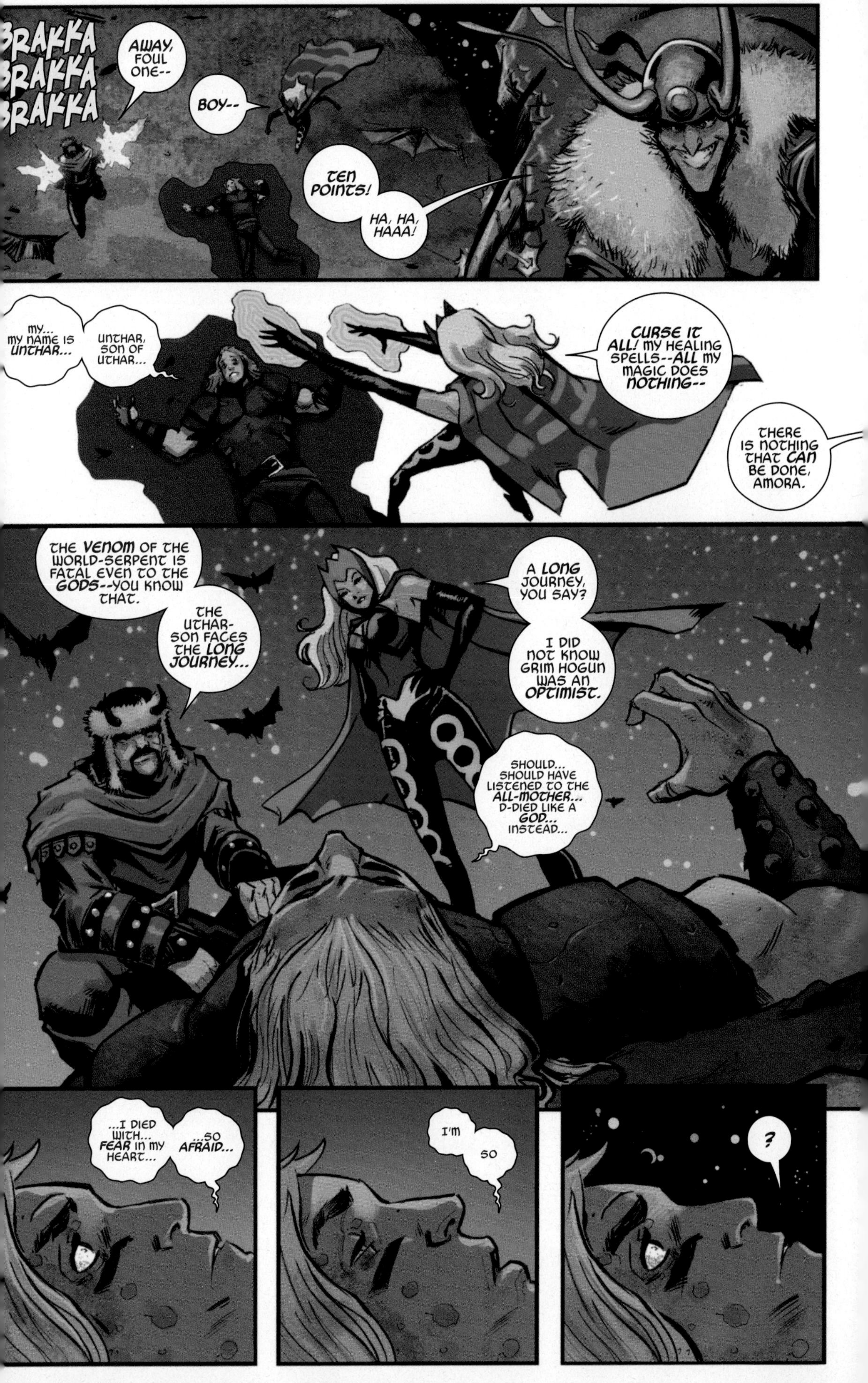
BRAKKA BRAKKA BRAKKA
AWAY, FOUL ONE--
BOY--
TEN POINTS!
HA, HA, HAAA!
MY... MY NAME IS UNTHAR...
UNTHAR, SON OF UTHAR...
CURSE IT ALL! MY HEALING SPELLS--ALL MY MAGIC DOES NOTHING--
THERE IS NOTHING THAT CAN BE DONE, AMORA.
THE VENOM OF THE WORLD-SERPENT IS FATAL EVEN TO THE GODS--YOU KNOW THAT.
THE UTHAR-SON FACES THE LONG JOURNEY...
A LONG JOURNEY, YOU SAY?
I DID NOT KNOW GRIM HOGUN WAS AN OPTIMIST.
SHOULD... SHOULD HAVE LISTENED TO THE ALL-MOTHER... D-DIED LIKE A GOD... INSTEAD...
...I DIED WITH... FEAR IN MY HEART...
...SO AFRAID...
I'M
SO
?

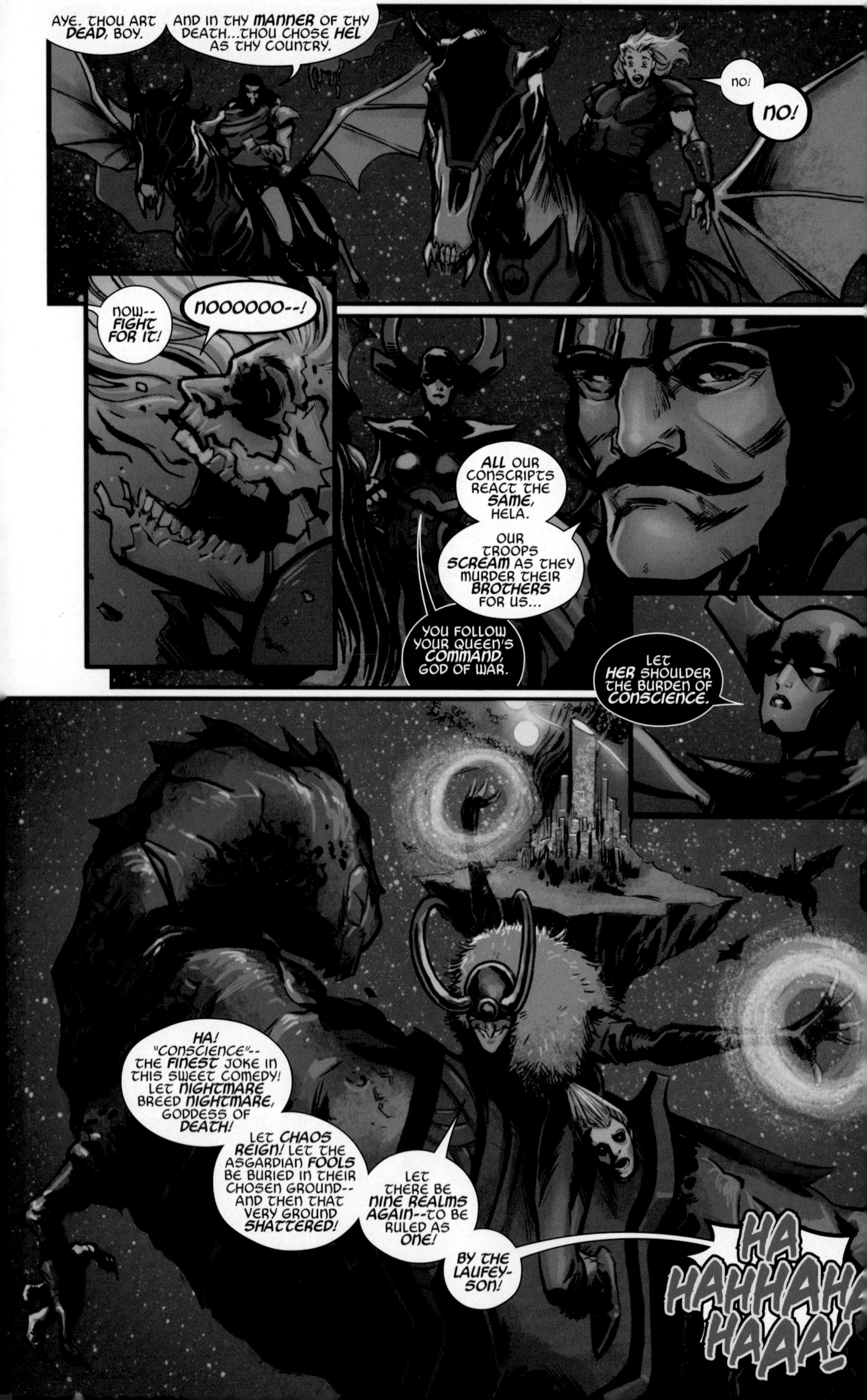
AYE. THOU ART DEAD, BOY.
AND IN THY MANNER OF THY DEATH...THOU CHOSE HEL AS THY COUNTRY.
NO!
NO!
NOW-- FIGHT FOR IT!
NOOOOOO--!
ALL OUR CONSCRIPTS REACT THE SAME, HELA.
OUR TROOPS SCREAM AS THEY MURDER THEIR BROTHERS FOR US...
YOU FOLLOW YOUR QUEEN'S COMMAND, GOD OF WAR.
LET HER SHOULDER THE BURDEN OF CONSCIENCE.
HA! "CONSCIENCE"-- THE FINEST JOKE IN THIS SWEET COMEDY! LET NIGHTMARE BREED NIGHTMARE, GODDESS OF DEATH!
LET CHAOS REIGN! LET THE ASGARDIAN FOOLS BE BURIED IN THEIR CHOSEN GROUND-- AND THEN THAT VERY GROUND SHATTERED!
LET THERE BE NINE REALMS AGAIN--TO BE RULED AS ONE!
BY THE LAUFEY-SON!
HA HAHHAH HAAA!

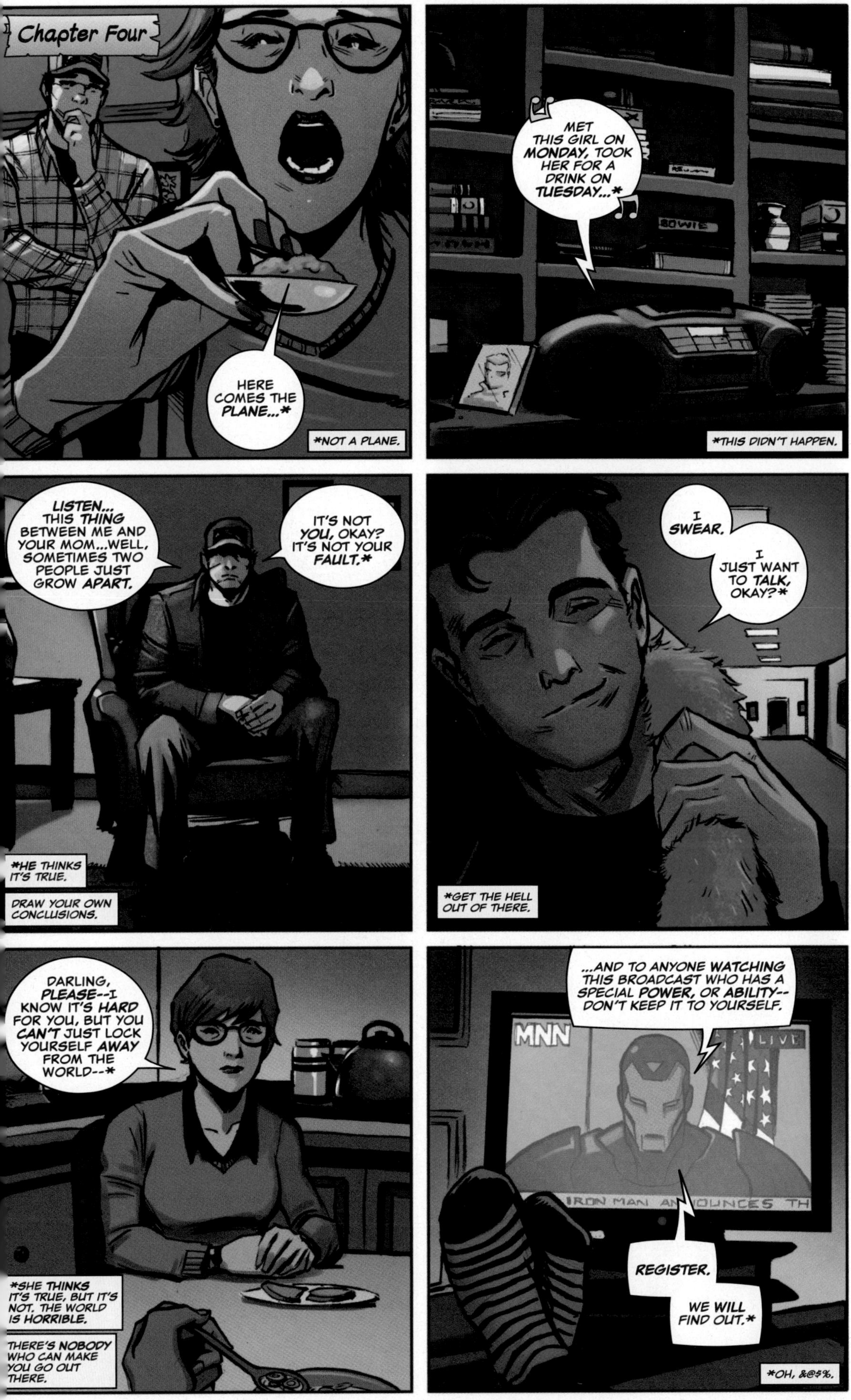
Chapter Four
HERE COMES THE PLANE...*
*NOT A PLANE.
MET THIS GIRL ON MONDAY, TOOK HER FOR A DRINK ON TUESDAY...*
*THIS DIDN'T HAPPEN.
LISTEN... THIS THING BETWEEN ME AND YOUR MOM...WELL, SOMETIMES TWO PEOPLE JUST GROW APART.
IT'S NOT YOU, OKAY? IT'S NOT YOUR FAULT.*
*HE THINKS IT'S TRUE.
DRAW YOUR OWN CONCLUSIONS.
I SWEAR.
I JUST WANT TO TALK, OKAY?*
*GET THE HELL OUT OF THERE.
DARLING, PLEASE--I KNOW IT'S HARD FOR YOU, BUT YOU CAN'T JUST LOCK YOURSELF AWAY FROM THE WORLD--*
*SHE THINKS IT'S TRUE, BUT IT'S NOT. THE WORLD IS HORRIBLE.
THERE'S NOBODY WHO CAN MAKE YOU GO OUT THERE.
...AND TO ANYONE WATCHING THIS BROADCAST WHO HAS A SPECIAL POWER, OR ABILITY--DON'T KEEP IT TO YOURSELF.
MNN
LIVE
IRON MAN AN OUNCES TH
REGISTER.
WE WILL FIND OUT.*
*OH, &@$%.

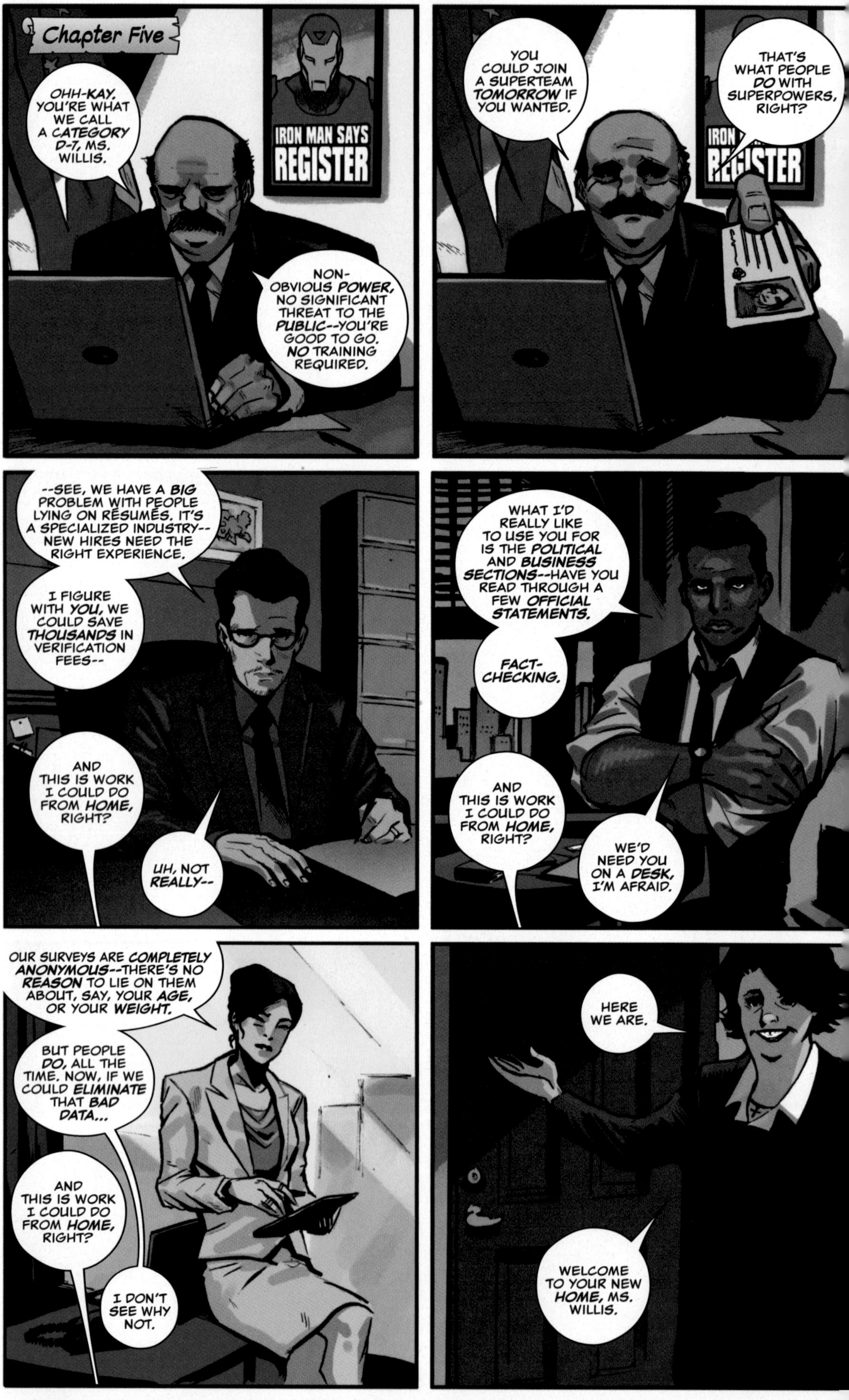
Chapter Five
OHH-KAY. YOU'RE WHAT WE CALL A CATEGORY D-7, MS. WILLIS.
IRON MAN SAYS REGISTER
NON-OBVIOUS POWER, NO SIGNIFICANT THREAT TO THE PUBLIC--YOU'RE GOOD TO GO. NO TRAINING REQUIRED.
YOU COULD JOIN A SUPERTEAM TOMORROW IF YOU WANTED.
THAT'S WHAT PEOPLE DO WITH SUPERPOWERS, RIGHT?
--SEE, WE HAVE A BIG PROBLEM WITH PEOPLE LYING ON RÉSUMÉS. IT'S A SPECIALIZED INDUSTRY--NEW HIRES NEED THE RIGHT EXPERIENCE.
I FIGURE WITH YOU, WE COULD SAVE THOUSANDS IN VERIFICATION FEES--
AND THIS IS WORK I COULD DO FROM HOME, RIGHT?
UH, NOT REALLY--
WHAT I'D REALLY LIKE TO USE YOU FOR IS THE POLITICAL AND BUSINESS SECTIONS--HAVE YOU READ THROUGH A FEW OFFICIAL STATEMENTS.
FACT-CHECKING.
AND THIS IS WORK I COULD DO FROM HOME, RIGHT?
WE'D NEED YOU ON A DESK, I'M AFRAID.
OUR SURVEYS ARE COMPLETELY ANONYMOUS--THERE'S NO REASON TO LIE ON THEM ABOUT, SAY, YOUR AGE, OR YOUR WEIGHT.
BUT PEOPLE DO, ALL THE TIME. NOW, IF WE COULD ELIMINATE THAT BAD DATA...
AND THIS IS WORK I COULD DO FROM HOME, RIGHT?
I DON'T SEE WHY NOT.
HERE WE ARE.
WELCOME TO YOUR NEW HOME, MS. WILLIS.

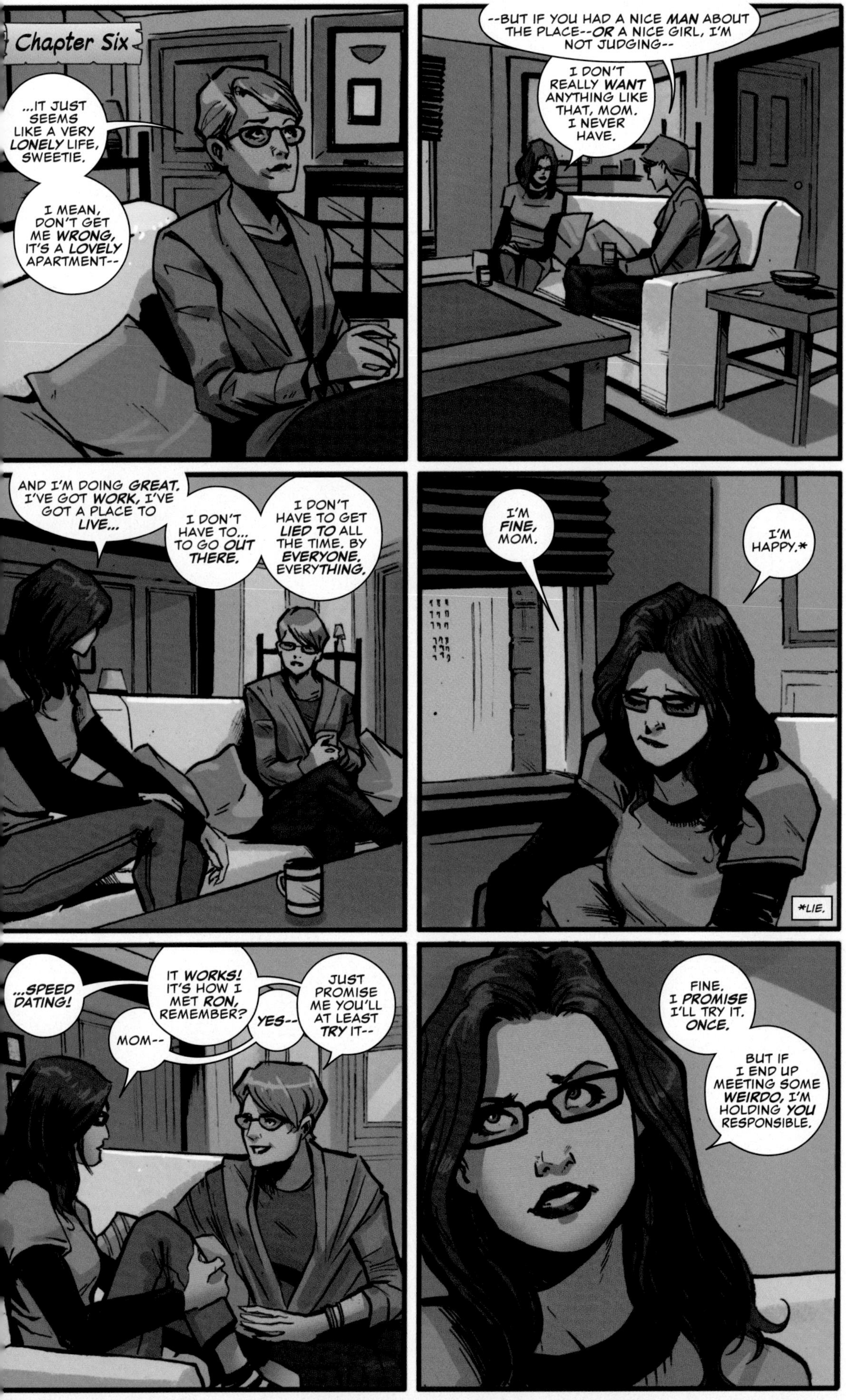
Chapter Six
...IT JUST SEEMS LIKE A VERY LONELY LIFE, SWEETIE.
I MEAN, DON'T GET ME WRONG, IT'S A LOVELY APARTMENT--
--BUT IF YOU HAD A NICE MAN ABOUT THE PLACE--OR A NICE GIRL, I'M NOT JUDGING--
I DON'T REALLY WANT ANYTHING LIKE THAT, MOM. I NEVER HAVE.
AND I'M DOING GREAT. I'VE GOT WORK, I'VE GOT A PLACE TO LIVE...
I DON'T HAVE TO... TO GO OUT THERE.
I DON'T HAVE TO GET LIED TO ALL THE TIME. BY EVERYONE. EVERYTHING.
I'M FINE, MOM.
I'M HAPPY.*
*LIE.
...SPEED DATING!
IT WORKS! IT'S HOW I MET RON, REMEMBER?
MOM--
YES--
JUST PROMISE ME YOU'LL AT LEAST TRY IT--
FINE. I PROMISE I'LL TRY IT. ONCE.
BUT IF I END UP MEETING SOME WEIRDO, I'M HOLDING YOU RESPONSIBLE.

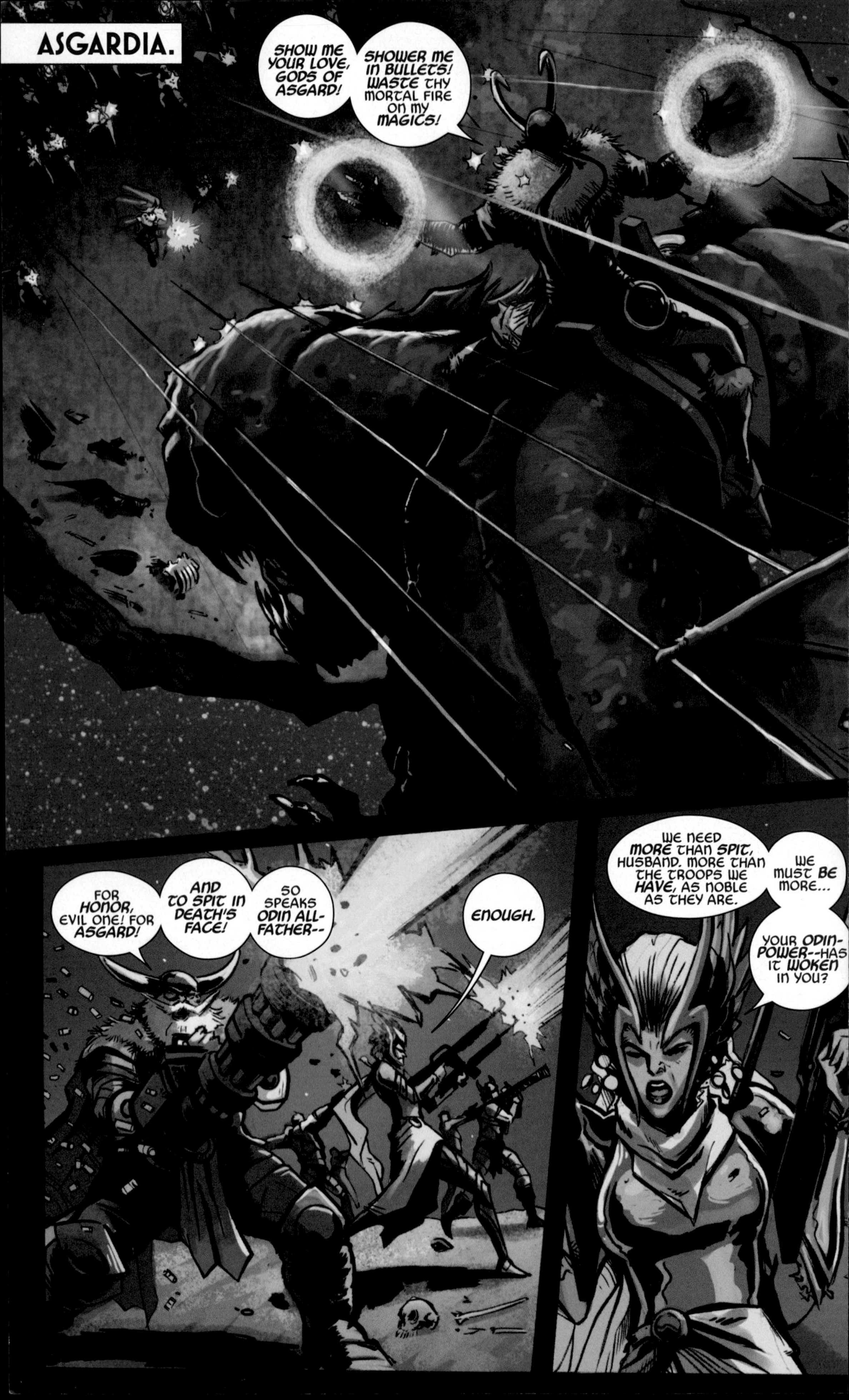
ASGARDIA.
SHOW ME YOUR LOVE, GODS OF ASGARD!
SHOWER ME IN BULLETS! WASTE THY MORTAL FIRE ON MY MAGICS!
FOR HONOR, EVIL ONE! FOR ASGARD!
AND TO SPIT IN DEATH'S FACE!
SO SPEAKS ODIN ALL-FATHER--
ENOUGH.
WE NEED MORE THAN SPIT, HUSBAND. MORE THAN THE TROOPS WE HAVE, AS NOBLE AS THEY ARE.
WE MUST BE MORE...
YOUR ODIN-POWER--HAS IT WOKEN IN YOU?

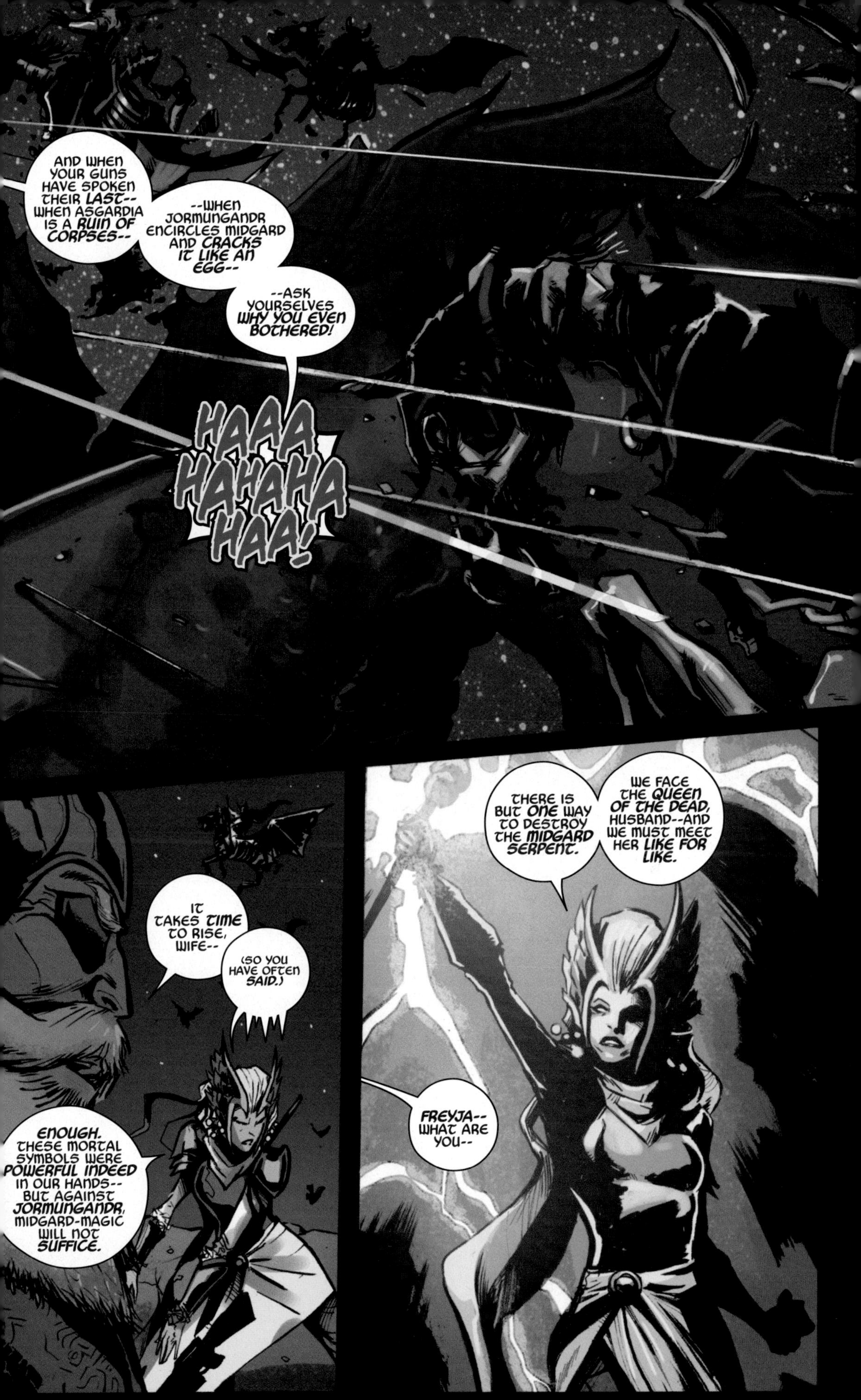
AND WHEN YOUR GUNS HAVE SPOKEN THEIR LAST-- WHEN ASGARDIA IS A RUIN OF CORPSES--
--WHEN JORMUNGANDR ENCIRCLES MIDGARD AND CRACKS IT LIKE AN EGG--
--ASK YOURSELVES WHY YOU EVEN BOTHERED!
HAAA HAHAHA HAA!
IT TAKES TIME TO RISE, WIFE--
(SO YOU HAVE OFTEN SAID.)
ENOUGH. THESE MORTAL SYMBOLS WERE POWERFUL INDEED IN OUR HANDS-- BUT AGAINST JORMUNGANDR, MIDGARD-MAGIC WILL NOT SUFFICE.
THERE IS BUT ONE WAY TO DESTROY THE MIDGARD SERPENT.
WE FACE THE QUEEN OF THE DEAD, HUSBAND--AND WE MUST MEET HER LIKE FOR LIKE.
FREYJA-- WHAT ARE YOU--

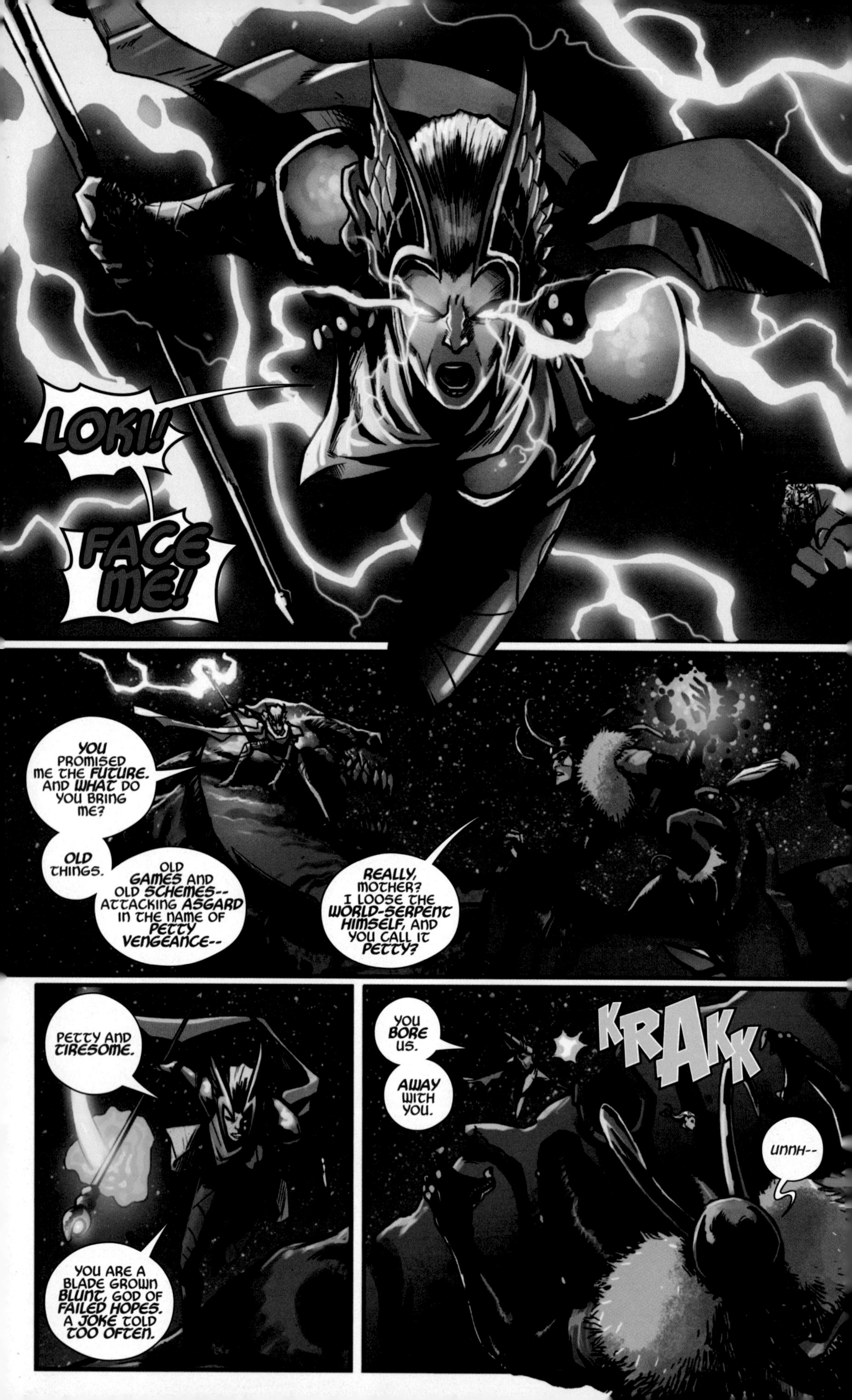
LOKI!
FACE ME!
YOU PROMISED ME THE FUTURE. AND WHAT DO YOU BRING ME?
OLD THINGS.
OLD GAMES AND OLD SCHEMES-- ATTACKING ASGARD IN THE NAME OF PETTY VENGEANCE--
REALLY, MOTHER? I LOOSE THE WORLD-SERPENT HIMSELF, AND YOU CALL IT PETTY?
PETTY AND TIRESOME.
YOU ARE A BLADE GROWN BLUNT, GOD OF FAILED HOPES. A JOKE TOLD TOO OFTEN.
YOU BORE US.
AWAY WITH YOU.
KRAKK
UNNH--

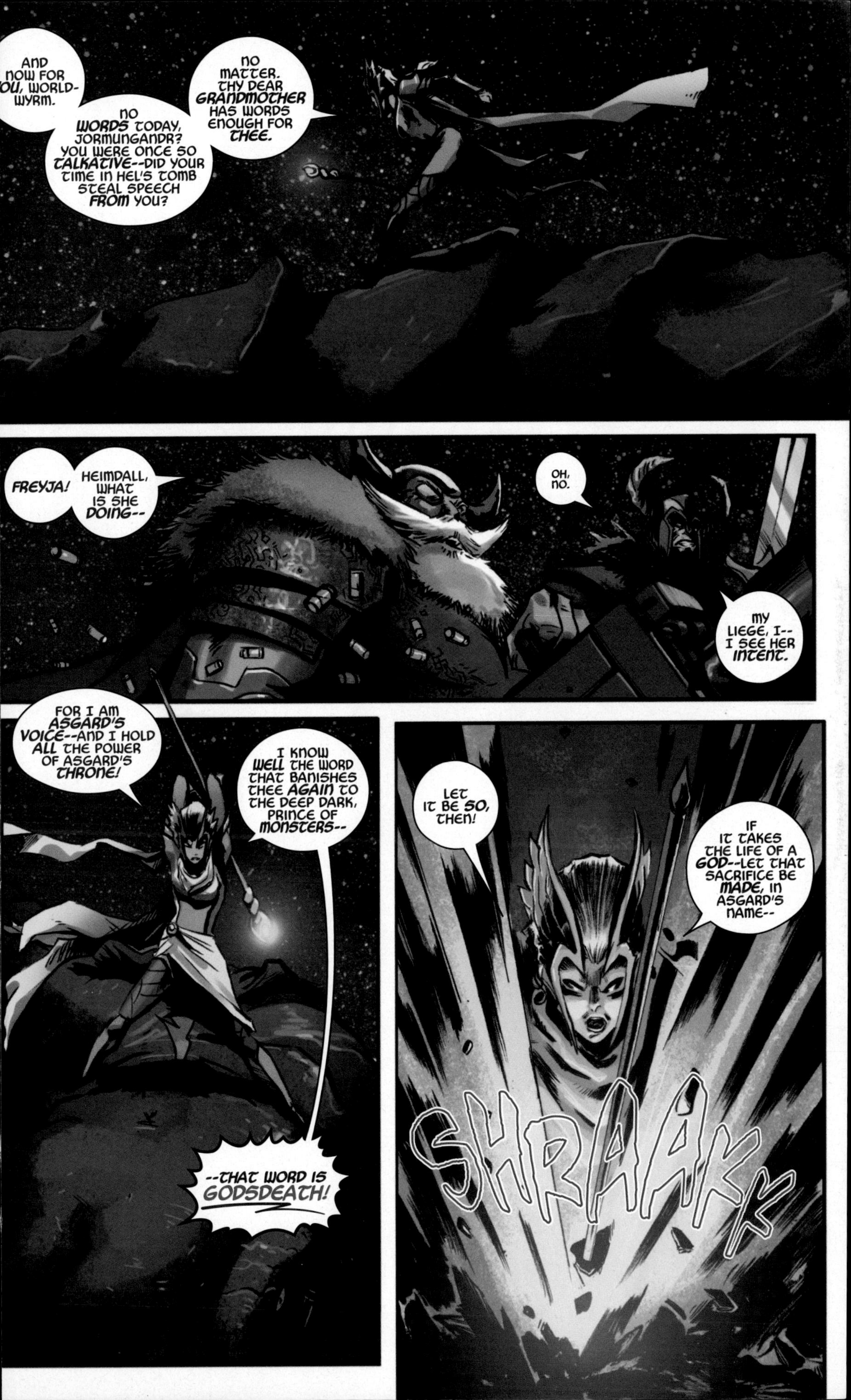
AND NOW FOR YOU, WORLD-WYRM.
NO WORDS TODAY, JORMUNGANDR? YOU WERE ONCE SO TALKATIVE--DID YOUR TIME IN HEL'S TOMB STEAL SPEECH FROM YOU?
NO MATTER. THY DEAR GRANDMOTHER HAS WORDS ENOUGH FOR THEE.
FREYJA!
HEIMDALL, WHAT IS SHE DOING--
OH, NO.
MY LIEGE, I-- I SEE HER INTENT.
FOR I AM ASGARD'S VOICE--AND I HOLD ALL THE POWER OF ASGARD'S THRONE!
I KNOW WELL THE WORD THAT BANISHES THEE AGAIN TO THE DEEP DARK, PRINCE OF MONSTERS--
--THAT WORD IS GODSDEATH!
LET IT BE SO, THEN!
IF IT TAKES THE LIFE OF A GOD--LET THAT SACRIFICE BE MADE, IN ASGARD'S NAME--
SHRAAKK

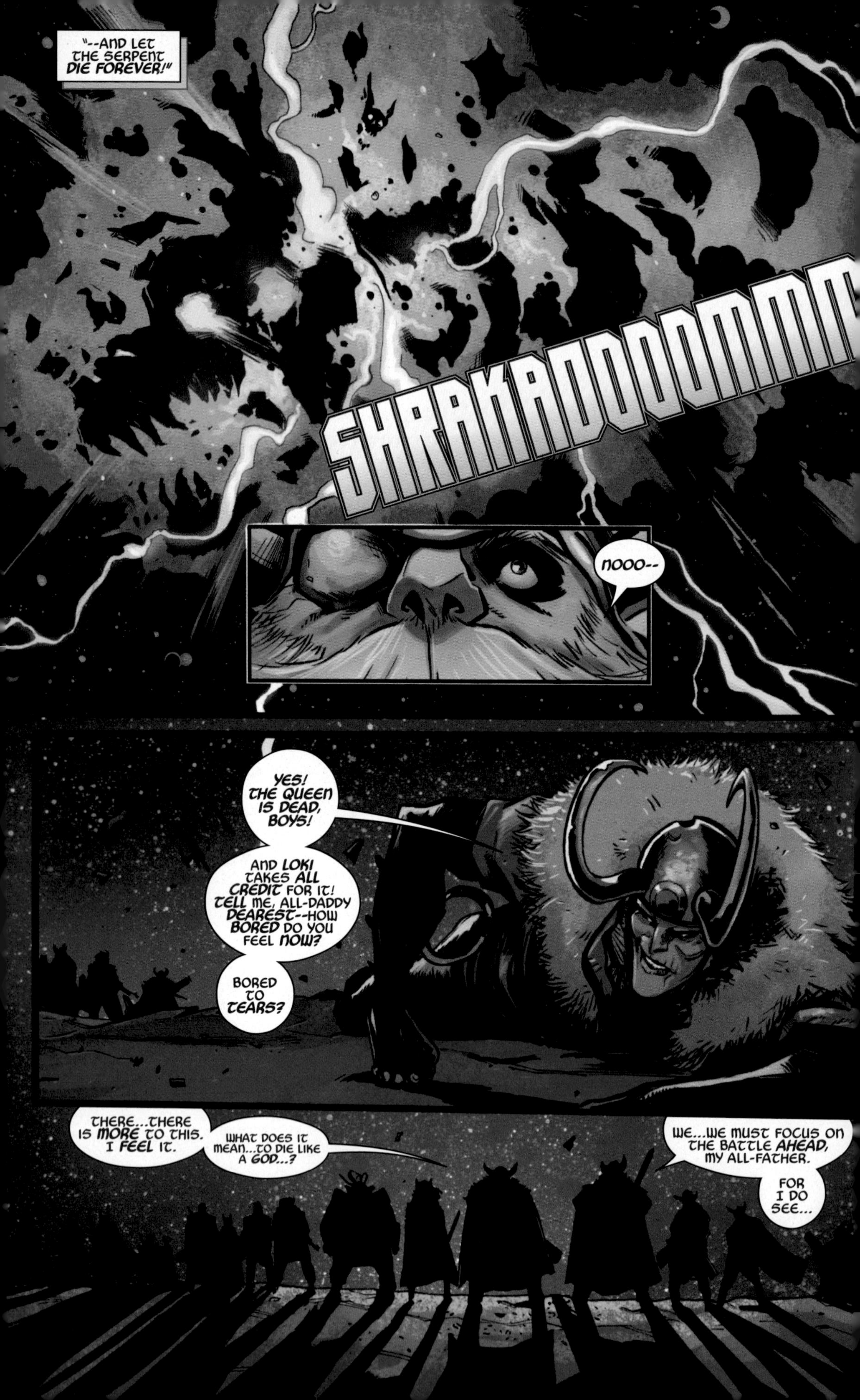
"--AND LET THE SERPENT DIE FOREVER!"
SHRAKADOOOMMM
NOOO--
YES! THE QUEEN IS DEAD, BOYS!
AND LOKI TAKES ALL CREDIT FOR IT! TELL ME, ALL-DADDY DEAREST--HOW BORED DO YOU FEEL NOW?
BORED TO TEARS?
THERE...THERE IS MORE TO THIS. I FEEL IT.
WHAT DOES IT MEAN...TO DIE LIKE A GOD...?
WE...WE MUST FOCUS ON THE BATTLE AHEAD, MY ALL-FATHER.
FOR I DO SEE...

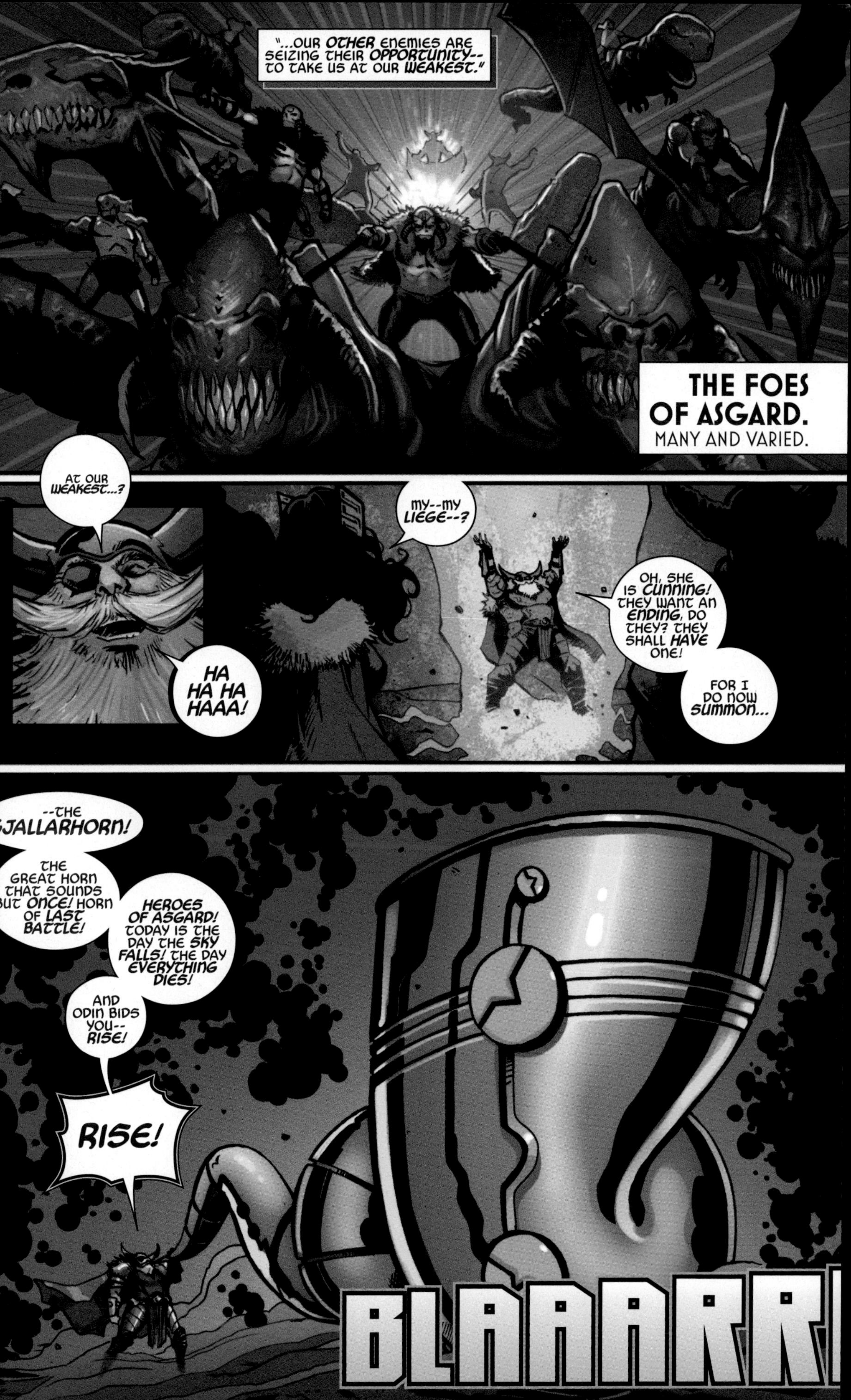
"...OUR OTHER ENEMIES ARE SEIZING THEIR OPPORTUNITY-- TO TAKE US AT OUR WEAKEST."
THE FOES OF ASGARD.
MANY AND VARIED.
AT OUR WEAKEST...?
HA HA HA HAAA!
MY--MY LIEGE--?
OH, SHE IS CUNNING! THEY WANT AN ENDING, DO THEY? THEY SHALL HAVE ONE!
FOR I DO NOW SUMMON...
--THE GJALLARHORN!
THE GREAT HORN THAT SOUNDS BUT ONCE! HORN OF LAST BATTLE!
HEROES OF ASGARD! TODAY IS THE DAY THE SKY FALLS! THE DAY EVERYTHING DIES!
AND ODIN BIDS YOU-- RISE!
RISE!
BLAAARR

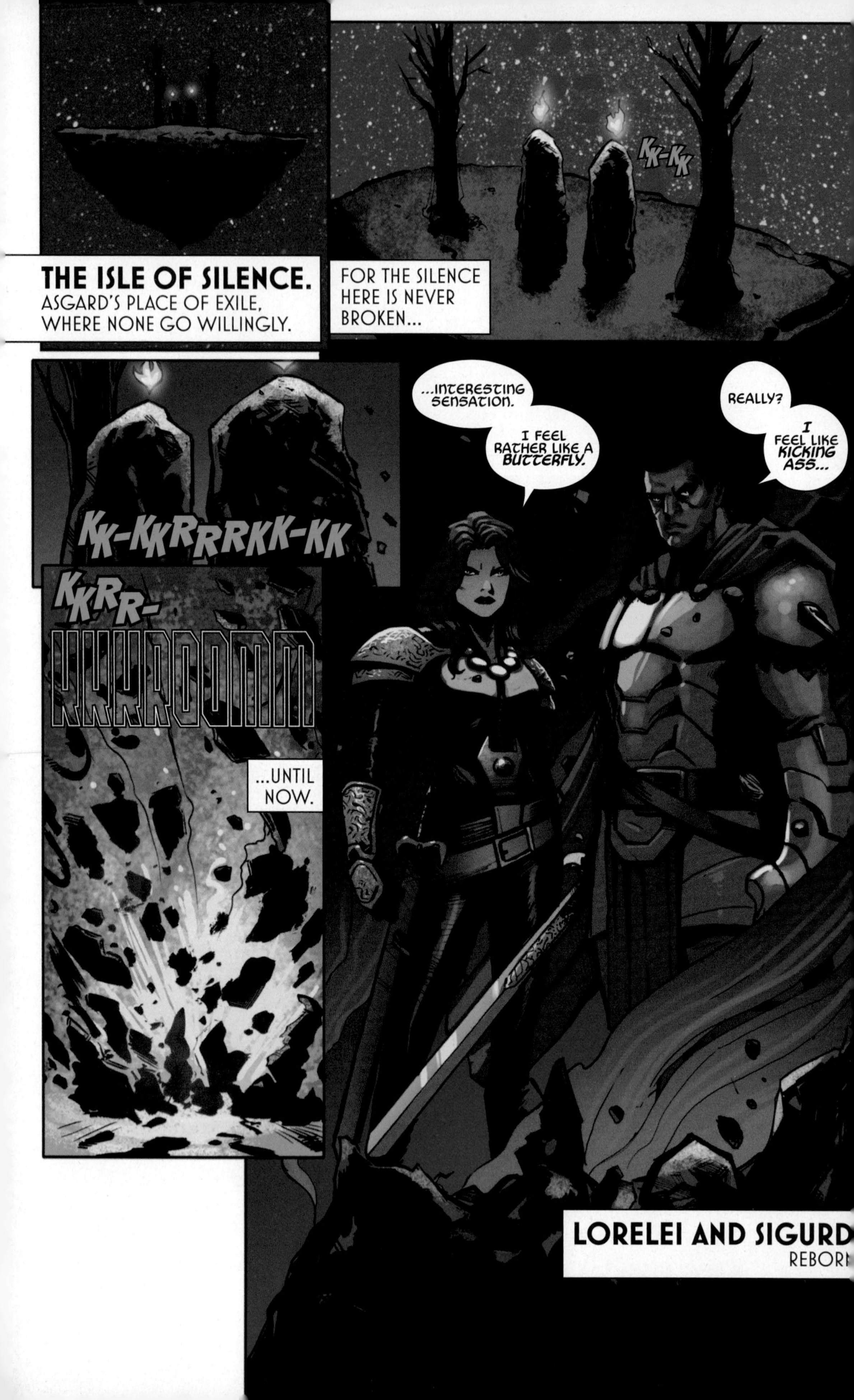
THE ISLE OF SILENCE.
ASGARD'S PLACE OF EXILE, WHERE NONE GO WILLINGLY.
FOR THE SILENCE HERE IS NEVER BROKEN...
KK-KK
KK-KKRRRKK-KK
KKRR-
KKKROOMM
...UNTIL NOW.
...INTERESTING SENSATION.
I FEEL RATHER LIKE A BUTTERFLY.
REALLY?
I FEEL LIKE KICKING ASS...
LORELEI AND SIGURD
REBORN

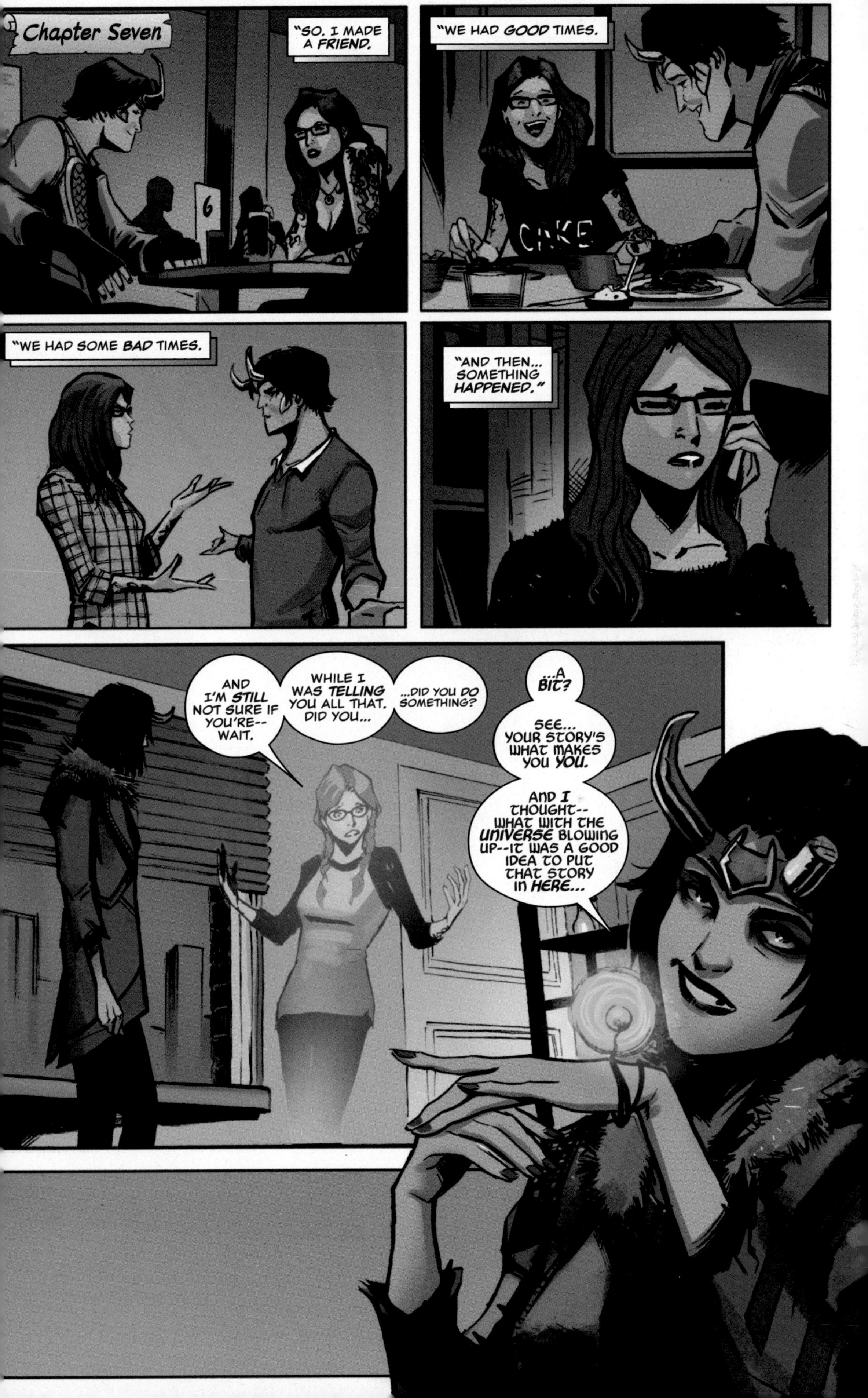
Chapter Seven
"SO. I MADE A FRIEND.
"WE HAD GOOD TIMES.
CAKE
"WE HAD SOME BAD TIMES.
"AND THEN... SOMETHING HAPPENED."
AND I'M STILL NOT SURE IF YOU'RE-- WAIT.
WHILE I WAS TELLING YOU ALL THAT. DID YOU...
...DID YOU DO SOMETHING?
...A BIT?
SEE... YOUR STORY'S WHAT MAKES YOU YOU.
AND I THOUGHT-- WHAT WITH THE UNIVERSE BLOWING UP--IT WAS A GOOD IDEA TO PUT THAT STORY IN HERE...

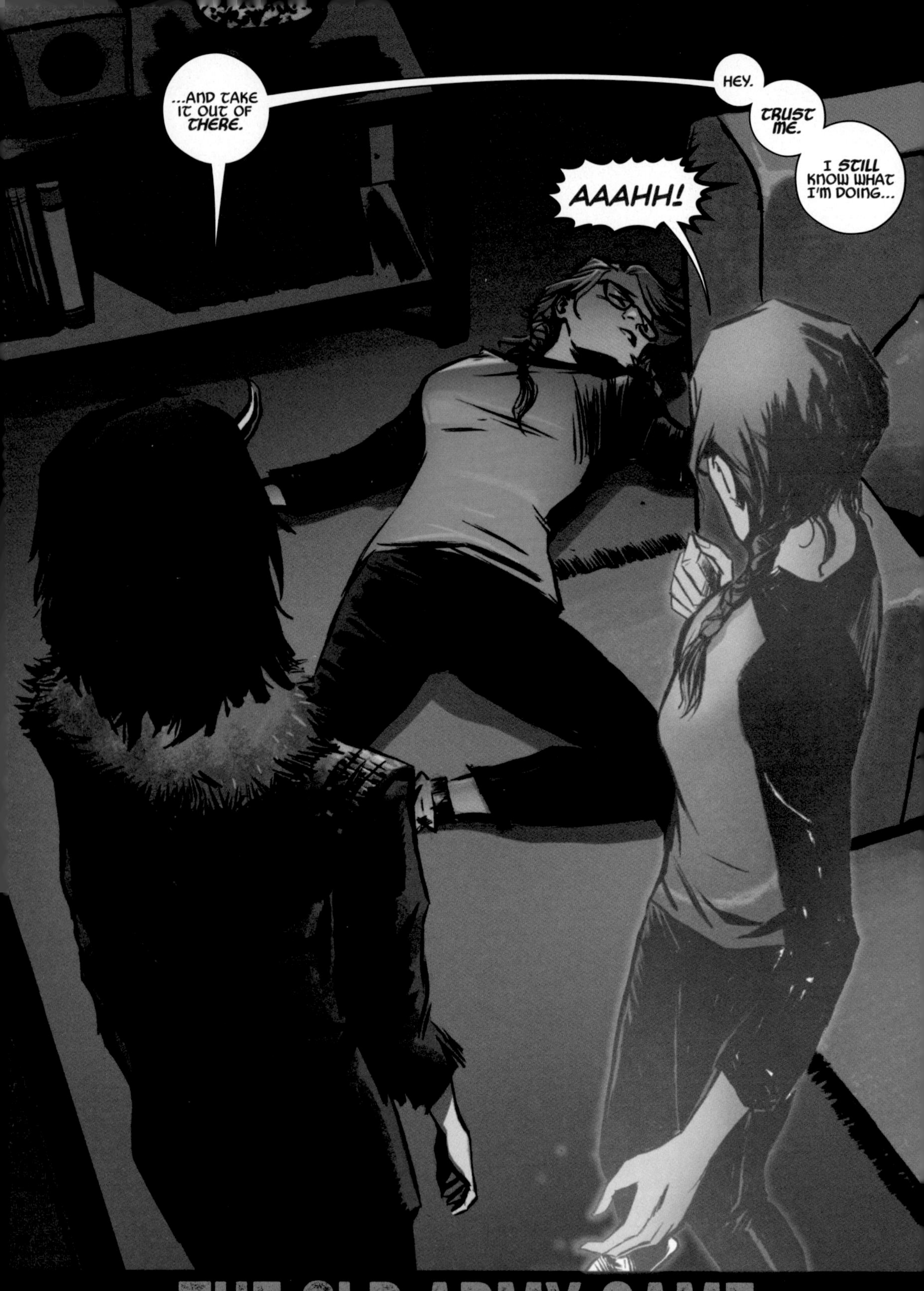
...AND TAKE IT OUT OF THERE.
HEY.
TRUST ME.
AAAHH!
I STILL KNOW WHAT I'M DOING...

THE OLD ARMY GAME

LOKI: AGENT OF ASGARD #3 VARIANT
by Olivier Coipel & Marte Gracia

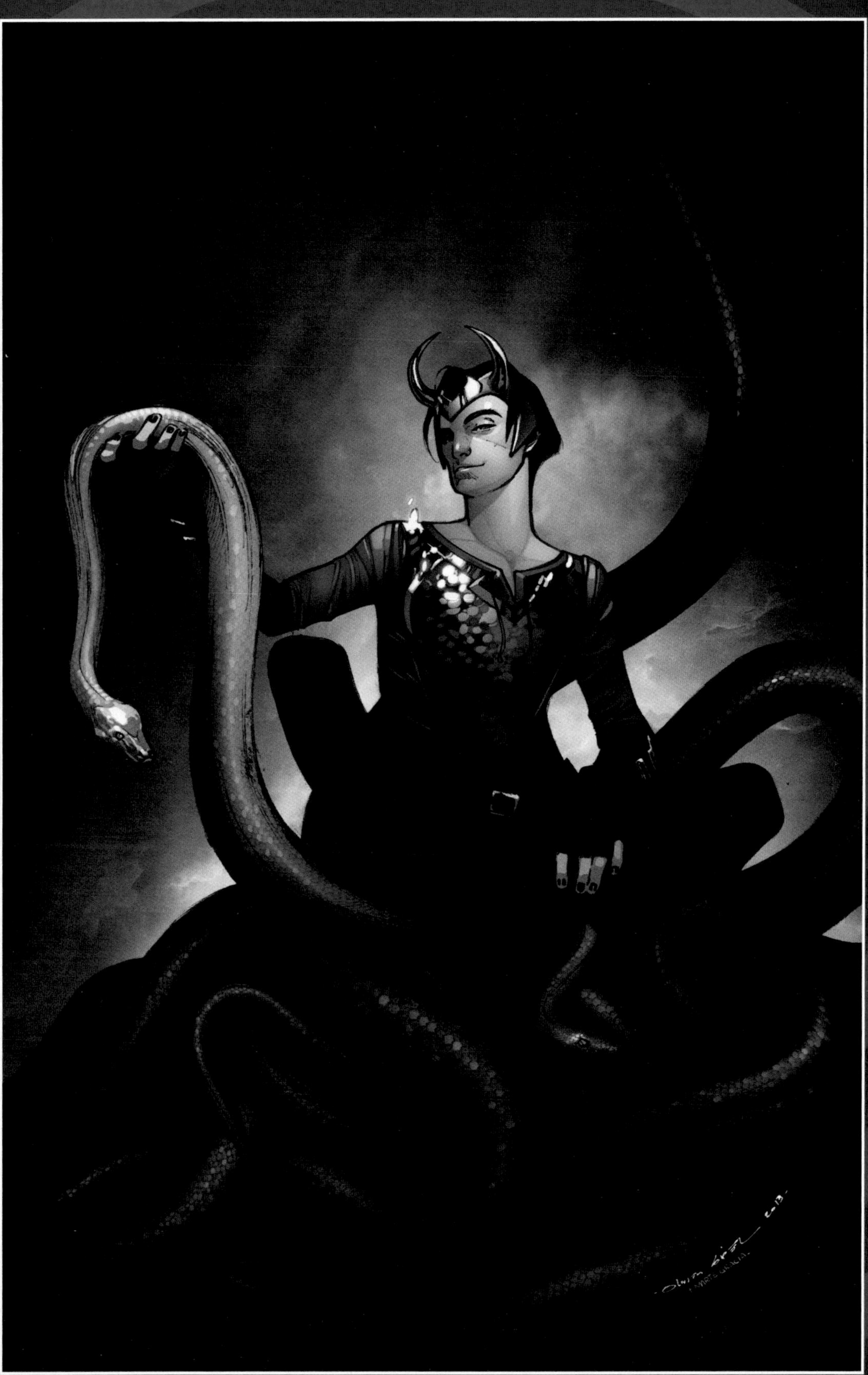

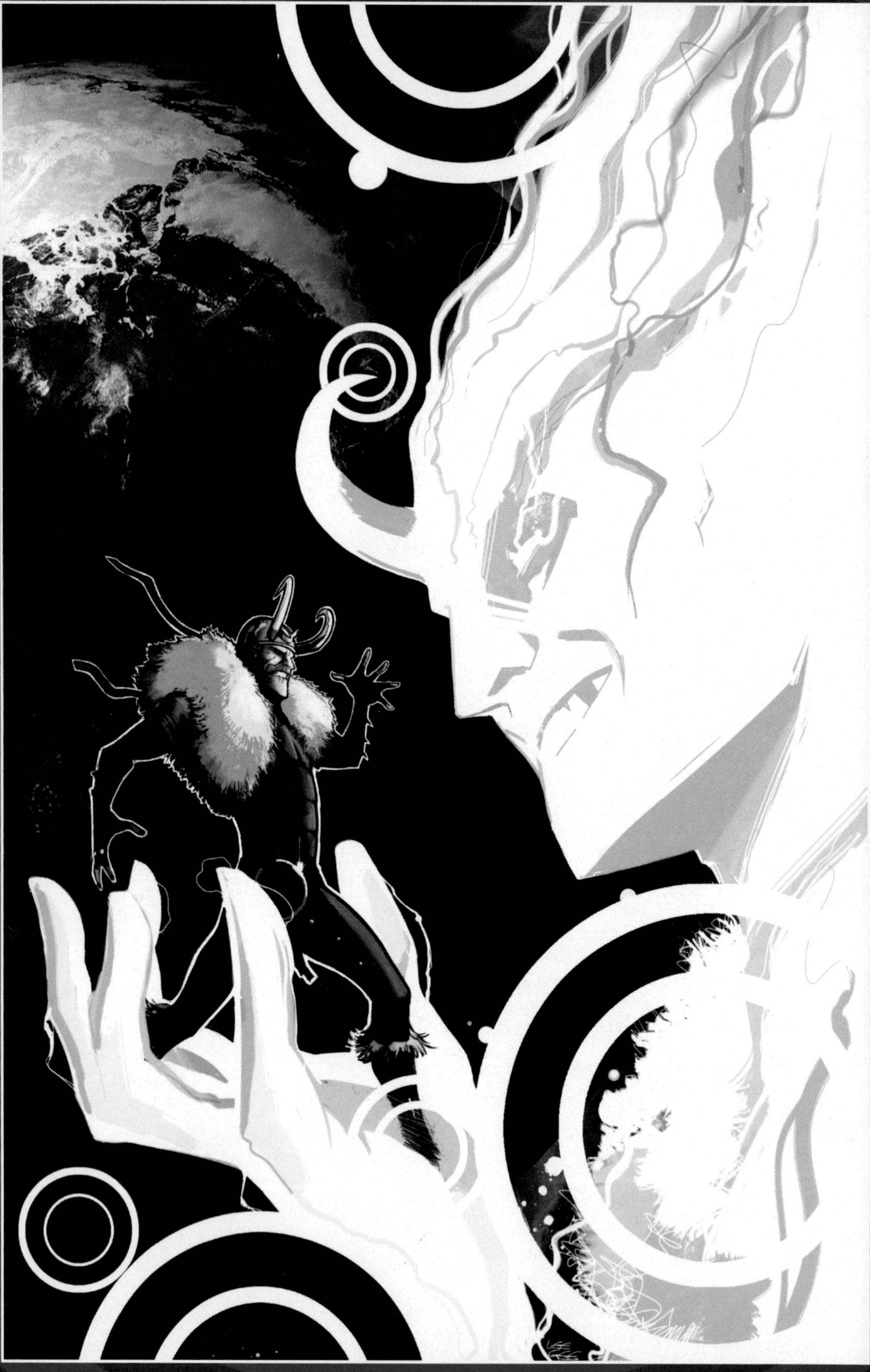

LOKI: AGENT OF ASGARD #16

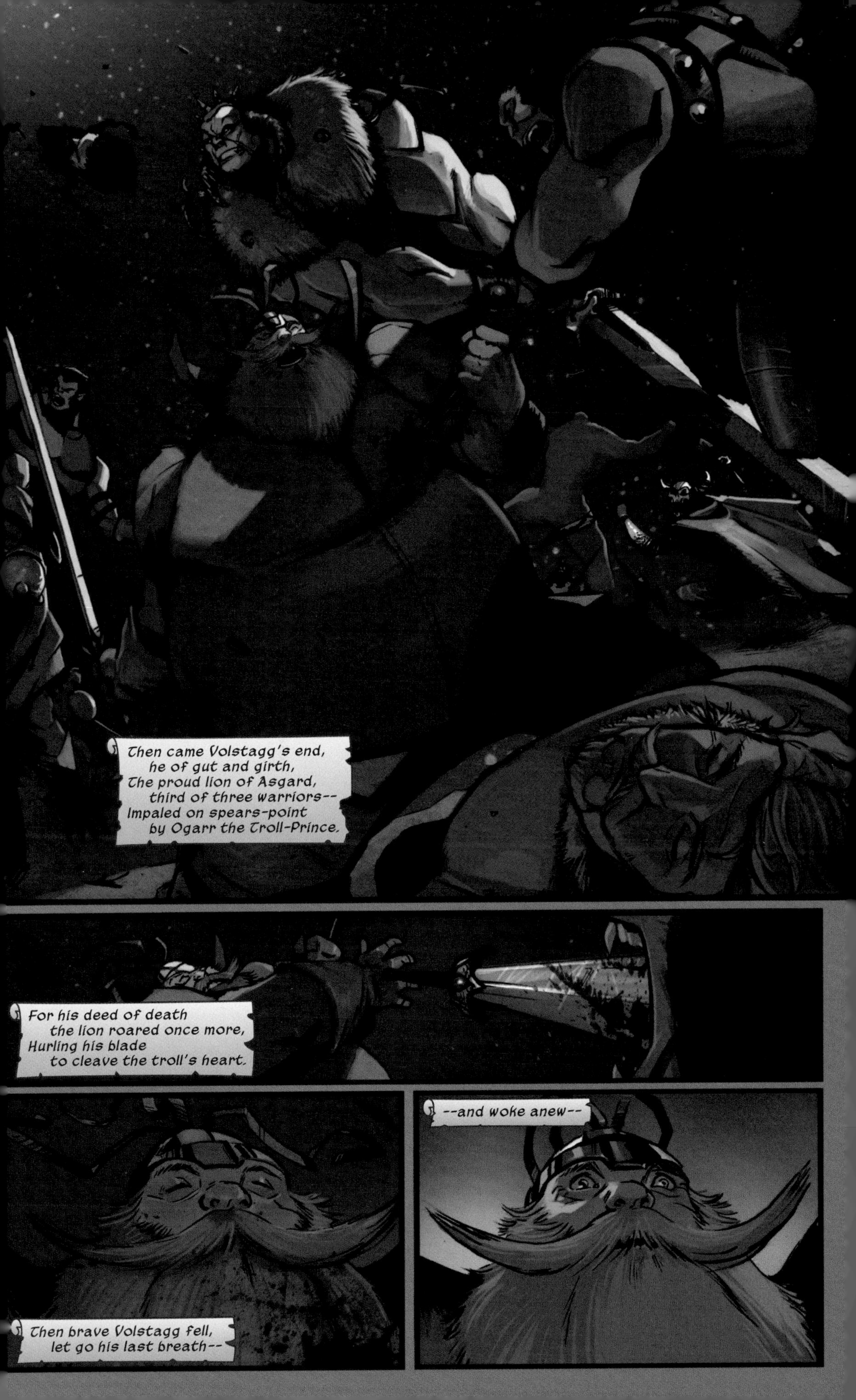
Then came Volstagg's end,
he of gut and girth,
The proud lion of Asgard,
third of three warriors--
Impaled on spears-point
by Ogarr the Troll-Prince.
For his deed of death
the lion roared once more,
Hurling his blade
to cleave the troll's heart.
Then brave Volstagg fell,
let go his last breath--
--and woke anew--

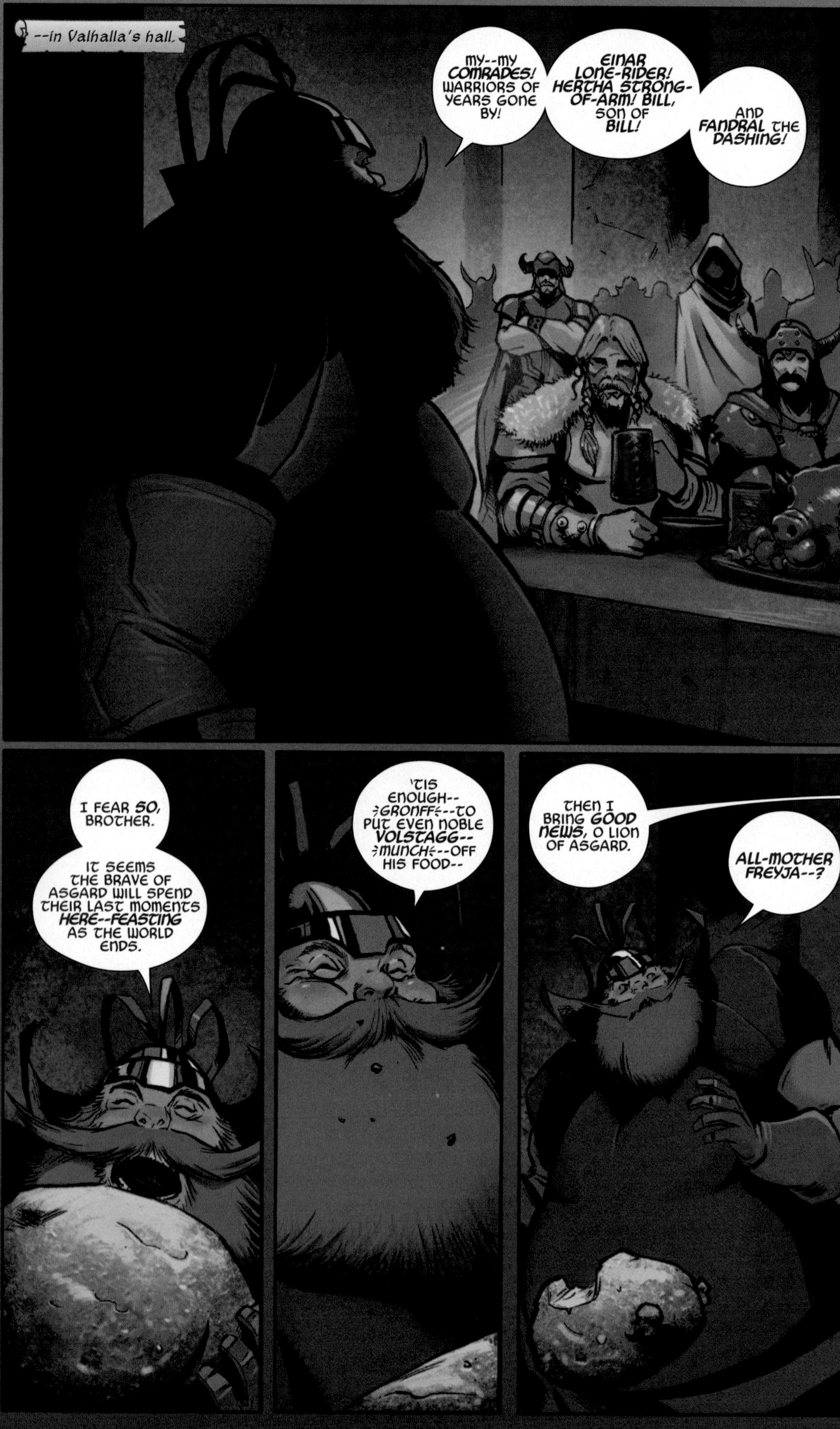
--in Valhalla's hall.
My--my COMRADES! Warriors of years gone by!
EINAR LONE-RIDER! HERTHA STRONG-OF-ARM! BILL, son of BILL!
And FANDRAL the DASHING!
I fear SO, brother.
It seems the brave of Asgard will spend their last moments HERE--FEASTING as the world ends.
'Tis enough-- *GRONFF* --to put even noble VOLSTAGG-- *MUNCH* --off his food--
Then I bring GOOD NEWS, O lion of Asgard.
ALL-MOTHER FREYJA--?

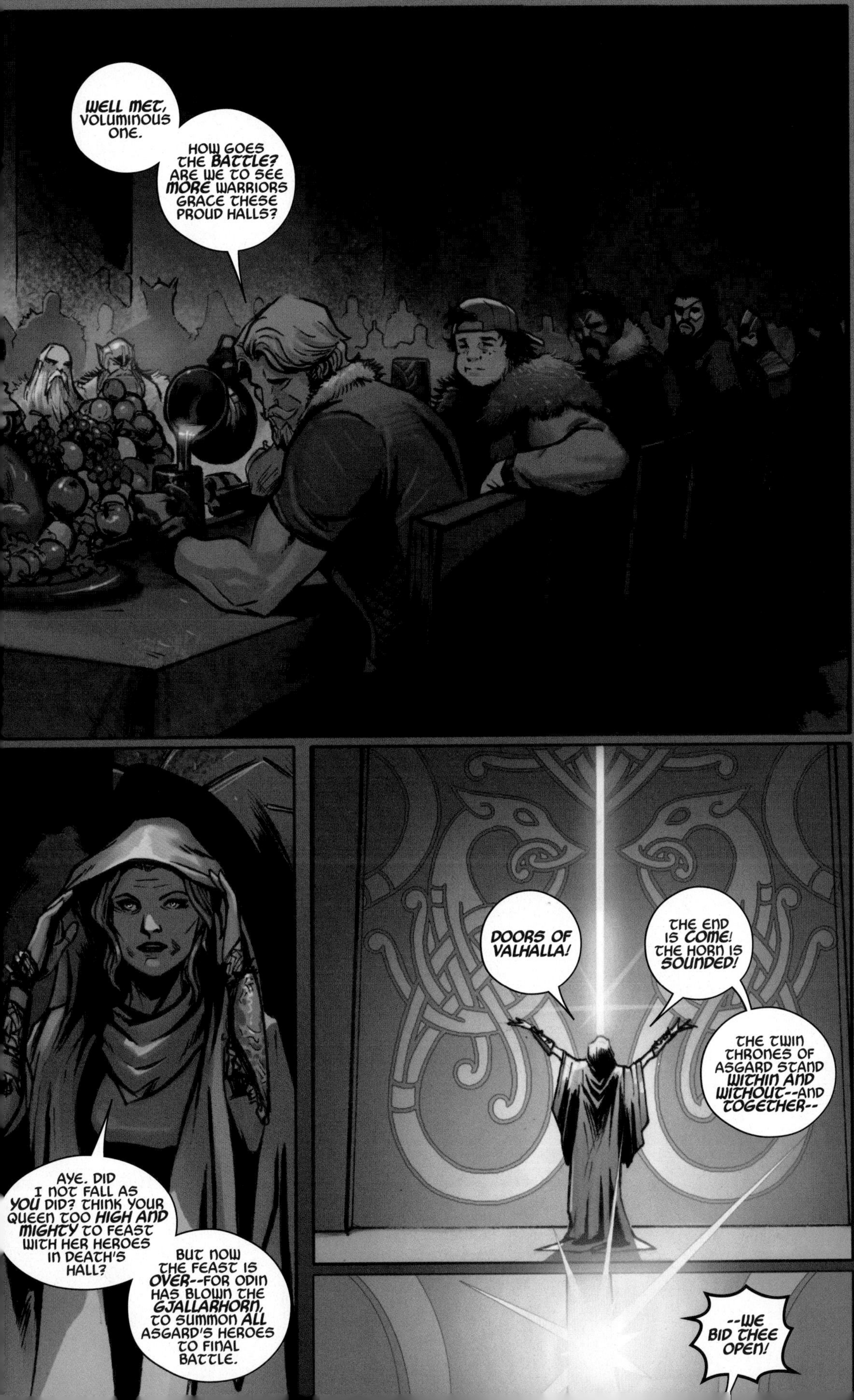

WELL MET, VOLUMINOUS ONE.
HOW GOES THE BATTLE? ARE WE TO SEE MORE WARRIORS GRACE THESE PROUD HALLS?
AYE. DID I NOT FALL AS YOU DID? THINK YOUR QUEEN TOO HIGH AND MIGHTY TO FEAST WITH HER HEROES IN DEATH'S HALL?
BUT NOW THE FEAST IS OVER--FOR ODIN HAS BLOWN THE GJALLARHORN, TO SUMMON ALL ASGARD'S HEROES TO FINAL BATTLE.
DOORS OF VALHALLA!
THE END IS COME! THE HORN IS SOUNDED!
THE TWIN THRONES OF ASGARD STAND WITHIN AND WITHOUT--AND TOGETHER--
--WE BID THEE OPEN!

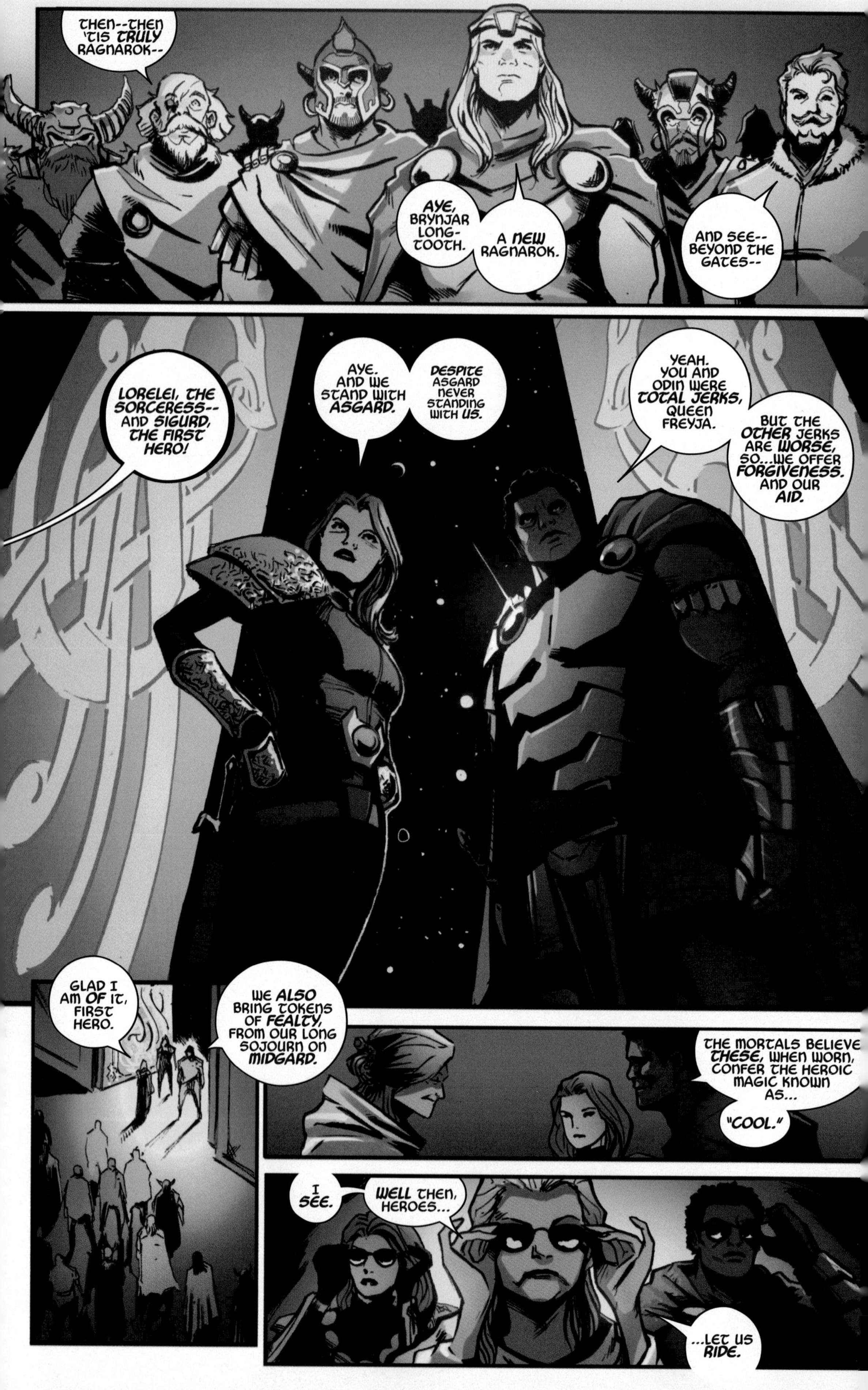
THEN--THEN 'TIS TRULY RAGNAROK--
AYE, BRYNJAR LONG-TOOTH.
A NEW RAGNAROK.
AND SEE--BEYOND THE GATES--
LORELEI, THE SORCERESS--AND SIGURD, THE FIRST HERO!
AYE. AND WE STAND WITH ASGARD.
DESPITE ASGARD NEVER STANDING WITH US.
YEAH. YOU AND ODIN WERE TOTAL JERKS, QUEEN FREYJA.
BUT THE OTHER JERKS ARE WORSE, SO...WE OFFER FORGIVENESS. AND OUR AID.
GLAD I AM OF IT, FIRST HERO.
WE ALSO BRING TOKENS OF FEALTY, FROM OUR LONG SOJOURN ON MIDGARD.
THE MORTALS BELIEVE THESE, WHEN WORN, CONFER THE HEROIC MAGIC KNOWN AS...
"COOL."
I SEE.
WELL THEN, HEROES...
...LET US RIDE.

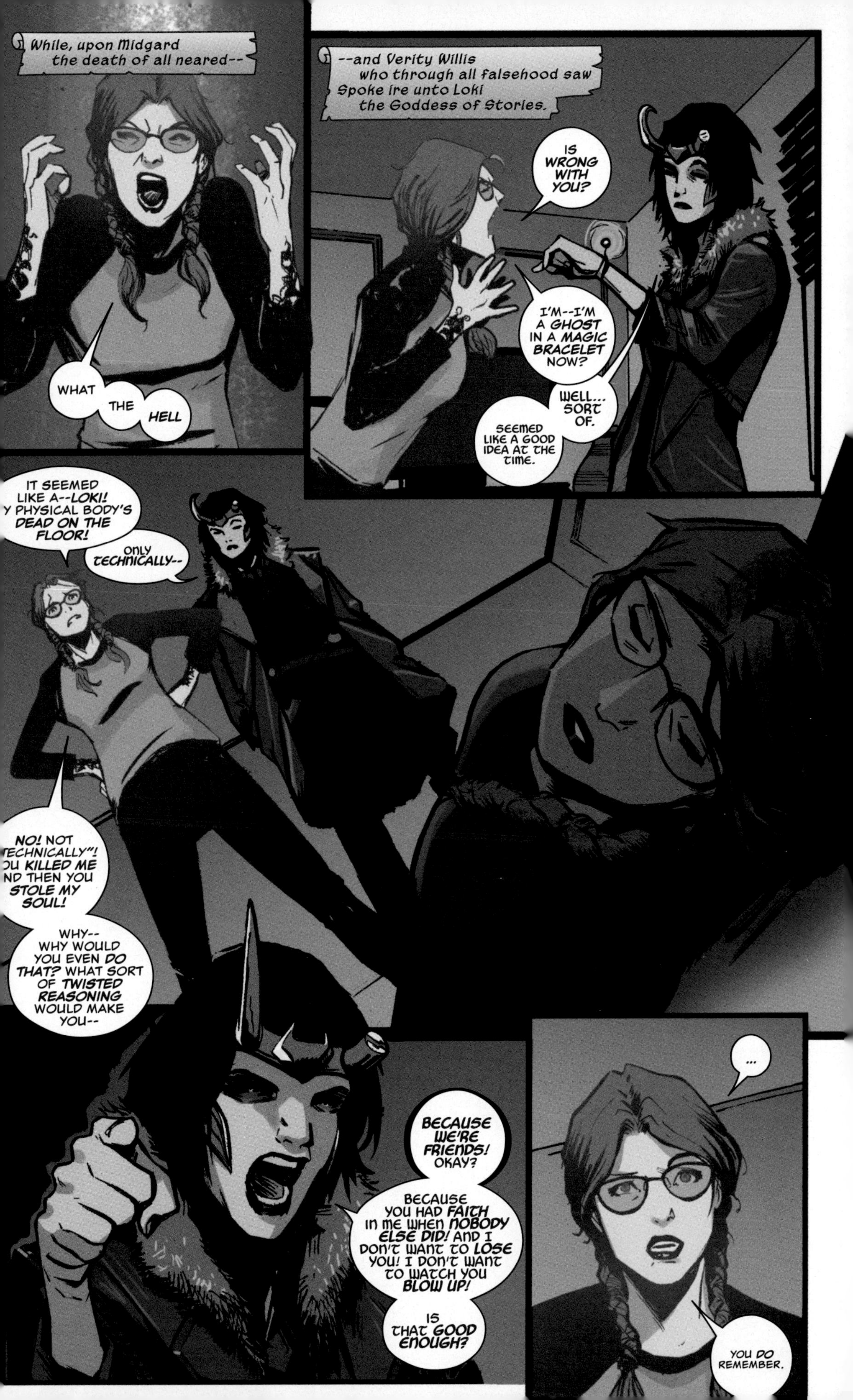

While, upon Midgard the death of all neared--
WHAT THE HELL
--and Verity Willis who through all falsehood saw Spoke ire unto Loki the Goddess of Stories.
IS WRONG WITH YOU?
I'M--I'M A GHOST IN A MAGIC BRACELET NOW?
WELL... SORT OF.
SEEMED LIKE A GOOD IDEA AT THE TIME.
IT SEEMED LIKE A--LOKI! Y PHYSICAL BODY'S DEAD ON THE FLOOR!
ONLY TECHNICALLY--
NO! NOT ECHNICALLY"! OU KILLED ME ND THEN YOU STOLE MY SOUL!
WHY-- WHY WOULD YOU EVEN DO THAT? WHAT SORT OF TWISTED REASONING WOULD MAKE YOU--
BECAUSE WE'RE FRIENDS! OKAY?
BECAUSE YOU HAD FAITH IN ME WHEN NOBODY ELSE DID! AND I DON'T WANT TO LOSE YOU! I DON'T WANT TO WATCH YOU BLOW UP!
IS THAT GOOD ENOUGH?
...
YOU DO REMEMBER.

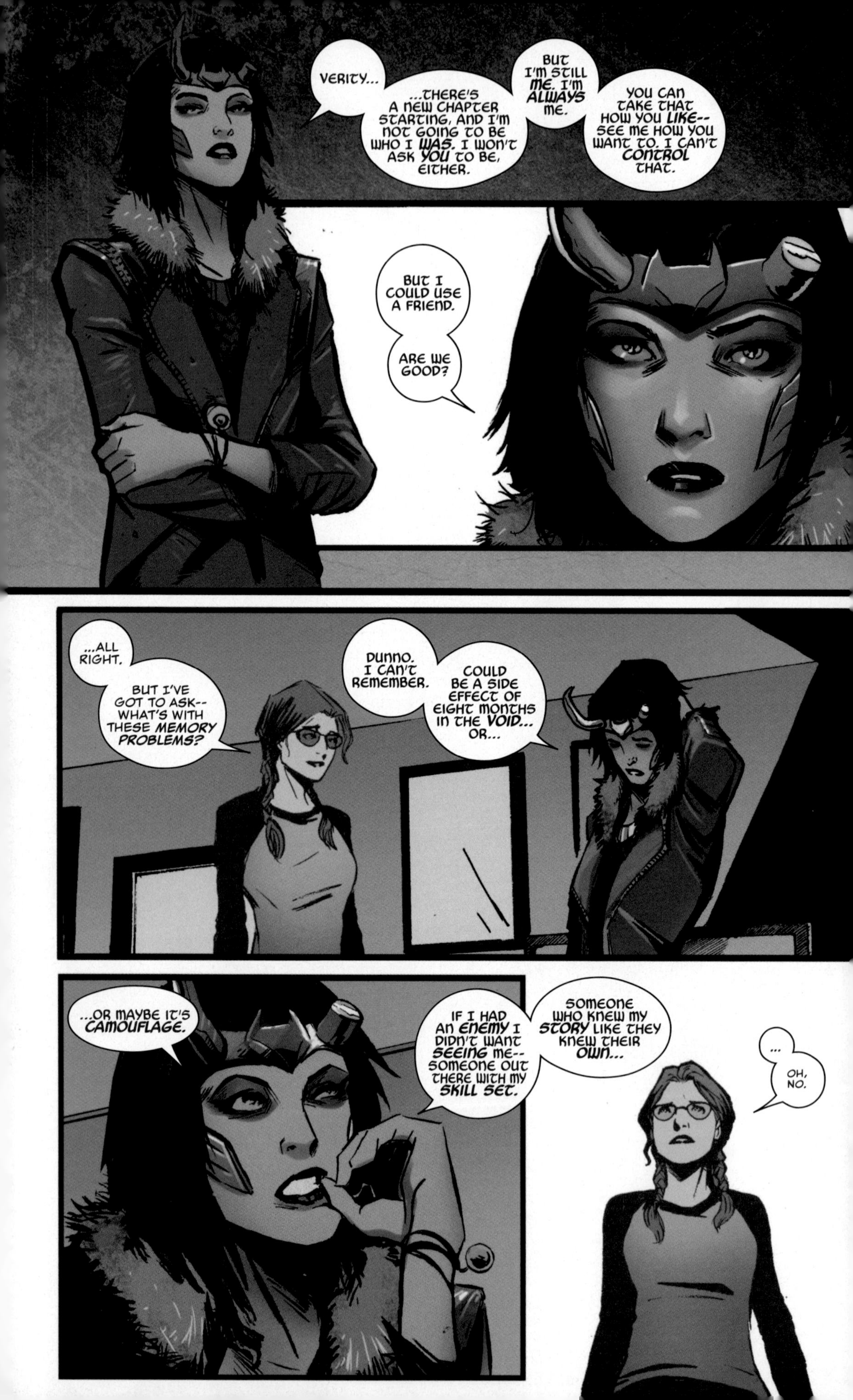
VERITY...
...THERE'S A NEW CHAPTER STARTING, AND I'M NOT GOING TO BE WHO I WAS. I WON'T ASK YOU TO BE, EITHER.
BUT I'M STILL ME. I'M ALWAYS ME.
YOU CAN TAKE THAT HOW YOU LIKE-- SEE ME HOW YOU WANT TO. I CAN'T CONTROL THAT.
BUT I COULD USE A FRIEND.
ARE WE GOOD?
...ALL RIGHT.
BUT I'VE GOT TO ASK-- WHAT'S WITH THESE MEMORY PROBLEMS?
DUNNO. I CAN'T REMEMBER.
COULD BE A SIDE EFFECT OF EIGHT MONTHS IN THE VOID... OR...
...OR MAYBE IT'S CAMOUFLAGE.
IF I HAD AN ENEMY I DIDN'T WANT SEEING ME-- SOMEONE OUT THERE WITH MY SKILL SET.
SOMEONE WHO KNEW MY STORY LIKE THEY KNEW THEIR OWN...
...
OH, NO.

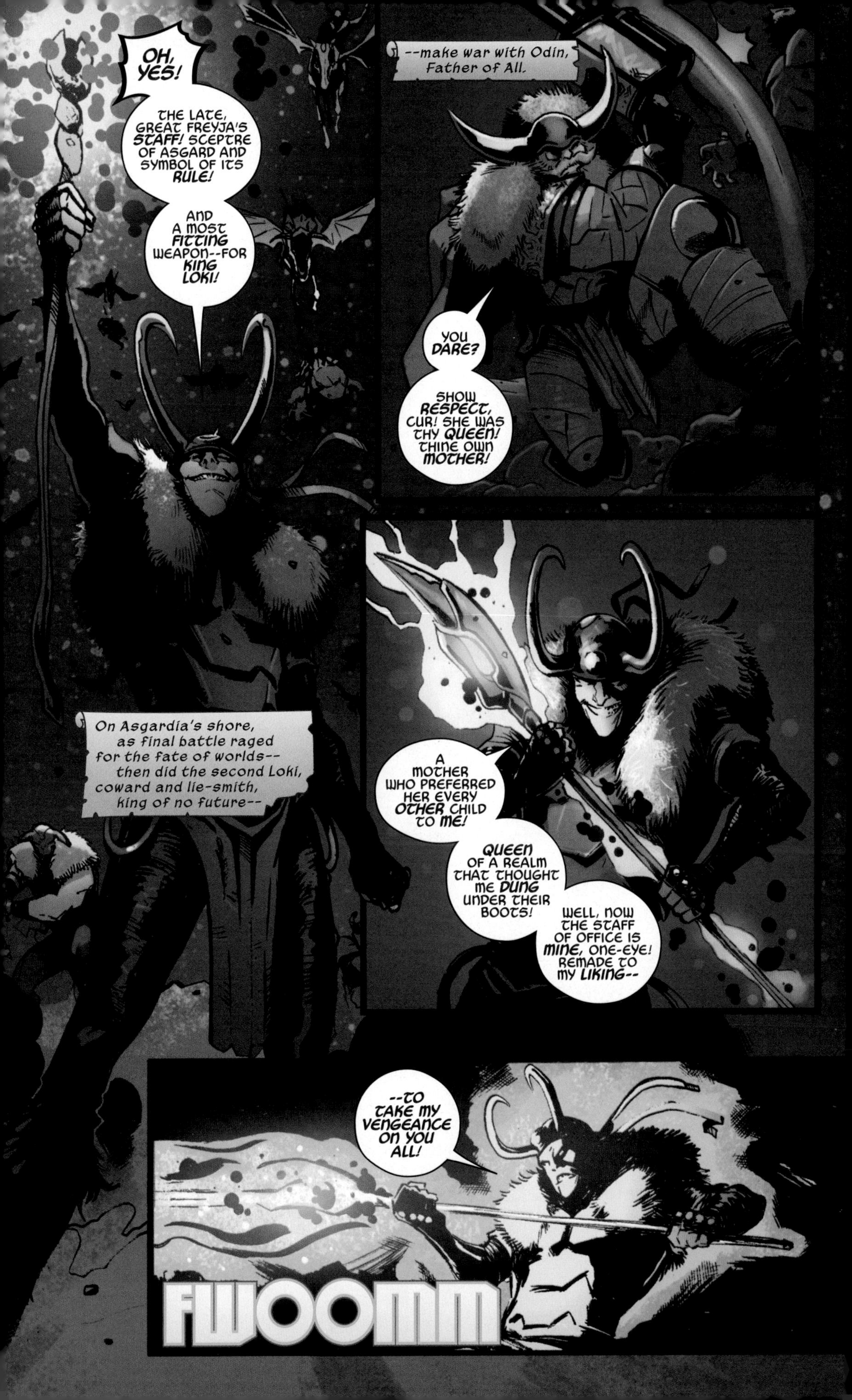
OH, YES!
THE LATE, GREAT FREYJA'S STAFF! SCEPTRE OF ASGARD AND SYMBOL OF ITS RULE!
AND A MOST FITTING WEAPON--FOR KING LOKI!
On Asgardia's shore, as final battle raged for the fate of worlds-- then did the second Loki, coward and lie-smith, king of no future--
--make war with Odin, Father of All.
YOU DARE?
SHOW RESPECT, CUR! SHE WAS THY QUEEN! THINE OWN MOTHER!
A MOTHER WHO PREFERRED HER EVERY OTHER CHILD TO ME!
QUEEN OF A REALM THAT THOUGHT ME DUNG UNDER THEIR BOOTS!
WELL, NOW THE STAFF OF OFFICE IS MINE, ONE-EYE! REMADE TO MY LIKING--
--TO TAKE MY VENGEANCE ON YOU ALL!
FWOOMM

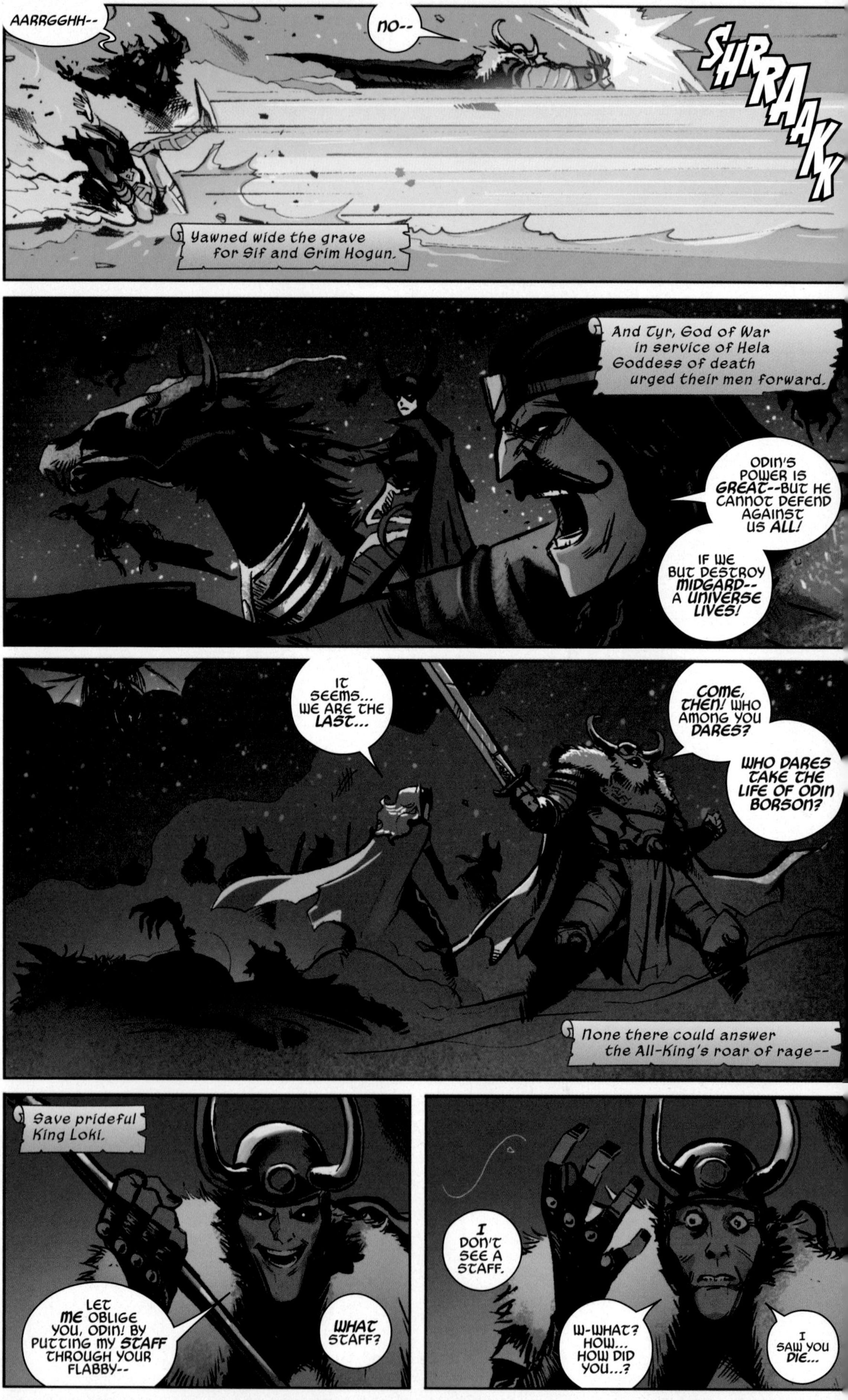
AARRGGHH--
no--
SHRRAAKK
Yawned wide the grave for Sif and Grim Hogun.
And Tyr, God of War in service of Hela Goddess of death urged their men forward.
ODIN'S POWER IS GREAT--BUT HE CANNOT DEFEND AGAINST US ALL!
IF WE BUT DESTROY MIDGARD-- A UNIVERSE LIVES!
IT SEEMS... WE ARE THE LAST...
COME, THEN! WHO AMONG YOU DARES?
WHO DARES TAKE THE LIFE OF ODIN BORSON?
None there could answer the All-King's roar of rage--
Save prideful King Loki.
LET ME OBLIGE YOU, ODIN! BY PUTTING MY STAFF THROUGH YOUR FLABBY--
WHAT STAFF?
I DON'T SEE A STAFF.
W-WHAT? HOW... HOW DID YOU...?
I SAW YOU DIE...

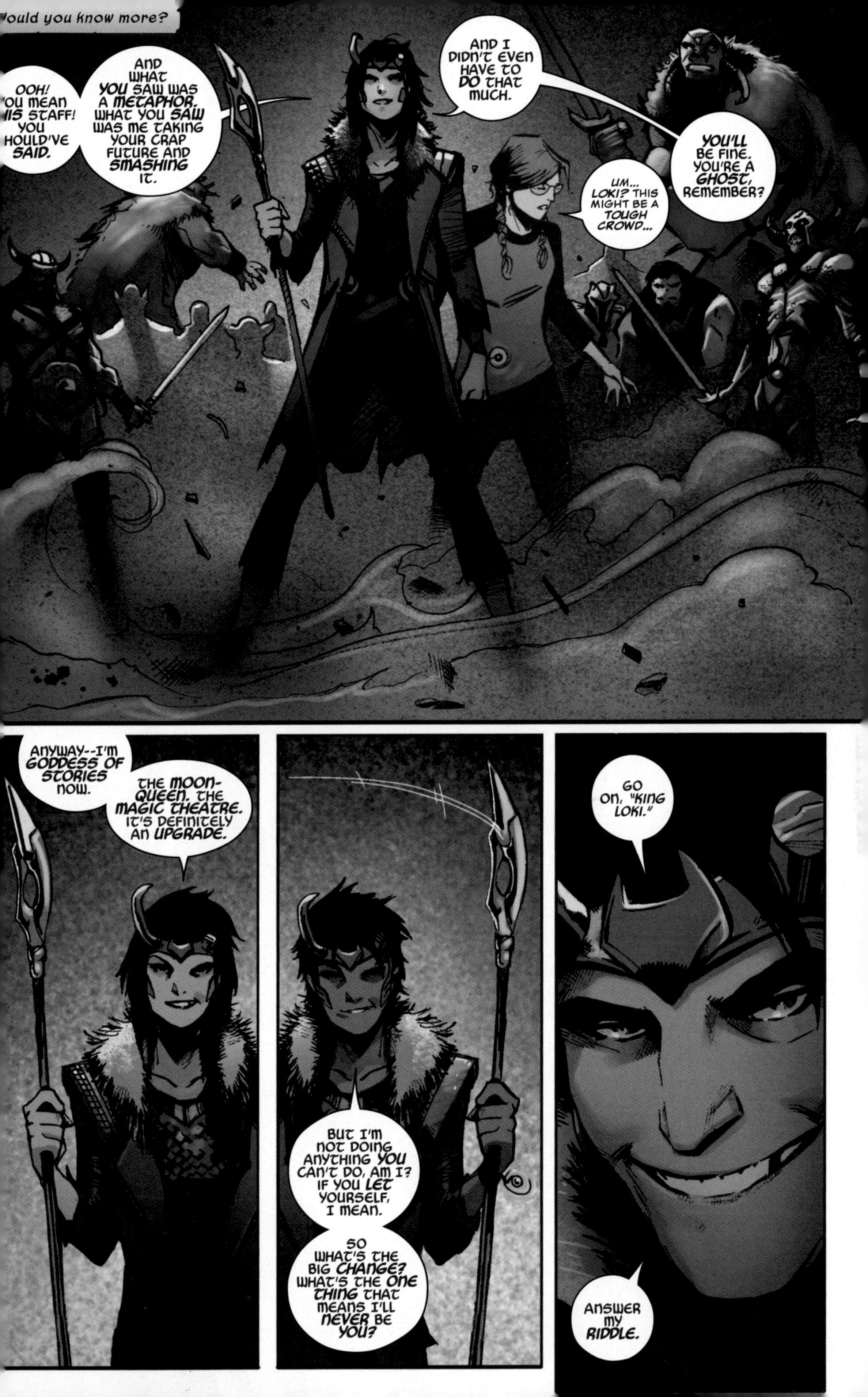

ould you know more?
OOH! 'OU MEAN IIS STAFF! YOU HOULD'VE SAID.
AND WHAT YOU SAW WAS A METAPHOR. WHAT YOU SAW WAS ME TAKING YOUR CRAP FUTURE AND SMASHING IT.
AND I DIDN'T EVEN HAVE TO DO THAT MUCH.
UM... LOKI? THIS MIGHT BE A TOUGH CROWD...
YOU'LL BE FINE. YOU'RE A GHOST, REMEMBER?
ANYWAY--I'M GODDESS OF STORIES NOW.
THE MOON-QUEEN. THE MAGIC THEATRE. IT'S DEFINITELY AN UPGRADE.
BUT I'M NOT DOING ANYTHING YOU CAN'T DO, AM I? IF YOU LET YOURSELF, I MEAN.
SO WHAT'S THE BIG CHANGE? WHAT'S THE ONE THING THAT MEANS I'LL NEVER BE YOU?
GO ON, "KING LOKI."
ANSWER MY RIDDLE.

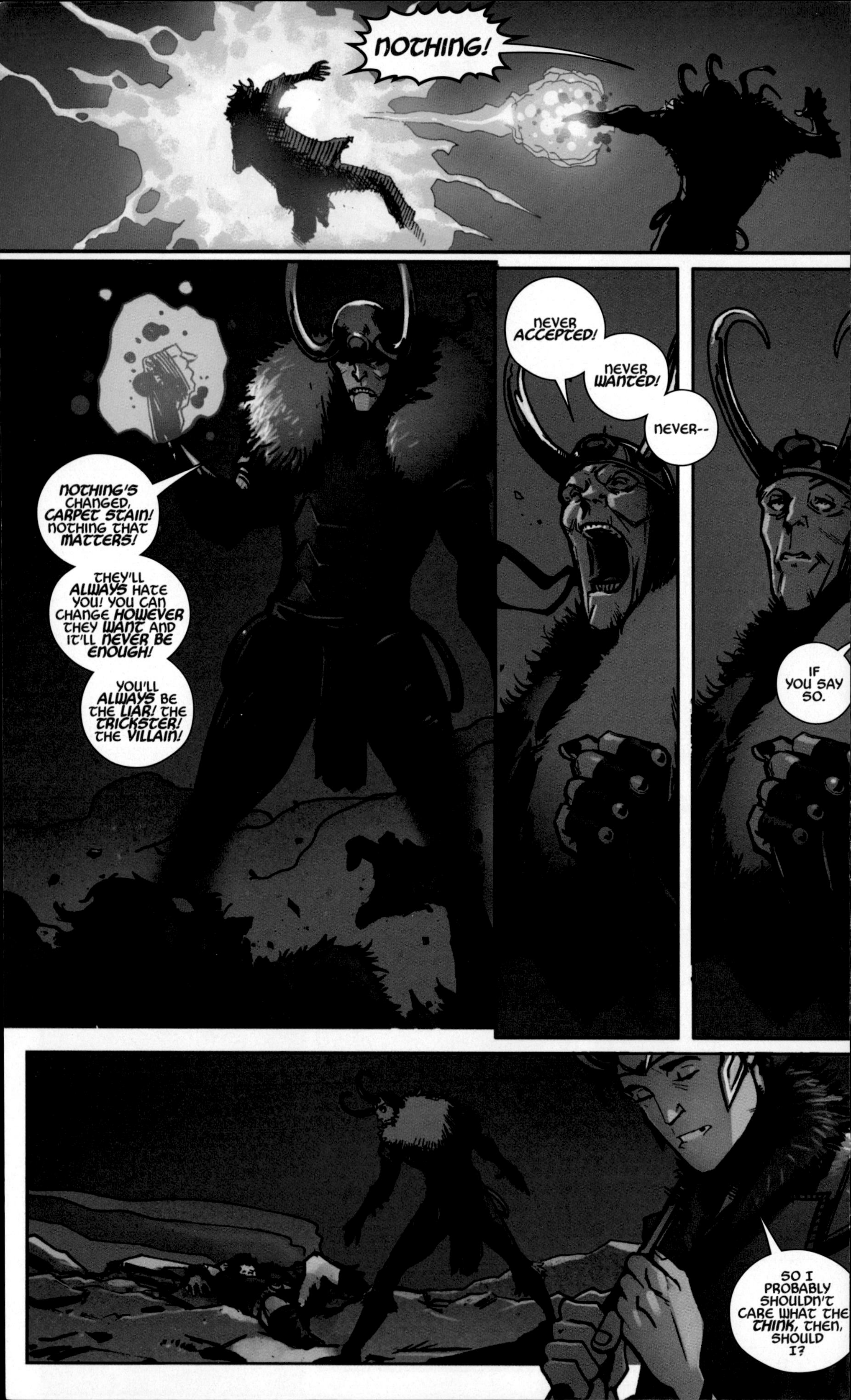
NOTHING!
NOTHING'S CHANGED, CARPET STAIN! NOTHING THAT MATTERS!
THEY'LL ALWAYS HATE YOU! YOU CAN CHANGE HOWEVER THEY WANT AND IT'LL NEVER BE ENOUGH!
YOU'LL ALWAYS BE THE LIAR! THE TRICKSTER! THE VILLAIN!
NEVER ACCEPTED!
NEVER WANTED!
NEVER--
IF YOU SAY SO.
SO I PROBABLY SHOULDN'T CARE WHAT THE THINK, THEN, SHOULD I?

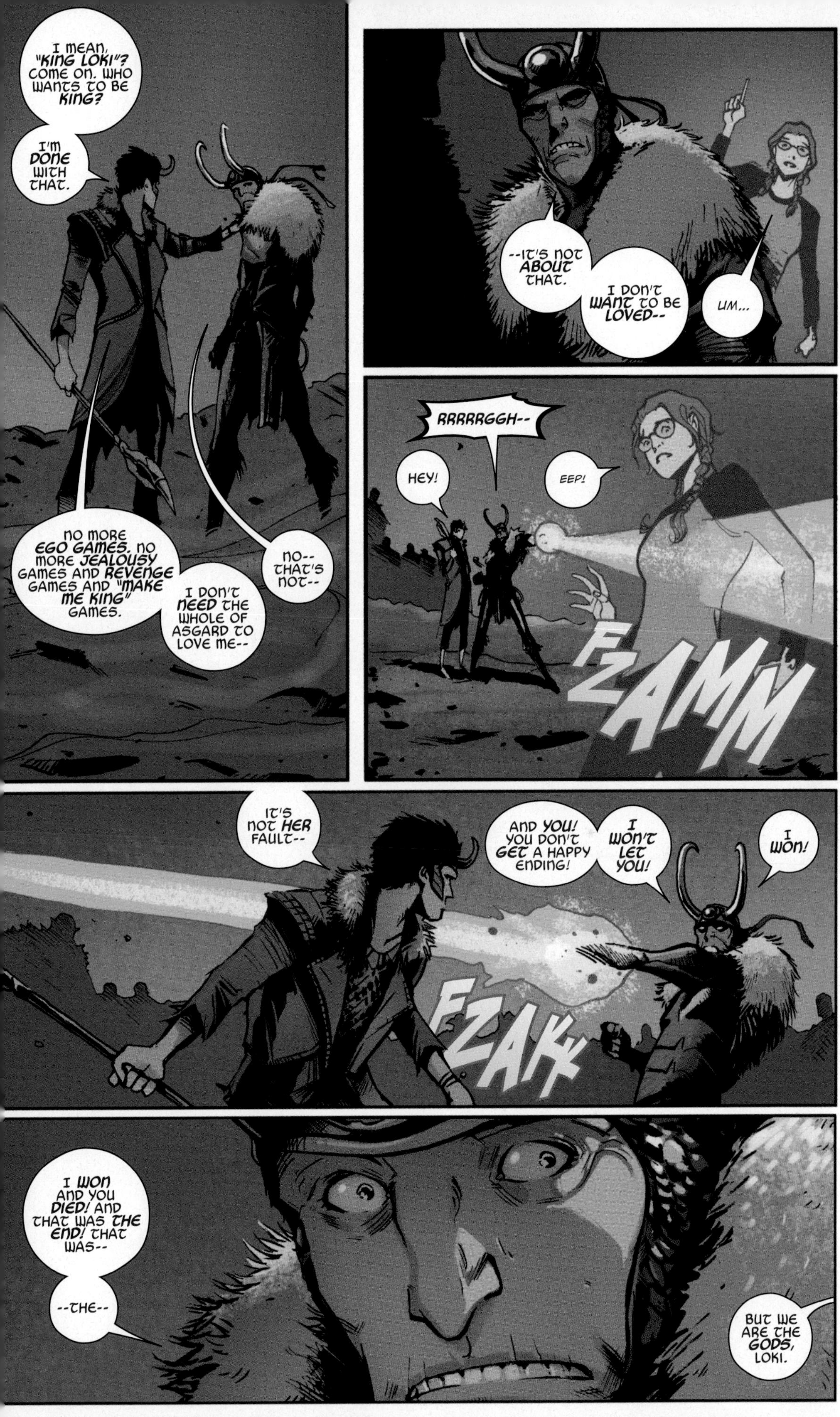
I MEAN, "KING LOKI"? COME ON. WHO WANTS TO BE KING?
I'M DONE WITH THAT.
NO MORE EGO GAMES. NO MORE JEALOUSY GAMES AND REVENGE GAMES AND "MAKE ME KING" GAMES.
I DON'T NEED THE WHOLE OF ASGARD TO LOVE ME--
NO--THAT'S NOT--
--IT'S NOT ABOUT THAT.
I DON'T WANT TO BE LOVED--
UM...
RRRRRGGH--
HEY!
EEP!
FZAMM
IT'S NOT HER FAULT--
AND YOU! YOU DON'T GET A HAPPY ENDING!
I WON'T LET YOU!
I WON!
FZAKK
I WON AND YOU DIED! AND THAT WAS THE END! THAT WAS--
--THE--
BUT WE ARE THE GODS, LOKI.

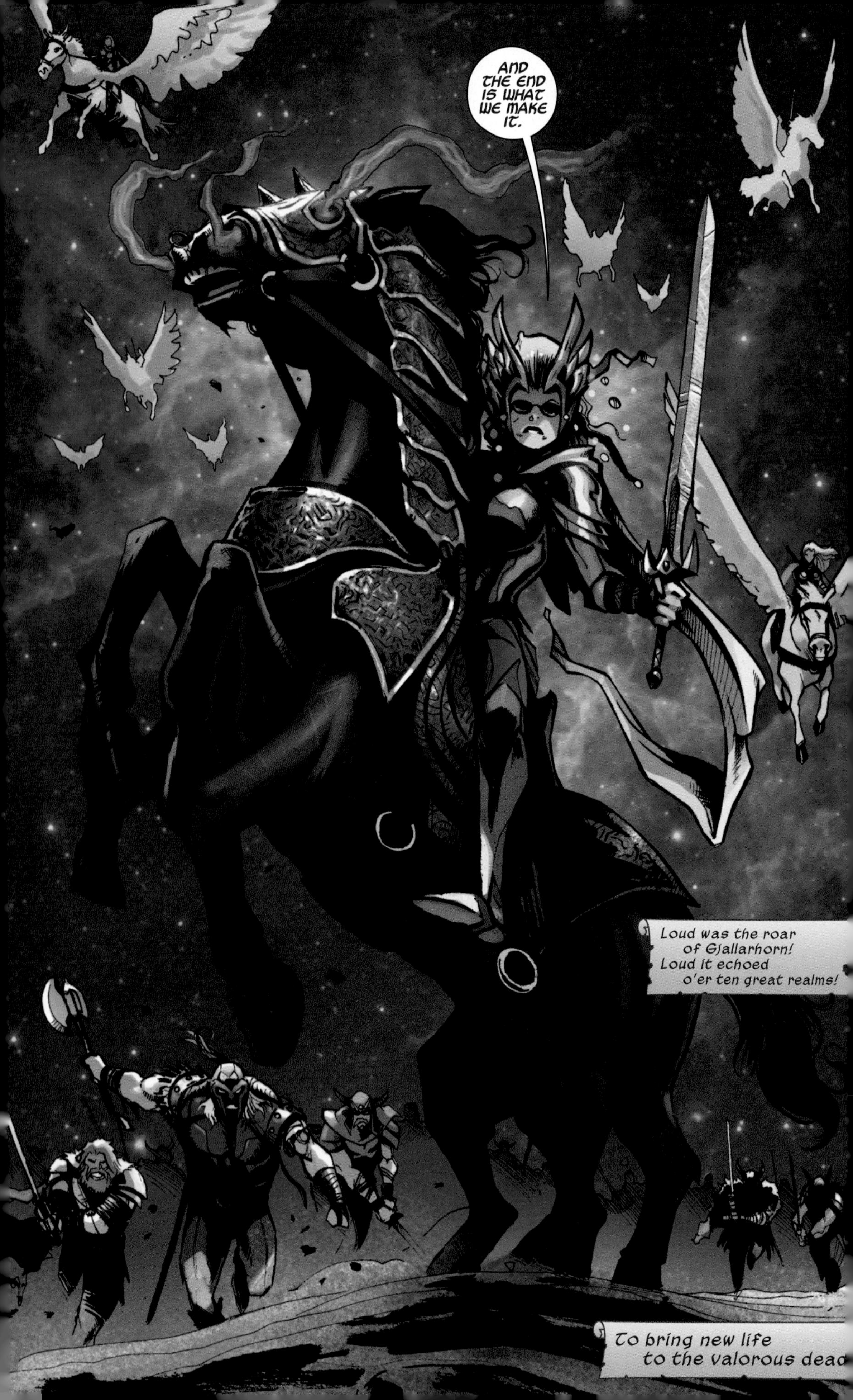
AND THE END IS WHAT WE MAKE IT.
Loud was the roar of Gjallarhorn! Loud it echoed o'er ten great realms!
To bring new life to the valorous dead

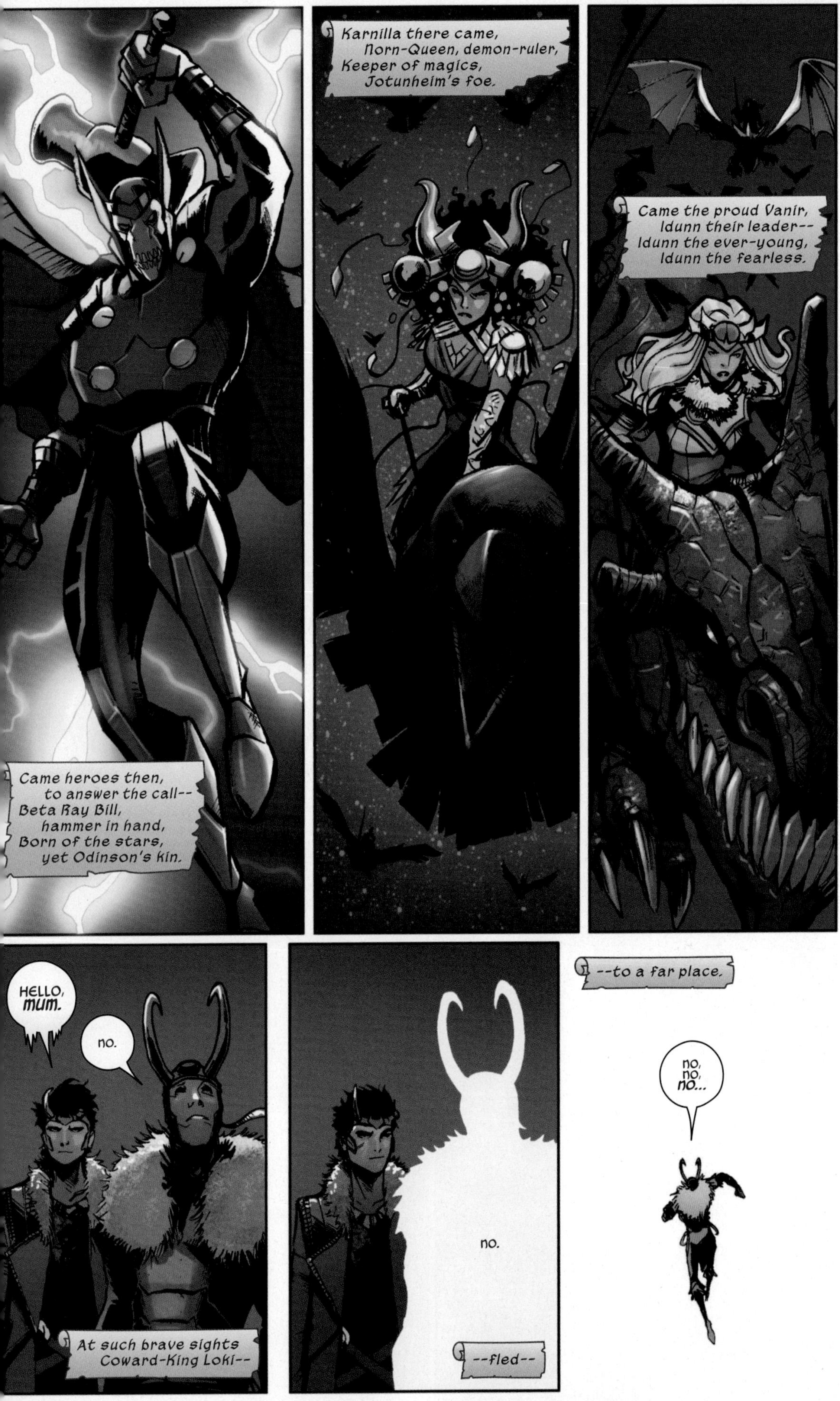
Came heroes then,
to answer the call--
Beta Ray Bill,
hammer in hand,
Born of the stars,
yet Odinson's kin.
Karnilla there came,
Norn-Queen, demon-ruler,
Keeper of magics,
Jotunheim's foe.
Came the proud Vanir,
Idunn their leader--
Idunn the ever-young,
Idunn the fearless.
HELLO, mum.
no.
At such brave sights
Coward-King Loki--
no.
--fled--
--to a far place.
no, no, no...

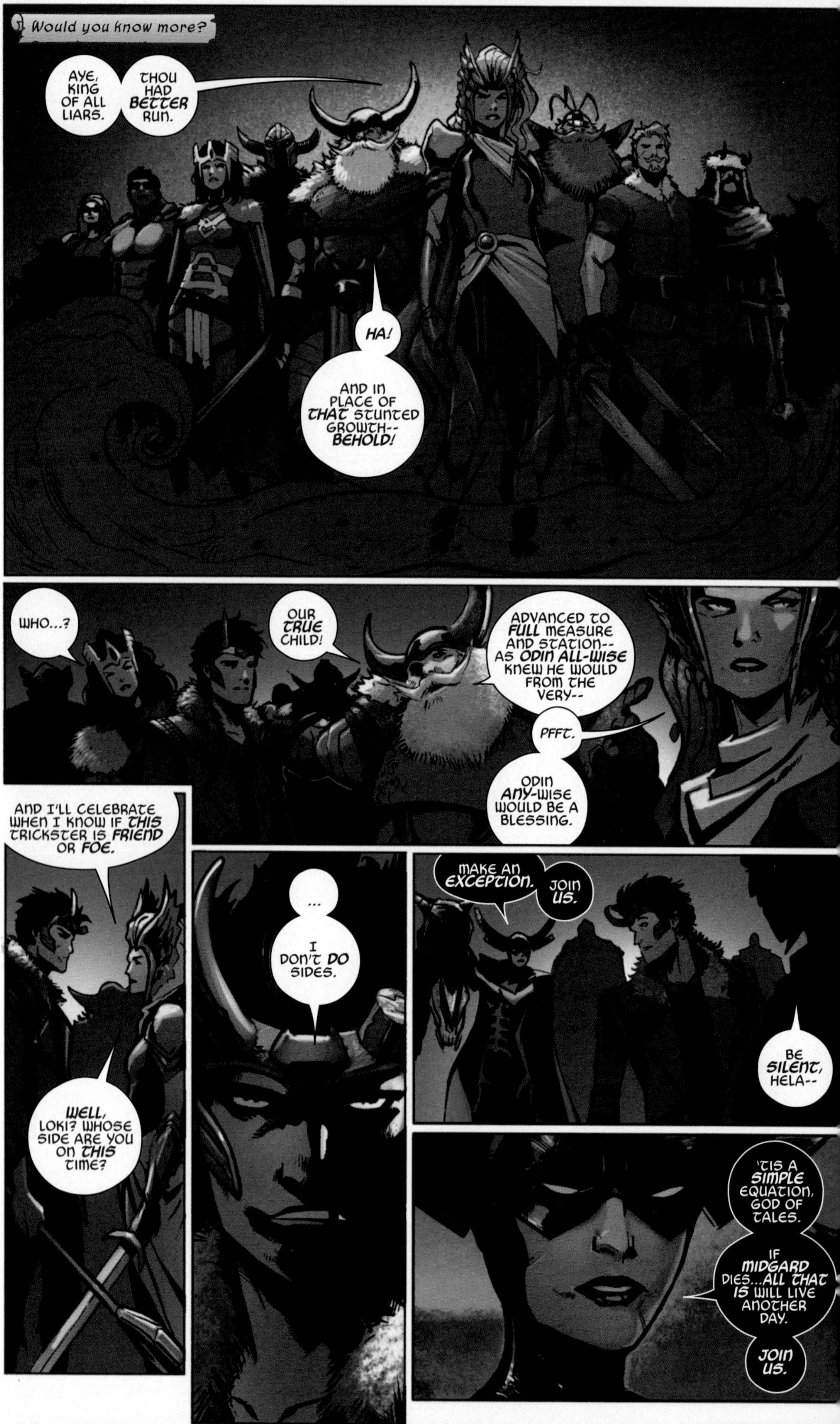
Would you know more?
AYE, KING OF ALL LIARS.
THOU HAD BETTER RUN.
HA!
AND IN PLACE OF THAT STUNTED GROWTH-- BEHOLD!
WHO...?
OUR TRUE CHILD!
ADVANCED TO FULL MEASURE AND STATION-- AS ODIN ALL-WISE KNEW HE WOULD FROM THE VERY--
PFFT.
ODIN ANY-WISE WOULD BE A BLESSING.
AND I'LL CELEBRATE WHEN I KNOW IF THIS TRICKSTER IS FRIEND OR FOE.
WELL, LOKI? WHOSE SIDE ARE YOU ON THIS TIME?
...
I DON'T DO SIDES.
MAKE AN EXCEPTION.
JOIN US.
BE SILENT, HELA--
'TIS A SIMPLE EQUATION, GOD OF TALES.
IF MIDGARD DIES...ALL THAT IS WILL LIVE ANOTHER DAY.
JOIN US.

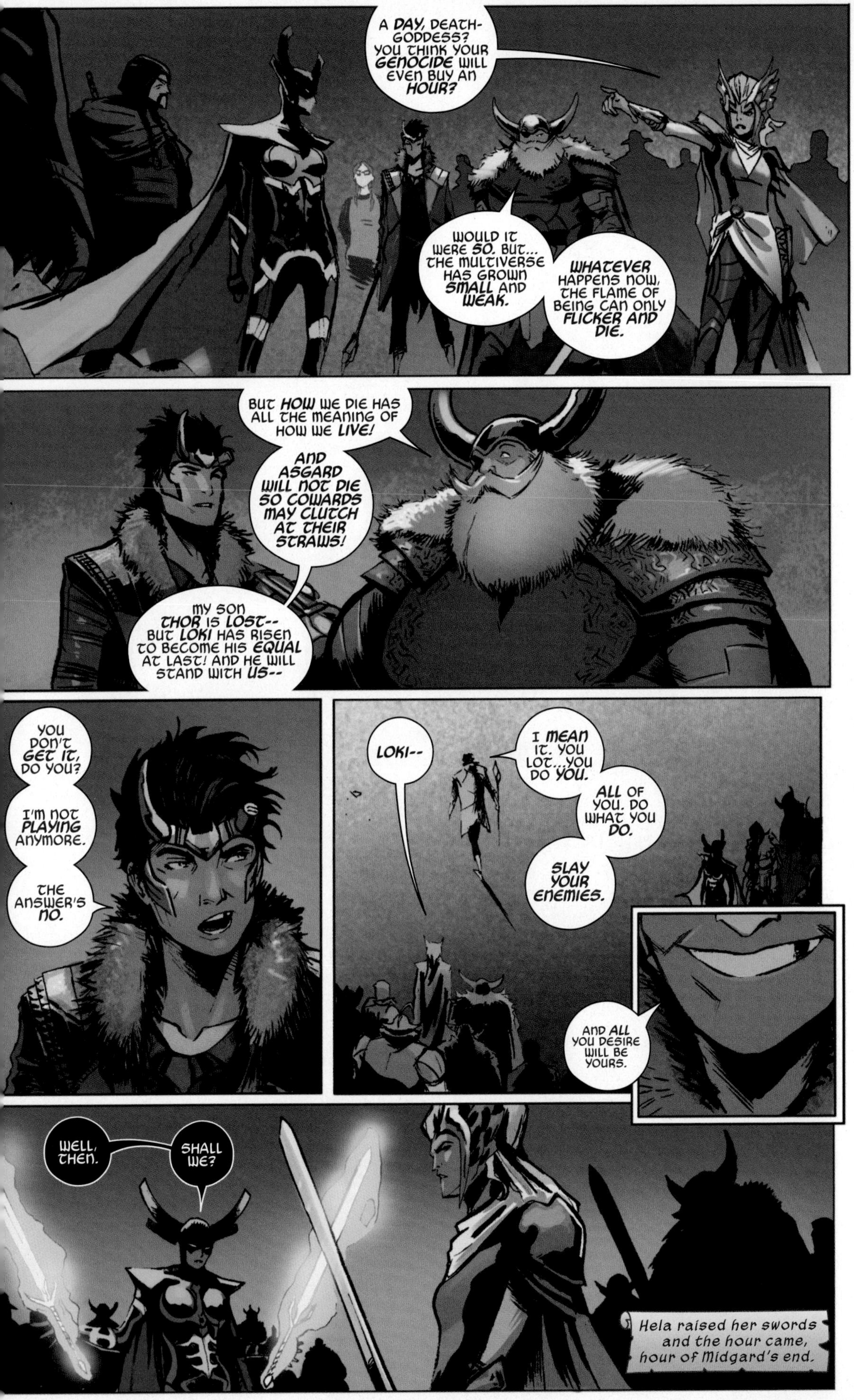
A DAY, DEATH-GODDESS? YOU THINK YOUR GENOCIDE WILL EVEN BUY AN HOUR?
WOULD IT WERE SO. BUT... THE MULTIVERSE HAS GROWN SMALL AND WEAK.
WHATEVER HAPPENS NOW, THE FLAME OF BEING CAN ONLY FLICKER AND DIE.
BUT HOW WE DIE HAS ALL THE MEANING OF HOW WE LIVE!
AND ASGARD WILL NOT DIE SO COWARDS MAY CLUTCH AT THEIR STRAWS!
MY SON THOR IS LOST-- BUT LOKI HAS RISEN TO BECOME HIS EQUAL AT LAST! AND HE WILL STAND WITH US--
YOU DON'T GET IT, DO YOU?
I'M NOT PLAYING ANYMORE.
THE ANSWER'S NO.
LOKI--
I MEAN IT. YOU LOT...YOU DO YOU.
ALL OF YOU. DO WHAT YOU DO.
SLAY YOUR ENEMIES.
AND ALL YOU DESIRE WILL BE YOURS.
WELL, THEN.
SHALL WE?
Hela raised her swords and the hour came, hour of Midgard's end.

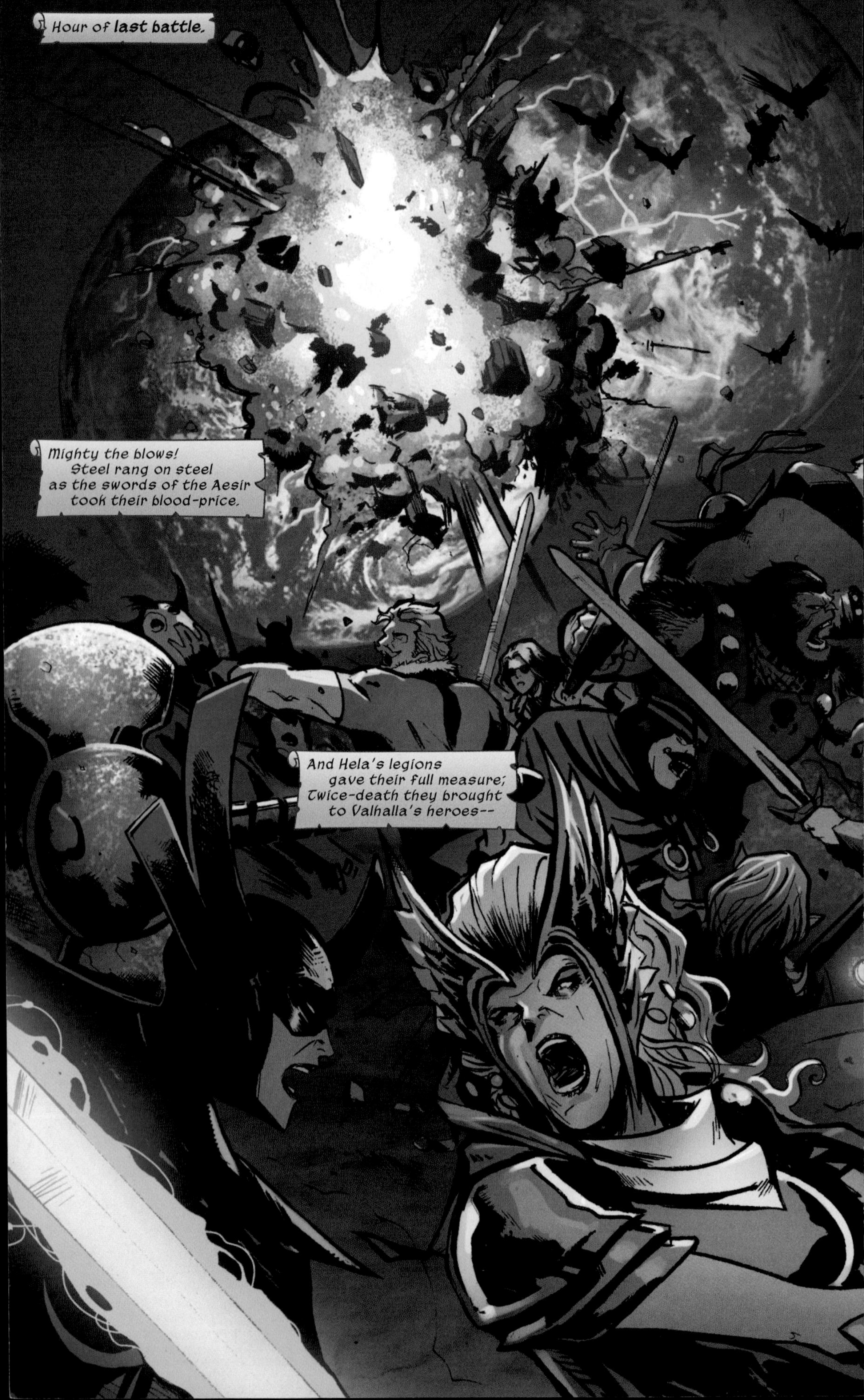
Hour of last battle.
Mighty the blows! Steel rang on steel as the swords of the Aesir took their blood-price.
And Hela's legions gave their full measure; Twice-death they brought to Valhalla's heroes--

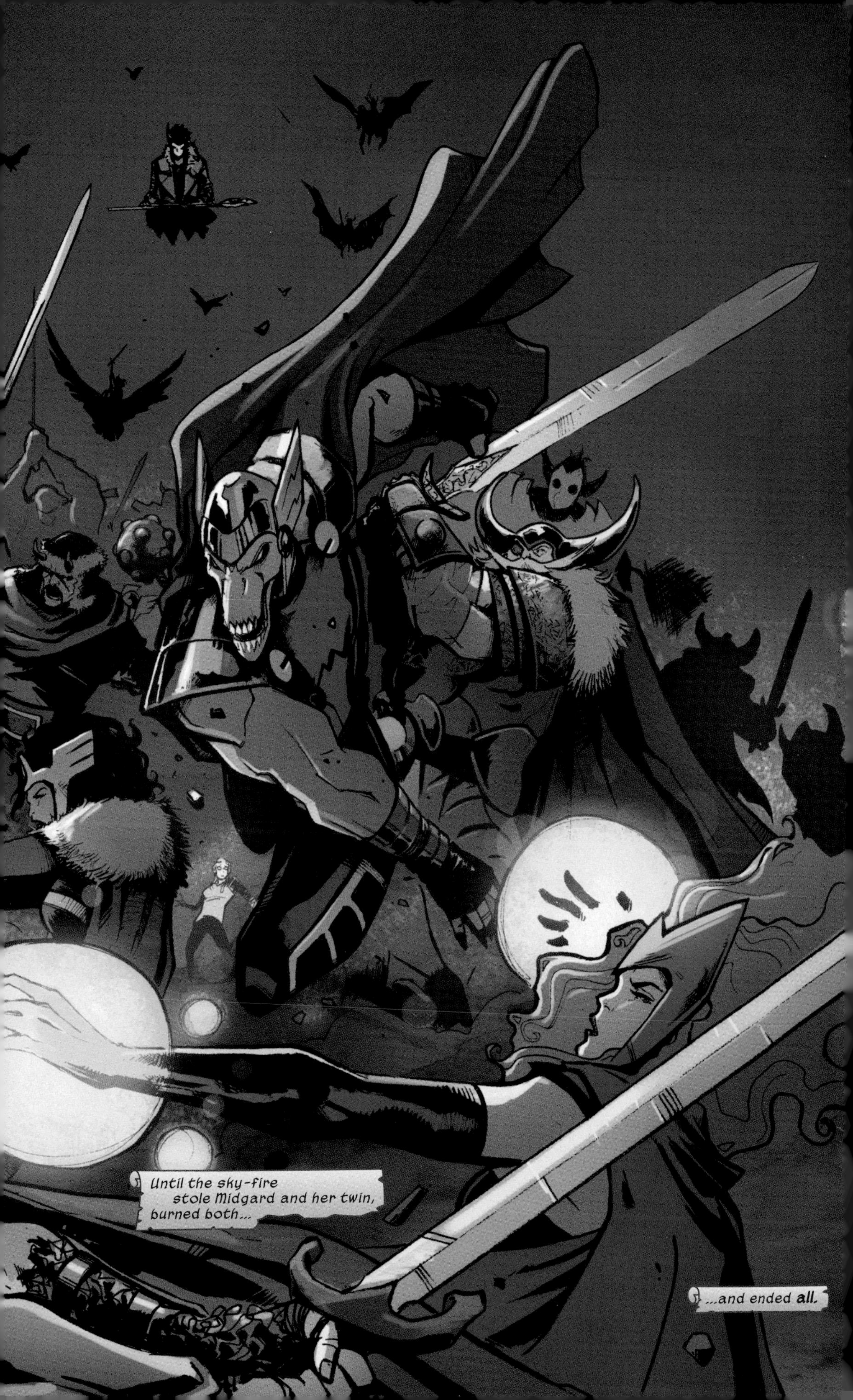
Until the sky-fire stole Midgard and her twin, burned both...
...and ended all.

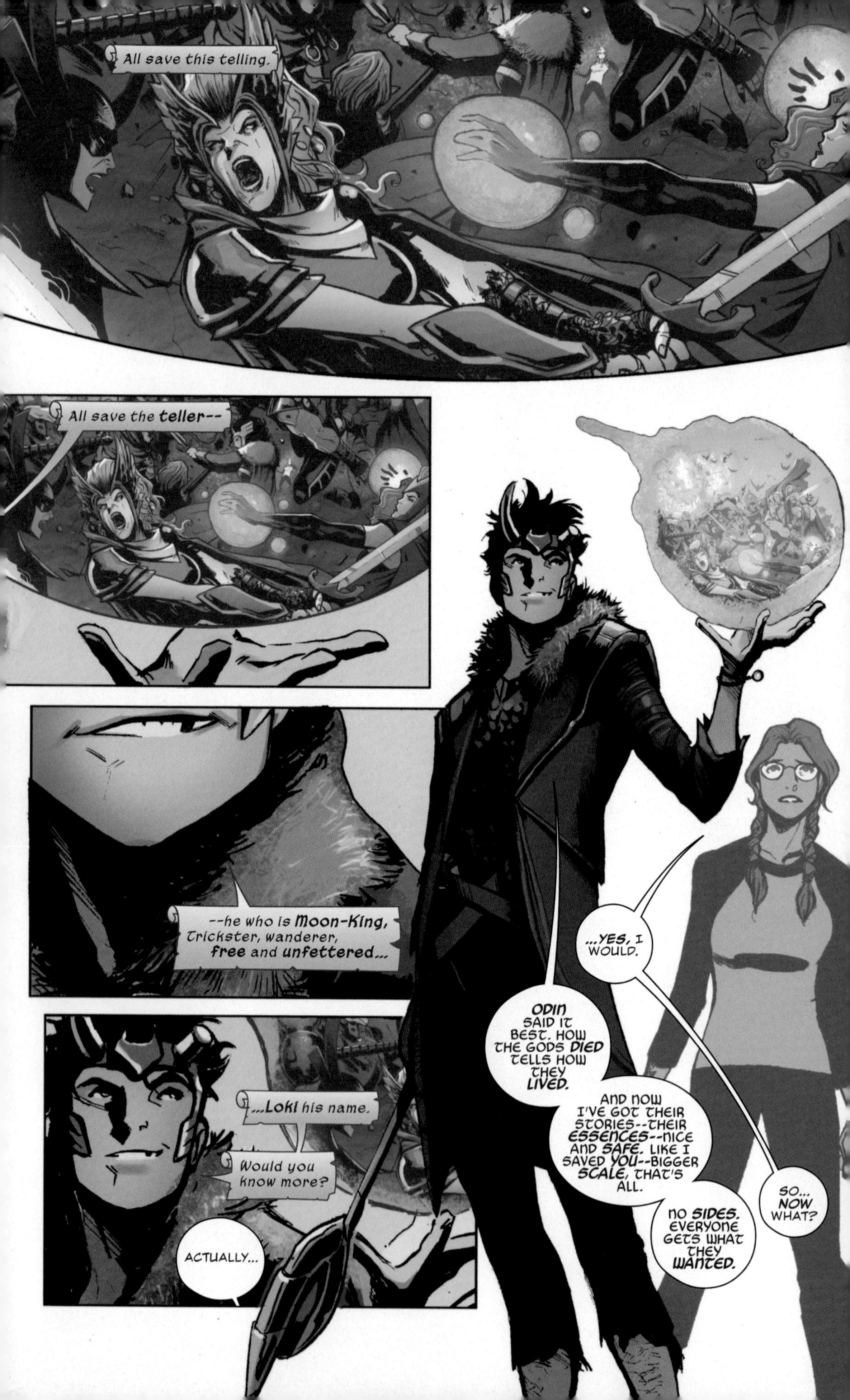
All save this telling.
All save the teller--
--he who is Moon-King, Trickster, wanderer, free and unfettered...
...Loki his name.
Would you know more?
ACTUALLY...
...YES, I WOULD.
ODIN SAID IT BEST. HOW THE GODS DIED TELLS HOW THEY LIVED.
AND NOW I'VE GOT THEIR STORIES--THEIR ESSENCES--NICE AND SAFE. LIKE I SAVED YOU--BIGGER SCALE, THAT'S ALL.
NO SIDES. EVERYONE GETS WHAT THEY WANTED.
SO... NOW WHAT?

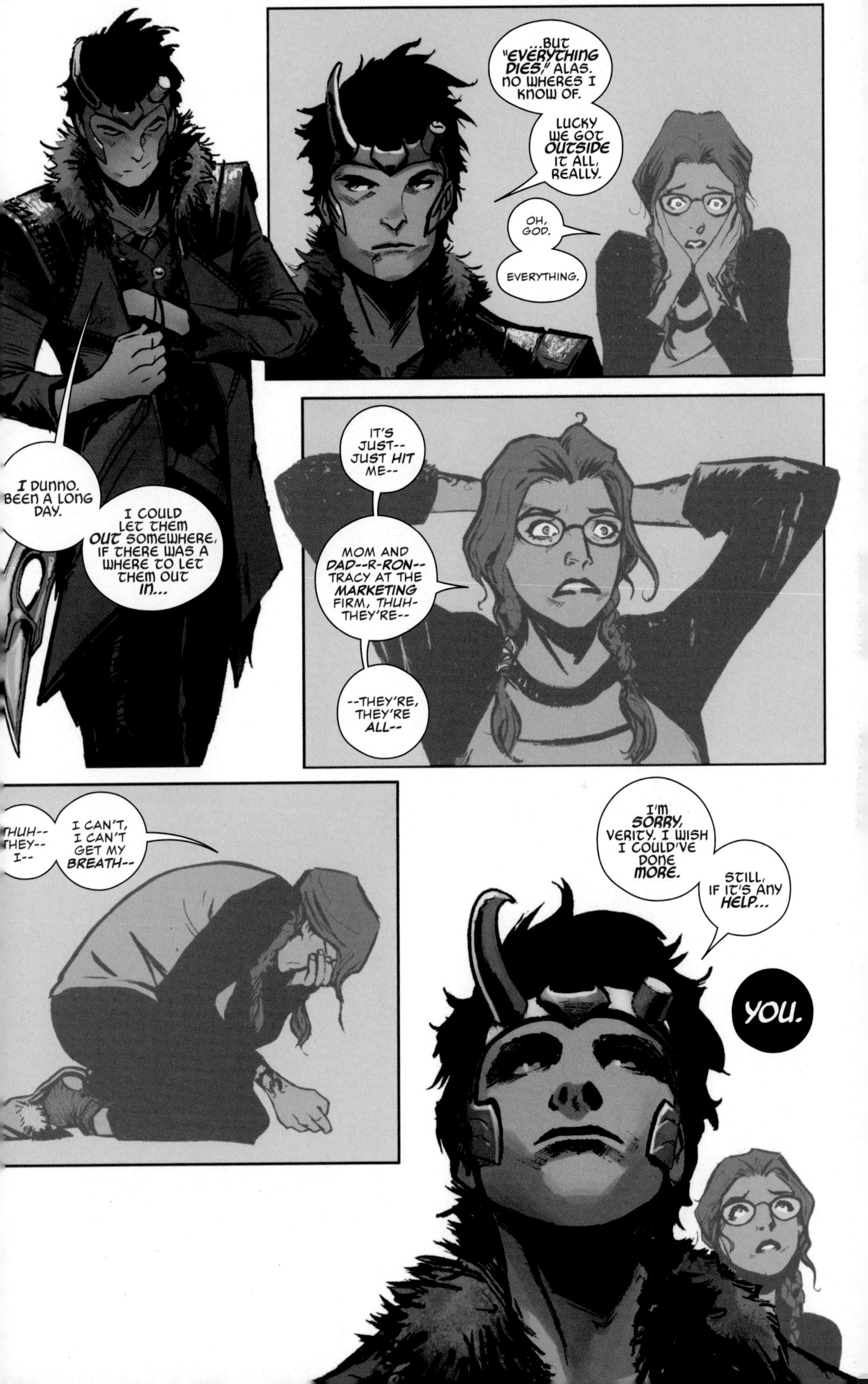
...BUT "EVERYTHING DIES," ALAS. NO WHERES I KNOW OF.
LUCKY WE GOT OUTSIDE IT ALL, REALLY.
OH, GOD.
EVERYTHING.
I DUNNO. BEEN A LONG DAY.
I COULD LET THEM OUT SOMEWHERE, IF THERE WAS A WHERE TO LET THEM OUT IN...
IT'S JUST-- JUST HIT ME--
MOM AND DAD--R-RON-- TRACY AT THE MARKETING FIRM, THUH-THEY'RE--
--THEY'RE, THEY'RE ALL--
THUH-- THEY-- I--
I CAN'T, I CAN'T GET MY BREATH--
I'M SORRY, VERITY. I WISH I COULD'VE DONE MORE.
STILL, IF IT'S ANY HELP...
YOU.

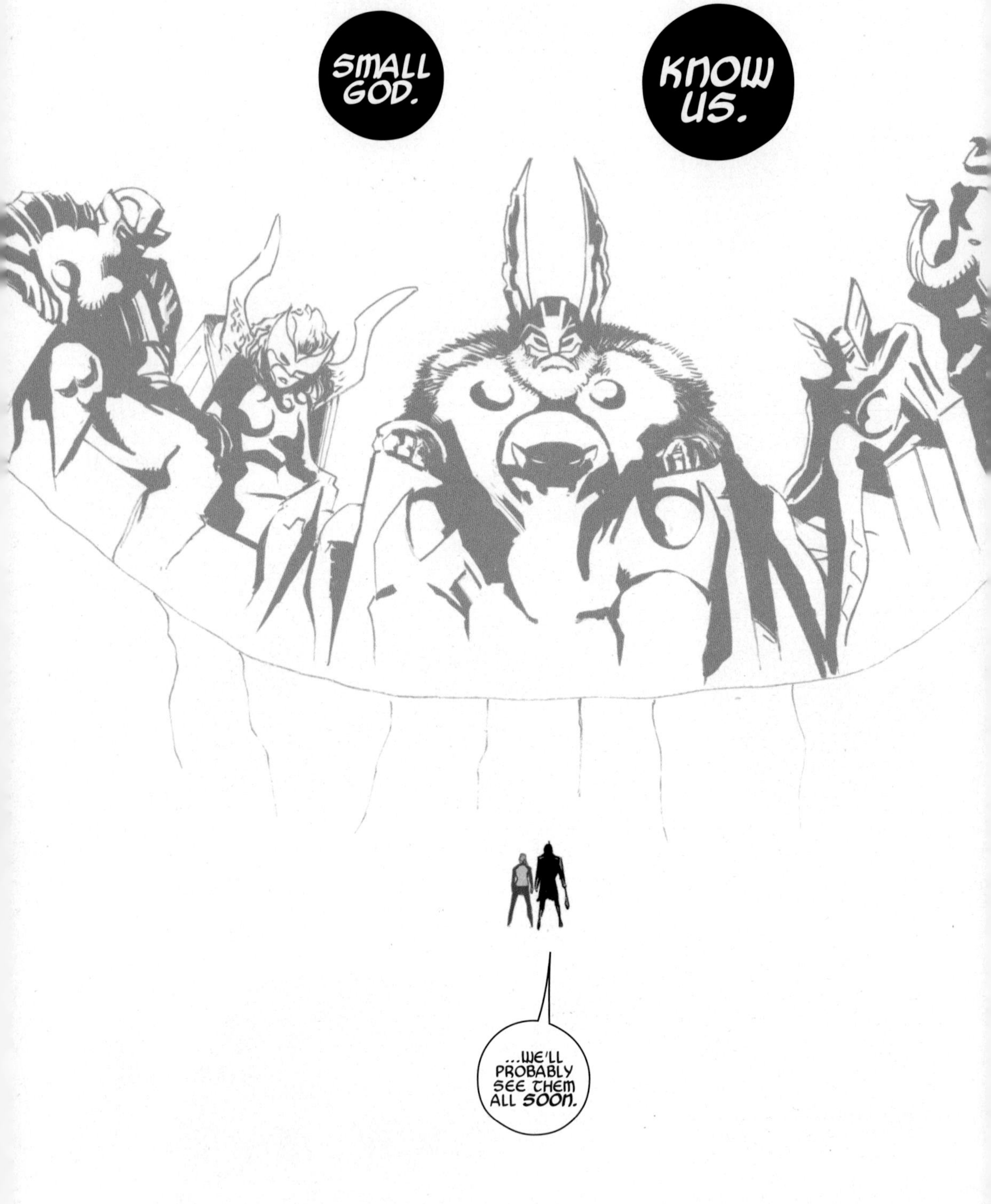
SMALL GOD.
KNOW US.
...WE'LL PROBABLY SEE THEM ALL SOON.

WOULD YOU KNOW MORE?

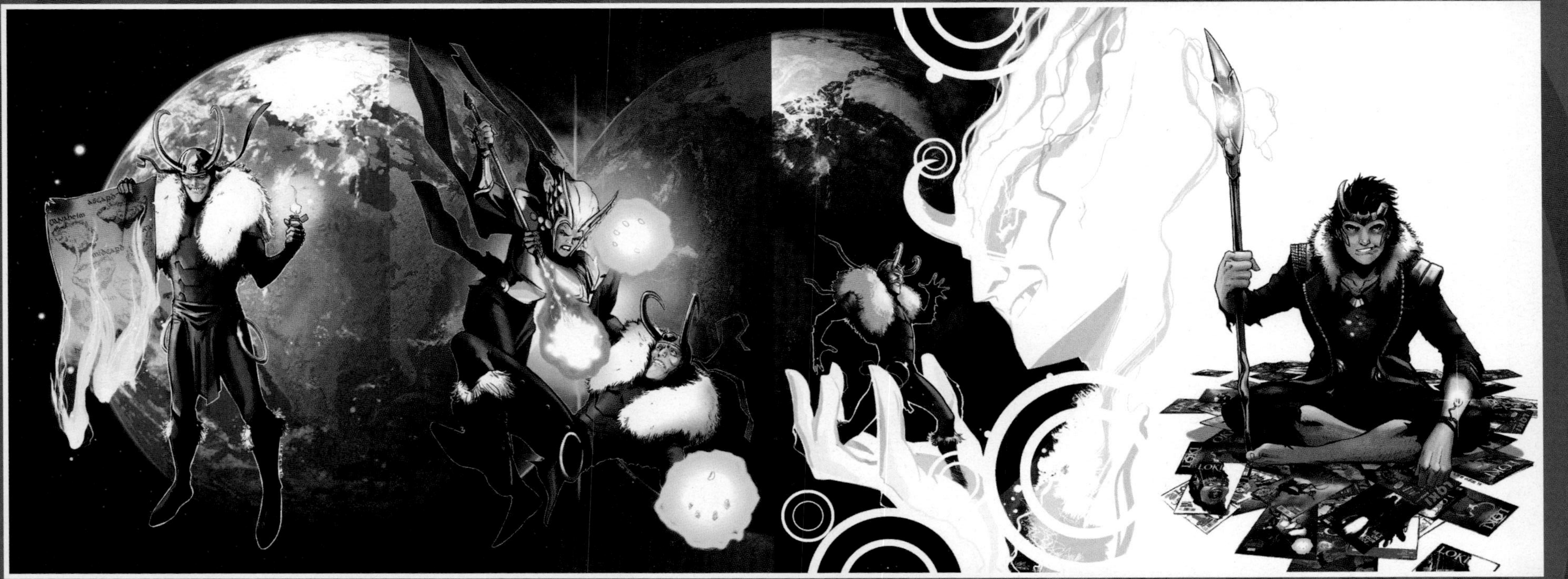

LOKI: AGENT OF ASGARD #14-17 COMBINED COVER ART
by Lee Garbett

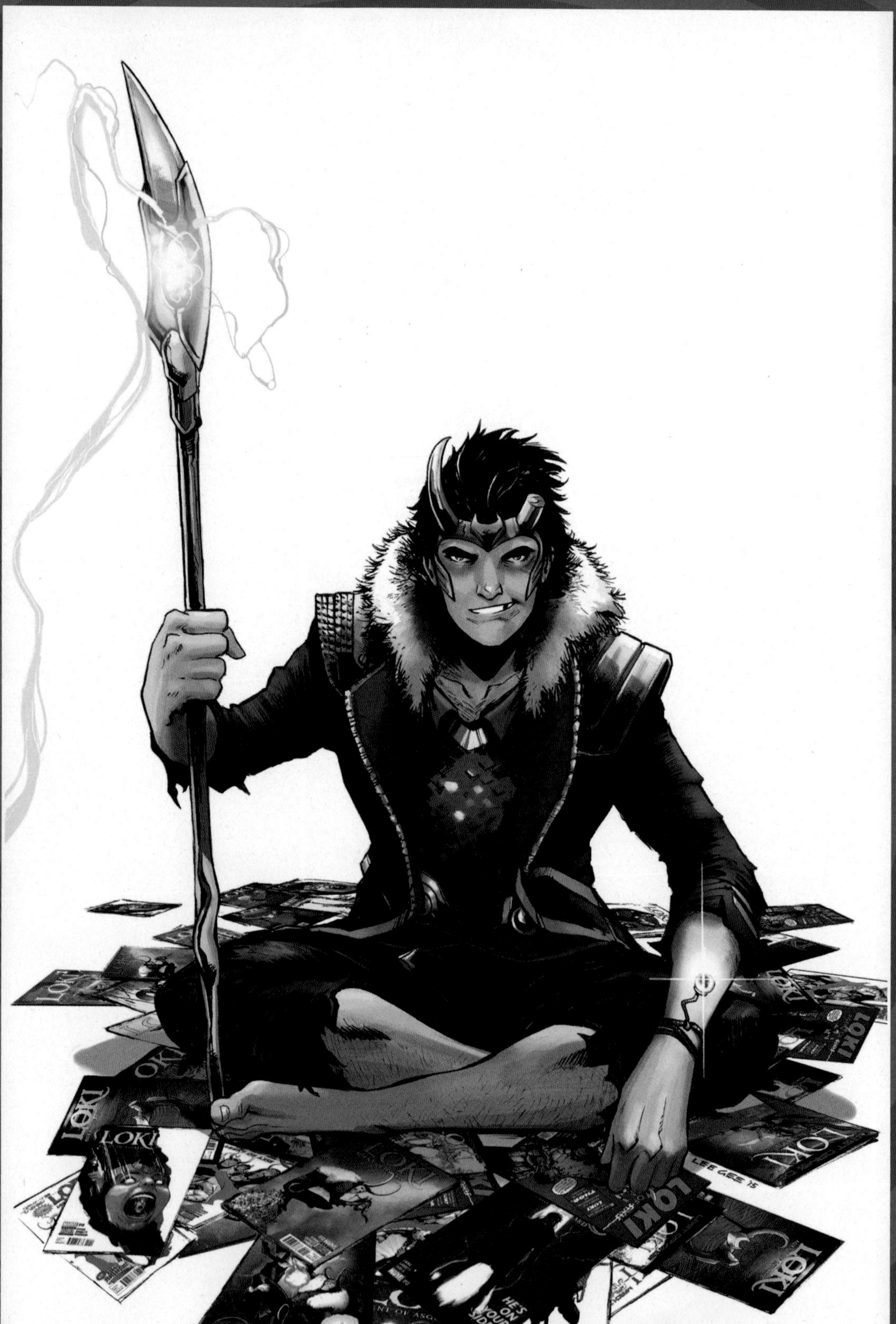
LOKI
HE'S ON YOUR SIDE...
LEE GEE 15

LOKI: AGENT OF ASGARD #17

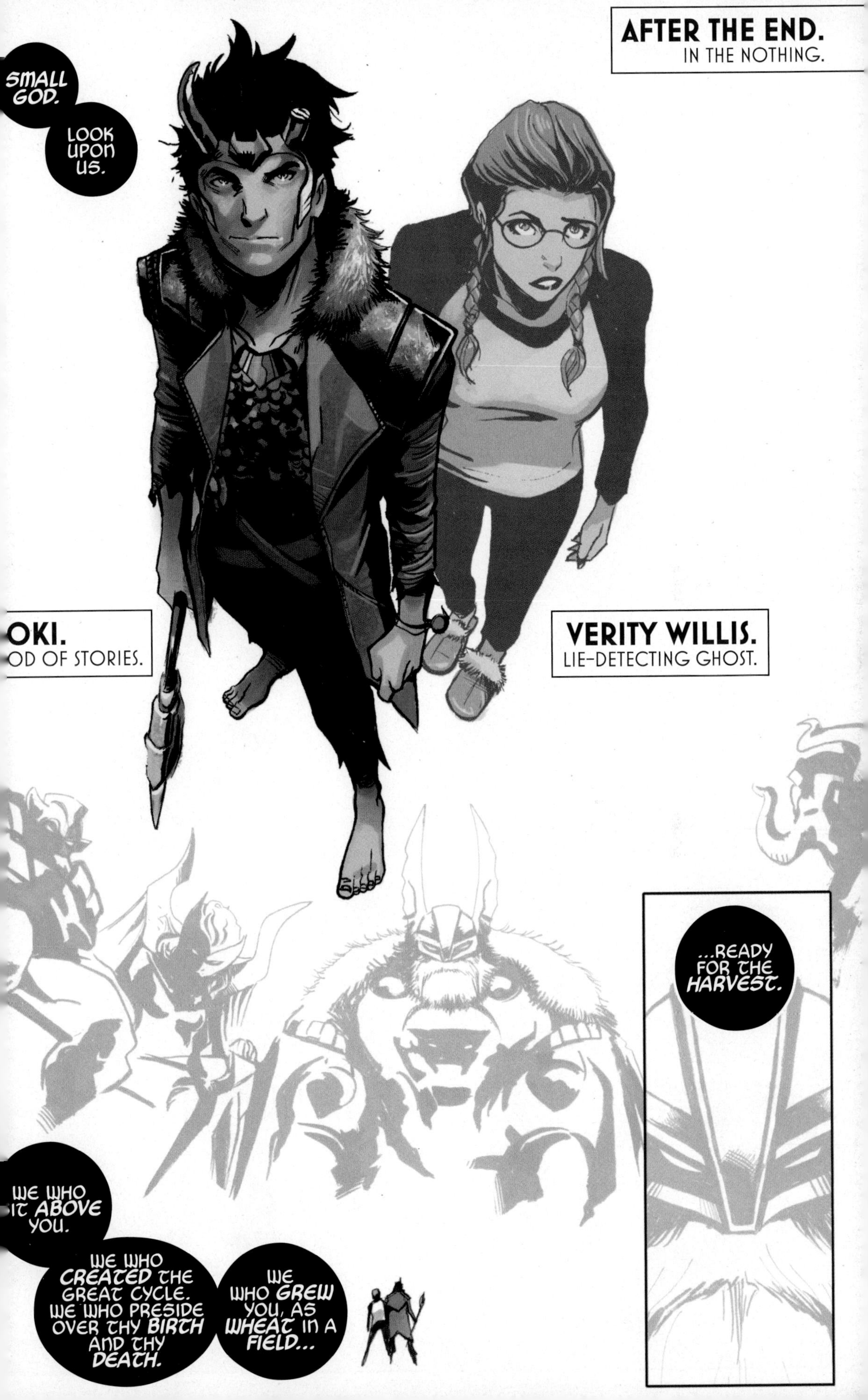
AFTER THE END.
IN THE NOTHING.
SMALL GOD.
LOOK UPON US.
OKI.
OD OF STORIES.
VERITY WILLIS.
LIE-DETECTING GHOST.
WE WHO IT ABOVE YOU.
WE WHO CREATED THE GREAT CYCLE. WE WHO PRESIDE OVER THY BIRTH AND THY DEATH.
WE WHO GREW YOU, AS WHEAT IN A FIELD...
...READY FOR THE HARVEST.

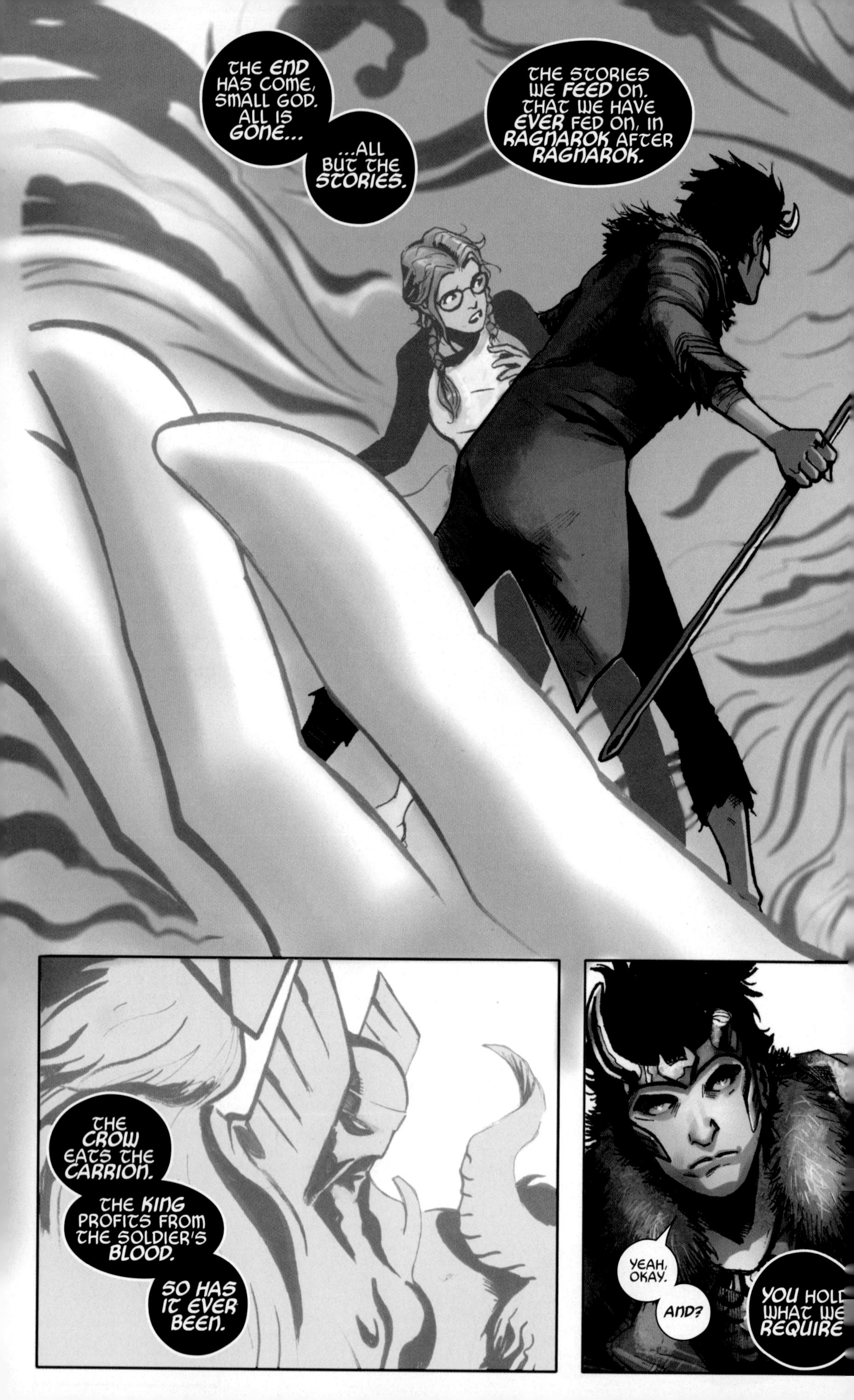
THE END HAS COME, SMALL GOD. ALL IS GONE...
...ALL BUT THE STORIES.
THE STORIES WE FEED ON. THAT WE HAVE EVER FED ON, IN RAGNAROK AFTER RAGNAROK.
THE CROW EATS THE CARRION.
THE KING PROFITS FROM THE SOLDIER'S BLOOD.
SO HAS IT EVER BEEN.
YEAH, OKAY.
AND?
YOU HOLD WHAT WE REQUIRE

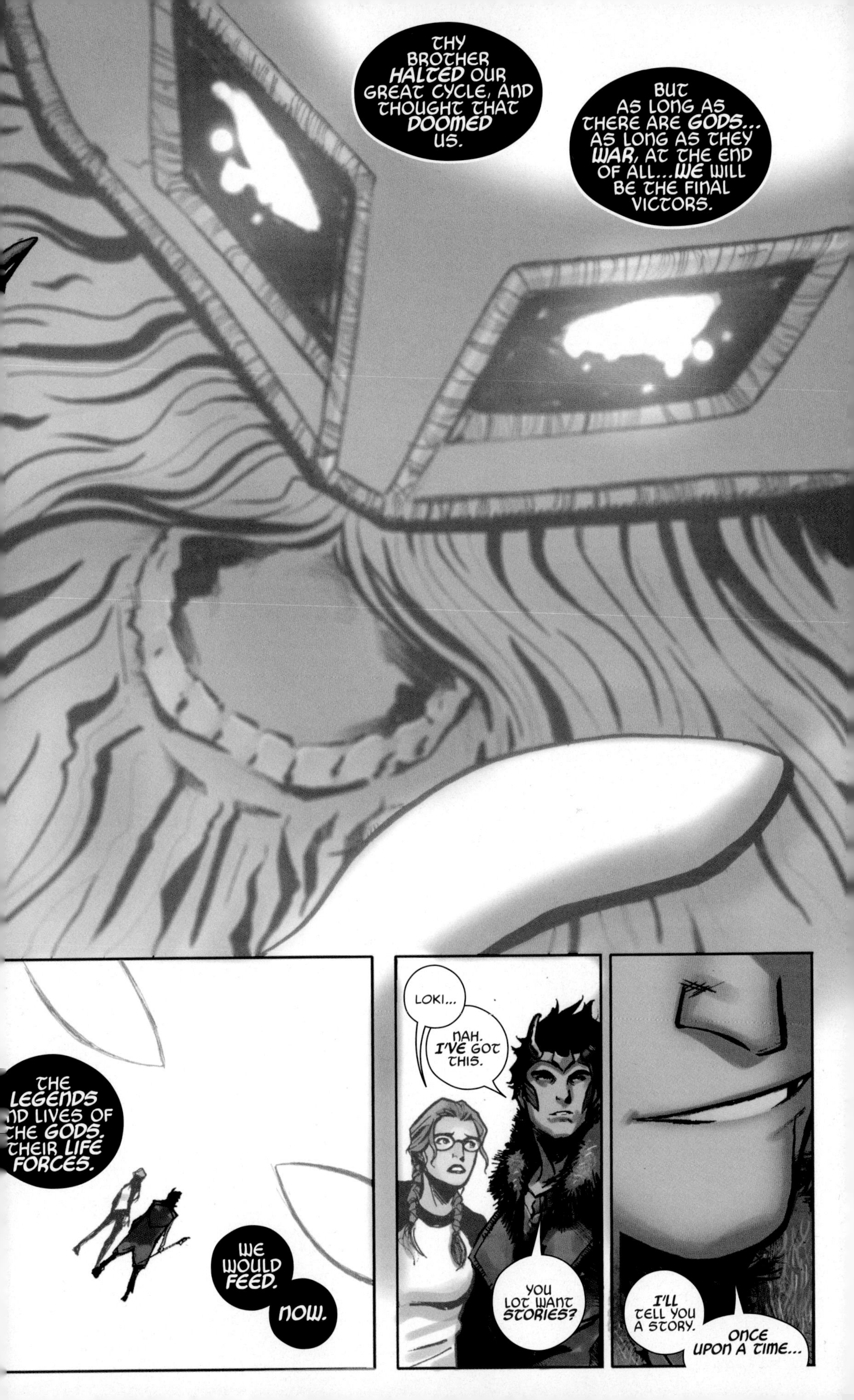

THY BROTHER HALTED OUR GREAT CYCLE, AND THOUGHT THAT DOOMED US.
BUT AS LONG AS THERE ARE GODS... AS LONG AS THEY WAR, AT THE END OF ALL... WE WILL BE THE FINAL VICTORS.
THE LEGENDS ND LIVES OF THE GODS. THEIR LIFE FORCES.
WE WOULD FEED.
NOW.
LOKI...
NAH. I'VE GOT THIS.
YOU LOT WANT STORIES?
I'LL TELL YOU A STORY.
ONCE UPON A TIME...

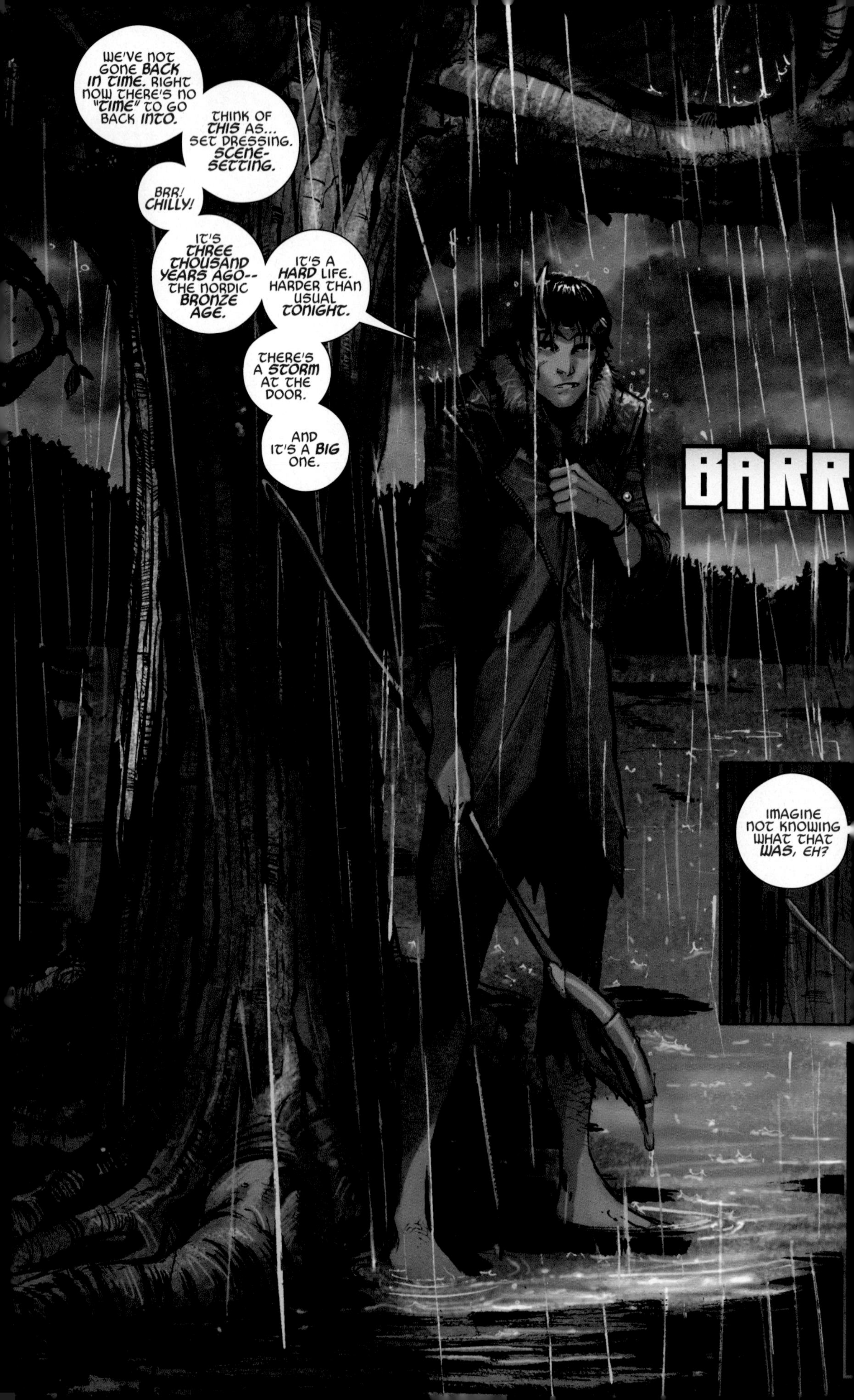

WE'VE NOT GONE BACK IN TIME. RIGHT NOW THERE'S NO "TIME" TO GO BACK INTO.
THINK OF THIS AS... SET DRESSING. SCENE-SETTING.
BRR! CHILLY!
IT'S THREE THOUSAND YEARS AGO-- THE NORDIC BRONZE AGE.
IT'S A HARD LIFE. HARDER THAN USUAL TONIGHT.
THERE'S A STORM AT THE DOOR.
AND IT'S A BIG ONE.
BARR
IMAGINE NOT KNOWING WHAT THAT WAS, EH?

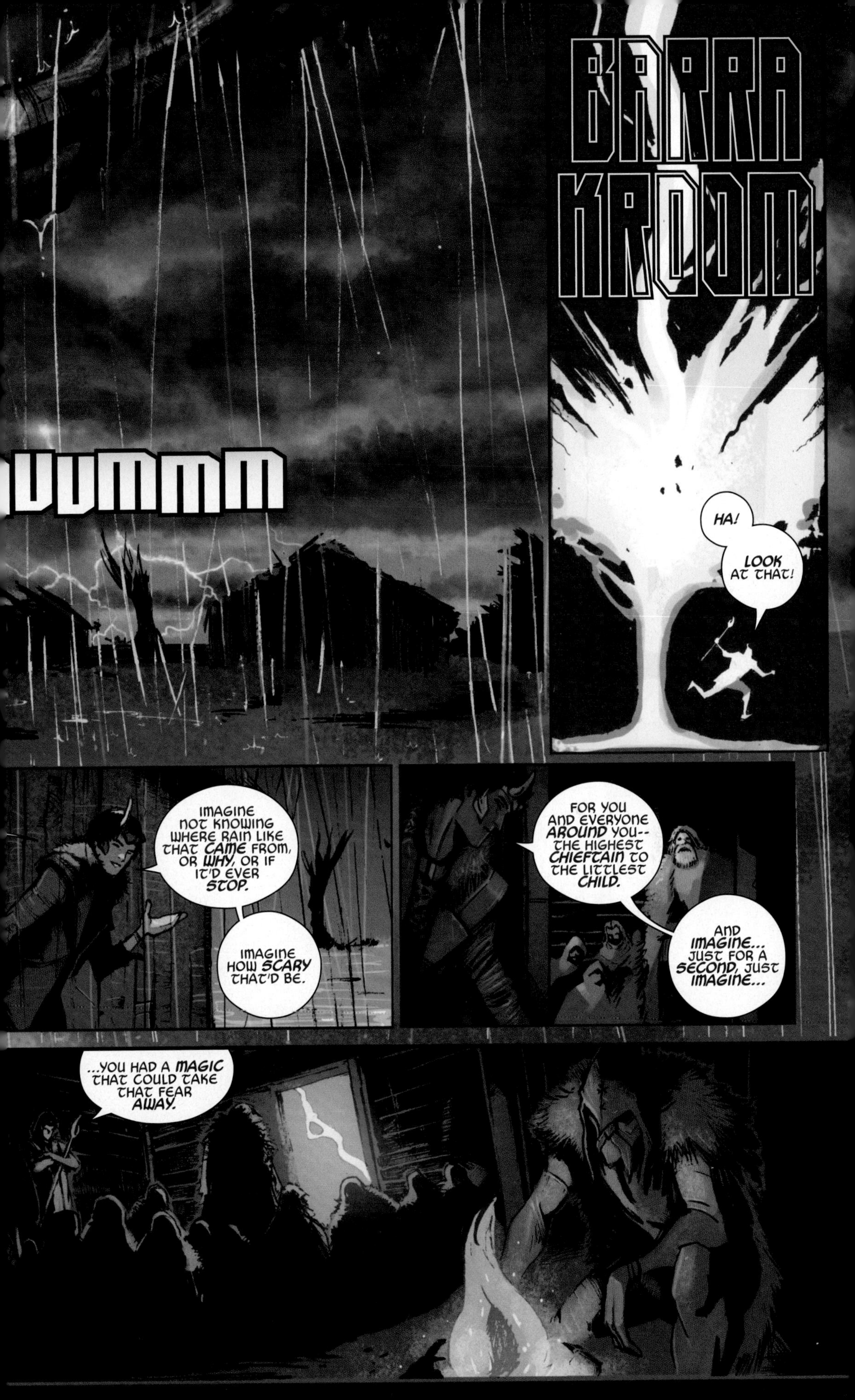
BRRRA KROOM
VUMMM
HA!
LOOK AT THAT!
IMAGINE NOT KNOWING WHERE RAIN LIKE THAT CAME FROM, OR WHY, OR IF IT'D EVER STOP.
IMAGINE HOW SCARY THAT'D BE.
FOR YOU AND EVERYONE AROUND YOU-- THE HIGHEST CHIEFTAIN TO THE LITTLEST CHILD.
AND IMAGINE... JUST FOR A SECOND, JUST IMAGINE...
...YOU HAD A MAGIC THAT COULD TAKE THAT FEAR AWAY.

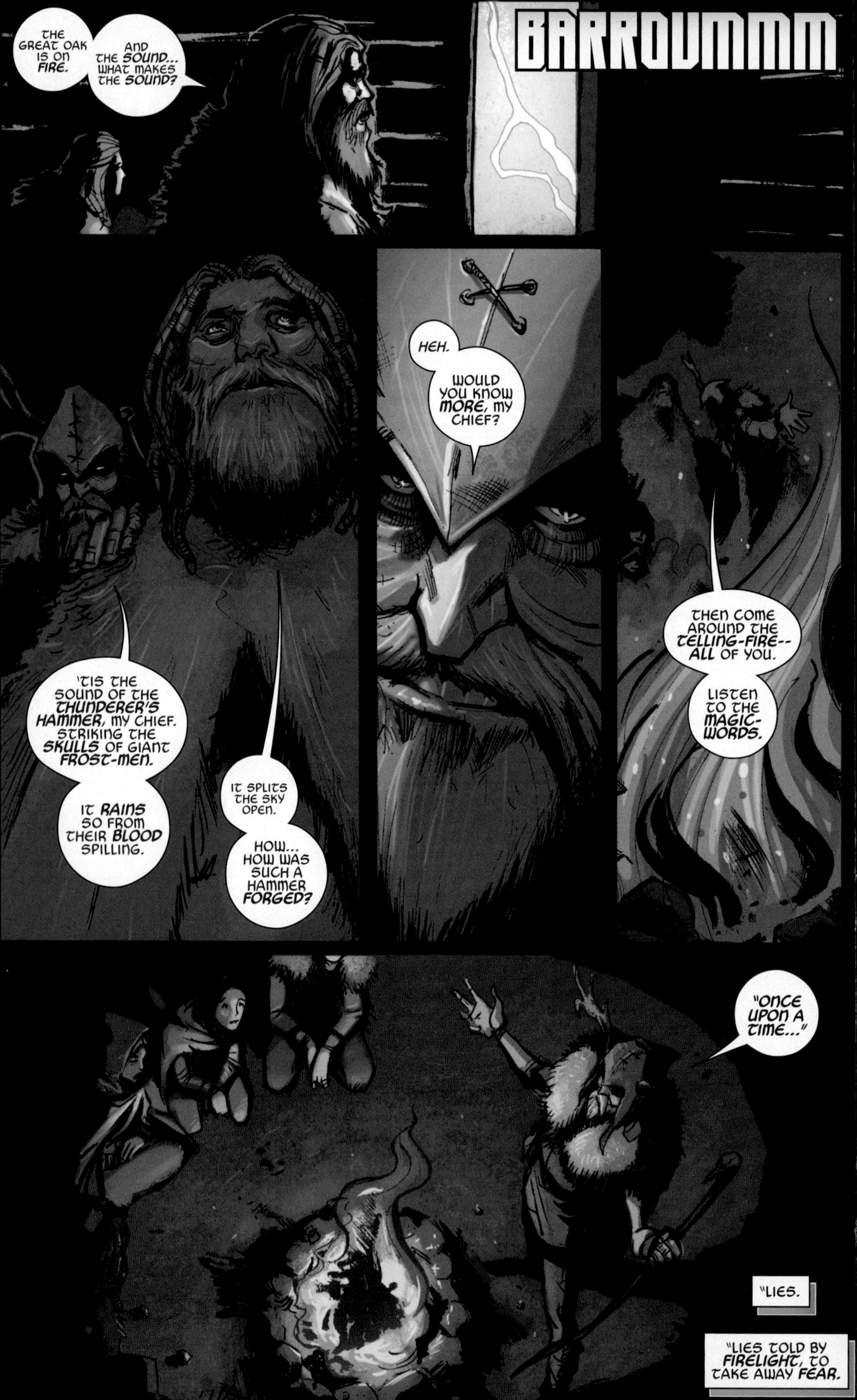
BARROUMMMM
THE GREAT OAK IS ON FIRE.
AND THE SOUND... WHAT MAKES THE SOUND?
'TIS THE SOUND OF THE THUNDERER'S HAMMER, MY CHIEF. STRIKING THE SKULLS OF GIANT FROST-MEN.
IT RAINS SO FROM THEIR BLOOD SPILLING.
IT SPLITS THE SKY OPEN.
HOW... HOW WAS SUCH A HAMMER FORGED?
HEH.
WOULD YOU KNOW MORE, MY CHIEF?
THEN COME AROUND THE TELLING-FIRE-- ALL OF YOU.
LISTEN TO THE MAGIC-WORDS.
"ONCE UPON A TIME..."
"LIES.
"LIES TOLD BY FIRELIGHT, TO TAKE AWAY FEAR.

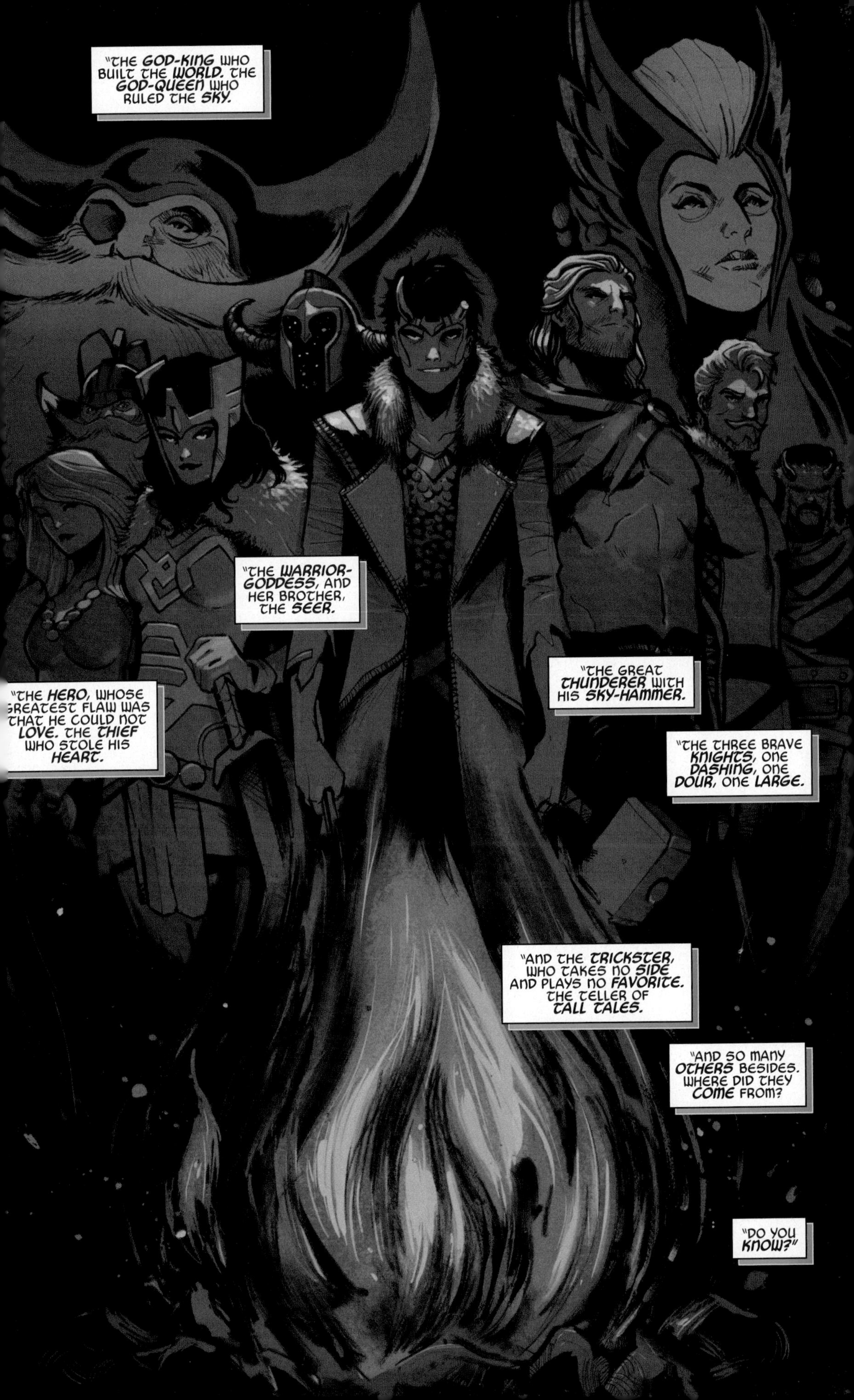
"THE GOD-KING WHO BUILT THE WORLD. THE GOD-QUEEN WHO RULED THE SKY.
"THE WARRIOR-GODDESS, AND HER BROTHER, THE SEER.
"THE HERO, WHOSE GREATEST FLAW WAS THAT HE COULD NOT LOVE. THE THIEF WHO STOLE HIS HEART.
"THE GREAT THUNDERER WITH HIS SKY-HAMMER.
"THE THREE BRAVE KNIGHTS, ONE DASHING, ONE DOUR, ONE LARGE.
"AND THE TRICKSTER, WHO TAKES NO SIDE AND PLAYS NO FAVORITE. THE TELLER OF TALL TALES.
"AND SO MANY OTHERS BESIDES. WHERE DID THEY COME FROM?
"DO YOU KNOW?"

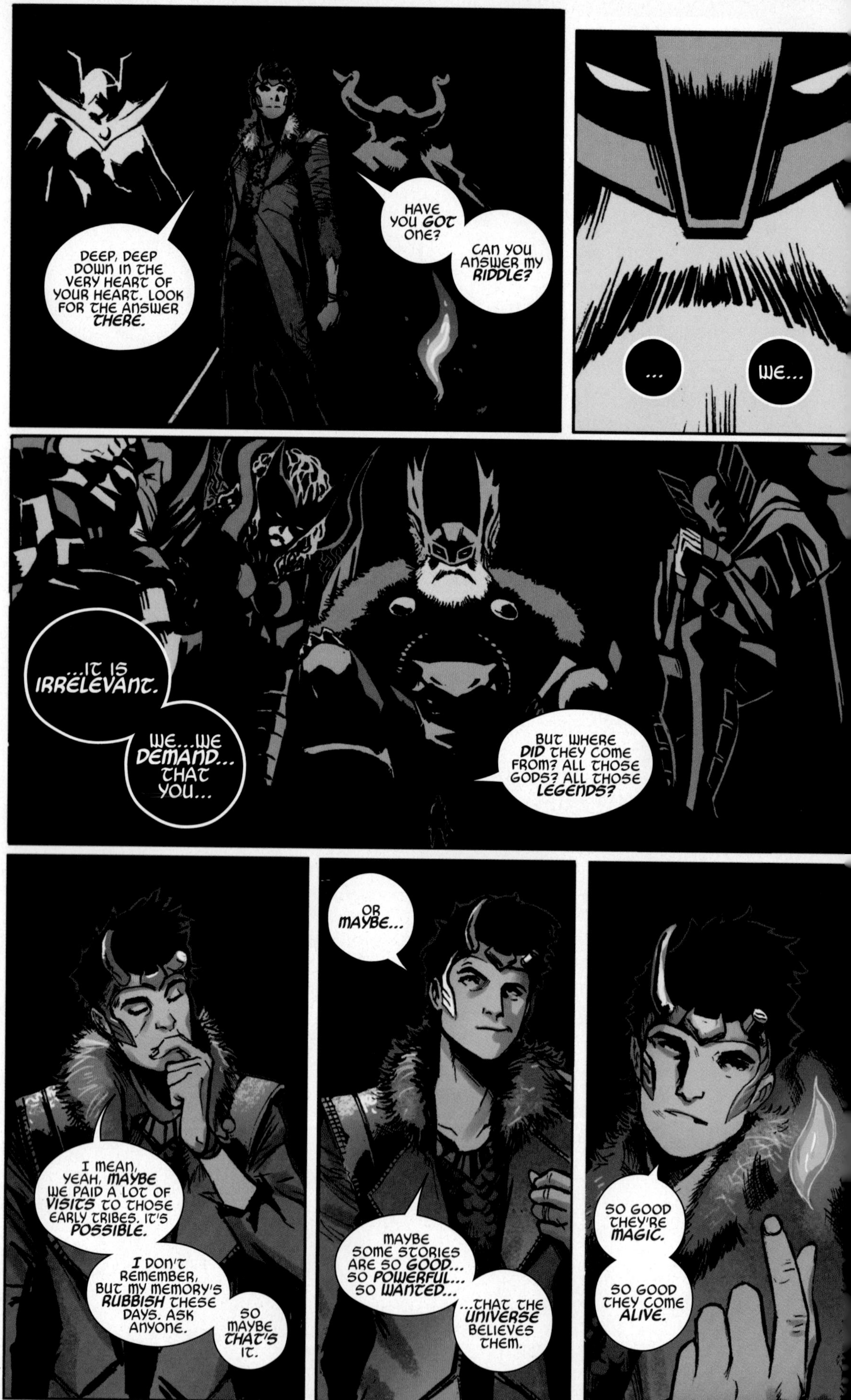
DEEP, DEEP DOWN IN THE VERY HEART OF YOUR HEART. LOOK FOR THE ANSWER THERE.
HAVE YOU GOT ONE?
CAN YOU ANSWER MY RIDDLE?
...
WE...
...IT IS IRRELEVANT.
WE...WE DEMAND... THAT YOU...
BUT WHERE DID THEY COME FROM? ALL THOSE GODS? ALL THOSE LEGENDS?
I MEAN, YEAH, MAYBE WE PAID A LOT OF VISITS TO THOSE EARLY TRIBES. IT'S POSSIBLE.
I DON'T REMEMBER, BUT MY MEMORY'S RUBBISH THESE DAYS. ASK ANYONE.
SO MAYBE THAT'S IT.
OR MAYBE...
MAYBE SOME STORIES ARE SO GOOD... SO POWERFUL... SO WANTED...
...THAT THE UNIVERSE BELIEVES THEM.
SO GOOD THEY'RE MAGIC.
SO GOOD THEY COME ALIVE.

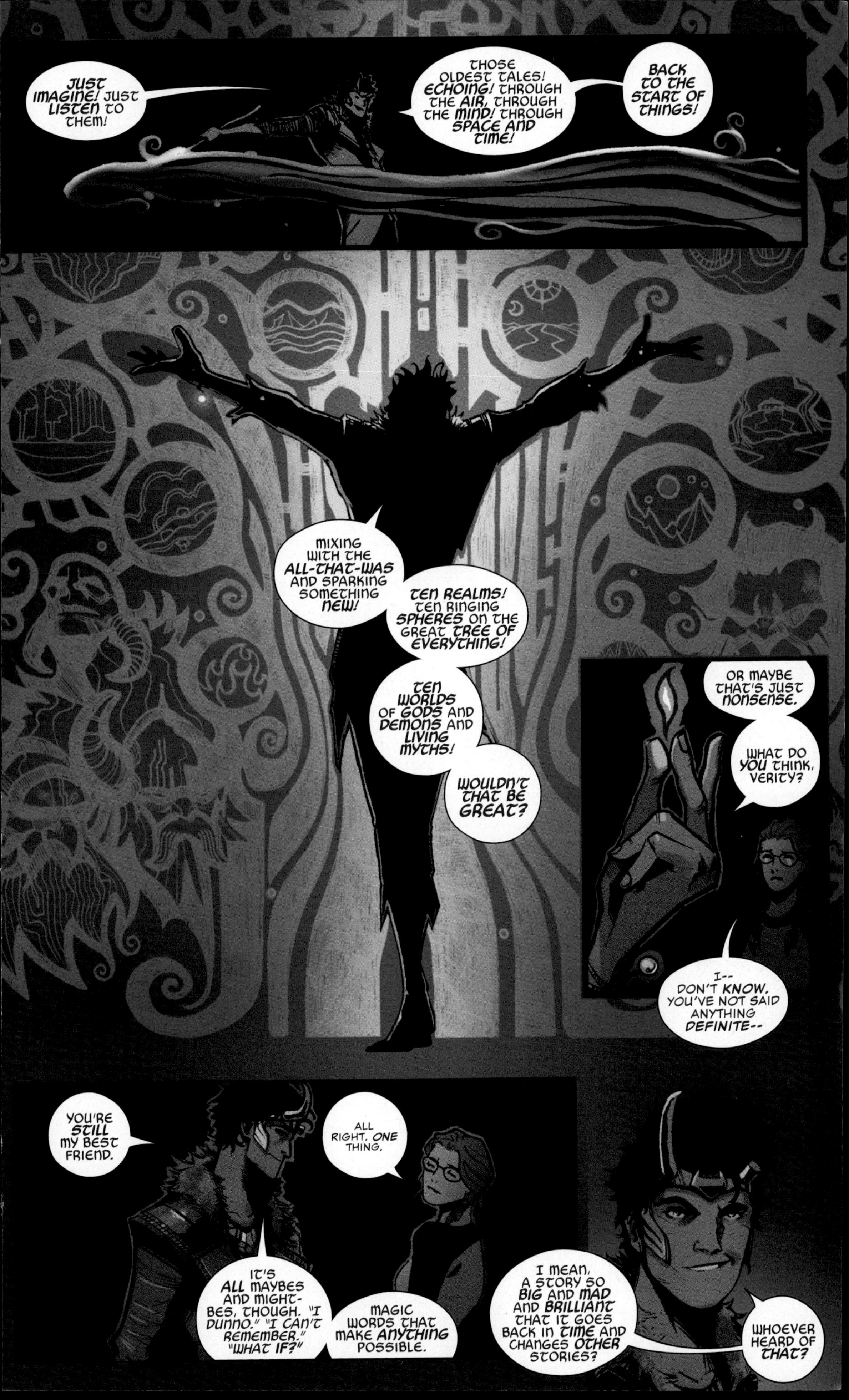

JUST IMAGINE! JUST LISTEN TO THEM!
THOSE OLDEST TALES! ECHOING! THROUGH THE AIR, THROUGH THE MIND! THROUGH SPACE AND TIME!
BACK TO THE START OF THINGS!
MIXING WITH THE ALL-THAT-WAS AND SPARKING SOMETHING NEW!
TEN REALMS! TEN RINGING SPHERES ON THE GREAT TREE OF EVERYTHING!
TEN WORLDS OF GODS AND DEMONS AND LIVING MYTHS!
WOULDN'T THAT BE GREAT?
OR MAYBE THAT'S JUST NONSENSE.
WHAT DO YOU THINK, VERITY?
I-- DON'T KNOW. YOU'VE NOT SAID ANYTHING DEFINITE--
YOU'RE STILL MY BEST FRIEND.
ALL RIGHT. ONE THING.
IT'S ALL MAYBES AND MIGHT-BES, THOUGH. "I DUNNO." "I CAN'T REMEMBER." "WHAT IF?"
MAGIC WORDS THAT MAKE ANYTHING POSSIBLE.
I MEAN, A STORY SO BIG AND MAD AND BRILLIANT THAT IT GOES BACK IN TIME AND CHANGES OTHER STORIES?
WHOEVER HEARD OF THAT?

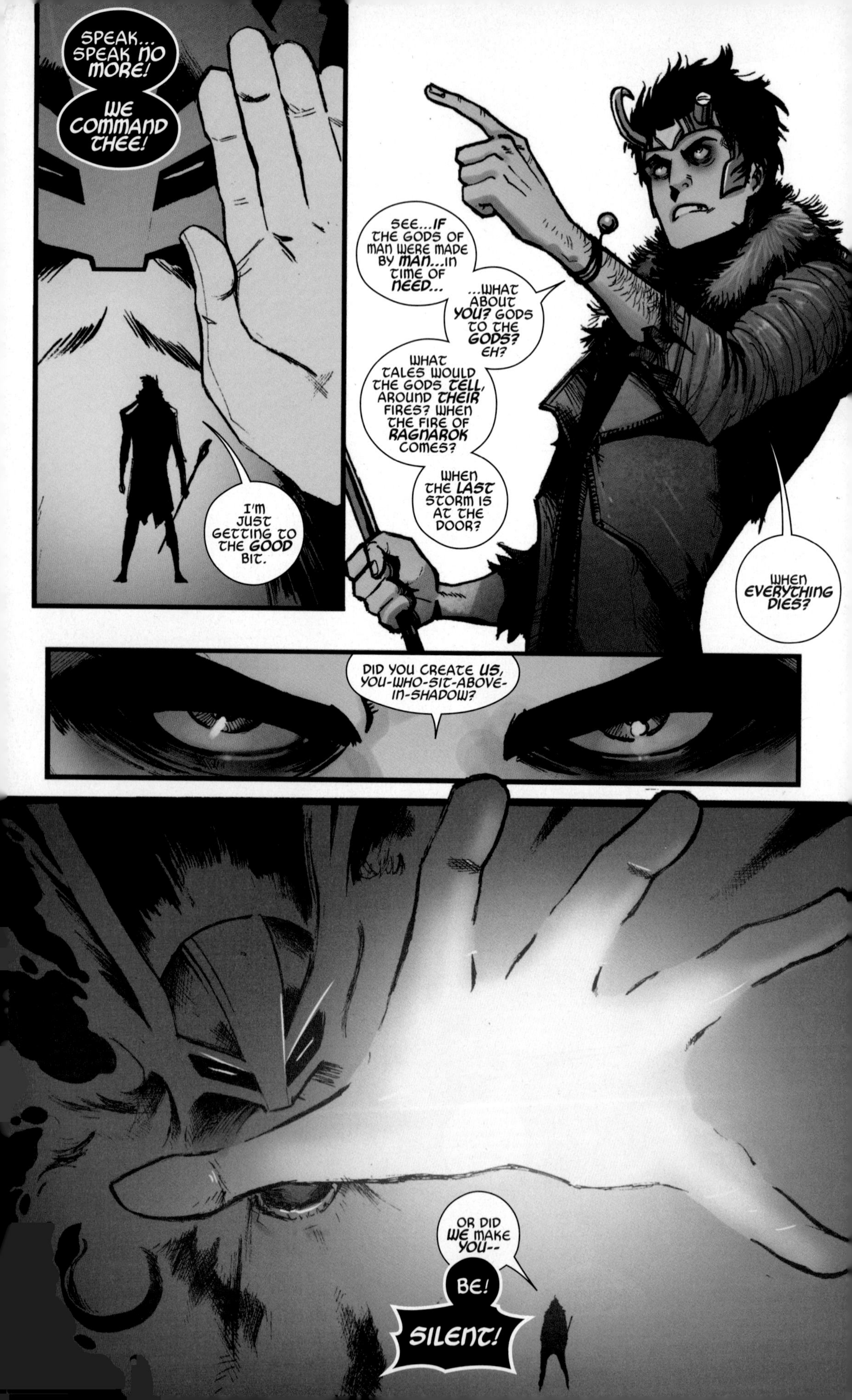
SPEAK... SPEAK NO MORE!
WE COMMAND THEE!
SEE...IF THE GODS OF MAN WERE MADE BY MAN...IN TIME OF NEED...
...WHAT ABOUT YOU? GODS TO THE GODS? EH?
WHAT TALES WOULD THE GODS TELL, AROUND THEIR FIRES? WHEN THE FIRE OF RAGNAROK COMES?
WHEN THE LAST STORM IS AT THE DOOR?
I'M JUST GETTING TO THE GOOD BIT.
WHEN EVERYTHING DIES?
DID YOU CREATE US, YOU-WHO-SIT-ABOVE-IN-SHADOW?
OR DID WE MAKE YOU--
BE!
SILENT!

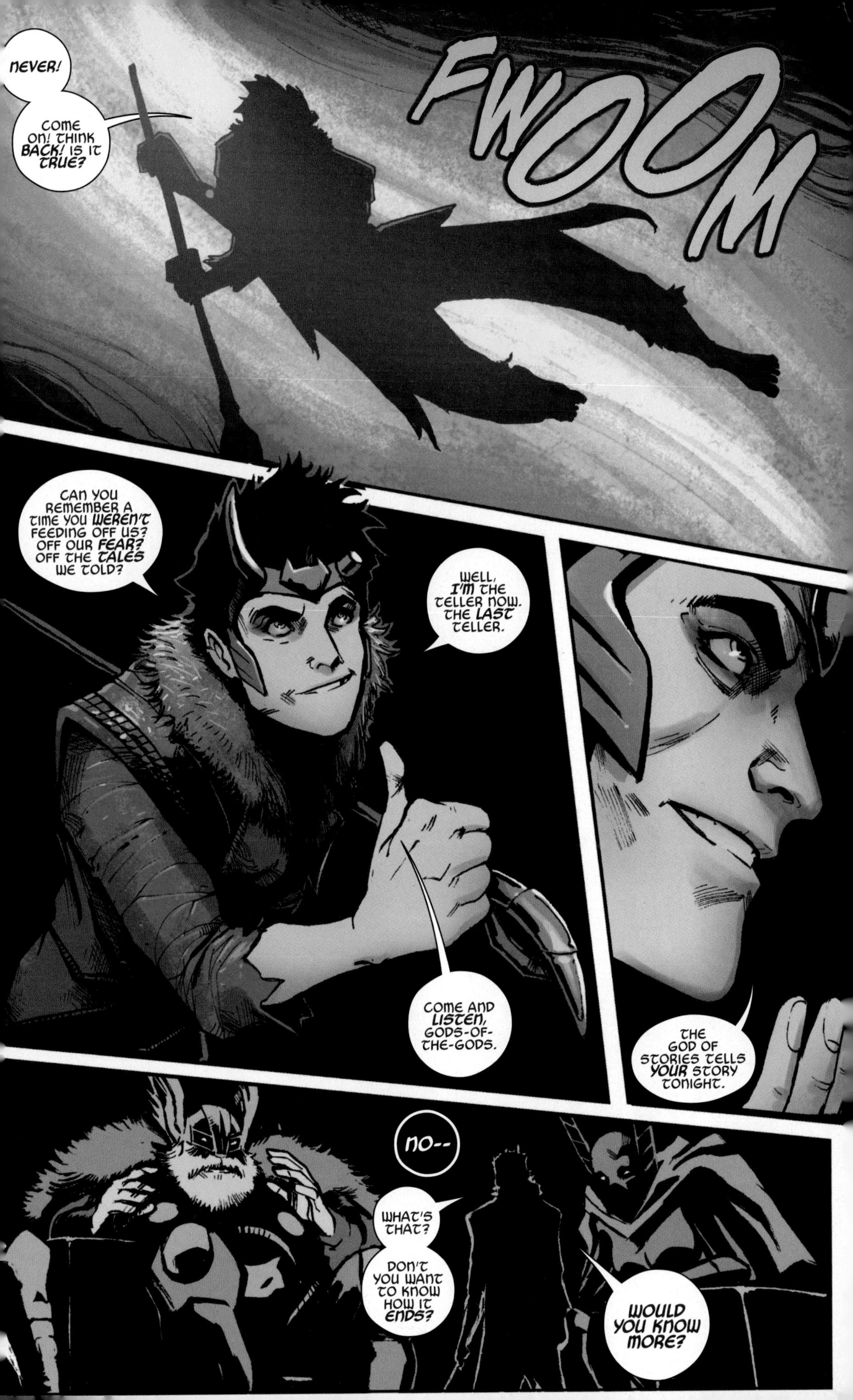
NEVER!
COME ON! THINK BACK! IS IT TRUE?
FWOOM
CAN YOU REMEMBER A TIME YOU WEREN'T FEEDING OFF US? OFF OUR FEAR? OFF THE TALES WE TOLD?
WELL, I'M THE TELLER NOW. THE LAST TELLER.
COME AND LISTEN, GODS-OF-THE-GODS.
THE GOD OF STORIES TELLS YOUR STORY TONIGHT.
NO--
WHAT'S THAT?
DON'T YOU WANT TO KNOW HOW IT ENDS?
WOULD YOU KNOW MORE?

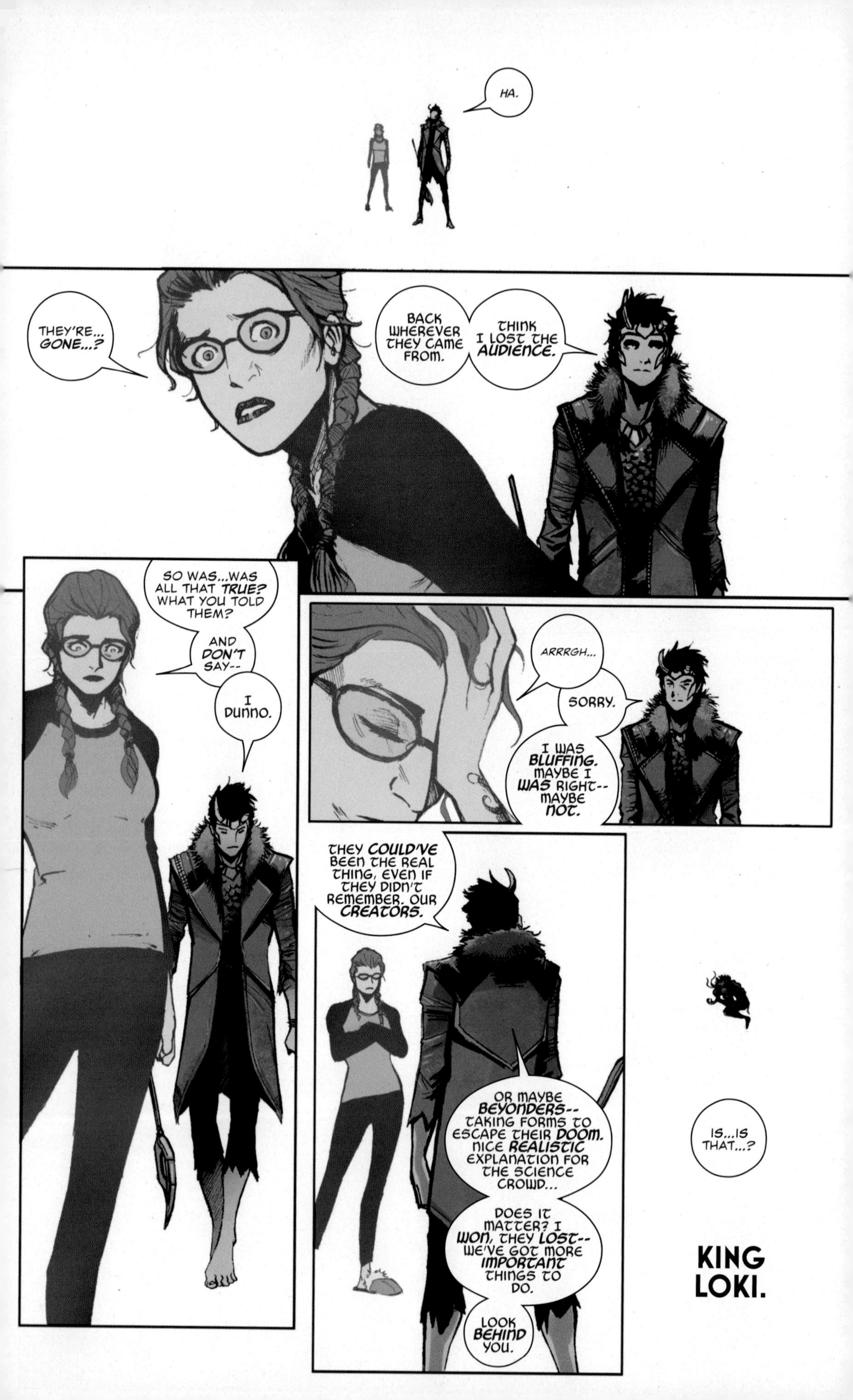
HA.
THEY'RE... GONE...?
BACK WHEREVER THEY CAME FROM.
THINK I LOST THE AUDIENCE.
SO WAS...WAS ALL THAT TRUE? WHAT YOU TOLD THEM?
AND DON'T SAY--
I DUNNO.
ARRRGH...
SORRY.
I WAS BLUFFING. MAYBE I WAS RIGHT--MAYBE NOT.
THEY COULD'VE BEEN THE REAL THING, EVEN IF THEY DIDN'T REMEMBER. OUR CREATORS.
OR MAYBE BEYONDERS--TAKING FORMS TO ESCAPE THEIR DOOM. NICE REALISTIC EXPLANATION FOR THE SCIENCE CROWD...
DOES IT MATTER? I WON, THEY LOST--WE'VE GOT MORE IMPORTANT THINGS TO DO.
LOOK BEHIND YOU.
IS...IS THAT...?
KING LOKI.

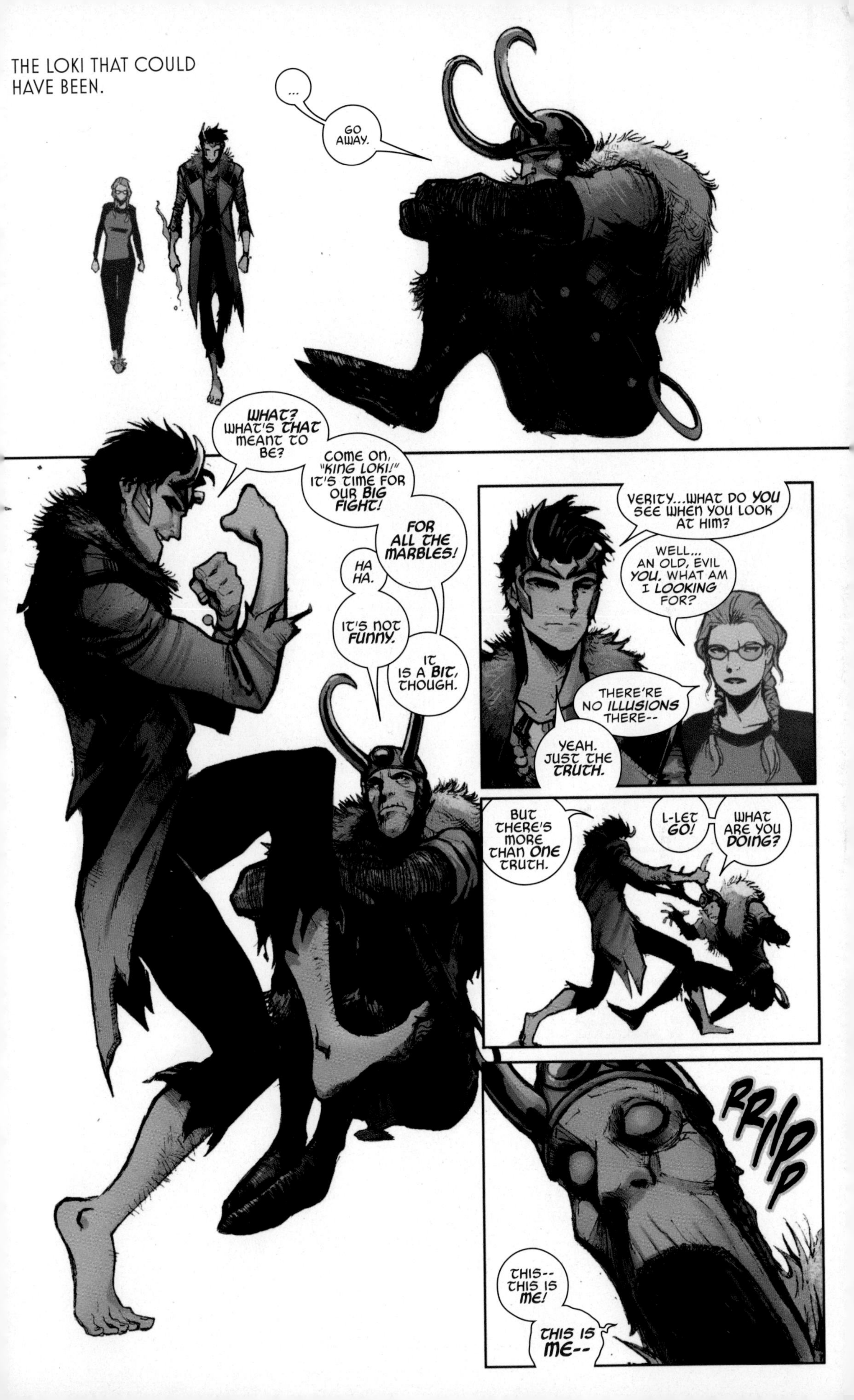
THE LOKI THAT COULD HAVE BEEN.
...
GO AWAY.
WHAT? WHAT'S THAT MEANT TO BE?
COME ON, "KING LOKI!" IT'S TIME FOR OUR BIG FIGHT!
FOR ALL THE MARBLES!
HA HA.
IT'S NOT FUNNY.
IT IS A BIT, THOUGH.
VERITY...WHAT DO YOU SEE WHEN YOU LOOK AT HIM?
WELL... AN OLD, EVIL YOU. WHAT AM I LOOKING FOR?
THERE'RE NO ILLUSIONS THERE--
YEAH. JUST THE TRUTH.
BUT THERE'S MORE THAN ONE TRUTH.
L-LET GO!
WHAT ARE YOU DOING?
RRIPP
THIS-- THIS IS ME!
THIS IS ME--

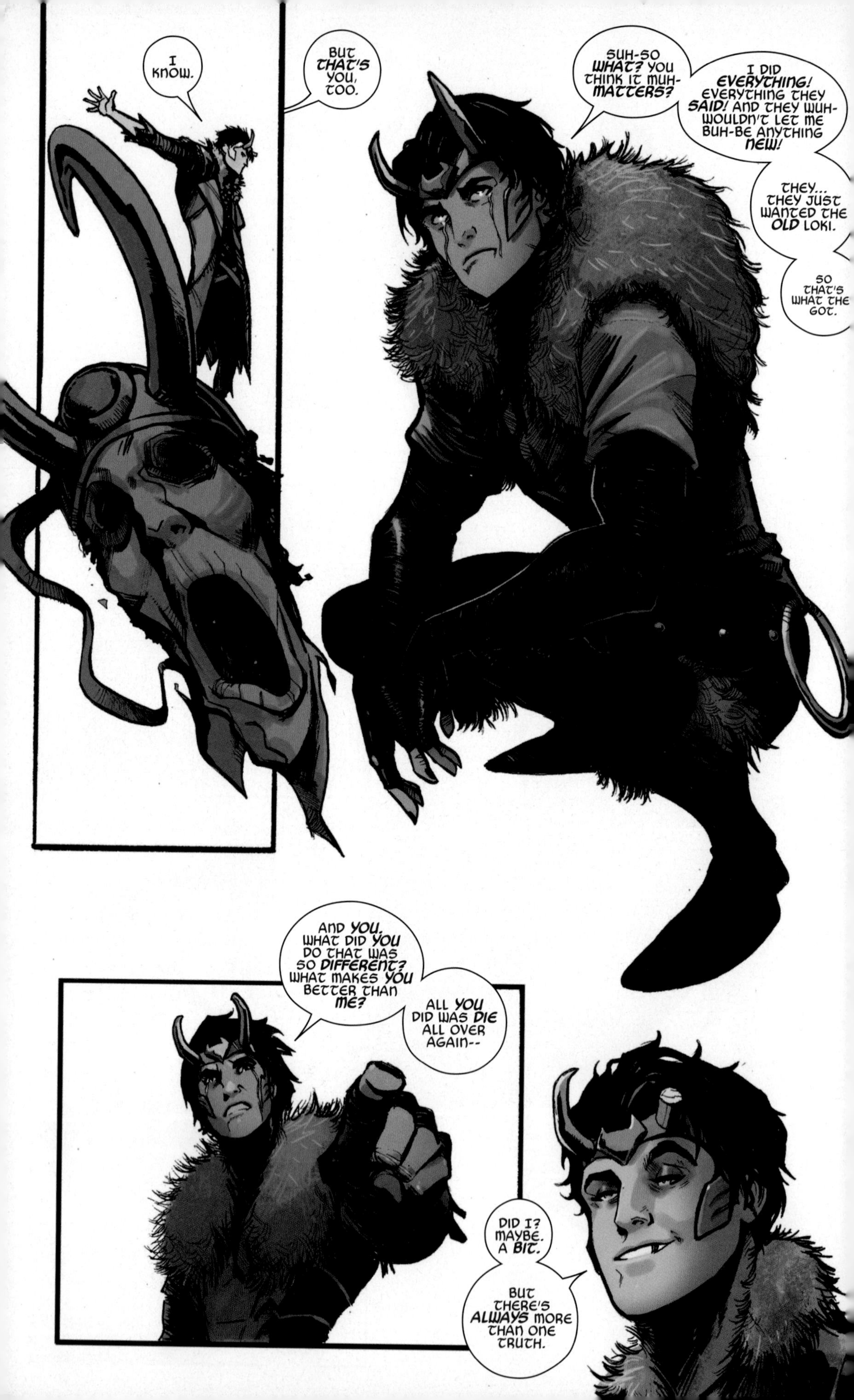
I KNOW.
BUT THAT'S YOU, TOO.
SUH-SO WHAT? YOU THINK IT MUH-MATTERS?
I DID EVERYTHING! EVERYTHING THEY SAID! AND THEY WUH-WOULDN'T LET ME BUH-BE ANYTHING NEW!
THEY... THEY JUST WANTED THE OLD LOKI.
SO THAT'S WHAT THE GOT.
AND YOU. WHAT DID YOU DO THAT WAS SO DIFFERENT? WHAT MAKES YOU BETTER THAN ME?
ALL YOU DID WAS DIE ALL OVER AGAIN--
DID I? MAYBE. A BIT.
BUT THERE'S ALWAYS MORE THAN ONE TRUTH.

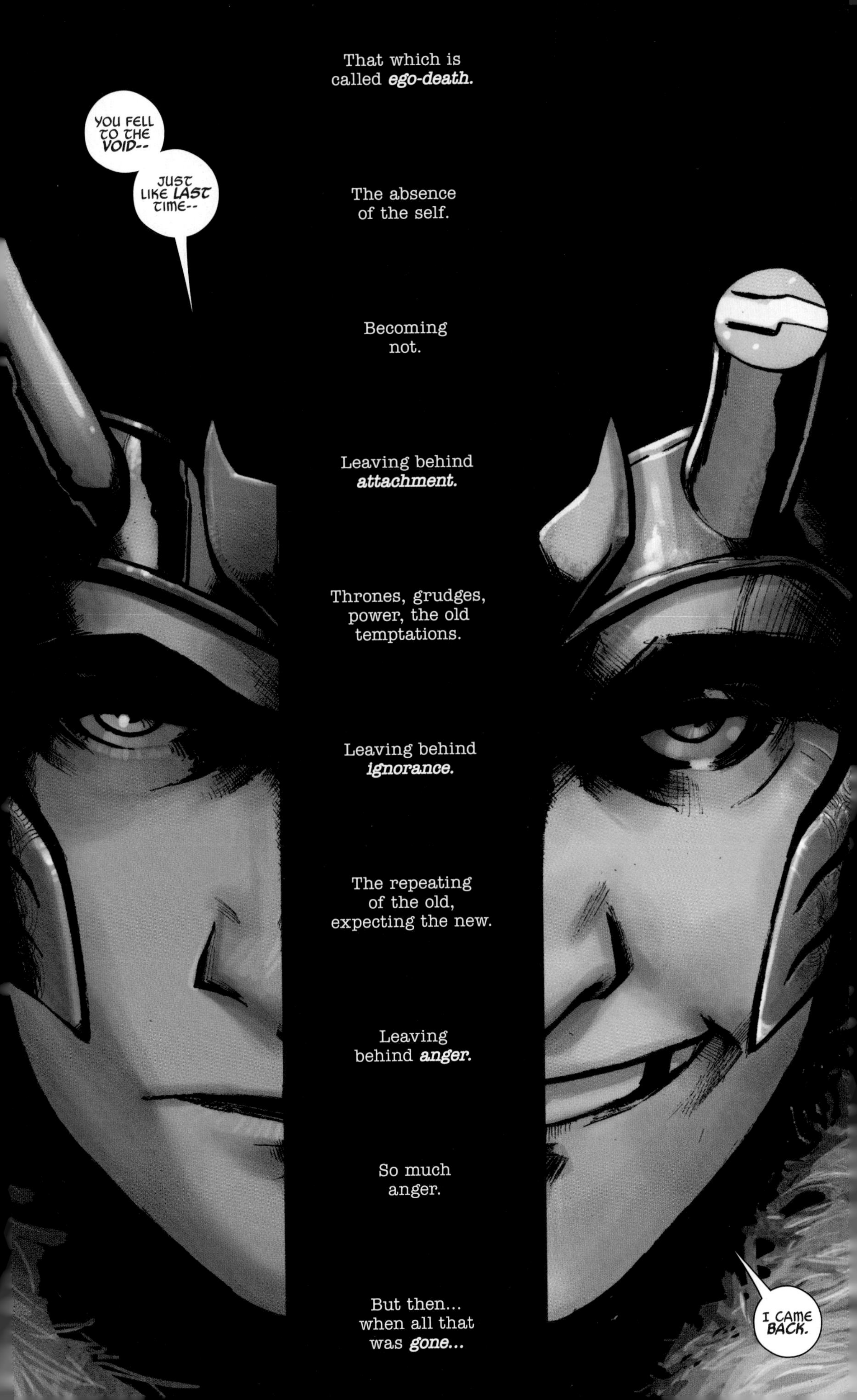
That which is called *ego-death.*
YOU FELL TO THE VOID--
JUST LIKE LAST TIME--
The absence of the self.
Becoming not.
Leaving behind *attachment.*
Thrones, grudges, power, the old temptations.
Leaving behind *ignorance.*
The repeating of the old, expecting the new.
Leaving behind *anger.*
So much anger.
But then... when all that was *gone...*
I CAME BACK.

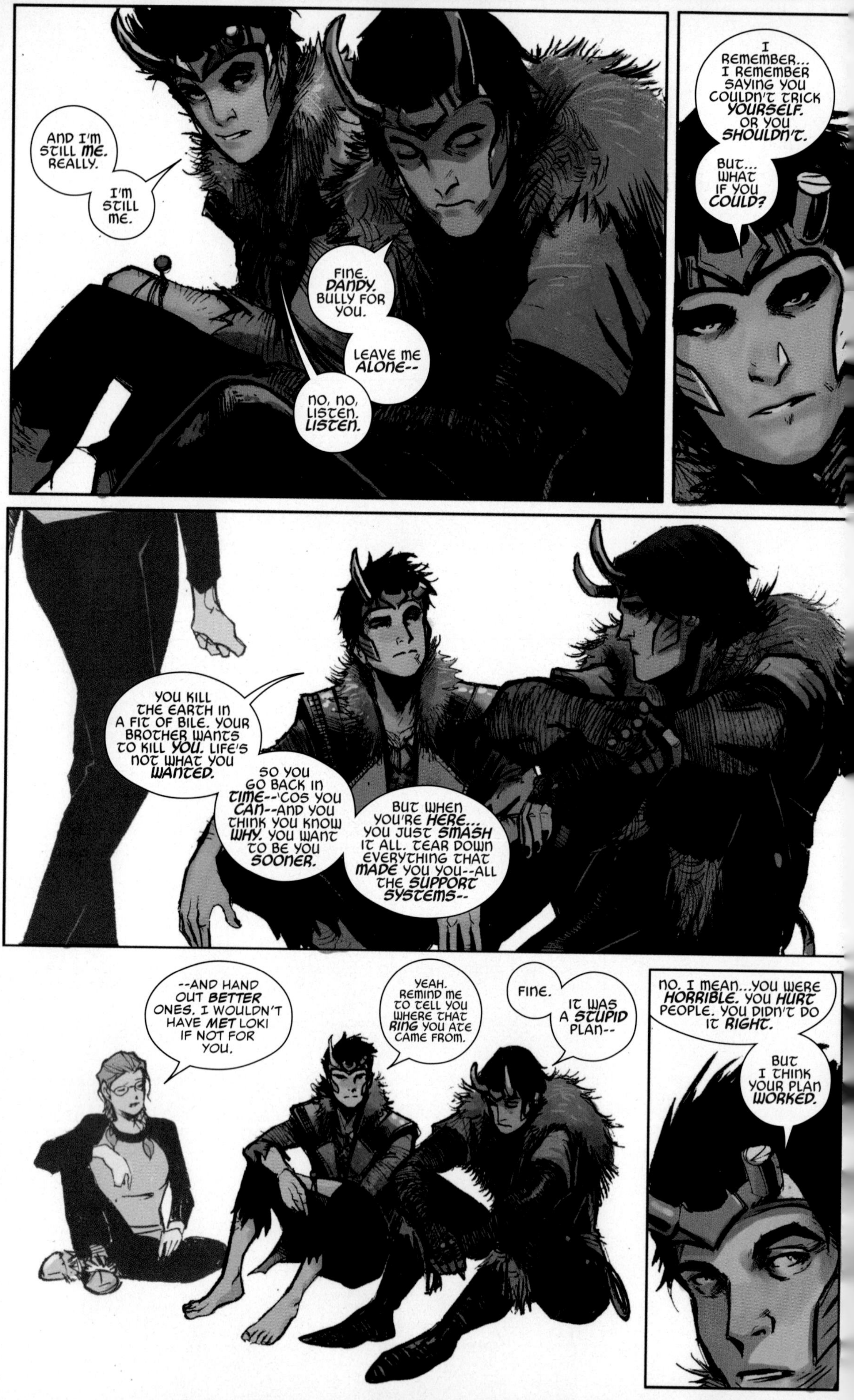
AND I'M STILL ME. REALLY.
I'M STILL ME.
FINE. DANDY. BULLY FOR YOU.
LEAVE ME ALONE--
NO, NO, LISTEN. LISTEN.
I REMEMBER... I REMEMBER SAYING YOU COULDN'T TRICK YOURSELF. OR YOU SHOULDN'T.
BUT... WHAT IF YOU COULD?
YOU KILL THE EARTH IN A FIT OF BILE. YOUR BROTHER WANTS TO KILL YOU. LIFE'S NOT WHAT YOU WANTED.
SO YOU GO BACK IN TIME--'COS YOU CAN--AND YOU THINK YOU KNOW WHY. YOU WANT TO BE YOU SOONER.
BUT WHEN YOU'RE HERE... YOU JUST SMASH IT ALL. TEAR DOWN EVERYTHING THAT MADE YOU YOU--ALL THE SUPPORT SYSTEMS--
--AND HAND OUT BETTER ONES. I WOULDN'T HAVE MET LOKI IF NOT FOR YOU.
YEAH. REMIND ME TO TELL YOU WHERE THAT RING YOU ATE CAME FROM.
FINE.
IT WAS A STUPID PLAN--
NO. I MEAN...YOU WERE HORRIBLE. YOU HURT PEOPLE. YOU DIDN'T DO IT RIGHT.
BUT I THINK YOUR PLAN WORKED.

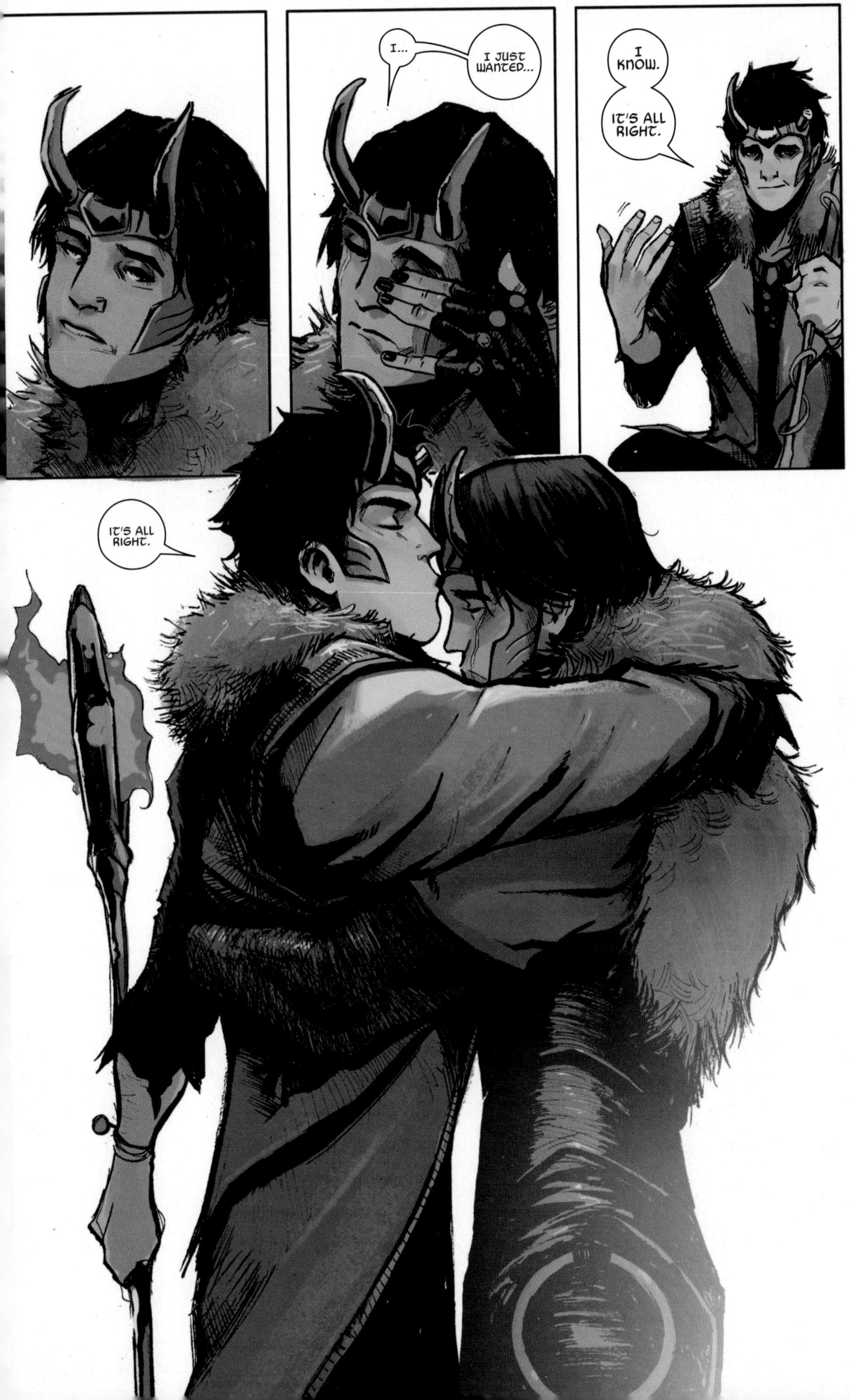
I...
I JUST WANTED...
I KNOW.
IT'S ALL RIGHT.
IT'S ALL RIGHT.

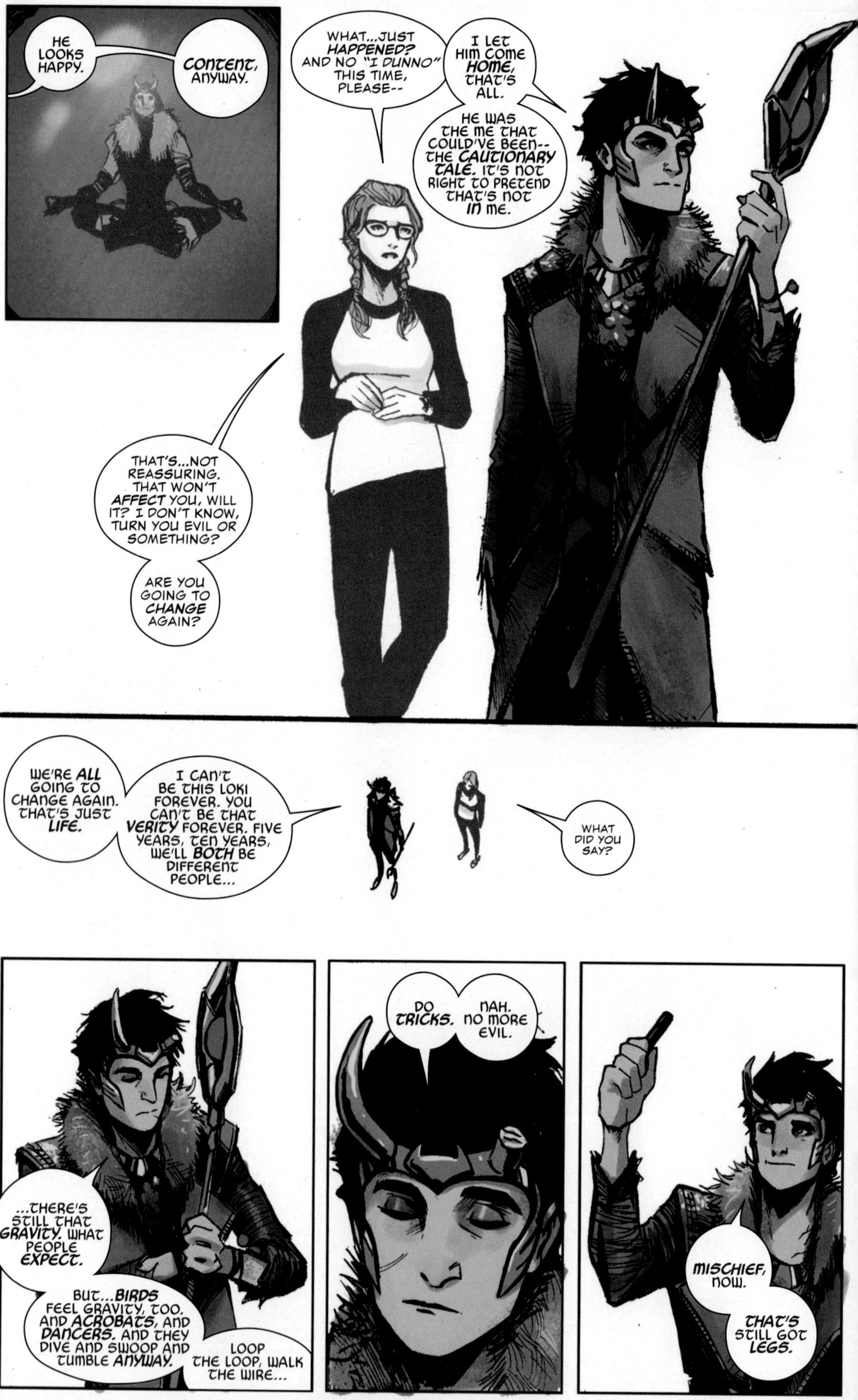
HE LOOKS HAPPY.
CONTENT, ANYWAY.
WHAT...JUST HAPPENED? AND NO "I DUNNO" THIS TIME, PLEASE--
I LET HIM COME HOME, THAT'S ALL.
HE WAS THE ME THAT COULD'VE BEEN-- THE CAUTIONARY TALE. IT'S NOT RIGHT TO PRETEND THAT'S NOT IN ME.
THAT'S...NOT REASSURING. THAT WON'T AFFECT YOU, WILL IT? I DON'T KNOW, TURN YOU EVIL OR SOMETHING?
ARE YOU GOING TO CHANGE AGAIN?
WE'RE ALL GOING TO CHANGE AGAIN. THAT'S JUST LIFE.
I CAN'T BE THIS LOKI FOREVER. YOU CAN'T BE THAT VERITY FOREVER. FIVE YEARS, TEN YEARS, WE'LL BOTH BE DIFFERENT PEOPLE...
WHAT DID YOU SAY?
...THERE'S STILL THAT GRAVITY. WHAT PEOPLE EXPECT.
BUT...BIRDS FEEL GRAVITY, TOO. AND ACROBATS, AND DANCERS. AND THEY DIVE AND SWOOP AND TUMBLE ANYWAY.
LOOP THE LOOP, WALK THE WIRE...
DO TRICKS.
NAH. NO MORE EVIL.
MISCHIEF, NOW.
THAT'S STILL GOT LEGS.

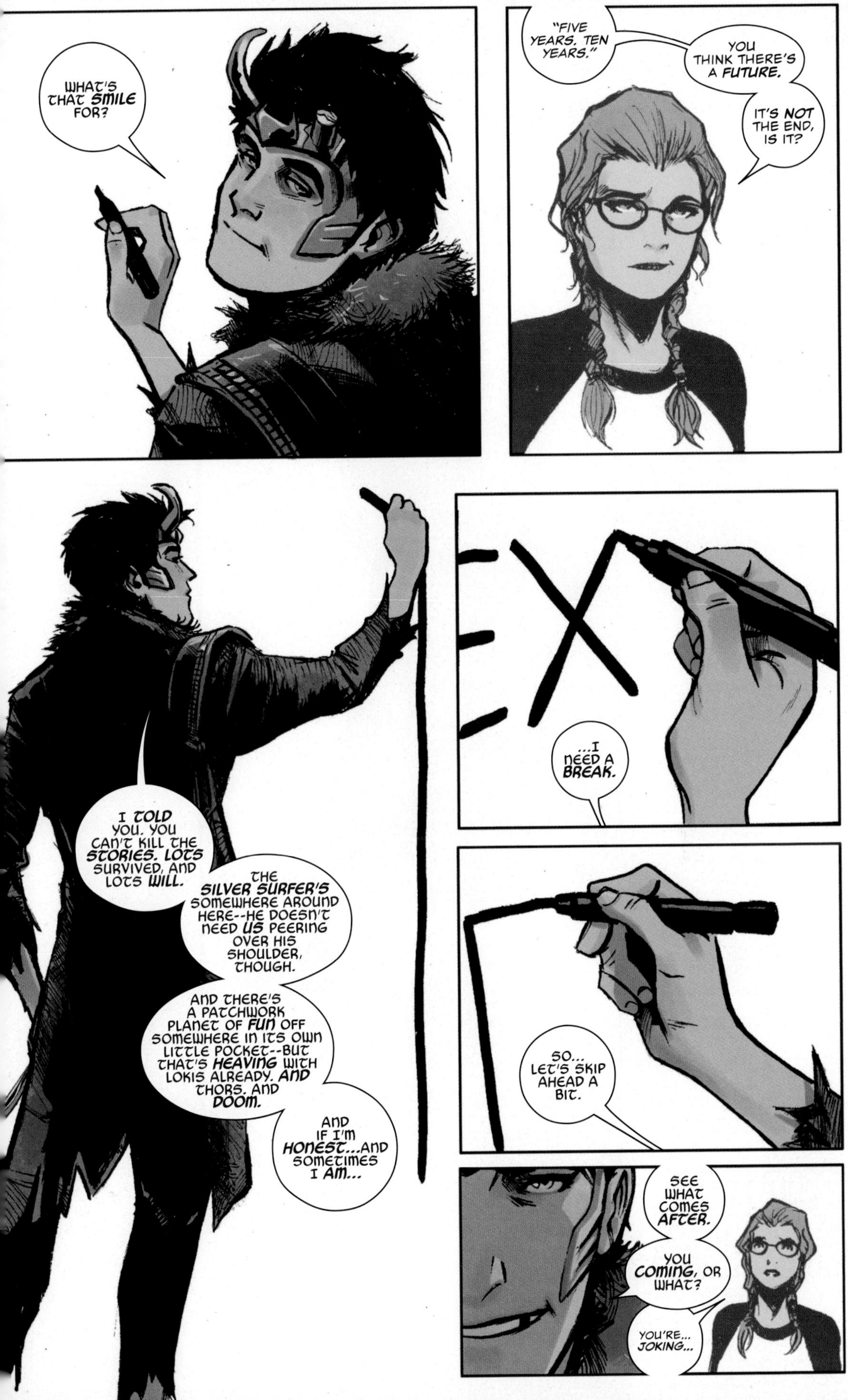
WHAT'S THAT SMILE FOR?
"FIVE YEARS. TEN YEARS."
YOU THINK THERE'S A FUTURE.
IT'S NOT THE END, IS IT?
I TOLD YOU. YOU CAN'T KILL THE STORIES. LOTS SURVIVED, AND LOTS WILL.
THE SILVER SURFER'S SOMEWHERE AROUND HERE--HE DOESN'T NEED US PEERING OVER HIS SHOULDER, THOUGH.
AND THERE'S A PATCHWORK PLANET OF FUN OFF SOMEWHERE IN ITS OWN LITTLE POCKET--BUT THAT'S HEAVING WITH LOKIS ALREADY. AND THORS. AND DOOM.
AND IF I'M HONEST...AND SOMETIMES I AM...
...I NEED A BREAK.
SO... LET'S SKIP AHEAD A BIT.
SEE WHAT COMES AFTER.
YOU COMING, OR WHAT?
YOU'RE... JOKING...

NEXT:

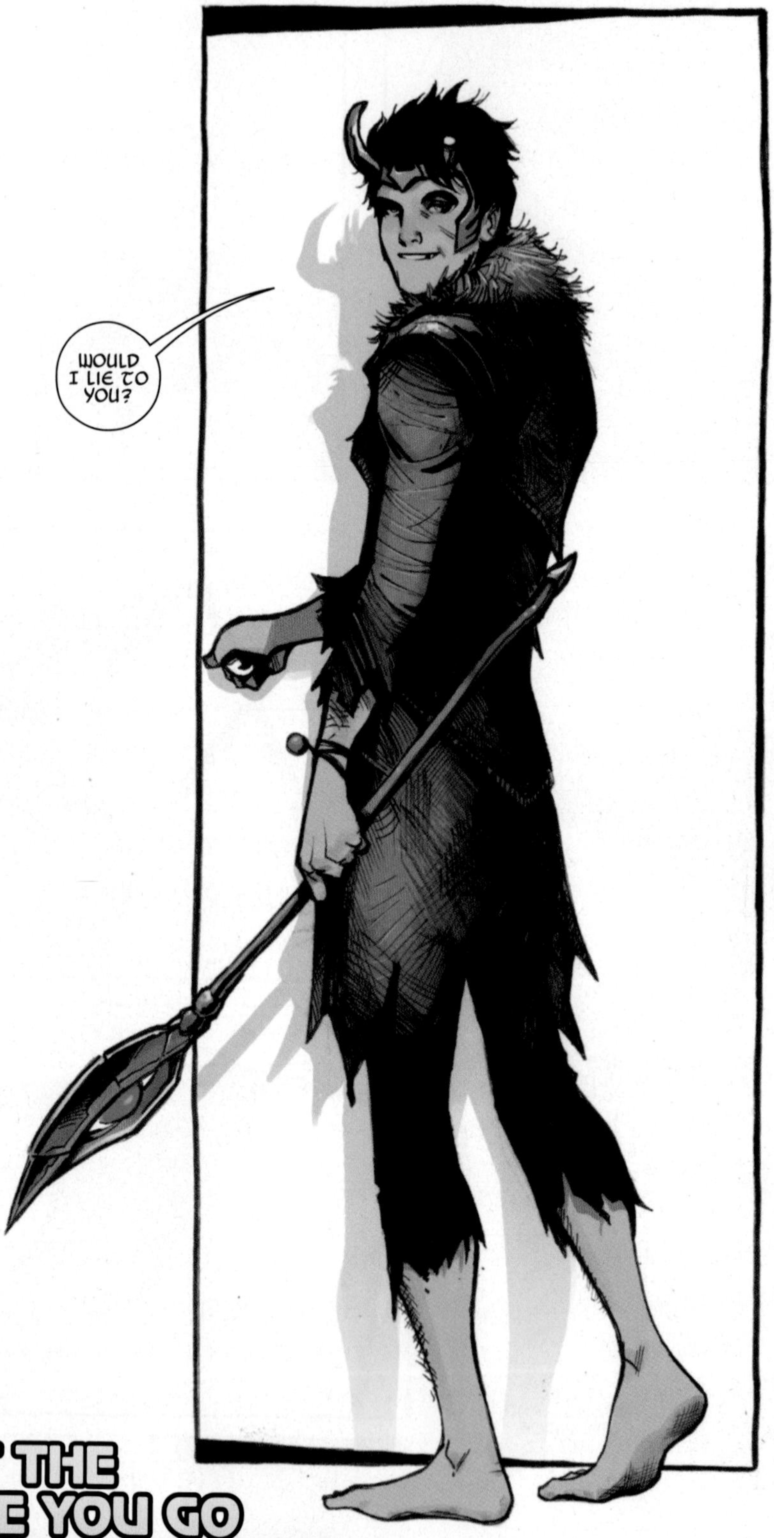
WOULD I LIE TO YOU?

OUT THE GATE YOU GO AND NEVER STOP

LOKI: AGENT OF ASGARD #6 COVER SKETCHES
by Lee Garbett

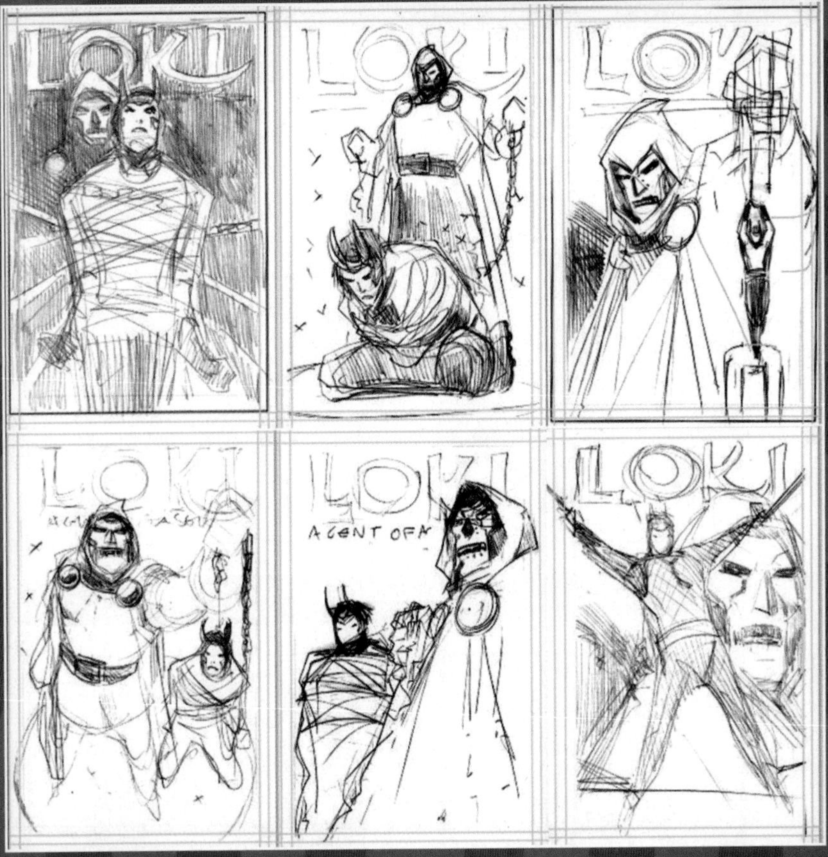
LOKI
AGENT OFA

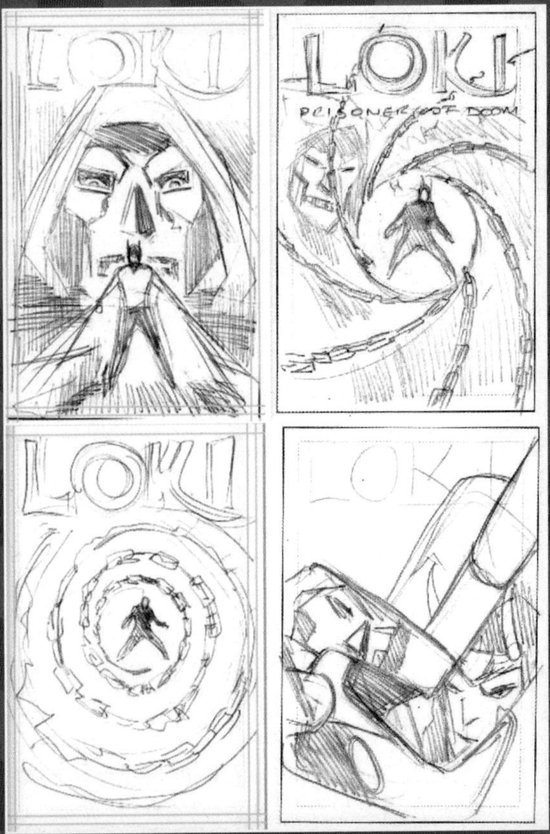
LOKI
PRISONER OF DOOM

LOKI: AGENT OF ASGARD #7 COVER SKETCHES
by Lee Garbett

1

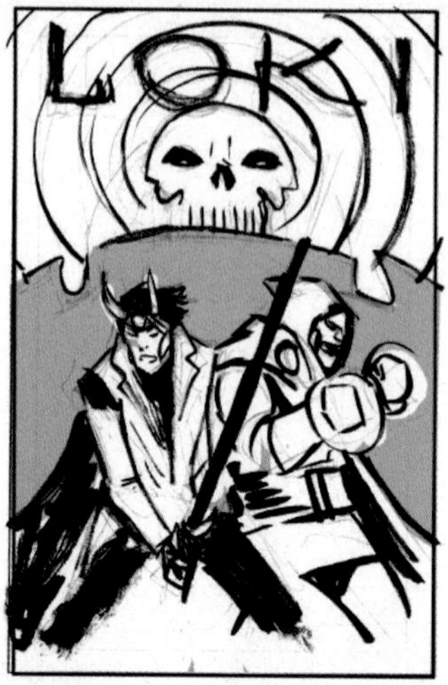
LOKI

2

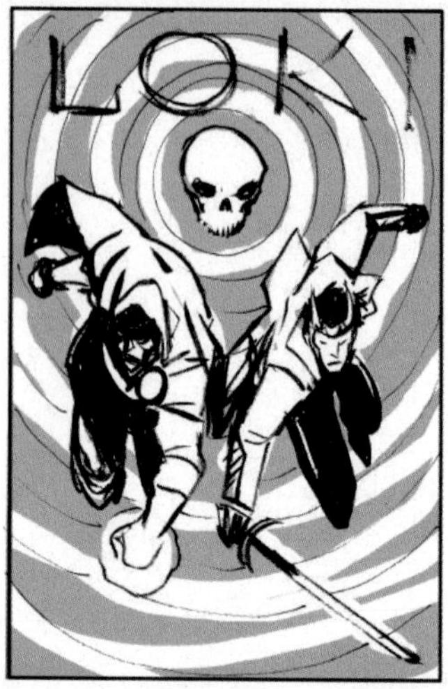
LOKI

3

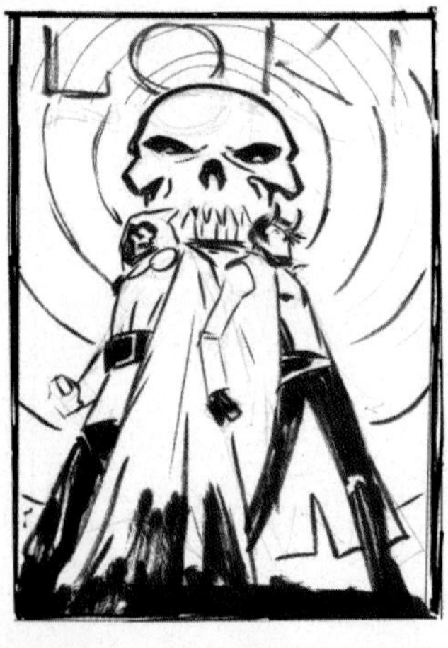

4

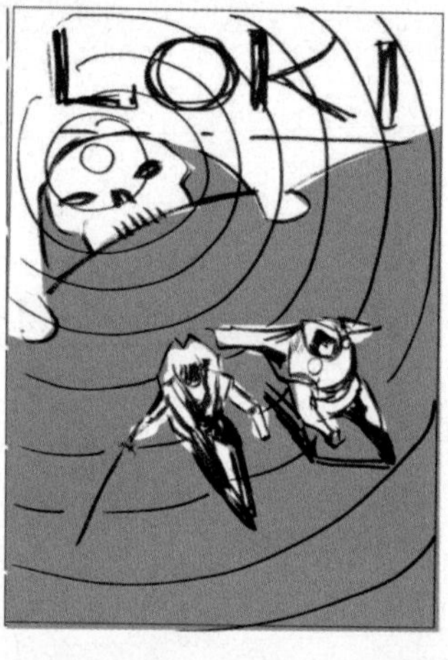
LOKI

5

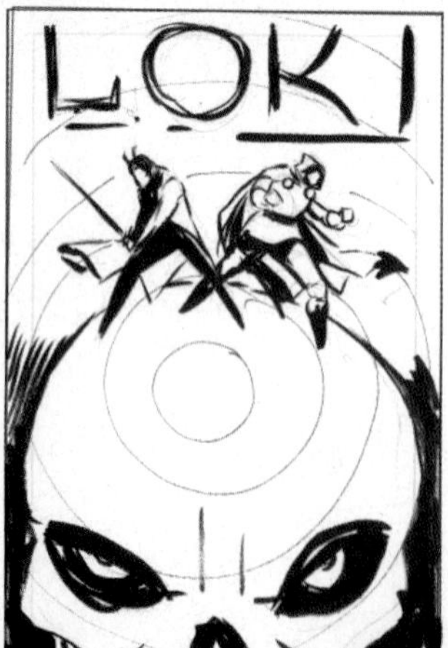
LOKI

6

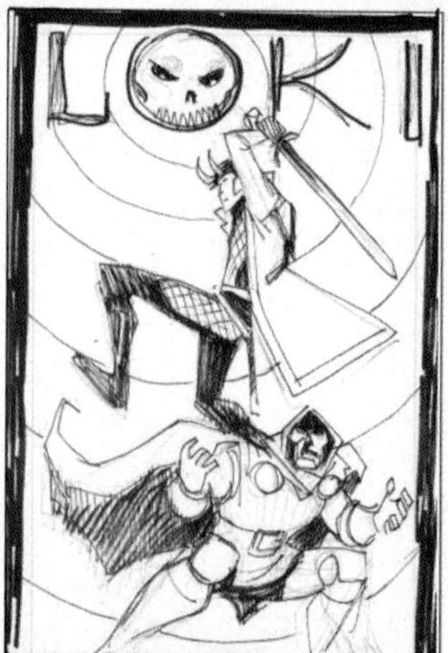

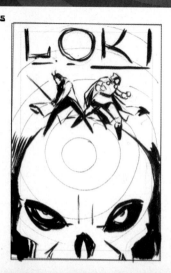

LOKI: AGENT OF ASGARD #7-8 COVER SKETCHES
by Lee Garbett

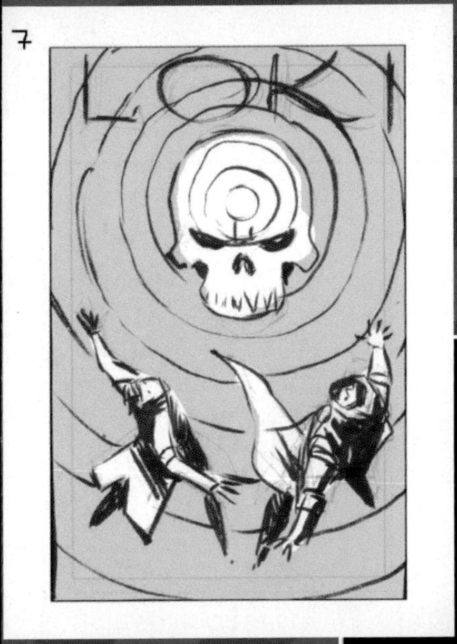
7
LOKI

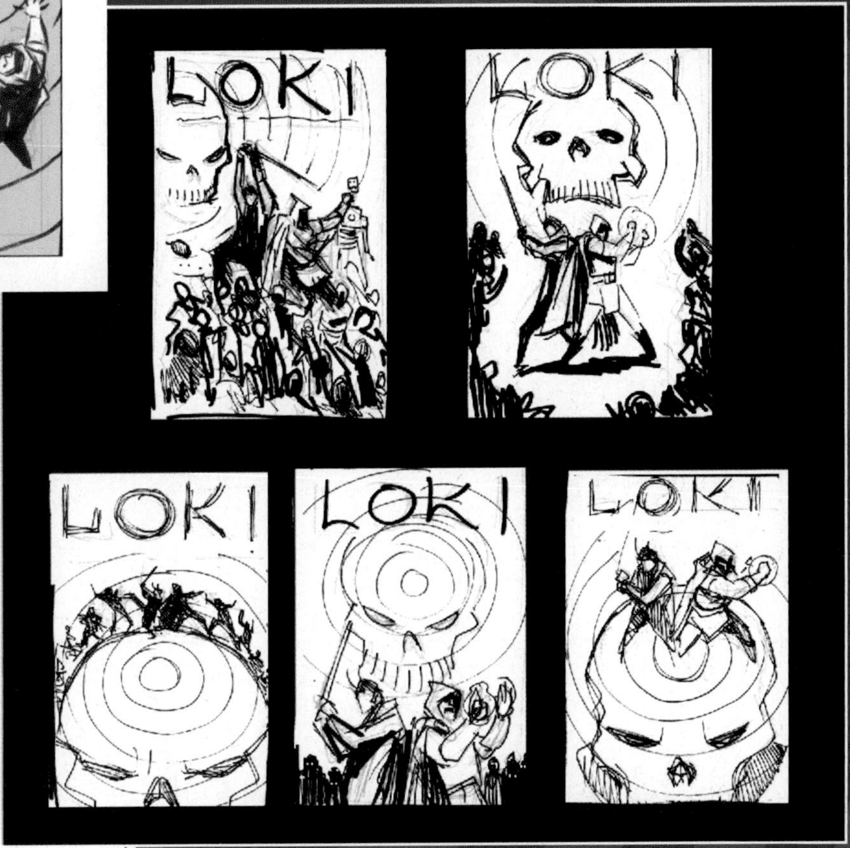
LOKI
LOKI
LOKI
LOKI
LOKI

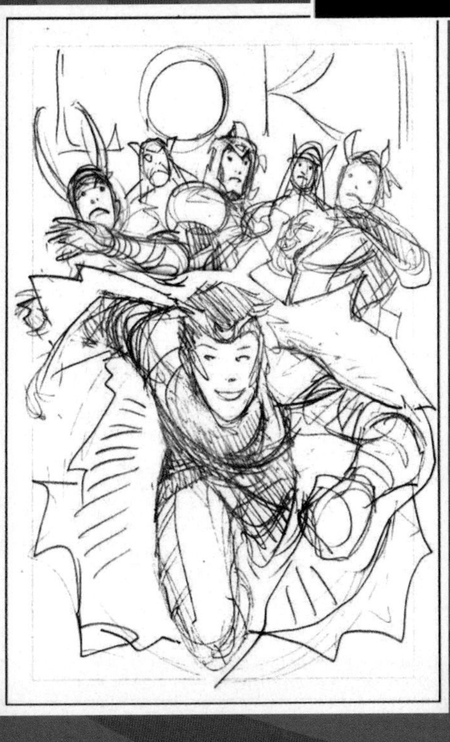
LOKI

LOKI: AGENT OF ASGARD #9 COVER SKETCHES
by Lee Garbett

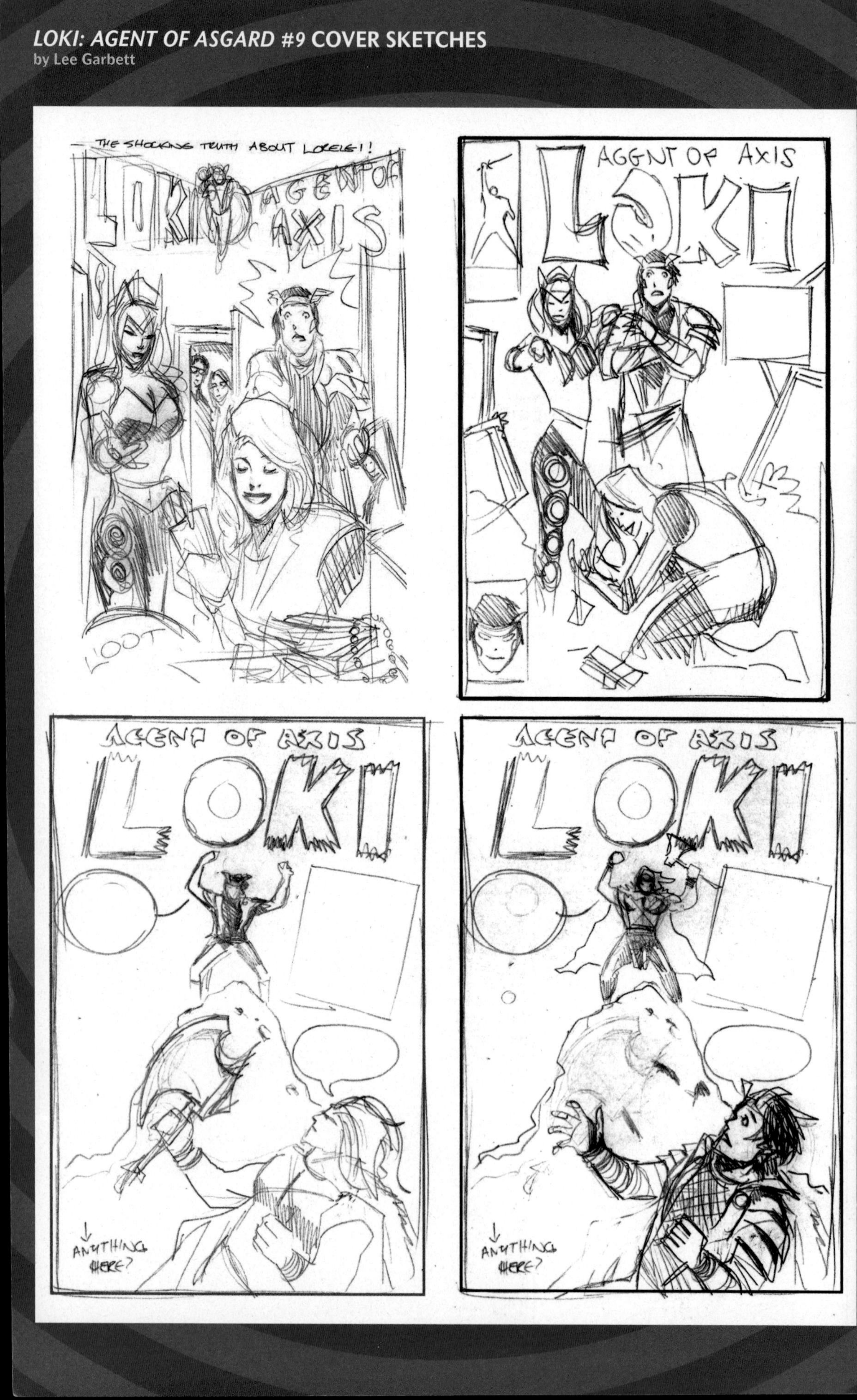
THE SHOCKING TRUTH ABOUT LORELEI!
LOKI AGENT OF AXIS
LOOT
AGENT OF AXIS
LOKI
AGENT OF AXIS
LOKI
ANYTHING HERE?
AGENT OF AXIS
LOKI
ANYTHING HERE?

LOKI: AGENT OF ASGARD #10 COVER SKETCHES

by Lee Garbett

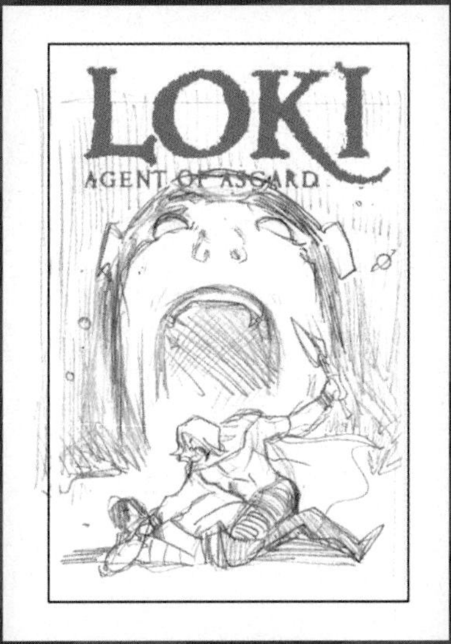
LOKI
AGENT OF ASGARD

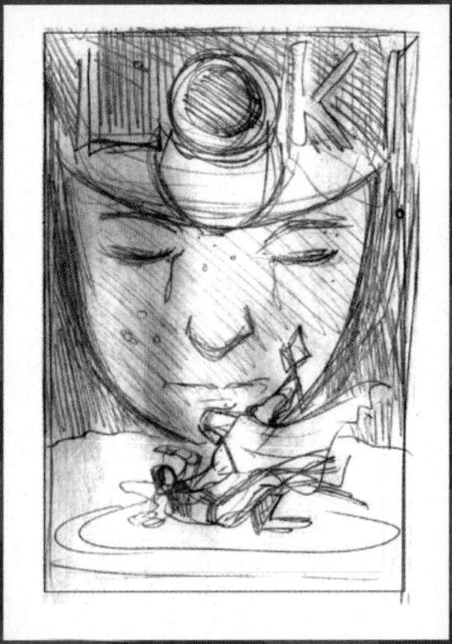
LOKI

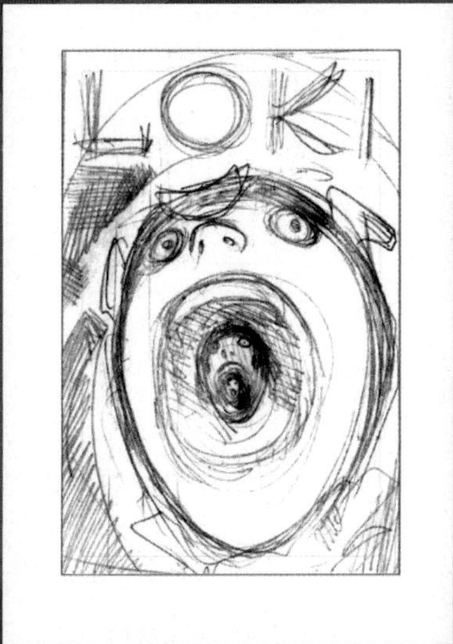
LOKI

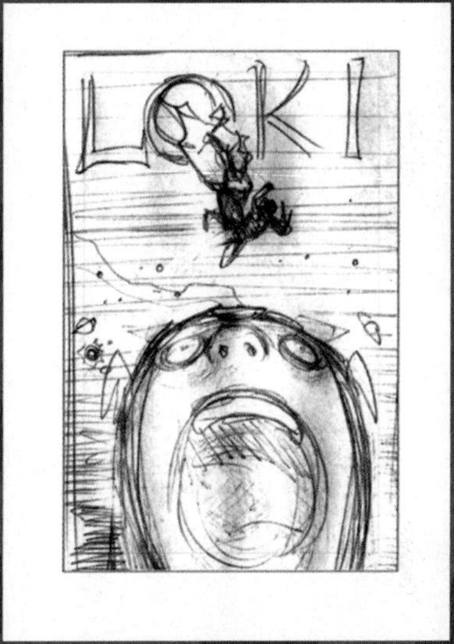
LOKI

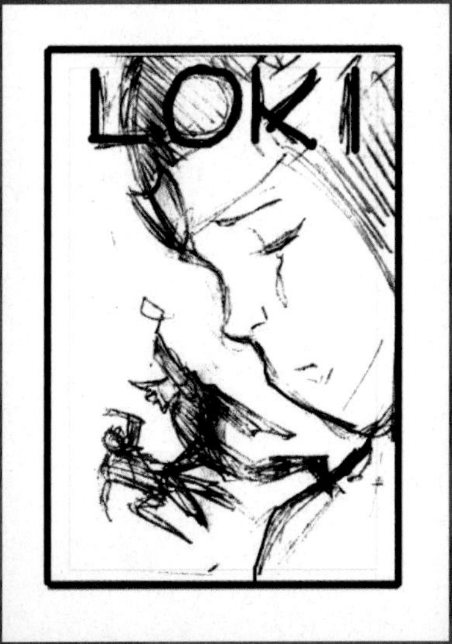
LOKI

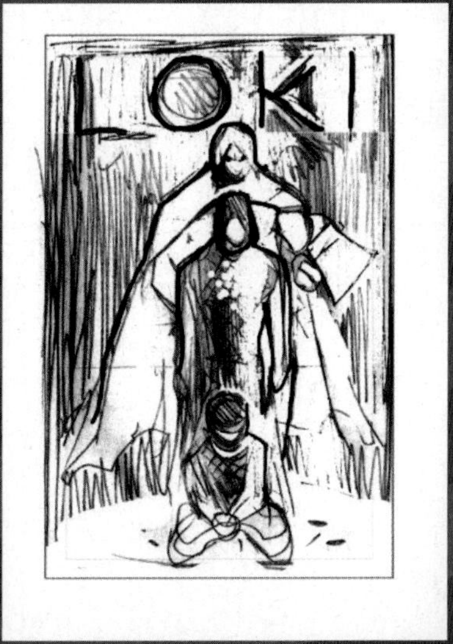
LOKI

LOKI: AGENT OF ASGARD #6 PAGES 10-13 LAYOUTS
by Jorge Coelho

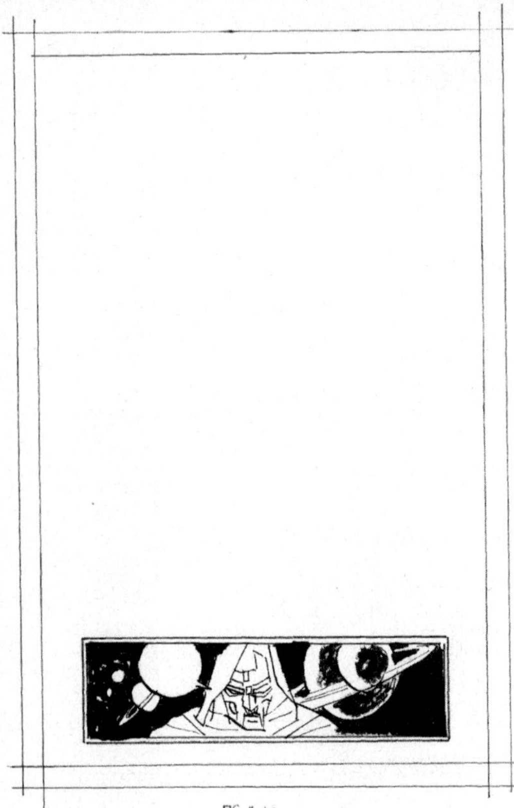

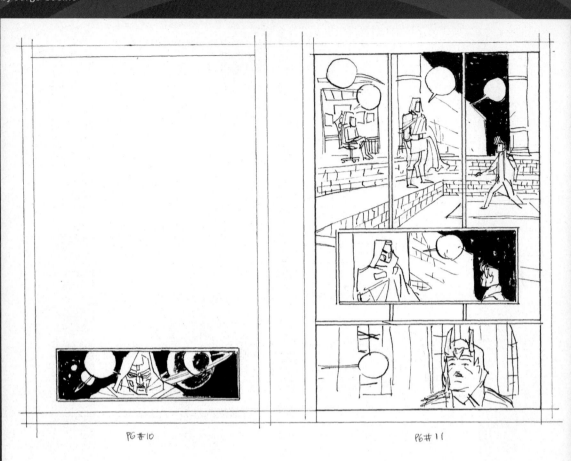

PG#10

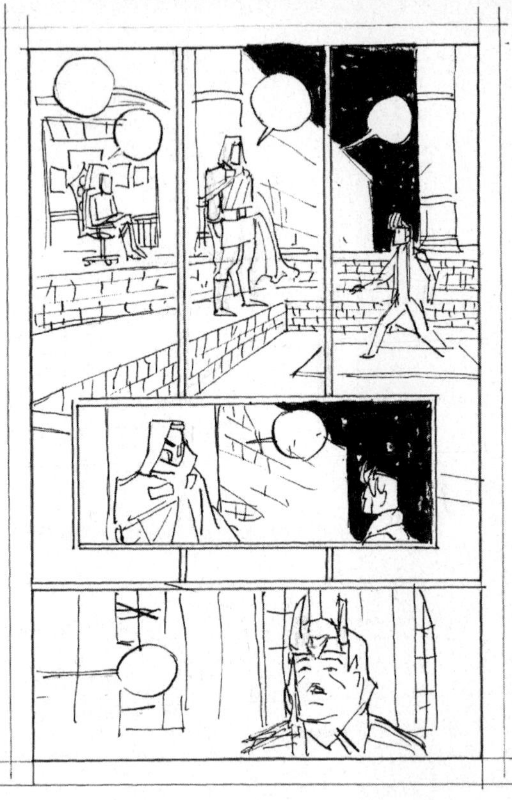

PG#11

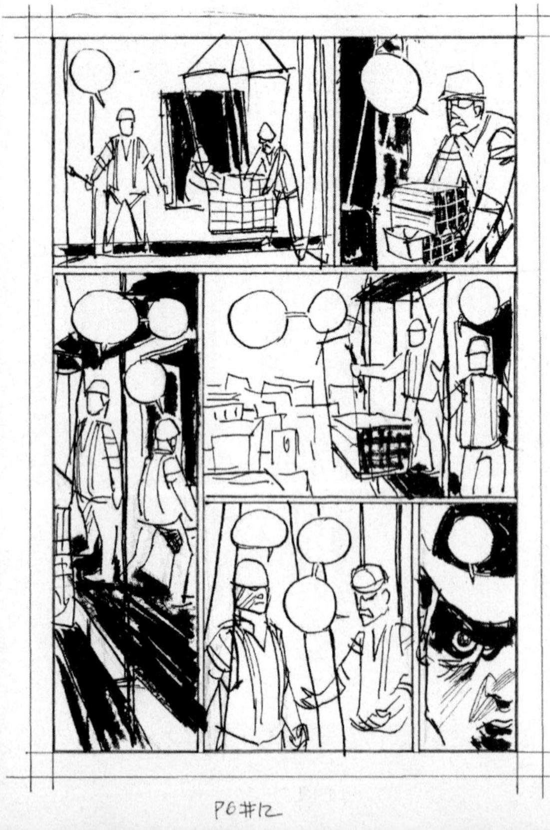

PG#12

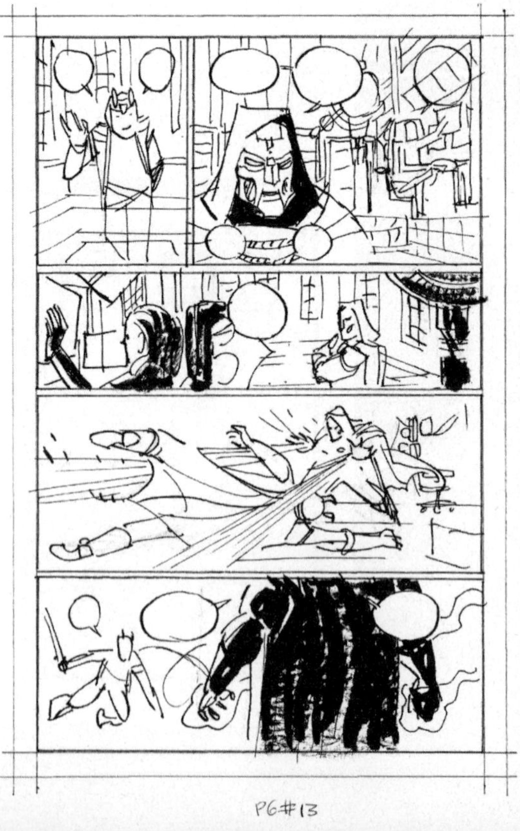

PG#13

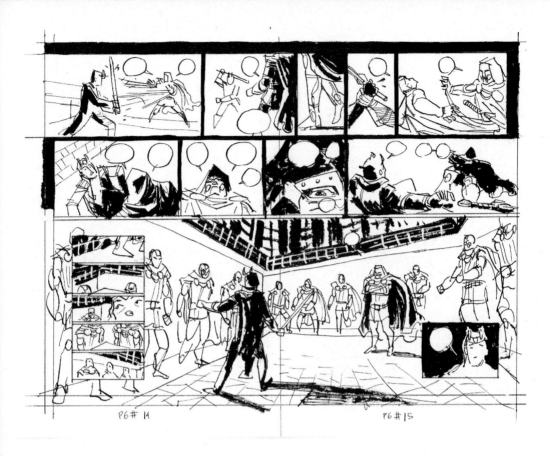

PG# 14   PG#15

PG #16

PG #17

LOKI: AGENT OF ASGARD #6, PAGES 18-2 LAYOUTS
by Jorge Coelho

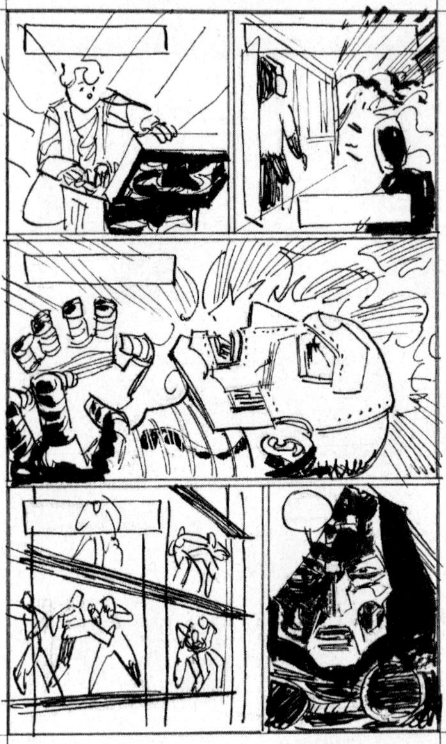

PG #18

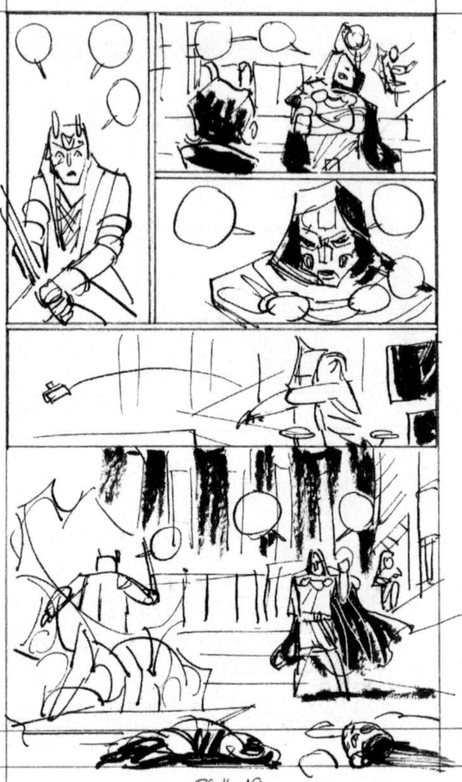

PG# 19

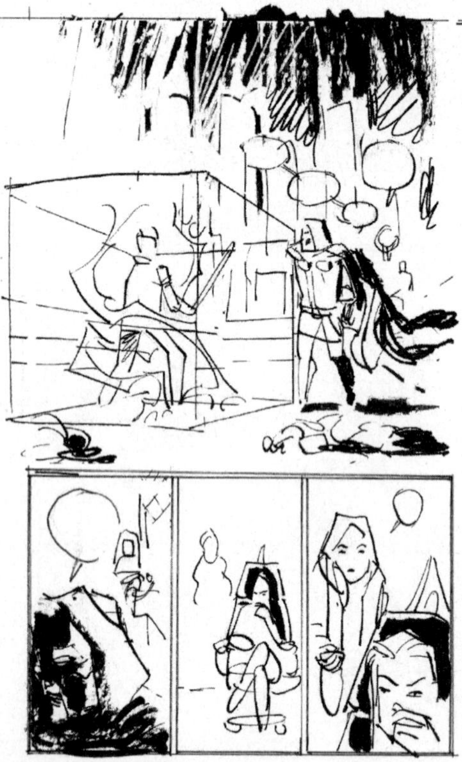

LOKI: AGENT OF ASGARD #7, PAGES 1-5 LAYOUTS
by Jorge Coelho

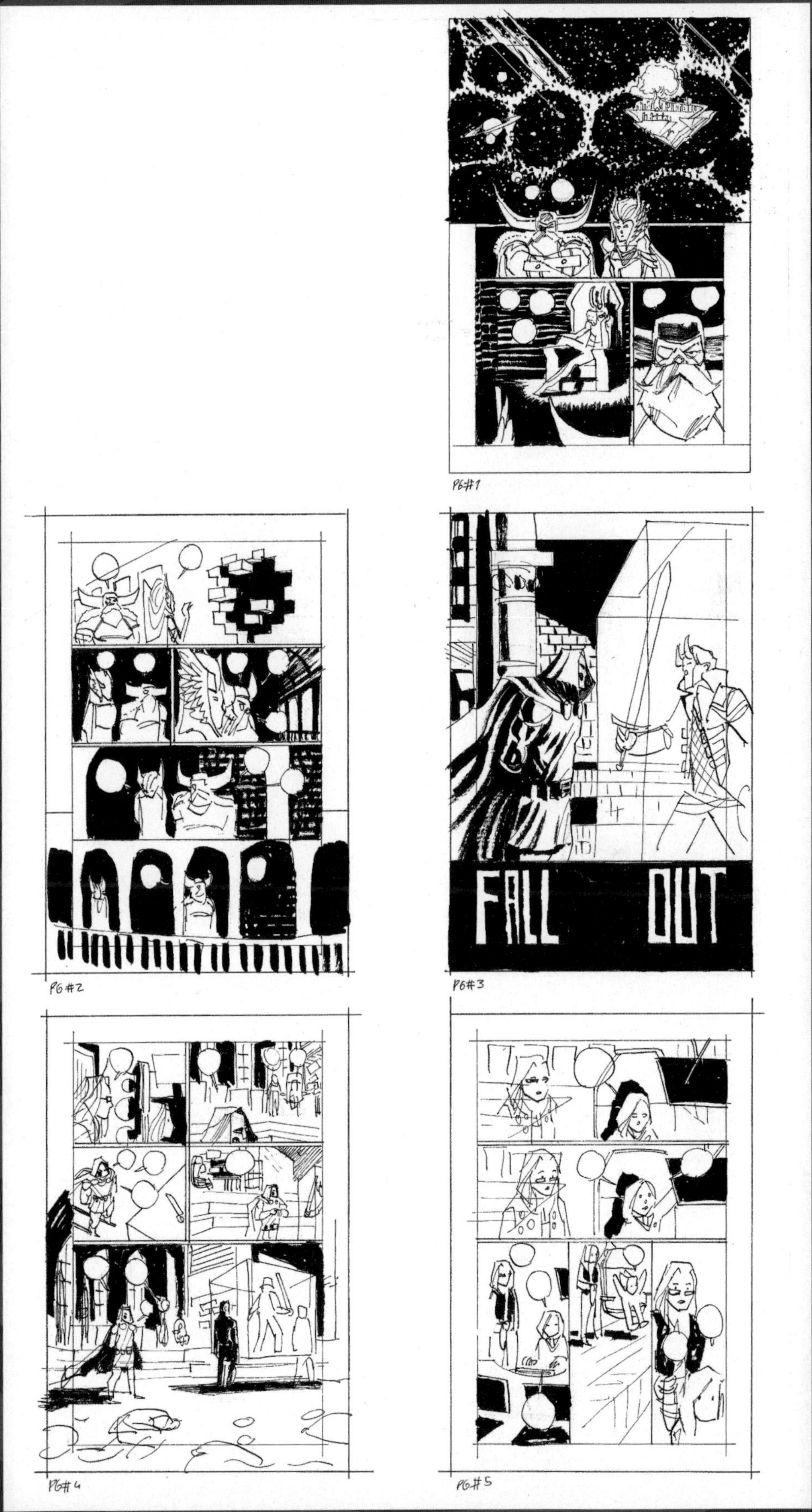
PG#1
PG#2
FALL OUT
PG#3
PG#4
PG#5

LOKI: AGENT OF ASGARD #7, PAGES 12-15 LAYOUTS

by Jorge Coelho

PG#6
PG# 7
PG#9
PG#11

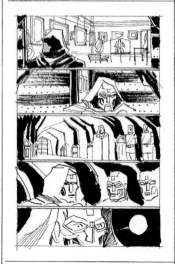

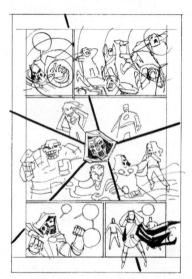

LOKI: AGENT OF ASGARD #7 PAGES 16-2 LAYOUTS
by Jorge Coelho

LOKi AGENT OF ASGARD #7, LAYOUTS #7

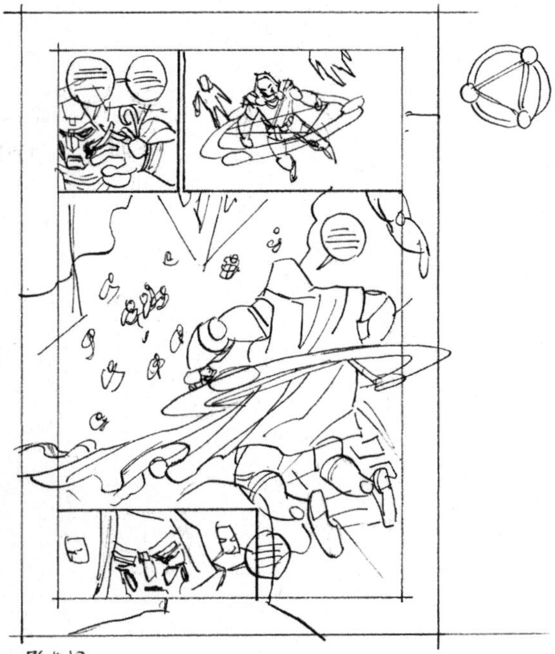

PG#12

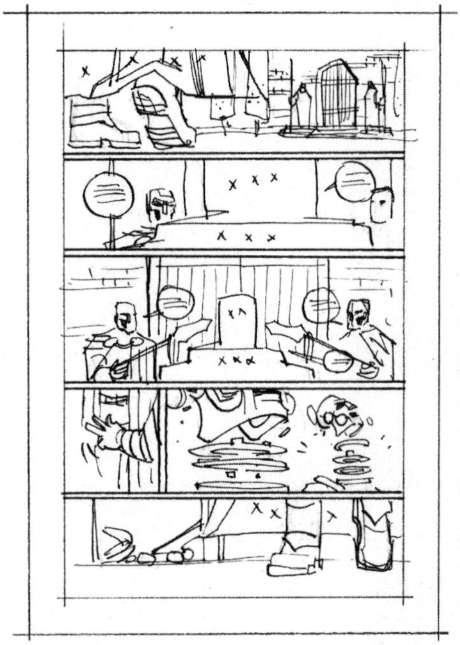

PG#13

LOKi AGENT OF ASGARD #7, LAYOUTS #8

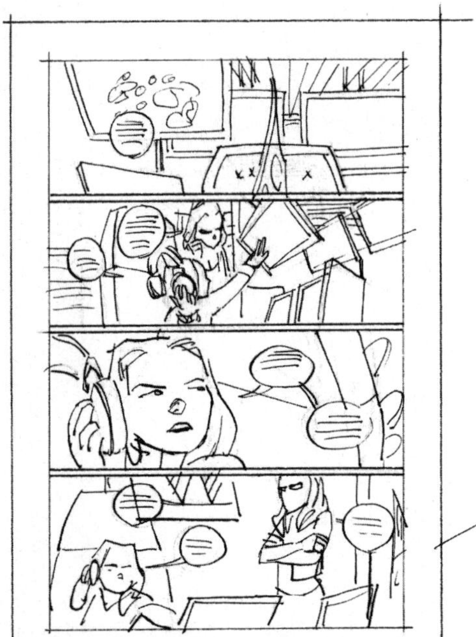

PG#14

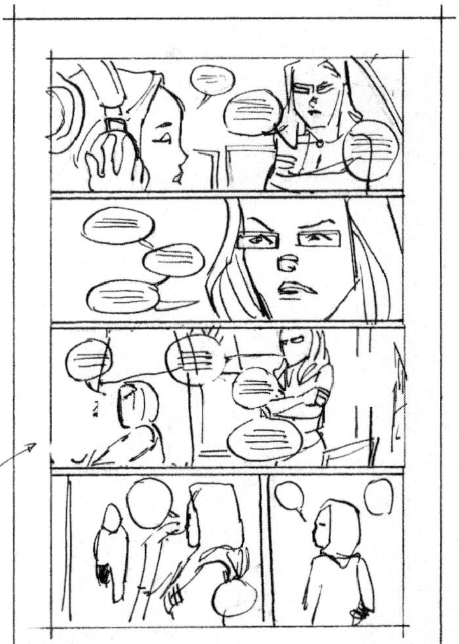

PG#15

LOKI: AGENT OF ASGARD #7, PAGES 16-20 LAYOUTS

by Jorge Coelho

LOKi AGENT OF ASGARd#7, LAYOUTS#9
PG#16
PG#17
LOKi AGENT OF ASGARd#7, LAYOUTS # 10
PG#18
PG#19
PG#20

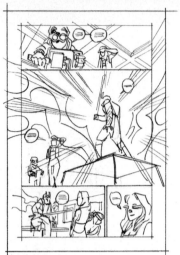

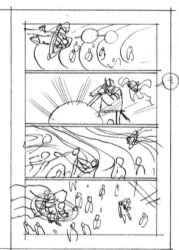

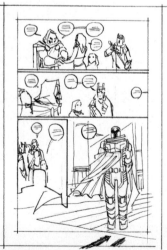

LOKI: AGENT OF ASGARD #9, PAGES 1-8 LAYOUTS
by Lee Garbett

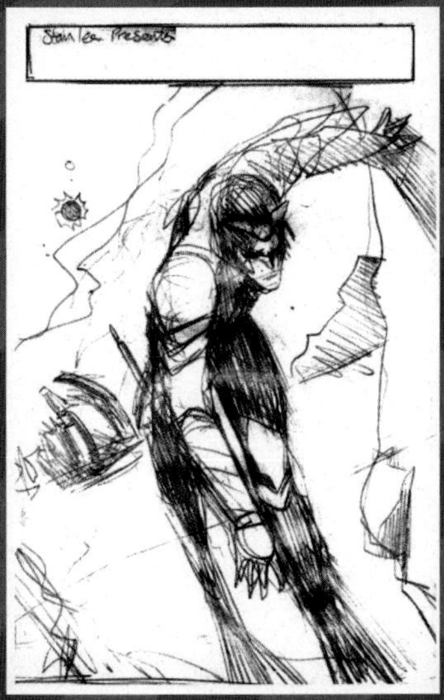
Stan Lee Presents

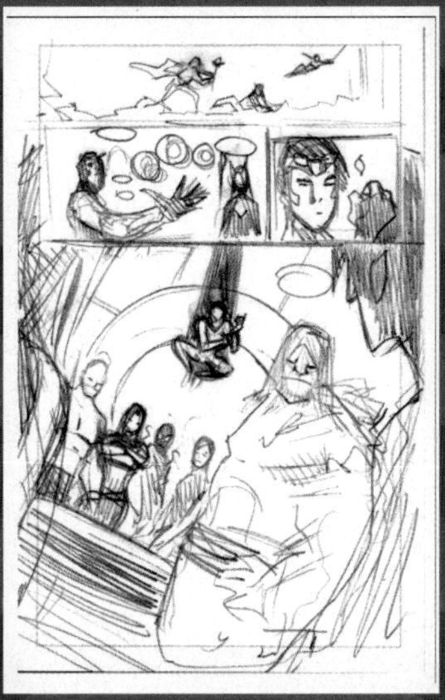

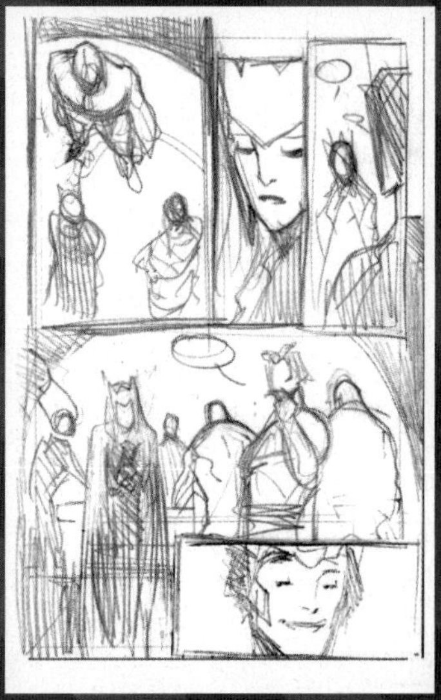

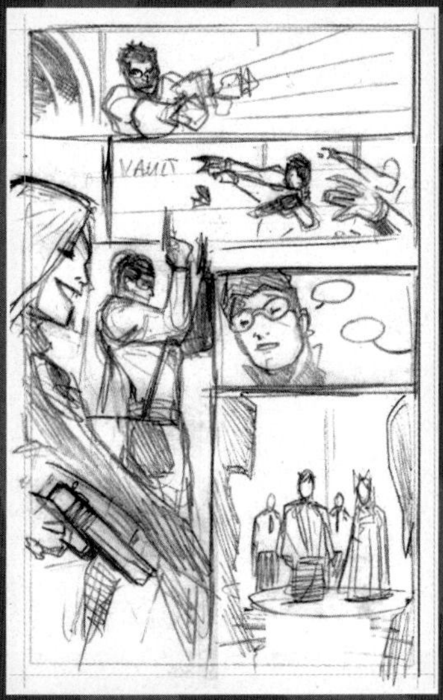
VAULT

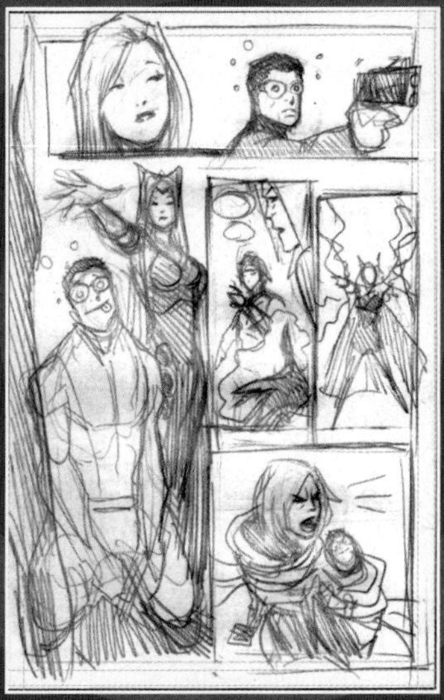

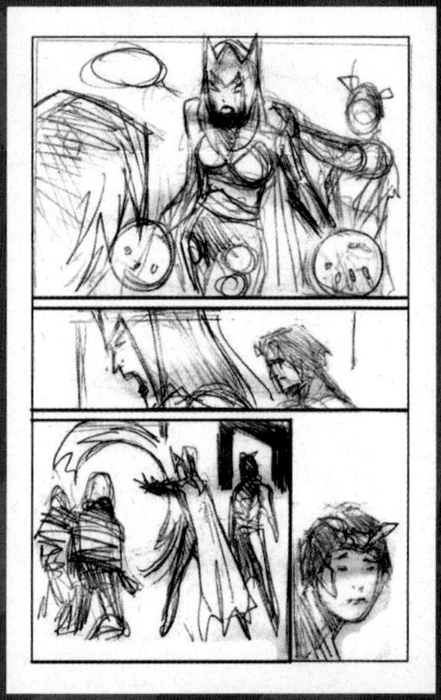

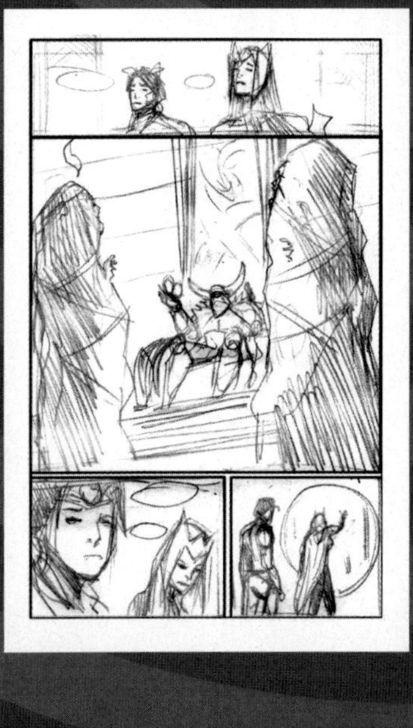

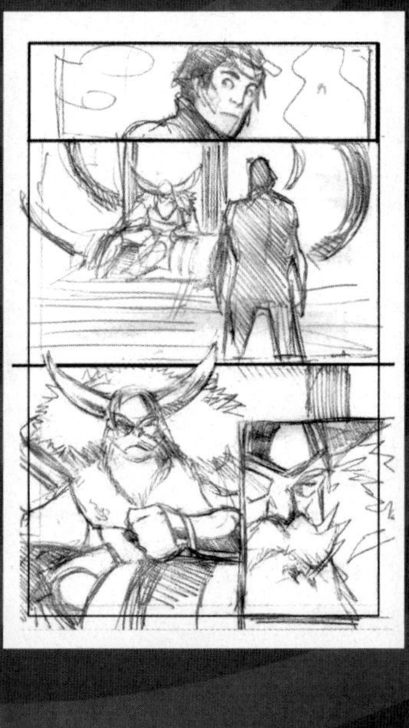

LOKI: AGENT OF ASGARD #9, PAGES 9-16 LAYOUTS
by Lee Garbett

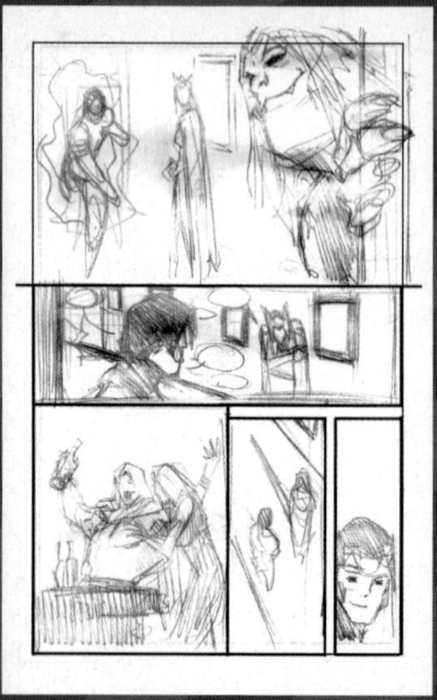

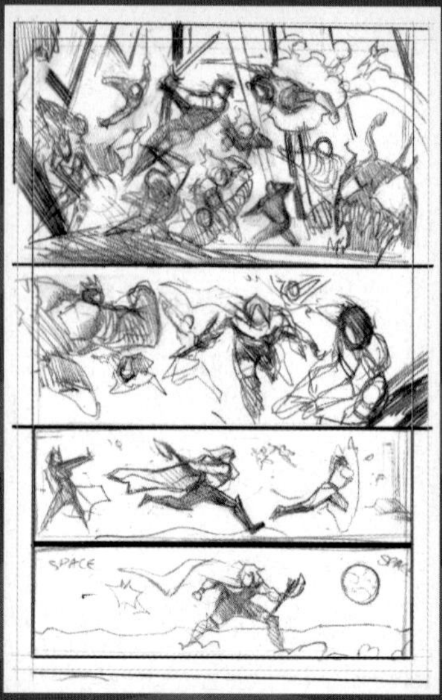
SPACE

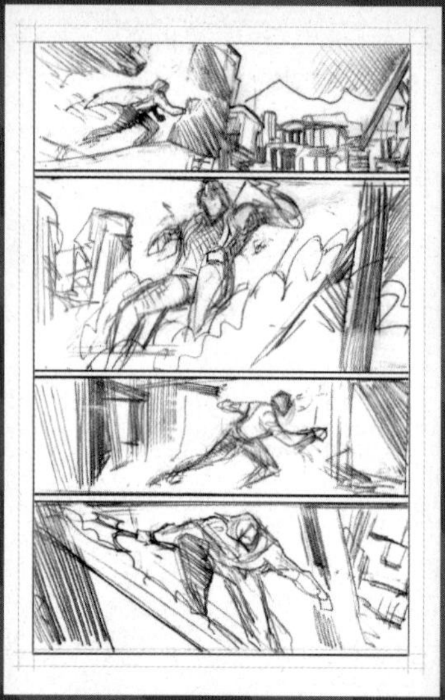

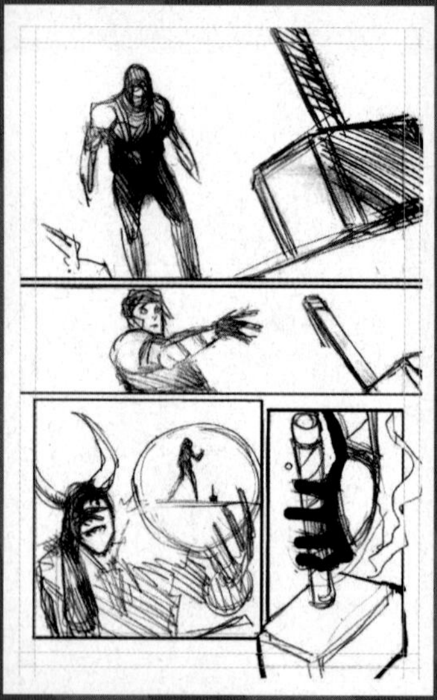

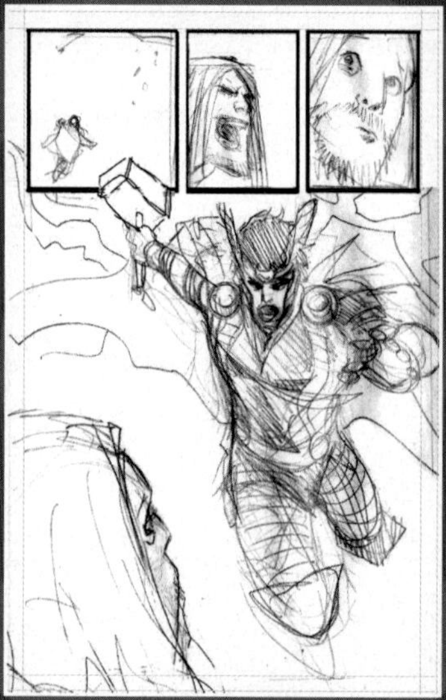

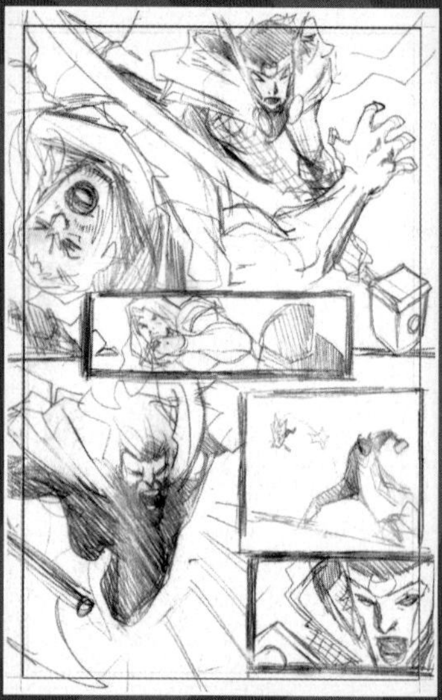

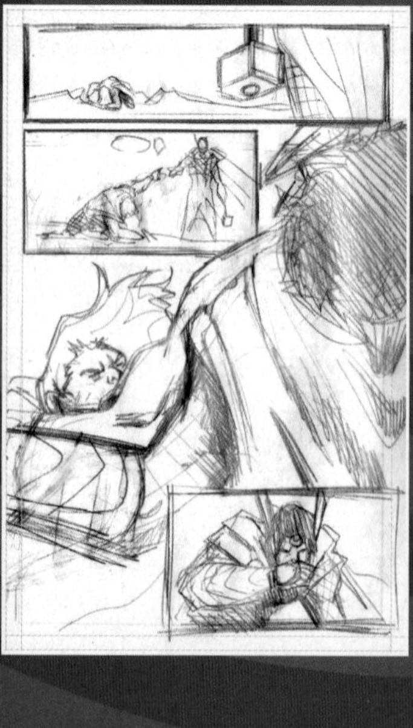

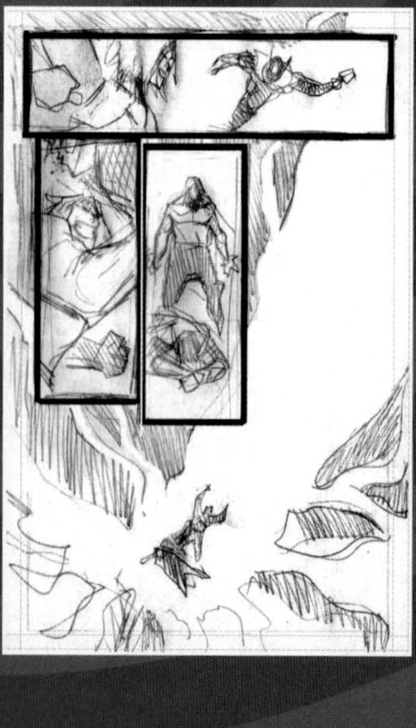

HERE'S LOKI-ING AT YOU

Send letters to MHEROES@MARVEL.COM. **Don't forget to mark "OKAY TO PRINT!"**

That's the title of this letter-column – until we die or YOU send us something better! While Lee and I and the rest of Team Loki cannot guarantee a response, every dreadful pun you send in will be groaned at by a panel of wincing experts. That's a promise – a LOKI promise! Trust us!

There's no letters to put in this column yet, mind – or none I've seen – so I thought I'd write a letter to YOU, dear reader. About Loki and my own experiences with him…

…which probably date back to roughly 1985 or so. Readers of MIGHTY AVENGERS will be familiar with this period – I was seven or eight years old, there was a newsagent next to a barber shop, and every time I got taken for a haircut I got to buy a couple of American comics.

So Walt Simonson's Loki was My First Loki – and that's a pretty good Loki to start on, you've got to admit. A swaggering, sneering rake, horns trimmed back and a cunning plan in every pocket – there's a sequence in which he tricks a pacifist Balder into chopping his head off, just for a laugh, which sticks firmly in my mind as particularly Loki-esque.

But in terms of this book, the standout issue was probably THOR #353 – the death of Odin. Now, I can't honestly swear to have read this when I was eight – this was before I knew what comic shops or back issues were, so if you missed an issue you just put up with it – but I definitely read it later. And there's that one moment, when Odin's making his final stand against Surtur, and Thor and Loki are at his side, and they all yell out their battle-cry…

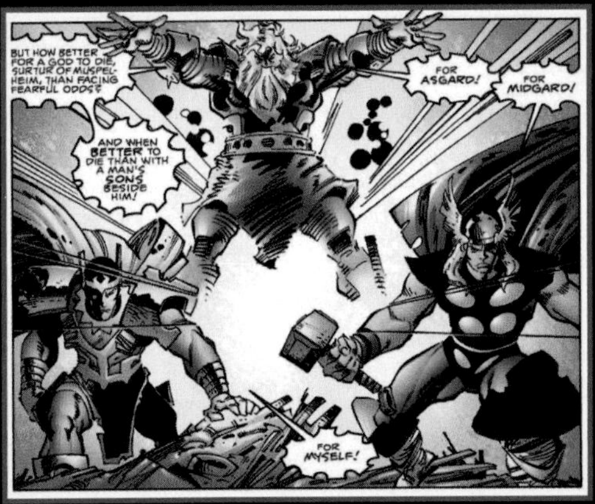
BUT HOW BETTER FOR A GOD TO DIE, SURTUR OF MUSPELHEIM, THAN FACING FEARFUL ODDS?
AND WHEN BETTER TO DIE THAN WITH A MAN'S SONS BESIDE HIM!
FOR ASGARD!
FOR MIDGARD!
FOR MYSELF!

It's a comedy moment, obviously. It's meant to show how selfish and venal Loki is – that even in this hour of peril, he's got nothing to swear himself to but his own skin.

But… when the whole of your reality would rather see you as someone you're not anymore…when the whole universe wants to crush you down into a little box with a label on it and nail the lid down…when your self' is a thing you have to fight the very cosmos to decide…

…well, suddenly it's not quite so funny.

Suddenly, it's almost kind of…heroic?

Uh-oh.

Welcome to LOKI: AGENT OF ASGARD – a comic about being For Yourself. And also about swordfights, espionage, casino heists, giant otters, speed dating and dragon-fighting, all beautifully delineated by art supremo "Lovely" Lee Garbett, a man who clearly "gets" Loki in a way that's hard to define but is – I think Loki fans will agree – extremely easy to appreciate.

Join us, why don't you?

- Al Ewing

P.S. If you're reading this after seeing that last page… no, we're not telling.

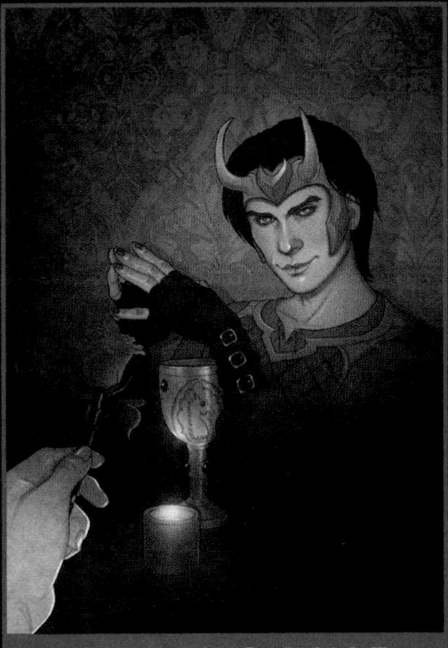

ISSUE #2 ON SALE MARCH 5, 2014!

LOKI: AGENT OF ASGARD #17 AFTERWORD

by Al Ewing & Lee Garbett

HERE'S LOKI-ING AT YOU

Send letters to MHEROES@MARVEL.COM. Don't bother to mark "OKAY TO PRINT!"

"It's all right. It's all right."

I wrote that yesterday, and I actually started crying.

Four pages from the end and he finally got me.

LOKI started off as a book about being For Yourself, and I feel like it's managed to end that way, too. Looking back, it's been a series about trying to be better – about finding some way to care for yourself despite everything. I don't know if we really answered that question of how that's done, in the end – but then it's all a hell of a lot easier said than done anyway. Everything's easier for stories.

I hope reading this book was better than not reading it. That's all I've got.

In terms of the writing – it was work I'm incredibly proud of, and work that could have been so much better, and sometimes I did good and sometimes I stumbled and failed and let everyone down. It was all of that. A whole lot of me went into this series and it took a lot out. If I'm honest, I need a break. I'll be glad to let it go.

I really, really hate to let it go.

But it wasn't just the writing, obviously. No comic is.

So – thanks to Lauren Sankovitch, who started all this rolling, and Wil Moss and Jon Moisan, the editorial team supreme. Thanks to Clayton Cowles for providing perfect lettering and never flying to the UK and strangling me, and thanks to Nolan Woodard, Lee Loughridge and Antonio Fabela for the matchless color work. Thanks to Jenny Frison for the gorgeousness of the first five covers. And thank you, Jorge Coelho, for being the perfect fill-in artist – I can't imagine the magic battle in #6 done by anyone else.

Who does that leave?

Lee.

I could talk about seventeen-and-a-half issues – fifteen of this and two-and-a-half of the TENTH REALM mini – done, pencil and ink, without a break under deadline pressures that even Ditko Spidey couldn't have stood the weight of. I could talk about putting up with my crap for month after month. I could talk about the pure clean beauty of his line, his mastery of expression, his storytelling instincts, all of which survived and thrived under the aforementioned Spidey-murdering pressure. But I'll just say this:

Lee is the only artist who could possibly have done this comic. He's a true friend. And we're not done. You'll be hearing more of us as a team sooner or later – it's just a question of when. The day will come.

Meanwhile, Loki's going to change again sooner or later, because that's what comics do to meet the times, and that's okay. That's how it should be. But right now, I think we've left him where he needed to be.

I hope you liked it. If I let you down, I'm sorry.

Thanks for reading.

-Al

Well…wow…

What a ride that was!

I'm so proud to have been a part of this book and so sad that it's come to a close - but if it has to end, then what better time to do it, eh?

I think this last arc has been the most beautiful of all for me, and I love that, despite being set against a backdrop of action-packed epic battles, worlds colliding and everything literally being obliterated, our final confrontation is actually one of gentleness and warmth.

Of acceptance and forgiveness.

Of course, there's still the odd trick or two, naturally. No one changes THAT much.

Speaking of which, we were also so lucky to have been given one of the rarest opportunities in comics these days, the chance to affect genuine change.

Will that change stick? Hopefully, for a while at least. Who needs shoes, right? But this is a character that has change written into his/her DNA, so it's inevitable, and correct, that change will occur somewhere down the line.

So I guess that leaves me to just say a big bunch of heartfelt thank yous!

Thank you to everyone who bought and supported the book and character so passionately and vocally along the way. It was always noticed and appreciated and I had all of you in mind when drawing this.

Thank you to the wonderful team behind LOKI. Marvel in general, but especially C.B. Cebulski for suggesting me in the first place and Lauren Sankovitch for putting the team together. Special thanks to Wil Moss and Jon Moisan, for being so fun, supportive, watchful and enthusiastic throughout. Thanks to lettering maestro Clayton Cowles and to Jenny Frison for those gorgeous covers! To Jorge Coelho for his safe hands and pitch perfect take on issues #6 and #7. Thanks to Nolan Woodard, Lee Loughridge and the wonderful Antonio Fabela for bringing this world to life with their stunning colors.

And last but not least: Al Ewing. The Al-Father. The All-Ewing.

Al and I go back a ways. He wrote the very first gig I had at 2000 AD. A one-page "Future Shock" and even that was whip-smart - but I think his LOKI is a masterpiece. It continually blew me away. Every time I'd get a new script I'd be reading it in stunned surprise at where he'd taken it, at how cleverly he'd laid it out, the emotional impact or wit of a scene, his understanding of the characters and their unique voices. I could tell when he'd had fun with something or when something had caused him genuine pain to get onto the page.

I think Al *is* Loki. A sweet, bearded Loki. Always five steps ahead of the game, sharp as a tack and capable of real magic.

He is also my friend.

So thank you, Al. Let's do this again, soon.

Finally, if I may, I would like to dedicate this book to my wonderful parents: My mom, Margaret, who passed away shortly before I started on LOKI, and my dad, Derrick, who passed away during its run. I know they would both have been very proud to see me fulfill my dream.

-Lee

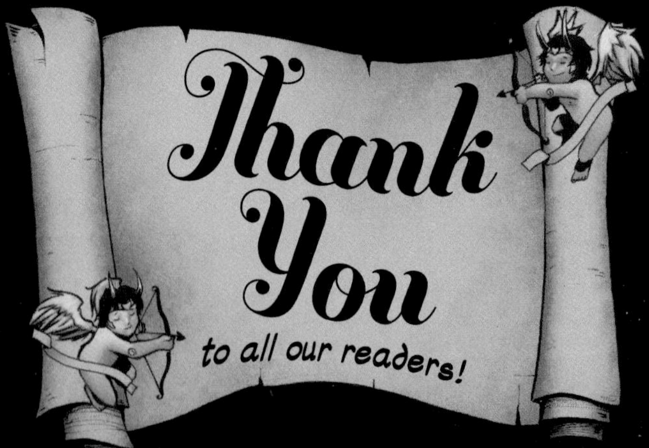
Thank You
to all our readers!